Conflict of Laws

Conflict of Laws
Cases and Materials

Fifth Edition

Lea Brilmayer
Howard M. Holtzmann Professor
of International Law
Yale University

Jack Goldsmith
Professor of Law
University of Chicago

76 Ninth Avenue, New York, NY 10011
http://lawschool.aspenpublishers.com

Aspen Publishers
Attn: Permissions Department
76 Ninth Avenue, 7th Floor
New York, NY 10011-5201

Printed in the United States of America

3 4 5 6 7 8 9 0

Library of Congress Cataloging-in-Publication Data
Brilmayer, Lea.
Conflict of laws : cases and materials / Lea Brilmayer, Jack Goldsmith.—5th ed.
p. cm.
ISBN 0-7355-2419-X
1. Conflict of laws—United States—Cases. I. Goldsmith, Jack L. II. Title.

KF410.M37 2002
342.73′042—dc21 2001053547

To Our Teachers and Students

Summary of Contents

Contents

Chapter 7. Conflicts in the International Setting 723

Chapter 8. Conflicts and the Internet 813

Preface to the Fifth Edition

Jack Goldsmith joins Lea Brilmayer in editing the fifth edition of this casebook begun by the late Professor James Martin in 1978. It has been almost seven years since the publication of the fourth edition of the casebook. Perhaps the most important change during this period has been the rise of the Internet, a communication technology that has generated many new and difficult conflicts problems. The importance of the Internet to conflict of laws is reflected in a new chapter (Chapter 8) devoted to the topic. The organization of the remainder of the book remains largely the same, but the chapters have been significantly updated to reflect changes during the past seven years. The following changes may be of particular note: The interstate (and federal-state) consequences of same-sex marriages are discussed in Chapters 1 and 6; Chapters 2 and 8 have more elaborate discussions of contractual choice-of-law; and Chapter 7 ("Conflicts in the International Setting") has been expanded a great deal. Many new cases and notes have been added to all of the other chapters as well. To make room for these changes, we have eliminated outdated material and we have cut down a bit on coverage in Chapter 4 ("The Jurisdiction of Courts over Persons and Property") on the theory that personal jurisdiction is thoroughly covered in the first-year civil procedure class. We hope that the book continues to meet the needs of teachers in the field and to attract curious students.

Lea Brilmayer
Jack Goldsmith

August 2001

Preface to the Second Edition

The teacher of conflicts already knows that it is a fascinating course. The student is about to find out. It is, moreover, one of those courses in which to be "theoretical" is to be "practical"; the supposed war between those two qualities is not even a skirmish in conflicts law, where changes have come (and will no doubt continue to come) so quickly that the only preparation is understanding, not memorization.

This book is organized to present the heart of conflicts first: choice-of-law problems. In the first chapter the "traditional" approach is exposed; in the second, the struggle of the courts and the commentators to come up with a more responsive (but not unduly complicated) approach. The remaining broad topics—constitutional limitations on choice of law, the *Erie* doctrine, personal jurisdiction, recognition of judgments, and conflicts in the international context—are considered in light of the wisdom derived from consideration of the basic choice-of-law problems. I have attempted to make the materials short enough so that they really can be covered in a three- or four-hour course, but we have all experienced the temptation to slow down and inspect in detail some of the particularly intriguing questions that are raised in conflicts.

Questions and comments at the ends of cases or case groupings tend to be brief, concentrating on the problems raised by the principal cases rather than adding notes about other cases. Occasionally the opinion of the editor may show through in questions and comments, but many questions that may seem to present a point of view are asked in the spirit of the devil's advocate.

Cases have been severely edited to eliminate citations. Thus, they do not read like real case reports, but they do read somewhat more smoothly. Citations are retained on some occasions when they refer to other important cases, when they refer to writings of important conflicts scholars, when they cite the editor of this casebook, or otherwise seem worthy of retention. Footnotes in cases and other quoted material have generally been eliminated without the use of ellipses. Those that have survived editing retain their original numbers, while the editor's footnotes employ asterisks and daggers.

Jim Martin

January 1984

Acknowledgments

Numerous people deserve thanks for their contributions to the publication of the fifth edition of this casebook. Our most enthusiastic thanks go to Jason Callen, a law student at the University of Chicago who provided truly outstanding assistance in research and editing. Jeannie Heffernan and Shelley Pierce, also law students at the University of Chicago, provided important research help as well. Kathie Kepchar provided invaluable typing, organizational, and moral support. Perry Dane, Ryan Goodman, Derek Jinks, Larry Kramer, Jonathan Nash, Erin O'Hara, Hank Perritt, Larry Ribstein, and Allan Stein provided helpful comments on various chapters. Professor Goldsmith thanks the extraordinary library staff at the University of Chicago Law School for its quick, reliable, and cheerful help, and the Russell Baker Scholars Fund for generous financial support.

We also thank the copyright holders who kindly granted their permission to reprint excerpts from the following materials.

American Law Institute, selections from Restatement, Conflict of Laws. Copyright 1934 by The American Law Institute. Reprinted with the permission of The American Law Institute.

———, selections from Restatement (Second), Conflict of Laws. Copyright 1971, 1989 by The American Law Institute. Reprinted with the permission of The American Law Institute.

———, selections from Restatement (Revised) of Foreign Relations Law. Copyright 1986 by The American Law Institute. Reprinted with the permission of The American Law Institute.

Currie, Comments on *Babcock vs. Jackson.* Copyright © 1983 by the Directors for the Columbia Law Review Association, Inc. All rights reserved. This article originally appeared at 63 Colum. L. Rev. 1242-1243, 1247 (1969). Reprinted by permission.

———, Selected Essays on the Conflict of Laws, Copyright © 1963 by Duke University Press.

Escher, drawing entitled "Tekenen." Copyright Beeldrecht, Amsterdam/VAGA, New York, Collection Haags Gemeenthmuseum—The Hague.

Goldsmith, Against Cyberanarchy, 65 U. Chi. L. Rev. 1199 (1998). Reprinted by permission of the University of Chicago Law Review.

Johnson & Post, Law and Borders—The Rise of Law in Cyberspace, 48 Stan. L. Rev. 1367 (1996). Reprinted with permission of David Johnson and David Post.

Lapres, translation of Licra and UEJF v. Yahoo! Inc. (Tribunal de Grande Instance de Paris, May 22, 2000), available at *www.lapres.net/html/yahen.html.* Reprinted with permission of the translator.

Leflar, Choice-of-Law Statutes, 44 Tenn. L. Rev. 951, 958 (1977). Reprinted by permission of the author and the Tennessee Law Review Association.

———, Conflicts Law: More on Choice-Influencing Considerations, 54 Cal. L. Rev. 1584 (1966). Copyright © 1966, California Law Review, Inc. Reprinted by permission.

Perritt, Dispute Resolution in Cyberspace: Demand for New Forms of ADR, 15 Oh. St. J. Dis. Res. 675 (2000). Reprinted with permission of Henry Perritt, Jr.

Perritt, Will the Judgment-proof Own Cyberspace? 32 Int'l Lawyer 1121 (1998). Reprinted with permission of Henry Perritt, Jr.

Reppy, Eclecticism in Choice of Law: Hybrid Method or Mishmash?, 34 Mercer L. Rev. 645 (1983). Copyright © 1983 Walter F. George School of Law, Mercer University.

Introduction

A (Very) Brief History of the Subject

Conflict of laws encompasses several related areas of law: choice of law, constitutional limitations on choice of law, jurisdiction of courts, recognition of sister-state judgments, and *Erie* problems.

Of these topics, choice of law is at the heart of the course. A choice-of-law problem arises in the selection of the governing law for a case with connections to two or more jurisdictions. Choice-of-law questions have arisen wherever people have been subject to the authority of more than one state, nation, or tribal law. The late Professor Yntema said that a choice-of-law rule was found on the wrappings of a crocodile mummy in Egypt. Yntema, The Historic Bases of Private International Law, 2 Am. J. Comp. L. 297, 300 (1953). The Corpus Juris of the Roman Empire tended to eliminate such problems by the direct method of eliminating all laws but one (namely, Roman law). Choice-of-law problems arose again in the Middle Ages, however, especially in Italy, which was divided into many commercially active city-states. The "statutists" of medieval Italy approached conflicts problems by dividing statutes into the "real" and "personal" category — the former applied only within the jurisdiction that promulgated it; the latter followed the person wherever he went. Unfortunately, the statutes were not labeled, and the crunch came in trying to determine which statutes were which. Overriding the Italian efforts in the area was the notion of what is now sometimes termed a "superlaw," which was based in part on the natural law and which was viewed as having more authority than the local laws in conflict.

In the 1600s, Holland became influential in choice-of-law theory. The greatest of the Dutch scholars was Ulric Huber, who took the position that states defer to the law of other states in appropriate cases not because some superlaw requires them to do so, but rather because of "comity" — a kind of golden rule among sovereigns. His book, *De Conflictu Legum Diversarum in Diversis Imperiis* [On The Conflict of Diverse Laws of Different States], translated in Ernest G. Lorenzen, Selected Articles on the Conflict of Laws 136 (1947), set forth three postulates from which he derived his solutions to conflicts problems:

> (1) The laws of each state have force within the limits of that government and bind all subjects to it, but not beyond.
>
> (2) All persons within the limits of a government, whether they live there permanently or temporarily, are deemed to be subjects thereof.
>
> (3) Sovereigns will so act by way of comity that rights acquired within the limits of a government retain their force everywhere so far as they do not cause prejudice to the power or rights of such government or of its subjects.

Lorenzen, *supra,* at 163.

Huber's work had a strong effect on Joseph Story, a Justice of the United States Supreme Court who was considered the foremost conflicts scholar in the English-speaking world in the nineteenth century. Story's approach was similar to Huber's and helped entrench the "comity" rather than "superlaw" orientation in the United States. Story's *Commentaries on the Conflict of Laws* (1834) was the most influential work in the field until A. V. Dicey, in England, produced his vested-rights theory at the turn of the century. In the United States, Professor Joseph Beale of the Harvard Law School took up Dicey's vested-rights theory, with strong doses of territorialism. The theory was enshrined in the American Law Institute's *Restatement of Conflict of Laws* (1934) and appeared for a time to be headed for apotheosis by the United States Supreme Court as a branch of the law of due process. Beale's system tended to select a governing law on the basis of where various critical acts occurred, such as where a contract was signed or where a tort was committed.

Beale's approach was heavily criticized by three outstanding scholars — Cook, Lorenzen, and Cavers. But these criticisms had little influence in the courts for many years. In the 1950s, Professor Brainerd Currie attacked the First Restatement approach and suggested in its place a system of conflicts known as "interest analysis." Currie's work influenced courts and provided a basis for others to build on. In 1971, the American Law Institute published the *Restatement (Second) of Conflict of Laws,* which tried to accommodate the policy-based insights of Currie and others. Today choice of law in the United States is something of a hodge-podge. In the context of torts and contracts, most states have rejected the traditional approach and have adopted one of a variety of policy-based approaches. But the traditional approach fares better in other contexts, such as marriage, corporate internal affairs, and real property.

About the Terminology

The late Professor Prosser once said, in an oft-quoted comment, that "[t]he realm of the conflict of laws is a dismal swamp, filled with quaking quagmires, and inhabited by learned but eccentric professors who theorize about mysterious matters in a strange and incomprehensible jargon. The ordinary court, or lawyer, is quite lost when engulfed and entangled in it." Prosser, Interstate Publication, 51 Mich. L. Rev. 959, 971 (1953). A small amount of introduction to the terminology may then be in order. *Comity,* a term already used above, indicates the nonmandatory acceptance by one jurisdiction of the law of another. *Vested rights* is a term with meaning very similar to its meaning in constitutional law and is used in connection with theories that indicate, for example, that the victim of a tort would acquire a vested right to recovery under the law of the place where the tort occurs, a right that thereafter accompanies the person and may be used as the basis for a lawsuit even in a jurisdiction that would not impose liability if the same events had taken place within its own borders. Closely connected with vested rights is the phrase *lex loci* and its children, *lex loci contractus* and *lex loci delicti. Lex loci* is simply "the law of the place," with *contractus* adding "of the contract" and *delicti* adding "of the tort." Another term important to your reading of the cases is *domicile,* which refers to the political jurisdiction (state, country, etc.) in which a person makes his or her permanent home. We will see many cases elaborating that sketchy definition.

Finally, you will probably already have noted that several terms are used interchangeably for the topic under discussion. "Conflicts of laws," "choice of law," and "private international law" are common labels for what you are about to study, although "choice of law" is often restricted to choice-of-law questions, excluding such other questions as jurisdiction and recognition of judgments.

Conflict of Laws

1

Traditional Approaches

The cases and rules in this first chapter represent the traditional approaches to choice of law that prevailed in the United States in the nineteenth century and first half of the twentieth century. Time has passed many of these rules by, especially with regard to choice-of-law problems related to tort and contract. New theories (discussed in Chapter 2) have emerged, and relatively few scholars defend the "old rules" as originally conceived. Nonetheless, ten or so states adhere to the traditional rules in the torts and contracts contexts, and many more states follow traditional approaches in other areas of law. Even in states that have abandoned traditional rules, these rules form the backdrop that makes the present state of the law more comprehensible.

A. Torts

1. Nonintentional Torts

Alabama Great Southern Railroad v. Carroll

97 Ala. 126, 11 So. 803 (1892)

McClellan, J.

The plaintiff W. D. Carroll is, and was at the time of entering into the service of the defendant, the Alabama Great Southern Railroad Company, and at the time of being injured in that service, a citizen of Alabama. The defendant is an Alabama corporation operating a railroad extending from Chattanooga in the State of Tennessee through Alabama to Meridian in the State of Mississippi. At the time of the casualty complained of, plaintiff was in the service of the defendant in the capacity of brakeman on freight trains running from Birmingham, Alabama, to Meridian, Mississippi, under a contract which was made in the State of Alabama. The injury was caused by the breaking of a link between two cars in a freight train which was proceeding from Birmingham to Meridian. The point at which the link broke and the injury was suffered was in the State of Mississippi. The evidence tended to show that the link which broke was a defective link and that it was in a defective condition when the train left Birmingham. . . . The evidence went also to show that the defect in this link consisted in or resulted from its having been bent while cold, that this tended to weaken the iron and in this instance had cracked the link somewhat on the outer curve of the bend, and that the link broke at the point of this crack. It was shown to be the duty of certain employees of defendant stationed along its line to inspect the links attached to cars to be put in trains or forming the couplings between cars in trains at Chattanooga, Birmingham, and some points between Birmingham and the place where this link broke, and also that it was the duty of the conductor of freight trains and the other trainmen to maintain such inspection as occasion afforded throughout the runs or trips of such trains; and the evidence affords ground for inference that there was a negligent omission on the part of such employees to perform this duty, or if performed, the failure to discover the defect in and to remove this link was the result of negligence. . . .

The only negligence, in other words and in short, which finds support by direction or inference in any tendency of the evidence, is that of persons whose duty it was to inspect the links of the train, and remove such as were defective and replace them with others which were not defective. This was the negligence not of the master, the defendant, but of fellow-servants of the plaintiff, for which at common-law the defendant is not liable. . . .

This being the common-law applicable to the premises as understood and declared in Alabama, it will be presumed in our courts as thus declared to be the common-law of Mississippi, unless the evidence shows a different rule to have been announced by the Supreme Court of the State as being the common-law thereof. The evidence adduced here fails to show any such thing; but to the contrary it is made to appear from the testimony of Judge Arnold and by the decisions of the Supreme Court of Mississippi which were introduced on the trial below that that court is in full accord with this one in this respect. Indeed, if anything, those decisions go further than this court has ever gone in applying the doctrine of fellow-servants to the exemption of railway companies from liability to one servant for injuries resulting from the negligence of another. . . .

It is, however, further contended that the plaintiff, if his evidence be believed, has made out a case for the recovery sought under the Employer's Liability Act of Alabama, it being clearly shown that there is no such, or similar law of force in the State of Mississippi. Considering this position in the abstract, that is dissociated from the facts of this particular case which are supposed to exert an important influence upon it, there cannot be two opinions as to its being unsound and untenable. So looked at, we do not understand appellee's counsel even to deny either the proposition or its application to this case, that there can be no recovery in one State for injuries to the person sustained in another unless the infliction of the injuries is actionable under the law of the State in which they were received. Certainly this is the well established rule of law subject in some jurisdictions to the qualification that the infliction of the injuries would also support an action in the State where the suit is brought, had they been received within that State. . . .

But it is claimed that the facts of this case take it out of the general rule which the authorities cited above abundantly support, and authorize the courts of Alabama to subject the defendant to the payment of damages under section 2590 of the Code, although the injuries counted on were sustained in Mississippi under circumstances which involved no liability on the defendant by the laws of that State.

This insistence is in the first instance based on that aspect of the evidence which goes to show that the negligence which produced the casualty transpired in Alabama, and the theory that wherever the consequence of that negligence manifested itself, a recovery can be had in Alabama. We are referred to no authority in support of this proposition, and exhaustive investigation on our part has failed to disclose any. . . .

The position [that the occurrence of the negligence in Alabama would not justify applying Alabama law] appears to us to be eminently sound in principle and upon logic. It is admitted, or at least cannot be denied, that negligence of duty unproductive of damnifying results will not authorize or support a recovery. Up to the time this train passed out of Alabama no injury had resulted. For all that occurred in Alabama, therefore, no cause of action whatever arose. The fact which created the right to sue, the injury without which confessedly no action would lie anywhere, transpired in the State of Mississippi. It was in that State, therefore, necessarily that the cause of action, if any, arose; and whether a cause of action arose and existed at all or not must in all reason be determined by the law which obtained at the time and place when and where the fact which is relied on to justify a recovery transpired. Section 2590 of the Code of Alabama had no efficacy beyond the lines of Alabama. It cannot be allowed to operate upon facts occurring in another State so as to evolve out of them rights and liabilities which do not exist under the law of the State which is of course paramount in the premises. Where the facts occur in Alabama and a liability becomes fixed in Alabama, it may be enforced in another State having like enactments, or whose policy is not opposed to the spirit of such enactments, but this is quite a different matter. This is but enforcing the statute upon facts to which it is applicable all of which occur within the territory for the government of which it was enacted. Section 2590 of the Code, in other words is to be interpreted in the light of universally recognized principles of private international or interstate law, as if its operation had been expressly limited to this State and as if its first line read as follows: "When a personal injury is *received in Alabama* by a servant or employee," &c., &c. The negligent infliction of an injury here under statutory circumstances creates a right of action here, which, being transitory, may be enforced in any other State or country the comity of which admits of it; but for an injury inflicted elsewhere than in Alabama our statute gives no right of recovery, and the aggrieved party must look to the local law to ascertain what his rights are. Under that law this plaintiff had no cause of action, as we have seen, and hence he has no rights which our courts can enforce, unless it be upon a consideration to be presently adverted to. We have not been inattentive to the suggestions of counsel in the connection, which are based upon that rule of the statutory and common criminal law under which a murderer is punishable where the fatal blow is delivered, regardless of the place where death ensues. This principle is patently without application here. There would be some analogy if the plaintiff had been stricken in Alabama and suffered in Mississippi, which is not the fact. There is, however, an analogy which is afforded by the criminal law, but which points away from the conclusion appellee's counsel desire us to reach. This is found in that well established doctrine of criminal law, that where the unlawful act is committed in one jurisdiction or State and takes effect—produces the result which it is the purpose of the law to prevent, or, it having ensued, punish for—in another jurisdiction or State, the crime is deemed to have been committed and is punished in that jurisdiction or State in which the result is manifested, and not where the act was committed.

Another consideration—that referred to above—it is insisted, entitles this plaintiff to recover here under the Employer's Liability Act for an injury inflicted beyond the territorial operation of that act. This is claimed upon the fact that at the time plaintiff was injured he was in the discharge of duties which rested on him by the terms of a contract between him and defendant which had been entered into in Alabama, and, hence, was an Alabama contract, in connection with the facts that plaintiff was and is a citizen of this State, and the defendant is an Alabama corporation. These latter facts—of citizenship and domicile respectively of plaintiff and defendant—are of no importance in this connection, it seems to us, further than this: they may tend to show that the contract was made here, which is not controverted, and if the plaintiff has a cause of action at all, he, by reason of them, may prosecute it in our courts. They have no bearing on the primary question of existence of a cause of action, and as that is the question before us, we need not further advert to the fact of plaintiff's citizenship or defendant's domicile.

The contract was that plaintiff should serve the defendant in the capacity of a brakeman on its freight train between Birmingham, Alabama, and Meridian, Mississippi, and should receive as compensation a stipulated sum for each trip from Birmingham to Meridian and return. The theory is that the

Employer's Liability Act became a part of this contract; that the duties and liabilities which it prescribes became contractual duties and liabilities, or duties and liabilities springing out of the contract, and that these duties attended upon the execution whenever its performance was required—in Mississippi as well as in Alabama—and that the liability prescribed for a failure to perform any of such duties attached upon such failure and consequent injury wherever it occurred, and was enforceable here because imposed by an Alabama contract notwithstanding the remission of duty and the resulting injury occurred in Mississippi, under whose laws no liability was incurred by such remission. The argument is that a contract for service is a condition precedent to the application of the statute, and that "as soon as the contract is made the rights and obligations of the parties, under the Employer's Act, became vested and fixed," so that "no subsequent repeal of the law could deprive the injured party of his rights nor discharge the master from his liabilities," &c., &c. If this argument is sound, and it is sound if the duties and liabilities prescribed by the act can be said to be contractual duties and obligations at all, it would lead to conclusions the possibility of which has not hitherto been suggested by any court or law writer, and which, to say the least, would be astounding to the profession. For instance: If the act of 1885 becomes a part of every contract of service entered into since its passage, just "as if such law were in so many words expressly included in the contract as a part thereof," as counsel insist it did, so as to make the liability of the master to pay damages from injuries to a fellow-servant of his negligent employee, a contractual obligation, no reason can be conceived why the law existing in this regard prior to the passage of that act did not become in like manner a part of every contract of service then entered into, so that every such contract would be deemed to contain stipulations for the non-liability of the master for injuries flowing from the negligence of a fellow-servant, and confining the injured servant's right to damage to a claim against his negligent fellow-servant—the former, in other words, agreeing to look alone to the latter. There were many thousands of such contracts existing in this country and England at the time when statutes similar to section 2590 of our Code were enacted, there were indeed many thousands of such contracts existing in Alabama when that section became the law of this State. Each of these contracts, if the position of plaintiff as to our statute being embodied into the terms of his contract so that its duties were contractual duties, and its liabilities contractual obligations to pay money can be maintained, involved the assurances of organic provisions, State and Federal, of the continued non-liability of the master for the negligence of his servants, notwithstanding the passage of such statutes. Yet these statutes were passed, and they have been applied to servants under pre-existing contracts as fully as to servants under subsequent contracts, and there has never been a suggestion even in any part of the common-law world that they were not rightly so applied. If plaintiff's contention is well taken, many a judgment has gone on the rolls in this State, and throughout the country, and has been satisfied, which palpably overrode vested rights without the least suspicion on the part of court or counsel that one of the most familiar ordinances of the fundamental law was being violated. Nay more, another result not heretofore at all contemplated would ensue. Contracts for service partly in Alabama might be now entered into in adjoining States where the common-law rule still obtains, as in Mississippi, for instance, where the servant has no right to recover for the negligence of his fellow, and the assumption of this risk under the law becoming, according to the argument of counsel, a contractual obligation to bear it, such contracts would be good in Alabama and as to servants entering into them, our statute would have no operation even upon negligence and resulting injury within its terms occurring wholly in Alabama. And on the other hand, if this defendant is under a contractual obligation to pay the plaintiff the damages sustained by him because of the injury inflicted in Mississippi, the contract could be of course enforced in Mississippi and damages there awarded by its courts, notwithstanding the law of that State provides that there can be no recovery under any circumstances whatever by one servant for the negligence of his fellow employee. We do not suppose that such a proposition ever has been or ever will be made in the courts of Mississippi. Yet that it should be made and sustained is the natural and necessary sequence of the position advanced in this case. These considerations demonstrate the infirmity of plaintiff's position in this connection, and serve to show the necessity and propriety of the conclusion we propose to announce on this part of the case. That conclusion is, that the duties and liabilities incident to the relation between the plaintiff and the defendant which are involved in this case, are not imposed by and do not rest in or spring from the contract between the parties. The only office of the contract, under section 2590 of the Code, is the establishment of a relation between them, that of master and servant; and it is upon that relation, that incident or consequence of the contract, and not upon the rights of the parties under the contract, that our statute operates. The law is not concerned with the contractual stipulations, except insofar as to determine from them that the relation upon which it is to operate exists. Finding this relation the statute imposes certain duties and liabilities on the parties to it wholly regardless of the stipulations of the contract as to the rights of the parties under it, and, it may be, in the teeth of such stipulations. It is the purpose of the statute and must be the limit of its operation to govern persons standing in the relation of master and servants to each other in respect of their conduct in certain particulars within the State of Alabama. Mississippi has the same right to establish governmental rules for such persons within her borders as Alabama; and she has established rules which are different from those of our law. And the conduct of such persons toward each other is, when its legality is brought in question, to be adjudged by the rules of the one or the other States as it falls territorially within the one or the other. The doctrine is like that which prevails in respect of other relations, as that of man and wife. Marriage is a contract. The entering into this contract raises up certain duties and imposes certain liabilities in all civilized countries. What these duties and liabilities are at the place of the contract are determinable by the law of that place; but when the parties go into other jurisdictions, the relation created by the contract under the laws of the place of its execution will be recognized, but the personal duties, obligations and liabilities incident to the relation are such as exist under the law of the jurisdiction in which an act is done or omitted as to the legality, effect or consequence of which the question arises. . . .

The only true doctrine is that each sovereignty, state or nation, has the exclusive power to finally determine and declare what acts or omission in the conduct of one to another, whether they be strangers or sustain relations to each other which the law recognizes, as parent and child, husband and wife, master and servant, and the like, shall impose a liability in damages for the consequent injury, and the courts of no other sovereignty can impute a damnifying quality to an act or omission which afforded no cause of action where it transpired.

Questions and Comments

(1) Why should Alabama pay any attention at all to the law of Mississippi? Why should it ever apply any state's law but its own? Doesn't a court have an obligation to achieve a "just" result? And if Alabama's law (including its conflicts rules) tells it to apply the law of Mississippi to a case, doesn't it follow either that (a) Alabama has erred, because it should apply its own law, which is more just, or (b) Mississippi law is more just, and Alabama should change its own law?

Justice Cardozo answered these questions in the course of a famous articulation of the same vested rights theory employed in *Carroll.* In a case in which the question was whether a New York court should apply Massachusetts or New York wrongful death law to an accident that occurred in Massachusetts, Cardozo explained why Massachusetts law would normally govern:

> A foreign statute is not law in this state, but it gives rise to an obligation, which, if transitory, follows the person and may be enforced wherever the person may be found. . . . [I]t is a principle of every civilized law that vested rights shall be protected. The plaintiff owns something, and we help him to get it. . . . Our own scheme of legislation may be different. We may even have no legislation on the subject. That is not enough to show that public policy forbids us to enforce the foreign right. A right of action is property. If a foreign statute gives the right, the mere fact that we do not give a like right is no reason for refusing to help the plaintiff in getting what belongs to him. We are not so provincial as to say that every solution of a problem is wrong because we deal with it otherwise at home.

Loucks v. Standard Oil Co., 224 N.Y. 99, 120 N.E. 198 (N.Y. 1918); *see also* Slater v. Mexican Nat'l R.R., 194 U.S. 120, 126 (1904) (Holmes, J.) ("The theory of the foreign suit is that although the act complained of was subject to no law having force in the forum, it gave rise to an obligation, an *obligatio,* which like other obligations follows that person, and may be enforced wherever the person may be found.").

Are these convincing arguments? By assuming that the right has vested in another state, does Cardozo beg the question of what law creates the right? What benefit, if any, does the forum get from enforcing a foreign-vested right? Why is it important to the vested rights theory to insist that courts apply foreign vested rights but not foreign law? For the classic theoretical defense of the vested rights theory in the United States, see Beale, 1 Conflict of Laws 1-86 (1935). For classic criticisms of Beale's vested rights theory, see Cook, The Logical and Legal Bases of the Conflict of Laws (1942); Currie, Selected Essays on the Conflict of Laws (1963); Lorenzen, Selected Articles on the Conflict of Laws (1947).

(2) What should be the goals of a body of conflicts law? The traditional answer is, for the most part, uniformity. "The purpose of a conflict-of-laws doctrine is to assure that a case will be treated in the same way under the appropriate law regardless of the fortuitous circumstances which often determine the forum." Lauritzen v. Larsen, 345 U.S. 571, 591 (1952). Such uniformity has been equated with "fairness to the parties." H. Goodrich & E. Scoles, Handbook of the Conflict of Laws 5 (1964). But the answer of uniformity, though facile and traditional, is dubious. As Professor Weintraub has put it, "After all, if the only purpose of choice-of-law rules is to make the result independent of forum choice, not only must there be choice-of-law rules, but also those rules must be uniform in each possible forum." R. Weintraub, Commentary on the Conflict of Laws 3 (2d ed. 1980).

The late Professor Currie suggested "[i]n all solemnity" that in certain cases the law of the state first in alphabetical order be applied. (In order to avoid discrimination and burdening the judges of the state lowest in order by making them determine foreign law all the time, he suggested that the inverse alphabetical order be used for transactions occurring in odd-numbered years.) Currie, Selected Essays on the Conflict of Laws 609 (1963).

It is clear, isn't it, that Currie's suggestion would achieve almost complete uniformity of result? (This is assuming, of course, that it will be noncontroversial which states have enough contact that their laws should be on the list for consideration.) Moreover predictability, the avoidance of forum-shopping, and ease of administration, three other goals sometimes mentioned, would be greatly enhanced.

What's so good about uniformity? If Missouri (or any other state) comes to a conclusion in a conflicts case that it thinks is the right and just result, what role should the desire for uniformity play? If uniformity is achieved by reaching the Missouri result, uniformity is merely superfluous. On the other hand, if Missouri is out of step with the results reached by other states, even after giving due deference to their reasoning, should it give up what is perceived as the just result in order to fall into line with the others? Wouldn't there have to be powerful arguments for uniformity in order to justify reaching what is seen as an unjust result?

It would seem, then, that there must be unarticulated goals of the conflicts system other than uniformity and its related concepts. Can we be any more specific about what those goals might be, other than to say that the court should reach a result that is "correct" or "just"? *See generally* Hay, Flexibility Versus Predictability and Uniformity in Choice of Law, 226 Recueil des Cours d'Academie de Droit International 285 (1991).

(3) A principle that may or may not be categorized as an ultimate goal of the conflicts system, but which pervades early conflicts cases, is that of territoriality: Generally speaking, a state has the right to control people and things located within its own borders.

A closely related—and less universally acknowledged—proposition is that states have the right to control the *effects* of people's behavior within their borders. For example, if *X* hits *Y* over the head with a baseball bat while in Missouri, it is reasonably clear that *X* may be subject to the criminal law of Missouri for that act. In many cases the law of Missouri will also be the only relevant law with respect to the civil effects of the act—but not always. Assume that *X* and *Y* are both citizens of Illinois, traveling into St. Louis only for shopping purposes. We might not be surprised to find that an Illinois court later considering the issue might apply Illinois law, rather than Missouri law, to the question whether one who kills a testator may take under the testator's will—especially if all the property to pass under the will is located in Illinois. Would Missouri even want its law to apply in such a case? Would the answer to such a question depend on whether it was Illinois or Missouri law that allowed a killer to profit from his own act? Should it matter whether or not Missouri would want its own law applied?

(4) The Section of the Alabama Code analyzed in *Carroll* provided:

> When a personal injury is received by a servant or employee in the service or business of the master or employer, the master or employer is liable to answer in damages to such servant or employee, as if he were a stranger, and not engaged in such service or employment, . . . [w]hen such injury is caused by reason of the negligence of *any person in the service or employment of the master or employer,* who has the charge or control of any signal, points, locomotive, engine, switch, car, or train upon a railway, or of any part of the track of a railway.

Alabama Civil Code, §2590(5) (1886) (emphasis added). On its face, doesn't this provision apply to the facts of *Carroll*? After all, it extends the master's liability to torts caused by "any" fellow servant, and it contains no geographical limitation. Why did the court read the statute's first sentence as if it included the words "personal injury is received *in Alabama*"? Was this a fair reading of the Alabama legislature's intent? Did the Alabama legislature have the territorial "principles of private international or interstate law" in mind when it enacted the statute? (Note that if the courts do not read some limiting principle into the statute, the statute would also apply to torts in Mississippi involving only Mississippi parties.) Or would the legislature have likely wanted the law to apply to people like Carroll—a citizen of Alabama, working for an Alabama railroad, entering a contract to do so in Alabama, and performing a good deal of the contract in Alabama? Do you think the legislature gave the choice-of-law question any thought at all? How should courts determine the geographical scope of a statute in the face of legislative silence?

(5) "The fact which created the right to sue, the injury . . . transpired in the State of Mississippi. It was in that State, *therefore*, necessarily that the cause of action, if any, arose. . . ." Why the "therefore"? Didn't the negligence equally create the right to sue, since an injury without negligence would not have been tortious? Which would you rather give up, your lungs or your heart? The "last act" may determine, of course, *when* the tort takes place (although not always) for such things as statute-of-limitations purposes.

If the court's reasoning is inadequate, how should you determine where a tort "occurs"? Can this question be answered without knowing why the place of occurrence supplies the governing law?

(6) What are the merits of the plaintiff's arguments that his contract with the defendant incorporated the Alabama statute? What is the court's answer to those arguments? "It is commonly said that existing laws at the time and place of the making of a contract enter into and form a part of the contract as fully as if expressly incorporated therein." Williston on Contracts §615 (3d ed. 1961). If the rule is applicable here, its effect may turn on two possible constructions of law: (a) The parties are in fact presumed to have intended the controlling law to be made part of their contract; or (b) regardless of their intentions, their contract will be interpreted to incorporate the law existing at the time of formation. If the first interpretation is correct, does it help Carroll? If the law of Alabama was to be incorporated into the contract, isn't it first necessary to interpret the law of Alabama—which the court decided did not apply to Mississippi accidents? On the other hand, if the second interpretation is correct and the incorporation rule is merely a fiction, imposed on the parties regardless of their true intent, should it be imposed regardless of where the accident occurred? Don't we need to know *why* the law was incorporated, despite the parties' intent, to know whether the rule would be applicable in a conflicts case?

Conceding, for a moment, that the contract may incorporate existing statutory law for conflicts purposes, why should the rule be, as Williston puts it, that the relevant laws are those "existing . . . at the time *and place* of the making of a contract"? If two Michiganders, both conducting business in Michigan, conclude a deal and sign a contract during a weekend at an Ontario hunting lodge, should the law of Ontario be presumed to be incorporated? Isn't it clear that the fiction of incorporation was designed without the subject of conflicts in mind and should not be mentioned further in this book?

But such is not to be. Consider the treatment given by another court to the question of what effect a statute should have on the interpretation of a contract. In Levy v. Daniels' U-Drive Auto Renting Co., 108 Conn. 333, 143 A. 163 (1928), the defendant had rented an auto in Connecticut, which by statute imposed vicarious liability on persons leasing cars for damages caused to others by the lessee. The lessee in *Levy* caused an accident in Massachusetts, which imposed no such liability on the lessor. The question was whether the law of Massachusetts, the place of the accident, or the law of Connecticut, the place of the rental, would apply. In deciding that the lessor was contractually obligated to the other party to the accident, the court said:

> If the liability of this defendant under this statute is contractual, no question can arise as to the plaintiff's right to enforce this contract. . . . The law inserted in the contract this provision. The statute did not create the liability; it imposed it in case the defendant voluntarily rented the automobile. Whether the defendant entered into this contract of hiring was his own voluntary act; if he did he must accept the condition upon which the law permitted the making of the contract.

108 Conn. at 333, 143 A. at 165.

So far we have talked about the contract theory as a means of avoiding the place-of-injury conflicts rule for torts. Assuming that the question is one of contracts, is it clear that Alabama law should control the contract, at least with respect to an accident occurring in Mississippi? The issue can probably be avoided by assuming that *if* it were clear that the contract was intended to incorporate the Alabama statute and make it applicable to Mississippi accidents, the contract law of Mississippi would probably recognize the cause of action.

(7) In the final paragraph of the court's opinion, a rather absolute rule is laid down with respect to whose law is to apply in cases like *Carroll.* Does the rule have an intuitive appeal? If so, what kinds of qualifications, if any, should be put on the rule? Should the *procedural* law of the place of injury apply? Including the size of the paper on which pleadings are typed? If the plaintiff in a tort case is a corporation and the forum state has a rule forbidding unregistered foreign corporations that do business in the state from using its courts (a common rule), should the more permissive rule of the state of injury apply to that issue?

Is there any way to characterize issues for which the law of the place of injury seems more appropriate, as opposed to those for which the law of the forum is more appealing?

Below (and throughout this chapter) are excerpts from the American Law Institute's Restatement of Conflict of Laws (1934). The Restatement's reporter and principal author, Harvard Law School professor Joseph Beale, was a proponent of the "vested rights" theory of which *Carroll* is an exemplar. While the Restatement gives a flavor of the traditional approach to choice of law in the American states, not all American jurisdictions embraced its principles in every respect.

Selections from the First Restatement of Conflicts, on Wrongs

§§377-379, 382, 384-387, 390-391, 398-399, 412, 421 (1934)

§377. The Place of Wrong

The place of wrong is in the state where the last event necessary to make an actor liable for an alleged tort takes place. . . .

NOTE: Summary of Rules in Important Situations Determining Where a Tort is Committed

1. Except in the case of harm from poison, when a person sustains bodily harm, the place of wrong is the place where the harmful force takes effect upon the body. . . .

2. When a person causes another voluntarily to take a deleterious substance which takes effect within the body, the place of wrong is where the deleterious substance takes effect and not where it is administered. [Why?]. . . .

3. When harm is caused to land or chattels, the place of wrong is the place where the force takes effect on the thing. . . .

4. When a person sustains loss by fraud, the place of wrong is where the loss is sustained, not where fraudulent representations are made. . . .

5. Where harm is done to the reputation of a person, the place of wrong is where the defamatory statement is communicated. . . .

§378. Law Governing Plaintiff's Injury

The law of the place of wrong determines whether a person has sustained a legal injury. . . .

§379. Law Governing Liability-Creating Conduct

Except as stated in §382, the law of the place of wrong determines

(a) whether a person is responsible for harm he has caused only if he intended it,

(b) whether a person is responsible for unintended harm he has caused only if he was negligent,

(c) whether a person is responsible for harm he has caused irrespective of his intention or the care which he has exercised. . . .

§382. Duty or Privilege to Act

(1) A person who is required by law to act or not to act in one state in a certain manner will not be held liable for the results of such action or failure to act which occur in another state.

(2) A person who acts pursuant to a privilege conferred by the law of the place of acting will not be held liable for the results of his act in another state. . . .

Illustrations. . . .

5. By the law of *X*, an attacked party may lawfully stand his ground and defend himself by killing if necessary; by the law of *Y*, he should retire without killing if it is safe to do so. *A*, in *X*, is attacked by *B* who apparently intends to kill *A*. *A* reasonably believes that the only way he can save his life without retiring is to shoot *B*. He stands his ground, shoots at *B*, misses him and hits *C* in state *Y*. If he shoots at *B* with reasonable care to avoid hitting third persons, he is not liable to *C*. . . .

Comment on Subsection (2). . . .

c. Significance of privilege as basis for immunity. The word "privilege" denotes the fact that conduct which, under ordinary circumstances, would subject an actor to liability, under particular circumstances does not subject him thereto (*see* Restatement of Torts, §10). It is necessary to distinguish between a situation in which an actor is not liable because of a privilege, and situations in which he is not liable because the policy of the law is not to impose liability for harm caused by a certain general type of conduct. Thus, one who intentionally shoots another is, unless privileged, liable for the harm caused. If the actor in such a case is privileged, he is not liable, but this is because of some particular circumstances which make the case exceptional. On the other hand, if a person while driving his car with due care strikes a pedestrian and injures him, he is not liable; but in this situation, the actor is immune from liability, not because of some particular circumstances which make the case an exception to the general rule, but because the general rule is that liability is imposed in such cases only when the actor has been at fault. This distinction is important in the Conflict of Laws because, as stated in §379, the general question of the liability-creating character of the actor's conduct is determined by the law of the place of wrong, while under the statement in Subsection (2) of this Section, the question of privilege is determined by the law of the place where the actor acts. . . .

[Question: Why is it any more significant that a state gives someone a "privilege," than that the policy of its law is not to impose liability for a certain type of conduct?]

§384. Recognition of Foreign Cause of Action

(1) If a cause of action in tort is created at the place of wrong, a cause of action will be recognized in other states.

(2) If no cause of action is created at the place of wrong, no recovery in tort can be had in any other state. . . .

§385. Contributory Negligence

Whether contributory negligence of the plaintiff precludes recovery in whole or in part in an action for negligent injury is determined by the law of the place of wrong.

§386. Liability to Servant for Tort of Fellow Servant

The law of the place of wrong determines whether a master is liable in tort to a servant for a wrong caused by a fellow servant. . . .

§387. Vicarious Liability

When a person authorizes another to act for him in any state and the other does so act, whether he is liable for the tort of the other is determined by the law of the place of wrong. . . .

§390. Survival of Actions

Whether a claim for damages for a tort survives the death of the tortfeasor or of the injured person is determined by the law of the place of wrong. . . .

§391. Right of Action for Death

The law of the place of wrong governs the right of action for death. . . .

[Question: Does this mean that if *X* shoots *Y* in Nebraska, which limits recoveries for wrongful death, *Y* ought to have himself transported to New York before he dies because New York has no such limitation?]

§398. Compensation under Act of State of Employment

A workman who enters into a contract of employment in a state in which a Workmen's Compensation Act is in force can recover compensation under the Act in that state for bodily harm arising out of and in the course of the employment, although the harm was suffered in another state, unless the Act provides in specific words or is so interpreted as to apply only to bodily harm occurring within the state. . . .

[Question: Does this provision boil down to anything more than that the person can recover unless he can't? If not, what is the meaning of the words, "unless the Act . . . is so interpreted as to apply only to bodily harm occurring within the state"? *Cf.* the treatment of this issue in the *Carroll* case above.]

§399. Compensation under Act of State of Harm

Except as stated in §401, a workman may recover in a state in which he sustains harm under the Workmen's Compensation Act of that state although the contract of employment was made in another state, unless the Act provides in specific words or is so interpreted as to apply only when the contract of employment is made within the state. . . .

§412. Measure of Damages for Tort

The measure of damages for a tort is determined by the law of the place of wrong. . . .

§421. Exemplary Damages

The right to exemplary damages is determined by the law of the place of wrong. . . .

2. Intentional Torts

Carroll involved an unintentional tort. Should the rules be different when the defendant's wrongful behavior is intentional? That question is considered in Marra v. Bushee.

Marra v. Bushee

317 F. Supp. 972 (D. Vt. 1970), *rev'd on other grounds,* 447 F.2d 1282 (2d Cir. 1971)

[The following statement of facts is taken from the opinion of the Court of Appeals: "Helen Marra, a resident of New York, brought this diversity action in the District Court for the District of Vermont against appellant Esther Bushee, a Vermont resident, to recover for the loss of consortium resulting from appellant's alienation of the affections of and criminal conversation with Allan Marra, the plaintiff's husband. The jury found in the plaintiff's favor and awarded her some $9,000 in damages. [The court] reverse[d] and remand[ed] for a new trial.

"During the latter years of their marriage Allan and Helen Marra seldom shared the same house. According to the plaintiff's testimony, her spouse's carousing, cohabitation with other women, and shifting employment took him from one locale to another, with only brief intervals of residence in her home. In July, 1968 Allan Marra returned to his wife's Granville, New York farm but left soon thereafter to take up residence in the Manchester, Vermont home of defendant Esther Bushee. During the months that followed, the defendant and the plaintiff's husband, ostensibly a boarder in the Bushee home, frequented Granville taverns, but Allan Marra did not, as before, return to his wife.

"At the close of the plaintiff's case, and again at the conclusion of all the evidence, the defendant moved for a directed verdict contending, inter alia, that under the applicable Vermont conflict-of-laws principle the law of New York, which has abolished causes of action arising from interference with the marital relationship, governed the substantive rights and liabilities of the litigants. It was the defendant's position that liability must be determined by the law of the place where the injury was incurred and that, in this instance, the loss of consortium occurred in New York, the state of the marital domicile."]

LEDDY, C.J.

This is an alienation of affections and criminal conversation case. Trial was by jury and on June 19, 1970, a verdict was returned for the plaintiff in the sum of nine thousand (9,000) dollars. At the close of the plaintiff's case, defendant moved for a directed verdict on the ground that under the applicable conflicts of law rule of the State of Vermont, the law of New York governs this cause of action and New York has abolished the cause of action of alienation of affections and criminal conversation. . . .

Although this court is inclined to agree with the defendant that the Vermont Supreme Court would follow the modern test, set out in Restatement 2d, Conflict of Laws §154 (Proposed Draft, Part II 1968), the problem is academic because under either of the two conflicts tests, Vermont law applies.

1. The Lex Loci Delecti Test

The traditional conflicts test, incorporated into the First Restatement, was that the law of the state where the wrong occurred governed the cause of action. The place of the wrong is in the state where the last event necessary to make an actor liable for an alleged tort takes place. Restatement of the Law of Conflict of Laws §377 (1934). In such a case, the last link in the chain of liability is the place where the injury was sustained. Defendant contends that if the traditional test is applied, this court should look to the place of the injury to determine whether or not the plaintiff has a cause of action for the intentional torts of alienation of affection and criminal conversation. Defendant further contends that because the injury is loss of consortium, the locus of the injury is the domicile of the plaintiff and the marital domicile, that is New York.

The first of these two contentions is based on the traditional Restatement view which looks to the place of the injury in a multistate tort situation. In 1960, the Supreme Court of Vermont adopted the "place of the injury" conflicts test in the context of a negligent tort. Goldman v. Beaudry. Without disturbing the law contained in *Goldman,* there is strong indication that considerations apart from the "place of injury" govern choice of law problems when certain types of intentional torts are involved. Although the Restatement *may* suggest otherwise, "[A]merican courts have always given, . . . preference to the law of the *place of conduct* over that of the place of harm, if the former (though not the latter) renders the defendant liable for an intentional tort." Ehrenzweig, The Place of Acting in Intentional Multistate Torts: Law and Reason Versus the Restatement, 36 Minn. L. Rev. 1, 5 (1951). (Emphasis added.) Ehrenzweig strenuously contends that there is a distinction for conflicts purposes between negligent torts which are primarily compensatory in character and properly subject to the place of the harm rule, and intentional torts, such as alienation of affections, which are primarily admonitory in character, closely related to the criminal sanction, requiring the application of the laws of the state in which the wrongful conduct has occurred.

The case of Gordon v. Parker offers a good illustration of this distinction. In *Gordon,*

> A domiciliary of Pennsylvania sued in the federal court in Massachusetts for the alienation of his wife's affections by acts committed in the state of the forum. Defendant moved for a summary judgment under a Pennsylvania statute barring actions of this type and alleged to be applicable as

> the law of the place where the defendant's act had its chief and indeed its final consequences.

36 U. Minn. L. Rev. 1, 3 (1951). Judge Wyzanski denied the defendant's motion, holding the law of Massachusetts applicable as the law of the state in which the defendant's conduct had concededly occurred.

He concluded that the major justification for the place of the harm rule is the protection of the compensatory element which buttresses a state's designation of negligence as "wrongful conduct." When this compensatory element is dominant as it is in the ordinary negligence action, the place of the harm rule is appropriate. However, when compensation is a secondary factor and the punitive element is dominant, a state finds conduct wrongful because its people regard it as sinful or offensive to public morals, and the conduct, not the injury, is critical for purposes of applying the applicable law.

Even if the "place of injury" is the touchstone for the tort of alienation of affections under the traditional rule, the law of Vermont would still be applied, because for the purposes of this tort Vermont is the "place of the injury." Section 377 of the first Restatement of the Law of Conflict of Laws posits the place of wrong in the state where the last event necessary to make an actor liable for an alleged tort takes place. The Restatement does not distinguish between negligent compensatory torts and intentional punitive torts in applying the place of harm rule, but it does conceptualize the place of the harm differently depending on the type of injury inflicted. The defendants in this case contend that without regard to where the wrongful acts occurred, the injury must be located in the state where the plaintiff and the matrimonial domicile were located when the alienation took place. If the injury to the consortium of the plaintiff was analogous to an injury against his person, the defendant's contention would be sound. *See* Restatement of the Law of Conflict of Laws §377 Note 1 (1935). If, however, injury to consortium is conceptually similar to an injury inflicted on things or chattels, then the place of harm is the place where the force takes effect on the thing injured. *See* Restatement of the Law of Conflict of Laws §377 Note 3 (1934). When this latter concept applies, both *wrongful conduct* and *harm* can quite regularly be localized at the situs of the thing injured. A good illustration of this point is found in Section 415, comment (b) of the Restatement where, in dealing with conversion, identity between the place of the harm and the place of the wrongful conduct is assumed. Restatement, Conflict of Laws §415, Comment (b) (1934).

Conceptualizing the locus of consortium, when it is injured is more difficult than positing the situs of personal injury, or injury to chattel. Consortium involves feelings and emotions which flow between two persons. Although it may be the husband's right to retain the consortium of his wife, it does not follow that the injury is inflicted at the situs of his person or the situs of the marriage when this consortium is damaged or cut off. On the contrary, it appears that the traditional conflicts test placed the situs of the injury with the wife or husband who was lured away. The 1928 Tentative Draft of the Restatement contained a specific provision governing the conflict of laws test applicable when rights incidental to relative status were injured. Relative status was defined as " . . . a relation in which one person has a legally recognized interest in another person." Restatement No. 4, Conflict of Laws §406, Comment (a) (Tentative Draft, 1928). The rule stated that:

> *Section 406.* Rights incidental to relative status are determined by the law of that state where the person in whom the right is asserted is at the time when the right is alleged to have been violated.

Restatement No. 4, Conflict of Laws §406 (Tentative Draft 1928). Illustration (b) accompanying Tentative Section 406 gave an example solution to an alienation of affections conflicts problem:

> (b) *A,* domiciled in state *X,* has a wife *B.* While *B* is visiting *C,* her mother, in state *Y, C* persuades *B* to leave *A.* Whether *A* has a cause of action against *C* depends on the law of *Y.*

Restatement No. 4, Conflict of Laws §406, Comment (a), Illustration (b) (Tentative Draft 1928). Professor Beale notes in his commentaries on the Tentative Draft above that: "Rights incidental to relative status are created by the law of the state where the person is whose status is concerned." Restatement No. 4, Conflict of Laws, Beale's Commentaries §405 (Tentative Draft 1928). So also whether the husband has a right of action against one who entices his wife from him, or a father has a right to defend the child against attack, depends upon the law of the state where the wife or child is at the time. Restatement No. 4, Conflict of Laws, Beale's Commentaries §405 (Tentative Draft 1928). Section 406 was not included in the Official Draft of the Restatement presumably because it was felt that the general place of the harm rule covered the various specific rules contained in the tentative draft. *See* the discussion of the No. 4 tentative draft in A.L.I. Proceedings, Vol. VI at 454-478 (1928) and A.L.I. Proceedings Vol. XI at 410-475 (1934). Although the traditional rule is less than clear in a case of this nature, it appears that consortium is properly recognized as being a right of the *plaintiff* spouse, but a right which is carried by the person of the spouse who is enticed away. Support for this view of "injury" in an alienation of affections case is found in Albert v. McGrath and Orr v. Sasseman.

In *Orr,* the plaintiff husband and his wife were residents of Illinois. They spent the 1954 Christmas holidays with the wife's parents in Atlanta, Georgia. The defendant was introduced to the plaintiff and his wife shortly after their arrival in Atlanta. On or about January 1, 1955, the plaintiff returned to Illinois. The plaintiff's wife remained in Georgia until February 5, 1955. The jury in the trial court found that during the period from January 1, 1955 to February 5, 1955, the defendant alienated the affections of the plaintiff's wife. The wife returned to Illinois on February 5, where she had subsequent contacts with the defendant.

The Illinois law on alienation of affections limited the recovery to actual damages. There was no such limitation under Georgia law. The defendant contended in *Orr* that Illinois law should apply because the evidence was insufficient to establish an alienation before February 5, 1955, and that no legal rights were violated until the wife returned to Illinois. The dispute in the case centered on where the *wife* was when the affections were alienated, not where the plaintiff husband was when the harm occurred. Judge Jones suggests that if the alienation took place before February 5, 1955, as the jury found it did, then it could not have occurred in Illinois because the defendant had not been ". . . in the company of the *plaintiff's wife* in the state as of that date." Although the plaintiff was in Georgia until January 1, 1955, it was not contended by either party at the trial that the alienation occurred before January 1, 1955, while the husband was in Georgia. Indeed the defendant contended that the plaintiff's wife returned from Georgia with her affection for her husband intact. Id. at 185. Both the trial court and the Circuit Court found the place of injury to be with the wife and the law of Georgia was applied when the jury found that the injury occurred while the wife was in Georgia, and not after she returned to Illinois. I am satisfied that under the traditional "place of the injury" test the locus of the harm in the tort of alienation of affections is the state where the alienated spouse is when the enticement occurs.

In summary, then, the traditional lex loci delecti rule points to Vermont for two reasons: (1) assuming that the place of injury controls as a general rule, the place of conduct controls in the context of an intentional tort when the punitive element of the tort is dominant and the place of conduct renders the defendant liable while the place of injury does not; (2) even if the distinction above is not adhered to, the place of the injury would be the place of the conduct (Vermont) in this case because consortium follows the alienated spouse through whom it is claimed and not the plaintiff.

Questions and Comments

(1) The Second Circuit reversed, 447 F.2d 1282 (2d Cir. 1971), on the basis that the factual question of the "territorial location of Esther Bushee's alluring conduct required a factual determination, and that that determination had to be made by the jury." The court distinguished factual questions necessary for determinations of personal jurisdiction, which it conceded were the proper province of the trial judge.

(2) The court of appeals not only determined that the location of the facts was a question for the jury, as indicated in note (1), but also made it clear that the determinative issue was where the defendant's conduct had "primarily occurred"—the state in which the conduct occurred would be the state whose law was applicable. Is that the only sensible way to resolve the

issue? Would it not be equally reasonable to say that if conduct occurred in both states and one of them, Vermont, made it tortious, that was enough to support a case based on the Vermont conduct? If so, what if there are two (or more) separate elements to a tort, and one occurs in a state that recognizes the tort while the other occurs in a state that does not?

(3) Does an intentional tort deserve any different analysis from that given an unintentional tort? The court emphasizes the intent of the state where the defendant was acting to discourage wrongful behavior. But what if the behavior had taken place in New York, which did not recognize the tort, while the harm occurred in Vermont, which did? Wouldn't Vermont's interest in compensation (apart from the question of whether it should be able to punish behavior occurring outside its borders) be enough to apply its own law? If so, is Vermont law getting applied too often, at the expense of New York law?

(4) Before applying the lex loci approach, the court in Marra v. Bushee states its opinion that the Supreme Court of Vermont would follow a more modern rule. As of the year 2000, only ten states continue to adhere to the First Restatement approach to choice of law for tort cases. *See* Symeonides, Choice of Law in the American Courts in 2000: As the Century Turns, 49 Am. J. Comp. L. 1, 12 (2001). Articulate modern decisions justifying this approach include Spinozzi v. ITT Sheraton Corp., 174 F.3d 842 (7th Cir. 1999) (Posner, J.); Paul v. National Life, 352 S.E.2d 550 (W. Va. 1986), reprinted at page 327 *infra;* Fitts v. Minnesota Mining & Mfg. Co., 581 So. 2d 819 (Ala. 1991); and Winters v. Maxey, 481 S.W.2d 755 (Tenn. 1972).

(5) A defense from a different quarter may be found in a book by Cavers, The Choice-of-Law Process (1965). The book, based on a series of lectures at the University of Michigan, states five imaginary cases and the opinions of various "judges," all prominent conflicts scholars. Each of the opinions was shown to the real-life professorial counterpart of the fictional judge and was revised to meet his reactions. Professor Griswold's defense of the traditional system more or less boils down to three points:

(a) If the applicable law is not independent of the forum in which the action is brought, lawyers will not be able to advise their clients as to what course to pursue.
(b) It might be advantageous to plaintiffs to forum-shop or file multiple lawsuits.
(c) The notion of "law" is unitary, and a system that allows results to differ on the basis of forum is therefore not law.

Do these criticisms stand up to close inspection? Take the first example. Presumably it is important for parties to know as much as possible about their prospects in court before they get to court. This allows planning and probably encourages out-of-court settlement. But how often will the plaintiff be able to obtain jurisdiction over the defendant in more than one or two states? And how often will the potential for differing results be realized—*i.e.*, won't courts from different states very often have the same opinion as to the just result, even if they abandon lex loci? And finally, if it is assumed that the plaintiff will choose the forum whose conflicts principles are most favorable to the plaintiff's position, isn't the only uncertainty remaining that of predicting what that particular forum will do? After a state has settled on the conflicts principles it prefers, is the uncertainty likely to be any greater than in any other kind of case?

(6) What's wrong with forum-shopping? We are all taught during our first year in law school that it is evil—and that Erie Railroad v. Tompkins conquered it. But there are obvious differences, aren't there, between the kind of forum-shopping that *Erie* prevents (federal versus state court) and the kind that Professor Griswold would like to do away with? For one, *Erie* rested in part on the absence of lawmaking authority in the federal courts—that is, by applying a federal common law to cases without federal issues in them, the federal courts were making law, even though the Constitution did not give the federal government power to make law in these areas (or, if it did, allocated that power to the Congress). But when the question is that of forum-shopping among states that have some connection with the underlying dispute, is there any question about lawmaking authority of both states?

None of the above, of course, demonstrates that forum-shopping is good; rather a mere distinction is made between two types of forum-shopping. What are the arguments against interstate forum-shopping? It may be felt that the plaintiff has an unfair advantage by being able to choose the forum with the favorable law. But doesn't the very fact that one forum's law favors the plaintiff legitimate the plaintiff's position? Assume plaintiff chooses State *A*, with favorable law. Presumably State *A* adheres to its law because it thinks that law is best. Assume further that State *B* is another possible forum for the plaintiff, and that forum *B* has law that is unfavorable to the plaintiff. Should State *A* deliberately choose what it sees as the wrong result in order to discourage the plaintiff from suing there?

Perhaps the arguments above, however, are wide of the mark. On a statistical basis, across the United States, forum-shopping by plaintiffs to obtain more favorable controlling law ought to increase the number of times plaintiffs recover, without increasing the intrinsic merits of their cases. Thus, while State *A* in the argument above might view State *B*'s choice-of-law rule as wrong, but essentially a problem for State *B*, a nationwide viewpoint might see things in terms of overall prejudices in favor of plaintiffs or defendants. Is there any way to choose between these two viewpoints?

Doesn't Professor Griswold's anxiety about the unitary nature of law arise not from our conflicts doctrines but from the fact that we have different political units that create law? Is this a fact to bemoan or to applaud?

(7) For very different but somewhat sympathetic accounts of a "rights-based" approach to choice of law, see Brilmayer, Rights, Fairness, and Choice

of Law, 99 Yale L.J. 1277 (1989); Dane, Vested Rights, Vestedness and Choice of Law, 96 Yale L.J. 1191 (1987).

B. Contracts

Selections from the First Restatement of Conflicts, on Contracts

§§311-312, 314-315, 323, 325-326, 332-336, 340, 355, 358, 360-361 (1934)

§311. Place of Contracting

The law of the forum decides as a preliminary question by the law of which state questions arising concerning the formation of a contract are to be determined, and this state is, in the Restatement of this Subject, called the "place of contracting." . . .

COMMENT . . .

d. *Determination of "place of contracting."* Under its Conflict of Laws rules, in determining the place of contracting, the forum ascertains the place in which, under the general law of Contracts, the principal event necessary to make a contract occurs. The forum at this stage of the investigation does not seek to ascertain whether there is a contract. It examines the facts of the transaction in question only so far as is necessary to determine the place of the principal event, if any, which, under the general law of Contracts, would result in a contract. Then, and not until then, does the forum refer to the law of such state to ascertain if, under that law, there is a contract, although of course there normally will be a contract unless the local law of Contracts of the state to which reference is thus made differs from the general law of Contracts as understood at the forum. . . .

[Question: Why does the forum use the general law of contracts rather than its own law or the law of some other jurisdiction? Is the general law of contracts superlaw? What is the general law of contracts? Would it matter if the states involved include Saudi Arabia or the People's Republic of China?]

§312. Formal Contract

Except as stated in §313, when a formal contract becomes effective on delivery, the place of contracting is where the delivery is made.

COMMENT

a. Formal contracts are contracts under seal, recognizances and negotiable instruments (*see* Restatement of Contracts, §7), and other contracts which are given by statute the character of formal contracts. . . .

§314. Formal Contract Completed by Mail or Carriage

When a document embodying a formal contract is to be delivered by mail or by a common carrier, the place of contracting is where the document is posted or is received by the carrier.

§315. Formal Contract Delivered by Agent

When a document embodying a formal contract is delivered through an agent of the promisor, the place of contracting is where the agent delivers it.

[Why this distinction between methods of delivery?]

§323. Informal Unilateral Contract

In the case of an informal unilateral contract, the place of contracting is where the event takes place which makes the promise binding.

ILLUSTRATIONS

1. An offer of reward for the arrest of a felon is published in state *X*. The felon is arrested in response to the offer, in state *Y*. The contract for reward is made in *Y*.

2. A father in state *X* promises his son $10,000 if he marries *M*. The son marries *M* in state *Y*. The contract for payment of the money is made in *Y*. . . .

§325. Informal Bilateral Contract

In the case of an informal bilateral contract, the place of contracting is where the second promise is made in consideration of the first promise.

Illustration

1. *A* and *B* being in state *X*, *A* offers to buy *B*'s horse for one hundred dollars, the offer to remain open for ten days. Five days later *A* meets *B* in state *Y* and *B* there accepts *A*'s offer. The contract for the sale of the horse is made in *Y*.

§326. Acceptance Sent from One State to Another

When an offer for a bilateral contract is made in one state and an acceptance is sent from another state to the first state in an authorized manner the place of contracting is as follows:

(a) If the acceptance is sent by an agent of the acceptor, the place of contracting is the state where the agent delivers it;

(b) if the acceptance is sent by any other means, the place of contracting is the state from which the acceptance is sent. . . .

Illustration

1. *A* in state *X* offers by mail to pay *B* in state *Y* $100 for a certain horse if *B* will agree to sell the horse. *B* mails a letter of acceptance in state *Z*. The letter is carried through the mails and delivered by a postman to *A* in *X*. The place of contracting for the sale of the horse is *Z*.

Comment . . .

b. *Acceptance by telegraph.* When an acceptance is authorized to be sent by telegraph, the place of contracting is where the message of acceptance is received by the telegraph company for transmission.

c. *Acceptance by telephone.* When an acceptance is to be given by telephone, the place of contracting is where the acceptor speaks his acceptance. . . .

§332. Law Governing Validity of Contract

The law of the place of contracting determines the validity and effect of a promise with respect to

(a) capacity to make the contract;

(b) the necessary form, if any, in which the promise must be made;

(c) the mutual assent or consideration, if any, required to make a promise binding;

(d) any other requirements for making a promise binding;

(e) fraud, illegality, or any other circumstances which make a promise void or voidable;

(f) except as stated in §358, the nature and extent of the duty for the performance of which a party becomes bound;

(g) the time when and the place where the promise is by its terms to be performed;

(h) the absolute or conditional character of the promise. . . .

§333. Capacity to Contract

The law of the place of contracting determines the capacity to enter into a contract.

Comment

a. *Distinction between capacity to make contract and capacity to transfer property.* There is a distinction between capacity to make a contract and capacity to transfer property. The capacity to transfer land is governed by the law of the state where the land is (*see* §216), but capacity to make a contract for the transfer of land is governed by the law of the place of contracting. So too, capacity to transfer a chattel is governed by the law of the state where the chattel is at the time of the conveyance (*see* §255), but capacity to make a contract for the transfer of a chattel is governed by the law of the place of contracting.

Illustrations

1. *A*, a married woman, contracts in state *X* to transfer to *B* land in state *Y*. By the law of *X*, a married woman has capacity to make such a contract; by the law of *Y*, she has no capacity to make such a contract, but she can transfer her land. The contract will be specifically enforced in a court of *Y*.

2. *A*, a married woman, contracts in state *X* to sell to *B* a horse then in state *Y*. By the law of *Y*, title to a chattel passes as the result of a valid contract to sell. By the law of *X*, a married woman has capacity to contract for the sale of a chattel; by the law of *Y*, she has not. Title to the horse passes to *B* who is obligated to pay for it according to the law of *X*.

§334. Formalities for Contracting

The law of the place of contracting determines the formalities required for making a contract.

COMMENT . . .

b. *Statutes of frauds.* The requirements of writing may be a requirement of procedure or a requirement of validity, or both. If, for instance, the statute of frauds of the place of contracting is interpreted as meaning that no evidence of an oral contract will be received by the court, it is a procedural statute, and inapplicable in the courts of any other state (*see* §598). If, however, the statute of frauds of the place of contracting is interpreted as making satisfaction of the statute essential to the binding character of the promise, no action can be maintained on an oral promise there made in that or any state; and if the statute of frauds of the place of contracting makes an oral promise voidable, and the promisor avoids such a promise, the same result follows. If the statute of frauds of the place of contracting is procedural only and that of the forum goes to substance only, an oral contract will be enforced though it does not conform to either statute.

§335. Sealed Instruments

The law of the place of contracting determines whether an instrument alleged to be a contract under seal is effectively sealed; whether it is duly executed and delivered; whether it is valid without consideration, and if not whether consideration has been given.

§336. Negotiable Instruments

The law of the place of contracting determines whether a mercantile instrument is negotiable, whether it is duly executed and delivered, whether it is valid without consideration, and if not, whether consideration has been given. . . .

§340. Contracts to Transfer or to Convey Land

The law of the place of contracting determines the validity of a promise to transfer or to convey land. . . .

§355. Place of Performance

The place of performance is the state where, either by specific provision or by interpretation of the language of the promise, the promise is to be performed.

COMMENT

a. The place of performance is often fixed by the contract. If the place of performance is not stated in specific words in the contract, it must be determined by construction and interpretation. A contract may be made up of several promises, each of which has its own place of performance which is different from that of the other promises. . . .

§358. Law Governing Performance

The duty for the performance of which a party to a contract is bound will be discharged by compliance with the law of the place of performance of the promise with respect to:

(a) the manner of performance;

(b) the time and locality of performance;

(c) the person or persons by whom or to whom performance shall be made or rendered;

(d) the sufficiency of performance;

(e) excuse for non-performance.

COMMENT

b. *Practical line separating question of obligation from question of performance.* While the law of the place of performance is applicable to determine the manner and sufficiency and conditions under which performance is to be made, it is not applicable to the point where the substantial obligation of the parties is materially altered. As stated in §332, Comment *c*, there is no logical line which separates questions of the obligation of the contract, which is determined by the law of the place of contracting, from questions of performance, determined by the law of the place of performance. There is, however, a practical line which is drawn in every case by the particular circumstances thereof. When the application of law of the place of contracting would extend to the determination of minute details of the manner, method, time and sufficiency of performance so that it would be an unreasonable regulation of acts in the place of performance, the law of the place of contracting will cease to control and the law of the place of performance will be applied. On the other hand, when the application of the law of the place of performance would extend to a regulation of the substance of the obligation to which the parties purported to bind themselves so that it would unreasonably determine the effect of an agreement made in the place of contracting, the law of the place of performance will give way to the law of the place of contracting. . . .

§360. Illegality of Performance

(1) If performance of a contract is illegal by the law of the place of performance at the time for performance, there is no obligation to perform so long as the illegality continues.

(2) If the legality of performance is temporary and the obligation of the contract still continues, whether the contract must be performed within a reasonable time after its performance becomes legal depends upon the law of the place of performance. . . .

§361. What Amounts to Performance

The law of the place of performance determines the details of the manner of performing the duty imposed by the contract.

Illustrations

1. *A* agrees to sell and *B* to buy goods to be inspected in state *X*. The law of *X* determines the method of inspection. . . .

Poole v. Perkins

126 Va. 33, 101 S.E. 240 (1919)

Kelly, J., delivered the opinion of the court.

On January 1, 1912, W. T. Poole and his wife F. D. Poole executed a joint promissory negotiable note to the order of Marvin Perkins. Poole and wife and Perkins at that time resided and were domiciled in the city of Bristol, Tennessee. More than a year after the execution of the note, but prior to the institution of this suit, all of the parties, makers and payee, became and since remained residents of and domiciled in Virginia. The note was dated, signed and delivered in Tennessee, but upon its face was payable at a bank in the city of Bristol, Virginia.

According to the laws of the State of Tennessee in force at the time of the execution and delivery of the note, and for some time thereafter, the contracts of a married woman were voidable and could not be enforced against her where there was a plea of coverture, but at the time of the institution of this suit the disability of coverture had been removed by statute in Tennessee so far as concerns the contracts of married women subsequent to the passage of the statute. This is a proceeding by notice of motion brought by Perkins against Mrs. F. D. Poole in the Circuit Court of Wythe county to recover judgment on the note. All matters of law and fact having been submitted to the court without the intervention of a jury, a judgment was rendered against her, and she thereupon obtained this writ of error.

There were other issues in the lower court, but the sole question before us is whether Mrs. Poole's common law disability of coverture at the time of the execution of the note can be successfully relied upon by her as a defense.

If the note had been made payable in Tennessee, it is clear that her plea of coverture would have been good. The reason and authority for this proposition are perfectly familiar and require no elaboration or citation. If the obligation can be enforced against her at all, it is because the note was payable in Virginia. Does the fact that it was so payable enable us to apply the law of this State in determining her capacity to make the contract? If so, it is conceded that she was liable, and that the judgment complained of is right.

It would be idle to say that the question is free from difficulty. There are substantial reasons for a difference of legal opinion and the authorities upon the subject are by no means in harmony. The exact question has never been decided in this State. It would be impossible in an opinion of reasonable length to review all of the authorities bearing upon the subject, and it would perhaps be unprofitable to do so if such a thing were feasible.

In the case of Freeman's Bank v. Ruckman, Judge Moncure announced the following general rule upon which there is practically no conflict of opinion:

> It is a general rule that every contract as to its validity, nature, interpretation and effect, or, as they may be called, the right, in contradistinction to the remedy, is governed by the law of the place where it is made, unless it is to be performed in another place, and then it is governed by the law of the place where it is to be performed.

This familiar and well settled rule, however, cannot be said to be conclusive of the instant case because as the same was applied by Judge Moncure, and as most commonly illustrated by decided cases, it does not relate specifically to the capacity of the parties to make a contract, but to the validity and effect of a contract made by concededly competent parties.

Prof. Raleigh C. Minor, in his excellent "Conflict of Laws," says at page 410:

> The only law that can operate to create a contract is the law of the place where the contract is entered into (lex celebrationis). If the parties enter into an agreement in a particular State the law of that State alone can determine whether a contract has been made. If by the law of that State no contract has been made, there is no contract. Hence, if by the lex celebrationis the parties are incapable of making a binding contract there is no contract upon which the law of any other State can operate. It is void ab initio.

And the author in support of the text quotes from the opinion in Campbell v. Crampton, 2 Fed. 417, 423, as follows:

> Upon principle, no reason can be alleged why a contract, void for want of capacity of the party at the place where it is made, should be held good because it provides that it shall be performed elsewhere, and nothing can be found in any adjudication or text book to support such a conclusion. It is a solecism to speak of that transaction as a contract which cannot be a contract because of the inability of the persons to make it such.

Strong support for the opinion thus advanced is also found in [several cases].

In opposition to the above view is the following pronouncement by one of the most eminent of Virginia law writers, Prof. John B. Minor:

> The law which is to govern in relation to the capacity of parties to enter into a contract is much disputed by the *continental* jurists of Europe. In general, however, they hold that *the law of the party's domicile* ought to govern. But the doctrine of the common law is well established both in England and America that the capacity of parties to contract is with some few exceptions determined by the lex loci contractus—that is, the law of the place *with reference to which the contract is made,* which is usually the place where *it is made,* unless it is to be performed *in another place or country,* and then the law of that country.

We are disposed to accept the latter as the rule applicable to the instant case, for reasons which we shall now point out.

It is to be observed, in the outset, that with practical unanimity the authorities, even those relied upon by the plaintiff in error, hold that the disability of coverture arising from the law of the married woman's domicile does not follow her into other States, and that if she goes into another State than that of her domicile and makes a contract *valid by and to be performed in accordance with the* laws of such other State, she will be bound thereby, even though she would not have been competent to make the contract according to the laws of her own State. In such a case the law of the place where the contract is made will be enforced wherever the suit is brought, even in the State of her domicile, subject only to the exception that if the suit is brought in a jurisdiction whose law imposes upon married women a total incapacity to bind themselves by any contract whatever, then perhaps for reasons of public policy the contract will not be enforced. It follows, therefore, beyond question, that if Mrs. Poole had merely stepped across the State line between Bristol, Tenn., and Bristol, Virginia, and signed the note in the latter State, she would be held liable thereon in a suit brought in any State where a married woman can contract, including now the State of Tennessee.

It will be found, too, from an examination of the authorities last above cited, to which many others of like tenor and effect might be added, that most of them concede that the actual bodily presence of the contracting party is not necessary to make the contract valid according to the laws of some other State than that of the domicile. If, for example, in the instant case Mrs. Poole had delivered the note to Perkins by mailing or sending it to him in Virginia, then by the clear weight of authority she would have bound herself in accordance with the laws of the State of Virginia as fully as if she had actually crossed the State line and signed and delivered the note in that jurisdiction. This is unmistakably implied even in the New York case of Union National Bank v. Chapman, *supra,* so strongly relied upon by the plaintiff in error.

We are brought, therefore, to this question: If Mrs. Poole had actually come into Virginia and signed the note, or had sent it here for delivery and acceptance, would there have been any substantial legal difference between the case as thus supposed and the case as it actually exists? We think not. It may be stated as settled law that when parties make contracts which upon their face are to be discharged in a State other than that in which they are executed, they are presumed, in the absence of anything to the contrary, to have intended the law of the State of performance, the lex loci solutionis, to control, and thus, if intention can do so, to have voluntarily constituted the law of that State the law of the contract, or, as often otherwise expressed, the proper law or the governing law. So unanimous are the authorities on this proposition that those advocating the actual situs of the parties as the test of contractual capacity concede that if the intent in such cases is effective then they are in error and the lex loci solutionis must be regarded as the governing law.

The adoption of the intention of the parties to the contract as the true criterion is consistent with the reason which Prof. Minor assigns for his opinion that *the proper law* is the law of the place where the contract is actually signed. He says:

> It may be regarded as certain that if the party enters into a contract in the State of his domicile, though the contract is to be performed elsewhere, the proper law governing his capacity to enter into the contract is the lex domicilii no matter where the suit may be brought. But if the contract is entered into in a State other than the party's domicile, he has not the same right to claim the protection of his domiciliary law. He has voluntarily entered into another State and has there made an agreement with persons who are relying upon the law under which he is acting. To that law he has submitted himself when he makes the contract there, and a just comity will ordinarily demand that the sovereignty of that State over all acts done there should be respected in other States.

(Conflict of Laws, p. 145.) If the parties, by the mere act of signing in a State other than their domicile can give validity to a contract which would not be valid in their own State, and if the reason for this is that they are presumed to contract with reference to the law of such other State, it would seem to follow that the actual situs of the parties is only important as a factor in determining the law with reference to which they intended to contract. In this view, all that is needed to divest a married woman of her domiciliary incapacity is an intention sufficiently evidenced or expressed to contract with reference to the laws of a State in which the contract is valid, and, as we have just seen, where the contract, like the one involved in the instant case, provides upon its face for performance in a State whose laws will uphold it, such provision is alone sufficient to evidence an intention to bring the contract within the influence of the laws of the latter State [citing cases]. These cases did not involve the question of contractual capacity, but granting that the intention of the parties determines the proper law, the decisions here cited are conclusive of the proposition that the note in litigation, by providing for payment in Virginia, sufficiently expressed such intention. Citations to the same effect might be multiplied indefinitely. . . .

We conclude, therefore, that the note sued on in this case must be construed as having been executed with reference to the laws of the State of Virginia; that it became to all legal intents and purposes, so far as its validity is concerned, as truly a Virginia note as if it had been signed and delivered here; that by the laws of this State, Mrs. Poole could have legally executed the same; and that, therefore, the lower court was right in holding her liable.

The judgment is accordingly affirmed.

Linn v. Employers Reinsurance Corp.

392 Pa. 58, 139 A.2d 638 (1958)

Opinion by COHEN, J.

Plaintiff insurance brokers brought this action in law to require the defendant insurance company to account and pay to them commissions on insurance premiums received since 1953 from a New Jersey company. At the close of plaintiff's evidence, the trial judge entered a nonsuit which the court en banc refused to remove, and this appeal followed.

From the undisputed evidence it appears that in 1926 the plaintiffs were engaged in the insurance brokerage business in Philadelphia. In that year plaintiffs offered to place risks undertaken by the Selected Risks Insurance Company of New Jersey for a consideration of five per cent of all premiums collected by the defendant on such policies. Plaintiff Linn went to New York City to negotiate an agreement with one William Ehmann, an agent of the defendant. Ehmann stated that he would first have to obtain authority to accept the offer from the defendant's home office in Kansas City. He promised that he would communicate with the plaintiff "as soon as he could get word from Kansas City." Linn then returned to Philadelphia, and subsequently received a telephone call from Ehmann accepting the offer.

The defendant entered into the required treaty with the New Jersey company which, as modified and renewed, continues in effect. From 1926 until 1953 the defendant paid the plaintiffs the agreed upon commissions. But in 1953, the defendant notified the plaintiffs that it did not consider itself obligated further under the contract and that it would discontinue accounting to the plaintiffs for the premiums received from the New Jersey company.

On this evidence the trial judge found that the contract was made in New York, and applying the New York Statute of Frauds, held that the agreement was unenforcible thereunder because it was not to be performed within one year from the date it was entered into. Wherefore, the court concluded that the defendant was under no duty to account.

We recognize that the formal validity of a contract is determined by the law of the state in which the contract was made. Since the provisions of the Statute of Frauds relate to formal validity, it is to the statute of the place of contracting that we must refer.[3] It is therefore necessary for us to determine in which state the contract was made.

When a principal authorizes an agent to accept an offer made by a third party, as the defendant authorized Ehmann in the present case, the place of contracting is where the agent accepts the offer. In the case of acceptance by mail or telegraph, the act of acceptance is held to be effective where the acceptance was posted, or received by the telegraph company for transmission.

This court has not heretofore been required to determine the place where an acceptance spoken over the telephone is effective.

Professor Williston and the Restatement of Contracts take the position that a contract made over the telephone is no different from a contract made where the parties orally address one another in each other's presence. In the latter case the offeror does not have the risk of hearing an acceptance addressed to him, and a contract is formed only if the acceptance is heard. Consequently, the place of contracting is where the acceptance is heard and not where the acceptance is spoken. While we agree that this analysis represents a sound theoretical view, the reported cases which consider this issue are uniform in holding that by analogy to the situations in which acceptance is mailed or telegraphed, an acceptance by telephone is effective, and a contract is created at the place where the acceptor speaks. Restatement, Conflict of Laws, *supra*, §326, comment *c*. In fact, where the federal courts are charged with the duty of applying Pennsylvania law they have reached this conclusion.

We believe that in this day of multistate commercial transactions it is particularly desirable that the determination of the place of contracting be the same regardless of the state in which suit is brought. The absence of uniformity makes the rights and liabilities of parties to a contract dependent upon the choice of the state in which suit is instituted and thus encourages "forum-shopping." For this reason we choose to follow the established pattern of decisions and hold that acceptance by telephone of an offer takes place where the words are spoken.

Applying this principle to the facts before us, we conclude that the state where the contract was made is the state from which Ehmann telephoned the defendant's acceptance to Linn. However, contrary to the trial court's deter-

---

3. The rules embodied in the Pennsylvania Statute of Frauds are matters of substance, not procedure, and apply only to contracts made in Pennsylvania.

mination, there is no evidence in the record to indicate from which state Ehmann spoke. It is likely that he telephoned from his New York office, but it is also possible that he called from Kansas City or even Philadelphia; we cannot substitute speculation for evidence. The record of this case, therefore, must be remitted to the court below for determination of this question.

Judgment reversed and record remanded for further proceedings in accordance with this opinion. Costs to abide the event.

[Upon remand the case was tried, and on a second appeal, 397 Pa. 153, 153 A.2d 638 (1958), the court went over some of the same ground and added the following discussion of the determination of where the contract was made.] The court below submitted the issue of where the contract was made to the jury:

> The question is simply this: Was this contract completed and made in New York? Was the acceptance made in New York? Whether that acceptance be by the spoken word over the telephone to Mr. Linn or whether it was by an act of Mr. Ehmann which was in the nature of an acceptance, could only be construed as an acceptance.
>
> If the acceptance was not in New York but was at any other place, your verdict should be for the plaintiffs. If, however, it was in New York, your verdict must be for the defendant.

The jury returned a verdict for the plaintiffs upon which the court entered an order for the accounting.

. . . At least the jury, by its verdict, has determined that defendant's contention as to the applicability of New York law has not been sustained by the evidence. Testimony was presented to them adequate to support their finding that a telephone call of acceptance was made and that the said telephone call was not made in the State of New York. While it is true that plaintiffs have the ultimate burden of proof in convincing the jury that a valid contract was entered into, the burden of producing evidence to show that this contract was made in New York was alleged and necessarily assumed by defendant.* This burden was not met. Since it was not established that the laws of New York are applicable, the laws of the forum, Pennsylvania, are presumed to apply. Unlike the New York Statute of Frauds the various provisions in the Pennsylvania statute do not require that an agreement of this sort be in writing even if it is not to be performed within a year. It has been said that the Statute of Frauds, where applicable, is not a mere rule of evidence, but rather, is a limitation of judicial authority to afford a remedy. Our statutes do not so limit the authority of this court to grant a remedy in this case. . . .

In the light of the disposition we make of this case it is unnecessary for us to consider plaintiff's contention that even if the New York Statute of

* What is the nature of the presumption the defendant must defeat?—Ed.

Frauds does apply its effect was waived by the admission of defendant's counsel that an oral agreement had been entered into.

Judgment affirmed.

Questions and Comments

(1) The *Poole* court's position seems to boil down to allowing the parties' intent to control resolution of the choice-of-law question. Why should intent control? What was the purpose of the common-law rule relied on by F. D. Poole as a defense against the obligation of her note? *Compare* Milliken v. Pratt, 125 Mass. 374, 382 (Mass. 1878) (stating that "continental jurists" maintain that "laws limiting the capacity of infants or of married women are intended for their protection, and cannot therefore be dispensed with by their agreement; that all civilized states recognize the incapacity of infants and married women."). Is it likely that a law that voided a married woman's efforts to obligate herself on a promissory note was meant to be applicable, or not, depending on her intent? Wasn't the law intended to frustrate her intent? Note, however, that not all (or even most) state contract laws are "mandatory" in the sense of placing limits on party intent. To the contrary, many contract issues are governed by state laws viewed as "defaults" that apply unless the parties vary them in the contract. Is the distinction between default and mandatory rules of contract law relevant to intent-based theories of choice of law for contract? How? What are the advantages and disadvantages of allowing party intent to control contractual choice-of-law issues?

Assuming that intent is the appropriate criterion, how should courts determine which state's law the parties intended to choose? If the contract contains a choice-of-law clause that recites that the contract is to be governed by the law of State *X*, the matter is not too difficult. But what if the contract contains no choice-of-law clause? Is it likely that the parties in *Poole* specifically intended Virginia law to operate by virtue of their choice of a Virginia bank as the place of payment? If the intent of the parties is to govern with respect to capacity, why not pick the state whose law upholds the contract? That is, in fact, the rule chosen by some jurisdictions, sometimes referred to as the *lex validitatis. See, e.g.*, Pritchard v. Norton, 106 U.S. 124 (1882).

(2) *Poole*'s intent-based approach for questions of contractual capacity is at odds with the First Restatement, which nowhere mentions the intent theory, but instead asserts that the "law of the place of contracting determines the capacity to enter into a contract." *See* Restatement §333 (reproduced *supra* page 26). *Poole* thus makes clear that there were many different, and sometimes incompatible, strands to the traditional approach to choice of law for contracts. Beale, the author of the First Restatement, believed that party intent was impossible to discern with certainty. More fundamentally, he thought that party intent (including party intent as embodied in a choice-of-

law clause) could not control because it would amount to "the power to do a legislative act"—a power that Beale believed private persons necessarily lacked. *See* 2 Beale, A Treatise on the Conflict of Laws §332.2 (1935). Do you agree with Beale? Is an intent-based rule inconsistent with a vested rights approach? Do you see why one committed to the "law of the place of the wrong" for torts might insist that the "law of the place of contract" governs contractual capacity issues? For an argument that the Restatement's approach to contracts is inconsistent with then-prevailing case law and theoretically unattractive, see Nussbaum, Conflict Theories of Contracts: Cases Versus Restatement, 51 Yale L. Rev. 893 (1942).

(3) Does *Poole*'s focus on intent suggest an important difference between choice of law for contract and for tort? How, if at all, should these differences translate into differences in the content of choice-of-law rules?

(4) A promissory note is said by the court to be "performed" at the place of payment. Although the opinion does not say so, presumably the Poole note was signed in return for the loan of money. Wasn't that lending by the lender the lender's performance? Why doesn't the court ask where the lender's performance took place? If Perkins lent the Pooles the money in Tennessee, should Tennessee law govern Perkins's obligations while Virginia law governs the Pooles' obligations?

(5) The *Poole* court cites another case at one point for the proposition that "every contract as to its validity . . . is governed by the law of the place where it is made, unless it is to be performed in another place, and then it is governed by the law of the place where it is to be performed." Wouldn't it be a trifle simpler to say, "every contract as to its validity . . . is governed by the law of the place where it is to be performed"? Isn't that observation so obvious that it makes you a little suspicious of the court's confidence in a rule it won't state simply?

(6) If some ambiguity exists as to where performance occurred, or whose performance is critical, or whether the law of the place of contracting or performance is the applicable law, is the resulting uncertainty necessarily bad? Consider the fact that the court adjudicating F. D. Poole's obligation was a Virginia court and Virginia had no coverture rule; F. D. Poole was trying to get out of an obligation that she had once (presumably) voluntarily undertaken; and the law of Tennessee had changed in the meanwhile. In Milliken v. Pratt, *supra,* the court hinted broadly that its decision was influenced by the fact that the law of Massachusetts, relied on there by a married woman to void her guaranty of her husband's debt, had been altered in the meanwhile by the legislature. Is a certain amount of flexibility in conflicts desirable in order to allow the court to reach the "right" result? If so, why not abandon the rules that need the oil of flexibility and use as rules (or method) the considerations that lead us to conclude that a particular result is "right"?

(7) In the *Poole* case the court said that it was clear that if Poole had signed the note in Virginia she would have been bound by Virginia law. It concluded that if she was going to be allowed to achieve that result by chang-

ing location, there was little reason to deny such an effect by having the parties determine the place of performance. If the court is speaking in practical terms, is its conclusion correct? How many parties far from the state line would actually make a trip elsewhere to settle a choice-of-law issue in signing their contracts?

(8) What was the purpose of the New York statute of frauds relied on by the defendant in the *Linn* case? Would its purpose vary with where the telephone call in question was made?

(9) Isn't it silly to make the entire result of an important business transaction like that in the *Linn* case turn on where the defendant's agent called from? Moreover, there are other possible problems arising from the *Linn* court's approach. Suppose that we had two scenarios of that telephone call, and suppose that the defendant's agent had in fact called from New York.

Scenario I

Linn: Bill, you ol' sun of a gun, is that you?
Ehmann: None other, Walt.
Linn: What have you heard from K.C.?
Ehmann: It's in the bag—they said OK to your offer.
Linn: Hey, baby, that's great.

Scenario II

Linn: Good morning Mr. Ehmann. How are you?
Ehmann: What's the matter, Walt? You aren't losing interest in the deal, are you?
Linn: Well . . .
Ehmann: Hey, come on, Walt. K.C. thinks it's a good idea. I could even offer you a free desk calendar every year.
Linn: How could I turn down a deal like that? Sold!
Ehmann: Hey, baby, that's great.

(Adapted from Cramton, Currie, & Kay, Conflict of Laws 25 (3d ed. 1981).) Where was the contract in Scenario I formed? In Scenario II? How well will the participants remember which of these two possible 1926 conversations took place when they go to court in 1953? Does it make sense to ignore how the parties dealt with each other for 27 years and determine their dispute by the *form* of a 1926 telephone conversation? Or is it unfair to judge a rule that works well in many cases on the basis of a possibly unusual fact situation?

(10) Note that it is the place of contract formation, and not the place of performance, that the court says determines the statute of frauds issue. Why should that be?

(11) Recall that the "last act" doctrine for torts is that the governing law is that of the state where the last act necessary for a *cause of action* occurs, while the last-act approach for contracts zeroes in on the law of the state where

the last act necessary for the formation of the contract occurs. Why not use the law of the place of breach in contracts cases, since that is the act necessary to give rise to a cause of action? It isn't necessary to do much violence to the language of the *Carroll* case to adopt a place-of-breach position for contracts that is "eminently sound in principle and upon logic":

> It is admitted, or at least cannot be denied, that [a contract without a breach] will not authorize or support a recovery. Up to the time [the breach occurred] no injury had resulted. For all that occurred in Alabama, therefore, no cause of action whatever arose. The fact which created the right to sue, the [breach] without which confessedly no action would lie anywhere, transpired in the State of Mississippi. It was in that State, therefore, necessarily that the cause of action, if any, arose; and whether a cause of action arose and existed at all or not must in all reason be determined by the law which obtained at the time and place when and where the fact which is relied on to justify a recovery transpired.

Fair?

An Exercise

On February 16, 1975, the New York Times carried an illustrated story on a case of food poisoning occurring on an international jet airliner. The following is the outline of events in the story:

(1) On February 1 a cook in Alaska handled ham to be served aboard the flight. The cook had blisters infected with staphylococcus. The ham was kept at room temperature for six hours during preparation.

(2) In Tokyo, 343 passengers boarded the flight. While the plane was flying toward Anchorage for refueling, the food trays were stored at 50° overnight. Staphylococcus multiplies at temperatures above 40° and produces a toxin that commonly causes food poisoning.

(3) The trays were loaded at Anchorage, and the plane took off for Copenhagen, its next stop.

(4) The trays were heated in a 300° oven for 15 minutes, a treatment that will not destroy the toxin, and the passengers were served. Those who ate the contaminated food began to experience the symptoms of food poisoning as the plane approached Copenhagen.

(5) In Copenhagen, 144 passengers disembarked ill. The rest flew on to Paris. Another 51 of these later became ill.

If Smith (a) arranged a tour of Japan by telephone from Michigan through American Express in New York and left from Detroit Metropolitan Airport for Japan, (b) arranged while she was in Tokyo, through the American Express office there to take a different flight and include Europe in her travels, (c) boarded in Tokyo, (d) ate the contaminated food, which was loaded in Anchorage, while flying over Canada, (e) landed in Copenhagen, where she began to feel ill but refused medical attention, and (f) continued on to Paris, where she became violently ill and died,

(1) Whose law would determine whether an action for wrongful death would be available?

(2) Whose law would determine whether negligence was a necessary part of the cause of action or whether strict liability would apply?

(3) Whose law would apply to determine whether Smith's refusal of medical assistance in Copenhagen constituted contributory negligence? Whose law would determine whether contributory negligence was a valid defense?

(4) If an action is brought by Smith's estate for violation of an implied provision of her contract of passage that she would be transported safely, whose law would apply to determine whether the airline's behavior constituted proper performance of its contract?

(5) Whose law would determine, in a contract action, whether Smith's refusal of medical assistance constituted a failure to mitigate damages, limiting her estate's recovery?

(6) Whose law should determine whether the proper action is one in tort or contract? If both are permitted, what should be done if the applicable tort law disallows recovery, while the applicable contract law (of a different jurisdiction) allows recovery?

C. Domicile

Selections from the First Restatement of Conflicts, on Domicile

§§9-16, 18-21, 23, 25, 27, 41 (1934)

§9. Domicil

Domicil is the place with which a person has a settled connection for certain legal purposes, either because his home is there, or because that place is assigned to him by the law.

§10. Domicil by What Law Determined

(1) A question of domicil as between the state of the forum and another state is determined by the law of the forum.

(2) A question of domicil as between one or another of several states other than the forum, the law of each which differs from that of the other and from that of the forum, is determined by the law of the forum.

§11. One and Only One Domicil

Every person has at all times one domicil, and no person has more than one domicil at a time.

§12. Relation between Domicil and Home

Except as stated in §§17 and 26 to 40, relating to domicil in a vehicle and to domicil by operation of law, when a person has one home and only one home, his domicil is the place where his home is.

§13. Home Defined

A home is a dwelling place of a person, distinguished from other dwelling places of that person by the intimacy of the relation between the person and the place.

§14. Domicil of Origin

(1) The domicil of origin is the domicil assigned to every child at its birth.

(2) Subject to the rule stated in §32 pertaining to divorce or separation of the parents, if the child is the legitimate child of its father, the domicil of the father at the time of its birth is assigned to it; if the child is not the legitimate child of its father, or is posthumous, the domicil assigned is that of its mother at the time of birth.

(3) Upon failure of proof of the domicil of the parent at the time of the child's birth, a court may accept as the domicil of origin the place to which a person can earliest be traced.

§15. Domicil of Choice

(1) A domicil of choice is a domicil acquired, through the exercise of his own will, by a person who is legally capable of changing his domicil.

(2) To acquire a domicil of choice, a person must establish a dwelling-place with the intention of making it his home.

(3) The fact of physical presence at a dwelling-place and the intention to make it a home must concur; if they do so, even for a moment, the change of domicil takes place.

(4) A person can acquire a domicil of choice only in one of three ways:

(a) having no home, he acquires a home in a place other than his former domicil;

(b) having a home in one place, he gives it up as such and acquires a new home in another place;

(c) having two homes, he comes to regard the one of them not previously his domicil as his principal home.

§16. Requisite of Physical Presence

To acquire a domicil of choice in a place, a person must be physically present there; but a home in a particular building is not necessary for the acquisition of a domicil.

§18. Requisite of Intention

A person cannot change his domicil by removal to a new dwelling-place without an intention to make the new dwelling place his home.

§19. Nature of Intention Required

The intention required for the acquisition of a domicil of choice is an intention to make a home in fact, and not an intention to acquire a domicil.

§20. Present Intention

For the acquisition of a domicil of choice the intention to make a home must be an intention to make a home at the moment, not to make a home in the future.

§21. Presence under Compulsion

A person cannot acquire a domicil of choice by any act done under legal or physical compulsion.

§23. Continuing Quality of Domicil

A domicil once established continues until it is superseded by a new domicil.

§25. Domicil in Dwelling-House Cut by Boundary Line

Where a person has his home in a dwelling-house which is situated upon a dividing line between political divisions of territory, his domicil is within that territorial division in which the preponderant part of his dwelling-house is situated; if there is no preponderance, the domicil is in the territorial division in which the principal entrance to the house is situated.

§27. Domicil of Married Woman

Except as stated in §28, a wife has the same domicil as that of her husband.

§41. Domicil of Corporation

A corporation is domiciled in the state where it was incorporated, and cannot acquire a domicil outside that state.

White v. Tenant

31 W. Va. 790, 8 S.E. 596 (1888)

SNYDER, J.

This is a suit brought December, 1886, in the Circuit Court of Monongalia county by William L. White and others against Emrod Tennant, administrator of Michael White deceased and Lucinda White, the widow of said Michael White, to set aside the settlement and distribution made by the administrator of the personal estate of said decedent, and to have the same settled and distributed according to the laws of the State of Pennsylvania, which State it is claimed was the domicile of said decedent, who died in this State intestate. On October 28, 1887, the court entered a decree dismissing the plaintiff's bill, and they have appealed.

The sole question presented for our determination is, whether the said Michael White at the time of his death, in May, 1885, had his legal domicile in this State or in the State of Pennsylvania. It is admitted to be the settled law, that the law of the State, in which the decedent had his domicile at the time of his death, will control the succession and distribution of his personal estate. Before referring to the facts proved in this cause, we shall endeavor to determine what in law is meant by "domicile."

Dr. Wharton says: "'Domicile' is a residence acquired as a final abode. To constitute it there must be (1) residence, actual or inchoate; (2) the nonexistence of any intention to make a domicile elsewhere." Whart. Confl. Law §21. . . . Two things must concur to establish domicile,—the fact of residence, and the intention of remaining. These two must exist, or must have existed, in combination. There must have been an actual residence. The character of the residence is of no importance; and, if domicile has once existed, mere temporary absence will not destroy it, however long continued. The original domicile continues until it is fairly changed for another. It is a legal maxim that every person must have a domicile somewhere; and he can have but one at a time for the same purpose. From this it follows that one can not be lost or extinguished until another is acquired. When one domicile is definitely abandoned and a new one selected and entered upon, length of time is not important; one day will be sufficient, provided the *animus* exists. Even when the point of destination is not reached, domicile may shift *in itinere*, if the abandonment of the old domicile and the setting out for the new are plainly shown. . . . A change of domicile does not depend so much upon the intention to remain in the new place for a definite or indefinite period as upon its being without an intention to return. . . . A domicile once acquired remains until a new one is acquired elsewhere, *facto et animo*. Story Confl. Law, §47.

The material facts in the case at bar are as follows: [In 1885, Michael White, a life-long West Virginia domiciliary, sold his farm in West Virginia. Michael had made arrangements with his family to move to a house on a forty-acre tract in Pennsylvania that was part of a larger family estate the main part of which, including the family mansion, was in West Virginia. On April 2, 1885, Michael, along with his wife Lucinda and their personal possessions, left the West Virginia home "with the declared intent and purpose of making the Pennsylvania house his home that evening." They arrived at the Pennsylvania house by sundown and unloaded their goods and stock. But because the house was cold and damp, and because Lucinda was feeling unwell, the couple returned to the mansion in West Virginia to spend the evening. When Lucinda White's illness turned out to be typhoid fever, Michael stayed at the West Virginia mansion to care for her, returning daily to the Pennsylvania home to look after it and care for the stock. Within two weeks Michael himself contracted typhoid fever and died intestate in the West Virginia mansion. Lucinda recovered, and the defendant, Emrod Tennant, Lucinda's father, administered Michael's estate in West Virginia and distributed the estate in accordance with West Virginia law, under which a widow received the decedent's entire personal estate. If the estate had been distributed under Pennsylvania law, the wife would receive only one-half of the estate, and Michael's brothers and sisters—the plaintiffs—would have received the other half.]

As the law of the State, in which the decedent had his domicile at the time of his death, must govern the distribution of his estate, the important question is, where, according to the foregoing facts, was the domicile of Michael at the time of his death? It is unquestionable, that prior to the 2d day of April, 1885, his domicile was and had been in the State of West Virginia. Did he on that day or at any subsequent day change his domicile to the State of Pennsylvania?

The facts in this case conclusively prove, that Michael White, the decedent, abandoned his residence in West Virginia with the intention and purpose not only of not returning to it, but for the expressed purpose of making a fixed place in the State of Pennsylvania his home for an indefinite time.

This fact is shown by all the circumstances as well as by his declarations and acts. He had sold his residence in West Virginia and surrendered its possession to the purchaser, and thereby made it impossible for him to return to it and make it his home. He rented a dwelling in Pennsylvania, for which he had no use except to live in and make it his home. In addition to all this, he had moved a part of his household goods into this house, and then, on the 2d of April, 1885, he with his family and the remainder of his goods and stock finally left his former home and the State of West Virginia, and moved into the State of Pennsylvania to his house in that State, and there put his goods in the house, and turned his stock loose on the premises. At the time he left his former home on that morning, and while he was on the way to his new home, his declared purpose and intention were to make that his home from that very day, and to occupy it that night. He arrived in Pennsylvania and at his new home with that intention; and it was only after he arrived there and for reasons not before known, which had no effect to change his purpose of making that his future home, that he failed to remain there from that time. There was no change in his purpose, except that after he arrived at his new home and unloaded and left his property there, he concluded on account of the condition of the house and the illness of his wife, that it would be better to go with his wife to remain one night with his relatives and return the next morning.

When he left his former home without any intention of returning and in pursuance of that intention did in fact move with his family and effects to his new home with the intention of making it his residence for an indefinite time, it is my opinion, that, when he and his wife arrived at his new home, it became *eo instanti* his domicile, and that his leaving there under the circumstances with the intention of returning the next day did not change the fact. The concurrence of his intention to make the Pennsylvania house his permanent residence with the fact, that he had actually abandoned his former residence and moved to and put his goods in the new one, made the latter his domicile. According to the authorities hereinbefore referred to he must of necessity have had a domicile somewhere. If he did not have one in Pennsylvania, where did he have one? The fact, that he left the Pennsylvania house, after he had moved to it with his family and goods, to spend the night, did not revive his domicile at his former residence on Day's run, because he had sold that, and left it without any purpose of returning there. By going from his new home to the house of his relatives to spend the night he certainly did not make the house thus visited his domicile; therefore, unless the Pennsylvania house was on the evening of April 2, 1885, his domicile, he was in the anomalous position of being without a domicile anywhere, which, as we have seen, is a legal impossibility; and, that house having become his domicile, there is nothing in this case to show, that he ever did in fact change or intend to change it or to establish a domicile elsewhere.

It follows, therefore, that that house remained his domicile up to and at the time of his death; and, that house being in the State of Pennsylvania, the laws of that State must control the distribution of his personal estate notwithstanding the fact, that he died in State of West Virginia. For these reasons the decree of the Circuit Court must be reversed, and the cause must be remanded to that court to be there further proceeded in according to the principles announced in this opinion and the rules of courts of equity.

Rodriguez Diaz v. Sierra Martinez

853 F.2d 1027 (1st Cir. 1988)

LEVIN H. CAMPBELL, C.J.

Plaintiff Wilfredo Rodriguez Diaz (Rodriguez Diaz) appeals from an order of the United States District Court for the District of Puerto Rico dismissing his complaint for negligence and medical malpractice for lack of diversity jurisdiction. Rodriguez Diaz brought this action in the district court following a motor vehicle accident in Puerto Rico when he was 17 years of age. All the defendants reside in Puerto Rico. However, between the time of the accident and the commencement of this action, Rodriguez Diaz moved from his family's home in Puerto Rico to New York, and attained his 18th birthday. He then sued in the United States District Court for the District of Puerto Rico, on his own behalf and through his parents as next friends, alleging that he is a citizen of New York and that there is diversity of citizenship under 28 U.S.C. §1332 (1982).

I

The facts relevant to the jurisdictional issue are these: On November 21, 1984, Rodriguez Diaz, while operating a motorcycle in Caguas, Puerto Rico, was in a collision with an automobile driven by Marcelo Sierra Martinez. Rodriguez Diaz suffered bodily injuries. He was immediately taken to the Hospital Regional de Caguas, from where he was transferred to the Centro Medico for emergency treatment. Rodriguez Diaz alleges in the present complaint that the treatment he received at the Centro Medico caused him to suffer a massive bone infection and aggravation of a leg injury. From Centro Medico he was transferred to Hospital General San Carlos where he alleges he also received improper treatment. Sometime later, Rodriguez Diaz was transferred to a hospital in New York City. He alleges he was living in New York at the time he brought this action in the United States District Court for the District of Puerto Rico. He further alleges in his complaint that he intends to remain in New York and make it his permanent home, and that he is now domiciled there. Rodriquez Diaz had turned 18 by the time he brought this action.[1] His parents were and still are residents and domiciliaries of Puerto Rico, where the age of majority is 21. P.R. Laws Ann. tit. 31, §971 (1967).

---

1. The age of majority in New York is 18. N.Y. Civ. Prac. L. & R. 105(j) (Supp. 1988).

The defendants in the action brought by Rodriguez Diaz were the driver of the automobile, Sierra Martinez, and two Puerto Rico hospitals, all of whom are residents and domiciliaries of Puerto Rico. The defendants moved in the United States District Court for the District of Puerto Rico where the action was brought to dismiss the complaint for lack of diversity jurisdiction. The district court concluded that, under Puerto Rico law, Rodriguez Diaz is a minor, and therefore, his domicile is that of his parents. Ruling that as a matter of law Rodriguez Diaz's domicile at the time of the filing of this action was Puerto Rico, the court dismissed the complaint for lack of diversity. This appeal followed.

In its decision, the district court observed that, for purposes of diversity jurisdiction under 28 U.S.C. §1332(a)(1), state citizenship and domicile are equivalents. The court also noted that in a diversity case the capacity of a person to sue or be sued is determined by the law of the state of the litigant's domicile. Fed R. Civ. P. 17(b). The court then made certain observations crucial to its analysis. These were that the citizenship of a minor was the citizenship of his parents, and that the latter's domicile determined whether the minor had become emancipated so that he could establish a domicile of choice elsewhere. On the basis of the foregoing, the district court concluded that the law of Puerto Rico—the home of Rodriguez Diaz's parents—controlled the issue of Rodriguez Diaz's present domicile. As under Puerto Rico law plaintiff was still a minor, being under 21 at the time of suit, and as he was unemancipated under Puerto Rico law, he could not establish a domicile of choice outside Puerto Rico. It followed that he was still a domiciliary of Puerto Rico, and that, therefore, there was no diversity of citizenship.

II

While the case is close, we disagree with the district court's conclusion that the domicile of Rodriguez Diaz's parents—Puerto Rico—is the jurisdiction whose law must necessarily determine his capacity to acquire a domicile of choice.

We begin with certain generally accepted principles: As the lower court correctly noted, state citizenship[2] for diversity purposes is ordinarily equated

---

2. Section 1332(a)(1) provides,

> The district courts shall have original jurisdiction of all civil actions where the matter in controversy exceeds the sum or value of $10,000, exclusive of interest and costs, and is between—
>
> (1) citizens of different States; . . .

Section 1332(d) provides,

> The word "States" as used in this section includes the Territories, the District of Columbia, and the Commonwealth of Puerto Rico.

with domicile. A person's domicile "is the place where he has his true, fixed home and principal establishment, and to which, whenever he is absent, he has the intention of returning." Domicile generally requires two elements: 1) physical presence in a state, and 2) the intent to make such a state a home. It is the domicile at the time the suit is filed which controls, and the fact that the plaintiff has changed his domicile with the purpose of bringing a diversity action in federal court is irrelevant. Thus, except for the possible effect of his being a minor under Puerto Rico law, plaintiff's settling in New York with the requisite domiciliary intent would make him a citizen of New York and entitle him to pursue this action.

The district court ruled that since plaintiff was under 21, the age of majority in Puerto Rico, he was a minor as a matter of law, and as such he could have only one domicile, that of his parents, which in this case is Puerto Rico. It so ruled even though the age of majority in[3] New York is 18, so that, in the eyes of New York, plaintiff could acquire a personal domicile of his own there. We shall assume for purposes of resolving the legal issue raised in this appeal that New York is plaintiff's "true, fixed home." . . . The question before us is whether this is enough for plaintiff to have acquired a New York domicile for diversity jurisdiction purposes.

The parties and the district court have framed the issue as one of choice of law: which law is applicable, Puerto Rico law or New York law. It is a general principle of common law, recognized also in Puerto Rico, that the domicile of an unemancipated minor is ordinarily that of his parents. The age of majority in Puerto Rico is 21, while in New York it is 18. Plaintiff was 18 when he filed this action in the United States District Court for the District of Puerto Rico. Depending on which law is applied, the argument goes, Rodriguez Diaz will be treated as an adult or as a minor, with the capacity or lack of capacity to establish his own independent domicile. Plaintiff argues that we have to apply New York law, because that was his "domicile" at the time the action was filed. Not surprisingly, defendants argued, and the district court agreed, that whether Rodriguez Diaz was an adult with capacity to establish his domicile of choice is governed by Puerto Rico law.

As we see it, resolution of the issue before us does not and should not turn solely upon a conflicts of laws analysis. Although federal courts have to apply the choice of law rules of the forum to determine the substantive law in diversity cases, the "determination of litigant's state citizenship for pur-

---

3. We emphasize, however, that the district court did not make a finding that Rodriguez Diaz (assuming he had the legal capacity to obtain a New York domicile) actually met the elements necessary to acquire a domicile there. To the extent there may be a genuine issue of fact as to plaintiff's "true, fixed home" and actual intention, our present assumption, arguendo, that his presence in New York meets these requirements, should not be taken as a final resolution of that issue. The only issue the district court addressed, and the only issue now before us, is whether, for diversity purposes, Rodriguez Diaz could have a domicile separate from that of his parents. We leave open the factual issue of whether plaintiff actually met the elements necessary to acquire a domicile of choice in New York.

poses of section 1332(a)(1) is controlled by federal common law, not by the law of any state." The issue of what substantive law applies in a diversity case "is surely a different problem from that of whether a litigant should have access to federal court, and it does not conduce to clarity of analysis to suppose that the same answers will suffice for different questions." . . . That does not mean that state law and state conflicts rules regarding domicile should be ignored. At very least, they are "useful in providing basic working definitions." Stifel v. Hopkins, 477 F.2d 1116, 1120 (6th Cir. 1973). However, as the Sixth Circuit pointed out in *Stifel,* the considerations undergirding state choice-of-law rules have often been "developed in such diverse contexts as probate jurisdiction, taxation of incomes or intangibles, or divorce laws." *Id.* Choice-of-law formulae, therefore, cannot be the sole guideposts when determining, for federal diversity purposes, whether a party is domiciled in one or another state. *Id.* at 1126. The ultimate decision must be such as will best serve the aims of the federal diversity statute and the perspectives of a nationwide judicial system.

III

In the case at bar, the district court noted that in a suit brought by the next friend, the minor's domicile was controlling for diversity purposes. The court went on to state,

> Under the common law, the citizenship of a minor is the citizenship of his parents, and to determine whether the minor has become emancipated so that he may establish a domicile of choice, we look to the law of the state of the citizenship of his parents.

After noting the dilemma caused by the fact Rodriguez Diaz had achieved majority status in New York, his present home, at age 18, while remaining a minor under Puerto Rico law, the court rejected plaintiff's argument that he had the capacity to acquire a domicile of choice in New York. The court stated, "[w]e have already concluded that the law of Puerto Rico controls the issue of Wilfredo's [Rodriguez Diaz's] domicile."

The district court went on to show that, by Puerto Rico's standards, plaintiff was unemancipated, given Puerto Rico's strict civil law requirement that emancipation occur by formal notarized document.

The difficulty with this rationale, as we see it, lies in the court's basic premise that the law of Puerto Rico controls. If Rodriguez Diaz were clearly a minor (under, say, both New York and Puerto Rico law), the court's analysis would be hard to fault. The domicile of a minor is commonly regarded as that of his parents; as Rodriguez Diaz's parents were domiciled in Puerto Rico, the law of Puerto Rico would ordinarily be controlling as to the means whereby, being a minor, he could be emancipated and so become free to acquire a domicile of choice.[4]

The problem here, however, is that the question is not whether, as a minor, plaintiff was emancipated, but whether *he is a minor.* That, in turn, depends upon a determination of where he is domiciled, the ultimate question. We do not, therefore, find the district court's analysis persuasive.

This is not to say that Puerto Rico may not properly believe that the interest it has in its own citizens includes a legitimate concern as to the age at which a minor child reaches majority. Whether and when a person has legal capacity to, among other things, sue in Puerto Rico's own courts, make contracts, dispose of property, and sustain himself without parental support or reciprocal duty owed to his parents, are all matters properly within the state's province. However, local interests of this character are not in issue here. Rodriguez Diaz's right of access to a federal court is "one uniquely of federal cognizance." Ziady v. Curley, 396 F.2d [873 (4th Cir. 1968)] at 874; and since Rodriguez Diaz is now physically present in New York, which regards him, at 18, as having the capacity to be its domiciliary, we must weigh a ruling that would extend Puerto Rico's less favorable policy towards 18 year olds against one that would accord to plaintiff the mature status he enjoys under the law of the state in which he now resides.

In any event, the court below erred in assuming at the very outset of its inquiry that Rodriguez Diaz was a minor and, on that basis, invoking the law of his parents' domicile in preference to that of his present physical residence, which does not view him as a minor.

A similar logical difficulty occurs when we turn to the alternative approaches urged by appellees. For example, appellees point to Section 9 of the Puerto Rico Civil Code providing that,

---

4. We agree that, ordinarily, if a person is under 18, federal courts should follow the common law principle that he is incapable of choosing his own domicile. There is a general understanding that a person under 18 lacks the full capacity to conduct his life as he will. The years between 18 and 21, however, are currently a twilight zone. The majority of the states have adopted 18 as the age of majority. . . . A person 18 or older has the constitutional right to vote in federal and state elections. U.S. Const. amendment XXVI. Nonetheless, some states, like Puerto Rico, still consider a person under 21, but 18 or older, to be incapable (unless formally emancipated) of conducting his personal life. Although this policy is entitled to respect in federal courts for substantive law purposes, we see no necessary reason to give it special deference for diversity jurisdictional purposes when it conflicts with another state's policy judgment that an 18 year old living within its borders is of legal age and fully capable of choosing the place he regards as home. Puerto Rico, in fact, recognizes that a child may be emancipated with parental consent and, thereafter, although under age, will be capable of choosing a domicile of his own. It is generally recognized that even persons lacking the capacity to enter into contracts and other legal arrangements may have sufficient capacity to select a domicile of choice. R. Weintraub, Commentary on the Conflicts of Laws §2.4, at 18 (1980).

> The laws relating to family rights and obligations or to the status, condition and *legal capacity* of persons, shall be binding upon the citizens of Puerto Rico, although they reside in a foreign country.

P.R. Laws Ann. tit. 31, §9 (1967) (emphasis supplied). Appellees argue that this article provides that the issue of plaintiff's legal capacity is governed by Puerto Rico law. The problem is, however, that the term "citizens of Puerto Rico" has been defined by the Supreme Court of Puerto Rico as equivalent to domicile. Therefore, whether Section 247 of the Civil Code, P.R. Laws Ann. tit. 31, §971—which provides that the majority age in Puerto Rico is 21—applies to Rodriguez Diaz will depend on where he is domiciled. Since this is the ultimate issue in contention, the approach does nothing to assist our resolution of the dispute.

The fact is, there is no purely logical way out of the dilemma. We cannot decide whether plaintiff is a minor under Puerto Rico law or an adult pursuant to New York law, without first determining where he is domiciled. On the other hand, we cannot make a determination whether he has the capacity to establish his own domicile without first knowing if he has reached the age of majority. We have, therefore, come full circle. To know if he has the legal capacity to establish his domicile of choice we need to know if he is an adult. But to determine whether he is an adult or a minor we first have to know where he is domiciled.

There is, to be sure, a possible way out of this circle under formal conflict of laws principles. We could apply forum law to determine Rodriguez Diaz's legal capacity. Restatement of the Law, Conflicts of Law (Second), §§13 and 15(a). (1971).[5] This might be a proper resolution had the question of plaintiff's domicile arisen in a Commonwealth of Puerto Rico court, where the question of domicile is likely to implicate local matters over which Puerto Rico has the final say. But we do not think the lex forum provides a satisfactory resolution where the overriding and ultimate question is plaintiff's *citizenship* for purposes of federal diversity jurisdiction. 28 U.S.C. §1332(a). Federal district courts sit throughout the nation. While it is unlikely a tort action like this, based on an accident in Puerto Rico, with all defendants residing there, could be pursued elsewhere than in the District of Puerto Rico, plaintiff could be involved in other federal diversity cases in other federal district courts, including the district courts located in New York. Were we to apply the rule of lex forum, Rodriguez Diaz could be viewed at one and the same time, and within the same judicial system, as both a citizen of New York

5. "[A] person cannot acquire a domicil of choice unless he has legal capacity to do so. Whether such legal capacity exists will be determined by the law of the forum." Restatement of the Law, Conflicts of Law (Second) §13, comment *d*.

and a citizen of Puerto Rico. That this is even theoretically possible suggests the unsatisfactoriness of determining state citizenship here, *for federal diversity purposes,* on the basis of lex forum. Rodriguez Diaz, we think, must be a "citizen" of one or the other state—not of both simultaneously.

We do not, moreover, see any compelling reasons of policy for adopting the law of the forum here. As pointed out already, while Puerto Rico doubtless has legitimate reasons for regulating persons such as plaintiff in respect to the making of contracts, property dispositions, support, and the like in Puerto Rico, it has little if any interest, based simply on the continuing presence of his parents in Puerto Rico, in denying to Rodriguez Diaz, while physically residing in New York, the right to sue under the diversity jurisdiction in a federal district court whether in Puerto Rico or elsewhere. While not crucial to our result, we also note that even plaintiff's parents have joined him in bringing this action: thus the parents' separate interests provide no reason to deny him the right to sue in a federal court.[6] In brief, a mechanical recourse to the lex forum does not strike us as a thoughtful solution to the current dilemma.

IV

Since neither pure logic nor conflict rules provide a meaningful solution, we feel free to make the choice we think fits best with the aims of the diversity statute and the national character of the federal judicial system. We hold that Rodriguez Diaz is a domiciliary of the State of New York—or, rather, that, if he can satisfy the district court that he meets the requisite factors of physical presence and intent, he is entitled to be a New York domiciliary for diversity purposes notwithstanding his minority status under Puerto Rico law. In reaching this result, we focus upon the physical and mental aspects of plaintiff's own situation, rather than imposing upon him a disability foreign to the law of the state where he now resides and having little meaning in this situation even to the place—Puerto Rico—whose law calls for it. To hold that one who meets all the domiciliary requirements (including capacity) of the state where he currently resides is a citizen of that state, seems clearly the most reasonable result here.

Our approach is consistent with that of other federal courts. . . . While in the ordinary case, relevant rules of state law provide the basis for the applicable federal common law, federal courts will deviate if necessary in order

6. There would, of course, be no diversity jurisdiction as to any claim of the parents, who reside in Puerto Rico. The parents sue here solely as next friends; their domicile is irrelevant in such circumstances.

to achieve the purposes of the diversity statute[7] and, sometimes, simply to achieve a more equitable and coherent result.[8] Not surprisingly, a number of cases have arisen from the tension, as here, between technical presumptions as to the domicile of a minor and the realities of the minor's actual situation.

In the present case, there are perhaps no urgent reasons of federal diversity policy comparable to those found [in other cases]. Since Rodriguez Diaz is recently from Puerto Rico, and his parents reside there, it is unlikely he would encounter prejudice were he forced to sue in Puerto Rico's own courts. The more realistic comparison, however, may be between the relative unfairness of denying a federal forum to Rodriguez Diaz while granting it to another young Puerto Rican of similar age whose parents moved to New York with him. Federal diversity jurisdiction exists as a matter of right for those who meet the statutory criteria, whether or not the plaintiff would actually encounter prejudice in the courts of another state. Federal courts should not, therefore, deny the right on the basis of pointless technicalities. In this case, if Rodriguez Diaz, being physically present in New York, qualifies under regular domiciliary rules as a domiciliary of New York, we do not think the difference in law between his former domicile, Puerto Rico, and New York concerning the age of majority should deny him right to sue as a citizen of New York in federal court.

Vacated and remanded for further proceedings not inconsistent herewith.

TORRUELLA, J. (dissenting).

With due respect I believe the majority has reached the wrong result, and that, by a circuitous route. Its conclusion is inevitable because its reasoning commences by "assum[ing] for purposes of resolving the legal issues raised in this appeal that New York is plaintiff's 'true, fixed home.'" I believe this is a fallacious assumption because it improperly shifts the focus of analysis.

Since the only undisputed fact in this case is that plaintiff was domiciled in Puerto Rico to begin with, it seems to me that the logical starting point is determining how plaintiff could change his domicile from Puerto Rico to New York. The answer to that question, in the context of this case, raises

---

7. See, e.g., Ziady v. Curley, 396 F.2d 873 (4th Cir. 1968) (in deciding infant plaintiff's domicile, the court took into account a major purpose of diversity jurisdiction, which is to protect a citizen of one state from parochialism if forced to litigate in another state).

8. Bjornquist v. Boston & A.R. Co., 250 F. 929 (1st Cir.), *cert. denied*, 248 U.S. 573 (1918). In this case, this circuit refused to follow the common-law rule that a minor could not establish his own domicile for diversity purposes: the minor's parents were dead, and plaintiff's domicile was technically that of his deceased father. Nonetheless, we found that he had acquired a Maine domicile when he moved there when 19 for a relatively brief sojourn with an aunt. *See also* Stifel v. Hopkins, 477 F.2d 1116 (6th Cir. 1973) (a prisoner may show a change of domicile to a state to which he was moved by his jailers notwithstanding old rule that the pre-incarceration domicile of a prisoner must continue during his imprisonment).

an issue of *capacity*, not one of intention. Since there is no case in which a change in domicile has taken place without, at the very least, a physical departure from the place of original domicile, and it is legally impossible to acquire a new domicile without first loosing the old one, we must determine the legal significance of such action in that jurisdiction; *i.e.*, Puerto Rico. The issue thus is what, if any, is the legal significance, for change of domicile purposes, of an 18 year old resident of Puerto Rico leaving that jurisdiction.

The answer under Puerto Rican law is clear: none. An 18 year old is considered a minor in Puerto Rico. The domicile of an unemancipated minor is that of his parents, or in appropriate cases, his guardian. A minor can be emancipated, thus allowing him to acquire a separate domicile from his parents or guardian, only by either parent (or both if they jointly exercise the patria potestas) appearing before a civil law notary in the presence of two witness, and, with the minor's consent, signing an emancipation deed. Unless this formal proceeding is effectuated *beforehand*, a Puerto Rico-domiciled minor *lacks legal capacity* to change his domicile from that of his parents, or in the appropriate case, his guardian. His moving away from his legal domicile (*i.e.*, that of his parents or guardian), be that to a different location down the street, or to another place in Puerto Rico, or to another jurisdiction, is legally irrelevant because he cannot gain a new domicile until one has licitly lost the old one.

That a state has a paramount interest in protecting, regulating and controlling its minor citizens is beyond cavil.

. . . This paramount interest of a state in regulating the conduct of its minors is not, of course, limited to Puerto Rico, and protective legislation may be found throughout the United States varying its content in a manner reflective of local interests and attitudes.

Because this is, as it should be, an area highly reflective of local attitudes, values and mores, it is particularly unsuited to federalized tinkering. Thus, the majority is mistaken in placing emphasis on the "right of access to a federal court" as the central issue raised by this appeal. . . .

The majority, however, finds all of this authority unpersuasive. Instead, it directs a district court sitting in Puerto Rico and adjudicating a case controlled by Puerto Rico law, concerning an incident occurring in Puerto Rico, and involving an individual who is unemancipated and still a minor under Puerto Rico law, to apply New York law to determine that the youth is no longer a minor (*i.e.*, emancipated) and thus able to invoke diversity jurisdiction in Puerto Rico. . . .

Perhaps most troubling about the decision of the majority is that it is presented without reliance on any rule of law. Is the majority saying that henceforth in this circuit the age of eighteen is the age of emancipation for choosing one's own domicile for purposes of diversity jurisdiction? If so, why is eighteen chosen instead of twenty-one or any other age? Or is the rule now that we will use the law of the jurisdiction to which the youth has moved, such that if a New York nineteen-year-old leaves his parents and moves to Puerto

Rico his domicile will remain in New York? Or is it that we use the law of the jurisdiction which has the youngest age of emancipation? Perhaps the rule is simply that we use the law of the jurisdiction which will create diversity jurisdiction.

Whatever the new rule is, I simply cannot see *why* it has been adopted at the expense of valid local interests—interests completely ignored by the majority. For instance, Puerto Rico may have a very legitimate interest in allowing parents to control the lawsuits of its citizens under the age of twenty-one. It may want parents deciding whether and in what court a suit is prosecuted, the Commonwealth allows parents better to control the expense and scope of litigation. In some situations, parents may decide that local court *is* the better alternative. Furthermore, Puerto Rico may have an interest in not encouraging a young person to leave home to establish domicile elsewhere so as to bring a suit in federal court contrary to the wishes of those ultimately responsible under its law for that youth. . . .

I dissent.

Questions and Comments

(1) Holmes stated: "[W]hat the law means by domicile is the one technically pre-eminent headquarters, which as a result of either fact or fiction every person is compelled to have in order that by aid of it certain rights and duties which have been attached to it by the law may be determined." Bergner & Engel Brewing Co. v. Dreyfus, 172 Mass. 154, 157 (1898).

(2) The domicile concept serves many purposes. As *White* shows, domicile provides the controlling law for questions of succession to personal property. Domicile was also the traditional choice-of-law criterion in contexts "related to personal status, such as marriage and divorce, legitimacy and adoption." 1 Beale, The Conflict of Laws §9.3, p. 91 (1935). As we shall see in Chapter 2, domicile is even more important for modern approaches to choice of law. Domicile also has uses beyond pure choice-of-law questions. As *Rodriguez Diaz* shows, domicile is typically equated with a natural person's citizenship for purposes of federal diversity jurisdiction. The domicile of at least one party provides the basis for divorce jurisdiction. Domicile also provides the basis for in personam jurisdiction and for determination of numerous taxation questions. There are many other functions of the domicile concept as well. Is it likely that all of these different purposes will be served by a unitary concept? *Compare* Toll v. Moreno, 284 Md. 425, 397 A.2d 1009 (1979) ("in Maryland, as in the majority of jurisdictions, the meaning and basic principles for determining domicile do not vary depending on the context").

(3) Is the use of domicile for choice-of-law purposes in tension with the First Restatement's emphasis on the place where events occur? Is domicile simply a different form of territorialism, focusing on where someone is from rather than where certain events occur? *See* Dane, Conflict of Laws, *in* A Companion to the Philosophy of Law and Legal Theory 209 (Patterson ed., 1996)

(distinguishing between "act-territorial" and "person-territorial" choice-of-law rules). Why do some traditional choice-of-law rules focus on act-territorialism while others focus on person-territorialism?

(4) What does *White* suggest about the relative priority of the "intent" and "presence" prongs of domicile? What would the court have done if Mr. White died in Pennsylvania before he ever entered the house? What if he died just before he crossed the border from West Virginia into Pennsylvania?

(5) The military poses a special problem precisely because it puts in question the intent of the putative domiciliary. Can an intent to make a place one's home really be formed if one is present because of orders and subject to being moved at any time because of further orders? The same question arose in Stifel v. Hopkins, 477 F.2d 116 (6th Cir. 1973), cited by the *Rodriguez Diaz* court, in which a prisoner in a federal prison in Pennsylvania sought to sue his attorney and parents, all residents of Ohio, in federal court. Jurisdiction was based on diversity. The lower court dismissed on the grounds that the plaintiff could not by law acquire a Pennsylvania domicile while in prison. The court of appeals reversed, indicating that a per se rule is inappropriate. On remand, the lower court was ordered to

> consider factors such as the possibility of parole for appellant, the manner in which appellant has ordered his personal and business transactions, and any other factors that are relevant to corroboration of appellant's statements. These factors must be weighed along with the policies and purposes underlying federal diversity jurisdiction to determine whether appellant has overcome the presumption that he has maintained his former domicile.

477 F.2d at 1127. If you were the district judge, what kind of questions would you like to hear answered before making a new finding that won't get reversed by the court of appeals? *Compare* Restatement (Second) of Conflict of Laws §17 (1986 Revision) (stating that a person "usually" does not acquire a domicile of choice by presence under physical or legal compulsion).

(6) An unusual domicile case is Blaine v. Murphy, 265 F. 324 (D. Mass. 1920), which was brought in federal court by virtue of federal diversity jurisdiction. The plaintiff was a citizen of New York and alleged that the defendants were citizens of Massachusetts. The defendants pleaded in abatement that they were also citizens of New York. Defendants ran a hotel called the State Line Hotel, through which ran the Massachusetts-New York line, as indicated by an old marker. A later survey sponsored by the two states, however, had shown that the marker was some 50 feet east of the true line. Thus, almost all of the hotel (where the defendants lived as well as worked) lay in Massachusetts. In particular, those portions of the building in which they ate and slept were in Massachusetts. The court did note that the outdoor

toilets were in New York. Nonetheless, the court invoked the rule, "The place where a person habitually eats, sleeps, and makes his home is his domicile." It was held not to be relevant that the parties had believed their domicile (as shown by numerous documents) to be New York for at least 40 years.

(7) According to a recent article in Nature Magazine discussing the appointment of Mr. Michael Sohlman as director of the Nobel Foundation, the Sohlman family connection with Alfred Nobel dated back to the turn of the century, when as Nobel's employee, Mr. Sohlman's grandfather was assigned the responsibility of moving all of the late inventor's personal assets from Paris to Sweden, where the estate was being administered. The reasoning behind locating administration of the estate in Sweden was that "French law at the time specified that a person's domicile was the place at which he kept his horses, which, in Nobel's case, was Sweden, not Paris." "Following Ancestral Footsteps," 360 Nature 514 (1992).

D. Marriage

Selections from the First Restatement of Conflicts, on Marriage and Legitimacy

§§121-123, 128-130, 132-134, 136-141 (1934)

§121. Law Governing Validity of Marriage

Except as stated in §§131 and 132, a marriage is valid everywhere if the requirements of the marriage law of the state where the contract of marriage takes place are complied with.

§122. Requirements of State of Celebration

A marriage is invalid everywhere if any mandatory requirement of the marriage law of the state in which the marriage is celebrated is not complied with.

§123. "Common Law" Marriage

A marriage without any formal ceremony is valid everywhere if the acts alleged to have created it took place in a state in which such a marriage is valid.

§128. Marriage in a Nomadic Tribe

If one or both of the parties to a marriage is a member of a tribe governed by tribal law, and the marriage takes place where the tribe is at the time located, and in accordance with the tribal law, the marriage is valid everywhere.

COMMENT . . .

c. *Gipsy, North American Indian, African and Esquimaux tribes.* Tribal law means the law of a tribe which by the law of the state in which it is located has its own law. The term would not be used, for instance, of the usages of a gipsy tribe not recognized by the state in which it is as having a right to a separate law. Tribal law is recognized as existing law in the case of Indian tribes in North America, of native African tribes, and of Esquimaux tribes.

§129. Evasion of Requirement of Domicil

If the requirements of the law of the state of celebration are complied with, the marriage is valid everywhere, except under the circumstances stated in §§131 and 132, although the parties of the marriage went to that state in order to evade the requirements of the law of their domicil.

§130. Remarriage after One Party to Divorce Forbidden to Remarry

If, by a decree of divorce validly granted in one state, one party is forbidden for a certain time or during his life to marry again, and he goes into another state and marries in accordance with the law of that state, the marriage, unless invalid for other reasons, is valid everywhere, even in the state in which the divorce was granted.

§132. Marriage Declared Void by Law of Domicil

A marriage which is against the law of the state of domicil of either party, though the requirements of the law of the state of celebration have been complied with, will be invalid everywhere in the following cases:

(a) polygamous marriage,

(b) incestuous marriage between persons so closely related that their marriage is contrary to a strong public policy of the domicil,

(c) marriage between persons of different races where such marriages are at the domicil regarded as odious,

(d) marriage of a domiciliary which a statute at the domicil makes void even though celebrated in another state.

§133. Effect of Foreign Marriage

Except as stated in §134, a state will give the same effect to a marriage created by the law of another state that it gives to a marriage created by its own law.

§134. Marriage Contrary to Public Policy

If any effect of a marriage created by the law of one state is deemed by the courts of another state sufficiently offensive to the policy of the latter state, the latter state will refuse to give that effect to the marriage.

§136. Law Governing Nullity

The law governing the right to a decree of nullity is the law which determined the validity of the marriage with respect to the matter on account of which the marriage is alleged to be null.

§137. Law Governing Legitimacy

The status of legitimacy is created by the law of the domicil of the parent whose relationship to the child is in question.

§138. Legitimacy at Birth

The legitimate kinship of a child to either parent from the time of the child's birth is determined by the law of the state of domicil of that parent at that time.

§139. Legitimacy from Birth

An act or event after the birth of a child who was born illegitimate may make it the legitimate child of either parent from birth if the law of the state of domicil of that parent at the time of the child's birth and the law of the parent's domicil at the time of the legitimating act so provide.

§140. Legitimation after Birth

An act done after the birth of an illegitimate child will legitimize the child as to a parent from the time of the act if the law of the state of domicil of that parent at that time so provides.

§141. Effect of Legitimacy Created by Foreign Law

The status of legitimacy, created by the law of a state having jurisdiction so to do, will be given the same effect in another state as is given by the latter state to the status when created by its own law.

In re May's Estate

305 N.Y. 486, 114 N.E.2d 4 (1953)

LEWIS, C. J.

In this proceeding, involving the administration of the estate of Fannie May, deceased, we are to determine whether the marriage in 1913 between the respondent Sam May and the decedent, who was his niece by the half blood—which marriage was celebrated in Rhode Island, where concededly such marriage is valid—is to be given legal effect in New York where statute law declares incestuous and void a marriage between uncle and niece.

The question thus presented arises from proof of the following facts: The petitioner Alice May Greenberg, one of six children born of the Rhode Island marriage of Sam and Fannie May, petitioned in 1951 for letters of administration of the estate of her mother Fannie May, who had died in 1945. Thereupon, the respondent Sam May, who asserts the validity of his marriage to the decedent, filed an objection to the issuance of petitioner of such letters of administration upon the ground that he is the surviving husband of the decedent and accordingly, under section 118 of the Surrogate's Court Act, he has the paramount right to administer her estate. Contemporaneously with, and in support of the objection filed by Sam May, his daughter Sirel Lenrow and his sons Harry May and Morris B. May—who are children of the challenged marriage—filed objections to the issuance of letters of administration to their sister, the petitioner, and by such objections consented that letters of administration be issued to their father Sam May.

The petitioner, supported by her sisters Ruth Weisbrout and Evelyn May, contended throughout this proceeding that her father is not the surviving spouse of her mother because, although their marriage was valid in Rhode Island, the marriage never had validity in New York where they were then resident and where they retained their residence until the decedent's death.

The record shows that for a period of more than five years prior to his marriage to decedent the respondent Sam May had resided in Portage, Wisconsin; that he came to New York in December, 1912, and within a month thereafter he and the decedent—both of whom were adherents of the Jewish faith—went to Providence, Rhode Island, where, on January 21, 1913, they entered into a ceremonial marriage performed by and at the home of a Jewish rabbi. The certificate issued upon that marriage gave the age of each party as twenty-six years and the residence of each as "New York, N.Y." Two weeks after their marriage in Rhode Island the respondent May and the decedent returned to Ulster County, New York, where they lived as man and wife for thirty-two years until the decedent's death in 1945. Meantime the six children were born who are parties to this proceeding.

A further significant item of proof—to which more particular reference will be made—was the fact that in Rhode Island on January 21, 1913, the date of the marriage here involved, there were effective statutes which prohibited the marriage of an uncle and a niece, *excluding*, however, those instances—of which the present case is one—where the marriage solemnized is between persons of the Jewish faith within the degrees of affinity and consanguinity allowed by their religion.

In Surrogate's Court, where letters of administration were granted to the petitioner, the Surrogate ruled that although the marriage of Sam May and the decedent in Rhode Island in 1913 was valid in that State, such marriage was not only void in New York as opposed to natural law but is contrary to the provisions of subdivision 3 of section 5 of the Domestic Relations Law. Accordingly the Surrogate concluded that Sam May did not qualify in this jurisdiction for letters of administration as the surviving spouse of the decedent.

At the Appellate Division the order of the Surrogate was reversed on the law and the proceeding was remitted to Surrogate's Court with direction that letters of administration upon decedent's estate be granted to Sam May who was held to be the surviving spouse of the decedent. In reaching that decision the Appellate Division concluded that the 1913 marriage of Sam May and the decedent in Rhode Island, being concededly valid in that State, is valid in New York where the degree of consanguinity of uncle and niece is not so close as to be repugnant to our concept of natural law, and that the statute, Domestic Relations Law, §5, subd. 3—which declares such a marriage to be incestuous and void—lacks express language which gives it extraterritorial force. The case comes to us upon appeal as of right by the petitioner and her two sisters Ruth Weisbrout and Evelyn May.

We regard the law as settled that, subject to two exceptions presently to be considered, and in the absence of a statute expressly regulating within the domiciliary State marriages solemnized abroad, the legality of a marriage between persons sui juris is to be determined by the law of the place where it is celebrated. . . .

In Van Voorhis v. Brintnall, *supra,* the decision turned upon the civil status in this State of a divorced husband and his second wife whom he had married in Connecticut to evade the prohibition of a judgment of divorce which, pursuant to New York law then prevailing, forbade his remarriage until the death of his former wife. In reaching its decision, which held valid the Connecticut marriage there involved, this court noted the fact that in the much earlier case of Decouche v. Savetier, . . . Chancellor Kent had recognized the general principle ". . . that the rights dependent upon nuptial contracts, are to be determined by the lex loci." Incidental to the decision in Van Voorhis v. Brintnall, *supra*, which followed the general rule that ". . . recognizes as valid a marriage considered valid in the place where celebrated," *id.*, 86 N.Y. at page 25, this court gave careful consideration to, and held against the application of two exceptions to that rule—*viz.*, cases within the prohibition of positive law; and cases involving polygamy or incest in a degree regarded generally as within the prohibition of natural law.

We think the Appellate Division in the case at bar rightly held that the principle of law which ruled Van Voorhis v. Brintnall and kindred cases cited, supra, was decisive of the present case and that neither of the two exceptions to that general rule is here applicable.

The statute of New York upon which the appellants rely is subdivision 3 of section 5 of the Domestic Relations Law which, insofar as relevant to our problem, provides:

> **§5. Incestuous and Void Marriages**
>
> A marriage is incestuous and void whether the relatives are legitimate or illegitimate between either. . . .
>
> 3. An uncle and niece or an aunt and nephew.
>
> If a marriage prohibited by the foregoing provisions of this section be solemnized it shall be void, and the parties thereto shall each be fined not less than fifty nor more than one hundred dollars and may, in the discretion of the court in addition to said fine, be imprisoned for a term not exceeding six months. Any person who shall knowingly and wilfully solemnize such marriage, or procure or aid in the solemnization of the same, shall be deemed guilty of a misdemeanor and shall be fined or imprisoned in like manner.

Although the New York statute quoted above declares to be incestuous and void a marriage between an uncle and a niece and imposes penal measures upon the parties thereto, it is important to note that the statute does not by express terms regulate a marriage solemnized in another State where, as in our present case, the marriage was concededly legal. In the case at hand, as we have seen, the parties to the challenged marriage were adherents of the Jewish faith which, according to Biblical law and Jewish tradition—made the subject of proof in this case—permits a marriage between an uncle and a niece; they were married by a Jewish rabbi in the State of Rhode Island where, on the date of such marriage in 1913 and ever since, a statute forbidding the marriage of an uncle and a niece was expressly qualified by the following statutory exceptions appearing in 1913 in Rhode Island General Laws:

> §4. The provisions of the preceding sections shall not extend to, or in any way affect, any marriage which shall be solemnized among the Jews, within the degrees of affinity or consanguinity allowed by their religion. . . .
>
> §9. Any marriage which may be had and solemnized among the people called Quakers, or Friends, in the manner and form used or practised in their societies, or among persons professing the Jewish religion, according to their rites and ceremonies, shall be good and valid in law; and wherever the words "minister" and "elder" are used in this chapter, they shall be held to include all of the persons connected with the society of Friends, or Quakers, and with the Jewish religion, who perform or have charge of the marriage ceremony according to their rites and ceremonies.

As section 5 of the New York Domestic Relations Law (quoted *supra*) does not expressly declare void a marriage of its domiciliaries solemnized in a foreign State where such marriage is valid, the statute's scope should not be extended by judicial construction. Van Voorhis v. Brintnall, *supra.* Indeed, had the Legislature been so disposed it could have declared by appropriate enactment that marriages contracted in another State—which if entered into here would be void—shall have no force in this State. Although examples of such legislation are not wanting, we find none in New York which serve to give subdivision 3 of section 5 of the Domestic Relations Law extraterritorial effectiveness. . . . Accordingly, as to the first exception to the general rule that a marriage valid where performed is valid everywhere, we conclude that, absent any New York statute expressing clearly the Legislature's intent to regulate within this State marriages of its domiciliaries solemnized abroad, there is no "positive law" in this jurisdiction which serves to interdict the 1913 marriage in Rhode Island of the respondent Sam May and the decedent.

As to the application of the second exception to the marriage here involved—between persons of the Jewish faith whose kinship was not in the direct ascending or descending line of consanguinity and who were not brother and sister—we conclude that such marriage, solemnized, as it was, in accord with the ritual of the Jewish faith in a State whose legislative body has declared such a marriage to be "good and valid in law," was not offensive to the public sense of morality to a degree regarded generally with abhorrence and thus was not within the inhibitions of natural law.

DESMOND, J. (dissenting).

It is fundamental that every State has the right to determine the marital status of its own citizens. . . . Exercising that right, New York has declared in section 5 of the Domestic Relations Law that a marriage between uncle and niece is incestuous, void and criminal. Such marriages, while not within

Left residence just to get married

the Levitical forbidden degrees of the Old Testament, have been condemned by public opinion for centuries (*see* 1 Bishop on Marriage, Divorce and Separation, §738), and are void, by statute in (it would seem) forty-seven of the States of the Union (all except Georgia, *see* Martindale-Hubbell, Law Digests, and except, also, that Rhode Island, one of the forty-seven, exempts from its local statute "any marriage which shall be solemnized among the Jews, within the degrees of affinity or consanguinity allowed by their religion," Gen. L. of R.I., ch. 415, §4). It is undisputed here that this uncle and niece were both domiciled in New York in 1913, when they left New York for the sole purpose of going to Rhode Island to be married there, and that they were married in that State conformably to its laws (*see* above) and immediately returned to New York and ever afterwards resided in this State. That Rhode Island marriage, between two New York residents, was, in New York, absolutely void for any and all purposes, by positive New York law which declares a strong policy of this State. *See* Penal Law, §1110.

The general rule that "a marriage valid where solemnized is valid everywhere" (*see* Restatement, Conflict of Laws, §121) does not apply. To that rule there is a proviso or exception, recognized, it would seem by all the States, as follows: "unless contrary to the prohibitions of natural law or the express prohibitions of a statute." Section 132 of the Restatement of Conflict of Laws states the rule apparently followed throughout America:

> A marriage which is against the law of the state or domicil of either party, though the requirements of the law of the state of celebration have been complied with, will be invalid everywhere in the following cases: . . . (b) incestuous marriage between persons so closely related that their marriage is contrary to a strong public policy of the domicil.

. . . The old and famous New York case of Wightman v. Wightman, . . . decided in 1820 when there were no marriage statutes in our State, says that marriages may be declared by "appropriate legislation," to be incestuous. New York, as a sovereign State with absolute powers over the marital status of its citizens, has enacted such legislation, but we, by this decision, are denying it efficacy.

Van Voorhis v. Brintnall . . . does not save this marriage. That case dealt not with a marriage void under section 5 of the Domestic Relations Law, but one forbidden by section 8 thereof. Section 8 forbids the guilty party, in a New York divorce judgement, to marry again within a certain time, and the Van Voorhis ruling was that, by section 8, the Legislature did not intend to make such marriages contracted outside this State absolutely void, but merely stated an in personam prohibition against the adjudged adulterer marrying, for a period of time. . . . This court's opinion in the *Van Voorhis* case, while stating the general rule that the validity of a marriage depends on the law of the place of marriage, noted that there are exceptions thereto in cases of incest, within the prohibition of natural law, and "prohibition by positive law."

Section 5 of the Domestic Relations Law, the one we are concerned with here, lists the marriages which are "incestuous and void" in New York, as being those between parent and child, brother and sister, uncle and niece, and aunt and nephew. All such misalliances are incestuous, and all, equally, are void. The policy, language, meaning and validity of the statute are beyond dispute. It should be enforced by the courts.

The order should be reversed and the proceedings remitted to the Surrogate for appropriate proceedings, with costs to abide the event. . . .

Decree affirmed.

Lanham v. Lanham

136 Wis. 360, 117 N.W. 787 (1908)

Sarah A. Lanham appealed to the county court for support out of the estate of James W. Lanham, deceased, as his widow. The application being denied, she appealed to the circuit court, where the application was granted, and Art Lanham and others, decedent's heirs, appeal. Reversed and remanded.

The plaintiff applied to the county court of Monroe county for an allowance for her support out of the estate of James W. Lanham, deceased, claiming that she was the widow of said deceased. The application was contested, and denied in the county court; but on appeal that judgment was reversed, and an allowance granted, and from this judgment the heirs of Lanham appeal. The facts are few and simple. On and prior to the 15th day of September, 1905, the plaintiff was a resident of this state and was the wife of one J. R. Sherman. On the day named she obtained a judgment of divorce from Mr. Sherman for the purpose of marrying the deceased, who was then a resident of Wisconsin and a man 84 years of age. After the divorce both parties learned that the law of Wisconsin prohibited the plaintiff from marrying again until the expiration of one year from the divorce. For the purpose of avoiding the effect of the law, they went to Menomonee, Mich., October 10, 1905, and were there married by a justice of the peace, and returned to Wisconsin on the following day. They immediately assumed the relations of husband and wife, and lived and cohabited together in Monroe county until Lanham's death, March 13, 1907. On March 8, 1907, the plaintiff made application to the county judge of Monroe county for a permit to marry Lanham; but he was then very ill, and no ceremony was ever performed. The circuit court concluded that there was a valid common-law marriage between the parties, resulting from their living and cohabiting together as man and wife after the expiration of one year from the date of the decree of divorce, and held that the plaintiff was the lawful widow of the deceased and entitled to an allowance as such. . . .

WINSLOW, C.J. (after stating the facts as above).

Section 2330, St. 1898, as amended by chapter 456, p. 785, Laws of 1905, provides, among other things, that

> it shall not be lawful for any person divorced from the bonds of matrimony by any court of this state to marry again within one year from the date of the entry of such judgment or decree and the marriage of any divorced person solemnized within one year from the date of the entry of any such judgment or decree of divorce shall be null and void.

A proviso to the section authorizes the circuit judge to grant permission to the divorced parties to remarry within the year, but this is of no moment here. The first question is whether the Michigan marriage was valid, notwithstanding the provisions of this law.

The general rule of law unquestionably is that a marriage valid where it is celebrated is valid everywhere. To this rule, however, there are two general exceptions, which are equally well recognized, namely: (1) Marriages which are deemed contrary to the law of nature as generally recognized by Christian civilized states; and (2) marriage which the lawmaking power of the forum has declared shall not be allowed validity on grounds of public policy. The first of these exceptions covers polygamous and incestuous marriages, and has no application here; and the question presented is whether the case comes within the second exception.

A state undoubtedly has the power to declare what marriages between its own citizens shall not be recognized as valid in its courts, and it also has the power to declare that marriages between its own citizens contrary to its established public policy shall have no validity in its courts, even though they be celebrated in other states, under whose laws they would ordinarily be valid. In this sense, at least, it has power to give extraterritorial effect to its laws. The intention to give such effect must, however, be quite clear. So the question must be, in the present case, whether our Legislature by the act quoted declared a public policy, and clearly indicated the intention that the law was to apply to its citizens wherever they may be at the time of their marriage. To our minds there can be no doubt that the law was intended to express a public policy. There have been many laws in other states providing that the guilty party in a divorce action shall not remarry for a term of years, or for life, and these laws have generally been regarded merely as intended to regulate the conduct of the divorced party within the state, and not as intended to follow him to another jurisdiction and prevent a marriage which would be lawful there; in other words, they impose a penalty local only in its effect. Under this construction the remarriage of such guilty party in another state has generally been held valid, notwithstanding the prohibition of the local statute. . . .

It is very clear, however, that the statute under consideration is in no sense a penal law. It imposes a restriction upon the remarriage of both parties, whether innocent or guilty. Upon no reasonable ground can this general restriction be explained, except upon the ground that the Legislature deemed that it was against public policy and good morals that divorced persons should be at liberty to immediately contract new marriages. The inference is unmistakable that the sacredness of marriage and the stability of the marriage lie at the very foundation of Christian civilization and social order; that divorce, while at times necessary, should not be made easy, nor should inducement be held out to procure it; that one of the frequent causes of marital disagreement and divorce actions is the desire on the part of one of the parties to marry another; that if there be liberty to immediately remarry an inducement is thus offered to those who have become tired of one union, not only to become faithless to their marriage vows, but to collusively procure the severance of that union under the forms of law for the purpose of experimenting with another partner, and perhaps yet another, thus accomplishing what may be called progressive polygamy; and, finally, that this means destruction of the home and debasement of public morals. In a word, the intent of the law plainly is to remove one of the most frequent inducing causes for the bringing of divorce actions. This means a declaration of public policy, or it means nothing. It means that the Legislature regarded frequent and easy divorce as against good morals, and that it proposed, not to punish the guilty party, but to remove an inducement to frequent divorce.

To say that the Legislature intended such a law to apply only while the parties are within the boundaries of the state, and that it contemplated that by crossing the state line its citizens could successfully nullify its terms, is to make the act essentially useless and impotent, and ascribe practical imbecility to the lawmaking power. A construction which produces such an effect should not be given it, unless the terms of the act make it necessary. The prohibitory terms are broad and sweeping: they declare, not only that it shall be unlawful for divorced persons to marry again within the year, but that any such marriage shall be null and void. There is no limitation as to the place of the pretended marriage in express terms, nor is language used from which such a limitation can naturally be implied. It seems unquestionably intended to control the conduct of the residents of the state, whether they be within or outside of its boundaries. Such being, in our opinion, the evident and clearly expressed intent of the Legislature, we hold that when persons domiciled in this state, and who are subject to the provisions of the law, leave the state for the purpose of evading those provisions, and go through the ceremony of marriage in another state, and return to their domicile, such pretended marriage is within the provisions of the law, and will not be recognized by the courts of this state. Further than this we are not required to go. . . .

Another view of the question, leading to the same result, has been suggested to our minds, which will be stated. The statute cited is an integral part of the divorce law of this state, and in legal effect enters into every judgment of divorce. This being so, must not any judgment of divorce be construed as containing an inhibition upon the parties, rendering them incapable of legal marriage within a year, which must be given "full faith and credit" in all other states, under section 1, art. 4, of the Constitution of the United States? And if it be entitled to receive such faith and credit, how can a marriage within another state be considered valid anywhere? Are not the parties incapable of contracting such a marriage anywhere, for the reason that they have not yet been relieved of their incapacity to marry another, resulting from their former marriage, or, in other words, for the reason that their divorce is not complete until the expiration of the year? We suggest these questions, without definitely expressing an opinion upon them or making them a ground of decision.

The Michigan marriage being held void, the question recurs whether the finding that there was a common-law marriage, resulting from the fact that the parties lived and cohabited together as man and wife for about six months, can be sustained. This must be answered in the negative. This court has held that, where cohabitation is illegal in its inception, the relation between the parties will not be transformed into marriage by evidence of continued cohabitation, or by any evidence which falls short of establishing either directly or circumstantially the fact of an actual contract of marriage after the bar has been removed. . . . There was no such evidence here. At most the evidence only shows that the parties continued to live together after the expiration of the year in the manner of husband and wife, and talked about a remarriage, which never took place on account of the husband's illness and death. The evidence in fact rebuts any inference of remarriage, rather than supports it.

Judgment reversed, and action remanded to the circuit court, with directions to affirm the judgment of the county court.

SIEBECKER, J., dissents.

Questions and Comments

(1) Haven't these two cases missed the real point? Is the ultimate issue the validity of the marriage—or is it who gets some money? In fact, few cases will arise directly attacking the validity of a marriage: A rare criminal conviction (*e.g.*, State v. Bell, 66 Tenn. 9 (1872)) will arise, and somewhat more often an action for annulment or for a declaratory judgment that no valid marriage ever existed.

In the *May's Estate* and *Lanham* cases, the putative spouses claimed the benefit of certain statutory provisions applying to spouses. Statutes giving special rights to surviving spouses may be indicative of the legislature's assumptions about the intent of the deceased, but are more likely to express a moral view about the surviving spouse's right to benefits. This is particularly clear in the case of statutes that give a surviving spouse a forced share of the decedent's estate, even if there is a will to the contrary. But even if such statutes are supposed to operate independently of the testator's intent, is it clear that the validity of the marriage per se is at issue? After two people have lived together for many years, might the legislature determine that the survivor is entitled to as much consideration whether the marriage was valid or not?

(2) Aren't the answers even easier in the line of cases (*see, e.g.*, Metropolitan Life Insurance Co. v. Holding, 293 F. Supp. 854 (E.D. Va. 1968)) in which the question is whether the person now claiming insurance proceeds was the "wife" or "husband" of the decedent as the term was used in the insurance contract? Is it likely that a decedent who thought that a marriage was valid and who bought insurance naming "my wife" or "my husband" as beneficiary would intend to benefit someone other than his or her cohabitant, whether or not the marriage was valid?

(3) Apart from questions about the "real" issue in these cases, are the considerations behind conflicts rules for marriage different from those for torts and contracts? Even an enemy of overemphasis on the desirability of uniformity would have to concede that uniformity is an attractive goal when the question is the validity of a marriage. Few people or states would wish to see marriages valid in some states while invalid in others, with cohabitants never sure of their status with respect to the criminal law, or the legitimacy of their children, etc.

In fact, the usual tendency is not merely to aim toward a uniform result but to aim for uniformity in favor of the marriage. For example, the *Holding* case, *supra,* (where the court, applying Virginia conflicts law, searched for a state in which the parties' common-law marriage was void) stated: "The public policy of Virginia is to uphold the validity of a marriage if at all possible." But if that is true, why does Virginia deny validity to its own domestic common-law marriages?

(4) Is Section 132 of the Restatement, *supra* page 58, an exception that swallows much of Section 121's "place of celebration" rule, see *supra* page 57? Consider:

> The First Restatement . . . does not merely contemplate that the domicile has a potential veto over a well-defined subset of issues. It recognizes in the domicile an absolute power, exercisable by statute or otherwise, to control for any reason the validity of its people's marriages celebrated anywhere. Put another way, if a marriage of a domiciliary conducted outside the domicile is valid, it is only by the permission of the domicile. This reading, in turn, requires a new look at section 121. . . . At first, section 121 had looked like a typical First Restatement rule—a second-order, territorially based, allocation of prescriptive jurisdiction. In truth, however, section 121 does not recognize in the place of celebration any independent power to validate marriages. Rather, it reflects the first-order substantive decision of domicile states to recognize, by their own law, most marriages performed in accordance with the law of the place of celebration.

Dane, Whereof One Cannot Speak: Legal Diversity and the Limits of a Restatement of Conflict of Laws, 75 Ind. L.J. 511, 514 (2000). Do you agree with this interpretation? What explains the elevation of domicile over the place of celebration? Why would the state of domicile ever defer to marriages performed elsewhere? Why does the First Restatement appear to give the state of domicile more say over marriage than over tort and contract? Is uniformity more important in the marriage context? Why or why not?

(5) Why are incestuous marriages forbidden? Is it merely a moral matter—or does the state have a legitimate fear of the biological effects of inbreeding? *See generally* Nagan, Conflict of Laws and Proximate Relations: A Policy-Science Perspective, 8 Rut.-Cam. L.J. 416 (1977).) In either case, what difference should it make to the state of New York *where* related persons are married, when the dangers arise from the cohabitation itself?

In Rhodes v. McAfee, 224 Tenn. 495, 457 S.W.2d 522 (1970), the court was faced with a case in which B. E. Plunk had divorced his second wife and later married Tula Boone Griggs, the woman's daughter, who was not related to him by blood. The court found the marriage to be a violation of the law both at the parties' domicile and at the place of celebration and suggested that the reason behind the ban on that particular kind of "incest" was the desire to preserve matrimonial harmony.

(6) Would it make sense for a state to recognize the validity of a marriage but forbid or punish cohabitation within its borders? In State v. Bell, 66 Tenn. 9 (1872), the state of Tennessee prosecuted a white man for cohabitation with his black wife. The marriage had taken place in Mississippi, which did not forbid interracial marriage, and the court seemed to assume that the marriage was valid. But the court nonetheless applied Tennessee's prohibition on interracial cohabitation, reasoning that the "place of celebration" rule applied to the capacity of parties to enter marriage, and not the "manner and form" of marriage. *Id.* at 10.

The California Court of Appeals in In re Dalip Singh Bir's Estate, 83 Cal. App. 2d 256, 188 P.2d 499 (1948), held that the state might prohibit cohabitation within its borders with more than one wife but that the reasons for such a policy would not apply when the question was one of succession to the dead husband's property. Two wives of the decedent, both of whose marriages were valid under Indian law, were allowed to split the dead husband's property.

(7) When a state's own residents are involved and they have gone to another state only to evade its laws and marry, does it ever make any sense to recognize the validity of the marriage? Some states have statutes specifically covering the situation—for example, the Arizona statute cited in In re Estate of Mortenson, 83 Ariz. 87, 316 P.2d 1106 (1957), which validated marriages valid by the law where contracted, subject to the proviso that parties who intended at the time of marriage to reside in Arizona would have their marriages treated as if they had taken place in Arizona.

Didn't *May's Estate* allow a blatant evasion of New York law? Although the court purports to be following the legislative mandate, didn't it attribute a rather bizarre policy to the legislature in doing so—forbidding incest unless the parties went through the ritual of stepping across state lines?

Sometimes a court interprets a statute to forbid parties from marrying, without invalidating the marriage itself. Is that a likely legislative intent?

Did New York application of the Rhode Island statute in *May's Estate* discriminate against the poor who could not afford to go to Rhode Island? Against the ignorant who didn't know about it? Didn't the Rhode Island statute discriminate in favor of Jews in violation of the First Amendment? Or did it guarantee freedom of religion, as required by the First Amendment?

(8) When residents of State *A* step across the state line into State *B* and marry, does State *B* have any desire at all to see its law applied to the marriage? If so, why?

(9) Many interesting questions have been raised about the interstate consequences of state same-sex marriage laws. Hawaii piqued interest in the question when its courts suggested that the state equal protection clause might require the state to legalize same-sex marriages, *see* Baehr v. Lewin, 852 P.2d 44 (Haw. 1993), but the state eventually passed a constitutional amendment giving the Hawaii legislature "the power to reserve marriage to opposite-sex couples." *See* Baehr v. Miike, 92 Haw. 634, 635 (Hawaii 1999). On April 26, 2000, however, the Vermont legislature, also under pressure from Vermont state courts, *see* Baker v. State, 744 A.2d 864 (Vt. 1999), enacted legislation recognizing civil unions between same-sex couples. See An Act Relating to Civil Unions, H.B. 847, 1999 Gen. Assem., Adjourned Sess. (Vt. 1999). The Vermont law provides that same-sex couples entering into civil unions will enjoy the same benefits and obligations that Vermont law provides for different-sex couples who enter into civil marriages.

Consider this hypothetical: A gay couple from Illinois, which does not permit marriages between persons of the same gender, *see* Ill. Comp. Stat. Ann. Ch. 750, §§5/201, 5/203(1), 212(a)(1), (2), (5), travels to Vermont and has a civil union ceremony there. They then return home to Illinois and attempt to file a joint tax return, or enroll in a health insurance plan for married couples, or move into a neighborhood zoned for single families. In the course of subsequent related litigation, the question arises whether the couple is married. Assuming that Illinois followed the First Restatement, would an Illinois court view the couple as married for purposes of taxation, health benefits, or zoning? Could the Illinois court refuse to recognize the marriage? Does the answer differ if the same-sex couple were longtime Vermont domiciliaries who moved to Illinois because of a job transfer?

In response to the possibility of state-sanctioned same-sex marriages, at least 30 states have enacted statutes that limit legally recognizable marriages to ones that include a man and a woman. *See* Coolidge & Duncan, Definition or Discrimination? State Marriage Recognition Statutes in the "Same-Sex Marriage" Debate, 32 Creighton L. Rev. 3 (1998). In addition, Congress in 1996 enacted the Defense of Marriage Act ("DOMA"), 28 U.S.C.

§1738(c), which provides: "No State . . . shall be required to give effect to any public act, record, or judicial proceeding of any other State . . . respecting a relationship between persons of the same sex that is treated as a marriage under the laws of such other State." Does a Vermont civil union couple lose all rights arising from their marriage as soon as they cross the Vermont border into one of these 30 states? We shall examine the constitutionality of these state and federal laws *infra* page 687.

There is an enormous literature on choice of law and same-sex marriages. Some of the better articles include Koppelman, Same-Sex Marriage, Choice of Law, and Public Policy, 76 Tex. L. Rev. 921 (1998); Fruehwald, Choice of Law and Same-Sex Marriage, 51 Fla. L. Rev 799 (1999); Kramer, Same-Sex Marriage, Conflict of Laws, and the Unconstitutional Public Policy Exception, 106 Yale L.J. 1965 (1997); Myers, Same-Sex "Marriage" and the Public Policy Doctrine, 32 Creighton L. Rev. 45 (1998).

E. Real Property

Selections from the First Restatement of Conflicts, on Real Property

§§211, 214, 216-223, 225-227, 237-238, 244-246, 248-251 (1934)

§211. Property in Tangible Thing: Where Created

The original creation of property in a tangible thing is governed by the law of the state where the thing is at the time of the events which create the interests.

§214. Legal Effect and Interpretation of Words Used in an Instrument of Conveyance

(1) Words used in an instrument of conveyance of an interest in land which, by the law of the state where the land is, have a given operative effect irrespective of the intent of the conveyor, will be accorded such effect in any state.

(2) Words used in an instrument of conveyance of an interest in land which, by the law of the state where the land is, have a given operative effect unless a contrary intent is shown by admissible evidence, will be accorded such effect in any state.

(3) The meaning of words used in an instrument of conveyance of an interest in land which, by the law of the state where the land is, are accorded neither of the effects described in Subsections (1) and (2), is in the absence

of controlling circumstances to the contrary, determined in accordance with usage at the domicile of the conveyor at the time of the conveyance.

§216. Capacity to Convey Interest in Land

Capacity to make a valid conveyance of an interest in land is determined by the law of the state where the land is.

§217. Formalities of Conveyance of Interest in Land

The formalities necessary for the validity of a conveyance of an interest in land are determined by the law of the state where the land is.

§218. Substantial Validity of Conveyance of Interest in Land

Whether a conveyance of an interest in land, which is in due form and is made by a party who has capacity to convey it, is in other respects valid, is determined by the law of the state where the land is.

§219. Capacity of Grantee to Take or Hold Land

Whether the grantee in a conveyance of an interest in land is capable of taking or holding the interest is determined by the law of the state where the land is.

§220. Effect of Conveyance of Interest in Land

The effect upon interests in land of a conveyance is determined by the law of the state where the land is.

§221. Nature of Interest Created by Conveyance of Land

The nature of the interest in land created by a conveyance is determined by the law of the state where the land is.

§222. Non-Possessory Interests in Land

The creation, transfer and termination of non-possessory interests in land are determined by the law of the state where the land is.

§223. Transfer of Interest in Land by Operation of Law

An interest in land can be transferred by operation of law only by the law of the state where the land is.

§225. Mortgage on Land; By What Law Determined

The validity and effect of a mortgage on land is determined by the law of the state where the land is. [*But* refer back to pages 24-30 *supra,* and read again comment (*a*) to §333 concerning contracts.]

§226. Assignment of Mortgage on Land

The validity and effect of an assignment of a mortgage on land are determined by the law of the state where the land is.

§227. Foreclosure of Mortgage on Land

The method and effect of the foreclosure of a mortgage on land are determined by the law of the state where the land is.

§237. Effect of Marriage on Existing Interests in Land

The effect of marriage upon interests in land owned by a spouse at the time of marriage is determined by the law of the state where the land is.

§238. Effect of Marriage on an Interest in Land Later Acquired

The effect of marriage upon an interest in land acquired by either or both of the spouses during coverture is determined by the law of the state where the land is.

§244. Equitable Conversion of Trust Property

Whether the interest of the beneficiary of a trust of land is real estate or whether, because of a direction to sell the land, it is personal property, is determined by the law of the state where the land is.

§245. Inheritance of Land

The law of the state where the land is determines its devolution upon the death of the owner intestate.

§246. Legitimacy of Claimant by Descent

A person who is heir by the law of the state where the land is, only if legitimate, is heir if, but only if, he is born legitimate as stated in §138 or has been legitimized as stated in §139 and §140.

§248. Share of Spouse in Land upon Termination of Marriage

(1) The existence and extent of a common law or statutory interest of a surviving spouse in the land of a deceased spouse are determined by the law of the state where the land is.

(2) The effect of divorce upon the interest of one spouse in the land of another is determined by the law of the state where the land is.

§249. Will of Land

The validity and effect of a will of an interest in land are determined by the law of the state where the land is.

§250. Revocation of Will of Land

The effectiveness of an intended revocation of a will of an interest in land is determined by the law of the state where the land is.

§251. Interpretation, Construction and Effect of Will of Land

(1) Words used in a devise of an interest in land which, by the law of the state where the land is, have a given operative effect irrespective of the intent of the testator, will be accorded such effect in any state.

(2) Words used in a devise of an interest in land which, by the law of the state where the land is, have a given operative effect unless a contrary intent is shown by admissible evidence, will be accorded such effect in any state.

(3) The meaning of words used in a devise of an interest in land which, by the law of the state where the land is, are accorded neither of the effects

described in Subsections (1) and (2), is, in the absence of controlling circumstances to the contrary, determined in accordance with usage at the domicile of the testator at the time when the will was made.

Burr v. Beckler

264 Ill. 230, 106 N.E. 206 (1914)

CARTWRIGHT, C.J.

The appellee, Shelton C. Burr, filed his bill in the circuit court of Cook county against Ednah J. Tobey (now Ednah J. Beckler), Charles H. Tobey, and William E. Church, trustee, to foreclose a trust deed dated March 11, 1905, made by Ednah J. Tobey and Charles H. Tobey, who was then her husband, conveying certain real estate in Chicago to secure a note of that date made by Ednah J. Tobey, payable to her own order five years after date, with interest, and endorsed by her. Ednah J. Tobey answered, alleging that she was induced to execute the note and trust deed by the false and fraudulent representation of her said husband, Charles H. Tobey; that Shelton C. Burr had notice of the fraud and was not a bona fide assignee of the note; and that the note and trust deed were void for the reason that they were executed in the state of Florida while she was a feme covert and incapable by the laws of Florida of executing the same. . . . The [intermediate appellate] court also concluded that the note and trust deed were not invalid because made in Florida while the maker was temporarily in that state, and because the note was dated at Chicago, Ill., and secured by real estate in this state, and the trust deed recited the residence of the grantors at Chicago. . . .

[I]f the note was void because executed in the state of Florida, the decree of the chancellor was in accordance with the law regardless of all other questions.

The validity, construction, force, and effect of instruments affecting the title to land depend upon the law of the state where the land lies. . . . But, if the note was void, the trust deed, which was incidental and intended to secure a performance of the obligation created by the note, could not be enforced. It is a universal rule that the validity of a contract is to be determined by the law of the place where it is made, and if it is not valid there it will not be enforced in another state in which it would have been valid if made there. . . .

A note takes effect from the time of its delivery and not from its date. Until the maker of a note parts with the possession and control of the instrument he may cancel it or dispose of it as he pleases, and a note is not executed until delivered. The note in this case was made in Florida, and the trust deed was signed at the same time and acknowledged before a notary public of the county of Dade, in that state. Charles H. Tobey had designated the United States mail as the means of transmission of the note and trust deed to him, and Ednah J. Tobey, in compliance with his request, deposited them in the mail in the state of Florida. When the note and trust deed were so deposited, Ednah J. Tobey, the maker, parted with the possession of and lost all control over the papers and all right to retake or reclaim them. Under such circumstances, the delivery was complete in Florida when the note and trust deed were placed in the mail, directed by Charles H. Tobey, trustee of the Ludington estate. . . . The fact that the domicile of Ednah J. Tobey was in Illinois did not enable her to execute a note in the state of Florida contrary to the laws of that state, under which she was not competent to enter into a contract. In Forsyth v. Barnes, *supra,* a man and his wife domiciled in the state of Illinois, made in Ohio a note and warrant of attorney authorizing the confession of a judgment. Judgment was taken in Ohio and an action of debt brought on the judgment in Illinois. It was held that the judgment entered on the warrant of attorney was void as against the wife, and subject to attack either directly or collaterally, because she was a feme covert, incapable at common law of executing the warrant, and in the absence of proof it would be presumed that the common law was in force in Ohio. The note was payable in Ohio, but that is not a ground of distinction, because the place where the contract is made determines its validity and the place of performance affects only the time, mode, and extent of the remedy. The law of the state of performance will govern in determining the rights of the parties and the effect of the contract, but if a party is not competent to make a contract, the contract is not valid and will not be enforced anywhere. The application of the rules of law in this case leads to the conclusion that the note was void.

The judgment of the Appellate Court is reversed, and the decree of the circuit court affirmed.

Thomson v. Kyle

39 Fla. 582, 23 So. 12 (1897)

A full statement of the numerous lengthy pleadings and depositions contained in this very voluminous record would fill many pages of our reports. For this reason we shall not attempt a complete history of the case, but will endeavor to state concisely the main facts bearing upon those assignments of error only which appellants have argued in their briefs here. The appellee (complainant below), on November 14, 1891, filed a bill in equity in the circuit court of Alachua county, praying foreclosure of a mortgage on certain real estate situated in that county. The mortgage debt was evidenced by a note executed by the appellants (defendants below) to complainant, under date January 18, 1890, for $2,932, due April 10, 1890, and payable in the city of Birmingham, Alabama. The mortgage given to secure this note was executed on the same day by the defendants. The defendant, Della K. Thomson, filed her plea on January 4, 1892, whereby she alleged that prior and subsequent to, and at the time of, the execution of the note and mortgage, she was a married woman, the wife of her codefendant, and seised and possessed of a statutory separate estate in her own individual right and control, part of which was embraced in the mortgage; that the note and mortgage were executed in the state of Alabama, and that all transactions out of which the mortgage debt arose occurred in said state; that the mortgage debt was the debt of her husband exclusively, and she executed the note and mortgage as security only, and upon no other consideration; that by the laws of Alabama the obligation of a married woman executed for her husband's debt was null and void, and incapable of enforcement, and that the note and mortgage, being void as to her in the state of Alabama, were likewise void in the state of Florida. This plea was, upon argument, overruled. . . .

CARTER, J. (after stating the facts).

I

The question presented by the plea of Della K. Thomson is an interesting one, and one upon which the authorities are not in entire accord. It is not denied by appellants that, had the mortgage sought to be foreclosed in this case been executed in this state, it would have been valid, and enforceable under our laws. Indeed, it has been held by this court, on more than one occasion, that a mortgage properly executed by a married woman and her husband, conveying the wife's separate statutory real estate as security for her husband's debt, is valid. . . . It is insisted, however, that under the laws of Alabama, a married woman is without capacity to bind herself or her property as security for the debt of her husband, and, as the mortgage sought to be enforced in this case was executed, and the debt secured thereby was payable, in that state, and all the parties were there domiciled, that those laws necessarily entered into and became a part of the contract, rendering it void in that state; and that, being void in Alabama, it is, by virtue of interstate law, void in Florida. It may be admitted that this argument has strong application to the note executed by Mrs. Thomson with her husband, which the mortgage was given to secure, for, the note being a general personal obligation, if void by the laws of the state in which it was executed and made payable, it ought likewise to be void in every other state where it is sought to be enforced. But it does not follow that because Mrs. Thomson is not bound by the note it is for that reason totally void. It still remains a valid obligation of her husband, which she can, in this state, secure by a mortgage of her separate statutory property. We do not understand that any principle of interstate law requires us to test the validity or sufficiency of conveyances of or liens upon real estate in this state by the laws of other states or nations, even though such contracts may have been executed, or given to secure the performance of some act, within their jurisdiction. The reasons why we should not are obvious. The subject-matter, with reference to the title of which the conveyance or lien is executed, being at the time of such execution an immovable thing, not only located beyond the control of that sovereignty within whose jurisdiction the contract is executed, and forever so to remain, but then within the exclusive jurisdiction of another independent sovereignty, and forever so to remain, the parties to such conveyance are presumed to have contracted, at least so far as the immovable thing is concerned, with reference to the laws of that jurisdiction within whose borders the thing is situated. And no sovereign state, without express legislative sanction, is presumed to surrender to owners of immovable property within its limits the power to incumber or charge the title thereto in any other manner than that pointed out by its laws. It is, therefore, almost universally held that so far as real estate or immovable property is concerned, we must look to the laws of the state where it is situated for the rules which govern its descent, alienation, and transfer, and for the construction, validity, and effect of conveyances thereof . . . ; and it is to the same law that we must look for the rules governing the capacity of the parties to such contracts or conveyances, and their rights under the same. . . . It would seem, therefore, that upon principle the mortgage in this case should be subjected to the laws of this state, in order to ascertain its validity, construction, and the capacity of the parties to execute it, rather than to the laws of the state of Alabama, within whose borders the real estate is not situated, and as to which her laws can have no extraterritorial effect. While a contrary opinion was entertained in Ohio, . . . it has been held in several well-considered cases that, although by the laws of the state of a married woman's domicile she has no capacity to execute a mortgage upon her separate estate as security for the debt of her husband, yet if she, in that state, executes a mortgage of that character upon real estate situated in another state, whose laws permit a married woman to mortgage her property to secure such a debt, the mortgage will, in the latter state, be held valid, and enforceable in its courts by appropriate proceedings. . . . We hold that, notwithstanding Mrs. Thomson's incapacity by the laws of Alabama to execute the mortgage sought to be foreclosed here, she was capable, under our laws, of executing in Alabama a mortgage upon her separate statutory real property in this state to secure her husband's debt, and that her plea was properly overruled. This conclusion also disposes of those portions of the cross bill and answer of the defendant John M. Thomson which cover the same matters as this plea.

The answer and cross bill of the defendant John M. Thomson alleged that there was included in the obligation evidencing the mortgage debt the sum of $300, which, under the laws of the state of Alabama, was usurious interest, and that under the laws of that state usury forfeited all interest upon the principal debt as to which unlawful interest was charged. As this obligation was a personal one, and it was executed and to be performed in the state of Alabama, having no reference to immovable property in this state, we think its validity and interpretation are governed by the laws of the former state. Perry vs. Lewis, 6 Fla. 555. Therefore, although in this state there were no laws against usury at the time of the execution of this obligation, yet, if it is tainted with usury by the laws of Alabama, where it was executed and made payable, and where all the parties resided at the time of its execution, we think the infirmity follows it to this state, even when secured by a mortgage on lands in this state. The authorities are not entirely unanimous on this point, but we think the weight of them, supported by principle, sustains the proposition that a note executed and payable in one state, though secured by a mortgage on lands in another, will be governed, as to the rate of interest it shall bear, by the laws of the former; and if, by such laws, all interest is forfeited for usury, the same result will follow, upon foreclosure of the mortgage securing it, in the state where the mortgaged lands are situated. . . .

Questions and Comments

(1) Do the *Burr* and *Thomson* cases reach inconsistent results? Would it have made a difference in *Burr* if Charles had joined Ednah in making the note for which foreclosure on the mortgage was sought?

(2) Was the purpose of the Florida common-law rule of coverture served by invalidating a note made by Ednah Tobey, an Illinois resident? Was the purpose of the Alabama coverture rule fulfilled in the *Thomson* case by allowing her to mortgage her Florida land? What purpose of Florida law might have been served by the ruling in the *Thomson* case?

(3) If Alabama, with its coverture rule, followed the same conflicts approach as Florida in the *Thomson* case, what would happen in an Alabama case in which a Florida woman had executed a guaranty of her husband's note in Florida, to be paid in Florida and secured by a mortgage of land in Alabama? Wouldn't the note be enforceable under the *Thomson* approach, while the mortgage would not be? But if the note was enforceable, could the resulting judgment be satisfied by execution against the Alabama land? If so, has striking down the mortgage been limited in effect to depriving the mortgage holder of priorities that it would have had over other creditors? Has it failed in its essential purpose of protecting the married woman from her husband's overreaching? If so, what good (to Alabama) would the *Thomson* rule be? Even if Alabama used such reasoning to reject the *Thomson* approach, couldn't the plaintiff in this hypothetical get a judgment in Florida, which would apply its own law to the note, and demand enforcement of the judgment against the land in Alabama under the full faith and credit clause of the Constitution? If so, is there any way for Alabama to protect its married women, or are the conflicts rules stacked against the Alabama policy in this situation?

(4) Why all of the emphasis on the situs of real property, especially when—as we shall see—no similar obsession is present with personal property? The situs rule is frequently criticized by proponents of modern approaches to choice of law. *See, e.g.*, Weintraub, Obstacles to Sensible Choice of Law for Determining Marital Property Rights on Divorce or in Probate: Hanau and the Situs Rule, 25 Hous. L. Rev. 1113 (1988); Leflar, American Conflicts Law 410-411 (1968). Professor Leflar defends the rule on the

grounds that our title recording systems are set up territorially, and a would-be purchaser needs to be able to rely on the applicability of situs law in performing a title search.

Other reasons that have been given include the fact that (a) only the state in which land is located has physical power over it (and, as we shall see in the chapter on full faith and credit to judgments, the principle is carried so far that a judgment of State *A*, purporting to affect title to land in State *B*, is ineffective even if there is jurisdiction over all the concerned parties); (b) real property is of greatest concern to the state in which it is located (though one may ask, for example, whether that has anything to do with whether an out-of-state wife can guaranty the debts of her husband); and (c) it is rare that there is any uncertainty as to the location of land. *See* Introductory Note to §214 of the Restatement of Conflict of Laws Second (Tent. Draft No. 5, April 24, 1959) (not contained in the final draft as promulgated).

For an unusual case in which the location of land itself was in question, *see* Durfee v. Duke, 375 U.S. 106 (1963), page 642 *infra,* in which title was disputed because the Missouri River, forming the border between Nebraska and Missouri, had changed course.

F. Corporations

Selections from the First Restatement of Conflicts, on Corporations

§§154, 155, 165, 166, 182, 183, 187, 188, 190-192, 205 (1934)

§154. Recognition of Foreign Corporation

The fact of incorporation by one state will be recognized in every other state.

§155. Questions of Incorporation

(1) Whether an association has been incorporated is determined by the law of the state in which an attempt to incorporate has been made.

(2) The effects of an unsuccessful attempt to incorporate are governed by the law of the state in which the attempt was made.

(3) Defects in the process of incorporation which may give the incorporating state a power to dissolve the corporation are governed by the law of such state.

§165. Powers of Foreign Corporation

A foreign corporation can legally perform any act within its corporate powers under the law of the state of incorporation unless the act is prohibited by the law of the state where it is to be performed.

§166. Law Governing Act of Foreign Corporation

The effect of an act directed to be done by a foreign corporation is governed by the law of the state where it is done.

§182. Law Governing Title to Share

Whether a person is a shareholder or other member of a corporation is determined by the law of the state of incorporation.

§183. Participation in Management and Profits

The right of a shareholder to participate in the administration of the affairs of the corporation, in the division of profits and in the distribution of assets on dissolution and his rights on the issuance of new shares are determined by the law of the state of incorporation.

§187. Director's or Shareholder's Liability

Except as stated in §188, the existence and extent of the liability of shareholders, officers or directors of a corporation to a creditor of the corporation for a violation of law by them, is determined by the law of the state of incorporation.

§188. Liability Imposed by State Where Corporation Acts

So far as the directors or agents are participants in acts done within the state, a state can impose liability upon the directors or agents of a foreign corporation doing business in the state for acts done within the state or for failure to do acts required by the law of the state as a condition of doing business within the state.

§190. Direct Liability of Shareholder Imposed by State of Incorporation

The state of incorporation can impose liability on a shareholder running directly to creditors, for debts of the corporation incurred in another state and this liability will be enforced in any state which has judicial jurisdiction over the shareholder.

§191. Direct Liability of Shareholder Imposed by Foreign State

Liability for an act caused by a foreign corporation to be done by its agent can be imposed on a shareholder by the law of the state where the act is done only if the shareholder

(a) is domiciled in the state, or

(b) has personally taken part in doing the act or causing it to be done, or

(c) has notice that the corporation was formed to do business there.

This liability will be enforced in any state having judicial jurisdiction over the shareholder.

§192. Action Concerning Shares

Except as stated in §193 and subject to the considerations stated in the Scope Note to this Topic, a court will usually not entertain a suit brought against a foreign corporation to obtain a decree against it requiring or enjoining the issuance, transfer, or cancellation of shares.

§205. Creation of Shares by Reincorporated Association

When an association already incorporated by one state is incorporated by another, the creation of shares is governed by the law of the state which first incorporates the association.

Vanderpoel v. Gorman

140 N.Y. 563, 35 N.E. 932 (1894)

PECKHAM, J.

The North River Lumber Company was a company incorporated under the laws of New Jersey, and transacting its business in the city of New York. On the 24th of February, 1891, the corporation made in this state a general assignment to the predecessor of the plaintiff of all its property for the benefit of its creditors, and without any preferences. Subsequent to the assignment, certain of its creditors commenced actions against it to recover the amounts of their debts, respectively, and in those actions attachments were issued and delivered to the defendant, who was the sheriff of New York county; and he subsequently levied, by virtue of such attachments, upon property which was alleged to belong to the corporation. The plaintiff, as its general assignee, has commenced this action to recover from the defendant the value of the property thus levied on by him. The question turns upon the validity of the general assignment of the corporation to the plaintiff. If it were a legal and valid act, it carried the title to the property in question to the plaintiff, and, if not, then the defendant was justified in his levy. The defendant, on the trial, objected to evidence of the assignment, and urged as grounds for his objection: (1) that a foreign corporation cannot, under the laws of this state, while insolvent, or in contemplation of insolvency, make a general assignment for the benefit of creditors; (2) that, if such corporation could make that kind of an assignment, it could not make it in the manner of this instrument, *viz.* by the signature of an alleged president and secretary; (3) there is no sufficient proof of any authority on the part of the persons executing this assignment to make a general assignment for the benefit of creditors. The trial court sustained the defendant's objections, and upon appeal the judgment entered in defendant's favor was affirmed by the general term of the New York common pleas. The plaintiff has appealed from such judgment of affirmance to this court.

The defendant's first ground of objection must mean that the courts of this state will not recognize as valid, so far as respects property within their jurisdiction, a general assignment of its property, made for the benefit of its creditors, by an insolvent foreign corporation. . . . As the common law permits such an assignment, and the state of New Jersey also permits it, and as it does not appear that the charter or by-laws of this particular corporation prohibit it, we are left to the question whether there is any statute or public policy in this state which would be violated if the courts should recognize the validity of an instrument good at common law, and good in the state which created the corporation. The power of the legislature to impose terms upon a foreign corporation as a condition for granting it leave to do business within another state is admitted.

The sole question now is as to what has been the legislative action of this state upon this subject. The defendant alleges that there is a statute of this state which prohibits such act on the part of a foreign corporation. . . . It provides, among other things, that no corporation shall make any transfer or assignment to any person whatever, in contemplation of its insolvency, and every such assignment is declared to be void. We have no doubt that this section refers solely to domestic corporations. . . . The legislature declares, as above stated, that certain transfers or assignments made by the corporation shall be void. What power had the legislature to enact any such provision as to a foreign corporation? There is nothing in the section limiting its scope and effect to such property as the foreign corporation might have within this state. It is a broad enactment, affecting every assignment made by a corporation under the circumstances mentioned. Can it be supposed that the legislature had in mind a foreign corporation, and intended to assume a jurisdiction to declare such an act, even when done outside this state, and in respect to property also outside of its boundaries, to be void and of no effect? This cannot be supposed, for we cannot impute to the legislature such ignorance upon the subject of its inability to give extraterritorial effect to its own laws. And if it had foreign corporations in mind, when proposing to legislate upon the subject, and knew it could not affect the validity of such transfers outside this state, and intended to provide that such transfers should not carry the title to property of the corporation held within this state, and subject to our jurisdiction, it must be clear that language somewhat appropriate to express such purpose would have been used. The language actually used was neither apt nor pertinent for this purpose. It is both appropriate and pertinent when applied to domestic corporations only. The language of the section clearly implies full and complete jurisdiction over the whole subject-matter. It implies the right to forbid absolutely. It also implies the right to declare the consequences of a violation of the prohibition, not in regard to some particular property, but generally and absolutely. The legislature has such jurisdiction in the case of domestic corporations, while in the case of foreign corporations it has not. To render the section applicable to foreign corporations would be to discard the plain meaning of the language used. The provisions of the Revised Statutes as to transfers by a corporation when insolvent or in contemplation of insolvency, prohibiting them when made with intent to give preferences, etc., were said to apply only to domestic corporations. We have no doubt of the correctness of the statement. The same reasons are applicable in both cases, and, if section 9 do [*sic*] not apply to foreign corporations, nothing can be found in the language of section 48 of the Laws of 1890, which would extend it to other than domestic corporations. As the prohibition is not contained in any statute of the state, we are unable to discover any public policy of the state which would stand in lieu of a positive statute, and prohibit our recognition of the validity of this transfer.

It is urged that such a policy is to be found in this same statute, even though it, in terms, applies only to domestic corporations. The argument is that, if the state refuses to its own corporations the privilege of making such an assignment, it surely cannot be consistent with its policy to permit the exercise of the same privilege by a foreign corporation. The statute, while only applicable to domestic corporations, is thus used as evidence of the public policy of the state with regard to foreign corporations. If it were a question of the simple grant of a privilege, it may well be that what this state denied to its own corporations it would not grant to those from a foreign state. It is not, however, the mere question of the exercise of a certain privilege, which is to be affirmatively granted in order to exist. The right to make such an assignment exists inherently in all corporations, unless specially forbidden. In regard to domestic corporations, it has been specially forbidden. Does that prohibition furnish any legitimate evidence of the existence of a public policy in this state, which forbids in the case of a foreign corporation the exercise of this inherent right? It seems to us that it does not. The two kinds of corporations, domestic and foreign, stand, with reference to this subject, in very different circumstances and positions towards the state. What might be proper or necessary in one case might be wholly inappropriate or impossible of complete execution in the other. As to domestic corporations, we assume certain responsibilities arising out of the very liberty given by the state for their creation or formation. We provide for their birth, for their regulation and government during life, and for their death. Upon their dissolution, which no other power than the state itself, acting through its legislature or its courts, can pronounce, the whole power of the corporation ceases, and the property which the corporation leaves passes under the dominion of the sovereignty which created it. Responsible for its creation, for its government, and for its death, the state has assumed, in such cases, complete and full jurisdiction over the corporation and its property; and accordingly the state has, in a series of statutory provisions, made certain that the corporate property shall be distributed in accordance with its own ideas of justice. On the other hand, in the case of a foreign corporation, the same kind of responsibility does not obtain. Our courts cannot dissolve it, nor can we, by virtue of our laws, in any way affect its property situated outside of the state, nor call it to any account therefor. . . . It is thus seen that there are differences of a marked character between a domestic and a foreign corporation in relation to this subject. The differences are so marked that the statute regarding domestic corporations can furnish no proof as to the existence of a public policy, which, in the case of foreign corporations, should stand in the place of, and be equivalent to, that statute.

Again, this assignment is valid by the law of New Jersey, which is the domicile of the corporation. It provides for an equal distribution of all the property of the corporation among all of its creditors, being in this respect in entire conformity with our own policy regarding the distribution of the property of insolvent domestic corporations. Is not the argument quite strong, under such circumstances, which favors the application of the general rule that an assignment of personal property, valid by the law of the domicile of the owner, will be recognized as valid everywhere? Can it be said, in such a case, that the interests of our own citizens are in any manner neglected by their own state, when they are to share equally in the assets with all the other creditors of the corporation? If it were a domestic corporation, they would get no more than an equal rate of division. Can they be said to be legally harmed when they get the same rate of division under such an assignment? Are we not, in such case, only following the general doctrine which refers the validity of the transfer of personal property to the law of the domicile of its owner? It is true that the assignment in this case was made by the corporation through its officers in New York, where it was doing business, but nevertheless it was a New Jersey corporation, and the assignment was valid by the law of that state. . . . The judgment should be reversed and a new trial ordered; costs to abide the event. All concur, except BARTLETT, J., not sitting.

Irving Trust Co. v. Maryland Casualty Co.

83 F.2d 168 (1936)

L. HAND, J.

This is an appeal from a decree, dismissing a bill in equity for lack of equity, filed by a trustee in bankruptcy against grantees and transferees of the bankrupt. The bankrupt is a Delaware company, doing business in New York under license of the Secretary of State; an involuntary petition was filed against it on the 13th of October, 1932; it was adjudicated, and the plaintiff was appointed its trustee in the following December. On January 6, 1932, it was indebted to four surety companies, with which on that day it entered into two contracts on separate dates by which it promised to transfer to the companies or their nominees in payment of its debts to them certain personal property, and to procure the transfer by three of its subsidiaries of certain other real and personal property. Most of the real property was within the state of New York, but one parcel with chattels upon it was in Missouri, one was in Florida, and two were in New Jersey. The chattels consisted of the supplies, furniture, and the like; the other personalty was made up of mortgages, mortgage bonds secured by real property, insurance policies, assignments of rent, accounts receivable, and cash. The bill alleged that at the time of the contracts the bankrupt was insolvent, or in imminent danger of insolvency; that the transfers were intended to prefer the surety companies, as they well knew or had cause to know; and that in performance of the contracts the subsidiaries conveyed the real property and chattels thereon to nominees of the surety companies, and the bankrupt transferred the bonds, mortgages, accounts, etc., to the companies themselves. The suit was against the companies and the nominees, and was based upon section 114 of the Stock Corporation Law (Consol. Laws N.Y. c.59) quoted in the margin.* . . . The judge decided that section 114 applied only to the liability of officers, directors, and stockholders of foreign companies and did not make unlawful the transfers themselves; for this reason he dismissed the bill. The plaintiff appealed.

Section 114 was confessedly passed to fill the gap left in section 15 when Vanderpoel v. Gorman construed that section as limited to domestic companies. The result was to put domestic companies at a disadvantage as compared with foreign companies licensed by the state to do business within its borders; and in 1897 the Legislature made up its mind to end the handicap. The report of the committee then appointed particularly mentioned among other things the desirability of subjecting foreign companies to the same limitations in favor of their creditors which applied to domestic; section 114, then section 60, was the result of their efforts. . . . A more troublesome question concerns the property outside New York. Although the bill does not say where the transfers were made, the contracts required them to be delivered in that state, and we are to assume that the parties performed as stipulated. The receipt of the deeds by the defendants was therefore a wrong, and any liabilities imposed as a remedy would be recognized and enforced elsewhere, for the law of the place where acts occur normally fixes their jural character. Restatement of Conflict of Laws, §384. The question here is whether it makes a difference that the wrong consisted in the conveyance of property in another state, under whose laws the conveyance might perhaps have been valid. . . . The doctrine is of course well settled, certainly as to real property, and, as we shall assume arguendo, equally at the present time as to personal, that the law of the situs absolutely determines the validity of conveyances wherever made. No title will pass and no interest will arise, save as that law prescribes. We have no doubt therefore that title passed by the deeds delivered in New York to property situated in those of the three states whose laws did not forbid such transfers; yet the law of New York might still make re-

---

* "Liabilities of Officers, Directors and Stockholders. Except as otherwise provided in this chapter, the officers, directors and stockholders of a foreign stock corporation transacting business in this state, except a moneyed or a railroad corporation, shall be liable under the provisions of this chapter, in the same manner and to the same extent as the officers, directors and stockholders of a domestic corporation, for the making of

1. Unauthorized dividends;
2. Unlawful loans to stockholders;
3. False certificates, reports or public notices;
4. Illegal transfers of the stock and property of such corporation, when it is insolvent or its insolvency is threatened.

Such liabilities may be enforced in the courts of this state, in the same manner as similar liabilities imposed by law upon the officers, directors and stockholders of domestic corporations."

ceipt of the deed a wrong and impose a liability upon the grantee though he got a good title. That would not trench upon the sovereignty of the state of the situs whose power over the res would remain wholly unimpaired. Nobody would question this so far as concerned the grantee's liability in damages; it would be but reasonable that he should become liable to the grantor's creditors just because his title was unimpeachable. In the case of contracts for the sale of land the lex loci contractus certainly controls. . . . Some of the relief asked by the bill cannot therefore be granted; the court cannot adjudge the transfers void as to land and chattels outside the state, except as the lex rei sitae is the same as section 114. But under his general prayer the plaintiff, if he proves his case, may have a decree as to any of the property transferred directing the defendants to reconvey it, and this he can enforce in personam. Of course he may also recover damages as a substitute if he so elects.

Decree reversed; defendants to answer over.

McDermott Inc. v. Lewis

531 A.2d 206 (Del. 1987)

Before Christie, C. J., Horsey and Moore, JJ.

Moore, J.:

We confront an important issue of first impression—whether a Delaware subsidiary of a Panamanian corporation may vote the share it holds in its parent company under circumstances which are prohibited by Delaware law, but not the law of Panama. Necessarily, this involves questions of foreign law, and applicability of the internal affairs doctrine under Delaware law.

Plaintiffs, Harry Lewis and Nina Altman, filed these consolidated suits in the Court of Chancery in December, 1982 seeking to enjoin or rescind the 1982 Reorganization under which McDermott Incorporated, a Delaware corporation ("McDermott Delaware"), became a 92%-owned subsidiary of McDermott International, Inc., a Panamanian corporation ("International"). Lewis and Altman are stockholders of McDermott Delaware, which emerged from the Reorganization owning approximately 10% of International's common stock. Plaintiffs challenged this aspect of the Reorganization, and the Court of Chancery granted partial summary judgment in their favor, holding that McDermott Delaware could not vote its stock in International.

We conclude that the trial court erred in refusing to apply the law of Panama to the internal affairs of International. There was no nexus between International and the State of Delaware. Moreover, plaintiffs concede that the issues here do not involve the internal affairs of McDermott Delaware. Thus, we decline to follow Norlin Corp. v. Rooney, Pace Inc., 744 F.2d 255 (2d Cir. 1984), which prohibited a similar device involving a Panamanian subsidiary seeking to vote the share it held in its Panamanian parent. Accordingly, we reverse. In so doing, we reaffirm the principle that the internal affairs doctrine is a major tenet of Delaware corporation law having important federal constitutional underpinnings.

I

International was incorporated in Panama on August 11, 1959, and is principally engaged in providing worldwide marine construction services to the oil and gas industry. Its executive offices are in New Orleans, Louisiana, and there are no operations in Delaware. International does not maintain offices in Delaware, hold meetings or conduct business here, have agents or employees in Delaware, or have any assets here.

McDermott Delaware and its subsidiaries operate throughout the United States in three principal industry segments: marine construction services, power generation systems and equipment, and engineered materials. McDermott Delaware's principal offices are in New Orleans.

Following the 1982 Reorganization, McDermott Delaware became a 92%-owned subsidiary of International. The public stockholders of International hold approximately 90% of the voting power of International, while McDermott Delaware holds about 10%.

The stated "principal purpose" of the reorganization, according to International's prospectus, was to enable the McDermott Group to retain, reinvest and redeploy earnings from operations outside the United States without subjecting such earnings to United States income tax. The prospectus also admitted that the 10% voting interest given to McDermott Delaware would be voted by International, "and such voting power could be used to oppose an attempt by a third party to acquire control of International if the management of International believes such use of the voting power would be in the best interests of the stockholders of International." An exchange offer, and thus the Reorganization, was supported by 89.59% of McDermott Delaware stockholders.

The applicable Panamanian law is set forth in the record by affidavits and opinion letters of Ricardo A. Durling, Esquire, and the deans of two Panamanian law schools, to support the claim that McDermott Delaware's retention of a 10% interest in International, and its right to vote those shares, is permitted by the laws of Panama. Significantly, the plaintiffs have not offered any contrary evidence. . . .

II

We note at the outset that if International were incorporated either in Delaware or Louisiana, its stock could not be voted by a majority-owned subsidiary. No United States jurisdiction of which we are aware permits that practice.

Relying on Norlin Corp. v. Rooney, Pace Inc., 744 F.2d 255 (2d Cir. 1984), the Court of Chancery concluded that Panama in effect would refrain from applying its laws under the facts of this case. On that basis, the trial court then concluded that since both Delaware and Louisiana law prohibit a majority-owned subsidiary from voting its parent's stock, the device was improper. We consider this an erroneous application of both Delaware and Panamanian law.

Our analysis requires a two-step inquiry. First, we must determine if Panamanian law, in the factual context addressed by the Court of Chancery, permits International to vote its own shares through the device of McDermott Delaware's ownership. If it does not, then the inquiry ends. However, if Panamanian law permits the practice, we must consider the multifaceted issues inherent in the application of the internal affairs doctrine.

A

It is apparent that under limited circumstances the laws of Panama permit a subsidiary to vote the shares of its parent. Article 35 of Panamanian Cabinet Decree No. 247 of July 16, 1970, which is part of the General Corporation Law of Panama, restricts the exercise of voting rights on shares of certain Panamanian corporations, but Article 37 limits the scope of Article 35 to "corporations registered in the National Securities Commission [of Panama] and those whose shares are sold on the market. . . ." Opinion of Ricardo A. Durling, *supra* p. 5. Based on the facts before the Court of Chancery, it is undisputed that International was not required to register, nor had it registered, with the National Securities Commission. Further, International's shares were not "sold on the market," as that term is defined by the Attorney General of Panama. Reading Articles 35 and 37 together, it is apparent that Article 35's prohibition did not apply to International.

B

Given the uncontroverted evidence of Panamanian law, establishing that a Panamanian corporation may place voting shares in a majority-owned subsidiary under the limited circumstances provided by Article 37, we turn to the fundamental issues presented by application of the internal affairs doctrine.

III

Internal corporate affairs involve those matters which are peculiar to the relationships among or between the corporation and its current officers, directors, and shareholders. It is essential to distinguish between acts which can be performed by both corporations and individuals, and those activities which are peculiar to the corporate entity.

Corporations and individuals alike enter into contracts, commit torts, and deal in personal and real property. Choice of law decisions relating to such corporate activities are usually determined after consideration of the facts of each transaction. *See* Reese and Kaufman, The Law Governing Corporate Affairs: Choice of Law and the Impact of Full Faith and Credit, 58 Colum. L. Rev. 1118, 1121 (1958) (hereinafter "Reese and Kaufman"). In such cases, the choice of law determination often turns on whether the corporation had sufficient contacts with the forum state, in relation to the act or transaction in question, to satisfy the constitutional requirements of due process. The internal affairs doctrine has no applicability in these situations. Rather, this doctrine governs the choice of law determinations involving matters *peculiar* to corporations, that is, those activities concerning the relationships inter se of the corporation, its directors, officers and shareholders.

The internal affairs doctrine requires that the law of the state of incorporation should determine issues relating to internal corporate affairs. Under Delaware conflict of laws principles and the United States Constitution, there are appropriate circumstances which mandate application of this doctrine.

A

Delaware's well established conflict of laws principles require that the laws of the jurisdiction of incorporation—here the Republic of Panama—govern this dispute involving McDermott International's voting rights.

The traditional conflicts rule developed by courts has been that internal corporate relationships are governed by the laws of the forum of incorporation. *See* Macey & Miller, Toward an Interest-Group Theory of Delaware Corporate Law, 65 Tex. L. Rev. 469, 495 (1987). As early as 1933, the Supreme Court of the United States noted:

> It has long been settled doctrine that a court—state or federal—sitting in one state will, as a general rule, decline to interfere with, or control by injunction or otherwise, the management of the internal affairs of a corporation organized under the laws of another state but will leave controversies as to such matters to the courts of the state of the domicile. . . .

Rogers v. Guaranty Trust Co. of New York, 288 U.S. 123, 130 (1933) (citations omitted).

However, in Western Air Lines, Inc. v. Sobieski, Cal. App., 191 Cal. App. 2d 399, 12 Cal. Rptr. 719 (1961), a California court upheld an order of the California Commissioner of Corporations directing a Delaware corporation having major contacts with California to follow the cumulative voting requirements imposed by California law. After the *Western Air* decision, commentators noted that the case signaled the alleged start of a "conflicts revolution." *See* Kozyris, Corporate Wars and Choice of Law, 1985 Duke L.J. 1 (hereinafter "Kozyris"); Kaplan, Foreign Corporations and Local Corporate Policy, 21 Vand. L. Rev. 433 (1968) (hereinafter "Kaplan"). . . .

A review of cases over the last twenty-six years, however, finds that in all but a few, the law of the state of incorporation was applied without any discussion. *Id.* at 17-18. In fact, twenty-six years after *Western Air* the following statement remains apt:

> The umbilical tie of the foreign corporation to the state of its charter is usually still religiously regarded as conclusive in determining the law to be applied in intracorporate disputes. The fundamental reexamination of the nature of conflict of laws over the past few years has virtually left foreign corporation matters remaining as a pocket of the past in a subject area which has otherwise been characterized by free inquiry, change and flux.

Kaplan, *supra* at 464.

The policy underlying the internal affairs doctrine is an important one, and we decline to erode the principle:

> Under the prevailing conflicts practice, neither courts nor legislatures have maximized the imposition of local corporate policy on foreign corporations but have consistently applied the law of the state of incorporation to the entire gamut of internal corporate affairs. In many cases, this is a wise, practical, and equitable choice. It serves the vital need for a single, constant and equal law to avoid the fragmentation of continuing, interdependent internal relationships. The lex incorporationis, unlike the lex loci delicti, is not a rule based merely on the priori concept of territoriality and on the desirability of avoiding forum-shopping. It validates the autonomy of the parties in a subject where the underlying policy of the law is enabling. It facilitates planning and enhances predictability. In fields like torts, where the typical dispute involves two persons and a single or simple one-shot issue and where the common substantive policy is to spread the loss through compensation and insurance, the preference for forum law and the emphasis on the state interest in forum residents which are the common denominators of the new conflicts methodologies do not necessarily lead to unacceptable choices. By contrast, applying local internal affairs law to a foreign corporation just because it is amenable to process in the forum or because it has some local shareholders or some other local contact is apt to produce inequalities, intolerable confusion, and uncertainty, and intrude into the domain of other states that have a superior claim to regulate the same subject matter. . . .

Kozyris, *supra* at 98. . . . In conclusion, the trial court erred as a matter of law in ignoring the uncontroverted Panamanian law, and in applying

Delaware and/or Louisiana law to the internal affairs of International contrary to established Delaware law and important constitutional principles. Accordingly the judgment of the Court of Chancery is reversed.

Questions and Comments

(1) The *McDermott* court also decided, in an omitted portion of its opinion, that its ruling was constitutionally compelled. For a discussion of the constitutional issues raised by the "internal affairs" doctrine requiring application of the law of the state of incorporation, *see* page 432 *infra.*

(2) Although most states continue to follow the internal affairs doctrine, some states have departed from the doctrine through statutory provision. California has been the most aggressive in subjecting the internal affairs of foreign-incorporated firms to portions of its corporate code. For example, if a foreign corporation does half its business in California and if half of its voting securities are held by California residents, California law governs issues such as director elections, inspection of books and records, distribution policy, and cumulative voting. *See* Cal. Corp. Code §2115 (2001). California courts have upheld this provision against numerous legal challenges. *See* Valtz v. Penta Inv. Corp., 139 Cal. App. 3d 803 (Cal. Ct. App. 1983) (upholding California's shareholders' right to inspect laws against a Delaware corporation); Wilson v. Louisiana-Pacific Resources, Inc., 138 Cal. App. 3d 216 (Cal. Ct. App. 1982) (upholding California's cumulative voting requirements as applied to a Utah corporation). New York also applies provisions of its corporate code to foreign corporations that do business in the state. *See* N.Y. Bus. Corp. §§1317, 1318, 1319 (2001); Norlin Corp. v. Rooney, Pace Inc., 744 F.2d 255 (2d Cir. 1984) (applying New York law forbidding subsidiaries from voting shares of the parent's stock to Panamanian corporation, and observing that "principles compelling a forum state to apply foreign law come into play only when a legitimate and substantial interest of another state would thereby be served").

(3) States have also applied local law on occasion to "pseudo-foreign" or "tramp" corporations that do all their business in one state while being formally incorporated in another. *See, e.g.*, Mansfield Hardwood Lumber Co. v. Johnson, 268 F.2d 317 (5th Cir. 1959). In Weede v. Iowa Southern Utilities Co. of Delaware, 231 Iowa 784, 2 N.W.2d 372, *opinion modified*, 4 N.W.2d 869 (1942), the Supreme Court of Iowa applied forum law designed to prevent "stock watering" to a foreign corporation operating a local utility plant. The corporation had argued that Iowa was without power to interfere with the corporation's internal affairs.

> In passing upon these propositions, it must be kept in mind that while the appellee is a corporation organized under the laws of Delaware, it is what the authorities or decisions speak of as a "tramp" or "migratory" corporation. "While this practice of taking out a charter in one state to

> do business solely in another is probably too general and too long recognized to be questioned, the courts of a state in which such business is to be done are ordinarily reluctant to adopt a construction of the local laws which would enable corporators, by resorting to such practice, to receive, by reason of foreign incorporation, more favorable treatment than similar domestic corporations." 23 Am. Jur. Section 123, p.127. Its promotors went from Iowa to Maine and first organized under the laws of the latter state. Later they reorganized under the laws of Delaware. They had no apparent intention of operating their utility plant, or of doing any other business in Maine or Delaware. Its officers, its plant and operating property, its assets, except a bank account or two, its business, almost all of its officers, its books and records, in fact, all of its physical manifestations, have always been, and are now in Iowa, within the jurisdiction of the courts of Iowa. . . . Its creation in Delaware was purely one of convenience, or other hoped for advantage. It was not for the purpose of becoming an actual, as well as a legal, resident of Delaware. While it was, and is, in law a legal resident of Delaware, and has its technical domicile there, its "commercial" or "economic" domicile is in Iowa. It was conceived in Iowa, born in Delaware, and has lived its entire life in Iowa. The foreignness of such a corporation has been spoken of as but a "metaphysical concept." Its existence in Delaware is an illusory mirage, more atmospheric, than real. Under the circumstances it is, in actuality, more domestic than foreign. The courts of this state have full jurisdiction of the parties and the subject matter with authority to grant all of the relief prayed for, and the power at hand to fully enforce such decree.

Is forum-shopping in this context good or bad? Does the answer turn on whether the rights of third parties are at stake, *i.e.*, persons who were in no way involved in the choice of where to incorporate? Aren't shareholders and managers in a different position than tort victims?

(4) Problems arise in defining the contours of "internal affairs." Is piercing the corporate veil a matter of internal affairs? *See, e.g.*, Jefferson Pilot Broadcasting Co. v. Hilary & Hogan, Inc., 617 F. 2d 133 (5th Cir. 1980) (law of place of incorporation governs decision whether to disregard corporate entity). What about enforcement requests to view the corporate books? *See, e.g.*, Jefferson Industrial Bank v. First Golden Bancorporation, 762 P.2d 768 (Colo. Ct. App. 1988) (Colorado law giving shareholders access to corporate records applies to Delaware corporation conducting substantial business within the state); Sadler v. NCR Corp., 928 F.2d 48 (4th Cir. 1991) (access to stockholder list is recognized exception to internal affairs doctrine).

(5) As *Irving Trust* suggests, there is a substantial possibility of collision between the rules of corporate capacity and those tort, property, or contract rules specifying the law of some place other than the place of incorporation. If the *ABC* Corp. injures someone in state *X*, is this a tort case governed by *X* law even if the plaintiff seeks to pierce the corporate veil and reach the assets of individual shareholders? In Pinney v. Nelson, 183 U.S. 144 (1901), the Supreme Court upheld application of forum law imposing

personal liability on shareholders by citing a contract rationale. By forming a corporation to do business in the forum, the shareholders had formed their "contract" of corporation with reference to forum law. Is this convincing?

It has been suggested recently that the doctrine of limited liability for corporate shareholders be abandoned. Hansmann and Kraakman, Toward Unlimited Shareholder Liability for Corporate Torts, 100 Yale L.J. 1879 (1991); Leebron, Limited Liability, Tort Victims, and Creditors, 91 Colum. L. Rev. 1565 (1991). But as has been pointed out, the feasibility of any one state abolishing the doctrine depends on whether it has a right to impose its laws on foreign corporations and shareholders, who may have little connection with the state. Alexander, Unlimited Shareholder Liability Through a Procedural Lens, 106 Harv. L. Rev. 387 (1992). Alexander argues that the issue would be treated as a question of "internal affairs" and would therefore be governed by the law of the state of incorporation; Hansmann and Kraakman, in a response, disagree. A Procedural Focus on Unlimited Shareholder Liability, 106 Harv. L. Rev. 446 (1992). Which side does *Pinney* support?

G. Personal Property and Trusts

Selections from the First Restatement of Conflicts, on Trusts of Personal Property

§§294-298 (1934)

§294. Validity of Trust of Movables Created Inter Vivos

(1) Except as stated in §263, the validity of a trust of chattels created by a settlement or other transaction inter vivos is determined as to each item by the law of the state in which the particular chattel is at the time of the creation of the trust.

(2) The validity of a trust of choses in action created by a settlement or other transaction inter vivos is determined by the law of the place where the transaction takes place.

§295. Validity of Trust Created by Will

The validity of a trust of movables created by a will is determined by the law of the testator's domicil at the time of his death.

§296. Interpretation of Trust Instrument

The meaning of the words used in an instrument creating a trust of movables is, in the absence of controlling circumstances to the contrary, determined in accordance with usage at the domicil of the settlor of the trust at the time of the execution of the instrument which created it.

§297. Administration of Trust of Movables Created Inter Vivos

A trust of movables created by an instrument inter vivos is administered by the trustee according to the law of the state where the instrument creating the trust locates the administration of the trust.

Comment

a. *What constitutes administration of trust.* As to the validity of a trust of movables, *see* §§294 and 295. Once it is determined that the trust is valid, many legal questions concerning the administration of the trust may arise. The administration by the trustee is the action of the trustee in carrying out the duties of the trust. In what securities can he invest? What interest should he receive on investment? To whom shall he pay the income? To whom shall he render an account? These are questions of administration and the rule stated in this Section is applicable to them.

§298. Administration of Trust of Movables Created by Will

A testamentary trust of movables is administered by the trustee according to the law of the state of the testator's domicil at the time of his death unless the will shows an intention that the trust should be administered in another state.

Hutchison v. Ross

262 N.Y. 381, 187 N.E. 65 (1933)

Lehman, J.

John Kenneth Ross, a resident of Montreal, married in Toronto in 1902. In anticipation of their marriage, the parties entered into an antenuptial agreement to regulate their property rights in accordance with the law of Quebec, where they intended to reside. They still do reside there. Under the civil law prevailing in that province, there is community of property between spouses, but the parties to a marriage may by antenuptial agreement provide that each shall continue to have separate property. They may also by such antenuptial agreement provide for gifts or trusts in favor of one or the other. After the marriage, such provisions in an antenuptial agreement may not be abrogated, modified, or enlarged. Neither husband nor wife may transfer to the other, directly or in trust, any substantial part of his or her fortune.

The antenuptial agreement made by Ross and his prospective wife provided that the property of each should be separate, and Ross agreed in addition to provide for the support of his wife and to establish either by deed or will a trust fund of $125,000 for the benefit of his wife and children. Since John Kenneth Ross was at that time a young man without personal fortune, though the only son of a very rich man, his father became a party to the antenuptial agreement and guaranteed a "donation" of $125,000 binding upon his estate.

The father of John Kenneth Ross died in 1913, leaving an estate of about $10,000,000 to his son. In 1916, during the World War, John Kenneth Ross, the son, decided that a provision of $125,000 for his family was insufficient, and he told his wife that he desired to provide for her more adequately by creating a trust fund of $1,000,000 the income to be paid to his wife for life, and the principal to go to their two children upon her death. One D. M. C. Hogg, a Scotchman [*sic*] learned in the law of Scotland, but perhaps not in the law of Quebec, had been the secretary and advisor of Ross' father. Ross, the son, had continued to employ him in the same capacity. Ross directed Hogg to prepare or have prepared appropriate instruments to transfer to the Equitable Trust Company in the city of New York a fund of $1,000,000, to be held in trust for his wife. Both father and son had kept bank deposits and had securities valued at more than half a million dollars in New York City, in the New York branch of the Bank of Montreal. Ross desired that such securities, with substitutions and additions sufficient to create a fund of $1,000,000, should constitute the corpus of the trust estate.

Hogg, in accordance with what he deemed his instructions, prepared a trust deed or agreement. The trustee was to pay the income to Mrs. Ross during her life, and after her death, to divide the principal among the children of the marriage, her surviving or their issue per stirpes, or to make other disposition thereof in accordance with the provisions of the instrument. The instrument was submitted to the trust company for approval. After the trust company had agreed to act as trustee, the instrument was sent to Montreal, where Ross and his wife executed it before the American Consul General. The Equitable Trust Company had not yet signed the indenture, but did so after the indenture was sent to it. Then the Bank of Montreal in New York City, acting as agent for Ross, delivered the securities to the trustee. The trust deed contains a recital that:

> Whereas Mr. Ross has become possessed of ample means and is desirous of making suitable provision for Mrs. Ross in lieu of the provisions in her favor contained in said contract of marriage settlement, and Mrs. Ross is

> willing to renounce and revoke the provisions of said marriage settlement in her favor and to accept in lieu thereof the provisions for her benefit and support hereinafter contained in this agreement.

Mrs. Ross then expressly revoked all conditions or provisions contained in the contract of marriage and all benefits which might accrue to her under the marriage contract.

For about ten years, the trustee carried out the provisions of the trust indenture. During that time no one questioned its validity. In 1926, Ross retained a Montreal barrister to draw up a will. He told the barrister of the provision he had already made for his family. The barrister promptly told Ross that the trust indenture was patently invalid under the law of Quebec, and so notified the trustee. By that time, most of the estate which Ross had received from his father had dissipated. Ross was deeply involved in speculations in oil stocks. He owed large sums to some Baltimore banks. He informed the Baltimore banks that the trust he had created was invalid, and, in consideration of his promise to bring legal proceedings to have the trust set aside and deliver the trust property to the banks as collateral, they agreed not only to extend the existing loans but to make new loans for Ross. He secured the signature of his wife and children to written consents to revoke the trust. Ross then began an action to set aside the trust on the ground that it was void at its inception and a second action for the revocation of the trust upon the consent of the interested parties.

After the actions were commenced, a petition in bankruptcy was filed against the plaintiff, and the trustee in bankruptcy was substituted in his place. The defendants in the first action assert that under the law of New York the conveyance is valid and should be enforced here. In the second action, they assert that the signatures to the consents to revoke the trust were obtained by misrepresentations and that issue of the settlor's children, born and unborn, have an interest in the trust. Both actions were tried together. They resulted in a judgment in favor of the plaintiff in the first action, and a judgment on the merits in favor of the defendants in the second action. Appropriate findings were made in each action. Upon appeal, the Appellate Division reversed the judgment in the first action, and upon new findings dismissed the complaint upon the merits. It affirmed the judgment in the second action.

The situs of personal property in a jurisdiction other than that where the owner of the property is domiciled has given rise to many difficulties and perplexities. The maxim "mobilia sequuntur personam" ["personal property follows the person"] cannot always be carried to its logical conclusion. Practical considerations often stand in the way. Physical presence in one jurisdiction is a fact; the maxim is only a juristic formula which cannot destroy the act. Within territorial limits, the jurisdiction of the courts of each state or nation is limited only by Constitution or treaty. The courts of each jurisdiction determine all judicial questions by the law of that jurisdiction. When the owner of personal property authorizes its removal from its domicile or acquires property elsewhere, he must be deemed to know that his property comes under the protection of, and subject to, the laws of the jurisdiction to which it has been removed, and that appeal may be made to the courts of that jurisdiction for the determination of conflicting rights in such property. The law of his domicile may be different from the law of the state or nation in which the personal property is placed. A conveyance of the property may be valid under the laws of one jurisdiction and void under the laws of the other jurisdiction. If the courts of each jurisdiction determine such questions according to their own law, then transfers of property become complicated and restricted in effect. A title, valid here, may be lost when the property is removed to another jurisdiction. Such a situation would obviously be intolerable. Therefore the rule has become ingrafted in the law of every jurisdiction that in some circumstances its courts must determine questions submitted to them by the rules of law applied in some other jurisdiction. To that extent foreign law is applied but as part of our own law. *See* articles by Professor Beale, 23 Harvard Law Review, 260, and 45 Harvard Law Review, 969. Though public policy and comity may be decisive in the determination of what law shall be applied in given circumstances,

> it does not belong to the judges to recognize or to deny the rights which individuals may claim under it, at their pleasure or caprice; but, it having obtained the force of law by use and acquiescence, it belongs only to the political government of the State to change it whenever a change becomes desirable.

Here, as in other branches of the law, there should be certainty of rule and uniformity of application, and we must look to the judicial decisions and legislative enactment for guidance.

The courts of the various jurisdictions have with substantial unanimity adopted certain rules. "Capacity to make a valid conveyance of a chattel is determined by the law of the State where the chattel is situated at the time of conveyance." American Law Institute, Tentative Restatement Conflict of Laws, §275. "The essential validity of a conveyance of a chattel is determined by the law of the state where the chattel is situated at the time of the conveyance." *Id.* §277. In this state these rules have long been applied to the conveyance of tangible chattels. More recently, we have indicated that the rule should be applied to negotiable paper instruments.

> Bills and notes were developed under the law merchant as convenient instrumentalities of trade and commerce. They pass from hand to hand by indorsement and delivery and properly are governed by the rule relating to the transfer of tangibles. The rule of international law, that the validity of a transfer of movable chattels must be governed by the law of the country in which the transfer takes place, applies to the transfer of checks or bills of exchange by indorsement. . . .

For the same reasons the rule should be and generally is applied to other tangible personal property, at least when "no one can get the benefits of ownership except through and by means of the paper" which evidences such intangible property. . . . Intangible property, like shares of corporate stock or debts, may for practical purposes be merged and embodied in documents like stock certificates or bonds, which like bills and notes are "instrumentalities of trade and commerce." "They pass from hand to hand and properly are governed by the rule relating to the transfer of tangibles." *Cf.* American Law Institute, Tentative Restatement Conflict of Laws, §§53, 57, 281, 282. Such documents and the personal property merged or embodied in them have, like tangible chattels, a situs apart from the domicile of the owners. . . .

Nevertheless the physical presence of such documents gives the state jurisdiction over them in other respects [besides taxation]. . . . Judicial decisions affecting the situs of choses in action or intangible property not embodied or merged in a mercantile document are not in point. . . . We are dealing with a conveyance in trust of documents which in the market place are treated as property and not merely evidence of property . . . and consider no other question.

The rules that both the capacity to make a valid conveyance of tangible chattels and securities and the essential validity of such conveyance are determined by the law of the state where the chattel is situated at the time of the conveyance have been generally applied to conveyances inter vivos. They are not generally applied to passage of title by will or the intestacy of a decedent owner. With possible limitations, not relevant to the question here presented . . . the rule is well established that the essential validity of a testamentary trust must be determined by the law of the decedent's domicile, and the same rule often is applied to trusts established as part of a marriage settlement. The plaintiff urges that the same rule should be applied to a conveyance in trust inter vivos, especially where such trust is established for the benefit of the wife and children of the settlor.

. . . Today the courts cannot close their eyes to the fact that trusts of personal property and securities are created by settlors during their lifetime for many purposes, and for the first time our court is called upon to decide directly the question whether conveyance in trust of securities made inter vivos shall be governed by the same rules as testamentary trusts or by the same rules as other conveyances inter vivos.

Analogy furnishes no satisfactory guide, for analogy in either case is imperfect and incomplete. Dicta in earlier opinions are certainly unreliable, because the rule announced is assumed rather than considered. Nevertheless the fact that the rule has been assumed is not without significance. . . .

In all the affairs of life there has been a vast increase of mobility. Residence is growing less and less the focal point of existence, and its practical effect is steadily diminishing. Men living in one jurisdiction often conduct their affairs in other jurisdictions, and keep their securities there. Trusts are created in business and financial centers by settlors residing elsewhere. A settlor, regardless of residence, cannot establish a trust to be administered here which offends our public policy. If we hold that a nonresident settlor may also not establish a trust of personal property here which offends the public policy of his domicile, we shackle both the nonresident settlor and the resident trustee.

Our courts have sought whenever possible to sustain the validity even of testamentary trusts to be administered in a jurisdiction other than the domicile of the testator. . . . In regard to other conveyances or alienations of personal property situated here, they have steadfastly applied the law of the jurisdiction where the personal property is situated. The maxim that movable personal property follows its owner is restricted to the field within which the state, where that property is found, chooses to apply other laws than its own, and modern conditions have caused a limitation of the field to narrow bounds. That is true in other jurisdictions as well as here. Where a nonresident settlor establishes here a trust of personal property intending that the trust should be governed by the law of this jurisdiction, there is little reason why the courts should defeat his intention by applying the law of another jurisdiction. . . .

The instrument creating the trust is not, in form, merely an assignment of personal property upon specified trusts, nor is it merely an agreement between the settlor and the trustee. Mrs. Ross is a party to the instrument, and at least in form it constitutes, in addition to a deed or conveyance in trust, an agreement between wife and husband whereby she consents to revoke any and all conditions or provisions for her benefit and support contained in the said contract of marriage settlement dated January 28, 1902, and does for herself, her heirs, executors and administrators and assigns renounce any and all benefits which might accrue to her under the provision of said marriage settlement.

Though the validity of the conveyance in trust be determined by the law of the state of New York, there can be no doubt that the validity of the provisions of the agreement for the revocation of the contract of marriage settlement and for the renunciation of the benefits which might accrue to the defendant under the marriage settlement must be determined by the law of Quebec. There the parties were domiciled, and there the marriage contract was made and will be enforced. In the province of Quebec these provisions of the agreement will be given no effect. The attempted renunciation of the marriage settlement is a futile act, and the courts of this state are powerless to give it effect. The parties to the contract by appeal to our courts have subjected themselves to the jurisdiction of those courts, but the decrees of our courts have no extraterritorial effect and cannot alter the domiciliary martial status of parties not domiciled here, or direct the courts of the jurisdiction where the parties are domiciled in the enforcement of marital rights there.

There is nevertheless no rule of law which would preclude the courts of this state from determining in accordance with the rules of law of this jurisdiction the validity of a conveyance of real or personal property contained in a bilateral agreement, even though the remainder of the agreement be governed by, and is void under, the law of another jurisdiction, provided the conveyance be separable from the other parts of the contract. Concededly that would be true if the conveyance were of real estate here. It is equally true of personal property situated within the jurisdiction of our courts. Here we are free to apply our law rather than the law of another jurisdiction.

The difficulty in this case is that on the face of the contract the conveyance in trust seems to have been made, at least partly, in consideration of the revocation of the provisions of the marriage contract and according to the recitals "in lieu of the provisions . . . contained in said contract of marriage settlement." Though an executed deed or conveyance in trust requires no consideration, . . . yet, if made for a promised consideration which fails, the conveyance may be revoked. Though apparently that question has never heretofore been presented to any court, it would seem clear that a conveyance valid under the law of New York, might be unenforceable and subject to rescission if the consideration fails because the laws of Quebec effectually preclude the enjoyment of the promised consideration. Upon the face of the agreement the wife's renunciation is the consideration for the husband's conveyance in trust. Invalidity in either, it is said, renders the other unenforceable or subject to rescission.

The Appellate Division has, however, found that the defendant Mrs. Ross never "knowingly consented to revoke any of the conditions or provisions for her benefit contained in the said marriage settlement, and never knowingly renounced any benefit which might accrue to her thereunder" and that "no consent to revoke, or agreement to renounce, or renunciation, by the defendant Ethel Adine Ross . . . was intended to induce, or did induce, the plaintiff Ross to transfer the securities" included in the trust. The evidence on this point was elicited from the parties themselves. . . .

The judgment in each action should be affirmed, with costs.

Wilmington Trust Co. v. Wilmington Trust Co.

26 Del. Ch. 397, 24 A.2d 309 (1942)

LAYTON, C.J.

The vexed question is one of conflict of law. Upon its determination depend the validity and effect of a deed of appointment under a power conferred by a trust agreement. The facts of the case and pertinent provisions of the writings involved have been fully stated in three opinions heretofore filed in the Court below. They will be restated in the briefest possible way.

On November 20, 1920, William H. Donner, hereinafter referred to as the donor, then domiciled in Buffalo, New York, executed a deed of trust, conveying to his wife, Dora Browing Donner, certain shares of stock in trust for the benefit of his wife and his five children for their respective lives. Subject to certain conditions, the trust to the extent of each child's interest therein was to cease at death; but it was provided that the property and securities held under the trust to produce the income for such deceased child should be transferred and delivered to such lawful child or children or other lawful lineal descendants of the donor then surviving, and in such proportions, as such deceased child should appoint and designate by last will and testament, or other instrument. . . . By the tenth paragraph of the trust agreement, a majority of the adult beneficiaries, subject to the approval of the donor during his lifetime, were authorized to change from time to time the trustee under the trust agreement, or under any of the separate trusts, to any trust company of any state, possessing certain qualifications, and in such event, it was directed that such successor trustee "shall hold the said trust estate to all the conditions herein to the same effect as though now named herein."

During the years 1921 to 1923, inclusive, the donor made substantial additions to the trust estate, and on January 16, 1924, the value of the securities held by the trustee exceeded $2,000,000.00.

By an instrument dated January 16, 1924, Dora Browing Donner, the wife of the donor and trustee under the trust agreement, Robert Newsom Donner and Joseph W. Donner, sons of the donor, they being all of the adult beneficiaries under the trust agreement, constituted and appointed Wilmington Trust Company as the trustee to succeed Dora Browing Donner; and she, as trustee, was authorized and directed to transfer and deliver to the successor trustee all of the money, securities and property held by her under the trust agreement. On February 16, 1924, the principal of the trust was delivered to Wilmington Trust Company as successor trustee at the City of Wilmington [Delaware]; and since that time it has administered the trust.

Subsequent to the appointment of the successor trustee, large additions were made to the trust fund. . . .

On October 9, 1929, Joseph W. Donner executed an instrument in which express reference was made to the power of appointment conferred on him by the trust agreement. He appointed and designated his two children, Joseph W. Donner, Jr. and Carroll E. Donner, Jr. to receive all of his interest and share in the trust fund. . . . It was provided that at the death of each of his children the trust was to cease to the extent of the deceased child's interest or share, and that all of the property and securities so held under the trust to produce income for such child should be transferred and delivered as such child should have devised or designated, or in default thereof, to his or her lawful lineal descendants, if any; otherwise to remain in trust for the benefit of the survivor of the children; and if there should be no survivor, the share would remain as part of the principal of the trust for the benefit of all of the cestui trustent thereunder.

On November 9, 1929, Joseph W. Donner died, leaving to survive him his widow, and the two children. The will was probated in Erie County, New York. . . .

In these circumstances, Wilmington Trust Company, as guardian for the two children of Joseph W. Donner, deceased, sued in the Court below to compel Wilmington Trust Company, as successor trustee under the trust agreement of the donor, to account for and to pay over to the complainant the property which is held in trust for the benefit of the deceased. . . .

At the first hearing before the late Chancellor no questions of conflict of law were raised. . . .

A rehearing was granted. Pertinent provisions of the statutes of the State of New York and decisions construing them were made a part of the record. It was contended that the trust was governed by the law of New York, and, therefore, the validity and effect of the deed of appointment were to be adjudged by that law. In this state of record, Chancellor Wolcott . . . held that the trust was governed by the law of New York; [and] that . . . the testator's attempt by the deed of appointment to appoint it in trust for his children for life remainder to their appointees or their lawful lineal descendants was void under the New York law against perpetuities. . . .

No decree had been signed by the late Chancellor at the time of his death. An informal request for a rehearing was at that time before him, and a rehearing was granted by his successor, the present Chancellor. . . . The Chancellor held . . . that on October 9, 1929, the date of the execution of the deed of appointment by Joseph W. Donner, the trust created by the donor was located in the State of Delaware; that the deed of appointment was a valid exercise of the power of appointment conferred on Joseph W. Donner by the terms of the trust deed of November 20, 1920; [and] that the appointment in trust for life for the benefit of the two children of Joseph W. Donner was a valid exercise of that power. . . .

From the decree entered, two appeals were taken. . . .

The power of appointment exercised by Joseph W. Donner for the benefit of his two children had its origin in the donor's deed of trust; the provisions of the deed of appointment were reviewed in law as though they had been embodied in that instrument; and the rights and interests appointed to the children are regarded as creations of the trust deed. . . . The validity of the deed of appointment and of the rights and interests assigned thereunder depend upon the law of the jurisdiction in which the trust had its seat when the power of appointment was exercised.

The diversity of judicial opinion with respect to the discovery of the jurisdiction under whose law the validity of a trust inter vivos of intangible personal property is to be determined is such that no useful purpose will be served by an attempted analysis of the decisions. Courts have variously looked to the domicile of the donor, the place of execution of the trust instrument, the situs of the trust property, the place of administration of the trust, the domicile of the trustee, the domicile of the beneficiaries, and to the intent or desire of the donor, or to a combination of some of these denominators, in deciding the troublesome question of conflict of law. In the case of a testamentary trust of personalty it is very generally held that the law of the testator's domicile is the governing law. In some jurisdictions the same rule is applied in the case of a living trust of personal property. Modern methods of transportation with a resulting change of business economy have tended, however, to obliterate state lines and to depreciate the importance of particular localities. The place of one's residence no longer is a sure indication of one's place of business; nor is ownership of property closely tied to residence. The domicile of the donor is, of course, a circumstance to be considered in the ascertainment of the seat of the trust; but courts, today, are not so much inclined to the uncompromising pursuit of abstract doctrine. They are disposed to take a more realistic and practical view of the problem; and the donor's domicile is no longer regarded as the decisive factor. The place of execution of the trust instrument and the domicile of the trustee and the place of administration of the trust—quite generally the same place—are important factors; and the intent of the donor, if that can be ascertained, has been increasingly emphasized. . . .

Contracting parties, within definite limits, have some right of choice in the selection of the jurisdiction under whose law their contract is to be governed. And where the donor in a trust agreement has expressed his desire, or if it pleases, his intent to have his trust controlled by the law of a certain state, there seems to be no good reason why his intent should not be respected by the courts, if the selected jurisdiction has a material connection with the transaction. More frequently, perhaps, the trust instrument contains no expression of choice of jurisdiction; but, again, there is no sufficient reason why the donor's choice should be disregarded if his intention in this respect can be ascertained from an examination of attendant facts and circumstances, provided that the same substantial connection between the transaction and the intended jurisdiction shall be found to exist. . . .

Originally the trust under consideration was a trust under the laws of the State of New York for the reason that every operative factor pointed solely to that State. But a change of trustee, not only as to character but as to location, was clearly contemplated and provided for in the trust instrument. At this point the divergence of view in the Court below is first manifested. The late Chancellor took his stand squarely on the ground that a mere change of domicile of the trustee accompanied by a change of the location of the trust property does not change the status of the trust. He found nothing in the language of the trust instrument, nor in the surrounding facts and circumstances, which, as he said, pointed to a fundamental modification of the terms and conditions of the trust. He emphasized the fact that a change of jurisdiction would affect the rights and privileges of the beneficiaries. Expressly, with reference to the phrase contained in the tenth paragraph, "*to the same effect as though now named herein,*" he refused to accord it any other or further significance than as referring to the conditions as stated and existing at the time the trust was created.

The present Chancellor took a more liberal view. He was of opinion that, at the least, the italicized phrase was susceptible to more than one interpretation. In his view the phrase pointed to something more than mere administrative action; and with the aid, perhaps, of the donor's testimony which is detailed in his opinion, he reached the conclusion that the donor had made provision for a shift of the situs of his trust, and for a re-creation of it under the laws of a jurisdiction to be selected by the adult beneficiaries with his approval.

There was no disagreement in the Court below with respect to the general rules. . . . The clash of opinion was with respect to a question of interpretation of language. We . . . are of the opinion that the narrow interpretation put upon the italicized phrase by the late Chancellor was unjustified.

. . . The donor was careful to provide for a change of trustee subject to his approval in his lifetime. In the event of such change he declared that the successor trustee should "hold the said trust estate subject to all the conditions herein *to the same effect as though now named herein*." . . . As we view the donor's language, he very plainly declared that if the trustee should be changed, the successor trustee should not only be bound by the same conditions as were expressed in the trust deed, but also that the successor trustee should have the same status, and should be considered in all respects, as an original appointee. The phrase, reasonably considered, can have no other significance unless it is to be dismissed as a mere redundancy. If the donor, domiciled in New York, had, in the first instance, named Wilmington Trust Company as the guardian of his trust, and had delivered to it in this State the original corpus, making substantial additions thereto from time to time, the late Chancellor, as we read his opinion, would readily have accepted these facts and circumstances as sufficient evidence of the donor's intention to submit his trust to the law of this jurisdiction. . . .

There is no substantial reason why a donor, in dealing with that which is his own, may not provide for a change in the location of his trust with a consequent shifting of the controlling law. In an era of economic uncertainty, with vanishing returns from investments and with tax laws approaching confiscation, such a provision would seem to amount to no more than common foresight and prudence. The rights of beneficiaries may, it is true, be disturbed by a shift of jurisdiction, but if such change has been provided for, they have no more cause to complain than other persons who are recipients of bounty under some condition or limitation.

The adult beneficiaries, with the donor's approval, transferred the seat of the trust from New York to Delaware. On October 9, 1929, when Joseph W. Donner availed himself of the power of appointment conferred on him by the trust agreement, the home of the trust was in the State, and, being subject then to local law, the validity and effect of his deed of appointment and of the rights and interests of the appointees thereunder are to be adjudged and determined by the law of Delaware. . . .

Question and Comments

(1) In the *Hutchison* case, did the court deal adequately with the problem created by the fact that New York law upheld the $1,000,000 trust while Quebec law forbade rescission of the original $125,000 trust? Assuming that

sufficient assets had been set aside in trust to fulfill the antenuptial agreement, why couldn't the New York court have revoked the New York trust to the amount of $125,000—that is, why does the New York decision have to be an all-or-nothing matter?

(2) How much respect did the New York court actually give the law of Quebec when it upheld a trust that was invalid under Quebec law? What specific reasons did the court state for applying its own law rather than that of the marital domicile to the trust question? What harm would be worked by "shackling" the New York trustee with the limitations of the settlor's domiciliary law? If in fact the trust business of New York financial institutions would be impaired by subjecting them to law other than that of New York, is that a valid consideration in determining whose law to apply in cases like *Hutchison?*

In Wyatt v. Fulrath, 16 N.Y.2d 169, 211 N.E.2d 637, 264 N.Y.S.2d 233 (1965), the Duke and Duchess of Arion had placed large amounts of money in New York bank accounts during the Spanish civil war. Both were domiciliaries of Spain, and neither had ever been in New York. The accounts were of the survivorship type; that is, upon the death of one of the parties, the other succeeded to ownership. But under the law of Spain (a community property jurisdiction), only half the property would go to the wife at the time of her husband's death. A statute protected the bank from liability for paying her the proceeds, so the only immediate interests were those of the claimants. The court chose to apply New York law and to recognize the "physical and legal submission of the property to our laws." "Thus we would at once honor their intentional resort to the protection of our laws and their recognition of the general stability of our Government which may well be deemed interrelated things." 16 N.Y.2d at 173, 211 N.E.2d at 639, 264 N.Y.S.2d at 236.

Are such arguments persuasive? "Physical submission" of the property obviously empowers the New York court to adjudicate the dispute and to apply whatever law it wants, but what does it have to do with whose law *should* apply? And why should intent be allowed to bypass Spanish succession law indirectly when it is ineffective to do so directly? Is there in fact a relationship between the bank deposit laws of New York and the "general stability of our Government"? Would the New York banks have lost these particular accounts, and perhaps many others, if the New York courts had not been so accommodating? Is that a worthy reason to frustrate Spanish law?

(3) In the *Wilmington Trust* case, the court allowed the parties to avoid the effects of the New York Rule Against Perpetuities. (For a long and amusing dissertation on how properly to capitalize the name of that rule, *see* Dukeminier, Perpetuities: Contagious Capitalization, 20 J. Legal Ed. 341 (1968).) What is the purpose of the rule? Is it fair to New York policy to allow the parties to escape the rule, or can the same arguments be made about this rule as were made about the formalities attendant to making wills in note (4) after In re Barrie's Estate?

(4) What has happened to the confident, syllogistic reasoning of the *Carroll* and Poole v. Perkins opinions? Is there a way to determine trust questions from neutral, a priori principles? Should principles of marital relations be applied in *Hutchison* because the settlor and chief beneficiary were married? Or should the case be considered one involving a gift of chattels? Should the *Wilmington Trust* case be viewed as a gift case or a testamentary matter?

Selections from the First Restatement of Conflicts, on Personal Property

§§255-258, 260-261, 289-291, 300-302, 306-307 (1934)

§255. Capacity to Convey Chattel

Capacity to make a valid conveyance of an interest in a chattel is determined by the law of the state where the chattel is at the time of the conveyance.

§256. Formalities of Conveyance of Chattel

The formal validity of a conveyance of an interest in a chattel is determined by the law of the state where the chattel is at the time of conveyance.

§257. Substantial Validity of Conveyance of Chattel

Whether a conveyance of a chattel which is in due form and is made by a party who has capacity to convey it is in other respects valid, is determined by the law of the state where the chattel is at the time of conveyance.

§258. Nature of Interest Created by Conveyance of Chattel

The nature and characteristics of an interest created by a conveyance of an interest in a chattel is determined by the law of the place where the chattel is at the time of the conveyance.

§260. Moving Chattels into Another State; Effect on Title

An interest in a chattel acquired in accordance with the law of the state in which the chattel is at the time when the interest is acquired will be recognized in a state into which the chattel is subsequently taken.

§261. Chattel Embodied in a Document

(1) Whether the title to a chattel is embodied in a document is determined by the law of the place where the chattel is at the time when the document is issued.

(2) The validity of a conveyance of a chattel, title to which is embodied in a document, depends upon the validity of the conveyance of the document.

(3) The validity of a conveyance of a document in which title to a chattel is embodied as stated in Subsection (1), is determined by the law of the place where the document is at the time of the conveyance.

§289. Effect of Marriage on Title to Existing Movables

At marriage the husband and wife respectively acquire such rights or other interests in movables then belonging to the other as are given by the law of the domicil of the husband at the time of marriage.

§290. Movables Acquired during Marriage

Interests of one spouse in movables acquired by the other during the marriage are determined by the law of the domicil of the parties when the movables are acquired.

§291. Removal of Movables of Spouses to Another State

Interests in movables acquired by either or both of the spouses in one state continue after the movables have been brought into another state until the interests are affected by some new dealings with the movables in the second state.

§300. Devolution of Chattels on Death of Owner

At the death of the owner of chattels the title to the chattels passes to the executor or administrator appointed by the court of the state in which the chattels are habitually kept.

§301. Right of Widow or Child Outside Will

The right or other interest of a widow, child, or other person to a share of the movables of a decedent in preference to legatees is determined by the law of the state in which the decedent died domiciled.

§302. Enforcement of Widow's Allowance in Another State

If a widow's allowance has been granted by a court in the state of domicile of her deceased husband, it constitutes a valid claim against movable assets in another state.

§306. Will of Movables

The validity and effect of a will of movables is determined by the law of the state in which the deceased died domiciled.

§307. Revocation of Will of Movables

Whether an act claimed to be a revocation of a will is effective to revoke it as a will of movables is determined by the law of the state in which the deceased was domiciled at the time of his death.

Morson v. Second National Bank of Boston

306 Mass. 588, 29 N.E.2d 19 (1940)

QUA, J.

This is a bill in equity by the administrator of the estate of Herbert B. Turner, late of Gloucester, alleging, in substance, that a certificate for one hundred and fifty shares of the stock of the defendant Massachusetts Mohair Plush Company, a Massachusetts corporation, had been originally issued to Herbert B. Turner, but had been delivered to the defendant bank as "transfer agent" of the plush company by the defendant Mildred Turner Copperman for transfer to her on the ground that Herbert B. Turner in his lifetime had made her a gift of the stock. The prayers are for injunctions against the transfer of the stock and for recovery of the certificate.

The judge carefully found all the materials facts in detail, upon which he ruled that there had been no completed gift of the stock for the plaintiff. The issue is whether the facts found show a valid gift of the stock, which should now be recognized by a transfer on the books of the corporation and the issuance of a new certificate to Mildred Turner Copperman. We think that they do.

Among the facts found are these: About September 20, 1937, while Turner and Mildred Turner Copperman were travelling together in Italy, Turner handed to Mildred Turner Copperman a sealed envelope previously marked by him "Property of Mildred Turner Copperman." As he did so he said, "These are yours." The certificate in his name, dated October 6, 1933, was in the envelope. He also said that he would have to sign the back of the certificate. Two days later a notary and two witnesses came to the hotel where the parties were staying. Mildred Turner Copperman produced the certificate, and "Turner signed his name on the back . . . and then he filled in the name of Miss Copperman and her address" and delivered the certificate to Mildred Turner Copperman, who "accepted it." Turner's intention at that time was "to make an absolute gift to Mildred Copperman to take effect at once."

It is provided by [Uniform Stock Transfer Act §1], that title

> to a certificate and to the shares represented thereby shall be transferred only—(a) By delivery of the certificate endorsed either in blank or to a specified person by the person appearing by the certificate to be the owner of the shares represented thereby; or (b) By delivery of the certificate and a separate document containing a written assignment of the certificate or a power of attorney to sell, assign or transfer the same or the shares represented thereby, signed by the person appearing by the certificate to be the owner of the shares represented thereby. Such assignment or power of attorney may be either in blank or to a specified person.

[Uniform Stock Transfer Act §22] defines "certificate" as "a certificate of stock in a corporation organized under the laws of this commonwealth or of another state whose laws are consistent with said sections." Plainly that which was done in Italy would have been sufficient, if it had been done in Massachusetts, to effect a transfer legal title to the shares.

But it is argued that the validity of the transfer is to be judged by the law of Italy, and that certain formalities required by that law for making of gifts in general were not observed. Doubtless it is true that whether or not there is a completed gift of an ordinary tangible chattel is to be determined by the law of the situs of the chattel. American Law Inst., Restatement, Conflict of Laws §§256, 257, 258. Shares of stock, however, are not ordinary tangible chattels. A distinction has been taken between the shares and the certificate, regarded as a piece of paper which can be seen and felt, the former being said to be subject to the jurisdiction of the state of incorporation and the latter subject to the jurisdiction of the state in which it is located. American Law Inst., Restatement, Conflict of Laws, §53. The shares are part of the structure of the corporation, all of which was erected and stands by virtue of the law of the state of incorporation. The law of that state determines the nature and attributes of the shares. If by the law of that state the shares devolve upon one who obtains ownership of the certificate, it may be that the law of the state of a purported transfer of the certificate will indirectly determine share ownership. But at least when the state of incorporation has seen fit in creating the shares to insert in them the intrinsic attribute or quality of being assignable in a particular manner it would seem that that state, and other states as well, should recognize assignments made in the specified manner wherever they are made, even though that manner involves dealing in some way with the certificate. Or the shares may be regarded for this purpose as remaining at home with the corporation, wherever the certificate may be—much as real estate remains at home when the deeds are taken abroad. Thus the American Law Institute in its Restatement of Conflict Laws, §53, comment *d,* says that shares created in a State which has adopted the Uniform Stock Transfer Act with its provision that title to a share can be transferred only by delivery of the certificate "may be transferred by delivery of the certificate as provided by the Act even though such delivery takes place in another state where such Act is not in force." This rule is precisely applicable to the present case. This rule has, in our opinion, the decided advantage of promoting convenience, certainty, and uniformity in the transfer of stock. We prefer to follow it.

Questions and Comments

(1) What is a "plush company"?

(2) Would it have made a difference to the outcome of this case if the gift had been a piece of antique art rather than a gift of shares? Should it make a difference? Would it make a difference if the Italian law the parties failed to comply with was designed to monitor ownership of antique art?

(3) The Restatement provisions quoted above point chiefly to the locus of the tangible item to determine questions about transfers. Exceptions are made with respect to testamentary dispositions and transfers between spouses. Are the reasons discussed previously for applying the law of the situs to questions involving real property as compelling for questions of personal property?

(4) A particularly troublesome aspect of chattels is that they can be moved. When that fact is added to the fact that valuable chattels are often the collateral for security interests, the opportunity for a great deal of mischief arises. The Uniform Commercial Code has spelled out a set of fairly specific rules for dealing with the perfection of security interests in movable goods and in intangibles. Provisions are made for accounts, "ordinary goods," "mobile goods," goods subject to certificate-of-title legislation, and several other categories of collateral. *In general,* ordinary goods are governed by the law of their location. Accounts and mobile goods, having no handily identifiable location, are governed by the law of the debtor's location—usually its place of business. Goods subject to a certificate of title are generally subject to the law of the state that issues the certificate of title. For each category, there are rules concerning the relocation of the collateral or debtor.

For the most part, the single most important choice of law question concerning goods under Article Nine is where to file a financing statement in order to perfect a security interest, and in the 1972 version of the UCC, the rules of section 9-103 are limited to rules on where to file. Note that this is an area in which certainty is not only the most important consideration but nearly the only consideration. UCC 1-103 governs other conflicts issues. (*See* Chapter 2H below.)

H. Wrinkles in the Theory

1. Characterization

In the first case in this book, *Carroll*, the plaintiff attempted to avoid the application of Mississippi's fellow-servant doctrine by arguing that the issue in the case was contractual (and governed by the law of Alabama where the contract was formed), rather than tortious (and governed by the law of the place where the tort occurred). The plaintiff was unsuccessful in that attempt, but the plaintiff in Levy v. Daniel's U-Drive Auto Renting Co., note (6), *supra* page 11, succeeded with a similar argument. Likewise, in Burr v. Beckler, *supra* page 76, the court had to choose between characterizing the case as one involving real property, to be governed by the law of the situs of the property, or involving the validity of a note, to be governed by the law of the place where the note was made. These cases and several others illustrate the general problem of *characterization:* Before the rules of the First Restatement may be applied, one must know whether the case is a tort case, a contract case, etc. The First Restatement says remarkably little about characterization. It does comment about determining whether a contract issue is one of obligation or performance (*see* comment *b* to §358, *supra* page 28) and has a few words on the difference between the capacity to make a contract to transfer property and the capacity to transfer property (*see* comment *a* to §333, *supra* page 26), but in general it doesn't offer too much help.

Haumschild v. Continental Casualty Co.

7 Wis. 2d 130, 95 N.W.2d 814 (Wis. 1959)

CURRIE, Justice.

[Mrs. Haumschild sued her husband for personal injuries she suffered in an automobile accident in California as a result of his negligence. Both parties were Wisconsin domiciliaries. The Wisconsin trial court dismissed the case under California's law prohibiting a wife from suing her husband in tort.]

This appeal presents a conflict of laws problem with respect to interspousal liability for tort growing out of an automobile accident. Which law controls, that of the state of the forum, the state of the place of wrong, or the state of domicile? Wisconsin is both the state of the forum and of the domicile while California is the state where the alleged wrong was committed. Under Wisconsin law a wife may sue her husband in tort. Under California law she cannot.

This court was first faced with this question in Buckeye v. Buckeye, 1931, 203 Wis. 248, 234 N.W. 342. In that case Wisconsin was the state of the forum and domicile, while Illinois was the state of the place of wrong. It was there held that the law governing the creation and extent of tort liability is that of the place where the tort was committed. From this premise it was further held that interspousal immunity from tort liability necessarily is governed by the law of the place of injury.

The principle enunciated in the *Buckeye* case and followed in subsequent Wisconsin cases, that the law of the place of wrong controls as to whether one spouse is immune from suit in tort by the other, is the prevailing view in the majority of jurisdictions in this country. It is also the rule adopted in Restatement, Conflict of Laws, p. 457, sec. 378, and p. 470, sec. 384(2). However, criticism of the rule of the *Buckeye* case . . . , and recent decisions by the courts of California, New Jersey, and Pennsylvania, have caused us to re-examine the question afresh.

The first case to break the ice and flatly hold that the law of domicile should be applied in determining whether there existed an immunity from suit for tort based upon family relationship is Emery v. Emery, 1955, 45 Cal. 2d 421, 289 P.2d 218. In that case two unemancipated minor sisters sued their unemancipated minor brother and their father to recover for injuries sustained in an automobile accident that occurred in the state of Idaho, the complaint alleging wilful misconduct in order to come within the provisions of the Idaho "guest" statute. All parties were domiciled in California. The opinion by Mr. Justice Traynor recognized that the California court, in passing on the question of whether an unemancipated minor child may sue the parent or an unemancipated brother, had a choice to apply the law of the place of wrong, of the forum, or of the domicile. It was held that the immunity issue was not a question of tort but one of capacity to sue and be sued, and rejected the law of the place of injury as "both fortuitous and irrelevant." In deciding whether to apply the law of the forum, or the law of the domicile, the opinion stated this conclusion:

> Although tort actions between members of the same family will ordinarily be brought in the state of the family domicile, the courts of another state will in some cases be a more convenient forum, and thus the question arises whether the choice of law rule should be expressed in terms of the law of the forum or that of the domicile. We think that disabilities to sue and immunities from suit because of a family relationship are more properly determined by reference to the law of the state of the family domicile. That state has the primary responsibility for establishing and regulating the incidents of the family relationship and it is the only state

> in which the parties can, by participation in the legislative processes, effect a change in those incidents. Moreover, it is undesirable that the rights, duties, disabilities, and immunities conferred or imposed by the family relationship should constantly change as members of the family cross state boundaries during temporary absences from their home.

The two reasons most often advanced for the common law rule, that one spouse may not sue the other, are the ancient concept that husband and wife constitute in law but one person, and that to permit such suits will be to foment family discord and strife. The Married Women's Acts of the various states have effectively destroyed the "one person" concept thereby leaving as the other remaining reason for the immunity the objective of preventing family discord. This is also the justification usually advanced for denying an unemancipated child the capacity to sue a parent, brother or sister. Clearly this policy reason for denying the capacity to sue more properly lies within the sphere of family law, where domicile usually controls the law to be applied, than it does tort law, where the place of injury generally determines the substantive law which will govern.

We are convinced that, from both the standpoint of public policy and logic, the proper solution of the conflict of laws problem, in cases similar to the instant action, is to hold that the law of the domicile is the one that ought to be applied in determining any issue of incapacity to sue based upon family relationship.

After most careful deliberation, it is our considered judgment that this court should adopt the rule that, whenever the courts of this state are confronted with a conflict of laws problem as to which law governs the capacity of one spouse to sue the other in tort, the law to be applied is that of the state of domicile. We, therefore, expressly overrule the cases of Buckeye v. Buckeye, *supra*.

Perhaps a word of caution should be sounded to the effect that the instant decision should not be interpreted as a rejection by this court of the general rule that ordinarily the substantive rights of parties to an action in tort are to be determined in the light of the law of the place of wrong. This decision merely holds that incapacity to sue because of marital status presents a question of family law rather than tort law.

The concurring opinion by Mr. Justice Fairchild protests that we should not adopt the conflict of laws rule, that interspousal immunity to suit in tort should be determined by the law of the domicile, because this was not urged in the briefs or arguments of counsel. . . . While the appellant's counsel did not request that we overrule Buckeye v. Buckeye, *supra*, and the subsequent Wisconsin case dealing with this particular conflict of laws problem, he did specifically seek to have this court apply California's conflict of laws principle, that the law of the domicile is determinative of interspousal capacity to sue, to this particular case. However, to do so would violate the well recognized principle of conflict of laws that, where the substantive law of another state is applied, there necessarily must be excluded such foreign state's law of conflict of laws.

The reason why the authorities on conflict of laws almost universally reject the renvoi doctrine (permitting a court of the forum state to apply the conflict of laws principle of a foreign state) is that it is likely to result in the court pursuing a course equivalent to a never ending circle. For example, in the instant case, if the Buckeye v. Buckeye line of Wisconsin cases is to be followed, the Wisconsin court first looks to the law of California to see whether a wife can sue her husband in tort. California substantive law holds that she cannot. However, California has adopted a conflict of laws principle that holds that the law of the domicile determines such question. Applying such principle the court is referred back to Wisconsin law because Wisconsin is the state of domicile. Again the court applies Wisconsin law and, under the prior holdings of the Buckeye v. Buckeye line of authorities, would have to again refer to California law because such line of cases does not recognize that the law of domicile has anything to do with interspousal immunity, but holds that the law of the state of injury controls.

Wisconsin certainly should not adopt the much criticized renvoi principle in order not to overrule the Buckeye v. Buckeye line of cases, and still permit the plaintiff to recover. Such a result we believe would contribute for more to produce chaos in the field of conflict of laws than to overrule the Buckeye v. Buckeye line of cases and adopt a principle the soundness of which has been commended by so many reputable authorities.

Judgment reversed and cause remanded for further proceedings not inconsistent with this opinion.

FAIRCHILD, J. (concurring):

I concur in the reversal of the judgment, but do not find it necessary to re-examine settled Wisconsin law in order to do so. A fundamental change in the law of Wisconsin such as the one announced by the majority in this case, which will importantly affect many people, should be made, if at all, in a case where the question is necessarily presented. Both parties assumed that their case would be decided under the principle which is being overturned by the majority, and accordingly, we have not had the benefit of brief or argument upon the validity of the principle.

1. *Solution of this case without overruling previous decisions.* Plaintiff wife alleges a personal injury tort cause of action arising in California against defendant husband. Defendant husband pleads that she has no cause of action because she was his wife. It has been the rule in Wisconsin that the existence or non-existence of immunity because of family relationship is substantive and not merely procedural, and is to be determined by the law of the locus state. The law of California is that the existence or non-existence of immunity is a substantive matter, but that it is an element of the law of status, not of tort. The tort law of California is no more concerned with immunity than is Wisconsin's. Thus it makes no difference under the facts of this

case whether we look directly to the law of Wisconsin to determine that immunity is not available as a defense or look to the law of Wisconsin only because California, having no general tort principle as to immunity, classifies immunity as a matter of status.

2. *Policy questions requiring full consideration.* Under the principle announced by the majority that the existence of nonexistence of immunity is a matter of status our courts must henceforth recognize immunity as a defense where the alleged tort occurred in Wisconsin, but the parties are married and are domiciled in an immunity state. This would mean that such an act is or is not a remedial wrong depending upon the state where the parties happen to be domiciled.

The determination of domicil is not always easy, yet the courts will henceforth be required to determine it in many cases where it has heretofore been considered immaterial. A good many married couples who may have domicil in other states are in Wisconsin for extended periods. Some for example, are students at colleges and universities, some stationed here for military duty, some temporarily assigned here by employers, and some vacationing. Under the rule abandoned by the majority, a tortious act done in Wisconsin by a nonresident and injuring his spouse gave rise to the same civil liability as if done by a permanent resident.

The problem involved apparently has its principal impact because of injuries sustained in automobile accidents where members of a family travel together across state lines. Under the new rule Wisconsin courts will not countenance the defense of immunity for a Wisconsin husband when sued by his wife for an injury occurring in an immunity state. I concede there is some merit to the logic relied upon and that there may be some practical benefit to Wisconsin people. It is to be remembered, however, that under the law of many states a wife will have no cause of action for simple negligence of her husband because she will be a gratuitous guest. The fact that she and her husband are domiciled in Wisconsin and that they are on a family trip which began in Wisconsin will not exempt her from that principle of tort law. Thus the purely practical benefit to Wisconsin people which might appear at first blush to arise from the new rule will be limited.

Questions and Comments

(1) The rigidity of the First Restatement's rules, combined with its silence on the characterization issue, provided an opportunity for manipulation of characterization to achieve results that courts think are fair or desirable. For this reason, characterization is sometimes known as an "escape device." But is *this* characterization fair? After all, if there are no rules for characterization, how can characterization be used to "escape" an otherwise-mandated result?

(2) Are you convinced by *Haumschild*'s reasons for concluding that "incapacity to sue because of marital status presents a question of family law

rather than tort law"? How should a court resolve the characterization problem? What law should it apply in making this decision? Is *Haumschild*'s inquiry into the purposes of the interspousal immunity rule a fruitful approach? How did the *Carroll* court decide that the case involved a tort rather than a contract?

(3) Doesn't the characterization problem make it harder for the First Restatement to achieve its desired choice-of-law uniformity? Unless courts in different states would characterize the same case in the same way, uniformity will likely be defeated.

(4) Note that in *Haumschild*, the court appeared to commit itself to applying California law on tort issues such as negligence even though it applied Wisconsin's law rejecting interspousal immunity. The process of dividing a case up into various issues governed by potentially different laws is known as *dépecage.* Is such characterization at the level of issue rather than case appropriate? Is it consistent with the provisions of the First Restatement that you have read? Whether it is or not, does it make sense?

2. Renvoi

First Restatement choice-of-law rules pick out *the law* of the place of the wrong, the contract, the property, etc. But when the chosen law is the law of another state, does the chosen "law" include the foreign state's choice-of-law rules? This is the sticky problem of renvoi. As the majority opinion in *Haumschild* suggests, the inclusion of choice-of-law rules within the law chosen by a choice-of-law rule can lead to intractable problems, and for that reason is usually—but not always—avoided. The First Restatement generally rejected the renvoi doctrine except in cases involving title to land or the validity of a decree of divorce. *See* First Restatement, §§7-8. Consider whether these exceptions make sense as you read the cases below.

In re Estate of Damato

86 N.J. Super. 107, 206 A.2d 171 (1965)

LABRECQUE, J.A.D.

This is an appeal from a judgment of the Probate Division awarding the balance in two out-of-state bank accounts to decedent's son Philip Damato.

The facts are not in dispute. Decedent died on November 6, 1960, a resident of Paterson, New Jersey. Although he had been engaged in the wastepaper business in the Paterson area for many years, he also had business interests in Florida, including the operation of a small stable of race horses. His will was admitted to probate by the Surrogate of Passaic County, his son James Damato qualifying as the executor thereof. On July 26, 1962, the executor filed a verified complaint praying, inter alia, for instructions as to the disposition of the balances remaining in two savings accounts in the Bank of Hollywood, Hollywood, Florida, which are the subject of the present controversy. . . .

Both Philip and James Damato were sons of the decedent. Philip worked for his father in the Paterson business and never knew of the accounts until after the death of his father. The passbooks for both accounts remained in decedent's possession and were found among his papers in Florida.

In awarding the balance in each account to Philip, the trial judge held that the transactions were governed by the law of Florida, their situs, and since Florida had adopted the rule of In re Totten, they were effective to pass the balance in each account to Philip upon the death of the decedent. . . .

The law is well settled that the creation of an inter vivos trust in money or securities, as distinguished from a testamentary trust, is governed by the law of the situs of the money or securities. The validity of an inter vivos trust of choses in action is determined by the law of the place where the transaction takes place.

The savings bank trust doctrine which the trial judge found to be dispositive of the issue before him was set forth in its present form in In re Totten, *supra,* to the effect that:

> A deposit by one person of his own money in his own name and as trustee for another, standing alone, does not establish an irrevocable trust during the lifetime of the depositor. It is a tentative trust merely, revocable at will, until the depositor dies or completes the gift in his lifetime by some unequivocal act or declaration, such as delivery of the passbook or notice to the beneficiary. In case the depositor dies before the beneficiary without revocation, or some decisive act or declaration of disaffirmance, the presumption arises that an absolute trust is created as to the balance on hand at the death of the depositor.

In Cutts v. Najdrowski the court held that where a New Jersey resident opened an account in a New York savings bank in his name in trust for another, since the transaction was effective there, it was effective here to pass title to the balance in the account at the depositor's death, to the other person named, under the *Totten* trust doctrine. It was so held notwithstanding that such a transaction, had it been consummated here by a New Jersey resident, would have been invalid to *pass title* as violative of our statute of wills or as an ineffective gift inter vivos. Since then, however, N.J.S.A. 17:9A-216 has been held effective to pass valid title to the balance, at death, in such an account, to the beneficiary named. . . . *Cutts* was followed in Conry v. Maloney, where a New York savings account was again involved and, through application of the law of situs, it was held that the cestui, a niece, took the balance in an account opened by the decedent "in trust for" her, to the exclusion of the decedent's widow.

The trial judge, following *Cutts* and *Conry,* held that the law of Florida applied. Concluding that the *Totten* trust doctrine had been adopted in Florida, he found that title to the bank balances passed to respondent. In so doing, he applied the substantive law of Florida as found in Seymour v. Seymour. . . .

Appellant urges that in thus applying Florida substantive law, instead of Florida conflict of laws, the trial judge fell into error. Specifically, it is argued that in *Seymour* the court was passing upon the validity, as a trust, of an account established by a domiciliary of Florida in a Florida bank, whereas we are here concerned with an account opened in Florida by a domiciliary of New Jersey. Under Florida conflicts law, the argument continues, the doctrine of mobilia sequuntur personam would be applied. Hanson v. Denckla, 100 So. 2d 378 (Fla. Sup. Ct. 1956), *reversed on grounds of lack of jurisdiction* in Hanson v. Denckla, 357 U.S. 235 (1958). Turning, then, to the law of decedent's domicile, New Jersey, appellant invokes Swetland v. Swetland as holding the transaction to be ineffective as a trust of the accounts in question. Appellant thus seeks to invoke the doctrine of renvoi to defeat respondent's claim. . . .

However, we find it unnecessary to determine the Florida conflicts rule which would be applicable in view of the conclusions which follow.

We are satisfied that the trial judge correctly ruled that the substantive law of Florida should be applied to the transaction in question. In neither *Cutts* nor *Conry* did our courts proceed any further than to apply the internal law of the place where the transaction took place. The transaction rule was also followed in Hooton v. Needl, *supra.* In the Restatement, Conflict of Laws, §7, p.11 (1934), the rule as to conflicts is set forth as follows:

> Except as stated in §8 [concerning matters involving title to land and the validity of divorce decrees], when there is a difference in the Conflict of Laws of two states whose laws are involved in a problem, the rule of Conflict of Laws of the forum is applied: (a) in all cases where as a preliminary to determining the choice of law it is necessary to determine the quality and character of legal ideas, these are determined by the forum according to its law; (b) where in making the choice of law to govern a certain situation the law of another state is to be applied, since the only Conflict of Laws used in the determination of the case is the Conflict of Laws of the forum, the foreign law to be applied is the law applicable to the matter in hand and not the Conflict of Laws of the foreign state.

In comment (d) to subsection (b) the learned authors note that, under the rule stated, the court of the forum, in a matter involving a contract, applies only the contract law of the other state, and this "may result in a decision contrary to that which would be reached by a court in that state, the law of which is being applied, by reason of the fact that a different Conflict of Laws rule prevails in the latter state."

The rule set forth in the Restatement seems grounded in reason for, if appellant's views were to be upheld, the courts would be faced with a possible unending circuity. Thus, if the Florida conflicts rule would refer the matter back to New Jersey, New Jersey, applying its full body of law, including its conflict rules, would again refer to the law of Florida because of the holdings in *Cutts, Conry* and *Hooton.* The circular process would then begin anew and continue ad infinitum. Such was the problem posed In re Tallmadge, 109 Misc. 696, 181 N.Y.S. 336 (Surr. Ct. 1919), where application of the renvoi doctrine was denied on account of its inconsistency with common law theory of the conflict of laws, its fundamental unsoundness and the chaos which would result from its application to conflicts arising between the laws of the several states. (181 N.Y.S., at p. 348)

Accordingly, we hold that where, in a proceeding in this State, the validity of a transaction in a foreign state—except one involving title to land or the validity of a divorce, as to which we make no determination—is, by virtue of our conflict of laws principles, made to depend upon the laws of such state, the foreign law to be applied is the law applicable to the matter in hand not the conflict of laws of the foreign state. . . .

University of Chicago v. Dater

277 Mich. 653, 270 N.W. 175 (1936)

[The facts are taken from the dissenting opinion of Justice Sharpe.]

In November, 1928, negotiations were commenced to secure a loan in the sum of $75,000 on a piece of property in Chicago. The property was owned by George R. Dater and John R. Price of Benton Harbor, Mich., and they appointed H. S. Gray, an attorney of Benton Harbor, as their agent in the matter. Plaintiff agreed to make the loan if it could be assured that the title was good. A trust deed and certain promissory notes were drawn up with George R. Dater and Nellie E. Dater, his wife, and John R. Price and Clara A. Price, his wife, as parties of the first part, and the Chicago Title & Trust Company, as trustee, and as party of the second part. The notes were payable in the city of Chicago and at such place as the legal holder might appoint. The trust mortgage and notes were sent by mail to the Benton Harbor State Bank for the signature of the parties involved. The papers were signed in Benton Harbor, Mich., about December 8, 1928, and mailed to plaintiff's agent in the city of Chicago where the trust deed was placed on record, then it was found that there were some objections to certain delinquent taxes of 1927. Further negotiations followed, and finally on January 3, 1929, and after the tax objections were cleared in the title, the loan was actually made and the money paid over by check made payable to Mr. and Mrs. Dater and Mr. and Mrs. Price and cashed in Chicago, Ill.

January 29, 1929, John R. Price died, and it is conceded that Mrs. Price became the actual and record owner of at least one-half of the property after the death of her husband. Subsequent to December 1, 1933, foreclosure proceedings were commenced on the property and the property purchased at chancery sale. Suit was filed in Michigan before the foreclosure suit was completed in Chicago. The cause was heard November 7, 1934, and on June 18, 1935, judgment was rendered in favor of plaintiff against George R. Dater in the amount of $15,536.32 and from which no appeal has been taken. On the same date judgment was entered in favor of Clara Price of no cause for action, from which judgment plaintiff appeals.

WIEST, J.

The obligation in suit was executed in this state by defendant Clara A. Price, a married woman, and bore no relation to her separate estate, and, without more, carried no personal liability when sued upon in this jurisdiction. But, it is claimed, that the obligation was accepted in the state of Illinois, and was there payable and, by the law of the state, Mrs. Price is not saved from liability by reason of want of capacity under the Michigan law of coverture.

As pointed out later in this opinion, personal liability of Mrs. Price could not be enforced in Illinois under the theory of an Illinois contract.

In the case at bar negotiations for the loan, to be secured by mortgage, had reached the state where the lender prepared the note and mortgage in Illinois and sent the same to an agent in Michigan, with direction as to execution by defendants in this state, and, when executed, to be returned by such agent to the mortgagee in Illinois. Mrs. Price, at the request of the agent, executed the instruments and the agent mailed the same to the mortgagee.

The instant case does not involve conflict of laws relative to the construction, force, and effect of the instruments, signed or executed in one state to be performed in another, but that of capacity of Mrs. Price to enter into such an obligation in this state.

It is well said in a note, 26 L.R.A. (N.S.) 773:

> While there are almost numberless cases which state, with slight variations, Story's general proposition that, where the contract is either expressly or tacitly to be performed in some place other than that where it is made, the general rule is, in conformity to the presumed intention of the parties, that the contract, as to its validity, nature, obligation, and interpretation, is to be governed by the law of the place of performance, none of them can be regarded as express authority for the application of that rule to the question of the capacity of a married woman to contract. Few of them can be relied upon for the application of that rule to any question relating to the existence of a contract as distinguished from its interpretation or obligation or essential validity.

It must be agreed that this case is governed by the law of Michigan or of Illinois. If by the law of Michigan, it is clear, and is not disputed, that defendant has no personal liability on the note, recoverable from her separate estate.

Assuming, however, that by the Michigan law of the forum that case is governed by the law of Illinois, it presents the unique situation in the realm of conflict of laws that by the law of Illinois, Burr v. Beckler [page 76 *supra*] the case is governed by the law of Michigan.

In Burr v. Beckler, the wife, a resident of Illinois, was sojourning temporarily in Florida. Her husband owed a concern in Illinois, of which he was treasurer, on an overdraft. He informed his wife that he could borrow the necessary money to pay the overdraft from an estate of which he was trustee. The wife executed a note and trust deed in Florida and mailed them to her husband, as trustee, at Chicago, Ill., as he had directed her to do. The husband also signed the trust deed, but the opinion does not state when. The court held that delivery of the note and trust deed by the wife was complete in Florida, the law of that state governed her capacity to contract, and, because she was not competent to enter into a contract under the law of Florida, her note and trust deed were void.

The question is not whether the decision is in harmony with the law of Michigan, but whether it governs this case. Here, manual delivery was as complete as in the *Burr* case because it was made to a bank which had been designated by the mortgagee for that purpose.

In neither case had there been a binding engagement by the mortgagee to make the loan prior to delivery. In neither case had the money been paid in advance of the delivery or contemporaneously therewith. There is nothing in the *Burr* Case to indicate that the mortgagee could not have refused to make the loan or that the mortgagors could not have refused to take the money or could not have abandoned the matter after the wife deposited the papers in the mail. The *Burr* opinion indicated no circumstance fixing the effect of the manual delivery which is not present here. The *Burr* Case is directly applicable, and, consequently, under the law of Illinois, it must be held that the capacity of defendant Clara A. Price is governed by the law of Michigan. Under the law of Michigan, a married woman cannot bind her separate estate through personal engagement for the benefit of others. Defendant Price is not liable.

Affirmed, with costs to defendant Price.

North, C.J., and Fead and Toy, JJ., concurred with Wiest, J.

Sharpe, J. (dissenting).

It is conceded that under the law of Illinois a married woman is as free to contract as a man, while in Michigan a married woman has not the legal capacity to bind herself or her separate estate by signing these notes. . . .

The plaintiff contends that the contract was an Illinois contract; that the signing of the notes in Michigan was not the final act in the making of the contract, but rather a preliminary step, the delivery of the note being conditional upon defendant's producing a satisfactory title, the approval of the title in Illinois was the last act necessary to make a legal delivery.

The general rule is well stated in John A. Tolman Co. v. Reed, where the court said:

> The law is well settled that contracts must be construed and their validity determined by the law of the country where they were made, unless the contracting parties clearly appear to have had some other law in view.
>
> The general rule is that the law of the place where the instrument was executed and delivered so as to become binding as a contract . . . governs the rights and liabilities of the parties thereto, except in so far as they are controlled by the law of the place where the instrument is payable. . . .

8 C.J. 87, §145.

> There is good authority for the broad proposition, however, that when a note is executed by a married woman in the state of her domicile but made payable in another state, if under the law of the former state she could not have entered into the contract but could have done so under the law of the latter state, it will be presumed that it was the intention of the parties that the note should be governed by the law of the latter state and being valid under such law should be enforced against her even in the state of her domicile. . . .
>
> It is a general rule that every contract as to its validity, nature, interpretation and effect, or, as they may be called, the right, in contradistinction to the remedy, is governed by the law of the place where it is made, unless it is to be performed in another place; and then it is governed by the law of the place where it is to be performed.

Poole v. Perkins [*supra* page 29].

The next question that presents itself in the case at bar is the place where the contract was made.

> A contract is deemed to have been made in the state where the last act necessary to make it a binding agreement takes place.

Goodrich, Conflict of Laws, 218.

> When the contract is made in one jurisdiction to be performed in another the case presents a more complicated question, the rule being that if the parties to a contract are in different jurisdictions, the place where the last act is done which is necessary to the validity of the contract is the place where the contract is entered into.

5 R.C.L. 935.

In the case at bar all of the negotiations for the loan occurred in Chicago, the property upon which the mortgage was placed was located in Chicago, and no money was to be paid by plaintiff until such time as the defendants could show good title to the property. We think the mailing of the papers to Chicago was for the purpose of enabling the plaintiff to ascertain if the title to the real estate was satisfactory and was but a preliminary step in the whole transaction. The final act in the making of the loan was the payment of the money in Chicago. This concluded the negotiations and made it an Illinois contract.

BUSHNELL, J., concurred with SHARPE, J.

BUTZEL, J. (dissenting).

I concur in the result reached by Justice Sharpe. The place of contracting controls the question of capacity of the parties to contract. Palmer National Bank v. Van Doren, 260 Mich. 310, 244 N.W. 485; American Law Institute Restatement of the Conflict of Laws, §333. The notes were dated and payable at Chicago and secured by Chicago real estate. The loan was made in Chicago 25 days after the notes had been signed and not until an actual cloud on the title to the realty had been removed. These circumstances leave no doubt that the notes in question constituted Illinois contracts. . . . The facts are entirely different from those in Re Estate of Lucas . . . in which the loan was solicited by residents of Michigan, the moneys were first received in Michigan by the borrowers, and subsequently the note was dated and signed in Michigan and was payable in Michigan. The place of contracting is where the note is first delivered for value. In Beale on Conflict of Laws, page 1047, it is said:

> Delivery, however, is not the only requisite to the creation of a contract on a negotiable instrument. Value must be given, and until, therefore, there has been a delivery for value, the instrument cannot be said to have had any inception. . . .
>
> It follows that the place of contracting of a contract on a negotiable instrument, be it the obligation of the maker, the drawer or the endorser, is the place where, after the signature of the party in question, the instrument is first delivered for value.

It is true that the physical act of signing the note in the instant case took place in Michigan and the notes were mailed to plaintiff in Chicago, but there was no absolute delivery until the plaintiff had satisfied itself of the status of the title to the mortgaged property and until an actual cloud had been removed. Until that time the transaction was conditional and the notes of no binding force and effect.

The rule is stated in Beale on Conflicts of Laws, p. 1045, as follows: "The phrase 'place of contracting' and its equivalents, the place of making or the place where the contract is made, properly mean the place in which the final act was done which made the promise or promises binding" . . .

We do not believe that the case of Burr v. Beckler . . . should in any way be controlling on this court in determining the lex loci contractus. The problem in the instant case is termed by the authorities as one of "qualifications." The prevailing view in answer to the problem is that the law of the forum should control on the question of lex loci contractus. An excellent treatment of the entire subject may be found in an article entitled, "The Theory of Qualifications and Conflict of Laws," by Professor Lorenzen in 20 Columbia Law Review, p. 247.

Were we not to be controlled by our own law and obliged each time to ascertain what a foreign state would have held under similar circumstances, our decisions would be in hopeless confusion, and it would be necessary each time to examine the decisions of other states in determining the lex loci contractus. The question, however, is foreclosed in this state, as we held in the case of Ohio v. Purse, *supra,* that the law of the place of contracting is to be determined in accordance with the law of the forum.

The judgment should be reversed, with costs to plaintiff.

BUSHNELL, J., concurred with BUTZEL, J.

Questions and Comments

(1) Terminology: *whole law* = conflicts rules + internal law.

(2) In the *Damato* case, why does New Jersey's conflicts rule refer to the law of the situs of the trust money? If the answer is that the situs state has the right to control the disposition of trust funds, doesn't the decision in the case deny that right by reaching a result that the courts of the situs would not have reached? On the other hand, of course, one could ask the same question about why Florida conflicts law defers to the state of the settlor's domicile. If it is because that state has the right to control the disposition of the money (in Florida's view), then we are in trouble, with neither state claiming the right.

(3) Wouldn't the simple answer to such a non-conflict be to say that where neither state is particularly interested, the intent of the parties ought to control, or lacking any obvious intent, the forum ought to apply its own law by default? Isn't it a bit strange that under the court's approach, New Jersey ends up applying the law of Florida, which it presumably thinks is inferior (since it has not adopted the *Totten* trust doctrine—a matter that has traditionally been a function for the courts rather than for the legislatures), while Florida would end up applying the law of New Jersey, which it thinks is inferior? Isn't this the least satisfactory solution?

(4) Why is the doctrine of renvoi accepted in American law for real property and marriage questions but not generally for other matters? With respect to the real property half of the question, some of the traditional justifications are thin. For example, the courts of State *A* will not (for jurisdictional reasons) determine matters directly affecting title to land in State *B*. Thus, our

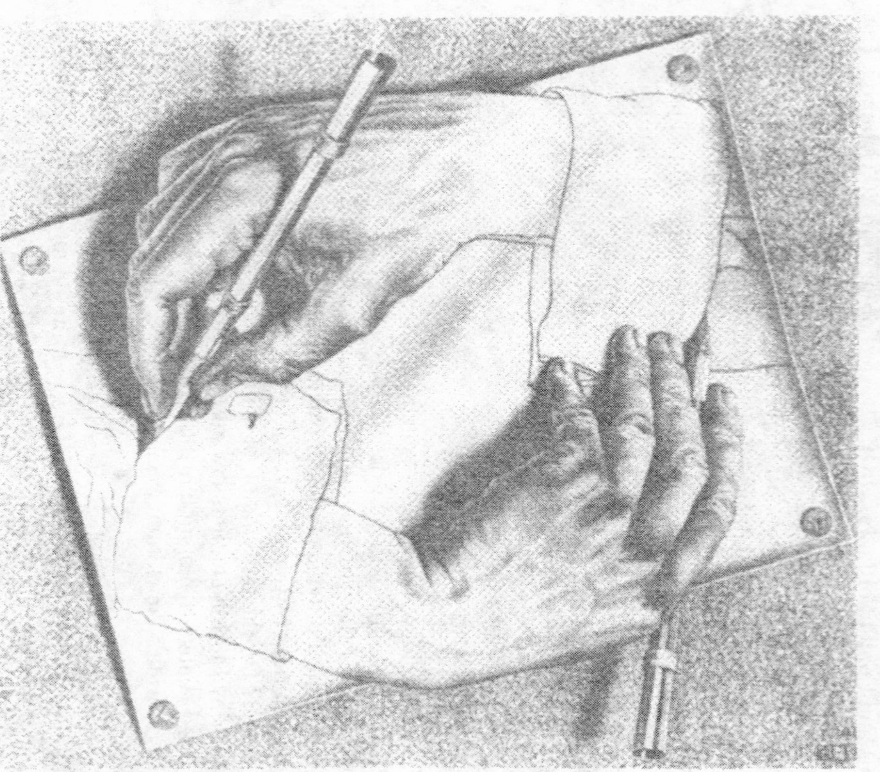

M. C. Escher, "Tekenen"

traditional concern for the poor title searcher need not concern us in a renvoi case. If the reason for renvoi with respect to real property is deference to the situs state's political control over its own land, isn't that reason weakened by the fact that in a renvoi case, by hypothesis, the situs state has already relinquished political control over its own land by applying the law of another state, rather than its own, to that land?

(5) A renvoi situation can come about in several different ways. First, the two states may have choice-of-law rules that agree but may characterize the case differently (one calling it a tort case, the other a contract case, for example). Second, the two states may simply have two different choice-of-law rules (place of execution vs. place of performance, for example). Third, the two states may use the same concept but define it differently (e.g., domicile). Should it make any difference to the renvoi analysis which of these situations is responsible for the problem?

(6) The court in the *Dater* case seems at one point (though it is not clear) to be saying either (a) the law of Michigan applies or (b) the law of Illinois applies and it makes the law of Michigan apply. But if one mixes one's *a*'s and *b*'s, one could say either (a) the law of Illinois applies or (b) the law of Michigan applies and it makes the law of Illinois apply.

Isn't the basic flaw of the court's reasoning the fact that it fails to note the shift in meaning of "law" between the two halves of its dichotomy? That is, when it says that the law of Michigan may apply, it means the internal law, while it means the whole law of Illinois when it says that the law of Illinois may apply. Granted these different meanings of "law," the court's reasoning is correct, but its assumptions contain its conclusion—that is, the decision to refer to Illinois whole law rather than Illinois internal law is the central issue of the case, isn't it?

3. Substance vs. Procedure

There are certain rules and principles of conflicts that cut across various substantive areas like torts or contracts. For example, the question whether a particular issue is substantive or procedural can arise in a tort, contract, or any other kind of case.

That procedure should be governed by the law of the forum is, at least in the most basic cases, obvious. It would be strange to conclude that the size of paper required in the courts of the state whose substantive law controls would be the size required in another state adjudicating the case. But as soon as we leave the precinct of such safely "procedural" topics, the question becomes more obscure. As you read the following Restatement selections and cases, keep in mind the question why the law of the forum should apply to procedural issues as a yardstick for determining whether a particular issue should be called "procedural."

Selections from the First Restatement of Conflicts, on Procedure

§§584-585, 588, 591, 594-597, 599-601, 606 (1934)

§584. Determination of Whether Question Is One of Procedure

The court at the forum determines according to its own Conflict of Laws rule whether a given question is one of substance or procedure.

§585. What Law Governs Procedure

All matters of procedure are governed by the law of the forum.

§588. Parties

The law of the forum determines who may and who must sue and be sued.

§591. Commencement of Action

The law of the forum determines at what moment action is begun.

§594. Mode of Trial

The law of the forum determines whether an issue of fact shall be tried by the court or by a jury.

§595. Proof of Facts

(1) The law of the forum governs the proof in court of a fact alleged.

(2) The law of the forum governs presumptions and inferences to be drawn from evidence.

§596. Witnesses

The law of the forum determines the competency and the credibility of witnesses.

§597. Evidence

The law of the forum determines the admissibility of a particular piece of evidence.

§599. Integrated Contracts

When a contract is integrated in a writing by the law of the place of contracting, no variation of the writing can be shown in another state which could not be shown in a court in the place of contracting under the law of that state, whatever the law of the other state as to integrated contracts.

§600. Execution of Judgment

The law of the forum determines matters pertaining to the execution of a judgment, and what property of a judgment defendant within the state is exempt from execution and on what property within the state execution can be levied, and the priorities among competing execution creditors.

§601. Freedom from Fault

If the law of the forum makes it a condition of maintaining an action that the party bringing the action show himself free from fault, the condition must be fulfilled though there is no such requirement in the state where the cause of action arose.

§606. Limitation of Amount Recoverable

If a statute of the forum limits the amount which in any action of a certain class may be recovered in its courts, no greater amount can be recovered though under the law of the state which created the cause of action, a greater recovery would be justified or required.

Sampson v. Channell

110 F.2d 754 (1st Cir.), *cert. denied,* 310 U.S. 650 (1940)

MAGRUDER, J.

On this appeal the question presented may be stated simply, but the answer is not free from difficulty. A car driven by defendant's testator collided in Maine with a car driven by the plaintiff, injuring both the plaintiff and his wife, who was a passenger. The wife sued and recovered judgment. We affirm that judgment. . . . In this, the husband's action, the jury found specially that the plaintiff's injury was caused by the negligence of defendant's testator, but brought in a general verdict for the defendant on the issue of contributory negligence. Judgment was entered for the defendant.

The action was brought in the federal district court for Massachusetts, there being the requisite diversity of citizenship. On the issue of contributory negligence the plaintiff requested the court to charge the jury, in accordance with the local Massachusetts rule, that "the burden of proving lack of care on the part of the plaintiff is on the defendant." This the court declined to do, but upon the contrary charged, in accordance with the Maine law, that the burden was upon the plaintiff to show affirmatively that no want of ordinary care on his part contributed to cause his injuries. The sole question raised is as to the correctness of this charge, and refusal to charge as requested.

Inquiry must first be directed to whether a federal court, in a diversity of citizenship case, must follow the applicable state rule as to incidence of burden of proof. If the answer is in the affirmative, the further point to be considered is whether the applicable state rule here is that of Massachusetts, where the action was brought, or Maine, where the accident occurred.

It would be an over-simplification to say that the case turns on whether burden of proof is a matter of substance or procedure. These are not clean-cut categories. During the reign of Swift v. Tyson the federal courts in diversity of citizenship cases consistently held that the defendant had the burden of proving the plaintiff's contributory negligence, even though the suit arose in a state whose local rule was the contrary. They avoided having to apply the local rule under the Conformity Act by saying that burden of proof was not a mere matter of procedure but concerned substantive rights, as to which the federal courts on a matter of "general law" were free to take their own view. . . . The question of classification also arose where suit was brought in one state on an alleged tort committed in another state. But here it was generally held, in the state courts at least, that burden of proof as to contributory negligence was a matter of procedure; hence the rule of the forum would be applied despite a contrary rule of the locus delicti. In these two groups of cases the courts were talking about the same thing and labelling it differently, but in each instance the result was the same; the court was choosing the appropriate classification to enable it to apply its own familiar rule.

In another and quite different setting the question of classification has frequently arisen, namely, in cases involving the constitutionality of statutes shifting from the plaintiff to the defendant the burden of proof on the issue of contributory negligence, as applied retroactively to alleged torts committed before the date of the enactment. Here the courts, federal as well as state, have upheld the statutes as so applied. . . . The courts say that such statutes introduce no change of the substantive law rule that contributory negligence is a complete bar to liability, but pertain only to the procedure by which the fact as to contributory negligence is to be established. In Easterling Lumber Co. v. Pierce, a state statute, applicable to railroads, provided that from the proof of the happening of an accident there should arise a prima facie presumption of negligence. Referring to this statute, the U.S. Supreme Court said,

> The objection to the . . . statute is that it was wanting in due process because retroactively applied to the case since the statute was enacted after the accident occurred. But the court below held that the statute cut off no substantive defense but simply provided a rule of evidence controlling the burden of proof. That as thus construed it does not violate the Fourteenth Amendment to the Constitution of the United States is also so conclusively settled as to again require nothing but a reference to the decided cases.

It is apparent, then, that burden of proof does not fall within either category of "substance" or "procedure" by virtue of any intrinsic compulsion, but the matter has been made to turn upon the purpose at hand to be served by the classification. Therefore, inasmuch as the older decisions in the federal courts, applying in diversity cases the federal rule as to burden of proof as a matter of "general law," are founded upon an assumption no longer valid since Erie Railroad Co. v. Tompkins, their classification of burden of proof as a matter of substance should be re-examined in the light of the objective and policy disclosed in the *Tompkins* case.

The opinion in that case sets forth as a moving consideration of policy that it is unfair and unseemly to have the outcome of litigation substantially affected by the fortuitous existence of diversity of citizenship. Hence, the greater likelihood there is that litigation would come out one way in the federal court and another way in the state court if the federal court failed to apply a particular local rule, the stronger the urge would be to classify the rule as not a mere matter of procedure but one of substantive law falling within the mandate of the *Tompkins* case. There will be, inescapably, a twilight zone between the two categories where a rational classification could be made either way, and where Congress directly, or the Supreme Court under authority of the Act of June 19, 1934 . . . , would have power to prescribe a so-called rule of procedure for the federal courts. Thus, if Rule 8(c) of the Federal Rules of Civil Procedure, 28 U.S.C.A. following section 723c, could be construed as imposing upon the defendant the burden of proof of contributory negligence, it seems that this would be valid and conclusive of the case at bar, despite the contrary intimation in Francis v. Humphrey. Rule 8(c) speaks of contributory negligence as an "affirmative defense," a phrase implying that the burden of proof is on the defendant. Yet the only rule laid down is one of *pleading;* the defendant must affirmatively plead contributory negligence. It is not inconsistent to require the defendant to plead contributory negligence if he wants to raise the issue, and yet to put the burden of proof on the plaintiff if the issue is raised. Since Rule 8(c) contains no prescription as to burden of proof, we must look elsewhere for the answer.

It seems to be said in Francis v. Humphrey and was suggested by counsel in the case at bar, that the question whether in diversity of citizenship cases burden of proof is to be classified as a matter of procedure or substantive law is to be determined by following the classification made by the courts of the state. No doubt we should look to those courts to tell us what their rule is and how it operates in local litigation. But once that is determined, the rule is the same whether it is labeled substantive law or procedure. Furthermore, as already pointed out, such a classification by the state court for one purpose does not mean that the classification is valid for another purpose. Surely the question whether a particular subject-matter falls within the power of the Supreme Court to prescribe rules of procedure under the Act of 1934, or is a matter of substantive law governed by the doctrine of the *Tompkins* case, cannot be foreclosed by the label given to the subject-matter by the state courts.

The inquiry then must be: considering the policy underlying Erie Railroad Co. v. Tompkins, *supra,* would that policy best be served by classifying burden of proof as to contributory negligence as a matter of procedure or substantive law? The incidence of burden of proof may determine the outcome of the case. This is true where the evidence is conflicting and the jury is not convinced either way. It is more pointedly true where, as sometimes happens, the injured person dies and no evidence is available on the issue of contributory negligence. If, in such a case, the burden of proof is on the defendant, the plaintiff wins, assuming the other elements of the cause of action are established. . . . If the burden is on the plaintiff, however, the defendant wins. . . . Assuming the state rule to be one way and the federal rule the other, then the accident of citizenship becomes decisive of the litigation. The situation seems to call for the application of the rule in the *Tompkins* case. There is no important counterconsideration here, for the state rule can be easily ascertained and applied by the federal court without any administrative inconvenience. In thus concluding that for this purpose the incidence of the burden of proof as to contributory negligence is to be classified as a matter of substantive law, we are in harmony with the spirit of the *Tompkins* case, and at the same time are adhering to the classification maintained in an unbroken line of federal court decisions under Swift v. Tyson, *supra.* Federal courts in other circuits have held, since the *Tompkins* decision, that the state rule as to burden of proof must now be applied in diversity of citizenship cases. . . .

Thus far, the case has been discussed as though suit had been brought in the federal court sitting in the state where the alleged tort occurred. But there is the complicating factor that the accident occurred in Maine and suit was brought in Massachusetts. This makes it necessary to consider three further points:

First, if the plaintiff had sued in a Massachusetts state court, would the Massachusetts Supreme Judicial Court have allowed the application of the Maine rule as to burden of proof? The answer is, no. The court would have said that burden of proof is a matter of procedure only, and would have applied the Massachusetts rule that the burden is on the defendant to establish the plaintiff's contributory negligence. Such was the holding in Levy v. Steiger and Smith v. Brown.

Second, would such a decision by the Supreme Judicial Court of Massachusetts be subject to reversal by the Supreme Court of the United States? Presumably we are permitted under the *Tompkins* case thus to attack the decision of a state court collaterally, so to speak, for the Supreme Court would hardly require the federal courts to follow a local decision which, had it been appealed, would have been reversed by the Supreme Court on constitutional grounds. . . .

Whatever the eventual development of this line of cases may be, we know of no decision indicating that the Supreme Court at the present time would reverse a decision of a state court in a case like Levy v. Steiger, *supra*, applying the lex fori rather than the lex loci delicti in the matter of burden of proof. Numerous decisions to this effect have been rendered by state courts, and it has never seemed to occur to anyone that a federal question was involved. Furthermore, in Levy v. Steiger, *supra*, the Massachusetts court was applying not its common law (which put the burden of proof on the plaintiff), but a statute providing that "In all actions, civil or criminal, to recover damages for injuries to the person or property or for causing the death of a person, the person injured or killed shall be presumed to have been in the exercise of due care, and contributory negligence on his part shall be an affirmative defense to be set up in the answer and proved by the defendant." . . . To hold that this statute is unconstitutional, as applied in Levy v. Steiger, *supra*, to a foreign tort, one would have to find somewhere in the Constitution an implied prohibition to the effect that no state shall pass any law altering an assumed nationally applicable body of doctrine concerning the conflict of laws, the final interpreter of which is the Supreme Court of the United States.

It follows, therefore, that the unimpeachable law of Massachusetts in the case at bar is that in a suit brought in Massachusetts the burden of proof as to contributory negligence is on the defendant, despite the contrary rule applicable in Maine where the accident occurred.

Third, this being Massachusetts law, there remains the inquiry, what law must be applied in the federal court in Massachusetts when jurisdiction is invoked on the ground of diversity of citizenship? Under Erie Railroad v. Tompkins, *supra*, is it the Massachusetts or the Maine rule? We know of no considered decision by the Supreme Court on this point. In the *Tompkins* case, suit was brought in the federal court in New York on a tort alleged to have been committed in Pennsylvania. The question was whether the railroad owed a duty of care to an undiscovered pedestrian walking on a much-used path along the right of way near the tracks. The Supreme Court held that the lower court was in error in treating this question as a matter of "general law," and sent the case back for determination in accordance with the common law of Pennsylvania as declared by its highest court. There is no doubt that in this situation the state courts of New York would have applied the same rule of conflict of laws, and would have looked to the lex loci delicti. The decision in the *Tompkins* case manifestly tended to produce a uniformity in result in that particular situation, whether action on the Pennsylvania tort were brought in a New York state court or New York federal court. . . .

Until the point is finally ruled upon by the Supreme Court, lower courts must piece out as best they can the implications of the *Tompkins* case. The theory is that the federal court in Massachusetts sits as a court coordinate with the Massachusetts state courts to apply the Massachusetts law in diversity of citizenship cases. . . . The powerful argument by Holmes, J., dissenting, in Black & White Taxi Co. v. Brown & Yellow Taxi Co., cited with approval by the majority opinion in the *Tompkins* case, seems to be applicable to that portion of the Massachusetts common law relating to conflict of laws quite as much as to the common law of contracts or torts. Except in the limited range of cases, already alluded to above, where state court decisions on points of conflict of law are subject to reversal by the United States Supreme Court under the federal constitution, the rules applicable to conflict of laws are not "a transcendental body of law outside of any particular state but obligatory within it. If the federal court in Massachusetts on points of conflict of laws may disregard the law of Massachusetts as formulated by the Supreme Judicial Court and take its own view as a matter of "general law," then the ghost of Swift v. Tyson, *supra,* still walks abroad, somewhat shrunken in size, yet capable of much mischief. In the case at bar, it is difficult to see that any gain in the direction of uniformity would be achieved by creating a discrepancy between the rules of law applicable in the Massachusetts state and federal courts, respectively, in order to bring the law of the Massachusetts federal court in harmony with the law that would be applied in the state courts of Maine.

Our conclusion is that the court below was bound to apply the law as to burden of proof as it would have been applied by the state courts in Massachusetts.

This result may seem to present a surface incongruity, viz., the deference owing to the substantive law of Massachusetts as pronounced by its court requires the federal court in that state to apply a Massachusetts rule as to burden of proof which the highest state court insists is procedural only. The explanation is that reasons of policy, set forth in the *Tompkins* case, make it desirable for the federal court in diversity of citizenship cases to apply the state rule, because the incidence of burden of proof is likely to have a decisive influence on the outcome of litigation; and this is true regardless of whether the state court characterizes the rule as one of procedure or substantive law. Certainly the federal court in Massachusetts cannot treat burden of proof as a matter of procedure in order to disregard the Massachusetts rule, and then treat it as substantive law in order to apply the Maine rule. Under the conclusion we have reached, if suit were brought in Massachusetts, the state and federal courts there would be in harmony as to burden of proof; and if suit were brought in Maine, the state and federal courts there would likewise be in harmony on this important matter. It is true that the rule applied in the Maine courts would not be the same as the rule applied in the Massachusetts courts. But this is a disparity that existed prior to Erie Railroad v. Tompkins, *supra,* and cannot be corrected by the doctrine of that case. It is a disparity that exists because Massachusetts may constitutionally maintain a rule of conflict of laws to the effect that the incidence of burden of proof is a matter of "procedure" to be governed by the law of the forum. Levy v. Steiger, *supra.*

For error in the instructions given to the jury on the burden of proof, the judgment must be reversed and the cause remanded for further proceedings not inconsistent with this opinion.

O'Leary v. Illinois Terminal Railroad

299 S.W.2d 873 (Mo. 1957)

HOLLINGSWORTH, J.

Plaintiff recovered judgment against defendant in the Circuit Court of the City of St. Louis for the sum of $7,000 for personal injuries sustained when an automobile in which she was a passenger was struck by defendant's electric railway train in Granite City, Illinois. Upon appeal by defendant to the St. Louis Court of Appeals, the several assignments of error there asserted were decided adversely to defendant and the judgment of the trial court was affirmed. . . . Among the assignments considered by the Court of Appeals was defendant's contention that the trial court erred in giving plaintiff's Instruction No. 10, which casts upon defendant the burden of proving its affirmatively pleaded defense for contributory negligence on the part of plaintiff in bar of any right of recovery she otherwise might have.

In determining that question, the Court of Appeals took judicial notice that the law of Illinois made it incumbent upon plaintiff to allege and prove that she was in the exercise of ordinary care for her own safety at the time of the collision. . . . It then undertook to determine "whether the Illinois requirement that the plaintiff allege and prove that she was in the exercise of due care was a substantive and essential element of her right to recover or was merely a procedural matter to be determined by the law of Missouri." At that point, the court was confronted with a situation which it aptly described as "difficult and delicate." . . .

. . . The Court of Appeals of its own motion, transferred the case here to the end "that the law on the subject should be re-examined." . . . The parties have briefed the question anew. The importance of the question impels us to give it first consideration before discussion of the other assignments of error asserted by defendant in this court.

Plaintiff insists that the overwhelming weight of authority is that the burden of proof is a rule of evidence and as such is procedural, not substantive [citing] cases from several states, and several Missouri cases which the *Redick* case had purported to overrule and to which reference will be hereinafter made. Plaintiff has also invoked the rule of stare decisis and insists that "under this time-honored rule this court should refrain from disturbing the existing law until an authoritative court of Illinois should declare that the burden of proof as to contributory negligence is substantive and not procedural, and thereby demonstrate that the present law is 'clearly erroneous or manifestly wrong.' " . . .

We have carefully considered the cases and authorities cited by both of the parties in the instant case and the cases and authorities upon which the *Redick* case was decided. Unquestionably, there is a conflict of authority upon this subject. Oftentimes, however, a careful analysis of the precise question presented in these cases reveals that the conflict is more seeming than real. The rule applied in the more closely reasoned cases is thus stated in 11 Am. Jur., Conflict of Laws, §203, p. 523:

> Even in those jurisdictions which recognize that ordinarily matters concerning presumptions of evidence and burden of proof relate to the remedy, where the remedy prescribed by that rule of the lex loci, which attaches the burden of proof to one of the parties, is so inseparably connected with, and incorporated in, the substantive rule creating the right that to ignore that remedy and substitute therefor the rule of the forum would destroy, prejudice, or render ineffective the right to which it is attached, substituting a local cause of action for the one arising in another state, the lex loci in its entirety will be given effect in preference to the contrary rule of the lex fori. It is sometimes stated that the burden of proof is not determinable by the lex fori if it is made a substantial part of the right of action by the laws of the jurisdiction under which it arose.

No purpose will be served by further discussion. We are convinced that the authorities upon which the decision in the *Redick* case was reached are sound. Hence we affirm that portion of the *Redick* case . . . reading:

> Is the Illinois requirement that plaintiff prove he was in the exercise of due care substantive or merely procedural? In Barker v. St. Louis County, . . . we quoted with approval from Jones v. Erie R. Co., . . . as follows: "The distinction between substantive law and procedural law is that 'substantive law relates to rights and duties which give rise 'to a cause of action,' while procedural law 'is the machinery for carrying on the suit.' "
>
> We think that the Illinois requirement is substantive, just as much as is the requirement that plaintiff plead and prove the negligence of defendant. No one would argue that the latter was not substantive. Both are

essential elements of plaintiff's *right to recover* under the law of Illinois. Plaintiff suggests, however, that our courts are not obligated to involuntarily have the laws of another state engrafted into our jurisprudence, . . . and that it will be Missouri rules of law that determine whether a given question is substance or procedure. . . . But certainly we should not determine the matter by mere whim or fiat. "In administering the substantive laws of a sister state we administer *them,* not our own; and we should not administer them either more or less blandly than do our sister's courts." . . .

The Restatement, Conflict of Laws, Sec. 595, ch. 12, states that

> if a requirement concerning proof of freedom from fault exists in the law of the place of injury and if such condition is there interpreted as a condition of the cause of action itself, . . . the court at the forum will apply the rule of the foreign state. . . . In such a case, the remedial and substantive portions of the foreign law are so bound together that the application of the usual procedural rule of the forum would seriously alter the effect of the operative facts under the law of the appropriate foreign state.

The illustration following the comment is:

> *A,* in state *X,* is injured by the alleged negligence of *B. A* sues *B* in state *Y.* By the law of *X,* a plaintiff has no cause of action until he has shown that his own negligence did not contribute to his injury. By the law of *Y,* contributory negligence is an affirmative defense to be pleaded and proved by the defendant. *A* must show his freedom from contributory negligence.

The *Redick* case continues . . . :

> We are convinced that, to the extent the *Menard* case holds that the Illinois rule is remedial and not substantive and to the extent it holds that Missouri courts will adhere to their rule of placing the burden of proving contributory negligence upon the defendant in a case arising in another state wherein the law of that state is as it is in Illinois, it should no longer be followed. The distinction is that the Missouri law makes a plaintiff's contributory negligence a matter of defense only, the proof of which will defeat an existing claim. But in Illinois, the plaintiff's due care, or his freedom from contributory negligence, is not a matter of defense, defeating a claim, but an essential element which must exist before there is a cause of action in the first instance.

For the reasons stated, the rule announced in the *Menard* and subsequent cases was clearly erroneous and manifestly wrong. The rule of stare decisis is never applied to prevent the repudiation of decisions that are patently wrong and destructive of substantive rights. . . .

The judgment is reversed and the cause remanded.
All concur.

Questions and Comments

(1) Why does a court apply its own procedural rules even though it may be applying the substantive law of another jurisdiction? Presumably the answer lies in the desire of the forum not to complicate its task unduly. If domestic procedure can be applied without affecting the foreign rights asserted by way of foreign law, there seems little reason to borrow foreign procedure as well. On the other hand, if a matter is one that will clearly affect the outcome of the case, the tendency is to call it substantive and apply the foreign rule. Two considerations muddy the waters, however: First, it isn't always clear whether a particular rule will affect the outcome of the case (for example, the burden of proof when the question comes up on appeal by way of an attack on jury instructions); second, the forum may wish to apply its own "procedural" rule even though the outcome of a case will be affected in one respect or another because the adoption of the foreign procedure is too burdensome. This second point is particularly strong when the first factor is also operating—the adoption of troublesome foreign procedure when its effect on the outcome is doubtful is not always attractive to the forum.

Outcome determination and ease of application are not always the sole considerations, however. If the issue is the right to a jury trial, for example, the forum may have rejected trial by jury for a particular cause of action because it feels that the judge is a more reliable finder of fact for the particular kind of action in question. Thus, although there might be no difficulty in empaneling a jury in the action in question (since the forum uses juries in other types of actions), the forum might nonetheless refuse to do so on the grounds that the foreign cause of action is *better* served by forum procedure than by foreign procedure. Similarly, forum rules concerning the scope of cross-examination, competency of witnesses and documents, etc., may appeal to the forum as superior and unrelated to its obligation to apply foreign law, even though they may affect the outcome of the case. Evidentiary privileges may further complicate matters since the privilege asserted (doctor-patient privilege, for example) may have little to do either with the forum or the state whose substantive law is applicable if the communication took place in a third state.

Finally, might there be sound analytical reasons, especially in the traditional choice-of-law framework, for distinguishing between primary rights that attach normative judgments to out-of-court behavior, and adjective rights that regulate how primary rights get adjudicated? On this latter distinction, see Dane, Vested Rights, Vestedness and Choice of Law, 96 Yale L.J. 1191 (1987). And for an intelligent general discussion of the substance/procedure distinction, see Risinger, "Substance" and "Procedure" Revisited, 30 U.C.L.A. L. Rev. 189 (1982).

(2) Some of the common issues that provoke controversy as to proper categorization are:

(a) Statutes of fraud. These statutes have frequently been categorized as substantive or procedural depending on their precise wording, the search being for words that forbid *enforcement* of the obligation (procedural) as against words that forbid *creation* of the obligation (substantive). When they analyze the matter, cases taking the former view concentrate on preventing perjury in the forum's courts, while cases taking the latter view concentrate on the rights of the parties.
(b) Statutes of limitations. These are considered in the following subsection.
(c) Burdens of proof, privilege, and other evidentiary questions, including the parol evidence rule.
(d) Joinder, counterclaim, setoff, impleader, right to jury trial, and other matters usually thought of as "procedural" without regard to the conflicts controversy.
(e) Survival or revival of a cause of action.
(f) The availability of equitable relief, installment judgments, etc., and other "remedy" questions such as measure of damages.

(3) *Sampson* was cited with apparent approval by the Supreme Court in Klaxon Co. v. Stentor Manufacturing Co., 313 U.S. 487 (1941), page 577, *infra*. Does the *Sampson* opinion do a convincing job of arguing that the issue there is substantive for *Erie* purposes and procedural as a matter of state law? What if two states were involved instead of a state and a federal court? That is, assume that State *A* is the forum and State *B* is the place of injury. If State *A* decides that a particular matter is substantive and that the law of State *B*, the locus delicti, therefore ought to apply to the issue, what should be done if the law of State *B* characterizes the issue as procedural?

(4) Assuming that a state places the burden of proof with respect to contributory negligence on the plaintiff because of a suspicion of negligence actions, is it likely that this extra bit of help for the defendant is important enough, in a case that actually gets to the jury, that reversal is merited when the wrong conflicts principle is applied and the plaintiff gets the extra help instead? In other words, how often does the burden of proof affect the "normal" case? Should reversals be limited to cases in which evidence is lacking and the burden issue is therefore determinative of the outcome?

Grant v. McAuliffe

41 Cal. 2d 859, 264 P.2d 944 (1953)

TRAYNOR, J.

On December 17, 1949, plaintiffs W. R. Grant and R. M. Manchester were riding west on U.S. Highway 66 in an automobile owned and driven by plaintiff D. O. Jensen. Defendant's decedent, W. W. Pullen, was driving his automobile east on the same highway. The two automobiles collided at a point approximately 15 miles east of Flagstaff, Arizona. Jensen's automobile was badly damaged and Jensen, Grant, and Manchester suffered personal injuries. Nineteen days later, on January 5, 1950, Pullen died as a result of injuries received in the collision. Defendant McAuliffe was appointed administrator of his estate and letters testamentary were issued by the Superior Court of Plumas County. All three plaintiffs, as well as Pullen, were residents of California at the time of the collision. After the appointment of defendant, each plaintiff presented his claim for damages. He rejected all three claims, and on December 14, 1950, each plaintiff filed an action against the estate of Pullen to recover damages for the injuries caused by the alleged negligence of the decedent. Defendant filed a general demurrer and a motion to abate each of the complaints. The trial court entered an order granting the motion in each case. Each plaintiff has appealed. The appeals are based on the same ground and have therefore been consolidated.

The basic question is whether plaintiffs' causes of action against Pullen survived his death and are maintainable against his estate. The statutes of this state provide that causes of action for negligent torts survive the death of the tortfeasor and can be maintained against the administrator or executor of his estate. Defendant contends, however, that the survival of a cause of action is a matter of substantive law, and that the courts of this state must apply the law of Arizona governing survival of causes of action. There is no provision for survival of causes of action in the statutes of Arizona, although there is a provision that in the event of the death of a party to a pending proceeding his personal representative can be substituted as a party to the action . . . if the cause of action survives. The Supreme Court of Arizona has held that if a tort action has not been commenced before the death of the tortfeasor a plea in abatement must be sustained.

Thus, the answer to the question whether the causes of action against Pullen survived and are maintainable against his estate depends on whether Arizona or California law applies. In actions on torts occurring abroad, the courts of this state determine the substantive matters inherent in the cause of action by adopting as their own the law of the place where the tortious acts occurred, unless it is contrary to the public policy of this state. "[N]o court can enforce any law but that of its own sovereign, and, when a suitor comes to a jurisdiction foreign to the place of the tort, he can only invoke an obligation of its own as nearly homologous as possible to that arising in the place where the tort occurs." Learned Hand, J., in Guinness v. Miller. But the forum does not adopt as its own the procedural law of the place where the tortious acts occur. It must, therefore, be determined whether survival of causes of action is procedural or substantive for conflict of laws purposes.

This question is one of first impression in this state. The precedents in other jurisdictions are conflicting. In many cases it has been held that the survival of a cause of action is a matter of substance and that the law of the place where the tortious acts occurred must be applied to determine the question. The Restatement of the Conflict of Laws, section 390, is in accord. It should be noted, however, that the majority of the foregoing cases were decided after drafts of the Restatement were first circulated in 1929. Before that time, it appears that the weight of authority was that survival of causes of action is procedural and governed by the domestic law of the forum. Many of the cases, decided both before and after the Restatement, holding that survival is substantive and must be determined by the law of the place where the tortious acts occurred, confused the problems involved in survival of causes of action with those in causes of action for wrongful death. The problems are not analogous. *See* Schumacher, "Rights of Action Under Death and Survival Statutes," 23 Mich. L. Rev. 114, 116-117, 124-125. A cause of action for wrongful death is statutory. It is a new cause of action vested in the widow or next of kin, and arises on the death of the injured person. Before his death, the injured person himself has a separate and distinct cause of action and, if it survives, the same cause of action can be enforced by the personal representative of the deceased against the tortfeasor. The survival statutes do not create a new cause of action, as do the wrongful death statutes. The English courts have reached the same result in construing similar statutes. They merely prevent the abatement of the cause of action of the injured person, and provide for its enforcement by or against the personal representative of the deceased. They are analogous to statutes of limitation, which are procedural for conflict of laws purposes and are governed by the domestic law of the forum. Thus, a cause of action arising in another state, by the laws of which an action cannot be maintained thereon because of lapse of time, can be enforced in California by a citizen of this state, if he has held the cause of action from the time it accrued.

Defendant contends, however, that the characterization of survival of causes of action as substantive or procedural is foreclosed by Cort v. Steen, where it was held that the California survival statutes were substantive and therefore did not apply retroactively. The problem in the present proceeding, however, is not whether the survival statutes apply retroactively, but whether they are substantive or procedural for purposes of conflict of laws. " 'Substance' and 'procedure,' . . . are not legal concepts of invariant content." [A] statute or other rule of law will be characterized as substantive or procedural according to the nature of the problem for which a characterization must be made.

Defendant also contends that a distinction must be drawn between survival of causes of action and revival of actions, and that the former are substantive but the latter procedural. On the basis of this distinction, defendant concludes that many of the cases cited above as holding that survival is procedural and is governed by the domestic law of the forum do not support this position, since they involved problems of "revival" rather than "survival." The distinction urged by defendant is not a valid one. Most of the statutes involved in the cases cited provided for the "revival" of a pending proceeding by or against the personal representative of a party thereto should he die while the action is still pending. But in most "revival" statutes, substitution of a personal representative in place of a deceased party is expressly conditioned on the survival of the cause of action itself. If the cause of action dies with the tortfeasor, a pending proceeding must be abated. A personal representative cannot be substituted in the place of a deceased party unless the cause of action is still subsisting. In cases where this substitution has occurred, the courts have looked to the domestic law of the forum to determine whether the cause of action survives as well as to determine whether the personal representative can be substituted as a party to the action. Defendant's contention would require the courts to look to their local statutes to determine "revival" and to the law of the place where the tort occurred to determine "survival," but we have found no case in which this procedure was followed.

Since we find no compelling weight of authority for either alternative, we are free to make a choice on the merits. We have concluded that survival of causes of action should be governed by the law of the forum. Survival is not an essential part of the cause of action itself but relates to the procedures available for the enforcement of the legal claim for damages. Basically the question is one of administration of decedent's estates, which is a purely local proceeding. The problem here is whether the causes of action that these plaintiffs had against Pullen before his death survive as liabilities of his estate. . . . Decedent's estate is located in this state, and letters of administration were issued to defendant by the courts of this state. The responsibilities of defendant, as administrator of Pullen's estate, for injuries inflicted by Pullen before his death are governed by the laws of this state. This approach has been followed in a number of well-reasoned cases. It retains control of the administration of estates by the local legislature, and avoids the problems involved in determining the administrator's amenability to suit under the laws of other states. The common law doctrine *actio personalis moritur cum persona* had its origin in a penal concept of tort liability. *See* Prosser, Law of Torts 950-951. Today, tort liabilities of the sort involved in these actions are regarded as compensatory. When, as in the present case, all of the parties were residents of this state, and the estate of the deceased tortfeasor is being administered in this state, plaintiff's right to prosecute their causes of action is governed by the laws of this state relating to administration of estates.

[A dissenting opinion is omitted.]

Questions and Comments

(1) Can calling the survival issue of this case "procedural" be justified on the basis of ease of administrability of the forum? Wouldn't dismissal on the basis of the Arizona nonsurvival rule be much easier?

(2) Why did Arizona allow abatement of the action against a dead tortfeasor? The *Grant* court cites the ancient origin of the tort law and its origi-

nal penal purpose: Presumably the decedent is not significantly punished by a judgment against his estate. Professor Brainerd Currie, in writing about this case, concluded that the most probable reason for the Arizona rule was inertia in moving away from its common-law origins, but he also proposed another possible rationale for the rule: "that the living should not be mulcted for the wrongs of the dead: that the interests represented in the estate of the tort-feasor—his heirs, next of kin, devisees, legatees, creditors—should not suffer because of what he did." Currie, Selected Essays on the Conflict of Laws 143, 144 (1963).

Do these considerations make the rule look procedural?

(3) In the same article Professor Currie speculated as to what "really" went on in the decision of the *Grant* case:

> The judges fed the data into the machine in the usual way, but, when the machine's answer came out, they couldn't swallow it. They rebelled against the machine. They *adjudicated* the case. . . . Doubtless they felt a bit uncomfortable. . . . So they went back to the machine and fed the same data into it again, this time using a somewhat different procedure. After pressing the button marked "Procedure is governed by the law of the forum, substance by the law of the place of the wrong," they pressed the button marked "Procedural" instead of the one marked "Substantive." This time the machine came up with the answer that the court had arrived at independently.

Id. at 138-139.

(4) "We have concluded that survival of the causes of action should be governed by the law of the forum." "Decedent's estate is located in this state, and letters of administration were issued to the defendant by the courts of this state. The responsibilities of defendant, as administrator of Pullen's estate, for injuries inflicted by Pullen before his death are governed by the laws of this state."

Question: What happens when the forum is other than the state of administration of the decedent's estate—because, for example, the decedent had property elsewhere that serves as the basis for jurisdiction? Which rule governs—that of the forum, or that of the state of administration?

(5) Justice Traynor later commented on the decision in this case: "I do not regard it as ideally articulated, developed as it had to be against the brooding background of a petrified forest. Yet I would make no more apology for it than that in reaching a rational result it was less deft than it might have been to quit itself of the familiar speech of choice of law." Traynor, Is This Conflict Really Necessary?, 37 Tex. L. Rev. 657, 670 n.35 (1959).

What are the reasons that led Justice Traynor to believe that he had reached a "rational" result?

4. Statutes of Limitations

Selections from the First Restatement of Conflicts, on Statutes of Limitations

§§603-605 (1934)

§603. Statute of Limitations of Forum

If action is barred by the statute of limitations of the forum, no action can be maintained though action is not barred in the state where the cause of action arose.

§604. Foreign Statute of Limitations

If action is not barred by the statute of limitations of the forum, an action can be maintained, though action is barred in the state where the cause of action arose.

§605. Time Limitations on Cause of Action

If by the law of the state which has created a right of action, it is made a condition of the right that it shall expire after a certain period of limitation has elapsed, no action begun after the period has elapsed can be maintained in any state.

Duke v. Housen

589 P.2d 334 (Wyo.), *cert. denied,* 444 U.S. 863 (1979)

In the appeal now before the court, appellant-defendant challenges the jury verdict and district court judgment entered against him awarding the appellee-plaintiff, based upon defendant's alleged grossly negligent infection of plaintiff with venereal disease, compensatory and punitive damages in the sum of $1,300,000. Through this appellate challenge, defendant raises the following questions:

1. Is the action barred by the statute of limitations? . . .

For the reasons stated in detail herein, we shall reverse on the ground that the action is barred by the statue of limitations and not consider the other issues.

In early April, 1970, plaintiff was living, working, and going to college part-time in the Washington, D.C. area. On April 4 of that year she was introduced by her brother to defendant; and on the same night and early morning of April 5, following dinner and dancing plus moderate drinking, engaged in sexual intercourse with defendant in the front seat of his pickup truck. On April 8th, at least partially in response to defendant's sudden and convincing professions of love and desire to marry, plaintiff met defendant at the LaGuardia airport in New York and subsequently traveled by truck with him from New York to Denver, Colorado, engaging on and off in acts of sexual intercourse with defendant along the way. Upon reaching Denver, defendant, having lost interest in plaintiff, lodged her in a local hotel and left for his home in Meeteetse, Wyoming. Plaintiff, after contacting her brother and waiting for him to arrive, subsequently traveled to Meeteetse and confronted defendant concerning his behavior. As a result, it was agreed that defendant would accompany plaintiff and her brother back to Washington, D.C. and apologize to the family; yet after arriving in Washington and discussing the situation with her family, plaintiff for some reason which is neither totally clear nor probably capable of elucidation, accompanied the defendant to New York, there occupying a hotel room together and engaged once more in sexual intercourse with him. Finally, on the next morning of April 21, 1970, defendant broke off his relationship with the plaintiff and informed her for the first time that he had venereal disease, gonorrhea, and that now she probably had it too.

At trial, through the presentation of voluminous testimony by both parties, it was established that at some time prior to March 22, 1970, defendant had become aware that he was probably infected with venereal disease for on that day he visited a doctor in Dallas, Texas, complaining of pain and a urethral discharge. In response, the examining physician took a sample of the discharge for testing and administered a large dosage of fast-acting penicillin, telling defendant to return the next day for the test results. When defendant returned on March 23, 1970, the test results for gonorrhea having been found positive, a larger dose of a longer-acting penicillin was administered and defendant was advised to see his own doctor for further treatment. Defendant then left by plane for New York, arriving the same day, March 23, where immediately upon arrival he contacted his own physician, who after an external examination, stated that he could find no "clinical evidence of gonorrhea"—defendant had no current urethral discharge. On the basis of the previous treatment and this current information, defendant asserted at trial that it was his belief that as of his first sexual contact with the plaintiff on the night of April 4-5, 1970, his infection with gonorrhea had been cured.

Plaintiff, after being told by defendant on April 21, 1970, that she had probably contracted gonorrhea from him and should see a doctor, left New York for Washington, D.C. and the following day, April 22, 1970, visited her personal physician who through a smear test confirmed that gonorrhea was present. In response to medication, plaintiff's infection with what her physician described as a "classic case of asymptomatic gonorrhea" was arrested by May 14, 1970, but more serious problems were to develop. Beginning in January, 1973, plaintiff noticed a pain in her lower right side which by March, 1973, had become so severe and constant as to require medical attention.

After various external medical tests provided negative results and antibiotic medication proved ineffective, major exploratory surgery was performed in July, 1973. As a result, plaintiff's physician found that because of the gonorrhea infection, and possibly other related secondary infections as well, scar tissue adhesions had formed within a number of areas of appellee's lower abdomen. He testified that although he had lysed (loosed or detached by surgical procedures) the adhesions, thus somewhat relieving temporarily the severe pain, because of the nature of the scar tissue involved, new adhesions would eventually form and the pain would very probably return again and continue in this cyclical manner for the remainder of plaintiff's life. He further advised that because of the scarring involved, plaintiff's ability to bear children had been greatly reduced. . . .

Plaintiff filed this new action on April 19, 1974, seeking hospital expenses, doctor's expenses, wage loss, future medical expense, as well as damages for pain and suffering, present and future. In addition, based on an allegation that defendant was guilty of gross negligence when he infected her with gonorrhea, plaintiff requested $1 million in exemplary damages. By interrogatory, the jury found that defendant had been infected with gonorrhea at the time of his relations with plaintiff between April 4 and April 21, 1970; and by verdict awarded plaintiff $300,000.00 in compensatory damages, and $1,000,000.00 in exemplary or punitive damages. Following denial of various posttrial motions, the appeal herein was filed.

By way of both the answer filed in response to plaintiff's complaint as well as by motions prior, during and after trial, defendant alleged and strongly argued that based upon applicable statutes and case law, plaintiff's cause of action had been barred by the passage of time and her complaint should therefore be dismissed. Rule 8(c), W.R.C.P. requires that the statute of limitations be specifically set forth as an affirmative defense. In response, the trial judge ruled that inasmuch as plaintiff's scar adhesions had not been discovered until a date much later than when the infection itself had occurred, the applicable time period for limitation of action purposes was to be computed only from discovery of the adhesions; and defendant's assertion was thus denied.

Statutes of limitation have long been a part of the jurisprudence of the United States, all its states and the State of Wyoming. They are pragmatic devices to save courts from stale claim litigation and spare citizens from having to defend when memories have faded, witnesses are unavailable by death or disappearance and evidence is lost. Statutes of limitation are arbitrary by their very nature and do not discriminate between the just and unjust claim. They are not judicially made but represent legislative and public policy controlling the right to litigate. The statutes operate against even the most meritorious of claims and courts have no right to deny their application. When considering the statute of limitations, the nature of injury, its extent, the amount of money damages involved, social considerations, and the emotional appeal the facts may have must pass to the background. The circumstances are only significant in the bearing they may have on where the cause of action arose, when it arose and when the time expired for pursuing the applicable judicial remedy.

[W]hile the basic claim raised by plaintiff, albeit an unusual one, sounds in tort, the circumstance of its pursuance in Wyoming is somewhat unique. Since, as the evidence points up, there was no sexual contact between plaintiff and defendant in Wyoming, nor any tortious injury in this state, simple logic reveals that there could be no tortious conduct, no negligent exposure of plaintiff's body to disease by defendant in this, the forum state. There can be no question that plaintiff's cause of action could only be found as having arisen elsewhere.

. . . The heavy weight of authority in interstate tort cases such as here with elements in different jurisdictions, is that the law of the place where the plaintiff sustains injury to her person controls. Restatement of Conflict of Laws, §377; 2 Harper and James, §30.4, p. 1961.

At common law, the limitation period of the forum jurisdiction, the lex fori, generally controlled the time within which causes of action had to be pursued, regardless of the fact that the cause itself in all its elements may have accrued outside the forum jurisdiction. Only when the limitation of action statute of the foreign jurisdiction in which the cause arose could be deemed substantive law rather than procedural would the foreign statute be applied by the forum court. Ehrenzweig, Conflict of Laws §161 (1962); Vernon, Statutes of Limitation in the Conflict of Laws; Borrowing Statutes, 32 Rocky Mtn. L. Rev. 287 (1960). In order to avoid the confusion and problems associated with attempting to determine when a foreign limitation of action statute was substantive or procedural, a majority of states, including Wyoming, enacted what are referred to as "borrowing" statutes. Section 1-3-117, W.S. 1977, which we find to be controlling in this regard, is simple and clear:

> If by the laws of the state or country where the cause of action arose the action is barred, it is also barred in this state.

The plaintiff takes an unusual position that since the case is tried in Wyoming, it must be tried under Wyoming law as a whole, including §1-3-105, W.S. 1977, prescribing a period of limitation of four years "after the cause of action accrues," pertaining to causes of action arising in Wyoming. She then asserts that under the statutory section, since she discovered she was infected with gonorrhea "around April 22, 1970," her action was timely brought within the Wyoming four year period by filing her complaint on April 19, 1974. She elects to ignore the borrowing statute, §1-3-117, *supra.* She then relies upon [two cases] to support a 51 Am. Jur. 2d, Limitation of Actions, §66, p.645 statement as follows:

> . . . the statutes of limitation of the place where the action is brought and the remedy is sought to be enforced, and not those of the place where the

> contract was made, the right in tort arose, or the plaintiff resides, or of the domicil of one or the other of the persons affected by the litigation, control in the event of a conflict of laws. . . .

We have no argument with that rule in the case before us but we have no conflict of laws to make it applicable. Any conflict has been erased by the legislature by enactment of the "borrowing" statute fixing the statute of limitations of this state to be the same as that of the jurisdiction in which the cause of the action arose. That is explained in the next section (67) of the Am. Jur. 2d, *supra,* quote. The limitations law of the jurisdiction in which a cause of action arises is the law of this state and has been ever since territorial days, even though a defendant is properly before a Wyoming court, the place where he may be personally served with process and a remedy found. . . .

. . . Cope v. Anderson, 331 U.S. 461 (1947), points out that the bottom line purpose of a state's borrowing statute is to require its courts to bar suits if the right to sue had already expired in another jurisdiction where the crucial combination of circumstances giving the right to sue had taken place, the existence of which affords a party a right to judicial interference in his behalf.

Plaintiff also argues, and the trial judge so held, that the statute of limitations did not commence to run until October, 1973, when adhesions resulting from the infection were discovered because it is the injury therefrom for which the damages are sought. That position is not the accepted rule. . . .

The jury found as a fact that the defendant was the bearer of gonorrhea during the period April 4, 1970 to April 21, 1970. The plaintiff's testimony, admitted by the defendant, is that sexual intercourse between the plaintiff and defendant took place on the dates and in other state jurisdictions in accordance with an itinerary as follows:

> April 4-5, 1970. State of Virginia.
> April 7-8, 1970. Tuxedo, New York.
> April 8-9, 1970. Erie, Pennsylvania.
> April 9-10, 1970. State of Iowa.
> April 10-11, 1970. Ogallala, Nebraska.
> April 20-21, 1970. New York City, New York.

There is no evidence of sexual intercourse taking place in the State of Wyoming. We must therefore look elsewhere for a jurisdiction in which the cause arose. While it is perhaps unusual that the defendant perpetrated his negligent acts and caused injury to plaintiff's body in several different states and which may give an appearance of complexity, an application of settled rules of tort law in the jurisdictions involved clears away any suggestion of obscurity.

The limitation of action statute of the foreign jurisdiction in which the cause in question arose is applied by the forum court irregardless [*sic*] of whether or not the foreign limitation could be characterized as substantive or procedural. Thus, in almost all instances, if a plaintiff's cause of action is time-barred in the jurisdiction in which the cause of action arose, it would be barred by the passage of time in the forum court as well. Such a rule not only clears up any substantive procedural conflict problem, but eliminates as well the possibility of the plaintiff shopping for a favorable forum in which to revive a dead claim. It thus becomes of acute importance in the situation at bar to specifically determine, for limitation of action purposes, where and when plaintiff's cause of action arose. In making such a determination based upon a borrowed limitational period, in all jurisdictions having a borrowing statute, with the exception of Ohio, not only is the specific prescriptive period utilized, but all of its accouterments as well whether in the form of additional statutory provisions or interpretive judicial decisions. Ester, Borrowing Statutes of Limitation and Conflict of Laws, 15 U. of Fla. Law Rev. 33, 57 (1962). As the court in Devine v. Rook has very aptly stated:

> But when such [limitational] statute is so borrowed, it is not wrenched bodily out of its own setting, but taken along with it are the court decisions of its own state which interpret and apply it, and the comparison statutes which limit and restrict its operation. This we think is the general law.

(Bracketed material added, footnote omitted.) Thus, in applying a "borrowed" statute, we must consider not only the borrowed limitation of action statute itself, but also any applicable tolling or other statutes as well as pertinent court cases. In effect, plaintiff's cause must be viewed as if filed in the state where under the laws of that state a cause of action accrued.[7]

We find and hold that a cause of action arose in the state of New York on April 8, 1970 and April 21, 1970. New York City, New York was the place where the defendant committed his second and last acts of negligence in communicating disease to the plaintiff. In New York it has long been the rule that in classic actions of negligence, damage is the gist and essence of a plaintiff's cause, Schwartz v. Heyden Newport Chemical Corporation, and the

---

7. During the remaining course of this opinion, we shall be citing and quoting from the statutes of other states. As allowed by the law of the State of Wyoming, we shall take judicial notice of those considered.

Section 1-12-303, W.S. 1977: "Every court of this state shall take judicial notice of the common law and statutes of every state, territory and other jurisdiction of the United States."

Section 1-12-303, W.S. 1977: "The court may inform itself of foreign laws in such manner as it deems proper, and the court may call upon counsel to aid it in obtaining such information."

Counsel for defendant informed the trial judge of his reliance on the statutes of limitation of other states. The statutes we set out are those applicable at the time of the occurrence herein and are found in the Wyoming State Law Library, Cheyenne.

statute of limitations commences to run at the time of injury is produced (in personal injury cases) and there is damage to the structure of the body. *Schwartz* holds that the cause of action is complete when the invasion of the body by injury takes place "independently of any actual pecuniary damage." The injury is considered a trespass upon the person of the injured plaintiff. . . .

The *Schmidt* doctrine as applied to this case means that a cause of action arose in New York when the defendant had sexual intercourse with the plaintiff at the Motel in the Mountains in Tuxedo, New York on the morning of April 8, 1970. At that time he introduced into the body of the plaintiff infectious pus producing bacteria known as gonococci, which causes the disease of gonorrhea. There is no question but that under the law of New York the defendant was guilty of a tortious act of negligence and the plaintiff was injured by the placement in her body of deleterious matter. Then on the morning of April 21, 1970, the defendant once again at a hotel in New York City, New York repeated the tortious act and once again in the same fashion introduced into the body of plaintiff the bacteria of gonococci. . . .

Having concluded a cause of action accrued in the State of New York, the "borrowing" statute of Wyoming controls the determination of whether or not plaintiff's action has been barred. Under New York law, an action to recover damages for personal injury, unless involving certain specific causes of action not relevant here, must be commenced within three years.

Plaintiff's cause of action accrued in New York at the latest on April 21, 1970, the date of last sexual contact between the parties. Disregarding for the moment any other possibly applicable statute, plaintiff's action not having been filed until April 19, 1974, it appears to be barred, and defendant has so asserted. In response, plaintiff has urged that because of defendant's absence from New York following his tortious conduct, the applicable limitation period has by statute been tolled. N.Y. CPLR §207. We, as did the New York Supreme Court in a recent case, must disagree with the plaintiff. Burwell v. Whitmoyer, 1977, 56, A.D.2d 950, 392 N.Y.S.2d 512, 513:

> We now pass to plaintiff's contention that the statute of limitations was tolled pursuant to CPLR 207. While that section does provide for the tolling of the statute where a defendant is out of the state for more than four months after the action has accrued, subdivision 3 provides for an exception where the jurisdiction over the person can be obtained without personal delivery of the summons to him within the state. . . .

Under the provisions of N.Y. CPLR §302, the defendant, although a nondomiciliary of the state of New York, was still subject to the personal jurisdiction of the courts of that state based upon his commission of a tortious act within the confines of the state itself.

Once found subject to the court's jurisdiction, service of process could have been made upon defendant notwithstanding his absence from the state. . . . It would thus seem clear that had plaintiff brought this action against defendant in New York, the situs of its accrual, by the statutes and authorities of that state, her cause of action would be barred. The limitational period having run in New York, it has run in this, the forum state, as well. §1-3-117, W.S. 1977, *supra.*

In other jurisdictions in which defendant committed his acts of negligence, the cause of action is likewise either barred by a statute of limitations or no cause of action there arose. The defendant's first installment of negligence, April 4-5, 1970, was in the State of Virginia. Arguably, under the law of that state, the cause of action could have arisen there; if indeed it did, it is likewise barred by the state's limitations. In Virginia, the appropriate limitational period for personal injuries of the kind sustained herein is two years, and even though the defendant did not then and does not now reside in Virginia, he was still subject to the personal jurisdiction of its courts through its long arm statutes because of his allegedly tortious conduct within the state.

. . . On the other hand, if we follow the holding of the Virginia court's *Street* case, that the statute begins to run upon the date of last exposure, then the cause of action arose in New York City, New York, on April 22, 1970 where the last act of sexual intercourse took place. In the first instance, the plaintiff is barred in Virginia by its two year statute of limitations. In the other no cause of action arose in Virginia.

Even if it could be considered that a cause of action arose in Pennsylvania, its statute of limitations bars any action there. The Pennsylvania statute of limitations, 12 P.S. §34, provides that a personal injury action "must be brought within two years from the time when the injury was done and not afterwards." The tolling statute of Pennsylvania, 12 P.S. §40, applies only to residents. . . . The presence of plaintiff and defendant in Pennsylvania was only transient.

We must also conclude that no cause of action arose in Iowa. Iowa follows the Restatement, Conflict of Laws, §377 rule that: "The place of wrong is in the state where the last event necessary to make an actor liable for an alleged tort takes place." Since Iowa follows the discovery rule, as noted, it would appear that it was in Washington, D.C. that the cause of action accrued as far as that state is concerned because it was in the District of Columbia that plaintiff discovered that she had in fact suffered injury by virtue of the negligent conduct of the defendant.

[The court rejected application of the Nebraska statute for reasons discussed in connection with the statutes of other states.]

We foreclose Washington, D.C. as the place where a cause of action arose because no tortious act was committed there, nor was that a place where the plaintiff was injured by the implanting of infection by the defendant. It is true that Washington, D.C. was the place where plaintiff incurred medical expense for diagnosis and treatment of the injury inflicted upon her but has no controlling force as to where the cause arose. While she had money damages in the District of Columbia, her physical injury of contracting gonorrhea took place elsewhere. . . .

We therefore must conclude after extensive research that by virtue of Wyoming's borrowing statute, the filing of plaintiff's complaint on April 19, 1974 was untimely.

Reversed with directions to vacate the judgment for plaintiff and enter judgment for the defendant.

THOMAS, J., concurring.

I concur in the result in this case that was reached by the majority of the Court. I would, however, reach that result in a different manner. In my view this action was barred by the three-year statute of limitations of the District of Columbia, which is the place where the cause of action arose and to which we are directed by §1-3-117, W.S. 1977. The District of Columbia, like our state, follows a discovery rule with respect to the accrual of an action in tort. . . .

I am impressed with the reference in the majority opinion and the dissenting opinion to A.L.I. Restatement, Conflict of Laws, §377 (1934), which sets forth the rule as follows:

> §377. *The Place of Wrong.* The place of wrong is in the state where the last event necessary to make an actor liable for an alleged tort takes place.

As I understand the thrust of the majority opinion that place is determined to be the state of New York. Included within §377 is a section entitled "Summary of Rules in Important Situations Determining Where a Tort is Committed," and included within that section is a rule set forth as follows:

> 2. When a person causes another voluntarily to take a deleterious substance which takes effect within the body, the place of wrong is where the deleterious substance takes effect and not where it is administered.
>
> *Illustration:*
>
> 2. *A*, in state *X*, mails to *B* in state *Y* a package containing poisoned candy. *B* eats the candy in state *Y* and gets on a train to go to state *W*. After the train has passed into state *Z*, he becomes ill as a result of the poison and eventually dies from the poison in state *W*. The place of wrong is state *Z*.

This illustration seems peculiarly applicable to the factual situation herein in which the infection could have been transmitted in any one of a number of states. The plaintiff did not manifest any symptoms of the disease, and the illness was identified in Washington, D.C., upon physical examination. I have no quarrel with the general discussion of the law relative to statutes of limitations set forth in the majority opinion, but those concepts are designed to reach a degree of certainty in the law, albeit arbitrarily. Their application in this instance identifies the District of Columbia as the place of wrong. . . .

McClintock, J., dissenting.

In brief outline of the basis of my dissent, I agree with the majority that under the common law, limitations of actions are governed by the law of the forum. Section 1-3-117, W.S. 1977, the so-called borrowing statute, changes that rule only to the extent that we are required to apply the limitation of another state if it is determined that the "cause of action arose" in that other state. The majority recognize that both a wrongful act and a resulting injury are necessary to effect an actionable tort, and that the "law of the place where the plaintiff sustains injury to her person controls." The record does not disclose and neither the jury nor this court could find the specific state where either the wrongful act took place or the plaintiff sustained injury to her person. An essential prerequisite to application of our borrowing statute, namely, that there be a state from which to borrow, is then lacking. However, it might be logically consistent with §1-3-117 to hold the action barred if, by the law of *all* the states where the action *might possibly* have arisen, the action is barred. That is not the situation here, since Nebraska and Wyoming, both of which are states where the injury could have taken place, have four-year statutes and both are discovery states. My essential disagreement with both the majority and concurring opinions is with their concept that discovery of the wrongful act and resulting injury is an essential condition to the existence of an actionable tort. I would hold that discovery is of importance only in determining when a statute of limitations begins to run. I would then hold that defendant, who bears the burden of proving facts bringing the case within an applicable statute of limitations, has failed in that burden. I would therefore not dismiss the action. . . .

[Justice McClintock stated his opinion that the wrong was committed only when the disease was "communicated" to the plaintiff, and discussed incubation periods.]

. . . Consistently with the proper holding of the majority that it is the law of the state of injury and not of the wrongful act that determines whether a tort has been committed, it is possible that the tort could have become complete in any one of 11 states in which the plaintiff, in the company of the defendant, or separately, found herself during the 18-day sojourn between the first contact and confirmation of the existence of the disease in plaintiff in Washington on April 22.

I think it fairly obvious that our §1-3-117 was not adopted with this type of tort in mind and it is true that in most cases the state where the action arose is not too difficult to determine. In products liability cases, for example, where the negligence occurs in one state and the product is purchased and used in another state, with injury to the user, there is a clear demarcation. But in this case, which I think we all agree is one of first impression in its interstate nature, the place of injury is obscure and all we know is that at some time and place the plaintiff was injured through negligent act of the defendant. This has been found by the jury. I do not think that we can properly conclude that our legislature has said that if the action would be barred in *one* of a number of *possible* states, it is likewise barred in this state. The statute of no one state may be adopted unless it is clearly established that it was the place of injury.

Although it is the law of the place of injury that governs, the majority briefly and I think arbitrarily dismiss Wyoming as a possible place of wrong because no sexual act took place therein. If transmission of the disease through sexual intercourse is not certain and if there is an incubation period, then it is possible that transmission and planting of the infection occurred in one state and took effect in another. . . .

. . . I therefore conclude that it is only in the application of the statute of limitations to the remedy to be sought for an accrued cause of action that the question of discovery becomes of importance. It is only in connection with the question of limitations that we find judicial statements that the action has accrued upon "discovery" of the wrong or injury. It appears that this is a developing concept. In 2 Wood on Limitations, 4th Ed. 1916, §276c(1), pp. 1408-1410, we find this broad statement:

> Mere ignorance of the existence of a cause of action does not prevent the running of the statute of limitations unless there has been fraudulent concealment on the part of those invoking the benefit of the statute. . . .

I concede that I have referred to possibilities. If those possibilities concerned whether defendant had committed an actionable tort against plaintiff, it might well be said that plaintiff did not sustain the burden of proof resting upon her. However, defendant has not contended in his brief or upon oral argument that the evidence was insufficient to support the verdict of negligence rendered by the jury. The bar of the statute of limitations is one sought to be raised by the defendant in avoidance of established liability. In such case, "[t]he party pleading the statute of limitations has the burden of proving that the action is barred." . . .

Defendant does not plead the statute of limitations of any particular state, and claims only that the action is barred by the provisions of our borrowing statutes, §1-3-117, W.S. 1977. In this court he relies on the District of Columbia three-year statute. I would hold that statute inapplicable on the basis already discussed, and since he has shown no other statute which governs and has not shown that the statutes of all possible places of wrong have run, he has failed in his burden. From this, it follows that the action should not be dismissed. . . .

Questions and Comments

(1) A well known exception to the usual principle that forum statutes of limitations automatically apply in the absence of a borrowing statute is Bournias v. Atlantic Maritime Co., 220 F.2d 152 (2d Cir. 1955) (Harlan, J.—later Justice Harlan). There the question was whether the one-year limitations period of the Panamanian code or the longer period under American maritime law would apply in a case arising under the Panamanian Labor Code. The forum was the United States District Court, not an individual state, because federal maritime jurisdiction had been invoked. The United States has no borrowing statute. The court said that the Panamanian limitation would be applied if it were substantive but not if it were procedural. It then discussed the various tests for distinguishing substantive from procedural statutes of limitations, expressed a lack of satisfaction with all of them, and settled on what appeared to be the most acceptable: Statutes of limitations will be presumed to be procedural unless they are contained in the same statute that creates the substantive right. Under that test, the court said, the Panamanian statute was procedural (since it did not deem the broad Panamanian Labor Code to be a single statute). Did such a test ever make sense? Why should a United States court wish to entertain an action that arose under Panamanian law but that could not be brought in Panama?

So-called "statutes of repose," in contrast to statutes of limitations, are likely to be treated as substantive, at least if they are deemed substantive by the states adopting them. *See, e.g.*, Bonti v. Ford Motor Co., 898 F. Supp. 391, 397 (S.D. Miss. 1995), *aff'd*, 85 F.3d 625 (5th Cir. 1996) (North Carolina's products liability statute of repose is substantive rather than procedural). Does consultation of the other state's characterization violate the principle embodied in section 584, reprinted at page 130 *supra?*

(2) As in *Duke*, most states have adopted some kind of borrowing statute to determine when the forum will apply its own statute of limitations statute to a case and when it will apply the limitations statute of another state. The Wyoming statute at issue in *Duke* is typical in borrowing the statute of limitations of the state where the cause of action "arose." Will this criterion always be appropriate, even in simple cases? What if the claim "arose" in State *A* but is to be governed by the law of State *B*?

(3) The *Duke* opinion at one point refers to the "*Schmidt* doctrine" to determine that the cause of action arose in New York, thus triggering the Wyoming borrowing statute (which applies when the cause of action "arose" in another state or country.) But *Schmidt* was a New York case. Shouldn't the court have applied *Wyoming* law to determine where, for purposes of a Wyoming statute, the cause of action arose?

After the court decides that the cause of action arose in another jurisdiction, what law governs issues such as tolling and accrual? *See* Uniform Conflict of Laws Limitations §3 (1982) ("If the statute of limitations of another state applies to the assertion of a claim in this State, the other state's relevant statutes and other rules of law governing tolling and accrual apply in computing the limitations period, but its statutes and other rules governing conflict of laws do not apply").

(4) In several other places the court, in discussing the law of various states, concluded that under the law of the state being discussed, the claim accrued only when it was discovered. The court therefore ignored the laws of those states since the claim was discovered in the District of Columbia. Isn't the dissent right in saying that the majority was confusing the issue of *when* a claim arose and *where* it accrued? Specifically, could Wyoming do the following:

(a) determine that the claim had "arisen," say, in Virginia, and
(b) therefore apply the law of Virginia, under which the statute would begin to run when the claim was discovered, no matter where it was discovered?

(5) What would the *Duke* majority have done if it determined that wrongs had been committed in several states against the plaintiff and that actions were barred under the laws of some of those states but not others?

5. Public Policy

Selection from the First Restatement of Conflicts, on Public Policy

§612 (1934)

§612. Action Contrary to Public Policy

No action can be maintained upon a cause of action created in another state the enforcement of which is contrary to the strong public policy of the forum.

(1948 Supp.) Likewise, a distinction has to be noted between the situation dealt with in this Section and the situation where a party sets up a defense which is contrary to the strong public policy of the forum. The latter situation involves more than a matter of denial of access to the court. The plaintiff is asking for a judgment even though there is a defense otherwise valid. It is, therefore, not within the scope of the rule of this Section.

Marchlik v. Coronet Insurance Co.

40 Ill. 2d 327, 239 N.E.2d 799 (1968)

House, J.

This is an appeal from an order of the circuit court of Cook County dismissing the complaint of plaintiff, Christine Marchlik, against two Illinois insurance companies, Coronet Insurance Company and State Farm Mutual Automobile Insurance Company. Constitutional questions are raised.

Plaintiff, a resident of Wisconsin, was injured when the automobile of Henry Tapio, in which she was riding, was involved in a collision with one driven by Edward Trombley on U.S. Highway 51 in Iron County, Wisconsin. She received hospital and medical care in Wisconsin. Tapio was a resident of Bessemer, Michigan, Trombley was a Wisconsin resident, and the automobile driven by him bore Wisconsin registration. Tapio's liability policy was issued by Coronet and Trombley's by State Farm. Each policy was issued in Illinois, and they contained practically identical "no action" clauses prohibiting direct action against the carrier until final judgment had been entered against the insured.

The action was commenced under the Wisconsin "Direct Action" statutes . . . which authorize original suits against insurance companies provided the injuries were sustained in Wisconsin. . . .

The issues as stated by the parties are whether the public policy of Illinois precludes direct action against an insurer for tort liability of the insured where the policy has a "no action" clause and when the statutory law of the place where the tort occurs allows direct action and, if so, does the full-faith-and-credit clause of the Constitution of the United States force a State to enforce a foreign statute.

The preliminary approach to these issues is whether Wisconsin's direct action statutes are procedural or substantive. If procedural or remedial, it is well settled that the lex fori, or law of the jurisdiction in which relief is sought, will govern. . . . On the other hand, the lex loci delictus or law of the place of wrong generally governs where the substantive rights of the parties will be affected. But, even this is an oversimplification for, if entertaining a foreign cause (such as this direct action suit against casualty insurers) is contrary to the public policy of the forum, its courts may bar enforcement of the foreign remedy, provided, of course, such a bar is not in contravention of the full-faith-and-credit clause of the Federal constitution. . . .

In commenting on the two sections the Wisconsin court said:

> Sec. 204.30(4) is substantive and creates direct liability between the injured third person and the insurer while sec. 260.11(1) is procedural and determines when the insurer can be made a party to the action despite the presence of a no-action clause in the policy. . . .

While passing on the question of the effect of no-action provisions the Supreme Court of Minnesota in Kertson v. Johnson. . . . held the Wisconsin direct action statute . . . to be substantive. In Oltarsh v. Aetna Insurance Co. . . . it was said that the Puerto Rican direct action statute, which resembled section 260.11(1) of the Wisconsin statute, was substantive in character and even though New York had no similar statute the insured injured in Puerto Rico could maintain her action directly against the insurance carrier. Mr. Justice

Traynor, speaking for the California court in Grant v. McAuliffe . . . recognized that the courts of that State determine substantive matters by adopting as their law the law of the place where the tortious acts occurred, unless contrary to the public policy of the State. The question of first impression there was whether survival of causes of action was procedural or substantive for conflict-of-laws purposes. It was carefully pointed out that survival statutes do not create a new cause of action and are analogous to statutes of limitations, whereas the wrongful death statutes do create new causes of action and are substantive.

We adopt the view that this direct action statute is substantive and, as such, is entitled to comity, provided there is no compelling public policy of this State to the contrary.

Public policy has been defined as "judicial decisions, legislation and constitutions as well as customs, morals and notions of justice which may prevail in a state." (Speidel, Extra-territorial Assertion of the Direct Action Statute: Due Process, Full Faith and Credit and the Search for Government Interest, 53 Northwestern U. Law Review 179, 200.) The author in developing the thesis that the direct action statute contravenes Illinois public policy said:

> An exclusionary policy which is directed at the nature of the right sought to be enforced and is predicated upon protecting the outcome of litigation from prejudice and error reflects a peculiar local interest. . . . This argument becomes even more compelling when it is realized that the direct action statute is an innovation which has been adopted by only three states [Wisconsin, Louisiana, and Rhode Island]. While uniform enforcement in general may be a desirable goal, it should not foist the experimental whims of other states upon the place of trial.

(P.203) An examination of Illinois law and customs will, we believe, demonstrate that entertaining direct action suits is contrary to a firmly-fixed public policy.

First, while there is no direct legislation prohibiting such actions as in Michigan . . . section 25 of the Civil Practice Act . . . which provided for the filing of a third party complaint, expresses a legislative policy by adding the admonition:

> Nothing herein applies to liability insurers or creates any substantive right to contribution among tortfeasors or against any insurer or other person which has not heretofore existed.

Section 388 of the Insurance Code . . . provides that policies shall contain a privilege for suit against an insurer where the insured becomes insolvent or bankrupt and execution has been returned unsatisfied. These statutory provisions definitely indicate to us a legislative policy against direct actions against insurers before judgment.

In Pohlman v. Universal Mutual Casualty Co. . . . section 388 was interpreted as expressing a legislative policy against direct action against insurers until after liability had been established and judgment rendered against an insured. In Mutual Service Casualty Insurance Co. v. Prudence Mutual Casualty Co. . . . the appellate court refused to permit the plaintiff company to maintain an action to enforce a repayment of the amount it had to pay under Wisconsin's comparative negligence statute. The decision was based squarely upon the theory that public policy of this State prohibited direct actions against insurers.

. . . Disclosure of liability coverage at a trial against an insured for injuries resulting from his negligence constitutes prejudicial error in this State, contrary to the rule prevailing in Wisconsin. . . . The Wisconsin direct action statute is indirect contravention of no action clauses in policies which are recognized in this State. . . .

Foreign substantive law is not, of course, unenforceable as being contrary to public policy just because it differs from our own law, but the differences here are such as to be against our public policy. Our courts and juries would be hard put to cope with the complex problems posed by other aspects of Wisconsin law if these direct actions are permitted. Wisconsin's lack of a guest statute such as we have, and its interpretation of policy language, would result in confusion and possibly injustice. If this case is entertained by our courts, many more will follow with their attendant appeals. Eventually two bodies of law would be built up, one relating to domestic cases and the other based on our interpretation of Wisconsin law.

Public policy of Illinois precludes the use of our courts as the forum for cases under the Wisconsin direct action statutes and application of the exclusionary rule does not violate the full-faith-and-credit provisions of the Federal Constitution.

The judgment of the circuit court of Cook County is affirmed.

WARD, J. (concurring in the result).

The majority say that it would be contrary to the public policy of this State to entertain an action under the Wisconsin statute concerned and that such denial of access to our courts does not violate the full-faith-and-credit provision of the constitution of the United States.

While I agree that this cause should not be entertained in Illinois, I am not fully persuaded that the rationale of the majority is beyond proper challenge. . . .

I judge that the complaint and cause should have been dismissed on the basis of forum non conveniens. Under this doctrine a court may, exercising sound discretion, decline to assume jurisdiction of an action brought before it if it deems that the cause may more conveniently and at no sacrifice of full justice be litigated in another court to which it may be brought after the declining court's refusal to entertain jurisdiction. . . .

Holzer v. Deutsche Reichsbahn-Gesellschaft

277 N.Y. 474, 14 N.E. 2d 798 (1938)

PER CURIAM.

The complaint alleges two causes of action arising out of a contract between plaintiff, a German national, and Schenker & Co. G.m.b.H., a German corporation, for services to be performed by plaintiff for three years from January 1, 1932, in Germany and in other locations outside this state. Defendants, German corporations, controlled either through stock ownership or otherwise, the transportation system known as Schenker & Co.

Both causes of action allege that the contract provides that "in the event the plaintiff should die or become unable, without fault on his part, to serve during the period of the contract the defendants would pay to him or his heirs the sum of 120,000 marks, in discharge of their obligations under the hiring aforesaid."

The first cause of action alleges that on June 21, 1933, defendants discharged plaintiff as of October 31, 1933, upon the sole ground that he is a Jew and that as the result of such discharge he was damaged in a sum upwards of $50,000.

The second cause of action alleges that in April, 1933, the German government incarcerated plaintiff in prison and in a concentration camp for about six months, that his imprisonment was not brought about by any act or fault of plaintiff but solely by reason of the policy of the government which required the elimination of all persons of Jewish blood from leading commercial, industrial, and transportation enterprises, that as a result "plaintiff became unable, without any fault on his part, to continue his services from the month of April, 1933," and has been damaged in the sum of $50,000.

The second separate defense of defendant Deutsche Reichsbahn-Gesellschaft alleges that the contract of hiring was made and was to be performed in Germany, was terminated in Germany and is governed by the laws of Germany, that subsequent to April 7, 1933, the government of Germany adopted and promulgated certain laws, decrees, and orders which required persons of non-Aryan descent, of whom plaintiff is one, to be retired.

The Special Term granted plaintiff's motion to strike out this defense, the Appellate Division affirmed and certified these questions: "(1) Is the second separate defense contained in the answer of the defendant, Deutsche Reichsbahn-Gesellschaft, sufficient in law upon the face thereof? (2) Does the complaint herein state facts sufficient to constitute a cause of action?"

The courts of this state are empowered to entertain jurisdiction of actions between citizens of foreign countries or other states of this Union based upon contracts between nonresidents to be performed outside this state. . . . Under the decisions of this court and of the Supreme Court of the United States, the law of the country or state where the contract was made and was to be performed by citizens of that country or state governs. . . .

Within its own territory every government is supreme . . . and our courts are not competent to review its actions. . . . We have so held, "however objectionable" we may consider the conduct of a foreign government. Dougherty v. Equitable Life Assur. Soc. of United States. . . . "Every sovereign State is bound to respect the independence of every other sovereign State, and the courts of one country will not sit in judgment on the acts of the government of another done within its own territory." Oetjen v. Central Leather Co. . . . In the *Dougherty* Case . . . we have held: "It cannot be against the public policy of this State to hold nationals to the contracts which they have made in their own country to be performed there according to the laws of the country."

Therefore, in respect to the first cause of action, we are bound to decide, as a matter of pleading, that the complaint does not state facts sufficient to constitute a cause of action and that the second separate defense of the answer is sufficient in law upon its face. Defendants did not breach their contract with plaintiff. They were forced by operation of law to discharge him.

In respect to the second cause of action, the result is necessarily different. We are dealing merely with pleadings. Assuming, as alleged, that plaintiff became unable without any fault on his part to continue his services subsequent to April, 1933, that part of the agreement which is alleged to provide "that in the event the plaintiff should die or become unable, without fault on his part, to serve during the period of the contract the defendants would pay to him or his heirs the sum of 120,000 marks, in discharge of their obligations, under the hiring aforesaid," must be interpreted according to German law and the meaning of German words. What that law is depends upon the solution of questions of fact which must be determined on the trial. If the English words "become unable" are a correct translation of the German words employed in the contract, then they would not appear to be limited to inability caused by physical illness but might be intended to apply to any factor which might prevent his service. . . .

Questions and Comments

(1) The classic definition of "public policy" is found in Loucks v. Standard Oil Co. of New York, 224 N.Y. 99, 120 N.E. 198, 202 (1918) (Cardozo, J.):

> The courts are not free to refuse to enforce a foreign right at the pleasure of the judges, to suit the individual notion of expediency or fairness. They do not close their doors unless help [to the other state] would violate some fundamental principle of justice, some prevalent conception of good morals, some deep-rooted tradition of the common weal.

With the due process clause to strike down the most serious abuses, and with a fairly uniform sense of fairness throughout the country, should there be many instances in which laws meet the criteria of the *Loucks* case?

(2) What did the *Marchlik* court have in mind when it said, "Our courts and juries would be hard put to cope with the complex problems posed by other aspects of the Wisconsin law if these direct actions are permitted"? Although Wisconsin courts have more experience in applying Wisconsin law, how can one differentiate between Wisconsin juries and Illinois juries? Are people from Wisconsin smarter than people from Illinois? Isn't the court engaging in a great deal of speculation about the possible mischief to be posed by the Wisconsin statute? As long as Illinois would permit an action based on a Wisconsin accident against the tortfeasor and would permit an action by the tortfeasor against his insurer, why should a suit directly against the tortfeasor's insurer introduce significant complications?

On the other hand, even if the *Marchlik* court is not adept at identifying the source of its unease over the direct-action statute of Wisconsin, isn't there room for legitimate concern that juries who know that the defendant is an insurer will be more willing to find in favor of the plaintiff, even in the absence of negligence? Or do juries assume that everyone is insured? (And, of course, do they assume that the amount of coverage will be sufficient to cover whatever verdict they return?) Note the court's statement that disclosure of the fact of insurance in Illinois constitutes reversible error.

(3) Does it make a difference in *Marchlik* that the policies were issued in Illinois? If the companies had been Wisconsin companies and the policies had been issued there, would any Illinois concern for the possibility of sympathy-induced verdicts be an officious interest? Or does Illinois have an automatic justified interest in the quality of justice dispensed in its courts, even when the defendants are from Wisconsin, and even when Wisconsin is satisfied with the factfinding that occurs when the jury knows of the insurance?

(4) The concurring opinion in the *Marchlik* case suggests a forum non conveniens dismissal. What is the difference between such a dismissal and what the court actually did? What should be the res judicata effect of the *Marchlik* opinion? Should the same plaintiff be able to sue the same defendants on the same cause of action in *Wisconsin?* Ordinarily, of course, the mere fact that State *A* must make a choice of law to rule against the plaintiff will not allow State *B* to enter a later inconsistent judgment between the same parties on the basis of a different choice of law. Res judicata principles and the full faith and credit clause of the Constitution would forbid such a result. But isn't there something different about the decision in *Marchlik*—that is, can it really be said that the decision is "on the merits"?

(5) In Mertz v. Mertz, 271 N.Y. 466, 3 N.E.2d 597 (1936), Emmy sued Fred for damages resulting from his negligent use of an automobile in the state of Connecticut. Both were residents of New York, which forbade such suits between spouses. The law of Connecticut contained no such bar. The New York Court of Appeals apparently concluded that Connecticut provided the applicable law to the interspousal immunity issue but went on to refuse application of the Connecticut rule because it was against the public policy

of New York. (In the alternative, the court found that questions of capacity—such as interspousal immunity—are matters for the forum.)

In light of the *Mertz* and *Holzer* cases, is it fair to say that interspousal suits are against the public policy of New York but that racial persecution is not?

(6) Was the *Holzer* court somehow condoning racial discrimination in its opinion, or is it significant that the defendant was required by law to fire Holzer? If someone held a gun against *A*'s head and required her to commit a tort against *B*, would it be condoning the tort not to hold *A* liable?

(7) Assume that Germany had a prewar statute providing (a) that Jewish people were not allowed to hold positions in industry, (b) that it was the duty of every German citizen to report every Jewish person remaining in an industrial position after January 1, 1937, and (c) that the first person making such a report was entitled to a bounty of one tenth of the victim's wealth. If the victim owned property in New York, would the *Holzer* court have applied the principles applied in *Holzer*—that "[w]ithin its own territory every government is supreme . . . and our courts are not competent to review its actions"? Note that under the hypothetical statute, as in *Holzer*, the offending party was required to behave as it did.

(8) Should it make a difference whether public policy is invoked to defeat a foreign cause of action or invoked to defeat a defense to a foreign cause of action?

In Bradford Electric Light Co. v. Clapper, 286 U.S. 145, 160 (1932), Justice Brandeis said:

> A State may, on occasion, decline to enforce a foreign cause of action. In so doing, it merely denies a remedy, leaving unimpaired the plaintiff's substantive right, so that he is free to enforce it elsewhere. But to refuse to give effect to a substantive defense under the applicable law of another State . . . subjects the defendant to irremediable liability. This may not be done.

Is sending the parties away adequate vindication of a state's public policy, or should it try to make its judgment res judicata? In other words, is public policy merely a kind of clean-hands doctrine for the state, or does it represent the desire to see a particular result in the case no matter where it is finally decided?

(9) Brainerd Currie didn't think much of the argument made by Justice Brandeis (and termed it the "Brandeis fallacy" even though it had been voiced by others). The chief difficulty he found was that it assumes that parties can go elsewhere when the public-policy doctrine is sued to bar a cause of action. Often plaintiffs cannot get jurisdiction elsewhere, he said, and consequently the effect of dismissal on public-policy grounds is often the equivalent of denying a defense on public-policy grounds. Currie, Selected Essays on the Conflicts of Laws 211-212 (1963).

(10) Paulsen and Sovern, in a careful study of the public policy principle ("Public Policy" in the Conflict of Laws, 56 Colum. L. Rev. 969 (1956)), found that "[t]he overwhelming number of cases which have rejected foreign law on public policy grounds are cases with which the forum had some important connection." They concluded that the evil of public policy overuse was not provincialism, to which it had often been equated, but its use as a "substitute for analysis" in cases where the forum was in fact justified in applying its own law on other grounds.

6. Penal Laws

Selections from the First Restatement of Conflicts, on Penal Laws and Tax Claims

§§610-611 (1934)

§610. Action on Foreign Public Right

No action can be maintained on a right created by the law of a foreign state as a method of furthering its own governmental interests.

(1948 Supp.) *Caveat:* The Institute expresses no opinion whether an action can be maintained by a foreign state on a claim for taxes.

§611. Action for a Penalty

No action can be maintained to recover a penalty the right to which is given by the law of another state.

Paper Products Co. v. Doggrell

195 Tenn. 581, 261 S.W.2d 127 (1953)

TOMLINSON, J.

Appellees, Doggrell, and Konz, together with one Van E. Whitaker, Jr., were the sole stockholders in an Arkansas corporation formed by them under the name of Forrest City Wood Products, Inc. with principal office to be located in St. Francis County, Arkansas.

The Arkansas statute requires the articles of incorporation to be filed (1) with the Secretary of State and (2) thereafter in the office of the County Clerk of the County in which the corporations' principal place of business is to be located.

Doggrell and Konz, Tennessee residents, left the management of the corporation entirely to the third stockholder, Whitaker, a resident of Arkansas. The lawyer in Memphis who prepared the charter directed Whitaker to file it with the Secretary of State and then with the Clerk of the County Court of St. Francis County, Arkansas. Whitaker inadvertently failed to file it with the Clerk of the County Court of St. Francis County. It was not filed with this clerk until after the account which gave rise to this suit had been made. Neither Doggrell or Konz were [*sic*] aware of the fact that the charter had not been filed in St. Francis County as required by the Arkansas statute. Neither has received any dividends or profits or remuneration from the corporation.

Under the decisions of the Arkansas Court of last resort the stockholders of a corporation are liable as partners when the charter is not filed as required by the Arkansas statute in the county where the principal office of the corporation is to be maintained. Based on those decisions of the Arkansas Supreme Court, Whitaker, the third stockholder in the aforementioned corporation, has been adjudged by the Arkansas Court liable for a debt made by this corporation before this charter was filed in St. Francis County. . . . The Arkansas Court rendered no judgment in that case against Doggrell and Konz because no service had been had on these Tennessee residents.

Whitaker who operated and managed the business of the corporation purchased goods in the name of the corporation from Paper Products Company and issued the company's note payable in thirty days. Paper Products Company in this transaction dealt with the Forrest City Wood Products, Inc. as such and not through the personal credit of Doggrell and Konz. These two stockholders knew nothing whatever about the account in question.

Forrest City Wood Products, Inc. became bankrupt. A substantial balance of its note issued to Paper Products Company remains unpaid. Accordingly, Paper Products Company instituted this suit in Shelby County, Tennessee Circuit Court against Doggrell and Konz. It seeks a recovery against them individually because of the Arkansas law holding stockholders personally liable as partners for the accounts made by a corporation whose charter has not been filed in the County where its principal office is located.

It was the judgment of the Shelby County Circuit Court that Doggrell and Konz are not liable individually, or as partners, for this obligation of Forrest City Wood Products, because this Arkansas rule "is penal in its nature, and will not be enforced in the State Courts of Tennessee." Paper Products Company has appealed and insists that (1) the Arkansas rule is not penal in nature and (2) under the law of comity the Arkansas rule should be applied in this case.

Under Tennessee decisions, the liability of a stockholder for the debts of his corporation is determined by the law of the State in which that corporation is domiciled unless such law is contrary to the legislation or public policy of Tennessee, or is penal in nature. Under these circumstances such law of a sister State will not be enforced in Tennessee.

When a Tennessee Court is called upon to enforce the civil law of a sister jurisdiction it will determine whether such law is penal in nature or contrary to the public policy of the law of Tennessee in which it is sought to be enforced. . . . Whether the aforementioned law of Arkansas, therefore, is contrary to our public policy or penal in nature is a matter to be determined in this case by the Tennessee Court since it is in that Court that it is sought to enforce this Arkansas rule.

The Arkansas statute heretofore referred to provides that "upon the filing with the Secretary of State of articles of incorporation, *the corporate existence shall begin.*" Ark. Stats. §64-103. (Emphasis supplied.) It follows that the corporate existence of Forrest City Wood Products, Inc. had begun prior to the inadvertent failure of Whitaker to file the corporation's charter in the office of the County Court of St. Francis County, Arkansas. The Arkansas rule, therefore, is that an inadvertent failure to comply with some detail in a bona fide effort to comply with the law chartering corporations is a failure which makes the stockholders liable in Arkansas for those debts of the corporation made prior to the compliance with such required detail.

This Arkansas rule is contrary to the public policy of Tennessee, wherein the rule is that the stockholders are not liable for the debts of their corporation in a case where there has been "made a bona fide effort to comply with the provisions of law," but "have inadvertently failed in some particular, and in good faith have exercised the franchises of such corporation." . . . It is a commonly known fact that one of the purposes of organizing a corporation for the carrying on of a business is to relieve stockholders of individual liability for the debts of the corporation. That fact is well known to those dealing with corporations. The Tennessee rule forwards the accomplishment of that purpose.

In ascertaining whether the Arkansas statute is penal in nature it is well to observe again that under the Arkansas rule the stockholders of the corporation are liable as partners for the mere failure, after the commencement of corporate existence, to file its charter in the Arkansas County of its principal office. This liability is imposed without regard to the fact that a creditor is not prejudiced by the failure to comply with this detail and was not misled thereby. There is no escape from the conclusion, therefore, that this rule prescribes a penalty in order to enforce compliance with the law of Arkansas as to the registering of a charter in the county where the principal office of the corporation is maintained. "Penalties prescribed by one state to enforce a compliance with its law will not be enforced by the courts of another state." . . .

A case directly in point is Woods v. Wicks, cited in appellees' brief. A statute of Kentucky was involved in that suit. That statute required the directors of a corporation to file and record within a specified time in a certain office a certificate stating the amount of the capital stock fixed and paid in. Stockholders were arbitrarily made liable in double the amount of their stock for failure to file such certificate. The Tennessee Court refused to hold such stockholders liable for the failure to file such certificate. In rejecting such a suit our Court said that "no court of another sovereignty can be expected to enforce such a penalty." . . .

The judgment must be affirmed with costs taxed to Paper Products Company and its surety.

On Petition to Rehear

The case of Doggrell v. Great Southern Box Company, Inc., was decided by the United States Court of Appeals for the 6th Circuit on July 9, 1953. 206 F.2d 671.* It came to that Court by appeal from the Federal District Court for the Western District of Tennessee. That case involved the identical Arkansas law and question decided by this Court in the instant case on July 17, 1953.

Preceded by well considered remarks unnecessary here to detail, the conclusion of the United States Court of Appeals in that case is that the Arkansas law in question is not penal within the meaning of the full faith and credit clause of our Federal Constitution, Article 4, §1; hence, that "the courts of Tennessee, including a United States District Court sitting in that state, are bound" to give effect to this Arkansas law in proceedings brought by a creditor of the Arkansas corporation to recover a personal money judgment against some of the stockholders of that Arkansas corporation. In the instant case this Court reached the opposite conclusion. Judge McAllister, in a dissenting opinion in the Federal case, reached the same conclusion as that reached by this Court with reference to the penal nature of this Arkansas law.

Because of the majority opinion of the United States Court of Appeals in its case, *supra*, Paper Products Company, appellant in the instant case, has filed in the instant case its petition to rehear. . . .

The expression Arkansas "law," rather than Arkansas "statute," is used by this Court because it is a decision of the Arkansas Supreme Court as to the effect which must be given a failure to comply with the Arkansas statute requiring a copy of the corporation's charter to be filed in the office of the County Clerk of the county in which the corporation's principal place of business is located. Its decision is that such failure, ipso facto, renders each stockholder of such Arkansas corporation liable for every debt incurred by that corporation prior to such filing in such county, notwithstanding the fact that such charter had been filed with the Arkansas Secretary of State, whereby, under the express language of the statute, its "corporate existence shall begin."

This Court was of the opinion that the instant case fell within the ruling of Woods v. Wicks . . . wherein this Court refused to give effect to a very similar Kentucky statute because of its penal nature. The United States Court of Appeals thought its case to be distinguishable from Woods v. Wicks because the incorporation of the Tennessee organization had been completed whereas such incorporation of the Arkansas organization lacked completion, so it is

---

* This decision was later set aside. 208 F.2d 310 (6th Cir. 1953)—ED.

said, to the extent that a copy of its charter had not been filed in the Arkansas county of its principal office.

Apparently, in considering material such above stated distinction between the Kentucky and Arkansas organizations, the United States Court of Appeals inadvertently failed to give effect to the fact that in Tennessee the stockholders of a de facto corporation are not liable for its debts, and that corporations de facto are "those which have made a bona fide effort to comply with the provisions of law and have inadvertently failed in some particular, and in good faith have exercised the franchises of such corporation." . . . Judge McAllister calls attention to the fact that the Arkansas organization was also a de facto corporation in Arkansas. . . .

The United States Court of Appeals felt that its case fell within Huntington v. Attrill, 146 U.S. 657. In that case it was held that the full faith and credit clause of our Federal Constitution required the Maryland Court to give effect to a New York statute said to be penal in character. Compliance with that statute, however, was clearly intended for the protection of creditors of corporations created pursuant to its provisions. The court can find no purpose of the Arkansas law other than that of better procuring compliance with a technical requirement of the Arkansas statute by inflicting a penalty merely because of a failure to so comply.

The above stated distinction between the instant case and Huntington v. Attrill, *supra,* makes it unnecessary to consider the further fact that the proceedings in the Maryland Court were to enforce a New York judgment based on a statute said to be penal in nature. In the case at bar the effort is to procure a judgment in a Tennessee Court based on an Arkansas law which the Tennessee Court regards as penal in nature and contrary to the public policy of its State.

Whether the full faith and credit clause requires the Courts of one state to enforce the law of another state penal in some respects "depends upon the question whether its purpose is to punish an offense against the public justice of the state, or to afford a private remedy to a person injured by the wrongful act." Huntington v. Attrill, *supra.* . . .

As heretofore stated, this Court thinks that there is no escape from the conclusion that the sole purpose of the Arkansas law in question is to procure a compliance with its statute as to a formal or technical requirement. But, pursuing further the immediately above stated test furnished by Huntington v. Attrill, there is particularly applicable the statement in Judge McAllister's dissenting opinion in Doggrell v. Great Southern Box Company, *supra* [206 F.2d 682], that:

> There was no wrong committed against any individual in not filing the articles with the County Clerk. To subject an innocent party, who happens to be an incorporator or original stockholder, to what may prove great financial losses or ruin, in being obliged to pay personally all the debts of the corporation merely because someone who should have complied with

this technical requirement failed to do so, seems to me to subject appellant to a liability that is clearly penal in its nature.

On principal, as well as under the test pronounced by the United States Supreme Court, this Court is of the opinion that the penal nature of the Arkansas law in question is such that the Tennessee Court is not required by the full faith and credit clause of our Federal Constitution to give it effect.

The rule of comity does not apply because the Arkansas law is contrary to the law and public policy of this State. . . .

Questions and Comments

(1) Why shouldn't confessedly penal laws be enforced by other jurisdictions? If the basis for enforcing the law of other jurisdictions is some kind of comity, or respect for the sovereignty of another state, shouldn't penal laws, which obviously express some particularly strong state interest, be the *first* to be enforced?

(2) The oft-cited case defining a "penal" law is Huntington v. Attrill, 146 U.S. 657 (1892), which involved an attempt in Maryland to enforce a New York judgment based on a New York statute that imposed personal liability on directors and stockholders of a corporation for its debts when papers falsely stating the capital position of the corporation were filed. The Court determined that the law in question was not penal and that Maryland was required to enforce the judgment. The mark of a penal statute, the Court said, was that it appeared to the forum "to be, in its essential character and effect, a punishment of an offense against the public." Section 611, comment *a,* of the Restatement defines a penalty as a "sum of money exacted as punishment for a civil wrong as distinguished from compensation for the loss suffered by the injured party."

Was the Arkansas statute penal by this standard?

Note that the *Huntington* case allows a state to ignore not only the law of another jurisdiction but its judgments as well.

See generally Kutner, Judicial Identification of "Penal Laws" in the Conflict of Laws, 31 Okla. L. Rev. 590 (1978).

(3) Finding that filing with the secretary of state was enough to cause de facto corporate existence made it easy for the court to determine that the penalty for failure to file with the local clerk was penal. But would the Tennessee courts come to a different conclusion in a case with similar facts if the Arkansas legislature, in reaction to the *Paper Products* opinion, amended its statutes to provide that de facto corporate existence was not possible in Arkansas? Note that the effect would be to impose liability on each of the partners in a partnership—not exactly a result that appears "penal."

(4) Is it fair to make the Arkansas partner (against whom an Arkansas judgment was rendered) bear the entire burden? Isn't that the effect of the

Paper Products decision, since judgment was rendered against the third partner in Arkansas? If the Arkansas partner, after paying the Arkansas judgment, brought an action against the Tennessee partners for contribution, would the attractiveness of using the penal-law exception be as great?

(5) What would have been the result in the *Paper Products* case if Tennessee had had a law identical to that of Arkansas? Surely under those circumstances Tennessee would not have been able to find that the Arkansas law violated Tennessee public policy. But would the fact that Tennessee had an identical law make the Arkansas law any less "penal"? Do you really think that the Tennessee court would have come out the same way (refusing enforcement of the Arkansas law) if Tennessee law had been identical?

(6) In Campbell v. Mitsubishi Aircraft International, 452 F. Supp. 930 (W.D. Pa. 1978), the court, applying Pennsylvania law, found a Texas usury statute to be penal and refused to apply it. The Texas statute provided for penalties of twice the amount of interest provided for by the contract, plus attorney fees, when the interest rate charged exceeded that allowed in Texas. The federal district court said that under Pennsylvania law it was bound by Texas's characterization of its own statute as penal and cited several Texas cases that referred to the amount the plaintiff could recover as a "penalty."

Since Texas would obviously never refuse enforcement to its own statute on the grounds that it was penal, doesn't it follow that Texas's characterization of the statute must have been for purposes other than conflicts purposes? And doesn't it follow from that that the Texas characterization of the statute should be, at most, persuasive and not binding?

(7) Closely related to the traditional prohibition on enforcing foreign penal laws was a prohibition on enforcing foreign revenue laws. *See* First Restatement §610 comment c (1934) ("No action can be maintained by a foreign state to enforce its license of revenue laws, or claims for taxes."). Learned Hand justified this prohibition (as well as the penal law prohibition) on the following grounds:

> While the origin of the exception in the case of penal liabilities does not appear in the books, a sound basis for it exists, in my judgment, which includes liabilities for taxes as well. Even in the case of ordinary municipal liabilities, a court will not recognize those arising in a foreign state, if they run counter to the "settled public policy" of its own. Thus a scrutiny of the liability is necessarily always in reserve, and the possibility that it will be found not to accord with the policy of the domestic state. This is not a troublesome or delicate inquiry when the question arises between private persons, but it takes on quite another face when it concerns the relations between the foreign state and its own citizens or even those who may be temporarily within its borders. To pass upon the provisions for the public order of another state is, or at any rate should be, beyond the powers of a court; it involves the relations between the states themselves, with which courts are incompetent to deal, and which are entrusted to other authorities. It may commit the domestic state to a

> position which would seriously embarrass its neighbor. Revenue laws fall within the same reasoning; they affect a state in matters as vital to its existence as its criminal laws. No court ought to undertake an inquiry which it cannot prosecute without determining whether those laws are consonant with its own notions of what is proper.

Moore v. Mitchell, 30 F.2d 600, 604 (2d Cir. 1929). Is this reasoning an artifact of the vested rights theory? Why is it more offensive to refuse to apply a state's tort law than to refuse to apply a state's tax law? For criticism of the tax rule, see Oklahoma ex rel. Oklahoma Tax Commission v. Neely, 225 Ark. 230, 282 S.W. 2d 150 (1955); Leflar, Extrastate Enforcement of Penal and Governmental Claims, 46 Harv. L. Rev. 193 (1932).

I. Proof of Foreign Law

Tidewater Oil Co. v. Waller

302 F.2d 638 (10th Cir. 1962)

MURRAH, C.J.

This is an appeal from a judgment of a district court in Oklahoma in a diversity suit for damages for personal injuries allegedly caused by the appellant—Tidewater Oil Company's negligence in the country of Turkey. The basic facts are that the appellee, Waller, an employee of Spartan Aircraft Company, an Oklahoma manufacturer of mobile homes, was sent to Turkey to perform repair work on behalf of his Oklahoma employer on mobile homes belonging to a pipeline company. While in Turkey, Waller undertook on behalf of his Oklahoma employer, to perform similar work on the mobile homes of Tidewater Oil Company at a remote and isolated oil well drilling site. Waller was injured when Tidewater's plane in which he was being transported crashed while attempting to land at the drilling site where the repair work was to be done.

It seems agreed that Waller was injured in the course of his employment with Spartan, his Oklahoma employer, and that he was paid $35.00 per week in lieu of Oklahoma's workmen's compensation, and all hospital and medical care. After the commencement of this suit against Tidewater, Waller filed a workmen's compensation claim with the Oklahoma Workmen's Compensation Commission, and at the same time sought and obtained an order of the Commission holding the claim in abeyance pending the outcome of this litigation.

After alleging his Oklahoma employment and his undertaking to perform work in Turkey for Tidewater on behalf of his Oklahoma employer, Waller alleged that his injuries were caused by the unsafe condition of the airstrip where Tidewater's plane was required to land and the negligent operation of it. It was specifically alleged that his right to recover was to be determined by the laws of Turkey, under which Tidewater owed Waller the duty to use ordinary care in the operation of the aircraft, and to furnish a reasonably safe place on which to land it; and that res ipsa loquitur was recognized in Turkey and applicable here.

Tidewater admitted Waller's employment in Oklahoma and his undertaking to do certain work for it in Turkey as a loaned servant of Spartan, and that the rights and liabilities of the parties were governed by the laws of the country of Turkey. It denied the allegations of negligence or that res ipsa loquitur was applicable. As a separate and primary defense, Tidewater asserted that any claim or right of action is exclusively cognizable under either the workmen's compensation law of the country of Turkey, or of the State of Oklahoma, and in either event, Tidewater was secondarily and hence exclusively liable for workmen's compensation benefits; and that the Oklahoma court was therefore without jurisdiction to entertain this suit.

In the trial of the case, neither party offered any evidence of controlling and applicable Turkish law, and the court manifestly proceeded upon the factual premise that the tort laws of Turkey permitted recovery for the asserted wrong as if in Oklahoma. . . .

[The Oklahoma statute, as interpreted by the majority, allowed Waller either to proceed under Oklahoma's worker's compensation system or, in the case of accidents occurring elsewhere, to proceed under the law of the locus.]

. . . The decisive issue, as indeed the parties ultimately seem to agree, is whether Waller, having elected to pursue his remedy under the law of Turkey, where the injury occurred, may maintain this suit under and by virtue of such laws.

It is agreed that the law of Turkey is controlling and is a matter of fact of which the Oklahoma Court cannot take judicial notice; and, having pleaded Turkish law to sustain his right of recovery, Waller is under the burden of going forward with proof of it at the risk of nonpersuasion. *See* Vol. 3 Beale, Conflict of Laws, p. 1663, §621. . . .

Tidewater takes the position that since there was no evidence of controlling Turkish law, Oklahoma law, including its workmen's compensation statutes, is applicable; and that under Section II thereof, as construed in the Mid-Continent case, it is secondarily and exclusively liable under the provisions of the Workmen's Compensation Act, as if the accident had occurred in Oklahoma. . . .

In the absence of proof of applicable foreign law, courts of the forum have rather unevenly followed three alternative courses: (1) dismissed the claim for failure to make out a prima facie case; (2) conveniently applied the law of the forum; and (3) indulged in certain presumptions as to the foreign law and applied it accordingly. . . . Courts which arbitrarily apply the law of the forum do so as a rule of convenience in disregard of the evidentiary rule of burden of proof, or going forward with the evidence at the risk of nonpersuasion. Courts which indulge in the presumption of foreign law do so by first taking judicial notice of the fundamental system of jurisprudence in the foreign country, and having noticed that its system is fundamentally the same, will indulge in the presumption that applicable law is similar and apply it accordingly. If, however, having judicially noticed that the systems of the two are fundamentally different, it will not indulge in any presumption of similarity, except the juridical principles which may be assumed to inhere in the laws of all civilized countries. . . . Oklahoma, whose conflicts rule we apply, has recognized the factual quality of applicable general law, and along with most other states has statutorily provided for the admissibility of such laws. . . . It has embraced the theory that in the absence of pleading and proof of applicable law of sister state, it will apply its own law, both general and statutory, on the convenient assumption that the law of the sister state is the same as its own. . . .

We have found no cases in which the Oklahoma courts have been confronted with application of the law of a foreign country in the absence of any proof of it, except some early cases in which they declined to take judicial notice of the laws of the Five Civilized Tribes. . . . Since the legal system prevailing in Turkey is judicially known not to be the same as Oklahoma, but is wholly different, it does not seem reasonable to presume under any circumstances that the general law of Turkey is the same or similar to Oklahoma, much less the workmen's compensation law. . . . There is a rational and, we think, admissible basis, however, for presuming that as a civilized country with a juridical system based upon civil law, Turkey recognizes the universal fundamental principle which embraces the legal duty of one to exercise due care not to injure another, and that its courts of justice will grant compensable redress for the unexcused violation of that duty. . . .

Of course if Oklahoma law is to be transplanted to Turkey and applied to a Turkish employment contract, it cannot be doubted that Waller was injured in the course of his employment under the Turkish contract; and, making application of the Oklahoma Workmen's Compensation Act as Turkish law, Tidewater would doubtlessly be primarily exclusively liable under its Turkish employment contract; for, in these circumstances, we should have no difficulty saying as a matter of law, that the maintenance of the mobile homes at the remote drilling site, was a necessary and integral part of Tidewater's hazardous business of drilling oil wells. . . . In that respect, it is important to note that Tidewater's liability is in no wise governed by Waller's Oklahoma employment contract with Spartan to which it was not a party, but rather, under the Turkey employment contract to which it was a party, and which must condition the rights of the parties.

Obviously, this suit was not tried and submitted to the jury on the theory that applicable Turkish law embraced a workmen's compensation act identical to or even similar to that of Oklahoma. Nor does the record before us indicate that either party had any such farfetched factual theory in mind at the time of trial. Rather, as we have seen, it is clear that the case was tried on the factual premise that Turkish law recognized the acts complained of as redressable wrongs. There is no suggestion that the asserted remedy is contrary to the public policy of the State of Oklahoma. Moreover, Section 4 of the Oklahoma Workmen's Compensation Act, *supra*, which grants the election to claim extra-territorial benefits, specifically provides that such right of election shall not preclude an injured employee from pursuing his remedy under the laws of the state where the injury occurred. Having accorded this right of election, we should not presume that Oklahoma would close the doors of its courts to the assertion of the remedy, even though it would have been unavailable if the injury had occurred in the State. . . . There being nothing in the public policy of the State of Oklahoma to forbid a remedy, the Oklahoma courts will enforce the right in accordance with the prevailing forms of practice and procedure. It was on this factual basis that the court formulated the law of the case and submitted it to the jury in accordance with the rules of evidence, standard of care and measure of damages prevailing in Oklahoma. . . . Inasmuch as the instructions of the court are not in issue, we will of course assume that they correctly stated the law of the case, and the judgment of the court based upon the jury verdict is sustained.

Federal Rule of Civil Procedure 44.1 provides:

> A party who intends to raise an issue concerning the law of a foreign country shall give notice by pleadings or other reasonable written notice. The court, in determining foreign law, may consider any relevant material or source, including testimony, whether or not submitted by a party or admissible under the Federal Rules of Evidence. The court's determination shall be treated as a ruling on a question of law.

The present form of the Rule dates from July 1, 1966. It was given exhaustive treatment (136 pages) in Miller, Federal Rule 44.1 and the "Fact" Approach to Determining Foreign Law: Death-Knell for a Die-Hard Doctrine, 65 Mich. L. Rev. 615 (1967).

Questions and Comments

(1) Similar facts yielded the opposite result in Walton v. Arabian American Oil Co., 233 F.2d 541 (2d Cir. 1956), a case in which the injury occurred in Saudi Arabia, the action was tried in New York, and the plaintiff refused to offer proof concerning Arabian law. The trial judge directed a verdict in favor of the defendant for failure of the plaintiff to prove his case. The Court of Appeals affirmed, rejecting plaintiff's invocation of the rule that the forum may apply its own law when the injury occurs in an uncivilized place that has no law or legal system. (Note the date of the case and the fact that knowledge about Saudi Arabia in the outside world was substantially more limited than today.)

The trial judge in the *Walton* case gave plaintiff's counsel an opportunity to prove Arabian law and indicated that he would rule against plaintiffs without such proof. Plaintiff's counsel declined. What would lead the lawyer to behave in such a way? If the lawyer had accepted the opportunity where should he or she have turned to find out about Arabian law? Should it have made a difference that the defendant was a rich corporation with more knowledge of Arabian law and more resources, financial and otherwise, for finding out more about it?

(2) How would *Waller* and *Walton* have been handled under Fed. R. Civ. P. 44.1, set out above?

(3) *See generally* Currie, On the Displacement of the Law of the Forum, in Selected Essays on the Conflict of Laws 3-4 (1963). Currie favored a presumption in favor of the application of forum law. Other commentators, even those generally sympathetic to his assumptions, disagree. *See* Kramer, Interest Analysis and the Presumption of Forum Law, 56 U. Chi. L. Rev. 1301 (1989).

(4) Tidewater Oil Co. v. Waller considered using a presumption of forum law because there was insufficient evidence of what foreign law said. But there are other ways that presumptions might come in handy. Recall Linn v. Employers Reinsurance Corp., page 33 *supra,* in which the court did not know which state the phone call of acceptance originated from. A similar situation arose in Doe v. Roe, 841 F. Supp. 444 (D.D.C. 1994), where the plaintiff alleged the defendant had infected her with the herpes simplex virus after misrepresenting his health status; recovery would have been allowed under District of Columbia law, but not under Virgina law. There had been equal opportunities for infection in both states, and it was scientifically impossible for the court to determine in which state the disease had actually been transmitted.

The court followed, in effect, the strategy advocated by Professor Kramer in the article cited in note (3), above. Kramer argues that the plaintiff always has the burden of demonstrating a cause of action, so that in the absence of reason to apply the plaintiff-favoring rule, the defendant must win. The *Doe* court reasoned, analogously, that "recovery would be possible only if plaintiff could trace her injury to the District encounter. Because we conclude that no reasonable trier of fact could determine which encounter resulted in infection, we are forced to grant defendant's motion for summary judgment. We regret this unfortunate result which, if plaintiff's allegations are true, shields from liability conduct which is not only despicable, but at the least is highly irresponsible. We hope plaintiff will appeal our determination that we are unable to grant the relief she seeks." 841 F. Supp. at 449.

(5) Rule 44.1 of the Federal Rules of Civil Procedure was applied in Vishipco Line v. Chase Manhattan Bank, 660 F.2d 854 (2d Cir. 1981). Until April 24, 1975, Chase had operated a branch office in Saigon; plaintiffs had maintained demand deposit accounts in piastres at that branch. On the eve of the fall of Saigon, Chase closed the branch without permitting an opportunity to withdraw deposits. The communist regime confiscated all accounts upon taking the city, and plaintiffs sued in New York to recover the dollar

value of their accounts. The district and appellate courts agreed that Vietnamese law governed; but the parties were unable to muster much evidence about the content of Vietnamese law.

> Chase here first contends that plaintiffs' claims were dismissible for failure to prove that under Vietnamese law they were entitled to recover. We disagree. The district court largely agreed with Chase's contention, stating:
>
> > When foreign law is an issue in a case, that law must be proved as a fact. Plaintiffs, however, presented no evidence concerning the law of Vietnam. Such failure has resulted in dismissal of a plaintiff's claims. However, since defendant has shouldered plaintiffs' burden and offered proof of Vietnamese law, there is no need to dismiss for lack of evidence on which to determine Vietnamese law.
>
> Although this statement reflects the law as it existed prior to the adoption of Rule 44.1 F.R. Civ. P. in 1966, it no longer governs the manner in which questions of foreign law are to be dealt with in the federal courts. Prior to 1966 foreign law questions were regarded as questions of fact, 9 C. Wright & A. Miller, Federal Practice and Procedure §2441 (1971), and, as the district court's citations indicate, a number of courts took the position that a failure to prove foreign law was fatal to a claim, even if the parties had not raised the issue of the applicability of foreign law on their own. Even in this state of the law, however, federal courts frequently refused to dismiss where they were sitting in a state which provided for judicial notice of foreign law.
>
> Rule 44.1 of the Federal Rules of Civil Procedure, which became effective in 1966, put to rest the idea that foreign law is a question of fact which has to be proven by the claimant in order to recover. It declared that "[t]he court's determination shall be treated as a ruling on a question of law."
>
> Chase nevertheless contends that even under the more liberal standards of Rule 44.1, plaintiffs' claims should have been dismissed for failure to provide evidence of foreign law after it became clear that under New York's choice of law rules the entire case would normally be governed by Vietnamese law.
>
> This assumes that the forum's choice of law rules are mandatory rather than permissive. However, with the decline of the vested rights theory, *see* Currie, On the Displacement of the Law of the Forum, 58 Colum. L. Rev. 964, 1001 (1958), the movement has been away from a mandatory application of the forum's choice of law rules and toward the adoption of a discretionary rule. While, as the Advisory Committee's notes to Rule 44.1 make clear, a court is still permitted to apply foreign law even if not requested by a party, we believe that the law of the forum may be applied here, where the parties did not at trial take the position that plaintiffs were required to prove their claims under Vietnamese law, even though the forum's choice of law rules would have called for the appli-

cation of foreign law. This reflects the view adopted by ourselves and other federal courts since 1966.

While Chase invoked foreign law under Rule 44.1 with respect to its own affirmative defenses only, neither party invoked foreign law with respect to Chase's basic obligations to its depositors and holders of certificates of deposit. Nor did Chase ever suggest that under Vietnamese law those obligations would not have formed a basis for recovery. Therefore, while Vietnamese law as invoked by Chase will be applied to those affirmative defenses which rest on Vietnamese law, the parties' failure to invoke foreign law with respect to the underlying obligations themselves would not mandate dismissal of the claims. Under New York law it is clear that, unless relieved of liability under one or more of the affirmative defenses asserted by it, Chase was obligated under its contracts with plaintiffs to pay them the amounts deposited with it.

660 F.2d 859-860. When the court wrote of "Vietnamese law" did it mean the law of the pro-American Saigon government or of the new revolutionary regime? How much law on international banking do you think the revolutionary regime had promulgated?

(6) The approach that American courts take to the law of another state or American jurisdiction is considerably different from the approach they take to the law of other countries or their subdivisions. The full faith and credit clause of the Constitution requires some deference to the law of other states (a topic to be discussed more fully in Chapter 3). Most states, but not all (*see, e.g.*, Retirement Credit Plan, Inc. v. Melnick, 139 Ga. App. 570, 228 S.E.2d 740 (1976)), take judicial notice of the laws of other states. But what should a court of State *A* do when faced with a question about the law of State *B* and with no answer in the case law of State *B?* One solution is set out below.

(7) Through certification or some related procedure, 45 states, the District of Columbia, and Puerto Rico allow their high courts to answer questions about their law posed by a court in another jurisdiction (including another state). *See* Kaye & Weissman, Interactive Judicial Federalism: Certified Questions in New York, 69 Fordham L. Rev. 373, 422-423 (2000) (Appendix A). Is this a general solution to the problem of proving foreign law, at least in the interstate context? It certainly helps one court avoid errors in the interpretation of another state's law. But is this a feasible process in the run-of-the-mill choice-of-law case? Does the court to which certification is directed really want to expend its limited resources to decide a pure question of law in another court? For discussion of these issues, see Robbins, Interstate Certification of Questions of Law: A Valuable Process in Need of Reform, 76 Judicature 125 (1992); Corr & Robbins, Interjurisdictional Certification and Choice of Law, 41 Vand. L. Rev. 411 (1988).

The full faith and credit clause provides weak limitations on one state court's (mis)interpretation of another state's law. *See* Sun Oil v. Wortman, 486 U.S. 717 (1988), reproduced *infra* page 383.

2

The New Learning

In a remarkable series of essays beginning in the 1920s and eventually collected in book form in The Logical and Legal Bases of the Conflict of Laws, Professor Walter Wheeler Cook undertook an examination of the foundations of Conflicts. Much of the book attacked the position of the First Restatement. One of the main themes of the book is that the Restatement is logically inconsistent in its "jurisdictional" approach, derived from fundamental principles. The theoretical basis for the Restatement, Cook said, is that a sovereign has the right to control events within its territory, and that other sovereigns ought to recognize that right. In some simple cases that principle is violated. He used the example of a fire set in State *A* that escapes, without any negligence on the part of the defendant, and spreads across the nearby border into State *B*, where it destroys a building owned by the plaintiff. The law of State *A* does not impose liability in domestic cases for such an occurrence. The domestic law of State *B* does impose liability, on a strict-liability theory. If an action is brought in State *A*, and that state follows the last act approach of the Restatement, it will be referred to the "law" of State *B*. But what is the "law" of State *B* with respect to this case? It must be how State *B* would decide this particular case—not a domestic case. That, however, was clearly not what the drafters of the Restatement had in mind. They meant to refer to the *internal* law of State *B*. Cook's argument was not with the imprecise wording of the Restatement, nor with the result, since he did not favor the complications caused by renvoi. He pointed out, however, that the reference to the internal law of

State *B* was inconsistent with the right of State *B*, as a sovereign, to control the effects of the events which took place within its borders. State *B* "controls" such effects only if other states' courts will reach the same decision reached by the courts of *B*. The territorial principle, purportedly derived fairly directly from fundamentals such as sovereignty, was being rejected in application by its chief proponents.

The other half of Cook's attack was broader and deeper. He rejected the entire notion of determining legal principles by deduction from fundamentals. Instead, he suggested that the methodology of science be used, whereby (1) observations are made, (2) a tentative principle is formed and matched against observations already made, and (3) if successful so far, the tentative principle is used to make predictions about future observations, against which it is also tested. The "observations" for the lawyer are case decisions (and not necessarily the reasons that judges give for their decisions). Thus the idea was to look at the cases to find out what the real rules were, instead of looking for *a priori* rules to decide the cases. Once rules were arrived at, they could be used to assist (but only assist) in the decision of new cases. Whether the facts of a new case brought it within the old rule would be determined by the same process one would use to determine whether, for example, a new tort case should fall within the usual rule, or be distinguished on the basis of different facts.

Cook's analogy between the proposed methodology of conflicts and the methodology of science is obviously imperfect. Events subject to scientific observation are not affected by the beliefs or acts of the observer (except as to events small enough to fall within the range of Heisenberg's Uncertainty Principle), while case decisions can very much be affected by judges' beliefs in one theory or another. In a sense, however, that point enhances the credibility of Cook's approach, for if we find that the theory being mouthed by the judges is not influential enough to control the outcome of cases in a predictable way, then the ground is fertile for the introduction of a theory that better accords with the outcome reached by way of judicial intuition.

The intellectual excellence of Cook's work has been widely recognized. Professor Brainerd Currie, for example, said that it "discredited the vested-rights theory as thoroughly as the intellect of one man can ever discredit the intellectual product of another." Currie, Selected Essays on the Conflict of Laws 6 (1963). Yet Cook's efforts did not have immediate effect. The first real cracks in the theoretical monopoly of the territorialists in the courts did not occur until the early 1950s.

A. The Evolution of a Modern Approach

Most states have departed from the First Restatement rules, at least in the torts and contracts contexts. Unfortunately, numerous approaches have been proposed in place of the First Restatement, and none has established itself as superior to the rest. Some of these approaches are refinements or elaborations of others. Some are fundamentally inconsistent. To make things worse, some courts profess adherence to more than one approach, not recognizing the differences (and sometimes they are few in terms of actual decisions) or wishing to use the time-honored technique of covering one's derrière by invoking multiple justifications for the same conclusion.* Finally, many states' approaches to conflicts problems have changed over time. By the nature of the case method, one can only guess what the law is at any given time: A new approach to tort cases, for example, may or may not imply an analogous new approach to contract cases. Only the next contract case—with just the right facts—will tell with certainty.

New York was the first state to experiment with explicit departure from the First Restatement. As the following cases illustrate, the progress—if progress it was—was sometimes halting. We look first at the evolution of a new approach in New York and return in subsequent sections to ideas raised in the New York cases but not considered fully, and to other ideas altogether.

Haag v. Barnes

9 N.Y.2d 554, 175 N.E.2d 441, 216 N.Y.S.2d 65 (1961)

FULD, J.

This appeal is concerned with the effect in New York of an agreement made in another State for the support of a child born out of wedlock.

The complainant Dorothy Haag alleges that in 1947 she moved from Minnesota and took up residence in New York City and that since then she has been a resident of this State. The defendant Norman Barnes, on the other hand, is now and was, during the period involved in this litigation, a resident of Illinois.

According to the statements contained in the complainant's affidavits, she met the defendant in the spring of 1954 in New York. She was a law secretary and had been hired by the defendant through an agency to do work for him while he was in New York on one of his business trips. The relationship between the man and the girl soon "ripened into friendship" and, on the basis of representations that he loved her and planned to divorce his wife and marry her, she was "importuned" into having sexual relations with him.

The complainant further alleges that she became pregnant as a result of having sexual relations with the defendant and that, upon being informed of this, he asked her to move to Illinois to be near him. She refused and, instead, went to live in California with her sister to await the birth of her child. Fearing that the defendant was losing interest in her, however, she returned to Chicago before the child was born and, upon attempting to communicate

---

* This phenomenon is well (and amusingly) documented in Reppy, Eclecticism in Choice of Law: Hybrid Method or Mishmash?, 34 Mercer L. Rev. 645 (1983).

with the defendant, was referred to his attorney. The latter told Dorothy to choose a hospital in Chicago, which she did, and the baby was born there in December, 1955, the defendant paying the expenses.

Shortly after the birth of the child, her attempts to see the defendant in New York failed and she was advised by his attorney to return to Chicago in order that an agreement might be made for the support of her and her child. Returning to that city, she procured an attorney, recommended by a friend in New York, and signed an agreement on January 12, 1956. The agreement provides, in pertinent part, as follows:

1. It recites payment to the complainant by the defendant of $2,000 between September, 1955 and January, 1956 and a willingness on his part to support her child in the future, on condition that such payments "shall not constitute an admission" that he is the child's father;

2. The defendant promises to pay $50 a week and $75 a month, i.e., a total of $275 a month, "continuing while [the child] is alive and until she attains the age of sixteen years";

3. The complainant agrees "to properly support, maintain, educate, and care for [the child]";

4. The complainant agrees to keep the child in Illinois for at least two years, except if she marries within that period;

5. The complainant "remise[s], release[s] and forever discharge[s] Norman Barnes . . . from all manner of actions . . . which [she] now has against [him] or ever had or which she . . . hereafter can, shall or may have, for, upon or by reason of any matter, cause or thing whatsoever . . . including . . . the support of [the child]", and

6. The parties agree that their agreement "shall in all respects be interpreted, construed and governed by the laws of the State of Illinois."

Shortly after the agreement was signed, the complainant received permission, pursuant to one of its provisions, to live in California where she remained for two years. She then returned to New York where she and her child have ever since been supported by the defendant in full compliance with the terms of his agreement. In fact, he has provided sums far in excess of his agreement; all told, we were informed on oral argument, the defendant has paid the complainant some $30,000.

The present proceeding was instituted in 1959 by the service of a complaint and the defendant was thereafter arrested pursuant to section 64 of the New York City Criminal Courts Act. A motion, made by the defendant, to dismiss the proceeding was granted by the Court of Special Sessions and the resulting order was affirmed by the Appellate Division.

The ground urged for dismissal was that the parties had entered into an agreement providing for the support of the child which has been fully performed; that in this agreement the complainant relinquished the right to bring any action for the support of the child; and that, in any event the action is precluded by the law of the State of Illinois which, the parties expressly agreed, would govern their rights under the agreement. In opposition, the complainant contended that New York, not Illinois, law applies; that the agreement in question is not a sufficient basis for a motion to dismiss under either section 63 of the New York City Criminal Courts Act or section 121 of the Domestic Relations Law, since both of these provisions provide that "An agreement or compromise made by the mother . . . shall be binding only when the court shall have determined that adequate provision has been made"; and that, even were the Illinois law to apply, it does not bar the present proceeding.

The motion to dismiss was properly granted; the complainant may not upset a support agreement which is itself perfectly consistent with the public policy of this State, which was entered into in Illinois with the understanding that it would be governed by the laws of that State and which constitutes a bar to a suit for further support under Illinois law.

The complainant is correct in her position that, since the agreement was not court approved, it may not be held to be a bar to her suit under New York internal law. . . . On the other hand, it is clear that the agreement is a bar under the internal law of Illinois since it provides, in the language of that State's statute, for a "sum not less than eight hundred dollars." . . . The simple question before us, therefore, is whether the law of New York or of Illinois applies.

The traditional view was that the law governing a contract is to be determined by the intention of the parties. . . . The more modern view is that "courts, instead of regarding as conclusive the parties' intention or the place of making or performing, lay emphasis rather upon the law of the place 'which has the most significant contacts with the matter in dispute.'" *See* Auten v. Auten. . . . Whichever of these views one applies in this case, however, the answer is the same, namely, that Illinois law applies.

The agreement, in so many words, recites that it "shall in all respects be interpreted, construed and governed by the laws of the State of Illinois" and, since it was also drawn and signed by the complainant in Illinois, the traditional conflicts rule would, without doubt, treat these factors as conclusive and result in applying Illinois law. But, even if the parties' intention and the place of the making of the contract are not given decisive effect, they are nevertheless to be given heavy weight in determining which jurisdiction " 'has the most significant contacts with the matter in dispute.' " Auten v. Auten. . . . And, when these important factors are taken together with other of the "significant contacts" in the case, they likewise point to Illinois law. Among these other Illinois contacts are the following: (1) both parties are designated in the agreement as being "of Chicago, Illinois," and the defendant's place of business is and always has been in Illinois; (2) the child was born in Illinois; (3) the persons designated to act as agents for the principals (except for a third alternate) are Illinois residents, as are the attorneys for both parties who drew the agreement; and (4) all contributions for support always have been, and still are being, made from Chicago.

Contrasted with these Illinois contacts, the New York contacts are of far less weight and significance. Chief among these is the fact that child and mother presently live in New York and that part of the "liaison" took place in New York. When these contacts are measured against the parties' clearly expressed intention to have their agreement governed by Illinois law and the more numerous and more substantial Illinois contacts, it may not be gainsaid that the "center of gravity" of this agreement is Illinois and that, absent compelling public policy to the contrary (*see* F. S. Straus & Co. v. Canadian Pacific Ry. Co., 254 N.Y. 407, 414, 173 N.E. 564, 567), Illinois law should apply.

As to the question of public policy, we would emphasize that the issue is *not* whether the New York statute reflects a different public policy from that of the Illinois statute, but rather whether enforcement of the particular agreement before us under Illinois law represents an affront to our public policy. . . . It is settled that the New York Paternity Law requires something more than the provision of "the bare necessities otherwise required to be supplied by the community," that, "although providing for indemnification of the community, [it] is chiefly concerned with the welfare of the child." . . . In our judgment, enforcement of the support agreement in this case under Illinois law and the refusal to allow its provisions to be reopened in the present proceeding does not do violence to this policy.

As matter of fact, the agreement before us clearly goes beyond "indemnification of the community" and the provision of "bare necessities." Whether we read it as a whole, or look only to the financial provisions concerned ($275 a month until the child reaches the age of 16), we must conclude that "the welfare of the child" is fully protected. . . . The public policy of this State having been satisfied, there is no reason why we should not enforce the provisions of the parties' support agreement under Illinois law and treat the agreement as a bar to the present action for support.

The order of the Appellate Division should be affirmed.

DESMOND, C.J., and DYE, FROESSEL, VAN VOORHIS, BURKE and FOSTER, JJ., concur.

Order affirmed.

Questions and Comments

(1) The reception to Haag v. Barnes was not particularly warm. Professor Brainerd Currie, for example, noted one obvious point about the methodology of the "grouping of contacts" approach:

> The "grouping of contacts" theory provides no standard for determining what "contacts" are significant, or for appraising the relative significance of the respective groups of "contacts." . . . The process of "grouping contacts" . . . deals in broad generalities about the "interest" of a state in applying its law without inquiry into how the "contacts" in question relate to the policies expressed in specific laws. One "contact" seems to be about as good as another for almost any purpose. The "contacts" are totted up

> and a highly subjective fiat is issued to the effect that one group of contacts or the other is more significant. The reasons for the conclusion are too elusive for objective evaluation. State interests are quite likely to be thwarted in the confusion.

Currie, Selected Essays on the Conflict of Laws 727-728 (1963). Professor Ehrenzweig commented, in passing:

> We may hope, however, that this decision was primarily determined by what the court may have considered an inequitable and possibly extortionist demand for additional support, and that this ruling will not be construed to put the forum's policy regarding the absolute right to the establishment of paternity at the mercy of any foreign law that appears to permit the purchase of this right by the father.

Ehrenzweig, The "Bastard" in the Conflict of Laws—A National Disgrace, 29 U. Chi. L. Rev. 498, 503 (1962).

(2) One of the court's recitations of "other Illinois contacts" is that the agreement recites that the parties are of Chicago, Illinois. It would seem that either they are from Chicago, or they are not. If they are not, the fact that the contract says so doesn't change the situation. If they are, of what significance is the contract's affirmation of the fact?

Of what significance should it be that the persons who are designed "to act as agents for the principals" were from Illinois or that the parties' lawyers were from Illinois? Would the citizenship of the plaintiff's grandmother or of her lawyer's sister also be relevant? What have any of these things to do with the purpose of the New York legislation? Or is the court saying that the purpose of the New York legislation is irrelevant until it is established that New York is the more concerned jurisdiction?

What possible difference does it make that the defendant's place of business was Illinois? Why isn't the mother's place of business important?

Did the court do the best possible job of looking for New York contacts? Consider the following partial list (in contrast with the list supplied by the court for Illinois contacts): (a) The plaintiff was from New York, and her place of occupation was there until the affair and pregnancy. (b) The plaintiff is now a New York resident. (c) The child is a New York resident. (d) The child was conceived in New York. (e) The defendant induced the plaintiff to leave New York. (f) Contributions for support are to be made to her in New York. (g) If support is insufficient, mother and child will be a public charge in New York.

How does the court know that these aren't the significant contacts? How does a court avoid artificially multiplying contacts—for example, by listing the domicile of parties' lawyers, which is likely to be the same as the domicile of at least one of the parties?

(3) One kind of "contact" listed by the court may be singled out for particular attention. Is it a "contact" at all that the parties "intended," according to their contract, to make Illinois law govern? Since the New York law

was clearly intended to operate despite the contracting parties' intent, how can that intent be significant, whether or not it is labeled a "contact"? Isn't it about time to deemphasize the parties' intent because (a) when the substantive legal rule in question is one the parties have the right to control, their expressed intent ought to control despite all other factors (save fraud, overreaching, and the like); (b) when the rule is one the parties have the right to control but their intent is not expressed, actual intent ought to control if it is discernible; and (c) when the rule is one that parties have no right to control, such as the court-approval rule in *Haag*, their intent ought to be irrelevant?

Or was the court really thinking about some kind of legitimate expectation on the parties' part when it talked about their intent?

(4) The precursor of Haag v. Barnes was Auten v. Auten, 308 N.Y. 155, 124 N.E.2d 99 (1954). There, Judge Fuld initiated the "grouping of contacts" theory that was applied in *Haag*. *Auten* involved a couple married in England. After fourteen years of marriage, the husband deserted the wife and two children and went to the United States. The wife traveled to New York to find him and there signed a separation agreement. She returned to England, but was eventually forced to bring suit in New York to collect. The court applied English law to allow her to recover, relying primarily on a "center of gravity," or "most significant relationship" approach, but also asserting that traditional learning would provide the same result; England was the place of performance.

Babcock v. Jackson

12 N.Y.2d 473, 191 N.E.2d 279, 240 N.Y.S.2d 743 (1963)

FULD, J.

On Friday, September 16, 1960, Miss Georgia Babcock and her friends, Mr. and Mrs. William Jackson, all residents of Rochester, left that city in Mr. Jackson's automobile, Miss Babcock as guest, for a weekend trip to Canada. Some hours later, as Mr. Jackson was driving in the Province of Ontario, he apparently lost control of the car; it went off the highway into an adjacent stone wall, and Miss Babcock was seriously injured. Upon her return to the State, she brought the present action against William Jackson, alleging negligence on his part in operating his vehicle.

At the time of the accident, there was in force in Ontario a statute providing that

> the owner or driver of a motor vehicle other than a vehicle operated in the business of carrying passengers for compensation, is not liable for any loss or damages resulting from bodily injury to, or the death of any person being carried in . . . the motor vehicle. . . .

Even though no such bar is recognized under this State's substantive law of torts . . . the defendant moved to dismiss the complaint on the ground that the law of the place where the accident occurred governs and that Ontario's guest statute bars recovery. The court at Special Term, agreeing with the defendant, granted the motion and the Appellate Division over a strong dissent by Justice Halpern affirmed the judgment of dismissal without option.

The question presented is simply drawn. Shall the law of the place of the tort *invariably* govern the availability of relief for the tort or shall the applicable choice of law rule also reflect a consideration of other factors which are relevant to the purposes served by the enforcement or denial of the remedy? . . .

Comparison of the relative "contacts" and "interests" of New York and Ontario in this litigation, vis-à-vis the issue here presented, makes it clear that the concern of New York is unquestionably the greater and more direct and that the interest of Ontario is at best minimal. The present action involves injuries sustained by a New York guest as the result of the negligence of a New York host in the operation of an automobile, garaged, licensed and undoubtedly insured in New York, in the course of a weekend journey which began and was to end there. In sharp contrast, Ontario's sole relationship with the occurrence is the purely adventitious circumstance that the accident occurred there.

New York's policy of requiring a tort-feasor to compensate his guest for injuries caused by his negligence cannot be doubted—as attested by the fact that the Legislature of this State has repeatedly refused to enact a statute denying or limiting recovery in such cases . . . and our courts have neither reason nor warrant for departing from that policy simply because the accident, solely affecting New York residents and arising out of the operation of a New York based automobile, happened beyond its borders. Per contra, Ontario has no conceivable interest in denying a remedy to a New York guest against his New York host for injuries suffered in Ontario by reason of conduct which was tortious under Ontario law. The object of Ontario's guest statute, it has been said, is "to prevent the fraudulent assertion of claims by passengers, in collusion with the drivers, against insurance companies" (Survey of Canadian Legislation, 1 U. Toronto L.J. 358, 366) and, quite obviously, the fraudulent claims intended to be prevented by the statute are those asserted against Ontario defendants and their insurance carriers. Whether New York defendants are imposed upon or their insurers defrauded by a New York plaintiff is scarcely a valid legislative concern of Ontario simply because the accident occurred there, any more so than if the accident had happened in some other jurisdiction.

It is hardly necessary to say that Ontario's interest is quite different from what it would have been had the issue related to the manner in which the defendant had been driving his car at the time of the accident. Where the defendant's exercise of due care in the operation of his automobile is in issue, the jurisdiction in which the allegedly wrongful conduct occurred will usually have a predominant, if not exclusive, concern. In such a case, it is appropriate to look to the law of the place of the tort so as to give effect to that jurisdiction's interest in regulating conduct within its borders, and it would be almost unthinkable to seek the applicable rule in the law of some other place.

The issue here, however, is not whether the defendant offended against a rule of the road prescribed by Ontario for motorists generally or whether he violated some standard of conduct imposed by that jurisdiction, but rather whether the plaintiff, because she was a guest in the defendant's automobile, is barred from recovering damages for a wrong concededly committed. As to that issue, it is New York, the place where the parties resided, where their guest-host relationship arose and where the trip began and was to end, rather than Ontario, the place of the fortuitous occurrence of the accident, which has the dominant contacts and the superior claim for application of its law. Although the rightness or wrongness of defendant's conduct may depend upon the law of the particular jurisdiction through which the automobile passes, the rights and liabilities of the parties which stem from their guest-host relationship should remain constant and not vary and shift as the automobile proceeds from place to place. Indeed, such a result, we note, accords with "the interests of the host in procuring liability insurance adequate under the applicable law, and the interests of his insurer in reasonable calculability of the premium." (Ehrenzweig, Guest Statutes in the Conflict of Laws, 69 Yale L.J. 595, 603.)

Although the traditional rule has in the past been applied by this court in giving controlling effect to the guest statute of the foreign jurisdiction in which the accident occurred . . . it is not amiss to point out that the question here posed was neither raised nor considered in those cases and that the question has never been presented in so stark a manner as in the case before us with a statute so unique as Ontario's. Be that as it may, however, reconsideration of the inflexible traditional rule persuades us, as already indicated, that, in failing to take into account essential policy considerations and objectives, its application may lead to unjust and anomalous results. This being so, the rule, formulated as it was by the courts, should be discarded.[14]

In conclusion, then, there is no reason why all issues arising out of a tort claim must be resolved by reference to the law of the same jurisdiction. Where the issue involves standards of conduct, it is more than likely that it is the law of the place of the tort which will be controlling but the disposition of other issues must turn, as does the issue of the standard of conduct itself, on the law of the jurisdiction which has the strongest interest in the resolution of the particular issue presented.

The judgment appealed from should be reversed, with costs, and the motion to dismiss the complaint denied.

VAN VOORHIS, J. (dissenting).

. . . The case of Auten v. Auten, . . . involving a separation agreement between English people and providing for the support of a wife and children

14. It of course follows from our decision herein that, given the facts of the present case, the result would be the same and the law of New York applied where the foreign guest statute requires a showing of gross negligence.

to continue to live in England, accomplished no such revolution in the law as the present appeal. Auten v. Auten dealt with contracts, the agreement was held to be governed by the law of the country where it was mainly to be performed, which had previously been the law, and the salient expression "center of gravity," "grouping of contacts," and similar catchwords were employed as a shorthand reference to the reconciliation of such rigid concepts in the conflict of laws as the formulae making applicable the place where the contract was signed or where it was to be performed—rules which themselves were occasionally in conflict with one another. In the course of the opinion it was stated that "even if we were not to place our emphasis on the law of the place with the most significant contacts, but were instead simply to apply the rule that matters of performance and breach are governed by the law of the place of performance, the same result would follow." . . . The decision in Auten v. Auten rationalized and rendered more workable the existing law of contracts. The name "grouping of contacts" was simply a label to identify the rationalization of existing decisions on the conflict of laws in contract cases which were technically inconsistent, in some instances. The difference between the present case and Auten v. Auten is that *Auten* did not materially change the law, but sought to formulate what had previously been decided. The present case makes substantial changes in the law of torts. The expressions "center of gravity," "grouping of contacts," and "significant contacts" and catchwords which were not employed to define and are inadequate to define a principle of law, were neither applied to nor are they applicable in the realm of torts.

Any idea is without foundation that cases such as the present render more uniform the laws of torts in the several States of the United States. Attempts to make the law or public policy of New York State prevail over the laws and policies of other States where citizens of New York State are concerned are simply a form of extraterritoriality which can be turned against us wherever actions are brought in the courts of New York which involve citizens of other States. This is no substitute for uniform State laws or for obtaining uniformity by covering the subject by Federal Law. Undoubtedly ease of travel and communication, and the increase in inter-state business have rendered more awkward discrepancies between the laws of the States in many respects. But this is not a condition to be cured by introducing or extending principles of extraterritoriality, as though we were living in the days of the Roman or British Empire, when the concepts were formed that the rights of a Roman or an Englishman were so significant that they must be enforced throughout the world even where they were otherwise unlikely to be honored by "lesser breeds without the law." Importing the principles of extraterritoriality into the conflicts of laws between the States of the United States can only make confusion worse confounded. If extraterritoriality is to be the criterion, what would happen, for example, in case of an automobile accident where some of the passengers came from or were picked up in States or countries where causes of action against the driver were prohibited, others where gross negligence needed to be shown, some, perhaps, from States where contributory negligence and others where comparative negligence prevailed? In the majority opinion it is said that "Where the defendant's exercise of due care in the operation of his automobile is in issue, the jurisdiction in which the allegedly wrongful conduct occurred will usually have a predominant, if not exclusive, concern." This is hardly consistent with the statement in the footnote that gross negligence would not need to be established in an action by a passenger if the accident occurred in a State whose statute so required. If the status of the passenger as a New Yorker would prevent the operation of a statute in a sister State or neighboring country which granted immunity to the driver in suits by passengers, it is said that it would also prevent the operation of a statute which instead of granting immunity permits recovery only in case of gross negligence. There are passenger statutes or common-law decisions requiring gross negligence or its substantial equivalent to be shown in 29 States. One wonders what would happen if contributory negligence were eliminated as a defense by statute in another jurisdiction? Or if comparative negligence were established as the rule in the other State?

In my view there is no overriding consideration of public policy which justifies or directs this change in the established rule or renders necessary or advisable the confusion which such a change will introduce.

The judgment dismissing the complaint should be affirmed.

Tooker v. Lopez

24 N.Y.2d 569, 249 N.E.2d 394, 301 N.Y.S.2d 519 (1969)

KEATING, J.

On October 16, 1964, Catharina Tooker, a 20-year-old coed at Michigan State University, was killed when the Japanese sports car in which she was a passenger overturned after the driver had lost control of the vehicle while attempting to pass another car. The accident also took the life of the driver of the vehicle, Marcia Lopez, and seriously injured another passenger, Susan Silk. The two girls were classmates of Catharina Tooker at Michigan State University and lived in the same dormitory. They were en route from the university to Detroit, Michigan, to spend the weekend.

Catharina Tooker and Marcia Lopez were both New York domiciliaries. The automobile which Miss Lopez was driving belonged to her father who resided in New York, where the sports car he had given his daughter was registered and insured.

This action for wrongful death was commenced by Oliver P. Tooker, Jr., the father of Catharina Tooker, as the administrator of her estate. The defendant asserted as an affirmative defense the Michigan "guest statute" which permits recovery by guests only by showing willful misconduct or gross negligence of the driver. The plaintiff moved to dismiss the affirmative defense on the ground that under the governing choice-of-law rules it was New York law rather than Michigan law which applied. The motion was granted by the Special Term Justice who concluded that: "New York State 'has the greatest concern with the specific issue raised in the litigation' and New York law should apply." The Appellate Division (Third Department) agreed with "the cogent argument advanced by Special Term" but felt "constrained" by the holding in Dym v. Gordon to apply the Michigan guest statute.

We are presented here with a choice-of-law problem which we have had occasion to consider in several cases since our decision in Babcock v. Jackson rejected the traditional rule which looked invariably to the law of the place of wrong. Unfortunately, as we recently had occasion to observe, our decisions subsequent to rejection of the lex loci delictus rule "have lacked a precise consistency." This case gives us the opportunity to resolve those inconsistencies in a class of cases which have been particularly troublesome. . . .

[The court discussed previous guest statute cases and their lack of consistency, opting for the approach of *Babcock.*]

Viewed in the light of the foregoing discussion, the instant case is one of the simplest in the choice-of-law area. If the facts are examined in light of the policy considerations which underlie the ostensibly conflicting laws it is clear that New York has the only real interest in whether recovery should be granted and that the application of Michigan law "would defeat a legitimate interest of the forum State without serving a legitimate interest of any other State."

The policy of this State with respect to all those injured in automobile accidents is reflected in the legislative declaration which prefaces New York's compulsory insurance law:

> The legislature is concerned over the rising toll of motor vehicle accidents and the suffering and loss thereby inflicted. The legislature determines that it is a matter of grave concern that motorists shall be financially able to respond in damages for their negligent acts, so that innocent victims of motor vehicle accidents may be recompensed for the injury and financial loss inflicted upon them.

(Vehicle and Traffic Laws, Consol. Laws, c.71, §310.)

Neither this declaration of policy nor the standard required provisions for an auto liability insurance policy makes any distinction between guests, pedestrians or other insured parties.

New York's "grave concern" in affording recovery for the injuries suffered by Catharina Tooker, a New York domiciliary, and the loss suffered by her family as a result of her wrongful death, is evident merely in stating the policy which our law reflects. On the other hand, Michigan has no interest in whether a New York plaintiff is denied recovery against a New York defendant where the car is insured here.[1] The fact that the deceased guest and

1. The Michigan courts have suggested that the purpose of their guest statute is to protect the owner of the vehicle. . . .

driver were in Michigan for an extended period of time is plainly irrelevant. Indeed, the Legislature, in requiring that insurance policies cover liabilities for injuries regardless of where the accident takes place (Vehicle & Traffic Law, §311, subd. 4) has evinced commendable concern not only for residents of this State, but residents of other States who may be injured as a result of the activities of New York residents. Under these circumstances we cannot be concerned with whether Miss Tooker or Miss Lopez were [*sic*] in Michigan for a summer session or for a full college education.

The argument that the choice of law in tort cases should be governed by the fictional expectation of the parties has been rejected unequivocally by this court. In Miller v. Miller we wrote:

> We reject the argument . . . that the choice of applicable law in this tort action should be determined on the basis of the expectations of the parties as derived from their contact with the State of the place of the accident. Such a determination of the applicable law is based upon an obvious fiction having little to do with the laws in conflict. . . . "Though our nation is divided into fifty-one separate legal systems, our people act most [of] the time as if they lived in a single one. [They suffer from a] chronic failure to take account of differences in state laws." . . . It is for this reason that "[f]ew speculations are more slippery than assessing the expectations of parties as to the laws applicable to their activities, and especially is this true where the expectations relate to the law of torts." Cavers, [Choice-of-Law Process], p. [119], 302. . . .

Moreover, when the Legislature has chosen to compel an owner of an automobile to provide a fund for recovery for those who will be injured, and thus taken the element of choice and expectation out of the question, it seems unreasonable to look to that factor as a basis for a choice of law. And, even if we were to engage in such fictions as the expectations of the parties, it seems only fair to infer that the owner of the vehicle by purchasing a New York insurance policy which provided for the specific liability "intended to protect [the] passenger against negligent injury, as well as to secure indemnity for liability, in whatever state an accident might occur." . . .

Applying the choice-of-law rule which we have adopted, it is not an "implicit consequence" [as claimed by the dissent] that the Michigan passenger injured along with Miss Lopez should be denied recovery. Under the reasoning adopted here, it is not at all clear that Michigan law would govern. We do not, however, find it necessary or desirable to conclusively resolve a question which is not now before us. It suffices to note that any anomaly resulting from the application of Michigan law to bar an action brought by Miss Silk is "the implicit consequence" of a Federal system which, at a time when we have truly become one nation, permits a citizen of one State to recover for injuries sustained in an automobile accident and denies a citizen of another State the right to recover for injuries sustained in a similar accident. The anomaly does not arise from any choice-of-law rule. . . .

[Chief Judge FULD concurred in the opinion but also suggested some rules, which appear in his majority opinion in Neumeier v. Kuehner, below. Judge Breitel dissented, adhering to the "seat of the relationship" concept and finding that Michigan was the seat of the relationship.]

Questions and Comments

(1) While *Haag* addressed "center of gravity" and "most significant relationship," *Babcock* and *Tooker* focus on the "policies" and "interests" that a state has in the application of its laws. Is it any easier to determine whether a state is the center of gravity or whether it has a policy interest? How are the policies of a state determined in a conflict-of-laws case? How does the forum ascertain the policies of the other state? Should it matter that Ontario or Michigan thinks that it has an interest in having its law applied?

(2) Should it matter that the New Yorkers in *Tooker* were away from New York for an extended period, while the New Yorkers in *Babcock* were on a brief auto trip? Should it matter whether the New Yorkers left their home state together rather than meeting outside the state, near the scene of the accident? Is *Tooker* consistent with *Haag?*

(3) What should the court have done if Silk, a Michigan domiciliary, had joined as plaintiff? Should she be treated differently because New York has a lesser interest in non-New York plaintiffs? Or should that approach be rejected because it is discriminatory? If Silk would collect, isn't the effect a windfall for the Michigan driver who happens to be struck in Michigan by a driver from New York rather than a fellow Michigander? A somewhat similar situation is addressed in Hurtado v. Superior Court, *infra* page 228.

Neumeier v. Kuehner

31 N.Y.2d 121, 286 N.E.2d 454, 335 N.Y.S.2d 64 (1972)

FULD, C.J.

A domiciliary of Ontario, Canada, was killed when the automobile in which he was riding, owned and driven by a New York resident, collided with a train in Ontario. That jurisdiction has a guest statute, and the primary question posed by this appeal is whether in this action brought by the Ontario passenger's estate, Ontario law should be applied and the New York defendant permitted to rely on its guest statute as a defense.

The facts are quickly told. On May 7, 1969, Arthur Kuehner, the defendant's intestate, a resident of Buffalo, drove his automobile from that city to Fort Erie in the Province of Ontario, Canada, where he picked up Amie Neumeier, who lived in that town with his wife and their children. Their trip was to take them to Long Beach, also in Ontario, and back again to Neumeier's home in Fort Erie. However, at a railroad crossing in the Town of Sherkston—on the way to Long Beach—the auto was struck by a train of the defendant Canadian National Railway Company. Both Kuehner and his guest-passenger were instantly killed.

Neumeier's wife and administratrix, a citizen of Canada and a domiciliary of Ontario, thereupon commenced this wrongful death action in New York against both Kuehner's estate and the Canadian National Railway Company. The defendant estate pleaded, as an affirmative defense, the Ontario guest statute and the defendant railway also interposed defenses in reliance upon it. In substance, the statute provides that the owner or driver of a motor vehicle is not liable for damages resulting from injury to, or the death of, a guest-passenger unless he was guilty of gross negligence. . . . It is worth noting, at this point, that, although our court originally considered that the sole purpose of the Ontario statute was to protect Ontario defendants and their insurers against collusive claims . . . , "[f]urther research . . . has revealed the distinct possibility that one purpose, and perhaps the only purpose, of the statute was to protect owners and drivers against ungrateful guests." . . .

The plaintiff, asserting that the Ontario statute "is not available . . . in the present action," moved, pursuant to CPLR 3211 (subd. [b]), to dismiss the affirmative defenses pleaded. The court at Special Term, holding the guest statute applicable, denied the motions . . . , but, on appeal, a closely divided Appellate Division reversed and directed dismissal of the defenses. . . . It was the court's belief that this result was dictated by Tooker v. Lopez. . . .

In reaching that conclusion, the Appellate Division misread our decision in the *Tooker* case—a not unnatural result in light of the variant views expressed in the three separate opinions written on behalf of the majority. It is important to bear in mind that in *Tooker*, the guest-passenger and the host-driver were both domiciled in New York, and our decision—that New York law was controlling—was based upon, and limited to, that fact situation. Indeed, two of the three judges who wrote for reversal—Judge Keating . . . and Judge Burke . . . expressly noted that the determination then being made left open the question whether New York law would be applicable if the plaintiff passenger happened to be a domiciliary of the very jurisdiction which had a guest statute. Thus, Tooker v. Lopez did no more than hold that, when the passenger and driver are residents of the same jurisdiction and the car is there registered and insured, its law, and not the law of the place of the accident, controls and determines the standard of care which the host owes to his guest.

What significantly and effectively differentiates the present case is the fact that, although the host was a domiciliary of New York, the guest, for whose death recovery is sought, was domiciled in Ontario, the place of the accident and the very jurisdiction which had enacted the statute designed to protect the host from liability for ordinary negligence. It is clear that although New York has a deep interest in protecting its own residents, injured in a foreign state, against unfair or anachronistic statutes of that state, it has no legitimate interest in ignoring the public policy of a foreign jurisdiction—such as Ontario—and in protecting the plaintiff guest domiciled and injured there from legislation obviously addressed, at the very least, to a resident riding in a vehicle traveling within its borders.

To distinguish *Tooker* on such a basis is not improperly discriminatory. It is quite true that, in applying the Ontario guest statute to the Ontario-domiciled passenger, we, in a sense, extend a right less generous than New York extends to a New York passenger in a New York vehicle with New York insurance. That, though, is not a consequence of invidious discrimination; it is, rather, the result of the existence of disparate rules of law in jurisdictions that have diverse and important connections with the litigants and the litigated issue.

The fact that insurance policies issued in this State on New York-based vehicles cover liability, regardless of the place of the accident . . . certainly does not call for the application of internal New York law in this case. The compulsory insurance requirement is designed to *cover* a carowner's liability, not *create* it; in other words, the applicable statute was not intended to impose liability where none would otherwise exist. This being so, we may not properly look to the New York insurance requirement to dictate a choice-of-law rule which would invariably impose liability. As Justice Moule wrote in the course of his dissenting opinion below,

> The statute . . . does not purport to impose liability where none would otherwise exist. We must observe that Judge Keating's statement . . . that the legislature "has evinced commendable concern not only for the residents of this State, but residents of other States who may be injured as a result of the activities of New York residents" was in the context, not of proving that New York had a governmental interest in overriding foreign rules of liability, but of demonstrating that it was immaterial in that case that the driver and passenger, while domiciliaries of New York, were attending college in Michigan. While New York may be a proper forum for actions involving its own domiciliaries, regardless of where the accident happened, it does not follow that we should apply New York law simply because some may think it is a better rule, where doing so does not advance any New York interest, nor the interest of any New York State domiciliary.

When in Babcock v. Jackson we rejected the mechanical place of injury rule in personal injury cases because it failed to take account of underlying policy considerations, we were willing to sacrifice the certainty provided by the old rule for the more just, fair and practical result that may best be achieved by giving controlling effect to the law of the jurisdiction which has the greatest concern with, or interest in, the specific issue raised in the litigation. . . . In consequence of the change effected—and this was to be anticipated—our decisions in multi-state highway accident cases, particularly in those involving guest-host controversies, have, it must be acknowledged, lacked consistency. This stemmed, in part, from the circumstance that it is frequently difficult to discover the purposes or policies underlying the relevant local law rules of the respective jurisdictions involved. It is even more difficult, assuming that these purposes or policies are found to conflict, to determine on some principled basis which should be given effect at the expense of the others.

The single all-encompassing rule which called, inexorably, for selection of the law of the place of injury was discarded, and wisely, because it was too broad to prove satisfactory in application. There is, however, no reason why choice-of-law rules, more narrow than those previously devised, should not be successfully developed, in order to assure a greater degree of predictability and uniformity, on the basis of our present knowledge and experience. . . . "The time has come," I wrote in *Tooker,* "to endeavor to minimize what some have characterized as an ad hoc case-by-case approach by laying down guidelines, as well as we can, for the solution of guest-host conflicts problems." *Babcock* and its progeny enable us to formulate a set of basic principles that may be profitably utilized, for they have helped us uncover the underlying values and policies which are operative in this area of law. To quote again from the concurring opinion in *Tooker,* "Now that these values and policies have been revealed, we may proceed to the next state in the evolution of the law—the formulation of a few rules of general applicability, promising a fair level of predictability." Although it was recognized that no rule may be formulated to guarantee a satisfactory result in every case, the following principles were proposed as sound for situations involving guest statutes in conflicts settings:

> 1. When the guest-passenger and the host-driver are domiciled in the same state, and the car is there registered, the law of the state should control and determine the standard of care which the host owes to his guest.
>
> 2. When the driver's conduct occurred in the state of his domicile and that state does not cast him in liability for that conduct, he should not be held liable by reason of the fact that liability would be imposed upon him under the tort law of the state of the victim's domicile. Conversely, when the guest was injured in the state of his own domicile and its law permits recovery, the driver who has come into that state should not—in the absence of special circumstances—be permitted to interpose the law of his state as a defense.
>
> 3. In other situations, when the passenger and the driver are domiciled in different states, the rule is necessarily less categorical. Normally, the applicable rule of decision will be that of the state where the accident occurred but not if it can be shown that displacing that normally applicable rule will advance the relevant substantive law purposes without impairing the smooth working of the multi-state system or pro-

ducing great uncertainty for litigants. (*Cf.* Restatement, 2d, Conflict of Laws, P.O.D., pt. II, §§146, 159 [later adopted and promulgated May 23, 1969.])

The variant views expressed not only in *Tooker* but by Special Term and the divided Appellate Division in this litigation underscore and confirm the need for these rules. Since the passenger was domiciled in Ontario and the driver in New York, the present case is covered by the third stated principle. The law to be applied is that of the jurisdiction where the accident happened unless it appears that "displacing [the] normally applicable rule will advance the relevant substantive law purposes" of the jurisdictions involved. Certainly, ignoring Ontario's policy requiring proof of gross negligence in a case which involves an Ontario-domiciled guest at the expense of a New Yorker does not further the substantive law purposes of New York. In point of fact, application of New York law would result in the exposure of this State's domiciliaries to a greater liability than that imposed upon resident users of Ontario's highways. Conversely, the failure to apply Ontario's law would "impair"—to cull from the rule set out above—"the smooth working of the multi-state system [and] produce great uncertainty for litigants" by sanctioning forum shopping and thereby allowing a party to select a forum which could give him a larger recovery than the court of his own domicile. In short, the plaintiff has failed to show that this State's connection with the controversy was sufficient to justify displacing the rule of lex loci delictus.

Professor Willis Reese, the Reporter for the current Conflict of Laws Restatement, expressed approval of rules such as those suggested above; they are, he wrote, "the sort of rules at which the courts should aim." Indeed, in discussing the present case following the determination at Special Term that Ontario law should govern, he expressed the opinion that any other result would have been highly unreasonable. . . .

> So far as the New York law was concerned, Judge Keating had argued in Tooker v. Lopez that New York's motor vehicle compulsory insurance law revealed a "commendable concern" not only for New York residents but also for non-residents injured by New Yorkers. On this basis, it could perhaps be argued that New York policy would be furthered by application of the New York rule imposing upon the driver the duty of exercising ordinary care for the protection of his guest. But could this argument really be made with a straight face in support of an Ontario guest picked up in Ontario and who enjoyed no similar protection under Ontario law? Was the New York rule really intended to be manna for the entire world? One can well understand the relief with which the trial judge seized upon Judge Fuld's third rule and followed it by holding the Ontario statute applicable. . . .

[A concurring opinion is omitted.]

BERGAN, J. (dissenting).

The doctrine of lex loci delictus, whatever its other shortcomings may be, including a somewhat abrasive effect on inconsistent law of the forum, had at least the virtues of certainty and reckonability.

But the operation of the guest statutes of other jurisdictions worked out so differently—unjustly by New York standards—that in a series of highly debatable and debated decisions from Babcock v. Jackson to Tooker v. Lopez this court refused to follow the rule of lex loci delictus in special situations and applied New York law in New York litigation to motor vehicle torts occurring in other jurisdictions.

The rationale of departure from the settled rule was that New York had a greater "concern" or "interest" in the controversy or the parties; or had closer "contacts" than the jurisdiction of the situs of the accident. The direction taken and justified by the rationale of "interest" or "contact," however, necessarily started with the court's preference for the local rule and a belief in its greater justice.

There is a difference of fundamental character between justifying a departure from lex loci delictus because the court will not, as a matter of policy, permit a New York owner of a car licensed and insured in New York to escape a liability that would be imposed on him here; and a departure based on the fact a New York resident makes the claim for injury. The first ground of departure is justifiable as sound policy; the second is justifiable only if one is willing to treat the rights of a stranger permitted to sue in New York differently from the way a resident is treated. Neither because of "interest" or "contact" nor any other defensible ground is it proper to say in a court of law that the rights of one man whose suit is accepted shall be adjudged differently on the merits on the basis of where he happens to live. . . .

. . . What the court is deciding today is that although it will prevent a New York car owner from asserting the defense of a protective foreign statute when a New York resident in whose rights it has an "interest" sues; it has no such "interest" when it accepts the suit in New York of a non-resident. This is an inadmissible distinction.

The order should be affirmed.

Schultz v. Boy Scouts of America, Inc.

65 N.Y.2d 189, 480 N.E.2d 679, 491 N.Y.S.2d 90 (1985)

SIMONS, J.

Plaintiffs, Richard E. and Margaret Schultz, instituted this action to recover damages for personal injuries they and their sons, Richard and Christopher, suffered because the boys were sexually abused by defendant Edmund Coakeley and for damages sustained as a result of Christopher's wrongful death after he committed suicide. Coakeley, a brother in the Franciscan order, was the boys' school teacher and leader of their scout troop. Plaintiffs allege

Damages & wrongful death

that the sexual abuse occurred while Coakeley was acting in those capacities and the causes of action before us on this appeal charge defendants Boy Scouts of America, Inc., and the Brothers of the Poor of St. Francis, Inc. (sued as Franciscan Brothers of the Poor, Inc.), with negligently hiring and supervising him.

Plaintiffs are domiciled in New Jersey and some of the injuries were sustained there. Thus, a choice-of-law issue is presented because New Jersey recognizes the doctrine of charitable immunity and New York does not. Defendants contend New Jersey law governs this litigation and that its courts have already determined that plaintiffs' claims are barred in a separate action against the Roman Catholic Archdiocese of Newark (*see* Schultz v. Roman Catholic Archdiocese, 95 N.J. 530, 472 A.2d 531). Following the rationale of Babcock v. Jackson, 12 N.Y.2d 473, 240 N.Y.S.2d 743, 191 N.E.2d 279, and similar cases, we hold that New Jersey law applies and that plaintiffs are precluded from relitigating its effect on the claims they assert.

I

In 1978 plaintiffs were residents of Emerson, New Jersey, where their two sons, Richard, age 13, and Christopher, age 11, attended Assumption School, an institution owned and operated by the Roman Catholic Archdiocese of Newark. By an agreement with the Archdiocese, defendant Brothers of the Poor of St. Francis, Inc., supplied teachers for the school. One of those assigned was Brother Edmund Coakeley, who also served as the scoutmaster of Boy Scout Troop 337, a locally chartered Boy Scout troop sponsored and approved by defendant Boy Scouts of America. Richard and Christopher attended Coakeley's class and were members of his scout troop.

In July 1978 Coakeley took Christopher Schultz to Pine Creek Reservation, a Boy Scout camp located in upstate New York near the Oneida County community of Foresport. The camp was located on land owned by Peter Grandy, who was also a resident of Emerson, New Jersey. The complaint alleges that while at the camp, Coakeley sexually abused Christopher, that he continued to do so when Christopher returned to Assumption School in New Jersey that fall and that he threatened Christopher with harm if he revealed what had occurred. The complaint also alleges that Coakeley sexually abused Richard Schultz and made similar threats to him during a scout trip to Pine Creek Reservation on Memorial Day weekend in 1978. Plaintiffs claim that as a result of Coakeley's acts both boys suffered several psychological, emotional and mental pain and suffering and that as a result of the distress Coakeley's acts caused, Christopher Schultz committed suicide by ingesting drugs on May 29, 1979. They charge both defendants with negligence in assigning Coakeley to positions of trust where he could molest young boys and in failing to dismiss him despite actual or constructive notice that

Coakeley had previously been dismissed from another Boy Scout camp for similar improper conduct. . . .

II

A

The choice-of-law question presented in the action against defendant Boy Scouts of America is whether New York should apply its law in an action involving codomiciliaries of New Jersey when tortious acts were committed in New York. This is the posture of the appeal although defendant is a Federally chartered corporation created exclusively for educational and charitable purposes pursuant to an act of Congress (*see*, 36 U.S.C. §21) that originally maintained its national headquarters in New Brunswick, New Jersey, but moved to Dallas, Texas, in 1979. New Jersey is considered defendant's domicile because its national headquarters was in that State. . . . Its change of domicile after the commission of the wrongs from New Jersey to Texas, which no longer recognizes the doctrine of charitable immunity, provides New York with no greater interest in this action than it would have without the change. Our decision recognizing a postaccident change in domicile in Miller v. Miller, 22 N.Y.2d 12, 290 N.Y.S.2d 734, 237 N.E.2d 877, is distinguishable because in that case the defendant's domicile was changed to New York, which was the forum and also the plaintiff's domicile.

The question presented in the action against defendant Franciscan Brothers is what law should apply when the parties' different domiciles have conflicting charitable immunity rules. The Franciscan order is incorporated in Ohio and it is a domiciliary of that State. . . . At the time these causes of action arose Ohio, like New Jersey, recognized charitable immunity. . . . The Ohio rule denied immunity in actions based on negligent hiring and supervision, however, . . . whereas New Jersey does not. . . . For this reason, no doubt, defendant Franciscan Brothers does not claim Ohio law governs and the choice is between the law of New York and the law of New Jersey.

As for the locus of the tort, both parties and the dissent implicitly assume it is New York because most of Coakeley's acts were committed here. Under traditional rules, the law of the place of the wrong governs all substantive issues in the action . . . but when the defendant's negligent conduct occurs in one jurisdiction and the plaintiff's injuries are suffered in another, the place of the wrong is considered to be the place where the last event necessary to make the actor liable occurred. . . . Thus, the locus in this case is determined by where the plaintiffs' injuries occurred.

The first and fourth causes of action, the wrongful death of Christopher and plaintiffs' own psychological and other injuries respectively, allege injuries inflicted in New Jersey. New York's only interests in these claims are as the forum State and as the jurisdiction where the tortious conduct underlying plaintiffs' claims against defendants, *i.e.*, the negligent assignment and failure to dismiss Coakeley, occurred. Standing alone, these interests are insufficient to warrant application of New York law, at least when the relevant issue is a loss-distribution rule, like charitable immunity, rather than one regulating conduct. . . . The second and third causes of action seek damages for the psychological, emotional and physical injuries suffered by Christopher and Richard Schultz, injuries which occurred in both New York and New Jersey, because a fair reading of the complaint indicates that both boys suffered injuries when Coakeley molested them and also after they returned home. These two causes of action sufficiently implicate New York's interests to require a resolution of the choice-of-law problem in the case.

B

Historically, choice-of-law conflicts in tort actions have been resolved by applying the law of the place of the wrong. In Babcock v. Jackson, we departed from traditional doctrine, however, and refused to invariably apply the rule of lex loci delicti to determine the availability of relief for commission of a tort.

The analysis [in *Babcock*] was flexible and to the extent that it may have placed too much emphasis on contact-counting without specifying the relative significance of those contacts, the necessary refinements were added in later decisions of this court. In four of the five subsequent tort cases presenting the same *Babcock*-style fact pattern of common New York domiciliaries and a foreign locus having loss-distribution rules in conflict with those of New York we reached results consistent with *Babcock* and applied New York law. . . . In each of the five cases, however, the court rejected the indiscriminate grouping of contacts, which in *Babcock* had been a consideration coequal to interest analysis, because it bore no reasonable relation to the underlying policies of conflicting rules of recovery in tort actions. . . . Interest analysis became the relevant analytical approach to choice of law in tort actions in New York. "[T]he law of the jurisdiction having the greatest interest in the litigation will be applied and . . . the [only] facts or contacts which obtain significance in defining State interests are those which relate to the purpose of the particular law in conflict." . . . Under this formulation, the significant contacts are, almost exclusively, the parties' domiciles and the locus of the tort. . . .

Thus, under present rules, most of the nondomicile and nonlocus contacts relied on in Babcock v. Jackson (*supra*), such as where the guest-host relationship arose and where the journey was to begin and end, are no longer controlling in tort actions involving guest statutes. . . . Both *Tooker* and

Neumeier continued to place some importance on where the automobile involved was insured . . . but this is not inconsistent with the present rule because usually a defendant host's automobile will be insured in the State of his domicile and also because it reflects a recognition that the insurer, rather than the individually named defendant, is often "the real party in interest." . . . Insofar as issues of liability insurance might also be relevant in a case such as the one before us involving charitable immunity, the record provides no relevant information on the subject.

These decisions also establish that the relative interests of the domicile and locus jurisdictions in having their laws apply will depend on the particular tort issue in conflict with the case. Thus, when the conflicting rules involve the appropriate standards of conduct, rules of the road, for example, the law of the place of the tort "will usually have a predominant, if not exclusive, concern" . . . because the locus jurisdiction's interests in protecting the reasonable expectations of the parties who relied on it to govern their primary conduct and in the admonitory effect that applying its law will have on similar conduct in the future assume critical importance and outweigh any interests of the common-domicile jurisdiction. . . .

. . . Conversely, when the jurisdictions' conflicting rules relate to allocating losses that result from admittedly tortious conduct, as they do here, rules such as those limiting damages in wrongful death actions, vicarious liability rules, or immunities from suit, considerations of the State's admonitory interest and party reliance are less important. Under those circumstances, the locus jurisdiction has at best a minimal interest in determining the right of recovery or the extent of the remedy in an action by a foreign domiciliary for injuries resulting from the conduct of a codomiciliary that was tortious under the laws of both jurisdictions. . . . Analysis then favors the jurisdiction of common domicile because of its interest in enforcing the decisions of both parties to accept both the benefits and the burdens of identifying with that jurisdiction and to submit themselves to its authority.[2] These considerations made the need for change in the lex loci delicti rule obvious in *Babcock*, but the validity of this interest analysis is more clearly demonstrated in the split domicile case of Neumeier v. Kuehner. In *Neumeier* we applied Ontario's guest statute in an action on behalf of an Ontario decedent against a New York defendant at least in part because the Ontario statute, which contained reciprocal benefits and burdens depending on one's status as either host or guest, was "obviously addressed" to Ontario domiciliaries such as plaintiff's decedent (*id.*). In *Babcock* New York had an important interest in protecting its own residents injured in a foreign State against unfair or anachronistic

---

2. New York's rule holding charities liable for their tortious acts, or its rule of nonimmunity as the dissent characterizes it, is also a loss-allocating rule, just as New Jersey's charitable immunity statute is.

statutes of that State but it had no similar interest in *Neumeier* in protecting a guest domiciled in Ontario and injured there.

C

As to defendant Boy Scouts, this case is but a slight variation of our *Babcock* line of decisions and differs from them on only two grounds: (1) the issue involved in charitable immunity rather than a guest statute, and (2) it presents a fact pattern which one commentator has characterized as a "reverse" *Babcock* case because New York is the place of the tort rather than the jurisdiction of the parties' common domicile (*see*, Korn, The Choice-of-Law Revolution: A Critique, 83 Colum. L. Rev. 772, 789).

Although most of our major choice-of-law decisions after *Babcock* involved foreign guest statutes in actions for personal injuries, we have not so limited them, but have applied the *Babcock* reasoning to other tort issues as well. . . . Nor is there any logical basis for distinguishing guest statutes from other loss-distributing rules because they all share the characteristic of being postevent remedial rules designed to allocate the burden of losses resulting from tortious conduct in which the jurisdiction of the parties' common domicile has a paramount interest. There is even less reason for distinguishing *Babcock* here where the conflicting rules involve the defense of charitable immunity. . . .

Both plaintiffs and defendant Boy Scouts in this case have chosen to identify themselves in the most concrete form possible, domicile, with a jurisdiction that has weighed the interests of charitable tort-feasors and their victims and decided to retain the defense of charitable immunity. Significantly, the New Jersey statute excepts from its protection actions by nonbeneficiaries of the charity who suffer injuries as a result of the negligence of its employees or agents (*see*, N.J. Stat. Ann. §2A:53A-7). Plaintiffs and their sons, however, were beneficiaries of the Boy Scouts' charitable activities in New Jersey and should be bound by the benefits and burdens of that choice. Additionally, the State of New Jersey is intimately interested in seeing that the parties' associational interests are respected and its own loss-distributing rules are enforced so that the underlying policy, which is undoubtedly to encourage the growth of charitable work within its borders, is effectuated.

Thus, if this were a straight *Babcock* fact pattern, rather than the reverse, we would have no reason to depart from the first *Neumeier* rule and would apply the law of the parties' common domicile. Because this case presents the first case for our review in which New York is the forum-locus rather than the parties' common domicile, however, we consider the reasons most often advanced for applying the law of the forum-locus and those supporting application of the law of the common domicile.

The three reasons most often urged in support of applying the law of the forum-locus in cases such as this are: (1) to protect medical creditors who provided services to injured parties in the locus State, (2) to prevent injured tort victims from becoming public wards in the locus State and (3) the deterrent effect application of locus law has on future tort-feasors in the locus State. . . . The first two reasons share common weaknesses. First, in the abstract, neither reason necessarily requires application of the locus jurisdiction's law, but rather invariably mandates application of the law of the jurisdiction that would either allow recovery or allow the greater recovery. . . . They are subject to criticism, therefore, as being biased in favor of recovery. Second, on the facts of this case neither reason is relevant since the record contains no evidence that there are New York medical creditors or that plaintiffs are or will likely become wards of this State. Finally, although it is conceivable that application of New York's law in this case would have some deterrent effect on future tortious conduct in this State, New York's deterrent interest is considerably less because none of the parties is a resident and the rule in conflict is loss-allocating rather than conduct-regulating.

Conversely, there are persuasive reasons for consistently applying the law of the parties' common domicile. First, it significantly reduces forum-shopping opportunities, because the same law will be applied by the common-domicile and locus jurisdictions, the two most likely forums. Second, it rebuts charges that the forum-locus is biased in favor of its own laws and in favor of rules permitting recovery. Third, the concepts of mutuality and reciprocity support consistent application of the common-domicile law. In any given case, one person could be either plaintiff or defendant and one State could be either the parties' common domicile or the locus, and yet the applicable law would not change depending on their status. Finally, it produces a rule that is easy to apply and brings a modicum of predictability and certainty to an area of the law needing both.

As to defendant Franciscan Brothers, this action requires an application of the third of the rules set forth in *Neumeier* because the parties are domiciled in different jurisdictions with conflicting loss-distribution rules and the locus of the tort is New York, a separate jurisdiction. In that situation the law of the place of the tort will normally apply, unless displacing it " 'will advance the relevant substantive law purposes without impairing the smooth working of the multi-state system or producing great uncertainty for litigants' " (Neumeier v. Kuehner). For the same reasons stated in our analysis of the action against defendant Boy Scouts, application of the law of New Jersey in plaintiffs' action against defendant Franciscan Brothers would further that State's interest in enforcing the decision of its domiciliaries to accept the burdens as well as the benefits of that State's loss-distribution tort rules and its interest in promoting the continuation and expansion of defendant's charitable activities in that State. Conversely, although application of New Jersey's law may not affirmatively advance the substantive law purposes of New York, it will not frustrate those interests because New York has no significant interest in applying its own law to this dispute. Finally, application of New Jersey law will enhance "the smooth working of the multistate system" by actually reducing the incentive for forum shopping and it will provide certainty for the litigants whose only reasonable expectation[3] surely would have been that the law of the jurisdiction where plaintiffs are domiciled and defendant sends its teachers would apply, not the law of New York where the parties had only isolated and infrequent contacts as a result of Coakeley's position as Boy Scout leader. Thus, we conclude that defendant Franciscan Brothers has met its burden of demonstrating that the law of New Jersey, rather than the law of New York, should govern plaintiffs' action against it.

III

Plaintiffs contend that even if the New Jersey charitable immunity statute is applicable to this action, it should not be enforced because it is contrary to the public policy of New York.

The public policy doctrine is an exception to implementing an otherwise applicable choice of law in which the forum refuses to apply a portion of foreign law because it is contrary or repugnant to its State's own public policy. . . . The doctrine is considered only after the court has determined that the applicable substantive law under relevant choice-of-law principles is not the forum's law. Having found that, the court must enforce the foreign law "unless some sound reason of public policy makes it unwise for us to lend our aid." . . . The party seeking to invoke the doctrine has the burden of proving that the foreign law is contrary to New York public policy. It is a heavy burden for public policy is not measured by individual notions of expediency and fairness or by a showing that the foreign law is unreasonable or unwise. . . . Public policy is found in the State's Constitution, statutes and judicial decisions and the proponent of the exception must establish that to enforce the foreign law "would violate some fundamental principle of justice, some prevalent conception of good morals, some deep-rooted tradition of the common weal" expressed in them. . . . In addition, the proponent must establish that there are enough important contacts between the parties, the occurrence and the New York forum to implicate our public policy and thus preclude enforcement of the foreign law. . . .

When we have employed the exception in the past and refused to enforce otherwise applicable foreign law, the contacts between the New York forum, the parties and the transaction involved were substantial enough to

3. As the dissent notes, we rejected the notion that the parties' reasonable expectations of the applicable law was [*sic*] determinative in Miller v. Miller and Tooker v. Lopez. Our discussion here is limited to application of the "uncertainty" standard of the third of the *Neumeier* rules to defendant Franciscan Brothers.

threaten our public policy. Thus, in Kilberg v. Northeast Airlines we found the law of the place of tort, Massachusetts, appropriate to a wrongful death action but refused to apply its statutory limit on damages because it was contrary to New York public policy, expressed in our State Constitution, prohibiting limitations on such damages. Insofar as the decedent was a resident, who had purchased his ticket and boarded his flight in New York and the defendant carried on extensive operations here, New York's interest in providing its residents with full compensation for wrongful death was jeopardized and led us to reject the Massachusetts limitation.

Similarly, in Mertz v. Mertz and Straus & Co. v. Canadian Pac. Ry. Co., this State's public policy was seriously threatened because it was intimately connected to the parties and the transaction. In *Mertz* we refused to follow Connecticut law that permitted a wife to sue her husband for negligently inflicted injuries caused there because New York's law was just the opposite and the parties were both New York domiciliaries. In *Straus & Co.*, we refused to enforce a contractual provision releasing the defendant shipper from liability for its own negligence, valid under otherwise applicable British law but invalid under the laws of New York, when the plaintiff was a New York company, the final place of shipment was New York, and the defendant had chosen to do business here by way of shipping goods into the State.

Thus, although New York discarded the doctrine of charitable immunity long ago . . . and enforcement of New Jersey's statute might well run counter to our fundamental public policy, we need not decide that issue because there are not sufficient contacts between New York, the parties and the transactions involved to implicate our public policy and call for its enforcement. . . .

Jasen, J. (dissenting).

I respectfully dissent. In my view, the majority overstates the significance of New Jersey's interests in having its law apply in this case and understates the interests of New York. . . .

New Jersey's interests, denominated by the majority as loss-distribution, are hardly pressing under the circumstances. While it is true that laws providing for charitable immunity typically are intended to serve the purpose of protecting and promoting the charities incorporated within a state's jurisdiction, that function is virtually irrelevant in this case. Presently, neither corporate defendant is a resident of New Jersey. The Brothers of the Poor of St. Francis (the Franciscan Brothers) has at all relevant times been a resident of the State of Ohio, a jurisdiction which recognizes only a limited charitable immunity that does not extend to negligence in the selection and retention of personnel. . . . The Boy Scouts of America, although originally incorporated in New Jersey at the time of its alleged tortious conduct, has since relocated in Texas, a State which has wholly rejected charitable immunity. . . .

. . . While ordinarily a change in residence subsequent to the events upon which a lawsuit is predicated ought not to affect the rights and liabilities of the parties in order to avoid forum-shopping, there is no such reason to deny giving effect to the change in residence here. Rather, a defendant's post-tort change in residence—as opposed to that of a plaintiff—is often critical insofar as it affects state interest analysis. . . . Indeed, as this court stated in Miller v. Miller:

> To the extent that the [foreign State's] limitation evinced a desire to protect its residents in wrongful death actions, that purpose cannot be defeated here since no judgment in this action will be entered against a . . . resident [of that State. It] would have no concern with the nature of the recovery awarded against defendants who are no longer residents of that State and who are, therefore, no longer proper objects of its legislative concern. It is true that, at the time of the accident, the defendants were residents of [that State] but they would have no vested right to the application of the law of their former residence unless it could be demonstrated that they had governed their conduct in reliance upon it—reliance which is neither present nor claimed in the case at bar. Any claim that [the foreign State] has a paternalistic interest in protecting its residents against liability for acts committed while they were in [that State] should they move to another jurisdiction, is highly speculative.

It simply cannot be disputed that New Jersey presently has a much diminished interest, if any at all, in shielding the Boy Scouts of America from liability—let alone the Franciscan Brothers which has never been a New Jersey resident. The majority does not question that conclusion, but merely states that the change in residence does not enhance New York's interest. . . . While the latter may be true in the abstract, the point, of course, is that New Jersey's interest in the application of its charitable immunity law has been substantially reduced.

Consequently, because the majority cannot in actuality rely upon New Jersey's interest in protecting resident charities—into which category neither corporate defendant now falls—the decision today is, in effect, predicated almost exclusively upon the plaintiffs' New Jersey domicile. What emerges from the majority's holding is an entirely untoward rule that nonresident plaintiffs are somehow less entitled to the protections of this State's law while they are within our borders. Besides smacking of arbitrary and injudicious discrimination against guests in this State and before our courts (*see*, Ely, Choice of Law and the State's Interest in Protecting Its Own, 23 Wm. & Mary L. Rev. 173, 186-187) . . . such a position, without more, has severely limited, if any, validity in resolving conflicts questions. . . . This is especially so where, as here, the defendants' contacts with the foreign State are insignificant for the purposes of interest analysis while, at the same time, the parties' contacts with New York are so clear and direct, and the resulting interests of this State so strong.

There can be no question that this State has a paramount interest in preventing and protecting against injurious misconduct within its borders. This interest is particularly vital and compelling where, as here, the tortious misconduct involves sexual abuse and exploitation of children, regardless of the residency of the victims and the tort-feasors. . . . Despite the majority's denial, New York's law in question is intimately connected to this overriding interest.

Padula v. Lilarn Properties Corporation

644 N.E.2d 1001, 620 N.Y.S.2d 310 (N.Y. Ct. App. 1994)

SMITH, J.

Plaintiff is a resident of New York and defendant is a corporation incorporated under the laws of New York. Defendant owns property in Massachusetts, at which plaintiff was working, under a subcontracting agreement. Plaintiff sustained injuries when he fell from a scaffold while performing work on a construction project in Massachusetts. Plaintiff brought this action for damages, alleging violations of sections 200, 240 (1) and 241 (6) of the New York Labor Law and the rules and regulations thereunder. The issue here is the applicability of these sections of the Labor Law to this accident.

Defendant's motion for partial summary judgment dismissing plaintiff's causes of action alleging violations of the New York State Labor Law and various rules and regulations thereunder was granted by Supreme Court and affirmed by the Appellate Division. Supreme Court thereafter granted defendant's motion for summary judgment dismissing the remainder of plaintiff's complaint. This Court granted leave from the Supreme Court judgment to bring up for review the prior nonfinal Appellate Division order.

We reject plaintiff's contention that New York law should apply here. New York's choice-of-law principles govern the outcome of this matter. In the context of tort law, New York utilizes interest analysis to determine which of two competing jurisdictions has the greater interest in having its law applied in the litigation. The greater interest is determined by an evaluation of the "facts or contacts which . . . relate to the purpose of the particular law in conflict" (Schultz v. Boy Scouts, 65 N.Y. 2d 189, 197). Two separate inquiries are thereby required to determine the greater interest: (1) what are the significant contacts and in which jurisdiction are they located; and, (2) whether the purpose of the law is to regulate conduct or allocate loss (*id.* at 198).

As to the first inquiry concerning the significant contacts and the jurisdiction in which they are located, both the plaintiff employee and the defendant owner of the Massachusetts property are domiciliaries of New York State. The other relevant actors are not parties to this lawsuit. They include the plaintiff's employer (a subcontractor which is a New York domiciliary), the tenant of the property (a Massachusetts domiciliary who contracted with the general contractor), and the general contractor (a domiciliary of Vermont). The tort occurred in Massachusetts.

As to the second inquiry, a distinction must be made between a choice-of-law analysis involving standards of conduct and one involving the allocation of losses (Schultz v. Boy Scouts, 65 N.Y.2d 189, 198, *supra*). In the former case the law of the place of the tort governs. As we stated in *Schultz:*

> Thus, when the conflicting rules involve the appropriate standards of conduct, rules of the road, for example, the law of the place of the tort 'will usually have a predominant, if not exclusive, concern' . . . because the locus jurisdiction's interests in protecting the reasonable expectations of the parties who relied on it to govern their primary conduct and in the admonitory effect that applying its law will have on similar conduct in the future assume critical importance and outweigh any interests of the common-domicile jurisdiction." (*Schultz,* 65 N.Y.2d, at 198; *see also* Cooney v. Osgood Mach., 81 N.Y.2d 66, 72.)

Conduct-regulating rules have the prophylactic effect of governing conduct to prevent injuries from occurring. "If conflicting conduct-regulating laws are at issue, the law of the jurisdiction where the tort occurred will generally apply because that jurisdiction has the greatest interest in regulating behavior within its borders" (Cooney v. Osgood Mach., 81 N.Y.2d 66, 72, *supra*).

Loss allocating rules, on the other hand, are those which prohibit, assign, or limit liability after the tort occurs, such as charitable immunity statutes (*e.g.*, Schultz v. Boy Scouts, *supra*), guest statutes (*e.g.*, Dym v. Gordon, 16 N.Y.2d 120), wrongful death statutes (*e.g.*, Miller v. Miller, 22 N.Y.2d 12), vicarious liability statutes (*e.g.*, Farber v. Smolack, 20 N.Y.2d 198), and contribution rules (*e.g.*, Cooney v. Osgood Mach., *supra*). Where the conflicting rules at issue are loss allocating and the parties to the lawsuit share a common domicile, the loss allocation rule of the common domicile will apply (*see* Cooney v. Osgood Mach., *supra,* at 73 [setting forth the three *Neumeier* rules (Neumeier v. Kuehner, 31 N.Y.2d 121) which address the "common domicile" situation in rule No. 1]).

Thus, the fundamental question in this case, where the parties share a common domicile, is whether Labor Law §§240 and 241 are primarily conduct-regulating or loss-allocating. The relevant Labor Law provisions, sections 240 and 241, embody both conduct-regulating and loss-allocating functions requiring worksites be made safe (conduct-regulating) and failure to do so results in strict and vicarious liability of the owner of the property or the general contractor. We hold however, that sections 240 and 241 of the Labor Law are primarily conduct-regulating rules, requiring that adequate safety measures be instituted at the worksite and should not be applied to the resolution of this tort dispute arising in Massachusetts. Thus, Massachusetts law was properly applied.

Accordingly, the judgment of Supreme Court appealed from and the order of the Appellate Division brought up for review should be affirmed, with costs.

[Judge TITONE filed a concurring opinion]

Questions and Comments

(1) How would you describe the methodological differences between *Padula*, *Schultz*, and *Neumeier*, on the one hand, and *Babcock* and *Tooker*, on the other? How do both differ from *Haag*? Would you expect to see the New York courts stay with the *Padula-Schultz-Neumeier* approach, or would you expect to see still another set of gyrations? Or is there some unifying theme with which all of these decisions are consistent? For a general critique of this line of cases, *see* Simson, The *Neumeier-Schultz* Rules: How Logical A "Next Stage in the Evolution of the Law" after *Babcock*?, 56 Alb. L. Rev. 913 (1993).

(2) The distinction between conduct-regulating and loss-allocating rules is crucial in *Schultz* and *Padula*. Is the distinction useful? Won't most laws, as *Padula* put it, "embody both conduct-regulating and loss-allocating functions"? Are you convinced by *Padula*'s conclusion that §§240-241 of New York's Labor law are "primarily conduct regulating"? Doesn't the conduct-regulation/loss-allocation distinction raise a new and intractable characterization problem?

Scholars disagree about the validity and usefulness of the distinction. Professor Symeonides applauds it:

> Although it is often difficult to draw a precise line between the two categories, this distinction is both necessary and useful in that it provides the vehicle for attaining the necessary equilibrium between the two perennially competing principles: territoriality and personality of the laws. Indeed, to a large extent, the story of private international law can be described as a contest between these two grand principles, with the pendulum swinging from the one to the other principle in different periods in history. In this country, Joseph Beale had pulled the pendulum all the way towards territoriality, and then Brainerd Currie pulled it almost all the way back towards personality. It is time to acknowledge that neither Beale nor Currie was entirely wrong or entirely right, and to attempt a new equilibrium between these two principles.

Symeonides, The Need for a Third Conflicts Restatement (And a Proposal for Tort Conflicts), 75 Ind. L.J. 437, 452-453 (2000); *see also* Borchers, The Return of Territorialism to New York's Conflicts Law: Padula v. Lilarn Properties Corp., 58 Alb. L. Rev. 775 (1995) (suggesting that the distinction, though not always easy to draw, is essential and serviceable). Others are critical of the distinction:

> [T]he distinction breaks down in practice. For example, a comparative negligence rule might be either conduct-regulating or loss-allocating. Although damage caps may appear to be about loss-allocation, they can affect repeat-player tortfeasors. Limiting the funds available to compensate the families of children who die from vaccination profoundly affected drug companies' willingness to produce the vaccines

O'Hara & Ribstein, From Politics to Efficiency in Choice of Law, 67 U. Chi. L. Rev. 1151 (2000); *see also* Perdue, A Reexamination of the Distinction between "Loss-Allocating" and "Conduct-Regulating Rules," 60 La. L. Rev. 1251, 1252 (arguing that "most tort rules are both and that the compensation and deterrence goals ascribed to the tort system cannot be separated") (citation and internal quotations removed); Hay & Ellis, Bridging the Gap Between Rules and Approaches in Tort Choice of Law in the United States: A Survey of Current Case Law, 27 Intl. Law 369, 382 (1993) ("distinction creates more trouble than it's worth").

(3) Another important New York Court of Appeals' choice-of-law decision is Cooney v. Osgood Machinery, Inc., 81 N.Y.2d 66,612 N.E.2d 277, 595 N.Y.S.2d 919 (1993). There the *Neumeier* rules were held to require application of Missouri law barring contribution claims against employers subject to workers' compensation laws. New York law permitted contribution. The party requesting contribution, Osgood, was a New York sales agent who, 35 years earlier, had assisted in the purchase of a piece of equipment to shape large pieces of metal. The equipment found its way to Missouri "in some unknown manner," where it injured Cooney, an employee of defendant Mueller. After recovering in Missouri under the workers' compensation law, Cooney sued Osgood (who would not have been amenable to jurisdiction in Missouri) in New York on a products liability theory. Osgood then sought contribution from Mueller.

The court noted that contribution rules are loss-allocating, not conduct-regulating, and that the case was one of split domicile. The interests of Missouri and New York, moreover, were "manifestly . . . irreconcilable" so that a true conflict was presented. Missouri law was applied "because, although the interests of the respective jurisdictions are irreconcilable, the accident occurred in Missouri, and unavailability of contribution would more closely comport with the reasonable expectations of both parties in conducting their business affairs." The court also held that application of Missouri law would not violate fundamental New York public policy.

Note the unusual situation presented by this case: The New York party has no connection with Missouri, and the Missouri party has no connection with New York. Is any solution to this problem likely to seem completely fair? *See* Silberman, *Cooney v. Osgood Machinery, Inc.*: A Less Than Complete "Contribution," in Symposium—*Cooney v. Osgood Machinery, Inc.*, 59 Brook. L. Rev. 1323 (1994).

(4) After *Schultz, Padula,* and *Cooney,* doesn't New York's choice-of-law rule for torts boil down to: Apply the law of the place of injury unless the issue involves a loss-allocation dispute between common domiciliaries, in which case apply the law of the domicile? If this is correct, then the New York "revolution" amounts to nothing more than the First Restatement with a narrow exception for common domicile cases involving loss-allocation issues. Was it necessary to walk the tortured path from *Haag* to *Padula* to reach this destination? Doesn't *Padula* suggest that the New York approach is as wooden, jurisdiction-selecting, and "blind" as the traditional approach? Is there perhaps virtue in these qualities? Professor Hill has argued that the choice-of-law revolution is virtually unique in its willingness to discard the common sense of centuries and blaze new trails on a case-by-case basis. He points out that there was much more to traditional thinking than Beale's dogma and that some traditional thinking might be worth consulting. Hill, The Judicial Function in Choice of Law, 85 Colum. L. Rev. 1585 (1985). Does the line of cases from *Haag* to *Padula* support Hill's view? What does this line of cases suggest about the capacities of courts to view choice-of-law as about the pursuit of "state interests"?

(5) *Schultz* states that the Boy Scouts' post-transaction move to Texas (which doesn't recognize charitable immunity) "provides New York with no greater interest in this action than it would have without the change." But isn't the dissent correct that the relevance of the move, instead, lies in its impact on the interests of New Jersey and Texas? Shouldn't the argument be that there is now a false conflict because New York and Texas have the same law, and there is no longer a New Jersey defendant?

(6) Where did the tort at issue in *Schultz* "occur"? Why shouldn't the locus of the tort be the place where the negligent hiring occurred? With its talk of "the last event necessary to make the actor liable," is the court harking back to the First Restatement?

(7) The court lists three reasons sometimes advanced for applying the law of the forum locus. The first two—protecting local medical creditors and preventing injured parties from becoming public wards of the state—are rejected as reasons for applying New York law in part because they are "biased in favor of recovery." But aren't all underlying policies biased in this sense, either favoring recovery (if pro-plaintiff) or denying it (if pro-defendant)? What is left of the new methodology once we discard such "biased" policies? And with regard to the third reason—deterrence—why is New York's interest less where the parties are not residents? Are nonresidents supposed to be immune from local conduct-regulating rules while in New York?

(8) Regarding the Franciscan Brothers, why would New Jersey have an interest in forcing its domiciliaries to bear the costs as well as the benefits of local law? Does a state have an interest generally in applying its disadvantageous rules to locals?

(9) Why are there insufficient contacts with New York for New York to invoke its public policy? Should contacts be required?

B. Interest Analysis: In Theory and in Practice

1. Theoretical Foundations of Interest Analysis

Currie, Notes on Methods and Objectives in the Conflict of Laws

Selected Essays on the Conflict of Laws 177, 183-187 (1963)

We would be better off without choice-of-law rules. We would be better off if Congress were to give some attention to problems of private law, and were to legislate concerning the choice between conflicting state interests in some of the specific areas in which the need for solutions is serious. In the meantime, we would be better off if we would admit the teachings of sociological jurisprudence into the conceptualistic precincts of conflict of laws. This would imply a basic method along the following lines:

1. Normally, even in cases involving foreign elements, the court should be expected, as a matter of course, to apply the rule of decision found in the law of the forum.

2. When it is suggested that the law of a foreign state should furnish the rule of decision, the court should, first of all, determine the governmental policy expressed in the law of the forum. It should then inquire whether the relation of the forum to the case is such as to provide a legitimate basis for the assertion of an interest in the application of that policy. This process is essentially the familiar one of construction or interpretation. Just as we determine by that process how a statute applies in time, and how it applies to marginal domestic situations, so we may determine how it should be applied to cases involving foreign elements in order to effectuate the legislative purpose.

3. If necessary, the court should similarly determine the policy expressed by the foreign law, and whether the foreign state has an interest in the application of its policy.

4. If the court finds that the forum state has no interest in the application of its policy, but that the foreign state has, it should apply the foreign law.

5. If the court finds that the forum state has an interest in the application of its policy, it should apply the law of the forum, even though the foreign state also has an interest in the application of its contrary policy, and, a fortiori, it should apply the law of the forum if the foreign state has no such interest.

A probable by-product of such a method is the elimination of certain classical problems that are wholly artificial, being raised merely by the form of choice-of-law rules. The problem of characterization is ubiquitous in the law and can never be wholly avoided. Without choice-of-law rules, however, there would be no occasion for the specialized function of characterization as the mode of discriminating among the available prefabricated solutions of a problem. . . . And, though I make this suggestion with some trepidation, it seems clear that the problem of the renvoi would have no place at all in the analysis that has been suggested. Foreign law would be applied only when the court has determined that the foreign state has a legitimate interest in the application of its law and policy to the case at bar and that the forum has none. Hence, there can be no question of applying anything other than the internal law of the foreign state. The closest approximation to the renvoi problem that will be encountered under the suggested method is the case in which neither state has an interest in the application of its law and policy; in that event, the forum would apply its own law simply on the ground that that is the more convenient disposition. Is it possible that this is, in fact, all that is involved in the typical renvoi situation?

It will be said that it is no great trick to dispose of the characteristic problems of a system by destroying the system itself. But my basic point is that the system itself is at fault. We have invented an apparatus for the solution of problems of conflicting interest that obscures the real problems, deals with them blindly and badly, and creates problems of its own which, in their way, are as troublesome as the ones we originally set out to solve. Professor Yntema has suggested that Walter Wheeler Cook, instead of attempting to eliminate the weeds of dogma from the garden of conflict of laws, might have been well advised to reduce the whole garden to ashes, from which a phoenix might in time arise. If I may vary this classic metaphor, we would indeed do well to scrap the system of choice-of-law rules for determining the rule of decision, though without entertaining vain hopes that a new "system" will arise to take its place. We shall have to go back to the original problems, and to the hard task of dealing with them realistically by ordinary judicial methods, such as construction and interpretation, and by neglected political methods.

The suggested analysis does not imply the ruthless pursuit of self-interest by the states.

In the first place, the states of the Union are significantly restrained in the pursuit of their respective interests by the Privileges and Immunities Clause of article IV and by the Equal Protection Clause. . . .

In the second place, there is no need to exclude the possibility of rational altruism: for example, when a state has determined upon the policy of placing upon local industry all the social costs of the enterprise, it may well decide to adhere to this policy regardless of where the harm occurs and who the victim is.

In the third place, there is room for restraint and enlightenment in the determination of what state policy is and where state interests lie. An excellent example is furnished by Nebraska's experience with small-loan contracts. After first taking a position consistent with a rather rigid interpretation of its policy, denying effect to a foreign contract providing for somewhat higher interest rates than were permitted by local law, Nebraska reversed itself and conceded validity to such contracts where the law of the foreign state was "similar in principle" to the Nebraska small-loan act. The policy of Nebraska was not to protect its residents against any exaction of interest in excess of a particular rate, but to protect them against exactions in excess of a reasonable range of rates, based upon the common principle underlying such acts. This sensible approach to the delineation of policy could find wide application, especially to laws relating to formalities. It is, in fact, this kind of thinking that supports such legislation as section 7 of the Model Execution of Wills Act. This is not so much a rule of alternative reference to the law of the state of execution, or of domicile, as it is a recognition that the policies of all the states are substantially the same and may be fulfilled by compliance with any—not just a particular one—of the formal requirements. Similar analysis may be expected to yield satisfactory results in the handling of the problem of consideration in the conflict of laws concerning contracts.

I have been told that I give insufficient recognition to governmental policies other than those that are expressed in specific statutes and rules: the policy of promoting a general legal order, that of fostering amicable relations with other states, that of vindicating reasonable expectations, and so on. If this is so, it is not, I hope, because of a provincial lack of appreciation of the worth of those ideals, but because of a felt necessity to emphasize the obstacles that the present system interposes to any intelligent approach to the problem. Let us first clear away the apparatus that creates false problems and obscures the nature of the real ones. Only then can we effectively set about ameliorating the ills that arise from a diversity of laws by bringing to bear all of the resources of jurisprudence, politics, and humanism—each in its appropriate way.

Currie later restated his principles and added provisions dealing with the "disinterested forum" and objections that had been raised by others. In Currie, Comments on *Babcock v. Jackson*, 63 Colum. L. Rev. 1233, 1242-1243 (1963), he said:

> If I were asked to restate the law of conflict of laws I would decline the honor. A descriptive restatement with any sort of internal consistency is impossible. Much of the existing law, or pseudo law, of the subject is irrational; profound changes destructive of the fundamental tenets of the traditional system are gathering momentum. On the assumption that the project admits of a statement of what is reasonable in existing law and what may reasonably be desired for the future, however, I volunteer the following as a substitute for all that part of the Restatement dealing with choice of law (for the purpose of finding the rule of decision):
>
> §1. When a court is asked to apply the law of a foreign state different from the law of the forum, it should inquire into the policies expressed in the respective laws, and into the circumstances in which it is reasonable for the respective states to assert an interest in the application of

> those policies. In making these determinations the court should employ the ordinary processes of construction and interpretation.
>
> §2. If the court finds that one state has an interest in the application of its policy in the circumstances of the case and the other has none, it should apply the law of the only interested state.
>
> §3. If the court finds an apparent conflict between the interests of the two states it should reconsider. A more moderate and restrained interpretation of the policy or interest of one state or the other may avoid conflict.
>
> §4. If, upon reconsideration, the court finds that a conflict between the legitimate interests of the two states is unavoidable, it should apply the law of the forum.
>
> §5. If the forum is disinterested, but an unavoidable conflict exists between the laws of the two other states, and the court cannot with justice decline to adjudicate the case, it should apply the law of the forum—until someone comes along with a better idea.
>
> §6. The conflict of interest between states will result in different dispositions of the same problem, depending on where the action is brought. If with respect to a particular problem this appears seriously to infringe a strong national interest in uniformity of decision, the court should not attempt to improvise a solution sacrificing the legitimate interest of its own state, but should leave to Congress, exercising its powers under the full faith and credit clause, the determination of which interest shall be required to yield.
>
> The explanatory note might run a little longer. [Footnotes omitted.]

This restatement is notable for, among other things, Currie's suggestion that the forum should not automatically apply its law when it had an interest but should reconsider whether a more moderate interpretation of its law might not be feasible. Principle 3 of his "Restatement" thus represents a change from rule 5 of his earlier outline.

Currie's analysis has been enormously influential. If nothing else, it has led to a whole new terminology. Instead of determining the parties' "vested rights" under a set of specified territorial rules, the court was supposed to determine which states had "interests" through an application of the various state policies. Courts were supposed to do this by construing the statutes vying for application just as they would in a domestic case. Once they had ascertained the relevant policies or interests, the case would be seen to be either a false conflict, a true conflict, or an unprovided-for case.

Babcock and *Tooker* are generally conceded to be false conflicts because only one state had an interest. New York was interested in providing recovery for its domiciliary, while Ontario and Michigan had no interest in denying recovery simply because the accident occurred there. Currie's method requires application of the law of the only interested state.

True conflicts and unprovided-for cases involve disputes where two states and no states, respectively, have an interest in application of local law. Here, Currie's solution of applying forum law seems less than irresistible. *Neumeier* was probably an unprovided-for case because Ontario had no interest in protecting a New York defendant, while there was no reason to apply New York law to the benefit of an Ontario plaintiff. The court solved the problem through the special rules it developed. *See generally* Twerski, *Neumeier v. Kuehner:* Where Are the Emperor's Clothes?, 1 Hofstra L. Rev. 104 (1973). Currie's solution—to apply forum law—was adopted in Erwin v. Thomas, 264 Or. 454, 506 P.2d 494 (1973).

The next three cases illustrate the tribulations of courts dealing with true conflicts and unprovided-for cases.

2. Judicial Applications

a. *True Conflicts*

Lilienthal v. Kaufman

239 Or. 1, 395 P.2d 543 (1964)

DENECKE, J.

This is an action to collect two promissory notes. The defense is that the defendant maker has previously been declared a spendthrift by an Oregon court and placed under a guardianship and that the guardian has declared the obligations void. The plaintiff's counter is that the notes were executed and delivered in California, that the law of California does not recognize the disability of a spendthrift, and that the Oregon court is bound to apply the law of the place of the making of the contract. The trial court rejected plaintiff's argument and held for the defendant.

This same defendant spendthrift was the prevailing party in our recent decision in Olshen v. Kaufman, 235 Or. 423, 385 P.2d 161 (1963). In that case the spendthrift and the plaintiff, an Oregon resident, had gone into a joint venture to purchase binoculars for resale. For this purpose plaintiff had advanced moneys to the spendthrift. The spendthrift had repaid plaintiff by his personal check for the amount advanced and for plaintiff's share of the profits of such venture. The check had not been paid because the spendthrift had had insufficient funds in his account. The action was for the unpaid balance of the check.

The evidence in that case showed that the plaintiff had been unaware that Kaufman was under a spendthrift guardianship. The guardian testified that he knew Kaufman was engaging in some business and had bank accounts and that he had admonished him to cease these practices; but he could not control the spendthrift.

The statute applicable in that case and in this one is ORS 126.335:

> After the appointment of a guardian for the spendthrift, all contracts, except for necessaries, and all gifts, sales and transfers of real or personal

> estate made by such spendthrift thereafter and before the termination of the guardianship are voidable.

(Repealed 1961, ch. 344, §109, now ORS 126.280). [*I.e.*, the statute was recodified but is still in effect.] We held in that case that the voiding of the contract by the guardian precluded recovery by the plaintiff and that the spendthrift and the guardian were not estopped to deny the validity of plaintiff's claim. Plaintiff does not seek to overturn the principle of that decision but contends it has no application because the law of California governs, and under California law the plaintiff's claims are valid.

The facts here are identical to those in Olshen v. Kaufman, *supra*, except for the California locale for portions of the transaction. The notes were for the repayment of advances to finance another joint venture to sell binoculars. The plaintiff was unaware that defendant had been declared a spendthrift and placed under guardianship. The guardian, upon demand for payment by the plaintiff, declared the notes void. The issue is solely one involving the principles of conflict of laws. . . .

Before entering the choice-of-law area of the general field of conflict of laws, we must determine whether the laws of the states having a connection with the controversy are in conflict. Defendant did not expressly concede that under the law of California the defendant's obligation would be enforceable, but his counsel did state that if this proceeding were in the courts of California, the plaintiff probably would recover. We agree.

At common law a spendthrift was not considered incapable of contracting. Incapacity of a spendthrift to contract is a disability created by the legislature. California has no such legislation. In addition, the Civil Code of California provides that all persons are capable of contracting except minors, persons judicially determined to be of unsound mind, and persons deprived of civil rights. §1556. Furthermore, §1913 of the California Code of Civil Procedure provides: ". . . that the authority of a guardian . . . does not extend beyond the jurisdiction of the Government under which he was invested with his authority."

Plaintiff contends that the substantive issue of whether or not an obligation is valid and binding is governed by the law of the place of making, California. This court has repeatedly stated that the law of the place of contract "must govern as to the validity, interpretation, and construction of the contract. . . ." Restatement 408, Conflict of Laws, §332, so announced and specifically stated that "capacity to make the contract" was to be determined by the law of the place of contract. . . .

There is no need to decide that our previous statements that the law of the place of contract governs were in error. Our purpose is to state that this portion of our decision is not founded upon that principle because of our doubt that it is correct if the *only* connection of the state whose law would govern is that it was the place of making.

In this case California has more connection with the transaction than being merely the place where the contract was executed. The defendant went to San Francisco to ask the plaintiff, a California resident, for money for the defendant's venture. The money was loaned to defendant in San Francisco, and by the terms of the note, it was to be repaid to plaintiff in San Francisco.

On these facts, apart from lex loci contractus, other accepted principles of conflict of laws lead to the conclusion that the law of California should be applied. Sterrett v. Stoddard Lumber Co. rests, at least in part, on the proposition that the validity of a note is determined by the law of the place of payment. Tentative Draft No. 6, p. 30, Restatement (Second), Conflict of Laws, §332b(a) states:

> If the place of contracting and the place of performance are in the same state, the local law of this state determines the validity of the contract. . . .

. . . The place of payment, unlike the place of making, is usually not determined fortuitously. The place is usually selected by the payee and the payee normally selects his place of business or the location of his bank. The parties at the time of contract normally do not have in mind the problem of what law should govern. If they did, it is our belief that the payee would intend the law of the place of payment to be governing.

There is another conflict principle calling for the application of California law. Ehrenzweig calls it the "Rule of Validation." Ehrenzweig, Conflict of Laws 353 (1962). Mr. Justice Harlan, speaking for the majority in Kossick v. United Fruit Co., stated such a rule and cited Ehrenzweig. The "rule" is that, if the contract is valid under the law of any jurisdiction having significant connection with the contract, *i.e.,* place of making, place of performance, etc., the law of that jurisdiction validating the contract will be applied. This would also agree with the intention of the parties, if they had any intentions in this regard. They must have intended their agreement to be valid.

Thus far all signs have pointed to applying the law of California and holding the contract enforceable. There is, however, an obstacle to cross before this end can be logically reached. In Olshen v. Kaufman, *supra,* we decided that the law of Oregon, at least as applied to persons domiciled in Oregon contracting in Oregon for performance in Oregon, is that spendthrifts' contracts are voidable. Are the choice-of-law principles of conflict of laws so superior that they overcome this principle of Oregon law?

To answer this question we must determine, upon some basis, whether the interests of Oregon are so basic and important that we should not apply California law despite its several intimate connections with the transaction. The traditional method used by this court and most others is framed in the terminology of "public policy." The court decides whether or not the public policy of the forum is so strong that the law of the forum must prevail although another jurisdiction, with different laws, has more and closer contacts with the transaction. Included in "public policy" we must consider the economic and social interests of Oregon. When these factors are included in a consideration of whether the law of the forum should be applied this traditional approach is very similar to that advocated by many legal scholars. This latter theory is "that choice-of-law rules should rationally advance the policies or interests of the several states (or of the nations in the world community)."

The traditional test this court and many others have used in determining whether the public policy of the forum prevents the application of otherwise applicable conflict of laws principles is stated in the oft-quoted opinion of Mr. Justice Cardozo in Loucks v. Standard Oil Co. of New York. Foreign law will not be applied if it ". . . would violate some fundamental principle of justice, some prevalent conception of good morals, some deeprooted tradition of the common weal." . . .

How "deep rooted [the] tradition of the common weal," particularly regarding spendthrifts, is illustrated by our decisions on foreign marriages. This court has decided that Oregon's policy voiding spendthrifts' contracts is not so strong as to void an Oregon spendthrift's marriage contract made in Washington. Sturgis v. Sturgis . . . was a suit for divorce and alimony. Defendant had been declared a spendthrift by an Oregon court. The guardian refused to consent to the spendthrift's marriage. The spendthrift got married in Washington. The marriage was held valid. Although the case involved a spendthrift's contract, and therefore, is persuasive in this case, it should not be considered determinative since marriage contracts are unique and the law applicable to marriage contracts does not necessarily apply to other types of contracts. . . .

However, as previously stated, if we include in our search for the public policy of the forum a consideration of the various interests that the forum has in this litigation, we are guided by more definite criteria. In addition to the interests of the forum, we should consider the interests of the other jurisdictions which have some connection with the transaction.

Some of the interests of Oregon in this litigation are set forth in Olshen v. Kaufman, *supra*. The spendthrift's family which is to be protected by the establishment of the guardianship is presumably an Oregon family. The public authority which may be charged with the expense of supporting the spendthrift or his family, if he is permitted to go unrestrained upon his wasteful way, will probably be an Oregon public authority. These, obviously, are interests of some substance.

Oregon has other interests and policies regarding this matter which were not necessary to discuss in Olshen. As previously stated, Oregon, as well as all other states, has a strong policy favoring the validity and enforceability of contracts. This policy applies whether the contract is made and to be performed in Oregon or elsewhere.

The defendant's conduct—borrowing money with the belief that the repayment of such loan could be avoided—is a species of fraud. Oregon and all other states have a strong policy of protecting innocent persons from fraud. "The law . . . is intended as a protection to even the foolishly credulous, as against the machinations of the designedly wicked." . . .

It is in Oregon's commercial interest to encourage citizens of other states to conduct business with Oregonians. If Oregonians acquire a reputation for not honoring their agreements, commercial intercourse with Oregonians will be discouraged. If there are Oregon laws, somewhat unique to Oregon, which permit an Oregonian to escape his otherwise binding obligations, persons may well avoid commercial dealings with Oregonians.

The substance of these commercial considerations, however, is deflated by the recollection that the Oregon Legislature has determined, despite the weight of these considerations, that a spendthrift's contracts are voidable.

California's most direct interest in this transaction is having its citizen creditor paid. As previously noted, California's policy is that any creditor, in California or otherwise, should be paid even though the debtor is a spendthrift. California probably has another, although more intangible, interest involved. It is presumably to every state's benefit to have the reputation of being a jurisdiction in which contracts can be made and performance be promised with the certain knowledge that such contracts will be enforced. Both of these interests, particularly the former, are also of substance.

We have, then, two jurisdictions, each with several close connections with the transaction, and each with a substantial interest, which will be served or thwarted, depending upon which law is applied. The interests of neither jurisdiction are clearly more important than those of the other. We are of the opinion that in such a case the public policy of Oregon should prevail and the law of Oregon should be applied; we should apply that choice-of-law rule which will "advance the policies or interests of" Oregon. . . .

Courts are instruments of state policy. The Oregon legislature has adopted a policy to avoid possible hardship to an Oregon family of a spendthrift and to avoid possible expenditure of Oregon public funds which might occur if the spendthrift is required to pay his obligations. In litigation Oregon courts are the appropriate instrument to enforce this policy. The mechanical application of choice-of-law rules would be the only apparent reason for an Oregon court not advancing the interests of Oregon. The present principles of conflict of laws are not favorable to such mechanical application.

We hold that the spendthrift law of Oregon is applicable and the plaintiff cannot recover.

Judgment affirmed.

[There were also a dissent and a concurring opinion.]

b. True Conflicts vs. Apparent Conflicts

Bernkrant v. Fowler

55 Cal. 2d 588, 360 P.2d 906, 12 Cal. Rptr. 266 (1961)

TRAYNOR, J.

Plaintiffs appeal on the clerk's transcript from a judgment for defendant as executrix of the estate of John Granrud. They contend that the findings of fact do not support the judgment.

Some time before 1954 plaintiffs purchased the Granrud Garden Apartments in Las Vegas, Nevada. In 1954 the property was encumbered by a first deed of trust given to secure an installment note payable to Granrud at $200 per month plus interest. Granrud's note and deed of trust provided for subordination to a deed of trust plaintiffs might execute to secure a construction loan. In July 1954, there remained unpaid approximately $11,000 on the note secured by the first deed of trust and approximately $24,000 on the note payable to Granrud. At that time Granrud wished to buy a trailer park and asked plaintiffs to refinance their obligations and pay a substantial part of their indebtedness to him. At a meeting in Las Vegas he stated that if plaintiffs would do so, he would provide by will that any debt that remained on the purchase price at the time of his death would be canceled and forgiven. Plaintiffs then arranged for a new loan of $25,000, the most they could obtain on the property, secured by a new first deed of trust. They used the proceeds to pay the balance of the loan secured by the existing first deed of trust and $13,114.20 of their indebtedness to Granrud. They executed a new note for the balance of $9,227 owing Granrud, payable in installments of $175 per month secured by a new second deed of trust. This deed of trust contained no subordination provision. The $13,114.20 was deposited in Granrud's bank account in Covina, California and subsequently used by him to buy a trailer park. Plaintiffs incurred expenses of $800.90 in refinancing their obligations.

Granrud died testate on March 4, 1956, a resident of Los Angeles County. His will, dated January 23, 1956, was admitted to probate, and defendant was appointed executrix of his estate. His will made no provision for cancelling the balance of $6,425 due on the note at the time of his death. Plaintiffs have continued to make regular payments of principal and interest to defendant under protest.

Plaintiffs brought this action to have the note cancelled and discharged and the property reconveyed to them and to recover the amounts paid defendant after Granrud's death. The trial court concluded that the action was barred by both the Nevada and the California statute of frauds; that to remove the bar of the statutes, the action must be one for quasi-specific performance in which an heir or beneficiary under the will would be an indispensable party; and that defendant was not estopped to rely on the statutes of frauds.

Probate Code, §573 provides that

> Actions for the recovery of any property, real or personal, or for the possession thereof, or to quiet title thereto, or to enforce a lien thereon, or to determine any adverse claim thereon, and all actions founded upon contracts . . . may be maintained by and against executors and administrators in all cases in which the cause of action whether arising before or after death is one which would not abate upon the death of their respective testators or intestates. . . .

Since the present action is founded on contract and involves an adverse claim to an interest in real property, it was properly brought against the executrix pursuant to this section. Moreover, since plaintiffs do not seek to enforce a trust against any of the beneficiaries of the estate, none of the beneficiaries is an indispensable party. . . . Apart from seeking the recovery of sums paid directly to defendant to protect their interests pending the action, plaintiffs seek only a determination that pursuant to their contract with Granrud their liability on the note has been discharged and the security interest in the property thereby released. Under these circumstances defendant represents all those interested in the estate just as she would had she brought an action to enforce the note and been met with the defense that it had been discharged. . . .

Moreover, since plaintiffs do not seek a money judgment payable out of the assets of the estate but only a determination that their obligations have been discharged, they were not required to file a claim against the estate . . . and were not precluded . . . from testifying to events occurring before Granrud's death. . . .

Subdivision 6 of section 1624 of the Civil Code provides that "An agreement which by its terms is not to be performed during the lifetime of the promisor, or an agreement to devise or bequeath any property, or to make any provision for any person by will" is "invalid, unless the same, or some note or memorandum thereof, is in writing, and subscribed by the party to be charged or by his agent." *See also* Code Civ. Proc. §1973, subd. 6. Plaintiffs concede that in the absence of an estoppel, the contract in this case would be invalid under this provision if it is subject thereto. They contend, however, that only the Nevada statute of frauds is applicable and point out that the Nevada statute has no counterpart to subdivision 6. Defendant contends that the California statute of frauds is applicable, and that if it is not, the Nevada statute of frauds covering real property transactions invalidates the contract.

We have found no Nevada case in point. We believe, however, that Nevada would follow the general rule in other jurisdictions, that an oral agreement providing for the discharge of an obligation to pay money secured by an interest in real property is not within the real property provision of the statute of frauds, on the ground that the termination of the security interest is merely incidental to and follows by operation of law from the discharge of the principal obligation. . . .

We are therefore confronted with a contract that is valid under the law of Nevada but invalid under the California statute of frauds if that statute is applicable. We have no doubt that California's interest in protecting estates being probated here from false claims based on alleged oral contracts to make wills is constitutionally sufficient to justify the Legislature's making our statute of frauds applicable to all such contracts sought to be enforced against such estates. . . . The Legislature, however, is ordinarily concerned with enacting laws to govern purely local transactions, and it has not spelled out the extent to which the statute of frauds is to apply to a contract having substantial contacts with another state. Accordingly, we must determine its scope in the light of applicable principles of the law of conflict of laws. . . .

In the present case plaintiffs were residents of Nevada, the contract was made in Nevada, and plaintiffs performed it there. If Granrud was a resident of Nevada at the time the contract was made, the California statute of frauds, in the absence of a plain legislative direction to the contrary, could not reasonably be interpreted as applying to the contract even though Granrud subsequently moved to California and died there. . . . The basic policy of upholding the expectations of the parties by enforcing contracts valid under the only law apparently applicable would preclude an interpretation of our statute of frauds that would make it apply to and thus invalidate the contract because Granrud moved to California and died here. Such a case would be analogous to People v. One 1953 Ford Victoria . . . where we held that a Texas mortgagee of an automobile mortgaged in Texas did not forfeit his interest when the automobile was subsequently used to transport narcotics in California although he failed to make the character investigation of the mortgagor required by California law. A mortgagee entering into a purely local transaction in another state could not reasonably be expected to take cognizance of the law of all the other jurisdictions where the property might possibly be taken, and accordingly, the California statute requiring an investigation to protect his interest could not reasonably be interpreted to apply to such out of state mortgagees. Another analogy is found in the holding that the statute of frauds did not apply to contracts to make wills entered into before the statute was enacted. . . . Just as parties to local transactions cannot be expected to take cognizance of the law of other jurisdictions, they cannot be expected to anticipate a change in the local statute of frauds. Protection of rights growing out of valid contracts precludes interpreting the general language of the statute of frauds to destroy such rights whether the possible applicability of the statute arises from the movement of one or more of the parties across state lines or subsequent enactment of the statute. . . .

In the present case, however, there is no finding as to where Granrud was domiciled at the time the contract was made. Since he had a bank account in California at that time and died a resident here less than two years later it may be that he was domiciled here when the contract was made. Even if he was, the result should be the same. The contract was made in Nevada and performed by plaintiffs there, and it involved the refinancing of obligation arising from the sale of Nevada land and secured by interests therein. Nevada has a substantial interest in the contract and in protecting the rights of its residents who are parties thereto, and its policy is that the contract is valid and enforceable. California's policy is also to enforce lawful contracts. That policy, however, must be subordinated in the case of any contract that does not meet the requirements of an applicable statute of frauds. In determining whether the contract herein is subject to the California statute of frauds, we must consider both the policy to protect the reasonable expectations of the parties and the policy of the statute of frauds. . . . It is true that if Granrud was domiciled here at the time the contract was made, plaintiffs may have been alerted to the possibility that the California statute of frauds might apply. Since California, however, would have no interest in applying its own statute of frauds unless Granrud remained here until his death, plaintiffs were not bound to know that California's statute might ultimately be invoked against them. Unless they could rely on their own law, they would have to look to the laws of all the jurisdictions to which Granrud might move regardless of where he was domiciled when the contract was made. We conclude, therefore, that the contract herein does not fall within our statute of frauds. . . . Since there is thus no conflict between the law of California and the law of Nevada, we can give effect to the common policy of both states to enforce lawful contracts and sustain Nevada's interest in protecting its residents and their reasonable expectations growing out of a transaction substantially related to that state without subordinating any legitimate interest of this state.

The judgment is reversed.

Questions and Comments

(1) Is it clear that *Lilienthal* is a true conflict case? Would Currie have concurred because the Oregon court followed §4 of his "Restatement" or would he have dissented because the court failed to follow §3 by looking for some accommodation of the interests of Oregon and California?

Is *Bernkrant* a true conflict case? Is the dividing line between true and false conflict cases becoming more or less clear?

(2) Is there any less danger in the *Bernkrant* case than in a purely domestic California case of fraud on the estate of the deceased? If not, what justification is there for submerging the apparent California policy against enforcement of alleged oral agreements?

(3) One of the greatest points of attack on Currie's theory involved the principle contained in §4 of his "Restatement," since it disallowed a weighing of state interests. Currie's rationale was that the judge, as an appointed or elected official of a given state, had no right to declare the policy of another state to be more important. On the other hand, yielding somewhat to his critics, Currie added §3 of his "Restatement" to encourage judges to take a second look at the interests of the forum when an "apparent" conflict was found. But Currie was not altogether clear as to how far a court should go in being altruistic or in softening the interests of the forum when measured against the interests of other states.

Is there a difference between weighing and being altruistic or avoiding "ruthlessness"? Does Currie's position melt down to the self-evident proposition that a court faced with a conflicts problem should not go further in yielding on state interests than the legislature would want, but that it should not assume a totally provincial legislature? (That is self-evident, isn't it?) Under Currie's approach, is it possible (or likely) that reinspection of a state interest could produce the conviction that a weak state interest was in fact present—an interest that Currie would have the forum apply, even in the face of a strong interest of another state?

Regardless of Currie's attitude, most others have engaged in some sort of weighing. As the late Professor Ehrenzweig put it: "As far as I can see, *all* courts and writers who have professed acceptance of Currie's interest language have transformed it by indulging in that very weighing and balancing of interests from which Currie refrained." Ehrenzweig, A Counter-Revolution in Conflicts Laws? From Beale to Cavers, 80 Harv. L. Rev. 377, 389 (1966). Is this true of the *Lilienthal* case?

(4) Are you satisfied that the *Lilienthal* court did an adequate job of determining the interests of Oregon when it invoked the proposition that the legislature had already balanced the competing factors by passing the spendthrift law? Assuming, as we have since Alabama Great Southern Railroad v. Carroll, page 1 *supra,* that legislatures usually pass statutes with only domestic cases in mind, doesn't the court's reasoning in effect deny that the factors involved in a domestic spendthrift case are identical to those in an interstate conflicts case? Won't the court's approach mean that the forum will always apply its own statute if there is any basis at all for doing so?

c. Unprovided-For Cases

Hurtado v. Superior Court

11 Cal. 3d 574, 522 P.2d 666, 114 Cal. Rptr. 106 (1974)

SULLIVAN, J.

In this proceeding, petitioner Manuel Cid Hurtado seeks a writ of mandate directing respondent superior court to vacate its ruling that the applicable measure of damages in the underlying action for wrongful death was that prescribed by California law without any maximum limitation, rather than that prescribed by the law of Mexico which limits the amount of recovery. We have concluded that the trial court correctly chose the law of California. We deny the writ.

Real parties in interest, the widow and children of Antonio Hurtado (hereinafter plaintiffs) commenced against Manuel Hurtado and Jack Rexius (hereafter defendants) the underlying action for damages for wrongful death, arising out of an automobile accident occurring in Sacramento County on January 19, 1969. Plaintiffs' decedent was riding in an automobile owned and operated by his cousin, defendant Manuel Hurtado. Defendant Hurtado's vehicle, while being driven along a two-lane paved road, collided with a pickup truck, owned and operated by defendant Rexius, which was parked partially on the side of the road and partially on the pavement on which defendant Hurtado was driving. Upon impact, the truck in turn collided with an automobile parked in front of it, owned by Rexius and occupied by his son. Decedent died as a result of the collision.

At all material times plaintiffs were, and now are residents and domiciliaries of the State of Zacatecas, Mexico. Decedent, at the time of the accident, was also a resident and domiciliary of the same place and was in California temporarily and only as a visitor. All three vehicles involved in the accident were registered in California; Manuel Hurtado, Jack Rexius and the latter's son were all residents of California. Both defendants denied liability.

Defendant Hurtado moved respondent court for a separate trial of the issue whether the measure of damages was to be applied according to the law of California or the law of Mexico. The motion was granted and at the ensuing trial of this issue the court took judicial notice (Evid. Code, §§452, 453) of the relevant Mexican law prescribing a maximum limitation of damages for wrongful death. As a result it was established that the maximum amount recoverable under Mexican law would be 24,334 pesos or $1,946.72 at the applicable exchange rate of 12.5 pesos to the dollar. After submission of the issue on briefs, the trial court announced its intended decision and filed a memorandum opinion, ruling in substance that it would apply a measure of damages in accordance with California law and not Mexican law. Defendant Hurtado then sought a writ of mandate in the Court of Appeal to compel the trial court to vacate its ruling and to issue a ruling that Mexico's limitation of damages for wrongful death be applied. The Court of Appeal granted an alternative writ and thereafter issued a peremptory writ of mandate so directing the trial court. We granted a hearing in this court upon the petition of plaintiffs. . . .

In the landmark opinion authored by former Chief Justice Traynor for a unanimous court in Reich v. Purcell (1967) 67 Cal. 2d 551, 63 Cal. Rptr. 31, 432 P.2d 727 (*see* Symposium, Comments on *Reich v. Purcell* (1968) 15 U.C.L.A. L. Rev. 551-654), we renounced the prior rule, adhered to by courts for many years, that in tort actions the law of the place of the wrong was the applicable law in a California forum regardless of the issues before the court. We adopted in its place a rule requiring an analysis of the respective interests of the states involved (governmental interest approach) the objective of which is "to determine the law that most appropriately applies to the issue involved." . . .

The issue involved in the matter before us is the measure of damages in the underlying action for wrongful death. Two states or governments are implicated: (1) California—the place of the wrong, the place of defendants' domicile and residence, and the forum; and (2) Mexico—the domicile and residence of both plaintiffs and their decedent. . . .

In the case at bench, California as the forum should apply its own measure of damages for wrongful death, unless Mexico has an interest in having its measure of damages applied. Since, as we have previously explained, Mexico has no interest whatsoever in the application of its limitation of damages rule to the instant case, we conclude that the trial court correctly chose California law.

To recapitulate, we hold that where as here in a California action both this state as the forum and a foreign state (or country) are potentially concerned in a question of choice of law with respect to an issue in tort and it appears that the foreign state (or country) has no interest whatsoever in having its own law applied, California as the forum should apply California law. Since this was done, we deny the writ.

Nevertheless, although our holding disposes of the mandamus proceeding before us, we deem it advisable to consider the argument addressed by defendant to the interest of California in applying its measure of damages for wrongful death. We do this because the argument reflects a serious misreading of *Reich* which apparently has not been confined to the parties before us.

First, defendant contends the California has no interest in applying its measure of damages in this case because Reich v. Purcell determined that the interest of a state in the law governing damages in wrongful death actions is "in determining the distribution of proceeds to the beneficiaries and that interest extends only to local decedents and beneficiaries." Decedent and plaintiffs were residents of Mexico and not "local decedents and beneficiaries" in California. Therefore, so the argument runs, California has *no* interest whatever in how plaintiff survivors, residents of Mexico, should be compensated for the wrongful death of their decedent, also a resident of Mexico, and conversely Mexico *does* have an interest.

Defendant's reading of *Reich* is inaccurate. It confuses two completely independent state interests: (1) the state interest involved in *creating* a cause of action for wrongful death so as to provide *some* recovery; and (2) the state interest involved in *limiting* the *amount* of that recovery. In *Reich* this court carefully separated these two state interests, although it referred to them in the same paragraph. The state interest in creating a cause of action for wrongful death is in "determining the distribution of proceeds to the beneficiaries"; the state interest in limiting damage is "to avoid the imposition of excessive financial burdens on them [defendants]."

In the case at bench, the entire controversy revolves about the choice of an appropriate rule of decision on the issue of the proper *measure* of damages; there is no contention that plaintiffs are not entitled under the applicable rules of decision to *some* recovery in wrongful death. The Mexican rule is a rule limiting damages. Thus, the interest of Mexico at stake is one aimed at protecting resident defendants in wrongful death actions and, as previously explained, is inapplicable to this case, because defendants are not Mexican residents. Mexico's interest in limiting damages is not concerned with providing compensation for decendent's beneficiaries. It is Mexico's interest in creating wrongful death actions which is concerned with distributing proceeds to the beneficiaries and that issue has not been raised in the case at bench.

The creation of wrongful death actions "insofar as plaintiffs are concerned" is directed toward compensating decedent's beneficiaries. California does not have this interest in applying its wrongful death statute here because plaintiffs are residents of Mexico. However, the creation of wrongful death actions is not concerned solely with plaintiffs. As to defendants the state interest in creating wrongful death actions is to deter conduct. We made this clear in *Reich:* "Missouri [as the place of wrong] is concerned with conduct within her borders and as to such conduct she has the predominant interest of the states involved." We went on to observe that the predominant interest of the state of the place of the wrong in conduct was not in rules concerning the *limitation* of damages: "Limitations of damages for wrongful death, however, have little or nothing to do with conduct. They are concerned not with how people should behave but with how survivors should be compensated." Since it was not involved in *Reich*, we left implicit in our conclusion the proposition that the predominant interest of the state of the place of the wrong in conduct is in the creation of a cause of action for wrongful death.

It is manifest that one of the primary purposes of a state in creating a cause of action in the heirs for the wrongful death of the decedent is to deter the kind of conduct within its borders which wrongfully takes life. It is also abundantly clear that a cause of action for wrongful death without any limitation as to the amount of recoverable damages strengthens the deterrent aspect of the civil sanction: "the sting of unlimited recovery . . . more effectively penalize[s] the culpable defendant and deter[s] it and others similarly situated from such future conduct." Therefore when the defendant is a resident of California and the tortious conduct giving rise to the wrongful death action occurs here, California's deterrent policy of full compensation is clearly advanced by application of its own law. This is precisely the situation in the case at bench. California has a decided interest in applying its own law to California defendants who allegedly caused wrongful death within its borders. On the other hand, a state which prescribes a limitation on the measure of damages modifies the sanction imposed by a countervailing concern to protect local defendants against excessive financial burdens for the conduct sought to be deterred.

It is important, therefore, to recognize the three distinct aspects of a cause of action for wrongful death: (1) compensation for survivors, (2) deterrence of conduct and (3) limitation, or lack thereof, upon the damages recoverable. Reich v. Purcell recognizes that all three aspects are primarily local in character. The first aspect, insofar as *plaintiffs* are concerned, reflects the state's interest in providing for compensation and in determining the distribution of the proceeds, said interest extending only to local decedents and local beneficiaries; the second, insofar as *defendants* are concerned, reflects the state's interest in deterring conduct, said interest extending to all persons present within its border; the third, insofar as *defendants* are concerned, reflects the state's interest in protecting resident defendants from excessive financial burdens. In making a choice of law, these three aspects of wrongful death must be carefully separated. The key step in this process is delineating the issue to be decided. . . .

Defendant's final contention is that California has no interest in extending to out-of-state residents greater rights than are afforded by the state of residence, citing Ryan v. Clark Equipment Co., *supra.* Defendant urges seemingly as an absolute choice of law principle that plaintiffs in wrongful death actions are not entitled to recover more than they would have recovered under the law of the state of their residence. In effect defendant argues that the state of plaintiffs' residence has an overriding interest in denying their own residents unlimited recovery.

Limitations of damages express no such state interest. A policy of limiting recovery in wrongful death actions "does not reflect a preference that widows and orphans should be denied full recovery." . . .

Because Mexico has no interest in applying its limitation of damages in wrongful death actions to nonresident defendants or in denying full recovery to its resident plaintiffs, the trial court both as the forum, and as an interested state, correctly looked to its own law.

The alternative writ of mandate is discharged and the petition for a peremptory writ is denied.

Questions and Comments

(1) Is there any way to take seriously the court's contention that California's refusal to place a limitation on wrongful death liability represented an affirmative policy of deterrence? Is someone likely to be (a) aware of the law and (b) insufficiently aware of the dangerousness of his own behavior to be deterred by application of the law when he is not also deterred by the danger to his own life? Even if the California refusal to place a limitation on wrongful death recoveries serves some deterrent purpose, is that deterrence likely to be diminished when the rule is not applied to victims from states with limitations? That is, is the driver-to-be-deterred likely to determine the domicile of his victim before making a decision on how careful to be?

(2) The clue to "solving" both true conflicts and unprovided-for cases would seem to be to turn them into false conflicts, a food that interest analysis can easily digest. With true conflicts, this means making one of the interests go away (as in *Bernkrant*); the artificiality of some courts' ingenious efforts to turn true conflicts into false ones is dissected in Singer, Facing Real Conflicts, 24 Cornell Intl. L.J. 197 (1991). With unprovided-for cases this means uncovering a new interest to fill the void. Two likely sources of interests are territorially triggered conduct regulating interests (as in *Hurtado*) and interests in burdening locals even when they are acting outside the territory. Recall, for example, the "interest," alluded to in Schultz v. Boy Scouts of America, page 200 *supra,* that New Jersey was said to have in imposing the burden of its no-recovery rule even though the New Jersey plaintiff was injured in New York.

Such interests are convenient when they turn unprovided-for cases into false conflicts. But won't recognizing them risk turning some false conflicts into true conflicts? If two Ontario residents are driving in New York when an accident occurs, is this a true conflict because New York has an interest in deterring unsafe driving by allowing recovery by a guest against a host? Doesn't the *Hurtado* analysis suggest as much?

(3) Another possible approach to unprovided-for cases is based upon Professor Robert Sedler's discussion of *Neumeier.* Sedler says that while neither state has an interest in applying its law on the issue of guest-host immunity, the two states have a common policy of compensating the victims of negligence. That makes *Neumeier* an "easy case." Whether the policy of the guest statute is to protect drivers from ungrateful guests, to protect insurance companies from fraud, or to keep insurance rates down, neither state has an interest in applying such a policy in favor of this particular defendant. Thus, the common policy of compensation should be applied. Sedler, Interstate Accidents and the Unprovided for Case: Reflections on *Neumeier v. Kuehner,* 1 Hofstra L. Rev. 125, 137-139 (1973). In *Hurtado,* one might discern a similar shared policy of allowing compensation.

Isn't Sedler getting off the hook a bit too easily? If the "ingratitude" policy is the right one, doesn't it reflect a desire not only to protect the defendant but also to keep the plaintiff from recovery on the grounds that one should not bite the hand that feeds? Dean Ely's criticism of Sedler's argument is that Ontario had no policy (shared or otherwise) for allowing a New Yorker to recover under a cause of action that it refused to recognize, while New York policy simply did not extend to Ontario plaintiffs at all. Ely, Choice of Law and the State's Interest in Protecting Its Own, 23 Wm. & Mary L. Rev. 173, 202-203 (1981). Does this theory of "common policies" make any sense?

3. Recent Theoretical Criticisms of Interest Analysis

Almost from its inception, interest analysis has been subject to criticism from the academy. The critics have recently gathered speed, however, and supporters of interest analysis have come to its defense. There are those who find the whole debate of little consequence, *see* Sterk, The Marginal Relevance of Choice of Law Theory, 142 U. Pa. L. Rev. 949 (1994), but by and large the criticisms and responses continue unabated. There are several different lines of attack, which fall into roughly three categories. The first we have already seen; namely, that interest analysis has no good resolution of true conflicts. This is probably the least fundamental, because it accepts Currie's basic definition of interests and his identification of false conflicts. We have outlined his solution to true conflicts above, and our discussion below of other modern theories will describe the resolution that other authors have proposed.

The second criticism acknowledges the role that "policies" might play in choice-of-law analysis, but denies that Currie's methods for identifying interests are appropriate. In particular, a number of authors disagree with

Currie's suggestion that a state has an interest in applying its law when doing so would protect a local defendant or compensate a local plaintiff. *See, e.g.*, Corr, Interest Analysis and Choice of Law: The Dubious Dominance of Domicile, 4 Utah L. Rev. 651 (1983). Professor Ely has been an especially forceful proponent of the idea that it is wrong to define a state's interests this way. Ely, Choice of Law and the State's Interest in Protecting Its Own, 23 Wm. & Mary L. Rev. 173 (1981). For one thing, this definition of "interests" seems somewhat discriminatory—a problem that we will return to in our discussion of constitutional doctrine in Chapter 3; for another, defining interests this way has certain surprising consequences. As Ely notes, this definition of interests turns all common domicile cases into false conflicts (as it does all cases where the parties are from different states with identical laws). Ely, *supra,* at pages 206-207. The reason is that if only domiciliary factors can trigger interests and if the parties share a domicile, there is only one state that can have an interest. False conflicts are easy to resolve because once a court decides to disregard all connecting variables other than domicile, and if all remaining variables point toward the same state, the answer is obvious.

When the parties are from states with different laws, then the case is either a true conflict or an unprovided-for case, depending on whether each party prefers home-state law (as in *Lilienthal*) or each party prefers the law of the other party's home state (as in *Hurtado*). Currie's original solution was to apply forum law, and his whole method can therefore be summarized in a single sentence: In cases of shared domicile, apply that jurisdiction's law, but otherwise apply forum law. If one starts with a presumption that local law is designed to benefit local people, then one does not need to investigate policies at length, or even to know the content of the competing laws. One can select which jurisdiction's law to apply based on only one fact: whether the litigants come from states with the identical legal rule. Brilmayer, Rights, Fairness, and Choice of Law, 99 Yale L.J. 1277, 1315 (1989).

Allowing greater flexibility in the definition of interests presents its own problems, however. The result is that the method may be so amorphous that almost any contact can be used to explain why forum law applies. One European author who started with an initial inclination in favor of interest analysis concluded after surveying numerous tort cases that the method was unworkable. The legislation itself gives no clue as to issues of territorial scope, and the policies that courts uncover in their attempts to interpret statutes are often designed simply to further preconceived results. T. de Boer, Beyond Lex Loci Delicti (1987). "Due to the lack of objective criteria for interest identification," de Boer concludes ". . . interest analysis can never be the 'rational' choice of law method it aspires to be." *Id.* at 478. *See also* Maier, Finding the Trees in Spite of the Metaphorist: the Problem of State Interests in Choice of Law, 56 Alb. L. Rev. 753 (1993).

Obviously, much of the work in analyzing governmental interests is done by making such assumptions about what factors give rise to interests in the first place. Professor Robert Sedler denies that interest analysis defines "interests" in terms of whether the benefiting party is a local resident, but then adds that "[i]n the typical accident case, the relevant interests are compensatory and protective ones, and a state's interest in applying its law in order to implement those policies indeed depends on a party's residence in that state, *since the consequences of the accident and of imposing or denying liability will be felt by the parties and the insurer in the parties' home state.*" Sedler, Interest Analysis and Forum Preference in the Conflict of Laws: A Response to the "New Critics," 34 Mercer L. Rev. 593, 620 (1983) (emphasis in the original). Does this adequately rebut the complaint?

The third line of criticism of interest analysis goes beyond the argument that the definition of interests incorporates a preference for local residents. It attacks the notion that the goal of modern choice-of-law theory is, and ought to be, the effectuation of legislative policy. On the question of whether the method actually effectuates legislative policy, it has been argued that, as carried out, Currie's notion of interests did not reflect *legislative* policy but, rather, Currie's own peculiar normative vision about how far legislation ought to reach. Brilmayer, Interest Analysis and the Myth of Legislative Intent, 78 Mich. L. Rev. 392 (1980). *See also* Borchers, Professor Brilmayer and the Holy Grail, 1991 Wis. L. Rev. 465, 473 (1991). Sedler responds by explaining the idea of legislative policy as follows:

> One reason that the critics of interest analysis have seen such difficulty in determining the policies behind the laws of the involved states is their failure to distinguish between legislative purpose and legislative motivation. Legislative purpose refers to the objectives a law is designed to accomplish, while legislative motivation may be defined as factors stimulating enactment of a law. For example, if the legislature imposes a limit on the amount recoverable for wrongful death, its purpose obviously is to limit damages awards in such cases, and the policy reflected in such a law is to protect defendants and insurers from what the legislature considers to be excessive liability. Motivation, however, may vary from one legislator to the next. Some may have feared excessive verdicts in wrongful death cases and believed that such verdicts would be unjust. Others may have been concerned about rising insurance premiums. Others simply may have responded to the pressures of the insurance lobby.
>
> In determining, both in the conflicts and non-conflicts situation, the policy behind a rule of substantive law, what is relevant is legislative purpose, not legislative motivation. That purpose can be determined from the provisions of the law itself, viewed functionally and in relation to other laws of the state dealing with the same subject. As the example above indicates, a collective motivation cannot be ascribed to the legislature, but a collective purpose can. That purpose must be found in the provisions of the law that the legislature has enacted. It is this collective purpose that determines the policy behind a rule of substantive law under interest analysis.

Sedler, The Governmental Interest Approach to Choice of Law: An Analysis and Reformulation, 25 UCLA L. Rev. 181, 197 (1977). Does this mean that any actual legislative preferences about the intended territorial scope of a statute are irrelevant in determining whether an interest exists? *See* Weintraub, Interest Analysis in the Conflict of Laws as an Application of Sound Legal Reasoning, 35 Mercer L. Rev. 629, 631 (1984), Posnak, Choice of Law: Interest Analysis and Its "New Crits," 36 Am. J. Comp. L. 681, 687 n.42 (1988). If so, then how is the process of ascertaining "interests" simply the usual domestic process of statutory construction, as Currie asserted?

The most articulate attempt to reformulate governmental interest analysis is found in the prolific writings of Professor Larry Kramer. Kramer begins with one of Currie's central assumptions: that determining the proper territorial scope of a statute is not an essentially different enterprise from determining the statute's scope in domestic controversies. From this assumption follow the usual categories of false conflict, true conflict, and unprovided-for case (or, as he puts it, cases where one law provides a right, two laws provide a right, or no law provides a right). *See generally* Kramer, Rethinking Choice of Law, 90 Colum. L. Rev. 277 (1990). His analysis departs from Currie's in that he takes a much broader and more open-minded view about which connecting factors might give rise to a reason for applying local law. In particular, as will be discussed at page 312 *infra,* he advises the court to defer to another state's definition of its own interests, even when that state defines its interests in old-fashioned territorial terms. Kramer is therefore not bound to rigid notions about statutory application being tied to providing benefits for locals. He also rejects Currie's argument that forum law should presumptively apply, unless affirmative arguments can be given for displacing it. Interest Analysis and the Presumption of Forum Law, 56 U. Chi. L. Rev. 1301 (1989). His suggestions have not yet found widespread acceptance among interest analysts.

We will return to the problems of domicile and of ascertaining interests; for these problems are common to other modern choice-of-law theory as well. See page 303 *infra.* On the jurisprudential issue of whether choice of law ought simply to address the implementation of legislative substantive policy, *see* Dane, Vested Rights, Vestedness, and Choice of Law, 96 Yale L.J. 1191 (1987); Brilmayer, Rights, Fairness, and Choice of Law, 99 Yale L.J. 1277 (1989). For a defense that modern choice of law should, and does, concern itself with which state will experience the consequences of the judgment, *see* Weintraub, An Approach to Choice of Law that Focuses on Consequences, 56 Alb. L. Rev. 701 (1993).

4. A Short Note on Interest Analysis in Other Nations

Other countries have choice-of-law problems, of course, to at least as great a degree as the United States, although the problems mainly concern choice between the laws of different nations rather than the laws of different states. In many countries, there is keen academic and judicial attention to developments in choice-of-law theory, and the events of the last few decades in the United States have provoked a fair amount of controversy.

While generalizations are made at one's peril, it is fair to say that most European countries (and many countries in other parts of the world) start with a substantial fundamental commitment to what Americans would view as traditional choice-of-law rules. The reason has nothing to do with protection of "vested rights," for European countries are more likely to have been influenced philosophically by Savigny's theory of "seat of the relationship."[1] Instead, it has, in part, to do with the fact that many conflicts problems in other countries are dealt with through treaty or convention; the process of drafting a treaty or convention encourages its authors to identify specific factors in advance and to specify how they should be taken into account—to formulate rules, in other words. In addition, the civil law system on which many European legal institutions are grounded is said to be more suspicious of assigning a judge the flexibility and discretion to set policy in what might be thought an essentially ad hoc manner. Finally, European legal systems are less likely to rely on legislative history, a tool that might prove particularly useful in applying modern policy theory. *See generally* Jayme, The American Conflicts Revolution and its Impact on European Private International Law, in T. de Boer (ed.), Forty Years On: The Evolution of Postwar Private International Law in Europe (1990).

The new methods have nonetheless provoked considerable interest around the world. A Canadian author, Professor William Maslechko, concedes that the new methods are relatively foreign to Canadian jurisprudence, but believes that Canadian courts are increasingly approaching choice-of-law problems in a functional manner, and he applauds this development. Revolution and Counterrevolution: An Examination of the Continuing Debate over 'Interest Analysis' in the United States and its Relevance to Canadian Conflict of Laws, 44 U. Toronto L. Rev. 57 (1986). Another enthusiast is Professor Strikwerda of the Netherlands. "Interest analysis," he writes, "is a well-founded and rational approach to the choice-of-law problem." Interest Analysis: No More than a 'Protest Song'?, in Mathilde Sumampouw, Law and Reality: Essays on National and International Procedural Law 301 (1992). "Clearly, the interest approach to choice of law has been the catalyst of the renovation in this field of law, even in Europe. And in my view benefits can still be reaped from interest analysis in present-day choice-of-law problems." *Id.* at 313. This is not to say that the Dutch view is uniformly positive; Professor Ted de Boer's exhaustive study of choice of law, Beyond Lex Loci Delicti (1987), which studied American practice in great detail, was noticeably less positive.

---

1. F. Von Savigny, System des Heutigen Romischen Rechts (1849).

A French author states that the influence of American choice-of-law theory is "incontestable." Hanotiau, The American Conflicts Revolution and European Tort Choice of Law Thinking, in Symposium, 30 Am. J. Comp. L. 1, 713 (1982). He includes the Restatement of Conflicts Second and other modern theories in this assessment.

> The new American approach to tort choice of law has raised great interest in most European countries. Various courses and monographs have been devoted at least in part to the subject. Many scholars have found in the new theories the necessary inspiration to criticize their own conflicts provisions and to propose a more flexible approach. The lex loci remains the general rule, but its displacement is advocated in cases where the consequences of the wrongful act belong to the legal sphere of another country, for instance, where the parties share a common nationality and/or there was a special relation between them before the accident took place.

30 Am. J. Comp. L. at 88. Yet his conclusion is not shared universally. Another author, also French, concludes that the inroads modern American choice-of-law methods have made on traditional Continental thinking is "more limited than may generally be believed." Audit, A Continental Lawyer Looks at Contemporary American Choice-of-Law Principles, 27 Am. J. Comp. L. 589, 589 (1979). His reasoning is that modern methods were quite a change in the United States, where theory had been dominated by Beale; but on the Continent, the theories of Savigny were considerably closer to the modern methods from the very beginning, so that no revolution was necessary.

Perhaps not surprisingly, several authors have concluded that the modern methodology works better in torts than in other areas of the law. Professor Fawcett states that it is "only in tort choice of law that it has found favour in England." Is American Governmental Interest Analysis the Solution to English Tort Choice of Law Problems?, 31 Intl. & Comp. L.Q. 150, 150 (1982). Other authors also express caution about how widely useful interest analysis can be.

> Unlike the more extreme proponents of interest analysis, such as Brainerd Currie himself, the present writer would not favour its adoption by way of total replacement of the traditional system of 'mechanical' choice-of-law rules which select a particular country whose law is to govern, more or less regardless of the content of the chosen law. Rather, it is submitted that interest analysis should be used as a corrective device, in order to prevent over-board or unduly single-minded mechanical choice of law rules from producing particularly unwelcome results.

Lasok and Stone, Conflict of Laws in the European Community 392 (1987). Since modern methods first found acceptance in tort cases in this country, and continue to be somewhat less influential outside that area to this day, these outside observers seem to share the same reservations that motivate American judges and academics.

Yet some foreign authors seem to feel that what works in the United States is simply not likely to work for the rest of the world. One South African writer states flatly that the modern methods are "not for export elsewhere." Forsyth, Private International Law 50 (1990). Another writes,

> As far as the conflict of laws of contracts is concerned, it has not been possible for me to trace any influential or significant follower in Europe of the new American theories. I have not found any writer of renown who in this field has seriously advocated replacement of the traditional structure of the conflict-of-law rule with the new structures proposed by Cavers, Currie and other Americans of the same schools. Why have these ideas had so little impact upon European thinking? Although a number of European jurists may think in grooves, they are not *all* incapable of accepting new ideas.
>
> The explanation is probably that the new theories have been difficult to apply to the European situation.

Lando, New American Choice-of-Law Principles and the European Conflict of Laws of Contracts, 30 Am. J. Comp. L. 19, 25 (1982). He points to the familiar difficulties: the inability to determine the underlying policies and to attribute to them a territorial scope, the failure to take multistate and international policies into account, and the like. Another European author agrees:

> The difficulties about all this are formidable. The search for the 'just solution' on these lines may be entirely chimerical. There may be no particular policies behind, say, some of the rules of the law of tort of a country, and no legislation either. . . . The fairly predictable result of such a search is that the lex fori would most probably be applied. . . . It may not be too difficult for a court in the United States to proceed on the lines suggested by these American writers. . . . [But] it is obvious that the task of an English court in following these doctrines would be very much more difficult, if not impossible.
>
> In any event, the House of Lords, when pressed to adopt the 'new' tort conflict rules as propounded in the United States, proved singularly unwilling to do so.

Collier, Conflict of Laws 356-358 (1987).

Two Australian authors have, perhaps, the ultimate put-down.

> The need for [modernizing choice of law] has led to a welter of views from American writers among which are to be found emphasis on policy comparisons and evaluations, on 'governmental interests,' on the reconciliation of conflicts interests within a framework of 'conflicts justice,' on 'most significant contact,' on 'principles of preference' and so on. Many writers

> are fond of the word 'functional' and many seem to feel the job of solution is done once they have used this magic word and verbally discarded 'conceptual thinking' and 'mechanistic processes.' One is disposed to think that some kind of jumping on the band-waggon is involved.

Sykes and Prykes, Australian Private International Law 203 (3d ed. 1991).

C. Comparative Impairment

Most, but not all, current commentators accept Currie's concept of and resolution of false conflict cases. Though there are cases, as we have seen, that are not on one side or the other of a thin bright line, there are other cases in which there is simply no conflict between state policies. Thus, thinking since Currie has concentrated on solutions to the true conflict case. Currie initially said the law of the forum should be applied in a true conflict. Although he did not express his reasons in such a way, an element of game theory seems to run through Currie's thinking: If someone could propose a solution to the true conflict case which would, in the long run, advance the interests of all states, such a solution would be desirable. But in the absence of such a solution, the only proper thing for a judge to do is to be "true to his or her state." Approaches that categorize state law as good or bad must be rejected because they would elevate the judge above the local legislature. Similarly, approaches that weigh the importance of state law are rejected because it is improper for a judge to make the political decision that the interests of one's own state are less important than those of another.

Professor William Baxter produced a modification of interest analysis called "comparative impairment."* It directs a court in the true conflict situation to apply the law of the state whose policies would be most impaired (if such is determinable) by rejection of its rules. Weighing of the interests is rejected; but weighing of the harm that would be caused by refusing to carry out interests in particular cases is not. In the long run, such an approach, if engaged in by all jurisdictions, should result in benefit to each, since each will have "given in" in cases where the harm to its own interests was minimal, and "won" in cases where the harm would have been greater.

There has been increasing academic attention to the argument that all states might be made better off if courts resolved true conflicts by applying the law of the state with a greater concern. *See, e.g.*, Brilmayer, Conflict of

* Baxter, Choice of Law and the Federal System, 16 Stan. L. Rev. 1 (1963).

Laws: Foundations and Future Directions chapter 4 (1991); Kramer, Rethinking Choice of Law, 90 Colum. L. Rev. 277, 315 (1990). These arguments tend to rely on game theory analogies (such as to the game of Prisoners' Dilemma) and on the possibility of achieving mutual gains through cooperation; Currie, unlike Baxter and these new proposals, seemed to see choice of law in true conflict cases as a "zero sum game." Others doubt that the game theory analogy is appropriate; *see, e.g.*, Borchers, Professor Brilmayer and the Holy Grail, 1991 Wis. L. Rev. 465, 479 (1991); Weinberg, Against Comity, 80 Geo. L.J. 53, 55 (1991).

Bernhard v. Harrah's Club

16 Cal. 3d 313, 546 P.2d 719, 128 Cal. Rptr. 215 (1976)

SULLIVAN, J.

Plaintiff's complaint, containing only one count, alleged in substance the following: Defendant Harrah's Club, a Nevada corporation, owned and operated gambling establishments in the State of Nevada in which intoxicating liquors were sold, furnished to the public and given away for consumption on the premises. Defendant advertised for and solicited in California the business of California residents at such establishments knowing and expecting that many California residents would use the public highways in going to and from defendant's drinking and gambling establishments.

On July 24, 1971, Fern and Philip Myers, in response to defendant's advertisements and solicitations, drove from their California residence to defendant's gambling and drinking club in Nevada, where they stayed until the early morning hours of July 25, 1971. During their stay, the Myers were served numerous alcoholic beverages by defendant's employees, progressively reaching a point of intoxication rendering them incapable of safely driving a car. Nonetheless defendant continued to serve and furnish the Myers alcoholic beverages.

While still in this intoxicated state, the Myers drove their car back to California. Proceeding in a northeasterly direction on Highway 49, near Nevada City, California, the Myers' car, driven negligently by a still intoxicated Fern Myers, drifted across the center line into the lane of oncoming traffic and collided head-on with plaintiff Richard A. Bernhard, a resident of California, who was then driving his motorcycle along said highway. As a result of the collision plaintiff suffered severe injuries. Defendant's sale and furnishing of alcoholic beverages to the Myers, who were intoxicated to the point of being unable to drive safely, was negligent and was the proximate cause of the plaintiff's injuries in the ensuing automobile accident in California for which plaintiff prayed $100,000 in damages.

Defendant filed a general demurrer to the first amended complaint. In essence it was grounded on the following contentions: that Nevada law denies recovery against a tavern keeper by a third person for injuries proximately caused by the former by selling or furnishing alcoholic beverages to an intoxicated patron who inflicts the injuries on the latter; that Nevada law governed since the alleged tort was committed by defendant in Nevada; and that section 25602 of the California Business and Professions Code which established the duty necessary for liability under our decision in Vesely v. Sager was inapplicable to a Nevada tavern. The trial court sustained the demurrer without leave to amend and entered a judgment of dismissal. This appeal followed.

We face a problem in the choice of law governing a tort action. As we have made clear on other occasions, we no longer adhere to the rule that the law of the place of the wrong is applicable in California forum regardless of the issues before this court. (Hurtado v. Superior Court.) Rather we have adopted in its place a rule requiring an analysis of the respective interests of the states involved—the objective of which is "to determine the law that most appropriately applies to the issue involved." (*Hurtado, supra.*)

The issue involved in the case at bench is the civil liability of defendant tavern keeper to plaintiff, a third person, for injuries allegedly caused by the former by selling and furnishing alcoholic beverages in Nevada to intoxicated patrons who subsequently injured plaintiff in California. Two states are involved: (1) California—the place of plaintiff's residence and domicile, the place where he was injured, and the forum; and (2) Nevada—the place of defendant's residence and the place of the wrong.

We observe at the start that the laws of the two states—California and Nevada—applicable to the issue involved are not identical. California imposes liability on tavern keepers in this state for conduct such as here alleged. In Vesely v. Sager, *supra,* this court rejected the contention that

> civil liability for tavern keepers should be left to future legislative action. . . . First, liability has been denied in cases such as the one before us solely because of the judicially created rule that the furnishing of alcoholic beverages is not the proximate cause of injuries resulting from intoxication. As demonstrated, *supra,* this rule is patently unsound and totally inconsistent with the principles of proximate cause established in other areas of negligence law. . . . Second, the Legislature has expressed its intention in this area with the adoption of Evidence Code section 669, and Business and Professions Code section 25602. . . . It is clear that Business and Professions Code section 25602 [making it a misdemeanor to sell to an obviously intoxicated person] is a statute to which this presumption [of negligence, Evidence Code section 669] applies and that the policy expressed in the statute is to promote safety of the people of California. . . .

Nevada on the other hand refuses to impose such liability. In Hamm v. Carson City Nuggett, Inc., the court held it would create neither common law liability nor liability based on the criminal statute banning sale of alcoholic beverages to a person who is drunk, because "if civil liability is to be imposed, it should be accomplished by legislative act after appropriate surveys, hearings, and investigations to ascertain the need for it and the expected consequences to follow." It is noteworthy that in *Hamm* the Nevada court in relying on the common law rule denying liability cited our decision in Cole v. Rush, later overruled by us in *Vesely* to the extent that it was inconsistent with that decision.

Although California and Nevada, the two "involved states," have different laws governing the issue presented in the case at bench, we encounter a problem in selecting the applicable rule of law only if *both* states have an interest in having their respective laws applied. "[G]enerally speaking the forum will apply its own rule of decision unless a party litigant timely invokes the law of a foreign state. In such event he must demonstrate that the latter rule of decision will further the interest of the foreign state and therefore that it is an appropriate one for the forum to apply to the case before it." (*Hurtado, supra.*)

Defendant contends that Nevada has a definite interest in having its rule of decision applied in this case in order to protect its resident tavern keepers like defendant from being subjected to a civil liability which Nevada has not imposed either by legislative enactment or decisional law. It is urged that in Hamm v. Carson City Nuggett, *supra,* the Supreme Court of Nevada clearly delineated the policy underlying denial of civil liability of tavern keepers who sell to obviously intoxicated patrons:

> Those opposed to extending liability point out that to hold otherwise would subject the tavern owner to ruinous exposure every time he poured a drink and would multiply litigation endlessly in a claim-conscious society. Every liquor vendor visited by the patron who became intoxicated would be a likely defendant in subsequent litigation flowing from the patron's wrongful conduct. . . . Judicial restraint is a worthwhile practice when the proposed new doctrine may have implications far beyond the perception of the court asked to declare it. They urge that if civil liability is to be imposed, it should be accomplished by legislative act after appropriate surveys, hearings, and investigations. . . . We prefer this point of view.

Accordingly defendant argues that the Nevada rule of decision is the appropriate one for the forum to apply.

Plaintiff on the other hand points out that California also has an interest in applying its own rule of decision to the case at bench. California imposes on tavern keepers civil liability to third parties injured by persons to whom the tavern keeper has sold alcoholic beverages when they are obviously intoxicated "for the purpose of protecting members of the general public from injuries to person and damage to property resulting from the excessive use of intoxicating liquor." (Vesely v. Sager, *supra.*) California, it is urged, has a special interest in affording this protection to all California residents injured in California.

Thus, since the case at bench involves a California resident (plaintiff) injured in this state by intoxicated drivers and a Nevada resident tavern keeper (defendant) which served alcoholic beverages to them in Nevada, it is clear that each state has an interest in the application of its respective law of liability and nonliability. It goes without saying that these interests conflict. Therefore, unlike . . . Hurtado v. Superior Court, *supra,* where we were faced with "false conflicts," in the instant case for the first time since applying a governmental interest analysis as a choice of law doctrine in *Reich,* we are confronted with a "true" conflicts case. We must therefore determine the appropriate rule of decision in a controversy where each of the states involved has a legitimate but conflicting interest in applying its own law in respect to the civil liability of tavern keepers.

The search for the proper resolution of a true conflicts case, while proceeding within orthodox parameters of governmental interest analysis, has generated much scholarly examination and discussion. The father of the governmental interest approach,[2] Professor Brainerd Currie, originally took the position that in a true conflicts situation the law of the forum should always be applied. (Currie, Selected Essays on Conflicts of Laws (1963) p. 184.) However, upon further reflection, Currie suggested that when under the governmental interest approach a preliminary analysis reveals an apparent conflict of interest upon the forum's assertion of its own rule of decision, the forum should reexamine its policy to determine if a more restrained interpretation of it is more appropriate.

---

2. Traditionally the search for choice-of-law rules focused upon the interests of the immediate parties to the action in terms of their private rights. Thus, it concentrated "upon the same factors that would be dispositive in a similar case wholly internal to a single state. I cannot escape the conclusion that a search so oriented must prove unrewarding. Every choice-of-law case involves several parties, each of whom would prevail if the internal law of one rather than another state were applied. Each party is 'right,' 'worthy,' and 'deserving' and 'ought in all fairness' to prevail under one of the competing bodies of law and in the view of one of the competing groups of lawmakers. Fact situations which differ only in that they are internal to a single state have been assessed by the different groups of lawmakers, and each has reached a different value judgment on the rule best calculated to serve the overall interest of its community. If attention is confined to the circumstances of the immediate parties, the conflict between the internal laws and between the value judgments they are intended to implement cannot be resolved by the judge unless he is prepared to impose still another value judgment upon the controversy. . . .

"These difficulties can be avoided if normative criteria can be found which relate to the very aspects of a conflicts case that distinguish it from an analogous internal case. That such criteria can be elaborated in many, if not all, conflicts cases has been demonstrated by several writers who have urged that conflicts cases be resolved on the basis of the governmental interests involved. . . .

"[T]he process of resolving choice cases is necessarily one of allocating spheres of legal control among states. His [Professor Currie] thesis, like mine, is that the process of allocation should not be performed unconsciously, that the private interests in choice cases are necessarily in balance, and that the cases can be decided by viewing them as instances of conflicting states interests rather than of conflicting private interests." (Baxter, Choice of Law and the Federal System, *supra,* 16 Stan. L. Rev. 1, 5, 6, 22, fn. omitted.)

> To assert a conflict between the interests of the forum and the foreign state is a serious matter; the mere fact that a suggested broad conception of a local interest will conflict with that of a foreign state is a sound reason why the conception should be reexamined, with a view to a more moderate and restrained interpretation both of the policy and of the circumstances in which it must be applied to effectuate the forum's legitimate purpose. . . . An analysis of this kind . . . was brilliantly performed by Justice Traynor in Bernkrant v. Fowler.

(Currie, The Disinterested Third State (1963) 28 Law & Contemp. Prob., pp. 754, 757; *see also* Sedler in Symposium, Conflict of Laws Round Table, *supra,* 49 Texas L. Rev. 211, at (pp. 224-225.) This process of reexamination requires identification of a "real interest as opposed to a hypothetical interest" on the part of the forum (Sedler, Value of Principled Preferences, 49 Texas L. Rev. 224) and can be approached under principles of "comparative impairment." (Baxter, Choice of Law and the Federal System, *supra,* 16 Stan. L. Rev. 1-22.)

Once this preliminary analysis has identified a true conflict of the governmental interests involved as applied to the parties under the particular circumstances of the case, the "comparative impairment" approach to the resolution of such conflict seeks to determine which state's interest would be more impaired if its policy were subordinated to the policy of the other state. This analysis proceeds on the principle that true conflicts should be resolved by applying the law of the state whose interest would be the more impaired if its law were not applied. Exponents of this process of analysis emphasize that it is very different from a weighing process. The court does not

> "weigh" the conflicting governmental interests in the sense of determining which conflicting law manifested the "better" or the "worthier" social policy on the specific issue. An attempted balancing of conflicting state policies in that sense . . . is difficult to justify in the context of a federal system in which, within constitutional limits, states are empowered to mold their polices as they wish. . . . [The process] can accurately be described as . . . accommodation of conflicting state policies, as a problem of allocating domains of lawmaking power in multi-state contexts—limitations on the reach of state policies as distinguished from evaluating wisdom of those policies. . . . [E]mphasis is placed on the appropriate scope of conflicting state policies rather than on the "quality of those policies. . . ."

(Horowitz, The Law of Choice of Law in California—A Restatement, *supra,* 21 UCLA L. Rev. 719, 753; *see also* Baxter, Choice of Law and the Federal System, *supra,* 16 Stan. L. Rev. 1, 18-19.) However, the true function of this methodology can probably be appreciated only casuistically in its application to an endless variety of choice of law problems.

Although the concept and nomenclature of this methodology may have received fuller recognition at a later time, it is noteworthy that the core of its rationale was applied by Justice Traynor in his opinion for this court in People v. One 1953 Ford Victoria (1957). There in a proceeding to forfeit an automobile for unlawful transportation of narcotics we dealt with the question whether a chattel mortgage of the vehicle given in Texas and, admittedly valid both in that state and this, succumbed to the forfeiture proceedings. The purchaser of the car, having executed a note and chattel mortgage for the unpaid purchase price, without the consent of the mortgagee drove the vehicle to California where he used it to transport marijuana. Applicable California statutes made it clear that they did not contemplate the forfeiture of the interest of an innocent mortgagee, that is a person whose "interest was created after a reasonable investigation of the moral responsibility, character, and reputation of the purchaser, and without any knowledge that the vehicle was being, or was to be, used for the purpose charged. . . ." Texas had no similar statute; nor had the mortgagee, though proving that the mortgage was bona fide, also proved that he had made the above reasonable investigation of the mortgagor.

It was clear that Texas had an interest in seeing that valid security interests created upon the lawful purchase of automobiles in Texas be enforceable and recognized. California had an interest in controlling the transportation of narcotics. Each interest was at stake in the case, since the chattel mortgage had been validly created in Texas and the car was used to transport narcotics in California. The crucial question confronting the court was whether the "reasonable investigation" required by statute of a California mortgagee applied to the Texas mortgagee. Employing what was in substance a "comparative impairment" approach, the court answer the question in the negative.

> It is contended that a holding that the "reasonable investigation" requirement is not applicable to respondent will subvert the enforcement of California's narcotics laws. We are not persuaded that such dire consequences will ensue. The state may still forfeit the interest of the wrongdoer. It has done so in this case. Moreover, the Legislature has made plain its purpose not to forfeit the interests of innocent mortgagees. It has not made plain that "reasonable investigation" of the purchaser is such an essential element of innocence that it must be made even by an out-of-state mortgagee although such mortgagee could not reasonably be expected to make such investigation.

Mindful of the above principles governing our choice of law, we proceed to reexamine the California policy underlying the imposition of civil liability upon tavern keepers. At its broadest limits this policy would afford protection to all persons injured in California by intoxicated persons who have been sold or furnished alcoholic beverages while intoxicated regardless of where such beverages were sold or furnished. Such a broad policy would naturally embrace situations where the intoxicated actor had been provided with liquor by out-of-state tavern keepers. Although the State of Nevada does not impose such *civil* liability on its tavern keepers, nevertheless they are subject to *criminal* penalties under a statute making it unlawful to sell or give intoxicating liquor to any person who is drunk or known to be a habitual drunkard.

We need not, and accordingly do not here determine the outer limits to which California's policy should be extended, for it appears clear to us that it must encompass defendant, who as alleged in the complaint,

> advertis[es] for and otherwise solicit[s] in California the business of California residents at defendant Harrah's Club Nevada drinking and gambling establishments, knowing and expecting said California residents, in response to said advertising and solicitation, to use the public highways of the State of California in going and coming from defendant Harrah's Club Nevada drinking and gambling establishments.

Defendant by the course of its chosen commercial practice has put itself at the heart of California's regulatory interest, namely to prevent tavern keepers from selling alcoholic beverages to obviously intoxicated persons who are likely to act in California in the intoxicated state. It seems clear that California cannot reasonably effectuate its policy if it does not extend its regulation to include out-of-state tavern keepers such as defendant who regularly and purposely sell intoxicating beverages to California residents in places and under conditions in which it is reasonably certain these residents will return to California and act therein while still in an intoxicated state. California's interest would be very significantly impaired if its policy were not applied to defendant.

Since the act of selling alcoholic beverages to obviously intoxicated persons is already proscribed in Nevada, the application of California's rule of civil liability would not impose an entirely new duty requiring the ability to distinguish between California residents and other patrons. Rather the imposition of such liability involves an increased economic exposure, which, at least for businesses which actively solicit extensive California patronage, is a foreseeable and coverable business expense. Moreover, Nevada's interest in protecting its tavern keepers from civil liability of a boundless and unrestricted nature will not be significantly impaired when as in the instant case liability is imposed only on those tavern keepers who actively solicit California business.

Therefore, upon reexamining the policy underlying California's rule of decision and giving such policy a more restrained interpretation for the purpose of this case pursuant to the principles of the law of choice of law discussed above, we conclude that California has an important and abiding interest in applying its rule of decision to the case at bench, that the policy of this state would be more significantly impaired if such rule were not applied and that the trial court erred in not applying California law.

Defendant argues, however, that even if California law is applied, the demurrer was nonetheless properly sustained because the tavern keeper's duty stated in Vesely v. Sager, *supra,* is based on Business and Professions Code section 25602, which is a criminal statute and thus without extraterritorial effect. It is quite true, as defendant argues, that in *Vesely* we determined "that civil liability results when a vendor furnishes alcoholic beverages to a customer in violation of Business and Professions Code section 25602 and each of the conditions set forth in Evidence Code section 669, subdivision (a) is established."

It is also clear, as defendant's argument points out, that since, unlike the California vendor in *Vesely,* defendant was a Nevada resident which furnished the alcoholic beverage to the Myers in that state, the above California statute had no extraterritorial effect and that civil liability could not be posited on defendant's violation of a California criminal law. We recognize, therefore, that we cannot make the same determination as quoted above with respect to defendant that we made with respect to the defendant vendor in *Vesely.*

However, our decision in *Vesely* was much broader than defendant would have it. There, at the very outset of our opinion, we declared that the traditional common law rule denying recovery on the ground that the furnishing of alcoholic beverage is not the proximate cause of the injuries inflicted on a third person by an intoxicated individual "is patently unsound." (5 Cal. 3d at p.157, 95 Cal. Rptr. 623, 486 P.2d 151.) Observing that "[u]ntil fairly recently, it was uniformly held that [such] an action could not be maintained at common law" (*id.* 5 Cal. 3d at p.158, 95 Cal. Rptr. at p.627, 486 P.2d at p.155) and reviewing in detail the common law rule (*id.* 5 Cal. 3d at pp.158-164, 95 Cal. Rptr. at p.631, 486 P.2d at p.159) we concluded that "the furnishing of an alcoholic beverage to an intoxicated person may be a proximate cause of injuries inflicted by that individual upon a third person." We reasoned: "If such furnishing is a proximate cause, it is so because the consumption, resulting intoxication, and injury-producing conduct are foreseeable intervening causes, or at least the injury-producing conduct is one of the hazards which makes such furnishing negligent."

Proceeding to the question of the tavern keeper's duty in this respect and rejecting his contention that civil liability for tavern keepers should be left to future legislative action, we noted that

> liability has been denied in cases such as the one before us solely because of the judicially created rule that the furnishing of alcoholic beverages is not the proximate cause of injuries resulting from intoxication. As demonstrated, *supra,* this rule is patently unsound and totally inconsistent with the principles of proximate cause established in other areas of negligence law. Other common law tort rules which were determined

to be lacking in validity have been abrogated by this court and there is no sound reason for retaining the common law rule presented in this case.

In sum, our opinion in *Vesely* struck down the old common law rule of nonliability constructed on the basis that the consumption, not the sale, of alcoholic beverages was the proximate cause of injuries inflicted by the intoxicated person. Although we chose to impose liability on the *Vesely* defendant on the basis of his violating the applicable statute, the clear import of our decision was that there was no bar to civil liability under modern negligence law. Certainly, we said nothing in *Vesely* indicative of an intention to retain the former rule that an action at common law does not lie. The fact then, that in the case at bench, section 25602 of the Business and Professions Code is not applicable to this defendant in Nevada so as to warrant the imposition of civil liability on the basis of its violation, does not preclude recovery on the basis of negligence apart from the statute. Pertinent here is our observation in Rowland v. Christian. "It bears repetition that the basic policy of this state set forth by the Legislature in section 1714 of the Civil Code is that everyone is responsible for an injury caused to another by his want of ordinary care or skill in the management of his property."

The judgment is reversed and the cause is remanded to the trial court with directions to overrule the demurrer and to allow defendant a reasonable time within which to answer.

Questions and Comments

(1) Blamey v. Brown, 270 N.W.2d 844 (Minn. 1978), is a case similar, but not identical, to *Bernhard. Blamey* involved a one-car accident. The defendant, sole proprietor of a beer and liquor store, was in Wisconsin but within a few miles of the Minnesota border. Defendant's store sold beer to the driver of the car in which plaintiff was injured in Minnesota. The Minnesota court specifically found that "[d]efendant neither advertised in Minnesota nor attempted to attract Minnesota residents or young people [plaintiff was 15] to his establishment." The defendant did not have insurance to cover the kind of liability imposed by Minnesota since Wisconsin imposed no similar liability. The Minnesota court decided that the Minnesota statute imposing strict liability for sales of alcohol to minors was inapplicable by its own terms. But rather than apply the considerably milder Wisconsin statute (which would not have imposed liability), it applied Minnesota common-law negligence theory to hold the defendant liable while specifically holding that Wisconsin common law would not impose liability. The decision was based upon Minnesota interests and the "better law" approach, which is treated at page 252 *infra*.

(2) How would *Bernhard* have been decided under the First Restatement? *Cf.* note 2 to §377, quoted above at page 12, *supra*, which talks about applying the law of the place where a deleterious substance takes effect and

not where it is administered. Shouldn't that principle apply a fortiori when the deleterious effect is felt not by the person who has traveled but by the one who has never left California?

(3) Is comparative impairment anything more than what Currie suggested (restraint in the interpretation of domestic policies when there is an apparent conflict) plus some of what he condemned (weighing of interests)? Professor Kanowitz thinks it sounds a lot like the latter, and adds:

> Despite the elaborate stages of the comparative impairment method revealed in *Bernhard* . . . it is hard to avoid the impression that the technique is founded essentially on an interest-counting process. This process will, in the long run, prove no more satisfactory than the contact-counting prescribed by the Second Restatement of the Conflict of Laws.

Kanowitz, Comparative Impairment and Better Law: Grand Illusion in the Conflict of Laws, 30 Hast. L.J. 255, 277 (1978).

(4) Even if comparative impairment is a valid theory, Professor Reppy thinks that it was misapplied to the facts of *Bernhard:*

> The court in *Bernhard* then misapplied comparative impairment to permit recovery. Nevada's interest in protecting this class of defendants, tavern keepers, from what Nevada considered to be unfair liability for injuries caused by persons becoming drunk at the tavern would have been sacrificed one hundred percent by the application of California's law imposing liability. But California's interest in seeing a California tort victim receive compensation would not have been wholly sacrificed by the application of the Nevada law, since the victim already had a cause of action against the drunk tortfeasor or could recover against his own insurer if the drunk had no liability insurance. To have deprived the California victim of a second bite at the compensation apple would not have fully defeated California's interest.

Reppy, Eclecticism in Choice of Law: Hybrid Method or Mishmash?, 34 Mercer L. Rev. 645 (1983).

(5) If it is California's *regulatory* interest that is at stake (and not a compensatory interest), does it make any difference that the plaintiff was a California resident? *See* Brilmayer, Interest Analysis and the Myth of Legislative Intent, 78 Mich. L. Rev. 392, 406 (1980).

(6) Why did the court in *Bernhard* consider it appropriate to limit the scope of its holding to those Nevada tavern owners who "actively solicit extensive California patronage"? In product-liability cases, the usual rule has become application of the law of the place of injury, rather than of the place

of manufacture. Does a tavern owner anywhere within driving distance of the California border do any less to put the drunken driver into the "stream of commerce" than the manufacturer of a defective product? Doesn't the fact that the tavern owner's act was already criminal in Nevada, quite apart from his or her advertising in California, establish that Nevada's interest in protecting the tavern owner is a weak one?

(7) *See* Note, Comparative Impairment Reformed: Rethinking State Interests in the Conflict of Laws, 95 Harv. L. Rev. 1079, 1084-1085 (1982):

> Interest analysis insists that this kind of policy [seeking accommodation of various states' interests] can never be strong enough to override the forum state's interest, however weak it may be, in applying its own law. . . . [But a] regime in which every choice-of-law decision were [*sic*] calculated to achieve maximum effectuation of the policies of all interested states would give each state the greatest opportunity to attain its own policy objectives. Thus, a state bent on effectuating its purely internal policy to the greatest extent possible can easily sacrifice its own weak interests in a spirit of interstate comity, knowing that in a future case its sister state will do the same.

But if the appeal is to be on the basis of self-interest, isn't the forum better off by adhering to interest analysis while its neighbors adhere to comparative impairment?

(8) In 1978, the California legislature amended section 25602 of its Business and Professional Code, changing the former provision to subsection (a) and adding subsections (b) and (c). The entire statute now reads:

§25602. Sales to drunkard or intoxicated person; offense; civil liability

(a) Every person who sells, furnishes, gives, or causes to be sold, furnished, or given away, any alcoholic beverage to any habitual or common drunkard or to any obviously intoxicated person is guilty of a misdemeanor.

(b) No person who sells, furnishes, gives, or causes to be sold, furnished, or given away, any alcoholic beverage pursuant to subdivision (a) of this section shall be civilly liable to any injured person or the estate of such person for injuries inflicted on that person as a result of intoxication by the consumer of such alcoholic beverage.

(c) The Legislature hereby declares that this section shall be interpreted so that the holdings in cases such as Vesely v. Sager, Bernhard v. Harrah's Club and Coulter v. Superior Court be abrogated in favor of prior judicial interpretation finding the consumption of alcoholic beverages rather than the serving of alcoholic beverages as the proximate cause of injuries inflicted upon another by an intoxicated person.

D. The "Better Rule"

Leflar, Conflicts Law: More on Choice-Influencing Considerations

54 Calif. L. Rev. 1584, 1586-1588 (1966)

Major Choice-Influencing Considerations

A short restatement of the five summarized considerations is given here.

A. Predictability of Results

Uniformity of results, regardless of forum, has always been a major goal in choice-of-law theory. Achievement of this goal would enable parties entering into a consensual transaction to plan it with reference to a body of law that would give them the results they desired. As a result, their transactions would normally be validated and their justified expectations thus protected. This would further the broad social policies of most forum states by sustaining legal arrangements in which parties have in good faith engaged themselves. At the same time it would discourage "forum shopping."

B. Maintenance of Interstate and International Order

Both nations and states within a nation are interested in facilitating the orderly legal control of transactions that in any fashion cross their boundary lines. Smooth conduct of affairs between the peoples of different nations is essential to modern civilization; the easy movement of persons and things—free social and economic commerce—between states in a federal nation is essential to the very existence of the federation. There must be a minimum of mutual interference with claims or aspirations to sovereignty. No forum whose concern with a set of facts is negligible should claim priority for its law over the law of a state which has a clearly superior concern with the facts; nor should any state's choice-of-law system be based upon deliberate across-the-board "forum preference." Encouragement of that measure of interstate and international intercourse which is in keeping with the interests of the forum state and its people has always been a prime function of conflicts law.

C. Simplification of the Judicial Task

Courts do not like to do things the hard way if an easier way serves the ends of justice substantially as well. It would be utterly impractical for a court hearing a case brought on extrastate facts to apply the whole body of procedural law of the place where the facts occurred, and not much would be gained by doing so. Courts therefore use their own procedural rules. There are, however, some outcome-determinative rules, at times classified as procedural, which are so simple that one state's rule can be used as easily as another's, so that the substance-procedure dichotomy is not sensibly applicable to them. Purely mechanical rules for choice of substantive law are also easy for courts to apply, but other considerations may outweigh simplification of the judicial task where such rules are involved. Ease in judicial performance is ordinarily not of first importance among the choice-influencing considerations, but it is important in some choices.

D. Advancement of the Forum's Governmental Interests

If a forum state has a genuine concern with the facts in a given case, a concern discoverable from its strongly felt social or legal policy, it is reasonable to expect the state's courts to act in accordance with that concern. This refers to legitimate concerns, not just to the local occurrence of some facts, or to the local existence of some rule of law that could constitutionally be applied to the facts. A state's governmental interests in the choice-of-law sense need not coincide with its rules of local law, especially if the local rules, whether statutory or judgemade, are old or out of tune with the times. A state's total governmental interest in a case is to be discovered from all the considerations that properly motivate the state in its law-making and law-administering tasks, viewed as of the time when the question is presented. So viewed, the circumstances may show that the forum is truly interested in applying its own law to a set of facts. If they do show this, that conclusion becomes a major choice-influencing consideration.

E. Application of the Better Rule of Law

The better rule of law is the most controversial of the considerations, yet a potent one. If choice of law were purely a jurisdiction-selecting process, with courts first deciding which state's law should govern and checking afterward to see what that state's law was, this consideration would not be present. Everyone knows that this is not what courts do, nor what they should do. Judges know from the beginning between which rules of law, and not just which states, they are choosing. A state's "governmental interest" in a set of facts can be analyzed only by reference to the content of the competing rules of law. Choice of law is not wholly a choice between laws as distinguished from a choice between jurisdictions, but partly it is.

A judge's natural feeling that his own state's law is better than that of other states to some extent explains forum preference. Of course the local law is sometimes not better, and most judges are perfectly capable of realizing this. The inclination of any reasonable court will be to prefer rules of law which make good socio-economic sense for the time when the court speaks, whether they be its own or another state's rules. The law's legitimate concerns with "justice in the individual case," sometimes spoken of as a choice-of-law objective, and with that "protection of justified expectations of the parties," which often corresponds with Ehrenzweig's "basic rules of validation," are furthered by deliberate preference for the better rule of law. The preference is objective, not subjective. It has to do with preferred law, not preferred parties. It is "result selective" only in the same sense that in any non-conflicts case a determination of what the law is (presumably the "better law," if there was argument about the law) controls the results of litigation. In conflict cases, just as in other cases, courts have always taken the content of competing rules into account, but they have too often used characterization, renvoi, multiple-choice rules or the like as manipulative devices to cover up what they were really doing, when there was no need at all for any cover-up.

Milkovich v. Saari

295 Minn. 155, 203 N.W.2d 408 (1973)

Todd, J.

Defendants appeal from an order of the trial denying their motion to dismiss plaintiff's complaint for failure to state a cause of action because the law of Ontario, where plaintiff and defendants reside, has a guest statute requiring proof of gross negligence, which was not alleged. Defendants further appeal from the granting of plaintiff's motion to strike their affirmative defense that the law of Ontario should apply. The trial court certified the question as important and doubtful. We affirm.

Plaintiff and both defendants are residents of Thunder Bay (formerly Port Arthur), Ontario, Canada. On November 8, 1968, they left Thunder Bay for Duluth, Minnesota, to shop and attend a play. The car belonged to defendant Erma Saari, who drove the first part of the trip. At the United States

Customs House at Pigeon River, Minnesota, defendant Judith Rudd took over the driving, and about 40 miles south of the border the car left the road and crashed into rock formations adjacent to the road, causing the injuries to plaintiff. Plaintiff was hospitalized at Duluth for approximately 1½ months and thereafter returned to her home in Thunder Bay.

Defendant Saari's automobile was garaged, registered, and insured in the Province of Ontario, Canada. Ontario has a guest statute, and if the law of Ontario is to be applied in this case, plaintiff would have to establish gross negligence in order to recover. Minnesota does not have a guest statute, and the rulings of the court would be correct if Minnesota law is to apply.

The field of "conflict of laws" in tort matters has undergone dramatic change in the last decade. Prior to that time, most courts were willing to accept the doctrine of "lex loci," which proved to be easy to administer since the happening of an accident in any particular forum established that the law of the place of the accident would apply. Criticism of this entrenched doctrine mounted from all sides. The issue was met head on in Babcock v. Jackson.

While New York was experiencing its difficulties in the changing field of conflict of laws, a fact situation arose in a case appealed to the Supreme Court of New Hampshire, which allowed its learned Mr. Chief Justice Kenison to enunciate a doctrine which has been followed by many courts throughout the country, including our own Minnesota court. In Clark v. Clark, . . . a husband and wife had left their home in New Hampshire to proceed to another part of New Hampshire for a visit and were to return that evening. Part of their trip took them through Vermont, where the accident occurred. The plaintiff wife brought action in New Hampshire against her husband and sought an order of the court that the substantive law of New Hampshire governed the rights of the parties. New Hampshire had no guest statute and Vermont did. In a carefully reasoned opinion, Mr. Chief Justice Kenison traced the history and difficulty of the lex loci rule. He then proceeded to adopt five basic "choice-influencing considerations" to be applied in these cases. The basic premises for the considerations adopted by the court were first proposed by Professor Robert Leflar in his article, "Choice-Influencing Considerations in Conflicts Law," 41 N.Y.U.L. Rev. 267, 279, and briefly stated, the tests selected by the New Hampshire court are: (a) Predictability of results; (b) maintenance of interstate and international order; (c) simplification of the judicial task; (d) advancement of the forum's governmental interests; and (e) application of the better rule of law.

Predictability of results can be overlooked since basically this test relates to consensual transactions where people should know in advance what law will govern their act. Obviously, no one plans to have an accident, and, except for the remote possibility of forum shopping, this test is of little import in an automobile accident case. As to the second consideration, the court found little trouble since under this heading no more is called for than the court apply the law of no state which does not have substantial connection with the total facts and the particular issue being litigated. The third point, simplification of the judicial task, poses no problem since the courts are fully capable of administering the law of another forum if called upon to do so.

The court observed that in selecting the law of a particular case the last two considerations carry most weight. In the case before it, the court found adequate governmental interest in applying its state's law and concluded that the New Hampshire law was unquestionably the better law and should be applied. . . .

The facts of this case now complete the cycle. The choice-influencing considerations proposed by Professor Leflar and set forth by Mr. Chief Justice Kenison in Clark v. Clark were adopted by our court in Schneider v. Nichols indicating our preference for the better-law approach and our rejection of the guest statute concept of various jurisdictions. We have come to the conclusion in this case that plaintiff should be allowed to proceed with her action under our common law rules of negligence and should not be bound by the guest statute requirements of the Province of Ontario. . . .

On the consideration of governmental interest [in discussing Kell v. Henderson], Professor Leflar found adequate support for the decision rendered by the New York court. In so doing, he rejected the concept of the practical interest of the state in the supervision and safety of its state highways since the rule in question, unlike rules of the road and definitions of negligence, does not bear upon vehicle operation as such. Instead, he pointed out that the factor to be considered is the relevant effect the New York rule has on the duty of host to guest and the danger of collusion between them to defraud the host's insurer. New York's interest in applying its own law rather than Ontario law on these issues, he found to be based primarily on the status, as a justice-administering state. In that status it is strongly concerned with seeing that persons who come into New York courts to litigate controversies with substantial New York connections have these cases determined according to rules consistent with New York concepts of justice, or at least not inconsistent with them. That will be as true for nondomiciliary litigants as for domiciliaries. This interest will not manifest itself clearly if the out-of-state rule does not run contrary to some strong socio-legal policy of the forum, but it will become a major consideration if there is such a strong opposing local policy.

Professor Leflar then pointed out that this consideration leads to preference for what is regarded as the better rule of law, that New York has such a preference, and that it is a vigorous one. He concluded that the combination of the last two items, governmental interest and better rule of law, called for the application of New York law. His statements and reasoning apply equally to the facts of this case and lead to the conclusion that Minnesota should apply its better rule of law and should allow plaintiff to proceed with her action.

Strong support for the better-rule-of-law concept appears in an article by Professor Albert A. Ehrenzweig, "False Conflicts" and the "Better Rule":

Threat and Promise in Multistate Tort Laws, 53 Va. L. Rev. 847, 853, in which he wrote:

> Express recognition of the forum's right and duty to apply its own better rule as such is an ancient tradition which apparently succumbed to the 19th century's international conceptualism. We need only remember the priority given by early statutists to the statuta favorabilia of the forum against foreign statuta odiosa, or Master Aldricus' choice of the custom "potior et utilior," or Byzantium's *philanthropoteron.* The widespread disregard of foreign Sunday laws, fellow-servant rules, and married woman's incapacities, as well as statutes of frauds, and limitations on wrongful death damages, may serve as modern examples.
>
> Now, we shall, of course, not "ask the judge simply to express a preference between two rules." This would, indeed, "abolish our centuries-old subject." But we should face the "fact of life" that judges, our best judges, often take advantage of the "looseness in the joints of the [choice-of-law] apparatus," or employ "manipulative techniques such as characterization and renvoi," and all-purpose tools such as the "most significant relationship," in order to substitute a better foreign rule for much "that is archaic and foolish" in their own law. . . .
>
> Whether or not general express recognition of the "better-rule" approach can be justified at present, we must at least acknowledge the validity of the proposition advanced by Currie that transient ("disinterested") third states, having no incentive to follow the "stay-at-home" trend, are likely to choose what they consider the better of two foreign rules. Moreover, admiralty courts in their more forthright manner have sometimes acknowledged their bias toward a "better rule." And may we not ultimately in part explain the great willingness of American courts to permit parties to choose their own laws of a similar better-rule approach?
>
> Although the "better-rule" principle is not generally capable of replacing conflicts rules, I see little justification within the limits set by settled law for the prevailing horror against the recognition of that principle as one of many determining the growth of conflicts law. The very growth of common-law rules is based on the judge's choice between competing principles, choices expressed in the process of overruling or distinguishing earlier judicial pronouncements. In purely domestic cases open admission of this technique is often hampered by justified respect for "certainty" and the parties' expectations, a respect which also accounts, of course, for both legislative and judicial reluctance to act with retroactive effect. In cases involving foreign elements, however, this consideration often should be, and generally is, less relevant, and the path is open for the courageous judge to prepare the ground for a domestic reform by open preference for "better" foreign solutions. . . .

[I]n Conklin v. Horner the Wisconsin court was confronted with a fact situation again exactly on all fours with our situation. There the court, speaking through Mr. Justice Heffernan, adopted the better-rule approach which we have adopted here and, in a well-reasoned opinion, arrived at the same conclusion that this court has. In the Wisconsin case, the litigants were all residents of the State of Illinois; the automobile in question was licensed and garaged in Illinois; the trip originated in Illinois with the intent and purpose to return to Illinois; and the insurance policy was issued in the State of Illinois. Illinois has a guest statute; Wisconsin does not. The court in that case first considered the problem of labeling any procedure in determining rules of law to be applied, saying:

> *We emphasized that what we adopted was not a rule, but a method of analysis that permitted dissection of the jural bundle constituting a tort and its environment to determine what elements therein were relevant to a reasonable choice of law.*
>
> When the *Wilcox* case is so viewed, it is apparent that we cannot conclude that, when one set of facts leads logically to the law of the forum, the reverse, or the apparent reverse, of these facts will lead to the opposite conclusion. [Emphasis added.]

We, too, adopt this concept that what the court is considering is a methodology and not a rule.

The Wisconsin court then proceeded to adopt the choice-influencing considerations of Professor Leflar as expounded by Mr. Chief Justice Kenison in Clark v. Clark, *supra.* The court considered the various rules in the same manner that Professor Leflar applied them to Kell v. Henderson, *supra.* It should be noted that the Wisconsin court gave much more credence to the state interest in its highways and state regulations than Professor Leflar would ascribe. Following this reasoning process, the Wisconsin court concluded that the Wisconsin law was the better law to apply under the circumstances.

We find then that in *Conklin* the Wisconsin court, premising its choice-of-law methodology on the factors initially propagated by Professor Leflar and Mr. Chief Justice Kenison of New Hampshire, has resolved substantially the same fact situation as now appears before us by applying the common-law liability of the forum and place of the accident rather than the guest statute of the residence of the parties. *See also* Kell v. Henderson, *supra.* Since our methodology owes a similar debt to Professor Leflar and Mr. Chief Justice Kenison we find their reasoning relevant and persuasive.

We have already noted the relative unimportance of predictability of results to tort actions. Similarly, the simplification of the judicial task need not concern us to any great extent since we have no doubt our judicial system could in the appropriate case apply the guest statute rule of gross negligence as readily as our common-law rule. Interstate and international relations are maintained without harm where, as here, the forum state has a substantial connection with the facts and issues involved. This requirement is amply met by the fact that the accident occurred in Minnesota, as well as by the fact the plaintiff was hospitalized for well over a month in the state.

The compelling factors in this case are the advancement of the forum's governmental interests and the application of the better law. While there may be more deterrent effect in our common-law rule of liability as opposed to the guest statute requirements of gross negligence, the main governmental interest involved is that of any "justice-administering state." Leflar, Conflicts Law: More on Choice-Influencing Considerations, 54 Calif. L. Rev. 1584, 1594. In that posture, we are concerned that our courts not be called upon to determine issues under rules which, however accepted they may be in other states, are inconsistent with our own concept of fairness and equity. We might also note that persons injured in automobile accidents occurring within our borders can reasonably be expected to require treatment in our medical facilities, both public and private. In the instant case, plaintiff incurred medical bills in a Duluth hospital which have already been paid, but we are loath to place weight on the individual case for fear it might offer even minor incentives to "hospital shop" or to create litigation-directed pressures on the payment of debts to medical facilities. Suffice it to say that we recognize that medical costs are likely to be incurred with a consequent governmental interest that injured persons not be denied recovery on the basis of doctrines foreign to Minnesota.

In our search for the better rule, we are firmly convinced of the superiority of the common-law rule of liability to that of the Ontario guest statute. We can find little reason for the strict limitation of a host's liability to his guest beyond the fear of collusive suits and the vague disapproval of a guest "biting the hand that feeds him." Neither rationale is persuasive. We are convinced the judicial system can uncover collusive suits without such overinclusive rules, and we do not find any discomfort in the prospect of a guest suing his host for injuries suffered through the host's simple negligence.

Accordingly, we hold that Minnesota law should be applied to this lawsuit.

Affirmed.

PETERSON, J. (dissenting).

The "center-of-gravity-of-the-contacts" theory of conflict of laws has been adopted in this state, and we have applied it in situations where an automobile trip started and was intended to terminate in this state, where the host-guest relationship was formed in this state, or where the place of registration or garaging of the automobile was in this state. Until today, however, we have not considered the mere happening of an automobile accident in this state a sufficient contact with the forum to establish the center of gravity here. In my view, the center of gravity is in Ontario, not Minnesota.

The "choice-influencing factor" in the majority opinion is simply that Minnesota law is "better law" because, unlike Ontario law, this state has no guest statute. Notwithstanding our undoubted preference for this forum's standard of liability, I am not persuaded that decision should turn on that factor alone. We may assume that these Canadian citizens have concurred in the rule of law of their own government as just, so the law of this American forum is not for them the "better" standard of justice. The litigation, indeed, was first initiated by plaintiff in the courts of Ontario and was later commenced in Minnesota as an act of forum shopping.

Our own cases, of course, do not compel such a decision. Two cases from other jurisdictions that are "on all fours" are not persuasive. The New York case of Kell v. Henderson . . . is not the decision of that state's highest court and, in addition, is at odds with the later case of Arbuthnot v. Allbright. The Wisconsin case of Conklin v. Horner is a final expression of its highest court, based upon a well-written majority opinion of Mr. Justice Heffernan. I nevertheless am more persuaded by the dissenting opinion of two justices. Mr. Chief Justice Hallows, in dissent, appropriately observed that the so-called "methodology of analysis" is really little more than a mechanical application of the law of the forum. As he wrote: "If we are going to be consistent only in applying the law of the forum, then we are merely giving lip service to the new 'significant contacts' rule."

Questions and Comments

(1) Not too surprisingly, the most controversial part of Professor Leflar's approach is the "better rule" component. It is not 100 percent clear that Professor Leflar *advocated* a better-rule approach instead of simply stating that courts do in fact tend to choose what they consider to be the better rule. Professor Ehrenzweig, in the article quoted by the *Milkovich* court, seems to stand somewhere between description and advocacy, since he felt that conflicts rules should reflect what courts actually do in conflicts cases, rather than what scholars urge. In any event, it is clear that several courts have embraced explicit acceptance of the approach.

(2) Consider the posture of a lower court comparing forum law formulated by its state's supreme court to the law of another state. Presumably, if there is a supreme court decision in the forum holding that local law is "better" for a choice-of-law purposes, then this is binding. How is that any different from a state supreme court decision that the rule is "better" for substantive purposes? Why, in other words, isn't a substantive precedent also binding on choice of law issues—given that a choice-of-law precedent on "betterness" would be?

In Jepson v. General Casualty Co., 513 N.W. 2d 467 (Minn. 1994), the Minnesota Supreme Court held that a recent legislative amendment allowing insurance contracts to prevent stacking was not evidence that Minnesota's law was "better" in a case involving a contract signed in Minnesota for an out-of-state risk involved in an out-of-state accident. Would a choice-of-law provision in a statue be given effect if it declared that this substantive law was "better" in Leflar's terms? If so, then why doesn't the simple adoption of a substantive statute declare, in effect, that this rule is better for choice of law purposes? Doesn't this suggest that the only sort of rule that could be declared "worse" for choice-of-law purposes is one that is not authoritative for substantive purposes? For instance, a forum's common-law rule that was outdated or eroded by subsequent decisions could be declared "worse" for choice of law purposes. But if such a substantive decision is not authoritative, why not simply overrule it directly for domestic purposes as well?

(3) The *Milkovich* opinion states, at 526-527, that "we are concerned that our courts not be called upon to determine issues under rules which, however acceptable they may be in other states, are inconsistent with our own concept of fairness and equity." Couldn't that interest be much more rationally served in this case, and with much less disruption to the policy interests of Ontario, by a forum non conveniens dismissal? Wouldn't such an approach also have the advantage of not burdening the Minnesota courts? In light of the less drastic dismissal alternative, isn't the use of the quoted rationale to decide the issue an instance of meddling in Ontario interest?

(4) Is the determination of the "better rule" as objective as Professor Leflar tries to make it sound? In the article excerpt quoted before *Milkovich,* he says at one point that the "better rule" approach "has to do with preferred law, not preferred parties" and is therefore objective and not subjective. But isn't that just saying that it makes no nonobjective choice between parties, while leaving open the possibility that the choice between two laws is nonobjective?

In fact, if there is an objective way in a given conflicts case for a court to determine what the better rule is, why weren't the courts or the legislature of the state with the worse rule able to see that fact and change their rule?

(5) Professor Weintraub finds the use of the better-law criterion "commendable" if two limitations are observed: first, he would require that it be used only to resolve a true conflict; second, he would require that the selection of the better law be by objective standards. Such standards include rejecting the law that is an "anachronism" or is "aberrational." Weintraub, Commentary on the Conflict of Laws 328 (2d ed. 1980). Is that another way of saying that new laws are always better than old laws and that one should discriminate against experimentation among the states?

The better-rule approach was specifically limited to true conflict cases where the other considerations are in "near equipoise" in Fuerste v. Bemis, 156 N.W.2d 831 (Iowa 1968).

(6) It is a common observation that the better-rule approach for true conflict cases is little more than Currie's solution in disguise if the court determines that its own law is the better law. Moreover, as in *Milkovich*, courts routinely conclude that their own law is the better law. And yet not all courts do. *See, e.g.*, LaBounty v. American Ins. Co. , 451 A.2d 161 (N.H. 1982); Bigelow v. Halloran, 313 N.W. 2d 10 (Minn. 1981); *compare* Jepson v. General Casualty Co. of Wisconsin, 513 N.W.2d 467, 473 (Minn. 1994)("if it were true [that] forum law would always be the better law . . . this step in our choice of law analysis would be meaningless"). Moreover, an empirical study of tort conflict cases suggests that the better law approach does not lead to the application of forum law any more often than the other modern approaches (although the modern approaches as a group lead to the application of forum

law more frequently than the traditional approach). *See* Borchers, The Choice-of-Law Revolution: An Empirical Study, 49 Wash. & Lee L. Rev. 357 (1992).

(7) The attention that the better-rule factor has diverted from Professor Leflar's other choice-influencing considerations may be justified. Professor Reppy claims that the factors are really only two, not five. See Reppy, Eclecticism in Choice of Law: Hybrid Method or Mish-mash?, 34 Mercer L. Rev. 645 (1983). Factor 3, simplification of the judicial task, is most easily satisfied by applying the law of the forum and could never influence the court away from picking what it will usually pick under factor 5, the better law—forum law. No case has ever turned on factor 2, maintenance of interstate and international order, and it is hard to imagine a conflicts case threatening that order. Predictability might sometimes be a concern, but, Reppy says, it will lose, 2 to 1, to the factors that point toward application of forum law: better law and factor 4, advancement of the forum's governmental interests.

(8) In recent years Minnesota has backed away from the "better law" approach. In Nodak Mutual Ins. Co. v. Am. Fam. Mut. Ins. Co., 604 N.W. 2d 91, 96 (Min. 2000), the Minnesota Supreme Court noted that "this court has not placed any emphasis on the [better-law] factor in nearly twenty years," and described its approach instead as "the significant contacts test." *See also* Montpetit v. Allina Health System, Inc., 2000 Minn. App. LEXIS 1051 (Minn. App. 2000) (better rule approach "has been abandoned in recent years"). At least four states—Arkansas, New Hampshire, Rhode Island, and Wisconsin—still use some form of the better law approach for torts. *See* Symeonides, Choice of Law in the American Courts in 2000: As the Century Turns, 49 Am. J. Comp. L. 1 (2001). For a recent intelligent defense of the better law approach, see Singer, Pay No Attention to That Man Behind the Curtain: The Place of Better Law in a Third Restatement of Conflicts, 75 Indiana L. J. 659 (2000). For a symposium devoted to Leflar's conflicts theory, see 52 Ark. L. Rev. 1-232 (1999).

E. The Restatement Second and the Most Significant Relationship

The First Restatement was promulgated in 1934. Less than 20 years later the American Law Institute called for a new Restatement because of the perceived inadequacies of the old one. The first tentative draft of the Restatement Second appeared in 1953. The final product was completed and published in 1971.

The choice-of-law process contemplated by the (Second) Restatement generally works as follows. The centerpiece of the Second Restatement is a "most significant relationship" test. So, for example, the general choice-of-law rule for torts provides:

§145. The General Principle

(1) The rights and liabilities of the parties with respect to an issue in tort are determined by the local law of that state which, with respect to that issue, has the most significant relationship to the occurrence and the parties under the principles stated in §6.

(2) Contacts to be taken into account in applying the principles of §6 to determine the law applicable to an issue include:

(a) the place where the injury occurred,

(b) the place where the conduct causing the injury occurred,

(c) the domicil, residence, nationality, place of incorporation and place of business of the parties, and

(d) the place where the relationship, if any, between the parties is centered.

These contacts are to be evaluated according to their relative importance with respect to the particular issue.

The §6 referred to in Section 145 provides:

§6. Choice-of-Law Principles

(1) A court, subject to constitutional restrictions, will follow a statutory directive of its own state on choice of law.

(2) When there is no such directive, the factors relevant to the choice of the applicable rule of law include

(a) the needs of the interstate and international systems,

(b) the relevant policies of the forum,

(c) the relevant policies of other interested states and the relative interests of those states in the determination of the particular issue,

(d) the protection of justified expectations,

(e) the basic policies underlying the particular field of law,

(f) certainty, predictability and uniformity of result, and

(g) ease in the determination and application of the law to be applied.

There are obvious tensions between Sections 145 and 6. Section 145 looks like a blind, contacts-based jurisdiction-selecting approach (i.e., an approach that picks which state's law to apply without reference to the content of state laws), while Section 6 contemplates policy analysis. In addition,

Section 145 states a rule, even if a highly general one, while section 6 states an approach. *See* Reese, Choice of Law: Rules or Approach, 57 Cornell L. Rev. 315 (1972). For these reasons, there is a certain amount of schizophrenia built into the Second Restatement. To make matters more complicated, the Second Restatement also contains more specific sections that provide presumptive rules in discrete substantive contexts. For example, Section 154's presumptive choice-of-law rule for interference with marriage relationships provides:

§154. Interference with Marriage Relationship

The local law of the state where the conduct complained of principally occurred determines the liability of one who interferes with a marriage relationship, unless, with respect to the particular issue, some other state has a more significant relationship under the principles stated in §6 to the occurrence and the parties, in which event the local law of the other state will be applied.

Because of the Second Restatement's eclecticism, courts have done many different things under its banner. Sometimes they count contacts; sometimes they apply the law of the place of the injury; sometimes they perform interest analysis; often they mix several different approaches. As a result, the case that follows cannot be said to be a "typical" application of the Second Restatement. Excellent general discussions of the methodology of the Second Restatement may be found in Reppy, Eclecticism in Choice of Law: Hybrid Method or Mish-mash?, 34 Mercer L. Rev. 645, 655-666 (1983), and Kay, Theory into Practice, Choice of Law in the Courts, 34 Mercer L. Rev. 521, 552-562 (1983).

Phillips v. General Motors Corp.

995 P.2d 1002 (Mont. 2000)

Justice REGNIER delivered the opinion of the Court.

Factual Background

The vehicle which is the subject of this action was a 1985 Chevrolet pickup. The vehicle was originally sold by General Motors in North Carolina. Darrell Byrd subsequently purchased the pickup in or about February 1995 from Mike's Wholesale Cars in Newton, North Carolina. In doing so, he supplied a North Carolina address. The 1985 Chevrolet pickup truck was designed, tested, manufactured, and distributed by General Motors. The subject vehicle had fuel tanks mounted outside the frame rail.

On December 22, 1997, Darrell Byrd was driving with his family in the 1985 Chevrolet pickup truck from their home near Fortine, Montana, where Darrell Byrd was employed and where Timothy and Samuel Byrd attended school. The purpose of the trip was to spend Christmas vacation with family in North Carolina. The Byrds were domiciled in Montana before and at the time of the 1997 accident.

The wreck and fire which form the basis of this action occurred on December 22, 1997, on Interstate 70 near Russell, Kansas. A 1997 International semi-tractor trailer driven by Betty J. Kendall collided with the subject 1985 Chevrolet pickup truck driven by Darrell Byrd. A fire ensued. Darrell, Angela, and Timothy Byrd died. Samuel Byrd sustained personal injuries which required emergency treatment and hospitalization.

Before and at the time of the 1997 accident, Samuel, Timothy, Darrell, and Angela Byrd were Montana residents. The deceased, Darrell and Angela Byrd, were respectively the father and mother of the deceased, Timothy Byrd. Timothy was 13 years of age at the time of his death. Samuel Byrd, who survived the accident is also the son of the deceased, Darrell and Angela Byrd, and was 11 years old at the time of the 1997 accident.

Plaintiff Alvin Phillips is the legal guardian of Samuel Byrd and the personal representative of the estates of Angela Byrd, Darrell Byrd, and Timothy Byrd. Alvin Phillips resides in Newton, North Carolina. Samuel Byrd presently resides in North Carolina. Probate proceedings for the Estates of Timothy, Angela, and Darrell Byrd are filed with and pending in the Montana Nineteenth Judicial District Court, Lincoln County, Montana.

In these product liability cases, in which Plaintiffs raise claims of negligence and strict liability, Plaintiffs seek compensatory and punitive damages related to the deaths of Darrell, Angela, and Timothy Byrd and the personal injuries sustained by Samuel Byrd. General Motors denies all liability.

[The case was filed in federal district court in Montana, which certified three questions to the Montana state court.] According to the District Court's Order, the parties disagree about the substantive law that should be applied to this case. . . . Montana does not have a statutory provision governing choice of law nor has this Court reached a choice of law issue in a case involving conflicting tort rules. Absent a definitive determination of Montana's choice of law rule in tort cases, federal judges for the District of Montana have applied the "most significant relationship" test of the Restatement (Second) of Conflict of Laws.

The District Court observed that the instant case raised significant policy questions involving Montana's choice of law rules, that choice of law questions in tort cases are frequent in diversity litigation in federal court, and that it would be helpful in resolving this case and others to have a definitive determination of what the Montana choice of law rule is.

Question One

Whether, in a personal injury/product liability/wrongful death action, where there is a potential conflict of laws, Montana will follow the Restatement (Second) of Conflict of Laws, including the "most significant relationship" test set forth in §§146 and 6, in the determination of which state's substantive law to apply?

The traditional choice of law rule, known as *lex loci delicti commissi* (or the law of place where the wrong was committed), provides that the infliction of injury is actionable under the law of the state in which it was received. *See* Alabama Great S. R.R. Co. v. Carroll (Ala. 1892), 97 Ala. 126, 11 So. 803, 805. . . . The theoretical basis for the traditional rule was the "vested rights" theory propounded by Joseph H. Beale. The theory explained the forum's use of foreign legal rules in terms of the creation and enforcement of vested rights. According to Professor Beale's theory, the only law that can operate in a foreign territory is the law of the foreign sovereign. When an event occurred in a foreign territory (an injury caused by a defective product, for example), and under the laws of that territory that event gave rise to a right (damages), a right "vested" under that territory's law. The role of the forum court was simply to enforce the right which had vested in the foreign territory according to that territory's law. Crucial to this theory was a determination of where and when a right vested, because the law in place where the right vested would control the existence and content of the right. As evidenced by the decision in *Carroll*, courts have held that for tort claims a right vested where and when an injury occurred.

Traditional practice depends on a few broad, single-contact, jurisdiction-selecting rules. Traditionalist courts find the location of the last event necessary for a right to vest and apply the law of that location. As a result, courts following the traditional approach often choose the law of a state with no interest in the resolution of the dispute, like the choice of Mississippi law in *Carroll*.

The traditional rule has largely been justified on the basis of the practical advantages that it offers: certainty, predictability, and forum neutrality. However, problems inherent in its application as well as escape devices used to avoid results perceived to be arbitrary or unfair have greatly diminished the advantages the traditional rule supposedly provides. For example, the explicit public policy exception to the *lex loci* rule allows courts to avoid the law of the place of injury by concluding that it violates the public policy of the forum. Use of the public policy escape device by *lex loci* courts continues today.

The traditional rule also no longer affords consistency and predictability across jurisdictions. While some jurisdictions still cling to the traditional rule, the vast majority of states have rejected it. . . . Professor Symeonides observes:

> As the century draws to a close, the traditional theory in tort and contract conflicts in the United States finds itself in a very precarious state. This

> assessment is based not simply on the relatively low number of states that still adhere to that theory, but also on the shallowness of their commitment to it. Although the degree of commitment varies from state to state, it is fair to say that very few of these states are philosophically committed to the traditional theory. . . . More often, these rules remain in place only because [a] court is able to find a way to evade them by using one of the traditional escapes, such as characterization, substance versus procedure, renvoi, or, more often, the [public policy] exception.

Symeonides, [Choice of Law in American Courts in 1998: Twelfth Annual Survey, 47 Am. J. Comp. L. 327,] 345. The Restatement (Second) of Conflict of Laws largely abandoned the traditional rule in favor of an approach which seeks to apply the law of the state with the "most significant relationship to the occurrence and the parties." Restatement (Second) of Conflict of Laws §145(1) (1971) (hereinafter "Restatement (Second)"). In adopting a policy analysis approach, the drafters noted that "experience has shown that the last event rule does not always work well. Situations arise where the state of the last event (place of injury) bears only a slight relationship to the occurrence and the parties with respect to the particular issue." Restatement (Second), Introductory Note to Ch. 7, at 412.

In abandoning the *lex loci* rule in favor of the most significant relationship test, one court observed:

> The majority of courts which have considered the question have abandoned the *lex loci* rule in favor of a more flexible approach which permits analysis of the policies and interests underlying the particular issue before the court. Additionally, the commentators are overwhelmingly opposed to its retention and, although they disagree as to a substitute approach, all advocate a method which allows Courts to focus on the policies underlying the conflicting laws . . . and the governmental interests which would be advanced by their application.

In re Air Crash Disaster at Boston, Mass. on July 31, 1973 (D. Mass. 1975), 399 F. Supp. 1106, 1110. In determining the choice of law rules for contract disputes, we adopted the approach contained in the Restatement (Second) of Conflict of Laws. We see no reason to have one choice of law approach for contracts and another for torts. For the reasons set forth above, we now hereby adopt the "most significant relationship" approach to determine the applicable substantive law for issues of tort.

Question Two

Given the facts of this case, which state's law applies to plaintiff's various tort and damages claims under Montana's choice of law rules?

The Byrds claim that under the most significant relationship test Montana law applies. General Motors contends that under this same test, the law of Kansas applies. We agree with the Byrds.

At the outset, we note that many appellate courts that have analyzed the most significant relationship test have done so in a fairly conclusory fashion. Although the analysis that follows appears somewhat tedious, our attempt is to comply with the procedures set forth in the Restatement (Second) of Conflict of Laws. We also raise an additional caveat. Any analysis under the Restatement approach is necessarily driven by the unique facts, issues, applicable law, and jurisdictions implicated in a particular case.

A. Relevant Restatement Provisions

Any conflict of law analysis under the Restatement must begin with §6. [The court recites Section 6, reproduced *supra* page 263]. Since we have no statutory directive regarding choice of law, we turn to the specific section that relates to tort and personal injury actions. [The court recites Section 145, reproduced *supra* page 263.] These contacts are to be evaluated according to their relative importance with respect to the particular issue.

The Restatement also has more specific sections relating to personal injury and wrongful death actions. Sections 146 and 175 provide that the rights and liabilities of the parties are to be determined in accordance with the law of the state where the injury occurred unless, with respect to a particular issue, another state has a more significant relationship. Whether another state has a more significant relationship is determined under §145(2). We further note that issues such as the tortious character of conduct, available defenses, contributory fault, and damages are all to be determined by applying the most significant relationship rule of §145. *See, e.g.*, Restatement (Second) §§156 ("Tortious Character of Conduct"), 157 ("Standard of Care"), 161 ("Defenses"), 164 ("Contributory Fault"), and 171 ("Damages").

B. Most Significant Relationship Analysis

Under the Restatement (Second) approach, the local law of the place of injury, Kansas, is presumptively applicable in a product liability and wrongful death action unless, with respect to a particular issue, a different state has a more significant relationship. *See* Restatement (Second) §§146 and 175. In order to determine whether a state other than the place of injury has a more significant relationship, the contacts listed under §145(2) "are to be taken into account in applying the principles of §6." Restatement (Second) §145(2). Accordingly, we shall address each of the factors enumerated under §6(2), taking into account, when appropriate, the contacts of §145(2).

1. NEEDS OF THE INTERSTATE AND INTERNATIONAL SYSTEM

The first factor we must consider under §6(2) is the needs of the interstate and international system. Restatement (Second) §6(2)(a). The drafters stated,

> Choice-of-law rules, among other things, should seek to further harmonious relations between states and to facilitate commercial intercourse between them. In formulating rules of choice of law, a state should have regard for the needs and policies of other states and of the community of states. Rules of choice of law formulated with regard for such needs and policies are likely to commend themselves to other states and to be adopted by these states
>
> Restatement §6 cmt. d.

On the facts of this case, this factor does not point toward the importance of applying any particular state's law. Rather, this factor supports the application of the Restatement approach, namely the law of the state with the most significant relationship to an issue. We believe the Restatement approach fosters harmonious relationships between states by respecting the substantive law of other states when those states have a greater interest in the determination of a particular issue litigated in a foreign jurisdiction. The Restatement approach is preferable, in our view, to the traditional *lex loci* rule which applies the law of the place of the accident which may be fortuitous in tort actions. We further conclude that there is no need to evaluate the contacts listed in §145 to this issue.

2. THE POLICIES OF INTERESTED STATES

The second and third factors we must consider are the relevant policies of the forum state and other interested states. *See* Restatement (Second) §6(2)(b) and (c). In the case *sub judice*, these are the most important factors in our analysis. The drafters stated,

> Every Rule of Law, whether embodied in a statute or in a common law rule, was designed to achieve one or more purposes. A court should have regard for these purposes in determining whether to apply its own rule or the rule of another state in the decision of a particular issue. If the purposes sought to be achieved by a local statute or common law rule would be furthered by its application to out-of-state facts, this is a weighty reason why such application should be made.

Restatement (Second) §6 cmt. e. This principle requires us to consider whether applying the law of a state with a relevant contact would further the purpose that law was designed to achieve. Upon consideration of this principle, it is clear that Montana has the more significant relationship to the issues raised by this dispute for the reasons set forth below.

a. Place of Injury

As noted above, in product liability and wrongful death actions, the law of the place of injury is presumptively applicable unless another state has a more significant relationship. *See* Restatement (Second) §§146 and 175. The injury here occurred in Kansas. Kansas law provides for a cause of action against a manufacturer whose product causes harm as a result of its defective design. *See* Kan. Stat. Ann. §60-3302. The purpose of a state's product liability statute is to regulate the sale of products in that state and to prevent injuries incurred by that state's residents due to defective products. . . . Any conduct the state of Kansas may have been attempting to regulate through §60-3302 could not be implicated by the facts of this case as it involves neither a sale in Kansas nor an injury to a Kansas resident.

Kansas law provides for multiple defenses to a product liability claim. For example, Kansas law bars recovery for injuries occurring after "the time during which the product would be normally likely to perform or be stored in a safe manner." Kan. Stat. Ann. §60-3303(a)(1). Kansas law also allows a party defending a product liability claim to assert that the injury causing aspect of the product was in compliance with the regulatory standards relating to design or performance at the time of manufacture. *See* Kan. Stat. Ann. §60-3304(a). Once again, the overriding purpose of Kansas's product liability laws is to establish the level of safety of products sold either in Kansas or to a Kansas resident. Clearly, these rules regarding defenses were not enacted in order to grant a defense to a manufacturer when a non-Kansas resident is injured by a product not purchased in Kansas.

Under Kansas law, an award of damages for product liability may be diminished in proportion to the amount of negligence attributed to the plaintiff or decedent. General Motors asserts that the issue of comparative negligence turns upon conduct that occurred in Kansas and therefore Kansas law should apply because Kansas has an interest in regulating conduct which occurred within its borders. However, the record before us does not contain the substance of General Motors' allegations regarding the Byrds' allegedly negligent conduct. Therefore, there is no evidence that General Motors' allegations concerning the comparative negligence of the Byrds are limited to conduct occurring solely within Kansas.

Moreover, even if General Motors' allegations concerned conduct occurring solely in Kansas, the Kansas Supreme Court did not extend Kansas's comparative negligence statute to product liability causes of action in order to regulate conduct occurring in Kansas. In concluding that the comparative negligence statute applied to product liability actions, the Kansas Supreme Court stated:

> ***Comparative liability provides a system for allocating responsibility*** for an injury while still serving the social policy of not allowing a manufacturer or seller to escape liability for defective products merely because of slight culpability on the part of the product user in bringing about the injury.

[Kennedy v. City of Sawyer, 618 P. 2d 788, 796 (Kan. 1980) (emphasis added). It is clear from the *Kennedy* decision that the Kansas Supreme Court extended Kansas's comparative negligence standard to product liability cases in order to "allocate responsibility for an injury" due to a defective product, disallowing defenses such as "assumption of the risk," "product misuse," or "unreasonable use" from completely precluding recovery under Kansas product liability law. Kansas has no interest in allocating responsibility for the injuries suffered by Montana residents and caused by a product purchased in North Carolina. Again, the purpose of a state's product liability laws is to protect and provide compensation to its residents and regulate the sale of products within its borders.

Kansas law limits the total amount recoverable for "noneconomic loss" in a personal injury action to $250,000, and limits "nonpecuniary" damages in wrongful death actions to $100,000. Kan. Stat. Ann. §§60-19a02, 1903. Section 60-1903 was enacted in an effort to alleviate a perceived crisis in the availability and affordability of liability insurance. . . . The purpose of these limitations would be furthered if any damage award issued would affect the availability or affordability of liability insurance for Kansas residents. The purpose of these limitations would not be furthered by applying them to the instant case because an award of damages against General Motors which exceeded Kansas's statutory damage limitations would not affect the availability or affordability of liability insurance for Kansas residents.

Lastly, Kansas law allows for punitive damages, but limits them to the lesser of $5 million or the defendant's highest gross annual income earned during any one of the five years immediately before the act for which such damages are awarded. The purpose of the availability and extent of punitive damage awards is to punish or deter conduct deemed wrongful when the availability of a cause of action and compensatory damages are considered an insufficient punishment or deterrence. Accordingly, the purpose of Kansas's punitive damage provisions would only be furthered on a particular set of facts if it had an interest in punishing or deterring the conduct at issue. As noted above, the purpose of Kansas's cause of action for product liability would not be furthered by its application to these facts because the pickup was not sold in Kansas nor were the Byrds Kansas residents. Correspondingly, this case does not involve conduct which Kansas was attempting to punish or deter through its punitive damage provisions.

b. Place of Conduct

The Byrds purchased the vehicle in North Carolina. General Motors has made a general assertion that North Carolina might have an interest in having its law applied, but has not briefed us on which North Carolina laws might be applicable. Accordingly, our discussion will be somewhat general in nature. General Motors has argued that North Carolina has an interest because General Motors initially sold the truck in North Carolina, the Byrds subsequently purchased the truck in North Carolina, and the Byrds may have been North Carolina residents when they made this purchase.

The fact that the Byrds purchased the truck in North Carolina while residing there indicates that one of the purposes of North Carolina product liability law—the regulation of products sold within its borders—might be implicated by the facts of this case. However, we think it significant that a North Carolina court would not apply North Carolina law to these facts, even if the Byrds had remained in North Carolina; North Carolina still adheres to the traditional place of injury rule in tort cases. On the facts of this case, a North Carolina court would apply the law of Kansas because they still adhere to the "vested rights" theory that any right created by an injury is solely a product of the law of the territory in which that injury occurred. Accordingly, the scope of North Carolina product liability law does not include causes of action for products purchased in North Carolina by North Carolina residents which cause injury outside of North Carolina. This belies the significance of North Carolina's interest in having its law applied. We note, however, that the place of purchase may have had greater significance if North Carolina followed the Restatement's approach rather than the traditional place of injury rule.

General Motors asserts that Michigan has an interest in regulating conduct occurring in Michigan. We note that evidence of where the pickup truck was designed and manufactured is not in the record nor has General Motors briefed us on the content of the precise laws which it claims might be applicable to these facts. However, we do not believe that the purpose of any potentially applicable Michigan product liability law would be to regulate the design and manufacture of products within its borders. The purpose of product liability law is to regulate in-state sales or sales to residents and to set the level of compensation when residents are injured.

Significantly, Michigan courts have recognized that it would not further the purpose of Michigan product liability law to apply it to a similar set of facts. Michigan courts have not applied Michigan law under similar circumstances because Michigan has little interest in applying its law when its only contact with the dispute is the location of the manufacturer.

Other courts have observed that applying the law of the place of manufacture would be unfair because it would tend to leave victims under compensated as states wishing to attract and hold manufacturing companies would raise the threshold of liability and reduce compensation. We agree that stressing the importance of the place of manufacture for choice of law purposes in a product liability case would be unfair. The conclusion that the place of manufacture is a relatively unimportant factor in a product liability case is obvious when we consider a hypothetical case in which all of the relevant contacts are in the forum state except the location of the manufacturer (most likely the fact pattern for the vast majority of product liability cases). Applying the law of the place of manufacture to that case simply because the product was manufactured out-of-state would allow a state with a high concentration of industry to capture all of the benefits of a high threshold of liability and a low level of compensation. Specifically, the manufacturing state could enjoy the benefits associated with liability laws which favored manufacturers in order to attract and retain manufacturing firms and encourage business within its borders while placing the costs of its legislative decision, in the form of less tort compensation, on the shoulders of nonresidents injured by its manufacturers' products. This seems inherently unfair.

c. Residence of Parties

The Plaintiffs were residents of Montana at the time they were injured. Unlike the laws of the other states with relevant contacts under §145(2), the purposes sought to be achieved by Montana's product liability laws would be furthered by their application to this set of facts.[1] One of the central purposes of Montana's product liability scheme is to prevent injuries to Montana residents caused by defectively designed products. In contrast to Kansas, Montana has a direct interest in the application of its product liability laws because its residents were injured in this accident. Montana adopted a strict liability standard in order to afford "*maximum protection for consumers against dangerous defects in manufactured products with the focus on the condition of the product, and not on the manufacturer's conduct or knowledge.*" *See* Sternhagen v. Dow Co. (1997), 282 Mont. 168, 176, 935 P.2d 1139, 1144 (emphasis added).

As is clear from *Sternhagen,* the focus of Montana law is not only on the regulation of products sold in Montana, but also on providing the maximum protection and compensation to Montana residents with the focus on the condition of the product and not on the conduct of the manufacturer. Applying Montana's provisions guaranteeing strict liability and full compensation to a cause of action involving a Montana domiciliary injured by a defective product would further the purposes of Montana law by insuring that the costs to Montana residents due to injuries from defective products are fully borne by

1. In analyzing the place of manufacture, we fully addressed the relative significance of General Motors' principal place of business under this principle. Neither party asserts that Delaware, General Motors' place of incorporation, has any interest in having its product liability or wrongful death statutes apply to this case.

the responsible parties. It will also have the salutary effect of deterring future sales of defective products in Montana and encouraging manufacturers to warn Montana residents about defects in their products as quickly and as thoroughly as possible.

Likewise, the purposes of Montana's laws regarding the availability and extent of punitive damages in product liability actions would also be furthered by their application to these facts. This is because, as described more fully above, punitive damages serve to punish and deter conduct deemed wrongful—in this case, placing a defective product into the stream of commerce which subsequently injured a Montana resident.

Lastly, we must address whether the purpose underlying Montana's rules governing product liability would be furthered by their application in this case despite the fact that Samuel Byrd is no longer a Montana domiciliary. We believe that the application of Montana law to an injury received by a Montana domiciliary would further the purpose of that law regardless of the postaccident residency of the plaintiff. As discussed previously, the purpose of Montana product liability law is to regulate product sales in Montana and to compensate injured Montanans. Clearly, that concern arises as soon as a product is either sold in Montana or causes injury to a Montana resident. Consequently, the relevant residence of the plaintiff is the residence at the time of injury.

We note that the only reason Samuel Byrd is currently residing in North Carolina is because his parents died in the accident which forms the basis of the Plaintiffs' claims. The guarantee of full compensation for Montana residents who suffer injuries due to defective products certainly will not turn on such fortuitous circumstances as a postaccident move caused by the allegedly wrongful conduct of a defendant.

d. The Place Where the Relationship, If Any, between the Parties Is Centered

It doesn't appear that there is a place where the relationship, if any, between General Motors and the Byrds is centered. As one court described in similar circumstances:

Products liability arises out of the most casual "relationship" imaginable, the one-time purchase and sale of the product, and the plaintiff, as here, may have had no connection with it. The only "relationship" between the parties here is that of injured victim and alleged tortfeasor.

In sum, upon an analysis of the principle requiring us to consider the policies of interested states, it appears that Montana, as the domicile of the Byrds, has a significant relationship to the issues raised by this dispute. This is because, in general, the purpose of a state's product liability law is to regulate purchases made within its borders and to protect and compensate its residents. The policies underlying Montana product liability law would be furthered on these facts because the Byrds were Montana domiciliaries at the time they were injured. The policies underlying Kansas and Michigan law would not be furthered by their application to these facts because the product was not sold in either state, nor were the Plaintiffs domiciled in either state at the time they where injured. The purposes underlying North Carolina product liability law would not be furthered on these facts because, under North Carolina's vested rights approach to conflict of laws, North Carolina would apply the law of the jurisdiction where the injury occurred, whatever that law may be.

3. JUSTIFIED EXPECTATIONS

Although we are to consider the justified expectations of the parties, tort cases generally do not involve justified expectations. Particularly in the area of negligence, when parties act without giving thought to the legal consequences of their conduct or to the law to be applied, they have no justified expectations. *See* Restatement (Second) §6 cmt. g.

Automobile manufacturers do presumably give advance thought to the legal consequences of their conduct when designing and manufacturing their products. However, we note that the law of any state could potentially apply in a product liability action involving an automobile. For example, because North Carolina employs the traditional place of injury rule for choice of law purposes, if a North Carolina resident receives an injury from a defective vehicle while driving out-of-state, the law of the place of injury would govern that dispute. Accordingly, any expectation General Motors had that the law of North Carolina would govern a product liability suit involving a pickup truck it sold in North Carolina would not be justified. Furthermore, . . . automobiles are moveable and frequently resold and the maintenance of a product liability action does not require privity. For example, the pickup could have been subsequently resold by the initial purchaser in a state which does not adhere to the traditional *lex loci* rule. Therefore, any expectation General Motors had that a dispute concerning this pickup truck would be governed by North Carolina's place of injury rule would not be justified.

4. BASIC POLICIES UNDERLYING PARTICULAR FIELD OF LAW

We must also consider the relevant contacts in regard to the basic policies underlying the particular field of law. *See* Restatement (Second) §6(2)(e). The drafters state that:

> This factor is of particular importance in situations where the policies of the interested states are largely the same but there are nevertheless minor differences between their relevant local law rules. In such instances, there is good reason for the court to apply the local law of the state which will best achieve the basic policy, or policies, underlying the particular field of law involved.

Restatement (Second) §6(2) cmt. h. This is not a case in which the policies of interested states are basically the same except for minor differences in their local rules. For example, although under Kansas and Montana law, manufacturers of defective products are strictly liable for injuries, North Carolina law does not permit strict liability in tort in product liability actions. Instead, it appears that the various interested states have reached different conclusions concerning the right level of compensation and deterrence for injuries caused by defective products. Therefore, we need go no further in addressing this contact.

5. CERTAINTY, PREDICTABILITY, UNIFORMITY, EASE

We are also instructed to give consideration to the certainty, predictability and uniformity of result as well as the ease in the determination and application of the law to be applied. *See* Restatement (Second) §6(2)(f) and (g). The comments state:

> Predictability and uniformity of result are of particular importance in areas where parties are likely to give advance thought to the legal consequences of their transactions. It is partly on account of these factors that the parties are permitted within broad limits to choose the law that will determine the validity and effect of their contract. . . .

Restatement (Second) §6(2) cmt. i. A consideration of this principle does not indicate that any one state has a more significant relationship than any other. Applying the law of the place of injury would not increase certainty or predictability any more than applying the law of the plaintiff's residence at the time of accident.

C. CONCLUSION

Under the most significant relationship approach of the Restatement (Second), the local law of the place of injury, Kansas, governs the rights and liabilities of the parties to a product liability and wrongful death action unless, with respect to a particular issue, a different state has a more significant relationship. *See* Restatement (Second) §§146 and 175. In order to determine whether a state other than the place of injury has a more significant relationship, the contacts listed under §145(2) must be analyzed in relation to the principles enumerated under §6(2). However, the principles of §6(2) need not be given equal consideration in each case. Varying weight must be given to a particular factor, or group of factors, in different areas of choice of law. *See* Restatement (Second) §6 cmt. c. On the facts before us, we give most weight to the principles requiring us to consider the relevant policies of interested states. Restatement (Second) §6(2)(b) and (c). The other principles do not indicate the significance of any one contact.

Upon an analysis of the policies of interested states, it appears that the purposes of both Montana and North Carolina product liability law would presumably be furthered by their application to these facts. The place of purchase has an interest in regulating the safety of products sold within its borders; the place of the plaintiff's residence has an interest in deterring injuries to its residents and setting the level of compensation. Significantly, however, North Carolina law would not apply its own law to these facts, even if the Byrds had been North Carolina residents at the time of injury.

The purpose behind Montana product liability laws is clearly implicated by these facts. The following factors all point toward applying Montana law: the Byrds resided in Montana at the time of the accident, General Motors does business in Montana, Montana has a direct interest in preventing defective products from causing injuries to Montana residents as well as punishing and deterring manufacturers whose products injure Montana residents, and finally Montana is interested in fully compensating Montana residents. All of these factors would be furthered by applying Montana product liability, defenses, damages, and wrongful death statutes to the facts of this case.

Question Three

Does Montana recognize a "public policy" exception that would require application of Montana law even where Montana's choice of law rules dictate application of the laws of another state, and would such an exception apply in this case?

For choice of law purposes, the public policy of a state is simply the rules, as expressed in its legislative enactments and judicial decisions, that it uses to decide controversies. The purpose of a choice of law rule is to resolve conflicts between competing policies. Considerations of public policy are expressly subsumed within the most significant relationship approach. *See* Restatement (Second) §6(2)(b) and (c) (mandating consideration of the relevant policies of the forum state and other interested states). In order to determine which state has the more significant relationship, the public policies of all interested states must be considered. A "public policy" exception to the most significant relationship test would be redundant.

Accordingly, in answer to the questions certified, we adopt the Restatement (Second) of Conflict of Laws for tort actions. Under the analysis contained in the Restatement (Second), we conclude that given the facts as presented in the District Court's Order, the laws of Montana apply. Lastly, considerations of public policy are accounted for under the analysis contained in the Restatement (Second) of Conflict of Laws.

Questions and Comments

(1) The history of the drafting of the Second Restatement helps to explain its complex methodology. The project began in 1953 as a response to

the harsh criticisms of the First Restatement. The first tentative draft retained the First Restatement's jurisdiction-selecting approach but used the more flexible jurisdiction-selecting criteria of the "most significant relationship" test. Early drafts of the Second Restatement were heavily criticized by Currie and Ehrenzweig (among others) on the grounds that its rules focused too much on territorialism and ignored interest analysis. *See* Currie, The Disinterested Third State, 28 Law & Contemp. Probs. 754, 755 (1963); Ehrenzweig, The "Most Significant Relationship" in the Conflicts Law of Torts: Law and Reason Versus the Restatement Second, 28 Law & Contemp. Probs. 700, 700 (1963). Section 6 was a response to these criticisms. In the words of one writer, it was "a sop tossed . . . to members of the American Law Institute who were unhappy with a purely territorial methodology." Reppy, Eclecticism in Choice of Law: Hybrid Method or Mishmash?, 34 Mercer L. Rev. 645, 662 (1983).

(2) How would you characterize the Second Restatement as applied in *Phillips?* Was it a contacts-counting case akin to *Haag,* page 183 *supra?* Or was it more akin to the interest analysis cases that we have read? Does the Second Restatement allow a court to do either, or both?

(3) The Second Restatement is by far the most popular choice-of-law methodology in the United States. Approximately 22 states have formally embraced its approach to torts, and 24 have embraced it's approach to contracts. *See* Symeonides, Choice of Law in the American Courts in 2000: As the Century Turns, 49 Am. J. Comp. L. 1, 10 (2001). These numbers are misleading, however. As Professor Symeonides has noted, Second Restatement courts evince wildly varying "gradations of commitment to the Second Restatement," and perform many different choice-of-law analyses in its name. *See* Symeonides, The Judicial Acceptance of the Second Conflicts Restatement, A Mixed Blessing, 56 Md. L. Rev. 1248, 1261-1263 (1997). Some courts use the Second Restatement's specific presumptive rules to break a true conflict, *see, e.g.,* Reichhold Chemicals, Inc. v. Hartford Accident and Indemnity Co., 703 A. 2d 1132 (Ct. 1997) (applying §193 to break true conflict between New York and Washington law). Other courts ignore the Second Restatement's specific presumptive rules even when they are on point, *see, e.g.,* Allstate Insurance Co. v. Stolarz, 613 N.E.2d 936 (N.Y. 1993) (applying Second Restatement but ignoring §193 in case involving insurance stacking). Some courts use the Second Restatement to perform a "groupings-of-contacts" analysis, *see, e.g.,* Palmer v. ARCO Chem. Co., 904 P. 2d 1221 (Alaska 1995), others use it to curtail but not avoid interest analysis, *see, e.g.,* Nelson v. Hix, 522 N.E. 2d 1214 (Ill. 1988), and yet others use it in a manner akin to the First Restatement, *see, e.g.,* Hataway v. McKinley, 830 S.W. 2d 53, 58 (Tenn. 1992). There are many other possibilities. Is the discretion that the Second Restatement obviously gives judges the key to its widespread acceptance?

(4) One author's survey of Second Restatement cases led to the following conclusions:

> Some state courts routinely list [the Restatement's] relevant sections in their opinions and try to follow them; this task is easiest when the case is controlled by one of the Restatement Second's specific narrow rules. Other state courts have not been consistent in their terminology about what approach they are following, and others have retained primary emphasis on the place of the wrong in tort cases, even while abandoning the lex loci delicti for the Restatement Second. . . . This review of the cases suggests that, if the original Restatement was unsuccessful because of its dogmatic rigidity and its insistence on the uncritical application of a few specific rules, the Restatement Second may fail to provide enough guidance to the courts to produce even a semblance of uniformity among the states following its method. In the drafters' attempt to mollify their critics, they have created an umbrella for traditionalist and modern theorist alike: a fragile shelter that may prove itself unable to survive any but the most gentle of showers.

Kay, Theory Into Practice: Choice of Law in the Courts, 34 Mercer L. Rev. 521, 561-562 (1983). An Oregon court was less gentle, comparing the Second Restatement to "skeet shooting with a bow and arrow: a direct hit is likely to be a rarity, if not pure luck." Fisher v. Huck, 624 P. 2d 177, 178 (Or. 1981).

(5) Do the Second Restatement's specific "presumptive" rules (like §§146 and 175 at issue in *Phillips*) have any bite? Doesn't a court applying the Second Restatement with rigor always have to ensure that there is not a state with a "more significant relationship"? And doesn't this, in turn, push courts back into the conundrum of sorting out the relationship between §§6 and 145. Isn't this what happened in *Phillips?* Why, then, have the specific provisions?

(6) One of the problems with the First Restatement that the Restatement Second retains (apparently deliberately) is characterization. Characterization is one difficulty that other modern approaches seem to have dispensed with effectively. Although §6 sets out the general principles for all issues—substantive and procedural, tort and contract, and the like—the remainder of the Second Restatement attempts to provide more specific principles to deal with these separate categories. Resolution of the question of whether products liability or insurance indemnification (to name just two examples) should be analyzed according to §146 or §188 can determine the outcome of the choice-of-law process.

(7) For further analysis of the *Phillips* court's public policy analysis, see *infra* page 326-327. For further analysis of its use of renvoi, see *infra* page 311.

(8) For a 25-year retrospective symposium on the Second Restatement, see The Silver Anniversary of the Second Conflicts Restatement, 56 Md. L. Rev. 1193-1410 (1997). For a recent symposium on the possibility of a Third Restatement of Conflicts, with much critical analysis of the Second Restatement, see Preparing for the Next Century—a New Restatement of Conflicts?, 75 Indiana L. J. 399-686 (2000).

F. Contractual Choice of Law

As we saw in Chapter 1, *supra* page 36, the First Restatement made no provision for the enforcement of choice-of-law clauses, and Beale (as well as some courts) were hostile to them on the grounds that they involved "private legislation." As the provisions below make clear, the Second Restatement explicitly endorses party autonomy to choose the applicable law in a wide range of circumstances. These provisions are enormously popular among courts—including (as the first case below demonstrates) courts that do not otherwise follow the Second Restatement.

Selections from the Restatement (Second) of Conflicts

§§186-188, 203 (1969)

Contracts

§186. Applicable Law

Issues in contract are determined by the law chosen by the parties in accordance with the rule of §187 and otherwise by the law selected in accordance with the rule of §188.

§187. Law of the State Chosen by the Parties

(1) The law of the state chosen by the parties to govern their contractual rights and duties will be applied if the particular issue is one which the parties could have resolved by an explicit provision in their agreement directed to that issue.

(2) The law of the state chosen by the parties to govern their contractual rights and duties will be applied, even if the particular issue is one which the parties could not have resolved by an explicit provision in their agreement directed to that issue, unless either

(a) the chosen state has no substantial relationship to the parties or the transaction and there is no other reasonable basis for the parties' choice, or

(b) application of the law of the chosen state would be contrary to a fundamental policy of a state which has a materially greater interest than the chosen state in the determination of the particular issue and which, under the rule of §188, would be the state of the applicable law in the absence of an effective choice of law by the parties.

(3) In the absence of a contrary indication of intention, the reference is to the local law of the state of the chosen law. [Why are the parties allowed, under subsection (2)(b), to violate the "fundamental policy" of a state that has half, but not a "materially greater" interest in the issue at stake? If the issue is one which the parties could not have resolved by an explicit provi-

sion of their contract, why should a state with a "materially greater" interest in the case not get to apply its law, in the face of a contrary contractual provision, simply because the policy is merely important, and not fundamental? And as long as the forum is willing to allow parties to choose law other than its own, even when it has policies in point, why is the choice limited to the law of a state with "substantial connection?"]

§188. Law Governing in Absence of Effective Choice by the Parties

(1) The rights and duties of the parties with respect to an issue in contract are determined by the local law of the state which, with respect to that issue, has the most significant relationship to the transaction and the parties under the principles stated in §6.

(2) In the absence of an effective choice of law by the parties (*see* §187), the contacts to be taken into account in applying the principles of §6 to determine the law applicable to an issue include:

(a) the place of contracting,

(b) the place of negotiation of the contract,

(c) the place of performance,

(d) the location of the subject matter of the contract, and

(e) the domicil, residence, nationality, place of incorporation and place of business of the parties.

These contacts are to be evaluated according to their relative importance with respect to the particular issue.

(3) If the place of negotiating the contract and the place of performance are in the same state, the local law of this state will usually be applied, except as otherwise provided in §§189-199 and 203.

§203. Usury

The validity of a contract will be sustained against the charge of usury if it provides for a rate of interest that is permissible in a state to which the contract has a substantial relationship and is not greatly in excess of the rate permitted by the general usury law of the state of the otherwise applicable law under the rule of §188.

Nedlloyd Lines B.V. v. Superior Court of San Mateo County Seawinds Ltd.

834 P.2d 1148, 3 Cal. 4th 459, 11 Cal. Rptr. 2d 330 (1992)

Baxter, J.

We granted review to consider the effect of a choice-of-law clause in a contract between commercial entities to finance and operate an international shipping business. In our order granting review, we limited our consideration to the question whether and to what extent the law of Hong Kong, chosen in the parties' agreement, should be applied in ruling on defendant's demurrer to plaintiff's complaint.

We conclude the choice-of-law clause, which requires that the contract be "governed by" the law of Hong Kong, a jurisdiction having a substantial connection with the parties, is fully enforceable and applicable to claims for breach of the implied covenant of good faith and fair dealing and for breach of fiduciary duties allegedly arising out of the contract. Our conclusion rests on the choice-of-law rules derived from California decisions and the Restatement Second of Conflict of Laws, which reflect strong policy considerations favoring the enforcement of freely negotiated choice-of-law clauses. Based on our conclusion, we will reverse the judgments of the Court of Appeal and remand for further proceedings.

Plaintiff and real party in interest Seawinds Limited (Seawinds) is a shipping company, currently undergoing reorganization under chapter 11 of the United States Bankruptcy Code, whose business consists of the operation of three container ships. Seawinds was incorporated in Hong Kong in late 1982 and has its principal place of business in Redwood City, California. Defendants and petitioners Nedlloyd Lines B.V., Royal Nedlloyd Group N.V., and KNSM Lines B.V. (collectively referred to as Nedlloyd) are interrelated shipping companies incorporated in the Netherlands with their principal place of business in Rotterdam.

In March 1983, Nedlloyd and other parties (including an Oregon corporation, a Hong Kong corporation, a British corporation, three individual residents of California, and a resident of Singapore) entered into a contract to purchase shares of Seawinds' stock. The contract, which was entitled "Shareholders' Agreement in Respect of Seawinds Limited," stated that its purpose was "to establish [Seawinds] as a joint venture company to carry on a transportation operation." The agreement also provided that Seawinds would carry on the business of the transportation company and that the parties to the agreement would use "means reasonably available" to ensure the business was a success.

The shareholders' agreement between the parties contained the following choice-of-law and forum selection provision: "This agreement shall be governed by and construed in accordance with Hong Kong law and each party hereby irrevocably submits to the nonexclusive jurisdiction and service of process of the Hong Kong courts."

In January 1989, Seawinds sued Nedlloyd, alleging in essence that Nedlloyd breached express and implied obligations under the shareholders' agreement by: "(1) engaging in activities that led to the cancellation of charter hires that were essential to Seawinds' business; (2) attempting to interfere with a proposed joint service agreement between Seawinds and the East Asiatic Company, and delaying its implementation; (3) making and then reneging on commitments to contribute additional capital, thereby dissuading others from dealing with Seawinds, and (4) making false and disparaging statements about Seawinds' business operations and financial condition." Seawinds' original and first amended complaint included causes of action for breach of contract, breach of the implied covenant of good faith and fair dealing (in both contract and tort), and breach of fiduciary duty. This matter comes before us after trial court rulings on demurrers to Seawinds' complaints.

Nedlloyd demurred to Seawinds' original complaint on the grounds that it failed to state causes of action for breach of the implied covenant of good faith and fair dealing (either in contract or in tort) and breach of fiduciary duty. In support of its demurrer, Nedlloyd contended the shareholders' agreement required the application of Hong Kong law to Seawinds' claims. In opposition to the demurrer, Seawinds argued that California law should be applied to its causes of action. . . .

I

We have not previously considered the enforceability of a contractual choice-of-law provision. We have, however, addressed the closely related issue of the enforceability of a contractual choice-of-forum provision, and we have made clear that, "No satisfying reason of public policy has been suggested why enforcement should be denied a forum selection clause appearing in a contract entered into freely and voluntarily by parties who have negotiated at arm's length." Smith, Valentino & Smith, Inc. v. Superior Court (1976) 17 Cal. 3d 491, 495-496, 131 Cal. Rptr. 374, 551 P.2d 1206. The forum selection provision in *Smith* was contained within a choice-of-law clause, and we observed that, "Such choice of law provisions are usually respected by California courts." We noted this result was consistent with the modern approach of section 187 of the Restatement Second of Conflict of Laws (Restatement). Prior Court of Appeal decisions, although not always explicitly referring to the Restatement, also overwhelmingly reflect the modern, mainstream approach adopted in the Restatement.[1] We affirm this approach. In determining the enforceability of the arm's-length contractual choice-of-law provisions, California courts shall apply the principles set forth in Restatement section 187, which reflect a strong policy favoring enforcement of such provisions.

. . . [T]he proper approach under Restatement section 187, subdivision (2) is for the court first to determine either: (1) whether the chosen state has a substantial relationship to the parties or their transaction, or (2) whether there is any other reasonable basis for the parties' choice of law. If neither of

1. Federal courts applying California's conflicts law have also adhered to this approach. The mainstream nature of this approach is further reflected by a recent study indicating that 15 states other than California follow the general approach of the Restatement Second.

these tests is met, that is the end of the inquiry, and the court need not enforce the parties' choice of law.[4] If, however, either test is met, the court must next determine whether the chosen state's law is contrary to a *fundamental* policy of California.[5] If there is no such conflict, the court shall enforce the parties' choice of law. If, however, there is a fundamental conflict with California law, the court must then determine whether California has a "materially greater interest than the chosen state in the determination of the particular issue. . . ." (Rest., §187, subd. (2).) If California has a materially greater interest than the chosen state, the choice of law shall not be enforced, for the obvious reason that in such circumstance we will decline to enforce a law contrary to this state's fundamental policy.[6] We now apply the Restatement test to the facts of this case.

II

B

1

As to the first required determination, Hong Kong—"the chosen state"—clearly has a "substantial relationship to the parties." (Rest. §187, subd.

4. As noted above, a different result might obtain under Restatement section 187, subdivision (1), which appears to allow the parties *in some circumstances* to specify the law of a state that has no relation to the parties or their transaction. The Restatement gives these two illustrations: "4. In State *X*, *A* establishes a trust and provides that *B*, the trustee, shall be paid commissions at the highest rate permissible under the local law of state *Y*. *A and B are both domiciled in X, and the trust has no relation to any state but X*. In *X*, the highest permissible rate of commissions for trustees is 5 per cent. In *Y*, the highest permissible rate is 4 per cent. The choice-of-law provision will be given effect, and *B* will be held entitled to commissions at the rate of 4 per cent. 5. Same facts as in Illustration 4 except that the highest permissible rate of commissions in *X* is 4 per cent and in *Y* is 5 per cent. Effect will not be given to the choice-of-law provision since under *X* local law the parties lacked power to provide for a rate of commissions in excess of 4 per cent and *Y*, the state of the chosen law, has no relation to the parties or the trust." (Rest., §187, subd. (1), com. c., illus. 4 & 5, p. 564; italics added.)

5. To be more precise, we note that Restatement section 187, subdivision (2) refers not merely to the forum state—for example, California in the present case—but rather to the state ". . . which, under the rule of §188, would be the state of the applicable law in the absence of an effective choice of law by the parties." For example, there may be an occasional case in which California is the forum, and the parties have chosen the law of another state, but the law of yet a third state, rather than California's, would apply absent the parties' choice. In that situation, a California court will look to the fundamental policy of the third state in determining whether to enforce the parties' choice of law. The present case is not such a situation.

6. There may also be instances when the chosen state has a materially greater interest in the matter than does California, but enforcement of the law of the chosen state would lead to a result contrary to a fundamental policy of California. In some such cases, enforcement of the law of the chosen state may be appropriate despite California's policy to the contrary. Careful consideration, however, of California's policy and the other state's interest would be required. No such question is present in this case, and we thus need not and do not decide how Restatement section 187 would apply in such circumstances.

(2)(a).) The shareholders' agreement, which is incorporated by reference in Seawinds' first amended complaint, shows that Seawinds is incorporated under the laws of Hong Kong and has a registered office there. The same is true of one of the shareholder parties to the agreement—Red Coconut Trading Co. The incorporation of these parties in Hong Kong provides the required "substantial relationship" (*Id.*, com. f [substantial relationship present when "one of the parties is domiciled" in the chosen state].

Moreover, the presence of two Hong Kong corporations as parties also provides a "reasonable basis" for a contractual provision requiring application of Hong Kong law. "If one of the parties resides in the chosen state, the parties have a reasonable basis for their choice." The reasonableness of choosing Hong Kong becomes manifest when the nature of the agreement before us is considered. A state of incorporation is certainly at least one government entity with a keen and intimate interest in internal corporate affairs, including the purchase and sale of its shares, as well as corporate management and operations. (*See* Corp. Code, §102 [applying California's general corporation law to domestic corporations].)

2

We next consider whether application of the law chosen by the parties would be contrary to "a fundamental policy" of California. We perceive no fundamental policy of California requiring the application of California law to Seawinds' claims based on the implied covenant of good faith and fair dealing. The covenant is not a government regulatory policy designed to restrict freedom of contract, but an implied promise inserted in an agreement to carry out the presumed intentions of contracting parties.

Seawinds directs us to no authority exalting the *implied* covenant of good faith and fair dealing over the *express* covenant of these parties that Hong Kong law shall govern their agreement. We have located none. Because Seawinds has identified no fundamental policy of our state at issue in its essentially contractual dispute with Nedlloyd, the second exception to the rule of section 187 of the Restatement does not apply.

C

1

Seawinds contends that, whether or not the choice-of-law clause governs Seawinds' implied covenant claim, Seawinds' fiduciary duty claim is somehow independent of the shareholders' agreement and therefore outside the intended scope of the clause. Seawinds thus concludes California law must be applied to this claim. We disagree.

When two sophisticated, commercial entities agree to a choice-of-law clause like the one in this case, the most reasonable interpretation of their actions is that they intended for the clause to apply to all causes of action arising from or related to their contract. Initially, such an interpretation is supported by the plain meaning of the language used by the parties. The choice-of-law clause in the shareholders' agreement provides: "This agreement shall be *governed by* and construed in accordance with Hong Kong law and each party hereby irrevocably submits to the non-exclusive jurisdiction and service of process of the Hong Kong courts." (Italics added.)[7]

The phrase "governed by" is a broad one signifying a relationship of absolute direction, control, and restraint. Thus, the clause reflects the parties' clear contemplation that "the agreement" is to be completely and absolutely controlled by Hong Kong law. No exceptions are provided. In the context of this case, the agreement to be controlled by Hong Kong law is a shareholders' agreement that expressly provides for the purchase of shares in Seawinds by Nedlloyd and creates the relationship between shareholder and corporation that gives rise to Seawinds' cause of action. Nedlloyd's fiduciary duties, if any, arise from—and can exist only because of—the shareholders' agreement pursuant to which Seawinds' stock was purchased by Nedlloyd.

In order to control completely the agreement of the parties, Hong Kong law must also govern the stock purchase portion of that agreement and the legal duties created by or emanating from the stock purchase, including any fiduciary duties. If Hong Kong law were not applied to these duties, it would effectively control only part of the agreement, not all of it. Such an interpretation would be inconsistent with the unrestricted character of the choice-of-law clause.

Our conclusion in this regard comports with common sense and commercial reality. When a rational businessperson enters into an agreement establishing a transaction or relationship and provides that disputes arising from the agreement shall be governed by the law of an identified jurisdiction, the logical conclusion is that he or she intended that law to apply to *all* disputes arising out of the transaction or relationship. We seriously doubt that any rational businessperson, attempting to provide by contract for an efficient and businesslike resolution of possible future disputes, would intend that the laws of multiple jurisdictions would apply to a single controversy having its origin in a single, contract-based relationship. Nor do we believe such a person would reasonably desire a protracted litigation battle concerning only the threshold question of

---

7. As we have noted, the choice-of-law clause states: "This agreement shall be governed by and *construed in accordance with Hong Kong law*. . . . (Italics added.) The agreement, of course, includes the choice-of-law clause itself. Thus the question of whether that clause is ambiguous as to its scope (i.e., whether it includes the fiduciary duty claim) is a question of contract interpretation that in the normal course should be determined pursuant to Hong Kong law. The parties in this case, however, did not request judicial notice of Hong Kong law on this question of interpretation (Evid. Code, §452, subd. (f)) or supply us with evidence of the relevant aspects of that law (Evid. Code, §453, subd. (b)). The question therefore becomes one of California law.

what law was to be applied to which asserted claims or issues. Indeed, the manifest purpose of a choice-of-law clause is precisely to avoid such a battle.

Seawinds' view of the problem—which would require extensive litigation of the parties' supposed intentions regarding the choice-of-law clause to the end that the laws of multiple states might be applied to their dispute—is more likely the product of postdispute litigation strategy, not predispute contractual intent. If commercially sophisticated parties (such as those now before us) truly intend the result advocated by Seawinds, they should, in fairness to one another and in the interest of economy in dispute resolution, negotiate and obtain the assent of their fellow parties to explicit contract language specifying what jurisdiction's law applies to what issues.

For the reasons stated above, we hold a valid choice-of-law clause, which provides that a specified body of law "governs" the "agreement" between the parties, encompasses all causes of action arising from or related to that agreement, regardless of how they are characterized, including tortious breaches of duties emanating from the agreement or the legal relationships it creates.

2

Applying the test we have adopted we find no reason not to apply the parties' choice of law to Seawinds' cause of action for breach of fiduciary duty. As we have explained, Hong Kong, the chosen state, has a "substantial relationship to the parties" because two of those parties are incorporated there. Moreover, their incorporation in that state affords a "reasonable basis" for choosing Hong Kong law.

Seawinds identifies no fundamental public policy of this state that would be offended by application of Hong Kong law to a claim by a Hong Kong corporation against its allegedly controlling shareholder. We are directed to no California statute or constitutional provision designed to preclude freedom of contract in this context. Indeed, even in the absence of a choice-of-law clause, Hong Kong's overriding interest in the internal affairs of corporations domiciled there would in most cases require application of its law. (*See* Rest. §306 [obligations owed by majority shareholder to corporation determined by the law of the state of incorporation except in unusual circumstances not present here].

For strategic reasons related to its current dispute with Nedlloyd, Seawinds seeks to create a fiduciary relationship by disregarding the law Seawinds voluntarily agreed to accept as binding—the law of a state that also happens to be Seawinds' own corporate domicile. To allow Seawinds to use California law in this fashion would further no ascertainable fundamental policy of California; indeed, it would undermine California's policy of respecting the choices made by parties to voluntarily negotiated agreements.

LUCAS, C.J., and ARABIAN and GEORGE, JJ., concur.

PANELLI, J., concurring and dissenting.

I generally concur in the majority opinion's explanation of the standards controlling when a contractual choice-of-law provision will be honored by the courts of this state and with the majority's application of these standards to Seawinds' cause of action for breach of the covenant of good faith and fair dealing. I write separately to express my disagreement with the majority's conclusion, based on the record before us, that the choice-of-law clause in this case governs Seawinds' cause of action for breach of fiduciary duty. In my view, the majority's analysis of the scope of the choice-of-law clause is unsound.

The choice-of-law clause in this case reads in pertinent part: "This agreement shall be governed by and construed in accordance with Hong Kong law. . . ."[1] The majority determines that the scope of the choice-of-law clause, which was incorporated into the first amended complaint by attachment, extends to related, *noncontractual* causes of action, such as Seawinds' breach of fiduciary duty claim. In so doing, the majority opinion adopts the rule that "[w]hen two sophisticated, commercial entities agree to a choice-of-law clause like the one in this case, the most reasonable interpretation of their actions is that they intended for the clause to apply to all causes of action arising from or related to their contract." Without citing any authority, the majority opinion announces a binding rule of contractual interpretation, based solely upon "common sense and commercial reality."

. . . In this case, the language of the incorporated contract easily can be read to apply only to contractual causes of action: "*This agreement* shall be governed . . . by Hong Kong law."

In my view, the majority's mistaken construction of the choice-of-law clause is clear when the language used in the present contract is compared, as Nedlloyd urges us to do, with the language construed by this court in Smith, Valentino & Smith, Inc. v. Superior Court (1976) 17 Cal. 3d 491, 131 Cal. Rptr. 374, 551 P.2d 1206. In that case, this court determined that claims for unfair competition and intentional interference with advantageous business relationships were governed by a choice-of-forum clause as " 'actions or proceedings instituted by . . . [Smith] under this Agreement with respect to any matters arising under *or growing out of this agreement. . . .*' " In contrast to the language used by Nedlloyd and Seawinds in their agreement, the contractual language, "arising under or growing out of this agreement," which was used in *Smith,* explicitly shows an intent to embrace related noncontractual claims, as well as contractual claims. Although similar language was readily available to them, the sophisticated parties in the present case did

1. I agree with the majority that the scope of the choice-of-law clause in this contract is a question that would ordinarily be determined under Hong Kong law. I further agree with the majority that, since the parties neither produced any evidence of Hong Kong law relating to this subject nor requested judicial notice of any such law, we may apply California law to ascertain the scope of the clause.

not draft their choice-of-law clause to clearly encompass related noncontractual causes of action.[2] . . .

Finally, the majority's rule effectively subordinates the intent of the contracting parties to the need for predictability in commercial transactions. The majority strikes this balance despite the fact that our Legislature has commanded otherwise. Under California law, "[a] contract must be so interpreted as to give effect to the mutual intention of the parties as it existed at the time of contracting, so far as the same is ascertainable and lawful." (Civ. Code, §1636.) In contrast to this legislative command, the majority conclusively presumes that choice-of-law clauses entered into between or among commercial entities apply to related noncontractual causes of action regardless of whether the intent of the parties or the contract language (as in this case) shows otherwise. I believe that the departure by the majority from established California law is unwarranted and is unnecessary to further the goals of predictability in the enforcement of contracts and protection of the justified expectations of contracting parties. These goals can be adequately protected within the framework of the current law governing contractual interpretation by enforcing choice-of-law clauses in a manner consistent with the language of the contract and the intent of the parties.

I am keenly aware of the need for predictability in the enforcement of commercial contracts. Nevertheless, although courts and litigants may wish the law were otherwise, not every issue can be conclusively determined at the pleading stage. On the present record, the scope of the choice-of-law clause must be construed in favor of Seawinds.

Questions and Comments

(1) Choice-of-law clauses have become extremely popular in large commercial contracts, and even occur with increasing frequency in smaller scale consumer contracts. Sometimes they are included because the law of one specific state is thought particularly desirable by one of the parties. But in a surprising number of instances, the parties do not even bother to research the chosen law before they include a clause selecting it. This suggests that the parties may be as attracted by the avoidance of uncertainty and litigation expenses over choice-of-law matters, per se, as by the perceived benefits of any particular law. Note that the beneficiary of the increased certainty is likely to be the defendant, for it is typically the plaintiff who benefits from the chance to forum shop for a more desirable substantive law.

(2) Despite their obvious advantages in reducing uncertainty, choice-of-law clauses have not proven as trouble-free as one might think. They are,

2. Despite the majority's artfully crafted argument, the words "governed by" do not assist in defining what causes of action the choice-of-law clause was intended to address. Rather, the parties defined the scope of their choice-of-law clause by choosing the phrase "[t]his agreement."

themselves, increasingly a source of litigation, as the *Nedlloyd* case suggests. Under the Restatement Second test, there are two main sources of controversy, both illustrated by *Nedlloyd.* The first is the question of whether the clause should be enforced under subsections (1) and (2). A quick look at the wording of those two subsections uncovers fertile opportunity for dispute.

There is, at the outset, the issue of whether (1) or (2) is the applicable subsection; the former is much more permissive, while the latter imposes more onerous conditions before the clause will be enforced. The difference between the two is that (1) applies to issues on which the parties had the freedom to provide the same substantive result by explicitly substantive terms in the contract and simply chose to do so in a shorthand manner, namely by selecting a law that so provides. Many rules of contract law are default rules, which the parties can override by specific contract terms; as to these, they may select any state's law they choose, even if it has no connection to the controversy. Subsection (2), in contrast, deals with what are sometimes called "mandatory" rules, which the parties could not defeat by more detailed drafting of the substantive terms of the contract; this category would include, for example, rules prohibiting punitive damages or outlawing certain kinds of disclaimers. As to these, a reasonable basis for selecting the chosen state must be shown, and the chosen law must not offend a "materially greater interest" on the part of the state whose law must otherwise apply. These requirements are sufficiently vague to allow clever lawyers ample opportunity to challenge the applicability of the selected law. Note in particular that application of section 187(2) requires a prior determination of the law that would otherwise apply, which seems to be precisely the issue that a choice-of-law clause ought to help avoid.

(3) The second type of problem with application of section 187 is determining the scope of the choice-of-law clause. As *Nedlloyd* suggests, the parties' dispute may include claims that are not, strictly speaking, contractual; in addition to the sort of claim at issue there (breach of fiduciary duty), other examples include claims based on fraud or misrepresentation. Does the selected law govern these issues as well? The *Nedlloyd* solution is controversial in at least two respects. First, it states (in footnote 7) that the scope of the choice-of-law clause must be determined by consulting the chosen state's law. Given that section 187(3) states that the reference is to the chosen state's local law, and not its choice-of-law rules, this result is highly dubious. What reasons could be given for the court's result? Second, the court decided that under California law the clause should be read broadly, to include a claim for breach of fiduciary duty; in this respect, it was arguably in a minority. *See, e.g.*, Klock v. Lehman Bros. Kuhn Loeb, Inc., 584 F. Supp. 210 (S.D.N.Y. 1984); Carlock v. Pillsbury Co., 719 F. Supp. 791 (D. Minn. 1989).

(4) Another issue concerning the scope of choice-of-law clauses is whether selection of some state's laws requires application of that state's "pro-

cedural" rules, such as statutes of limitations. Should the fact that such issues are ordinarily resolved under forum law mean that the choice-of-law clause has no relevance to resolving them? Note that the parties might, if they so chose, specify in the contract a time period for bringing suit; does this cast doubt on the "procedural" characterization?

(5) New York has adopted legislation providing for virtually automatic enforcement of clauses choosing New York law. (Section 5-1402 of the General Obligations Law, analogously, provides for enforcement of clauses choosing New York as the forum). It provides:

§5-1401. Choice of Law

1. The parties to any contract, agreement or undertaking, contingent or otherwise, in consideration of, or relating to any obligation arising out of a transaction covering in the aggregate not less than two hundred fifty thousand dollars, including a transaction otherwise covered by subsection one of section 1-105 of the uniform commercial code, may agree that the law of this state shall govern their rights and duties in whole or in part, whether or not such contract, agreement or undertaking bears a reasonable relation to this state. This section shall not apply to any contract, agreement or undertaking (a) for labor or personal services, (b) relating to any transaction for personal, family or household services, or (c) to the extent provided to the contrary in subsection two of section 1-105 of the uniform commercial code.

2. Nothing contained in this section shall be construed to limit or deny the enforcement of any provision respecting choice of law in any other contract, agreement or undertaking.

Does the fact that it provides for enforcement of clauses choosing New York law, but not clauses choosing the law of other states, discriminate against sister states' laws? Is there any good reason for distinguishing between the two? Consult Hughes v. Fetter, page 394 *infra*.

Banek, Inc. v. Yogurt Ventures U.S.A., Inc.

6 F.3d 357 (6th Cir. 1993)

GUY, Circuit Judge.

In this interlocutory appeal, plaintiff, Banek, Inc., appeals the district court's ruling that a choice of law provision contained in the parties' franchise agreement was valid and enforceable. Upon review of the record and consideration of the arguments of the parties, we conclude that the district court's decision was correct and affirm.

I

Plaintiff, Banek, Inc., owned by Mr. and Mrs. Banek, entered into negotiations with defendant Yogurt Ventures U.S.A., Inc., a Georgia corporation owned by defendants John and Richard Stern, for the purchase of a Freshens Yogurt franchise to be located in Monroe, Michigan. After negotiating several changes in the agreement, the parties signed a "Franchise and Development Agreement" in February 1990. Sales at the Monroe location were not as expected, and Banek closed its Freshens franchise in March 1992. In October 1991, prior to shutting down, Banek filed suit in state court against Yogurt Ventures. The suit alleged breach of contract, various violations of the Michigan Franchise Investment Law (MFIL), violations of the Federal Trade Commission Franchise Rules, common law fraud and misrepresentation, and negligence. In May 1992, after closing the Monroe site, Banek filed a separate action against John and Richard Stern. These two cases were then consolidated. Following removal to federal court based on diversity jurisdiction, defendants moved for dismissal of all counts on various theories.

The district court granted defendants' motion in part and denied it in part. The court ruled that the choice of law provision in the parties' agreement, providing that Georgia law is to govern the rights and obligations of the parties, was valid and enforceable under Michigan law and thus dismissed plaintiff's claim alleging violations of the MFIL. . . . Only the ruling concerning the choice of law provision is before this court on interlocutory appeal.

II

The franchise agreement between these parties provides:

> This Agreement was made and entered into in the State [of] Georgia and all rights and obligations of the parties hereto shall be governed by and construed in accordance with the laws of the State of Georgia.

We see the issue in this appeal as involving three separate, sequential questions. First, is this a valid choice of law clause or is it a waiver of rights which is prohibited under the MFIL? Second, if the clause is valid, is this choice of law provision enforceable under Michigan choice of law rules? Third, if this provision is valid and enforceable, does Georgia law govern all claims between the parties or only contract claims?

We begin with answering the first question in the affirmative. Plaintiff . . . argue[s] that the choice of law provision in the agreement operates as a waiver of the rights and protections under the MFIL and thus is void under Mich. Comp. Laws Ann. §445.1527. That section provides:

Each of the following provisions is void and unenforceable if contained in any documents relating to a franchise:

> . . . (b) A requirement that a franchisee assent to a release, assignment, novation, waiver, or estoppel which deprives a franchisee of rights and protections provided in this act. This shall not preclude a franchisee, after entering into a franchise agreement, from settling any and all claims.
>
> . . . (f) A provision requiring that arbitration or litigation be conducted outside this state. This shall not preclude the franchisee from entering into an agreement, at the time of arbitration, to conduct arbitration at a location outside this state.

Plaintiff argues that the choice of law provision making Georgia law applicable acts as a waiver of "rights and protections" provided under the MFIL. We disagree.

The Michigan legislature was specific enough to include forum selection provisions in the list of void provisions, but did not specify choice of law provisions. Seemingly, the Michigan legislature understood that the burdens of being forced to arbitrate a claim in a foreign forum are significant, as subsection (f) makes arbitration or litigation forum selection clauses void. However, litigating in Michigan does not require that Michigan law must govern the dispute. The statute does not expressly void choice of law provisions, and we decline to imply such a prohibition. The Michigan legislature may have purposefully omitted choice of law provisions from those clauses prohibited because it may have realized that other states' laws might provide more protection to franchisees; thus, if a franchisee and franchisor want to choose a different state's law to govern any disputes, the parties may so contract. Providing that waivers and releases are void is not equivalent to voiding choice of law provisions. *See* Tele-Save Merchandising Co. v. Consumers Distrib. Co., 814 F.2d 1120, 1122-23 (6th Cir. 1987) (Ohio law voiding any waiver of the Ohio Business Opportunity Plans Act did not void choice of law provision).

The cases cited by plaintiff . . . are inapposite. As noted in Wright-Moore Corp. v. Ricoh Corp., 908 F.2d 128, 134 (7th Cir. 1990), "the strength of nonwaiver provisions among states varies." In *Wright-Moore,* the Indiana statute made it unlawful to enter into an agreement "limiting litigation brought for breach of the agreement in any manner whatsoever," Ind. Code §23-2-2.7-1(10), and thus the court held that the choice of law provision in the contract at issue was void. Other states expressly include choice of law provisions in the list of void and unenforceable provisions. *See, e.g.,* Minn. Stat. §80C.21. The Michigan statute is not so strongly worded, perhaps for the reason expressed above. Alternatively or additionally, the Michigan legislature may have recognized that requiring all franchises located in Michigan be governed by Michigan law, regardless of any agreement to the contrary, would make Michigan a less desirable target state for franchisors, making franchises in Michigan more expensive to own. This would be largely because of a national franchisor's need for uniformity in its business affairs. Having to comply with differing laws for each of the states in which it does business increases expenses. In any event, Michigan has not indicated a desire to bar choice of law provisions either expressly or implicitly.

That brings us to the second question: Should the valid choice of law provision be enforced under Michigan's choice of law rules? It is a well-accepted principle that a federal court in a diversity case must apply the conflict of law rules of the state in which it sits. Klaxon Co. v. Stentor Elec. Mfg. Co., 313 U.S. 487, 490 (1941). Therefore, this court must look to Michigan conflict of law principles to determine whether Michigan or Georgia law governs this dispute.

Michigan has adopted the approach articulated in Restatement (Second) of Conflict of Laws §187 (1971). Under section 187, a contractual choice of law provision will govern unless either:

> (a) the chosen state has no substantial relationship to the parties or the transaction and there is no other reasonable basis for the parties' choice, or
>
> (b) application of the law of the chosen state would be contrary to a fundamental policy of a state which has a materially greater interest than the chosen state in the determination of the particular issue and which, under the rule of §188, would be the state of the applicable law in the absence of an effective choice of law by the parties.

In the present case, the parties do not dispute that there is a substantial relationship with the State of Georgia. Assuming without deciding that under section 188 Michigan law would apply, plaintiff argues that to enforce the choice of law provision and apply Georgia law would violate Michigan's public policy, as expressed in the MFIL, to protect franchisees from overreaching by franchisors and from the superior bargaining power franchisors possess. Initially, we note that this is not a case of a take-it-or-leave-it adhesion contract. Banek successfully negotiated multiple changes in Yogurt Ventures' standard franchise agreement, dispelling the claim of unfair bargaining power.[2] As we have stated previously, we "move cautiously when asked to hold contract clauses unenforceable on public policy grounds. . . ." Moses v. Business Card Express, Inc., 929 F.2d 1131, 1139 (6th Cir.) (1991).

---

2. Banek was not forced into this investment decision, but chose to negotiate an agreement with the defendant. Having negotiated that agreement, including several changes beneficial to Banek's position, it is now attempting to escape one of the contract's provisions.

The price that Banek paid for its franchise reflected the terms of the agreement. We are hesitant to void the choice of law provision because that would mean Banek would be getting more than it bargained for.

While we agree with plaintiff that the comprehensive and paternalistic franchise investment law represents Michigan public policy,[3] that does not end the inquiry. The more central question in this case is whether the parties have selected, through their choice of law provision, a jurisdiction in which there is a substantial erosion of the quality of protection that the MFIL would otherwise provide. A court may not assume that, merely because Michigan has adopted a franchise statute, the application of Georgia's laws would be contrary to Michigan's public policy. *Tele-Save,* 814 F.2d at 1123.

"In order for the chosen state's law to violate the fundamental policy of [the forum state], it must be shown that there are significant differences in the application of the law of the two states." *Id.* Banek has failed to show any specific significant differences between the application of Georgia law and Michigan law to their claims. The main thrust of Banek's complaint in this case is that it was not provided with sufficient and accurate information in order for it to make an informed investment decision. The Georgia Sale of Business Opportunities Act provides disclosure standards similar but not identical to the MFIL.

Banek argues, without reference to a particular Georgia code section, that the protections of the Georgia Sale of Business Opportunities Act are only available to franchises located in Georgia or to residents of Georgia. The Georgia Sale of Business Opportunities Act applies to conduct occurring in Georgia regardless of the residence of the person solicited. The relevant section was amended to clarify that the act applies "even if solicitations are of nonresidents of Georgia." Ga. Code Ann. §10-1-410(3) (1992). Defendant has conceded and will be bound by its admission that "the alleged fraud occurred in Georgia." Thus, plaintiff's claim that it may not be able to seek recourse under the Georgia Act is incorrect.

Additionally, section 10-1-417(b) provides that any violation of part 3 of the Act, dealing with the sale of business opportunities, "shall constitute an unfair or deceptive act or practice in the conduct of a consumer act or practice or consumer transactions under Part 2 of this article, the 'Fair Business Practices Act of 1975,' and shall authorize an affected participant or purchaser to seek the remedies provided for in Code Section 10-1-399. . . ." Ga. Code Ann. §10-1-417(b). The remedies provided for under section 10-1-399 include attorney fees and treble damages for intentional violations. Furthermore, the statue of limitations for such actions is "two years after the

3. Various aspects of the MFIL evidence that it represents public policy of Michigan: provisions for enforcement by both public and private actions, Mich. Comp. Laws Ann. §§445.1531, 445.1535; the imposition of joint and several liability of owners, directors, officers, and employees of the franchisor, Mich. Comp. Laws Ann. §445.1532; recovery of attorney fees in private actions, Mich. Comp. Laws Ann. §445.1531; and the imposition of penalties and fines, including up to seven years imprisonment and up to $10,000 in fines, Mich. Comp. Laws Ann. §445.1538. Enforcement of the act's provisions by the attorney general would not be affected by a choice of law provision in a franchise contract.

person bringing the action knew or should have known of the occurrence of the alleged violation. . . ." Ga. Code Ann. §10-1-401.

In addition to its various remedies under the Georgia Act, plaintiff may also pursue common law claims for fraud. It is not sufficient for plaintiff to simply assert that Michigan law should apply "merely because a different result would be reached under" Georgia law. *Tele-Save*, 814 F.2d at 1123. . . . [P]laintiff has failed to demonstrate how application of Georgia law would violate a specific fundamental policy of Michigan. The choice of law provision in the parties' agreement provides that Georgia law is to be applied. The application of Georgia law in this context would not be violative of a public policy of Michigan and therefore should be enforced. We therefore will enforce the agreement of the parties embodied in the choice of law provision.

Finally, because the choice of law provision in the contract is valid and enforceable, we must determine its scope. Plaintiff contends that Georgia law should only govern contract claims, while defendant argues that all claims arising out of the parties franchise dealings should be governed under Georgia law. This court faced a similar question in *Moses* where the choice of law provision read: "This Franchise and License Agreement and the construction thereof shall be governed by the laws of the state of Michigan." We held that the clause clearly referred to more than just the construction of the agreement and extended to plaintiff's claims of fraud and misrepresentation. In the present case, the contract provides "this Agreement was made and entered into in the State [of] Georgia and all rights and obligations of the parties hereto shall be governed by and construed in accordance with the laws of the State of Georgia." As in *Moses,* we find that the choice of law provision is sufficiently broad so as to cover plaintiff's claims of fraud and misrepresentation. Had these claims only been tangentially related to the franchise relationship, we would be much more inclined to find the choice of law provision not applicable. The claims of fraud and misrepresentation that plaintiff has asserted here are directly related to the franchise agreement.

The order of the district court is affirmed.

Kipin Industries, Inc. v. Van Deilen International, Inc.

182 F. 3d 490 (6th Cir. 1999)

MOORE, Circuit Judge.

The question presented in this appeal is whether a lien-waiver provision in a contract between Plaintiff-Appellant Kipin Industries, Inc. ("Kipin") and Defendant-Appellee Van Deilen International, Inc. ("VDI") is enforceable. We hold that it is. Although the express waiver would be void under the substantive law of Michigan, which the parties selected to govern the contract, the waiver is valid under the law of Kentucky, which would govern the agreement in the absence of an express choice-of-law provision. Following the Michigan law of conflict of laws, we conclude that, although the substantive law of Michigan applies generally to this contract, Michigan's substantive law does not invalidate the express waiver in this circumstance. Accordingly, we affirm the judgment of the district court entered in favor of the defendants-appellees.

I

. . . In November 1995 Kipin and VDI entered into a contract under which Kipin agreed to perform certain work in Kentucky at a site owned by a third party, AK Steel, Inc. ("AK Steel"). Alleging that VDI had refused to pay $400,000 owed under the otherwise completed contract, Kipin filed an action in the Western District of Pennsylvania in September 1996 to recover the unpaid amount. In accordance with the contract forum-selection clause, this case subsequently was transferred to the Eastern District of Michigan. In October 1996 Kipin filed mechanic's liens against the AK Steel property. This step was taken in contravention of a clause in the contract with VDI that prohibited Kipin from filing such liens. VDI then filed bonds in the relevant Kentucky county clerks' offices that served to discharge Kipin's liens. Defendant-Appellee United Fidelity Corporation ("UFC") was listed as the surety on the bonds.

Kipin then filed the present action seeking to recover on the bonds. The district court properly exercised diversity jurisdiction pursuant to 28 U.S.C. §1332,[1] and the action was consolidated with the breach-of-contract action initially filed in Pennsylvania. Pointing to the lien-waiver provision of the contract, VDI moved to release the bonds. Kipin argued in response that the lien-waiver provision was void under governing Michigan law. Concluding that Michigan interests in the contract were minimal while Kentucky contacts were significant and, thus, that Kentucky law rather than Michigan law governed the contract, the district court held that the lien-waiver provision was enforceable and granted VDI's motion.

II

The substantive question in this case is whether the lien-waiver provision of the parties' contract is enforceable. The parties' contract states that it "shall be deemed to be executed in the State of Michigan, and should be construed according to Michigan Law," and that disputes "shall be adjudicated by a court of competent jurisdiction sitting in the State of Michigan." The contract also includes an explicit prohibition against the placement of

---

1. Kipin is a Pennsylvania corporation and citizen with its principal place of business in that state; VDI is a Michigan corporation and citizen with its principal place of business in Michigan; and UFC is a Cook Islands corporation with its principal place of business in Michigan.

liens by Kipin on the property of AK Steel. Section 8 of the agreement, entitled "Prohibition Against Liens," provides in relevant part:

> [Kipin] hereby acknowledges and agrees that no mechanic's liens, materialman's liens or other liens whatsoever shall be filed and no claim shall be maintained by [Kipin], any subcontractor, contractor, supplier, mechanic, materialman or other person or entity against AK Steel or any equipment belonging to AK Steel (including but not limited to, the Equipment covered by the Contract), for or on account of work or labor performed, or to be performed, or materials, machinery, equipment or other property of any kind furnished or to be furnished in relation to the Contract and/or the removal operation that is the subject matter of the Contract.

This prohibition or waiver of the right to file liens would be invalid under the statutory law of Michigan. Michigan law provides that "[a] person shall not require, as part of any contract for an improvement, that the right to a construction lien be waived in advance of work performed. A waiver obtained as part of a contract for an improvement is contrary to public policy, and shall be invalid. . . ." Mich. Comp. Laws Ann. §570.1115(1). Kentucky law does not forbid nor invalidate the pre-work waiver of the right to file mechanic's liens. By implication, Kentucky has accepted such waivers. *See* Ky. Rev. Stat. Ann. §376.070(3) (specifying that subsection is inapplicable "where persons . . . have waived in writing their right to file mechanics' or materialmen's liens").

In order to resolve the conflict between the contract and the substantive laws of Michigan and Kentucky on the issue of lien-waiver provisions, we must undertake a conflict-of-laws analysis. A federal court exercising diversity jurisdiction applies the choice-of-law or conflict rules of the forum state, in this case, Michigan. In resolving choice-of-law issues, Michigan courts follow §§187 and 188 of the Second Restatement of Conflict of Laws.

When the enforceability of a contractual provision is at issue, §187 provides that "the law of the state chosen by the parties to govern their contractual rights and duties will be applied" unless (1) there is no substantial relationship between the chosen state and the contract or other reasonable basis for the state's selection or (2) the application of the chosen state's law would violate a fundamental policy of a state which has a materially greater interest in the disputed issue and which would have supplied the governing law in the absence of the parties' selection. Restatement (Second) of Conflict of Laws §187(2) (1988 Revision).

Section 187 applies, of course, only when the parties have selected a state to supply the governing law. *See id.* cmt. a. As an initial matter, VDI might have argued that the contract does not specify the law that "governs" the contract under §187. The parties' choice-of-law provision states only that the contract "should be construed according to Michigan Law." To construe a contract is merely "to ascertain the meaning of language by a process of arrangement, interpretation and inference." Black's Law Dictionary 315 (6th ed. 1990). The law that governs a contract, on the other hand, regulates the contractual relationship, and, inter alia, determines the validity of the instrument as a whole or of specific provisions.

Read literally, the choice-of-law provision in the instant contract does not indicate that the parties wished to have their contract regulated under Michigan law. *See* Boat Town U.S.A., Inc. v. Mercury Marine Div. of Brunswick Corp., 364 So. 2d 15, 17 (Fla. Dist. Ct. App. 1978) (holding that the substantive law of Wisconsin was not applicable to a contract by virtue of clause stating that the document was "to be interpreted and construed according to" Wisconsin law). This court has rejected this argument in the past, however, holding that the same contract language at issue in Boat Town evidenced the parties' intention to be bound by the substantive law of the chosen state. See Boatland, Inc. v. Brunswick Corp., 558 F.2d 818, 821-22 (6th Cir. 1977) (noting that focusing on the technical distinction between "interpret/construe" and "govern" would yield an "unwarranted," "strained and narrow construction of the [contract] language"). Here, as in *Boatland*, there is no evidence that the parties did not intend their choice-of-law provision to invoke the substantive law of Michigan as well as its interpretive law (whatever that might be), and thus we conclude that §187 is applicable.

Kipin and the district court agreed that the applicability of Michigan law was to be tested under §187. However, Kipin disagrees with the district court's conclusion that Michigan law is inapplicable under the exceptions provided in §187(2). We conclude that the district court erred in determining that Michigan lacked a substantial relationship to the contract and that application of Michigan law would violate a fundamental policy of Kentucky. However, the district court's conclusion that the lien-waiver provision is enforceable must be affirmed on other grounds: Under the Restatement, the parties' choice of law is to be considered a mistake if the chosen law would invalidate an express provision of the contract. If, in such a situation, the express provision would be valid under the law of the state that would govern in the absence of an express choice-of-law provision, the mistaken choice-of-law provision should be ignored and the express contractual provision enforced.

As a threshold matter, we agree with Kipin that under Restatement §187 the parties' choice of Michigan substantive law should be respected generally. We agree that Michigan has a substantial relationship to the contract by virtue of VDI's residence and that application of Michigan law invalidating the lien-waiver provision would not run counter to a fundamental policy of Kentucky.

First, it is clear under the Restatement that a party's place of domicile is sufficient to meet the substantial relationship test of §187(2)(a). *See* Restatement §187 cmt. F. Second, although Kentucky may have a materially greater interest than Michigan regarding liens placed or not placed on real property within the state, one cannot reasonably assert that it is a fundamental policy of Kentucky to permit parties to waive the right to place liens. Although the Restatement does not closely define the term, "to be 'fundamental,' a policy must in any event be a substantial one." Restatement §187 cmt. g. By way of example, the Restatement provides that "a fundamental policy may be embodied in a statute which makes one or more kinds of contracts illegal. . . ." *Id.* Here, the relevant Kentucky statute does not even address the validity of a pre-work waiver of the right to place liens. Such waivers are not expressly forbidden, and they appear to be permitted by implication. However, this tolerance does not rise to a fundamental policy of permitting such waivers.

If the substantive laws of Michigan and Kentucky were reversed—if, in other words, lien-waiver provisions were valid in Michigan but invalid in Kentucky—our inquiry would be at an end. Express contractual provisions that are aligned with the substantive law of the state effectively selected by the parties to govern the contract simply are enforced. However, given the conflict here between the express contractual provision prohibiting the filing of liens and the otherwise effective background law which invalidates such prohibitions, we must delve further into the Restatement to resolve this issue. The Restatement indicates that where, as here, the express provision would be valid under the law of the state that would govern in the absence of a choice-of-law provision (the "default state"), the selection of an incompatible state's law to govern the contract is to be disregarded as a mistake of the parties.

The comments to the Restatement include the following discussion concerning mistaken choice-of-law provisions:

> On occasion, the parties may choose a law that would declare the contract invalid. In such situations, the chosen law will not be applied by reason of the parties' choice. To do so would defeat the expectations of the parties which it is the purpose of the present rule to protect. The parties can be assumed to have intended that the provisions of the contract would be binding upon them. . . . If the parties have chosen a law that would invalidate the contract, it can be assumed that they did so by mistake. If, however, the chosen law is that of the state of the otherwise applicable law under the rule of §188, this law will be applied even when it invalidates the contract.

Restatement §187 cmt. e n.4.

It is important to note that this doctrine applies to situations in which the selected law would invalidate an express provision of a contract as well as to situations in which the entire contract would be invalidated. *See* Infomax Office Sys., Inc. v. MBO Binder & Co. of America, 976 F. Supp. 1247, 1254 (S.D. Iowa 1997) (holding that "choice of law should be considered a mistake as to the invalidating portion of chosen state law").

Applying §187, the courts of Michigan would consider the choice of Michigan law in the present case to be mistaken to the extent this law invalidates the express lien-waiver provision. This conclusion does not end the analysis, however. Although the Restatement favors party autonomy, the parties are not permitted to avoid state law with regard to purely local transactions. Similarly, if an express provision would be invalid under the chosen state law as well as under the law of the default state, the doctrine of mistaken choice of law will not be employed to permit the parties to overcome the policy of both states. Thus, we must determine whether the lien-waiver provision would be valid under the law of the default state before we permit VDI to enforce the waiver provision.

Restatement §188(1) provides that in the absence of an effective choice by the parties a contract issue shall be governed by the law of the state that, "with respect to that issue, has the most significant relationship to the transaction and the parties." The contacts to be considered in evaluating state relationships to the contract include the locations of contracting, negotiation, performance, the subject matter of the contract, and the residence and business of the parties. See Restatement §188(2). Moreover, when a contract is for the rendition of services, §196 provides that the law of the state of performance shall apply unless another state has a more significant relationship to the contract.

Given the presumption created by §196, we conclude that a Michigan court would find that Kentucky law would apply in the absence of an effective choice by the parties. This contract entailed the rendition of services solely in the state of Kentucky. The particular issue in question, moreover, is the placement of a lien on property situated in Kentucky. Although the contract was deemed to have been executed in Michigan, it appears that the negotiation and contracting actually occurred through correspondence between a Michigan resident and a Pennsylvania resident. Thus, no state has a more significant relationship to the contract than does Kentucky.

The lien-waiver provision of the contract is valid under Kentucky law. Pursuant to Restatement §§187 and 188, the selection of Michigan law to govern the contract must be ignored with regard to this provision as a mistake of the parties. Accordingly, we conclude that the district court reached the correct result when it held that Kentucky law governed the parties' rights and obligations with respect to the lien-waiver provision and when it granted VDI's motion to release the bonds.

III

For the foregoing reasons, we **AFFIRM** the district court's order granting VDI's motion to release the bonds.

Questions and Comments

(1) Why does the *Banek, Inc.* court ask whether the choice-of-law clause is valid under the Michigan franchise law *before* performing a choice-of-law

analysis? Why does it assume the Michigan law governs this issue? Would the Michigan franchise law apply to a franchise agreement in Georgia between Georgia domiciliaries? What is the difference between the court's first and second "sequential questions"?

(2) Would the *Banek, Inc.* court have enforced the choice-of-law clause if the parties had not negotiated the contract and changed some of its terms? If the Michigan franchise law expressly prohibited choice-of-law clauses? If there were "significant differences" between the Michigan and Georgia franchise regimes? Which of these factors is most important under §187(2)(b)? More generally, how do courts determine when a state policy is "fundamental" within the meaning of §187(2)(b)? Is this the same inquiry as the traditional public policy exception to choice of law?

(3) What are the extraterritorial limits on a state's application of its franchise laws? In Instructional Systems, Inc. v. Computer Curriculum Corp., 614 A.2d 124 (N.J. 1992), a New Jersey firm (ISI) was the exclusive distributor in 11 Northeast states from 1974-1989 of an educational computer product made by a California firm (CCC). When their contract, which contained a California choice-of-law clause, expired in 1989, CCC offered ICI a new contract that reduced its marketing territory to three states. ISI sued CCC in New Jersey, alleging that the new contract imposed unreasonable performance standards in violation of the New Jersey Franchise Act. The court held that the New Jersey Franchise Act governed not only distribution activities in New Jersey, but also in other states included in the original contract. The court reasoned: "To the extent that it is applicable, the New Jersey Act regulates instate conduct that has out-of-state effects. . . . the State regulation is applicable . . . to specific transactions affecting New Jersey, *i.e.*, franchises that have a "place of business" in New Jersey." *Id.* at 368-389. The Third Circuit subsequently ruled that this holding did not violate constitutional limitations on interstate discrimination and extraterritorial regulation. *See* Instructional Sys. v. Computer Curriculum Corp., 35 F.3d 813 (3d Cir. 1994). We consider these limitations in detail in the next chapter.

(4) Do you agree with the court in *Kipin Industries* that the choice-of-law clause at issue here—providing that the contract should be "construed" according to Michigan law—was meant to include not only Michigan rules of contract interpretation, but rather all of Michigan substantive law? Under what law did the court interpret the choice-of-law clause to reach this conclusion? For a different view of a similar clause, *see* Heating & Air Specialists Inc. v. Jones, 180 F. 3d 923, 930 (8th Cir. 1999) (concluding that clause providing that "laws of the State of Texas shall govern [the contract's] interpretation" referred to Texas contract interpretation rules and did not preclude application of otherwise applicable Arkansas law).

(5) Why does the *Kipin Industries* court not enforce the Michigan choice-of-law clause with respect to lien-waiver provision? Was this really a "mistake" of the parties or just incompetent lawyering? Why should parties be relieved of the unfortunate and perhaps unforeseen consequences of a choice-

of-law clause in this context and not in others? Shouldn't the parties be held to their bargain? And isn't the choice of a law that invalidates a term of the contract different from a choice of law that invalidates the entire contract? Isn't the inference of mistake more powerful in the latter context?

(6) Professors O'Hara and Ribstein have argued that choice-of-law rules should be designed to maximize individual welfare rather than state interests. They view contractual choice of law as the paradigmatic method for achieving this end, and try to translate many disparate choice-of-law problems into issues of explicit or implicit party choice. They conclude that the expansion of party autonomy in choice of law both promotes individual welfare and pressures legislatures to enact efficient laws. *See* O'Hara & Ribstein, From Politics to Efficient in Choice of Law, 67 U. Chi. L. Rev, 1151 (2000); O'Hara, Opting Out of Regulation: A Public Choice Analysis of Contractual Choice of Law, 53 Vand. L. Rev. 1551 (2000); Kobayashi & Ribstein, Choosing Law by Contract, in The Fall and Rise of Freedom of Contract 325 (1999). For other related economic analyses of choice of law, *see* Guzman, Choice of Law: New Foundations, 90 Georgetown L.J. (forthcoming 2002); Stephan, The Political Economy of Choice of Law, 90 Georgetown L.J. (forthcoming 2002); Stephan, Regulatory Cooperation and Competition: The Search for Virtue, in Transatlantic Regulatory Cooperation—Legal Problems and Political Prospects (2000).

G. Wrinkles in the Theory

While modern choice-of-law theories are different from one another in many respects, they also have important similarities. The common attributes are the goal of implementing state substantive policies and the dislike of rigid rules of the First Restatement variety. Because of their substantial similarities, there are some problems that modern theories share. We have already examined some of the recent theoretical criticisms leveled against governmental interest analysis. The problems arising in the cases below are shared by modern theories generally; indeed, they are not very different from some of the issues raised by the First Restatement.

1. Domicile

The modern theories' assumption that state policies are often triggered by domicile makes domicile a key concept to the choice-of-law process. All of the problems that we saw in Chapter 1, pages 40 to 47, therefore also arise in the modern theories; indeed, they arise more frequently because domicile is important to a larger percentage of cases. In addition, there are problems about how to attribute a "domicile" to corporations, because it is not clear which states have interests in protecting a corporation: the state of incorporation? the principal place of business? The modern treatment of this issue is somewhat unsettled. *See generally* Note, Interest Analysis Applied to Corporations: The Unprincipled Use of a Choice of Law Method, 98 Yale L.J. 597 (1989).

One of the problems that plagues modern choice-of-law theories is that of after-acquired domicile.

Reich v. Purcell

67 Cal. 2d 551, 442 P.2d 727, 63 Cal. Rptr. 31 (1967)

TRAYNOR, C.J.

This wrongful death action arose out of a head-on collision of two automobiles in Missouri. One of the automobiles was owned and operated by defendant Joseph Purcell, a resident and domiciliary of California who was on his way to a vacation in Illinois. The other automobile was owned and operated by Mrs. Reich, the wife of plaintiff Lee Reich. The Reichs then resided in Ohio and Mrs. Reich and the Reich's two children, Jay and Jeffry, were on their way to California, where the Reichs were contemplating settling. Mrs. Reich and Jay were killed in the collision, and Jeffry was injured.

Plaintiffs, Lee Reich and Jeffry Reich, are the heirs of Mrs. Reich and Lee Reich is the heir of Jay Reich. Plaintiffs moved to California and became permanent residents here after the accident. The estates of Mrs. Reich and Jay Reich are being administered in Ohio.

The parties stipulated that judgment be entered in specified amounts for the wrongful death of Jay, for the personal injuries suffered by Jeffry, and for the damages to Mrs. Reich's automobile. For the death of Mrs. Reich they stipulated that judgment be entered for $55,000 or $25,000 depending on the court's ruling on the applicability of the Missouri limitation of damages to a maximum of $25,000. Neither Ohio nor California limit recovery in wrongful death actions. The trial court held that the Missouri limitation applied because the accident occurred there and entered judgment accordingly. Plaintiffs appealed. . . .

As the forum we must consider all of the foreign and domestic elements and interests involved in this case to determine the rule applicable. Three states are involved. Ohio is where the plaintiffs and their decedents resided before the accident and where the decedents' estates are being administered. Missouri is the place of the wrong. California is the place where defendant resides and is the forum. Although plaintiffs now reside in California, their residence and domicile at the time of the accident are the relevant residence and domicile. At the time of the accident the plans to change the family domicile were not definite and fixed, and if the choice of law were made to turn on events happening after the accident, forum shopping would be encouraged. Accordingly, plaintiffs' present domicile in California does not give this state any interest in applying its law, and since California has no limitation on damages, it also has no interest in applying its law on behalf of defendant. As a forum that is therefore disinterested in the only issue in dispute, we must decide whether to adopt the Ohio or the Missouri rule as the rule of decision for this case.

[The court concluded that Missouri, as the situs of the accident, had no interest in imposing limitations on a wrongful death recovery, while Ohio had an interest, presumably as former domiciliary state, in affording a full recovery. It therefore applied Ohio law.]

Questions and Comments

(1) Isn't the court guilty of a rather bald non sequitur in saying, "[F]orum shopping would be encouraged. Accordingly, plaintiffs' domicile in California does not give this state any interest in applying its law . . ."? Forum-shopping *may* be evil, and it may be something to be balanced against California's desire to see a full and fair recovery for its domiciliaries (especially when injured by another domiciliary), but can it accurately be said to prevent the existence of that interest in the first place?

(2) Does the mere possibility of forum-shopping justify the court's result? Aren't courts equipped to discover (within the bounds of acceptable uncertainty) states of mind in other courts? If forum-shopping is the only concern, shouldn't the plaintiffs have been allowed to show that they would have moved to California even if they had not contemplated litigation?

(3) Even if plaintiffs moved to California precisely to take advantage of its law, does California therefore have any less of an interest in their well-being? *Compare* Shapiro v. Thomson, 394 U.S. 618 (1969), in which the Supreme Court refused to allow New York to impose a one-year residency requirement for welfare benefits as a response (in part) to fears that New York's generosity would draw prospective welfare recipients. If forum-shopping is the only worry, and if (as suggested in note (2)), we can rely on the judicial process to weed out those who move to California solely to invoke its law while suing, can we be satisfied with giving higher judgments to those who seek out California for its sunny beaches or its lifestyle than for its law?

Might there be reasons not mentioned by the court for rejecting after-acquired domicile as providing a state with "interests"? For an argument that the real explanation for this attitude toward after-acquired domicile must be found outside the premises of modern policy analysis, *see* Brilmayer, Rights, Fairness, and Choice of Law, 99 Yale L.J. 1277, 1286-1287 (1989).

(4) Is the situation any different if it is the defendant who has acquired a new domicile? Is it any different if either party acquires a new domicile with law less favorable than that of the previous domicile? In Miller v. Miller,

22 N.Y.2d 12, 237 N.E.2d 877, 290 N.Y.S.2d 734 (1968), a New York resident was killed in a car accident in Maine. Maine limited recoveries for wrongful death; New York had a policy enshrined in its constitution against wrongful death limitations. The defendant, brother of the decedent, moved to New York a few months before suit was brought. (There was no evidence of collusion.) The case was complicated by the fact that Maine repealed its limitation after the accident. The Court of Appeals said,

> Having found no considerations present here arising out of fairness to the nominal or real party defendant, we turn next to the question of whether the application of New York law here will unduly interfere with a legitimate interest of a sister State in regulating the rights of its citizens, at least with regard to conduct within its borders. Here again we perceive no reason to deny application of our own law. To the extent that the Maine limitation evinced a desire to protect its residents in wrongful death actions, that purpose cannot be defeated here since no judgment in this action will be entered against a Maine resident. Maine would have no concern with the nature of the recovery awarded against defendants who are no longer residents of that State and who are, therefore, no longer proper objects of its legislative concern. It is true that, at the time of the accident, the defendants were residents of Maine but they would have no vested right to the application of the law of their former residence unless it could be demonstrated that they had governed their conduct in reliance upon it—a reliance which is neither present nor claimed in the case at bar. Any claim that Maine has a paternalistic interest in protecting its residents against liability for acts committed while they were in Maine, should they move to another jurisdiction, is highly speculative and ignores the fact that for the very same acts committed today Maine would now impose the same liability as New York.
>
> There may be times where policy considerations such as a desire to prevent forum shopping would require us to ignore changes in domicile after the accident (Gore v. Northeast Airlines; Reich v. Purcell). In the instant case, however, the change in domicile has nothing whatever to do with a desire to achieve a more favorable legal climate, and we see no reason to ignore the facts as they are presented at the time of the litigation. The two considerations urged in the dissenting opinion—the likelihood of discouraging wrongdoers from settling in this State lest they be held to respond for their wrongdoing and the possibility that wrongdoers will settle here in a collusive attempt to fix broader liability upon the insurer—contradict each other, are speculative and are insufficient to move us to disregard the change in domicile.

In Gore v. Northeast Airlines, 373 F.2d 717 (2d Cir. 1967), a federal court applying New York conflicts law held that a widow who moved away from New York would still be able to invoke New York's refusal to allow limitations on wrongful death recoveries, even though the state of her new domicile was less solicitous of her welfare. Does this mean a heads-I-win-tails-you-lose approach favoring forum law?

(5) In Clay v. Sun Insurance Office, Ltd., 377 U.S. 179 (1964), reproduced infra, page 352 the Supreme Court upheld the constitutionality (though of course did not pass on the wisdom) of application of a Florida statute providing for a minimum period during which suit could be brought on an insurance contract, despite a clause in the insurance contract providing for a shorter period. The contract had been purchased and paid for in Illinois by plaintiff, who was then a resident of Illinois. He later moved to Florida where the loss occurred, and sued after the contractual period had expired but before the Florida statutory period had expired.

Professor Currie said of *Clay:*

> It is vitally important that the Florida court answer one specific question: Assuming that the policy expressed in the statute is one designed "to preserve a fair opportunity for people who have bought and paid for insurance to go to court and collect it," is the evil which that policy is designed to alleviate so acute, and is the policy so exigent, that Florida believes it necessary to apply the statute from its effective date onward for the protection of the total population of Florida, including residents who had previously entered into domestic contracts containing such "suit clauses"? In other words, is the statute construed as having retroactive effect? If the answer is no, the Court's problem is solved. If Florida has no policy of protection for residents who entered into such contracts before they were protected by the statute, it has no policy that can rationally be applied to upset vested rights under contracts made under circumstances such that Florida then had no interest in them. If the answer is yes, the Court must determine a different question—probably an easier one, since it is an ordinary question of constitutional law rather than mixed with conflict-of-laws theory. Is such retroactive legislation a reasonable exercise of the lawmaking power under the Due Process and Contracts clauses?

Currie, The Verdict of the Quiescent Years, in Selected Essays on the Conflict of Laws 584, 625-626 (1963). Currie later modified this position by noting an important difference between retroactive legislation and situations like *Clay:* A state may forgo making legislation retroactive, even though it could do so, because the evils of prior law will diminish and disappear with time—eventually, for example, all current Florida insurance contracts will have been entered or renewed after the date of the Florida statute in question. On the other hand, insured parties may continue to travel ad infinitum from Illinois to Florida. The continuing nature of the latter problem might justify application of the state's new law even when the same had not been made retroactive in domestic cases. Currie, Conflict, Crisis and Confusion in New York, in Selected Essays on the Conflict of Laws 690, 739 (1963). For criticism of Currie's revised position, *see* Hancock, The Effect in Choice of Law Cases of the Acquisition of a New Domicile after the Commission of a Tort or Making of a Contract, 2 Hast. Intl. & Comp. L. Rev. 215, 220-223 (1979).

The Supreme Court again allowed a postaccident change of domicile to the forum to result in the application of forum law in Allstate Insurance Co. v. Hague, page 359 *infra.*

(6) The drafters of the Restatement Second were equally perplexed by the after-acquired domicile problem. The Introductory Note to Chapter 7 (Wrongs) says:

> Mention should here be made of a problem which runs through the entire area of choice of law. This problem is whether a change in a party's relationship to a state following the occurrence should ever affect choice of the applicable law. For example, let us suppose that at the time of an automobile accident in state *X* the plaintiff is domiciled in state *Y* and the defendant is domiciled in state *Z*, but that the plaintiff acquires a domicil in *Z* before bringing suit. Should this shift of the plaintiff's domicil from *Y* to *Z* have any impact on choice of the law governing any of the issues that might arise between the plaintiff and the defendant by reason of the accident? Presumably this change of domicil should have no effect upon the law governing most of the issues involving the accident. But is this necessarily true of all issues? The problem is not dealt with in the Restatement of this Subject because existing authority is too sparse to warrant doing so.

(7) Sometimes the change in domicile occurs after some of the events leading up to the litigation but before others. In Lange v. Penn Mutual Life Insurance Co., 843 F.2d 1175 (95th Cir. 1988), a court, applying the Restatement Second, was faced with a suit to recover a life insurance policy. Plaintiff had purchased the policy while a resident of Arizona, and this was where her husband died. She then moved to Iowa and was living there at the point that her insurance claim was denied. She was still in Iowa when her complaint was filed, but moved back to Arizona before the trial began.

(8) One of the chief problems of the First Restatement was that it singled out some unique territorial connecting factor, despite the fact that the litigation involved events in a number of different states in addition. Even if one was agreed that what mattered was the location of events, therefore, the choice of a single territorial event was arbitrary.

Do the modern theories have exactly the same problem with domiciliary connecting factors? First, some individuals and corporate entities have multiple connections (residence, domicile, place of incorporation, principal place of business, etc.). Second, these factors change over time. While the nemesis of the First Restatement was the case where *events* were widely scattered, the nemesis of the new learning is the case with widely scattered personal or corporate *affiliations.*

Should modern theories, just by fiat, choose a particular point in time at which to measure domicile? When should that be—the time when the cause of action "accrued" (*i.e.*, the time when the rights "vested")? Recall the problems with "vesting" discussed in Chapter 1, especially those in determining where or when the rights "accrued" for purpose of applying the forum's borrowing statute.

(9) Plaintiff is in the process of moving from State *A* to State *B*. On the way, she becomes involved in an auto accident. Which state has an "interest" in her? Doesn't her domicile at the time of the accident depend on where the accident occurred?

2. Renvoi

Pfau v. Trent Aluminum Co.

55 N.J. 511, 263 A.2d 129 (1970)

PROCTOR, J.

This appeal presents a conflict of laws problem regarding a host's liability to his guest for negligence arising out of an automobile accident. Plaintiff, a Connecticut domiciliary, was injured in Iowa while a passenger in an automobile driven by a New Jersey domiciliary and owned by a New Jersey corporation. Iowa has a guest statute which provides that a host-driver is not liable to his passenger-guest for ordinary negligence. . . .

The facts pertinent to this appeal are undisputed. Plaintiff, Steven Pfau, a domiciliary of Connecticut, was a student at Parsons College in Iowa, and the defendant, Bruce Trent, a domiciliary of New Jersey, was a student at the same college. The boys met for the first time at Parsons.

Following the Easter vacation in 1966, the defendant, Bruce Trent, drove the automobile involved in the accident back to Iowa for his use at college. The automobile was registered in New Jersey in the name of the Trent Aluminum Company, a New Jersey corporation owned by Bruce's father. Bruce was using the car with the owner-corporation's consent. The vehicle was insured in New Jersey by a New Jersey carrier.

About a month after Bruce's return to college and several days before the accident, he agreed to drive the plaintiff to Columbia, Missouri, for a weekend visit. They never reached their destination. Shortly after leaving Parsons on April 22, 1966, and while still in Iowa, Bruce failed to negotiate a curve and the car he was operating collided with an oncoming vehicle driven by Joseph Davis. Mr. Davis and his wife and child, who were Iowa domiciliaries, were injured in the accident. Their claims have now been settled by defendants' insurance carrier. The sole question presented by this appeal is whether the Iowa guest statute is applicable to this action.

[The court, following Babcock v. Jackson, page 188 *supra*, inspected the purposes behind the Iowa guest statute and determined that none of them was applicable to the facts of the case. The court then discussed the interests of Connecticut, the plaintiff's domicile, and New Jersey, the forum and defendant's domicile.]

In this case, however, we are faced with a more complex situation since plaintiff is a domiciliary of Connecticut. Thus, we must consider the law of both New Jersey and Connecticut. Connecticut long ago repealed its guest statute and now permits guest-passengers to recover from their host-drivers for ordinary negligence. There is no doubt that if this plaintiff-guest had been injured in a Connecticut accident by a Connecticut host-driver, there would be no bar to recover for ordinary negligence if suit were brought in that state.

Turning to New Jersey's law, we are led to Cohen v. Kaminetsky, where we held that the strong policy of this state is to allow a guest-passenger to be compensated by his host-driver in cases of ordinary negligence. Thus, the substantive laws of Connecticut and New Jersey are in accord. . . .

It would appear that Connecticut's substantive law allowing a guest to recover for his host's ordinary negligence would give it a significant interest in having that law applied to this case. Defendants argue, however, that if we apply Connecticut's substantive law, we should apply its choice-of-law rule as well. In other words, they contend Connecticut's interest in its domiciliaries is identified not only by its substantive law, but by its choice-of-law rule. Connecticut adheres to lex loci delicti and accordingly to its decisions would most likely apply the substantive law of Iowa in this case. Defendants contend that plaintiff should not be allowed to recover when he could not do so in either Iowa where the accident occurred or in Connecticut where he is domiciled. We cannot agree for two reasons. First, it is not definite that plaintiff would be unable to recover in either of those states.[4] More importantly, however, we see no reason for applying Connecticut's choice-of-law rule. To do so would frustrate the very goals of governmental-interest analysis. Connecticut's choice-of-law rule does not identify that state's interest in the matter. Lex loci delicti was born in an effort to achieve simplicity and uniformity, and does not relate to a state's interest in having its law applied to given issues in a tort case. It is significant that in Reich v. Purcell [page 304 *supra*], the California Supreme Court applied the substantive law of Ohio to the Missouri accident. The court did not apply Ohio's choice-of-law rule which was lex loci delicti, and would have called for application of the Missouri limitation on damages. Professor Kay in her comment on Reich v. Purcell was in agreement with the above authorities that only the foreign substantive law should be applied, and she agreed with the court in *Reich* that Ohio's choice-

---

4. We note in this connection that contrary to defendants' contention, it is not clear what substantive law Iowa would apply to this case. That state has recently departed from the traditional lex loci delicti rule, and it cannot be assumed that Iowa would apply its guest statute to this case. Additionally, although Connecticut remains a lex loci delicti state, it has in the past employed some of the traditional escape devices to avoid the doctrine's harsh results. . . . If, as defendants urge, we should look to Connecticut's whole law, *i.e.*, both its substantive law and its choice-of-law rule, why should not Connecticut look to Iowa's whole law if suit were brought in Connecticut? If it did look to Iowa's whole law, Connecticut might well be led back to its own substantive law.

of-law rule should be ignored. Kay, "Comment on Reich v. Purcell," 15 UCLA L. Rev., *supra* at 589 n.31.

We conclude that since Iowa has no interest in this litigation, and since the substantive laws of Connecticut and New Jersey are the same, this case presents a false conflict and the Connecticut plaintiff should have the right to maintain an action for ordinary negligence in our courts. In this situation principles of comity, and perhaps the equal protection and privileges and immunities clauses of the Constitution, dictate that we should afford the Connecticut plaintiff the same protection a New Jersey plaintiff would be given.

For the reasons expressed the order of the Appellate Division is reversed and the order of the trial court striking the separate defense of the Iowa guest statute is restated.

Questions and Comments

(1) Professor Currie would probably have approved the result in *Pfau*, since he thought that interest analysis virtually did away with the problem of renvoi:

> And, though I make this suggestion with some trepidation, it seems clear that the problem of renvoi would have no place at all [under interest analysis]. Foreign law would be applied only when the court has determined that that foreign state has a legitimate interest in the application of its law and policy to the case at bar and that the forum has none. Hence, there can be no question of applying anything other than the internal law of the foreign state. The closest approximation to the renvoi problem that will be encountered under the suggested method is the case in which neither state has an interest in the application of its law and policy; in that event, the forum would apply its own law simply on the ground that that is the more convenient disposition. Is it possible that this is, in fact, all that is involved in the typical renvoi situation?

Currie, Selected Essays on the Conflict of Laws 184-185 (1963) (footnotes omitted).

(2) Professor von Mehren has elaborated significantly on the idea only suggested by Currie—that a look at the conflicts rules of the other jurisdictions will shed significant light on the interests of that jurisdiction and thus be a considerable aid in applying interest analysis. That will be true, however, only when the other jurisdiction has itself adopted interest analysis, Professor von Mehren warns, since a territorial approach in the other jurisdiction is one that cannot be read as stating the other jurisdiction's interest or lack of interest in a problem. Von Mehren, The Renvoi and Its Relation to Various Approaches to the Choice-of-Law Problem, in XXth Century Comparative and Conflicts Law 380, 393-394 (1961). Recall that the court in *Phillips v. General Motors*, page 264 *supra*, disagreed with von Mehren because it referred to the lex loci attitude of North Carolina as evidence of that

state's lack of interest in applying its law to an accident in Kansas. In recent years many other courts using a modern choice-of-law methodology have employed this renvoi technique to measure the foreign state's interest. *See, e.g.*, Miller v. White, 702 A.2d 391 (Vt. 1997); Sutherland v. Kennington Truck Service Ltd., 562 N.W. 2d 466 (Mich. 1997); Braxton v. Anco Electric, Inc., 409 S.E. 2d 914 (N.C. 1991). Egnal, The "Essential" Role of Modern Renvoi in the Governmental Interest Analysis Approach to Choice of Law, 54 Temple L.Q. 237 (1981).

(3) Why should it be assumed that the other state's choice-of-law decisions would matter more if they conformed to tenets of governmental interest analysis? Isn't adoption of the First (or Second) Restatement a policy decision in its own right? Can't adherence to territorial rules be taken as a commitment to the goals of predictability, territorial sovereignty, and the like? Or perhaps a state adhering to an old-fashioned approach simply believes that its substantive policies are best advanced when the substantive rule is applied on a territorial basis. Why should the forum insist on remaking the policy choices of the other state? *See generally* Brilmayer, Conflict of Laws: Foundations and Future Directions 94-98 (1991).

(4) What should the forum do if it determines that another potentially interested state would not apply its own law because it uses the better-law approach? If it uses the most-significant-relationship approach? If it had a statutory provision declaring its law inapplicable? Professor Larry Kramer would consult the other state's choice-of-law rules whenever the rule defines the substantive scope of its law. Return of the Renvoi, 66 N.Y.U. L. Rev. 979, 1012 (1991).

Richards v. United States

369 U.S. 1 (1962)

[The action arose from an airplane crash in Missouri. The airplane had been en route from Tulsa, Oklahoma, to New York City. Plaintiffs were representatives of dead passengers. The government was named as a defendant on the theory that the Federal Aviation Agency had been negligent in failing to enforce relevant statutes and regulations concerning the practices of American Airlines in the Tulsa overhaul depot. The parties were generally agreed that the alleged negligence had occurred in Oklahoma and that the harmful effects had occurred in Missouri. Under the Federal Torts Claims Act, upon which the government's liability was premised, governmental liability would arise "under circumstances where the United States, if a private person, would be liable to the claimant in accordance with the law of the place where the act or omission occurred." 28 U.S.C. 1346. Three interpretations of this section were presented to the court and supported by lower court decisions: (1) That the whole law of the place of the negligence ought to control. (2) That the internal law of the place of negligence ought to control. (3) That the internal law of the place of injury ought to control. The Court rejected the last of these on the grounds that it was inconsistent with the language of the statute. It then noted that no choice could be made between the first two options solely on the basis of statutory language and that an analysis of the purpose of the act was necessary to resolve the dispute.]

We believe it fundamental that a section of a statute should not be read in isolation from the context of the whole Act, and that in fulfilling our responsibility in interpreting legislation, "we must not be guided by a single sentence or member of a sentence, but [should] look to the provisions of the whole law, and to its object and policy." We should not assume that Congress intended to set the courts completely adrift from state law with regard to questions for which it has not provided a specific and definite answer in an act such as the one before us which, as we have indicated, is so intimately related to state law. Thus, we conclude that a reading of the statute as a whole, with due regard to its purpose, requires application of the whole law of the State where the act or omission occurred.

We are led to our conclusion by other persuasive factors notwithstanding the fact that the very conflict among the lower federal courts that we must here resolve illustrates the also reasonable alternative view expressed by the petitioners. First, our interpretation enables the federal courts to treat the United States as a "private individual under like circumstances," and thus is consistent with the Act considered as a whole. The general conflict-of-laws rule, followed by a vast majority of the States, is to apply the law of the place of injury to the substantive rights of the parties. Therefore, where the forum State is the same as the one in which the act or omission occurred, our interpretation will enable the federal courts to treat the United States as an individual would be treated under like circumstances. Moreover, this interpretation of the Act provides a degree of flexibility to the law to be applied in federal courts that would not be possible under the view advanced either by the petitioners or by American. Recently there has been a tendency on the part of some States to depart from the general conflicts rule in order to take into account the interests of the State having significant contact with the parties to the litigation. We can see no compelling reason to saddle the Act with an interpretation that would prevent the federal courts from implementing this policy in choice-of-law rules where the State in which the negligence occurred has adopted it. Should the States continue this rejection of the older rule in those situations where its application might appear inappropriate or inequitable, the flexibility inherent in our interpretation will also be more in step with that judicial approach, as well as with the character of the legislation and with the purpose of the Act considered as a whole.

In the absence of persuasive evidence to the contrary, we do not believe that Congress intended to adopt the inflexible rule urged upon us by the petitioners. Despite the power of Congress to enact for litigation of this type a federal conflict-of-laws rule independent of the States' development of such rules, we should not, particularly in the type of interstitial legislation involved here, assume that it has done so. Nor are we persuaded to require such an independent federal rule by the petitioners' argument that there are other instances, specifically set forth in the Act, where the liability of the United States is not coextensive with that of a private person under state law. It seems sufficient to note that Congress has been specific in those instances where it intended the federal courts to depart completely from state law and, also, that this list of exceptions contains no direct or indirect modification of the principles controlling application of choice-of-law rules. Certainly there is nothing in the legislative history that even remotely supports the argument that Congress did not intend state conflict rules to apply to multistate tort actions brought against the Government. . . .

Our view of a State's power to adopt an appropriate conflict-of-laws doctrine in a situation touching more than one place has been indicated by our discussion in Part III of this opinion. Where more than one State has sufficiently substantial contact with the activity in question, the forum State, by analysis of the interests possessed by the States involved, could constitutionally apply to the decision of the case the law of one or another state having such an interest in the multistate activity. Thus, an Oklahoma state court would be free to apply either its own law, the law of the place where the negligence occurred, or the law of Missouri, the law of the place where the injury occurred, to an action brought in its courts and involving this factual situation. Both the Federal District Court sitting in Oklahoma, and the Court of Appeals for the Tenth Circuit, have interpreted the pertinent Oklahoma decisions, which we have held are controlling, to declare that an action for wrongful death is based on the statute of the place where the injury occurred that caused the death. Therefore, Missouri's statute controls the case at bar. It is conceded that each petitioner has received $15,000, the maximum amount recoverable under the Missouri Act, and the petitioners thus have received full compensation for their claims. Accordingly, the courts below were correct in holding that, in accordance with Oklahoma law, petitioners had failed to state claims upon which relief could be granted.

Questions and Comments

(1) Is it fair to say that *Richards* uses a kind of interest analysis since it concentrates on the policies of the Federal Tort Claims Act? If so, is the Court's decision to look to the whole law of the state where the negligence occurred inconsistent with Currie's conclusion that when foreign law was to be applied, it could only be internal law?

(2) Note that there are several differences between *Richards* and the typical renvoi case. First, there appears to be no substantive law of the deciding jurisdiction (the United States) on the tort liability issue. Thus, there must be reference to law other than the forum's, and if the conflicts rules would refer to the law of another jurisdiction, that cannot be taken as a sign of indifference justifying use of the forum's law. Also, unlike the common renvoi

case (to the extent that there is such a thing), the usual options are references to the internal law of the other jurisdiction or reference back to the forum. In the Tort Claims Act case, the reference, if any, will always be to the law of a third jurisdiction.

(3) How did Congress come to choose the conflicts rule in the Federal Tort Claims Act? Professor Leflar offers this explanation and commentary:

> Judge Goodrich learned that the draftsmen of the Act (not of course the members of Congress who enacted it) apparently thought that the quoted provision was in accord with settled conflicts law [citing Goodrich, Yielding Place to New: Rest Versus Motion in the Conflict of Laws, 50 Colum. L. Rev. 881, 894-895 (1950).] Even if the Act had been based on a correct understanding of the 1948 conflicts law, it would have produced a hard and fast rule contrary to the torts-conflicts law of most American states twenty-nine years later. Despite this fact, it is unlikely that Congress will correct the discrepancy between the Act and current state law. In Richards v. United States, the United States Supreme Court managed to salvage the conflicts rule of the Act by reading a kind of renvoi technique into the section so that it in effect reads "in accordance with the *conflict of laws* law of the place where the act or omission occurred." This interpretation makes the conflicts rule as up-to-date as that of the designated "place" at the time of the "act or omission" and would have been desirable, though unlikely, interpretation if the section had been drafted more knowingly to prescribe the law of the place of harmful impact. *As interpreted,* the statute becomes almost a model for federal enactments that should leave room for future growth and improvement in locally governing law. By their innocent error, the Tort Claims Act draftsmen created an opportunity for better law than they knew.

Leflar, Choice-of-Law Statutes, 44 Tenn. L. Rev. 951, 948 (1977).

(4) If the Act requires that the United States be treated as a private party would be, then in cases where the United States is a party, which states have an "interest" in applying their protective laws on its behalf?

3. Substance and Procedure

The substance-procedure dichotomy recognized even in territorialist thinking retains importance under interest analysis and related approaches. Assume that in a given case the forum has no interest but that another jurisdiction does. That situation calls for application of the other jurisdiction's substantive law. But on "truly" procedural questions, the forum *does* have an interest by virtue of the fact that its courts must involve themselves in the handling of the case. To borrow an example from the first chapter, the forum that uses 8½ × 11-inch paper has an interest in having the parties comply with that practice even though the courts of the state whose substantive law controls use 8½ × 14-inch paper. On a less trivial level, the forum also has an interest in requiring the parties to adhere to the forum's limits for the filing of pleadings and the like. These "conflicts" between the procedures of one state and another are more often false conflicts because the fact that the litigation is in State *A* rather than State *B* removes any procedural interest that State *B* may have from the issue. Since such procedures as have been discussed also fail to affect the substantive outcome of the case if the parties comply with them (compliance being possible and imposing a minimum burden), the conflict is truly false. Thus the traditional rule that the procedural law of the forum should apply seems quite consistent with interest analysis and its cousins.

The trouble, as usual, arises in determining what is procedural and what is substantive. Fortunately, the analysis above provides the answer to that question for the most part. Rules having to do with how the forum's courts handle cases, as opposed to how such cases come out, are procedural. Rules attempting to affect the parties' liabilities or their behavior are substantive. (This is a version of the test proposed by Justice Harlan in Hanna v. Plumer, 380 U.S. 460 (1965).) Thus, a rule of evidence requiring relevance is undoubtedly procedural since it is designed to save the time of the forum court, while a rule of privilege is substantive and more appropriately governed by the law of any of the states concerned with the reason for the privilege in the case at hand.

Occasionally, however, a procedural interest of the forum will conflict with a substantive interest of the only state interested in the substance of the case. In a variation on Cohen v. Beneficial Industrial Loan Corp., 337 U.S. 541 (1949), imagine a cause of action arising under the laws of State *A* but tried for some reason in State *B*. Imagine further that the cause of action is viewed with suspicion in State *A* and that a statute of State *A* requires the plaintiff to pay in to the clerk of the court a sum of money to be used to pay costs if the defendants prevail. The purpose of the requirement is to discourage plaintiffs with frivolous cases from bringing such suits in the hopes of getting at least minor settlements from defendants, which are viewed as particularly vulnerable to unjustified suits of the type in question. Assume further that State *B* has no general mechanism whereby money can be paid in to the clerk of the court for later purposes. A court of State *B* would be unlikely to allow its clerk to accept such money without bonding for the clerk, for which no statute of State *B* provides.

Here is a true conflict between the laws of the two states, even though State *B*'s objection to the bond is clearly procedural and State *A*'s requirement for it is clearly substantive in the sense of trying to shape people's behavior. There seems little doubt that the conflict will be resolved as Currie suggested—by applying the law of the forum.

Such cases are relatively easy to decide—cases in which the proposed procedure puts an extra burden on the forum. Much more difficult are cases in which a rule of the other state—the only one with a substantive interest in the outcome of the case—has clearly substantive effect even though its motivation seems to be more toward the procedural. Take, for example, the oft-seen justification for guest statutes—preventing fraud against insurance companies. If that is the true motivation for a given guest statute, and the state with the guest statute would otherwise impose tort liability on the driver for the usual motives, what should the forum confident of its ability to discover fraud do? Theoretically the forum could hold the trial and allow liability because the case would be a false conflict case—the antifraud interest of the other state would have been served (albeit by means different from those used by that state) and the underlying purpose of its substantive rule carried out. Similarly, there is no impairment of the procedural or substantive interests of the forum. Nonetheless, one is left with strong feelings of discomfort that a result is reached that is different from the one that the courts of the only substantively concerned jurisdiction would reach. Perhaps this is a case for application of Professor Cavers's idea that results must be comprehensible to lay people or Professor Twerski's notion that a rule developed for one purpose can give rise to expectations that deserve respect.

Professor Twerski has also pointed out the applicability of "process values" to the substance-procedure issue in conflicts law. His reference is to an idea put forward by Professor Robert Summers in Evaluating and Improving Legal Processes—A Plea for "Process Values," 60 Cornell L. Rev. 1 (1974), in which Professor Summers pointed out that processes can be judged not only in terms of their efficacy in producing good results, but also in terms of certain values having to do with the process itself, such as participatory governance, fairness, rationality, and humaneness. In commenting on the implications of Summers's observations, Twerski noted briefly:

> Professor Summers contends that we have placed inordinate emphasis on process as a means for obtaining good results, while very little emphasis has been placed on the intrinsic values to be achieved by the legal process itself. . . . He has . . . clearly identified a blind spot in our jurisprudential thinking. Its implications for the procedural-substantive dichotomy should be obvious. If we begin thinking of procedure qua procedure as implementing a broad range of social values, then we may have to reexamine the outcome-oriented approach that now dominates our thinking.

Twerski, Book Review, 61 Cornell L. Rev. 1045, 1061-1062 (1976).

Could Professor Twerski's concerns for process values rationally lead a court to apply its own state's guest statute if the announced purpose of that statute is to prevent fraud, on the grounds that the court does not want to countenance fraud in its process even if the other jurisdiction is more confident or less caring? Or are most process values of the kind we should be concerned with already encompassed in what we ordinarily call "procedure," so that the traditional rule directing the forum to apply its own procedure automatically accommodates the process values of the forum? Rules having to do with the reliability of admissibility of evidence, for example, which certainly relate directly to the fairness and rationality of a proceeding, are usually treated as procedural matters to be governed by the law of the forum. Is State *A*'s "liberal" statute of frauds, which shows a willingness to expose its residents (and perhaps others) to the risk of fraud in the interests of enforcing valid oral contracts, a process-or substance-oriented value? Would emphasis on process values add to the difficulty of classifying rules as substantive or procedural?

4. Statutes of Limitations

Ledesma v. Jack Stewart Produce, Inc.

816 F.2d 482 (9th Cir. 1987)

Before NELSON, WIGGINS and NOONAN, JJ.

NELSON, J.:

Alfonso Ledesma, Josephine Rodriguez, Rafaela Gaytan, and Jennifer Santiago seek review of the district court's dismissal of their personal injury claim on the ground that the statute of limitations had run. They argue that under the California choice-of-law rules the district court should not have applied the one-year California statute of limitations to their claim. They further argue that, even if the California statute of limitations was properly applied, the district court should have tolled it pursuant to Cal. Civ. Proc. Code §351 (West 1982). We agree with the first contention. Accordingly, we reverse and remand to the district court for further proceedings.

I

FACTS

On May 13, 1981, Alfonso Ledesma, Josephine Rodriguez, Rafaela Gaytan, and Jennifer Santiago ("plaintiffs"), all California residents, were injured on an Arizona highway when their van was allegedly struck by a tractor driven by defendant John Wayne Mize, an Arkansas resident, and owned by defendants Jack Stewart Produce, Inc., an Oklahoma corporation with its principal place of business in Oklahoma, and Jack Stewart, an Oklahoma resident ("defendants"). On April 7, 1983, plaintiffs filed a diversity action in the Eastern District of California, seeking damages arising out of the accident. The defendants filed a motion to dismiss under Fed. R. Civ. P. 12(b)(6), arguing that the one-year California statute of limitations applied and barred the action against them. *See* Cal. Civ. Proc. Code §340(3) (West Supp. 1987). The district court granted the defendants' motion to dismiss the action as time-barred. Plaintiffs appeal from the order of dismissal. . . .

It is well-settled that in diversity cases federal courts must apply the choice-of-law rules of the forum state. California has adopted a "governmental interest" approach to resolve choice-of-law problems. Under that approach, the court must first determine if the laws of the two jurisdictions differ. If they do differ, the court should determine whether both states have an interest in applying their respective law. If only one state has an interest, there is no "true conflict" of laws and the court should apply the law of the interested jurisdiction. If both states have an interest in having their differing laws applied, a true conflict arises; in that case the court should apply the law of the state whose interest would be more impaired if its law were not applied. . . . Nelson v. International Paint Co., 716 F.2d 640, 644 (9th Cir. 1983).

California's one-year statute of limitations clearly differs from the two-year statutes of limitations in effect in Arizona and Oklahoma and the three-year statute in Arkansas. . . . Therefore, we move to the second step of the analysis to determine whether each state has an interest in applying its law in this case. The district court, relying on *Nelson,* concluded that the governmental interest analysis invariably dictates that the statute of limitations of the forum state must apply. *Nelson* did not, however, set down a per se rule.

In *Nelson,* we were faced with a conflict between the one-year California statute of limitations and the two-year statutes of Texas and Alaska. A Texas plaintiff brought an action in California against a California defendant for injuries sustained in Alaska. Relying on the reasoning of Ashland Chemical Co. v. Provence, 129 Cal. App. 3d 790, 181 Cal. Rptr. 340 (1982), we found that, in the particular circumstance of the case, only California had an interest in applying its statute of limitations. We based this decision on the California court's explanation in *Ashland* that statutes of limitations " 'are designed to protect the enacting state's residents and courts from the burdens associated with the prosecution of stale cases. . . . California courts and a California resident would be protected by applying California's statute of limitations because California is the forum and the defendant is a California resident.' " *Nelson,* 716 F.2d at 644 (quoting *Ashland,* 129 Cal. App. 3d at 794, 181 Cal. Rptr. at 341). The *Ashland* court concluded that when both the forum and the defendant's residence were the same, no state other than California had an interest in having its statute applied. *See id.* at 644-645. We decided *Nelson* in accord with *Ashland* because *Nelson* "parallels *Ashland,* since the forum is in California and the only defendant is a California resident." *Id.* at 645.

The present case differs from *Nelson,* both on its facts and in its policy considerations. Unlike *Nelson,* this case involves California residents who are plaintiffs, not defendants, thereby weakening the forum state's interest in applying its own statute of limitations. Second, Arizona, the state in which the alleged injury occurred, has an interest in having its statute of limitations apply to cases involving accidents on its highways. Hence, this case presents a "true conflict" of law between California and Arizona.[3] We move accordingly to the third stage of the analysis as required by California law, to determine whether the interests of California or Arizona would be more impaired by application of the law of the other state.

The California statute of limitations serves two purposes: it protects state residents from the burden of defending cases " 'in which memories have faded and evidence has been lost,' " and it protects the courts of the state from the need to process stale claims. *Nelson*, 716 F.2d at 644 (quoting *Ashland*, 129 Cal. App. 3d at 794, 181 Cal. Rptr. at 341). The first interest does not apply here because there is no California defendant in this case. All of the defendants reside in states that do not consider twenty-three-month-old claims to be stale. Therefore, neither California, nor Oklahoma, nor Arkansas has an interest in applying its statute of limitations in order to protect the defendants. Furthermore, although California has an interest in protecting its courts from stale claims,[4] that interest is at least equally balanced by its interest in allowing its residents to recover for injuries sustained in a state that would recognize their claim as timely.

In addition, we note that the California statue of limitations is not inflexible when California plaintiffs are involved. Pursuant to Cal. Civ. Proc. Code §351, California courts will toll the statute of limitations during the time that a defendant is out of the state. That California is willing to toll its statute of limitations in order to assist resident plaintiffs in bringing claims for injury further indicates that little harm would be done to California's interest by applying the two-year statute of limitations for the benefit of the California plaintiffs. We find that, for the foregoing reasons, California's interests would not be greatly impaired by the application of Arizona's statute of limitations in this case.

We cannot say the same for Arizona. On the contrary, we find that Arizona's interest would be significantly impaired by a failure to apply its statute of limitations. The Arizona legislature has established a two-year statute of limitations for personal injury claims arising out of highway accidents. As the

---

3. There is no conflict between Arizona, Arkansas, and Oklahoma law in this case, because application of any of these states' statutes of limitations would not bar the plaintiff's suit. The case does not present a "true conflict" of law between California and either Arkansas or Oklahoma because neither of the latter two states has an interest in having its statute applied. The alleged wrong occurred in Arizona, the courts of Arkansas and Oklahoma are not involved, and any interest that these states might have in barring the plaintiffs' suit is satisfied in this case by the Arizona statute. Hence, we treat this case as primarily involving a choice between California and Arizona law.

4. While the processing of the claim in this case would affect a federal and not a California court, a federal court sitting in diversity applies the "governmental interest" analysis as would a California court. This approach ensures that "the accident of diversity of citizenship would [not] constantly disturb equal administration of justice in coordinate state and federal courts sitting side by side." *See* Klaxon Co. v. Stentor Elec. Mfg. Co., 313 U.S. 487, 496, 61 S. Ct. 1020, 1021, 85 L. Ed. 1477 (1941).

Supreme Court of California has recognized, "one of the primary purposes of a state in creating a cause of action . . . is to deter the kind of conduct within its borders which wrongfully [causes injury]." Hurtado v. Superior Court. Insofar as drivers tend to be more careful when their chances of incurring liability are more substantial, Arizona does have an interest in ensuring that its statute of limitations is applied in any case that arises from accidents occurring within its state borders. Were we to apply the California statute of limitations in this case, we would impede the legitimate interest of the state of Arizona in promoting highway safety by allowing a cause of action for a two-year period.

Applying the "governmental interest" analysis of California's choice-of-law rules, we conclude that Arizona's interests would be impaired by the failure to apply its statute of limitations more than California's interests would be impaired by the failure to apply its statute. California has little interest in applying its statute of limitations when no California defendant is involved and when California plaintiffs seek to recover for injuries that occurred in a state in which the claim was not time-barred. Arizona's legitimate government policy would be impaired by a failure to allow the cause of action that it has established for personal injury claims. Accordingly, we hold that the Arizona statute of limitations should apply in the present case and that the district court erred in dismissing the complaint.

We need not reach the plaintiffs' argument that the district court should have tolled the California statute of limitations during the period the defendants were out of the state.

Reversed and remanded.

NOONAN, J., dissenting;

The Restatement of the Law of Conflicts states as black letter law: "An action will not be maintained if it is barred by the Statute of Limitations of the forum. . . ." Restatement (Second) of Conflicts of Law, §142(i) (1971). California has followed this rule. Hall v. Copco Pacific Ltd., 224 F.2d 884 (9th Cir. 1955). If this normal rule is applied, Ledesma cannot proceed.

The landmark case in California adopting a "governmental interest" approach to the conflict of laws emphasized that the governmental interest should be weighed where "the substantive" laws of the states were in conflict. *Reich v. Purcell.* Chief Justice Traynor did not suggest that California departed from the normal rules on matters of procedure; nor did the Restatement, whose second edition came out four years later, acknowledge that *Reich* was a departure from established law.

California has characterized "an ordinary statute of limitations" as procedural, not substantive. Regents v. Hartford Accident & Indemnity Co., 21 Cal. 3d 624, 147 Cal. Rptr. 486, 581 P.2d 197 (1978). There is absolutely nothing to indicate that the statute before us is not "an ordinary statute of limitations."

There are at least two cases, as the opinion notes, which consider statutes of limitations under the California practice in the same way as substantive law choices: Nelson v. International Paint Co.; Ashland Chemical

Co. v. Provence. In both these cases, however, the result of the court's deliberations was to apply the California statute of limitations. Strictly speaking, the indication that some other statute of limitations might have been applied is dictum and need not be regarded as controlling here. . . .

Even if we should make the assumption that California would depart from the normal rule, it is difficult to see the California "interest" here. The California interest in not burdening its judicial system with stale claims is equally great whether the California resident is a defendant or a plaintiff. Consequently, even in terms of the interest of California, the California statute should apply.

Global Financial Corp. v. Triarc Corp.

93 N.Y.2d 525, 715 N.E.2d 482 (1999)

Chief Judge KAYE.

This appeal places before us a long-simmering question: where does a nonresident's contract claim accrue for purposes of the Statute of Limitations? [New York Civil Practice Law and Rules ("CPLR") Section 202] requires our courts to "borrow" the Statute of Limitations of a foreign jurisdiction where a nonresident's cause of action accrued, if that limitations period is shorter than New York's. The primary issue presented by this appeal is whether, for purposes of CPLR 202, the nonresident plaintiff's contract and quantum meruit claims accrued in New York, where most of the relevant events occurred, or in plaintiff's State of residence, where it sustained the economic impact of the alleged breach.

According to the complaint, by contract dated February 1, 1988, defendant retained plaintiff to perform certain consulting services. In March 1989 plaintiff located an investment company that agreed to purchase all of defendant's outstanding shares, and between February 1988 and August 1989, plaintiff additionally advised defendant regarding corporate planning. On November 6, 1989, plaintiff demanded payment of over nine million dollars for services rendered, which defendant refused the following week.

On November 9, 1995, plaintiff commenced an action in the United States District Court for the Southern District of New York to recover its commissions and fees. Because both parties were Delaware corporations, however, on April 10, 1996, the court dismissed the complaint for lack of subject matter jurisdiction. Three months later, plaintiff brought a substantially similar suit across the street, in Supreme Court, New York County. The parties do not dispute that this action is timely if the Federal action was timely when commenced on November 9, 1995 (CPLR 205).

Relying on CPLR 202, defendant sought dismissal of plaintiff's claims for failure to comply with the Statute of Limitations of Delaware (where plaintiff is incorporated) or Pennsylvania (where, according to the Federal complaint, plaintiff had its principal place of business). Plaintiff's claims would be time-barred in both States (*see* Del. Code Ann. tit. 10, §8106 [three-year limitations period for actions on a promise]; Del. Code Ann. tit. 10, §8111 [one year for actions for services]; 42 Pa. Cons. Stat. Ann. §5525 [four years for contract actions]). In opposing defendant's motion, plaintiff maintained that New York's six-year Statute of Limitations applied because most of the events relating to the contract took place in New York, and that the action was timely because the Federal action was commenced within six years after defendant refused plaintiff's demand for fees and commissions (*see* CPLR 213 [2]).

Supreme Court agreed with defendant and dismissed the complaint, holding that under the borrowing statute plaintiff's causes of action accrued where it suffered injury: its place of residence. In a separate order, Supreme Court denied plaintiff's motion to renew the motion to dismiss. The Appellate Division unanimously affirmed both Supreme Court orders (251 A.D. 2d 17), and this Court granted plaintiff leave to appeal so much of the Appellate Division order as affirmed the dismissal of the complaint, in order to resolve the issue definitively and eliminate the need for courts to engage in "guesswork" when determining the place of accrual for contract actions under CPLR 202 (*see* Siegel, N.Y. Prac. §57, at 70 [2d ed.]). Because we agree that plaintiff's cause of action accrued where it sustained its alleged injury, we now affirm.

When a nonresident sues on a cause of action accruing outside New York, CPLR 202 requires the cause of action to be timely under the limitation periods of both New York and the jurisdiction where the cause of action accrued.[2] This prevents nonresidents from shopping in New York for a favorable Statute of Limitations.

Plaintiff argues that the New York Statute of Limitations applies because its claims accrued in New York, where the contract was negotiated, executed, substantially performed and breached. In essence, plaintiff urges that we apply a "grouping of contacts" or "center of gravity" approach—used in substantive choice-of-law questions in contract cases—to determine where contract and quantum meruit causes of action accrue for purposes of CPLR 202.

At the threshold, however, there is a significant difference between a choice-of-law question, which is a matter of common law, and this Statute of Limitations issue, which is governed by particular terms of the CPLR. In using the word "accrued" in CPLR 202 there is no indication that the Legislature intended the term "to mean anything other than the generally accepted construction applied throughout CPLR Article 2—the time when, and

2. CPLR 202 states: "An action based upon a cause of action accruing without the state cannot be commenced after the expiration of the time limited by the laws of either the state or the place without the state where the cause of action accrued, except that where the cause of action accrued in favor of a resident of the state the time limited by the laws of the state shall apply."

the place where, the plaintiff first had the right to bring the cause of action" (1 Weinstein-Korn-Miller, N.Y. Civ. Prac. P 202.04, at 2-61).

CPLR 202 has remained substantially unchanged since 1902. While its predecessor, section 13 of the Civil Practice Act, used the word "arise" instead of "accrue," the Legislature intended no change in meaning when it adopted the present provision, in 1962, as part of the CPLR. The legislative purpose was simply to ensure that the language of CPLR 202 conformed with other CPLR provisions. Because earlier iterations of the borrowing statute predate the substantive choice-of-law "interest analysis" test used in tort cases (*see* Babcock v. Jackson, 12 N.Y.2d 473 [1963]) and the "grouping of contacts" or "center of gravity" approach used in contract cases (*see* Auten v. Auten, 308 N.Y. 155 [1954]), these choice-of-law analyses are inapplicable to the question of statutory construction presented by CPLR 202.

Indeed, while this Court has not addressed the issue in the context of a contract case, we have consistently employed the traditional definition of accrual—a cause of action accrues at the time and in the place of the injury—in tort cases involving the interpretation of CPLR 202. Martin v. Dierck Equip. Co. (43 N.Y.2d 583) is illustrative. There, the plaintiff was injured while operating a forklift at his employer's warehouse in Virginia. The forklift manufacturer and distributor were located in New York, and the forklift was sold to plaintiff's employer in New York. Plaintiff sued the manufacturer and distributor in negligence and strict products liability. The Court held that for purposes of the borrowing statute, the negligence causes of action as well as the cause of action which plaintiff labeled "breach of warranty" accrued in Virginia: "[p]laintiff possessed no cause of action, in tort or in contract, anywhere in the world until he was injured in Virginia" (*id.* at 588, 591).

When an alleged injury is purely economic, the place of injury usually is where the plaintiff resides and sustains the economic impact of the loss. Here, plaintiff's causes of action are time-barred whether one looks to its State of incorporation or its principal place of business. Thus, we need not determine whether it was in Delaware or Pennsylvania that plaintiff more acutely sustained the impact of its loss.

Plaintiff relies on Insurance Co. v. ABB Power Generation, 91 N.Y. 2d 180, 690 N.E. 2d 1249 (N.Y. 1997), for the proposition that the place where the relevant contacts are grouped, not the place of the injury, determines accrual for purposes of the borrowing statute. The question in *ABB Power* was whether plaintiff's cause of action could accrue in California, even though the parties in their contract chose the forum and law of New York. The Court answered in the affirmative, holding that a forum-selection clause, or inability to obtain personal jurisdiction over a defendant in a foreign jurisdiction, would not override CPLR 202. Once the Court decided that CPLR 202 applied, it was clear that California was the State of accrual, as California was the place of the injury as well as the place where "all of the operative facts" occurred (*id.* at 183). Thus, the Court did not have to decide whether to use a choice-of-law analysis or place-of-injury rule in order to determine where plaintiff's causes of action accrued.

Finally, as we underscored in *ABB Power*, " CPLR 202 is designed to add clarity to the law and to provide the certainty of uniform application to litigants" (*id.* at 187). This goal is better served by a rule requiring the single determination of a plaintiff's residence than by a rule dependent on a litany of events relevant to the "center of gravity" of a contract dispute.

Accordingly, the order of the Appellate Division should be affirmed, with costs.

Questions and Comments

(1) *Ledesma* ignores the traditional assumption that statutes of limitations are procedural rules governed by forum law, and instead treats the statute of limitations choice-of-law issue like any other issue that is subject to interest analysis. Are you satisfied with the analysis? Why does California have a "weaker" interest in applying its statute of limitations to California plaintiffs than California defendants? Is the California statute of limitations designed to promote recovery for Californians? Why does it matter that "[a]ll of the defendants reside in states that do not consider the twenty-three-month-old claims to be stale." Are statutes of limitations personal laws that travel with defendants wherever they may be sued? Why is it relevant to interest analysis that the "injuries [were] sustained in a state that would recognize their claim as timely"? Do you agree that Arizona's interest "would be significantly impaired by" a California court's failure to apply the Arizona statute of limitation in a case involving an accident in Arizona? Is it relevant that the year before *Ledesma,* the Arizona Supreme Court re-affirmed that under Arizona law, "statutes of limitation . . . are procedural and therefore governed by the law of the forum"? *See* Monroe v. Wood, 724 P. 2d 30, 31 (Ariz. 1986). Doesn't this suggest that Arizona does not view its statutes of limitations to be applicable in non-Arizona courts?

Professor Symeonides reports that, as of 1999, "seventeen states have abandoned the traditional procedural characterization of statutes of limitation and have applied to conflicts involving these statutes the same choice-of-law analysis applied to substantive issues." Symeonides, Choice of Law in the American Courts in 1999: One More Year, 48 Am. J. Comp. L. 143, 166 (2000). In light of *Ledesma,* is this a welcome trend?

(2) Is it incongruous for the New York Court of Appeals—a leader in the development of modern choice-of-law methodologies—to employ First Restatement criteria ("a cause of action accrues at the time and in the place of the injury") in determining where a cause of action accrued for purposes of a borrowing statute? If the court really believes that the goals of clarity and uniformity for the borrowing statute are better met by the place of injury criterion than by the "center of gravity" approach, why not apply the place of

injury in its common law choice-of-law decisions? Other courts that usually apply modern choice-of-law approaches but look to traditional criteria in interpreting a borrowing statute include Willits v. Peabody Coal Co., 188 F.3d 510 (6th Cir. 1999) (applying Kentucky conflicts law); Rajala v. Donnelly Meiners Jordan Kline P.C., 193 F.3d 925 (8th Cir. 1999) (applying Missouri conflicts law). For cases applying a modern conflicts analysis to determine where a cause of action accrues for borrowing statute purposes, see Kahn v. Royal Ins. Co., 709 N.E. 2d 822 (Mass. 1999) (applying most significant relationship test to determine where cause of action accrued); Celotex Corp. v. Meehan, 523 So. 2d 141 (Fla. 1988).

(3) The most recent (1988) revisions to the Restatement of Conflicts Second set out a new approach to statutes of limitations:

§142. Statute of Limitations

Whether a claim will be maintained against the defense of the statute of limitations is determined under the principles stated in §6. In general, unless the exceptional circumstances of the case make such a result unreasonable:

(1) The forum will apply its own statute of limitations barring the claim.

(2) The forum will apply its own statute of limitations permitting the claim unless:

(a) maintenance of the claim would serve no substantial interest of the forum; and

(b) the claim would be barred under the statute of limitations of a state having a more significant relationship to the parties and the occurrence.

5. Public Policy

In Chapter 1 we considered the public policy exception to the usual conflicts rules. Does such a principle have any place in the new theories? As noted in our earlier look at the topic, Paulsen & Sovern, "Public Policy" in the Conflict of Laws, 56 Colum. L. Rev. 969 (1956), found that the principle was invoked in cases in which there were substantial connections between the forum and the case itself in the "overwhelming number of cases." In such cases invocation of the principle ought to be unnecessary under interest analysis.

The forum, having an interest in the subject matter of the case itself, may simply impose its own law. For similar reasons, the public policy exception seems irrelevant to the Second Restatement approach. As the *Phillips* case, reproduced *supra* page 264, noted: "In order to determine which state has the more significant relationship, the public policies of all interested states must be considered. A public policy exception to the most significant relationship test would be redundant."

The New York Court of Appeals appears to believe, to the contrary, that an interest analysis court can in certain circumstances invoke the public policy exception. In *Cooney*, described *supra* page 213, the court stated: "In view of modern choice of law doctrine, resort to the public policy exception should be reserved for those foreign laws that are truly obnoxious." Does this make any sense? Should a court that lacks an interest in its law apply its law when foreign law is "truly obnoxious"? Should it dismiss the case on *forum non conveniens* grounds?

What about when there are factors connecting the case to the forum, but they do not give rise to an "interest" in the usual sense? This was the situation in *Schultz,* reproduced *supra* page 200, where the tort took place in New York but all other contacts pointed elsewhere, leading the New York Court of Appeals to rule that New Jersey's charitable immunity law governed. The *Schultz* court rejected a public policy argument, reasoning that although "New Jersey's statute might well run counter to our fundamental public policy," it need not decide the issue because there were in any event "insufficient contacts between the parties, transaction, and New York to warrant enforcement of New York public policy." Would the court reason the same way if it were asked to enforce a slavery contract made abroad? Does this suggest that the New Jersey statute does not in fact run afoul of New York public policy? What are the implications for the point made above about interest analysis not needing a public policy exception?

For commentary on the public policy exception under modern choice-of-law doctrines, see Comment, Choice of Law: A Fond Farewell to Comity and Public Policy, 74 Cal. L. Rev. 1447 (1986); Corr, Modern Choice of Law and Public Policy: The Emperor Has the Same Old Clothes, 39 U. Miami L. Rev. 647 (1985).

6. Postscript

Paul v. National Life

352 S.E.2d 550 (W. Va. 1986)

NEELY, J.:

In September of 1977 Eliza Vickers and Aloha Jane Paul, both West Virginia residents, took a weekend trip to Indiana. The two women were involved in a one-car collision on Interstate 65 in Indiana when Ms. Vickers lost control of the car. That collision took both women's lives. The administrator of Mrs. Paul's estate brought a wrongful death action against Ms. Vickers' estate and the National Life Accident Company in the Circuit Court of Kanawha County. Upon completion of discovery, the defendants below moved for summary judgment. Defendants' motion contended that: (1) the Indiana guest statute, which grants to a gratuitous host immunity from liability for the injury or death of a passenger unless that host was guilty of willful and wanton misconduct at the time of the accident, was applicable; and (2) that the record was devoid of any evidence of willful or wanton misconduct on the part of Ms. Vickers. By order dated 29 October 1984, the Circuit Court of Kanawha County entered summary judgment for the defendants below. The order of the circuit court held that our conflicts doctrine of lex loci delicti required that the law of the place of the injury, namely, Indiana, apply to the case, and that the record contained no evidence of willful or wanton misconduct on the part of Ms. Vickers. It is from this order that the plaintiffs below appeal.

The sole question presented in this case is whether the law of Indiana or of West Virginia shall apply. The appellees urge us to adhere to our traditional conflicts doctrine of lex loci delicti, while the appellants urge us to reject our traditional doctrine and to adopt one of the "modern" approaches to conflicts questions. Although we stand by lex loci delicti as our general conflicts rule, we nevertheless reverse the judgment of the court below.

I

Unlike other areas of the law, such as contracts, torts and property, "conflicts of law" as a body of common law is of relatively recent origin. Professor Dicey has written that he knew of no decisions in England considering conflicts of law points before the accession of James I, and it is generally acknowledged that the first authoritative work on conflicts did not appear until the publication of Joseph Story's Conflict of Laws in 1834. Accordingly, no conflicts of law doctrine has ever had any credible pretense to being "natural law" emergent from the murky mists of medieval mysticism. Indeed, the mention of conflicts of law and the jus naturale in the same breath would evoke a power guffaw in even the sternest scholar. In our post-Realist legal world, it is the received wisdom that judges, like their counterparts in the legislative branch, are political agents embodying social policy in law. Nowhere is this received wisdom more accurate than in the domain of conflict of laws.

Conflicts of law has become a veritable playpen for judicial policymakers. The last twenty years have seen a remarkable shift from the doctrine of lex loci delicti to more "modern" doctrines, such as the more flexible, manipulable Restatement "center of gravity" test. Of the twenty-five landmark cases cited by appellants in which a state supreme court rejected lex loci delicti and adopted one of the modern approaches, the great majority of them involved the application to an automobile accident case of a foreign state's guest statute, doctrine of interspousal or intrafamily immunity, or doctrine of contributory negligence. All but one of these landmark cases was decided in the decade between 1963 and 1973, when many jurisdictions still retained guest statutes, the doctrine of interspousal immunity, and the doctrine of contributory negligence. However, in the years since 1970, these statutes and doctrines have all but disappeared from the American legal landscape. . . .

Thus nearly half of the state supreme courts of the country have wrought a radical transformation of their procedural law of conflicts in order to sidestep perceived substantive evils, only to discover later that those evils had been exorcised from American law by other means. Now these courts are saddled with a cumbersome and unwieldy body of conflicts law that creates confusion, uncertainty and inconsistency, as well as complication of the judicial task. This approach has been like that of the misguided physician who treated a case of dandruff with nitric acid, only to discover later that the malady could have been remedied with medicated shampoo. Neither the doctor nor the patient need have lost his head.

The Restatement approach has been criticized for its indeterminate language and lack of concrete guidelines. Restatement of Conflicts Second of Law, Sec. 145-146 (1971) provides:

§145. The General Principle

(1) The rights and liabilities of the parties with respect to an issue in tort are determined by the local law of the state which, with respect to that issue, has the most significant relationship to the occurrence and the parties under the principle stated in §6.

(2) Contacts being taken into account in applying the principle of §6 to determine the law applicable to an issue include:

(a) the place where the injury occurred,

(b) the place where the conduct causing injury occurred,

(c) the domicile, residence, nationality, place of incorporation, and place of business of the parties, and

(d) the place where the relationship, if any, between the parties, is centered.

These contacts should be evaluated according to their relative importance with respect to the particular issues.

§146. Personal Injuries

In an action for a personal injury, the local law of the state where the injury occurred determines the *rights and liabilities* of the parties, unless, with respect to the particular issue, some other state has a more significant relationship under the principles stated in §6 to the occurrence and the parties, in which event the local law of the other state will be applied.

Section 6 of the Restatement lists the following factors as important choice of law considerations in all areas of law.

(a) The needs of the interstate and international systems;

(b) The relevant policies of the forum;

(c) The relevant policies of other interested states and relative interest of those states in the determination of the particular issue;

(d) The protection of justified expectations;
(e) The basic policies underlying the particular field of law;
(f) Certainty, predictability, and uniformity of results; and
(g) Ease in the determination and application of the law to be applied.

As Javolenus once said to Julian, *res ipsa loquitur.* The appellant cites with approval the description of the Restatement approach set forth in Conklin v. Horner, 38 Wis. 2d 468, 473, 157 N.W.2d 579, 581 (1968):

> We emphasized that what we adopted was not a rule, but a method of analysis that permitted dissection of the jural bundle constituting a tort and its environment to determine what elements therein were relevant to a reasonable choice of law.

That sounds pretty intellectual, but we still prefer a rule. The lesson of history is that methods of analysis that permit dissection of the jural bundle constituting a tort and its environment produce protracted litigation and voluminous, inscrutable appellate opinions, while rules get cases settled quickly and cheaply.

The manipulability inherent in the Restatement approach is nicely illustrated by two cases from New York, the first jurisdiction to make a clean break with lex loci delicti. The cases of Babcock v. Jackson, and Kell v. Henderson, are aptly discussed by the Supreme Court of Virginia:

> In *Babcock,* an automobile guest sued her host in New York for injuries sustained in Ontario caused by the defendant's ordinary negligence. Under New York law, the guest could recover for injuries caused by the host's lack of ordinary care, but the Ontario guest statute barred such a recovery. The court abandoned its adherence to the place-of-the-wrong rule and permitted recovery. It decided that, on the guest-host issue, New York had the "dominant contacts" because the parties were domiciled in New York, were on a trip which began in New York, and were traveling in a vehicle registered and regularly garaged in New York. The court noted that Ontario had no connection with the cause of action except that the accident happened to take place there.
>
> *Kell* presented the converse of *Babcock.* There, the question was also whether the New York ordinary negligence rule applied or whether the Ontario guest statute controlled. The guest was injured by the host's ordinary negligence while the parties, both residents of Ontario, were on a trip in New York which was to begin and end in Ontario. The New York court purported to follow *Babcock* but held that Ontario law would not apply.

McMillan v. McMillan, 219 Va. 1127, 253 S.E.2d 662, 664 (1979). It was perhaps recognition of just such gross disparities in result that prompted the Court of Appeals of New York to remark, in a towering achievement in the art of understatement, "candor requires the admission that our past decisions have lacked a precise consistency."

II

The appellant urges us in the alternative to adopt the "choice-influencing considerations approach" set forth by Professor Leflar in "Choice-Influencing Considerations and Conflicts of Law", 41 N.Y.U. L. Rev. 267 (1966). Professor Leflar has narrowed the list of considerations in conflicts cases to five:

(1) Predictability of results;
(2) Maintenance of interstate or international order;
(3) Simplification of the judicial task;
(4) Advancement of the forum's governmental interests;
(5) Application of the better rule of law.

Professor Leflar's approach has been adopted in the guest statute context in the landmark cases of Clark v. Clark, Milkovich v. Saari, and Conklin v. Horner. In practice the cases tend to focus more on the fourth and fifth considerations that the first three, and the upshot is that the courts of New Hampshire, Minnesota and Wisconsin simply will not apply guest statutes. This seems to us a perfectly intelligible and sensible bright-line rule. However, it seems unnecessary to scrap an entire body of law and dress the rule up in a newfangled five-factor costume when the same concerns can be addressed and the same result achieved through judicious employment of the traditional public policy exception to lex loci delicti.

III

Lex loci delicti has long been the cornerstone of our conflict of laws doctrine. The consistency, predictability, and ease of application provided by the traditional doctrine are not to be discarded lightly, and we are not persuaded that we should discard them today. The appellant contends that the various exceptions that have been engrafted onto the traditional rule have made it manipulable and have undermined the predictability and uniformity that were considered its primary virtues. There is certainly some truth in this, and we generally eschew the more strained escape devices employed to avoid the sometimes harsh effects of the traditional rule. Nevertheless, we remain convinced that the traditional rule, for all of its faults, remains superior to any of its modern competitors. Moreover, if we are going to manipulate conflicts doctrine in order to achieve substantive results, we might as well manipulate something we understand. Having mastered marble, we decline an apprenticeship in bronze. We therefore reaffirm our adherence to the doctrine of lex loci delicti today.

However, we have long recognized that comity does not require the application of the substantive law of a foreign state when that law contravenes the public policy of this State. West Virginia has never had an automobile guest passenger statute. It is the strong public policy of this State that persons injured by the negligence of another should be able to recover in tort. Accordingly, we have abolished the doctrine of interspousal immunity, Coffindaffer v. Coffindaffer, and we have adopted the doctrine of comparative negligence in preference to the harsh rule of contributory negligence. Bradley v. Appalachian Power Co. We abolished charitable immunity for hospitals in Adkins v. St. Francis Hospital. We held that there is no common law governmental immunity for municipal corporations in Higginbotham v. City of Charleston. And we abrogated the doctrine of parental immunity to permit an unemancipated minor child to sue for injuries received in a motor vehicle accident in Lee v. Comer. Today we declare that automobile guest passenger statutes violate the strong public policy of this State in favor of compensating persons injured by the negligence of others. Accordingly, we will no longer enforce the automobile guest passenger statutes of foreign jurisdictions in our courts.[14]

For the foregoing reasons, the order of the circuit granting summary judgment in favor of the appellees is hereby vacated, and the cause remanded for further proceedings not inconsistent with this opinion.

Reversed and remanded. . . .

Questions and Comments

(1) Is *Paul*'s indictment of modern choice-of-law doctrines fair? Is Judge Neely right to suggest that modern doctrines were an unfortunate overreaction to a few backward substantive law doctrines (such as guest statutes)? In light of his resolution of the case, is he hypocritical to criticize the manipulability of the modern approaches? Which is worse—manipulating the rigid traditional rules to reach the "just" result, or manipulating modern approaches that invite judges to reach the "just" result? Do you think a state's selection of a choice-of-law really affects decisional outcomes?

---

14. Although we intend this to be a rule of general application, we do not intend it as an invitation to flagrant forum shopping. For example, were a resident of a guest statute jurisdiction to sue another resident of a guest statute jurisdiction over an accident occurring in a guest statute jurisdiction, the simple fact that the plaintiff was able to serve process on the defendant within our State borders would not compel us to resist application of any relevant guest statute. The State must have some connection with the controversy above and beyond mere service of process before the rule we announce today will be applied. In other words, venue must be proper under some provision *other than W. Va. Code* 56-1-1(a)(4) [1986].

(2) Justice Neely is not the only judge who has decided to stick with tried-and-true methods, however imperfect. Two recent empirical studies have attempted to analyze the patterns of operation of the traditional as opposed to modern choice-of-law methods. *See* Solimine, An Economic and Empirical Analysis of Choice of Law, 24 Ga. L. Rev. 49 (1989); Borchers, The Choice-of-Law Revolution: An Empirical Study, 49 Wash. & Lee L. Rev. 357 (1992). In particular, these studies asked about possible biases in the new methods (their biases in favor of recovery, towards application of forum law, and on behalf of local parties and how the traditional methods fare, by comparison).

The Borchers study, interestingly, concluded that judges applying the First Restatement act in distinctly different ways from judges applying newer methods; in particular, they display less of the three biases just mentioned. However, courts applying any of the new methods do not act substantially different from one another. Since the new methods have rather different jurisprudential underpinnings, Borchers concludes that First Restatement judges are more sincere in their commitment to apply the method honestly than judges applying any of the newer methods: "Courts do *not* take the new approaches seriously." 49 Wash. & Lee L. Rev. at 379. Of course, if one does not like what the First Restatement prescribes, the fact that judges take it seriously is not a cause for celebration.

H. Statutory Resolution of Choice-of-Law Problems

Legislatures sometimes provide us with conflicts rules, especially in cases in which the courts have not produced satisfactory results.

It is doubtful that statutory conflicts rules are a general solution to the choice-of-law problem since legislators would face the same problems as the courts, the commentators, and the Restatement drafters. The Restatements in particular illustrate a central problem: The First Restatement offered a fair amount of certainty, but at the cost of fairness. The Restatement Second offers more flexibility, and thus potentially more fairness, but at the cost of certainty. How can a legislature do better?

Salavarria v. National Car Rental System, Inc.

705 So. 2d 809 (La. App. 4th Dist. 1998)

BYRNES, J.

The relator, National Car Rental System, Inc., filed a motion for summary judgment based on the rule in Louisiana that a self-insured car rental agency has the right to restrict the use of rental vehicles to "authorized users" and, therefore, cannot be held liable for accidents caused by unauthorized users. This motion was denied because the trial court found that Florida law applied. A reversal of the denial of the motion for summary judgment would terminate the litigation as to the relator. Therefore, we have consented to grant relator's application for writs, reverse the judgment of the trial court and render judgment dismissing plaintiffs' claims against relator.

This writ presents a conflicts of law issue. The plaintiffs were the driver and passengers in a car which collided with an automobile owned by National Car Rental Systems, Inc. in 1994. The car had been rented to Mitchell Brogdon, and the driver of the National car, Heather Trempe, was not an authorized driver of the car. The plaintiffs are Louisiana residents. Brogdon and Trempe are Florida residents. National is a Delaware corporation which was doing business in Florida. The contract was entered into in Florida. The accident occurred in Louisiana. National filed a motion for summary judgment arguing that Louisiana law applies. The trial court denied the motion, finding that Florida law controls the contractual obligations arising from National's rental agreement with Brogdon.

The Louisiana Supreme Court has ruled that a self-insured rental car company has the right to limit operation of its vehicles to only those individuals to whom it gives express permission, i.e., those individuals listed as authorized drivers in the rental agreement. Hearty v. Harris, 574 So. 2d 1234 (La. 1991). Florida law apparently does not distinguish between authorized and unauthorized users of rental cars because it simply holds owners vicariously liable for mere ownership of the vehicle under a dangerous instrumentality law. Relator argues that the trial court improperly ruled that because the National Car Rental System, Inc. car rental agreement was entered into in Florida, Florida law should apply. The relator argues that because Trempe was not a party to the contract, the existence of the contract and whether Florida law applies to the obligation between Brogdon and relator is of no moment in determining the relator's obligation to Trempe. The plaintiffs do not contest the applicability of Louisiana law to the issue of the liability of Trempe, but they contest the issue of the applicability of Louisiana law to the liability of the relator, as owner of the car.

The general conflict of law statute, LSA-C.C. art. 3515 provides:

> Except as otherwise provided in this Book, an issue in a case having contacts with other states is governed by the law of the state whose policies would be most seriously impaired if its law were not applied to that issue.
>
> That state is determined by evaluating the strength and pertinence of the relevant policies of all involved states in the light of: (1) the relationship of each state to the parties and the dispute; and (2) the policies and needs of the interstate and international systems, including the policies of upholding the justified expectations of parties and of minimizing the adverse consequences that might follow from subjecting a party to the law of more than one state.

LSA-C.C. art. 3542, the general conflict of law provision dealing specifically with delictual obligations would apply the:

> Law of the state whose policies would be most seriously impaired if its law were not applied to that issue.
>
> That state is determined by evaluating the strength and pertinence of the relevant policies of the involved states in light of: (1) the pertinent contacts of each state to the parties and the events giving rise to the dispute, including the place of conduct and injury, the domicile, habitual residence, or place of business of the parties, and the state in which the relationship, if any, between the parties was centered; and (2) the policies referred to in Article 3515, as well as policies of deterring wrongful conduct and of repairing the consequences of injurious acts.

Comment (b) to LSA-C.C. art. 3542 directs that the rules contained in Articles 3543 through 3546 are more specific, and where applicable, prevail over Article 3542. LSA-C.C. art 3543 provides that issues pertaining to standards of conduct and safety are governed by the law of the state in which the conduct occurred. In the instant case there is no dispute that the conduct that resulted in the plaintiffs' injuries occurred in Louisiana, and that Louisiana's standard of care must apply. Comment (a) to Article 3543 states, "by way of illustration, so-called 'rules of the road' establish or pertain to 'standards of conduct and safety,' whereas rules that impose a ceiling on the amount of compensatory damages or provide immunity from suit are 'rules of loss distribution and financial protection.'" Relator's derivative liability is a question of "loss distribution and financial protection." LSA-C.C. art. 3544 provides that issues of loss distribution and financial protections are governed, as between a person injured by an offense and the person who caused the injury, "by the law designated in the following order: . . . (2) If, at the time of the injury, the injured person and the person who caused the injury were domiciled in different states; (a) when *both the injury and the conduct that caused it occurred in one of those states, by the law of that state.*" (Emphasis added.) Since the injured persons in this case are Louisiana residents, and the person who caused the injury (Trempe) is a Florida resident, LSA-C.C. art. 3544(2)(a) is applicable. Since both the injury and the conduct that caused it occurred in Louisiana, and the plaintiffs are Louisiana domiciliaries, Louisiana law should be applied under LSA-C.C. art. 3544(2)(a).

Comment (g) under LSA-C.C. art. 3542(2)(a) reinforces the already clear language of LSA-C.C. art. 3542 in this regard:

> Domicile of either party. Subparagraph (2) deals with cases in which, at the time of the injury, the tortfeasor and the victim were not domiciled in the same state. Clause (a) of that subparagraph provides that when both the injurious conduct and the resulting injury occurred in a state where either the tortfeasor or the victim was domiciled, the law of that state shall apply,

> regardless of whether it provides for a higher or lower standard of financial protection than the law of the domicile of the other party. For rationale and supporting authority, see Symeonides, "Choice of Law for Torts", 453-56. When a person is injured in his home state by conduct in that state, his rights should be determined by the law of that state, even if the person who caused the injury happened to be from another state. The law of the latter state should not be interjected to the victim's detriment or benefit. By the same token, when a person acting within his home state causes injury in that state, he should be held accountable according to the law of that state, even if the injured person happened to be from another state. The law of the latter state should not be interjected to the tortfeasor's detriment or benefit.

The plaintiffs do not contend that relator, National Car Rental System, Inc., is liable to them by virtue of any provision in the rental car agreement. *If relator is liable to the plaintiffs, it is only by operation and application of Florida law, not by virtue of any contractual provision.* In fact, the terms of the rental contract specifically prohibit the use of the vehicle by any unauthorized driver. It is undisputed that Heather Trempe was not an authorized driver. In boldface uppercase type the rental agreement states:

> **I UNDERSTAND THAT IF THE VEHICLE IS OBTAINED OR USED FOR ANY PROHIBITED USE OR IN VIOLATION OF THIS AGREEMENT, THEN ANY LIMITATION OF MY RESPONSIBILITY UNDER THIS AGREEMENT SHALL BE VOID AND I SHALL BE FULLY RESPONSIBLE FOR ALL LOSS AND RESULTING DAMAGES, INCLUDING LOSS OF USE, CLAIMS PROCESSING FEES, ADMINISTRATIVE CHARGES, COSTS AND ATTORNEY'S FEES. ALSO, WHERE PERMITTED BY LAW, THE LAW OPTION SHALL BE VOID AND THE LIABILITY, PAI, PEC AND SLI INSURANCE SHALL BY VOID.**

We respectfully disagree with the analysis of the First Circuit in Oliver v. Davis, 95-1841 (La. App. 1 Cir. 8/12/96); 679 So. 2d 462, which involved a fact situation with much in common with the instant case. In *Oliver* the court stated that applying Florida's "dangerous instrumentality" theory of liability could be of benefit to the car rental agency:

> A rental agency would thereby be able to determine its risk of liability under the law of one state rather than having to determine the risk of liability under the laws of each state through which the vehicle travels.

Oliver, 679 So. 2d at 467.

The relator in this case resists having this unwanted "benefit" conferred upon it just as vigorously as did the rental agency in *Oliver*, leading this Court to conclude that it is not really a benefit to car rental agencies. The conclusion of this Court is supported by the language underlined in the boldface quoted above from the rental agreement ("**WHERE PERMITTED BY LAW**"). This language is a clear indication that the rental agency contemplated the potential application of different laws in different jurisdictions and sought to take advantage of those variations where permitted. We conclude that multi-state consistency of results for the benefit of the car rental agency is not a valid basis for preferring Florida law under the facts of this case.

The *Oliver* court suggested that we should also consider which state's policy would be most seriously impaired if its law were not applied to the issue pursuant to LSA-C.C. art. 3515. The *Oliver* court suggests that a Louisiana court might conclude that Florida's law of vicarious liability would be most seriously impaired if Louisiana law were not applied. But that is not what seriously impaired means. By that standard the state whose law is not applied would always be the most seriously impaired. "Seriously impaired" refers to the interest the state has in seeing its policies effectuated relative to the facts of the case, *i.e.*, does the state have such contacts with the cause of action that the failure to apply its laws results in a disproportionate frustration of that state's policies relative to the contacts with that state giving rise to the litigation. In the instant case, Louisiana's policies governing "loss distribution and financial protection" would be most seriously impaired by the application of Florida law because the overwhelming preponderance of the contacts out of which this litigation arises are with the state of Louisiana.

Oliver states that "the application of Florida law to the vicarious liability issue would not impair the policies promoted by Louisiana of protecting its injured citizens." *Id.*, 679 So. 2d at 468. The effect of this approach would be to apply the law of greatest recovery in all conflict situations, because affording the greatest recovery would never "impair the policies promoted by Louisiana of protecting its injured citizens." But that is not the proper standard. Comment (g) to LSA-C.C. art. 3544(2)(a) quoted above makes it clear that the choice is not to be based on either the benefit or detriment to the litigants.

The *Oliver* court treats the enforcement of Florida's "dangerous instrumentality" law as an end in itself from Florida's perspective. However, it is not the enforcement of any particular law that is at issue when "impairment of policies" is referred to in conflict of law situations. It is the state policies that those laws seek to effectuate that are at issue. We must determine what Florida is trying to achieve through the mechanism of its "dangerous instrumentality–vicarious liability law." If the goal of the Florida law is to make Florida roads safer, its application to the facts of this case will not achieve that purpose. The accident occurred in Louisiana. If the goal of the Florida law is to ensure recovery for Florida residents or those injured on Florida roads, its application to the facts of this case will not achieve that purpose. The injured parties are all Louisiana residents, injured in Louisiana. Florida's policies are only impaired if those policies include a concern for the safety of Louisiana roads, or a concern for the protection and recovery of Louisiana residents injured in Louisiana. Clearly Florida has no such policies or concerns, and any attempt by Florida to enact extra-territorial laws to effectuate such policies would represent an unconstitutional overreaching, and are obviously not the policies of the state of Florida. Neither *Oliver*, nor respondents have been able to articulate any genuine interest that Florida might have in the application of its law of vicarious liability to the facts of the instant case. Nor have the respondents any legitimate expectations that if injured while driving Louisiana roads that Florida law would apply.

There are no genuine issues of material fact. . . . Therefore, we reverse the judgment of the trial court and render judgment in favor of relator, National Car Rental Systems, Inc., dismissing plaintiff's claims against relator with prejudice at plaintiffs' cost, and remand for further proceedings consistent with this opinion.

Questions and Comments

(1) Louisiana's 1992 choice-of-law statute is the most ambitious state choice-of-law codification in the United States. The central principle of the Louisiana statute is set forth in article 3515, which calls for application of the law of "the state whose policies would be most impaired if its laws were not applied to that issue." *See also* La. Civ. Code §3542 (comparative impairment rule for torts); La. Civ. Code §3537 (comparative impairment rule for contracts). The rest of Louisiana's choice-of-law code explains how this general principle applies in specific substantive contexts. *See* Symeonides, Louisiana's New Law of Choice of Law for Torts: An Exegesis, 66 Tul. L. Rev. 677 (1992) (describing these more specific rules as "*a priori* legislative determinations of 'the state whose policies would be most impaired if not applied'"). As *Salavarria* makes clear, in the tort context these more specific rules incorporate the distinction between loss-allocation and conduct-regulating rules. *See* La. Civ. Code §§3543-3544. Finally, Article 3547 provides for escape from these more specific rules "if, from the totality of the circumstances of an exceptional case, it is clearly evident under the principles of Article 3542, that the policies of another state would be more seriously impaired if its laws were not applied to the particular issue." The Louisiana choice-of-law code's approach to torts thus seems like a mixture of comparative impairment, New York's approach, and the Second Restatement. One scholar has described this mixture as "an important effort to codify the best of modern conflicts understanding." Perdue, A Reexamination of the Distinction Between "Loss-Allocating" and "Conduct-Regulating Rules," 60 La. L. Rev. 1251, 1251 (2000). Do you agree?

(2) Does codification promote predictability in governing law? Does the answer depend on the content of the codified rules? Or does a codified rule necessarily reduce judicial discretion (and thus increase predictability) when compared to the same rule applied in a common law fashion? We have two empirical analyses of the operation of the Louisiana choice-of-law code, but they cut in two directions. Professor Borchers studied tort cases under the

code. He found that trial court choice-of-law decisions under the code were affirmed on appeal 76.2 percent of the time, as compared with a 52.9 percent affirmance rate in pre-code Louisiana conflicts cases. Viewing affirmance rates as a proxy for decisional predictability, Borchers concludes that the Louisiana choice-of-law code has increased predictability. *See* Borchers, Louisiana's Conflicts Codification: Some Empirical Observations Regarding Decisional Predictability, 60 La. L. Rev. 1061 (2000). Professor Weintraub studied the contracts provisions of the code and obtained less happy results. Of the thirty-two contractual choice of law cases decided under the Louisiana code, twenty-five or so make "fundamental" errors in applying the code. *See* Weintraub, Courts Flailing in the Waters of the Louisiana Conflicts Code: Not Waving But Drowning, 60 La. L. Rev. 1365, 1365-1366 (2000).

Assume that Borchers is right about the code increasing choice-of-law predictability. Is this attributable to the codification itself, or the content rules of the rules that happen to be codified? Even if the Louisiana code increased the *predictability* of Louisiana conflicts law, would this increase conflicts *uniformity?* Doesn't uniformity require national regulation?

(3) Professor Gottesman argues that we need a federal choice-of-law statute because our current decentralized system produces enormous waste, frustrates rational planning, and is unfair. *See* Gottesman, "Draining the Dismal Swamp": the Case for Federal Choice of Law Statutes, 80 Geo. L.J. 1 (1991). Gottesman is largely agnostic about the content of the federal statutory rules. He argues that within fairly large bounds, many choice-of-law rules codified at the national level would address the problems with the current system. But does Congress have the power to enact such rules? Is Congress institutionally competent to craft such rules? Would such a statute make every interstate case a federal question? Gottesman addresses these and many other questions, and surveys the literature.

(4) Oregon is in the process of developing statutory choice-of-law rules for tort and contract. *See* Nafziger, Oregon's Project to Codify Choice-of-Law Rules, 60 La. L. Rev. 1189 (2000). Why don't more state legislatures address choice-of-law problems?

(5) One of the most litigated statutory conflicts provisions has been Section 1-105(1) of the Uniform Commercial Code, which provides:

> *Except* as provided hereafter in this section, when a transaction bears a reasonable relation to this *state* and also to another *state* or nation the parties may agree that the law either of this state or of such other state or nation shall govern their rights and duties. Failing such agreement, this code [*i.e.* the law of this state] applies to transactions bearing an appropriate relation to this state.

Courts disagree about the meaning of the "appropriate relation" criterion. Some view it to permit application of local law on the basis of minimal contacts, regardless of whether another state has more significant contacts. *See, e.g.*, Whitaker v. Harvell-Kilgore Corp., 418 F. 2d 1010, 1016 (5th Cir. 1969). Most courts, however, equate the "appropriate relation" test with the Second Restatement's "most significant relationship" test. *See, e.g.*, In re Merritt Dredging Co., Inc., 839 F. 2d 203, 206-207 (4th Cir. 1988).

In April 2001, the National Conference of Commissioners on Uniform State Laws promulgated a draft comprehensive revision of Article 1 of the UCC, which included a revision of Section 1-105(1). The replacement provision, Section 1-301(c), provides in pertinent part, that "the rights and obligations of the parties are determined . . . by the law that would be selected by application of this State's conflict of laws principles." The official commentary states:

> Former Section 1-105(1), provided that the law of the forum (*i.e.*, the Uniform Commercial Code) applies if the transaction bears "an appropriate relation to this state." By using an "appropriate relation" test, rather than, say, requiring that the forum be the location of the "most significant" contact, Section 1-105(1) expressed a bias in favor of applying the forum's law. This bias, while not universally respected by the courts, was justifiable in light of the uncertainty that existed at the time of drafting as to whether the Uniform Commercial Code would be adopted by all the states; the pro-forum bias would assure that the Uniform Commercial Code would be applied so long as the transaction bore an "appropriate" relation to the forum. Inasmuch as the Uniform Commercial Code has been adopted, at least in part, in all U.S. jurisdictions, the vitality of this point is minimal in the domestic context, and international comity concerns militate against continuing the pro-forum, pro-UCC bias in transnational transactions. When the choice is between the law of two jurisdictions that have adopted the Uniform Commercial Code, but whose law differs (whether because of differences in enacted language or differing judicial interpretations), there is no strong justification for directing a court to apply different choice of law rules to its determination than it would apply if the matter were not governed by the Uniform Commercial Code. Similarly, given the wide variety of choice of law principles applied by the states, it would not be prudent to designate only one such principle as the proper one for transactions governed by the Uniform Commercial Code. Accordingly, in cases in which the parties have not made an effective choice of law, Section 1-301(a) simply directs the forum to apply its ordinary choice of law principles to determine which jurisdiction's law governs.

Will allowing each state to apply its own choice-of law-rules promote the uniformity aims of the UCC? How could these aims have better been promoted?

3

Constitutional Limitations

The due process and equal protection clauses of the Fourteenth Amendment:

[N]or shall any State deprive any person of life, liberty, or property, without due process of law; nor deny to any person within its jurisdiction the equal protection of the laws. . . . [U.S. Const. amend. XIV, §1.]

The full faith and credit clause and statute:

Full Faith and Credit shall be given in each State to the public Acts, records, and judicial Proceedings of every other State. And the Congress may by general laws prescribe the Manner in which such Acts, Records and Proceedings shall be proved, and the Effect thereof. [U.S. Const. art. IV, §1.]

Such Acts, records and judicial proceedings or copies thereof, so authenticated, shall have the same full faith and credit in every court within the United States and its Territories and Possessions as they have by law or usage in the courts of such State, Territory or Possession from which they are taken. [28 U.S.C. §1738.]

The privileges and immunities clause:

The Citizens of each State shall be entitled to all Privileges and Immunities of Citizens in the several States. [U.S. Const. art. IV, §2.]

The commerce clause:

The Congress shall have power . . . To regulate Commerce with foreign Nations, and among the several States and with the Indian Tribes. . . . [U.S. Const. art. I, §8.]

The major constitutional limitations on the choice-of-law process have been the federal due process clause and the full faith and credit clause. The commerce clause place limits on state regulation as well. In addition, both the equal protection and privileges and immunities clauses are of potential relevance to modern choice-of-law theory because they arguably limit a state's right to discriminate on the basis of where activities occur or where the litigants are domiciled.

It is unclear how these five constitutional provisions fit together. Do the due process clause and full faith and credit clause duplicate each others' choice-of-law functions precisely? Why does the Supreme Court sometimes rely on the commerce clause rather than on due process analysis in assessing the validity of state regulation? What is the connection between the equal protection clause and the privileges and immunities clause? And how can one tell in a particular case which constitutional provision to employ? Finding answers to these questions is further complicated by the fact that the scope and role of these clauses has changed over time.

A. Constitutional Limitations on Choice of Law

There was a point at which traditional principles of the kind found in the First Restatement appeared to be on the way to enshrinement in the Constitution (through Supreme Court interpretation). Thus, in New York Life Insurance Co. v. Dodge, 246 U.S. 357 (1918), the Court struck down application of a Missouri nonforfeiture statute to a life insurance policy bought in Missouri and covering a Missouri domiciliary, holding that the contract and an accompanying loan agreement were not in force until accepted by the company's home office in New York. Thus, the contract was formed in New York. Missouri, the Court said, was forbidden by the due process clause from denying the company rights that had vested under New York law. The Court backed off in result, though not in rhetoric, a few years later in an almost identical case, Mutual Life Insurance Co. v. Liebing, 259 U.S. 209 (1922), by finding that the loan agreement subject to the nonforfeiture statute was a separate agreement formed in Missouri and thus subject to Missouri law.

Even if the Constitution was not to be read as implementing every detailed traditional rule, attacks on parochial choice of law under the Constitution were not abandoned. The case that follows is still cited with approval in Supreme Court decisions.

Home Insurance Co. v. Dick

281 U.S. 397 (1930)

Justice BRANDEIS delivered the opinion of the Court.

Dick, a citizen of Texas, brought this action in a court of that State against Compania General Anglo-Mexicana de Seguros S.A., a Mexican corporation, to recover on a policy of fire insurance for the total loss of a tug. Jurisdiction was asserted in rem through garnishment, by ancillary writs issued against The Home Insurance Company and Franklin Fire Insurance Company, which reinsured, by contracts with the Mexican corporation, parts of the risk which it had assumed. The garnishees are New York corporations. Upon them, service was effected by serving their local agents in Texas appointed pursuant to Texas statutes, which require the appointment of local agents by foreign corporations seeking permits to do business within the State.

The controversy here is wholly between Dick and the garnishees. The defendant has never been admitted to do business in Texas; has not done any business there; and has not authorized anyone to receive service of process or enter an appearance for it in this cause. . . .

[The insurance companies'] defense rests upon the following facts. This suit was not commenced till more than one year after the date of the loss. The policy provided: "It is understood and agreed that no judicial suit or demand shall be entered before any tribunal for the collection of any claim under this policy, unless such suits or demands are filed within one year counted as from the date on which such damage occurs." This provision was in accord with the Mexican law to which the policy was expressly made subject. It was issued by the Mexican company in Mexico to one Bonner, of Tampico, Mexico, and was there duly assigned to Dick prior to the loss. It covered the vessel only in certain Mexican waters. The premium was paid in Mexico; and the loss was "payable in the City of Mexico in current funds of the United States of Mexico, or their equivalent elsewhere." At the time the policy was issued, when it was assigned to him, and until after the loss, Dick actually resided in Mexico, although his permanent residence was in Texas. The contracts of reinsurance were effected by correspondence between the Mexican company in Mexico and the New York companies in New York. Nothing thereunder was to be done, or was in fact done, in Texas.

In the trial court, the garnishees contended that since the insurance contract was made and was to be performed in Mexico, and the one year provision was valid by its laws, Dick's failure to sue within one year after accrual of the alleged cause of action was a complete defense to the suit on the policy; that this failure also relieved the garnishees of any obligation as reinsurers, the same defense being open to them, and that they, consequently, owed no debt to the Mexican company subject to garnishment. To this defense, Dick demurred, on the ground that Article 5545 of the Texas Revised Civil Statutes (1925) provides:

> No person, firm, corporation, association or combination of whatsoever kind shall enter into any stipulation, contract, or agreement, by reason whereof the time in which to sue thereon is limited to a shorter period than two years. And no stipulation, contract, or agreement for any such shorter limitation in which to sue shall ever be valid in this State.

The trial court sustained Dick's contention and entered judgment against the garnishees. On appeal, both in the Court of Civil Appeals and in the Supreme Court of the State, the garnishees asserted that, as construed and applied, the Texas statute violated the due process clause of the Fourteenth Amendment and the contract clause. Both courts treated the policy provision as equivalent to a foreign statute of limitation; held that Article 5545 related to the remedy available in Texas courts; concluded that it was validly applicable to the case at bar; and affirmed the judgment of the trial court. The garnishees appealed to this Court on the ground that the statute, as construed and applied, violated their rights under the Federal Constitution. Dick moved to dismiss the appeal for want of jurisdiction. Then the garnishees filed, also, a petition for a writ of certiorari. Consideration of the jurisdiction of this Court on the appeal, and of the petition for certiorari, was postponed to the hearing of the case on the merits.

First. Dick contends that this Court lacks jurisdiction of the action, because the errors assigned involve only questions of local law and of conflict of laws. The argument is that while a provision requiring notice of loss within a fixed period, is substantive because it is a condition precedent to the existence of the cause of action, the provision for liability only in case suit is brought within the year is not substantive because it relates only to the remedy after accrual of the cause of action; that while the validity, interpretation and performance of the substantive provisions of a contract are determined by the law of the place where it is made and is to be performed, matters which relate only to the remedy are unquestionably governed by the lex fori; and that even if the Texas court erred in holding the statute applicable to this contract, the error is one of state law or of the interpretation of the contract, and is not reviewable here.

The contention is unsound. There is no dispute as to the meaning of the provision in the policy. It is that the insurer shall not be liable unless suit is brought within one year of the loss. Whether the provision be interpreted as making the commencement of a suit within the year a condition precedent to the existence of a cause of action, or as making failure to sue within the year a breach of a condition subsequent which extinguishes the cause of action, is not of legal significance here. Nor are we concerned with the question whether the provision is properly described as relating to remedy or to substance. However characterized, it is an express term in the contract of the parties by which the right of the insured and the correlative obligation of the insurer are defined. If effect is given to the clause, Dick cannot recover from the Mexican corporation and the garnishees cannot be compelled to pay. If, on the other hand, the statute is applied to the contract, it admittedly abrogates a contractual right and imposes liability, although the parties have agreed that there should be none.

The statute is not simply one of limitation. It does not merely fix the time in which the aid of the Texas courts may be invoked. Nor does it govern only the remedies available in Texas courts. It deals with the powers and capacities of persons and corporations. It expressly prohibits the making of certain contracts. As construed, it also directs the disregard in Texas of contractual rights and obligations wherever created and assumed; and it commands the enforcement of obligations in excess of those contracted for. Therefore, the objection that, as applied to contracts made and to be performed outside of Texas, the statute violates the Federal Constitution, raises federal questions of substance; and the existence of the federal claim is not disproved by saying that the statute, or the one year provision in the policy, relates to the remedy and not to the substance.

Second. The Texas statute as here construed and applied deprives the garnishees of property without due process of law. A State may, of course, prohibit and declare invalid the making of certain contracts within its borders. Ordinarily, it may prohibit performance within its borders, even of contracts validly made elsewhere, if they are required to be performed within the State and their performance would violate its laws. But, in the case at bar, nothing in any way relating to the policy sued on, or to the contracts of reinsurance, was ever done or required to be done in Texas. All acts relating to the making of the policy were done in Mexico. All in relation to the making of the contracts of reinsurance were done there or in New York. And, likewise, all things in regard to performance were to be done outside of Texas. Neither the Texas laws nor the Texas courts were invoked for any purpose, except by Dick in the bringing of this suit. The fact that Dick's permanent residence was in Texas is without significance. At all times here material, he was physically present and acting in Mexico. Texas was, therefore, without power to affect the terms of contracts so made. Its attempt to impose a greater obligation than that agreed upon and to seize property in payment of the imposed obligation violates the guaranty against deprivation of property without due process of law.

The cases relied upon, in which it was held that a State may lengthen its statute of limitations, are not in point. In those cases, the parties had not stipulated a time limit for the enforcement of their obligations. It is true that a State may extend the time within which suit may be brought to its own courts, if, in doing so, it violates no agreement of the parties. And, in the absence of a contractual provision, the local statute of limitation may be applied to a right created in another jurisdiction even where the remedy in the latter is barred. In such cases, the rights and obligations of the parties are not varied. When, however, the parties have expressly agreed upon a time limit on their obligation, a statute which invalidates the agreement and directs enforcement of the contract after the time has expired increases their obligation and imposes a burden not contracted for.

It is true also that a State is not bound to provide remedies and procedure to suit the wishes of individual litigants. It may prescribe the kind of remedies to be available in its courts and dictate the practice and procedure to be followed in pursuing those remedies. Contractual provisions relating to these matters, even if valid where made, are often disregarded by the court of the forum, pursuant to statute or otherwise. But the Texas statute deals neither with the kind of remedy available nor with the mode in which it is to be pursued. It purports to create rights and obligations. It may not validly affect contracts which are neither made nor are to be performed in Texas.

Third. Dick urges that Article 5545 of the Texas law is a declaration of its public policy; and that a State may properly refuse to recognize foreign rights which violate its declared policy. Doubtless, a State may prohibit the enjoyment by persons within its borders of rights acquired elsewhere which violate its laws or public policy; and, under some circumstances, it may refuse to aid in the enforcement of such rights. But the Mexican corporation never was in Texas; and neither it nor the garnishees invoked the aid of the Texas courts or the Texas laws. The Mexican corporation was not before the court. The garnishees were brought in by compulsory process. Neither has asked favors. They ask only to be let alone. We need not consider how far the State may go in imposing restrictions on the conduct of its own residents, and of foreign corporations which have received permission to do business within its borders; or how far it may go in refusing to lend the aid of its courts to the enforcement of rights acquired outside its borders. It may not abrogate the rights of parties beyond its borders having no relation to anything done or to be done within them.

Fourth. Finally, it is urged that the Federal Constitution does not require the States to recognize and protect rights derived from the laws of foreign countries—that as to them, the full faith and credit clause has no application. The claims here asserted are not based upon the full faith and credit clause. They rest upon the Fourteenth Amendment. Its protection extends to aliens. Moreover, the parties in interest here are American companies. The defense asserted is based on the provision of the policy and on their contracts of reinsurance. The courts of the State confused this defense with that based on the Mexican Code. They held that even if the effort of the foreign statute was to extinguish the right, Dick's removal to Texas prior to the bar of the foreign statute, removed the cause of action from Mexico and subjected it to the Texas statute of limitation. And they applied the same rule to the provision in the policy. Whether or not that is a sufficient answer to the defense based on the foreign law, we may not consider; for, no issue under the full faith and credit clause was raised. But in Texas, as elsewhere, the contract was subject to its own limitations.

Reversed.

Questions and Comments

(1) Virtually all the contacts in this case were with Mexico. How did Dick get jurisdiction in Texas? The constitutionality of the quasi in rem jurisdiction the Court exercised was disposed of many years later in Rush v. Savchuk, 444 U.S. 320 (1980), page 564 *infra*. Should a state always be allowed to apply its own law if it has enough contacts to assert "normal" long-arm jurisdiction? *Compare* Phillips Petroleum Co. v. Shutts, page 376 *infra*.

(2) How persuasive is the Court's assertion that the statute in question is not merely one of limitation, and therefore not defensible under the exception for applying the forum's own procedural law? Is characterization a constitutional issue? What if the parties had omitted the contractual limitation in reliance on the Mexican one-year statute of limitations—the statute of the only jurisdiction with any contacts with the case? Would the result have been the same under the Court's reasoning? Would such a case be different in substance from the actual *Dick* case?

(3) Why didn't the defendants in *Dick* invoke the full faith and credit clause? Is there a good reason for state courts to pay more respect to the laws of sister-states than the laws of sovereign nations?

(4) Does the Court's discussion of public policy mean that a state may never invoke its public policy when it has insufficient contacts with a case? ("[Texas] may not abrogate the rights of parties beyond its borders having no relation to anything done or to be done within them.") Does the Court's position mean, for example, that Texas would be required by the due process clause to award damages for breach of a contract for the sale of slaves if the contract was legal in the country to which it was confined?

(5) What is the nature of the due process violation in the *Dick* case? Does due process incorporate some territorial principle per se? If so, where is that territorial principle to be found in the language of the clause or its legislative history? If the Court relies on some notion that the Mexican insurance company had some right to rely on the contractual clause not to be sued, and that such right was "property" protected by the due process clause, doesn't its reasoning beg the question? That is, the "right" in question can be "property" only if it really is a right, and it is a right under Mexican law

but not under Texas law. Thus, one must first decide that, *as a matter of constitutional law* concerning the due process clause, Mexican law was the only applicable law. We're back where we started. These matters are discussed at great length in Martin, Constitutional Limitations on Choice of Law, 61 Cornell L. Rev. 185, 188-191 (1976); Kirgis, The Roles of Due Process and Full Faith and Credit in Choice of Law, 62 Cornell L. Rev. 94 (1976); and Martin, A Reply to Professor Kirgis, *id.* at 62.

(6) What if the Texas law in question had disfavored Dick—would that have made a difference? In other words, is there any difference, from a due process perspective, between a state's applying its own law to aid a resident against a nonresident and a state's use of its own law to aid a nonresident against a resident?

(7) The Court in *Dick* states that Dick was "a citizen of Texas" and a "permanent residen[t]," and added that "[t]he fact that Dick's permanent residence was in Texas is without significance." Does this mean that Dick was domiciled in Texas? If so, does *Dick* stand for the proposition that a state's interest in applying its plaintiff-protecting law to a domiciliary is "without significance" to the validity, under the due process clause, of applying that law? What, then, are the implications of the due process clause for interest analysis? For discussion of these issues, see Rensberger, Who Was Dick? Constitutional Limitations on State Choice of Law, 1998 Utah L. Rev. 37. For an argument that considerations of fairness to the defendant should sometimes trump state interests in protecting plaintiffs, see Brilmayer, Rights, Fairness, and Choice of Law, 99 Yale L.J. 1277 (1989).

(8) Is there any pattern in the following cases, all decided within a few years after *Dick*?

(a) Delta & Pine Land Company had its principal place of business in Tennessee but did business in Mississippi. It entered an insurance contract against employee embezzlement with Hartford Accident & Indemnity Company, which was based in Connecticut but did business both in Mississippi and Tennessee. An employee of the land company embezzled some money in Mississippi. By the time of litigation, the land company had moved its chief place of business to Mississippi. The courts of Mississippi, where the action was brought, were asked to apply a Mississippi statute voiding contractual limitations on the period in which suit could be brought. The Supreme Court, in Hartford Accident & Indemnity Co. v. Delta & Pine Land Co., 292 U.S. 143 (1934), held that Mississippi could not apply its own statute. "Conceding that ordinarily a state may prohibit performance within its borders even of a contract validly made elsewhere, if the performance would violate its laws . . . it may not, on grounds of policy, ignore a right which has lawfully vested elsewhere, if, as here, the interest of the forum had but slight connection with the substance of the contract obligations." 292 U.S. at 149-150.

(b) A New Jersey resident allowed his car to be driven by another to New York, where the driver injured the plaintiff. The plaintiff sued the owner of the car, invoking a New York statute imposing vicarious liability on owners. This time the Supreme Court upheld the application of New York law as against a due process attack. Young v. Masci, 289 U.S. 253 (1933).

(c) In Skiriotes v. Florida, 313 U.S. 69 (1941), the Supreme Court upheld the right of Florida to prosecute a sponge fisher for using mechanical apparatuses (diving suits, etc.) in fishing for sponges outside but adjacent to Florida's territorial waters against a due process attack. The Court placed considerable emphasis on the fact that the defendant was a citizen of Florida and on the state's right to regulate the conduct of its citizens, even outside its borders. What if the complained-of activity had taken place within the territorial waters of an adjoining state, which encouraged the use of mechanical aids, rather than in international waters? What if the defendant had moved to another state before doing his sponge fishing?

Are these cases consistent with *Dick*?

As the Supreme Court continued to consider constitutional limitations on choice of law, it decided cases both under the due process clause and the full faith and credit clause. Although the distinction was not always clear, it appeared that the essence of the due process limitations was that a state had to have some minimal contacts in order to apply its own law under the due process clause. There was some indication that even a state with sufficient contacts to satisfy due process might be forbidden from applying its own law under full faith and credit if there were some strong reason to favor the law of another state—overwhelmingly stronger contacts, much greater interest, uniformity of treatment, or the like. In one case, Order of Commercial Travelers v. Wolfe, 331 U.S. 586 (1947), for example, the Court used the full faith and credit clause to strike down a state's application of its own law when there were clearly enough contacts to satisfy due process.

Nonetheless, the distinctions between the two constitutional limitations began to blur. *Wolfe* was confined to its particular subject matter, fraternal benefit organizations (where, arguably, all members, even from different states, should be subject to a single law in order to avoid unequal treatment). And in a pair of worker compensation cases that were widely viewed as stating principles of general applicability, the Court seemed to reject the notion that a state with enough contacts to satisfy due process could be prevented from applying its own law by the full faith and credit clause. The first case, Alaska Packers Association v. Industrial Accident Commission, 294 U.S. 532 (1935), ruled that the state where an employment relationship had been formed could apply its own worker compensation law to an employee injured in another state. The second case is reproduced below.

Pacific Employers Insurance Co. v. Industrial Accident Commission

306 U.S. 493 (1939)

Justice STONE delivered the opinion of the Court.

The question is whether the full faith and credit which the Constitution requires to be given to a Massachusetts workmen's compensation statute precludes California from applying its own workmen's compensation act in the case of an injury suffered by a Massachusetts employee of a Massachusetts employer while in California in the course of his employment.

The injured employee, a resident of Massachusetts, was regularly employed there under written contract in the laboratories of the Dewey & Almy Chemical Company as a chemical engineer and research chemist. In September, 1935, in the usual course of his employment he was sent by his employer to its branch factory in California, to act temporarily as technical adviser in the effort to improve the quality of one of the employer's products manufactured there.

[The injured employee] instituted the present proceeding before the California Commission for the award of compensation under the California Act for injuries received in the course of his employment in that state, naming petitioner as insurance carrier under that Act. The California Commission directed petitioner to pay the compensation prescribed by the California Act, including the amounts of lien claims filed in the proceeding for medical, hospital and nursing services and certain further amounts necessary for such services in the future.

By the applicable Massachusetts statute, §§24, 26, c. 152, Mass. Gen. Laws (Ter. Ed. 1932), an employee of a person insured under the Act, as was the employer in this case, is deemed to waive his "right of action at common law or under the law of any other jurisdiction" to recover for personal injuries unless he shall have given appropriate notice to the employer in writing that he elects to retain such rights. Section 26 directs that without the notice his right to recover be restricted to the compensation provided by the Act for injuries received in the course of his employment, "whether within or without the commonwealth."

Section 27 (a) [of the California Workmen's Compensation statute] provides that "No contract, rule, or regulation shall exempt the employer from liability for the compensation fixed by this act." And §58 provides that the commission shall have jurisdiction over claims for compensation for injuries suffered outside the state when the employee's contract of hire was entered into within the state. Both statutes are compensation acts, substituted for the common law remedy for negligence. The California Act is compulsory. The Massachusetts Act is similarly effective unless the employee gives notice not to be bound by it, which in this case he did not do.

[Petitioner] insists that since the contract of employment was entered into in Massachusetts and the employee consented to be bound by the Massachusetts Act, that, and not the California statute, fixes the employee's right to compensation whether the injuries were received within or without the state, and that the Massachusetts statute is constitutionally entitled to full faith and credit in the courts of California.

We may assume that these provisions are controlling upon the parties in Massachusetts, and that since they are applicable to a Massachusetts contract of employment between a Massachusetts employer and employee, they do not infringe due process. Similarly the constitutionality of the provisions of the California statute awarding compensation for injuries to an employee occurring within its borders, and for injuries as well occurring elsewhere, when the contract of employment was entered into within the state, is not open to question. Alaska Packers Assn. v. Industrial Accident Comm'n, 294 U.S. 532 (1935).

While in the circumstances now presented, either state, if its system for administering workmen's compensation permitted, would be free to adopt and enforce the remedy provided by the statute of the other, here each has provided for itself an exclusive remedy for a liability which it was constitutionally authorized to impose. But neither is bound, apart from the compulsion of the full faith and credit clause, to enforce the laws of the other; and the law of neither can by its own force determine the choice of law to be applied in the other.

To the extent that California is required to give full faith and credit to the conflicting Massachusetts statute it must be denied the right to apply in its own courts its own statute, constitutionally enacted in pursuance of its policy to provide compensation for employees injured in their employment within the state. It must withhold the remedy given by its own statute to its residents by way of compensation for medical, hospital and nursing services rendered to the injured employee, and it must remit him to Massachusetts to secure the administrative remedy which that state has provided. We cannot say that the full faith and credit clause goes so far.

While the purpose of that provision was to preserve rights acquired or confirmed under the public acts and judicial proceedings of one state by requiring recognition of their validity in other states, the very nature of the federal union of states, to which are reserved some of the attributes of sovereignty, precludes resort to the full faith and credit clause as the means for compelling a state to substitute the statutes of other states for its own statutes dealing with a subject matter concerning which it is competent to legislate. As was pointed out in Alaska Packers Assn. v. Industrial Accident Comm'n: "A rigid and literal enforcement of the full faith and credit clause, without regard to the statute of the forum, would lead to the absurd result that, wherever the conflict arises, the statute of each state must be enforced in the courts of the other, but cannot be in its own." And in cases like the present it would create an impasse which would often leave the employee remediless. Full faith and credit would deny to California the right to apply its own remedy, and its administrative machinery may well not be adapted to giving the remedy afforded by Massachusetts. Similarly, the full faith and credit demanded for the California Act would deny to Massachusetts the right to apply its own remedy, and its Department of Industrial Accidents may well be without statutory authority to afford the remedy provided by the California statute.

It has often been recognized by this Court that there are some limitations upon the extent to which a state may be required by the full faith and credit clause to enforce even the judgment of another state in contravention of its own statutes or policy. And in the case of statutes, the extrastate effect of which Congress has not prescribed, as it may under the constitutional provision, we think the conclusion is unavoidable that the full faith and credit clause does not require one state to substitute for its own statute, applicable to persons and events within it, the conflicting statute of another state, even though that statute is of controlling force in the courts of the state of its enactment with respect to the same persons and events.

This Court must determine for itself how far the full faith and credit clause compels the qualification or denial of rights asserted under the laws of one state, that of the forum, by the statute of another state. But there would seem to be little room for the exercise of that function when the statute of the forum is the expression of domestic policy, in terms declared to be exclusive in its application to persons and events within the state. Although Massachusetts has an interest in safeguarding the compensation of Massachusetts employees while temporarily abroad in the course of their employment, and may adopt that policy for itself, that could hardly be thought to support an application of the full faith and credit clause which would override the constitutional authority of another state to legislate for the bodily safety and economic protection of employees injured within it. Few matters could be deemed more appropriately the concern of the state in which the injury occurs or more completely within its power. Considerations of less weight led to the conclusion, in Alaska Packers Assn. v. Industrial Accident Comm'n, *supra,* that the full faith and credit clause did not require California to give effect to the Alaska Compensation Act in preference to its own. There this Court sustained the award by California of the compensation provided by its own statute for employees where the contract of employment was made within the state, although the injury occurred in Alaska, whose statute also provided compensation for the injury. Decision was rested explicitly upon the grounds that the full faith and credit exacted for the statute of one state does not necessarily preclude another state from enforcing in its own courts its own conflicting statute having no extra-territorial operation forbidden by the Fourteenth Amendment, and that no persuasive reason was shown for denying that right.

Here, California legislation not only conflicts with that of Massachusetts providing compensation for the Massachusetts employee if injured within the state of California, but it expressly provides, for the guidance of its own commission and courts, that "No contract, rule or regulation shall exempt the employer from liability for the compensation fixed by this Act." The Supreme

Court of California has declared in its opinion in this case that it is the policy of the state, as expressed in its Constitution and Compensation Act, to apply its own provisions for compensation, to the exclusion of all others, and that "It would be obnoxious to that policy to deny persons who have been injured in this state the right to apply for compensation when to do so might require physicians and hospitals to go to another state to collect charges for medical care and treatment given to such persons."

Full faith and credit does not here enable one state to legislate for the other or to project its laws across state lines so as to preclude the other from prescribing for itself the legal consequences of acts within it.

Questions and Comments

(1) What type of state laws are governed by the full faith and credit clause? There is a general consensus that the framers intended the clause to apply to state statutes (which is what they meant by "public acts"), but a continuing debate over whether they intended it to extend to common law rules. *Compare* Laycock, Equal Citizens of Equal and Territorial States: The Constitutional Foundations of Choice of Law, 92 Colum. L. Rev. 249, 290-295 (1992) (common law rules included within "judicial proceedings") *with* Whitten, The Constitutional Limitations on State Choice of Law: Full Faith and Credit, 12 Mem. St. U. L. Rev. 1, 56-60 (1981) (common law rules not included). *Pacific Employers* confirmed that the clause regulates state statutes. The Court later made clear that the clause applies to clashes of common law rules as well. *See* Carroll v. Lanza, 349 U.S. 408 (1955).

(2) What does it mean, for choice-of-law purposes, for a state to give full faith and credit to the laws of other states? Does the text of the clause suggest anything about which state choice-of-law rules are appropriate or acceptable? Most commentators believe that, as original matter, the clause incorporated traditional choice-of-rules law from international law, subject to Congress's implementation power under Article IV. *See* Sun Oil v. Wortman, 486 U.S. 717, 723 (1988), reproduced below at page 383; Rheinstein, The Constitutional Basis of Jurisdiction, 22 U. Chi. L. Rev. 775, 788-789, 816 (1955). But the Supreme Court did not actually regulate state choice-of-law rules under the full faith and credit clause until the twentieth century. *See* Whitten, The Constitutional Limits on State Choice of Law: Full Faith and Credit, 12 Mem. St. U. L. Rev. 1, 5 (1981).

(3) Does *Pacific Employers* stand for the proposition that any state with an interest in applying its law can do so, consistent with full faith and credit, even if other states have similar interests? How do we identify such state interests? *Pacific Employers* says that the state of injury has an interest in applying its law for full faith and credit purposes. The case that preceded it, *Alaska Packers,* discussed *supra* 349, held that the state where an employment relationship formed has an interest (for full faith and credit purposes) in applying its workmen compensation scheme, even if the injury took place in

another state. Do these decisions constitutionalize interest analysis or does the Court have a different conception of state interests in mind? Why does the full faith and credit clause focus on the interests of the state whose law is being applied instead of the interest of the state whose law is not being applied?

(4) How does the due process limitation on choice-of-law rules differ from the full faith and credit limitation? Is it correct to say that due process concerns the fairness of applying a particular state law to the defendant, while full faith and credit concerns the need to respect the sovereign prerogatives of other states? These two sets of considerations are contrasted in Kogan, Toward a Jurisprudence of Choice of Law: The Priority of Fairness over Comity, 62 N.Y.U. L. Rev. 651 (1987).

Watson v. Employers Liability Assurance Corp.

348 U.S. 66 (1954)

Justice BLACK delivered the opinion of the Court.

Louisiana has an insurance code which comprehensively regulates the business of insurance in all its phases. This case brings to us challenges to the constitutionality of certain provisions of that code allowing injured persons to bring direct actions against liability insurance companies that have issued policies contracting to pay liabilities imposed on persons who inflict injury. This is such a direct action brought by the appellants, Mr. and Mrs. Watson, in a Louisiana state court claiming damages against the appellee, Employers Liability Assurance Corporation, Ltd., on account of alleged personal injuries suffered by Mrs. Watson. The complaint charged that the injuries occurred in Louisiana when Mrs. Watson bought and used in that State "Toni Home Permanent" a hair-waving product alleged to have contained a highly dangerous latent ingredient put there by its manufacturer. The manufacturer is the Toni Company of Illinois, a subsidiary of the Gillette Safety Razor Company which has its headquarters in Massachusetts.

The particular problem presented with reference to enforcing the Louisiana statute in this case arises because the insurance policy sued on was negotiated and issued in Massachusetts and delivered in Massachusetts and Illinois.[1] This Massachusetts-negotiated contract contains a clause, recognized as binding and enforceable under Massachusetts and Illinois law, which prohibits direct actions against the insurance company until *after* final determination of the Toni Company's obligation to pay personal injury damages either by judgment or agreement. Contrary to this contractual "no action" clause, the challenged statutory provisions permit injured persons to sue an

1. The insurance policy was issued to "The Toni Company, a Division of the Gillette Safety Razor Company. . . ." Gillette is a Delaware Corporation with headquarters in Boston where the contract was negotiated with the Boston office of Employers. The Toni Company manufactures the hair-waving product in Chicago, Illinois.

insurance company *before* such final determination. As to injuries occurring in Louisiana, one provision of the State's direct action statute makes it applicable, even though, as here, an insurance contract is made in another state and contains a clause forbidding such direct actions. Another Louisiana statutory provision, with which Employers long ago complied, compels foreign insurance companies to consent to such direct suits in order to get a certificate to do business in the State. The basic issue raised by the attack on both these provisions is whether the Federal Constitution forbids Louisiana to apply its own law and compels it to apply the law of Massachusetts or Illinois.

Had the policy sued on been issued in Louisiana there would be no arguable due process question. But because the policy was bought, issued and delivered outside of Louisiana, Employers invokes the due process principle that a state is without power to exercise "extraterritorial jurisdiction," that is, to regulate and control activities wholly beyond its boundaries. Such a principle was recognized and applied in Home Ins. Co. v. Dick, a case strongly relied on by Employers.

Some contracts made locally, affecting nothing but local affairs, may well justify a denial to other states of power to alter those contracts. But, as this case illustrates, a vast part of the business affairs of this Nation does not present such simple local situations. Although this insurance contract was issued in Massachusetts, it was to protect Gillette and its Illinois subsidiary against damages on account of personal injuries that might be suffered by users of Toni Home Permanents anywhere in the United States, its territories, or in Canada. As a consequence of the modern practice of conducting widespread business activities throughout the entire United States, this Court has in a series of cases held that more states than one may seize hold of local activities which are part of multistate transactions and may regulate to protect interests of its own people, even though other phases of the same transactions might justify regulatory legislation in other states.

Louisiana's direct action statute is not a mere intermeddling in affairs beyond her boundaries which are no concern of hers. Persons injured or killed in Louisiana are most likely to be Louisiana residents, and even if not, Louisiana may have to care for them. Serious injuries may require treatment in Louisiana homes or hospitals by Louisiana doctors. The injured may be destitute. They may be compelled to call upon friends, relatives, or the public for help. Louisiana has manifested its natural interest in the injured by providing remedies for recovery of damages. It has a similar interest in policies of insurance which are designed to assure ultimate payment of such damages. Moreover, Louisiana courts in most instances provide the most convenient forum for trial of these cases. But modern transportation and business methods have made it more difficult to serve process on wrongdoers who live or do business in other states. In this case efforts to serve the Gillette Company were answered by a motion to dismiss on the ground that Gillette had no Louisiana agent on whom process could be served. If this motion is granted, Mrs. Watson, but for the direct action law, could not get her case tried without going to Massachusetts or Illinois although she lives in Louisiana and her claim is for injuries from a product bought and used there. What has been said is enough to show Louisiana's legitimate interest in safeguarding the rights of persons injured there. In view of that interest, the direct action provisions here challenged do not violate due process.

What we have said above goes far toward answering the Full Faith and Credit Clause contention. That clause does not automatically compel a state to subordinate its own contract laws to the laws of another state in which a contract happens to have been formally executed. Where, as here, a contract affects the people of several states, each may have interests that leave it free to enforce its own contract policies. We have already pointed to the vital interests of Louisiana in liability insurance that covers injuries to people in that State. Of course Massachusetts also has some interest in the policy sued on in this case. The insurance contract was formally executed in that State and Gillette has an office there. But plainly these interests cannot outweigh the interest of Louisiana in taking care of those injured in Louisiana. Since this is true, the Full Faith and Credit Clause does not compel Louisiana to subordinate its direct action provisions to Massachusetts contract rules. Pacific Employers Ins. Co. v. Commission.

Reversed.

Clay v. Sun Insurance Office, Ltd.

377 U.S. 179 (1964)

Justice DOUGLAS delivered the opinion of the Court.

This case, which invoked the diversity jurisdiction of the Federal District Court in a suit to recover damages under an insurance policy, was here before. . . . The initial question then as now is whether the 12-month-suit clause in the policy governs, in which event the claim is barred, or whether Florida's statutes nullifying such clauses if they require suit to be filed in less than five years are applicable and valid, in which event the suit is timely. The policy was purchased by petitioner in Illinois while he was a citizen and resident of that State. Respondent, a British company, is licensed to do business in Illinois, Florida, and several other States.

A few months after purchasing the policy, petitioner moved to Florida and became a citizen and resident of that State; and it was in Florida that the loss occurred two years later. When the case reached here, the majority view was that the underlying constitutional question—whether consistently with due process, Florida could apply its five-year statute to this Illinois contract—should not be reached until the Florida Supreme Court, through its certificate procedure, had construed that statute and resolved another local law question. On remand the Court of Appeals certified the two questions to the Florida Supreme Court, which answered both questions in petitioner's favor. Thereafter the Court of Appeals held that it was not compatible with due process for Florida to apply its five-year statute to this contract and that judgment should be entered for respondent. We again granted certiorari.

While there are Illinois cases indicating that parties may contract—as here—for a shorter period of limitations than is provided by the Illinois statute, we are referred to no Illinois decision extending that rule into other States whenever claims on Illinois contracts are sought to be enforced there. We see no difficulty whatever under either the Full Faith and Credit Clause or the Due Process Clause. We deal with an ambulatory contract on which suit might be brought in any one of several States. Normally, as the Court held in Pacific Employers Ins. Co. v. Industrial Accident Comm'n, a State having jurisdiction over a claim deriving from an out-of-state employment contract need not substitute the conflicting statute of the other State (workmen's compensation) for its own statute (workmen's compensation)—where the employee was injured in the course of his employment while temporarily in the latter State. We followed the same route in Watson v. Employers Liability Assurance Corp. where we upheld a state statute allowing direct actions against liability insurance companies in the State of the forum, even though a clause in the contract, binding in the State where it was made, prohibited direct action against the insurer until final determination of the obligation of the insured.

The Court of Appeals relied in the main on Hartford Accident & Indemnity Co. v. Delta & Pine Land Co., and Home Ins. Co. v. Dick. Those were cases where the activities in the State of the forum were thought to be too slight and too casual, as in the *Delta & Pine Land Co.* case, to make the application of local law consistent with due process, or wholly lacking, as in the *Dick* case. No deficiency of that order is present here. As Mr. Justice Black, dissenting, said when this case was here before:

> Insurance companies, like other contractors, do not confine their contractual activities and obligations within state boundaries. They sell to customers who are promised protection in States far away from the place where the contract is made. In this very case the policy was sold to Clay with knowledge that he could take his property anywhere in the world he saw fit without losing the protection of his insurance. In fact, his contract was described on its face as a "Personal Property Floater Policy (World Wide)." The contract did not even attempt to provide that the law of Illinois would govern when suits were filed anywhere else in the country. Shortly after the contract was made, Clay moved to Florida and there he lived for several years. His insured property was there all that time. The corporation knew this fact. Particularly since the company was licensed to do business in Florida, it must have known it might be sued there. . . .

. . . Florida has ample contacts with the present transaction and the parties to satisfy any conceivable requirement of full faith and credit or of due process.

Reversed.

Questions and Comments

(1) Is anything left of Home Ins. Co. v. Dick after *Watson* and *Clay?*

(2) Although in *Watson* the entire claim against Gillette arose in Louisiana, the claim against the insurance company necessarily derived in part from the contract between Gillette and the insurance company, entered into elsewhere. Is that fact irrelevant after *Pacific Employers* since that case is also one where a critical element—the employment relationship—was located outside the forum?

(3) What would the result in *Watson* have been if the insurance contract in question had not contained a clause requiring the insurance company to defend Gillette? Wouldn't allowing a suit against the insurance company in Louisiana seem more extreme—more unfair—under those circumstances?

(4) Are the factors listed by Justice Black in *Watson* in justification of the application of Louisiana law convincing? Consider:

(a) The first interest listed for Louisiana was the likelihood that persons injured in Louisiana would be Louisiana residents. Is that a sufficient reason for applying Louisiana law, however, in light of the fact that Dick was a resident of Texas and his residence did not justify application of Texas law in his case?

(b) The fact that there may be medical creditors in Louisiana for someone injured there may provide a desire on Louisiana's part to provide for local trial, but should medical creditors be singled out? Isn't it equally likely that there were Texas business creditors of Dick in the *Dick* case who would have benefited from a recovery by Dick? And if the concern is for the patient, isn't the danger of discouraging medical treatment by medical creditors likely to turn on more practical questions such as whether the patient is insured?

(c) Justice Black's third Louisiana interest—that of compensation, as manifested by Louisiana tort law—is more problematical. It should first be noted that Louisiana's interest in tort compensation is being invoked to allow it to control extra-state contractual relations between the insured and the insurer. Should a state's interest in *X* allow it to interfere with a relationship between *Y* and *Z?* Shouldn't the state be required first to find out if there are alternative means to accomplish the same goal? And wouldn't Louisiana be able to implement its tort law by allowing a suit directly against the tortfeasor, using a long-arm statute? Should the state's failure to provide itself with a constitutionally approved method of achieving its goals justify it in interfering with the third party's rights?

(d) The same questions may be raised about Louisiana's interest in providing a convenient Louisiana trial.

(5) If *Watson* fails to make an air-tight case for distinguishing *Dick*, can *Watson* nonetheless be justified on the grounds that the *effect* of the Louisiana statute is essentially no more than to change the place of trial, since the insurance company would have had to defend Gillette if Gillette had been sued in Massachusetts or Illinois?

On the other hand, even if *Watson* can be handled by this approach, what of *Clay*, in which the issue (extending a contractual limitation period) is exactly the same as in *Dick*?

(6) Is it relevant that in the *Clay* case the insurance premiums were paid lump-sum in Illinois? (The Supreme Court opinion makes no mention of the fact; it is found in the Court of Appeals decision, 265 F.2d 552, 554 (1959).) If two Americans had bet in the United States whether Chairman Mao could swim the Yangtze River, should the legality of the contract have been controlled by Chinese law? Should the result be different if the defendant had moved to China later? *Compare* State Board of Insurance v. Todd Shipyards Corp., 370 U.S. 451 (1962). *Todd Shipyards* declared it a violation of due process for Texas to tax or regulate an insurance policy issued out of state by an out-of-state insurer to an out-of-state insured. The only connection to Texas was that the insured property was located there. *Todd Shipyards* did not cite *Watson;* nor was it cited in *Clay*. Is taxation just somehow "different"?

The Supreme Court's due process holdings on a state's right to tax have followed a somewhat tortured path. In Quill Corp. v. North Dakota, 504 U.S. 298 (1992), it overruled earlier precedents and held that a state had a due process right to collect use taxes from mail order merchandisers with no physical presence within the state. A "use" tax is the functional equivalent of a sales tax; it is applied when the sale itself takes place outside the state, but the use occurs within. Prior to *Quill,* the Court had maintained that the state into which merchandise was sent had no right to impose a duty to collect the tax upon out-of-state sellers; the Court was unanimous in abandoning this holding, relying primarily on personal jurisdiction cases that expanded the reach of the state's long arm. The Court was split on whether such taxes violated the commerce clause; a majority held that they did. For a discussion of the commerce clause limits on state taxation, *see* page 432 *infra*.

Allstate Insurance Co. v. Hague

449 U.S. 302 (1981)

Justice BRENNAN announced the judgment of the Court and delivered an opinion, in which Justice WHITE, Justice MARSHALL, and Justice BLACKMUN joined.

This Court granted certiorari to determine whether the Due Process Clause of the Fourteenth Amendment or the Full Faith and Credit Clause of Art. IV, §1, of the United States Constitution bars the Minnesota Supreme Court's choice of substantive Minnesota law to govern the effect of a provision in an insurance policy issued to respondent's decedent. 444 U.S. 1070 (1980).

I

Respondent's late husband, Ralph Hague, died of injuries suffered when a motorcycle on which he was a passenger was struck from behind by an automobile. The accident occurred in Pierce County, Wis., which is immediately across the Minnesota border from Red Wing, Minn. The operators of both vehicles were Wisconsin residents, as was the decedent, who, at the time of the accident, resided with respondent in Hager City, Wis., which is one and one-half miles from Red Wing. Mr. Hague had been employed in Red Wing for the 15 years immediately preceding his death and had commuted daily from Wisconsin to his place of employment.

Neither the operator of the motorcycle nor the operator of the automobile carried valid insurance. However, the decedent held a policy issued by petitioner Allstate Insurance Co. covering three automobiles owned by him and containing an uninsured motorist clause insuring him against loss incurred from accidents with uninsured motorists. The uninsured motorist coverage was limited to $15,000 for each automobile.[3]

After the accident, but prior to the initiation of this lawsuit, respondent moved to Red Wing. Subsequently, she married a Minnesota resident and established residence with her new husband in Savage, Minn. At approximately the same time, a Minnesota Registrar of Probate appointed respondent personal representative of her deceased husband's estate. Following her appointment, she brought this action in Minnesota District Court seeking a declaration under Minnesota law that the $15,000 uninsured motorist coverage on each of her late husband's three automobiles could be "stacked" to provide total coverage of $45,000. Petitioner defended on the ground that whether the three uninsured motorist coverages could be stacked should be determined by Wisconsin law, since the insurance policy was delivered in Wisconsin, the accident occurred in Wisconsin, and all persons were Wisconsin residents at the time of the accident.

The Minnesota District Court disagreed. Interpreting Wisconsin law to disallow stacking, the court concluded that Minnesota's choice-of-law rules required the application of Minnesota law permitting stacking. The court refused to apply Wisconsin law as "inimical to the public policy of Minnesota" and granted summary judgment for respondent.

The Minnesota Supreme Court, sitting en banc, affirmed the District Court. The court, also interpreting Wisconsin law to prohibit stacking,[6] ap-

---

3. Ralph Hague paid a separate premium for each automobile including an additional separate premium for each uninsured motorist coverage.

6. Respondent has suggested that this case presents a "false conflict." The court below rejected this contention and applied Minnesota law. Even though the Minnesota Supreme Court's choice of Minnesota law followed a discussion of whether this case presents a false conflict, the fact is that the court chose to apply Minnesota law. Thus, the only question before this Court is whether that choice was constitutional.

plied Minnesota law after analyzing the relevant Minnesota contacts and interests within the analytical framework developed by Professor Leflar. . . .[7] Although stating that the Minnesota contacts might not be, "in themselves, sufficient to mandate application of [Minnesota] law,"[8] under the first four factors, the court concluded that the fifth factor—application of the better rule of law—favored selection of Minnesota law. The court emphasized that a majority of States allow stacking and that legal decisions allowing stacking "are fairly recent and well considered in light of current uses of automobiles." In addition, the court found the Minnesota rule superior to Wisconsin's "because it requires the cost of accidents with uninsured motorists to be spread more broadly through insurance premiums than does the Wisconsin rule." Finally, after rehearing en banc, the court buttressed its initial opinion by indicating "that contracts of insurance on motor vehicles are in a class by themselves" since an insurance company "knows the automobile is a movable item which will be driven from state to state." From this premise the court concluded that application of Minnesota law was "not so arbitrary and unreasonable as to violate due process."

II

It is not for this Court to say whether the choice-of-law analysis suggested by Professor Leflar is to be preferred or whether we would make the same choice-of-law decision if sitting as the Minnesota Supreme Court. Our sole function is to determine whether the Minnesota Supreme Court's choice of its own substantive law in this case exceeded federal constitutional limitations. Implicit in this inquiry is the recognition, long accepted by this Court, that a set of facts giving rise to a lawsuit, or a particular issue within a lawsuit, may justify, in constitutional terms, application of the law of more than one jurisdiction. *See, e.g.*, Watson v. Employers Liability Assurance Corp. *See generally* Clay v. Sun Insurance Office, Ltd. (hereinafter cited as *Clay II*). As a result, the forum State may have to select one law from among the laws of several jurisdictions having some contact with the controversy.

In deciding constitutional choice-of-law questions, whether under the Due Process Clause or the Full Faith and Credit Clause,[10] this Court has traditionally examined the contacts of the State, whose law was applied, with

---

7. Minnesota had previously adopted the conceptual model developed by Professor Leflar in Milkovich v. Saari [page 282 *supra*].

8. The court apparently was referring to sufficiency as a matter of choice of law and not as a matter of constitutional limitation on its choice-of-law decision.

10. This Court has taken a similar approach in deciding choice-of-law cases under both the Due Process Clause and the Full Faith and Credit Clause. In each instance, the Court has examined the relevant contacts and resulting interests of the State whose law was applied. *See, e.g.*, Nevada v. Hall [*infra* page 454]. Although at one time the Court required a more exacting standard under the Full Faith and Credit Clause than under the Due Process Clause for

the parties and with the occurrence or transaction giving rise to the litigation. *See Clay II, supra.* In order to ensure that the choice of law is neither arbitrary nor fundamentally unfair, *see* Alaska Packers Assn. v. Industrial Accident Commn., the Court has invalidated the choice of law of a State which has had no significant contact or significant aggregation of contacts, creating state interests, with the parties and the occurrence or transaction.[11]

Two instructive examples of such invalidation are Home Ins. Co. v. Dick, and John Hancock Mutual Life Ins. Co. v. Yates. In both cases, the selection of forum law rested exclusively on the presence of one nonsignificant forum contact. [The Court describes the facts and holding of *Dick.*]

The relationship of the forum State to the parties and the transaction was similarly attenuated in John Hancock Mutual Life Ins. Co. v. Yates. There, the insurer, a Massachusetts corporation, issued a contract of insurance on the life of a New York resident. The contract was applied for, issued, and delivered in New York where the insured and his spouse resided. After the insured died in New York, his spouse moved to Georgia and brought suit on the policy in Georgia. Under Georgia law, the jury was permitted to take into account oral modifications when deciding whether an insurance policy application contained material misrepresentations. Under New York law, however, such misrepresentations were to be evaluated solely on the basis of the written application. The Georgia court applied Georgia law. This Court reversed, finding application of Georgia law to be unconstitutional.

Dick and *Yates* stand for the proposition that if a State has only an insignificant contact with the parties and the occurrence or transaction, ap-

---

evaluating the constitutionality of choice-of-law decisions, *see* Alaska Packers Assn. v. Industrial Accident Commn. (interest of State whose law was applied was no less than interest of State whose law was rejected), the Court has since abandoned the weighting-of-interests requirement. Carrol v. Lanza; *see* Nevada v. Hall, *supra;* Weintraub, Due Process and Full Faith and Credit Limitations on a State's Choice of Law, 44 Iowa L. Rev. 449 (1959). Different considerations are of course at issue when full faith and credit is to be accorded to acts, records, and proceedings outside the choice-of-law area, such as in the case of sister state-court judgments.

11. Prior to the advent of interest analysis in the state courts as the "dominant mode of analysis in modern choice of law theory," the prevailing choice-of-law methodology focused on the jurisdiction where a particular event occurred. . . .

Hartford Accident & Indemnity Co. v. Delta & Pine Land Co. can, perhaps, best be explained as an example of that period. In that case, the Court struck down application by the Mississippi courts of Mississippi law which voided the limitations provision in a fidelity bond written in Tennessee between a Connecticut insurer and Delta, both of which were doing business in Tennessee and Mississippi. By its terms, the bond covered misapplication of funds "by an employee in any position, anywhere. . . ." After Delta discovered defalcations by one of its Mississippi-based employees, a lawsuit was commenced in Mississippi.

That case, however, has scant relevance for today. It implied a choice-of-law analysis which, for all intents and purposes, gave an isolated event—the writing of the bond in Tennessee—controlling constitutional significance, even though there might have been contacts with another State (here Mississippi) which would make application of its law neither unfair nor unexpected.

plication of its law is unconstitutional. *Dick* concluded that nominal residence—standing alone—was inadequate; *Yates* held that a post-occurrence change of residence to the forum State—standing alone—was insufficient to justify application of forum law. Although instructive as extreme examples of selection of forum law, neither *Dick* or *Yates* governs this case. For in contrast to those decisions, here the Minnesota contacts with the parties and the occurrence are obviously significant. Thus, this case is like *Alaska Packers* . . . and *Clay II*—cases where this Court sustained choice-of-law decisions based on the contacts of the State, whose law was applied, with the parties and occurrence.

The lesson from *Dick* and *Yates,* which found insufficient forum contacts to apply forum law, and from *Alaska Packers* . . . and *Clay II,* which found adequate contacts to sustain the choice of forum law, is that for a State's substantive law to be selected in a constitutionally permissible manner, that State must have a significant contact or significant aggregation of contacts, creating state interest, such that choice of its law is neither arbitrary nor fundamentally unfair. Application of this principle to the facts of this case persuades us that the Minnesota Supreme Court's choice of its own law did not offend the Federal Constitution.

III

Minnesota has three contacts with the parties and the occurrence giving rise to the litigation. In the aggregate, these contacts permit selection by the Minnesota Supreme Court of Minnesota law allowing the stacking of Mr. Hague's uninsured motorist coverages.

First, and for our purposes a very important contact, Mr. Hague was a member of Minnesota's work force, having been employed by a Red Wing, Minn., enterprise for the 15 years preceding his death. While employment status may implicate a state interest less substantial than does resident status, that interest is nevertheless important. The State of employment has police power responsibilities towards the nonresident employee that are analogous, if somewhat less profound, than towards residents. Thus, such employees use state services and amenities and may call upon state facilities in appropriate circumstances.

In addition, Mr. Hague commuted to work in Minnesota . . . , and was presumably covered by his uninsured motorist coverage during the commute. The State's interest in its commuting nonresident employees reflects a state concern for the safety and well-being of its work force and the concomitant effect on Minnesota employers.

That Mr. Hague was not killed while commuting to work or while in Minnesota does not dictate a different result. To hold that the Minnesota Supreme Court's choice of Minnesota law violated the Constitution for that reason would require too narrow a view of Minnesota's relationship with the parties and the occurrence giving rise to the litigation. An automobile accident need not occur within a particular jurisdiction for that jurisdiction to be connected to the occurrence.

Similarly, the occurrence of a crash fatal to a Minnesota employee in another State is a Minnesota contact. If Mr. Hague had only been injured and missed work for a few weeks, the effect on the Minnesota employer would have been palpable and Minnesota's interest in having its employee made whole would be evident. Mr. Hague's death affects Minnesota's interest still more acutely, even though Mr. Hague will not return to the Minnesota work force. Minnesota's work force is surely affected by the level of protection the State extends to it, either directly or indirectly. Vindication of the rights of the estate of a Minnesota employee, therefore, is an important state concern.

Mr. Hague's residence in Wisconsin does not—as Allstate seems to argue—constitutionally mandate application of Wisconsin law to the exclusion of forum law. If, in the instant case, the accident had occurred in Minnesota between Mr. Hague and an uninsured Minnesota motorist, if the insurance contract had been executed in Minnesota covering a Minnesota registered company automobile which Mr. Hague was permitted to drive, and if a Wisconsin court sought to apply Wisconsin law, certainly Mr. Hague's residence in Wisconsin, his commute between Wisconsin and Minnesota, and the insurer's presence in Wisconsin should be adequate to apply Wisconsin's law.[22] Employment status is not a sufficiently less important status than residence, when combined with Mr. Hague's daily commute across state lines and the other Minnesota contacts present, to prohibit the choice-of-law result in this case on constitutional grounds.

Second, Allstate was at all times present and doing business in Minnesota. By virtue of its presence, Allstate can hardly claim unfamiliarity with

---

22. Of course Allstate could not be certain that Wisconsin law would necessarily govern any accident which occurred in Wisconsin, whether brought in the Wisconsin courts or elsewhere. Such an expectation would give controlling significance to the wooden lex loci delicti doctrine. While the place of the accident is a factor to be considered in choice-of-law analysis, to apply blindly the traditional, but now largely abandoned, doctrine, would fail to distinguish between the relative importance of various legal issues involved in a lawsuit as well as the relationship of other jurisdictions to the parties and the occurrence or transaction. If, for example, Mr. Hague had been a Wisconsin resident and employee who was injured in Wisconsin and was then taken by ambulance to a hospital in Red Wing, Minn., where he languished for several weeks before dying, Minnesota's interest in ensuring that its medical creditors were paid would be obvious. Moreover, under such circumstances, the accident itself might be reasonably characterized as a bistate occurrence beginning in Wisconsin and ending in Minnesota. Thus, reliance by the insurer that Wisconsin law would necessarily govern any accident that occurred in Wisconsin, or that the law of another jurisdiction would necessarily govern any accident that did not occur in Wisconsin, would be unwarranted. *See* n.11, *supra*.

If the law of a jurisdiction other than Wisconsin did govern, there was a substantial likelihood, with respect to uninsured motorist coverage, that stacking would be allowed. Stacking was the rule in most States at the time the policy was issued. . . .

the laws of the host jurisdiction and surprise that the state courts might apply forum law to litigation in which the company is involved. "Particularly since the company was licensed to do business in [the forum], it must have known it might be sued there, and that [the forum] courts would feel bound by [forum] law."[24] Clay v. Sun Insurance Offices Ltd. (Black, J., dissenting). Moreover, Allstate's presence in Minnesota gave Minnesota an interest in regulating the company's insurance obligations insofar as they affected both a Minnesota resident and court-appointed representative—respondent—and a long-standing member of Minnesota's work force—Mr. Hague.

Third, respondent became a Minnesota resident prior to institution of this litigation. The stipulation facts reveal that she first settled in Red Wing, Minn., the town in which her late husband had worked. She subsequently moved to Savage, Minn., after marrying a Minnesota resident who operated an automobile service station in Bloomington, Minn. Her move to Savage occurred "almost concurrently," with the initiation of the instant case. There is no suggestion that Mrs. Hague moved to Minnesota in anticipation of this litigation or for the purpose of finding a legal climate especially hospitable to her claim.[28] The stipulated facts, sparse as they are, negate any such inference.

While John Hancock Mutual Life Ins. Co. v. Yates held that a post-occurrence change of residence to the forum State was insufficient in and of itself to confer power on the forum State to choose its law, that case did not hold that such a change of residence was irrelevant. Here, of course, respondent's bona fide residence in Minnesota was not the sole contact Minnesota had with this litigation. And in connection with her residence in Minnesota, respondent was appointed personal representative of Mr. Hague's estate by the Registrar of Probate for the County of Goodhue, Minn. Respondent's residence and subsequent appointment in Minnesota as personal representative of her late husband's estate constitute a Minnesota contact which gives Minnesota an interest in respondent's recovery, an interest which the court below identified as full compensation for "resident accident victims" to keep them "off welfare rolls" and able "to meet financial obligations."

---

24. There is no element of unfair surprise or frustration of legitimate expectations as a result of Minnesota's choice of its law. Because Allstate was doing business in Minnesota, and was undoubtedly aware that Mr. Hague was a Minnesota employee, it had to have anticipated that Minnesota law might apply to an accident in which Mr. Hague was involved. Indeed, Allstate specifically anticipated that Mr. Hague might suffer an accident either in Minnesota or elsewhere in the United States, outside of Wisconsin, since the policy it issued offered continental coverage. At the same time, Allstate did not seek to control construction of the contract since the policy contained no choice-of-law clause dictating application of Wisconsin law.

28. The dissent suggests that considering respondent's postoccurrence change of residence as one of the Minnesota contacts will encourage forum shopping. This overlooks the fact that her change of residence was bona fide and not motivated by litigation considerations.

In sum, Minnesota had a significant aggregation[29] of contacts with the parties and the occurrence, creating state interests, such that application of its law was neither arbitrary nor fundamentally unfair. Accordingly, the choice of Minnesota law by the Minnesota Supreme Court did not violate the Due Process Clause or the Full Faith and Credit Clause.

Affirmed.

Justice STEWART took no part in the consideration or decision of this case.

Justice STEVENS, concurring in the judgment.

As I view this unusual case—in which neither precedent nor constitutional language provides sure guidance—two separate questions must be answered. First, does the Full Faith and Credit Clause *require* Minnesota, the forum State, to apply Wisconsin law? Second, does the Due Process Clause of the Fourteenth Amendment *prevent* Minnesota from applying its own law? The first inquiry implicates the federal interest in ensuring that Minnesota respect the sovereignty of the State of Wisconsin; the second implicates the litigants' interest in a fair adjudication of their rights.[3]

I realize that both this court's analysis of clause questions and scholarly criticism of those decisions have treated these two inquiries as though they were indistinguishable. Nevertheless, I am persuaded that the two constitutional provisions protect different interests and that proper analysis requires separate consideration of each.

I

The Full Faith and Credit Clause is one of several provisions in the Federal Constitution designed to transform the several States from independent sovereignties into a single, unified Nation. The Full Faith and Credit Clause implements this design by directing that a State, when acting as the forum

29. We express no view whether the first two contacts, either together or separately, would have sufficed to sustain the choice of Minnesota law made by the Minnesota Supreme Court.

3. The two questions presented by the choice-of-law issue arise only after it is assumed or established that the defendant's contacts with the forum State are sufficient to support personal jurisdiction. Although the choice-of-law concerns—respect for another sovereign and fairness to the litigants—are similar to the two functions performed by the jurisdictional inquiry, they are not identical. In World-Wide Volkswagen Corp. v. Woodson, 444 U.S. 286, 291–292 (1980), we stated: "The concept of minimum contacts, in turn, can be seen to perform two related, but distinguishable, functions. It protects the defendant against the burdens of litigating in a distant or inconvenient forum. And it acts to ensure that the States, through their courts, do not reach out beyond the limits imposed on them by their status as coequal sovereigns in a federal system." While it has been suggested that this same minimum-contacts analysis be used to define the constitutional limitations on choice of law, the Court has made it clear over the years that the personal jurisdiction and choice-of-law inquiries are not the same. *See* Kulko v. California Superior Court; Shaffer v. Heitner; Hanson v. Denckla.

for litigation having multistate aspects or implications, respect the legitimate interests of other States and avoid infringement upon their sovereignty. The Clause does not, however, rigidly require the forum State to apply foreign law whenever another State has a valid interest in the litigation. On the contrary, in view of the fact that the forum State is also a sovereign in its own right, in appropriate cases it may attach paramount importance to its own legitimate interests. Accordingly, the fact that a choice-of-law decision may be unsound as a matter of conflicts law does not necessarily implicate the federal concerns embodied in the Full Faith and Credit Clause. Rather, in my opinion, the Clause should not invalidate a state court's choice of forum law unless that choice threatens the federal interest in national unity by unjustifiably infringing upon the legitimate interests of another State.

In this case, I think the Minnesota courts' decision to apply Minnesota law was plainly unsound as a matter of normal conflicts law. Both the execution of the insurance contract and the accident giving rise to the litigation took place in Wisconsin. Moreover, when both of those events occurred, the plaintiff, the decedent, and the operators of both vehicles were all residents of Wisconsin. Nevertheless, I do not believe that any threat to national unity or Wisconsin's sovereignty ensues from allowing the substantive question presented by this case to be determined by the law of another State.

The question on the merits is one of interpreting the meaning of the insurance contract. Neither the contract itself, nor anything else in the record, reflects any express understanding of the parties with respect to what law would be applied or with respect to whether the separate uninsured motorist coverage for each of the decedent's three cars could be "stacked." Since the policy provided coverage for accidents that might occur in other States, it was obvious to the parties at the time of contracting that it might give rise to the application of the law of States other than Wisconsin. Therefore, while Wisconsin may have an interest in ensuring that contracts formed in Wisconsin in reliance upon Wisconsin law are interpreted in accordance with that law, that interest is not implicated in this case.

Petitioner has failed to establish that Minnesota's refusal to apply Wisconsin law poses any direct or indirect threat to Wisconsin's sovereignty.[13] In the absence of any such threat, I find it unnecessary to evaluate the forum State's interest in the litigation in order to reach the conclusion that the Full Faith and Credit Clause does not require the Minnesota courts to apply Wisconsin law to the question of contract interpretation presented in this case.

---

13. . . . It is . . . clear that a state court's decision to apply its own law cannot violate the Full Faith and Credit Clause where the application of forum law does not impinge at all upon the interests of other States.

II

It may be assumed that a choice-of-law decision would violate the Due Process Clause if it were totally arbitrary or if it were fundamentally unfair to either litigant. I question whether a judge's decision to apply the law of his own State could ever be described as wholly irrational. For judges are presumably familiar with their own state law and may find it difficult and time consuming to discover and apply correctly the law of another State. The forum State's interest in the fair and efficient administration of justice is therefore sufficient, in my judgment, to attach a presumption of validity to a forum State's decision to apply its own law to a dispute over which it has jurisdiction.

The forum State's interest in the efficient operation of its judicial system is clearly not sufficient, however, to justify the application of a rule of law that is fundamentally unfair to one of the litigants. Arguably, a litigant could demonstrate such unfairness in a variety of ways. Concern about the fairness of the forum's choice of its own rule might arise if that rule favored residents over nonresidents, if it represented a dramatic departure from the rule that obtains in most American jurisdictions, or if the rule itself was unfair on its face or as applied.[15]

The application of an otherwise acceptable rule of law may result in unfairness to the litigants if, in engaging in the activity which is the subject of the litigation, they could not reasonably have anticipated that their actions would later be judged by this rule of law. A choice-of-law decision that frustrates the justifiable expectations of the parties can be fundamentally unfair. This desire to prevent unfair surprise to a litigant has been the central concern in this Court's review of choice-of-law decisions under the Due Process Clause.[16]

Neither the "stacking" rule itself, nor Minnesota's application of that rule to these litigants, raises any serious questions of fairness. As the plurality observes, "[s]tacking was the rule in most States at the time the policy was issued." Moreover, the rule is consistent with the economics of a contractual relationship in which the policyholder paid three separate premiums for insurance coverage for three automobiles, including a separate premium for each uninsured motorist coverage. Nor am I persuaded that the decision of the Minnesota courts to apply the "stacking" rule in this case can be said

15. Discrimination against nonresidents would be constitutionally suspect even if the Due Process Clause were not a check upon a State's choice-of-law decisions. Moreover, both discriminatory and substantively unfair rules of law may be detected and remedied without any special choice-of-law analysis; familiar constitutional principles are available to deal with both varieties of unfairness.

16. Upon careful analysis, most of the decisions of this Court that struck down on due process grounds a state court's choice of forum can be explained as attempts to prevent a State with a minimal contact with the litigation from materially enlarging the contractual obligations of one of the parties where that party had no reason to anticipate the possibility of such enlargement.

to violate due process because that decision frustrates the reasonable expectations of the contracting parties.

Contracting parties can, of course, make their expectations explicit by providing in their contract either that the law of a particular jurisdiction shall govern questions of contract interpretation, or that a particular substantive rule, for instance "stacking," shall or shall not apply.[20] In the absence of such express provisions, the contract nonetheless may implicitly reveal the expectations of the parties. For example, if a liability insurance policy issued by a resident of a particular State provides coverage only with respect to accidents within that State, it is reasonable to infer that the contracting parties expected that their obligations under the policy would be governed by that State's law.

In this case, no express indication of the parties' expectations is available. The insurance policy provided coverage for accidents throughout the United States; thus, at the time of contracting, the parties certainly could have anticipated that the laws of States other than Wisconsin would govern particular claims arising under the policy. By virtue of doing business in Minnesota, Allstate was aware that it could be sued in the Minnesota courts; Allstate also presumably was aware that Minnesota law, as well as the law of most States, permitted "stacking." Nothing in the record requires that a different inference be drawn. Therefore, the decision of the Minnesota courts to apply the law of the forum in this case does not frustrate the reasonable expectations of the contracting parties, and I can find no fundamental unfairness in that decision requiring the attention of this Court.[23]

---

20. . . . While such express provisions are obviously relevant, they are not always dispositive. In Clay v. Sun Insurance Office, Ltd., the Court allowed the lower court's choice of forum law to override an express contractual limitations period. The Court emphasized the fact that the insurer had issued the insurance policy with the knowledge that it would cover the insured property wherever it was taken. *Id.*, at 181-182. The Court also noted that the insurer had not attempted to provide in the policy that the law of another State would control. *Id.*, at 182.

In Watson v. Employers Liability Assurance Corp., the insurance policy expressly provided that an injured party could not maintain a direct action against the insurer until after the insured's liability had been determined. The Court found that neither the Due Process Clause nor the Full Faith and Credit Clause prevented the Louisiana courts from applying forum law to permit a direct action against the insurer prior to determination of the insured's liability. As in *Clay*, the Court noted that the policy provided coverage for injuries anywhere in the United States. . . .

23. Comparison of this case with Home Ins. Co. v. Dick, confirms my conclusion that the application of Minnesota law in this case does not offend the Due Process Clause. In *Home Ins. Co.*, the contract expressly provided that a particular limitations period would govern claims arising under the insurance contract and that Mexican law was to be applied in interpreting the contracts; in addition, the contract was limited in effect to certain Mexican waters. The parties could hardly have made their expectations with respect to the applicable law more plain. In this case, by way of contrast, nothing in the contract suggests that Wisconsin law should be applied or that Minnesota's "stacking" rule should not be applied. In this case, unlike *Home Ins. Co.*, the court's choice of forum law results in no unfair surprise to the insurer.

In terms of fundamental fairness, it seems to me that two factors relied upon by the plurality—the plaintiff's post-accident move to Minnesota and the decedent's Minnesota employment—are either irrelevant to or possibly even tend to undermine the plurality's conclusions. When the expectations of the parties at the time of contracting are the central due process concern, as they are in this case, an unanticipated post-accident occurrence is clearly irrelevant for due process purposes. The fact that the plaintiff became a resident of the forum State after the accident surely cannot justify a ruling in her favor that would not be made if the plaintiff were a nonresident. Similarly, while the fact that the decedent regularly drove into Minnesota might be relevant to the expectations of the contracting parties,[24] the fact that he did so because he was employed in Minnesota adds nothing to the due process analysis. The choice-of-law decision of the Minnesota courts is consistent with due process because it does not result in unfairness to either litigant, not because Minnesota now has an interest in the plaintiff as resident or formerly had an interest in the decedent as employee.

III

Although I regard the Minnesota courts' decision to apply forum law as unsound as a matter of conflicts law, and there is little in this record other than the presumption in favor of the forum's own law to support that decision, I concur in the plurality's judgment. It is not this Court's function to establish and impose upon state courts a federal choice-of-law rule, nor is it our function to ensure that state courts correctly apply whatever choice-of-law rules they have themselves adopted.[25] Our authority may be exercised in the choice-of-law area only to prevent a violation of the Full Faith and Credit or the Due Process Clause. For the reasons stated above, I find no such violation in this case.

---

24. Even this factor may not be of substantial significance. At the time of contracting, the parties were aware that the insurance policy was effective throughout the United States and that the law of any State, including Minnesota, might be applicable to particular claims. The fact that the decedent regularly drove to Minnesota, for whatever purpose, is relevant only to the extent that it affected the parties' evaluation, at the time of contracting, of the likelihood that Minnesota law would actually be applied at some point in the future. However, because the applicability of Minnesota law was perceived as possible at the time of contracting, it does not seem especially significant for due process purposes that the parties may also have considered it likely that Minnesota law would be applied. This factor merely reinforces the expectation revealed by the policy's national coverage.

25. In Kryger v. Wilson, after rejecting a due process challenge to a state court's choice of law, the Court stated: "The most that the plaintiff in error can say is that the state court made a mistaken application of doctrines of the conflict of laws in deciding that the cancellation of a land contract is governed by the law of the situs instead of the place of making and performance. But that, being purely a question of local common law, is a matter with which this court is not concerned."

Justice POWELL, with whom THE CHIEF JUSTICE and Justice REHNQUIST join, dissenting.

My disagreement with the plurality is narrow. I accept with few reservations Part II of the plurality opinion, which sets forth the basic principles that guide us in reviewing state choice-of-law decisions under the Constitution. The Court should invalidate a forum State's decision to apply its own law only when there are no significant contacts between the State and the litigation. This modest check on state power is mandated by the Due Process Clause of the Fourteenth Amendment and the Full Faith and Credit Clause of Art. IV, §1. I do not believe, however, that the plurality adequately analyzes the policies such review must serve. In consequence, it has found significant what appear to me to be trivial contacts between the forum State and the litigation.

I

. . . The significance of asserted contacts must be evaluated in light of the constitutional policies that oversight by this Court should serve. Two enduring policies emerge from our cases.

First, the contacts between the forum State and the litigation should not be so "slight and casual" that it would be fundamentally unfair to a litigant for the forum to apply its own State's law. Clay v. Sun Ins. Office, Ltd. The touchstone here is the reasonable expectation of the parties.

Second, the forum State must have a legitimate interest in the outcome of the litigation before it. Pacific Ins. Co. v. Industrial Accident Commn. The Full Faith and Credit Clause addresses the accommodation of sovereign power among the various States. Under limited circumstances, it requires one State to give effect to the statutory law of another State. To be sure, a forum State need not give effect to another State's law if that law is in "violation of its own legitimate public policy." Nonetheless, for a forum State to further its legitimate public policy by applying its own law to a controversy, there must be some connection between the facts giving rise to the litigation and the scope of the State's lawmaking jurisdiction.

Both the Due Process and Full Faith and Credit Clause ensure that the States do not "reach out beyond the limits imposed on them by their status as coequal sovereigns in a federal system." World-Wide Volkswagen Corp. v. Woodson (addressing Fourteenth Amendment limitation on state-court jurisdiction). As the Court stated in *Pacific Ins. Co., supra:* "[T]he full faith and credit clause does not require one state to substitute for its own statute, *applicable to persons and events within it,* the conflicting statute of another state." (Emphasis added.) The State has a legitimate interest in applying a rule of decision to the litigation only if the facts to which the rule will be applied have created effects within the State, toward which the State's public policy is directed. To assess the sufficiency of asserted contacts between the forum and the litigation, the court must determine if the contacts form a reasonable link between the litigation and a state policy. In short, examination of contacts addresses whether "the state has an interest in the application of its policy in this instance." Currie, The Constitution and the Choice of Law: Governmental Interests and the Judicial Function, in B. Currie, Selected Essays on the Conflict of Laws 188, 189 (1963). If it does, the Constitution is satisfied.

In summary, the significance of the contacts between a forum State and the litigation must be assessed in light of these two important constitutional policies.[3] A contact, or a pattern of contacts, satisfies the Constitution when it protects the litigants from being unfairly surprised if the forum State applies its own law, and when the application of the forum's law reasonably can be understood to further a legitimate public policy of the forum State.

II

Recognition of the complexity of the constitutional inquiry requires that this Court apply these principles with restraint. Applying these principles to the facts of this case, I do not believe, however, that Minnesota had sufficient contacts with the "persons and events" in this litigation to apply its rule permitting stacking. I would agree that no reasonable expectations of the parties were frustrated. The risk insured by petitioner was not geographically limited. The close proximity of Hager City, Wis., to Minnesota, and the fact that Hague commuted daily to Red Wing, Minn., for many years should have led the insurer to realize that there was a reasonable probability that the risk would materialize in Minnesota. Under our precedents, it is plain that Minnesota could have applied its own law to an accident occurring within its borders. The fact that the accident did not, in fact, occur in Minnesota is not controlling because the expectations of the litigants *before* the cause of action accrues provide the pertinent perspective.

The more doubtful question in this case is whether application of Minnesota's substantive law reasonably furthers a legitimate state interest. The plurality attempts to give substance to the tenuous contacts between Minnesota and this litigation. Upon examination, however, these contacts are either trivial or irrelevant to the furthering of any public policy of Minnesota.

3. The plurality today apparently recognizes that the significance of the contacts must be evaluated in light of the policies our review serves. It acknowledges that the sufficiency of the same contacts sometimes will differ in jurisdiction and choice-of-law questions. The plurality, however, pursues the rationale for the requirement of sufficient contacts in choice-of-law cases no further than to observe that the forum's application of its own law must be "neither arbitrary nor fundamentally unfair." *Ante*, at 313. But this general prohibition does not distinguish questions of choice of law from those of jurisdiction, or from much of the jurisprudence of the Fourteenth Amendment.

First, the postaccident residence of the plaintiff-beneficiary is constitutionally irrelevant to the choice-of-law question. John Hancock Mut. Life Ins. Co. v. Yates, *supra.* The plurality today insists that *Yates* only held that a postoccurrence move to the forum State could not "in and of itself" confer power on the forum to apply its own law, but did not establish that such a change of residence was irrelevant. *Ante,* at 319. What the *Yates* court held, however, was that "there was no occurrence, *nothing* done, to which the law of Georgia could apply." (Emphasis added.) Any possible ambiguity in the Court's view of the significance of a postoccurrence change of residence is dispelled by Home Ins. Co. v. Dick, *supra,* cited by the *Yates* Court, where it was held squarely that Dick's postaccident move to the forum State was "without significance."

This rule is sound. If a plaintiff could choose the substantive rules to be applied to an action by moving to a hospitable forum, the invitation to forum shopping would be irresistible. Moreover, it would permit the defendant's reasonable expectations at the time the cause of action accrues to be frustrated, because it would permit the choice-of-law question to turn on a postaccrual circumstance. Finally, postaccrual residence has nothing to do with facts to which the forum State proposes to apply its rule; it is unrelated to the substantive legal issues presented by the litigation.

Second, the plurality finds it significant that the insurer does business in the forum State. The State does have a legitimate interest in regulating the practices of such an insurer. But this argument proves too much. The insurer here does business in all 50 States. The forum State has no interest in regulating that conduct of the insurer unrelated to property, persons, or contracts executed within the forum State. The plurality recognizes this flaw and attempts to bolster the significance of the local presence of the insurer by combining it with the other factors deemed significant: the presence of the plaintiff and the fact that the deceased worked in the forum State. This merely restates the basic question in the case.

Third, the plurality emphasizes particularly that the insured worked in the forum State.[5] The fact that the insured was a nonresident employee in the forum State provides a significant contact for the furtherance of some local policies. The insured's place of employment is not, however, significant in this case. Neither the nature of the insurance policy, the events related to the

5. The plurality exacts double service from this fact, by finding a separate contact in that the insured commuted daily to his job. *Ante,* at 314-315. This is merely a repetition of the facts that the insured lived in Wisconsin and worked in Minnesota. The State does have an interest in the safety of all motorists who use its roads. This interest is not limited to employees, but extends to all nonresident motorists on its highways. This safety interest, however, cannot encompass, either in logic or in any practical sense, the determination whether a nonresident's estate can stack benefit coverage in a policy written in another State regarding an accident that occurred on another State's roads. . . .

accident, nor the immediate question of stacking coverage are in any way affected or implicated by the insured's employment status. The plurality's opinion is understandably vague in explaining how trebling the benefits to be paid to the estate of a nonresident employee furthers any substantial state interest relating to employment. Minnesota does not wish its workers to die in automobile accidents, but permitting stacking will not further this interest. The substantive issue here is solely one of compensation, and whether the compensation provided by this policy is increased or not will have no relation to the State's employment policies or police power.

Neither taken separately nor in the aggregate do the contacts asserted by the plurality today indicate that Minnesota's application of its substantive rule in this case will further any legitimate state interest. The plurality focuses only on physical contacts vel non, and in doing so pays scant attention to the more fundamental reasons why our precedents require reasonable policy-related contacts in choice-of-law cases. Therefore, I dissent.

Questions and Comments

(1) How important is the fact that the decedent's connection with the state of Minnesota was an employment connection? Would frequent visits to a relative—or to a bar—be enough? How does a court determine which contacts create interests? One possibility is to ask whether there is a substantive connection between the law in question (here, the stacking rule) and the contact (here, the Minnesota employment). *See generally* Brilmayer, Legitimate Interests in Multistate Problems: As Between State and Federal Law, 79 Mich. L. Rev. 1315 (1981); Martin, The Constitution and Legislative Jurisdiction, 10 Hofstra L. Rev. 133 (1981).

(2) May *Hague* at least be cited for the proposition that there is no longer any difference between due process and full faith and credit analysis of choice-of-law problems? Both the plurality and the dissenting opinions maintain that position.

(3) Both the plurality and the dissent in *Hague* concede that if the accident had taken place in Minnesota, Minnesota's stacking rule would have been applicable without difficulty. The plurality uses that point to establish (since the place of the accident could just as easily have been Minnesota) that there was no unfair surprise. Why should the fact that an accident takes place in Minnesota allow Minnesota to apply its law to the relationship between the driver and his insurance company—a relationship entered into in Wisconsin and with virtually no Minnesota contacts? Although the Court allowed an in-state incident to affect an essentially out-of-state relationship in Clay v. Sun Insurance Office, Ltd. and Watson v. Employers Liability Assurance Corp., the issue in both those cases was far less devastating to the insurer: the amount of time given the insured to sue in *Clay* and the place of suit in *Watson.* Do those cases apply when the effect of imposing forum law is to triple liability?

(4) Under Justice Stevens's rationale, isn't it arguable that application of Wisconsin law would have been unconstitutional—first, on the grounds that it is different from the rule applicable in most states, and second on the grounds that it is substantively unfair? Notice that Justice Stevens's criteria do not turn in any way on the nexus between the state whose law is applied and the involved parties or activities. The constitutionality of applying Wisconsin law, in other words, cannot be shown under his theory by identifying events or people located within Wisconsin. Even an entirely Wisconsin dispute, litigated in Wisconsin, could not be decided under Wisconsin law if that rule was a "dramatic departure" or seemed "substantively unfair." Can this possibly be correct?

(5) In McCluney v. Jos. Schlitz Brewing Co., 649 F.2d 578 (8th Cir. 1981), the plaintiff had worked for the defendant brewing company in Missouri for many years. Eventually he was offered a promotion in the form of a transfer to North Carolina, and thereafter a promotion and transfer to corporate headquarters in Milwaukee, Wisconsin. In Milwaukee a dispute arose when the plaintiff insisted that his secretary also be transferred from North Carolina. His employment was terminated. He claimed that he had been fired; the company claimed that he had resigned. He demanded severance pay due one who has been fired, as well as a "service letter" required by Missouri statute. The company answered with a letter stating that he had resigned. He sued the company and in a trial court won (a) severance pay, (b) $1 in damages for violation of the service letter statute (for misstating the reasons for termination), and (c) $400,000 in punitive damages for violation of the Missouri service letter statute. The Court of Appeals reversed with respect to the second and third items, holding that, despite *Hague*, contacts were insufficient to allow Missouri to apply its own law to a contract of employment arising out of a promotion granted in North Carolina and implemented in Wisconsin. A dissent noted that it was not unreasonable to characterize the entire employment as arising out of a single contract, formed in Missouri, which though modified from time to time was still subject to the Missouri statute. It noted further that the contacts could be viewed as stronger than those in *Hague:* (1) not just employment in the forum (as in *Hague*) but employment by the defendant; (2) later domicile in Missouri by the defendant when he moved back to that state; and (3) substantial business transacted in Missouri by the defendant. (Ironically, the dissent argued that punitive damages were inappropriate, thereby reducing its dispute with the majority to item (b) above—actual damages of $1.)

The Supreme Court affirmed without opinion in *McCluney*, thus not explaining why the majority was right and the dissent was wrong, and not explaining in particular why the extensive contacts between the plaintiff's early employment and the state of Missouri were inadequate to support legislative jurisdiction. 454 U.S. 1071 (1981). Can any sense be made of the Court's disposition of *McCluney?* If the real rationale for affirmance was the fact that the dollar difference between the majority and dissent was only $1, would the better course have been to dismiss "for want of a substantial federal question"?

Phillips Petroleum Co. v. Shutts

472 U.S. 797 (1985)

REHNQUIST, J., delivered the opinion of the Court, in which BURGER, C.J., and BRENNAN, WHITE, MARSHALL, BLACKMUN and O'CONNOR, JJ., joined, and in Parts I and II of which STEVENS, J., joined. STEVENS, J., filed an opinion concurring in part and dissenting in part. POWELL, J., took no part in the decision of the case.

Justice REHNQUIST delivered the opinion of the Court.

Petitioner is a Delaware corporation which has its principal place of business in Oklahoma. During the 1970's it produced or purchased natural gas from leased land located in 11 different States, and sold most of the gas in interstate commerce. Respondents are some 28,000 of the royalty owners possessing rights to the leases from which petitioner produced the gas; they reside in all 50 States, the District of Columbia, and several foreign countries. Respondents brought a class action against petitioner in the Kansas state court, seeking to recover interest on royalty payments which had been delayed by petitioner. They recovered judgment in the trial court, and the Supreme Court of Kansas affirmed the judgment over petitioner's contentions that the Due Process Clause of the Fourteenth Amendment prevented Kansas from adjudicating the claims of all the respondents, and that the Due Process Clause and the Full Faith and Credit Clause of Article IV of the Constitution prohibited the application of Kansas law to all of the transactions between petitioner and respondents. 235 Kan. 195, 679 P.2d 1159 (1984). We granted certiorari to consider these claims. 469 U.S. 879 (1984). We reject petitioner's jurisdictional claim, but sustain its claim regarding the choice of law.

Because petitioner sold the gas to its customers in interstate commerce, it was required to secure approval for price increases from what was then the Federal Power Commission, and is now the Federal Energy Regulatory Commission. Under its regulations the Federal Power Commission permitted petitioner to propose and collect tentative higher gas prices, subject to final approval by the Commission. If the Commission eventually denied petitioner's proposed price increase or reduced the proposed increase, petitioner would have to refund to its customers the difference between the approved price and the higher price charged, plus interest at a rate set by statute.

Although petitioner received higher gas prices pending review by the Commission, petitioner suspended any increase in royalties paid to the royalty owners because the higher price could be subject to recoupment by petitioner's customers. Petitioner agreed to pay the higher royalty only if the royalty owners would provide petitioner with a bond or indemnity for the increase, plus interest, in case the price increase was not ultimately approved and a refund was due to the customers. Petitioner set the interest rate on the indemnity agreements at the same interest rate the Commission would have required petitioner to refund to its customers. A small percentage of the royalty owners provided this indemnity and received royalties immediately from the interim price increases; these royalty owners are unimportant to this case.

The remaining royalty owners received no royalty on the unapproved portion of the prices until the Federal Power Commission approval of those prices became final. . . .

Respondents Irl Shutts, Robert Anderson, and Betty Anderson filed suit against petitioner in Kansas state court, seeking interest payments on their suspended royalties which petitioner had possessed pending the Commission's approval of the price increases. Shutts is a resident of Kansas, and the Andersons live in Oklahoma. Shutts and the Andersons own gas leases in Oklahoma and Texas. Over petitioner's objection the Kansas trial court granted respondents' motion to certify the suit as a class action under Kansas law. Kan. Stat. Ann. §60-223 et seq. (1983). The class as certified was comprised of 33,000 royalty owners who had royalties suspended by petitioner. The average claim of each royalty owner for interest on the suspended royalties was $100.

After the class was certified respondents provided each class member with notice through first-class mail. The notice described the action and informed each class member that he could appear in person or by counsel; otherwise each member would be represented by Shutts and the Andersons, the named plaintiffs. The notices also stated that class members would be included in the class and bound by the judgment unless they "opted out" of the lawsuit by executing and returning a "request for exclusion" that was included with the notice. The final class as certified contained 28,100 members; 3,400 had "opted out" of the class by returning the request for exclusion, and notice could not be delivered to another 1,500 members, who were also excluded. Less than 1,000 of the class members resided in Kansas. Only a minuscule amount, approximately one quarter of one percent, of the gas leases involved in the lawsuit were on Kansas land.

After petitioner's mandamus petition to decertify the class was denied, the case was tried to the court. The court found petitioner liable under Kansas law for interest on the suspended royalties to all class members. The trial court relied heavily on an earlier, unrelated class action involving the same nominal plaintiff and the same defendant, Shutts, Executor v. Phillips Petroleum Co., 222 Kan. 527, 567 P.2d 1292 (1977), *cert. denied*, 434 U.S. 1068 (1978). The Kansas Supreme Court had held in *Shutts, Executor* that a gas company owed interest to royalty owners for royalties suspended pending final Commission approval of a price increase. No federal statutes touched on the liability for suspended royalties, and the court in *Shutts, Executor* held as a matter of Kansas equity law that the applicable interest rates for computation of interest on suspended royalties were the interest rates at which the gas company would have had to reimburse its customers had its interim price increase been rejected by the Commission. The court in *Shutts, Executor* viewed these as the fairest interest rates because they were also the rates that petitioner required the royalty owners to meet in their indemnity agreements in order to avoid suspended royalties.

The trial court in the present case applied the rule from *Shutts, Executor,* and held petitioner liable for prejudgment and postjudgment interest on the suspended royalties, computed at the Commission rates governing petitioner's three price increases. . . .

Petitioner raised two principal claims in its appeal to the Supreme Court of Kansas. It first asserted that the Kansas trial court did not possess personal jurisdiction over absent plaintiff class members as required by International Shoe Co. v. Washington, 326 U.S. 310 (1945), and similar cases. Related to this first claim was petitioner's contention that the "opt-out" notice to absent class members, which forced them to return the request for exclusion in order to avoid the suit, was insufficient to bind class members who were not residents of Kansas or who did not possess "minimum contacts" with Kansas. Second, petitioner claimed that Kansas courts could not apply Kansas law to every claim in the dispute. The trial court should have looked to the laws of each State where the leases were located to determine, on the basis of conflict of laws principles, whether interest on the suspended royalties was recoverable, and at what rate.

The Supreme Court of Kansas held that the entire cause of action was maintainable under the Kansas class-action statute, and the court rejected both of petitioner's claims. First, it held that the absent class members were plaintiffs, not defendants, and thus the traditional minimum contacts test of *International Shoe* did not apply. The court held that nonresident class-action plaintiffs were only entitled to adequate notice, an opportunity to be heard, an opportunity to opt out of the case, and adequate representation by the named plaintiffs. If these procedural due process minima were met, according to the court, Kansas could assert jurisdiction over the plaintiff class and bind each class member with a judgment on his claim. The court surveyed the course of the litigation and concluded that all of these minima had been met.

The court also rejected petitioner's contention that Kansas law could not be applied to plaintiffs and royalty arrangements having no connection with Kansas. The court stated that generally the law of the forum controlled all claims unless "compelling reasons" existed to apply a different law. The court found no compelling reasons, and noted that "[t]he plaintiff class members have indicated their desire to have this action determined under the laws of Kansas." . . .

[The Court's opinion as to personal jurisdiction can be found at page 473 *infra.*]

III

The Kansas courts applied Kansas contract and Kansas equity law to every claim in this case, notwithstanding that over 99 percent of the gas leases and some 97 percent of the plaintiffs in the case had no apparent connection to the State of Kansas except for this lawsuit. Petitioner protested that the Kansas courts should apply the laws of the States where the leases were located, or at least apply Texas and Oklahoma law because so many of the leases came from those States. The Kansas courts disregarded this contention and found petitioner liable for interest on the suspended royalties as a matter of Kansas law, and set the interest rates under Kansas equity principles.

Petitioner contends that total application of Kansas substantive law violated the constitutional limitations on choice of law mandated by the Due Process Clause of the Fourteenth Amendment and the Full Faith and Credit Clause of Article IV, §1. We must first determine whether Kansas law conflicts in any material way with any other law which could apply.

[The Court next discussed the difference between Kansas law and the law of other states on the issue of interest rates.]

The conflicts on the applicable interest rates, alone—which we do not think can be labeled "false conflicts" without a more thoroughgoing treatment than was accorded them by the Supreme Court of Kansas—certainly amounted to millions of dollars in liability. We think that the Supreme Court of Kansas erred in deciding on the basis that it did that the application of its laws to all claims would be constitutional.

Four Terms ago we addressed a similar situation in Allstate Ins. Co. v. Hague, 449 U.S. 302 (1981).

The plurality in *Allstate* noted that a particular set of facts giving rise to litigation could justify, constitutionally, the application of more than one jurisdiction's laws. The plurality recognized, however, that the Due Process Clause and the Full Faith and Credit Clause provided modest restrictions on the application of forum law. These restrictions required "that for a State's substantive law to be selected in a constitutionally permissible manner, that State must have a significant contact or significant aggregation of contacts, creating state interests, such that choice of its law is neither arbitrary nor fundamentally unfair." *Id.*, at 312-313. The dissenting Justices were in substantial agreement with this principle. *Id.*, at 332 (opinion of POWELL, J., joined by BURGER, C. J., and REHNQUIST, J.).

Petitioner owns property and conducts substantial business in the State, so Kansas certainly has an interest in regulating petitioner's conduct in Kansas. Moreover, oil and gas extraction is an important business to Kansas, and although only a few leases in issue are located in Kansas, hundreds of Kansas plaintiffs were affected by petitioner's suspension of royalties; thus the court held that the State has a real interest in protecting "the rights of these royalty owners both as individual residents of [Kansas] and as members of this particular class of plaintiffs." The Kansas Supreme Court pointed out that Kansas courts are quite familiar with this type of lawsuit, and "[t]he plaintiff class members have indicated their desire to have this action determined under the laws of Kansas." Finally, the Kansas court buttressed its use of Kansas law by stating that this lawsuit was analogous to a suit against a "common fund" located in Kansas.

We do not lightly discount this description of Kansas' contacts with this litigation and its interest in applying its law. There is, however, no "common fund" located in Kansas that would require or support the application of only Kansas law to all these claims. As the Kansas court noted, petitioner commingled the suspended royalties with its general corporate accounts. There is no specific identifiable res in Kansas, nor is there any limited amount which may be depleted before every plaintiff is compensated. Only by somehow aggregating all the separate claims in this case could a "common fund" in any sense be created, and the term becomes all but meaningless when used in such an expansive sense.

We also give little credence to the idea that Kansas law should apply to all claims because the plaintiffs, by failing to opt out, evinced their desire to be bound by Kansas law. Even if one could say that the plaintiffs "consented" to the application of Kansas law by not opting out, plaintiff's desire for forum law is rarely, if ever controlling. In most cases the plaintiff shows his obvious wish for forum law by filing there. "If a plaintiff could choose the substantive rules to be applied to an action . . . the invitation to forum shopping would be irresistible." *Allstate, supra,* at 337 (opinion of Powell, J.). Even if a plaintiff evidences his desire for forum law by moving to the forum, we have generally accorded such a move little or no significance. John Hancock Mut. Life Ins. Co. v. Yates, 299 U.S. 178, 182 (1936); Home Ins. Co. v. Dick, 281 U.S. 397, 408 (1930). In *Allstate* the plaintiff's move to the forum was only relevant because it was unrelated and prior to the litigation. 449 U.S., at 318-319. Thus the plaintiffs' desire for Kansas law, manifested by their participation in this Kansas lawsuit, bears little relevance.

The Supreme Court of Kansas in its opinion in this case expressed the view that by reason of the fact that it was adjudicating a nationwide class action, it had much greater latitude in applying its own law to the transactions in question than might otherwise be the case:

> The general rule is that the law of the forum applies unless it is expressly shown that a different law governs, and in case of doubt, the law of the forum is preferred. . . . Where a state court determines it has jurisdiction over a nationwide class action and procedural due process guarantees of notice and adequate representation are present, we believe the law of the forum should be applied unless compelling reasons exist for applying a different law. . . . Compelling reasons do not exist to require this court to look to other state laws to determine the rights of the parties involved in this lawsuit. 235 Kan., at 221-222, 679 P.2d, at 1181.

We think that this is something of a "bootstrap" argument. The Kansas class-action statute, like those of most other jurisdictions, requires that there be "common issues of law or fact." But while a State may, for the reasons we have previously stated, assume jurisdiction over the claims of plaintiffs whose principal contacts are with other States, it may not use this assumption of jurisdiction as an added weight in the scale when considering the permissible constitutional limits on choice of substantive law. It may not take a transaction with little or no relationship to the forum and apply the law of the forum in order to satisfy the procedural requirement that there be a "common question of law." The issue of personal jurisdiction over plaintiffs in a class action is entirely distinct from the question of the constitutional limitations on choice of law; the latter calculus is not altered by the fact that it may be more difficult or more burdensome to comply with the constitutional limitations because of the large number of transactions which the State proposes to adjudicate and which have little connection with the forum.

Kansas must have a "significant contact or significant aggregation of contacts" to the claims asserted by each member of the plaintiff class, contacts "creating state interests," in order to ensure that the choice of Kansas law is not arbitrary or unfair. *Allstate*, 449 U.S., at 312-313. Given Kansas' lack of "interest" in claims unrelated to that State, and the substantive conflict with jurisdictions such as Texas, we conclude that application of Kansas law to every claim in this case is sufficiently arbitrary and unfair as to exceed constitutional limits.

When considering fairness in this context, an important element is the expectation of the parties. *See Allstate, supra,* at 333 (opinion of Powell, J.). There is no indication that when the leases involving land and royalty owners outside of Kansas were executed, the parties had any idea that Kansas law would control. Neither the Due Process Clause nor the Full Faith and Credit Clause requires Kansas "to substitute for its own [laws], applicable to persons and events within it, the conflicting statute of another state," Pacific Employees Ins. Co. v. Industrial Accident Comm'n, 306 U.S. 493, 502 (1939), but Kansas "may not abrogate the rights of parties beyond its borders having no relation to anything done or to be done within them." Home Ins. Co. v. Dick, *supra,* at 410.

Here the Supreme Court of Kansas took the view that in a nationwide class action where procedural due process guarantees of notice and adequate representation were met, "the law of the forum should be applied unless compelling reasons exist for applying a different law." Whatever practical reasons may have commended this rule to the Supreme Court of Kansas, for the reasons already stated we do not believe that it is consistent with the decisions of this Court. We make no effort to determine for ourselves which law must apply to the various transactions involved in this lawsuit, and we reaffirm our observation in *Allstate* that in many situations a state court may be free to apply one of several choices of law. But the constitutional limitations laid down in cases such as *Allstate* and Home Ins. Co. v. Dick, *supra,* must be respected even in a nationwide class action. . . .

Justice POWELL took no part in the decision of this case.

Justice STEVENS, concurring in part and dissenting in part. . . .

As the Court recognizes, there "can be no [constitutional] injury in applying Kansas law if it is not in conflict with that of any other jurisdiction connected to this suit." *Ante*, at 816. A fair reading of the Kansas Supreme Court's opinion in light of its earlier opinion in Shutts v. Phillips Petroleum Co., (hereinafter *Shutts I*), reveals that the Kansas court has examined the laws of connected jurisdictions and has correctly concluded that there is no "direct" or "substantive" conflict between the law applied by Kansas and the laws of those other States. Kansas has merely developed general common-law principles to accommodate the novel facts of this litigation—other state courts either agree with Kansas or have not yet addressed precisely similar claims. Consequently, I conclude that the Full Faith and Credit Clause of the Constitution did not require Kansas to apply the law of any other State, and the Fourteenth Amendment's Due Process Clause did not prevent Kansas from applying its own law in this case.

Questions and Comments

(1) The Court noted Phillips owned property and conducted substantial business in Kansas and concluded that therefore Kansas had an interest in regulating its conduct in Kansas. Why only in Kansas? Recall that in Allstate v. Hague, the plurality relied upon Allstate's unrelated business in the forum to justify imposition of forum law to a claim arising outside the forum. Why not do the same here?

(2) Does *Shutts* say anything new about the standard for applying forum law, or does it merely say that the forum may not automatically apply its own law? What guidance has been given to the court below on remand?

(3) Whose expectations is the Court referring to? If it is the defendant's, wasn't this answered in Allstate v. Hague, where the Court said that doing unrelated business in the forum should have made Allstate Insurance familiar with forum law and able to anticipate its application? The plaintiffs, on the other hand, are unlikely to complain about unfair surprise if Kansas law is applied; they actually *prefer* Kansas law. Moreover, are they any more likely to be surprised than Lavinia Hague was in *Allstate?*

(4) Even as to those plaintiffs that might claim the benefits of Kansas law—those with a Kansas oil lease, say—it is nevertheless conceivable that some other law would be more advantageous still. Assume, for instance, that Smith owns an oil lease executed at her home in Alaska and Alaskan law is even more generous to her. If Alaska would apply its law to her, and could do so constitutionally, then it is not to her advantage to be a member of the Kansas class. Doesn't it pose formidable problems of adequacy of representation, however, to bring an absent plaintiff into a class action that is against her interest? But how can a court determine where each particular plaintiff could get the best deal, without knowing plaintiff's contacts with all 50 states and performing detailed alternative choice-of-law analyses? Should a court merely notify potential class members of this possibility and suggest that each contact a lawyer?

(5) We still seem to know very little about what contacts would constitutionally justify application of forum law under the modern learning. Some academic writers continue to claim that the Court has adopted governmental interest analysis. Shreve, Interest Analysis as Constitutional Law, 48 Ohio St. L.J. 51 (1987). Does *Shutts* support this?

Sun Oil Co. v. Wortman

486 U.S. 717 (1988)

Justice SCALIA delivered the opinion of the Court.

[This case is related to *Shutts, supra,* and the facts are similar. Respondents, owners of property in Texas, Oklahoma, and Louisiana sued Sun Oil Company, a Delaware Company with its principal place of business in Texas, in Kansas state court to recover interest on previously suspended gas royalties. The action was barred by the statute of limitations in Texas, Oklahoma, and Louisiana, but it fell within Kansas's longer five-year statute of limitations. The Kansas courts applied the Kansas statute of limitations and rejected arguments that doing so violated the full faith and credit and due process clauses. The Kansas courts also rejected the claim that it had so misconstrued the substantive laws of Texas, Oklahoma, and Louisiana as to violate the full faith and credit and due process clauses.]

II

This Court has long and repeatedly held that the Constitution does not bar application of the forum State's statute of limitations to claims that in their substance are and must be governed by the law of a different State. We granted certiorari to reexamine this issue. We conclude that our prior holdings are sound.

A

The Full Faith and Credit Clause provides:

> Full Faith and Credit shall be given in each State to the public Acts, Records, and judicial Proceedings of every other State. And the Congress may by general Laws prescribe the Manner in which such Acts, Records and Proceedings shall be proved, and the Effect thereof.

The Full Faith and Credit Clause does not compel "a state to substitute the statutes of other states for its own statutes dealing with a subject matter concerning which it is competent to legislate." Pacific Employers Ins. Co. v. Industrial Accident Commn., 306 U.S. 493, 501 (1939). Since the procedural rules of its courts are surely matters on which a State is competent to legislate, it follows that a State may apply its own procedural rules to actions litigated in its courts. The issue here, then, can be characterized as whether a statute of limitations may be considered as a procedural matter for purposes of the Full Faith and Credit Clause.

Petitioner initially argues that M'Elmoyle v. Cohen, *supra,* was wrongly decided when handed down. The holding of *M'Elmoyle,* that a statute of limitations may be treated as procedural and thus may be governed by forum law even when the substance of the claim must be governed by another State's law, rested on two premises, one express and one implicit. The express premise was that this reflected the rule in international law at the time the Constitution was adopted. This is indisputably correct, and is not challenged by petitioner. The implicit premise, which petitioner does challenge, was that this rule from international law could properly have been applied in the interstate context consistently with the Full Faith and Credit Clause.

The first sentence of the Full Faith and Credit Clause was not much discussed at either the Constitutional Convention or the state ratifying conventions. However, the most pertinent comment at the Constitutional Convention, made by James Wilson of Pennsylvania, displays an expectation that it would be interpreted against the background of principles developed in international conflicts law. *See* 2 M. Farrand, The Records of the Federal Convention of 1787, p.488 (rev. ed. 1966). Moreover, this expectation was practically inevitable, since there was no other developed body of conflicts law to which courts in our new Union could turn for guidance.

The reported state cases in the decades immediately following ratification of the Constitution show that courts looked without hesitation to international law for guidance in resolving the issue underlying this case: which State's law governs the statute of limitations. The state of international law on that subject being as we have described, these early decisions uniformly concluded that the forum's statute of limitations governed even when it was longer than the limitations period of the State whose substantive law governed the merits of the claim. . . . By 1820, the use of the forum statute of limitations in the interstate context was acknowledged to be "well settled." . . . Obviously, judges writing in the era when the Constitution was framed and ratified thought the use of the forum statute of limitations to be proper in the interstate context. Their implicit understanding that the Full Faith and Credit Clause did not preclude reliance on the international law rule carries great weight.

Moreover, this view of statutes of limitation as procedural for purposes of choice of law followed quite logically from the manner in which they were treated for domestic-law purposes. At the time the Constitution was adopted the rule was already well established that suit would lie upon a promise to repay a debt barred by the statute of limitations—on the theory, as expressed by many courts, that the debt constitutes consideration for the promise, since the bar of the statute does not extinguish the underlying right but merely causes the remedy to be withheld. . . . This is the same theory, of course, underlying the conflicts rule: the right subsists, and the forum may choose to allow its courts to provide a remedy, even though the jurisdiction where the right arose would not.

Unable to sustain the contention that under the original understanding of the Full Faith and Credit Clause statutes of limitations would have been considered substantive, petitioner argues that we should apply the modern understanding that they are so. It is now agreed, petitioner argues, that the primary function of a statute of limitations is to balance the competing substantive values of repose and vindication of the underlying right; and we should apply that understanding here, as we have applied it in the area of choice of law for purposes of federal diversity jurisdiction, where we have held that statutes of limitation are substantive, *see* Guaranty Trust Co. v. York, 326 U.S. 99 (1945).

To address the last point first: *Guaranty Trust* itself rejects the notion that there is an equivalence between what is substantive under the *Erie* doctrine and what is substantive for purposes of conflict of laws. *Id.*, at 108. Except at the extremes, the terms "substance" and "procedure" precisely describe very little except a dichotomy, and what they mean in a particular context is largely determined by the purposes for which the dichotomy is drawn. In the context of our *Erie* jurisprudence, *see* Erie R. Co. v. Tompkins, 304 U.S. 64 (1938), that purpose is to establish (within the limits of applicable federal law, including the prescribed Rules of Federal Procedure) substantial uniformity of predictable outcome between cases tried in a federal court and cases tried in the courts of the State in which the federal court sits. *See Guaranty Trust, supra*, at 109; Hanna v. Plumer, 380 U.S. 460, 467, 471-474 (1965). The purpose of the substance-procedure dichotomy in the context of the Full Faith and Credit Clause, by contrast, is not to establish uniformity but to delimit spheres of state legislative competence. How different the two purposes (and hence the appropriate meanings) are is suggested by this: It is never the case under *Erie* that either federal *or* state law—if the two differ—can properly be applied to a particular issue, *cf. Erie, supra*, at 72-73; but since the legislative jurisdictions of the States overlap, it is frequently the case under the Full Faith and Credit Clause that a court can lawfully apply either the law of one State or the contrary law of another, *see Shutts III*, 472 U.S., at 823 ("in many situations a state court may be free to apply one of several choices of law"). Today, for example, we do not hold that Kansas must apply its own statute of limitations to a claim governed in its substance by another State's law, but only that it may.

But to address petitioner's broader point of which the *Erie* argument is only a part—that we should update our notion of what is sufficiently "substantive" to require full faith and credit: We cannot imagine what would be the basis for such an updating. As we have just observed, the words "substantive" and "procedural" themselves (besides not appearing in the Full Faith and Credit Clause) do not have a precise content, even (indeed especially) as their usage has evolved. And if one consults the purpose of their usage in the full-faith-and-credit context, that purpose is quite simply to give both the forum State and other interested States the legislative jurisdiction to which they are entitled. If we abandon the currently applied, traditional notions of such entitlement we would embark upon the enterprise of constitutionalizing choice-of-law rules, with no compass to guide us beyond our own perceptions of what seems desirable.[2] There is no more reason to consider recharacterizing statutes of limitations as substantive under the Full Faith and Credit Clause than there is to consider recharacterizing a host of other matters generally treated as procedural under conflicts law, and hence generally regarded as within the forum State's legislative jurisdiction. *See, e.g.*, Restatement (Second) of Conflict of Laws §131 (remedies available), §133 (placement of burden of proof), §134 (burden of production), §135 (sufficiency of the evidence), §139 (privileges) (1971).

In sum, long established and still subsisting choice-of-law practices that come to be thought, by modern scholars, unwise, do not thereby become unconstitutional. If current conditions render it desirable that forum States no longer treat a particular issue as procedural for conflict of laws purposes, those States can themselves adopt a rule to that effect, or it can be proposed that Congress legislate to that effect under the second sentence of the Full Faith and Credit Clause. It is not the function of this Court, however, to make departures from established choice-of-law precedent and practice constitutionally mandatory. We hold, therefore, that Kansas did not violate the Full Faith and Credit Clause when it applied its own statute of limitations.

B

Petitioner also makes a due process attack upon the Kansas court's application of its own statute of limitations.[3] Here again neither the tradition in

2. Contrary to Justice Brennan's concurrence, there is nothing unusual about our approach. This Court has regularly relied on traditional and subsisting practice in determining the constitutionally permissible authority of courts. . . . The concurrence's citation, of the criticism by the plurality opinion in Allstate Ins. Co. v. Hague, 449 U.S. 302 (1981), of Hartford Accident & Indemnity Co. v. Delta & Pine Land Co., 292 U.S. 143 (1934), is not to the contrary. That criticism merely rejected the view that the Constitution enshrines the rule that the law of the place of contracting governs validity of all provisions of the contract. By the time of *Allstate,* of course, such a rule could not have been characterized as a subsisting tradition, if it ever could have been, in light of escape devices such as the doctrine of public policy, characterization of an issue as procedural, and the rule that the law of the place of performance governs matters of performance.

3. Although petitioner takes up this issue after discussion of the full faith and credit claim, and devotes much less argument to it, we may note that, logically, the full faith and credit claim is entirely dependent upon it. It cannot possibly be a violation of the Full Faith and Credit Clause for a State to decline to apply another State's law in a case where that other State *itself* does not consider it applicable. Although in certain circumstances standard conflicts law considers a statute of limitations to bar the right and not just the remedy, *see* Restatement (Second) of Conflict of Laws §143 (1971), petitioner concedes that (apart from the fact that Kansas does not so regard the out-of-state statutes of limitations at issue here) Texas,

place when the constitutional provision was adopted nor subsequent practice supports the contention. At the time the Fourteenth Amendment was adopted, this Court had not only explicitly approved (under the Full Faith and Credit Clause) forum-state application of its own statute of limitations, but the practice had gone essentially unchallenged. And it has gone essentially unchallenged since. "If a thing has been practised for two hundred years by common consent, it will need a strong case for the Fourteenth Amendment to affect it." Jackman v. Rosenbaum Co., 260 U.S. 22, 31 (1922).

A State's interest in regulating the work load of its courts and determining when a claim is too stale to be adjudicated certainly suffices to give it legislative jurisdiction to control the remedies available in its courts by imposing statutes of limitations. Moreover, petitioner could in no way have been unfairly surprised by the application to it of a rule that is as old as the Republic. There is, in short, nothing in Kansas' action here that is "arbitrary or unfair," *Shutts III*, 472 U.S., at 821-822, and the due process challenge is entirely without substance.

III

In *Shutts III*, we held that Kansas could not apply its own law to claims for interest by nonresidents concerning royalties from property located in other States. The Kansas Supreme Court has complied with that ruling, but petitioner claims that it has unconstitutionally distorted Texas, Oklahoma, and Louisiana law in its determination of that law made in *Shutts IV* and applied to this case in *Wortman III*.

To constitute a violation of the Full Faith and Credit Clause or the Due Process Clause, it is not enough that a state court misconstrue the law of another State. Rather, our cases make plain that the misconstruction must contradict law of the other State that is clearly established and that has been brought to the court's attention. . . . We cannot conclude that any of the interpretations at issue here runs afoul of this standard.

[The Court then discussed the substantive laws of Texas, Oklahoma, and Louisiana.] For the reasons stated, the judgment of the Kansas Supreme Court is affirmed.

Justice KENNEDY took no part in the consideration or decision of this case.

Oklahoma, and Louisiana view their own statutes as procedural for choice-of-law purposes. A full faith and credit problem can therefore arise only if that disposition by those other States is invalid—that is, if they, as well as Kansas, are compelled to consider their statute of limitations substantive. The nub of the present controversy, in other words, is the scope of constitutionally permissible legislative jurisdiction, and it matters little whether that is discussed in the context of the Full Faith and Credit Clause, as the litigants have principally done, or in the context of the Due Process Clause. Since we are largely traversing ground already covered, our discussion of the due process claim can be brief.

Justice BRENNAN, with whom Justice MARSHALL and Justice BLACKMUN join, concurring in part and concurring in the judgment.

I join Parts I and III of the Court's opinion. Although I also agree with the result the Court reaches in Part II, I reach that result through a somewhat different path of analysis.

For 150 years, this Court has consistently held that a forum State may apply its own statute of limitations period to out-of-state claims even though it is longer or shorter than the limitations period that would be applied by the State out of which the claim arose. The main question presented in this case is whether this line of authority has been undermined by more recent case law concerning the constitutionality of state choice-of-law rules. *See* Phillips Petroleum Co. v. Shutts, 472 U.S. 797 (1985); Allstate Ins. Co. v. Hague, 449 U.S. 302 (1981). I conclude that it has not.

. . . The minimum requirements imposed by the Full Faith and Credit Clause[2] are that a forum State should not apply its law unless it has " 'a significant contact or significant aggregation of contacts, creating state interests, such that choice of its law is neither arbitrary nor fundamentally unfair,' " *Phillips Petroleum, supra,* at 818, quoting *Allstate, supra,* at 312-313 (plurality opinion of Brennan, J., joined by White, Marshall, and Blackmun, JJ.). The constitutional issue in this case is somewhat more complicated than usual because the question is not the typical one of whether a State can constitutionally apply its substantive law where both it and another State have certain contacts with the litigants and the facts underlying the dispute. Rather the question here is whether a forum State can constitutionally apply its limitations period, which has mixed substantive and procedural aspects, where its contacts with the dispute stem only from its status as the forum.

Were statutes of limitations purely substantive, the issue would be an easy one, for where, as here, a forum State has no contacts with the underlying dispute, it has no substantive interests and cannot apply its own law on a purely substantive matter. Nor would the issue be difficult if statutes of limitations were purely procedural, for the contacts a State has with a dispute by virtue of being the forum always create state procedural interests that make applications of the forum's law on purely procedural questions "neither arbitrary nor fundamentally unfair." *Phillips Petroleum,* 472 U.S., at 818. Statutes of limitations, however, defy characterization as either purely procedural or purely substantive. The statute of limitations a State enacts represents a balance between, on the one hand, its substantive interest in vindicating substantive claims and, on the other hand, a combination of its procedural interest in freeing its courts from adjudicating stale claims and its substantive interest in giving individuals repose from ancient breaches of law. A State that has enacted a particular limitations period has simply determined that after that period the interest in vindicating claims becomes out-

2. The minimum requirements imposed by the Due Process Clause are, in this context, the same as those imposed by the Full Faith and Credit Clause. . . .

weighed by the combination of the interests in repose and avoiding stale claims. One cannot neatly categorize this complicated temporal balance as either procedural or substantive.

Given the complex of interests underlying statutes of limitations, I conclude that the contact a State has with a claim simply by virtue of being the forum creates a sufficient procedural interest to make the application of its limitations period to wholly out-of-state claims consistent with the Full Faith and Credit Clause. This is clearest when the forum State's limitations period is shorter than that of the claim State. A forum State's procedural interest in avoiding the adjudication of stale claims is equally applicable to in-state and out-of-state claims. That the State out of which the claim arose may have concluded that at that shorter period its substantive interests outweigh its procedural interest in avoiding stale claims would not make any difference; it would be " 'neither arbitrary nor fundamentally unfair,' " *Phillips Petroleum, supra,* at 818, for the forum State to conclude that *its* procedural interest is more weighty than that of the claim State and requires an earlier time bar, as long as the time bar applied in a nondiscriminatory manner to in-state and out-of-state claims alike.

The constitutional question is somewhat less clear where, as here, the forum State's limitations period is longer than that of the claim State. In this situation, the claim State's statute of limitations reflects its policy judgment that at the time the suit was filed the combination of the claim State's procedural interest in avoiding stale claims and its substantive interest in repose outweighs its substantive interest in vindicating the plaintiff's substantive rights. Assuming, for the moment, that each State has an equal substantive interest in the repose of defendants, then a forum State that has concluded that its procedural interest is less weighty than that of the claim State does not act unfairly or arbitrarily in applying its longer limitations period. The claim State does not, after all, have any substantive interest in *not* vindicating rights it has created. Nor will it do to argue that the forum State has no interest in vindicating the substantive rights of nonresidents: the forum State cannot discriminate against nonresidents, and if it has concluded that the substantive rights of its citizens outweigh its procedural interests at that period then it cannot be faulted for applying that determination evenhandedly.

If the different limitations periods also reflect differing assessments of the substantive interests in the repose of defendants, however, the issue is more complicated. It is, to begin with, not entirely clear whether the interest in the repose of defendants is an interest the State has as a forum or wholly as the creator of the claim at issue. Even if one assumes the latter, determining whether application of the forum State's longer limitations period would thwart the claim State's substantive interest in repose requires a complex assessment of the relative weights of both States' procedural and substantive interests. For example, a claim State may have a substantive interest in vindicating claims that, at a particular period, outweighs its substantive interest in repose standing alone but not the combination of its interests in repose and avoiding the adjudication of stale claims. Such a State would not have its substantive interest in repose thwarted by the claim's adjudication in a State that professed no procedural interest in avoiding stale claims, even if the forum State had less substantive interest in repose than the claim State, because the forum State would be according the claim State's substantive interests all the weight the claim State gives them. Such efforts to break down and weigh the procedural and substantive components and interests served by the various States' limitations period would, however, involve a difficult, unwieldy and somewhat artificial inquiry that itself implicates the strong procedural interest any forum State has in having administrable choice-of-law rules.

In light of the forum State's procedural interests and the inherent ambiguity of any more refined inquiry in this context, there is some force to the conclusion that the forum State's contacts give it sufficient procedural interests to make it " 'neither arbitrary nor fundamentally unfair,' " *Phillips Petroleum*, 472 U.S., at 818, for the State to have a per se rule of applying its own limitations period to out-of-state claims—particularly where, as here, the states out of which the claims arise view their statutes of limitations as procedural. The issue, after all, is not whether the decision to apply forum limitations law is wise as a matter of choice-of-law doctrine but whether the decision is within the range of constitutionally permissible choices, and we have already held that distinctions similar to those offered above "are too unsubstantial to form the basis for constitutional distinctions." This conclusion may not be compelled, but the arguments to the contrary are at best arguable, and any merely arguable inconsistency with our current full faith and credit jurisprudence surely does not merit deviating from 150 years of precedent holding that choosing the forum State's limitations period over that of the claim State is constitutionally permissible.

The Court's technique of avoiding close examination of the relevant interests by wrapping itself in the mantle of tradition is as troublesome as it is conclusory. It leads the Court to assert broadly (albeit in dicta) that States do not violate the Full Faith and Credit Clause by adjudicating out-of-state claims under the forum's own law on, inter alia, remedies, burdens of proof, and burdens of production. The constitutionality of refusing to apply the law of the claim State on such issues was not briefed or argued before this Court, and whether, as the Court asserts without support, there are insufficient reasons for "recharacterizing" these issues (at least in part) as substantive is a question that itself presents multiple issues of enormous difficulty and importance which deserve more than the offhand treatment the Court gives them.

Even more troublesome is the Court's sweeping dicta that *any* choice-of-law practice that is "long established and still subsisting" is constitutional. *Ibid.* This statement on its face seems to encompass choice-of-law doctrines on purely substantive issues, and the blind reliance on tradition confuses and conflicts with the full faith and credit test we articulated just three years ago in *Phillips Petroleum*, 472 U.S., at 818. *See also Allstate*, 449 U.S., at

308-309, n.11 (plurality opinion of Brennan, J., joined by White, Marshall, and Blackmun, JJ.) (stating that a 1934 case giving "controlling constitutional significance" to a traditional choice-of-law test "has scant relevance for today"). That certain choice-of-law practices have so far avoided constitutional scrutiny by this Court is in any event a poor reason for concluding their constitutional validity. Nor is it persuasive that the practice reflected the rule applied by States or in international law around the time of the adoption of the Constitution, *see ante*, at 5–7, since "[t]he very purpose of the full faith and credit clause was to alter the status of the several states as independent foreign sovereignties," Milwaukee County v. M. E. White Co., 296 U.S. 268, 276-277 (1935), not to leave matters unchanged. The Court never offers a satisfactory explanation as to why tradition should enable States to engage in practices that, under our current test, are "arbitrary" or "fundamentally unfair." The broad range of choice-of-law practices that may, in one jurisdiction or another, be traditional are not before this Court and have not been surveyed by it, and we can only guess what practices today's opinion approves sight unseen. Nor am I much comforted by the fact that the Court opines on the constitutionality of traditional choice-of-law practices only to the extent they are "still subsisting," for few cases involve challenges to practices that no longer subsist. One wonders as well how future courts will determine which practices are traditional enough (or subsist strongly enough) to be constitutional, and about the utility of requiring courts to focus on such an uncertain and formalistic inquiry rather than on the fairness and arbitrariness of the choice-of-law rule at issue. Indeed, the disarray of the Court's test is amply demonstrated by the fact that two of the Justices necessary to form the Court leave open the issue of whether a forum State could constitutionally refuse to apply a shorter limitations period regarded as substantive by the foreign State, *see post* (O'Connor, J., joined by Rehnquist, C.J., concurring in part and dissenting in part), even though in many States the subsisting tradition of applying the forum's limitations period recognizes no exception for limitations periods considered substantive by the foreign State. *See generally* Restatement (Second) of Conflict of Laws §143 and Reporter's Note (1971) (collecting cases).

In short, I fear the Court's rationale will cause considerable mischief with no corresponding benefit.

Justice O'CONNOR, with whom THE CHIEF JUSTICE joins, concurring in part and dissenting in part.

The Court properly concludes that Kansas did not violate the Full Faith and Credit Clause or the Due Process Clause when it chose to apply its own statute of limitations in this case. Different issues might have arisen if Texas, Oklahoma, or Louisiana regarded its own shorter statute of limitations as substantive. Such issues, however, are not presented in this case, and they are appropriately left unresolved. Accordingly, I join Parts I and II of the Court's opinion.

In my view, however, the Supreme Court of Kansas violated the Full Faith and Credit Clause when it concluded that the three States in question would apply the interest rates set forth in the regulations of the Federal Power Commission (FPC). The Court correctly states that misconstruing those States' laws would not by itself have violated the Constitution, for the Full Faith and Credit Clause only required the Kansas court to adhere to law that was clearly established in those States and that had been brought to the Kansas court's attention. *See ante.* Under the standard the Court articulates, however, the Clause was violated. Each of the three States has a statute setting an interest rate that is different from the FPC rate, and the Supreme Court of Kansas offered no valid reason whatsoever for ignoring those statutory rates. Neither has this Court suggested a colorable argument that could support the Kansas court's decision, and its affirmance of that decision effectively converts an important constitutional guarantee into a precatory admonition.

[The opinion then discussed its view of Texas, Oklahoma, and Louisiana law.]

Today's decision discards important parts of our decision in *Shutts III*, 472 U.S. 797 (1985), and of the Full Faith and Credit Clause. Faced with the constitutional obligation to apply the substantive law of another State, a court that does not like that law apparently need take only two steps in order to avoid applying it. First, invent a legal theory so novel or strange that the other State has never had an opportunity to reject it; then, on the basis of nothing but unsupported speculation, "predict" that the other State would adopt that theory if it had the chance. To call this giving full faith and credit to the law of another State ignores the language of the Constitution and leaves it without the capacity to fulfill its purpose. Rather than take such a step, I would remand this case to the Supreme Court of Kansas with instructions to give effect to the interest rates established by law in Texas, Oklahoma, and Louisiana. I therefore respectfully dissent.

Questions and Comments

(1) *Wortman* must surely make one thing even clearer: that with regard to the issue of whether an adequate nexus exists for application of local law, the due process and full faith and credit limits are identical. Justice Scalia recognized this fact in footnote 3; and the concurring opinion of Justice Brennan agreed in its footnote 2. All members of the court who participated thus accepted the choice-of-law equivalence of the two clauses. While this result is in accord with earlier decisions, why (if they are identical) is the focus here primarily upon the interpretation of full faith and credit while earlier cases spoke in terms of due process?

What accounts for this interesting coincidence that these two rather different-sounding clauses just happen to turn out to have the identical scope in this context? Given his apparent interest in historical interpretation of constitutional provisions, why would Justice Scalia equate clauses from two different historical periods? Note that the argument that Kansas had denied other states' law full faith and credit through misinterpretation is discussed only in terms of full faith and credit and not also in due process terms. Why is this only a problem of the former, and not the latter? In the section of this chapter that follows, we will see additional problems that are amenable only to full faith and credit, and not to due process, analysis.

(2) By relying so extensively upon the understanding at the time that the Constitution was drafted, does Justice Scalia's opinion effectively give constitutional carte blanche to all First Restatement principles, or at least to all First Restatement rules adequately grounded in tradition? Has the *Wortman* majority constitutionalized the substance/procedure distinction? Did it, in footnote 3, constitutionalize renvoi? Has it constitutionalized international law, at least as it stood two hundred years ago?

(3) Is Justice Brennan's decidedly non-originalist approach any better? His concurrence draws heavily on the distinction between substantive and procedural interests. Is the substance/procedure distinction any more helpful here than it was in Chapters 1 and 2? Compare also the discussion of the *Erie* doctrine in Chapter 4. What precisely is the forum state's procedural interest in providing a longer statute of limitations than the claim state?

(4) Is Justice O'Connor's concern about opportunistic misinterpretation of foreign law a genuine one? Wouldn't it be worse for the Supreme Court to get into the business of closely scrutinizing the accuracy of state court interpretations of foreign law?

(5) Much speculation arose just prior to the 1992 presidential elections about the likely choice-of-law implications of a possible overruling of Roe v. Wade, 410 U.S. 113 (1973). If some states were allowed to criminalize abortions, would they also be permitted to penalize local individuals travelling to obtain abortions in other states, where the abortions were legal? Recall Skiriotes v. Florida, 313 U.S. 69 (1941), page 349 *supra*, recognizing a state's right to regulate its citizens' conduct outside the state in at least certain circumstances. The topic was the subject of a symposium in 67 Mich. L. Rev. (1992); Professors Kreimer and Brilmayer both concluded, although for different reasons, that extraterritorial prohibitions on abortion would be largely impermissible. Kreimer, The Law of Choice and Choice of Law: Abortion, the Right to Travel, and Extraterritorial Regulation in American Federalism, 67 Mich. L. Rev. 451 (1992); Brilmayer, Interstate Pre-emption: The Right to Travel, the Right to Life, and the Right to Die, 67 Mich. L. Rev. 873 (1992). Brilmayer argued that abortion is different from many other substantive areas, because the decision not to regulate abortion is typically a decision to afford women the affirmative freedom to make up their own minds, rather than a simple failure to regulate on the topic. *Compare* Bradford, What Happens if *Roe* is Overruled? Extraterritorial Regulation of Abortion by the States, 35 Ariz. L. Rev. 87 (1993) and Van Alstyne, Closing the Circle of Constitutional Review from *Griswold v. Connecticut* to *Roe v. Wade:* An Outline of Decision

Merely Overruling *Roe,* 1989 Duke L.J. 1677 (both concluding that extraterritorial regulation would be permissible).

B. The Obligation and the Right to Provide a Forum

Because the full faith and credit clause has come to require nothing more than the due process clause in the traditional choice-of-law context, its distinctive relevance to conflict of laws must be found elsewhere. One area of application is the interstate enforcement of judgments, a topic that will be addressed in Chapter 6. But there are nonjudgments contexts in which the clause has also been invoked and has provided the basis for invalidating state actions. The following cases address situations in which it is argued that the forum is according too little respect to the laws of another state. They deal with door-closing and localizing statutes pursuant to which either the forum declines to hear a foreign claim or refuses to respect the foreign state's wishes that its claim not be entertained in the forum. Why are such cases primarily a matter of full faith and credit, while choice-of-law cases can be treated equally well under either a due process or a full faith and credit analysis? *See generally* Brilmayer, Credit Due Judgments and Credit Due Laws: The Respective Roles of Due Process and Full Faith and Credit in the Interstate Context, 70 Iowa L. Rev. 95 (1984).

Hughes v. Fetter

341 U.S. 609 (1951)

Justice BLACK delivered the opinion of the Court.

Basing his complaint on the Illinois wrongful death statute, appellant administrator brought this action in the Wisconsin state court to recover damages for the death of Harold Hughes, who was fatally injured in an automobile accident in Illinois. The allegedly negligent driver and an insurance company were named as defendants. On their motion the trial court entered summary judgment "dismissing the complaint on the merits." It held that a Wisconsin statute, which creates a right of action only for deaths caused in that state, establishes a local public policy against Wisconsin's entertaining suits brought under the wrongful death acts of other states. The Wisconsin Supreme Court affirmed, notwithstanding the contention that the local statute so construed violated the Full Faith and Credit Clause of Art. IV, §1 of the Constitution. . . .

We are called upon to decide the narrow question whether Wisconsin, over the objection raised, can close the doors of its courts to the cause of action created by the Illinois wrongful death act.[4] Prior decisions have established that the Illinois statute is a "public act" within the provision of Art. IV, §1 that "Full Faith and Credit shall be given in each State to the public Acts . . . of every other State." It is also settled that Wisconsin cannot escape this constitutional obligation to enforce the rights and duties validly created under the laws of other states by the simple device of removing jurisdiction from courts otherwise competent. We have recognized, however, that full faith and credit does not automatically compel a forum state to subordinate its own statutory policy to a conflicting public act of another state; rather, it is for this Court to choose in each case between the competing public policies involved. The clash of interests in cases of this type has usually been described as a conflict between the public policies of two or more states. The more basic conflict involved in the present appeal, however, is as follows: On the one hand is the strong unifying principle embodied in the Full Faith and Credit Clause looking toward maximum enforcement in each state of the obligations or rights created or recognized by the statutes of sister states, on the other hand is the policy of Wisconsin, as interpreted by its highest court, against permitting Wisconsin courts to entertain this wrongful death action.

We hold that Wisconsin's policy must give way. That state has no real feeling of antagonism against wrongful death suits in general.[10] To the contrary, a forum is regularly provided for cases of this nature, the exclusionary rule extending only so far as to bar actions for death not caused locally.[11] The Wisconsin policy, moreover, cannot be considered as an application of the forum non conveniens doctrine, whatever effect that doctrine might be given if its use resulted in denying enforcement to public acts of other states. Even if we assume that Wisconsin could refuse, by reason of particular circumstances, to hear foreign controversies to which nonresidents were parties, the present case is not one lacking in close relationship with the state. For not only were appellant, the decedent, and the individual defendant all residents of Wisconsin, but also appellant was appointed administrator and the corporate defendant was created under Wisconsin laws. We also think it relevant, although not crucial here, that Wisconsin may well be the only jurisdiction in which service could be had as an original matter on the insurance company defendant. And while in the present case jurisdiction over

---

4. The parties concede, as they must, that if the same cause of action had previously been reduced to judgment, the Full Faith and Credit Clause would compel the courts of Wisconsin to entertain an action to enforce it. Kenney v. Supreme Lodge, 252 U.S. 411.

10. The present case is not one where Wisconsin, having entertained appellant's lawsuit, chose to apply its own instead of Illinois' statute to measure the substantive rights involved. This distinguishes the present case from those where we have said that "prima facie every state is entitled to enforce in its own courts its own statutes, lawfully enacted." Alaska Packers Assn. v. Industrial Act Commission.

11. It may well be that the wrongful death acts of Wisconsin and Illinois contain different provision in regard to such matters as maximum recovery and disposition of the proceeds of suit. Such differences, however, are generally considered unimportant.

the individual defendant apparently could be had in Illinois by substituted service, in other cases Wisconsin's exclusionary statute might amount to a deprivation of all opportunity to enforce valid death claims created by another state.

Under these circumstances, we conclude that Wisconsin's statutory policy which excludes this Illinois cause of action is forbidden by the national policy of the Full Faith and Credit Clause.[16] The judgment is reversed and the cause is remanded to the Supreme Court of Wisconsin for proceedings not inconsistent with this opinion.

Reversed and remanded.

Justice FRANKFURTER, whom Justice REED, Justice JACKSON, and Justice MINTON join, dissenting.

The Full Faith and Credit Clause was derived from a similar provision in the Articles of Confederation. Art. 4, §3. The only clue to its meaning in the available records of the Constitutional Convention is a notation in Madison's Debates that

> Mr. Wilson & Docr. Johnson [who became members of the committee to which the provision was referred] supposed the meaning to be that Judgments in one State should be the ground of actions in other States, & that acts of the Legislatures should be included, for the sake of Acts of insolvency &c—.

II Farrand, The Records of the Federal Convention, 447. This Court has, with good reason, gone far in requiring that the courts of a State respect judgments entered by courts of other States. But the extent to which a State must recognize and enforce the rights of action created by other States is not so clear.

In the tort action before us, there is little reason to impose a "state of vassalage" on the forum. The liability here imposed does not rest on a preexisting relationship between the plaintiff and defendant. There is consequently no need for fixed rules which would enable parties, at the time they enter into a transaction, to predict its consequences. . . .

This Court should certainly not require that the forum deny its own law and follow the tort law of another State where there is a reasonable basis for

---

16. In certain previous cases, *e.g.*, Pacific Ins. Co. v. Commission; Alaska Packers Assn. v. Commission, this Court suggested that under the Full Faith and Credit Clause a forum state might make a distinction between statutes and judgments of sister states because of Congress' failure to prescribe the extra-state effect to be accorded public acts. Subsequent to these decisions the Judicial Code was revised so as to provide: "*Such Acts* [of the legislature of any state] . . . and judicial proceedings . . . shall have the same full faith and credit in every court within the United States . . . as they have . . . in the courts of such State . . . from which they are taken." (Italics added.) 28 U.S.C. (1946 ed., Supp. III) §1738. In deciding the present appeal, however, we have not found it necessary to rely on any changes accomplished by the Judicial Code revision.

the forum to close its courts to the foreign cause of action. The decision of Wisconsin to open its courts to actions for wrongful deaths within the State but close them to actions for deaths outside the State may not satisfy everyone's notion of wise policy. But it is neither novel nor without reason. Wisconsin may be willing to grant a right of action where witnesses will be available in Wisconsin and the courts are acquainted with a detailed local statute and cases construing it. It may not wish to subject residents to suit where out-of-state witnesses will be difficult to bring before the court, and where the court will be faced with the alternative of applying a complex foreign statute—perhaps inconsistent with that of Wisconsin on important issues—or fitting the statute to the Wisconsin pattern. The legislature may well feel that it is better to allow the courts of the State where the accident occurred to construe and apply its own statute, and that the exceptional case where the defendant cannot be served in the State where the accident occurred does not warrant a general statute allowing suit in the Wisconsin courts. The various wrongful death statutes are inconsistent on such issues as beneficiaries, the party who may bring suit, limitations on liability, comparative negligence, and the measure of damages. . . . The measure of damages and the relation of wrongful death actions to actions for injury surviving death have raised extremely complicated problems, even for a court applying the familiar statute of its own State. These diversities reasonably suggest application by local judges versed in them.

No claim is made that Wisconsin has discriminated against the citizens of other States and thus violated Art. IV, §2 of the Constitution. Nor is a claim made that a lack of a forum in Wisconsin deprives the plaintiff of due process. Nor is it argued that Wisconsin is flouting a federal statute. The only question before us is how far the Full Faith and Credit Clause undercuts the purpose of the Constitution, made explicit by the Tenth Amendment, to leave the conduct of domestic affairs to the States. Few interests are of more dominant local concern than matters governing the administration of law. This vital interest of the States should not be sacrificed in the interest of a merely literal reading of the Full Faith and Credit Clause.

There is no support, either in reason or in the cases, for holding that this Court is to make a de novo choice between the policies underlying the laws of Wisconsin and Illinois. I cannot believe that the Full Faith and Credit Clause provided a "writer's inkhorn" so that this Court might separate right from wrong. "Prima facie every state is entitled to enforce in its own courts its own statutes, lawfully enacted. One who challenges that right, because of the force given to a conflicting statute of another state by the full faith and credit clause, assumes the burden of showing, upon some rational basis, that of the conflicting interests involved those of the foreign state are superior to those of the forum." Mr. Justice Stone, in Alaska Packers Assn. v. Commission. In the present case, the decedent, the plaintiff, and the individual defendant were residents of Wisconsin. The corporate defendant was created under Wisconsin law. The suit was brought in the Wisconsin courts. No reason is apparent—and none is vouchsafed in the opinion of the Court—why the interest of Illinois is so great that it can force the courts of Wisconsin to grant relief in defiance of their own law.

Finally, it may be noted that there is no conflict here in the policies underlying the statute of Wisconsin and that of Illinois. The Illinois wrongful death statute has a proviso that

> no action shall be brought or prosecuted in this State to recover damages for a death occurring outside of this State where a right of action for such death exists under the laws of the place where such death occurred and service of process in such suit may be had upon the defendant in such place.

The opinion of the Court concedes that "jurisdiction over the individual defendant apparently could be had in Illinois by substituted service." Thus, in the converse of the case at bar—if Hughes had been killed in Wisconsin and suit had been brought in Illinois—the Illinois courts would apparently have dismissed the suit. There is no need to be "more Roman than the Romans."

Wells v. Simonds Abrasive Co.

345 U.S. 514 (1953)

Chief Justice VINSON delivered the opinion of the Court.

Cheek Wells was killed in Alabama when a grinding wheel with which he was working burst. The wheel had been manufactured by the respondent, a corporation with its principal place of business in Pennsylvania. The administratrix of the estate of Cheek Wells brought an action for damages in the federal court for the Eastern District of Pennsylvania after one year, but within two years, after the death. Jurisdiction was based upon diversity of citizenship.

The section of the Alabama Code upon which petitioner predicated her action for wrongful death provided that action ". . . must be brought within two years from and after the death. . . ." The respondent moved for summary judgment on the ground the Pennsylvania wrongful death statute required suit to be commenced within one year. In an opinion on that motion, the district judge found that the Pennsylvania statute, which was analogous to the Alabama statute, had a one-year limitation. He further found that the Pennsylvania conflict of laws rule called for the application of its own limitation rather than that of the place of the accident. Deeming himself bound by the Pennsylvania conflicts rule, he ordered summary judgment for the respondent. The Court of Appeals for the Third Circuit affirmed.

Long ago, we held that applying the statute of limitations of the forum to a foreign substantive right did not deny full faith and credit. Recently we referred to ". . . the well-established principle of conflict of laws that 'If action is barred by the statute of limitations of the forum, no action can be maintained though action is not barred in the state where the cause of action arose.' Restatement, Conflict of Laws §603 (1934)." Order of United Commercial Travelers v. Wolfe.

The rule that the limitations of the forum apply (which this Court has said meets the requirements of full faith and credit) is the usual conflicts rule of the states. However, there have been divergent views when a foreign statutory right unknown to the common law has a period of limitations included in the section creating the right. The Alabama statute here involved creates such a right and contains a built-in limitation. The view is held in some jurisdictions that such a limitation is so intimately connected with the right that it must be enforced in the forum state along with the substantive right.

We are not concerned with the reasons which have led some states for their own purposes to adopt the foreign limitation, instead of their own, in such a situation. The question here is whether the Full Faith and Credit Clause compels them to do so. Our prevailing rule is that the Full Faith and Credit Clause does not compel the forum state to use the period of limitation of a foreign state. We see no reason in the present situation to graft an exception onto it. Differences based upon whether the foreign right was known to the common law or upon the arrangement of the code of the foreign state are too unsubstantial to form the basis of constitutional distinctions under the Full Faith and Credit Clause.

We agree with the respondent that Engel v. Davenport has no application here. It presented an entirely different problem. Congress had given a statutory cause of action to seamen for certain personal injuries, placing concurrent jurisdiction in the state and federal courts. In *Engel, supra*, the two-year federal limitation rather than the one-year California limitation for similar actions was held controlling in an action brought in the California courts. Once it was decided that the intention of Congress was that the two-year limitation was meant to apply in both federal and state courts under our Federal Constitution, that was the supreme law of the land.*

Our decisions in Hughes v. Fetter and First National Bank v. United Air Lines do not call for a change in the well-established rule that the forum state is permitted to apply its own period of limitation. The crucial factor in those two cases was that the forum laid an uneven hand on causes of action arising within and without the forum state. Causes of action arising in sister states were discriminated against. Here Pennsylvania applies her one-year limitation to all wrongful death actions wherever they may arise. The judgment is affirmed.

---

* "This Constitution, and the Laws of the United States which shall be made in Pursuance thereof; and all Treaties made, or which shall be made, under the Authority of the United States, shall be the supreme Law of the Land; and the Judges in every State shall be bound thereby, any Thing in the Constitution or Laws of any State to the Contrary notwithstanding." U.S. Const. art. VI, §2.—Ed.

Justice JACKSON, with whom Justice BLACK and Justice MINTON join, dissenting.

[T]he essence of the Full Faith and Credit Clause of the Constitution is that uniformities other than just those within the state are to be observed in a federal system. The whole purpose and the only need for requiring full faith and credit to foreign law is that it does differ from that of the forum. But that disparity does not cause the type of evil aimed at in Erie R. Co. v. Tompkins, *supra,* namely, that the same event may be judged by two different laws, depending upon whether a state court or a federal forum within that state is available. Application of the Full Faith and Credit Clause prevents this disparity by requiring that the law where the cause of action arose will follow the cause of action in whatever forum it is pursued.

The Court's decision, in contrast with our position, would enable shopping for favorable forums. Suppose this plaintiff might have obtained service of process in several different states—an assumption not extravagant in the case of many national corporations. Under the Court's holding, she could choose from as many varieties of laws as of forums. Under our theory, wherever she elected to sue (if she had a choice), she would take Alabama law with her. Suppose even now she can get service in a state with no statute of limitations or a long one; can she thereby revive a cause of action that has expired under Alabama law? The Court's logic would so indicate. The life of her cause of action is then determined by the fortuitous circumstances that enable her to make service of process in a certain state or states. . . .

We think that the better view of the case before us would be that it is Alabama law which giveth and only Alabama law that taketh away.

Questions and Comments

(1) In footnote 10 of *Hughes,* the Court mentioned that the case did not involve the typical choice-of-law problem in which the forum sought to supplant the law of the alternative state by applying its own law instead. What kind of problem is this, then? Note that the claim was that Wisconsin law was invalid rather than (as in the usual choice-of-law context) that it was a valid law that could not constitutionally be applied. Does this matter?

(2) Brainerd Currie found *Hughes* paradoxical because it compelled the forum to entertain the case but did not compel it to apply Illinois law. The Constitution and the "Transitory" Cause of Action, in Selected Essays on the Conflict of Laws 282, 282-283 (1963). Whether this is in fact paradoxical has been disputed. Martin, Constitutional Limits on Choice of Law, 61 Cornell L. Rev. 185, 219-220 (1976); Kirgis, The Roles of Due Process and Full Faith and Credit in Choice of Law, 62 Cornell L. Rev. 94, 118 (1976).

(3) Can *Hughes* be squared with Gulf Oil Co. v. Gilbert, 330 U.S. 501 (1947), in which the Supreme Court approved the doctrine of *forum non conveniens* for the federal courts? Are the federal courts and the Wisconsin courts different enough to require one court to entertain a cause of action and not

another? Or is *forum non conveniens* constitutional only when there are not as many contacts between the case and the forum as in *Hughes?* Or is the reason for the refusal to hear the case the critical factor? Can *Hughes* be squared with long-arm jurisdictional statutes that provide jurisdiction only where the cause of action accrued within the state?

(4) Shouldn't the recovery portions of the Illinois wrongful-death statute, to which *Hughes* said Wisconsin must give full faith and credit, be read together with that provision of the Illinois act (referred to in the last paragraph of the Frankfurter dissent and in the preceding note by Professor Currie), which would have done exactly the same thing that the Wisconsin courts attempted in *Hughes* if the facts had been reversed? In light of the no-foreign-accident provision of the Illinois statute, how can the Wisconsin courts be said to have ignored the policy of the Illinois statute?

(5) How does *Wells* compare with Sun Oil v. Wortman, reprinted at page 383 *supra?* Note that *Wortman* cannot be phrased in terms of whether the forum gave too little credit to the substantive cause of action under another state, for the forum limitations period in *Wortman* was longer, not shorter, as in *Wells.* At most, *Wortman* involves a claim of lack of respect for the foreign statute of limitations. That is, *Wortman* necessarily involves only a choice-of-law question (which limitations period to apply?), while *Wells* raises arguments about respect for both the limitations period *and* the substantive cause of action. The latter is not really a choice-of-law problem because the forum has already agreed to apply the other state's substantive law.

(6) Professor Kramer provocatively argues that the public policy exception in choice of law, discussed *supra* pages 158-166, 326-327, cannot survive *Hughes* and *Wells:*

> An accurate statement of the holding in *Hughes* would thus seem to be that state rules that discriminate against the laws of other states are subject to some form of intermediate constitutional scrutiny; that is, they must be justified by substantial reasons, and the discrimination must bear a substantial relationship to the state's objectives. . . . This antidiscrimination principle is, in fact, how the Court explained *Hughes* in its subsequent decision in *Wells,* which said that the result turned on the fact that "the forum laid an uneven hand on causes of action arising within and without the forum state. Causes of action arising in sister states were discriminated against." But if that is the test, the public policy doctrine must be unconstitutional. For surely "offensiveness" cannot be an appropriate reason under the Full Faith and Credit Clause for refusing to entertain a claim based on another state's law. It is difficult to think of a justification more at odds with the principal mission of the Clause. . . . [The Clause forbids] a state's refusal to apply another state's law, otherwise applicable under the forum's choice of law rules, on the ground that it promotes a policy the forum finds repugnant.

See Kramer, Same-Sex Marriage, Conflict of Laws, and the Unconstitutional Public Policy Exception, 106 Yale L.J. 1965, 1984-1987 (1997). Do you agree with this reasoning? Kramer goes on to argue that the purposes animating the full faith and credit clause—to bind states "more closely together," and to impose "mutual obligations to respect each other's laws and judgments," *id.* at 1986—are best served by elimination of the public policy exception. Couldn't one just as well argue that the public policy exception promotes interstate harmony by giving states a safety valve to avoid application of laws they deem unjust? Kramer thinks not. *See id.* at 1987-1991.

(7) *Hughes* concerns the constitutional obligation to provide a forum for a foreign cause of action. What if the state that created the cause of action does not want the action brought in another state's courts? In Tennessee Coal, Iron & Railroad Co. v. George, 233 U.S. 354 (1914), a plaintiff injured on the job in Alabama sued his employer in a Georgia state court under §3910 of the 1907 Alabama Code, which provided for vicarious liability under certain circumstances. A different section of the Alabama Code stated that all actions under §3910 must be brought "in a court of competent jurisdiction within the State of Alabama and not elsewhere." The defendant argues that the full faith and credit clause required the Georgia court to respect this provision and dismiss the case. The Supreme Court disagreed. After asserting that the right to sue was separable from the remedy, it stated that "a State cannot create a transitory cause of action and at the same time destroy the right to sue on the transitory cause of action in any court having jurisdiction. That jurisdiction is to be determined by the law of the court's creation and cannot be defeated by the extraterritorial operation of a statute of another State, even though it created the right of action." Is *Tennessee Coal* a First Restatement relic?

Tennessee Coal was followed in Crider v. Zurich Insurance Co., 380 U.S. 39 (1965). There the forum had disregarded a provision by the state creating the cause of action, which required that the cause of action be enforced only before a local administrative tribunal. The Court agreed, relying on the fact that the forum had an interest in providing a means of recovery for the plaintiff who was a forum resident. Should such an interest be a necessary condition for entertaining the cause of action? How can the forum have an "interest" in providing recovery under another state's law?

State of Nevada v. Hall

440 U.S. 410 (1979)

Justice STEVENS delivered the opinion of the Court.

In this tort action arising out of an automobile collision in California, a California court has entered a judgment against the State of Nevada that Nevada's own courts could not have entered. We granted certiorari to decide whether federal law prohibits the California courts from entering such a judgment or, indeed, from asserting any jurisdiction over another sovereign State.

The respondents are California residents. They suffered severe injuries in an automobile collision on a California highway on May 13, 1968. The driver of the other vehicle, an employee of the University of Nevada, was killed in the collision. It is conceded that he was driving a car owned by the State, that he was engaged in official business, and that the University is an instrumentality of the State itself.

. . . A Nevada statute places a limit of $25,000 on any award in a tort action against the State pursuant to its statutory waiver of sovereign immunity. Nevada argued that the Full Faith and Credit Clause of the United States Constitution required the California courts to enforce that statute. Nevada's motion was denied, and the case went to trial.

The jury concluded that the Nevada driver was negligent and awarded damages of $1,150,000. The Superior Court entered judgment on the verdict and the Court of Appeal affirmed. After the California Supreme Court denied review, the State of Nevada and its University successfully sought a writ of certiorari.

Despite its importance, the question whether a State may claim immunity from suit in the courts of another State has never been addressed by this court. The question is not expressly answered by any provision of the Constitution; Nevada argues that it is implicitly answered by reference to the common understanding that no sovereign is amenable to suit without its consent—an understanding prevalent when the Constitution was framed and repeatedly reflected in this Court's opinions. In order to determine whether that understanding is embodied in the Constitution, as Nevada claims, it is necessary to consider (1) the source and scope of the traditional doctrine of sovereign immunity; (2) the impact of the doctrine on the framing of the Constitution; (3) the Full Faith and Credit Clause; and (4) other aspects of the Constitution that qualify the sovereignty of the several States.

II

Unquestionably the doctrine of sovereign immunity was a matter of importance in the early days of independence. Many of the States were heavily indebted as a result of the Revolutionary War. They were vitally interested in the question whether the creation of a new federal sovereign, with courts of its own, would automatically subject them, like lower English lords, to suits in the courts of the "higher" sovereign.

But the question whether one State might be subject to suit in the courts of another State was apparently not a matter of concern when the new Constitution was being drafted and ratified. Regardless of whether the Framers were correct in assuming, as presumably they did, that prevailing notions of comity would provide adequate protections against the unlikely prospect of an attempt by the courts of one State to assert jurisdiction over another, the need for constitutional protection against that contingency was not discussed.

The debate about the suability of the States focused on the scope of the judicial power of the United States authorized by Art. III. In The Federalist,

Hamilton took the position that this authorization did not extend to suits brought by an individual against a nonconsenting State. The contrary position was also advocated and actually prevailed in this Court's decision in Chisholm v. Georgia.

The *Chisholm* decision led to the prompt adoption of the Eleventh Amendment. That Amendment places explicit limits on the powers of federal courts to entertain suits against a State.[19]

The language used by the Court in cases construing these limits, like the language used during the debates on ratification of the Constitution, emphasized the widespread acceptance of the view that a sovereign State is never amenable to suit without its consent. But all of these cases, and all of the relevant debate, concerned questions of federal court jurisdiction and the extent to which the States, by ratifying the Constitution and creating federal courts, had authorized suits against themselves in those courts. These decisions do not answer the question whether the Constitution places any limit on the exercise of one State's power to authorize its courts to assert jurisdiction over another State. Nor does anything in Art. III authorizing the judicial power of the United States, or in the Eleventh Amendment limitation on that power, provide any basis, explicit or implicit, for this Court to impose limits on the powers of California exercised in this case. A mandate for federal-court enforcement of interstate comity must find its basis elsewhere in the Constitution.

III

Nevada claims that the Full Faith and Credit Clause of the Constitution requires California to respect the limitations on Nevada's statutory waiver of its immunity from suit. That waiver only gives Nevada's consent to suits in its own courts. Moreover, even if the waiver is treated as a consent to be sued in California, California must honor the condition attached to that consent and limit respondent's recovery to $25,000, the maximum allowable in an action in Nevada's courts.

The Full Faith and Credit Clause does require each State to give effect to official acts of other States. A judgment entered in one State must be respected in another provided that the first State had jurisdiction over the par-

---

19. The Eleventh Amendment provides: "The Judicial power of the United States shall not be construed to extend to any suit in law or equity, commenced or prosecuted against one of the United States by Citizens of another State, or by Citizens or Subjects of any Foreign State."

Even as so limited, however, the Eleventh Amendment has not accorded the States absolute sovereign immunity in federal court actions. The States are subject to suit by both their sister States and the United States. Further, prospective injunctive and declaratory relief is available against States in suits in federal court in which state officials are the nominal defendants.

ties and the subject matter. . . . But this Court's decision in Pacific Insurance Co. v. Industrial Accident Commission clearly establishes that the Full Faith and Credit Clause does not require a State to apply another State's law in violation of its own legitimate public policy. . . . The interest of California afforded such respect in the *Pacific Insurance* case was in providing for "the bodily safety and economic protection of employees injured within it." In this case, California's interest is the closely related and equally substantial one of providing "full protection to those who are injured on its highways through the negligence of both residents and nonresidents." To effectuate this interest, California has provided by statute for jurisdiction in its courts over residents and nonresidents alike to allow those injured on its highways through the negligence of others to secure full compensation for their injuries in the California courts.

In further implementation of that policy, California has unequivocally waived its own immunity from liability for the torts committed by its own agents and authorized full recovery even against the sovereign. As the California courts have found, to require California either to surrender jurisdiction or to limit respondents' recovery to the $25,000 maximum of the Nevada statute would be obnoxious to its statutorily based policies of jurisdiction over nonresident motorists and full recovery. The Full Faith and Credit Clause does not require this result.[24]

IV

Even apart from the Full Faith and Credit Clause, Nevada argues that the Constitution implicitly establishes a Union in which the States are not free to treat each other as unfriendly sovereigns, but must respect the sovereignty of one another. While sovereign nations are free to levy discriminatory taxes on the goods of other nations or to bar their entry altogether, the States of the Union are not. Nor are the States free to deny extradition of a fugitive when a proper demand is made by the executive of another State. And the citizens in each State are entitled to all privileges and immunities of citizens in the several States.

Each of these provisions places a specific limitation on the sovereignty of the several States. Collectively they demonstrate that ours is not a union of 50 wholly independent sovereigns. But those provisions do not imply that any one State's immunity from suit in the courts of another State is anything

---

24. California's exercise of jurisdiction in this case poses no substantial threat to our constitutional system of cooperative federalism. Suits involving traffic accidents occurring outside of Nevada could hardly interfere with Nevada's capacity to fulfill its own sovereign responsibilities. We have no occasion, in this case, to consider whether different state policies, either of California or of Nevada, might require a different analysis or a different result.

other than a matter of comity. Indeed, in view of the Tenth Amendment's reminder that powers not delegated to the Federal Government nor prohibited to the States are reserved to the States or to the people, the existence of express limitations on state sovereignty may equally imply that caution should be exercised before concluding that unstated limitations on state power were intended by the Framers.

In the past, this Court has presumed that the States intended to adopt policies of broad comity toward one another. But this presumption reflected an understanding of state policy, rather than a constitutional command. As this Court stated in Bank of Augusta v. Earle,

> The intimate union of these states, as members of the same great political family; the deep and vital interests which bind them so closely together; should lead us, in the absence of proof to the contrary, to presume a greater degree of comity, and friendship, and kindness towards one another, than we should be authorized to presume between foreign nations. And when (as without doubt must occasionally happen) the interest of policy of any state requires it to restrict the rule, it has but to declare its will, and the legal presumption is at once at an end.

In this case, California has "declared its will"; it has adopted as its policy full compensation in its courts for injuries on its highways resulting from the negligence of others, whether those others be residents or nonresidents, agents of the State, or private citizens. Nothing in the Federal Constitution authorizes or obligates this Court to frustrate that policy out of enforced respect for the sovereignty of Nevada.[29] In this Nation each sovereign governs only with the consent of the governed. The people of Nevada have consented to a system in which their State is subject only to limited liability in tort. But the people of California, who have had no voice in Nevada's decision, have adopted a different system. Each of these decisions is equally entitled to our respect.

It may be wise policy, as a matter of harmonious interstate relations, for States to accord each other immunity or to respect any established limits on liability. They are free to do so. But if a federal court were to hold, by inference from the structure of our Constitution and nothing else, that California is not free in this case to enforce its policy of full compensation, that holding would constitute the real intrusion on the sovereignty of the States—and the power of the people—in our Union.

The judgment of the California Court of Appeal is affirmed.

---

29. *Cf.* Georgia v. Chattanooga, 264 U.S. 472, 480 ("Land acquired by one State in another State is held subject to the laws of the latter and to all the incidents of private ownership. The proprietary right of the owning State does not restrict or modify the power of eminent domain of the State wherein the land is situated").

Justice BLACKMUN, with whom THE CHIEF JUSTICE and Justice REHNQUIST join, dissenting.

[T]he Court paints with a very broad brush, and I am troubled by the implications of its holding. Despite a fragile footnote disclaimer, *ante* . . . n.24, the Court's basic and undeniable ruling is that what we have always thought of as a "sovereign State" is now to be treated in the courts of a sister State, once jurisdiction is obtained, just as any other litigant. I fear the ultimate consequences of that holding, and I suspect that the Court has opened the door to avenues of liability and interstate retaliation that will prove unsettling and upsetting for our federal system. Accordingly, I dissent.

It is important to note that at the time of the Constitutional Convention, as the Court concedes, there was "widespread acceptance of the view that a sovereign State is never amenable to suit without its consent." . . . The Court also acknowledges that "the notion that immunity from suit is an attribute of sovereignty is reflected in our cases." . . . Despite these concessions, the Court holds that the sovereign immunity doctrine is a mere matter of "comity" which a State is free to reject whenever its "policy" so dictates. . . .

There is no limit to the breadth of the Court's rationale, which goes beyond the approach taken by the California Court of Appeal in this case. That court theorized that Nevada was not "sovereign" for purposes of this case because sovereignty ended at the California-Nevada line. . . .

That reasoning finds no place in this Court's opinion. Rather, the Court assumes that Nevada is "sovereign," but then concludes that the sovereign-immunity doctrine has no *constitutional* source. Thus, it says, California can abolish the doctrine at will. . . .

The Court, by its footnote 24 . . . purports to confine its holding to traffic-accident torts committed outside the defendant State, and perhaps even to traffic "policies." Such facts, however, play absolutely no part in the reasoning by which the Court reaches its conclusion. . . . If, indeed, there is "[n]othing in the Federal Constitution" that allows frustration of California's policy, it is hard to see just how the Court could use a different analysis or reach a different result in a different case. . . .

I must agree with the Court that if the judgment of the California Court of Appeal is to be reversed, a constitutional source for Nevada's sovereign immunity must be found. I would find that source not in an express provision of the Constitution but in a guarantee that is implied as an essential component of federalism. . . .

. . . The Court's acknowledgment, referred to above, that the Framers must have assumed that States were immune from suit in the courts of their sister States lends substantial support. The only reason why this immunity did not receive specific mention is that it was too obvious to deserve mention. The prompt passage of the Eleventh Amendment nullifying the decision in Chisholm v. Georgia, is surely significant. If the Framers were indeed concerned lest the States be haled before the federal courts—as the courts of a

" 'higher' sovereign,"—how much more must they have reprehended the notion of a State's being haled before the courts of a sister State. The concept of sovereign immunity prevailed at the time of the Constitutional Convention. It is, for me, sufficiently fundamental to our federal structure to have implicit constitutional dimension. Indeed, if the Court means what it implies in its footnote 24—that *some* state policies might require a different result—it must be suggesting that there are some federalism constraints on a State's amenability to suit in the courts of another State. If that is so, the only question is whether the facts of this case are sufficient to call the implicit constitutional right of sovereign immunity into play here. I would answer that question in the affirmative. . . .

Justice REHNQUIST, with whom THE CHIEF JUSTICE joins, dissenting.

I am . . . concerned about the practical implications of this decision. The federal system as expressed in the Constitution—with the exception of representation in the House—is built on notions of state parity. No system is truly federal otherwise. This decision cannot help but induce some "Balkanization" in state relationships as States try to isolate assets from foreign judgments and generally reduce their contacts with other jurisdictions. That will work to the detriment of smaller States—like Nevada—who are more dependent on the facilities of a dominant neighbor—in this case, California.

The problem of enforcement of a judgment against a State creates a host of additional difficulties. Assuming Nevada has no seizable assets in California, can the plaintiff obtain enforcement of California's judgment in Nevada courts? Can Nevada refuse to give the California judgment "full faith and credit" because it is against state policy? Can Nevada challenge the seizure of its assets by California in this Court? If not, are the States relegated to the choice between the gamesmanship and tests of strength that characterize international disputes, on the one hand, and the midnight seizure of assets associated with private debt collection on the other? . . .

Questions and Comments

(1) States may ordinarily apply their own law to the collection of judgments—for example, a state's homestead exemption applies not only to its own judgments but to judgments it renders to enforce the judgments of other states with different homestead exemptions. Such rules may not, of course, discriminate in favor of in-state judgment debtors or against out-of-state judgment creditors. What would happen if Nevada withdrew its assets from California to avoid judgment collection there and further provided that state assets were exempt within Nevada? Such a statute would not clearly run afoul of prescriptions against discrimination since presumably even Nevada judgments against the state cannot be satisfied by seizure and sale of the state capitol. Could other states also exempt the assets of any state, thus keeping California from seizing Nevada assets elsewhere?

Could a similar result be accomplished by making the University of Nevada a separate legal entity, so that assets belonging to the state of Nevada and deposited in California bank accounts would not belong to the defendant? Under such circumstances, wouldn't the California plaintiff have to try to collect its judgment in Nevada, subject to Nevada collection laws? Or could California also ignore the law of Nevada making the university a separate legal entity? Note that the court justifies the application of California law in *Hall* because of the significant connection between the issue and the state of California and the physical intrusion of Nevada activity into California. The University's separate legal identity could not be said, of course, to intrude physically into California.

The Nevada legislature petitioned Congress to begin the process of amending the Constitution to add the following:

> Each state of the United States shall be immune from any suits in law or equity commenced or prosecuted in the courts of another state by citizens of any other state or by citizens or subjects of any foreign state except to the extent that any state has waived its sovereign immunity in its own courts or has waived its immunity as a matter of comity with any other state.

Assembly Joint Resolution, No. 29, 1979. Isn't that resolution a bit of overkill? Can't Congress, *by statute*, achieve the same effect under the implementing authority of the full faith and credit clause, by requiring states to give full faith and credit to the law of the defendant state on sovereign immunity?

(2) Why is there no due process objection to subjecting Nevada to suit in California? Both as a matter of personal jurisdiction and as a matter of choice of law, isn't it clear that California has adequate authority under the due process clause? If there were no issue of sovereign immunity (because, for example, Nevada had waived its immunity) would there be any plausible due process objection to application of, say, California traffic rules?

Would there be any full faith and credit objection, in such an example, to application of California traffic rules? Then wasn't Nevada's argument really a claim that sovereign immunity is different, for full faith and credit purposes, from all other rules of substantive law? Is this plausible, as a matter of full faith and credit?

(3) Would the result in *Hall* have been the same if California law retained California's immunity but did not honor the immunity of other states? Note that such discrimination would be hard to criticize under the equal protection clause of the Fourteenth Amendment, which refers to "persons," or under the privileges and immunities clause of Article IV, which protects "citizens." Would such "discrimination" be more vulnerable under full faith and credit than the even-handed rule that California applied here?

(4) Why didn't the Court rely on the argument, used by the California courts, that Nevada was simply not sovereign when it acted outside its territory? Wouldn't that allow holding Nevada liable even if both the involved states retained sovereign immunity for domestic purposes?

(5) If, contrary to the holding of *Hall,* California had been required to apply Nevada's limitation on state liability, could it also be required to yield to a Nevada statute requiring claims against the state to be brought in the Nevada Court of Claims?

(6) In Great Western United Corporation v. Kidwell, 577 F.2d 1257 (5th Cir. 1978), the court held that an action to declare an Idaho law unconstitutional on the grounds of preemption by the Securities Exchange Act of 1934 and the commerce clause could be brought in a federal district court in Texas. The defendant was the attorney general of Idaho and personal jurisdiction was asserted under the Texas long-arm statute on the grounds that the objected-to application of the law in question had had foreseeable effects in Texas. Could a similar action have been maintained (for damages, rather than to have a law declared unconstitutional) under Texas law, using *Hall* to support the proposition that as long as the activity in question by an Idaho official had an effect in Texas, Texas was free to apply its own law rather than that of Idaho even though the activity in question took place in Idaho? Has Pandora struck again?

(The Supreme Court reversed *Kidwell* sub nom. Leroy v. Great Western United Corp., 443 U.S. 173 (1979), on federal venue grounds. It specifically refused to reach the question of in personam jurisdiction in Texas.)

(7) In Underwood v. University of Kentucky, 390 So. 2d 433 (Fla. App. 1980), a Kentucky resident sued the University of Kentucky in Florida, alleging that he had been libeled in a book published by the University. The majority dismissed on jurisdictional grounds, finding insufficient contacts between the university and the state of Florida. A concurring opinion, however, would have decided the case on sovereign immunity grounds, finding the university to be the alter ego of the state of Kentucky. Nevada v. Hall was distinguished on the grounds that it involved and was limited to a case involving "California's interest in providing protection to those who are injured on its highways through the negligence of both residents and nonresidents." 390 So. 2d at 436. Is the distinction consistent with the majority's reasoning?

(8) An excellent critique of Nevada v. Hall can be found in Rogers, Applying the International Law of Sovereign Immunity to the States of the Union, 1981 Duke L.J. 449.

C. Constitutional Limitations on Interstate Discrimination

Two sources of constitutional limitation on choice of law, other than due process and full faith and credit, are the equal protection clause and the privileges and immunities clause. These provisions place limits on interstate discrimination, as do the commerce clause (discussed in Section D below) and the right to travel. In general, the First Restatement avoided equal protection and other discrimination problems by concentrating on places rather than people. The opportunity arose under interest analysis, however, to make arguments that equal protection was being denied. For example, if a driver from State *A*, with a guest statute, carries one passenger from State *A*, and one from State *B*, which has no guest statute, and is involved in an accident in State *B*, Judge Fuld's first rule would seem to dictate that the first passenger could not recover from the driver, while Judge Fuld's second rule would seem to allow the second passenger to recover. The different treatment received by the two passengers involved in the same accident strongly suggests a denial of equal protection. The cases do not yet seem to have addressed this problem, but Professors Brainerd Currie and Herma Hill Kay concluded that there are some situations in which discrimination on the basis of one's home state's law may be upheld against attack under the privileges and immunities clause. Since that clause is designed to prevent discrimination based on state citizenship, the suggestion would seem equally pertinent for equal protection. *See* Currie, Selected Essays on the Conflict of Laws 503-511 (1963). In response, it has been forthrightly argued that the domiciliary-based discrimination-of-interest analysis is unconstitutional. Laycock, Equality and the Citizens of Sister States, 15 Fla. St. L. Rev. 431 (1987) and Equal Citizens of Equal and Territorial States: The Constitutional Foundations of Choice of Law, 92 Colum. L. Rev. 249 (1992).

The problem is more complicated than might first appear. First, some of the old-style First Restatement rules relied upon domiciliary-connecting factors. *See,* for example, White v. Tenant, *supra* page 43. Arguably, these rules are different from modern choice-of-law theory in the way that they use the parties' domicile. Under the Restatement, the local person is as likely to be hurt as helped by application of local law, while under modern theory, a state may have an "interest" only if local law is of benefit to the local person.

Second, it is not always unconstitutional to give locals an advantage; different treatment is acceptable where there is an adequate justification, as the cases below demonstrate.

Third, choice of law necessarily involves the making of differentiations. The forum is not entitled simply to apply forum law to every case that comes before it. These discriminations must obviously turn on either the location of events or on the personal affiliations of individuals. Why are domiciliary connections the suspect factors? It would be possible to argue in the alternative that First Restatement rules are the ones that are unconstitutional because they treat people differently depending on "obviously irrelevant" factors, such as where an accident occurs. This view was set forth by Professors Currie and Kay in Currie, Selected Essays in the Conflict of Laws (1963), at 454-455 (privileges and immunities) and 575-583 (equal protection). Discrimination based on territorial factors and discrimination based on the domicile of the benefited party are therefore constitutional competitors of one another; at least one *must* be constitutional, and it is possible that *only one* is. *See generally* Gergen, Equality and the Conflict of Laws, 73 Iowa L. Rev. 893 (1988).

Both sides of the dispute tend to argue that the differentiation that they favor is simply a result of our having a federal system of government. Division into fifty states means a division of lawmaking power, and thus a difference in treatment. To this date, courts have not been convinced that an equal protection or privileges violation results from reliance on territorial factors. Given the Supreme Court's recent approval of traditional choice-of-law rules in Sun Oil Co. v. Wortman, *supra* page 383, one suspects that the Currie analysis of equal protection is unlikely to be adopted. Discrimination on the basis of personal affiliation, on the other hand, has long been thought problematic. The cases below survey some interstate discrimination principles and suggest that in at least certain circumstances, discrimination against nonresidents is unconstitutional.

Austin v. New Hampshire

420 U.S. 656 (1975)

Justice Marshall delivered the opinion of the Court.

Appellants are residents of Maine who were employed in New Hampshire during the 1970 tax year and as such were subject to the New Hampshire Commuters Income Tax. On behalf of themselves and others similarly situated, they petitioned the New Hampshire Superior Court for a declaration that the tax violates the Privileges and Immunities and Equal Protection Clauses of the Constitutions of New Hampshire and of the United States. The cause was transferred directly to the New Hampshire Supreme Court, which upheld the tax. We noted probable jurisdiction of the federal constitutional claims, 419 U.S. 822 (1974), and on the basis of the Privileges and Immunities Clause of Art. IV, we now reverse.

I

The New Hampshire Commuters Income Tax imposes a tax on nonresidents' New Hampshire-derived income in excess of $2,000. The tax rate is 4% except that if the nonresident taxpayer's State of residence would impose a lesser tax had the income been earned in that State, the New Hampshire tax is reduced to the amount of the tax that the State of residence would impose. Employers are required to withhold 4% of the nonresident's income, however, even if his home State would tax him at less than the full 4%. Any excess tax withheld is refunded to the nonresident upon his filing a New

Hampshire tax return after the close of the tax year showing that he is entitled to be taxed at a rate less than 4%.

The Commuters Income Tax initially imposes a tax of 4% as well on the income earned by New Hampshire residents outside the State. It then exempts such income from the tax, however: (1) if it is taxed by the State from which it is derived; (2) if it is exempted from taxation by the State from which it is derived; or (3) if the State from which it is derived does not tax such income. The effect of these imposition and exemption features is that no resident of New Hampshire is taxed on his out-of-state income. Nor is the domestic earned income of New Hampshire residents taxed. In effect, then, the State taxes only the incomes of nonresidents working in New Hampshire; it is on the basis of this disparate treatment of residents and nonresidents that appellants challenge New Hampshire's right to tax their income from employment in that State.

II

The Privileges and Immunities Clause of Art. IV, §2, cl. 1, provides:

> The Citizens of each State shall be entitled to all Privileges and Immunities of Citizens in the several States.

The Clause thus establishes a norm of comity without specifying the particular subjects as to which citizens of one State coming within the jurisdiction of another are guaranteed equality of treatment. The origins of the Clause do reveal, however, the concerns of central import to the Framers. During the preconstitutional period, the practice of some States denying to outlanders the treatment that its citizens demanded for themselves was widespread. The fourth of the Articles of Confederation was intended to arrest this centrifugal tendency with some particularity. It provided:

> The better to secure and perpetuate mutual friendship and intercourse among the people of the different States in this Union, the free inhabitants of each of these States, paupers, vagabonds and fugitives from justice excepted, shall be entitled to all privileges and immunities of free citizens in the several States; and the people of each State shall have free ingress and regress to and from any other State, and shall enjoy therein all the privileges of trade and commerce, subject to the same duties, impositions and restrictions as the inhabitants thereof respectively.

The discriminations at which the Clause was aimed were by no means eradicated during the short life of the Confederation, and the provision was carried over into the comity article of the Constitution in briefer form but with no change of substance or intent, unless it was to strengthen the force of the Clause in fashioning a single nation. Thus, in the first, and long the leading, explication of the Clause, Mr. Justice Washington, sitting as Circuit Justice, deemed the fundamental privileges and immunities protected by the Clause to be essentially coextensive with those calculated to achieve the purpose of forming a more perfect Union, including "an exemption from higher taxes or impositions than are paid by the other citizens of the state."

In resolving constitutional challenges to state tax measures this Court has made it clear that "in taxation, even more than in other fields, legislatures possess the greatest freedom in classification." Our review of tax classifications has generally been concomitantly narrow, therefore, to fit the broad discretion vested in the state legislatures. When a tax measure is challenged as an undue burden on an activity granted special constitutional recognition, however, the appropriate degree of inquiry is that necessary to protect the competing constitutional value from erosion.

This consideration applies equally to the protection of individual liberties and to the maintenance of our constitutional federalism. The Privileges and Immunities Clause, by making noncitizenship or nonresidence[8] an improper basis for locating a special burden, implicates not only the individual's right to nondiscriminatory treatment but also, perhaps more so, the structural balance essential to the concept of federalism. Since nonresidents are not represented in the taxing State's legislative halls, judicial acquiescence in taxation schemes that burden them particularly would remit them to such redress as they could secure through their own State; but "to prevent [retaliation] was one of the chief ends sought to be accomplished by the adoption of the Constitution." Our prior cases, therefore, reflect an appropriately heightened concern for the integrity of the Privileges and Immunities Clause by erecting a standard of review substantially more rigorous than that applied to state tax distinctions among, say, forms of business organizations or different trades and professions.

The first such case was Ward v. Maryland, 12 Wall. 418 (1871), challenging a statute under which nonresidents were required to pay $300 per year for a license to trade in goods not manufactured in Maryland, while resident traders paid a fee varying from $12 to $150, depending upon the value of their inventory. The State attempted to justify this disparity as a response to the practice of "runners" from industrial States selling by sample in Maryland, free from local taxation and other overhead expenses incurred by resident merchants. It portrayed the fee as a "tax upon a particular business or trade, carried on in a particular mode," rather than a discrimination against traders from other States. Although the tax may not have been "palpably ar-

---

8. For purposes of analyzing a taxing scheme under the Privileges and Immunities Clause the terms "citizen" and "resident" are essentially interchangeable. Travis v. Yale & Towne Mfg. Co., 252 U.S. 60, 79 (1920) ("a general taxing scheme . . . if it discriminates against all nonresidents, has the necessary effect of including in the discrimination those who are citizens of other States"); Smith v. Loughman, 245 N.Y. 486, 492, 157 N.E. 753, 755, *cert. denied,* 275 U.S. 560 (1927); *see* Toomer v. Witsell, 334 U.S. 385, 397 (1948).

bitrary," the discrimination could not be denied and the Court held that it violated the guarantee of the Privileges and Immunities Clause against "being subjected to any higher tax or excise than that exacted by law of . . . permanent residents."

In Travelers' Insurance Co. v. Connecticut, 185 U.S. 364 (1902), the Court considered a tax laid on the value of stock in local insurance corporations. The shares of nonresident stockholders were assessed at their market value, while those owned by residents were assessed at market value less the proportionate value of all real estate held by the corporation and on which it had already paid a local property tax. In analyzing the apparent discrimination thus worked against nonresidents, the Court took account of the overall distribution of the tax burden between resident and nonresident stockholders. Finding that nonresidents paid no local property taxes, while residents paid those taxes at an average rate approximating or exceeding the rate imposed by the State on nonresidents' stock, the Court upheld the scheme. While more precise equality between the two classes could have been obtained, it was "enough that the State has secured a reasonably fair distribution of burdens, and that no intentional discrimination has been made against non-residents." Their contribution to state and local property tax revenues, that is, was no more than the ratable share of their property within the State.

The principles of *Ward* and *Travelers'* were applied to taxes on nonresidents' local incomes in Shaffer v. Carter, 252 U.S. 37 (1920), and Travis v. Yale & Towne Mfg. Co., *supra. Shaffer* upheld the Oklahoma tax on income derived from local property and business by a nonresident where the State also taxed the income—from wherever derived—of its own citizens. Putting aside "theoretical distinctions" and looking to "the practical effect and operation" of the scheme, the nonresident was not treated more onerously than the resident in any particular, and in fact was called upon to make no more than his ratable contribution to the support of the state government. The New York tax on residents' and nonresidents' income at issue in *Travis*, by contrast, could not be sustained when its actual effect was considered. The tax there granted personal exemptions to each resident taxpayer for himself and each dependent, but it made no similar provision for nonresidents. The disparity could not be "deemed to be counterbalanced" by an exemption for nonresidents' interest and dividend income because it was not likely "to benefit non-residents to a degree corresponding to the discrimination against them." Looking to "the concrete, the particular incidence" of the tax, therefore, the Court said of the many New Jersey and Connecticut residents who worked in New York:

> They pursue their several occupations side by side with residents of the State of New York—in effect competing with them as to wages, salaries, and other terms of employment. Whether they must pay a tax upon the first $1,000 or $2,000 of income, while their associates and competitors

> who reside in New York do not, makes a substantial difference. . . . This is not a case of occasional or accidental inequality due to circumstances personal to the taxpayer . . . but a general rule, operating to the disadvantage of all non-residents . . . and favoring all residents. . . .

252 U.S., at 80-81 (citations omitted).

III

Against this background establishing a rule of substantial equality of treatment for the citizens of the taxing State and nonresident taxpayers, the New Hampshire Commuters Income Tax cannot be sustained. The overwhelming fact, as the State concedes, is that the tax falls exclusively on the income of nonresidents; and it is not offset even approximately by other taxes imposed upon residents alone. Rather, the argument advanced in favor of the tax is that the ultimate burden it imposes is "not more onerous in effect," Shaffer v. Carter, *supra,* on nonresidents because their total state tax liability is unchanged once the tax credit they receive from their State of residence is taken into account. *See* n.4, *supra* [omitted]. While this argument has an initial appeal, it cannot be squared with the underlying policy of comity to which the Privileges and Immunities Clause commits us.

According to the State's theory of the case, the only practical effect of the tax is to divert to New Hampshire tax revenues that would otherwise be paid to Maine, an effect entirely within Maine's power to terminate by repeal of its credit provision for income taxes paid to another State. The Maine Legislature could do this, presumably, by amending the provision so as to deny a credit for taxes paid to New Hampshire while retaining it for the other 48 States. Putting aside the acceptability of such a scheme, and the relevance of any increase in appellants' home state taxes that the diversionary effect is said to have, we do not think the possibility that Maine could shield its residents from New Hampshire's tax cures the constitutional defect of the discrimination in that tax. In fact, it compounds it. For New Hampshire in effect invites appellants to induce their representatives, if they can, to retaliate against it.

A similar, though much less disruptive, invitation was extended by New York in support of the discriminatory personal exemption at issue in *Travis.* The statute granted the nonresident a credit for taxes paid to his State of residence on New York-derived income only if that State granted a substantially similar credit to New York residents subject to its income tax. New York contended that it thus "looked forward to the speedy adoption of an income tax by the adjoining States," which would eliminate the discrimination "by providing similar exemptions similarly conditioned." To this the Court responded in terms fully applicable to the present case. Referring to the anticipated legislative response of the neighboring States, it stated:

> This, however, is wholly speculative; New York has no authority to legislate for the adjoining States; and we must pass upon its statute with respect to its effect and operation in the existing situation. . . . A State may not barter away the right, conferred upon its citizens by the Constitution of the United States, to enjoy the privileges and immunities of citizens when they go into other States. Nor can discrimination be corrected by retaliation; to prevent this was one of the chief ends sought to be accomplished by the adoption of the Constitution.

252 U.S., at 82.[12]

Nor, we may add, can the constitutionality of one State's statutes affecting nonresidents depend upon the present configuration of the statutes of another State.

Since we dispose of this case under Art. IV, §2, of the Constitution, we have no occasion to address the equal protection arguments directed at the disparate treatment of residents and nonresidents and at that feature of the statute that causes the rate of taxation imposed upon nonresidents to vary among them depending upon the rate established by their State of residence.

Reversed.

Justice DOUGLAS took no part in the consideration or decision of this case.

Justice BLACKMUN, dissenting.

For me, this is a noncase. I would dismiss the appeal for want of a substantial federal question. We have far more urgent demands upon our limited time than this kind of litigation.

Because the New Hampshire income tax statutes operate in such a way that no New Hampshire resident is ultimately subjected to the State's income tax, the case at first glance appears to have some attraction. That attraction, however, is superficial and, upon careful analysis, promptly fades and disappears entirely. The reason these appellants, who are residents of Maine, not of New Hampshire, pay a New Hampshire tax is because the Maine Legislature—the appellant's own duly elected representatives—has given New Hampshire the option to divert this increment of tax (on a Maine resident's income earned in New Hampshire) from Maine to New Hampshire, and New Hampshire willingly has picked up that option. All that New Hampshire has done is what Maine specifically permits and, indeed, invites it to do. If Maine should become disenchanted with its bestowed bounty, its legislature may change the Maine statute. The crux is the statute of Maine, not the statute of New Hampshire. The appellants, therefore, are really complaining about their own statute. It is ironic that the State of Maine, which

12. Neither *Travis* nor the present case should be taken in any way to denigrate the value of reciprocity in such matters. The evil at which they are aimed is the unilateral imposition of a disadvantage upon nonresidents, not reciprocally favorable treatment of nonresidents by States that coordinate their tax laws.

allows the credit, had made an appearance in this case as an amicus urging, in effect, the denial of the credit by an adjudication of unconstitutionality of New Hampshire's statute. It seems to me that Maine should be here seeking to uphold its own legislatively devised plan or turn its attention to its own legislature. . . .

One wonders whether this is just a lawyers' lawsuit. Certainly, the appellants, upon prevailing today, have no direct or apparent financial gain. Relief for them from the New Hampshire income tax results only in a corresponding, pro tanto, increase in their Maine income tax. Dollarwise, they emerge at exactly the same point. The single difference is that their State, Maine, enjoys the tax on the New Hampshire-earned income, rather than New Hampshire. Where, then, is the injury? If there is an element of injury, it is Maine-imposed.

We waste our time, therefore, theorizing and agonizing about the Privileges and Immunities Clause and equal protection in this case. But if that exercise in futility is nevertheless indicated, I see little merit in the appellants' quest for relief. It is settled that absolute equality is not a requisite under the Privileges and Immunities Clause. And I fail to perceive unconstitutional unequal protection on New Hampshire's part. If inequality exists, it is due to differences in the respective income tax rates of the States that border upon New Hampshire.

I say again that this is a noncase, made seemingly attractive by high-sounding suggestions of inequality and unfairness. The State of Maine has the cure within its grasp, and if the cure is of importance to it and to its citizens, such as appellants, it and they should be about adjusting Maine's house rather than coming here complaining of a collateral effect of its own statute.

Questions and Comments

(1) Under interest analysis it is assumed that the forum has an interest in the well-being of its own residents but not, generally, in the well-being of nonresidents. When forum law favors a resident, it is to be applied under the Currie approach (either because the forum is the only interested jurisdiction or because forum law applies in the face of a true conflict). On the other hand, if we substitute a nonresident for the resident, the forum interest may disappear, and the analysis may yield application of a different state's law. That looks a lot like discrimination on the basis of state citizenship, forbidden by the privileges and immunities clause. That worried Currie, and he addressed the problem at length (with co-author Herma Kay) in Chapter 10 of Currie, Selected Essays on the Conflict of Laws (1963). The basic answer was that such "discrimination" was acceptable if it merely resulted in subjecting the nonresident to the law of his home state.

Does *Austin* undermine the Currie solution? Professor Ely thinks so: "If *Austin* is right as written, the dominant contemporary choice-of-law theory is unconstitutional." Ely, Choice of Law and the State's Interest in Protecting Its Own, 23 Wm. & Mary L. Rev. 173, 186-187 (1981).

Ely notes two possible ways of avoiding that conclusion. First, *Austin* may be wrong: If the purpose of the privileges and immunities clause is to protect people from legislatures and courts of other states, with whom they have no political influence, adequate protection is afforded by treating them the way that their own legislature and courts would—*i.e.*, applying their own home state's law to them. Note, however, that under interest analysis, the nonresident is not *always* treated according to home-state law, because if the forum has an interest in applying its own law, it will do so. The nonresident, in other words, is held to his or her home-state law only in those circumstances where it is disadvantageous. Where home-state law *helps* the nonresident, its application is not guaranteed. Second, Ely says, the Court was obviously unaware of the conflicts implication of its decision in *Austin* since the plurality in *Hague*, page 359 *supra*, seemed to uphold the legitimacy of Minnesota's interest in one who had acquired a domicile in Minnesota. Such an interest should not both be a defense of applying Minnesota law against a due process attack and the basis for a privileges and immunities attack (because Minnesota would have "discriminated" against someone who had not acquired Minnesota residency by not applying its law to such a person). Ely, at 187-189.

(2) *Austin*'s implications for interest analysis might be further limited by noting: (a) In *Austin*, New Hampshire applied New Hampshire law, which itself discriminated on the basis of state residency; in a conflicts case, the forum is not applying its own law, with two different results depending on residency, but in a sense is applying two different states' laws, each of which has a legitimate claim to appliation; and (b) the privileges and immunities cases decided by the Supreme Court involve the state as litigant (tax cases, etc.), while conflicts cases involve the state merely as arbitrator. Are these observations enough to save interest analysis from constitutional invalidity?

(3) In Pennsylvania v. New Jersey, 426 U.S. 660 (1976), the Court turned down a suit to recover taxes "diverted" from the treasuries of the plaintiff states to the treasury of New Jersey by a New Jersey scheme virtually identical to that condemned in *Austin.*

The heart of the Court's reasoning lay in the fact that

> In neither of the suits at bar has the defendant State inflicted any injury upon the Plaintiff States through the imposition of the taxes held [or] alleged . . . to be unconstitutional. The injuries to the plaintiffs' fiscs were self-inflicted, resulting from decisions by their respective legislatures. [N]othing prevents Pennsylvania from withdrawing that credit for taxes paid to New Jersey. No State can be heard to complain about damage inflicted by its own hand.

426 U.S. at 664.

The Court went on to say that the equal protection and privileges and immunities clauses protect "people, not states." *Id.* at 664-665. The right of a state to maintain actions of this nature as parens patriae was rejected as carrying the potential of converting any private suit desired by the state into a case within the original jurisdiction of the Supreme Court.

(4) In Baldwin v. Montana Fish & Game Commission, 436 U.S. 371 (1978), the Supreme Court rejected a privileges and immunities attack on a Montana law that charged a substantially higher fee for nonresidents than residents for fishing and hunting licenses. Only those privileges and immunities that bear on the vitality of the nation as a whole were deemed to be within the protection of the clause. But very shortly thereafter, the Court struck down Alaska's law preferring state residents for jobs arising out of oil and gas leases or permits for oil and gas pipelines to which the state was a party. Hicklin v. Orbeck, 437 U.S. 518 (1978). Justice Brennan, who had dissented in *Baldwin,* wrote for a unanimous Court in rejecting an earlier line of cases (*e.g.*, Corfield v. Coryell, 6 F. Cas. 546 (C.C.E.D. Pa. 1823)) that had allowed states to discriminate with respect to benefits derived from state-owned property. Can *Baldwin* be squared with *Orbeck?*

(5) In Zobel v. Williams, 457 U.S. 55 (1982), the Supreme Court struck down on equal protection grounds an Alaskan plan that distributed state oil revenues to citizens on the basis of how long they had been state residents. Justice O'Connor concurred but urged a privileges and immunities rationale—forbidding discrimination because of *past* noncitizenship. Would her approach require a court in an ordinary conflicts case to treat one with after-acquired domicile the same as one with pre-acquired domicile?

(6) In 1997, Texas amended its procedural law to discourage out-of-state plaintiffs from filing claims in Texas on the basis of out-of-state injuries. It enacted a borrowing statute that required a non-resident plaintiff suing in Texas on a claim that arose in another state to satisfy the statute of limitations of both Texas and the state where the claim arose. And it amended its forum non conveniens statute to permit dismissal of out-of-state asbestos exposure claims unless the claim is brought by a legal resident of Texas. The Texas Supreme Court rejected a challenge to these statutes based on the privileges and immunities clause. *See* Owens Corning v. Carter, 997 S.W.2d 560 (Tex. 1999). Is this decision consistent with *Austin?*

(7) The Supreme Court invalidated on privileges and immunity grounds two statutes imposing residency requirements for admission to the bar. Supreme Court of Virginia v. Friedman, 487 U.S. 59 (1988) (invalidating a Virginia rule requiring out-of-state lawyers to become permanent residents in order to be admitted without examination); Barnard v. Thorstenn, 489 U.S. 546 (1989) (invalidating requirement that applicants live in Virgin Islands one year prior to admission and declare intention to reside in the Virgin Islands thereafter).

(8) Another issue that involves the treatment of citizens based upon their relationship with a state is that of residency requirements. The issue is not within the purview of the privileges and immunities clause because a residency requirement denies a privilege to those who may have acquired state citizenship before the end of the required residency period. Nonetheless, in Shapiro v. Thompson, 394 U.S. 618 (1969), the Court struck down one-year residency requirements for welfare benefits based on the right to travel (a right that has never been tied firmly to specific language of the of the Constitution). In Dunn v. Blumstein, 405 U.S. 330 (1972), the Court also struck down a year's residency requirement before voter registration. In Vlandis v. Kline, 412 U.S. 441 (1973), the Court invalidated a Connecticut statute that prevented a person from becoming a resident (for in-statute tuition purposes) while a student. And most recently in Saenz v. Roe, 526 U.S. 489 (1999), the Court struck down a California statute limiting welfare benefits during the recipient's first year of state residence. *Saenz* is important because it grounded the right to travel in the Fourteenth Amendment's privileges *or* immunities clause, a constitutional provision that most commentators viewed as moribund. For commentary, see Tribe, *Saenz* Sans Prophecy: Does the Privileges Or Immunities Revival Portend the Future—Or Reveal the Structure of the Present?, 113 Harv. L. Rev. 110 (1999); Hills, Poverty, Residency, and Federalism: States' Duty of Impartiality Toward Newcomers, 1999 Sup. Ct. Rev. 277.

The decisions from *Shapiro* through *Saenz* do not deny that states have interests that are served by residency requirements. Rather, they hold that financial and administration interests are not "compelling" interests that warrant restriction of the right to travel. The Court recognized such a compelling interest in Sosna v. Iowa, 419 U.S. 393 (1975), which upheld an Iowa statute requiring one year of state residence prior to obtaining a divorce from state courts. The Court differentiated this durational residency requirement from the one struck down in *Shapiro* on the ground that Iowa's requirement did not deprive the applicant of the benefit altogether. The Court reasoned that while the welfare benefits denied by the statute in *Shapiro* were irretrievably lost, the right to file for a divorce was only temporarily delayed by the Iowa statute. The Court also noted that significant social consequences were likely to follow from divorce and that the State has interests both in protecting itself from use as a "divorce mill" and in protecting its judgment from collateral attacks in other states.

G. D. Searle & Co. v. Cohn

455 U.S. 404 (1982)

Justice Blackmun delivered the opinion of the Court.

A New Jersey statute, N.J. Stat. Ann. §2A:14-22 (West) (1952), tolls the limitation period of an action against a foreign corporation that is amenable to jurisdiction in New Jersey courts but that has in New Jersey no person or officer upon whom process may be served. The United States Court of Appeals for the Third Circuit in this case held that the statute does not violate the Equal Protection and Due Process Clauses of the Fourteenth Amendment. We agree, but we vacate the Court of Appeals' Judgment and remand the case for consideration of petitioner's Commerce Clause challenge to the statute.

I

Respondents, Susan and Walter Cohn, are husband and wife. In 1963, Susan Cohn suffered a stroke. Eleven years later, in 1974, the Cohns sued petitioner, G. D. Searle & Co., in the Superior Court of New Jersey, Essex County, alleging that Susan Cohn's stroke was caused by her use of an oral contraceptive manufactured by petitioner. Petitioner was served under New Jersey's long-arm rule, N.J. Ct. Rule 4:4-4(c)(1) (1969). Petitioner removed the suit to federal court and thereafter moved for summary judgment based upon New Jersey's two-year statute of limitation, N.J. stat. Ann. §2A:14-2 (West) (1952), governing an "action at law for an injury to the person caused by . . . wrongful act." Respondents countered with §2A:14-22. That section tolls the statute of limitation for a cause of action against a foreign corporation that "is not represented" in New Jersey "by any person or officer upon whom summons or other original process may be served."

The District Court ruled that petitioner was not represented in New Jersey for the purposes of the tolling provision. Nevertheless, it held that respondents' suit was barred. According to the District Court, the tolling provision had operated to preserve only causes of action against corporate defendants that were not subject to in personam jurisdiction in New Jersey. With the enactment of New Jersey's long-arm rule, now N.J. Ct. Rule 4:4-4(c), the rationale for the pre-existing tolling provision ceased to exist. On this reasoning, the court held that the tolling provision served no logical purpose, found it invalid under the Equal Protection Clause, and ruled that the two-year statute of limitation therefore barred respondent's suit.

Respondents appealed. Before the Court of Appeals reached a decision, however, the Supreme Court of New Jersey decided Velmohos v. Maren Engineering Corp. That court ruled, as a matter of New Jersey law, that the tolling provision continued in force despite the advent of long-arm jurisdiction. In addition, the court concluded that the tolling provision did not violate the Equal Protection or Due Process Clauses of the Fourteenth Amendment, because the increased difficulty of out-of-state service provided a rational basis for tolling the statute of limitation in a suit against an unrepresented foreign corporation.

The Court of Appeals then followed the New Jersey Supreme Court's lead and reversed the District Court. Summing up what it felt to be the rational basis for the tolling provision, the Court of Appeals explained:

> Since service of process under the long-arm statute is more difficult and time-consuming to achieve than service within the state, and since out-of-state, non-represented corporate defendants may be difficult to locate let alone serve, tolling the statute of limitations protects New Jersey plaintiffs and facilitates their lawsuits against such defendants.

Because of the novel and substantial character of the federal issue involved, we granted certiorari.

II

Like the Court of Appeals, we conclude that the New Jersey statute does not violate the Equal Protection Clause. In the absence of a classification that is inherently invidious or that impinges upon fundamental rights, a state statute is to be upheld against equal protection attack if it is rationally related to the achievement of legitimate governmental ends. The New Jersey tolling provision need satisfy only this constitutional minimum. As the Court explained in Chase Securities Corp. v. Donaldson:

> [Statutes of limitation] represent a public policy about the privilege to litigate. Their shelter has never been regarded as what now is called a "fundamental" right or what used to be called a "natural" right of the individual. He may, of course, have the protection of the policy while it exists, but the history of pleas of limitation shows them to be good only by legislative grace and to be subject to a relatively large degree of legislative control.

See also Campbell v. Holt.[6]

Petitioner insists that the tolling statute no longer is rationally related to a legitimate state objective. Repeating the argument it made below, petitioner claims that the statute's only purpose was to preserve causes of action for those New Jersey plaintiffs unable to obtain in personam jurisdiction over unrepresented foreign corporations. With the presence now of long-arm jurisdiction, petitioner contends, there is no longer a valid reason for tolling the limitation period for a suit against an amenable foreign corporation without a New Jersey representative.

---

6. Before the Court of Appeals, petitioner conceded that the tolling provision does not implicate a suspect classification. Before this court, petitioner argues for a heightened level of scrutiny because it is a corporation not doing business in New Jersey and therefore is without a voice in the New Jersey legislature. Only a rational basis, however, is required to support a distinction between foreign and domestic corporations. Western & S.L.I. Co. v. Bd. of Equalization, 451 U.S. 648 (1981). The same is true here where the tolling provision treats an unrepresented foreign corporation differently from a domestic corporation and from a foreign corporation having a New Jersey representative.

We note at the outset, and in passing, that petitioner's argument fails as a matter of state law. The New Jersey Supreme Court disagreed with petitioner's interpretation of the statute. That court observed that the State's original tolling provision did not mention corporations and thus treated them like all other defendants. In 1949, the state legislature amended the statute and exempted corporations except those foreign corporations "not represented" in New Jersey. Consequently, the court reasoned, the tolling provision was not rendered meaningless by the subsequent acceptance of long-arm jurisdiction. As construed by the highest judicial authority on New Jersey law, the meaning of the tolling statute cannot be confined as narrowly as petitioner would like.

When the statute is examined under the Equal Protection Clause, it survives petitioner's constitutional challenge because rational reasons support tolling the limitation period for unrepresented foreign corporations despite the institution of long-arm jurisdiction in New Jersey. First, the unrepresented foreign corporation remains potentially difficult to locate. Long-arm jurisdiction does not alleviate this problem, since a New Jersey plaintiff must find the unrepresented foreign corporation before it can be served. It is true, of course, that respondents had little or no trouble locating this particular, well-known defendant-petitioner, but the tolling provision is premised on a reasonable assumption that unrepresented foreign corporations, as a general rule, may not be so easy to find and serve.

Second, the institution of long-arm jurisdiction in New Jersey has not made service upon an unrepresented foreign corporation the equivalent of service upon a corporation with a New Jersey representative. The long-arm rule, N.J. Ct. Rule 4:4-4(c)(1) (1969), prescribes conditions upon extraterritorial service to ensure that New Jersey's long-arm jurisdiction has been properly invoked. In *Velmohos*, the New Jersey Supreme Court explained:

> Under our rules, extra-territorial service is not simply an alternative to service within the State. Plaintiffs may not resort to out-of-state service unless proper efforts to effect service in New Jersey have failed. The rule imposes a further burden on a plaintiff by requiring him to gather sufficient information to satisfy a court that service is "consistent with due process of law."

Thus, there are burdens a plaintiff must bear when he sues a foreign corporation lacking a New Jersey representative that he would not bear if the defendant were a domestic corporation or a foreign corporation with a New Jersey representative.

In response to these rationales for treating unrepresented foreign corporations differently from other corporations, petitioner argues that the tolling provision is unnecessary. Petitioner cites N.J. Ct. Rule 4:2-2 and contends that a plaintiff can preserve his cause of action against a hard-to-locate corporate defendant by filing a complaint and thereby halting the running of the limitation period. But this is not an adequate substitute for the tolling provision. A court may dismiss a case if it has not been prosecuted after six months, N.J. Ct. Rule 1:13-7, or if summons is not issued within 10 days of the filing of the complaint, N.J. Ct. Rule 4:4-1. In any event, a State may provide more than one solution for a perceived problem. The Court of Appeals appropriately commented: "Nothing in law or logic prevents the New Jersey legislature from providing New Jersey plaintiffs with a mechanism for relief from the burdens of suits against nonrepresented foreign corporations which is additional to any mechanism found in the Court Rules."

Petitioner also argues that a New Jersey plaintiff's burdens do not justify leaving a defendant open to suit without any time limit. In *Velmohos*, however, the New Jersey Supreme Court expressly authorized an unrepresented foreign corporation to plead another defense in response to a tardy suit. While the tolling provision denies an unrepresented foreign corporation the benefit of the statute of limitation, the corporation, the court stated flatly, remains free to plead laches. "If a plaintiff's delay is inexcusable and has resulted in prejudice to the defendant, the latter may raise the equitable defense of laches to bar the claim." Thus, under New Jersey law, an amenable, unrepresented foreign corporation may successfully raise a bar to a plaintiff's suit if the plaintiff's delay cannot be excused and the corporation has suffered "prejudice."

In sum, because of the burdens connected with serving unrepresented foreign corporations, we agree with the Court of Appeals and the New Jersey Supreme Court that the tolling provision does not deprive an unrepresented foreign corporation of the equal protection of the laws.[7]

[The Court remands for consideration of a Commerce Clause challenge to the New Jersey statute.]

[Justice Powell, joined by Chief Justice Burger, concurred in parts I and II of the Court's opinion but dissented from Part III, feeling that it was appropriate for the Court to consider and determine the commerce clause issue. They expressed no opinion, however, on the merits of that issue.]

---

7. Petitioner also presses a due process claim. In the Court of Appeals, petitioner argued that the tolling statute violates due process "by unfairly and irrationally denying certain foreign corporations the benefit of the Statute of Limitations without furthering any legitimate societal interest." The Court of Appeals rejected petitioner's due process challenge to the statute at the same time that it rejected petitioner's equal protection contention. Indeed, this due process argument is nothing more than a restatement of petitioner's equal protection claim.

In this Court, petitioner has attempted to put forward a new due process argument. Petitioner notes that it can obtain the benefit of the statute of limitation by appointing an agent to accept service. Fearing that appointment of an agent might subject it to suit in New Jersey when there otherwise would not be the minimum contacts required for suit in the State under the Due Process Clause, *see* International Shoe Co. v. Washington, petitioner insists that New Jersey law violates due process by conditioning the benefit of the limitiation period upon the appointment of a New Jersey agent. Because petitioner did not present this argument to the Court of Appeals, we do not address it.

Justice STEVENS, dissenting.

The equal protection question in this case is novel. I agree with the Court that there is a rational basis for treating unregistered foreign corporations differently from registered corporations because they are somewhat more difficult to locate and to serve with process. Thus, a provision that merely gave a plaintiffs a fair opportunity to overcome these difficulties—for example, a longer period of limitations for suits against such corporations, or a tolling provision limited to corporations that had not filed their current address with the Secretary of State—would unquestionably be permissible. But does it follow that it is also rational to deny such corporations the benefit of any statute of limitations? Because there is a rational basis for *some* differential treatment, does it automatically follow that *any* differential treatment is constitutionally permissible? I think not; in my view the Constitution requires a rational basis for the special burden imposed on the disfavored class as well as a reason for treating that class differently.

The Court avoids these troubling questions by noting that the New Jersey Supreme Court has stated that an unrepresented foreign corporation may plead the defense of laches in an appropriate case. But there are material differences between laches—which requires the defendant to prove inexcusable delay and prejudice—and the bar of limitations, which requires no such proof. Thus, the availability of this alternative defense neither eliminates the differential treatment nor provides a justification for it; the defense merely lessens its adverse consequences.

I can find no legitimate state purpose to justify the special burden imposed on unregistered foreign corporations by the challenged statute. I would reverse the judgment of the Court of Appeals.

Questions and Comments

(1) What is the difference between the privileges and immunities clause and the equal protection clauses as they bear on discrimination on the basis of state citizenship? Professor Ely implies that the rational-basis test might always be satisfied when a state treats nonresidents differently because they are nonresidents, making equal protection irrelevant, while the privileges and immunities clause is directed specifically at such discrimination. *See* Ely, Choice of Law and the State's Interest in Protecting its Own, 23 Wm. & Mary L. Rev. 173, 181 (1981). Do the opinions in *Austin* and *G. D. Searle, supra* pages 412, 421, support this view? Another difference is that corporations cannot benefit from the privileges and immunities clause because they are not "citizens." Blake v. McClung, 172 U.S. 239 (1898).

(2) Are the distinctions between laches and a statute of limitations mentioned in Justice Stevens' dissent enough to establish his point that the discrimination against unrepresented foreign corporations is too great (even

though some discrimination may be justified)? Does the majority's reference to the applicability of the laches doctrine concede the underlying point that discrimination may not be too severe, even under a rational-basis test (while denying the applicability of the point to the facts of the case)?

(3) In Burlington Northern Railroad Co. v. Ford, 504 U.S. 648 (1992), the Supreme Court rejected an equal protection challenge to a Montana venue provision that made venue in cases brought against out-of-state corporate defendants proper in any county in the state but which restricted venue in cases brought against local corporate defendants to the county of their principal place of business. The rationale for the statute, which was upheld under a rational-basis test, was that with local defendants there was a substantial convenience justification for limiting venue to the principal place of business, but with out-of-state defendants there was very little convenience reason to favor one place of trial over another.

D. "Extraterritorial" and "Inconsistent" Regulations

The Supreme Court has long invoked the "dormant" commerce clause as a basis for judicial preemption of state law that unduly burdens interstate commerce clause. The Court has devised a number of tests to serve this end. The central prohibition of the dormant commerce clause, like the prohibitions of the privileges and immunities and equal protection clauses, concerns state legislation that discriminates against out-of-staters. *See* CTS Corp. v. Dynamics Corp. of Am., 481 U.S. 69, 87 (1987). If a state law discriminates against out-of-staters, it is subject to "the strictest scrutiny of any purported legitimate local purpose and of the absence of nondiscriminatory alternatives." Hughes v. Oklahoma, 441 U.S. 322, 337 (1979). A second dormant commerce clause test applies when a state law is nondiscriminatory on its face but nonetheless significantly burdens interstate commerce. In this context the Court applies a balancing test: "Where the statute regulates evenhandedly to effectuate a legitimate local public interest, and its effects on interstate commerce are only incidental, it will be upheld unless the burden imposed on such commerce is clearly excessive in relation to the putative local benefits." Pike v. Bruce Church, Inc., 397 U.S. 137, 142 (1970).

The Supreme Court has also said that the dormant commerce clause prohibits certain state laws that regulate extraterritorially and others that lead to inconsistent regulatory burdens. These aspects of the dormant commerce clause are unsettled and poorly understood. But they are most relevant to conflict of laws and thus are the focus of the cases below.

Brown-Forman Distillers Corp. v. New York State Liquor Authority

476 U.S. 573 (1986)

Justice MARSHALL delivered the opinion of the Court.

The State of New York requires every liquor distiller or producer that sells liquor to wholesalers within the State to sell at a price that is no higher than the lowest price the distiller charges wholesalers anywhere else in the United States. The issue in this case is whether that requirement violates the Commerce Clause of the Constitution.

I

New York extensively regulates the sale and distribution of alcoholic beverages within its borders. The State's Alcoholic Beverage Control Law (ABC Law) prohibits the manufacture and sale of alcoholic beverages within the State without the appropriate licenses, ABC Law §100(1) (McKinney 1970), and regulates the terms of all sales. . . .

This litigation concerns §101-b(3)(d) of the ABC Law, which requires any distiller or agent that files a schedule of prices to include an affirmation that "the bottle and case price of liquor to wholesalers set forth in such schedule is no higher than the lowest price at which such item of liquor will be sold by such [distiller] to any wholesaler anywhere in any other state of the United States or in the District of Columbia, or to any state (or state agency) which owns and operates retail liquor stores" during the month covered by the schedule. . . .

II

This Court has adopted what amounts to a two-tiered approach to analyzing state economic regulation under the Commerce Clause. When a state statute directly regulates or discriminates against interstate commerce, or when its effect is to favor in-state economic interests over out-of-state interests, we have generally struck down the statute without further inquiry. When, however, a statute has only indirect effects on interstate commerce and regulates evenhandedly, we have examined whether the State's interest is legitimate and whether the burden on interstate commerce clearly exceeds the local benefits. We have also recognized that there is no clear line separating the category of state regulation that is virtually per se invalid under the Commerce Clause, and the category subject to the Pike v. Bruce Church balancing approach. In either situation the critical consideration is the overall effect of the statute on both local and interstate activity.

A

Appellant does not dispute that New York's affirmation law regulates all distillers of intoxicating liquors evenhandedly, or that the State's asserted interest—to assure the lowest possible prices for its residents—is legitimate. Appellant contends that these factors are irrelevant, however, because the lowest-price affirmation provision of the ABC Law falls within that category of direct regulations of interstate commerce that the Commerce Clause wholly forbids. This is so, appellant contends, because the ABC Law effectively regulates the price at which liquor is sold in other States. By requiring distillers to affirm that they will make no sales anywhere in the United States at a price lower than the posted price in New York, appellant argues, New York makes it illegal for a distiller to reduce its price in other States during the period that the posted New York price is in effect. Appellant contends that this constitutes direct regulation of interstate commerce. The law also disadvantages consumers in other States, according to appellant, and is therefore the sort of "simple economic protectionism" that this Court has routinely forbidden. . . .

B

This Court has once before examined the extraterritorial effects of a New York affirmation statute. In Joseph E. Seagram & Sons, Inc. v. Hostetter, 384 U.S. 35 (1966), the Court considered the constitutionality, under the Commerce and Supremacy Clauses, of the predecessor to New York's current affirmation law. That law differed from the present version in that it required the distiller to affirm that its prices during a given month in New York would be no higher than the lowest price at which the item had been sold elsewhere during the *previous* month. The Court recognized in that case, as we have here, that the most important issue was whether the statute regulated out-of-state transactions. It concluded, however, that "[t]he mere fact that [the statute] is geared to appellants' pricing policies in other States is not sufficient to invalidate the statute." The Court distinguished [Baldwin v. Seelig, 294 U.S. 511 (1935)], *supra*, by concluding that any effects of New York's ABC Law on a distiller's pricing policies in other States were "largely matters of conjecture," *ibid.*

Appellant relies on United States Brewers Assn. v. Healy, 692 F.2d 275 (CA2 1982), *aff'd*, 464 U.S. 909 (1983), in seeking to distinguish the present case from *Seagram.* In *Healy*, the Court of Appeals for the Second Circuit considered a Connecticut price-affirmation statute for beer sales that is not materially different from the current New York ABC Law. The Connecticut statute, like the ABC Law, required sellers to post prices at the beginning of a month, and proscribed deviation from the posted prices during that month. The statute also required brewers to affirm that their prices in

Connecticut were as low as the price at which they would sell beer in any bordering State during the effective month of the posted prices. The Court of Appeals distinguished *Seagram* based on the "prospective" nature of this affirmation requirement. It concluded that the Connecticut statute made it impossible for a brewer to lower its price in a bordering State in response to market conditions so long as it had a higher posted price in effect in Connecticut. By so doing, the statute "regulate[d] conduct occurring wholly outside the state," 692 F.2d, at 279, and thereby violated the Commerce Clause. We affirmed summarily, 464 U.S. 909 (1983).

C

We agree with appellants and with the *Healy* court that a "prospective" statute such as Connecticut's beer affirmation statute, or New York's liquor affirmation statute, regulates out-of-state transactions in violation of the Commerce Clause. Once a distiller has posted prices in New York, it is not free to change its prices elsewhere in the United States during the relevant month. Forcing a merchant to seek regulatory approval in one State before undertaking a transaction in another directly regulates interstate commerce. While New York may regulate the sale of liquor within its borders, and may seek low prices for its residents, it may not "project its legislation into [other States] by regulating the price to be paid" for liquor in those States.

That the ABC Law is addressed only to sales of liquor in New York is irrelevant if the "practical effect" of the law is to control liquor prices in other States. Southern Pacific Co. v. Arizona ex rel. Sullivan, 325 U.S. 761, 775 (1945). We cannot agree with New York that the practical effects of the affirmation law are speculative. It is undisputed that once a distiller's posted price is in effect in New York, it must seek the approval of the New York State Liquor Authority before it may lower its price for the same item in other States. It is not at all counter-intuitive, as the dissent maintains, to assume that the Liquor Authority would not permit appellant to reduce its New York price after the posted price has taken effect . . .

Moreover, the proliferation of state affirmation laws following this Court's decision in *Seagram* has greatly multiplied the likelihood that a seller will be subjected to inconsistent obligations in different States. The ease with which New York's lowest-price regulation can interfere with a distiller's operations in other States is aptly demonstrated by the controversy that gave rise to this lawsuit. By defining the "effective price" of liquor differently from other States, New York can effectively force appellant to abandon its promotional allowance program in States in which that program is legal, or force those other States to alter their own regulatory schemes in order to permit appellant to lower its New York prices without violating the affirmation laws of those States. Thus New York has "project[ed] its legislation" into other States, and directly regulated commerce therein, in violation of *Seelig, supra.*[6]

Questions and Comments

(1) How broadly should *Brown-Forman* be read? The opinion seems to suggest that there could be a commerce clause violation whenever a statute regulates conduct occurring wholly outside the state. *See also* Healy v. Beer Institute Inc., 491 U.S. 324, 336 (1989) (similar case to *Brown-Forman,* asserting that "a statute that directly controls commerce occurring wholly outside the boundaries of a State exceeds the inherent limits of the enacting State's authority and is invalid regardless of whether the statute's extraterritorial reach was intended by the legislature"). Is the Court constitutionalizing territorialism? Should a commerce clause argument have been made in Allstate v. Hague, *supra* page 359? Doesn't the application of one state's law to a cross-border transaction or event always indirectly regulate conduct in another state?

(2) Note the Court's concern about potential proliferation of state laws, leading to possible inconsistent regulations. This problem is present also in garden variety choice-of-law problems, is it not? Again, what about *Allstate?* Compare the Court's concern about proliferation of inconsistent regulation in International Paper Co. v. Harmel Ouellette, discussed page 635 *infra.*

(3) Professors Goldsmith and Sykes note that it is commonplace in our federal system for one state's laws to have effects in another, and for multistate actors to face different regulations across states. They argue that the "extraterritoriality" and "inconsistency" prongs of the dormant commerce clause are best viewed as disguised forms of the Supreme Court's traditional dormant commerce clause "balancing" test. *See* Goldsmith & Sykes, The Internet and the Dormant Commerce Clause, 110 Yale L.J. 785, 803-808 (2001).

(4) Why are some cases perceived as choice-of-law problems, while others (like *Brown-Forman*) are analyzed without reference to traditional choice-of-law reasoning? Would the present case look more like a choice-of-law problem if there were a private right of action in which some plaintiff sought to recover damages for violation of liquor pricing laws? If the defendant then claimed that its sales in other states could be regulated only under that state's laws, would this constitute a due process claim?

---

6. While we hold that New York's prospective price affirmation statute violates the Commerce Clause, we do not necessarily attach constitutional significance to the difference between a prospective statute and the retrospective statute at issue in *Seagram.* Indeed, one could argue that the effects of the statute in *Seagram* do not differ markedly from the effects of the statute at issue in the present case. If there is a conflict between today's decision and the *Seagram* decision, however, there will be time enough to address that conflict should a case arise involving a retrospective statute. Because no such statute is before us now, we need not consider the continuing validity of *Seagram.*

(5) The Supreme Court addressed the Commerce Clause issue left open in *G. D. Searle & Co., supra* page 421, in Bendix Autolite Corp. v. Midwesco Enterprises, Inc., 486 U.S. 888 (1988). Ohio's four-year statute of limitations was tolled for any corporation not "present" in Ohio, and to be present a foreign corporation had to appoint an agent for service of process, thereby consenting to the general jurisdiction of Ohio courts. The Court invalidated the Ohio statute on the ground that it "imposes a greater burden on out-of-state companies than it does on Ohio companies, subjecting the activities of foreign and domestic corporations to inconsistent regulations." *Id.* at 894. The Court distinguished *G. D. Searle & Co.,* stating: "State interests that are legitimate for equal protection or due process purposes may be insufficient to withstand Commerce Clause scrutiny." *Id.* Why should commerce clause scrutiny be more demanding than equal protection and due process scrutiny? The *Bendix Autolite* case is also discussed prominently in Sternberg v. O'Neil, *infra* page 463.

(6) While *Brown-Forman* uses the commerce clause to invalidate state regulatory action that is "extraterritorial," the due process clause is occasionally used to similar effect. In BMW of North America, Inc. v. Gore, 517 U.S. 559 (1996), the Court struck down an Alabama award of punitive damages that was designed to change defendant BMW's lawful conduct in other states. Invoking the due process clause, the Court explained that "Alabama may insist that BMW adhere to a particular disclosure policy in that State," but it "does not have the power . . . to punish BMW for conduct that was lawful where it occurred and that had no impact on Alabama or its residents. *Id.* at 572-573. In State Board of Insurance v. Todd Shipyards, 370 U.S. 451 (1962), the Court relied upon due process in holding that a state might not tax or regulate insurance contracts where its only connection to the contact was that the insured risk was located in the state. The Court could not have based its decision upon the commerce clause because the business of insurance has been left to state regulation under the McCarran-Ferguson Act, 15 U.S.C. §§1011-1012.

(7) The commerce clause imposes limits on a state's power to tax activities and property that are located primarily in another state or in a foreign nation. Quill Corp. v. North Dakota, 504 U.S. 298 (1992) invalidated on commerce clause grounds a state effort to tax out-of-state mail order businesses with no physical presence within the state. (As noted above, page 359, the Court in *Quill* reversed earlier holdings that such taxation was also a violation of the due process clause.) The Court applied a four-part test derived from Complete Auto Transit, Inc. v. Brady, 430 U.S. 274 (1977), upholding a tax where it "[1] is applied to an activity with a substantial nexus with the taxing State, [2] is fairly apportioned, [3] does not discriminate against interstate commerce, and [4] is fairly related to the services provided by the State." This test blends elements of antidiscrimination analysis with elements of extraterritoriality analysis. Note that one consequence of invalidating the state tax under the commerce clause rather than the due process clause is that Congress has the power to overrule the Court's commerce clause decisions, a fact on which the opinion relied.

CTS Corp. v. Dynamics Corporation of America

481 U.S. 69 (1987)

Justice POWELL delivered the opinion of the Court.

These cases present the questions whether the Control Share Acquisitions Chapter of the Indiana Business Corporation Law, Ind. Code §23-1-42 1 et seq. (Supp. 1986), is pre-empted by the Williams Act, 82 Stat. 454, as amended, 15 U.S.C. §§78m(d)-(e) and 78n(d)-(f) (1982 ed. and Supp. III), or violates the Commerce Clause of the Federal Constitution, Art. I, §8, cl. 3.

I

A

On March 4, 1986, the Governor of Indiana signed a revised Indiana Business Corporation Law, Ind. Code §23-1-17-1 et seq. (Supp. 1986). That law included the Control Share Acquisitions Chapter (Indiana Act or Act). Beginning on August 1, 1987, the Act will apply to any corporation incorporated in Indiana, §23-1-17-3(a), unless the corporation amends its articles of incorporation or bylaws to opt out of the Act, §23-1-42-5. Before that date, any Indiana corporation can opt into the Act by resolution of its board of directors. §23-1-17-3(b). The Act applies only to "issuing public corporations." The term "corporation" includes only businesses incorporated in Indiana. *See* §23-1-20-5. An "issuing public corporation" is defined as:

> a corporation that has:
> (1) one hundred (100) or more shareholders;
> (2) its principal place of business, its principal office, or substantial assets within Indiana;
> and
> (3) either:
> (A) more than ten percent (10%) of its shareholders resident in Indiana;
> (B) more than ten percent (10%) of its shares owned by Indiana residents; or
> (C) ten thousand (10,000) shareholders resident in Indiana.

§23-1-42-4(a).

The Act focuses on the acquisition of "control shares" in an issuing public corporation. Under the Act, an entity acquires "control shares" whenever it acquires shares that, but for the operation of the Act, would bring its voting power in the corporation to or above any of three thresholds: 20%, 33 ⅓%, or 50%. §23-1-42-1. An entity that acquires control shares does not necessarily acquire voting rights. Rather, it gains those rights only "to the extent granted by resolution approved by the shareholders of the issuing public corporation." §23-1-42-9(a). Section 23-1-42-9(b) requires a majority vote of all disinterested shareholders holding each class of stock for passage of such a resolution. The practical effect of this requirement is to condition acquisition of control of a corporation on approval of a majority of the pre-existing disinterested shareholders.

The shareholders decide whether to confer rights on the control shares at the next regularly scheduled meeting of the shareholders, or at a specially scheduled meeting. The acquiror can require management of the corporation to hold such a special meeting within 50 days if it files an "acquiring person statement," requests the meeting, and agrees to pay the expenses of the meeting. *See* §23-1-42-7. If the shareholders do not vote to restore voting rights to the shares, the corporation may redeem the control shares from the acquiror at fair market value, but it is not required to do so. §23-1-42-10(b). Similarly, if the acquiror does not file an acquiring person statement with the corporation, the corporation may, if its bylaws or articles of incorporation so provide, redeem the shares at any time after 60 days after the acquiror's last acquisition. §23-1-42-10(a).

B

On March 10, 1986, appellee Dynamics Corporation of America (Dynamics) owned 9.6% of the common stock of appellant CTS Corporation, an Indiana corporation. On that day, six days after the Act went into effect, Dynamics announced a tender offer for another million shares in CTS; purchase of those shares would have brought Dynamics' ownership interest in CTS to 27.5%. Also on March 10, Dynamics filed suit in the United States District Court for the Northern District of Illinois, alleging that CTS had violated the federal securities laws in a number of respects no longer relevant to these proceedings. On March 27, the board of directors of CTS, an Indiana corporation, elected to be governed by the provisions of the Act, see §23-1-17-3.

Four days later, on March 31, Dynamics moved for leave to amend its complaint to allege that the Act is pre-empted by the Williams Act, 15 U.S.C. §§78m(d)-(e) and 78n(d)-(f) (1982 ed. and Supp. III), and violates the Commerce Clause, Art. I, §8, cl. 3. Dynamics sought a temporary restraining order, a preliminary injunction, and declaratory relief against CTS' use of the Act. On April 9, the District Court ruled that the Williams Act pre-empts the Indiana Act and granted Dynamics' motion for declaratory relief. 637 F. Supp. 389 (ND Ill. 1986). Relying on Justice White's plurality opinion in Edgar v. MITE Corp., 457 U.S. 624 (1982), the court concluded that the Act "wholly frustrates the purpose and objective of Congress in striking a balance between the investor, management, and the takeover bidder in takeover contests." 637 F. Supp., at 399. A week later, on April 17, the District Court issued an opinion accepting Dynamics' claim that the Act violates the Commerce Clause. This holding rested on the court's conclusion that "the substantial interference with interstate commerce created by the [Act] outweighs the articulated local benefits so as to create an impermissible indirect burden on interstate commerce." *Id.*, at 406. The District Court certified its decisions on the Williams Act and Commerce Clause claims as final under Federal Rule of Civil Procedure 54(b). *Ibid.*

CTS appealed the District Court's holdings on these claims to the Court of Appeals for the Seventh Circuit. Because of the imminence of CTS' annual meeting, the Court of Appeals consolidated and expedited the two appeals. On April 23—23 days after Dynamics first contested application of the Act in the District Court—the Court of Appeals issued an order affirming the judgment of the District Court. The opinion followed on May 28. 794 F.2d 250 (1986).

After disposing of a variety of questions not relevant to this appeal, the Court of Appeals examined Dynamics' claim that the Williams Act preempts the Indiana Act . . .

The court next addressed Dynamic's Commerce Clause challenge to the Act. Applying the balancing test articulated in Pike v. Bruce Church, Inc., 397 U.S. 137 (1970), the court found the Act unconstitutional:

> Unlike a state's blue sky law the Indiana statute is calculated to impede transactions between residents of other states. For the sake of trivial or even negative benefits to its residents Indiana is depriving nonresidents of the valued opportunity to accept tender offers from other nonresidents.
>
> . . . Even if a corporation's tangible assets are immovable, the efficiency with which they are employed and the proportions in which the earnings they generate are divided between management and shareholders depends on the market for corporate control—an interstate, indeed international, market that the State of Indiana is not authorized to opt out of, as in effect it has done in this statute.

794 F.2d, at 264.

Finally, the court addressed the "internal affairs" doctrine, a "principle of conflict of laws . . . designed to make sure that the law of only one state shall govern the internal affairs of a corporation or other association." *Ibid.* It stated:

> We may assume without having to decide that Indiana has a broad latitude in regulating those affairs, even when the consequence may be to make it harder to take over an Indiana corporation . . . But in this case the effect on the interstate market in securities and corporate control is direct, intended, and substantial . . . [T]hat the mode of regulation involves jiggering with voting rights cannot take it outside the scope of judicial review under the commerce clause.

Ibid. Accordingly, the court affirmed the judgment of the District Court.

Both Indiana and CTS filed jurisdictional statements. We noted probable jurisdiction under 28 U.S.C. §1254(2), 479 U.S. 810 (1986), and now reverse.

[The Court then discussed why the Indiana statute was not preempted by the Williams Act.]

III

As an alternative basis for its decision, the Court of Appeals held that the Act violates the Commerce Clause of the Federal Constitution. We now address this holding. On its face, the Commerce Clause is nothing more than a grant to Congress of the power "[t]o regulate Commerce . . . among the several States . . . ," Art. I, §8, cl. 3. But it has been settled for more than a century that the Clause prohibits States from taking certain actions respecting interstate commerce even absent congressional action. *See, e.g.*, Cooley v. Board of Wardens, 12 How. 299 (1852). The Court's interpretation of "these great silences of the Constitution," H. P. Hood & Sons, Inc. v. Du Mond, 336 U.S. 525, 535 (1949), has not always been easy to follow. Rather, as the volume and complexity of commerce and regulation have grown in this country, the Court has articulated a variety of tests in an attempt to describe the difference between those regulations that the Commerce Clause permits and those regulations that it prohibits. *See, e.g.*, Raymond Motor Transportation, Inc. v. Rice, 434 U.S. 429, 441, n.15 (1978).

A

The principal objects of dormant Commerce Clause scrutiny are statutes that discriminate against interstate commerce. *See, e.g.*, Lewis v. BT Investment Managers, Inc., 447 U.S. 27, 36-37 (1980) . . . The Indiana Act is not such a statute. It has the same effects on tender offers whether or not the offeror is a domiciliary or resident of Indiana. Thus, it "visits its effects equally upon both interstate and local business," Lewis v. BT Investment Managers, Inc., *supra*, at 36.

Dynamics nevertheless contends that the statute is discriminatory because it will apply most often to out-of-state entities. This argument rests on the contention that, as a practical matter, most hostile tender offers are launched by offerors outside Indiana. But this argument avails Dynamics little. "The fact that the burden of a state regulation falls on some interstate companies does not, by itself, establish a claim of discrimination against interstate commerce." Exxon Corp. v. Governor of Maryland, 437 U.S. 117, 126 (1978). *See* Minnesota v. Clover Leaf Creamery Co., 449 U.S. 456, 471-472 (1981) (rejecting a claim of discrimination because the challenged statute "regulate[d] evenhandedly . . . without regard to whether the [commerce came] from outside the State"); Commonwealth Edison Co. v. Montana, 453 U.S. 609, 619 (1981) (rejecting a claim of discrimination because the "tax burden [was] borne according to the amount . . . consumed and not according to any distinction between in-state and out-of-state consumers"). Because nothing in the Indiana Act imposes a greater burden on out-of-state offerors than it does on similarly situated Indiana offerors, we reject the contention that the Act discriminates against interstate commerce.

B

This Court's recent Commerce Clause cases also have invalidated statutes that adversely may affect interstate commerce by subjecting activities to inconsistent regulations. *E.g.*, Brown-Forman Distillers Corp. v. New York State Liquor Authority, Edgar v. MITE Corp., Kassel v. Consolidated Freightways Corp. *See* Southern Pacific Co. v. Arizona, 325 U.S. 761, 774 (1945) (noting the "confusion and difficulty" that would attend the "unsatisfied need for uniformity" in setting maximum limits on train lengths); Cooley v. Board of Wardens, *supra,* at 319 (stating that the Commerce Clause prohibits States from regulating subjects that "are in their nature national, or admit only of one uniform system, or plan of regulation"). The Indiana Act poses no such problem. So long as each State regulates voting rights only in the corporations it has created, each corporation will be subject to the law of only one State. No principle of corporation law and practice is more firmly established than a State's authority to regulate domestic corporations, including the authority to define the voting rights of shareholders. *See* Restatement (Second) of Conflict of Laws §304 (1971) (concluding that the law of the incorporating State generally should "determine the right of a shareholder to participate in the administration of the affairs of the corporation"). Accordingly, we conclude that the Indiana Act does not create an impermissible risk of inconsistent regulation by different States.

C

The Court of Appeals did not find the Act unconstitutional for either of these threshold reasons. Rather, its decision rested on its view of the Act's potential to hinder tender offers. We think the Court of Appeals failed to appreciate the significance for Commerce Clause analysis of the fact that state regulation of corporate governance is regulation of entities whose very existence and attributes are a product of state law. As Chief Justice Marshall explained:

> A corporation is an artificial being, invisible, intangible, and existing only in contemplation of law. Being the mere creature of law, it possesses only those properties which the charter of its creation confers upon it, either expressly, or as incidental to its very existence. These are such as are supposed best calculated to effect the object for which it was created.

Trustees of Dartmouth College v. Woodward, 4 Wheat, 518, 636 (1819). *See* First National Bank of Boston v. Bellotti, 435 U.S. 765, 822-824 (1978) (Rehnquist, J., dissenting). Every State in this country has enacted laws regulating corporate governance. By prohibiting certain transactions, and regulating others, such laws necessarily affect certain aspects of interstate commerce. This necessarily is true with respect to corporations with shareholders in States other than the State of incorporation. Large corporations that are listed on national exchanges, or even regional exchanges, will have shareholders in many States and shares that are traded frequently. The markets that facilitate this national and international participation in ownership of corporations are essential for providing capital not only for new enterprises but also for established companies that need to expand their business. This beneficial free market system depends at its core upon the fact that a corporation—except in the rarest situations—is organized under, and governed by, the law of a single jurisdiction, traditionally the corporate law of the State of its incorporation.

These regulatory laws may affect directly a variety of corporate transactions. Mergers are a typical example. In view of the substantial effect that a merger may have on the shareholders' interests in a corporation, many States require supermajority votes to approve mergers. *See, e.g.*, MBCA §73 (requiring approval of a merger by a majority of all shares, rather than simply a majority of votes cast); RMBCA §11.03 (same). By requiring a greater vote for mergers than is required for other transactions, these laws make it more difficult for corporations to merge. State laws also may provide for "dissenters' rights" under which minority shareholders who disagree with corporate decisions to take particular actions are entitled to sell their shares to the corporation at fair market value. *See, e.g.*, MBCA §§80, 81; RMBCA §13.02. By requiring the corporation to purchase the shares of dissenting shareholders, these laws may inhibit a corporation from engaging in the specified transactions.[12]

12. Numerous other common regulations may affect both nonresident and resident shareholders of a corporation. Specified votes may be required for the sale of all of the corporation's assets. *See* MBCA §79; RMBCA §12.02. The election of directors may be staggered over a period of years to prevent abrupt changes in management. *See* MBCA §37; RMBCA §8.06. Various classes of stock may be created with differences in voting rights as to dividends and on liquidation. *See* MBCA §15; RMBCA §6.01(c). Provisions may be made for cumulative voting. *See* MBCA §33, par. 4; RMBCA §7.28; n.9, *supra*. Corporations may adopt restrictions on payment of dividends to ensure that specified ratios of assets to liabilities are maintained for the benefit of the holders of corporate bonds or notes. *See* MBCA §45 (noting that a corporation's articles of incorporation can restrict payment of dividends); RMBCA §6.40 (same). Where the shares of a corporation are held in States other than that of incorporation, actions taken pursuant to these and similar provisions of state law will affect all shareholders alike wherever they reside or are domiciled.

Nor is it unusual for partnership law to restrict certain transactions. For example, a purchaser of a partnership interest generally can gain a right to control the business only with the consent of other owners. *See* Uniform Partnership Act §27, 6 U.L.A. 353 (1969); Uniform Limited Partnership Act §19 (1916 draft), 6 U.L.A. 603 (1969); Revised Uniform Limited Partnership Act §§702, 704 (1976 draft), 6 U.L.A. 259, 261 (Supp. 1986). These provisions—in force in the great majority of the States—bear a striking resemblance to the Act at issue in this case.

It thus is an accepted part of the business landscape in this country for States to create corporations, to prescribe their powers, and to define the rights that are acquired by purchasing their shares. A State has an interest in promoting stable relationships among parties involved in the corporations it charters, as well as in ensuring that investors in such corporations have an effective voice in corporate affairs.

There can be no doubt that the Act reflects these concerns. The primary purpose of the Act is to protect the shareholders of Indiana corporations. It does this by affording shareholders, when a takeover offer is made, an opportunity to decide collectively whether the resulting change in voting control of the corporation, as they perceive it, would be desirable. A change of management may have important effects on the shareholders' interests; it is well within the State's role as overseer of corporate governance to offer this opportunity. The autonomy provided by allowing shareholders collectively to determine whether the takeover is advantageous to their interests may be especially beneficial where a hostile tender offer may coerce shareholders into tendering their shares.

Appellee Dynamics responds to this concern by arguing that the prospect of coercive tender offers is illusory, and that tender offers generally should be favored because they reallocate corporate assets into the hands of management who can use them most effectively . . . As indicated *supra,* at 82-83, Indiana's concern with tender offers is not groundless. Indeed, the potentially coercive aspects of tender offers have been recognized by the SEC, see SEC Release No. 21079, p.86,916, and by a number of scholarly commentators . . . The Constitution does not require the States to subscribe to any particular economic theory. We are not inclined "to second-guess the empirical judgments of lawmakers concerning the utility of legislation," Kassel v. Consolidated Freightways Corp., 450 U.S., at 679 (Brennan, J., concurring in judgment). In our view, the possibility of coercion in some takeover bids offers additional justification for Indiana's decision to promote the autonomy of independent shareholders.

Dynamics argues in any event that the State has " 'no legitimate interest in protecting the nonresident shareholders.' " Dynamics relies heavily on the statement by the *MITE* Court that "[i]nsofar as the . . . law burdens out-of-state transactions, there is nothing to be weighed in the balance to sustain the law." 457 U.S., at 644. But that comment was made in reference to an Illinois law that applied as well to out-of-state corporations as to in-state corporations. We agree that Indiana has no interest in protecting nonresident shareholders of *nonresident corporations.* But this Act applies only to corporations incorporated in Indiana. We reject the contention that Indiana has no interest in providing for the shareholders of its corporations the voting autonomy granted by the Act. Indiana has a substantial interest in preventing the corporate form from becoming a shield for unfair business dealing. Moreover, unlike the Illinois statute invalidated in *MITE,* the Indiana Act applies only to corporations that have a substantial number of shareholders in Indiana. *See* Ind. Code §23-1-42-4(a)(3) (Supp. 1986). Thus, every application of the Indiana Act will affect a substantial number of Indiana residents, whom Indiana indisputably has an interest in protecting.

D

Dynamics' argument that the Act is unconstitutional ultimately rests on its contention that the Act will limit the number of successful tender offers. There is little evidence that this will occur. But even if true, this result would not substantially affect our Commerce Clause analysis. We reiterate that this Act does not prohibit any entity—resident or nonresident—from offering to purchase, or from purchasing, shares in Indiana corporations, or from attempting thereby to gain control. It only provides regulatory procedures designed for the better protection of the corporations' shareholders. We have rejected the "notion that the Commerce Clause protects the particular structure or methods of operation in a . . . market." The very commodity that is traded in the securities market is one whose characteristics are defined by state law. Similarly, the very commodity that is traded in the "market for corporate control"—the corporation—is one that owes its existence and attributes to state law. Indiana need not define these commodities as other States do; it need only provide that residents and nonresidents have equal access to them. This Indiana has done. Accordingly, even if the Act should decrease the number of successful tender offers for Indiana corporations, this would not offend the Commerce Clause.[14]

IV

On its face, the Indiana Control Share Acquisitions Chapter evenhandedly determines the voting rights of shares of Indiana corporations. The Act does not conflict with the provisions or purposes of the Williams Act. To the limited extent that the Act affects interstate commerce, this is justified by the State's interests in defining the attributes of shares in its corporations and in protecting shareholders. Congress has never questioned the need for state regulation of these matters. Nor do we think such regulation offends the Constitution. Accordingly, we reverse the judgment of the Court of Appeals.

It is so ordered.

Justice SCALIA, concurring in part and concurring in the judgment.

---

14. CTS also contends that the Act does not violate the Commerce Clause—regardless of any burdens it may impose on interstate commerce—because a corporation's decision to be covered by the Act is purely "private" activity beyond the reach of the Commerce Clause. Because we reverse the judgment of the Court of Appeals on other grounds, we have no occasion to consider this argument.

I join Parts I, III-A, and III-B of the Court's opinion. However, having found, as those Parts do, that the Indiana Control Share Acquisitions Chapter neither "discriminates against interstate commerce" nor "create[s] an impermissible risk of inconsistent regulation by different States," I would conclude without further analysis that it is not invalid under the dormant Commerce Clause. While it has become standard practice at least since Pike v. Bruce Church, Inc., 397 U.S. 137 (1970), to consider, in addition to these factors, whether the burden on commerce imposed by a state statute "is clearly excessive in relation to the putative local benefits," *id.*, at 142, such an inquiry is ill suited to the judicial function and should be undertaken rarely if at all. This case is a good illustration of the point. Whether the control shares statute "protects shareholders of Indiana corporations," or protects incumbent management seems to me a highly debatable question, but it is extraordinary to think that the constitutionality of the Act should depend on the answer. Nothing in the Constitution says that the protection of entrenched management is any less important a "putative local benefit" than the protection of entrenched shareholders, and I do not know what qualifies us to make that judgment—or the related judgment as to how effective the present statute is in achieving one or the other objective—or the ultimate (and most ineffable) judgment as to whether, given importance-level *x*, and effectiveness-level *y*, the worth of the statute is "outweighed" by impact-on-commerce *z*.

One commentator has suggested that, at least much of the time, we do not in fact mean what we say when we declare that statutes which neither discriminate against commerce nor present a threat of multiple and inconsistent burdens might nonetheless be unconstitutional under a "balancing" test. *See* Regan, The Supreme Court and State Protectionism: Making Sense of the Dormant Commerce Clause, 84 Mich. L. Rev. 1091 (1986). If he is not correct, he ought to be. As long as a State's corporation law governs only its own corporations and does not discriminate against out-of-state interests, it should survive this Court's scrutiny under the Commerce Clause, whether it promotes shareholder welfare or industrial stagnation. Beyond that, it is for Congress to prescribe its invalidity . . .

I do not share the Court's apparent high estimation of the beneficence of the state statute at issue here. But a law can be both economic folly and constitutional. The Indiana Control Share Acquisitions Chapter is at least the latter. I therefore concur in the judgment of the Court.

Justice WHITE, with whom Justice BLACKMUN and Justice STEVENS join as to Part II, dissenting.

The majority today upholds Indiana's Control Share Acquisitions Chapter, a statute which will predictably foreclose completely some tender offers for stock in Indiana corporations. I disagree with the conclusion that the Chapter is neither pre-empted by the Williams Act nor in conflict with the Commerce Clause. The Chapter undermines the policy of the Williams Act by effectively preventing minor shareholders, in some circumstances, from acting in their own best interests by selling their stock. In addition, the Chapter will substantially burden the interstate market in corporate ownership, particularly if other States follow Indiana's lead as many already have done. The Chapter, therefore, directly inhibits interstate commerce, the very economic consequences the Commerce Clause was intended to prevent. The opinion of the Court of Appeals is far more persuasive than that of the majority today, and the judgment of that court should be affirmed.

I

[The dissenting opinion then discussed the William Act.]

II

Given the impact of the Control Share Acquisitions Chapter, it is clear that Indiana is directly regulating the purchase and sale of shares of stock in interstate commerce. Appellant CTS' stock is traded on the New York Stock Exchange, and people from all over the country buy and sell CTS' shares daily. Yet, under Indiana's scheme, any prospective purchaser will be effectively precluded from purchasing CTS' shares if the purchaser crosses one of the Chapter's threshold ownership levels and a majority of CTS' shareholders refuse to give the purchaser voting rights. This Court should not countenance such a restraint on interstate trade.

The United States, as amicus curiae, argues that Indiana's Control Share Acquisitions Chapter

> is written as a restraint on the *transferability* of voting rights in specified transactions, and it could not be written in any other way without changing its meaning. Since the restraint on the transfer of voting rights is a restraint on the transfer of shares, the Indiana Chapter, like the Illinois Act [in *MITE*], restrains "transfers of stock by stockholders to a third party."

Brief for Securities and Exchange Commission and United States as Amici Curiae 26. I agree. The majority ignores the practical impact of the Chapter in concluding that the Chapter does not violate the Commerce Clause. The Chapter is characterized as merely defining "the attributes of shares in its corporations," *ante*, at 94. The majority sees the trees but not the forest.

The Commerce Clause was included in our Constitution by the Framers to prevent the very type of economic protectionism Indiana's Control Share Acquisitions Chapter represents:

> The few simple words of the Commerce Clause—"The Congress shall have Power . . . To regulate Commerce . . . among the several States

> . . ."—reflected a central concern of the Framers that was an immediate reason for calling the Constitutional Convention: the conviction that in order to succeed, the new Union would have to avoid the tendencies toward economic Balkanization that had plagued relations among the Colonies and later among the States under the Articles of Confederation.

Hughes, supra, at 325-326.

The State of Indiana, in its brief, admits that at least one of the Chapter's goals is to protect Indiana corporations. The State notes that the Chapter permits shareholders "to determine . . . whether [a tender offeror] will liquidate the company or remove it from the State." Brief for Appellant in No. 86-97, p.19. The State repeats this point later in its brief: "The Statute permits shareholders (who may also be community residents or employees or suppliers of the corporation) to determine the intentions of any offeror concerning the liquidation of the company or its possible removal from the State." *Id.*, at 90. A state law which permits a majority of an Indiana corporation's stockholders to prevent individual investors, including out-of-state stockholders, from selling their stock to an out-of-state tender offeror and thereby frustrate any transfer of corporate control, is the archetype of the kind of state law that the Commerce Clause forbids.

Unlike state blue sky laws, Indiana's Control Share Acquisitions Chapter regulates the purchase and sale of stock of Indiana corporations in interstate commerce. Indeed, as noted above, the Chapter will inevitably be used to block interstate transactions in such stock. Because the Commerce Clause protects the "interstate market" in such securities, Exxon Corp. v. Governor of Maryland, 437 U.S. 117, 127 (1978), and because the Control Share Acquisitions Chapter substantially interferes with this interstate market, the Chapter clearly conflicts with the Commerce Clause.

With all due respect, I dissent.

Questions and Comments

(1) As the opinion indicates, *CTS* was preceded by Edgar v. MITE Corp., 457 U.S. 624 (1982), which invalidated a state antitakeover law that was by its terms applicable to companies not incorporated locally. It should not be surprising that state laws that have a significant effect in other states are often faced with pre-emption challenges as well as commerce clause challenges; for large-scale commercial transactions are often regulated by federal substantive law. *See, e.g.*, Capital Cities Cable, Inc. v. Crisp, 467 U.S. 691 (1984) (inconsistency between FCC regulation and attempts by Oklahoma to regulate broadcasting certain kinds of television advertising).

(2) The commerce clause cases in the area of corporate takeovers have generated a substantial literature. In addition to discussions of the common-law internal affairs doctrine (page 81 *supra*), *see* Pinto, The Constitution and the Market for Corporate Control: State Takeover Statutes After *CTS Corp.*, 29

Wm. & Mary L. Rev. 699 (1988); Regan, Siamese Essays: (I) *CTS Corp. v. General Dynamics Corp. of America* and Dormant Commerce Clause Doctrine; (II) Extraterritorial State Legislation, 85 Mich. L. Rev. 1865 (1985); Langevoort, The Supreme Court and the Politics of Corporate Takeovers: A Comment on *CTS Corp. v. General Dynamics Corp. of America,* 101 Harv. L. Rev. 96 (1987); Buxbaum, The Threatened Constitutionalization of the Internal Affairs Doctrine in Corporation Law, 75 Cal. L. Rev. 29 (1987). For a criticism of the Regan article that is not limited to the topic of corporate takeovers, *see* Gergen, Territoriality and the Perils of Formalism, 86 Mich. L. Rev. 1735 (1988).

(3) *CTS* is in one respect a case of public regulation because the Indiana Act represents a direct attempt to regulate the transfer of corporate control. From another point of view, however, the transaction in question was simply a private contract to sell shares of stock. If one focuses on the "private" characterization of the case, the *CTS* resembles more nearly a typical choice-of-law dispute. The question is simply, which state's law may constitutionally be applied to the sale of stock in an Indiana corporation? The answer then seems to be, "only Indiana's." Is this correct? Does *CTS* have any relevance for private contracts for a sale of stock?

(4) To what other sorts of substantive problems might you expect the *MITE/CTS* analysis to apply? In what substantive areas is there a serious threat of inconsistent regulation?

(5) Should there be a general prohibition on extraterritorial injunctions? For a discussion of the dormant commerce clause authority bearing on this issue, *see* Welkowitz, Preemption, Extraterritoriality, and the Problem of State Antidilution Laws, 67 Tul. L. Rev. 1 (1992). The author's main concern is with multistate tort litigation, such as antidilution actions, in which state courts have granted nationwide injunctions. The article also discusses other possible objections to extraterritorial injunctions, based on due process and jurisdiction to tax principles.

(6) The "extraterritoriality" and "inconsistent regulations" prongs of the dormant commerce clause have been invoked a great deal in recent years in litigation over the validity of state regulation of the Internet. We explore these issues *infra* page 858.

4

The Jurisdiction of Courts over Persons and Property

The right of a particular court to adjudicate a claim involves a number of different legal issues. There must be a state (or federal) long-arm statute authorizing the court to assert jurisdiction over the parties; the defendant must receive adequate notice and an opportunity to defend; venue must be appropriate; and the forum must be sufficiently convenient that the litigation avoids dismissal on the grounds of forum non conveniens. Many of these issues have been alluded to, more or less directly, in earlier chapters. And they constitute an important part of an introductory course on civil procedure.

Much of personal jurisdiction centers on assessments of "fairness," a notoriously spongy notion. Frequently, what seems eminently fair to one person seems outrageously unfair to the next. Some of the institutions undergirding the Supreme Court's notions of fairness, however, are oddly familiar. We will see below that one of the chief bases for jurisdictional fairness is the consent of the party objecting to forum authority. Consent arguments are commonplace in liberal political theory; philosophers from Locke to Rawls to Nozick have treated it as one of the most convincing justifications for state authority. Another argument traceable to Locke is the claim that an individual subjects him- or herself to state authority (either explicitly or implicitly) by entering into the state's territory. This theme, too, finds its way into the personal jurisdiction cases, for a defendant whose entrance into the forum and activities there gives rise to the cause of action will be subject to suit. The parallels between political theory and jurisdictional theory are discussed in Brilmayer, Jurisdictional Due Process and Political Theory, 39 U. Fla. L. Rev. 293 (1987); *see also* Cappalli, Locke as the Key: A Unifying and Coherent Theory of In Personam Jurisdiction, 43 UCLA L. Rev. 99 (1992).

The discussion below is directed toward the constitutional limitations on exercising long-arm jurisdiction over a case that has attenuated connections with the forum. That is, primarily, a question of due process. At one time, due process limitations were satisfied through the expedient of serving process within the forum state's territory. Pennoyer v. Neff, 95 U.S. 714 (1877). Another alternative was to obtain jurisdiction by attaching the defendant's local property. Harris v. Balk, 198 U.S. 215 (1905). The conceptual basis for assertions of state court jurisdiction was drastically rewritten in International Shoe Co. v. Washington, 326 U.S. 310 (1945), which stated that assertions of jurisdiction are constitutional where they are based upon "minimum contacts" adequate to establish "fair play and substantial justice." This standard, as we will see, has hardly been self-explanatory.

The first basis for jurisdiction that we will examine—the defendant's consent or waiver of right to object—has not changed very substantially over the historical development of the due process clause. In other respects, however, we've come a long way since the days of *Pennoyer* and *Balk*.

A. Consent and Waiver

1. Consent

The Bremen v. Zapata Off-Shore Co.

407 U.S. 1 (1972)

Chief Justice BURGER delivered the opinion of the Court.

We granted certiorari to review a judgment of the United States Court of Appeals for the Fifth Circuit declining to enforce a forum-selection clause governing disputes arising under an international towage contract between petitioners and respondent. The circuits have differed in their approach to such clauses. For the reasons stated hereafter, we vacate the judgment of the Court of Appeals.

In November 1967, respondent Zapata, a Houston-based American corporation, contracted with petitioner Unterweser, a German corporation, to tow Zapata's ocean-going, self-elevating drilling rig *Chaparral* from Louisiana to a point off Ravenna, Italy, in the Adriatic Sea, where Zapata had agreed to drill certain wells.

Zapata had solicited bids for the towage, and several companies including Unterweser had responded. Unterweser was the low bidder and Zapata requested it to submit a contract, which it did. The contract submitted by Unterweser contained the following provision, which is at issue in this case:

> Any dispute arising must be treated before the London Court of Justice.

In addition the contract contained two clauses purporting to exculpate Unterweser from liability for damages to the towed barge.

After reviewing the contract and making several changes, but without any alteration in the forum-selection or exculpatory clauses, a Zapata vice president executed the contract and forwarded it to Unterweser in Germany, where Unterweser accepted the changes, and the contract became effective.

On January 5, 1968, Unterweser's deep sea tug *Bremen* departed Venice, Louisiana, with the *Chaparral* in tow bound for Italy. On January 9, while the flotilla was in international waters in the middle of the Gulf of Mexico, a severe storm arose. The sharp roll of the *Chaparral* in Gulf waters caused its elevator legs, which had been raised for the voyage, to break off and fall into the sea, seriously damaging the *Chaparral.* In this emergency situation Zapata instructed the *Bremen* to tow its damaged rig to Tampa, Florida, the nearest port of refuge.

On January 12, Zapata, ignoring its contract promise to litigate "any dispute arising" in the English courts, commenced a suit in admiralty in the United States District Court at Tampa, seeking $3,500,000 damages against Unterweser in personam and the *Bremen* in rem, alleging negligent towage and breach of contract. . . .

We hold, with the six dissenting members of the Court of Appeals, that far too little weight and effect were given to the forum clause in resolving this controversy. For at least two decades we have witnessed an expansion of overseas commercial activities by business enterprises based in the United States. The barrier of distance that once tended to confine a business concern to a modest territory no longer does so. Here we see an American company with special expertise contracting with a foreign company to tow a complex machine thousands of miles across seas and oceans. The expansion of American business and industry will hardly be encouraged if, notwithstanding solemn contracts, we insist on a parochial concept that all disputes must be resolved under our laws and in our courts. Absent a contract forum, the considerations relied on by the Court of Appeals would be persuasive reasons for holding an American forum convenient in the traditional sense, but in an era of expanding world trade and commerce, the absolute aspects of the doctrine of the *Carbon Black* case have little place and would be a heavy hand indeed on the future development of international commercial dealings by Americans. We cannot have trade and commerce in world markets and international waters exclusively on our terms, governed by our laws, and resolved in our courts.

Forum-selection clauses have historically not been favored by American courts. Many courts, federal and state, have declined to enforce such clauses on the ground that they were "contrary to public policy," or that their effect was to "oust the jurisdiction" of the court. Although this view apparently still has considerable acceptance, other courts are tending to adopt a more hospitable attitude toward forum-selection causes. This view, advanced in the well-reasoned dissenting opinion in the instant case, is that such clauses are prima facie valid and should be enforced unless enforcement is shown by the resisting party to be "unreasonable" under the circumstances. We believe this is the correct doctrine to be followed by federal district courts sitting in admiralty. It is merely the other side of the proposition recognized by this Court in National Equipment Rental, Ltd. v. Szukhent, holding that in federal courts a party may validly consent to be sued in a jurisdiction where he cannot be found for service of process through contractual designation of an "agent" for receipt of process in that jurisdiction. In so holding, the Court stated: "[I]t is settled . . . that parties to a contract may agree in advance to submit to the jurisdiction of a given court, to permit notice to be served by the opposing party, or even to waive notice altogether." This approach is substantially that followed in other common-law countries including England. It is the view advanced by noted scholars and that adopted by the Restatement [Second] of the Conflict of Laws. It accords with ancient concepts of freedom of contract and reflects an appreciation of the expanding horizons of American contractors who seek business in all parts of the world. Not surprisingly, foreign businessmen prefer, as we do, to have disputes resolved in their own courts, but if that choice is not available, then in a neutral forum with expertise in the subject matter. Plainly, the courts of England meet the standards of neutrality and long experience in admiralty litigation. The choice of that forum was made in an arm's-length negotiation by experienced and sophisticated businessmen, and absent some compelling and countervailing reason it should be honored by the parties and enforced by the courts.

The argument that such clauses are improper because they tend to "oust" a court of jurisdiction is hardly more than a vestigial legal fiction. It appears to rest at core on historical judicial resistance to any attempt to reduce the power and business of a particular court and has little place in an era when all courts are overloaded and when businesses once essentially local now operate in world markets. It reflects something of a provincial attitude regarding the fairness of other tribunals. No one seriously contends in this case that the forum-selection clause "ousted" the District Court of jurisdiction over Zapata's action. The threshold question is whether that court should have exercised its jurisdiction to do more than give effect to the legitimate expectations of the parties, manifested in their freely negotiated agreement, by specifically enforcing the forum clause.

There are compelling reasons why a freely negotiated private international agreement, unaffected by fraud, undue influence, or overweening bargaining power, such as that involved here, should be given full effect. In this case, for example, we are concerned with a far from routine transaction between companies of two different nations contemplating the tow of an extremely costly piece of equipment from Louisiana across the Gulf of Mexico and the Atlantic Ocean, through the Mediterranean Sea to its final destination in the Adriatic Sea. In the course of the voyage, it was to traverse the waters of many jurisdictions. The *Chaparral* could have been damaged at any point along the route, and there were countless possible ports of refuge. That the accident occurred in the Gulf of Mexico and the barge was towed to Tampa in an emergency were mere fortuities. It cannot be doubted for a moment that the parties sought to provide for a neutral forum for the resolution of any disputes arising during the tow. Manifestly much uncertainty and possibly great inconvenience to both parties could arise if a suit could be maintained in any jurisdiction in which an accident might occur or if jurisdiction were left to any place where the *Bremen* or Unterweser might happen to be found.[15] The elimination of all such uncertainties by agreeing in advance on a forum acceptable to both parties is an indispensable element in international trade, commerce, and contracting. There is strong evidence that the forum clause was a vital part of the agreement, and it would be unrealistic to think that the parties did not conduct their negotiations, including fixing the monetary terms, with the consequences of the forum clause figuring prominently in their calculations. Under these circumstances, as Justice Karminski reasoned in sustaining jurisdiction over Zapata in the High Court of Justice, "[t]he force of an agreement for litigation in this country, freely entered into between two competent parties, seems to me to be very powerful."

Thus, in the light of present-day commercial realities and expanding international trade we conclude that the forum clause should control absent a strong showing that it should be set aside. Although their opinions are not altogether explicit, it seems reasonably clear that the District Court and the Court of Appeals placed the burden on Unterweser to show that London would be a more convenient forum than Tampa, although the contract expressly resolved that issue. The correct approach would have been to enforce the forum clause specifically unless Zapata could clearly show that enforcement would be unreasonable and unjust, or that the clause was invalid for such reasons as fraud or overreaching. Accordingly, the case must be remanded for reconsideration.

We note, however, that there is nothing in the record presently before us that would support a refusal to enforce the forum clause. The Court of Appeals suggested that enforcement would be contrary to the public policy of the forum under Bisso v. Inland Waterways Corp., because of the prospect

---

15. At the very least, the clause was an effort to eliminate all uncertainty as to the nature, location, and outlook of the forum in which these companies of differing nationalities might find themselves. Moreover, while the contract here did not specifically provide that the substantive law of England should be applied, it is the general rule in English courts that the parties are assumed, absent contrary indication, to have designated the forum with the view that it should apply its own law. It is therefore reasonable to conclude that the forum clause was also an effort to obtain certainty as to the applicable substantive law.

that the English courts would enforce the clauses of the towage contract purporting to exculpate Unterweser from liability for damages to the *Chaparral.* A contractual choice-of-forum clause should be held unenforceable if enforcement would contravene a strong public policy of the forum in which suit is brought, whether declared by statute or by judicial decision. It is clear, however, that whatever the proper scope of the policy expressed in *Bisso,* it does not reach this case. *Bisso* rested on considerations with respect to the towage business strictly in American waters, and those considerations are not controlling in an international commercial agreement. . . .

Courts have also suggested that a forum clause, even though it is freely bargained for and contravenes no important public policy of the forum, may nevertheless be "unreasonable" and unenforceable if the chosen forum is *seriously* inconvenient for the trial of the action. Of course, where it can be said with reasonable assurance that at the time they entered the contract, the parties to a freely negotiated private international commercial agreement contemplated the claimed inconvenience, it is difficult to see why any such claim of inconvenience should be heard to render the forum clause unenforceable. We are not here dealing with an agreement between two Americans to resolve their essentially local disputes in a remote alien forum. In such a case, the serious inconvenience of the contractual forum to one or both of the parties might carry greater weight in determining the reasonableness of the forum clause. The remoteness of the forum might suggest that the agreement was an adhesive one, or that the parties did not have the particular controversy in mind when they made their agreement; yet even there the party claiming should bear a heavy burden of proof. Similarly, selection of a remote forum to apply differing foreign law to an essentially American controversy might contravene an important public policy of the forum. For example, so long as *Bisso* governs American courts with respect to the towage business in American waters, it would quite arguably be improper to permit an American tower to avoid that policy by providing a foreign forum for resolution of his disputes with an American towee.

This case, however, involves a freely negotiated international commercial transaction between a German and an American corporation for towage of a vessel from the Gulf of Mexico to the Adriatic Sea. As noted, selection of a London forum was clearly a reasonable effort to bring vital certainty to this international transaction and to provide a neutral forum experienced and capable in the resolution of admiralty litigation. Whatever "inconvenience" Zapata would suffer by being forced to litigate in the contractual forum as it agreed to do was clearly foreseeable at the time of contracting. In such circumstances it should be incumbent on the party seeking to escape his contract to show that trial in the contractual forum will be so gravely difficult and inconvenient that he will for all practical purposes be deprived of his day in court. Absent that, there is no basis for concluding that it would be unfair, unjust, or unreasonable to hold that party to his bargain. . . .

Zapata's remaining contentions do not require extended treatment. It is clear that Unterweser's action in filing its limitation complaint in the District Court in Tampa was, so far as Zapata was concerned, solely as a defensive measure made necessary as a response to Zapata's breach of the forum clause of the contract. . . .

Justice DOUGLAS, dissenting. . . .

Respondent is a citizen of this country. Moreover, if it were remitted to the English court, its substantive rights would be adversely affected. Exculpatory provisions in the towage control provide (1) that petitioners, the masters and the crews "are not responsible for defaults and/or errors in the navigation of the tow" and (2) that "[d]amages suffered by the towed object are in any case for account of its Owners."

Under our decision in Dixilyn Drilling Corp. v. Crescent Towing & Salvage Co., "a contract which exempts the tower from liability for its own negligence" is not enforceable, though there is evidence in the present record that it is enforceable in England. That policy was first announced in Bisso v. Inland Waterways Corp. Although the casualty occurred on the high seas, the *Bisso* doctrine is nonetheless applicable.

Moreover, the casualty occurred close to the District Court, a number of potential witnesses, including respondent's crewmen, reside in that area, and the inspection and repairwork were done there. The testimony of the tower's crewmen, residing in Germany, is already available by way of depositions taken in the proceedings.

All in all, the District Court judge exercised his discretion wisely in enjoining petitioners from pursuing the litigation in England.

I would affirm the judgment below.

Carnival Cruise Lines, Inc. v. Shute

499 U.S 585 (1991)

Justice BLACKMUN delivered the opinion of the Court.

In this admiralty case we primarily consider whether the United States Court of Appeals for the Ninth Circuit correctly refused to enforce a forum-selection clause contained in tickets issued by petitioner Carnival Cruise Lines, Inc., to respondents Eulala and Russel Shute.

I

The Shutes, through an Arlington, Wash., travel agent, purchased passage for a 7-day cruise on petitioner's ship, the *Tropicale.* Respondents paid the fare to the agent who forwarded the payment to petitioner's headquarters in Miami, Fla. Petitioner then prepared the tickets and sent them to respondents in the State of Washington. The face of each ticket, at its left-hand lower corner, contained this admonition:

"SUBJECT TO CONDITIONS OF
CONTRACT ON LAST PAGES
IMPORTANT! PLEASE READ CONTRACT
—ON LAST PAGES 1, 2, 3" App. 15.

The following appeared on "contract page 1" of each ticket:

TERMS AND CONDITIONS OF PASSAGE CONTRACT TICKET

. . . .

> 3. (a) The acceptance of this ticket by the person or persons named hereon as passengers shall be deemed to be an acceptance and agreement by each of them of all of the terms and conditions of this Passage Contract Ticket.
>
> . . . .
>
> 8. It is agreed by and between the passenger and the Carrier that all disputes and matters whatsoever arising under, in connection with or incident to this Contract shall be litigated, if at all, in and before a Court located in the State of Florida, U.S.A., to the exclusion of the Courts of any other state or country."

Id., at 16.

The last quoted paragraph is the forum-selection clause at issue.

II

Respondents boarded the *Tropicale* in Los Angeles, Cal. The ship sailed to Puerto Vallarta, Mexico, and then returned to Los Angeles. While the ship was in international waters off the Mexican coast, respondent Eulala Shute was injured when she slipped on a deck mat during a guided tour of the ship's galley. Respondents filed suit against petitioner in the United States District Court for the Western District of Washington, claiming that Mrs. Shute's injuries had been caused by the negligence of Carnival Cruise Lines and its employees. *Id.*, at 4.

Petitioner moved for summary judgment, contending that the forum clause in respondents' tickets required the Shutes to bring their suit against petitioner in a court in the State of Florida. Petitioner contended, alternatively, that the District Court lacked personal jurisdiction over petitioner because petitioner's contacts with the State of Washington were insubstantial. The District Court granted the motion, holding that petitioner's contacts with Washington were constitutionally insufficient to support the exercise of personal jurisdiction.

The Court of Appeals reversed. Reasoning that "but for" petitioner's solicitation of business in Washington, respondents would not have taken the cruise and Mrs. Shute would not have been injured, the court concluded that petitioner had sufficient contacts with Washington to justify the District Court's exercise of personal jurisdiction. 897 F.2d 377, 385-386 (9th Cir. 1990).

Turning to the forum-selection clause, the Court of Appeals acknowledged that a court concerned with the enforceability of such a clause must begin its analysis with The Bremen v. Zapata Off-Shore Co., 407 U.S. 1 (1972), where this Court held that forum-selection clauses, although not "historically . . . favored," are "prima facie valid." *Id.*, at 9-10. *See* 897 F.2d, at 388. The appellate court concluded that the forum clause should not be enforced because it "was not freely bargained for." *Id.*, at 389. As an "independent justification" for refusing to enforce the clause, the Court of Appeals noted that there was evidence in the record to indicate that "the Shutes are physically and financially incapable of pursuing this litigation in Florida" and that the enforcement of the clause would operate to deprive them of their day in court and thereby contravene this Court's holding in *The Bremen.* 897 F.2d, at 389.

We granted certiorari to address the question whether the Court of Appeals was correct in holding that the District Court should hear respondents' tort claim against petitioner. 498 U.S. 807-808 (1990). Because we find the forum-selection clause to be dispositive of this question, we need not consider petitioner's constitutional argument as to personal jurisdiction. . . .

III

We begin by noting the boundaries of our inquiry. First, this is a case in admiralty, and federal law governs the enforceability of the forum-selection clause we scrutinize. *See* Archawski v. Hanioti, 350 U.S. 532, 533 (1956); The Moses Taylor, 4 Wall. 411, 427 (1867); Tr. of Oral Arg. 36-37, 12, 47-48. *Cf.* Stewart Organization, Inc. v. Ricoh Corp., 487 U.S. 22, 28-29 (1988). Second, we do not address the question whether respondents had sufficient notice of the forum clause before entering the contract for passage. Respondents essentially have conceded that they had notice of the forum-selection provision. Additionally, the Court of Appeals evaluated the enforceability of the forum clause under the assumption, although "doubtful," that respondents could be deemed to have had knowledge of the clause.

Within this context, respondents urge that the forum clause should not be enforced because, contrary to this Court's teachings in *The Bremen*, the clause was not the product of negotiation, and enforcement effectively would deprive respondents of their day in court. Additionally, respondents contend that the clause violates the Limitation of Vessel Owner's Liability Act, 46 U.S.C. App. §183c. We consider these arguments in turn.

IV

A

Both petitioner and respondents argue vigorously that the Court's opinion in *The Bremen* governs this case, and each side purports to find ample support for its position in that opinion's broad-ranging language. This seeming paradox derives in large part from key factual differences between this case and *The Bremen*, differences that preclude an automatic and simple application of *The Bremen*'s general principles to the facts here.

[The Court discusses the facts and holding of *The Bremen*, reproduced *supra* page 451.]

In applying *The Bremen*, the Court of Appeals in the present litigation took note of the foregoing "reasonableness" factors and rather automatically decided that the forum-selection clause was unenforceable because, unlike the parties in *The Bremen*, respondents are not business persons and did not negotiate the terms of the clause with petitioner. Alternatively, the Court of Appeals ruled that the clause should not be enforced because enforcement effectively would deprive respondents of an opportunity to litigate their claim against petitioner.

The Bremen concerned a "far from routine transaction between companies of two different nations contemplating the tow of an extremely costly piece of equipment from Louisiana across the Gulf of Mexico and the Atlantic Ocean, through the Mediterranean Sea to its final destination in the Adriatic Sea." *Id.*, at 13. These facts suggest that, even apart from the evidence of negotiation regarding the forum clause, it was entirely reasonable for the Court in *The Bremen* to have expected Unterweser and Zapata to have negotiated with care in selecting a forum for the resolution of disputes arising from their special towing contract.

In contrast, respondents' passage contract was purely routine and doubtless nearly identical to every commercial passage contract issued by petitioner and most other cruise lines. In this context, it would be entirely unreasonable for us to assume that respondents—or any other cruise passenger—would negotiate with petitioner the terms of a forum-selection clause in an ordinary commercial cruise ticket. Common sense dictates that a ticket of this kind will be a form contract the terms of which are not subject to negotiation, and that an individual purchasing the ticket will not have bargaining parity with the cruise line. But by ignoring the crucial differences in the business contexts in which the respective contracts were executed, the Court of Appeals' analysis seems to us to have distorted somewhat this Court's holding in *The Bremen*.

In evaluating the reasonableness of the forum clause at issue in this case, we must refine the analysis of *The Bremen* to account for the realities of form passage contracts. As an initial matter, we do not adopt the Court of Appeals' determination that a nonnegotiated forum-selection clause in a form ticket contract is never enforceable simply because it is not the subject of bargaining. Including a reasonable forum clause in a form contract of this kind well may be permissible for several reasons: First, a cruise line has a special interest in limiting the fora in which it potentially could be subject to suit. Because a cruise ship typically carries passengers from many locales, it is not unlikely that a mishap on a cruise could subject the cruise line to litigation in several different fora. *See The Bremen*, 407 U.S., at 13. Additionally, a clause establishing ex ante the forum for dispute resolution has the salutary effect of dispelling any confusion about where suits arising from the contract must be brought and defended, sparing litigants the time and expense of pretrial motions to determine the correct forum and conserving judicial resources that otherwise would be devoted to deciding those motions. *See Stewart Organization*, 487 U.S., at 33 (concurring opinion). Finally, it stands to reason that passengers who purchase tickets containing a forum clause like that at issue in this case benefit in the form of reduced fares reflecting the savings that the cruise line enjoys by limiting the fora in which it may be sued.

We also do not accept the Court of Appeals' "independent justification" for its conclusion that *The Bremen* dictates that the clause should not be enforced because "[t]here is evidence in the record to indicate that the Shutes are physically and financially incapable of pursuing this litigation in Florida." 897 F.2d, at 389. We do not defer to the Court of Appeals' findings of fact. In dismissing the case for lack of personal jurisdiction over petitioner, the District Court made no finding regarding the physical and financial impediments to the Shutes' pursuing their case in Florida. The Court of Appeals' conclusory reference to the record provides no basis for this Court to validate the finding of inconvenience. Furthermore, the Court of Appeals did not place in proper context this Court's statement in *The Bremen* that "the serious inconvenience of the contractual forum to one or both of the parties might carry greater weight in determining the reasonableness of the forum clause." 407 U.S. at 17. The Court made this statement in evaluating a hypothetical "agreement between two Americans to resolve their essentially local disputes in a remote alien forum." *Ibid.* In the present case, Florida is not a "remote alien forum," nor—given the fact that Mrs. Shute's accident occurred off the coast of Mexico—is this dispute an essentially local one inherently more suited to resolution in the State of Washington than in Florida. In light of these distinctions, and because respondents do not claim lack of notice of the forum clause, we conclude that they have not satisfied the "heavy burden of proof," *ibid.*, required to set aside the clause on grounds of inconvenience.

It bears emphasis that forum-selection clauses contained in form passage contracts are subject to judicial scrutiny for fundamental fairness. In this case, there is no indication that petitioner set Florida as the forum in which disputes were to be resolved as a means of discouraging cruise passengers from pursuing legitimate claims. Any suggestion of such a bad-faith motive is belied by two facts: Petitioner has its principal place of business in

Florida, and many of its cruises depart from and return to Florida ports. Similarly, there is no evidence that petitioner obtained respondents' accession to the forum clause by fraud or overreaching. Finally, respondents have conceded that they were given notice of the forum provision and, therefore, presumably retained the option of rejecting the contract with impunity. In the case before us, therefore, we conclude that the Court of Appeals erred in refusing to enforce the forum-selection clause.

[The Court then rejected the respondents' argument based on the Limitation of Vessel Owner's Liability Act.]

The judgment of the Court of Appeals is reversed.

It is so ordered.

Justice STEVENS, with whom Justice MARSHALL joins, dissenting.

The court prefaces its legal analysis with a factual statement that implies that a purchaser of a Carnival Cruise Lines passenger ticket is fully and fairly notified about the existence of the choice of forum clause in the fine print on the back of the ticket. Even if this implication were accurate, I would disagree with the Court's analysis. But, given the Court's preface, I begin my dissent by noting that only the most meticulous passenger is likely to become aware of the forum-selection provision. I have therefore appended to this opinion a facsimile of the relevant text, using the type size that actually appears in the ticket itself. A careful reader will find the forum-selection clause in the 8th of the 25 numbered paragraphs.

Of course, many passengers, like the respondents in this case, *see ante*, at 587, will not have an opportunity to read paragraph 8 until they have actually purchased their tickets. By this point, the passengers will already have accepted the condition set forth in paragraph 16(a), which provides that "[t]he Carrier shall not be liable to make any refund to passengers in respect of . . . tickets wholly or partly not used by a passenger." Not knowing whether or not that provision is legally enforceable, I assume that the average passenger would accept the risk of having to file suit in Florida in the event of an injury, rather than canceling—without a refund—a planned vacation at the last minute. The fact that the cruise line can reduce its litigation costs, and therefore its liability insurance premiums, by forcing this choice on its passengers does not, in my opinion, suffice to render the provision reasonable. *Cf.* Steven v. Fidelity & Casualty Co. of New York, 58 Cal. 2d 862, 883, 377 P.2d 284, 298 (1962) (refusing to enforce limitation on liability in insurance policy because insured "must purchase the policy before he even knows its provisions").

Forum-selection clauses in passenger tickets involve the intersection of two strands of traditional contract law that qualify the general rule that courts will enforce the terms of a contract as written. Pursuant to the first strand, courts traditionally have reviewed with heightened scrutiny the terms of contracts of adhesion, form contracts offered on a take-or-leave basis by a party with stronger bargaining power to a party with weaker power. Some commentators have questioned whether contracts of adhesion can justifiably be enforced at all under traditional contract theory because the adhering party generally enters into them without manifesting knowing and voluntary consent to all their terms. *See., e.g.*, Rakoff, Contracts of Adhesion: An Essay in Reconstruction, 96 Harv. L. Rev. 1173, 1179-1180 (1983); Slawson, Mass Contracts: Lawful Fraud in California, 48 S. Cal. L. Rev. 1, 12-13 (1974); K. Llewellyn, The Common Law Tradition 370-371 (1960).

The common law, recognizing that standardized form contracts account for a significant portion of all commercial agreements, has taken a less extreme position and instead subjects terms in contracts of adhesion to scrutiny for reasonableness. Judge J. Skelly Wright set out the state of the law succinctly in Williams v. Walker-Thomas Furniture Co., 121 U.S. App. D.C. 315, 319-320, 350 F.2d 445, 449-450 (1965) (footnotes omitted):

> Ordinarily, one who signs an agreement without full knowledge of its terms might be held to assume the risk that he has entered a one-sided bargain. But when a party of little bargaining power, and hence little real choice, signs a commercially unreasonable contract with little or no knowledge of its terms, it is hardly likely that his consent, or even an objective manifestation of his consent, was ever given to all of the terms. In such a case the usual rule that the terms of the agreement are not to be questioned should be abandoned and the court should consider whether the terms of the contract are so unfair that enforcement should be withheld.

See also Steven, 58 Cal. 2d, at 879-883, 377 P.2d, at 295-297; Henningsen v. Bloomfield Motors, Inc., 32 N.J. 358, 161 A.2d 69 (1960).

The second doctrinal principle implicated by forum-selection clauses is the traditional rule that "contractual provisions, which seek to limit the place or court in which an action may . . . be brought, are invalid as contrary to public policy." *See* Dougherty, Validity of Contractual Provision Limiting Place or Court in Which Action May Be Brought, 31 A.L.R. 4th 404, 409, §3 (1984). *See also* Home Insurance Co. v. Morse, 20 Wall. 445, 451 (1874). Although adherence to this general rule has declined in recent years, particularly following our decision in The Bremen v. Zapata Off-Shore Co., 407 U.S. 1 (1972), the prevailing rule is still that forum-selection clauses are not enforceable if they were not freely bargained for, create additional expense for one party, or deny one party a remedy. *See* 31 A.L.R. 4th, at 409-438 (citing cases). A forum-selection clause in a standardized passenger ticket would clearly have been unenforceable under the common law before our decision in *The Bremen, see* 407 U.S., at 9, and n.10, and, in my opinion, remains unenforceable under the prevailing rule today.

The Bremen, which the Court effectively treats as controlling this case, had nothing to say about stipulations printed on the back of passenger tickets. That case involved the enforceability of a forum-selection clause in a freely negotiated international agreement between two large corporations providing for the towage of a vessel from the Gulf of Mexico to the Adriatic Sea.

The Court recognized that such towage agreements had generally been held unenforceable in American courts but held that the doctrine of those cases did not extend to commercial arrangements between parties with equal bargaining power.

Questions and Comments

(1) Isn't what's really at stake in *The Bremen* the enforceability of the contractual clauses exculpating Unterweser from liability for damages? What does this suggest about the relationship between choice-of-forum clauses and choice of law? What about Justice Douglas's argument that if a contractual term would be unenforceable in a U.S. court but enforceable in a London court, the parties should not be allowed to evade the application of U.S. law by litigating in London? *Compare* Richards v. Lloyd's of London, 135 F. 3d 1289 (9th Cir. 1998) (in case alleging violations of U.S. Securities laws, court enforces English forum-selection and choice-of-law clauses even though U.S. Securities law contain an explicit anti-waiver provision).

(2). In support of its holding, *The Bremen* makes much of the fact that the choice-of-forum clause was negotiated at arm's length. *Carnival Cruise*, by contrast, suggests that this factor is not particularly important. Which view is right? The dissent in *Carnival Cruise* is suspicious of contract clauses that are not individually bargained for. But isn't the price term of this sort of contract often presented on a "take it or leave it" basis? The buyer can shop around for a better price, as he or she can shop for a cruise line without forum-selection clauses, but in many cases does not bargain with a particular seller for either a price reduction or for omitting the clause. Does that mean the dissent thinks that the Shutes should be able to go on the cruise and then refuse to pay more than a "fair" price for it?

(3). The majority in *Carnival Cruise* suggests that it need not consider the claim that the Shutes did not have adequate notice of the provision because the notice issue had been conceded by the Shute's brief. What would the majority do in cases in which the consumer did not see the fine print in time? *Compare* Oxman v. Amoroso, 659 N.Y.S.2d 963, 967 (City Ct. 1997) (forum-selection and choice-of law-clauses unenforceable because written in small and undistinguishable print unfit for consumer transactions) *with* Cross v. Kloster Cruise Lines, 897 F. Supp. 1304 (D. Or. 1995) (forum-selection clause on ticket enforceable despite being in very fine print with smudged pages since the plaintiff admitted that she noticed provision and demonstrated her ability to do so on the record).

Does a party even need to view a forum selection clause for it to be binding? The Seventh Circuit thought not in Hill v. Gateway 2000, 105 F.3d 1147 (7th Cir. 1997), a case involving the enforceability of an arbitration agreement contained in the Statement of Terms that accompanied a computer ordered by telephone. The plaintiffs saw the Statement of Terms but never read them closely and never laid eyes on the arbitration agreement. Writing for the court, Judge Easterbrook reasoned:

> A contract need not be read to be effective; people who accept [the computer] take the risk that the unread terms may in retrospect prove unwelcome. Terms inside Gateway's box stand or fall together. If they constitute the parties' contract because the Hills had an opportunity to return the computer after reading them, then all must be enforced. . . . Payment preceding the revelation of full terms is common for air transportation, insurance, and many other endeavors. Practical considerations support allowing vendors to enclose the full legal terms with their products. Cashiers cannot be expected to read legal documents to customers before ringing up sales. If the staff at the other end of the phone for direct-sales operations such as Gateway's had to read the four-page statement of terms before taking the buyer's credit card number, the droning voice would anesthetize rather than enlighten many potential buyers. Others would hang up in a rage over the waste of their time. And oral recitation would not avoid customers' assertions (whether true or feigned) that the clerk did not read term X to them, or that they did not remember or understand it. Writing provides benefits for both sides of commercial transactions. Customers as a group are better off when vendors skip costly and ineffectual steps such as telephonic recitation, and use instead a simple approve-or-return device. Competent adults are bound by such documents, read or unread.

Id. at 1148-1149. Is this reasoning persuasive? Does it apply to court choice-of-forum clauses in addition to arbitration agreements? Is it consistent with *Carnival Cruise?* Does the answer depend on whether the parties bound by the clause had the opportunity to cancel the contract without penalty? *Compare* Johnson v. Holland America Line-Westours, Inc., 206 Wis. 2d 562, 572 (Wis. Ct. App. 1996) (forum-selection clause not enforceable since plaintiffs received cruise tickets less than 45 days before departure and would have forfeited half of purchase price if they had thereafter canceled their trip); Corna v. American Hawaii Cruises, Inc., 794 F. Supp. 1005, 1012 (D. Haw. 1992) (refusing to enforce forum-selection clause where plaintiffs had no opportunity to reject the forum-selection clause without forfeiture of purchase price and additional penalties).

(4) *Carnival Cruise* also declined to consider the claim that the Shutes were unable to sue in Florida because the claim was supported by an inadequate factual record. What if it is prohibitively expensive or otherwise very inconvenient for parties to travel to the selected forum? Consider Sudduth v. Occidental Peruana, Inc., 70 F. Supp. 2d 691 (E.D. Texas 1999), a lawsuit in the United States between U.S. employees and their U.S. employer for unpaid benefits under a contract for work in the Peruvian jungle. The court declined to enforce the Peruvian forum-selection clause in the contract, reasoning:

> The Defendants provided transportation to and from the foreign country and were fully aware that the only contact the Plaintiffs had with the forum was the completion of the project. All material facts and witnesses are located in the United States. The contracts were mailed from California to Texas and Louisiana, a majority of the documents were signed in Texas, and the breach of contract occurred when the correct salary due was not placed in the Plaintiffs' bank accounts. In addition: the Plaintiffs' employment was initially sought within the United States; Plaintiffs worked in Peru for a limited time period; salaries were paid by United States banks; transportation to and from South America was paid by the Defendants; and an inconvenient forum was surreptitiously chosen by the Defendant. This Court holds the Plaintiffs will be "deprived of their day in court" because of the grave inconvenience and unfairness in the enforcement of the forum selection clause. The inconvenience of trying this case extends past the difficulties in travel. Plaintiffs' financial status and failing health require that the case should be tried in the Eastern District of Texas. . . . In addition, there is evidence that six of the eight Plaintiffs cannot afford the cost of travel to Peru, the expense of a trial in Peru, and the heavy burden of requiring a translator to translate communications between the Peruvian attorney and at the trial proceedings. The enforcement of the forum selection clause would be unfair because it would require every American party to travel to a foreign country to litigate an essentially local dispute.

Id. at 696-697. Is this reasoning consistent with *Carnival Cruise?* Should physical or financial inability to travel to the selected forum be a defense to the forum-selection clause's enforcement? Does the court here mistakenly view its inquiry as whether the selected forum is the most convenient? Or is it performing a "fundamental fairness" analysis? For a different view of the relevance of convenience and expense to the enforcement of forum selection clauses, see Design Strategy Corp. v. Nghiem, 14 F. Supp. 2d 298, 14 F. Supp. 2d 298 (S.D.N.Y. 1998).

(5) Much of the commentary on *Carnival Cruise* has been critical. *See, e.g.*, Borchers, Forum Selection Agreements in the Federal Courts After Carnival Cruise: A Proposal for Congressional Reform, 67 Wash. L. Rev. 55 (1992); Mullenix, Another Easy Case, Some More Bad Law: Carnival Cruise Lines and Contractual Personal Jurisdiction, 27 Tex. Intl. L.J. 323 (1992); Purcell, Geography as a Litigation Weapon: Consumers, Forum-Selection Clauses and the Rehnquist Court, 40 U.C.L.A. L. Rev. 423 (1992). This commentary focuses on the unfairness to the Shutes of being required to litigate in a distant forum against a wealthy corporation. Scholars have also attacked the Court's economic analysis: "The [forum-selection clause] is not negotiated, the specific market is noncompetitive, the issue of forum choice is of trivial importance to an individual passenger ex ante, and the unadvised passenger cannot be expected to assign a suitable value to the clause; hence, the savings resulting from the enforcement of the clause went straight to the bottom line of Carnival Lines." Carrington and Haagen, Contract and Jurisdiction, 1996 Sup. Ct. Rev. 331, 356.

A more sympathetic view of *Carnival Cruise* can be found in Solimine, Forum-Selection Clauses and the Privatization of Procedure, 25 Cornell Intl. L.J. 51 (1992). Solimine downplays the lack of bargaining power of purchasers, points out that form contracts reduce transaction costs, and notes that some studies show that Americans do not like bargaining; he additionally notes that the Shutes ought to be able to retain Florida counsel without much difficulty. 25 Cornell Intl. L.J. at 83-84 & n.201.

Judge Posner, who is usually an enthusiastic defender of contractual freedom, takes an intermediate position:

> Why might a court be more suspicious of a forum selection clause contained in a contract than of the contract itself? There are two reasons, one bad, one good. The bad reason is that courts used to look askance at agreements to "oust" their jurisdiction. . . . All this nonsense was swept away by *Bremen.*
>
> Yet there really is something special about forum selection clauses after all. They could interfere with the orderly allocation of judicial business and injure other third-party interests (that is, interests of persons other than the parties to the contract containing the clause) as well. Suppose, to take an extreme but illustrative example, that the state and federal courts in Alaska became immensely popular forums for litigating contract disputes and as a result thousands of contracts were signed designating Alaska as the forum in the event of suit. Not only would these clauses impose great burdens on the courts in Alaska; they would impose great burdens on witnesses who were not employees of the parties (the inconvenience to employees would have been taken into account when the clause was drafted). The burdens on the Alaska courts would include not only the obvious ones but also the difficulty of having always to be applying other states' laws, one of the considerations that has been thought to justify limiting parties' power to specify by contract the law to be applied to their dispute if one arises. Restatement (Second) of Conflict of Laws §187(2)(a).
>
> [T]he only good reason for treating a forum selection clause differently from any other contract (specifically, from the contract in which the clause appears) is the possibility of adverse effects on third parties. Where that possibility is slight, the clause should be treated like any other contract. What is more, if any inconvenience to third parties can be cured by a change of venue under section 1404(a), that is the route to follow, rather than striking down the clause. This approach enables a clean separation between issues of general contract validity and the third-party consequences which alone justify treating the validity of a forum selection clause differently from that of the contract that contains it.

Northwestern Natl. Ins. Co. v. Donovan, 916 F.2d 372, 376 (7th Cir 1990); *see also id.* ("If ever there was a case for stretching the concept of fraud in the name of unconscionability, it was *Shute;* and perhaps no stretch was necessary.").

(6) In addition to her criticisms based on contract unconscionability, Mullenix chastises the majority for failing to take into account the fact that

the plaintiffs had no other contact with Florida and were thus effectively deprived of their legal rights unless they were willing to litigate in a state with which they had no minimum contacts. 27 Tex. Intl. L.J. at 365-366. This argument has been labeled the "reciprocal contacts" theory in other contexts, for it sometimes happens that the defendant has little contact with the plaintiff's chosen forum, but the plaintiff also has little contact with the defendant's chosen forum. Brilmayer, How Contacts Count: Due Process Limitations on State Court Jurisdiction, 1980 Sup. Ct. Rev. 77, 110 (making the argument in the context of World-Wide Volkswagen v. Woodson, page 524 *infra*). Should it be argued that it is in precisely such cases that forum-selection clauses are valuable because there is no other fair way to decide where suit should be brought? Or is this "symmetry" argument about the analogous postures of the plaintiff and the defendant out of touch with a reality in which defendants are strong and plaintiffs are weak?

(7) In Smith, Valentino, & Smith, Inc. v. Superior Court, 17 Cal. 3d 491, 551 P.2d 1206,131 Cal. Rptr. 374 (1976), the parties had agreed to a more interesting version of a forum-selecting and forum-ousting provision. The contract between a Pennsylvania corporation and a California corporation appointed as its agent for various purposes provided that if the California party brought suit it must be in Philadelphia, and if the Pennsylvania party brought suit it had to be in Los Angeles. The California party brought suit in California, and the Supreme Court of California refused to set aside an order of the lower court staying the proceedings. The court found nothing against public policy in such an agreement.

(8) The Supreme Court has held that denials of dismissal motions based on contractual forum selection clauses are not immediately appealable in federal court. Lauro Lines s.r.l. v. Chasser, 490 U.S. 495 (1989) (no immediate appeal). The case involved a suit arising out of the hijacking of the Achille Lauro, and the District Court had refused to enforce the clause because the ticket gave insufficient notice to passengers that they were waiving their opportunity to sue in a domestic forum.

(9) If *The Bremen* and *Carnival Cruise* were not admiralty cases but rather diversity cases in the federal court, would state or federal law apply? *Compare* In re Air Crash Disaster Near New Orleans, page 612 *infra, and* Stewart Organization v. Ricoh Corp., page 600 *infra.*

(10) The Supreme Court has shown increasing willingness to enforce arbitration clauses. In large part this is because the Federal Arbitration Act, 9 U.S.C. §1 *et seq.* contains a powerful commitment to such enforcement. A prominent decision is Mitsubishi Motor Corp. v. Soler Chrysler-Plymouth, 473 U.S. 614 (1985), which in the context of enforcing an arbitration agreement in an international antitrust dispute, stated:

> [C]oncerns of international comity, respect for capacities of foreign and transnational tribunals, and sensitivity to the need of the international commercial system for predictability in the resolution of disputes require

> that we enforce the parties' agreement, even assuming that a contrary result would be forthcoming in a domestic context.

Id. at 629. In Rodriguez de Quijas v. Shearson/American Express Inc., 490 U.S. 477 (1989), the Supreme Court overruled an earlier decision, Wilko v. Swan, 346 U.S. 427 (1953), in holding enforceable an agreement to arbitrate claims under the Securities Acts. *See also* Vimar Seguros y Reaseguros, S.A. v. M/V Sky Reefer, 515 U.S. 528 (1995) (arbitration clauses contained in maritime bills of lading enforceable despite Carriage of Goods by Sea Act). Should the standards for enforcement of arbitration clauses be higher or lower than the standards for enforcement of forum-selection clauses choosing a foreign judicial forum?

(We return to the issue of choice-of-forum clauses in Chapter 8's discussion of the Internet.)

Sternberg v. O'Neil

550 A.2d 1105 (Del. 1988)

HOLLAND, J.:

The appellant, Richard Sternberg ("Sternberg"), brought a double derivative suit[1] against GenCorp Inc. ("GenCorp"), its wholly owned subsidiary, RKO General, Inc. ("RKO General"), and certain past and present officers and directors of both corporations. GenCorp is an Ohio corporation qualified to do business in Delaware under 8 Del. C. §371. RKO General is a Delaware corporation. The Court of Chancery found "that the complaint does not allege a constitutionally permissible basis for the assertion of personal jurisdiction over either GenCorp or those individual defendants who are not directors of RKO General." The Court of Chancery also found that GenCorp was an indispensable party. It, therefore, held that "the complaint must be dismissed as to all defendants."

On appeal, we conclude on two bases, that the Court of Chancery erred, as a matter of law, when it determined that it lacked personal jurisdiction over GenCorp. First, when GenCorp registered to do business in Delaware and appointed an agent in Delaware to receive service of process, it consented to the general jurisdiction of Delaware courts. Second, we hold alternatively, that GenCorp's ownership of a Delaware corporation, whose alleged mismanagement is the subject of the double derivative suit, constitutes a "minimum contact" with Delaware which satisfies due process and enables Delaware courts to exercise specific personal jurisdiction over GenCorp in this matter. Therefore, we reverse the

---

1. A "double derivative" action is a derivative action maintained by the shareholders of a parent corporation or holding company on behalf of a subsidiary company. *See* 13 W. Fletcher, Cyclopedia of the Law of Private Corporations §5977 (rev. perm. ed. Supp. 1988). The wrongs addressed include wrongs directly incurred by the parent corporation as well as those indirectly incurred, because of wrongs suffered by the subsidiary company. *Id.*

Court of Chancery's decision to dismiss the complaint as to GenCorp. However, we affirm the dismissal of the complaint as to the individual nonresident defendants, who are not directors of RKO General.

Facts

GenCorp, an Ohio corporation, has its principal place of business in Akron, Ohio, and was known as The General Tire & Rubber Company until 1984 when it changed its name. GenCorp is qualified to conduct business in Delaware as a foreign corporation. RKO General, a Delaware corporation, has its principal place of business in New York, New York. All of RKO General's common stock has been owned by GenCorp since it was acquired in 1955. Sternberg is a shareholder of GenCorp.

Sternberg's complaint in the Court of Chancery alleged, *inter alia,* that the directors and officers of RKO General and GenCorp breached their fiduciary duties to the GenCorp shareholders when they made numerous false and misleading statements and omissions to the Federal Communications Commission ("FCC") about an investigation of GenCorp by the Securities and Exchange Commission ("SEC"). . . . Sternberg's double derivative claim is premised upon his allegation that the individual defendants, officers and directors of GenCorp and RKO General, failed to manage the affairs of GenCorp and RKO General in a "fair, careful and prudent manner" and that such failure constitutes a breach of their fiduciary duties.

General Jurisdiction and Consent

The first question that we must address is whether Delaware courts may assert general personal jurisdiction over a foreign corporation[3] upon the basis of that corporation's qualification to do business in Delaware and its appointment of an agent to receive service of process in Delaware pursuant to a registration statute. If we determine that such registration can constitute consent to the general jurisdiction of the Delaware courts, we must then analyze the constitutional validity of that consent. Although parties may not waive subject matter jurisdiction, they may waive personal jurisdiction. Insurance Corp. of Ireland v. Compagnie des Bauxites de Guinee, 456 U.S. 694, 703 (1982). Therefore, consent has been recognized as a basis for the exercise of general personal jurisdiction. In fact, "[a] variety of legal arrangements have been taken to represent express or implied consent to the personal jurisdiction of the Court." *Id.*[4]

---

3. A "foreign" corporation is one that is organized under the laws of another state.

4. A party may submit to a given court's jurisdiction by contractual consent. National Equip. Rental, Ltd. v. Szukhent, 375 U.S. 311 (1964). Parties may stipulate to personal jurisdiction. Petrowski v. Hawkeye-Security Insurance Co., 350 U.S. 495 (1956).

EXPRESS STATUTORY CONSENT

Express consent has been found to be a basis for jurisdiction when a foreign corporation appoints an agent for service of process.[5] *See* Neirbo Co. v. Bethlehem Shipbuilding Corp., 308 U.S. 165, 170-71 (1939); Pennsylvania Fire Ins. Co. v. Gold Issue Mining & Milling Co., 243 U.S. 93, 95 (1917). In *Pennsylvania Fire Ins. Co.*, the United States Supreme Court ruled that a foreign corporation, which authorizes an agent to receive service of process in compliance with the requirements of a state registration statute, has consented to the exercise of general personal jurisdiction in that state. *Id.* The unanimous opinion, written by Justice Holmes, held that Missouri could constitutionally exercise general jurisdiction over the defendant foreign corporation, and "not deprive the defendant of due process," even though its only apparent contact with Missouri was its designation of the Missouri Superintendent of Insurance as its registered agent. *Id.*

IMPLIED CONSENT

Implied consent has also been found to be a basis for jurisdiction over a foreign corporation. International Shoe Co. v. Washington, 326 U.S. 310 (1945). In fact, the Supreme Court's decision in *International Shoe* has become a landmark case because it established the modern doctrine of in personam jurisdiction by implied consent for state courts over foreign corporations (and non-resident defendants) when it held that:

> due process requires only that in order to subject a defendant to a judgment in personam, if he not be present within the territory of the forum, he have certain minimum contacts with it such that the maintenance of the suit does not offend "traditional notions of fair play and substantial justice."

Id. at 316 (emphasis added). As a result of *International Shoe,* "long arm" statutes have been passed in every state. These statutes are legislative enactments describing those contacts between the forum and the defendant by which the nonresident defendant has implicitly consented to the exercise of personal jurisdiction by the courts of the forum state. *Id.*

---

5. Currently, all fifty states and the District of Columbia require the appointment of a local agent as a condition for transacting certain kinds of business within their boundaries. *See* R. Casad, Jurisdiction in Civil Actions §3.02[2][a](1983).

QUESTIONS RAISED BY *INTERNATIONAL SHOE*

It would appear that the due process holdings of *Pennsylvania Fire Ins. Co.* (express consent by registration) and *International Shoe* (implied consent by minimum contact) complement one another and are neither inconsistent nor mutually exclusive. However, many legal scholars are of the view that the "due process" basis for the *Pennsylvania Fire Ins. Co.* decision (statutory consent in the absence of any other contact) would no longer be viable under the "due process" standards of *International Shoe* and its progeny (requiring minimum contacts). *See, e.g.*, Walker Foreign Corporation Laws: A Current Account, 47 N.C.L. Rev. 733, 734-38 (1969); Brilmayer, Haverkamp, Logan, Lynch, Neuwirth & O'Brien, A General Look at General Jurisdiction, 66 Tex. L. Rev. 721, 758-59 (1988). The United States Supreme Court has not *directly* examined its holding in *Pennsylvania Fire Ins. Co.*, since its decision in *International Shoe.* The state and federal courts that have examined the due process basis for the holding in *Pennsylvania Fire Ins. Co.* in light of *International Shoe* are divided as to whether statutory registration can operate as an express consent to personal jurisdiction in the absence of "minimum contacts." Thus, according to one scholar "the law regarding out-of-state claims against a foreign corporation is in disarray." Hill, Choice of Law and Jurisdiction in the Supreme Court, 81 Colum. L. Rev. 960, 982 (1981).

The debate about the continued viability of the holding in *Pennsylvania Fire Ins. Co.* after *International Shoe* is now before this Court. Sternberg argues that GenCorp., by qualifying to do business in Delaware as a foreign corporation, and by appointing an agent for service of process, has expressly consented to the general jurisdiction of the Delaware courts. GenCorp argues that, independent of its compliance with the Delaware qualification statute, the extent of its consent, if any, to the jurisdiction of Delaware's courts, must be examined in light of the *International Shoe* due process "minimum contact" requirements.

EXPRESS STATUTORY CONSENT TO JURISDICTION AND DUE PROCESS

We are of the opinion that express consent is a valid basis for the exercise of general jurisdiction in the absence of any other basis for the exercise of jurisdiction, *i.e.*, "minimum contacts." In particular, we are of the view that after *International Shoe*, a state still has power to exercise general judicial jurisdiction over a foreign corporation which has expressly consented to the exercise of such jurisdiction.

Not long after its decision in *International Shoe*, the United States Supreme Court upheld the constitutional validity of an exercise of in personam general jurisdiction with respect to a claim unrelated to the foreign corporation defendant's forum activity. Perkins v. Benguet Consol. Mining Co., 342 U.S. 437 (1952). The Court of Chancery relied upon a portion of the *Perkins* decision which stated:

> The corporate activities of a foreign corporation which, under state statute, make it necessary for it to secure a license and to designate a statutory agent upon whom process may be served provide a helpful but not a conclusive test.

The context of this quoted language was a search for "minimum contacts" which would support the legal fiction of implied consent to jurisdiction. It was necessary for the *Perkins* Court to conduct a minimum contact analysis before it could find an *implied consent* to the general jurisdiction of Ohio because *the foreign corporation was not qualified* in Ohio and *had not appointed an agent* for service of process. Nevertheless, *Perkins* reaffirmed the principle that there would have been no need to search for minimum contacts to support an implied consent to jurisdiction, if express consent had been given:

> Today if an authorized representative of a foreign corporation be physically present in the state of the forum and be there engaged in activities appropriate to accepting service and receiving notice on its behalf, we recognize that there is no unfairness in subjecting that corporation to the jurisdiction of the courts of that state through such service of process upon that representative.

Perkins v. Benguet Consol. Mining Co., 342 U.S. at 444.

The United States Supreme Court continued to acknowledge that the due process considerations are different when state court jurisdiction is based on implied consent and when such jurisdiction is based on express consent in Burger King Corp. v. Rudzewicz, 471 U.S. 462 (1985). When jurisdiction is based on implied consent, "[t]he Due Process Clause protects an individual's liberty interest in not being subject to the binding judgments of a forum with which he has established no meaningful 'contacts, ties, or relations.' " *Id.* at 471-72 (citing International Shoe Co. v. Washington, 326 U.S. at 319). However, immediately after stating this general proposition in *Burger King Corp.*, the Court reiterated its longstanding position that the personal jurisdiction requirement is a waivable right. Burger King Corp. v. Rudzewicz, 471 U.S. at 472 n. 14. Therefore, the Court held that "[w]here a forum seeks to assert specific jurisdiction over an out-of-state defendant *who has not consented* to suit there," due process is satisfied if the defendant has minimum contacts with the forum. *Id.* at 472 (emphasis added). Thus, in *Burger King Corp.*, as in *Perkins*, the Supreme Court found that in the absence of express consent, due process requires minimum contacts for a finding of implied consent to a forum's jurisdiction. *Id.* Conversely, due process is satisfied by express consent, since express consent constitutes a waiver of all other personal jurisdiction requirements. *See id.*

STATUTORY CONSENT REMAINS A VALID BASIS FOR JURISDICTION

We also find continuing support for the recognition of statutory consent as a basis for general jurisdiction in the Supreme Court's very recent decision in Bendix Autolite Corp. v. Midwesco Enterprises, 486 U.S. 888 (1988). The issue in *Bendix Autolite Corp.*, as in *Perkins,* involved an unregistered foreign corporation and an attempted assertion of jurisdiction over the foreign corporation by the state of Ohio. In *Bendix Autolite Corp.*, the Court appeared to accept the rationale, explicitly stated in the Ohio statute, that the appointment of an agent for service of process would operate as a consent to general jurisdiction in any cause of action, "including those in which it did not have minimum contacts necessary for supporting personal jurisdiction," without offending the requirements of due process. *Id.* 486 U.S. at 892. In a preamble to its ultimate holding, the Court stated:

> [D]esignation of an agent subjects the foreign corporation to the general jurisdiction of the Ohio courts in matters to which Ohio's tenuous relation would not otherwise extend. The Ohio statutory scheme thus forces a corporation to choose between exposure to the general jurisdiction of Ohio courts or forfeiture of the limitations defense, remaining subject to suit in Ohio and perpetuity. Requiring a foreign corporation to appoint an agent for service in all cases and to defend itself with reference to all transactions, including those in which it did not have the minimum contacts necessary for supporting personal jurisdiction, is a significant burden.

Id.

In our opinion, the holdings of the United States Supreme Court which involved foreign corporations, following *International Shoe,* are entirely consistent with the continued viability of its earlier holding in *Pennsylvania Fire Ins. Co.* If a foreign corporation has not expressly consented to a state's jurisdiction by registration, "minimum contacts" with that state can provide a due process basis for finding an implied consent to the state's jurisdiction. . . . If a foreign corporation has expressly consented to the jurisdiction of a state by registration, due process is satisfied and an examination of "minimum contacts" to find implied consent is unnecessary. . . . However, these due process conclusions do not mean that foreign corporations are without any federal constitutional protection from the registration requirements of fifty different states and the District of Columbia.

STATUTORY CONSENT TO JURISDICTION AND THE COMMERCE CLAUSE

In *Bendix Autolite Corp.*, the Court held that "[s]tate interests that are legitimate for equal protection or due process purposes may be insufficient to withstand Commerce Clause scrutiny." 486 U.S. at 904. Therefore, in the present case, although GenCorp's consent to the general personal jurisdiction of Delaware courts by qualifying as a foreign corporation satisfies due process, we must also determine if the Delaware statute places an unreasonable burden on interstate commerce. *Id.*

In *Bendix Autolite Corp.*, the Court was called upon to review an Ohio registration statute which tolled the statute of limitations for any period of time that the foreign corporation was not "present" in the state. To be present in Ohio, a foreign corporation had to appoint an agent for service of process which, by statute, made the corporation subject to the general jurisdiction of the Ohio courts. Thus, the Ohio tolling statute forced a foreign corporation to choose between exposure to the general jurisdiction of the Ohio courts, if it appointed an agent to receive process, and forfeiture of the statute of limitations defense if it did not make the appointment. The Court concluded that the tolling provision placed an undue burden on interstate commerce and thus violated the Commerce Clause. Specifically, the Court found that the burdens imposed on interstate commerce by Ohio's coercive statutory scheme was not outweighed by Ohio's interest in protecting its citizens from out-of-state corporations.

It is clear after *Bendix Autolite Corp.* that any statute which causes a foreign corporation to register and thereby consent to the general jurisdiction of a state, or in the absence of that registration and consent, to be subjected to regulations that are inconsistent with those for domestic corporations, is a burden that violates the federal commerce clause. *Id.* However, the Delaware statutory scheme contains no coercive penalties or inconsistent regulations for foreign corporations that chose not to register.

The right of an unregistered foreign corporation to defend an action in Delaware *and* to raise a statute of limitations defense deserves particular attention in view of *Bendix Autolite Corp.* In Delaware, the statute of limitations continues to run even with respect to foreign corporations that transact business in this State and have not qualified to do business under Section 371. This Court has specifically held that there is no tolling effect on the applicable statute of limitations in any action when the nonresident defendant in the suit is subject to substituted service of process. Substituted service of process on nonqualifying foreign corporations is provided for in 8 Del. C. §382(a). Therefore, a foreign corporation which transacts business in this State and does not qualify to do business under Section 371, still has an absolute right to raise the statute of limitations as a defense in any action. It is clear that, unlike Midwesco in *Bendix Autolite Corp.*, GenCorp faced no Hobson's choice in the Delaware statutory scheme which caused it to decide to qualify as a foreign correspondent. In fact, GenCorp did not argue that it had been coerced into qualifying as a foreign corporation, even though, following the oral argument in this case, the parties were directed to address the implications for this appeal of the decision of *Bendix Autolite Corp.*

SCOPE OF GENCORP'S EXPRESS STATUTORY CONSENT

GenCorp qualified as a foreign corporation in Delaware pursuant to 8 Del. C. §371(b).[15] Service of process upon a foreign corporation which has qualified under Section 371 is made upon its registered agent. In its final legal memorandum, although GenCorp did not argue that Sections 371 and 376 were coercive, it did contend that these sections "simply provided a method for service of process, giving fair notice to a foreign corporation that an action had been filed against it, but reserving unto that foreign corporation all rights to contest jurisdiction on due process grounds." GenCorp was also under the impression that Sections 371 and 376 had never been construed to operate as consent to the general jurisdiction of Delaware courts.

However, we have found that similar arguments were rejected by the United States District Court for the District of Delaware more than a decade ago, in D'Angelo v. Petroleos Mexicanas, 378 F. Supp. 1034 (D. Del. 1974), when it had occasion to address the scope of Section 376:

> Section 376 does not in [its] terms limit the amenability of service of a qualified corporation to one which does business in Delaware or with respect to a cause of action arising in Delaware. By the generality of its terms, a foreign corporation qualified in Delaware is subject to service of process in Delaware on any transitory cause of action.

Id. at 1039. The District Court held that by qualifying as a foreign corporation, the Mobil Oil Corporation could be *served* and *sued* in Delaware on a transitory cause of action *Id.*

We agree with the Delaware District Court's interpretation in *D'Angelo* of the effect of registration as a foreign corporation in Delaware. We find that

---

15. 8 Del. C. §371(b) reads as follows:

> (b) No foreign corporation shall do any business in this State, through or by branch offices, agents or representatives located in this State, until it shall have paid to the Secretary of State of this State for the use of this State, $50, and shall have filed in the office of the Secretary of State:
>
> (1) A certificate issued by an authorized officer of the jurisdiction of its incorporation evidencing its corporate existence. If such certificate is in a foreign language, a translation thereof, under oath of the translator, shall be attached thereto.
>
> (2) A statement executed by an authorized officer of each corporation setting forth (i) the name and address of its registered agent in this State, which agent shall be either an individual resident in this State when appointed or another corporation authorized to transact business in this State, (ii) a statement, as of a date not earlier than [six] months prior to the filing date, of the assets and liabilities of the corporation, and (iii) the business it proposes to do in this State and a statement that it is authorized to do that business in the jurisdiction of its incorporation. The statement shall be acknowledged in accordance with [section] 103 of this title.

when GenCorp qualified as a foreign corporation, pursuant to 8 Del. C. §371, and appointed a registered agent for the service of process, pursuant to 8 Del. C. §376, GenCorp consented to the exercise of general jurisdiction by the Courts of Delaware.[19] . . .

Questions and Comments

(1) Not all courts have reached the same conclusion as Sternberg v. O'Neill. *See, e.g.*, Wenche Siemer v. Learjet Acquisitions Corp., 966 F.2d 179, 183 (5th Cir. 1992):

> Not only does the mere act of registering an agent not create Learjet's general business presence in Texas, it also does not act as consent to be hauled into Texas courts on any dispute with any party anywhere concerning any matter. The Texas Business Corporation Act provides that service on a registered foreign corporation may be effected by serving its president, any vice president, or the registered agent of the corporation. . . . No Texas state court decision has held that this provision acts as a consent to jurisdiction over a corporation in a case such as ours—that is where plaintiffs are non-residents and the defendant is not conducting substantial activity within the state. . . . [T]he appointment of an agent for process has not been a waiver of its right to due process protection. . . . In short, a foreign corporation that properly complies with the Texas registration statute only consents to personal jurisdiction where such jurisdiction is constitutionally permissible.

The Third and Eighth Circuits, by contrast, agree with *Sternberg* and view registration as sufficient basis for subjecting a corporation to general jurisdiction. *See* Bane v. Netlink, 925 F.2d 637, 640 (3d Cir. 1991); Knowlton v. Allied Van Lines, Inc., 900 F.2d 1196, 1200 (8th Cir. 1990). The Second Restatement appears to agree, stating that the only issue is the interpretive one of whether registration statutes actually give forum courts authority to exercise general jurisdiction. Restatement (Second) of Conflict of Laws §44 cmt. c (1971).

Like *Sternberg*, most courts that uphold general jurisdiction on the basis of statutory consent rely on the pre-*International Shoe* case of Pennsylvania Fire Insurance Co. v. Gold Issue Mining and Milling Co., 243 U.S. 93 (1917). In *Pennsylvania Fire Insurance*, the Court (per Justice Holmes) held that the appointment of an agent in Missouri constituted consent to suits that had no other connection to Missouri, and that such consent satisfied due process. Does this reasoning survive *International Shoe*'s "minimum contacts" requirement? Does the requirement of statutory consent to general jurisdiction

19. "[W]hen a power actually is conferred by a document, the party executing it takes the risk of the interpretation that may be put upon it by the courts." Pennsylvania Fire Ins. Co. v. Gold Issue Mining & Milling Co., 243 U.S. at 96.

amount to an unconstitutional condition? For analysis of the problem, see Riou, General Jurisdiction over Foreign Corporations: All That Glitters Is Not Gold Issue Mining, 14 Rev. Litig. 741 (1995); Kipp, Inferring Express Consent: The Paradox of Permitting Registration Statutes to Confer General Jurisdiction, 9 Rev. Litg. 1 (1990); Brilmayer et al., A General Look at General Jurisdiction, 66 Tex. L. Rev. 721, 758-759 (1988).

(2) How does the statutory waiver in *Sternberg* compare with jurisdictional waivers in forum-selection clauses? Aren't statutory waivers more problematic because general jurisdiction is at issue? Is it relevant that contractual waivers often involve consumers while statutory waivers involve corporations doing multi-state business matter? *Compare* Ocepek v. Corporate Transport, Inc., 950 F.2d 556, 560 (8th Cir. 1991) (statutory waiver cases rest on assumption that "companies which do business nationwide can more easily defend themselves in any of those state in which they do business, than individual citizens can bring suit outside their home states, perhaps at great distances").

(3) If GenCorp did in fact "consent" to jurisdiction in Delaware, then why did it do so? If the court is correct that no coercion is involved in this Delaware statutory scheme, then why would a defendant unilaterally subject itself to this burden? Given that the statute cited in footnote 15 states that "[n]o foreign corporation shall do any business in this State . . . until it shall have filed . . . a statement . . . setting forth the name and address of its registered agent," how can the court claim that no compulsion is involved? Is the Delaware Supreme Court really counseling foreign corporations to ignore such statutes? Isn't it penalizing law-abiding corporations that meet registration requirements all along? If you were a Delaware resident, wouldn't you want your court to *encourage* foreign corporations to register, to make them easier to locate and to serve process upon?

(4) Portions of the omitted section of the opinion, discussing the distinction between general and specific jurisdiction and jurisdiction based on the corporate parent/subsidiary relationship, are discussed at page 556 *infra.*

(5) When did GenCorp file the statement appointing an agent? If its filing was prior to the judicial decision holding such an appointment a consent to general jurisdiction, then is this fair?

(6) What interest of Delaware's is served by asserting jurisdiction over this dispute?

(7) If an unregistered corporation wishes to file suit in Delaware, then according to the statute cited in the opinion, 8 Del. C. §383(a), it must at that point comply with the registration rules, pay back taxes and franchise fees, and so forth. Presumably, the consent to general jurisdiction then becomes effective. Is it retroactive; that is, can the corporation now be sued for an earlier cause of action? And how far into the future does the consent extend? Is it irrevocable? Doesn't this provision essentially coerce a defendant into consenting to general jurisdiction?

(8) The *Bendix Autolite* case is discussed at page 432 *supra;* G.D. Searle v. Cohn is discussed at page 421 *supra.*

(9) If in fact the consent to jurisdiction was purely gratuitous—there was no benefit that the state withheld from corporations that did not consent but granted to those that did—then should the consent be invalid for a lack of "consideration"? *See generally* Brilmayer, Consent, Contract, and Territory, 74 Minn. L. Rev. 1 (1989), discussing consent as a basis for personal jurisdiction in comparison with consent as a basis for political obligation.

Phillips Petroleum Co. v. Shutts

472 U.S. 797 (1985)

[The facts of the case can be found in a portion of the opinion excerpted at page 376 *supra.*]

II

Reduced to its essentials, petitioner's argument is that unless out-of-state plaintiffs affirmatively consent, the Kansas courts may not exert jurisdiction over their claims. Petitioner claims that failure to execute and return the "request for exclusion" provided with the class notice cannot constitute consent of the out-of-state plaintiffs; thus Kansas courts may exercise jurisdiction over these plaintiffs only if the plaintiffs possess the sufficient "minimum contacts" with Kansas as that term is used in cases involving personal jurisdiction over out-of-state defendants. *E.g.*, International Shoe Co. v. Washington, 326 U.S. 310 (1945); Shaffer v. Heitner, 433 U.S. 186 (1977); World-Wide Volkswagen Corp. v. Woodson, 444 U.S. 286 (1980). Since Kansas had no prelitigation contact with many of the plaintiffs and leases involved, petitioner claims that Kansas has exceeded its jurisdictional reach and thereby violated the due process rights of the absent plaintiffs.

Although the cases like *Shaffer* and *Woodson* which petitioner relies on for a minimum contacts requirement all dealt with out-of-state defendants or parties in the procedural posture of a defendant, *cf.* New York Life Ins. Co. v. Dunlevy, 241 U.S. 518 (1916); Estin v. Estin, 334 U.S. 541 (1948), petitioner claims that the same analysis must apply to absent class-action plaintiffs. In this regard petitioner correctly points out that a chose in action is a constitutionally recognized property interest possessed by each of the plaintiffs. Mullane v. Central Hanover Bank & Trust Co., 339 U.S. 306 (1950). An adverse judgment by Kansas courts in this case may extinguish the chose in action forever through res judicata. Such an adverse judgment, petitioner claims, would be every bit as onerous to an absent plaintiff as an adverse judgment on the merits would be to a defendant. Thus, the same due process protections should apply to absent plaintiffs: Kansas should not be able to exert jurisdiction over the plaintiffs' claims unless the plaintiffs have sufficient minimum contacts with Kansas.

We think petitioner's premise is in error. The burdens placed by a State upon an absent class-action plaintiff are not of the same order or magnitude as those it places upon an absent defendant. An out-of-state defendant summoned by a plaintiff is faced with the full powers of the forum State to render judgment *against* it. The defendant must generally hire counsel and travel to the forum to defend itself from the plaintiff's claim, or suffer a default judgment. The defendant may be forced to participate in extended and often costly discovery, and will be forced to respond in damages or to comply with some other form of remedy imposed by the court should it lose the suit. The defendant may also face liability for court costs and attorney's fees. These burdens are substantial, and the minimum contacts requirement of the Due Process Clause prevents the forum State from unfairly imposing them upon the defendant.

A class-action plaintiff, however, is in quite a different posture. The Court noted this difference in Hansberry v. Lee, 311 U.S. 32, 40-41 (1940), which explained that a "class" or "representative" suit was an exception to the rule that one could not be bound by judgment in personam unless one was made fully a party in the traditional sense. *Ibid.*, citing Pennoyer v. Neff, 95 U.S. 714 (1878). As the Court pointed out in *Hansberry*, the class action was an invention of equity to enable it to proceed to a decree in suits where the number of those interested in the litigation was too great to permit joinder. The absent parties would be bound by the decree so long as the named parties adequately represented the absent class and the prosecution of the litigation was within the common interest.[1] 311 U.S., at 41.

Modern plaintiff class actions follow the same goals, permitting litigation of a suit involving common questions when there are too many plaintiffs for proper joinder. Class actions also may permit the plaintiffs to pool claims which would be uneconomical to litigate individually. For example, this lawsuit involves claims averaging about $100 per plaintiff; most of the plaintiffs would have no realistic day in court if a class action were not available.

In sharp contrast to the predicament of a defendant haled into an out-of-state forum, the plaintiffs in this suit are not haled anywhere to defend themselves upon pain of a default judgment.

A plaintiff class in Kansas and numerous other jurisdictions cannot first be certified unless the judge, with the aid of the named plaintiffs and defendants, conducts an inquiry into the common nature of the named plaintiffs'

1. The holding in *Hansberry*, of course, was that petitioners in that case had not a sufficient common interest with the parties to a prior lawsuit such that a decree against those parties in the prior suit would bind the petitioners. But in the present case there is no question that the named plaintiffs adequately represent the class, and that all members of the class have the same interest in enforcing their claims against the defendant.

and the absent plaintiffs' claims, the adequacy of representation, the jurisdiction possessed over the class, and any other matters that will bear upon proper representation of the absent plaintiffs' interest. *See, e.g.*, Kan. Stat. Ann. §60-223 (1983); Fed. Rule Civ. Proc. 23. Unlike a defendant in a civil suit, a class-action plaintiff is not required to fend for himself. *See* Kan. Stat. Ann. §60-223(d) (1983). The court and named plaintiffs protect his interests. Indeed, the class-action defendant itself has a great interest in ensuring that the absent plaintiffs' claims are properly before the forum. In this case, for example, the defendant sought to avoid class certification by alleging that the absent plaintiffs would not be adequately represented and were not amenable to jurisdiction. *See* Phillips Petroleum v. Duckworth, No. 82-54608 (Kan., June 28, 1982).

The concern of the typical class-action rules for the absent plaintiffs is manifested in other ways. Most jurisdictions, including Kansas, require that a class action, once certified, may not be dismissed or compromised without the approval of the court. In many jurisdictions such as Kansas the court may amend the pleadings to ensure that all sections of the class are represented adequately. Kan. Stat. Ann. §60-223(d) (1983); *see also, e.g.*, Fed. Rule Civ. Proc. 23(d).

Besides this continuing solicitude for their rights, absent plaintiff class members are not subject to other burdens imposed upon defendants. They need not hire counsel or appear. They are almost never subject to counterclaims or cross-claims, or liability for fees or costs.[2] Absent plaintiff class members are not subject to coercive or punitive remedies. Nor will an adverse judgment typically bind an absent plaintiff for any damages, although a valid adverse judgment may extinguish any of the plaintiff's claims which were litigated.

Unlike a defendant in a normal civil suit, an absent class-action plaintiff is not required to do anything. He may sit back and allow the litigation to run its course, content in knowing that there are safeguards provided for his protection. In most class actions an absent plaintiff is provided at least with an opportunity to "opt out" of the class, and if he takes advantage of that opportunity he is removed from the litigation entirely. This was true of the Kansas proceedings in this case. The Kansas procedure provided for the mailing of a notice to each class member by first-class mail. The notice, as we have previously indicated, described the action and informed the class member that he could appear in person or by counsel, in default of which he would

---

2. Petitioner places emphasis on the fact that absent class members might be subject to discovery, counterclaims, cross-claims, or court costs. Petitioner cites no cases involving any such imposition upon plaintiffs, however. We are convinced that such burdens are rarely imposed upon plaintiff class members, and that the disposition of these issues is best left to a case which presents them in a more concrete way.

be represented by the named plaintiffs and their attorneys. The notice further stated that class members would be included in the class and bound by judgment unless they "opted out" by executing and returning a "request for exclusion" that was included in the notice.

Petitioner contends, however, that the "opt out" procedure provided by Kansas is not good enough, and that an "opt in" procedure is required to satisfy the Due Process Clause of the Fourteenth Amendment. Insofar as plaintiffs who have no minimum contacts with the forum State are concerned, an "opt in" provision would require that each class member affirmatively consent to his inclusion within the class.

Because States place fewer burdens upon absent class plaintiffs than they do upon absent defendants in nonclass suits, the Due Process Clause need not and does not afford the former as much protection from state-court jurisdiction as it does the latter. The Fourteenth Amendment does protect "persons," not "defendants," however, so absent plaintiffs as well as absent defendants are entitled to some protection from the jurisdiction of a forum State which seeks to adjudicate their claims. In this case we hold that a forum State may exercise jurisdiction over the claim of an absent class-action plaintiff, even though that plaintiff may not possess the minimum contacts with the forum which would support personal jurisdiction over a defendant. If the forum State wishes to bind an absent plaintiff concerning a claim for money damages or similar relief at law,[3] it must provide minimal procedural due process protection. The plaintiff must receive notice plus an opportunity to be heard and participate in the litigation, whether in person or through counsel. The notice must be the best practicable, "reasonably calculated, under all the circumstances, to apprise interested parties of the pendency of the action and afford them an opportunity to present their objections." *Mullane*, 339 U.S., at 314-315; *cf.* Eisen v. Carlisle & Jacquelin, 417 U.S. 156, 174-175 (1974). The notice should describe the action and the plaintiffs' rights in it. Additionally, we hold that due process requires at a minimum that an absent plaintiff be provided with an opportunity to remove himself from the class by executing and returning an "opt out" or "request for exclusion" form to the court. Finally, the Due Process Clause of course requires that the named plaintiff at all times adequately represent the interests of the absent class members. *Hansberry*, 311 U.S., at 42-43, 45.

We reject petitioner's contention that the Due Process Clause of the Fourteenth Amendment requires that absent plaintiffs affirmatively "opt in" to the class, rather than be deemed members of the class if they do not "opt

---

3. Our holding today is limited to those class actions which seek to bind known plaintiffs concerning claims wholly or predominately for money judgments. We intimate no view concerning other types of class actions, such as those seeking equitable relief. Nor, of course, does our discussion of personal jurisdiction address class actions where the jurisdiction is asserted against a *defendant* class.

out." We think that such a contention is supported by little, if any precedent, and that it ignores the differences between class-action plaintiffs, on the one hand, and defendants in nonclass civil suits on the other. Any plaintiff may consent to jurisdiction. Keeton v. Hustler Magazine, Inc., 465 U.S. 770 (1984). The essential question, then, is how stringent the requirement for a showing of consent will be.

We think that the procedure followed by Kansas, where a fully descriptive notice is sent first-class mail to each class member, with an explanation of the right to "opt out," satisfies due process. Requiring a plaintiff to affirmatively request inclusion would probably impede the prosecution of those class actions involving an aggregation of small individual claims, where a large number of claims are required to make it economical to bring suit. *See, e.g., Eisen, supra,* at 161. The plaintiff's claim may be so small, or the plaintiff so unfamiliar with the law, that he would not file suit individually, nor would he affirmatively request inclusion in the class if such a request were required by the Constitution. If, on the other hand, the plaintiff's claim is sufficiently large or important that he wishes to litigate it on his own, he will likely have retained an attorney or have thought about filing suit, and should be fully capable of exercising his right to "opt out."

In this case over 3,400 members of the potential class did "opt out," which belies the contention that "opt out" procedures result in guaranteed jurisdiction by inertia. Another 1,500 were excluded because the notice and "opt out" form was undeliverable. We think that such results show that the "opt out" procedure provided by Kansas is by no means *pro forma,* and that the Constitution does not require more to protect what must be the somewhat rare species of class member who is unwilling to execute an "opt out" form, but whose claim is nonetheless so important that he cannot be presumed to consent to being a member of the class by his failure to do so. Petitioner's "opt in" requirement would require the invalidation of scores of state statutes and of the class-action provision of the Federal Rules of Civil Procedure, and for the reasons stated we do not think that the Constitution requires the State to sacrifice the obvious advantages in judicial efficiency resulting from the "opt out" approach for the protection of the *rara avis* portrayed by petitioner.

We therefore hold that the protection afforded the plaintiff class members by the Kansas statute satisfies the Due Process Clause. The interests of the absent plaintiffs are sufficiently protected by the forum State when those plaintiffs are provided with a request for exclusion that can be returned within a reasonable time to the court. *See Insurance Corp. of Ireland,* 456 U.S., at 702-703, and n.10. Both the Kansas trial court and the Supreme Court of Kansas held that the class received adequate representation, and no party disputes that conclusion here. We conclude that the Kansas court properly asserted personal jurisdiction over the absent plaintiffs and their claims against petitioner.

Questions and Comments

(1) For an authoritative account by two authors of briefs on the case, *see* Miller and Crump, Jurisdiction and Choice of Law in Multistate Class Actions after *Phillips Petroleum Co. v. Shutts,* 96 Yale L.J. 1 (1986).

(2) If none of the plaintiff class members were from Kansas, and none of the leases were signed there or involved property there, should Kansas still be able to entertain this multistate class action? Does *Shutts* present problems of a race to the courthouse in one state by eager members of the plaintiff's bar who located a single class member? Should Kansas be allowed to provide local attorneys with business in this way, by imposing upon persons not otherwise subject to its legislative authority a duty to opt out according to the procedures that Kansas law prescribes? What if Kansas class action law provides a contingent fee of 50 percent as to all class members who do not opt out in time? As a general matter, can Kansas simply notify people throughout the nation that unless they object they will be subject to Kansas law? How does this square with the Court's choice-of-law analysis, page 376 *supra? See* Kennedy, The Supreme Court Meets the Bride of Frankenstein: *Phillips Petroleum Co. v. Shutts* and the State Multistate Class Action, 34 U. Kan. L. Rev. 255, 294 (1985). On the other hand, it is arguable in *Shutts* that there is no choice-of-law problem in applying Kansas "opt out" law to nonresident class members, because their home states probably also have class-action rules with "opt out" rather than "opt in" procedures.

(3) Normally, of course, it is not necessary for the *plaintiff* to consent to jurisdiction, for the plaintiff has chosen the forum (a form of consent in and of itself). Why is plaintiff consent relevant here?

(4) Certain sorts of class actions, of course, do not guarantee class members a right to opt out. *See, e.g.,* Fed. R. Civ. P. 23(b)(2), involving class claims for equitable relief. In footnote 3, the Court's opinion declined to address class actions other than those wholly or predominately for money judgments. What result, then, in a 23(b)(2) action? May a multistate class action proceed even without offering a right to opt out? Or does *Shutts* suggest instead that the class action is improper because other than in money judgment actions where a right to opt out is provided, jurisdiction over absent class plaintiffs is improper? *See* Avagliano v. Sumitomo Shoji America, 107 F.R.D. 749 (1987); In re Jackson Lockdown/MCO Cases, 107 F.R.D. 703 (1987); In re Asbestos School Litigation, 620 F. Supp. 873 (E.D. Pa. 1985).

Brown v. Ticor Title Insurance, 982 F.2d 386 (9th Cir. 1992) dealt with a case involving both money damage and injunctive relief; earlier multidistrict litigation had been certified under Fed. R. Civ. P. 23(b)(1) and (b)(2) (as to which no "opt out" right exists) and the question was whether the current plaintiff was bound by res judicata. The court held that Brown might be bound by the earlier action insofar as he requested injunctive relief, but not as to his money damages claim. *See also* In re Real Estate and Settlement Servs.

Antitrust Litig., 869 F.2d 760 (3d Cir. 1989). The Supreme Court initially agreed to hear Brown v. Ticor, but then in a per curiam opinion dismissed the case as moot on the grounds that a settlement had been reached, and because a majority felt that a non-constitutional basis for decision would have been available but for the res judicata effect of an earlier holding on the scope of Rule 23. 114 S. Ct. 1359 (1994).

(5) If an absent class member does not comply with discovery requests that would bear on whether he or she had minimum contacts with the forum, then may a court hold that jurisdiction exists under *Insurance Corp. of Ireland*, page 480 *infra?*

(6) Would a better solution be to restrict multistate class actions to federal courts? If so, apparently Snyder v. Harris, 394 U.S. 332 (1969) (prohibiting aggregation to meet the $10,000 amount in controversy requirement), and Zahn v. International Paper Co., 414 U.S. 291 (1973) (prohibiting pendent jurisdiction over claims not meeting amount in controversy requirement), would have to be overruled by the Supreme Court or Congress.

Some courts believe that Congress has in fact overruled *Snyder* and *Zahn* in the Judicial Improvements Act of 1990, 28 U.S.C. §1367. Section 1367(a) extends supplemental jurisdiction of the federal courts to "all other claims that are so related to claims in the action within such original jurisdiction that they form part of the same case or controversy under Article III of the United States Constitution." Section 1367(b) then restricts this grant by precluding the exercise of supplemental jurisdiction in diversity cases when joinder is accomplished pursuant to Fed. R. Civ. P. 14, 19, 20, or 24. Since 1367(b) makes no mention of Rule 23 (class actions), some courts have held that 1367(a) extends supplemental jurisdiction to diversity class members who do not meet the amount in controversy requirement. *See, e.g.*, Stromberg Metal Works v. Press Mechanical, 77 F.3d 928, 930 (7th Cir. 1996); In re Abbott Labs, 51 F.3d 524 (5th Cir. 1995), *aff'd by an equally divided court,* Free v. Abbott Labs, Inc., 529 U.S. 333 (2000) (per curiam). Other courts have held that *Snyder* and *Zahn* survive §1367. *See, e.g.*, Spielman v. Genzyme Corp., 251 F.3d 1, 11 (1st Cir. 2001). For analysis of the significance of this debate for class action practice, see Steinman, Crosscurrents: Supplemental Jurisdiction, Removal, and the ALI Revision Project, 74 Ind. L.J. 75 (1998); Baldassare, Comment, Pandora's Box or Treasure Chest?: Circuit Courts Face 28 U.S.C. 1367's Effect on Multi-Plaintiff Diversity Actions, 27 Seton Hall L. Rev. 1497 (1997). For commentary on the proper meaning of §1367, see Freer, Toward a Principled Statutory Approach to Supplemental Jurisdiction in Diversity of Citizenship Cases, 74 Ind. L.J. 5 (1998).

(7) Is the "consent" in *Shutts* express consent or implied consent? Is the answer that the consent at issue in *Shutts* is "real" implied consent rather than fictitious implied consent? Compare the distinction between implied-in-fact and implied-in-law contracts.

2. Waiver

Insurance Corp. of Ireland v. Compagnie des Bauxites de Guinee

456 U.S. 694 (1982)

Justice WHITE delivered the opinion of the Court.

Rule 37(b), Federal Rules of Civil Procedure, provides that a District Court may impose sanctions for failure to comply with discovery orders. Included among the available sanctions is:

> An order that the matters regarding which the order was made or any other designated facts shall be taken to be established for the purposes of the action in accordance with the claim of the party obtaining the order.

Rule 37(b)(2)(A).

The question presented by this case is whether this rule is applicable to facts that form the basis for personal jurisdiction over a defendant. May a District Court, as a sanction for failure to comply with a discovery order directed at establishing jurisdictional facts, proceed on the basis that personal jurisdiction over the recalcitrant party has been established? Petitioners urge that such an application of the Rule would violate Due Process: If a court does not have jurisdiction over a party, then it may not create that jurisdiction by judicial fiat. They contend also that until a court has jurisdiction over a party, that party need not comply with orders of the court; failure to comply, therefore, cannot provide the ground for a sanction. In our view, petitioners are attempting to create a logical conundrum out of a fairly straightforward matter.

[Plaintiff/respondent Compagnie des Bauxites de Guinee (CBG) arranged to obtain various kinds of insurance, including "excess" insurance against business interruption. When such an interruption allegedly occurred and the insurers, including the excess insurers, refused to pay, CBG brought suit. The regular insurer did not contest jurisdiction, but the excess insurers, a group of foreign insurance companies, did. Plaintiff made certain requests for discovery in the action, which was brought in a Pennsylvania federal district court. The excess insurers refused to comply on the grounds that the requests were too burdensome. CBG sought an order to comply, which the district court granted. A series of further moves failed to produce the required material. Finally the district court warned the defendants that it would assume that there was jurisdiction, as a sanction pursuant to Rule 37, unless there was compliance. There was not, and the court entered an order finding in personam jurisdiction.]

II

The validity of an order of a federal court depends upon that court's having jurisdiction over both the subject matter and the parties. [The Court discussed the nature of subject matter jurisdiction, including its nonwaivability and the fact that it may be raised sua sponte by the court.]

None of this is true with respect to personal jurisdiction. The requirement that a court have personal jurisdiction flows not from Art. III, but from the Due Process Clause. The personal jurisdiction requirement recognizes and protects an individual liberty interest. It represents a restriction on judicial power not as a matter of sovereignty, but as a matter of individual liberty.[10] Thus, the test for personal jurisdiction requires that "the maintenance of the suit . . . not offend 'traditional notions of fair play and substantial justice.'" International Shoe v. Washington, quoting Milliken v. Meyers.

Because the requirement of personal jurisdiction represents first of all an individual right, it can, like other such rights, be waived. In McDonald v. Mabee, *supra,* the Court indicated that regardless of the power of the state to serve process, an individual may submit to the jurisdiction of the Court by appearance. A variety of legal arrangements have been taken to represent express or implied consent to the personal jurisdiction of the court. In National Rental v. Szukhent, we stated that "parties to a contract may agree in advance to submit to the jurisdiction of a given court," and in Petrowski v. Hawkeye-Security Co., the Court upheld the personal jurisdiction of a district court on the basis of a stipulation entered into by the defendant. In addition, lower federal courts have found such consent implicit in agreements to arbitrate. Furthermore, the Court has upheld state procedures which find constructive consent to the personal jurisdiction of the state court in the voluntary use of certain state procedures. Finally, unlike subject matter jurisdiction, which even an appellate court may review sua sponte, under Rule 12(h), Fed. Rules Civ. Proc., "a defense of lack of jurisdiction over the person . . . is waived" if not timely raised in the answer or a responsive pleading.

---

10. It is true that we have stated that the requirement of personal jurisdiction, as applied to state courts, reflects an element of federalism and the character of state sovereignty vis-à-vis other states. . . . Contrary to the suggestion of Justice Powell, *post,* at 5-6, our holding today does not alter the requirement that there be "minimum contacts" between the nonresident defendant and the forum state. Rather, our holding deals with how the facts needed to show those "minimum contacts" can be established when a defendant fails to comply with court-ordered discovery. The restriction on state sovereign power described in *World-Wide Volkswagen Corp.,* however, must be seen as ultimately a function of the individual liberty interest preserved by the Due Process Clause. That clause is the only source of the personal jurisdiction requirement and the clause itself makes no mention of federalism concerns. Furthermore, if the federalism concept operated as an independent restriction on the sovereign power of the court, it would not be possible to waive the personal jurisdiction requirement: Individual actions cannot change the powers of sovereignty, although the individual can subject himself to powers from which he may otherwise be protected.

In sum, the requirement of personal jurisdiction may be intentionally waived, or for various reasons a defendant may be estopped from raising the issue. These characteristics portray it for what it is—a legal right protecting the individual. The plaintiff's demonstration of certain historical facts may make clear to the court that it has personal jurisdiction over the defendant as a matter of law—*i.e.*, certain factual showings will have legal consequences—but this is not the only way in which the personal jurisdiction of the court may arise. The actions of the defendant may amount to a legal submission to the jurisdiction of the court, whether voluntary or not.

The expression of legal rights is often subject to certain procedural rules: The failure to follow those rules may well result in a curtailment of the rights. Thus, the failure to enter a timely objection to personal jurisdiction constitutes, under Rule 12(h)(1), a waiver of the objection. A sanction under Rule 37(b)(2)(A) consisting of a finding of personal jurisdiction has precisely the same effect. As a general proposition, the Rule 37 sanction applied to a finding of personal jurisdiction creates no more of a due process problem than the Rule 12 waiver. Although "a court cannot conclude all persons interested by its mere assertion of its own power," not all rules that establish legal consequences to a party's own behavior are "mere assertions" of power.

Rule 37(b)(2)(a) itself embodies the standard established in Hammond Packing Co. v. Arkansas, 212 U.S. 322 (1909), for the Due Process limits on such rules. There the Court held that it did not violate due process for a state court to strike the answer and render a default judgment against a defendant who failed to comply with a pretrial discovery order. Such a rule was permissible as an expression of

> the undoubted right of the lawmaking power to create a presumption of fact as to the bad faith and untruth of an answer begotten from the suppression of failure to produce the proof ordered. . . . [T]he preservation of due process was secured by the presumption that the refusal to produce evidence material to the administration of due process was but an admission of the want of merit in the asserted defense.

The situation in *Hammond* was specifically distinguished from that in Hovey v. Elliot, 167 U.S. 409 (1897), in which the Court held that it did violate due process for a court to take similar action as "punishment" for failure to obey an order to pay into the registry of the court a certain sum of money. Due process is violated only if the behavior of the defendant will not support the *Hammond Packing* presumption. A proper application of Rule 37(b)(2) will, as a matter of law, support such a presumption. *See* Société Internationale v. Rogers, 357 U.S. 197, 209-213 (1958). If there is no abuse of discretion in the application of the Rule 37 sanction, as we find to be the case here (*see* §III), then the sanction is nothing more than the invocation of a legal presumption, or what is the same thing, the finding of a constructive waiver.

Petitioners argue that a sanction consisting of a finding of personal jurisdiction differs from all other instances in which a sanction is imposed, including the default judgment in *Hammond Packing*, because a party need not obey the orders of a court until it is established that the court has personal jurisdiction over that party. If there is no obligation to obey a judicial order, a sanction cannot be applied for the failure to comply. Until the court has established personal jurisdiction, moreover, any assertion of judicial power over the party violates due process.

This argument again assumes that there is something unique about the requirement of personal jurisdiction, which prevents it from being established or waived like other rights. A defendant is always free to ignore the judicial proceedings, risk a default judgment and then challenge that judgment on jurisdictional grounds in a collateral proceeding. By submitting to the jurisdiction of the court for a limited purpose of challenging jurisdiction, the defendant agrees to abide by that court's determination on the issue of jurisdiction: That decision will be res judicata on that issue in any further proceedings. As demonstrated above, the manner in which the court determines whether it has personal jurisdiction may include a variety of legal rules and presumptions, as well as straight forward fact-finding. A particular rule may offend the due process standard of *Hammond Packing*, but the mere use of procedural rules does not in itself violate the defendant's due process rights.

[The Court concluded by finding that the sanction imposed by the district court was not an abuse of discretion under the facts of the case.]

Justice POWELL, concurring in the judgment.

In my view the Court's broadly theoretical decision misapprehends the issues actually presented for decision. Federal courts are courts of limited jurisdiction. Their personal jurisdiction, no less than their subject matter jurisdiction, is subject both to constitutional and to statutory definition. When the applicable limitations on federal jurisdiction are identified, it becomes apparent that the Court's theory could require a sweeping but largely unexplicated revision of jurisdictional doctrine. This revision could encompass not only the personal jurisdiction of federal courts but "sovereign" limitations on state jurisdiction as identified by World-Wide Volkswagen Corp. v. Woodson. Fair resolution of this case does not require the Court's broad holding. Accordingly, although I concur in the Court's judgment, I cannot join its opinion.

I . . .

Rule 37(b) is not, however, a jurisdictional provision. As recognized by the Court of Appeals, the governing jurisdictional statute remains the long-arm statute of the State of Pennsylvania. In my view the Court fails to make clear the implications of this central fact: that the District Court in this case relied on state law to obtain personal jurisdiction.

As courts of limited jurisdiction, the federal district courts possess no warrant to create jurisdictional law of their own. Under the Rules of Decision Act, 28 U.S.C. §1652, 62 Stat. 944, they must apply state law "except where the Constitution or treaties of the United States or Acts of Congress otherwise require or provide. . . ." *See generally* Erie R. Co. v. Tompkins, 304 U.S. 64 (1938). Thus, in the absence of a federal rule or statute establishing a federal basis for the assertion of personal jurisdiction, the personal jurisdiction of the district courts is determined in diversity cases by the law of the forum State.

As a result of the District Court's dependence on the law of Pennsylvania to establish personal jurisdiction—a dependence mandated by Congress under 28 U.S.C. §1652—its jurisdiction in this case normally would be subject to the same due process limitations as a state court. Thus, the question arises how today's decision is related to cases restricting the personal jurisdiction of the States. . . .

A

Under traditional principles, the due process question in this case is whether "minimum contacts" exist between petitioners and the forum State that would justify the State in exercising personal jurisdiction. By finding that the establishment of minimum contacts is not a prerequisite to the exercise of jurisdiction to impose sanctions under Fed. Rule Civ. Proc. 37, the Court may be understood as finding that "minimum contacts" no longer is a constitutional requirement for the exercise by the state court of personal jurisdiction over an unconsenting defendant. Whenever the Court's notions of fairness are not offended, jurisdiction apparently may be upheld.

Before today, of course, our cases had linked minimum contacts and fair play as *jointly* defining the "sovereign" limits on state assertions of personal jurisdiction over unconsenting defendants. *See* World-Wide Volkswagen Corp. v. Woodson, Hanson v. Deckla. The Court appears to abandon the rationale of these cases in a footnote. *See* n.10. But it does not address the implications of its action. By eschewing reliance on the concept of minimum contacts as a "sovereign" limitation on the power of States—for, again, it is the State's long-arm statute that is invoked to obtain personal jurisdiction in the District Court—the Court today effects a potentially substantial change of law. For the first time it defines personal jurisdiction solely by reference to abstract notions of fair play. And, astonishingly to me, it does so in a case in which this rationale for decision was neither argued nor briefed by the parties.

B

Alternatively, it is possible to read the Court opinion, not as affecting the state jurisdiction, but simply as asserting that Rule 37 of the Federal Rules of Civil Procedure represents a congressionally approved basis for the exercise of personal jurisdiction by a federal district court. On this view Rule 37 vests the federal district courts with authority to take jurisdiction over persons not in compliance with discovery orders. This of course would be a more limited holding. Yet the Court does not cast its decision in these terms. And it provides no support for such an interpretation, either in the language or in the history of the Federal Rules.

In the absence of such support, I could not join the Court in embracing such a construction of the Rules of Civil Procedure. There is nothing in Rule 37 to suggest that it is intended to confer a grant of personal jurisdiction. Indeed, the clear language of Rule 82 seems to establish that Rule 37 should *not* be construed as a jurisdictional grant: "These rules shall not be construed to extend . . . the jurisdiction of the United States district courts or the venue of actions therein." Moreover, assuming that minimum contacts remain a constitutional predicate for the exercise of a State's in personam jurisdiction over an unconsenting defendant, constitutional questions would arise if Rule 37 were read to permit a plaintiff in a diversity action to subject a defendant to a "fishing expedition" in a foreign jurisdiction. A plaintiff is not entitled to discovery to establish essentially speculative allegations necessary to personal jurisdiction. Nor would the use of Rule 37 sanctions to enforce discovery orders constitute a mere abuse of discretion in such a case. For me at least, such a use of discovery would raise serious questions as to the constitutionality as well as the statutory authority of a federal court—in a diversity case—to exercise personal jurisdiction absent some showing of minimum contacts between the unconsenting defendant and the forum State.

II

In this case the facts alone—unaided by broad jurisdictional theories—more than amply demonstrate that the District Court possessed personal jurisdiction to impose sanctions under Rule 37 and otherwise to adjudicate this case. I would decide the case on this narrow basis. . . .

Questions and Comments

(1) The majority, as Justice Powell notes, does not seem to base its decision purely on a sanction rationale: Instead it invokes Hammand Packing Co. v. Arkansas for the proposition that a presumption that the facts giving rise to actual jurisdiction actually exist may be drawn from the defendants'

silence. Is such an inference credible? What if the defendants truly thought the requests for documents were excessively burdensome?

(2) Could the result of the case be rested on a sanction rationale? Or is it improper to impose a sanction on a party over whom the court has no jurisdiction?

(3) If the defendants had made no appearance at all, even to contest jurisdiction, the court might have entered a judgment against them, but it would have been subject to collateral attack—*i.e.*, a second court, asked to enforce the judgment, would be required to inspect the jurisdictional contacts afresh and make its own judgment. In the actual case, however, collateral attack is presumably not permitted. How can the Court justify worse treatment for the defendants who show up but don't cooperate fully as against those who don't cooperate at all by failing to show up?

(4) Waiver of the right to assert lack of jurisdiction may also occur under the federal rules if the defendant makes a preliminary motion and the motion does not include objection to lack of jurisdiction. Fed. R. Civ. P. 12(h). (The defendant may choose instead to include the defense in its answer.)

In some pleading systems the defense of lack of jurisdiction may not be joined with a defense on the merits; instead one must make a "special appearance" for the purpose of contesting jurisdiction. If the merits are contested, the jurisdictional issue is waived. May a court provide that *any* kind of appearance will constitute a waiver, that is, give the defendant the choice between showing up and litigating on the merits (despite a possibly meritorious jurisdictional defense) or staying away and suffering a default judgment that, if the defendant was wrong on the jurisdictional defense, will be binding and will preclude consideration of the merits? The Supreme Court said yes in York v. Texas, 137 U.S. 15 (1890), saying that the availability of collateral attack was sufficient to ensure due process.

B. Activities as a Basis for Jurisdiction

It has long been taken for granted that an individual is subject to suit in the state of his or her domicile on any cause of action whatsoever. *See, e.g.*, Milliken v. Meyer, 311 U.S. 457 (1940). By the same token, a corporation is subject to suit generally at the place of its incorporation or its principal place of business. In Perkins v. Benguet Consolidated Mining Co., 342 U.S. 437 (1952), jurisdiction over a cause of action unrelated to the defendant's forum activities was justified by the very substantial amount of business that the defendant transacted in the forum.

But the Supreme Court has repeatedly held that the forum affiliation need not be so extensive where the cause of action arises out of the defendant's forum activities. McGee v. International Life Insurance Co., 355 U.S. 220 (1957), upheld, for instance, an assertion of jurisdiction based upon the solicitation and writing of a single life insurance contract for a forum resident. Such holdings create an incentive for plaintiffs to argue that their cause of action arises out of or is related to the defendant's forum activities, for then the amount of contact shown need not be as great. Such assertions of "specific jurisdiction" are differentiated from "general jurisdiction" over all causes of action involving the particular defendant, based upon extensive contacts such as domicile or place of incorporation.

1. General and Specific Jurisdiction

Helicopteros Nacionales de Colombia, S.A. v. Hall

466 U.S. 408 (1983)

Justice BLACKMUN delivered the opinion of the Court.

We granted certiorari in this case, 460 U.S. 1021 (1983), to decide whether the Supreme Court of Texas correctly ruled that the contacts of a foreign corporation with the state of Texas were sufficient to allow a Texas state court to assert jurisdiction over the corporation in a cause of action not arising out of or related to the corporation's activities within the State.

I

Petitioner Helicopteros Nacionales de Colombia, S.A. (Helicol), is a Colombian corporation with its principal place of business in the city of Bogota in that country. It is engaged in the business of providing helicopter transportation for oil and construction companies in South America. On January 26, 1976, a helicopter owned by Helicol crashed in Peru. Four United States citizens were among those who lost their lives in the accident. Respondents are the survivors and representatives of the four decedents.

At the time of the crash, respondents' decedents were employed by Consorcio, a Peruvian consortium, and were working on a pipeline in Peru. Consorcio is the alter ego of a joint venture named Williams-Sedco-Horn (WSH). The venture had its headquarters in Houston, Tex. Consorcio had been formed to enable the venturers to enter into a contract with Petro Peru, the Peruvian state-owned oil company. Consorcio was to construct a pipeline for Petro Peru running from the interior of Peru westward to the Pacific Ocean. Peruvian law forbade construction of the pipeline by any non-Peruvian entity.

Consorcio/WSH needed helicopters to move personnel, materials, and equipment into and out of the construction area. In 1974, upon request of Consorcio/WSH, the chief executive officer of Helicol, Francisco Restrepo, flew to the United States and conferred in Houston with representatives of the three joint venturers. At that meeting, there was a discussion of prices, availability, working conditions, fuel, supplies, and housing. Restrepo represented that Helicol could have the first helicopter on the job in 15 days. The Consorcio/WSH representatives decided to accept the contract proposed by Restrepo. Helicol began performing before the agreement was formally signed in Peru on November 11, 1974.[3] The contract was written in Spanish on official government stationery and provided that the residence of all the parties would be Lima, Peru. It further stated that controversies arising out of the contract would be submitted to the jurisdiction of Peruvian courts. In addition, it provided that Consorcio/WSH would make payments to Helicol's account with the Bank of America in New York City.

Aside from the negotiation session in Houston between Restrepo and the representatives of Consorcio/WSH, Helicol had other contacts with Texas. During the years 1970-1977, it purchased helicopters (approximately 80% of its fleet), spare parts, and accessories for more than $4 million from Bell Helicopter Company in Fort Worth. In that period, Helicol sent prospective pilots to Fort Worth for training and to ferry the aircraft to South America. It also sent management and maintenance personnel to visit Bell Helicopter in Fort Worth during the same period in order to receive "plant familiarization" and for technical consultation. Helicol received into its New York City and Panama City, Fla., bank accounts over $5 million in payments from Consorcio/WSH drawn upon First City National Bank of Houston.

Beyond the foregoing, there have been no other business contacts between Helicol and the State of Texas. Helicol never has been authorized to do business in Texas and never has had an agent for the service of process within the State. It never has performed helicopter operations in Texas or sold any product that reached Texas, never solicited business in Texas, never signed any contract in Texas, never had any employee based there, and never recruited an employee in Texas. In addition, Helicol never has owned real or personal property in Texas and never has maintained an office or establishment there. Helicol has maintained no records in Texas and has no shareholders in that State. None of the respondents or their decedents were domiciled in Texas . . . ,[5] but all of the decedents were hired in Houston by Consorcio/WSH to work on the Petro Peru pipeline project.

Respondents instituted wrongful-death actions in the District Court of Harris County, Tex., against Consorcio/WSH, Bell Helicopter Company, and Helicol. Helicol filed special appearances and moved to dismiss the actions

---

3. Respondents acknowledge that the contract was executed in Peru and not in the United States. Tr. of Oral Arg. 22-23. *See* App. 79a; Brief for Respondents 3.

5. Respondents' lack of residential or other contacts with Texas of itself does not defeat otherwise proper jurisdiction. Keeton v. Hustler Magazine, Inc., 465 U.S. 770, 780 (1984); Calder v. Jones, 465 U.S. 783, 788 (1984). We mention respondents' lack of contacts merely to show that nothing in the nature of the relationship between respondents and Helicol could possibly enhance Helicol's contacts with Texas. The harm suffered by respondents did not occur in Texas. Nor is it alleged that any negligence on the part of Helicol took place in Texas.

for lack of *in personam* jurisdiction over it. The motion was denied. After a consolidated jury trial, judgment was entered against Helicol on a jury verdict of $1,141,200 in favor of respondents. . . . In ruling that the Texas courts had in personam jurisdiction, the Texas Supreme Court first held that the State's long-arm statute reaches as far as the Due Process Clause of the Fourteenth Amendment permits. Thus, the only question remaining for the court to decide was whether it was consistent with the Due Process Clause for Texas courts to assert in personam jurisdiction over Helicol.

II

The Due Process Clause of the Fourteenth Amendment operates to limit the power of a State to assert in personam jurisdiction over a nonresident defendant. Pennoyer v. Neff, 95 U.S. 714 (1878). Due process requirements are satisfied when in personam jurisdiction is asserted over a nonresident corporate defendant that has "certain minimum contacts with [the forum] such that the maintenance of the suit does not offend 'traditional notions of fair play and substantial justice.' " International Shoe Co. v. Washington, 326 U.S. 310, 316 (1945), quoting Milliken v. Meyer, 311 U.S. 457, 463 (1940). When a controversy is related to or "arises out of" a defendant's contacts with the forum, the Court has said that a "relationship among the defendant, the forum, and the litigation" is the essential foundation of in personam jurisdiction. Shaffer v. Heitner, 433 U.S. 186, 204 (1977).[8]

Even when the cause of action does not arise out of or relate to the foreign corporation's activities in the forum State,[9] due process is not offended by a State's subjecting the corporation to its *in personam* jurisdiction when there are sufficient contacts between the State and the foreign corporation. Perkins v. Benguet Consolidated Mining Co., 342 U.S. 437 (1952); *see* Keeton v. Hustler Magazine, Inc., 465 U.S. 770, 779-780 (1984). In *Perkins*, the Court addressed a situation in which state courts had asserted general jurisdiction over a defendant foreign corporation. During the Japanese occupation of the Philippine Islands, the president and general manager of a Philippine mining corporation maintained an office in Ohio from which he conducted activities on behalf of the company. He kept company files and held directors' meetings in the office, carried on correspondence relating to

---

8. It has been said that when a State exercises personal jurisdiction over a defendant in a suit arising out of or related to the defendant's contacts with the forum, the State is exercising "specific jurisdiction" over the defendant. *See* Von Mehren and Trautman, Jurisdiction to Adjudicate: A Suggested Analysis, 79 Harv. L. Rev. 1121, 1144-1164 (1966).

9. When a State exercises personal jurisdiction over a defendant in a suit not arising out of or related to the defendant's contacts with the forum, the State has been said to be exercising "general jurisdiction" over the defendant. *See* Brilmayer, How Contacts Count: Due Process Limitations on State Court Jurisdiction, 1980 S. Ct. Rev. 77, 80-81; Von Mehren and Trautman, 79 Harv. L. Rev., at 1136-1144; Calder v. Jones, 465 U.S., at 786.

the business, distributed salary checks drawn on two active Ohio bank accounts, engaged an Ohio bank to act as transfer agent, and supervised policies dealing with the rehabilitation of the corporation's properties in the Philippines. In short, the foreign corporation, through its president, "ha[d] been carrying on in Ohio a continuous and systematic, but limited, part of its general business," and the exercise of general jurisdiction over the Philippine corporation by an Ohio court was "reasonable and just." 342 U.S., at 438, 445.

All parties to the present case concede that respondents' claims against Helicol did not "arise out of," and are not related to, Helicol's activities within Texas.[10] We thus must explore the nature of Helicol's contacts with the State of Texas to determine whether they constitute the kind of continuous and systematic general business contacts the Court found to exist in *Perkins.* We hold that they do not.

It is undisputed that Helicol does not have a place of business in Texas and never has been licensed to do business in the State. Basically, Helicol's contacts with Texas consisted of sending its chief executive officer to Houston for a contract-negotiation session; accepting into its New York bank account checks drawn on a Houston bank; purchasing helicopters, equipment, and training services from Bell Helicopter for substantial sums; and sending personnel to Bell's facilities in Fort Worth for training.

The one trip to Houston by Helicol's chief executive officer for the purpose of negotiating the transportation-services contract with Consorcio/WSH cannot be described or regarded as a contact of a "continuous and systematic" nature, as *Perkins* described it, *see also* International Shoe Co. v. Washington, 326 U.S., at 320, and thus cannot support an assertion of in personam jurisdiction over Helicol by a Texas court. Similarly, Helicol's acceptance

---

10. Because the parties have not argued any relationship between the cause of action and Helicol's contacts with the State of Texas, we, contrary to the dissent's implication, assert no "view" with respect to that issue.

The dissent suggests that we have erred in drawing no distinction between controversies that "relate to" a defendant's contacts with a forum and those that "arise out of" such contacts. *Post,* at 420. This criticism is somewhat puzzling, for the dissent goes on to urge that, for purposes of determining the constitutional validity of an assertion of specific jurisdiction, there really should be no distinction between the two.

We do not address the validity or consequences of such a distinction because the issue has not been presented in this case. Respondents have made no argument that their cause of action either arose out of or is related to Helicol's contacts with the state of Texas. Absent any briefing on the issue, we decline to reach the questions (1) whether the terms "arising out of" and "related to" describe different connections between a cause of action and a defendant's contacts with a forum, and (2) what sort of tie between a cause of action and a defendant's contacts with a forum is necessary to a determination that either connection exists. Nor do we reach the question whether, if the two types of relationship differ, a forum's exercise of personal jurisdiction in a situation where the cause of action "relates to," but does not "arise out of," the defendant's contacts with the forum should be analyzed as an assertion of specific jurisdiction.

from Consorcio/WSH of checks drawn on a Texas bank is of negligible significance for purposes of determining whether Helicol had sufficient contacts in Texas. There is no indication that Helicol ever requested that the checks be drawn on a Texas bank or that there was any negotiation between Helicol and Consorcio/WSH with respect to the location or identity of the bank on which checks would be drawn. Common sense and everyday experience suggest that, absent unusual circumstances, the bank on which a check is drawn is generally of little consequence to the payee and is a matter left to the discretion of the drawer. Such unilateral activity of another party or a third person is not an appropriate consideration when determining whether a defendant has sufficient contacts with a forum State to justify an assertion of jurisdiction. *See* Kulko v. California Superior Court, 436 U.S. 84, 93 (1978) (arbitrary to subject one parent to suit in any State where other parent chooses to spend time while having custody of child pursuant to separation agreement); Hanson v. Denckla, 357 U.S. 235, 253 (1958) ("The unilateral activity of those who claim some relationship with a nonresident defendant cannot satisfy the requirement of contact with the forum State").

The Texas Supreme Court focused on the purchases and the related training trips in finding contacts sufficient to support an assertion of jurisdiction. We do not agree with that assessment, for the Court's opinion in Rosenberg Bros. & Co. v. Curtis Brown Co., 260 U.S. 516 (1923) (Brandeis, J., for a unanimous tribunal), makes clear that purchases and related trips, standing alone, are not a sufficient basis for a State's assertion of jurisdiction.

The defendant in *Rosenberg* was a small retailer in Tulsa, Okla., who dealt in men's clothing and furnishings. It never had applied for a license to do business in New York, nor had it at any time authorized suit to be brought against it there. It never had an established place of business in New York and never regularly carried on business in that State. Its only connection with New York was that it purchased from New York wholesalers a large portion of the merchandise sold in its Tulsa store. The purchases sometimes were made by correspondence and sometimes through visits to New York by an officer of the defendant. The Court concluded: "Visits on such business, even if occurring at regular intervals, would not warrant the inference that the corporation was present within the jurisdiction of [New York]" *Id.*, at 518.

This Court in *International Shoe* acknowledged and did not repudiate its holding in *Rosenberg*. *See* 326 U.S., at 318. In accordance with *Rosenberg*, we hold that mere purchases, even if occurring at regular intervals, are not enough to warrant a State's assertion of in personam jurisdiction over a nonresident corporation in a cause of action not related to those purchase transactions.[12] Nor can we conclude that the fact that Helicol sent personnel into

12. This Court in *International Shoe* cited *Rosenberg* for the proposition that "the commission of some single or occasional acts of the corporate agent in a state sufficient to impose an obligation or liability on the corporation has not been thought to confer upon the state authority to enforce it." 326 U.S., at 318. Arguably, therefore, *Rosenberg* also stands for the proposition that mere purchases are not a sufficient basis for either general or specific jurisdiction.

Texas for training in connection with the purchase of helicopters and equipment in that State in any way enhanced the nature of Helicol's contacts with Texas. The training was a part of the package of goods and services purchased by Helicol from Bell Helicopter. The brief presence of Helicol employees in Texas for the purpose of attending the training sessions is no more a significant contact than were the trips to New York made by the buyer for the retail store in *Rosenberg*.

III

We hold that Helicol's contacts with the State of Texas were insufficient to satisfy the requirements of the Due Process Clause of the Fourteenth Amendment.[13] Accordingly, we reverse the judgment of the Supreme Court of Texas.

It is so ordered.

Justice BRENNAN, dissenting.

I

The Court expressly limits its decision in this case to "an assertion of general jurisdiction over a foreign defendant." Having framed the question in this way, the Court is obliged to address our prior holdings in Perkins v. Benguet Consolidated Mining Co., 342 U.S. 437 (1952), and Rosenberg Bros. & Co. v. Curtis Brown Co., *supra.* In *Perkins,* the Court considered a State's assertion of general jurisdiction over a foreign corporation that "ha[d] been carrying on . . . a continuous and systematic, but limited, part of its general business" in the forum. 342 U.S., at 438. Under the circumstances of that case, we held that such contacts were constitutionally sufficient "to make it

---

Because the case before us is one in which there has been an assertion of general jurisdiction over a foreign defendant, we need not decide the continuing validity of *Rosenberg* with respect to an assertion of specific jurisdiction, *i.e.,* where the cause of action arises out of or relates to the purchases by the defendant in the forum State.

13. As an alternative to traditional minimum-contacts analysis, respondents suggest that the Court hold that the State of Texas had personal jurisdiction over Helicol under a doctrine of "jurisdiction by necessity." *See* Shaffer v. Heitner, 433 U.S. 186, 211, n.37 (1977). We conclude, however, that respondents failed to carry their burden of showing that all three defendants could not be sued together in a single forum. It is not clear from the record, for example, whether suit could have been brought against all three defendants in either Colombia or Peru. We decline to consider adoption of a doctrine of jurisdiction by necessity—a potentially far-reaching modification of existing law—in the absence of a more complete record.

reasonable and just to subject the corporation to the jurisdiction" of that State. *Id.*, at 445 (citing *International Shoe, supra,* at 317-320). Nothing in *Perkins* suggests, however, that such "continuous and systematic" contacts are a necessary minimum before a State may constitutionally assert general jurisdiction over a foreign corporation.

The Court therefore looks for guidance to our 1923 decision in *Rosenberg, supra,* which until today was of dubious validity given the subsequent expansion of personal jurisdiction that began with *International Shoe, supra,* in 1945. In *Rosenberg,* the Court held that a company's purchases within a State, even when combined with related trips to the State by company officials, would not allow the courts of that State to assert general jurisdiction over all claims against the nonresident corporate defendant making those purchases. Reasoning by analogy, the Court in this case concludes that Helicol's contacts with the State of Texas are no more significant than the purchases made by the defendant in *Rosenberg.* The Court makes no attempt, however, to ascertain whether the narrow view of in personam jurisdiction adopted by the Court in *Rosenberg* comports with "the fundamental transformation of our national economy" that has occurred since 1923. This failure, in my view, is fatal to the Court's analysis.

The vast expansion of our national economy during the past several decades has provided the primary rationale for expanding the permissible reach of a State's jurisdiction under the Due Process Clause. By broadening the type and amount of business opportunities available to participants in interstate and foreign commerce, our economy has increased the frequency with which foreign corporations actively pursue commercial transactions throughout the various States. In turn, it has become both necessary and, in my view, desirable to allow the States more leeway in bringing the activities of these nonresident corporations within the scope of their respective jurisdictions. . . .

As a foreign corporation that has actively and purposefully engaged in numerous and frequent commercial transactions in the State of Texas, Helicol clearly falls within the category of nonresident defendants that may be subject to that forum's general jurisdiction. Helicol not only purchased helicopters and other equipment in the State for many years, but also sent pilots and management personnel into Texas to be trained in the use of this equipment and to consult with the seller on technical matters. Moreover, negotiations for the contract under which Helicol provided transportation services to the joint venture that employed the respondents' decedents also took place in the State of Texas. Taken together, these contacts demonstrate that Helicol obtained numerous benefits from its transaction of business in Texas. In turn, it is eminently fair and reasonable to expect Helicol to face the obligations that attach to its participation in such commercial transactions. Accordingly, on the basis of continuous commercial contacts with the forum, I would conclude that the Due Process Clause allows the State of Texas to assert general jurisdiction over petitioner Helicol.

II

The Court also fails to distinguish the legal principles that controlled our prior decisions in *Perkins* and *Rosenberg*. In particular, the contacts between petitioner Helicol and the State of Texas, unlike the contacts between the defendant and the forum in each of those cases, are significantly related to the cause of action alleged in the original suit filed by the respondents. Accordingly, in my view, it is both fair and reasonable for the Texas courts to assert specific jurisdiction over Helicol in this case.

By asserting that the present case does not implicate the specific jurisdiction of the Texas courts, the Court necessarily removes its decision from the reality of the actual facts presented for our consideration.[3] Moreover, the Court refuses to consider any distinction between contacts that are "related to" the underlying cause of action and contacts that "give rise" to the underlying cause of action. In my view, however, there is a substantial difference between these two standards for asserting specific jurisdiction. Thus, although I agree that the respondents' cause of action did not formally "arise out of" specific activities initiated by Helicol in the State of Texas, I believe that the wrongful-death claim filed by the respondents is significantly related to the undisputed contacts between Helicol and the forum. On that basis, I would conclude that the Due Process Clause allows the Texas courts to assert specific jurisdiction over this particular action.

The wrongful-death actions filed by the respondents were premised on a fatal helicopter crash that occurred in Peru. Helicol was joined as a defendant in the lawsuits because it provided transportation services, including the particular helicopter and pilot involved in the crash, to the joint venture that employed the decedents. Specifically, the respondent Hall claimed in her original complaint that "Helicol is . . . legally responsible for its own negligence through its pilot employee." App. 6a. Viewed in light of these allegations, the contacts between Helicol and the State of Texas are directly and significantly related to the underlying claim filed by the respondents. The negotiations that took place in Texas led to the contract in which Helicol agreed to provide the precise transportation services that were being used at the time of the crash. Moreover, the helicopter involved in the crash was purchased by Helicol in Texas, and the pilot whose negligence was alleged to have caused the crash was actually trained in Texas. This is simply not a case, therefore, in which a state court has asserted jurisdiction over a nonresident defendant on the basis of wholly unrelated contacts with the forum. Rather, the contacts between Helicol and the forum are directly related to the negligence that was alleged in the respondent Hall's original com-

3. Nor do I agree with the Court that the respondents have conceded that their claims are not related to Helicol's activities within the State of Texas. Although no parts of their written and oral arguments before the Court proceed on the assumption that no such relationship exists, other portions suggest just the opposite. . . .

plaint.[4] Because Helicol should have expected to be amenable to suit in the Texas courts for claims directly related to these contacts, it is fair and reasonable to allow the assertion of jurisdiction in this case.

Despite this substantial relationship between the contacts and the cause of action, the Court declines to consider whether the courts of Texas may assert specific jurisdiction over this suit. Apparently, this simply reflects a narrow interpretation of the question presented for review. It is nonetheless possible that the Court's opinion may be read to imply that the specific jurisdiction of the Texas courts is inapplicable because the cause of action did not formally "arise out of" the contacts between Helicol and the forum. In my view, however, such a rule would place unjustifiable limits on the bases under which Texas may assert its jurisdictional power.[5]

Limiting the specific jurisdiction of a forum to cases in which the cause of action formally arose out of the defendant's contacts with the State would subject constitutional standards under the Due Process Clause to the vagaries of the substantive law or pleading requirements of each State. For example, the complaint filed against Helicol in this case alleged negligence based on pilot error. Even though the pilot was trained in Texas, the Court assumes that the Texas courts may not assert jurisdiction over the suit because the cause of action "did not 'arise out of,' and [is] not related to," that training. If, however, the applicable substantive law required that negligent training of the pilot was a necessary element of a cause of action for pilot error, or if the respondents had simply added an allegation of negligence in the training provided for the Helicol pilot, then presumably the Court would concede that the specific jurisdiction of the Texas courts was applicable.

Our interpretation of the Due Process Clause has never been so dependent upon the applicable substantive law or the State's formal pleading requirements. At least since International Shoe Co. v. Washington, 326 U.S. 310 (1945), the principal focus when determining whether a forum may constitutionally assert jurisdiction over a nonresident defendant has been on fairness and reasonableness to the defendant. To this extent, a court's specific jurisdiction should be applicable whenever the cause of action arises out of *or* relates to the contacts between the defendant and the forum. It is eminently fair and reasonable, in my view, to subject a defendant to suit in a forum with which it has significant contacts directly related to the underlying cause of

---

4. The jury specifically found that "the pilot failed to keep the helicopter under proper control," that "the helicopter was flown into a treetop fog condition, whereby the vision of the pilot was impaired," that "such flying was negligence," and that "such negligence . . . was a proximate cause of the crash." On the basis of these findings, Helicol was ordered to pay over $1 million in damages to the respondents.

5. *Compare* Von Mehren and Trautman, Jurisdiction to Adjudicate: A Suggested Analysis, 79 Harv. L. Rev. 1121, 1144-1163 (1966), *with* Brilmayer, How Contacts Count: Due Process Limitations on State Court Jurisdiction, 1980 S. Ct. Rev. 77, 80-88. *See also* Lilly, Jurisdiction Over Domestic and Alien Defendants, 69 Va. L. Rev. 85, 100-101, and n.66 (1983).

action. Because Helicol's contacts with the State of Texas meet this standard, I would affirm the judgment of the Supreme Court of Texas.

Questions and Comments

(1) What does it mean to say that the controversy "arises out of" or "relates to" the defendant's activities in the forum? Are these the same? In the Supreme Court Review article cited in the majority's footnote 9, the author argued that specific jurisdiction should be based upon contacts that were themselves of substantive relevance to the dispute. In rejecting this suggestion, did the dissent have an alternative conception of what "relating to" means, how it is different from "arising out of," and how both differ from total unrelatedness? Isn't this crucial if different types of contacts are to be weighted differently?

This issue has provoked considerable discussion in the courts and in the academic literature. Sternberg v. O'Neil, 550 A.2d 1105 (Del. 1988), excerpted at page 463 *supra,* contained a serious discussion of specific jurisdiction as it related to the court's differentiation between implied and express consent, 550 A.2d at 1116-1117. Different definitions of the requirement that a cause of action "arise from" the local contacts can be found in: Hexacomb Corp. v. Damage Prevention Products Corp., 905 F. Supp. 557 (N.D. Ind. 1995) (defendant's contacts with the forum must be substantively related to the cause of action); Creech v. Roberts, 908 F.2d 75 (6th Cir. 1990) (contacts must be related to the "operative facts" of the controversy); Pizzaro v. Hoteles Concorde Intl., C.A., 907 F.2d 1256 (1st Cir. 1990) (in applying proximate cause test, the court examined whether the facts constituting the defendant's contacts were relevant to the proof of the elements of the plaintiff's cause of action); Nowak v. Tak How Invs., Ltd., 94 F.3d 708 (1st Cir. 1996) (court deviates from proximate cause test to exercise jurisdiction where meaningful link exists between defendant's contacts and harm suffered by plaintiff); Shopper's Food Warehouse v. Moreno, 746 A.2d 320 (D.D.C. 2000) (contacts must have a substantial connection with plaintiff's claim); Vons Companies, Inc. v. Seabest Foods, Inc., 926 P.2d 1085 (Cal. 1996) (rejecting proximate cause test as too narrow and "but for" test as too broad, and holding that there must be a substantial nexus or connection between the defendant's forum activities and the plaintiff's claim); In re Oil Spill by Amoco Cadiz Off Coast of France, 699 F.2d 909 (7th Cir. 1983) (applying "in the wake of" test to state long-arm statute).

The lower court opinion in Carnival Cruise v. Shute, reprinted at page 451 *supra,* addressed the question of whether the injury arose out of the defendant's advertising activities in the forum, answering the question in the affirmative after applying a "but for" test. Shute v. Carnival Cruise Lines, 863 F.2d 1437 (9th Cir. 1988); *see also* Ballard v. Savage, 65 F.3d 1495, 1500 (9th Cir. 1995) (reaffirming "but for" test). Many observers hoped when the Supreme Court agreed to hear the case that its decision would clarify the issue; instead, the issue was avoided by the Court's holding that jurisdiction existed on the basis of the forum selection clause.

For academic discussion of these and other possible tests, *see* Twitchell, The Myth of General Jurisdiction, 101 Harv. L. Rev. 610 (1988); Brilmayer, Related Contacts and Personal Jurisdiction, 101 Harv. L. Rev. 1444 (1988); Twitchell, A Rejoinder to Professor Brilmayer, 101 Harv. L. Rev. 1465 (1988). For an analysis of the Ninth Circuit's "but for" test, *see* Comment, Related Contacts and Personal Jurisdiction: The "But For" Test, 82 Cal. L. Rev. 1545 (1994); Comment, Specific Personal Jurisdiction and the "Arise From Or Relate To" Requirement: What Does It Mean?, 50 Wash. & Lee L. Rev. 1265 (1993).

(2) Why should purchases be treated qualitatively differently from other sorts of unrelated contacts? Would unrelated purchases really be constitutionally distinguishable from, for example, unrelated sales? From unrelated visits? Ought the volume of unrelated purchases be important? Does the Court really mean that no quantity of unrelated purchases could ever support general jurisdiction?

(3) Even if the majority is correct that the plaintiffs did not argue that the cause of action is related to the contacts, why does it follow that this is a problem of general jurisdiction? Why not say, in other words, that unless the defendant shows why the contacts are unrelated, it will be assumed that the problem is one of specific jurisdiction?

(4) Is it possible to have hybrid jurisdiction, where some unrelated contacts that would themselves be insufficient are combined with either some somewhat related contacts or some related contacts that would also, by themselves, be insufficient? *See* Richman, Review Essay (Part II, A Sliding Scale to Supplement the Distinction Between General and Specific Jurisdiction), 72 Calif. L. Rev. 1328 (1984). In Camelback Ski Corp. v. Behning, 539 A.2d 1107 (Md. 1988), the court denied jurisdiction over a Pennsylvania ski resort for injuries sustained by plaintiff while skiing.

> Camelback is principally a "day"[2] resort, although it does receive some "destination business." Its market area, to which it devotes one hundred percent of its advertising budget, is comprised of those parts of Pennsylvania, New York, and New Jersey lying within a 100-mile radius of the resort. On one occasion in 1982, for a period of one or two days, a sales representative of Camelback called on travel agencies and military installations in Maryland, in an attempt to stimulate mid-week destination business. This effort was unsuccessful, and was not repeated.

---

2. This term refers to the fact that a majority of the resort's clientele comes to the area for a day of skiing and then returns home. In contrast, a "destination" resort is one which attracts skiers for extended periods of time. Camelback has no facilities for lodging guests. It has made available to some local hotels and motels discount ski lift tickets, but it has not participated in the advertising efforts of those establishments.

Camelback was aware that some of its customers came from Maryland. The record does not disclose what percentage of Camelback's customers were from this State, or whether Camelback had any means of obtaining information concerning the State of residence of its customers. Behning's trip to Camelback did not result from any solicitation by Camelback within this State.

. . . The Behnings correctly assert that forcing all cases into a rigid classification as either "general jurisdiction" or "specific jurisdiction" cases, and then mechanically applying a fixed standard for the quantum of contacts required to support personal jurisdiction in each class, would be inappropriate. We agree that the quality and quantity of contacts required to support the exercise of personal jurisdiction will depend upon the nature of the action brought and the nexus of the contacts to the subject matter of the action. We further agree that the spectrum of cases may be generally divided into those involving general jurisdiction (the cause of action is unrelated to the contacts), and those involving specific jurisdiction (the cause of action arises out of the conduct which constitutes the contacts). Generally speaking, when the cause of action does not arise out of, or is not directly related to, the conduct of the defendant within the forum, contacts reflecting continuous and systematic general business conduct will be required to sustain jurisdiction. . . . On the other hand, when the cause of action arises out of the contacts that the defendant had with the forum, it may be entirely fair to permit the exercise of jurisdiction as to that claim.

Some cases fit neatly into one or the other category. . . . McGee v. International Life Ins. Co., 355 U.S. 220 (1957), involved a claim arising out of the issuance and delivery of a single life insurance policy by a Texas insurance company to a California resident, and was therefore a case involving specific jurisdiction. By way of contrast, Perkins v. Benguet Mining Co., 342 U.S. 437 (1952) involved a cause of action that did not arise out of, or relate to, the activities of the defendant in the forum State, and was therefore a general jurisdiction case. The concept of specific and general jurisdiction is a useful tool in the sometimes difficult task of detecting how much contact is enough, and most cases will fit nicely into one category or the other. If, however, the facts of a given case do not naturally place it at either end of the spectrum, there is no need to jettison the concept, or to force-fit the case. In that instance, the proper approach is to identify the approximate position of the case on the continuum that exists between the two extremes, and apply the corresponding standard, recognizing that the quantum of required contacts increases as the nexus between the contacts and the cause of action decreases.

This case does not fit the classic mold of specific jurisdiction, and we find that the contacts required to support jurisdiction more nearly resemble those of a general jurisdiction case. Behning was not injured by any product Camelback sent into Maryland. There is no evidence that Behning went from Maryland to Pennsylvania in response to solicitation by Camelback. Yet, the Behnings argue the cause of action is not totally divorced from the contacts they rely upon, because Behning was one of a number of Maryland residents coming to Camelback to ski, and thus formed a part of a stream of commerce from which Camelback knew it derived economic advantage. The argument, though innovative, is not persuasive.

(5) Note the *Helicopteros* majority's apparently disapproving characterization, in footnote 13, of jurisdiction by necessity as a "potentially farreaching modification of existing law." What sort of more complete record would have encouraged the Court to address the argument? Merely a showing that the defendants could not all be sued in the same forum? That fact alone would not single out Texas as an appropriate place to litigate, would it? After all, if the three defendants could not all be sued in either Peru, Colombia, or Texas, then Texas is not better situated in this regard than Peru or Colombia.

(6) At what point in time ought the defendant's contacts be measured? Should the defendant's domicile (or business contacts) be assessed as of the time that the cause of action arose or as of the time that the suit was filed? Or, are *both* relevant? *See, e.g.*, Schneider v. Linkfield, 389 Mich. 608, 209 N.W.2d 225 (1973) (defendants resided in the forum at the time of the accident; jurisdiction upheld); Greene v. Sha-Na-Na, 637 F. Supp. 591 (D. Conn. 1986) (defendant's activities subsequent to filing of complaint not counted toward personal jurisdiction).

Burnham v. Superior Court of California

495 U.S. 604 (1990)

Justice SCALIA announced the judgment of the Court and delivered an opinion in which THE CHIEF JUSTICE and Justice KENNEDY join, and in which Justice WHITE joins with respect to Parts I, II-A, II-B, and II-C.

The question presented is whether the Due Process Clause of the Fourteenth Amendment denies California courts jurisdiction over a nonresident, who was personally served with process while temporarily in that State, in a suit unrelated to his activities in the State.

I

Petitioner Dennis Burnham married Francie Burnham in 1976, in West Virginia. In 1977 the couple moved to New Jersey, where their two children were born. In July 1987 the Burnhams decided to separate. They agreed that Mrs. Burnham, who intended to move to California, would take custody of the children. Shortly before Mrs. Burnham departed for California that same month, she and petitioner agreed that she would file for divorce on grounds of "irreconcilable differences."

In October 1987, petitioner filed for divorce in New Jersey state court on grounds of "desertion." Petitioner did not, however, obtain an issuance of summons against his wife, and did not attempt to serve her with process. Mrs.

Burnham, after unsuccessfully demanding that petitioner adhere to their prior agreement to submit to an "irreconcilable differences" divorce, brought suit for divorce in California state court in early January 1988.

In late January, petitioner visited southern California on business, after which he went north to visit his children in the San Francisco Bay area, where his wife resided. He took the older child to San Francisco for the weekend. Upon returning the child to Mrs. Burnham's home on January 24, 1988, petitioner was served with a California court summons and a copy of Mrs. Burnham's divorce petition. He then returned to New Jersey.

Later that year, petitioner made a special appearance in the California Superior Court, moving to quash the service of process on the ground that the court lacked personal jurisdiction over him because his only contacts with California were a few short visits to the State for the purposes of conducting business and visiting his children. The Superior Court denied the motion, and the California Court of Appeal denied mandamus relief, rejecting petitioner's contention that the Due Process Clause prohibited California courts from asserting jurisdiction over him because he lacked "minimum contacts" with the State. The court held it to be "a valid jurisdictional predicate for in personam jurisdiction" that the "defendant [was] present in the forum state and personally served with process." App. to Pet. for Cert. 5. We granted certiorari. 493 U.S. 807 (1989).

II

A

The proposition that the judgment of a court lacking jurisdiction is void traces back to the English Year Books, *see* Bowser v. Collins, Y.B. Mich. 22 Edw. 4, f. 30, pl. 11, 145 Eng. Rep. 97 (1482), and was made settled law by Lord Coke in Case of the Marshalsea, 10 Co. Rep. 68b, 77 Eng. Rep. 1027, 1041 (K.B. 1612). Traditionally that proposition was embodied in the phrase coram non judice, "before a person not a judge"—meaning, in effect, that the proceeding in question was not a *judicial* proceeding because lawful judicial authority was not present, and could therefore not yield a *judgment.* American courts invalidated, or denied recognition to, judgments that violated this common-law principle long before the Fourteenth Amendment was adopted. In Pennoyer v. Neff, 95 U.S. 714, 732 (1878) we announced that the judgment of a court lacking personal jurisdiction violated the Due Process Clause of the Fourteenth Amendment as well.

To determine whether the assertion of personal jurisdiction is consistent with due process, we have long relied on the principles traditionally followed by American courts in marking out the territorial limits of each State's authority. That criterion was first announced in Pennoyer v. Neff, *supra,* in which we stated that due process "mean[s] a course of legal proceedings according to those rules and principles which have been established in our systems of jurisprudence for the protection and enforcement of private rights," *id.*, at 733, including the "well-established principles of public law respecting the jurisdiction of an independent State over persons and property," *id.*, at 722. In what has become the classic expression of the criterion, we said in International Shoe Co. v. Washington, 326 U.S. 310 (1945), that a State court's assertion of personal jurisdiction satisfies the Due Process Clause if it does not violate " 'traditional notions of fair play and substantial justice.' " Since *International Shoe,* we have only been called upon to decide whether these "traditional notions" permit States to exercise jurisdiction over absent defendants in a manner that deviates from the rules of jurisdiction applied in the 19th century. We have held such deviations permissible, but only with respect to suits arising out of the absent defendant's contacts with the State.[1] *See, e.g.*, Helicopteros Nacionales de Colombia v. Hall, 466 U.S. 408, 414 (1984). The question we must decide today is whether due process requires a similar connection between the litigation and the defendant's contacts with the State in cases where the defendant is physically present in the State at the time process is served upon him.

B

Among the most firmly established principles of personal jurisdiction in American tradition is that the courts of a State have jurisdiction over nonresidents who are physically present in the State. The view developed early that each State had the power to hale before its courts any individual who could be found within its borders, and that once having acquired jurisdiction over such a person by properly serving him with process, the State could retain jurisdiction to enter judgment against him, no matter how fleeting his visit. *See, e.g.*, Potter v. Allin, 2 Root 63, 67 (Conn. 1793); Barrell v. Benjamin, 15 Mass. 354 (1819). That view had antecedents in English common-law practice, which sometimes allowed "transitory" actions, arising out of

---

1. We have said that "[e]ven when the cause of action does not arise out of or relate to the foreign corporation's activities in the forum State, due process is not offended by a State's subjecting the corporation to its in personam jurisdiction when there are sufficient contacts between the State and the foreign corporation." Helicopteros Nacionales de Colombia v. Hall, 466 U.S., at 414. Our only holding supporting that statement, however, involved "regular service of summons upon [the corporation's] president while he was in [the forum State] acting in that capacity." *See* Perkins v. Benguet Consolidated Mining Co., 342 U.S. 437, 440 (1952). It may be that whatever special rule exists permitting "continuous and systematic" contacts, *id.*, at 438, to support jurisdiction with respect to matters unrelated to activity in the forum, applies *only* to corporations, which have never fitted comfortably in a jurisdictional regime based primarily upon "de facto power over the defendant's person." International Shoe Co. v. Washington, 326 U.S. 310, 316 (1945). We express no views on these matters—and, for simplicity's sake, omit reference to this aspect of "contacts"-based jurisdiction in our discussion.

events outside the country, to be maintained against seemingly nonresident defendants who were present in England. *See, e.g.*, Mostyn v. Fabrigas, 98 Eng. Rep. 1021 (K.B. 1774); Cartwright v. Pettus, 22 Eng. Rep. 916 (Ch. 1675). Justice Story believed the principle, which he traced to Roman origins, to be firmly grounded in English tradition: "[B]y the common law[,] personal actions, being transitory, may be brought in any place, where the party defendant may be found," for "every nation may . . . rightfully exercise jurisdiction over all persons within its domains." Story, Commentaries on the Conflict of Laws §§543, 554 (1846). *See also* §§530-538; Picquet v. Swan, *supra,* at 611-612 (Story, J.) ("Where a party is within a territory, he may justly be subjected to its process, and bound personally by the judgment pronounced, on such process, against him").

Recent scholarship has suggested that English tradition was not as clear as Story thought, see Hazard, A General Theory of State-Court Jurisdiction, 1965 Sup. Ct. Rev. 241, 253-260; Ehrenzweig, The Transient Rule of Personal Jurisdiction: The "Power" Myth and Forum Conveniens, 65 Yale L.J. 289 (1956). Accurate or not, however, judging by the evidence of contemporaneous or near-contemporaneous decisions one must conclude that Story's understanding was shared by American courts at the crucial time for present purposes: 1868, when the Fourteenth Amendment was adopted. . . .

Decisions in the courts of many States in the 19th and early 20th centuries held that personal service upon a physically present defendant sufficed to confer jurisdiction, without regard to whether the defendant was only briefly in the State or whether the cause of action was related to his activities there.

Although research has not revealed a case deciding the issue in every State's courts, that appears to be because the issue was so well settled that it went unlitigated. Opinions from the courts of other States announced the rule in dictum. Most States, moreover, had statutes or common-law rules that exempted from service of process individuals who were brought into the forum by force or fraud, *see, e.g.*, Wanzer v. Bright, 52 Ill. 35 (1869), or who were there as a party or witness in unrelated judicial proceedings, *see, e.g.*, Burroughs v. Cocke & Willis, 56 Okla. 627, 156 P. 196 (1916); Malloy v. Brewer, 7 S.D. 587, 64 N.W. 1120 (1895). These exceptions obviously rested upon the premise that service of process conferred jurisdiction. Particularly striking is the fact that, as far as we have been able to determine, *not one* American case from the period (or, for that matter, not one American case until 1978) held, or even suggested, that in-state personal service on an individual was insufficient to confer personal jurisdiction. Commentators were also seemingly unanimous on the rule.

This American jurisdictional practice is, moreover, not merely old; it is continuing. It remains the practice of, not only a substantial number of the States, but as far as we are aware *all* the States and the federal government—if one disregards (as one must for this purpose) the few opinions since 1978 that have erroneously said, on grounds similar to those that petitioner presses here, that this Court's due-process decisions render the practice unconstitutional. We do not know of a single State or federal statute or a single judicial decision resting upon State law, that has abandoned in-State service as a basis of jurisdiction. Many recent cases reaffirm it.

C

Despite this formidable body of precedent, petitioner contends, in reliance on our decisions applying the *International Shoe* standard, that in the absence of "continuous and systematic" contacts with the forum, *see* note 1, *supra,* a nonresident defendant can be subjected to judgment only as to matters that arise out of or relate to his contacts with the forum. This argument rests on a thorough misunderstanding of our cases.

The view of most courts in the 19th century was that a court simply could not exercise in personam jurisdiction over a nonresident who had not been personally served with process in the forum. Pennoyer v. Neff, while renowned for its statement of the principle that the Fourteenth Amendment prohibits such an exercise of jurisdiction, in fact set that forth only as dictum, and decided the case (which involved a judgment rendered more than two years before the Fourteenth Amendment's ratification) under "well-established principles of public law." 95 U.S., at 722. Those principles, embodied in the Due Process Clause, required (we said) that when proceedings "involve[e] merely a determination of the personal liability of the defendant, he must be brought within [the court's] jurisdiction by service of process within the State, or his voluntary appearance." *Id.,* at 733. We invoked that rule in a series of subsequent cases, as either a matter of due process or a "fundamental principal[e] of jurisprudence."

Later years, however, saw the weakening of the *Pennoyer* rule. In the late 19th and early 20th centuries, changes in the technology of transportation and communication, and the tremendous growth of interstate business activity, led to an "inevitable relaxation of the strict limits on state jurisdiction" over nonresident individuals and corporations.

States required, for example, that nonresident corporations appoint an in-state agent upon whom process could be served as a condition of transacting business within their borders, *see, e.g.,* St. Clair v. Cox, 106 U.S. 350 (1882), and provided in-state "substituted service" for nonresident motorists who caused injury in the State and left before personal service could be accomplished, *see, e.g.,* Kane v. New Jersey, 242 U.S. 160 (1916); Hess v. Pawloski, 274 U.S. 352 (1927). We initially upheld these laws under the Due Process Clause on grounds that they complied with *Pennoyer*'s rigid requirement of either "consent," *see, e.g.,* Hess v. Pawloski, *supra,* at 356, or "presence," *see, e.g.,* Philadelphia & Reading R. Co. v. McKibbin, 243 U.S. 264, 265, (1917). As many observed, however, the consent and presence were purely fictional.

Our opinion in *International Shoe* cast these fictions aside, and made explicit the underlying basis of these decisions: due process does not necessarily *require* the States to adhere to the unbending territorial limits on jurisdiction set forth in *Pennoyer*. The validity of assertion of jurisdiction over a nonconsenting defendant who is not present in the forum depends upon whether "the quality and nature of [his] activity" in relation to the forum, 326 U.S., at 319, renders such jurisdiction consistent with "traditional notions of fair play and substantial justice." *Id.*, at 316 (citation omitted). Subsequent cases have derived from the *International Shoe* standard the general rule that a State may dispense with in-forum personal service on nonresident defendants in suits arising out of their activities in the State. *See generally* Helicopteros Nacionales de Colombia v. Hall, 466 U.S., at 414-415. As *International Shoe* suggests, the defendant's litigation-related "minimum contacts" may take the place of physical presence as the basis for jurisdiction:

> Historically the jurisdiction of courts to render judgment in personam is grounded on their de facto power over the defendant's person. Hence his presence within the territorial jurisdiction of a court was prerequisite to its rendition of a judgment personally binding on him. Pennoyer v. Neff, 95 U.S. 714, 733. But now that the capias ad respondendum has given way to personal service of summons or other form of notice, due process requires only that in order to subject a defendant to a judgment in personam, if he be not present within the territory of the forum, he have certain minimum contacts with it such that the maintenance of the suit does not offend "traditional notions of fair play and substantial justice."

326 U.S., at 316 (citations omitted).

Nothing in *International Shoe* or the cases that have followed it, however, offers support for the very different proposition petitioner seeks to establish today: that a defendant's presence in the forum is not only unnecessary to validate novel, nontraditional assertions of jurisdiction, but is itself no longer sufficient to establish jurisdiction. That proposition is unfaithful to both elementary logic and the foundations of our due process jurisprudence. The distinction between what is needed to support novel procedures and what is needed to sustain traditional ones is fundamental, as we observed over a century ago:

> [A] process of law, which is not otherwise forbidden, must be taken to be due process of law, if it can show the sanction of settled usage both in England and in this country; but it by no means followed that nothing else can be due process of law. . . . [That which], in substance, has been immemorially the actual law of the land . . . therefor[e] is due process of law. But to hold that such a characteristic is essential to due process of law, would be to deny every quality of the law but its age, and to render it incapable of progress or improvement. It would be to stamp upon our jurisprudence the unchangeableness attributed to the laws of the Medes and Persians.

Hurtado v. California, 110 U.S. 516, 528-529 (1884).

The short of the matter is that jurisdiction based on physical presence alone constitutes due process because it is one of the continuing traditions of our legal system that define the due process standard of "traditional notions of fair play and substantial justice." That standard was developed by *analogy* to "physical presence," and it would be perverse to say it could now be turned against that touchstone of jurisdiction.

D

Petitioner's strongest argument, though we ultimately reject it, relies upon our decision in Shaffer v. Heitner, 433 U.S. 186 (1977). . . .

It goes too far to say, as petitioner contends, that *Shaffer* compels the conclusion that a State lacks jurisdiction over an individual unless the litigation arises out of his activities in the State. *Shaffer,* like *International Shoe,* involved jurisdiction over an *absent defendant,* and it stands for nothing more than the proposition that when the "minimum contact" that is a substitute for physical presence consists of property ownership it must, like other minimum contacts, be related to the litigation. Petitioner wrenches out of its context our statement in *Shaffer* that "all assertions of state-court jurisdiction must be evaluated according to the standards set forth in *International Shoe* and its progeny," 433 U.S., at 212. When read together with the two sentences that preceded it, the meaning of this statement becomes clear:

> The fiction that an assertion of jurisdiction over property is anything but an assertion of jurisdiction over the owner of the property supports an ancient form without substantial modern justification. Its continued acceptance would serve only to allow state-court jurisdiction that is fundamentally unfair to the defendant.
>
> We *therefore conclude* that all assertions of state-court jurisdiction must be evaluated according to the standards set forth in *International Shoe* and its progeny.

Ibid. (emphasis added).

Shaffer was saying, in other words, not that all bases for the assertion of in personam jurisdiction (including, presumably, in-state service) must be treated alike and subjected to the "minimum contacts" analysis of *International Shoe;* but rather that quasi in rem jurisdiction, that fictional "ancient form," and in personam jurisdiction, are really one and the same and must be treated alike—leading to the conclusion that quasi in rem jurisdiction, *i.e.,* that form of in personam jurisdiction based upon a "property ownership" contact and by definition unaccompanied by personal, in-state service, must satisfy the litigation-relatedness requirement of *International Shoe.* The logic of *Shaffer*'s holding—which places all suits against absent nonresidents on the same constitutional footing, regardless of whether a separate Latin label is attached to one particular basis of contact—does not compel the conclusion that physically present defendants must be treated identically to absent ones. As we have demonstrated at length, our tradition has treated the two classes of defendants quite differently, and it is unreasonable to read *Shaffer* as casually obliterating that distinction. *International Shoe* confined its "minimum contacts" requirement to situations in which the defendant "be not present within the territory of the forum," 326 U.S., at 316, and nothing in *Shaffer* expands that requirement beyond that.

It is fair to say, however, that while our holding today does not contradict *Shaffer*, our basic approach to the due process question is different. We have conducted no independent inquiry into the desirability or fairness of the prevailing in-state service rule, leaving that judgment to the legislatures that are free to amend it; for our purposes, its validation is its pedigree, as the phrase "*traditional notions* of fair play and substantial justice" makes clear. *Shaffer* did conduct such an independent inquiry, asserting that "traditional notions of fair play and substantial justice" can be as readily offended by the perpetuation of ancient forms that are no longer justified as by the adoption of new procedures that are inconsistent with the basic values of our constitutional heritage." 433 U.S., at 212. Perhaps that assertion can be sustained when the "perpetuation of ancient forms" is engaged in by only a very small minority of the States.[4] Where, however, as in the present case, a jurisdictional principle is both firmly approved by tradition and still favored, it is impossible to imagine what standard we could appeal to for the judgment that it is "no longer justified." While in no way receding from or casting doubt upon the holding of *Shaffer* or any other case, we reaffirm today our time-honored approach. For new procedures, hitherto unknown, the Due Process Clause requires analysis to determine whether "traditional notions of fair play and substantial justice" have been offended. *International Shoe*, 326 U.S., at 316. But a doctrine of personal jurisdiction that dates back to the adoption of the Fourteenth Amendment and is still generally observed unquestionably meets that standard.

III

A few words in response to Justice Brennan's concurrence: It insists that we apply "contemporary notions of due process" to determine the constitutionality of California's assertion of jurisdiction. But our analysis today com-

4. *Shaffer* may have involved a unique state procedure in one respect: Justice Stevens noted that Delaware was the only State that treated the place of incorporation as the situs of corporate stock when both owner and custodian were elsewhere. *See* 433 U.S., at 218 (opinion concurring in judgment).

ports with that prescription, at least if we give it the only sense allowed by our precedents. The "contemporary notions of due process" applicable to personal jurisdiction are the enduring "*traditional* notions of fair play and substantial justice" established as the test by *International Shoe.* By its very language, that test is satisfied if a state court adheres to jurisdictional rules that are generally applied and have always been applied in the United States.

But the concurrence's proposed standard of "contemporary notions of due process" requires more: it measures state-court jurisdiction not only against traditional doctrines in this country, including current state-court practice, but against each Justice's subjective assessment of what is fair and just. Authority for that seductive standard is not to be found in any of our personal jurisdiction cases. It is, indeed, an outright break with the test of "traditional notions of fair play and substantial justice," which would have to be reformulated "*our* notions of fair play and substantial justice."

The subjectivity, and hence inadequacy, of this approach becomes apparent when the concurrence tries to explain *why* the assertion of jurisdiction in the present case meets its standard of continuing-American-tradition-*plus*-innate-fairness. Justice Brennan lists the "benefits" Mr. Burnham derived from the State of California—the fact that, during the few days he was there, "his health and safety [were] guaranteed by the State's police, fire, and emergency medical services; he [was] free to travel on the State's roads and waterways; he likely enjoy[ed] the fruits of the State's economy." Three days' worth of these benefits strike us as powerfully inadequate to establish, as an abstract matter, that it is "fair" for California to decree the ownership of all Mr. Burnham's worldly goods acquired during the ten years of his marriage, and the custody over his children. We daresay a contractual exchange swapping those benefits for that power would not survive the "unconscionability" provision of the Uniform Commercial Code. Even less persuasive are the other "fairness" factors alluded to by Justice Brennan. It would create "an asymmetry," we are told, if Burnham were *permitted* (as he is) to appear in California courts as a plaintiff, but were not *compelled* to appear in California courts as defendant; and travel being as easy as it is nowadays, and modern procedural devices being so convenient, it is no great hardship to appear in California courts. The problem with these assertions is that they justify the exercise of jurisdiction over *everyone, whether or not* he ever comes to California. The only "fairness" elements setting Mr. Burnham apart from the rest of the world are the three-days' "benefits" referred to above—and even those, do not set him apart from many other people who have enjoyed three days in the Golden State (savoring the fruits of its economy, the availability of its roads and police services) but who were fortunate enough not to be served with process while they were there and thus are not (simply by reason of that savoring) subject to the general jurisdiction of California's courts. *See, e.g.,* Helicopteros Nacionales de Colombia v. Hall, 466 U.S., at 414-416. In other words, even if one agreed with Justice Brennan's conception of an equitable bargain, the "benefits" we have been discussing would explain why it is "fair" to assert general jurisdiction over Burnham-returned-to-New-Jersey-after-service only at the expense of proving that it is also "fair" to assert general jurisdiction over Burnham-returned-to-New-Jersey-*without*-service—which we *know* does not conform with "contemporary notions of due process."

There is, we must acknowledge, one factor mentioned by Justice Brennan that *both* relates distinctively to the assertion of jurisdiction on the basis of personal in-state service *and* is fully persuasive—namely, the fact that a defendant voluntarily present in a particular State has a "reasonable expectatio[n]" that he is subject to suit there. By formulating it as a "reasonable expectation" Justice Brennan makes that seem like a "fairness" factor; but in reality, of course, it is just tradition masquerading as "fairness." The only reason for charging Mr. Burnham with the reasonable expectation of being subject to suit is that the States of the Union assert adjudicatory jurisdiction over the person, and have always asserted adjudicatory jurisdiction over the person, by serving him with process during his temporary physical presence in their territory. That continuing tradition, which anyone entering California should have known about, renders it "fair" for Mr. Burnham, who voluntarily entered California, to be sued there for divorce—at least "fair" in the limited sense that he has no one but himself to blame. Justice Brennan's long journey is a circular one, leaving him, at the end of the day, in complete reliance upon the very factor he sought to avoid: The existence of a continuing tradition is not enough, fairness also must be considered; fairness exists here because there is a continuing tradition.

While Justice Brennan's concurrence is unwilling to confess that the Justices of this Court can possibly be bound by a continuing American tradition that a particular procedure is fair, neither is it willing to embrace the logical consequences of that refusal—or even to be clear about what consequences (logical or otherwise) it does embrace. Justice Brennan says that "[f]or these reasons [*i.e.*, because of the reasonableness factors enumerated above], as a rule the exercise of personal jurisdiction over a defendant based on his voluntary presence in the forum will satisfy the requirements of due process." The use of the word "rule" conveys the reassuring feeling that he is establishing a principle of law one can rely upon—but of course he is not. Since Justice Brennan's only criterion of constitutionality is "fairness," the phrase "as a rule" represents nothing more than his estimation that, *usually*, all the elements of "fairness" he discusses in the present case will exist. But what if they do not? Suppose, for example, that a defendant in Mr. Burnham's situation enjoys not three days' worth of California "benefits," but fifteen minutes' worth. Or suppose we remove one of those "benefits"—"enjoy[ment of] the fruits of the State's economy"—by positing that Mr. Burnham had not come to California on business, but only to visit his children. Or suppose that Mr. Burnham were demonstrably so impecunious as to be unable to take advantage of the modern means of transportation and communication that Justice Brennan finds so relevant. Or suppose, finally, that the California courts lacked the "variety of procedural devices," *post*, at 2125, that Justice Brennan says can reduce the burden upon out-of-state litigants. One may also make additional suppositions, relating not to the absence of the factors that Justice Brennan discusses, but to the presence of additional factors bearing upon the ultimate criterion of "fairness." What if, for example, Mr. Burnham were visiting a sick child? Or a dying child? *Cf.* Kulko v. California Superior Court, 436 U.S. 84, 93 (1978) (finding the exercise of long-arm jurisdiction over an absent parent unreasonable because it would "discourage parents from entering into reasonable visitation agreements"). Since, so far as one can tell, Justice Brennan's approval of applying the in-state service rule in the present case rests on the presence of *all* the factors he lists, and on the absence of any others, every different case will present a different litigable issue. Thus, despite the fact that he manages to work the word "rule" into his formulation, Justice Brennan's approach does not establish a rule of law at all, but only a "totality of the circumstances" test, guaranteeing what traditional territorial rules of jurisdiction were designed precisely to avoid: uncertainty and litigation over the preliminary issue of the forum's competence. It may be that those evils, necessarily accompanying a freestanding "reasonableness" inquiry, must be accepted at the margins, when we evaluate *non*-traditional forms of jurisdiction newly adopted by the states, *see, e.g.*, Asahi Metal Industry Co., Ltd. v. Superior Court of California, 480 U.S. 102 (1987). But that is no reason for injecting them into the core of our American practice, exposing to such a "reasonableness" inquiry the ground of jurisdiction that has hitherto been considered the very *baseline* of reasonableness, physical presence.

. . . . Nothing we say today prevents individual States from limiting or entirely abandoning the in-state-service basis of jurisdiction. And nothing prevents an overwhelming majority of them from doing so, with the consequence that the "traditional notions of fairness" that this Court applies may change. But the states have overwhelmingly declined to adopt such limitation or abandonment, evidently not considering it to be progress.[5] The question is whether armed with no authority other than individual Justices' perceptions of fairness that conflict with both past and current practice, this Court can compel the states to make such a change on the ground that "due process" requires it. We hold that it cannot. . . .

---

5. I find quite unacceptable as a basis for this Court's decisions Justice Brennan's view that "the *raison d'être* of various constitutional doctrines designed to protect out-of-staters such as the Art. IV Privileges and Immunities Clause and the Commerce Clause," *post*, at 2125, n.13, entitles this Court to brand as "unfair," and hence unconstitutional, the refusal of all fifty states "to limit or abandon bases of jurisdiction that have become obsolete," *post*, at 2125, n.13. "Due process" (which is the constitutional text at issue here) does not mean that process which shifting majorities of this Court feel to be "due"; but that process which American society—self-interested American society, which expresses its judgments in the laws of self-interested states—has traditionally considered "due." The notion that the Constitution, through some penumbra emanating from the Privileges and Immunities Clause and the Commerce Clause, establishes this Court as a platonic check upon the society's greedy adherence to its traditions can only be described as imperious.

Because the Due Process Clause does not prohibit the California courts from exercising jurisdiction over petitioner based on the fact of in-state service of process, the judgment is

Affirmed.

Justice WHITE, concurring in part and concurring in the judgment.

I join Part I and Parts II-A, II-B, and II-C of Justice Scalia's opinion and concur in the judgment of affirmance. The rule allowing jurisdiction to be obtained over a non-resident by personal service in the forum state, without more, has been and is so widely accepted throughout this country that I could not possibly strike it down, either on its face or as applied in this case, on the ground that it denies due process of law guaranteed by the Fourteenth Amendment. Although the Court has the authority under the Amendment to examine even traditionally accepted procedures and declare them invalid, *e.g.*, Shaffer v. Heitner, 433 U.S. 186 (1977), there has been no showing here or elsewhere that as a general proposition the rule is so arbitrary and lacking in common sense in so many instances that it should be held violative of Due Process in every case. Furthermore, until such a showing is made, which would be difficult indeed, claims in individual cases that the rule would operate unfairly as applied to the particular non-resident involved need not be entertained. At least this would be the case where presence in the forum state is intentional, which would almost always be the fact. Otherwise, there would be endless, fact-specific litigation in the trial and appellate courts, including this one. Here, personal service in California, without more, is enough, and I agree that the judgment should be affirmed.

Justice BRENNAN, with whom Justice MARSHALL, Justice BLACKMUN, and Justice O'CONNOR join, concurring in the judgment.

I

I believe that the approach adopted by Justice Scalia's opinion today—reliance solely on historical pedigree—is foreclosed by our decisions in International Shoe Co. v. Washington, 326 U.S. 310 (1945), and Shaffer v. Heitner, 433 U.S. 186 (1977). In *International Shoe*, we held that a state court's assertion of personal jurisdiction does not violate the Due Process Clause if it is consistent with " 'traditional notions of fair play and substantial justice.' "[2] In *Shaffer*, we stated that "*all* assertions of state-court jurisdiction must be evaluated according to the standards set forth in *International Shoe* and its progeny." The critical insight of *Shaffer* is that all rules of ju-

---

2. Our reference in *International Shoe* to " 'traditional notions of fair play and substantial justice,' " 326 U.S., at 316, meant simply that those concepts are indeed traditional ones, not that, as Justice Scalia's opinion suggests, *see ante*, at 2116, 2117, their specific *content* was to be determined by tradition alone. We recognized that contemporary societal norms must

risdiction, even ancient ones, must satisfy contemporary notions of due process. No longer were we content to limit our jurisdictional analysis to pronouncements that "[t]he foundation of jurisdiction is physical power," McDonald v. Mabee, 243 U.S. 90, 91 (1917), and that "every State possesses exclusive jurisdiction and sovereignty over persons and property within its territory." Pennoyer v. Neff, 95 U.S. 714, 722 (1878). While acknowledging that "history must be considered as supporting the proposition that jurisdiction based solely on the presence of property satisfie[d] the demands of due process," we found that this factor could not be "decisive." 433 U.S., at 211-212. We recognized that " '[t]raditional notions of fair play and substantial justice' can be as readily offended by the perpetuation of ancient forms that are no longer justified as by the adoption of new procedures that are inconsistent with the basic values of our constitutional heritage." *Id.*, at 212 (citations omitted). I agree with this approach and continue to believe that "the minimum-contacts analysis developed in *International Shoe* . . . represents a far more sensible construct for the exercise of state-court jurisdiction than the patchwork of legal and factual fictions that has been generated from the decision in Pennoyer v. Neff." *Id.*, at 219 (citation omitted) (Brennan, J., concurring in part and dissenting in part).

II

Tradition, though alone not dispositive, is of course *relevant* to the question whether the rule of transient jurisdiction is consistent with due process.[7] Tradition is salient not in the sense that practices of the past are automatically reasonable today; indeed, under such a standard, the legitimacy of transient jurisdiction would be called into question because the rule's historical "pedigree" is a matter of intense debate. The rule was a stranger to the common law and was rather weakly implanted in American jurisprudence "at the crucial time for present purposes: 1868, when the Fourteenth Amendment was adopted." *Ante,* at 2111. For much of the 19th century, American courts did not uniformly recognize the concept of transient jurisdiction, and it appears that the transient rule did not receive wide currency until well after our decision in Pennoyer v. Neff, 95 U.S. 714 (1878).

---

play a role in our analysis. *See, e.g.*, 326 U.S., at 317 (considerations of "reasonable[ness], in the context of our federal system of government").

7. I do not propose that the "contemporary notions of due process" to be applied are no more than "each Justice's subjective assessment of what is fair and just." *Ante,* at 2117. Rather, the inquiry is guided by our decisions beginning with International Shoe Co. v. Washington, 326 U.S. 310 (1945), and the specific factors that we have developed to ascertain whether a jurisdictional rule comports with "traditional notions of fair play and substantial justice." This analysis may not be "mechanical or quantitative," *International Shoe,* 326 U.S., at 319, but neither is it "freestanding," *ante,* at 2119, or dependent on personal whim. Our experience with this approach demonstrates that it is well within our competence to employ.

Rather, I find the historical background relevant because, however murky the jurisprudential origins of transient jurisdiction, the fact that American courts have announced the rule for perhaps a century (first in dicta, more recently in holdings) provides a defendant voluntarily present in a particular state *today* "clear notice that [he] is subject to suit" in the forum. World-Wide Volkswagen Corp. v. Woodson, 444 U.S. 286, 297 (1980). Regardless of whether Justice Story's account of the rule's genesis is mythical, our common understanding *now,* fortified by a century of judicial practice, is that jurisdiction is often a function of geography. The transient rule is consistent with reasonable expectations and is entitled to a strong presumption that it comports with due process.

By visiting the forum State, a transient defendant actually "avail[s]" himself, *Burger King,* of significant benefits provided by the State. His health and safety are guaranteed by the State's police, fire, and emergency medical services; he is free to travel on the State's roads and waterways; he likely enjoys the fruits of the State's economy as well. Moreover, the Privileges and Immunities Clause of Article IV prevents a state government from discriminating against a transient defendant by denying him the protections of its law or the right of access to its courts. Subject only to the doctrine of forum non conveniens, an out-of-state plaintiff may use state courts in all circumstances in which those courts would be available to state citizens. Without transient jurisdiction, an asymmetry would arise: a transient would have the full benefit of the power of the forum State's courts as a plaintiff while retaining immunity from their authority as a defendant. *See* Maltz, Sovereign Authority, Fairness, and Personal Jurisdiction: The Case for the Doctrine of Transient Jurisdiction, 66 Wash. U. L.Q. 671, 698-699 (1988).

The potential burdens on a transient defendant are slight. " '[M]odern transportation and communications have made it much less burdensome for a party sued to defend himself' " in a State outside his place of residence. That the defendant has already journeyed at least once before to the forum—as evidenced by the fact that he was served with process there—is an indication that suit in the forum likely would not be prohibitively inconvenient. Finally, any burdens that do arise can be ameliorated by a variety of procedural devices. For these reasons, as a rule the exercise of personal jurisdiction over a defendant based on his voluntary presence in the forum will satisfy the requirements of due process.

In this case, it is undisputed that petitioner was served with process while voluntarily and knowingly in the State of California. I therefore concur in the judgment.

Justice STEVENS, concurring in the judgment.

As I explained in my separate writing, I did not join the Court's opinion in Shaffer v. Heitner, 433 U.S. 186 (1977), because I was concerned by its unnecessarily broad reach. *Id.,* at 217-219 (opinion concurring in judgment). The same concern prevents me from joining either Justice Scalia's or

Justice Brennan's opinion in this case. For me, it is sufficient to note that the historical evidence and consensus identified by Justice Scalia, the considerations of fairness identified by Justice Brennan, and the common sense displayed by Justice White, all combine to demonstrate that this is, indeed, a very easy case.* Accordingly, I agree that the judgment should be affirmed.

Questions and Comments

(1) Which way do you think Justice Scalia would have voted, had he been on the Court, in Shaffer v. Heitner, page 546 *infra*? In Erie Railroad v. Tompkins, page 565 *infra*? Compare his opinion for the Court in Sun Oil v. Wortman, page 383 *supra*. Is there any real reason that due process should be more tied to tradition than any other constitutional provision? Or is it simply a result of the coincidence that the justices who penned certain important personal jurisdiction precedents happened "subjectively" to choose to phrase the test in terms of tradition?

(2) In response to Justice Scalia's charges of subjectivity, Professor Weintraub offers one objective basis for rejecting transient jurisdiction: "the use of the defendant's temporary presence in the forum as grounds for personal jurisdiction is contrary to the consensus of civilized nations and, if used against foreigners, may violate international law." Weintraub, An Objective Basis for Rejecting Transient Jurisdiction, in The Future of Personal Jurisdiction: a Symposium on *Burnham v. Superior Court*, 22 Rutgers L.J. 611 (1991).

(3) In Grace v. MacArthur, 170 F. Supp. 442 (E.D. Ark. 1959) jurisdiction was based on service of process while in an airplane flying over the territory. Would such service meet Justice Scalia's test of tradition? Would it satisfy the test set out in the 1986 revisions to the Restatement Second, cited in the opinion?

(4) "Tag" jurisdiction is exercised regularly in human rights litigation between alien plaintiffs against alien defendants alleging human rights abuses committed abroad. For example, in Kadic v. Karadzic, 70 F.3d 232 (2d Cir. 1995), Radovan Karadzic, President of the self-proclaimed Bosnian-Serb republic of "Srpska," was served in New York while attending a conference at the United Nations. Karadzic left New York soon thereafter, and a jury returned a default judgment worth $4.5 billion. To date the judgment has not been enforced.

(5) Most courts refrain from exercising "tag jurisdiction" when the defendant is brought into the state by fraud or unlawful force for the purpose of service of process. *See, e.g.*, May Dept. Stores Co. v. Wilansky, 900 F. Supp. 1154 (E.D. Mo. 1995); Wyman v. Newhouse, 93 F.2d 313 (2d Cir. 1937); *see also* Restatement (Second) of Conflict of Laws §82 (1971); *compare* Coyne v.

* Perhaps the adage about hard cases making bad law should be revised to cover easy cases.

Grupo Industrial Trieme, S.A. de C.V., 105 F.R.D. 627, 630 n.6 (D.D.C. 1985) (extending immunity from service given defendants lured into the jurisdiction by fraud to any later attempts to serve the defendant pursuant to a long-arm statute). Courts disagree about the legal basis for this rule. Most courts hold that jurisdiction cannot be acquired when service of process is obtained fraudulently. *See, e.g., Wyman*, 93 F.2d at 315. Some courts, as well as the Restatement, conclude that jurisdiction is technically satisfied but that courts should refrain from exercising jurisdiction in favor of one who has obtained service of his summons by unlawful means. *See, e.g.*, Economy Electric Co. v. Automatic Electric Co., 118 S.E. 3 (N.C. 1923); Restatement §82 cmt. f (1971). Does anything turn on this distinction?

Apart from its seaminess, what is objectionable about fraudulent inducement into the jurisdiction? Is basing judicial jurisdiction upon presence procured by fraud any worse than basing it on presence completely unrelated to the lawsuit? Is the difference that the defendant who enters the jurisdiction voluntarily and without fraudulent inducement knows the danger that may befall him and therefore waives the right to be free of suit by entering?

2. Purposeful Availment and Foreseeability

World-Wide Volkswagen Corp. v. Woodson

444 U.S. 286 (1980)

Justice White delivered the opinion of the Court.

The issue before us is whether, consistently with the Due Process Clause of the Fourteenth Amendment, an Oklahoma court may exercise in personam jurisdiction over a nonresident automobile retailer and its wholesale distributor in a products liability action, when the defendants' only connection with Oklahoma is the fact that an automobile sold in New York to New York residents became involved in an accident in Oklahoma.

I

Respondents Harry and Kay Robinson purchased a new Audi automobile from petitioner Seaway Volkswagen, Inc. (Seaway) in Massena, N.Y., in 1976. The following year the Robinson family, who resided in New York, left that State for a new home in Arizona. As they passed through the State of Oklahoma, another car struck their Audi in the rear, causing a fire which severely burned Kay Robinson and her two children.[1]

The Robinsons subsequently brought a products liability action in the District Court for Creek County, Okla., claiming that their injuries resulted

1. The driver of the other automobile does not figure in the present litigation.

from defective design and placement of the Audi's gas tank and fuel system. They joined as defendants the automobile's manufacturer, Audi NSU Auto Union Aktiengesellschaft (Audi); its importer, Volkswagen of America, Inc. (Volkswagen); its regional distributor, petitioner World-Wide Volkswagen Corporation (World-Wide); and its retail dealer, petitioner Seaway. Seaway and World-Wide entered special appearances,[3] claiming that Oklahoma's exercise of jurisdiction over them would offend the limitations on the State's jurisdiction imposed by the Due Process Clause of the Fourteenth Amendment.

The facts presented to the District Court showed that World-Wide is incorporated and has its business office in New York. It distributes vehicles, parts and accessories, under contract with Volkswagen, to retail dealers in New York, New Jersey, and Connecticut. Seaway, one of these retail dealers, is incorporated and has its place of business in New York. Insofar as the record reveals, Seaway and World-Wide are fully independent corporations whose relations with each other and with Volkswagen and Audi are contractual only. Respondents adduced no evidence that either World-Wide or Seaway does any business in Oklahoma, ships or sells any products to or in that State, has an agent to receive process there, or purchases advertisements in any media calculated to reach Oklahoma. In fact, as respondents' counsel conceded at oral argument, there was no showing that any automobile sold by World-Wide or Seaway has ever entered Oklahoma with the single exception of the vehicle involved in the present case.

Despite the apparent paucity of contacts between petitioners and Oklahoma, the District Court rejected their constitutional claim and reaffirmed that ruling in denying petitioners' motion for reconsideration. Petitioners then sought a writ of prohibition in the Supreme Court of Oklahoma to restrain the District Judge, respondent Charles S. Woodson, from exercising in personam jurisdiction over them. They renewed their contention that because they had no "minimal contacts," with the State of Oklahoma, the actions of the District Judge were in violation of their rights under the Due Process Clause.

The Supreme Court of Oklahoma denied the writ, holding that personal jurisdiction over petitioners was authorized by Oklahoma's "Long-Arm" Statute, Okla. Stat., Tit. 12, §1701.3(a)(4) (1961). Although the Court noted that the proper approach was to test jurisdiction against both statutory and constitutional standards, its analysis did not distinguish these questions, probably because §1701.03(a)(4) has been interpreted as conferring jurisdiction to the limits permitted by the United States Constitution. The Court's rationale was contained in the following paragraph:

---

3. Volkswagen also entered a special appearance in the District Court, but unlike World-Wide and Seaway did not seek review in the Supreme Court of Oklahoma and is not a petitioner here. Both Volkswagen and Audi remain as defendants in the litigation pending before the District Court in Oklahoma.

> In the case before us, the product being sold and distributed by the petitioners is by its very design and purpose so mobile that petitioners can foresee its possible use in Oklahoma. This is especially true of the distributor, who has the exclusive right to distribute such automobile [*sic*] in New York, New Jersey and Connecticut. The evidence presented below demonstrated that goods sold and distributed by the petitioners were used in the State of Oklahoma, and under the facts we believe it reasonable to infer, given the retail value of the automobile, that the petitioners derive substantial income from automobiles which from time to time are used in the State of Oklahoma. This being the case, we hold that under the facts presented, the trial court was justified in concluding that the petitioners derive substantial revenue from goods used or consumed in this State.

We granted certiorari to consider an important constitutional question with respect to state-court jurisdiction and to resolve a conflict between the Supreme Court of Oklahoma and the highest courts of at least four other States. We reverse.

II

As has long been settled, and as we reaffirm today, a state court may exercise personal jurisdiction over a nonresident defendant only so long as there exist "minimum contacts" between the defendant and the forum State. International Shoe Co. v. Washington. The concept of minimum contacts, in turn, can be seen to perform two related, but distinguishable functions. It protects the defendant against the burdens of litigating in a distant or inconvenient forum. And it acts to ensure that the States, through their courts, do not reach out beyond the limits imposed on them by their status as coequal sovereigns in a federal system.

The protection against inconvenient litigations is typically described in terms of "reasonableness" or "fairness." We have said that the defendant's contacts with the forum State must be such that maintenance of the suit "does not offend 'traditional notions of fair play and substantial justice.' " International Shoe Co. v. Washington, quoting Milliken v. Meyer. The relationship between the defendant and the forum must be such that it is "reasonable . . . to require the corporation to defend the particular suit which is brought there." Implicit in this emphasis on reasonableness is the understanding that the burden on the defendant, while always a primary concern, will in an appropriate case be considered in light of other relevant factors, including the forum State's interest in adjudicating the dispute, *see* McGee v. International Life Ins. Co.; the plaintiff's interest in obtaining convenient and effective relief, *see* Kulko v. Superior Court, at least when that interest is not adequately protected by the plaintiff's power to choose the forum, *cf.* Shaffer v. Heitner; the interstate judicial system's interest in obtaining the most efficient resolution of controversies; and the shared interest of the several States in furthering fundamental substantive social policies, *see* Kulko v. Superior Court.

The limits imposed on state jurisdiction by the Due Process Clause, in its role as a guarantor against inconvenient litigation, have been substantially relaxed over the years. As we noted in McGee v. International Life Ins. Co., this trend is largely attributable to a fundamental transformation in the American economy:

> Today many commercial transactions touch two or more States and may involve parties separated by the full continent. With this increasing nationalization of commerce has come a great increase in the amount of business conducted by mail across state lines. At the same time modern transportation and communication have made it much less burdensome for a party sued to defend himself in a State where he engages in economic activity.

The historical developments noted in *McGee,* of course, have only accelerated in the generation since that case was decided.

Nevertheless, we have never accepted the proposition that state lines are irrelevant for jurisdictional purposes, nor could we and remain faithful to the principles of interstate federalism embodied in the Constitution. The economic interdependence of the States was foreseen and desired by the Framers. In the Commerce Clause, they provided that the Nation was to be a common market, a "free trade unit" in which the States are debarred from acting as separable economic entities. But the Framers also intended that the States retain many essential attributes of sovereignty, including, in particular, the sovereign power to try causes in their courts. The sovereignty of each State, in turn, implied a limitation on the sovereignty of all of its sister States—a limitation express or implicit in both the original scheme of the Constitution and the Fourteenth Amendment.

Thus, the Due Process Clause "does not contemplate that a state may make binding a judgment in personam against an individual or corporate defendant with which the state has no contacts, ties, or relations." International Shoe Co. v. Washington. Even if the defendant would suffer minimal or no inconvenience from being forced to litigate before the tribunals of another State; even if the forum State has a strong interest in applying its law to the controversy; even if the forum State is the most convenient location for litigation, the Due Process Clause, acting as an instrument of interstate federalism, may sometimes act to divest the State of its power to render a valid judgment. Hanson v. Denkla.

III

Applying these principles to the case at hand, we find in the record before us a total absence of those affiliating circumstances that are a necessary predicate to any exercise of state-court jurisdiction. Petitioners carry on no activity whatsoever in Oklahoma. They close no sales and perform no services there. They avail themselves of none of the privileges and benefits of Oklahoma law. They solicit no business there either through salespersons or through advertising reasonably calculated to reach the State. Nor does the record show that they regularly sell cars at wholesale or retail to Oklahoma customers or residents or that they indirectly, through others, serve or seek to serve the Oklahoma market. In short, respondents seek to base jurisdiction on one, isolated occurrence and whatever inferences can be drawn therefrom: the fortuitous circumstance that a single Audi automobile, sold in New York to New York residents, happened to suffer an accident while passing through Oklahoma.

It is argued, however, that because an automobile is mobile by its very definition and purpose it was "foreseeable" that the Robinsons' Audi would cause injury in Oklahoma. Yet "foreseeability" alone has never been a sufficient benchmark for personal jurisdiction under the Due Process Clause. . . . In Kulko v. Superior Court, *supra,* it was surely "foreseeable" that a divorced wife would move to California from New York, the domicile of the marriage, and that a minor daughter would live with the mother. Yet we held that California could not exercise jurisdiction in a child-support action over the former husband who had remained in New York.

If foreseeability were the criterion, a local California tire retailer could be forced to defend in Pennsylvania when a blowout occurs there: *see* Erlanger Mills, Inc. v. Cohoes Fibre Mills, Inc.; a Wisconsin seller of a defective automobile jack could be haled before a distant court for damage caused in New Jersey; or a Florida soft drink concessionaire could be summoned to Alaska to account for injuries happening there. Every seller of chattels would in effect appoint the chattel his agent for service of process. His amenability to suit would travel with the chattel. We recently abandoned the outworn rule of Harris v. Balk, that the interest of a creditor in a debt could be extinguished or otherwise affected by any State having transitory jurisdiction over the debtor. Shaffer v. Heitner. Having interred the mechanical rule that a creditor's amenability to a quasi in rem action travels with his debtor, we are unwilling to endorse an analogous principle in the present case.[11]

This is not to say, of course, that foreseeability is wholly irrelevant. But the foreseeability that is critical to due process analysis is not the mere likelihood that a product will find its way into the forum State. Rather, it is that

---

11. Respondents' counsel, at oral argument, sought to limit the reach of the foreseeability standard by suggesting that there is something unique about automobiles. It is true that automobiles are uniquely mobile, that they did play a crucial role in the expansion of personal jurisdiction through the fiction of implied consent, *e.g.*, Hess v. Pawloski, and that some of the cases have treated the automobile as a "dangerous instrumentality." But today, under the regime of *International Shoe,* we see no difference for jurisdictional purposes between an automobile and any other chattel. The "dangerous instrumentality" concept apparently was never used to support personal jurisdiction; and to the extent it has relevance today it bears not on jurisdiction but on the possible desirability of imposing substantive principles of tort law such as strict liability.

the defendant's conduct and connection with the forum State are such that he should reasonably anticipate being haled into court there. The Due Process Clause, by ensuring the "orderly administration of the laws," gives a degree of predictability to the legal system that allows potential defendants to structure their primary conduct with some minimum assurance as to where that conduct will and will not render them liable to suit.

When a corporation "purposefully avails itself of the privilege of conducting activities within the forum State," it has clear notice that it is subject to suit there, and can act to alleviate the risk of burdensome litigation by procuring insurance, passing the expected costs on to customers, or, if the risks are too great, severing its connection with the State. Hence if the sale of a product of a manufacturer or distributor such as Audi or Volkswagen is not simply an isolated occurrence, but arises from the efforts of the manufacturer or distributor to serve, directly or indirectly, the market for its product in other States, it is not unreasonable to subject it to suit in one of those States if its allegedly defective merchandise has there been the source of injury to its owners or to others. The forum State does not exceed its powers under the Due Process Clause if it asserts personal jurisdiction over a corporation that delivers its products into the stream of commerce with the expectation that they will be purchased by consumers in the forum State. *Compare* Gray v. American Radiator & Standard Sanitary Corp.

But there is no such or similar basis for Oklahoma jurisdiction over World-Wide or Seaway in this case. Seaway's sales are made in Massena, N.Y. World-Wide's market, although substantially larger, is limited to dealers in New York, New Jersey, and Connecticut. There is no evidence of record that any automobiles distributed by World-Wide are sold to retail customers outside this tri-State area. It is foreseeable that the purchasers of automobiles sold by World-Wide and Seaway may take them to Oklahoma. But the mere "unilateral activity of those who claim some relationship with a nonresident defendant cannot satisfy the requirement of contact with the forum State." Hanson v. Denkla.

In a variant on the previous argument, it is contended that jurisdiction can be supported by the fact that petitioners earn substantial revenue from goods used in Oklahoma. The Oklahoma Supreme Court so found, drawing the inference that because one automobile sold by petitioners had been used in Oklahoma, others might have been used there also. While this inference seems less than compelling on the facts of the instant case, we need not question the Court's factual findings in order to reject its reasoning.

This argument seems to make the point that the purchase of automobiles in New York, from which the petitioners earn substantial revenue, would not occur *but for* the fact that the automobiles are capable of use in distant States like Oklahoma. Respondents observe that the very purpose of an automobile is to travel, and that travel of automobiles sold by petitioners is facilitated by an extensive chain of Volkswagen service centers throughout the

Country, including some in Oklahoma.[12] However, financial benefits accruing to the defendant from a collateral relation to the forum State will not support jurisdiction if they do not stem from a constitutionally cognizable contact with that State. *See* Kulko v. Superior Court. In our view, whatever marginal revenues petitioners may receive by virtue of the fact that their products are capable of use in Oklahoma is far too attenuated a contact to justify that State's exercise of in personam jurisdiction over them.

Because we find that petitioners have no "contacts, ties, or relations" with the State of Oklahoma, the judgment of the Supreme Court of Oklahoma is reversed.

Justice BRENNAN, dissenting.

The Court's opinions focus tightly on the existence of contacts between the forum and the defendant. In so doing, they accord too little weight to the strength of the forum State's interest in the case and fail to explore whether there would be any actual inconvenience to the defendant. The essential inquiry in locating the constitutional limits on state court jurisdiction over absent defendants is whether the particular exercise of jurisdiction offends "traditional notions of fair play and substantial justice." The clear focus in *International Shoe* was on fairness and reasonableness. The Court specifically declined to establish a mechanical test based on the quantum of contacts between a State and the defendant. . . . The existence of contacts, so long as there were some, was merely one way of giving content to the determination of fairness and reasonableness.

Another consideration is the actual burden a defendant must bear in defending the suit in the forum. Because lesser burdens reduce the unfairness to the defendant, jurisdiction may be justified despite less significant contacts. The burden, of course, must be of constitutional dimension. Due process limits on jurisdiction do not protect a defendant from all inconvenience of travel, and it would not be sensible to make the constitutional rule turn solely on the number of miles the defendant must travel to the courtroom.[1] Instead, the constitutionally significant "burden" to be analyzed relates to the mobility of the defendant's defense. For instance, if having to travel to a foreign forum would hamper the defense because witness or evidence of the defendant himself were immobile, or if there were a disproportionately large number of witnesses or amount of evidence that would have to be transported at the defendant's expense, or if being away from home for the duration of the trial would work some special hardship on the defendant, then the Constitution would require special consideration for the defendant's interests.

That considerations other than contacts between the forum and the defendant are relevant necessarily means that the Constitution does not require

12. As we have noted, petitioners earn no direct revenues from these service centers.

1. In fact, a courtroom just across the state line from a defendant may often be far more convenient for the defendant than a courtroom in a distant corner of his own State.

that trial be held in the State which has the "best contacts" with the defendant. The defendant has no constitutional entitlement to the best forum or, for that matter, to any particular forum. Under even the most restrictive view of *International Shoe,* several States could have jurisdiction over a particular cause of action. We need only determine whether the forum States in these cases satisfy the constitutional minimum. . . .

B

[T]he interest of the forum State and its connection to the litigation is strong. The automobile accident underlying the litigation occurred in Oklahoma. The plaintiffs were hospitalized in Oklahoma when they brought suit. Essential witnesses and evidence were in Oklahoma. *See* Shaffer v. Heitner. The State has a legitimate interest in enforcing its laws designed to keep its highway system safe, and the trial can proceed at least as efficiently in Oklahoma as anywhere else.

The petitioners are not unconnected with the forum. Although both sell automobiles within limited sales territories, each sold the automobile which in fact was driven to Oklahoma where it was involved in an accident.[8] It may be true, as the Court suggests, that each sincerely intended to limit its commercial impact to the limited territory, and that each intended to accept the benefits and protection of the laws only of those States within the territory. But obviously these were unrealistic hopes that cannot be treated as an automatic constitutional shield.[9]

An automobile simply is not a stationary item or one designed to be used in one place. An automobile is *intended* to be moved around. Someone in the business of selling large numbers of automobiles can hardly plead ignorance of their mobility or pretend that the automobiles stay put after they are sold. It is not merely that a dealer in automobiles foresees that they will move. The dealer actually intends that the purchasers will use the automobiles to travel to distant States where the dealer does not directly "do business." The sale of an automobile does *purposefully* inject the vehicle into the stream of interstate commerce so that it can travel to distant States.

---

8. On the basis of this fact the state court inferred that the petitioners derived substantial revenue from goods used in Oklahoma. The inference is not without support. Certainly, were use of goods accepted as a relevant contact a plaintiff would not need to have an exact count of the number of petitioners' cars that are used in Oklahoma.

9. Moreover, imposing liability in this case would not so undermine certainty as to destroy an automobile dealer's ability to do business. According jurisdiction does not expand liability except in the marginal case where a plaintiff cannot afford to bring an action except in the plaintiff's own State. In addition, these petitioners are represented by insurance companies. They not only could, but did, purchase insurance to protect them should they stand trial and lose the case. The costs of insurance no doubt are passed on to customers.

The Court accepts that a State may exercise jurisdiction over a distributor which "serves" that State "indirectly" by "deliver[ing] its products into the stream of commerce with the expectation that they will [be] purchased by consumers in other States." It is difficult to see why the Constitution should distinguish between a case involving goods which reach a distant State through a chain of distribution and a case involving goods which reach the same State because a consumer, using them as the dealer knew the customer would, took them there.[11] In each case the seller purposefully injects the goods into the stream of commerce and those goods predictably are used in the forum State.

Furthermore, an automobile seller derives substantial benefits from States other than its own. A large part of the value of automobiles is the extensive, nationwide network of highways. Significant portions of that network have been constructed by and are maintained by the individual States, including Oklahoma. The States, through their highway programs, contribute in a very direct and important way to the value of petitioner's business. Additionally, a network of other related dealerships with their service departments operate throughout the country under the protection of the laws of the various States, including Oklahoma, and enhance the value of petitioners' businesses by facilitating their customers' traveling.

Thus, the Court errs in its conclusion (emphasis added) that "petitioners have *no* 'contacts, ties, or relations' " with Oklahoma. There obviously are contacts, and given Oklahoma's connection to the litigation, the contacts are sufficiently significant to make it fair and reasonable for the petitioners to submit to Oklahoma's jurisdiction.

III

It may be that affirmance of the judgments in these cases would approach the outer limits of *International Shoe's* jurisdictional principle. But that principle, with its almost exclusive focus on the rights of defendants, may be outdated. As Mr. Justice Marshall wrote in Shaffer v. Heitner, " '[T]raditional notions of fair play and substantial justice' can be as readily offended by the perpetuation of ancient forms that are no longer justified as by the adoption of new procedures." . . .

The Court opinion suggests that the defendant ought to be subject to a State's jurisdiction only if he has contacts with the State "such that he should reasonably anticipate being haled into court there."[18] There is nothing un-

11. For example, I cannot understand the constitutional distinction between selling an item in New Jersey and selling an item in New York expecting it to be used in New Jersey.

18. The Court suggests that this is the critical foreseeability rather than the likelihood that the product will go to the forum State. But the reasoning begs the question. A defendant cannot know if his actions will subject him to jurisdiction in another State until we have declared what the law of jurisdiction is.

reasonable or unfair, however, about recognizing commercial reality. Given the tremendous mobility of goods and people, and the inability of businessmen to control where goods are taken by customers (or retailers), I do not think that the defendant should be in complete control of the geographical stretch of his amenability to suit. Jurisdiction is no longer premised on the notion that nonresident defendants have somehow impliedly consented to suit. People should understand that they are held responsible for the consequences of their actions and that in our society most actions have consequences affecting many States. When an action in fact causes injury in another State, the actor should be prepared to answer for it there unless defending in that State would be unfair for some reason other than that a State boundary must be crossed.[19]

In effect the Court is allowing defendants to assert the sovereign rights of their home States. The expressed fear is that otherwise all limits on personal jurisdiction would disappear. But the argument's premise is wrong. I would not abolish limits on jurisdiction or strip state boundaries of all significance; I would still require the plaintiff to demonstrate sufficient contacts among the parties, the forum, and the litigation to make the forum a reasonable State in which to hold the trial.

Justice MARSHALL, with whom Justice BLACKMUN joins, dissenting. . . .

This is a difficult case, and reasonable minds may differ as to whether respondents have alleged a sufficient "relationship among the defendant[s], the forum, and the litigation," Shaffer v. Heitner, to satisfy the requirements of *International Shoe.* I am concerned, however, that the majority has reached its result by taking an unnecessarily narrow view of petitioners' forum-related conduct. The majority asserts that "respondents seek to base jurisdiction on one, isolated occurrence and whatever inferences can be drawn therefrom: the fortuitous circumstance that a single Audi automobile, sold in New York to New York residents, happened to suffer an accident while passing through Oklahoma." If that were the case, I would readily agree that the minimum contacts necessary to sustain jurisdiction are not present. But the basis for the assertion of jurisdiction is not the happenstance that an individual over whom petitioners had no control made a unilateral decision to take a chattel with him to a distant State. Rather, jurisdiction is premised on the deliberate and purposeful actions of the defendants themselves in choosing to become part of a nationwide, indeed a global, network for marketing and servicing automobiles.

Petitioners are sellers of a product whose utility derives from its mobility. . . .

---

19. One consideration that might create some unfairness would be if the choice of forum also imposed on the defendant an unfavorable substantive law which the defendant could justly have assumed would not apply.

To be sure, petitioners could not know in advance that this particular automobile would be driven to Oklahoma. They must have anticipated, however, that a substantial portion of the cars they sold would travel out of New York. Seaway, a local dealer in the second most populous State, and World-Wide, one of only seven regional Audi distributors in the entire country, would scarcely have been surprised to learn that a car sold by them had been driven to Oklahoma on Interstate 44, a heavily traveled transcontinental highway. In the case of the distributor, in particular, the probability that some of the cars it sells will be driven in every one of the contiguous States must amount to a virtual certainty. This knowledge should alert a reasonable businessman to the likelihood that a defect in the product might manifest itself in the forum State—not because of some unpredictable, aberrant, unilateral action by a single buyer, but in the normal course of the operation of the vehicles for their intended purpose.

It is misleading for the majority to characterize the argument in favor of jurisdiction as one of " 'foreseeability' alone." As economic entities petitioners reach out from New York, knowingly causing effects in other States and receiving economic advantage both from the ability to cause such effects themselves and from the activities of dealers and distributors in other States. While they did not receive revenue from making direct sales in Oklahoma, they intentionally became part of an interstate economic network, which included dealerships in Oklahoma, for pecuniary gain. In light of this purposeful conduct I do not believe it can be said that petitioners "had no reason to expect to be haled before a[n Oklahoma] court." . . .

[The dissenting opinion of Justice BLACKMUN is omitted.]

Questions and Comments

(1) Why did the Robinsons pursue the question of jurisdiction over the dealership and the regional distributor all the way to the Supreme Court when they knew that the court had jurisdiction over the manufacturer and the international distribution by the latter's acquiescence? Why wouldn't a judgment against them have been sufficient since, as Justice Blackmun noted (in an opinion not reproduced above), they are presumably solvent? For everything you ever wanted to know about the real story of *World-Wide Volkswagen, see* Adams, *World-Wide Volkswagen v. Woodson*—the Rest of the Story, 72 Neb. L. Rev. 1122 (1993).

(2) How can a Court that is so blasé about overreaching in choice of law (as in *Hague*, page 359 *supra*) be so concerned about jurisdiction? Doesn't a state do more harm when it does the former than when it does the latter? The irony was put into sharp relief when the Minnesota Supreme Court, which decided *Hague* at the state level, ruled that it had no jurisdiction in a case in which a Wisconsin border-city tavern had served alcohol to a Minnesota resident who subsequently had an accident in Minnesota. West American In-

surance Co. v. Westin, Inc., 337 P.2d 676 (Minn. 1983). *Cf.* Meyers Kallestead, 476 N.W.2d 65 (Iowa 1991) (same, citing *World-Wide Volkswagen*). Isn't the effect of *Hague* and *World-Wide Volkswagen,* taken together, to subject defendants to marginal choices of law when and only when they have substantial *un*related contacts with the forum state? *See* Martin, Personal Jurisdiction and Choice of Law, 78 Mich. L. Rev. 872 (1980), and Silberman, *Shaffer v. Heitner:* The End of an Era, 53 N.Y.U.L. Rev. 33, 79-90 (1978).

(3) What would have been the outcome of the case if the Robinsons had been moving to Oklahoma and not merely passing through it on their way to Arizona? If they already lived in Oklahoma at the time of the accident? If they had lived in Oklahoma when they bought the car but the dealership did not know that fact? If they had lived in Oklahoma at the time they bought the car and the dealership did know that fact, but they were the only Oklahoma customers of the dealership? (If you find in favor of jurisdiction in the last hypothetical, would it extend to the regional distributor, which had no dealings with the Robinsons?) What if a moderate number of sales were made to Oklahoma residents and that fact was known to the dealership, but those sales had not been solicited by the dealership?

(4) What is the answer to Justice Brennan's question of why there is a difference between the case where the chain of distribution takes the car to a distant state and the case where the customer takes it there and that fact could have been predicted? Could the difference be based on the concept of *benefit?* Consider: If the state of Oklahoma were to disappear tomorrow, the effect on the defendant dealer's sales would probably be zero. (Recall that the Robinsons were New York residents when they purchased their car.) But if the product in question were one that went through a chain of distribution to Oklahoma (like the valve in Gray v. American Radiator, 22 Ill. 2d 432, 176 N.E.2d 761 (1961)), the disappearance of the state of Oklahoma would decrease sales of the product. Thus, the amount of benefit that the defendant derives from a state, in a pecuniary sense, turns very much on whether the customer or the chain of distribution takes the product into that state.

(5) In footnote 19, Justice Brennan's dissent suggests that application of an unfavorable substantive law that the defendant could not have anticipated might be a factor, under his scheme, for denying jurisdiction. But does it make sense to say that an unfair choice of law will result in a denial of jurisdiction where that choice of law itself is constitutional? Consider, for example, defendants *A* and *B,* both of whom might be subject to unfair and surprising law in State *X* if jurisdiction is asserted there. Would it be rational to deny jurisdiction and allow defendant *A* to escape the law of State *X* while subjecting defendant *B* to that same unfair and surprising law because *B,* through "substantial contacts" with State *X,* totally unrelated to the cause of action, is subject to the general in personam jurisdiction of that state?

(6) In Ohio v. Wyandotte Chemicals Corp., 401 U.S. 493 (1971), the Supreme Court refused to exercise original jurisdiction of a complaint by the state of Ohio against Michigan and Canadian corporations alleged to be polluting Lake Erie. Though it found that it had such jurisdiction, it found the exercise of the jurisdiction unnecessary because alternative forums were available, including Ohio state courts. The Court found explicitly that Ohio courts could exercise in personam jurisdiction over the out-of-state defendants for a direct intrusion of pollutants causing physical harm within the state. Is *World-Wide Volkswagen* distinguishable because the presence of the automobile in Oklahoma, unlike the presence of the pollutants in Ohio, was due to an "intervening human agency"? Or is the distinction a narrower one—that the presence of the automobile in Oklahoma was due to the activities of the plaintiff, and the plaintiff's unilateral activities should not be able to create jurisdiction? If the latter distinction is the appropriate one, does it follow that jurisdiction should exist in Oklahoma for a suit brought by the driver of the other car if he, too, happened to have been injured by the burning of the Robinson car's gas tank (on the grounds that the other driver was not instrumental in getting the Robinson vehicle into Oklahoma)?

(7) Isn't it fairer to make the Robinsons travel to New York to litigate than to require these defendants to go to Oklahoma? The Robinsons, after all, are the ones responsible for the extra interstate costs of litigation. *See* Brilmayer, How Contacts Count: Due Process Limitations on State Court Jurisdiction, 1980 S. Ct. Rev. 77.

(8) The Supreme Court provoked a fair amount of interest with its discussion of state sovereignty as an essential element of jurisdiction. Recall the discussion in *Insurance Co. of Ireland,* page 480 *supra. See generally* Stein, Styles of Argument and Interstate Federalism in the Law of Personal Jurisdiction, 65 Tex. L. Rev. 689 (1987). Isn't the dichotomy between sovereignty analysis and individual liberty analysis really a false one, though? Isn't the defendant's individual liberty claim essentially a claim that the forum has exceeded the reach of the power legitimately accorded it in a world of territorially limited states?

(9) If foreseeability is the issue, then Doe v. National Medical Services, 974 F.2d 143 (10th Cir. 1992), presents an interesting test case. The Colorado plaintiff was an employee who had been discharged after a Pennsylvania testing laboratory reported (allegedly, negligently) that his urine sample had tested positive for drugs. (He was required to submit to random drug testing by his employer because he had recently completed a substance abuse program.) The urine sample had been collected in Colorado and was then sent to Smith-Kline Bio-Sciences in Van Nuys, California; from there it was sent to NMS in Pennsylvania. NMS did not know that the sample was from a Coloradan; indeed, they could not have known because the sample was identified only by a bar code. Nor did they know that the results would be communicated to a Colorado employer. What should the court decide on the personal jurisdiction motion?

Kulko v. Superior Court

436 U.S. 84 (1978)

Justice MARSHALL delivered the opinion of the court.

[Appellant Ezra Kulko and appellee Sharon Kulko Horn were New York domiciliaries when they got married during a brief stay in California. They returned to New York where their two children, Darwin and Ilsa, were born. The couple and their two children resided in New York until they separated in 1972. Sharon and the children moved to California. Sharon returned briefly to New York to sign a separation agreement specifying that Ezra would pay alimony and that the children would remain with Ezra during the school year and visit Sharon on holidays. Immediately after execution of the separation agreement, Sharon flew to Haiti, where she secured a divorce decree that incorporated the terms of the separation agreement.

Subsequently, each of the children expressed their desire to live with their mother in California. Ezra acquiesced, purchased a one-way plane ticket for Ilsa, and later paid for Darwin's move. Once both children arrived, Sharon instituted a civil action in California to establish the Haitian divorce as a California judgment, to modify the judgment so as to award her full custody of the children, and to increase appellant's child support obligations. Ezra was served with process under the California long-arm statute that allows state courts to assert jurisdiction on any basis not inconsistent with the Constitution. He challenged the court's jurisdiction under the due process clause. The California Supreme Court rejected his argument and held that jurisdiction was proper because appellant had "caused an effect in [California]" by purposefully sending Ilsa into the state.]

A

In reaching its result, the California Supreme Court did not rely on appellant's glancing presence in the State some 13 years before the events that led to this controversy, nor could it have. Appellant has been in California on only two occasions, once in 1959 for a three-day military stopover on his way to Korea and again in 1960 for a 24-hour stopover on his return from Korean service. To hold such temporary visits to a State a basis for the assertion of in personam jurisdiction over unrelated actions arising in the future would make a mockery of the limitations on state jurisdiction imposed by the Fourteenth Amendment. Nor did the California court rely on the fact that appellant was actually married in California on one of his two brief visits. We agree that where two New York domiciliaries, for reasons of convenience, marry in the State of California and thereafter spend their entire married life in New

York, the fact of their California marriage by itself cannot support a California court's exercise of jurisdiction over a spouse who remains a New York resident in an action relating to child support.

Finally, in holding that personal jurisdiction existed, the court below carefully disclaimed reliance on the fact that appellant had agreed at the time of separation to allow his children to live with their mother three months a year and that he had sent them to California each year pursuant to this agreement. [T]o find personal jurisdiction in a State on this basis, merely because the mother was residing there, would discourage parents from entering into reasonable visitation agreements. Moreover, it could arbitrarily subject one parent to suit in any State of the Union where the other parent chose to spend time while having custody of their offspring pursuant to a separation agreement. As we have emphasized,

> The unilateral activity of those who claim some relationship with a nonresident defendant cannot satisfy the requirement of contact with the forum State. . . . [I]t is essential in each case that there be some act by which the defendant purposefully avails [him]self of the privilege of conducting activities within the forum State. . . .

The "purposeful act" that the California Supreme Court believed did warrant the exercise of personal jurisdiction over appellant in California was his "actively and fully consent[ing] to Ilsa living in California for the school year . . . and . . . send[ing] her to California for that purpose." We cannot accept the proposition that appellant's acquiescence in Ilsa's desire to live with her mother conferred jurisdiction over appellant in the California courts in this action. A father who agrees, in the interests of family harmony and his children's preferences, to allow them to spend more time in California than was required under a separation agreement can hardly be said to have "purposefully availed himself" of the "benefits and protection" of California's laws.[7]

Nor can we agree with the assertion of the court below that the exercise of in personam jurisdiction here was warranted by the financial benefit appellant derived from his daughter's presence in California for nine months of the year. This argument rests on the premise that, while appellant's liability for support payments remained unchanged, his yearly expenses for supporting the child in New York decreased. But this circumstance, even if true, does not support California's assertion of jurisdiction here. Any diminution in appellant's household costs resulted, not from the child's presence in California, but rather from her absence from appellant's home.

---

7. The court below stated that the presence in California of appellant's daughter gave appellant the benefit of California's "police and fire protection, its school system, its hospital services, its recreational facilities, its libraries and museums. . . ." But, in the circumstances presented here, these services provided by the State were essentially benefits to the child, not the father, and in any event were not benefits that appellant purposefully sought for himself.

B

In light of our conclusion that appellant did not purposefully derive benefit from any activities relating to the State of California, it is apparent that the California Supreme Court's reliance on appellant's having caused an "effect" in California was misplaced. This "effects" test is derived from the American Law Institute's Restatement (Second) of Conflict §37 (1971), which provides:

> A state has power to exercise judicial jurisdiction over an individual who causes effects in the state by an act done elsewhere with respect to any cause of action arising from these effects unless the nature of the effects and of the individual's relationship to the state make the exercise of such jurisdiction unreasonable.

While this provision is not binding on this Court, it does not in any event support the decision below. As is apparent from the examples accompanying §37 in the Restatement, this section was intended to reach wrongful activity outside of the State causing injury within the State, *see, e.g.*, Comment *a*, p. 157 (shooting bullet from one State into another), or commercial activity affecting the state residents, *ibid.* Even in such situations, moreover, the Restatement recognizes that there might be circumstances that would render "unreasonable" the assertion of jurisdiction over the nonresident defendant.

The circumstances in this case clearly render "unreasonable" California's assertion of personal jurisdiction. There is no claim that appellant has visited physical injury on either property or persons within the State of California. The cause of action herein asserted arises, not from the defendant's commercial transactions in interstate commerce, but rather from his personal, domestic relations. It thus cannot be said that appellant has sought a commercial benefit from solicitation of business from a resident of California that could reasonably render him liable to suit in state court; appellant's activities cannot fairly be analogized to an insurer's sending an insurance contract and premium notices into the State to an insured resident of the State. Furthermore, the controversy between the parties arises from a separation that occurred in the State of New York; appellee Horn seeks modification of a contract that was negotiated in New York and that she flew to New York to sign. As in Hanson v. Denckla, the instant action involves an agreement that was entered into with virtually no connection with the forum State.

Finally, basic considerations of fairness point decisively in favor of appellant's State of domicile as the proper forum for adjudication of this case, whatever the merits of appellee's underlying claim. It is appellant who has remained in the State of the marital domicile, whereas it is appellee who has moved across the continent. Appellant has at all times resided in New York State, and, until the separation and appellee's move to California, his entire family resided there as well. As noted above, appellant did no more than acquiesce in the stated preference of one of his children to live with her mother in California. This single act is surely not one that a reasonable parent would expect to result in the substantial financial burden and personal strain of litigating a child-support suit in a forum 3,000 miles away, and we therefore see no basis on which it can be said that appellant could reasonably have anticipated being "haled before a [California] court." To make jurisdiction in a case such as this turn on whether appellant bought his daughter her ticket or instead unsuccessfully sought to prevent her departure would impose an unreasonable burden on family relations, and one wholly unjustified by the "quality and nature" of appellant's activities in or relating to the State of California.

III

In seeking to justify the burden that would be imposed on appellant were the exercise of in personam jurisdiction in California sustained, appellee argues that California has substantial interests in protecting the welfare of its minor residents and in promoting to the fullest extent possible a healthy and supportive family environment in which the children of the State are to be raised. These interests are unquestionably important. But while the presence of the children and one parent in California arguably might favor application of California law in a lawsuit in New York, the fact that California might be the " 'center of gravity' " for choice of law purposes does not mean that California has personal jurisdiction over the defendant. And California has not attempted to assert any particularized interest in trying such cases in its courts by, *e.g.*, enacting a special jurisdictional statute.

California's legitimate interest in ensuring the support of children resident in California without unduly disrupting the children's lives, moreover, is already being served by the State's participation in the Uniform Reciprocal Enforcement of Support Act of 1968. This statute provides a mechanism for communication between court systems in different States, in order to facilitate the procurement and enforcement of child-support decrees where the dependent children reside in a State that cannot obtain personal jurisdiction over the defendant. California's version of the Act essentially permits a California resident claiming support from a nonresident to file a petition in California and have its merits adjudicated in the State of the alleged obligor's residence, without either party having to leave his or her own State. Cal. Code Civ. Proc. §1650 et seq. New York State is a signatory to a similar act. Thus, not only may plaintiff-appellee here vindicate her claimed right to additional child support from her former husband in a New York court, but the uniform acts will facilitate both her prosecution of a claim for additional support and collection of any support payments found to be owed by appellant.

It cannot be disputed that California has substantial interests in protecting resident children and in facilitating child-support actions on behalf of those children. But these interests simply do not make California a "fair forum," Shaffer v. Heitner, in which to require appellant, who derives no personal or commercial benefit from his child's presence in California and who lacks any other relevant contact with the State, either to defend a child-support suit or to suffer liability by default.

IV

Accordingly, we conclude that the appellant's motion to quash service, on the ground of lack of personal jurisdiction, was erroneously denied by the California courts. The judgment of the California Supreme Court is, therefore, reversed.

Justice BRENNAN, with whom Justice WHITE and Justice POWELL join, dissenting.

The Court properly treats this case as presenting a single narrow question. That question is whether the California Supreme Court correctly "weighed" "the facts" . . . of this particular case in applying the settled "constitutional standard," that before state courts may exercise in personam jurisdiction over a nonresident, nondomiciliary parent of minor children domiciled in the State, it must appear that the nonresident has "certain minimum contacts [with the forum state] such that the maintenance of the suit does not offend 'traditional notions of fair play and substantial justice.' " International Shoe Co. v. Washington. The Court recognizes that "this determination is one in which few answers will be written 'in black and white.' " . . . I cannot say that the Court's determination against state court in personam jurisdiction is implausible, but, though the issue is close, my independent weighing of the facts leads me to conclude, in agreement with the analysis and determination of the California Supreme Court, that appellant's connection with the State of California was not too attenuated, under the standards of reasonableness and fairness implicit in the Due Process Clause, to require him to conduct his defense in the California courts. I therefore dissent.

Questions and Comments

(1) Why was it so clear that the marriage of the parties in California did not provide an adequate basis for jurisdiction needed for modifying child support? What if the children had been conceived during a layover in California? What if they had been born during a brief stop there? *Cf.* Poston v. Poston, 624 A.2d 853 (Vt. 1993) (no in personam jurisdiction in state of original marital domicile and birth of first child).

(2) Would it have made a difference if Kulko had urged Horn to move to California because it was a better place for the children to spend the summer? Would it have made a difference if Kulko, rather than the children, had been the instigator of their permanent move to residence with their mother?

(3) The Court emphasizes that the divorce and separation agreement were centered in New York. If Kulko had moved from New York to Florida, would New York still be an appropriate place to sue him? If not, would California then become appropriate—*i.e.,* is California jurisdiction rejected because it is altogether inappropriate, or merely because, as the facts stand, New York is a much better place to litigate (which might not be so if Kulko moved)?

(4) In McGee v. International Life Insurance Co., 355 U.S. 220 (1957), California jurisdiction over an out-of-state insurance company was upheld, despite a lack of any evidence that the company had any contacts with California apart from its solicitation of the deceased and its subsequent collection of premiums he mailed from California. In Hanson v. Denckla, 357 U.S. 235 (1958), however, the Court rejected Florida jurisdiction over a Delaware trustee of a trust established by a decedent who had moved to Florida after the trust was established, despite continued contact between the decedent and the trustee. In the latter case the trustee had not "purposefully availed itself of the privilege of conducting activities within the forum State"; *McGee* was further distinguished as a case in which the state of California had manifested strong interests in insurance by its special legislation in the area. Isn't California even more interested in the welfare of its resident children than in the insurance business? And in any event, if the standards are fair play and substantial justice and minimum contacts, what does the interest of the state have to do with either?

(5) Justice White joined in the brief dissenting opinion in *Kulko,* which declares that jurisdictional cases such as *Kulko* are close calls but that the dissenters would weigh the facts slightly differently than would the *Kulko*-majority. Does his majority opinion in *World-Wide Volkswagen* give any satisfactory method for resolving the ambiguities? Is it possible in such cases to do anything but produce vague verbal formulas and apply them to specific factual situations in the hope that the lower courts will get a feeling for what the Supreme Court thinks goes too far? Do *Kulko* and *World-Wide Volkswagen* represent anything more than a signal to the lower courts that they had begun to drift too far toward asserting jurisdiction since *International Shoe, McGee,* and Hanson v. Denckla?

(6) Is the real point of *Kulko* that the relaxations in the law of jurisdiction that bloomed in the *International Shoe* opinion were a result of the expansion of commercial transactions to a national scale, while personal relations, though they may have changed somewhat since the days of *Pennoyer,* have not changed in a similar manner? After all, the increased cost of litigation in a distant place can be passed on to the customer in the business setting, while the same cannot be said about the cost of inconvenience in litigation of personal matters.

(7) What effect ought it have on the existence of personal jurisdiction that the substantive cause of action is of one sort rather than another? If *Kulko* is in part explained by the fact that it is a domestic relations dispute, then are there other types of substantive disputes as to which special jurisdictional

standards apply? In both Keeton v. Hustler Magazine, Inc., 465 U.S. 770 (1984), and Calder v. Jones, 465 U.S. 783 (1984), the Court stated in no uncertain terms that it did not matter, for purposes of personal jurisdiction, that the case was a multistate defamation action in which assertion of jurisdiction might "chill" First Amendment rights. It stated that the First Amendment had no bearing on personal jurisdiction.

Is this correct or desirable? What if a state enacted a longer long arm for cases brought against Republican defendants than for cases against Democratic defendants? What if it had a longer long arm for defamation actions than for personal injury actions? *See generally* Pielemeier, Constitutional Limits on Choice of Law: The Special Case of Multistate Defamation, 133 U. Pa. L. Rev. 381 (1985).

In Connolly v. Burt, 757 F.2d 242 (10th Cir. 1986), the court relied on *Keeton* and *Calder* in asserting jurisdiction over a Nebraska doctor who had written a letter of recommendation about a former student to a Colorado hospital at the hospital's request. The defendant, Connolly, had written, "In reply to your inquiry about Dr. Burt, he did spend time here as an Orthopaedic Resident from 1974-1977. His performance was well below average and he has consequently not been recommended for Board eligibility. I think he might serve adequately in some field of medicine, but not that of Orthopaedic Surgery." The Supreme Court agreed to review the case, 474 U.S. 1004 (1985), but after the defendant filed his brief on the merits the plaintiff dropped the case and it was dismissed as moot. 475 U.S. 1063 (1986).

(8) Is the following generalization accurate about the impact on personal jurisdiction of the substantive nature of the dispute? Usually, where the cause of action arises out of the defendant's in-state activities, these activities are (at least alleged to be) actionable and therefore the state has an interest in determining them. Imposing extra "jurisdictional" costs on the defendant by making him or her litigate in this distant forum thus serves state substantive interests by placing the costs upon the party that brought about the tortious (or otherwise wrongful) activity within the state.

This argument does not apply, however, when the plaintiff was the one responsible for bringing the instrumentality into the state, as in *World-Wide Volkswagen.* In *Kulko,* similarly, the presence of the children in California was not really the defendant's responsibility, since he was merely passively acquiescent. Neither does it apply when the conduct serving as the basis for jurisdiction is not itself wrongful, as in *Kulko.* Where the conduct used as a basis for jurisdiction is substantively desirable, asserting jurisdiction imposes the wrong incentives. In *Keeton,* in contrast, the conduct upon which jurisdiction is founded (sending defamatory material into the forum) has First Amendment aspects, but is nonetheless wrongful and the forum may validly discourage it. *Cf.* Klinghoffer v. S.N.C. Achille Lauro, 937 F.2d 44 (2d Cir. 1991) (declining to base jurisdiction over P.L.O. on its involvement in U.N. activities in New York on the grounds that this would place an undue burden on participation in U.N. affairs).

Asahi Metal Industry Co. v. Superior Court of California

480 U.S. 102 (1987)

Justice O'CONNOR announced the judgment of the Court and delivered the unanimous opinion of the Court with respect to Part I, the opinion of the Court with respect to Part II-B, in which The CHIEF JUSTICE, Justice BRENNAN, Justice WHITE, Justice MARSHALL, Justice BLACKMUN, Justice POWELL, and Justice STEVENS join, and an opinion with respect to Parts II-A and III, in which THE CHIEF JUSTICE, Justice POWELL, and Justice SCALIA join.

I

On September 23, 1978, on Interstate Highway 80 in Solano County, California, Gary Zurcher lost control of his Honda motorcycle and collided with a tractor. Zurcher was severely injured, and his passenger and wife, Ruth Ann Moreno, was killed. In September 1979, Zurcher filed a product liability action in the Superior Court of the State of California in and for the County of Solano. Zurcher alleged that the 1978 accident was caused by a sudden loss of air and an explosion in the rear tire of the motorcycle, and alleged that the motorcycle tire, tube, and sealant were defective. Zurcher's complaint named, *inter alia,* Cheng Shin Rubber Industrial Co., Ltd. (Cheng Shin), the Taiwanese manufacturer of the tube. Cheng Shin in turn filed a cross-complaint seeking indemnification from its codefendants and from petitioner, Asahi Metal Industry Co., Ltd. (Asahi), the manufacturer of the tube's valve assembly. Zurcher's claims against Cheng Shin and the other defendants were eventually settled and dismissed, leaving only Cheng Shin's indemnity action against Asahi.

California's long-arm statute authorizes the exercise of jurisdiction "on any basis not inconsistent with the Constitution of this state or of the United States." Cal. Code Civ. Proc. Ann. §410.10 (West 1973). Asahi moved to quash Cheng Shin's service of summons arguing the State could not exert jurisdiction over it consistent with the Due Process Clause of the Fourteenth Amendment.

In relation to the motion, the following information was submitted by Asahi and Cheng Shin. Asahi is a Japanese corporation. It manufactures tire valve assemblies in Japan and sells the assemblies to Cheng Shin, and to several other tire manufacturers, for use as components in finished tire tubes. Asahi's sales to Cheng Shin took place in Taiwan. The shipments from Asahi to Cheng Shin were sent from Japan to Taiwan. Cheng Shin bought and incorporated into its tire tubes 150,000 Asahi valve assemblies in 1978; 500,000 in 1979; 500,000 in 1980; 100,000 in 1981; and 100,000 in 1982. Sales to Cheng Shin accounted for 1.24 percent of Asahi's income in 1981 and 0.44 percent in 1982. Cheng Shin alleged that approximately 20 percent of its sales in the United States are in California. Cheng Shin purchases valve assemblies from other suppliers as well, and sells finished tubes throughout the world.

In 1983 an attorney for Cheng Shin conducted an informal examination of the valve stems of the tire tubes sold in one cyclery in Solano County. The attorney declared that of the approximately 115 tire tubes in the store, 97 were purportedly manufactured in Japan or Taiwan, and of those 97, 21 valve stems were marked with the circled letter "A," apparently Asahi's trademark. Of the 21 Asahi valve stems, 12 were incorporated into Cheng Shin tire tubes. The store contained 41 other Cheng Shin tubes that incorporated the valve assemblies of other manufacturers. An affidavit of a manager of Cheng Shin whose duties included the purchasing of component parts stated: " 'In discussions with Asahi regarding the purchase of valve stem assemblies the fact that my Company sells tubes throughout the world and specifically the United States has been discussed. I am informed and believe that Asahi was fully aware that valve stem assemblies sold to my Company and to others would end up throughout the United States and in California.' " 39 Cal. 3d 35, 48 n.4, 702 P.2d 543, 549-550 n.4 (1985). An affidavit of the president of Asahi, on the other hand, declared that Asahi " 'has never contemplated that its limited sales of tire valves to Cheng Shin in Taiwan would subject it to lawsuits in California.' " *Ibid.*

Primarily on the basis of the above information, the Superior Court denied the motion to quash summons, stating that "Asahi obviously does business on an international scale. It is not unreasonable that they defend claims of defect in their product on an international scale." Order Denying Motion to Quash Summons, Zurcher v. Dunlop Tire & Rubber Co., No. 76180 (Super. Ct., Solano County, Cal., Apr. 20, 1983).

The Court of Appeal of the State of California issued a peremptory writ of mandate commanding the Superior Court to quash service of summons. The court concluded that "it would be reasonable to require Asahi to respond in California solely on the basis of ultimately realized foreseeability that the product into which its component was embodied would be sold all over the world including California." App. to Pet. for cert. B5-B6.

The Supreme Court of the State of California reversed and discharged the writ issued by the Court of Appeal. 39 Cal. 3d 35, 702 P.2d 543 (1985).

We granted certiorari, 475 U.S. 1044 (1986), and now reverse.

II

A

The Due Process Clause of the Fourteenth Amendment limits the power of a state court to exert personal jurisdiction over a nonresident defendant. "[T]he constitutional touchstone" of the determination whether an exercise of personal jurisdiction comports with due process "remains whether the defendant purposefully established 'minimum contacts' in the forum State."

Burger King Corp. v. Rudzewicz, 471 U.S. 462, 474 (1985), quoting International Shoe Co. v. Washington, 326 U.S. 310, 316 (1945).

Applying the principle that minimum contacts must be based on an act of the defendant, the Court in World-Wide Volkswagen Corp. v. Woodson, 444 U.S. 286 (1980), rejected the assertion that a *consumer's* unilateral act of bringing the defendant's product into the forum State was a sufficient constitutional basis for personal jurisdiction over the defendant. It had been argued in *World-Wide Volkswagen* that because an automobile retailer and its wholesale distributor sold a product mobile by design and purpose, they could foresee being haled into court in the distant States into which their customers might drive. The Court rejected this concept of foreseeability as an insufficient basis for jurisdiction under the Due Process Clause. *Id.*, at 295-296. The Court disclaimed, however, the idea that "foreseeability is wholly irrelevant" to personal jurisdiction, concluding that "[t]he forum State does not exceed its powers under the Due Process Clause if it asserts personal jurisdiction over a corporation that delivers its products into the stream of commerce with the expectation that they will be purchased by consumers in the forum State." *Id.*, 297-298 (citation omitted).

In *World-Wide Volkswagen* itself, the state court sought to base jurisdiction not on any act of the defendant, but on the foreseeable unilateral actions of the consumer. Since *World-Wide Volkswagen*, lower courts have been confronted with cases in which the defendant acted by placing a product in the stream of commerce, and the stream eventually swept defendant's product into the forum State, but the defendant did nothing else to purposefully avail itself of the market in the forum state. Some courts have understood the Due Process Clause, as interpreted in *World-Wide Volkswagen*, to allow an exercise of personal jurisdiction to be based on no more than the defendant's act of placing the product in the stream of commerce. Other courts have understood the Due Process Clause and the above-quoted language in *World-Wide Volkswagen* to require the action of the defendant to be more purposefully directed at the forum State than the mere act of placing a product in the stream of commerce.

The reasoning of the Supreme Court of California in the present case illustrates the former interpretation of *World-Wide Volkswagen*. The Supreme Court of California held that, because the stream of commerce eventually brought some valves Asahi sold Cheng Shin into California, Asahi's awareness that its valves would be sold in California was sufficient to permit California to exercise jurisdiction over Asahi consistent with the requirements of the Due Process Clause.

Other courts, however, have understood the Due Process Clause to require something more than that the defendant was aware of its product's entry into the forum State through the stream of commerce in order for the state to exert jurisdiction over the defendant. In the present case, for example, the State Court of Appeals did not read the Due Process Clause, as interpreted by *World-Wide Volkswagen*, to allow "mere foreseeability that the product will enter the forum state [to] be enough by itself to establish jurisdiction over the distributor and retailer." In Humble v. Toyota Motor Co., Ltd., 727 F.2d 709 (C.A.8 1984), an injured car passenger brought suit against Arakawa Auto Body Company, a Japanese corporation that manufactured car seats for Toyota. Arakawa did no business in the United States; it had no office, affiliate, subsidiary, or agent in the United States; it manufactured its component parts outside the United States and delivered them to Toyota Motor Company in Japan. The Court of Appeals, adopting the reasoning of the District Court in that case, noted that although it "does not doubt that Arakawa could have foreseen that its product would find its way into the United States," it would be "manifestly unjust" to require Arakawa to defend itself in the United States. *Id.*, at 710-711, quoting 578 F. Supp. 530, 533 (N.D. Iowa 1982).

We now find this latter position to be consonant with the requirements of due process. The "substantial connection," *Burger King*, 471 U.S., at 475; *McGee*, 355 U.S., at 223, between the defendant and the forum State necessary for a finding of minimum contacts must come about by an action of the defendant purposefully directed toward the forum State. *Burger King, supra,* 471 U.S., at 476; Keeton v. Hustler Magazine, Inc., 465 U.S. 770, 774 (1984). The placement of a product into the stream of commerce, without more, is not an act of the defendant purposefully directed toward the forum State. Additional conduct of the defendant may indicate an intent or purpose to serve the market in the forum State, for example, designing the product for the market in the forum State, advertising in the forum State, establishing channels for providing regular advice to customers in the forum State, or marketing the product through a distributor who has agreed to serve as the sales agent in the forum State. But a defendant's awareness that the stream of commerce may or will sweep the product into the forum State does not convert the mere act of placing the product into the stream into an act purposefully directed toward the forum State.

Assuming, arguendo, that respondents have established Asahi's awareness that some of the valves sold to Cheng Shin would be incorporated into tire tubes sold in California, respondents have not demonstrated any action by Asahi to purposefully avail itself of the California market. Asahi does not do business in California. It has no office, agents, employees, or property in California. It does not advertise or otherwise solicit business in California. It did not create, control, or employ the distribution system that brought its valves to California. There is no evidence that Asahi designed its product in anticipation of sales in California. On the basis of these facts, the exertion of personal jurisdiction over Asahi by the Superior Court of California* exceeds the limits of Due Process.

---

* We have no occasion here to determine whether Congress could, consistent with the Due Process Clause of the Fifth Amendment, authorize federal court personal jurisdiction over alien defendants based on the aggregate of *national* contacts, rather than on the contacts between the defendant and the State in which the federal court sits. *See* Max Daetwyler Corp. v.

B

The strictures of the Due Process Clause forbid a state court from exercising personal jurisdiction over Asahi under circumstances that would offend "traditional notions of fair play and substantial justice." International Shoe Co. v. Washington, 326 U.S., at 316, quoting Milliken v. Meyer, 311 U.S., at 463.

We have previously explained that the determination of the reasonableness of the exercise of jurisdiction in each case will depend on an evaluation of several factors. A court must consider the burden on the defendant, the interests of the forum state, and the plaintiff's interest in obtaining relief. It must also weigh in its determination "the interstate judicial system's interest in obtaining the most efficient resolution of controversies; and the shared interest of the several States in furthering fundamental substantive social policies." *World-Wide Volkswagen,* 444 U.S., at 292 (citations omitted).

A consideration of these factors in the present case clearly reveals the unreasonableness of the assertion of jurisdiction over Asahi, even apart from the question of the placement of goods in the stream of commerce.

Certainly the burden on the defendant in this case is severe. Asahi has been commanded by the Supreme Court of California not only to traverse the distance between Asahi's headquarters in Japan and the Superior Court of California in and for the County of Solano, but also to submit its dispute with Cheng Shin to a foreign nation's judicial system. The unique burdens placed upon one who must defend oneself in a foreign legal system should have significant weight in assessing the reasonableness of stretching the long arm of personal jurisdiction over national borders.

When minimum contacts have been established, often the interests of the plaintiff and the forum in the exercise of jurisdiction will justify even the serious burdens placed on the alien defendant. In the present case, however, the interests of the plaintiff and the forum in California's assertion of jurisdiction over Asahi are slight. All that remains is a claim for indemnification asserted by Cheng Shin, a Taiwanese corporation, against Asahi. The transaction on which the indemnification claim is based took place in Taiwan; Asahi's components were shipped from Japan to Taiwan. Cheng Shin has not demonstrated that it is more convenient for it to litigate its indemnification claim against Asahi in California rather than in Taiwan or Japan.

Because the plaintiff is not a California resident, California's legitimate interests in the dispute have considerably diminished. The Supreme Court of California argued that the State had an interest in "protecting its consumers by ensuring that foreign manufacturers comply with the state's safety standards." 39 Cal. 3d, at 49, 702 P.2d, at 550. The State Supreme Court's defi-

---

R. Meyer, 762 F.2d 290, 293-295 (C.A.3 1985); DeJames v. Magnificence Carriers, Inc., 654 F.2d 280, 283 (3d Cir. 1981); *see also* Born, Reflections on Judicial Jurisdiction in International Cases, in 17 Ga. J. Int'l & Comp. L. 1 (1987); Lilly, Jurisdiction Over Domestic and Alien Defendants, 69 Va. L. Rev. 85, 127-145 (1983).

nition of California's interest, however, was overly broad. The dispute between Cheng Shin and Asahi is primarily about indemnification rather than safety standards. Moreover, it is not at all clear at this point that California law should govern the question whether a Japanese corporation should indemnify a Taiwanese corporation on the basis of a sale made in Taiwan and a shipment of goods from Japan to Taiwan. Phillips Petroleum v. Shutts, 472 U.S. 797, 821-822 (1985); Allstate Insurance Co. v. Hague, 449 U.S. 302, 312-313 (1981). The possibility of being haled into a California court as a result of an accident involving Asahi's components undoubtedly creates an additional deterrent to the manufacture of unsafe components; however, similar pressures will be placed on Asahi by the purchasers of its components as long as those who use Asahi components in their final products, and sell those products in California, are subject to the application of California tort law.

World-Wide Volkswagen also admonished courts to take into consideration the interests of the "several States," in addition to the forum state, in the efficient judicial resolution of the dispute and the advancement of substantive policies. In the present case, this advice calls for a court to consider the procedural and substantive policies of other *nations* whose interests are affected by the assertion of jurisdiction by the California court. The procedural and substantive interests of other nations in a state court's assertion of jurisdiction over an alien defendant will differ from case to case. In every case, however, those interests, as well as the Federal interest in its foreign relations policies, will be best served by a careful inquiry into the reasonableness of the assertion of jurisdiction in the particular case, and an unwillingness to find the serious burdens on an alien defendant outweighed by minimal interests on the part of the plaintiff or the forum State. "Great care and reserve should be exercised when extending our notions of personal jurisdiction into the international field." United States v. First National City Bank, 379 U.S. 378, 404 (1965) (Harlan, J., dissenting). *See* Born, Reflections on Judicial Jurisdiction in International Cases, in 17 Ga. J. Int'l & Comp. L. 1 (1987).

Considering the international context, the heavy burden on the alien defendant, and the slight interests of the plaintiff and the forum State, the exercise of personal jurisdiction by a California court over Asahi in this instance would be unreasonable and unfair.

III

Because the facts of this case do not establish minimum contacts such that the exercise of personal jurisdiction is consistent with fair play and substantial justice, the judgment of Supreme Court of California is reversed, and the case is remanded for further proceedings not inconsistent with this opinion.

It is so ordered.

Justice BRENNAN, with whom Justice WHITE, Justice MARSHALL, and Justice BLACKMUN join, concurring in part and in the judgment.

I do not agree with the plurality's interpretation of the stream-of-commerce theory, nor with its conclusion that Asahi did not "purposely avail itself of the California market." I do agree, however, with the Court's conclusion in Part II-B that the exercise of personal jurisdiction over Asahi in this case would not comport with "fair play and substantial justice," International Shoe Co. v. Washington, 326 U.S. 310, 320 (1945). This is one of those rare cases in which "minimum requirements inherent in the concept of 'fair play and substantial justice' . . . defeat the reasonableness of jurisdiction even [though] the defendant has purposefully engaged in forum activities." Burger King Corp. v. Rudzewicz, 471 U.S. 462, 477-478 (1985). I therefore join Parts I and II-B of the Court's opinion, and write separately to explain my disagreement with Part II-A.

. . . The stream of commerce refers not to unpredictable currents or eddies, but to the regular and anticipated flow of products from manufacture to distribution to retail sale. As long as a participant in this process is aware that the final product is being marketed in the forum State, the possibility of a lawsuit there cannot come as a surprise. Nor will the litigation present a burden for which there is no corresponding benefit. A defendant who has placed goods in the stream of commerce benefits economically from the retail sale of the final product in the forum State, and indirectly benefits from the State's laws that regulate and facilitate commercial activity. These benefits accrue regardless of whether that participant directly conducts business in the forum State, or engages in additional conduct directed toward that State. Accordingly, most courts and commentators have found that jurisdiction premised on the placement of a product into the stream of commerce is consistent with the Due Process Clause, and have not required a showing of additional conduct.

The plurality's endorsement of what appears to be the minority view among Federal Courts of Appeals represents a marked retreat from its analysis in World-Wide Volkswagen v. Woodson, 444 U.S. 286 (1980) . . .

The Court in *World-Wide Volkswagen* . . . took great care to distinguish "between a case involving goods which reach a distant State through a chain of distribution and a case involving goods which reach the same State because a consumer . . . took them there." 444 U.S., at 306-307 (Brennan, J., dissenting). The California Supreme Court took note of this distinction, and correctly concluded that our holding in *World-Wide Volkswagen* preserved the stream-of-commerce theory.

In this case, the facts found by the California Supreme Court support its finding of minimum contacts. The Court found that "[a]lthough Asahi did not design or control the system of distribution that carried its valve assemblies into California, Asahi was aware of the distribution system's operation, and it knew that it would benefit economically from the sale in California of products incorporating its components." Accordingly, I cannot join the plurality's determination that Asahi's regular and extensive sales of component parts to a manufacturer it knew was making regular sales of the final product in California is insufficient to establish minimum contacts with California.

Justice STEVENS, with whom Justice WHITE and Justice BLACKMUN join, concurring in part and concurring in the judgment.

The judgment of the Supreme Court of California should be reversed for the reasons stated in Part II-B of the Court's opinion. While I join Parts I and II-B, I do not join Part II-A for two reasons. First, it is not necessary to the Court's decision. An examination of minimum contacts is not always necessary to determine whether a state court's assertion of personal jurisdiction is constitutional. *See* Burger King Corp. v. Rudzewicz, 471 U.S. 462, 476-478 (1985). Part II-B establishes, after considering the factors set forth in World-Wide Volkswagen Corp. v. Woodson, 444 U.S. 286, 292 (1980), that California's exercise of jurisdiction over Asahi in this case would be "unreasonable and unfair." This finding alone requires reversal; this case fits within the rule that "minimum requirements inherent in the concept of 'fair play and substantial justice' may defeat the reasonableness of jurisdiction even if the defendant has purposefully engaged in forum activities." *Burger King*, 471 U.S., at 477-478 (quoting International Shoe Co. v. Washington, 326 U.S., 310, 320 (1945)). Accordingly, I see no reason in this case for the Court to articulate "purposeful direction" or any other test as the nexus between an act of a defendant and the forum State that is necessary to establish minimum contacts.

Second, even assuming that the test ought to be formulated here, Part II-A misapplies it to the facts of this case. The Court seems to assume that an unwavering line can be drawn between "mere awareness" that a component will find its way into the forum State and "purposeful availment" of the forum's market. Over the course of its dealings with Cheng Shin, Asahi has arguably engaged in a higher quantum of conduct than "[t]he placement of a product into the stream of commerce, without more. . . ." Whether or not this conduct rises to the level of purposeful availment requires a constitutional determination that is affected by the volume, the value, and the hazardous character of the components. In most circumstances I would be inclined to conclude that a regular course of dealing that results in deliveries of over 100,000 units annually over a period of several years would constitute "purposeful availment" even though the item delivered to the forum State was a standard product marketed throughout the world.

Questions and Comments

(1) Would the Zurchers have been able to sue Asahi directly if they had chosen to name it as defendant in the litigation? If so, presumably Cheng Shin's claim against Asahi would also be subject to jurisdiction in a California court. Would Cheng Shin be allowed to bring Asahi into the litigation if

the Zurchers did not name Asahi as defendant but their suit against Cheng Shin had not settled so that California retained some interest in the litigation?

(2) Is Cheng Shin in the same position as the Robinsons were in *World-Wide Volkswagen*, in the sense that the defective product was only in the forum because Cheng Shin sent it there?

(3) What is the relationship between parts IIA and IIB of the opinion? If, as Part IIA seems to indicate, jurisdiction violates due process because no action of the defendant was purposefully directed toward the forum state, then of what relevance is the discussion in IIB of the defendant's burden and the state's and plaintiff's interests? Conversely, with a majority joining IIB, why did a group of justices find it necessary to address the stream-of-commerce argument in IIA?

(4) Note the majority's suggestion in IIB that the federal interest in foreign relations ought to be considered in the due process calculus. It has been argued that choice of law and jurisdiction in international cases perhaps ought to reflect such federal concerns because of the exclusive federal power over international affairs. Brilmayer, Extraterritorial Application of American Law: A Methodological and Constitutional Appraisal, 50 Law & Contemp. Probs. 11 (1987).

(5) In Burger King Corp. v. Rudzewicz, 471 U.S. 462 (1984), the Court upheld Florida's assertion of jurisdiction over Michigan franchises. Defendants had applied for a franchise to Burger King's Michigan district office, and their application was forwarded to the Miami headquarters. One of the defendants, MacShara, attended a training course in Miami, and both defendants communicated directly with the Miami office over the contract provisions, especially after they encountered financial problems. The Court stated that jurisdiction is appropriate where a defendant "purposefully directs" his activities toward forum residents and where "the contacts proximately result from actions by the defendant *himself* that create a 'substantial connection' with the forum state." (Emphasis in original.)

> Once it has been decided that a defendant purposefully established minimum contacts within the forum State, these contacts may be considered in light of other factors to determine whether the assertion of personal jurisdiction would comport with "fair play and substantial justice." International Shoe Co. v. Washington, 326 U.S., at 320. Thus courts in "appropriate case[s]" may evaluate "the burden on the defendant," "the forum State's interest in adjudicating the dispute," "the plaintiff's interest in obtaining convenient and effective relief," "the interstate judicial system's interest in obtaining the most efficient resolution of controversies," and the "shared interest of the several States in furthering fundamental substantive social policies." World-Wide Volkswagen Corp. v. Woodson, 444 U.S., at 292. These considerations sometimes serve to establish the reasonableness of jurisdiction upon a lesser showing of minimum contacts than would otherwise be required. *See, e.g.*, Keeton v. Hustler Magazine, Inc., *supra*, at 780; Calder v. Jones, *supra*, at 788-789;

> McGee v. International Life Insurance Co., *supra,* at 223-224. On the other hand, where a defendant who purposefully has directed his activities at forum residents seeks to defeat jurisdiction, he must present a compelling case that the presence of some other considerations would render jurisdiction unreasonable. Most such considerations usually may be accommodated through means short of finding jurisdiction unconstitutional. For example, the potential clash of the forum's law with the "fundamental substantive social policies" of another State may be accommodated through application of the forum's choice-of-law rules. Similarly, a defendant claiming substantial inconvenience may seek a change of venue. Nevertheless, minimum requirements inherent in the concept of "fair play and substantial justice" may defeat the reasonableness of jurisdiction even if the defendant has purposefully engaged in forum activities. World-Wide Volkswagen Corp. v. Woodson, *supra,* at 292; *see also* Restatement (Second) of Conflict of Laws §§36-37 (1971). As we previously have noted, jurisdictional rules may not be employed in such a way as to make litigation "so gravely difficult and inconvenient" that a party unfairly is at a "severe disadvantage" in comparison to his opponent. The Bremen v. Zapata Off-Shore Co., 407 U.S. 1, 18 (1972) (*re* forum-selection provisions); McGee v. International Life Insurance Co., *supra,* at 223-224.

471 U.S. at 476-478.

The Court then cited a number of factors in support of its affirmance of jurisdiction such as the defendant's refusal to make contractually required payments in Miami, the fact that the defendant deliberately affiliated himself with a Florida company, and the presence of a contract clause choosing Florida law. The Court rejected the argument that Burger King was such a large corporation that it could conveniently litigate anywhere in the country and that Burger King was guilty of misrepresentation, fraud, or duress. Justices Stevens and White dissented on the grounds that the defendant was a purely local Michigan operation, and that franchise relationships characteristically display a disparity of bargaining power.

(6) *Asahi, Burger King,* and the requirement of purposeful availment have provoked extensive critical academic scrutiny. *See, e.g.,* Sheehan, Predicting the Future: Personal Jurisdiction for the Twenty-First Century, 66 U. Cin. L. Rev. 385 (1998); Stewart, A New Litany of Personal Jurisdiction, 60 U. Colo. L. Rev. 5 (1989); Symposium, *Asahi Metal Industry Co. v. Superior Court* and the Future of Personal Jurisdiction, 39 S.C.L. Rev. 815 (1988); Dessem, Personal Jurisdiction after *Asahi:* The Other (International) Shoe Drops, 55 Tenn. L. Rev. 41 (1987); Weintraub, *Asahi* Sends Personal Jurisdiction Down the Tubes, 23 Texas Intl. L.J. 55 (1988); Cox, The Interrelationship of Personal Jurisdiction and Choice of Law: Forging New Theory Through *Asahi Metal Industry Co. v. Superior Court,* 49 U. Pitt. L. Rev. 189 (1987).

(7) "Stream of commerce" cases are common, especially in the products liability area. In addition to *World-Wide Volkswagen* and *Asahi, see* Grange

Insurance Associates v. State, 110 Wash. 2d 752, 757 P.2d 933 (1988), in which it was held that there was no jurisdiction over Idaho for negligence in certifying as free of brucellosis livestock destined for immediate sale to a Washington buyer. The veterinarian's certificate specified a Washington destination for the cattle; should such conduct satisfy the *Asahi* test? *See also* Clune v. Alimak AB, 233 F.3d 538 (8th Cir. 2000); Alpine View Co. v. Atlas Copco AB, 205 F.3d 208 (5th Cir. 2000); Pennzoil Prods. Co. v. Colelli & Assocs., 149 F.3d 197 (3rd Cir. 1998); Viam Corp. v. Iowa Export-Import Trading Co., 84 F.3d 424 (Fed. Cir. 1996); In re Celotex Corp. v. Rapid American Corp., 124 F.3d 619 (4th Cir. 1997); CMMC v. Salinas, 929 S.W.2d 435 (Tex. 1996).

(8) In footnote * of *Asahi,* the Court states that it has "no occasion to determine whether Congress could, consistent with the Due Process Clause of the Fifth Amendment, authorize federal court personal jurisdiction over alien defendants based on the aggregate of *national* contacts, rather than on the contacts between the defendant and the State in which the federal court sits." *See also* Omni Capital Intl. v. Rudolf Wolff & Co., 484 U.S. 97, 103 n. 5 (1987) (same). Many courts have held that a national contacts test satisfies the Fifth Amendment due process clause. *See, e.g.*, Go-Video, Inc. v. Akai Elec. Co., 885 F. 2d 1406 (9th Cir. 1989). Other courts have tempered this conclusion by insisting that due process requires not only minimum contacts with the nation, but also that the venue for the suit be fair and reasonable. *See, e.g.*, Peay v. Bellsouth Medical Assistance Plan, 205 F.3d 1206, 1212 (10th Cir. 2000).

A 1993 Amendment to Federal Rule of Civil Procedure 4 provides a federal long-arm statute authorization in cases arising under federal laws which themselves lack a long-arm statute. It provides: "If the exercise of jurisdiction is consistent with the Constitution and laws of the United States, serving a summons or filing a waiver of service is also *effective,* with respect to claims arising under federal law, to establish personal jurisdiction over the person of any defendant who is not subject to the jurisdiction of the courts of general jurisdiction of any state." Fed. R. Civ. P. 4(k)(2). Under Rule 4(k)(2), federal courts may exercise jurisdiction over a defendant (a) against whom a federal claim is asserted, (b) who has nationwide contacts; and (c) who is not subject to personal jurisdiction in any state. U.S.A. v. Swiss American Bank, 191 F.3d 30, 38 (7th Cir. 1999).

In addition to the question of the constitutionality of using nationwide contacts for personal jurisdiction in federal question cases, Rule 4(k)(2) raises two additional difficulties. The first is whether it exceeds the Rules Enabling Act's prohibition on Rules that "abridge, enlarge, or modify any substantive rights." 28 U.S.C. §2072(b). The Advisory Committee on the Civil Rules worried that it might. *See* H.R. Doc. No. 103-74, at 154-55 (1993). The second problem concerns the conundrum of establishing Rule 4(k)(2)'s requirement that the defendant lacks adequate contacts for personal jurisdiction in any particular state. The general rule is that the burden of proof lies with the party attempting to assert jurisdiction. But it is very hard for a plaintiff to demonstrate that the defendant lacks adequate contacts in each of the 50 states, especially since the defendant controls much of the relevant information. *See Swiss American Bank,* 191 F.3d at 40. On the other hand, shifting the burden to the defendant requires the defendant to either concede amenability to suit in either federal court (by admitting that no state court has jurisdiction) or in a state court (arguing that it has sufficient contacts with some state). *Id.* at 40-41. Courts have resolved this problem in different ways. Most courts follow the traditional rule and require the plaintiff to prove no jurisdiction in any of the fifty states. *See, e.g.,* CFMT Inc. v. Steag Microtech, Inc., 1997 WL 313161 (D. Del. 1997). The Seventh Circuit, by contrast, assigns the burden to the defendant; on this view, a defendant who wishes to defeat personal jurisdiction under Rule 4(k)(2) must name some state court in which the suit could proceed. *See* ISI Intl., Inc. v. Borden Ladner Gervais Llp, 2001 U.S. App. LEXIS 15026 (7th Cir. 2001). The First Circuit, by contrast, shifts the burden to the defendant only after the plaintiff has made a prima facie for the applicability of Rule 4(k)(2). *See Swiss American Bank,* 191 F.3d at 26. For commentary on these and other aspects of Rule 4(k)(2), see Burbank, The United States' Approach to International Civil Litigation: Recent Developments in Forum Selection, 19 U. Pa. J. Intl. Econ. L. 1, 13 (1998).

(9) Transactions on the Internet raise significant challenges for the "minimum contacts" test. We discuss these issues *infra* pages 816-826.

C. Jurisdiction Based on Property

In Harris v. Balk, 198 U.S. 215 (1905), the famous bête noir of first-year civil procedure students, Harris and Balk were from North Carolina. Harris owed Balk $180. Harris visited Maryland, where Epstein "seized" the debt owed to Balk to help satisfy a claim that Epstein had against Balk for a greater amount. The action proceeded against Harris in Maryland. He put up no defense, admitting that he owed the money to Balk and not involving himself in the merits of the dispute between Epstein and Balk. Epstein won the Maryland judgment and collected the $180. When Harris returned to North Carolina, Balk sued him for the $180. Harris claimed the Maryland judgment in bar. The Supreme Court upheld the defense. Note that two holdings were necessary to reach the result in Harris v. Balk: (1) A debt, though intangible property, is subject to seizure like tangible property; and (2) the debt is "located" where the debtor is (and not where the creditor-owner is) because that is where the debtor can be sued and the debt realized.

Perhaps the cleverest use ever made of the doctrine of Harris v. Balk occurred in Siro v. American Express Co., 99 Conn. 95, 121 A. 280 (1923).

Plaintiff had a claim against American Express but either could not or did not bother to obtain personal jurisdiction over American Express in Connecticut. Instead, plaintiff's lawyers had another lawyer go to the bank and buy $620 worth of travelers' checks. He made no representation to the bank about the purpose of his purchase. As soon as he left the bank, a deputy sheriff served garnishment papers on the bank—by accepting the lawyer's money, it became indebted to American Express under the agreement by which the bank sold American Express travelers' checks. The lawyer who bought the checks had done so with money supplied by the plaintiff's attorneys, and shortly after buying them he deposited them at another bank to the account of the plaintiff's attorneys. The court upheld jurisdiction on the basis of Harris v. Balk and ruled that there had been no fraudulent inducement of assets into the state because no misrepresentations had been made. The court added, "If the defendant has a good defense to the plaintiff's suit, it should rather welcome its determination by a judicial tribunal than seek to avoid or postpone the issue by a technicality."

The doctrine of Harris v. Balk survived until surprisingly recent times.

Shaffer v. Heitner

433 U.S. 186 (1977)

Justice MARSHALL delivered the opinion of the Court.

The controversy in this case concerns the constitutionality of a Delaware statute that allows a court of that State to take jurisdiction of a lawsuit by sequestering any property of the defendant that happens to be located in Delaware. Appellants contend that the sequestration statute as applied in this case violates the Due Process Clause of the Fourteenth Amendment both because it permits the state courts to exercise jurisdiction despite the absence of sufficient contacts among the defendants, the litigation, and the State of Delaware and because it authorizes the deprivation of defendants' property without providing adequate procedural safeguards. We find it necessary to consider only the first of these contentions.

I

Appellee Heitner, a nonresident of Delaware, is the owner of one share of stock in the Greyhound Corporation, a business incorporated under the laws of Delaware with its principal place of business in Phoenix, Ariz. On May 22, 1974, he filed a shareholder's derivative suit in the Court of Chancery for New Castle County, Del., in which he named as defendants Greyhound, its wholly owned subsidiary Greyhound Lines, Inc. and 28 present or former officers or directors of one or both of the corporations. In essence Heitner alleged that the individual defendants had violated their duties to Greyhound by causing it and its subsidiaries to engage in actions that resulted in the corporation's being held liable for substantial damages in a private antitrust suit and a large fine in a criminal contempt action. The activities which led to these penalties took place in Oregon.

Simultaneously with his complaint, Heitner filed a motion for an order of sequestration of the Delaware property of the individual defendants pursuant to 10 Del. C. §366. This motion was accompanied by a supporting affidavit of counsel which stated that the individual defendants were nonresidents of Delaware. The affidavit identified the property to be sequestered as

> common stock, 3% Second Cumulative Preferred Stock and stock unit credits of the Defendant Greyhound Corporation, a Delaware corporation, as well as all options and all warrants to purchase said stock issued to said individual Defendants and all contractual obligations, all rights, debts or credits due or accrued to or for the benefit of any of the said Defendants under any type of written agreement, contract, or other legal instrument of any kind whatever between any of the individual Defendants and said corporation.

The requested sequestration order was signed the day the motion was filed. Pursuant to that order, the sequestrator "seized" approximately 82,000 shares of Greyhound common stock belonging to 19 of the defendants, and options belonging to another two defendants. These seizures are accomplished by placing "stop transfer" orders or their equivalents on the books of the Greyhound Corporation. So far as the record shows, none of the certificates representing the seized property was physically present in Delaware. The stock was considered to be in Delaware, and so subject to seizure, by virtue of a Del. C. §169, which makes Delaware the situs of ownership of all stock in Delaware corporations.

All 28 defendants were notified of the initiation of the suit by certified mail directed to their last known addresses and by publication in a New Castle County newspaper. The 21 defendants whose property was seized (hereafter referred to as appellants) responded by entering a special appearance for the purpose of moving to quash service of process and to vacate the sequestration order. They contended that the ex parte sequestration procedure did not accord them due process of law and that the property seized was not capable of attachment in Delaware. In addition, appellants asserted that under the rule of International Shoe Co. v. Washington, they did not have sufficient contacts with Delaware to sustain the jurisdiction of that State's courts.

The Court of Chancery rejected these arguments. . . .

On appeal, the Delaware Supreme Court affirmed the judgment of the court of chancery. . . .

We noted probable jurisdiction. We reverse.

II

The Delaware courts rejected appellants' jurisdictional challenge by noting that this suit was brought as a quasi in rem proceeding. Since quasi in rem jurisdiction is traditionally based on attachment or seizure of property present in the jurisdiction, not on contacts between the defendant and the State, the courts considered appellants' claimed lack of contacts with Delaware to be unimportant. This categorical analysis assumes the continuous soundness of the conceptual structure founded on the century-old case of Pennoyer v. Neff. . . .

III

The case for applying to jurisdiction in rem the same test of "fair play and substantial justice" as governs assertions of jurisdiction in personam is simple and straightforward. It is premised on recognition that "[t]he phrase, 'judicial jurisdiction over a thing,' is a customary elliptical way of referring to jurisdiction over the interests of persons in a thing." Restatement (Second) of Conflict of Laws §56, introductory note. This recognition leads to the conclusion that in order to justify an exercise of jurisdiction in rem, the basis for jurisdiction must be sufficient to justify exercising "jurisdiction over the interests of persons in a thing." The standard for determining whether an exercise of jurisdiction over the interests of persons is consistent with the Due Process Clause is the minimum contacts standard elucidated in *International Shoe.*

This argument, of course, does not ignore the fact that the presence of property in a State may bear on the existence of jurisdiction by providing contacts among the forum State, the defendant, and the litigation. For example, when claims to the property itself are the source of the underlying controversy between the plaintiff and the defendant,[24] it would be unusual for the State where the property is located not to have jurisdiction. In such cases, the defendant's claim to property located in the State would normally indi-

---

24. This category includes true in rem actions and the first type of quasi in rem proceedings. *See* n.17 [which follows:]

[17. "A judgment in rem affects the interests of all persons in designated property. A judgment quasi in rem affects the interests of particular persons in designated property. The latter is of two types. In one the plaintiff is seeking to secure a pre-existing claim in the subject property and to extinguish or establish the nonexistence of similar interests of particular persons. In the other the plaintiff seeks to apply what he concedes to be the property of the defendant to the satisfaction of a claim against him. Restatement, Judgments, 5-9." Hanson v. Denckla, 357 U.S. 235, 246 n.12.

As did the Court in *Hanson,* we will for convenience generally use the term "in rem" in place of "in rem and quasi in rem."]

cate that he expected to benefit from the State's protection of his interest. The State's strong interests in assuring the marketability of property within its borders and in providing a procedure for peaceful resolution of disputes about the possession of that property could also support jurisdiction, as would the likelihood that important records and witnesses will be found in the State.[28] The presence of property may also favor jurisdiction in cases, such as suits for injury suffered on the land of an absentee owner, where the defendant's ownership of the property is conceded but the cause of action is otherwise related to rights and duties growing out of that ownership.

It appears, therefore, that jurisdiction over many types of actions which now are or might be brought in rem would not be affected by a holding that any assertion of state court jurisdiction must satisfy the *International Shoe* standard.[30] For the type of quasi in rem action typified by Harris v. Balk and the present case, however, accepting the proposed analysis would result in significant change. These are cases where the property which now serves as the basis for state court jurisdiction is completely unrelated to the plaintiff's cause of action. Thus, although the presence of the defendant's property in a State might suggest the existence of other ties among the defendant, the State, and the litigation, the presence of the property alone would not support the State's jurisdiction. If those other ties did not exist, cases over which the State is now thought to have jurisdiction could not be brought in that forum.

Since acceptance of the *International Shoe* test would most affect this class of cases, we examine the arguments against adopting that standard as they relate to this category of litigation. Before doing so, however, we note that this type of case also presents the clearest illustration of the argument in favor of assessing assertions of jurisdiction by a single standard. For in cases such as *Harris* and this one, the only role played by the property is to provide the basis for bringing the defendant into court. Indeed, the express purpose of the Delaware sequestration procedure is to compel the defendant to enter a personal appearance. In such cases, if a direct assertion of personal jurisdiction over the defendant would violate the Constitution, it would seem that an indirect assertion of that jurisdiction should be equally impermissible.

The primary rationale for treating the presence of property as a sufficient basis for jurisdiction to adjudicate claims over which the State would not have jurisdiction if *International Shoe* applied is that a wrongdoer "should not be able to avoid payment of his obligations by the expedient of removing

---

28. We do not suggest that these illustrations include all the factors that may affect the decision, nor that the factors we have mentioned are necessarily decisive.

30. *Cf.* Smit, The Enduring Utility of In Rem Rules: A Lasting Legacy of *Pennoyer v. Neff*, 48 Brooklyn L. Rev. 600 (1977). We do not suggest that jurisdictional doctrines other than those discussed in text, such as the particularized rules governing adjudications of status, are inconsistent with the standard of fairness.

his assets to a place where he is not subject to an in personam suit." Restatement (Second) of Conflicts §66, comment *a.* This justification, however, does not explain why jurisdiction should be recognized without regard to whether the property is present in the State because of an effort to avoid the owner's obligations. Nor does it support jurisdiction to adjudicate the underlying claim. At most, it suggests that a State in which property is located should have jurisdiction to attach that property, by use of proper procedures, as security for a judgment being sought in a forum where the litigation can be maintained consistently with *International Shoe.* Moreover, we know of nothing to justify the assumption that a debtor can avoid paying his obligations by removing his property to a State in which his creditor cannot obtain personal jurisdiction over him. The Full Faith and Credit Clause, after all, makes the valid in personam judgment of one State enforceable in all other States.[36]

It might also be suggested that allowing in rem jurisdiction avoids the uncertainty inherent in the *International Shoe* standard and assures a plaintiff of a forum.[37] We believe, however, that the fairness standard of *International Shoe* can be easily applied in the vast majority of cases. Moreover, when the existence of jurisdiction in a particular forum under *International Shoe* is unclear, the cost of simplifying the litigation by avoiding the jurisdictional question may be the sacrifice of "fair play and substantial justice." That cost is too high.

We are left, then, to consider the significance of the long history of jurisdiction based solely on the presence of property in a State. Although the theory that territorial power is both essential to and sufficient for jurisdiction has been undermined, we have never held that the presence of property in a State does not automatically confer jurisdiction over the owner's interest in that property. This history must be considered as supporting the proposition that jurisdiction based solely on the presence of property satisfies the demands of due process, but it is not decisive. "[T]raditional notions of fair play and substantial justice" can be as readily offended by the perpetuation of ancient forms that are no longer justified as by the adoption of new procedures that are inconsistent with the basic values of our constitutional heritage. The fiction that an assertion of jurisdiction over property is anything but an assertion of jurisdiction over the owner of the property supports an ancient form without substantial modern justification. Its continued acceptance would

---

36. Once it has been determined by a court of competent jurisdiction that the defendant is a debtor of the plaintiff, there would seem to be no unfairness in allowing an action to realize on that debt in a State where the defendant has property, whether or not that State would have jurisdiction to determine the existence of the debt as an original matter.

37. This case does not raise, and we therefore do not consider, the question whether the presence of a defendant's property in a State is a sufficient basis for jurisdiction when no other forum is available to the plaintiff.

serve only to allow state court jurisdiction that is fundamentally unfair to the defendant.

We therefore conclude that all assertions of state court jurisdiction must be evaluated according to the standards set forth in *International Shoe* and its progeny.[39]

IV

The Delaware courts based their assertion of jurisdiction in this case solely on the statutory presence of appellants' property in Delaware. Yet that property is not the subject matter of this litigation, nor is the underlying cause of action related to the property. Appellants' holdings in Greyhound do not, therefore, provide contacts with Delaware sufficient to support the jurisdiction of that State's courts over appellants. If it exists, that jurisdiction must have some other foundation.

Appellee Heitner did not allege and does not now claim that appellants have ever set foot in Delaware. Nor does he identify any act related to his cause of action as having taken place in Delaware. Nevertheless, he contends that appellants' positions as directors and officers of a corporation chartered in Delaware provide sufficient "contacts, ties, or relations," International Shoe Co. v. Washington, with that State to give its courts jurisdiction over appellants in this stockholder's derivative action. This argument is based primarily on what Heitner asserts to be the strong interest of Delaware in supervising the management of a Delaware corporation. That interest is said to derive from the role of Delaware law in establishing the corporation and defining the obligations owed to it by its officers and directors. In order to protect this interest, appellee concludes, Delaware's courts must have jurisdiction over corporate fiduciaries such as appellants.

This argument is undercut by the failure of the Delaware Legislature to assert the state interest appellee finds so compelling. Delaware law bases jurisdiction not on appellants' status as corporate fiduciaries, but rather on the presence of their property in the State. Although the sequestration procedure used here may be most frequently used in derivative suits against officers and directors, the authorizing statute evinces no specific concern with such actions. Sequestration can be used in any suit against a nonresident, and reaches corporate fiduciaries only if they happen to own interests in a Delaware corporation, or other property in the State. But as Heitner's failure to secure jurisdiction over seven of the defendants named in his complaint demonstrates, there is no necessary relationship between

39. It would not be fruitful for us to re-examine the facts of cases decided on the rationales of *Pennoyer* and *Harris* to determine whether jurisdiction might have been sustained under the standard we adopt today. To the extent that prior decisions are inconsistent with this standard, they are overruled.

holding a position as a corporate fiduciary and owning stock or other interests in the corporation. If Delaware perceived its interest in securing jurisdiction over corporate fiduciaries to be as great as Heitner suggests, we would expect it to have enacted a statute more clearly designed to protect that interest.

Moreover, even if Heitner's assessment of the importance of Delaware's interest is accepted, his argument fails to demonstrate that Delaware is a fair forum for this litigation. The interest appellee has identified may support the application of Delaware law to resolve any controversy over appellants' actions in their capacities as officers and directors.[44] But we have rejected the argument that if a State's law can properly be applied to a dispute, its courts necessarily have jurisdiction over the parties to that dispute.

Appellee suggests that by accepting positions as officers or directors of a Delaware corporation, appellants performed the acts required by Hanson v. Denckla. He notes that Delaware law provides substantial benefits to corporate officers and directors, and that these benefits were at least in part the incentive for appellants to assume their positions. It is, he says, "only fair and just" to require appellants, in return for these benefits, to respond in the State of Delaware when they are accused of misusing their powers.

But like Heitner's first argument, this line of reasoning establishes only that it is appropriate for Delaware law to govern the obligations of appellants to Greyhound and its stockholders. It does not demonstrate that appellants have "purposefully avail[ed themselves] of the privilege of conducting activities within the forum State," Hanson v. Denckla, in a way that would justify bringing them before a Delaware tribunal. Appellants have simply had nothing to do with the State of Delaware. Moreover, appellants had no reason to expect to be haled before a Delaware court. Delaware, unlike some States, has not enacted a statute that treats acceptance of a directorship as consent to jurisdiction in the State. And "[i]t strains reason . . . to suggest that anyone buying securities in a corporation formed in Delaware 'impliedly consents' to subject himself to Delaware's . . . jurisdiction on any cause of action." Appellants, who were not required to acquire interests in Greyhound in order to hold their positions, did not by acquiring those interests surrender their right to be brought to judgment only in States with which they had had "minimum contacts."

---

44. In general, the law of the State of incorporation is held to govern the liabilities of officers or directors to the corporation and its stockholders. *See* Restatement (Second) of Conflict of Laws §309. *But see* Cal. Corp. Code §2115 (West Supp. 1976). The rationale for the general rule appears to be based more on the need for a uniform and certain standard to govern the internal affairs of a corporation than on the perceived interest of the state of incorporation.

The judgment of the Delaware Supreme Court must, therefore, be reversed.

It is so ordered.

Justice REHNQUIST took no part in the consideration or decision of this case.

Justice POWELL, concurring.

I agree that the principles of International Shoe Co. v. Washington should be extended to govern assertions of in rem as well as in personam jurisdiction in state court. I also agree that neither the statutory presence of appellants' stock in Delaware nor their positions as directors and officers of a Delaware corporation can provide sufficient contacts to support the Delaware courts' assertion of jurisdiction in this case.

I would explicitly reserve judgment, however, on whether the ownership of some forms of property whose situs is indisputably and permanently located within a State may, without more, provide the contacts necessary to subject a defendant to jurisdiction within the State to the extent of the value of the property. In the case of real property, in particular, preservation of the common law concept of quasi in rem jurisdiction arguably would avoid the uncertainty of the general *International Shoe* standard without significant cost to "traditional notions of fair play and substantial justice."

Subject to that reservation, I join the opinion of the Court.

Justice STEVENS, concurring in the judgment.

The Due Process Clause affords protection against "judgments without notice." International Shoe Co. v. Washington (opinion of Black, J.). Throughout our history the acceptable exercise of in rem and quasi in rem jurisdiction has included a procedure giving reasonable assurance that actual notice of the particular claim will be conveyed to the defendant. Thus, publication, notice by registered mail, or extraterritorial personal service has been an essential ingredient of any procedure that serves as a substitute for personal service within the jurisdiction.

The requirement of fair notice also, I believe, includes fair warning that a particular activity may subject a person to the jurisdiction of a foreign sovereign. If I visit another state, or acquire real estate or open a bank account in it, I knowingly assume some risk that the state will exercise its power over my property or my person while there. My contact with the state, though minimal, gives rise to predictable risks.

Perhaps the same consequences should flow from the purchase of stock of a corporation organized under the laws of a foreign state, because to some limited extent one's property and affairs then become subject to the laws of the state of domicile of the corporation. As a matter of international law, that suggestion might be acceptable because a foreign investment is sufficiently unusual to make it appropriate to require the investor to study the ramifications of his decision. But a purchase of securities in the domestic market is an entirely different matter.

One who purchases shares of stock on the open market can hardly be expected to know that he has thereby become subject to suit in a forum remote from his residence and unrelated to the transaction. As a practical matter, the Delaware Sequestration Statute created an unacceptable risk of judgment without notice. Unlike the 49 other States, Delaware treats the place of incorporation as the situs of the stock, even though both the owner and the custodian of the shares are elsewhere. Moreover, Delaware denies the defendant the opportunity to defend the merits of the suit unless he subjects himself to the unlimited jurisdiction of the court. Thus, it coerces a defendant either to submit to personal jurisdiction in a forum which could not otherwise obtain such jurisdiction or to lose the securities which have been attached. If its procedure were upheld, Delaware would, in effect, impose a duty of inquiry on every purchaser of securities in the national market. For unless the purchaser ascertains both the state of incorporation of the company whose shares he is buying, and also the idiosyncrasies of its law, he may be assuming an unknown risk of litigation. I therefore agree with the Court that on the record before us no adequate basis for jurisdiction exists and that the Delaware statute is unconstitutional on its face.

How the Court's opinion may be applied in other contexts is not entirely clear to me. I agree with Mr. Justice Powell that it should not be read to invalidate in rem jurisdiction where real estate is involved. I would also not read it as invalidating other long accepted methods of acquiring jurisdiction over persons with adequate notice of both the particular controversy and also that their local activities might subject them to suit. My uncertainty as to the reach of the opinion, and my fear that it purports to decide a great deal more than is necessary to dispose of this case, persuade me merely to concur in the judgment.

Justice BRENNAN, concurring and dissenting.

I join Parts I-III of the Court's opinion. I fully agree that the minimum-contacts analysis developed in International Shoe Co. v. Washington represents a far more sensible construct for the exercise of state court jurisdiction than the patchwork of legal and factual fictions that has been generated from the decision in Pennoyer v. Neff. It is precisely because the inquiry into minimum contacts is now of such overriding importance, however, that I must respectfully dissent from Part IV of the Court's opinion. . . .

II

. . . While evidence derived through discovery might satisfy me that minimum contacts are lacking in a given case, I am convinced that as a general rule a state forum has jurisdiction to adjudicate a shareholder derivative action centering on the conduct and policies of the directors and officers of a corporation chartered by that State. Unlike the Court, I therefore would not foreclose Delaware from asserting jurisdiction over appellants were it persuaded to do so on the basis of minimum contacts.

It is well settled that a derivative lawsuit as presented here does not inure primarily to the benefit of the named plaintiff. Rather, the primary beneficiaries are the corporation and its owners, the shareholders. "The cause of action which such a plaintiff brings before the court is not his own but the corporation's. . . . Such a plaintiff may represent an important public and stockholder interest in bringing faithless managers to book."

Viewed in this light, the chartering State has an unusually powerful interest in insuring the availability of a convenient forum for litigating claims involving a possible multiplicity of defendant fiduciaries and for vindicating the State's substantive policies regarding the management of its domestic corporations. I believe that our cases fairly establish that the State's valid substantive interests are important considerations in assessing whether it constitutionally may claim jurisdiction over a given cause of action.

In this instance, Delaware can point to at least three interrelated public policies that are furthered by its assertion of jurisdiction. First, the State has a substantial interest in providing restitution for its local corporations that allegedly have been victimized by fiduciary misconduct, even if the managerial decisions occurred outside the State. . . . I, of course, am not suggesting that Delaware's varied interests would justify its acceptance of jurisdiction over any transaction touching upon the affairs of its domestic corporations. But a derivative action which raises allegations of abuses of the basic management of an institution whose existence is created by the State and whose powers and duties are defined by state law fundamentally implicates the public policies of that forum.

To be sure, the Court is not blind to these considerations. It notes that the State's interests "may support the application of Delaware law to resolve any controversy over appellants' actions in their capacities as officers and directors." But this, the Court argues, pertains to choice of law, not jurisdiction. I recognize that the jurisdictional and choice-of-law inquiries are not identical. Hanson v. Denckla. But I would not compartmentalize thinking in this area quite so rigidly as it seems to me the Court does today, for both inquiries "are often closely related and to a substantial degree depend upon similar considerations." *Id.* (Black, J. dissenting). In either case an important linchpin is the extent of contacts between the controversy, the parties, and the forum state. While constitutional limitations on the choice of law are by no means settled, *see, e.g.*, Home Ins. Co. v. Dick, important considerations certainly include the expectancies of the parties and the fairness of governing the defendants' acts and behavior by rules of conduct created by a given jurisdiction. *See, e.g.*, Restatement (Second) Choice of Law §6. These same factors bear upon the propriety of a State's exercising jurisdiction over a legal dispute. At the minimum, the decision that it is fair to bind a defendant by a State's laws and rules should prove to be highly relevant to the fairness of permitting that same State to accept jurisdiction for adjudicating the controversy. . . .

I, therefore, would approach the minimum contacts analysis differently than does the Court. Crucial to me is the fact that appellants voluntarily associated themselves with the State of Delaware, "invoking the benefits and protections of its laws," Hanson v. Denckla; International Shoe Co. v. Washington, by entering into a long term and fragile relationship with one of its domestic corporations. They thereby elected to assume powers and to undertake responsibilities wholly derived from that State's rules and regulations, and to become eligible for those benefits that Delaware law makes available to its corporations' officials. *E.g.*, 8 Del. C. §§143 (interest-free loans); 145 (indemnification). While it is possible that countervailing issues of judicial efficiency and the like might clearly favor a different forum, they do not appear on the meager record before us; and, of course, we are concerned solely with "minimum" contacts, not the "best" contacts. I thus do not believe that it is unfair to insist that appellants make themselves available to suit in a competent forum that Delaware might create for vindication of its important public policies directly pertaining to appellants' fiduciary associations with the State.

Sternberg v. O'Neil

550 A.2d 1105 (Del. 1988)

[The facts of the case can be found in a portion of the opinion excerpted at page 463 *supra.*]

In the first portion of this opinion, we concluded that GenCorp has expressly consented to the general jurisdiction of the State of Delaware. However, for the purpose of discerning any implied consent to Delaware's jurisdiction, we will limit our inquiry to GenCorp's implicit consent to specific jurisdiction in the double derivative action brought by Sternberg. The question which we will address is whether a foreign corporation's ownership of a Delaware corporate subsidiary, constitutes a due process minimum contact which permits Delaware courts to assert specific jurisdiction over the foreign parent corporation in a double derivative action.

. . . [W]hether the requisite minimum contacts exist is determined by examining the relationship between the defendant, the forum and the litigation. Shaffer v. Heitner, 433 U.S. at 204. Our analysis of GenCorp's implied consent to Delaware's specific jurisdiction in this case must focus, therefore, upon the relationship between GenCorp, Delaware, and Sternberg's lawsuit.

GenCorp is an Ohio corporation. For more than thirty years, GenCorp has owned 100% of the issued and outstanding shares of RKO General, a Delaware corporation. Sternberg's action is a double derivative suit. One aspect of the suit alleges mismanagement and breaches of fiduciary duty on the part of the directors of RKO General, the Delaware corporation, resulting in detriment to that corporation and therefore to GenCorp, the sole stockholder of that Delaware corporation. The other aspect of the Sternberg suit alleges mismanagement and breaches of fiduciary duty on the part of the GenCorp directors. Sternberg's complaint alleges that as a result of the breaches of fiduciary duty by the directors and officers of each of the corporations, RKO General has lost its radio and television broadcast licenses or the value thereof, to the detriment of both GenCorp and RKO General.

We must decide whether or not Delaware has specific jurisdiction to hear this controversy. The Court of Chancery concluded that GenCorp's ownership of a Delaware subsidiary was an insufficient contact with this State to establish a basis for personal jurisdiction. . . . The Court of Chancery ruled that Delaware had no authority to exercise in personam jurisdiction over GenCorp and that since GenCorp was an indispensable party, the entire case must be dismissed. On appeal, GenCorp argues that this conclusion was correct and is mandated by the holding in *Shaffer*.

[The Court discusses the facts and holding of *Shaffer*.]

. . . As one legal scholar has observed "whatever its nuances, the obvious impact of *Shaffer* is to limit jurisdiction where the property of a nonresident is seized in order to provide a basis for prosecuting an unrelated claim." Lilly, Jurisdiction over Domestic and Alien Defendants, 69 Va. L. Rev. 85, 98 (1983).

Shaffer Distinguished

One of the first *in rem* actions to come before this Court after *Shaffer* involved the attachment of a parent-foreign corporation's stock interest in a wholly owned Delaware subsidiary. Papendick v. Bosch, Del. Supr., 410 A.2d 148 (1979), *cert. denied*, 446 U.S. 909, 100 S. Ct. 1837 (1980). In *Papendick*, the litigation involved an alleged breach of contract. The parent foreign corporation had formed a Delaware subsidiary for the purpose of executing the contract which was in dispute. This Court found that a foreign corporation which had formed a Delaware subsidiary for the purpose of implementing a contract, had implicitly consented to the jurisdiction of the Delaware courts in an action brought against both corporations alleging a breach of that contract. *Id.* at 152. In *Papendick*, this Court followed the directive of *Shaffer* to focus upon the defendant, the forum, and the litigation *Id.*

In *Papendick*, after distinguishing the facts in *Shaffer*, this Court acknowledged its obligations to apply the *International Shoe* minimum contact standard, in accordance with the *Shaffer* holding. This Court was not only aware that the standards of *International Shoe* were to be applied, but that "[t]he requirements of *International Shoe* . . . must be met as to each defendant over whom a state court exercises jurisdiction." *Rush v. Savchuk*. Jurisdiction over a wholly owned Delaware subsidiary does not automatically establish jurisdiction over the parent corporation in *any* forum. *Cf.* Cannon Mfg. Co. v. Cudahy Packing Co., 267 U.S. 333 (1925).[28] Therefore, both the parent and the subsidiary corporation's contacts with the forum state must be assessed individually.

The decision of the foreign parent corporation to maintain a direct and continuing connection between Delaware and itself, as the owner of a Delaware subsidiary, was found to be a "minimum contact" of paramount importance in the specific jurisdictional analysis of *Papendick:*

> We do not believe that the *International Shoe* "minimum contact" due process standards were intended to deprive Delaware courts of jurisdiction by permitting an alien corporation to come into this State to create a Delaware corporate subsidiary for the purpose of implementing a contract under the protection of and pursuant to powers granted by the laws of Delaware, and then be heard to say, in a suit arising from the very contract which the subsidiary was created to implement, that the only contact between it and Delaware is the "mere" ownership of stock of the subsidiary.
>
> The latter point is most significant in applying *International Shoe* standards. There is a controlling distinction, for present purposes, between the ownership of shares of stock acquired by purchase or grant as in *Shaffer*, on the one hand, and ownership arising from the purposeful utilization of the benefits and protections of the Delaware Corporation Law in activities related to the underlying cause of action, on the other hand. [The appellee] purposefully availed itself of the benefits and protections of the laws of the State of Delaware for financial gain in activities related to the cause of action [by forming a Delaware subsidiary]. Therein lies the "minimum contact" sufficient to sustain the jurisdiction of Delaware's courts over [the appellee].

Papendick v. Bosch, 410 A.2d at 152. . . .

GenCorp seeks to distinguish *Papendick* on two grounds. First, it alleges that GenCorp did not *form* RKO General as a subsidiary corporation but instead purchased it after it had already been formed. Second, GenCorp argues that in *Papendick*, it was appropriate for Delaware to assert jurisdiction over the contract dispute but that in the present case, Delaware has little or no connection with Sternberg's double derivative action. We do not find either of GenCorp's arguments to be persuasive.

---

28. For a discussion of the "*Cannon* Doctrine," *see* Brilmayer & Paisley, Personal Jurisdiction and Substantive Legal Relations: Corporations, Conspiracies and Agency, 74 Calif. L. Rev. 1, 2-8 (1986). For a case distinguishing *Cannon, see* Waters v. Deutz Corp., Del. Supr., 479 A.2d 273, 275 (1984).

GenCorp and Delaware

Although GenCorp did not *form* RKO General as a Delaware subsidiary, it knew at the time of its acquisition that RKO General was incorporated under the laws of the State of Delaware. The record reflects that GenCorp has owned and operated RKO General as a Delaware subsidiary since 1955—more than 30 years. We find that the difference between creating a wholly owned subsidiary in Delaware and purchasing a Delaware subsidiary is a distinction without significance, when the subsidiary is not thereafter reincorporated in another state.

The decision to reincorporate or not to reincorporate in a particular jurisdiction is a deliberate one. The majority stockholders in a parent corporation can vote to change the state of incorporation of the parent, or of a subsidiary, anytime there is a preference to be governed by the laws of another jurisdiction. In fact, after the United States Supreme Court decision in *Shaffer*, the Delaware corporation involved in that litigation, Greyhound, reincorporated in Arizona. Conversely, it is well known that many corporations have chosen to incorporate or reincorporate in the State of Delaware, although the reasons for the decision have been debated. These competing positions are discussed at length in Macey & Miller, Toward an Interest-Group Theory of Delaware Corporate Law, 65 Tex. L. Rev. 469 (1987).

. . . Although scholars may debate its motivation, the fact remains that for more than thirty years, GenCorp has made the conscious decision to operate RKO General, its subsidiary, as a *Delaware* corporation. For more than thirty years, GenCorp has benefited from the protections of the Delaware law in operating RKO General for commercial gain, including the benefits afforded to it directly as a shareholder of a Delaware corporation. We conclude that GenCorp intentionally established and maintained minimum contacts with Delaware by its decision to continue to operate its wholly owned subsidiary, RKO General, as a Delaware corporation.

. . . Delaware has a legitimate interest in Sternberg's double derivative claim. . . . In this case, GenCorp used the benefits and protections of the State of Delaware to maintain a corporate subsidiary. Sternberg's double derivative suit alleges that the operation of RKO General, the wholly owned Delaware subsidiary, has caused damage to RKO General, GenCorp and the GenCorp stockholders. Delaware has an interest in holding accountable those responsible for the operation of a Delaware corporation. Moreover, just as the internal affairs doctrine mandates the application of Ohio law to the internal operations of GenCorp, that same doctrine mandates the application of Delaware law to the internal operation of RKO General. It is a basic principle of Delaware corporation law that the directors of Delaware corporations are subject to fiduciary duties. Specifically, the Delaware law provides that "in a parent and wholly owned subsidiary context, the directors of the subsidiary are obligated only to manage the affairs of the subsidiary in the best interests of the parent and its shareholders."

The United States Supreme Court has recognized that "[a] State has an interest in promoting stable relationships among parties involved in the corporation it charters." CTS Corp. v. Dynamics Corp. of America, 481 U.S. 69 (1987). In particular, the Supreme Court noted that states have "a substantial interest in preventing the corporate form from becoming a shield for unfair business dealing." *Id.* 107. In this case, Delaware has a legitimate interest in providing a forum for hearing and applying Delaware law to a double derivative claim related to the internal operation of a wholly owned Delaware subsidiary. . . . In this case, Delaware also has an interest in providing a forum for efficiently litigating, in a single proceeding, all issues and damages arising out of a double derivative claim alleging harm based upon the foreign parent corporation's maintenance of a Delaware subsidiary.

In a shareholder's derivative suit, the shareholder sues on behalf of the corporation for harm done to the corporation. Therefore, the damages recovered in the suit are paid to the corporation. R. Clark, Corporate Law, 639-640 (1986).[41] In a single derivative suit the corporation is an indispensable party. The presence of the corporation is required so that it can receive the monetary award in the event of recovery. The same logic has been held to apply in a double derivative suit. The parent corporation is an indispensable party in a double derivative suit against a subsidiary because any recovery for losses suffered by the subsidiary that were being sued upon would go to the parent. Thus, the Court of Chancery was correct in concluding that if it did not have jurisdiction over the parent corporation, the entire double derivative suit must be dismissed.

Delaware has more than an interest in providing a sure forum for shareholder derivative litigation involving the internal affairs of its domestic corporations. Delaware has an obligation to provide such a forum. All "traditional notions of fair play and substantial justice" would be offended if Delaware permitted GenCorp to use its laws to maintain a Delaware subsidiary and then declined to exercise jurisdiction over GenCorp in a double derivative suit, where GenCorp was an indispensable party.

We conclude that fairness and justice permit jurisdiction to be asserted by Delaware under the totality of the circumstances of this case. We find that the exercise of specific jurisdiction in this case is consistent with the requirements of due process. We hold that GenCorp's ownership of RKO General is a minimum contact with Delaware which is sufficient to support an

---

41. The normal derivative suit was "two suits in one: (1) The plaintiff brought a suit in equity against the corporation seeking an order against it; (2) to bring a suit for damages or other legal injury for damages or other relief against some third person who had caused legal injury to the corporation." R. Clark, Corporate Law, 639-640 (1986).

exercise of specific jurisdiction by the Delaware Courts over GenCorp to hear and decide Sternberg's double derivative complaint.[45] This holding is an independent and alternative basis for reversing the Court of Chancery's decision not to exercise specific jurisdiction over GenCorp.

[The court then decided that the individual directors of RKO were subject to jurisdiction, while the officers and directors of GenCorp were not.]

---

45. We note that legal scholars have suggested two ways of establishing jurisdiction over the parent *based on jurisdiction over the subsidiary:*

> These two methods for establishing jurisdiction involve showing either that the absent parent instigated the subsidiary's local activities or that the absent parent and the subsidiary are in fact a single legal entity. The first method we call *attribution,* the second *merger.* They are obviously similar in that both involve disregarding separate entity status and shifting responsibility for the subsidiary's actions onto the parent. The difference between attribution and merger lies in the extent of this shifting of responsibility. Under the attribution theory, only the precise conduct shown to be instigated by the parent is attributed to the parent; the rest of the subsidiary's actions still pertain only to the subsidiary. The two corporations remain distinct entities. If merger is shown, however, all of the activities of the subsidiary are by definition activities of the parent. Merger requires a greater showing of interconnectedness than attribution, but once shown, its scope is broader. Under both theories, the parent is declared responsible for in-state activities of the subsidiary, but in attribution the responsibility results from causing a separate legal entity to act while in merger there is no separate legal entity at all.

Brilmayer & Paisley, Personal Jurisdiction and Substantive Legal Relations: Corporations, Conspiracies and Agency, 74 Calif. L.R. 1, 12 (1986) (emphasis in original). The allegations in Sternberg's double derivative law suit appear to fit into the attribution method for establishing jurisdiction. In this double derivative action, Sternberg alleges that the parent-subsidiary relationship was simply the vehicle by which GenCorp caused RKO General to carry out its own wishes, which then ultimately led to the injury to GenCorp. The attribution principle is mentioned in a footnote in *Burger King Corp.*, where the United States Supreme Court said,

> [w]e have previously noted that when commercial activities are "carried on on behalf of" an out-of-state party, those activities may sometimes be ascribed to the party, . . . at least where he is a "primary participant[t]" in the enterprise and has acted purposefully in directing those activities.

Burger King Corp. v. Rudzewicz, 471 U.S. at 479 n.22, (citing International Shoe Co. v. Washington, 326 U.S. 310, 320 (1945); Calder V. Jones, 465 U.S. 783, 790 (1984).

Sternberg also argues that the corporate existence of GenCorp and RKO General should be ignored. In essence, Sternberg argues for the merger method of establishing jurisdiction based upon the findings of the FCC. *Cf.* Lucas v. Gulf & Western Industries, Inc., 666 F.2d 800, 806 (1981). Our analysis makes it unnecessary to base a finding of specific jurisdiction upon either one of these theories. However, we recognize the merit of both approaches if the facts in a given case support their applicability. *See* Waters v. Deutz Corp., Del. Supr., 479 A.2d 273 (1984); Japan Petroleum Co. (Nigeria) Ltd. v. Ashland Oil, Inc., 456 F. Supp. 831, 839 (D. Del. 1978); *Cf.* Akzona, Inc. v. E. I. Du Pont De Nemours & Co., 607 F. Supp. 227, 237-240 (D. Del. 1984).

Questions and Comments

(1) *Shaffer* purports to lay down the same standards for in personam and quasi in rem jurisdiction, citing *International Shoe* as the source for the former standards. But *International Shoe* required minimum contacts between the defendant and the forum state, while *Shaffer* requires minimum contacts among the forum state, the litigation, and the defendant. Can the apparent distinction be eliminated?

(2) If, as suggested in note (1) *supra,* the standards are now the same for in personam and quasi in rem jurisdiction, doesn't it follow that whenever a long-arm statute, if it existed, would be constitutional, quasi in rem jurisdiction would also be constitutional, and conversely, that if quasi in rem jurisdiction is not constitutional, a long-arm statute would not be either? If that proposition is true, was the Delaware statute that it discussed unconstitutional? On the other hand, if a long-arm statute would not be constitutional under the facts of *Shaffer,* why did the majority opinion say, "If Delaware perceived its interest in securing jurisdiction over corporate fiduciaries to be as great as Heitner suggests, we would expect it to have enacted a statute more clearly designed to protect that interest"? And why did it say, "Delaware, unlike some States, has not enacted a statute that treats acceptance of a directorship as consent to jurisdiction in the State"? Of what relevance are these observations unless such a statute would be constitutional?

Moreover, wasn't the whole "implied consent" line of reasoning rejected in *International Shoe*—the very basis for the *Shaffer* holding? ("True, some of the decisions holding the corporation amenable to suit have been supported by resort to the legal fiction that it has given its consent to service and suit, consent being implied from its presence in the state through the acts of its authorized agents. But more realistically it may be said that those authorized acts were of such a nature as to justify the fiction.") Doesn't it follow that if Delaware could have exacted consent, it can simply declare that it has jurisdiction over the corporate officers (though admittedly it did not do so here)?

Has Delaware solved these problems with the statute and analysis in *Sternberg?*

(3) As *Sternberg* suggests, there is increasing litigation over the effect on jurisdictional analysis of corporate ties. *See, e.g.,* Miller v. Honda Motor Co. Ltd., 779 F.2d 769 (1st Cir. 1985). In Keeton v. Hustler, 465 U.S. 770 n.13 (1984), the Supreme Court made clear that jurisdiction could not be predicated merely upon the fact of corporate ownership. The defendants were Hustler magazine, which was subject to jurisdiction in New Hampshire, and its parent corporation and sole owner, LFP Inc. and Larry Flynt. The fact that the magazine was subject to jurisdiction did not automatically subject the others; as to each party, jurisdiction had to be established. This is sometimes known as the *Cannon* doctrine from Cannon Manufacturing Co. v. Cudahy Packing Co., 267 U.S. 333 (1925). Where the parent controls the subsidiary's

forum activities, however, jurisdiction over the parent may be appropriate. *See, e.g.*, Hill by Hill v. Showa Denko, K.K., 425 S.E.2d 609 (W. Va. 1992). *See generally* Blumberg, The Increasing Recognition of Enterprise Principles in Determining Parent and Subsidiary Corporation Liabilities, 28 Conn. L. Rev. 295 (1996); Alexander, Unlimited Shareholder Liability Through a Procedural Lens, 106 Harv. L. Rev. 387 (1992); Brilmayer & Paisley, Personal Jurisdiction and Substantive Legal Relations: Corporations, Conspiracy, and Agency, 74 Cal. L. Rev. 1 (1986).

(4) Is *Sternberg* consistent with *Shaffer?* Can it be explained as consistent on the grounds that the defendant, GenCorp, owned property in Delaware that was "related to" the controversy? Is the test for "related" or specific jurisdiction the same for assets as it is for activities, as discussed in section B, *supra?* Was the property in *Shaffer* any less closely related to the controversy than the property in *Sternberg?* Is there any more of a Delaware interest in one case than in the other?

In Anderson v. Heartland Oil and Gas, Inc., 819 P.2d 1192 (Kan. 1991), the court upheld jurisdiction over two Colorado defendants whose only connection with the forum was that they were corporate directors and officers of a Kansas corporation. "Jurisdiction over individual officers, directors, and employees of a domestic corporation, for claims that may result in personal liability, is predicated merely upon jurisdiction over the corporation itself." 819 P.2d at 1200. Note that the rationale—that there is jurisdiction over the corporation—seems potentially quite expansive. Wouldn't it extend even to directors of a *nonresident* corporation that happened to be subject to forum jurisdiction for some other reason (*e.g.*, because it had committed a tort or breached a contract there, or because it carried on substantial unrelated business)? Is the rationale consistent with Shaffer v. Heitner?

(5) Footnote 37 of the *Shaffer* opinion suggests that quasi in rem jurisdiction might yet be available when "no other forum is available to the plaintiff." When might such circumstances occur? When the defendant is domiciled outside the country? Would that be discriminating against foreign defendants? Should the fact that a claim is barred by the statutes of limitations of other states bring it within the rationale of footnote 37 and allow a forum with otherwise inadequate contacts to assert jurisdiction? Compare footnote 13 in *Helicopteros*, page 487 *supra*, where the Court declined to adopt the theory of jurisdiction by necessity, which it apparently deemed rather novel.

(6) In Grand Bahama Petroleum Co. v. Canadian Transportation Agencies, 450 F. Supp. 447 (W.D. Wash. 1978), the court upheld garnishment of a bank account in a district having no contacts with the defendant other than the bank account. The case involved a claim for services to a ship, and the court distinguished *Shaffer* on those grounds. It noted that attachment jurisdiction has traditionally been the keystone of admiralty litigation, that such litigation usually involves people in commerce who are away from home for long periods of time, that admiralty has always been treated separately, as indicated by the separate listing of admiralty in Article III of the Constitu-

tion as a basis for federal jurisdiction, and the fact that maritime attachment jurisdiction does not trace back to Pennoyer v. Neff but has its own long history recognizing such attachment.

(7) Some states authorize quasi in rem jurisdiction after *Shaffer*. In these states, attachment plus notice authorize the court to exercise jurisdiction over a foreign defendant and limit the extent of the judgment to the value of the property attached. This exercise of jurisdiction is limited by the constitutional "minimum contacts" test and largely operates in states that have not extended their long arm to the limits of the Constitution. *See, e.g.*, Cargill Inc. v. Sabine Trading & Shipping Co., 756 F.2d 224 (2d Cir. 1984) (New York's limited appearance statutes apply in diversity action where the sole basis of jurisdiction was quasi in rem); Campbell v. Landmark First National Bank of Fort Lauderdale, 421 So. 2d 813 (Fla. 1982) (denying motion to quash constructive service in quasi in rem claim seeking imposition of a constructive trust and on accounting); Britton v. Howard Savings Bank, 727 F.2d 315 (1984) (upholding writ of attachment under amended New Jersey statute allowing prejudgment jurisdictional attachment where it conforms with due process).

(8) Traditionally, judgments of courts lacking jurisdiction over either person or property are considered void and thus not entitled to full faith and credit or res judicata effect. After *Shaffer,* what would be the remedy for a person who suffered a quasi in rem judgment *before Shaffer* was decided? Would a default judgment based on quasi in rem jurisdiction give rise to actions to recover the property?

(9) In Rush v. Savchuk, 444 U.S. 320 (1980), the Supreme Court applied the logic of *Shaffer* to invalidate quasi-in-rem jurisdiction over a defendant on the basis of attachment of the contractual obligation of his insurer to defend and indemnify him in the suit. This so-called *Seider* jurisdiction (the doctrine was derived from Seider v. Roth, 17 N.Y.2d 111 (N.Y. 1966)) allowed plaintiffs to attach the defendants insurance policy, and thus sue, in any state in which the insurance company did business. In *Rush,* the Court reasoned that because *International Shoe*'s minimum contacts analysis applied to each defendant separately, and because the contacts of the insurer could not be attributed to the insured, *Seider* jurisdiction is unconstitutional unless the insured had minimum contacts with the forum.

Rush insinuated that direct action statutes—which allow an injured party to sue the tortfeasor's insurance company directly instead of proceeding first against the tortfeasor—are constitutional. *See* 444 U.S. at 331-332. The Court distinguished direct action statutes from *Seider* jurisdiction on the basis of the fact that the former requires that the nominal defendant (the insured) have minimum contacts with the forum as a prerequisite to bringing suit against the insurer. *See id.; compare Watson* v. *Employers Liability Assurance Corp.*, 348 U.S. 66 (1954), reproduced *supra* page 354, which upheld the constitutionality of applying a direct action statute to an out-of-state insurance company.

(10) Interesting and difficult questions about *in rem* jurisdiction have arisen in connection with intangible property on the Internet. We discuss these cases *infra* page 826.

5

Conflict of Laws in the Federal System

To this point, our discussion has implicitly assumed, by and large, that conflict of laws involves only problems of relations between the states. But of course, the United States contains an additional set of courts and substantive laws, namely those of the federal system. This raises the question of how conflicts analysis might change when a conflicts issue arises in litigation in federal, rather than state, court. In particular, one might ask what effect this fact might have, first, on the choice of which state's substantive law applies, and second, on the choice of the location for litigation. Problems of this sort are usually dealt with under the rubric of "the *Erie* doctrine." One might also want to know whether federal substantive law might not sometimes preempt state law that impinges on the harmonious relations between the states. This preemption issue is dealt with under the rubric of federal common law.

A. The *Erie* Doctrine

Erie Railroad v. Tompkins

304 U.S. 64 (1938)

Justice BRANDEIS delivered the opinion of the Court.

The question for decision is whether the oft-challenged doctrine of Swift v. Tyson shall now be disapproved.

Tompkins, a citizen of Pennsylvania, was injured on a dark night by a passing freight train of the Erie Railroad Company while walking along its right of way at Hughestown in that State. He claimed that the accident occurred through negligence in the operation, or maintenance, of the train; that he was rightfully on the premises as licensee because he was on a commonly used beaten footpath which ran for a short distance alongside the tracks; and that he was struck by something which looked like a door projecting from one of the moving cars. To enforce that claim he brought an action in the federal court for southern New York, which had jurisdiction because the company is a corporation of that State. It denied liability; and the case was tried by a jury.

The Erie insisted that its duty to Tompkins was no greater than that owed to a trespasser. It contended, among other things, that its duty to Tompkins, and hence its liability, should be determined in accordance with the Pennsylvania law; that under the law of Pennsylvania, as declared by its highest court, persons who use pathways along the railroad right of way—that is a longitudinal pathway as distinguished from a crossing—are to be deemed trespassers; and that the railroad is not liable for injuries to undiscovered trespassers resulting from its negligence, unless it be wanton or wilful. Tompkins denied that any such rule had been established by the decisions of the Pennsylvania courts; and contended that, since there was no statute of the State on the subject, the railroad's duty and liability is to be determined in federal courts as a matter of general law.

The trial judge refused to rule that the applicable law precluded recovery. The jury brought in a verdict of $30,000; and the judgment entered thereon was affirmed by the Circuit Court of Appeals, which held that it was unnecessary to consider whether the law of Pennsylvania was as contended, because the question was one not of local, but of general law and that

> upon questions of general law the federal courts are free, in the absence of a local statute, to exercise their independent judgment as to what the law is; and it is well settled that the question of the responsibility of a railroad for injuries caused by its servants is one of general law. Where the public has made open and notorious use of a railroad right of way for a long period of time and without objection, the company owes to persons on such permissive pathway a duty of care in the operation of its trains. It is likewise generally recognized law that a jury may find that negligence exists toward a pedestrian using a permissive path on the railroad right of way if he is hit by some object projecting from the side of the train.

The Erie had contended that application of the Pennsylvania rule was required, among other things, by §34 of the Federal Judiciary Act of September 24, 1789, c.20, 28 U.S.C. §725, which provides:

> The laws of the several States, except where the Constitution, treaties, or statutes of the United States otherwise require or provide, shall be re-

> garded as rules of decision in trials at common law, in the courts of the United States, in cases where they apply.

Because of the importance of the question whether the federal court was free to disregard the alleged rule of the Pennsylvania common law, we granted certiorari.

First. Swift v. Tyson held that federal courts exercising jurisdiction on the ground of diversity of citizenship need not, in matters of general jurisprudence, apply the unwritten law of the State as declared by its highest court; that they are free to exercise an independent judgment as to what the common law of the State is—or should be; and that, as there stated by Mr. Justice Story:

> [T]he true interpretation of the thirty-fourth section limited its application to state laws strictly local, that is to say, to the positive statutes of the state, and the construction thereof adopted by the local tribunals, and to rights and titles to things having a permanent locality, such as the rights and titles to real estate, and other matters immovable and intraterritorial in their nature and character. It never has been supposed by us, that the section did apply, or was intended to apply, to questions of a more general nature, not at all dependent upon local statutes or local usages of a fixed and permanent operation, as, for example, to the construction of ordinary contracts or other written instruments, and especially to questions of general commercial law, where the state tribunals are called upon to perform the like functions as ourselves, that is, to ascertain upon general reasoning and legal analogies, what is the true exposition of the contract of instrument, or what is the just rule furnished by the principles of commercial law to govern the case.

The Court in applying the rule of §34 to equity cases, in Mason v. United States said: "The statute, however, is merely declarative of the rule which would exist in the absence of the statute." The federal courts assumed, in the broad field of "general law," the power to declare rules of decision which Congress was confessedly without power to enact as statutes. Doubt was repeatedly expressed as to the correctness of the construction given §34, and as to the soundness of the rule which it introduced. But it was the more recent research of a competent scholar, who examined the original document, which established that the construction given to it by the Court was erroneous; and that the purpose of the section was merely to make certain that, in all matters except those in which some federal law is controlling, the federal courts exercising jurisdiction in diversity of citizenship cases would apply as their rules of decision the law of the State, unwritten as well as written.

Criticism of the doctrine became widespread after the decision of Black & White Taxicab Co. v. Brown & Yellow Taxicab Co. There, Brown and Yellow, a Kentucky corporation owned by Kentuckians, and the Louisville and Nashville Railroad, also a Kentucky corporation, wished that the former should have the exclusive privilege of soliciting passenger and baggage transportation at the Bowling Green, Kentucky, railroad station; and that the Black and White, a competing Kentucky corporation, should be prevented from interfering with that privilege. Knowing that such a contract would be void under the common law of Kentucky, it was arranged that the Brown and Yellow reincorporate under the law of Tennessee, and that the contract with the railroad should be executed there. The suit was then brought by the Tennessee corporation in the federal court for Western Kentucky to enjoin competition by the Black and White; an injunction issued by the District Court was sustained by the Court of Appeals; and this Court, citing many decisions in which the doctrine of Swift v. Tyson had been applied, affirmed the decree.

Second. Experience in applying the doctrine of Swift v. Tyson had revealed its defects, political and social; and the benefits expected to flow from the rule did not accrue. Persistence of state courts in their own opinions on questions of common law prevented uniformity; and the impossibility of discovering a satisfactory line of demarcation between the province of general law and that of local law developed a new well of uncertainties.

On the other hand, the mischievous results of the doctrine had become apparent. Diversity of citizenship jurisdiction was conferred in order to prevent apprehended discrimination in state courts against those not citizens of the State. Swift v. Tyson introduced grave discrimination by non-citizens against citizens. It made rights enjoyed under the unwritten "general law" vary according to whether enforcement was sought in the state or in the federal court; and the privilege of selecting the court in which the right should be determined was conferred upon the non-citizen. Thus, the doctrine rendered impossible equal protection of the law. In attempting to promote uniformity of law throughout the United States, the doctrine had prevented uniformity in the administration of the law of the State.

The discrimination resulting became in practice far-reaching. This resulted in part from the broad province accorded to the so-called "general law" as to which federal courts exercised an independent judgment. In addition to questions of purely commercial law, "general law" was held to include the obligations under contracts entered into and to be performed within the State, the extent to which a carrier operating within a State may stipulate for exemption from liability for his own negligence or that of his employee; the liability for torts committed within the State upon persons resident or property located there, even where the question of liability depended upon the scope of a property right conferred by the State; and the right to exemplary or punitive damages. Furthermore, state decisions construing local deeds, mineral conveyances, and even devises of real estate were disregarded.

In part the discrimination resulted from the wide range of persons held entitled to avail themselves of the federal rule by resort to the diversity of citizenship jurisdiction. Through this jurisdiction individual citizens willing to remove from their own State and become citizens of another might avail themselves of the federal rule. And, without even change of residence, a corporate citizen of the State could avail itself of the federal rule by re-incorporating under the laws of another State, as was done in the Taxicab case.

The injustice and confusion incident to the doctrine of Swift v. Tyson have been repeatedly urged as reasons for abolishing or limiting diversity of citizenship jurisdiction. Other legislative relief has been proposed. If only a question of statutory construction were involved, we should not be prepared to abandon a doctrine so widely applied throughout nearly a century. But the unconstitutionality of the course pursued has now been made clear and compels us to do so.

Third. Except in matters governed by the Federal Constitution or by Acts of Congress, the law to be applied in any case is the law of the State. And whether the law of the State shall be declared by its Legislature in a statute or by its highest court in a decision is not a matter of federal concern. There is no federal general common law. Congress has no power to declare substantive rules of common law applicable in a State whether they be local in their nature or "general," be they commercial law or a part of the law of torts. And no clause in the Constitution purports to confer such a power upon the federal courts. As stated by Mr. Justice Field when protesting in Baltimore & Ohio R. Co. v. Baugh, against ignoring the Ohio common law of fellow servant liability:

> I am aware that what has been termed the general law of the country—which is often little less than what the judge advancing the doctrine thinks at the time should be the general law on a particular subject—has been often advanced in judicial opinions of this court to control a conflicting law of a State. I admit that learned judges have fallen into the habit of repeating this doctrine as a convenient mode of brushing aside the law of a State in conflict with their views. And I confess that, moved and governed by the authority of the great names of those judges, I have, myself, in many instances, unhesitatingly and confidently, but I think now erroneously, repeated the same doctrine. But, notwithstanding the great names which may be cited in favor of the doctrine, and notwithstanding the frequency with which the doctrine has been reiterated, there stands, as a perpetual protest against its repetition, the Constitution of the United States, which recognizes and preserves the autonomy and independence of the States—independence in their legislative and independence in their judicial departments. Supervision over either the legislative or the judicial action of the States is in no case permissible except as to matters by the Constitution specifically authorized or delegated to the United States. Any interference with either, except as thus permitted, is an invasion of the authority of the State and, to that extent, a denial of its independence.

The fallacy underlying the rule declared in Swift v. Tyson is made clear by Mr. Justice Holmes. The doctrine rests upon the assumption that there is "a transcendental body of law outside of any particular State but obligatory within it unless and until changed by statute," that federal courts have the power to use their judgment as to what the rules of common law are; and that in the federal courts "the parties are entitled to an independent judgment on matters of general law":

> [B]ut law in the sense in which courts speak of it today does not exist without some definite authority behind it. The common law so far as it is enforced in a State, whether called common law or not, is not the common law generally but the law of that State existing by the authority of that State without regard to what it may have been in England or anywhere else. [T]he authority and only authority is the State, and if that be so, the voice adopted by the State as its own [whether it be of its Legislature or of its Supreme Court] should utter the last word.

Thus the doctrine of Swift v. Tyson is, as Mr. Justice Holmes said, "an unconstitutional assumption of powers by courts of the United States which no lapse of time or respectable array of opinion should make us hesitate to correct." In disapproving that doctrine we do not hold unconstitutional §34 of the Federal Judiciary Act of 1789 or any other Act of Congress. We merely declare that in applying the doctrine this Court and the lower courts have invaded rights which in our opinion are reserved by the Constitution to the several States.

Fourth. The defendant contended that by the common law of Pennsylvania as declared by its highest court in Falchetti v. Pennsylvania R. Co., 307 Pa. 203; 160 A. 859, the only duty owed to the plaintiff was to refrain from wilful or wanton injury. The plaintiff denied that such is the Pennsylvania law. In support of their respective contentions the parties discussed and cited many decisions of the Supreme Court of the State. The Circuit Court of Appeals ruled that the question of liability is one of general law; and on that ground declined to decide the issue of state law. As we hold this was error, the judgment is reversed and the case remanded to it for further proceedings in conformity with our opinion.

Reversed.

[A concurring opinion of Justice Reed is omitted.]

Questions and Comments

(1) The Court makes it clear in *Erie* that it is handing down a constitutional decision. But what clause of the Constitution does the Court interpret in its opinion?

(2) Justice Brandeis's opinion says at one point "Congress has no power to declare substantive rules of common law applicable in a State whether they be local in their nature or 'general,' be they commercial law or a part of the law of torts." Much has happened since the *Erie* decision. Is it likely that today's Supreme Court would strike down a federal statute purporting to establish rules for liability for injury along the right-of-way of a railroad engaged in interstate commerce? If not, should *Erie* be overruled because its underlying assumptions have been eroded, or is it possible to uphold *Erie*

even if one assumes that there was federal power to declare substantive law in the case of Tompkins's injury?

(3) Assuming that Congress constitutionally could have legislated the rules of liability involved in Tompkins's accident, could Congress have delegated to the Court the task of making up such substantive rules? In Textile Workers Union of America v. Lincoln Mills, 353 U.S. 448 (1957), the Supreme Court was faced with an attack on the constitutionality of §301 of the Taft-Hartley Act, 29 U.S.C. §85 (1976). The basis for the attack was the statute's purporting to confer jurisdiction on the federal courts for disputes arising between employers and labor unions, even though no substantive rules to govern these disputes were suggested by the legislation. The problem arose because there was no obvious federal-question jurisdiction, and diversity of citizenship was absent. The Court rejected a "protective jurisdiction" theory, which suggested that Congress could give the federal courts jurisdiction in areas of federal concern even though diversity was absent and no specific substantive federal rules of decision were involved. But that did not mean that the statute conferred unconstitutional jurisdiction on the federal courts. Instead, the Court said, Congress must have intended by the grant of jurisdiction in §301 to give the federal courts substantive rulemaking power in the area—in other words, the courts were to develop a federal common law under the Taft-Hartley Act (often by borrowing from state contract law and the like).

(4) In light of *Lincoln Mills,* could Congress amend the Rules of Decision Act to provide that the federal courts can form their own common law? Or is a narrower grant, limited to a single field like labor law, a necessary condition for such a delegation?

(5) If congressional silence on the law concerning Tompkins's injury is taken as indicating a lack of federal policy in the area, is *Erie* a true or false conflict case? If it is a false conflict, is the result in *Erie* (as long as Congress has not legislated) required by the Court's reasoning in Home Insurance Co. v. Dick? Or is the fact that the accident took place within the geographical borders of the United States enough to take *Erie* out of the scope of *Dick?* Does *Dick* forbid a state to apply its own law when it has no interest or when it has no contact, or when it has neither? Note that if it is assumed that the First Restatement rules are constitutional, analogies to the constitutionality of interstate conflicts resolutions will fail to sort out the *Erie* problem, since only in a system in which two sovereigns both have jurisdiction over the same land can an accident be "within" one jurisdiction that has no interest, in the traditional sense, in its resolution.

(6) Much of the Court's discussion is devoted to the evils of forum-shopping. What's wrong with forum-shopping, anyway? If a federal judge believes that he or she has come up with the just and proper solution to a particular legal problem, doesn't it deny justice to the parties to rule to the contrary simply to imitate the state court's predicted result? Isn't that behaving as if two wrongs will somehow make a right?

(7) The earlier draft of the Rules of Decision Act discovered by Professor Warren provided: "the Statute law of the several States in force for the time being and their unwritten or common law now in use, whether by adoption from the common law of England, the ancient statutes of the same or otherwise" should be rules of decision in the federal courts. In the legislative process, the quoted phrase was shortened to "laws of the several states." Is it clear that this new phrase is simply a substitute for the earlier language?

(8) *Erie* was the first civil case heard by Judge Mandelbaum, the trial judge. Judge Mandelbaum, born in Poland, was a product of Tammany politics and, over strong protest from the bar, was appointed to the bench by President Roosevelt. Before his appointment, he had visited the federal court house only once, to see what it looked like. A somewhat ungrammatical comment was penned in the margin of his copy of the Supreme Court's *Erie* opinion as reported in Younger, Observation: What Happened in *Erie,* 56 Tex. L. Rev. 1011 (1978): "Because the *Swift Tyson* case although before this case I never knew of its existence to be truthful and for the confusion this decision brought about, it might have been better to leave it alone and stand by good old Swifty."

Note: *Erie* and Substance vs. Procedure

As all veterans of Civil Procedure know, the "real" *Erie* problem is substance vs. procedure. The problem first reared its ugly head in Guaranty Trust Co. v. York, 326 U.S. 99 (1945), where the question was whether to apply a state statute of limitations or federal laches doctrine to a diversity action brought in federal court. The Court assumed that the *Erie* principle would not apply to issues that are "procedural" rather than "substantive," presumably for the same reason that that distinction is made in ordinary conflicts cases where the substantive, but not the procedural, law of State *B* may be applied in the courts of State *A.* (Recall the double play on this issue in Sampson v. Channell, page 131 *supra,* where a federal court decided that the burden of proof was "substantive" for *Erie* purposes and therefore applied the law of the state in which it was sitting—whose law declared the issue "procedural" for conflicts purposes.)

To determine whether an issue is substantive or procedural, Justice Frankfurter produced his famous (or infamous) outcome-determination test:

> [D]oes it significantly affect the result of a litigation for a federal court to disregard a law of a State that would be controlling in an action upon the same claim by the same parties in a State court? [T]he outcome of the litigation in federal court should be substantially the same, so far as legal rules determine the outcome of a litigation, as it would be if tried in a State court.

326 U.S. at 109.

Subsequent Supreme Court cases wrestling with *Erie* and the substance/procedure dichotomy include:

(a) Ragan v. Merchants Transfer Co., 337 U.S. 530 (1949), which held that state law, rather than federal, would determine when an action was "commenced" for purposes of satisfying the state statute of limitations. Federal Rule 3 provides that an action is commenced by filing a complaint; the state rule provided that a case was commenced by service of process on the defendant. *Guaranty Trust* was invoked as controlling.

(b) Woods v. Interstate Realty Co., 337 U.S. 535 (1949), which held that a state statute closing the doors of the state courts to out-of-state corporations that had not qualified to do business in Mississippi would bar the Mississippi federal courts to those same corporations.

(c) Cohen v. Beneficial Industrial Loan Corp., 337 U.S. 541 (1949), which held that federal diversity cases must apply a state statute allowing a corporation to require a bond for the expenses of defense in a shareholders' derivative suit if the plaintiff should be unsuccessful. The purpose of the bond and requirement that the plaintiff was to pay expenses was to discourage so-called strike suits, brought to coerce settlements rather than win on the merits.

(d) Bernhardt v. Polygraphic Co., 350 U.S. 198 (1956), which narrowly construed the federal arbitration statute and held, on *Erie*-type grounds, that state law concerning the enforceability of arbitration agreements should control in a diversity action.

(e) Byrd v. Blue Ridge Rural Electric Cooperative, Inc., 356 U.S. 525 (1958), which held that federal law, rather than state law, controlled as to the division of authority between judge and jury to determine whether a person was a "statutory employee" for purposes of a state workers' compensation scheme. In this first pro-federal ruling after a long line of cases favoring state law, the Court referred to "countervailing considerations"—in this case, the federal court's interest in how it reached its own decisions. The Court also referred to "the influence—if not the command—of the Seventh Amendment." 356 U.S. at 537. Even without "countervailing considerations," is the *chance* that a jury will come out differently than a judge on an issue the kind of outcome-determinative factor that Justice Frankfurter had in mind in the *Guaranty Trust* case? Should the test be how much we should expect plaintiffs' lawyers to be enticed or repelled by the federal practice because of the effect they think it will have on the outcome of a case?

(f) Hanna v. Plumer, 380 U.S. 460 (1965), in which a state rule required personal in-hand service on an executor or administrator of an estate, while Federal Rule 4(d)(1) required only one of several options, including leaving service with a person of suitable age and discretion at the defendant's dwelling place. The federal rule was held to prevail, in an opinion that stressed that procedure was the key. In particular, the majority opinion noted that *Erie* had never been successfully invoked to void a federal rule. Justice Harlan's concurring opinion suggested that the test should be whether "the choice of a rule would substantially affect those primary decisions respecting human conduct which our constitutional system leaves to state regulation." 380 U.S. at 475. Speaking perhaps somewhat more plainly than the majority about the majority's own stand, Justice Harlan said,

> So long as a reasonable man could characterize any duly adopted federal rule as "procedural," the Court, unless I misapprehend what is said, would have it apply no matter how seriously it frustrated a State's substantive regulation of the primary conduct and affairs of its citizens. Since the members of the Advisory Committee, the Judicial Conference, and this Court who formulated the Federal Rules are presumably reasonable men, it follows that the integrity of the Federal Rules is absolute.

Id. at 476.

(g) Walker v. Armco Steel Corp., 446 U.S. 740 (1980), in which the *Ragan* question (in (a) above) was reexamined. Justice Harlan's concurring opinion in *Hanna* had questioned *Ragan*, and the supremacy of the Federal Rules announced in *Hanna* made its holding dubious. Nonetheless *Armco* reaffirmed *Ragan*. A major reason for the holding was stare decisis, but the Court also tried to square *Ragan* with *Hanna: Hanna* indicated that if a matter is in the Federal Rules, it controls. But Rule 3 states only how an action is "commenced," not the effect of that commencement on satisfying the statute of limitations. (The Court failed to specify any other reason for having a rule on when an action is commenced. Are there any?)

Fearing that *Armco* might be used to whittle down the holding of *Hanna* the Court added a warning in a footnote that *Armco* does not mean that the Federal Rules are to be read narrowly in order to avoid clashes with state law; instead they are to be given their "plain meaning." Two footnotes later, the Court reserved judgment on the question whether Rule 3 might indicate when a federal statute of limitations is satisfied in a federal-question case. If Rule 3 might have that meaning in a federal-question case but doesn't have that meaning in a diversity case like *Armco*, wouldn't that mean that Rule 3 was being read narrowly in order to avoid a clash with state law?

(h) Gasperini v. Center for Humanities, Inc., 518 U.S. 415 (1996), which involved the compatibility of (a) a state statute that empowered appellate courts to review jury verdicts and to order new trials when the jury's award "deviates materially from what would be reasonable compensation," and (b) the federal court's more lenient practice of reviewing excessive jury verdicts under a "shocks the conscience" standard. The Court first noted that the state statute was motivated by the "substantive" purpose of limiting excessive awards and was "outcome-effective" in the sense that it led to different results than the federal standard. The Court also noted, however, that deferential appellate review of a trial court's denial of a motion to set aside a jury verdict was an "essential characteristic" of the federal court system that was informed by the Seventh Amendment's reexamination clause, which states that "no fact, tried by a jury, shall be otherwise reexamined in any Court of the United States, than according to the rules of the common law." The Court concluded that, unlike in *Byrd,* it could reconcile the state and federal interests without exclusively choosing either rule. It accordingly held that federal district courts should apply the state "deviates materially" standard subject to appellate review under the federal abuse of discretion standard. For criticism of *Gasperini, see* Floyd, *Erie* Awry: A Comment on Gasperini v. Center for Humanities, Inc., 1997 B.Y.U. L. Rev. 267 (1997).

Questions and Comments

(1) Professor Sedler has noted a relationship between the substance/procedure dichotomy in *Erie* and conflicts cases:

> It is submitted that the *Erie* outcome test can furnish [a conflicts] guide, for *the underlying rationale for the application of the state law in an* Erie *situation is substantially the same as the rationale for the application of the lex loci in a conflicts situation.* The sole purpose of a federal court in a diversity case is to furnish an impartial forum. The only purpose of a court in a conflicts case, once it has decided that it will look to the law of another state, is to serve as a forum of convenience. In each situation the court should use as a model as much of the law of the reference point as will materially affect the outcome. [Emphasis in original.]

Sedler, The *Erie* Outcome Test as a Guide to Substance and Procedure in the Conflicts of Laws, 37 N.Y.U. L. Rev. 813, 821-822 (1962).

(2) And conflicts learning can be used on *Erie* cases as well. In Leathers, *Erie* and Its Progeny as Choice of Law Cases, 11 Hous. L. Rev. 791 (1974), the author suggests that the post-*Erie* cases can best be analyzed under interest analysis, and that for the most part they turn out to be false conflict cases. The substance-procedure dichotomy as such is rejected because the distinction between the two shifts as the use to which the distinction is being put changes. For other arguments on behalf of cross-fertilization between *Erie* and interstate conflicts, *see* Bauer, The *Erie* Doctrine Revisited: How a Conflicts Perspective Can Aid the Analysis, 74 Notre Dame L. Rev. 1235 (1999); and Weinberg, The Federal-State Conflict of Laws: "Actual" Conflicts, 70 Tex. L. Rev. 1743 (1992).

(3) In a perceptive article, Professor John Ely has cast considerable light on the "*Erie* problem." Ely, The Irrepressible Myth of *Erie*, 87 Harv. L. Rev. 693 (1974). Ely's thesis is that there are three separate but related questions raised in the various cases that have been identified with the *Erie* label: First is the *Erie* principle itself, considered as a constitutional issue. Second is the Rules of Decision Act of 1789, 28 U.S.C. §1652 (1970), which provides,

> The laws of the several states, except where the Constitution or treaties of the United States or Acts of Congress otherwise require or provide, shall be regarded as rules of decision in civil actions in the courts of the United States, in cases where they apply.

The third is the Rules Enabling Act of 1934, 28 U.S.C. §2072 (1970), which provides in part,

> The Supreme Court shall have the power to prescribe by general rules . . . the practice and procedure of the district courts. . . . Such rules shall not abridge, enlarge, or modify any substantive right. . . .

Disputing what he calls the "enclave" theory of states' rights—that there are rights reserved to the states other than those which remain after enumerated federal rights—Ely starts with the proposition that the Constitution, by providing for federal jurisdiction, justifies the federal courts in following any rules which are in fact procedural at least in part, even if they have substantive effect. A constitutional limitation in the *Erie* case was applied there because the rule in question—the standard of care owed by the railroad—was in no sense a procedural matter. The Constitution, however, should stay in the background until Congress prescribes a rule of decision in diversity cases by statute, since the Rules of Decision Act (as interpreted in *Erie* and *York*) protects state law as much as the Constitution does. When a federal rule is involved, however, the Rules Enabling Act is the relevant legislation.

The difference between the two acts is this: Outcome determination, properly defined, is the standard for the Rules of Decision Act. (The proper test, Ely says, is whether the litigant will get a different result in state court, playing by state court rules, than he will get in federal court, playing by the federal rules in question.) Whether a rule affects "substantive" rights, properly defined, is the standard for the Rules Enabling Act. Thus, for example, a federal practice (not embodied in a federal rule) that allowed extensive pretrial discovery where the same was not allowed in state court would have to be viewed as outcome-determinative and thus forbidden by the Rules of Decision Act (as interpreted by *Erie* and *York*). But if the federal practice is made a federal rule, the Rules Enabling Act takes over and allows the rule if it (a) is procedural (it is) and (b) does not abridge substantive rights (it doesn't, even though it may affect the outcome, since the *reason* for the state's failure to have discovery almost undoubtedly represents a judgment about proper procedure, and not how people's lives should be governed). The Constitution would be satisfied merely by showing that the rule was in part procedural, even if it does affect substantive rights.

Although agreeing with much of Professor Ely's general analysis, Professor Chayes disagreed with many of his applications in an article entitled The Bead Game, 87 Harv. L. Rev. 741 (1974); followed by Ely, The Necklace, 87 Harv. L. Rev. 753 (1974); followed by Mishkin, The Thread, 87 Harv. L. Rev. 1682 (1974).

1. *Erie* and Choice of Law

Klaxon Co. v. Stentor Electric Manufacturing Co.

313 U.S. 487 (1941)

Justice REED delivered the opinion of the Court.

The principal question in this case is whether in diversity cases the federal courts must follow conflict of laws rules prevailing in the states in which they sit. We left this open in Ruhlin v. New York Life Insurance Co. The frequent recurrence of the problem, as well as the conflict of approach to the problem between the Third Circuit's opinion here and that of the First Circuit in Sampson v. Channell [page 131 *supra*] led us to grant certiorari.

In 1918, respondent, a New York corporation, transferred its entire business to petitioner, a Delaware corporation. Petitioner contracted to use its best efforts to further the manufacture and sale of certain patented devices covered by the agreement, and respondent was to have a share of petitioner's profits. The agreement was executed in New York, the assets were transferred there, and petitioner began performance there although later moved its operations to other states. Respondent was voluntarily dissolved under New York law in 1919. Ten years later it instituted this action in the United States District Court for the District of Delaware, alleging that petitioner had failed to perform its agreement to use its best efforts. Jurisdiction rested on diversity of citizenship. In 1939 respondent recovered a jury verdict of $100,000, upon which judgment was entered. Respondent then moved to correct the judgment by adding interest at the rate of six percent from June 1, 1929, the date the action had been brought. The basis of the motion was the provision in §480 of the New York Civil Practice Act directing that in contract actions interest be added to the principal sum "whether theretofore liquidated or unliquidated." The District Court granted the motion, taking the view that the rights of the parties were governed by New York law and that under New York law the addition of such interest was mandatory. The Circuit Court of Appeals affirmed and we granted certiorari, limited to the question whether §480 of the New York Civil Practice Act is applicable to an action in the federal court in Delaware.

The Circuit Court of Appeals was of the view that under New York law the right to interest before verdict under §480 went to the substance of the obligation, and that proper construction of the contract in suit fixed New York as the place of performance. It then concluded that §480 was applicable to the case because

> it is clear by what we think is undoubtedly the better view of the law that the rules for ascertaining the measure of damages are not a matter of procedure at all, but are matters of substance which should be settled by reference to the law of the appropriate state according to the type of case being tried in the forum. The measure of damages for breach of contract is determined by the law of the place of performance; Restatement, Conflict of Laws §413.

The court referred also to §418 of the Restatement, which makes interest part of the damages to be determined by the law of the place of performance. Application of the New York statute apparently followed from the court's independent determination of the "better view" without regard to Delaware law, for no Delaware decision or statute was cited or discussed.

We are of opinion that the prohibition declared in Erie R. Co. v. Tompkins against such independent determinations by the federal courts, extends to the field of conflict of laws. The conflict of laws rules to be applied by the federal court in Delaware must conform to those prevailing in Delaware's state courts.[2] Otherwise, the accident of diversity of citizenship would constantly disturb equal administration of justice in coordinate state and federal courts sitting side by side. *See* Erie R. Co. v. Tompkins. Any other ruling would do violence to the principle of uniformity within a state, upon which the *Tompkins* decision is based. Whatever lack of uniformity this may produce between federal courts in different states is attributable to our federal system, which leaves to a state, within the limits permitted by the Constitution, the right to pursue local policies diverging from those of its neighbors. It is not for the federal courts to thwart such local policies by enforcing an independent "general law" of conflict of laws. Subject only to review by this Court on any federal question that may arise, Delaware is free to determine whether a given matter is to be governed by the law of the forum or some other law. . . . This Court's views are not the decisive factor in determining the applicable conflicts rule. . . . And the proper function of the Delaware federal court is to ascertain what the state law is, not what it ought to be.

Respondent makes the further argument that the judgment must be affirmed because, under the full faith and credit clause of the Constitution, the state courts of Delaware would be obliged to give effect to the New York statute. The argument rests mainly on the decision of this Court in John Hancock Mutual Life Ins. Co. v. Yates, where a New York statute was held such an integral part of a contract of insurance, that Georgia was compelled to sustain the contract under the full faith and credit clause. Here, however, §480 of the New York Civil Practice Act is in no way related to the validity of the contract in suit, but merely to an incidental item of damages, interest, with respect to which courts at the forum have commonly been free to apply their own or some other law as they see fit. Nothing in the Constitution en-

---

2. An opinion in Sampson v. Channell [page 131 *supra*] reaches the same conclusion. . . .

sures unlimited extraterritorial recognition of all statutes or of any statute under all circumstances. Pacific Employers Insurance Co. v. Industrial Accident Comm'n. The full faith and credit clause does not go so far as to compel Delaware to apply §480 if such application would interfere with its local policy.

Accordingly, the judgment is reversed and the case remanded to the Circuit Court of Appeals for decision in conformity with the law of Delaware.

Reversed.

Questions and Comments

(1) *Compare* Judge Friendly in Nolan v. Transocean Airlines, 276 F.2d 280, 281 (2d Cir. 1960): "Our principal task . . . is to determine what New York courts would think California courts would think on an issue about which neither has thought."

(2) In *Klaxon* Justice Reed's opinion says, at the very end, "The full faith and credit clause does not go so far as to compel Delaware to apply §480 if such application would interfere with its local policy." What local policy? If the Delaware courts applied New York substantive law to the merits, what is the *Delaware* policy concerning the assessment of interest after the case has been brought but before judgment has been entered? Traditionally, of course, the interest issue could be called "procedural," but what is the procedural interest in this interest? A rule granting interest, like New York's, might discourage delaying tactics by the defendant, but what procedural policy could lie behind a rule denying interest during the suit? Surely it is not too hard to calculate. And is it fair to say, as Justice Reed does, that the question is only one of "incidental" damages, when the amount of interest is 6 percent of $100,000 for ten years?

(3) If the Court's upholding of the possibility of applying Delaware law means that Delaware has some kind of interest in the issue, doesn't that make *Klaxon* a true conflict case with respect to the interest issue? If so, doesn't that fact put it outside the rationale for *Erie* developed in note (2) at page 575 *supra?* In other words, isn't there a fundamental difference between diversity cases raising issues of internal law and diversity cases raising conflicts issues, because in the former there is only one interested jurisdiction (the state) and a disinterested forum, while in the latter there are two interested jurisdictions (two states) and a disinterested forum? Granting that a federal court may not impose a nonexistent federal interest over an actual state interest, does it follow that a federal court may not choose between two state interests? As a neutral, isn't the federal court in a better position to choose than are the courts of either state?

(4) If the lack of federal interest or constitutional power is the basis for *Erie* and you aren't convinced by the arguments in the previous note, doesn't the full faith and credit clause remain as a basis for a contrary conclusion in *Klaxon?*

(5) Even if *Klaxon* is not constitutionally compelled by *Erie* principles, it has the virtue, for what it's worth, of avoiding forum-shopping. Even that latter virtue was absent, however, in Griffin v. McCoach, 313 U.S. 498 (1941), an interpleader action involving claimants in different states. There, because no state had jurisdiction over all the defendants, the action could only be brought in federal court (using the nationwide jurisdiction provided by the federal interpleader act). Without the possibility of suing in state court, there was no danger of forum-shopping. Nonetheless, the Court, following *Klaxon*, applied Texas conflicts rules, since the action had been brought in a Texas federal court. Even if there are occasional cases like *Griffin* where neither the constitutional reasoning of *Erie* nor the desire to avoid forum-shopping are present, are they numerous enough to justify the agonies of developing federal conflicts laws to govern them?

(6) The desire for uniformity and to avoid forum-shopping remain as policies promoted by *Erie* whether or not its decision is constitutionally mandated. But does *Klaxon* promote uniformity? At least in the case of a true conflict, isn't it almost assured that there will be another jurisdiction where suit could have been brought? In other words, don't recent developments in long-arm jurisdiction make inte*r*state forum-shopping as likely as int*ra*state forum-shopping? Is one worse than the other? And given the result in Van Dusen v. Barrack (page 582 *infra*), which rules that a case transferred under §1404 will take the transferor state's law with it, will it be possible to avoid the evils of forum-shopping, whatever they are, with enough regularity to make the quest worthwhile?

(7) Academics have continued to argue that choice of law is an appropriate subject for federal regulation either by statute, *see* Gottesman, Draining the Dismal Swamp: The Case for Federal Choice of Law Statutes, 80 Geo. L.J. 1 (1991), or by incremental federal common, *see* Trautman, Toward Federalizing Choice of Law, 70 Tex. L. Rev. 1715 (1992). One area particularly ripe for federal regulation might be choice of law in complex litigation. In 1993, the American Law Institute proposed to federalize many choice-of-law and choice-of-forum issues that arise in complex litigation. Chapter 6 of the 1993 Proposed Final Draft of its Complex Litigation Project outlines certain federal choice-of-law principles to be applied to complex litigation in the federal courts. The introductory notes recognize the disuniformity between state and federal courts that this innovation would create, but state that the possibility would dissipate if consolidation procedures were adopted to bring state and federal court cases together into the same court. As to the disuniformity that would then still persist between large complex cases (which would fall under the new federal standard) and smaller litigation (that would fall under *Klaxon*), "the need to achieve justice among the litigants by assuring the uniform and economical treatment of their dispute justifies this difference."

Do you agree? *See generally* Symposium on Problems in Disposition of Mass Related Cases and Proposals for Change, 10 Rev. Litg. 209 (1991). For critical discussions *see* Mullenix, Federalizing Choice of Law for Mass-Tort Litigation, 70 Tex. L. Rev. 1623 (1992); Steinman, Reverse Removal, 78 Iowa L. Rev. 1030 (1993); Sedler, Interest Analysis, State Sovereignty, and Federally Mandated Choice of Law in "Mass Tort" Cases, 56 Alb. L. Rev. 855 (1993); and Weber, Complex Litigation and the State Courts: Constitutional and Practical Advantages of the State Forum Over the Federal Forum in Mass Tort Cases, 21 Hastings Const. L.Q. 216 (1994).

(8) If *Klaxon* should not be followed, of course, it becomes necessary to consider what to do in its absence. Professor Baxter's comparative-impairment approach was announced in the context of an article urging the development of federal choice-of-law rules:

> Baseball's place as the favorite American pastime would not long survive if the responsibilities of the umpire were transferred to the first team member who managed to rule on a disputed event. Responsibility for allocating spheres of legal control among member states of a federal system cannot sensibly be placed elsewhere than with the federal government. . . .
>
> . . . At least after *Erie*, the full-faith-and-credit clause should have been interpreted to dictate the initial choice-of-law reference in every case, whether in a state or federal court. . . . Choice cases cannot be resolved on the basis of private interests except by super-value judgments. Regardless of the criteria used to decide choice cases, the inevitable result of their resolution is an allocation of spheres of legal control. Governmental interests can be identified in choice cases, and the unavoidable allocation of spheres of control ought to be made as those interests dictate by applying the principle of comparative impairment. The process of allocation ought to be committed to the federal government; for the alternative is to place that responsibility, not in the hands of the states, but ad hoc in the hands now of this state, now of that, as determined by promptitude of private party action and the expanding limits of service of process. . . .

Baxter, Choice of Law and the Federal System, 16 Stan. L. Rev. 1, 23, 33 (1963).

Assuming that eventual federal control over choice-of-law questions is appropriate, is the time yet ripe? How about a less drastic (though perhaps sweeping) approach, in which federal courts would apply state conflicts rules only in cases of true conflicts? Precisely such an approach, without much discussion or fanfare, seems to have been taken in Lester v. Aetna Life Ins. Co., 433 F.2d 844 (5th Cir. 1970), *cert. denied*, 402 U.S. 909 (1971).

But *Lester's* potential for a new approach to conflicts proved short-lived. In Day & Zimmerman, Inc. v. Challoner, 423 U.S. 3, 4 (1975), the Supreme Court said of *Lester:*

> We believe that the Court of Appeals either misinterpreted our longstanding decision in *Klaxon,* or else determined for itself that it was no

> longer of controlling force in a case such as this. We are of the opinion that *Klaxon* is by its terms applicable here [in a case similar to *Lester*] and should have been adhered to by the Court of Appeals.
>
> . . . A federal court in a diversity case is not free to engraft onto those state [conflicts] rules exceptions or modifications which may commend themselves to the federal court, but which have not commended themselves to the State in which the federal court sits.

The apparent effect of the Court's decision was to require the application of Cambodian law to a case involving the premature explosion in Cambodia of a 105-millimeter howitzer round, even though the defendant manufacturer and the injured plaintiff were American. Is that a result that the Court would impose if it were not serious about the *Klaxon* rule?

(9) In Harris v. Polskie Linie Lotnicze, 820 F.2d 1000 (9th Cir. 1987), plaintiffs sued LOT, the Polish national airline, after a crash occurring near Warsaw, Poland. The case arose under the Warsaw Convention and jurisdiction was based upon the Foreign Sovereign Immunities Act. In the effort to determine which substantive law to apply, the court stated that usually *Klaxon* would apply in a Warsaw Convention case, but only where the case was in federal court by reason of diversity of citizenship. *Klaxon* did not apply where jurisdiction was based on the F.S.I.A. It therefore developed a federal common law of choice of law, influenced by the Second Restatement. *Compare* Wang Laboratories v. Kagan, 990 F.2d 1126 (9th Cir. 1993) (applying federal rule on enforcement of choice-of-law clause in ERISA case).

Is this an accurate characterization of the range of *Klaxon's* applicability? What if a case contains a federal question sufficient to establish jurisdiction, but there are also state law elements in the case? Should the federal court fashion a federal choice-of-law rule to deal with the state law issues? What about the Rules of Decision Act? *See* Western & Lehman, Is There Life for *Erie* after the Death of Diversity?, 78 Mich. L. Rev. 311 (1980).

Van Dusen v. Barrack

376 U.S. 612 (1964)

Justice GOLDBERG delivered the opinion of the Court.

This case involves the construction and application of §1404(a) of the Judicial Code of 1948. Section 1404(a), which allows a "change of venue" within the federal judicial system, provides that:

> For the convenience of parties and witnesses, in the interest of justice, a district court may transfer any civil action to any other district or division where it might have been brought.

28 U.S.C. §1404(a).

The facts, which need but brief statement here, reveal that the disputed change of venue is set against the background of an alleged mass tort. On October 4, 1960, shortly after departing from a Boston airport, a commercial airliner, scheduled to fly from Boston to Philadelphia, plunged into Boston Harbor. As a result of the crash, over 150 actions for personal injury and wrongful death have been instituted against the airline, various manufacturers, the United States, and, in some cases, the Massachusetts Port Authority. In most of these actions the plaintiffs have alleged that the crash resulted from the defendant's negligence in permitting the aircraft's engines to ingest some birds. More than 100 actions were brought in the United States District Court for the District of Massachusetts, and more than 45 actions in the United States District Court for the Eastern District of Pennsylvania.

The present case concerns 40 of the wrongful death actions brought in the Eastern District of Pennsylvania by personal representatives of victims of the crash.[1] The defendants, petitioners in this Court, moved under §1404(a) to transfer these actions to the District of Massachusetts, where it was alleged that most of the witnesses resided and where over 100 other actions are pending. The District Court granted the motion, holding that the transfer was justified regardless of whether the transferred actions would be governed by the laws and choice-of-law rules of Pennsylvania or of Massachusetts. The District Court also specifically held that transfer was not precluded by the fact that the plaintiffs had not qualified under Massachusetts law to sue as representatives of the decedents. The plaintiffs, respondents in this Court, sought a writ of mandamus from the Court of Appeals and successfully contended that the District Court erred and should vacate its order to transfer. The Court of Appeals held that a §1404(a) transfer could be granted only if at the time the suits were brought, the plaintiffs had qualified to sue in Massachusetts, the State of the transferee District Court. The Court of Appeals relied in part upon its interpretation of Rule 17(b) of the Federal Rules of Civil Procedure.[2]

---

1. The plaintiffs are "Pennsylvania fiduciaries representing the estates of Pennsylvania decedents."

2. Rule 17(b), Fed. Rules Civ. Proc., 28 U.S.C.: "*Capacity to Sue or Be Sued.* The capacity of an individual, other than one acting in a representative capacity, to sue or be sued shall be determined by the law of his domicile. The capacity of a corporation to sue or be sued shall be determined by the law under which it was organized. In all other cases capacity to sue or be sued shall be determined by the law of the state in which the district court is held, except (1) that a partnership or other unincorporated association, which has no such capacity by the law of such state, may sue or be sued in its common name for the purpose of enforcing for or against it a substantive right existing under the Constitution or laws of the United States, and (2) that the capacity of a receiver appointed by a court of the United States to sue or be sued in a court of the United States is governed by Title 28, U.S.C., §§754 and 959(a)."

We granted a certiorari to review important questions concerning the construction and operation of §1404(a). 372 U.S. 964. For reasons to be stated below, we hold that the judgment of the Court of Appeals must be reversed, that both the Court of Appeals and the District Court erred in their fundamental assumptions regarding the state law to be applied to an action transferred under §1404(a), and that accordingly the case must be remanded to the District Court.

[The Court then determined that Massachusetts was a place "where (the action) might have been brought" even though the administrator was not qualified under state law.]

II. "The Interest of Justice": Effect of a Change of Venue upon Applicable State Law

A

The plaintiffs contend that the change of venue ordered by the District Court was necessarily precluded by the likelihood that it would be accompanied by a highly prejudicial change in the applicable state law. The prejudice alleged is not limited to that which might flow from the Massachusetts laws governing capacity to sue. Indeed, the plaintiffs emphasize the likelihood that the defendants' "ultimate reason for seeking transfer is to move to a forum where recoveries for wrongful death are restricted to sharply limited punitive damages rather than compensation for the loss suffered." It is argued that Pennsylvania choice-of-law rules would result in the application of laws substantially different from those that would be applied by courts sitting in Massachusetts. The District Court held, however, that transfer could be ordered regardless of the state laws and choice-of-law rules to be applied in the transferee forum and regardless of the possibility that the laws applicable in the transferor State would significantly differ from those applicable in the transferee State. This ruling assumed that transfer to a more convenient forum may be granted on a defendant's motion even though that transfer would seriously prejudice the plaintiff's legal claim. If this assumption is valid, the plaintiffs argue, transfer is necessarily precluded—regardless of convenience and other considerations—as against the "interest of justice" in dealing with plaintiffs who have either exercised the venue privilege conferred by federal statutes, or had their cases removed from state into federal court.

If conflict of laws rules are laid aside, it is clear that Massachusetts (the State of the transferee court) and Pennsylvania (the State of the transferor court) have significantly different laws concerning recovery for wrongful death. The Massachusetts Death Act provides that one who negligently causes the death of another "shall be liable in damages in the sum of not less than two thousand nor more than twenty thousand dollars, to be assessed with reference to the degree of his culpability. . . ." By contrast, under Pennsylvania law the recovery of damages (1) is based upon the more common principle of compensation for losses rather than upon the degree of the tortfeasor's culpability and (2) is not limited to $20,000. Some of the defendants urge, however, that these differences are irrelevant to the present case because Pennsylvania state courts, applying their own choice of law rules, would require that the Massachusetts Death Act be applied in its entirety, including its culpability principle and damage limitation. It follows that a federal district court sitting in Pennsylvania, and referring, as is required by Klaxon Co. v. Stentor Elec. Mfg. Co., Inc., to Pennsylvania choice of law rules, would therefore be applying the same substantive rules as would a state or federal court in Massachusetts if the actions had been commenced there. This argument highlights the fact that the most convenient forum is frequently the place where the cause of action arose and that the conflict-of-laws rules of other States may often refer to the substantive rules of the more convenient forum. The plaintiffs, however, point to the decision of the New York Court of Appeals in Kilberg v. Northeast Airlines, Inc. and the decision of the Court of Appeals for the Second Circuit in Pearson v. Northeast Airlines, Inc. as indicating that Pennsylvania, in light of its laws and policies, might not apply the culpability and damage limitation aspects of the Massachusetts statute. The District Court, in ordering that the actions be transferred, found it both undesirable and unnecessary to rule on the question of whether Pennsylvania courts would accept the right of action provided by the Massachusetts statute while at the same time denying enforcement of the Massachusetts measure of recovery.[24] The District Court found it undesirable to resolve this question because the Pennsylvania courts had not yet considered it and because they would, in view of similar pending cases, soon have an opportunity to do so. The District Court, being of the opinion that the District of Massachusetts was in any event a more convenient place for trial, reasoned that the transfer should be granted forthwith and that the transferee court could proceed to the trial of the actions and postpone consideration of the Pennsylvania choice of law rule as to damage until a later time at which the Pennsylvania decisions might well have supplied useful guidance. Fundamentally, however, the transferring District Court assumed that the Pennsylvania choice of law rule was irrelevant because the transfer would be permissible and justified even if accompanied by a significant change of law.

The possibilities suggested by the plaintiffs' argument illustrate the difficulties that would arise if a change of venue, granted at the motion of a defendant, were to result in a change of law. Although in the present case the contentions concern rules relating to capacity to sue and damages, in other cases the transferee forum might have a shorter statute of limitations or might

---

24. The defendants, rejecting the view adopted by the Second Circuit in Pearson v. Northeast Airlines, Inc., contend that the Full Faith and Credit Clause requires Pennsylvania courts to follow all the terms of the Massachusetts Death Act. We intimate no view concerning this contention.

refuse to adjudicate a claim which would have been actionable in the transferor State. In such cases a defendant's motion to transfer could be tantamount to a motion to dismiss. In light, therefore, of this background and the facts of the present case, we need not and do not consider the merits of the contentions concerning the meaning and proper application of Pennsylvania's laws and choice of laws rules. For present purposes it is enough that the potential prejudice to the plaintiffs is so substantial as to require review of the assumption that a change of state law would be a permissible result of transfer under §1404(a).

There is nothing . . . in the language or policy of §1404(a) to justify its use by defendants to defeat the advantages accruing to plaintiffs who have chosen a forum which, although it was inconvenient, was a proper venue. In this regard the transfer provisions of §1404(a) may be compared with those of §1406(a). Although both sections were broadly designed to allow transfer instead of dismissal, §1406(a) provides for transfer from forums in which venue is wrongly or improperly laid, whereas, in contrast, §1404(a) operates on the premise that the plaintiff has properly exercised his venue privilege. This distinction underlines the fact that Congress, in passing §1404(a), was primarily concerned with the problems arising where, despite the propriety of the plaintiff's venue selection, the chosen forum was an inconvenient one.

The legislative history of §1404(a) certainly does not justify the rather startling conclusion that one might "get a change of law as a bonus for a change of venue." Indeed, an interpretation accepting such a rule would go far to frustrate the remedial purposes of §1404(a). If a change of law were in the offing, the parties might well regard the section primarily as a forum-shopping instrument. And, more importantly, courts would at least be reluctant to grant transfers, despite considerations of convenience, if to do so might conceivably prejudice the claim of a plaintiff who had initially selected a permissible forum. We believe, therefore, that both the history and purposes of §1404(a) indicate that it should be regarded as a federal judicial housekeeping measure, dealing with the placement of litigation in the federal courts and generally intended, on the basis of convenience and fairness, simply to authorize a change of courtrooms.

Although we deal here with a congressional statute apportioning the business of the federal courts, our interpretation of that statute fully accords with and is supported by the policy underlying Erie R. Co. v. Tompkins. This Court has often formulated the *Erie* doctrine by stating that it establishes "the principle of uniformity within a state," Klaxon Co. v. Stentor Elec. Mfg. Co., Inc., and declaring that federal courts in diversity of citizenship cases are to apply the laws "of the states in which they sit," Griffin v. McCoach. A superficial reading of these formulations might suggest that a transferee federal court should apply the law of the State in which it sits rather than the law of the transferor State. Such a reading, however, directly contradicts the fundamental *Erie* doctrine which the quoted formulations were designed to express. As this Court said in Guaranty Trust Co. v. York:

> Erie R. Co. v. Tompkins was not an endeavor to formulate scientific legal terminology. It expressed a policy that touches vitally the proper distribution of judicial power between State and federal courts. . . . The nub of the policy that underlies Erie R. Co. v. Tompkins is that for the same transaction the accident of a suit by a non-resident litigant in a federal court instead of in a State court a block away should not lead to a substantially different result.

Applying this analysis to §1404(a), we should ensure that the "accident" of federal diversity jurisdiction does not enable a party to utilize a transfer to achieve a result in federal court which could not have been achieved in the courts of the State where the action was filed. This purpose would be defeated in cases such as the present if nonresident defendants, properly subjected to suit in the transferor State (Pennsylvania), could invoke §1404(a) to gain the benefits of the laws of another jurisdiction (Massachusetts). What *Erie* and the cases following it have sought was an identity or uniformity between federal and state courts; and the fact that in most instances this could be achieved by directing federal courts to apply the laws of the States "in which they sit" should not obscure that, in applying the same reasoning to §1404(a), the critical identity to be maintained is between the federal district court which decides the case and the courts of the State in which the action was filed.

We conclude, therefore, that in cases such as the present, where the defendants seek transfer, the transferee district court must be obligated to apply the state law that would have been applied if there had been no change of venue. A change of venue under §1404(a) generally should be, with respect to state law, but a change of courtrooms.[40]

We, therefore, reject the plaintiff's contention that the transfer was necessarily precluded by the likelihood that a prejudicial change of law would result. In also ruling, however, we do not and need not consider whether in all cases §1404(a) would require the application of the law of the transferor, as opposed to the transferee, State.[41] We do not attempt to determine whether, for example, the same considerations would govern if a plaintiff sought transfer under §1404(a) or if it was contended that the transferor State would simply have dismissed the action on the ground of forum non conveniens. . . .

---

40. Of course the transferee District Court may apply its own rules governing the conduct and dispatch of cases in its court. We are only concerned here with those state laws of the transferor State which would significantly affect the outcome of the case.

41. We do not suggest that the application of transferor state law is free from constitutional limitations. *See, e.g.*, Watson v. Employers Liability Assurance Corp. Ltd.; Hughes v. Fetter; Pacific Employers Ins. Co. v. Industrial Accident Commn.; Alaska Packers Assn. v. Industrial Accident Commn.; Home Ins. Co. v. Dick.

Questions and Comments

(1) The Court justifies its result in *Van Dusen* by observing that 28 U.S.C. §1404 was intended only to change the courthouse, and nothing else. But what if such a desire is impossible to accomplish? Doesn't §1404 plus the decision in *Van Dusen* give plaintiffs a right they never had before—the right to choose an inconvenient forum with favorable law, secure in the knowledge that §1404 will allow transfer to a convenient forum? Did Congress intend to give plaintiffs this advantage in passing §1404? Thus interpreted, won't §1404 *encourage* federal-state forum-shopping by plaintiffs (by removing the limitation of convenience), thus countering the only justification for *Klaxon?*

(2) How should a similar case be treated if transfer were sought under §1406, which allows transfer when venue is improperly laid? In Martin v. Stokes, 623 F.2d 469 (6th Cir. 1980), the court held that the law of the transferee forum would apply in cases transferred under 28 U.S.C. §1406 (transfer where venue lacking in original forum). Correct? What should be the result under a §1404 transfer if the courts of the state in which suit was originally brought would have dismissed the case on forum non conveniens grounds? Would *Erie* principles then dictate a change in law accompanying the transfer? If so and if there were *two* possible transferee forums with different choice-of-law rules, how should the transferor court choose between them?

(3) Should the *Van Dusen* principle be applied to a §1404 or §1407 transfer in a federal question case when the transfer is to a different circuit with a different interpretation of federal law controlling an issue in the case? Judge (now Justice) Ruth Bader Ginsburg believes that "[this] is a question meriting attention from a Higher Authority." In re Korean Air Lines Disaster of September 1, 1983, 829 F.2d 1171, 1174 (D.C. Cir. 1987). In the absence of guidance from Congress, the Supreme Court, and the Judicial Panel on Multidistrict Litigation, she concluded that in a §1407 transfer, the transferee court should use its own best judgment on matters of federal law. *Compare* Eckstein v. Balcor Film Investors, 8 F.3d 1121 (7th Cir. 1993), holding that this is usually the right result.

(4) A perceptive discussion of the general *Van Dusen* problem may be found in Note, Choice of Law in Federal Court after Transfer of Venue, 63 Cornell L. Rev. 149 (1977). The piece asserts that "[i]n the few reported cases where plaintiffs moved for transfer from proper forums, however, the defendants argued for the law of the transferor. This suggests that plaintiff-transferors often blunder in selecting an initial forum." *Id.* at 156 (footnote omitted). Should the blundering plaintiff have the right to the law of the transferee forum if it favors him, on the ground that he could have filed there in the first place? *Compare* Ferens v. Deere & Co., immediately below.

(5) In Scott v. Eastern Airlines, 399 F.2d 14 (3d Cir. 1967), the Third Circuit ruled that neither Pennsylvania nor Massachusetts law applied to the air crash involved in *Van Dusen* because the crash had occurred in navigable waters, making federal maritime law applicable.

Ferens v. John Deere Co.

494 U.S. 516 (1989)

Justice KENNEDY delivered the opinion of the Court.

Section 1404(a) of Title 28 states: "For the convenience of parties and witnesses, in the interest of justice, a district court may transfer any civil action to any other district or division where it might have been brought." 28 U.S.C. §1404(a) (1982 ed.). In Van Dusen v. Barrack, 376 U.S. 612 (1964), we held that, following a transfer under §1404(a) initiated by a defendant, the transferee court must follow the choice-of-law rules that prevailed in the transferor court. We now decide that, when a plaintiff moves for the transfer, the same rule applies.

I

Albert Ferens lost his right hand when, the allegation is, it became caught in his combine harvester, manufactured by Deere & Company. The accident occurred while Ferens was working with the combine on his farm in Pennsylvania. For reasons not explained in the record, Ferens delayed filing a tort suit, and Pennsylvania's 2-year limitations period expired. In the third year, he and his wife sued Deere in the United States District Court for the Western District of Pennsylvania, raising contract and warranty claims as to which the Pennsylvania limitations period had not yet run. The District Court had diversity jurisdiction, as Ferens and his wife are Pennsylvania residents, and Deere is incorporated in Delaware with its principal place of business in Illinois.

Not to be deprived of a tort action, the Ferenses in the same year filed a second diversity suit against Deere in the United States District Court for the Southern District of Mississippi, alleging negligence and products liability. Diversity jurisdiction and venue were proper. The Ferenses sued Deere in the District Court in Mississippi because they knew that, under Klaxon Co. v. Stentor Electric Mfg. Co., 313 U.S. 487, 496 (1941), the federal court in the exercise of diversity jurisdiction must apply the same choice-of-law rules that Mississippi state courts would apply if they were deciding the case. A Mississippi court would rule that Pennsylvania substantive law controls the personal injury claim but that Mississippi's own law governs the limitation period.

Although Mississippi has a borrowing statute which, on its face, would seem to enable its courts to apply statutes of limitations from other jurisdictions, *see* Miss. Code Ann. §15-1-65 (1972), the State Supreme Court has said that the borrowing statute "only applies where a nonresident [defendant] in whose favor the statute has accrued afterwards moves into this state." Louisiana & Mississippi R. Transfer Co. v. Long, 159 Miss. 654, 667, 131 So.

84, 88 (1930). The borrowing statute would not apply to the Ferenses' action because, as the parties agree, Deere was a corporate resident of Mississippi before the cause of action accrued. The Mississippi courts, as a result, would apply Mississippi's 6-year statute of limitations to the tort claim arising under Pennsylvania law and the tort action would not be time barred under the Mississippi statute. *See* Miss. Code Ann. §15-1-49 (1972).

The issue now before us arose when the Ferenses took their forum shopping a step further: having chosen the federal court in Mississippi to take advantage of the State's limitations period, they next moved, under §1404(a), to transfer the action to the federal court in Pennsylvania on the ground that Pennsylvania was a more convenient forum. The Ferenses acted on the assumption that, after the transfer, the choice-of-law rules in the Mississippi forum, including a rule requiring application of the Mississippi statute of limitations, would continue to govern the suit.

Deere put up no opposition, and the District Court in Mississippi granted the §1404(a) motion. The court accepted the Ferenses' arguments that they resided in Pennsylvania; that the accident occurred there; that the claim had no connection to Mississippi; that a substantial number of witnesses resided in the Western District of Pennsylvania but none resided in Mississippi; that most of the documentary evidence was located in the Western District of Pennsylvania but none was located in Mississippi; and that the warranty action pending in the Western District of Pennsylvania presented common questions of law and fact.

The District Court in Pennsylvania consolidated the transferred tort action with the Ferenses' pending warranty action but declined to honor the Mississippi statute of limitations as the District Court in Mississippi would have done. It ruled instead that, because the Ferenses had moved for transfer as plaintiffs, the rule in *Van Dusen* did not apply. Invoking the 2-year limitations period set by Pennsylvania law, the District Court dismissed their tort action. Ferens v. Deere & Co., 639 F. Supp. 1484 (W.D. Pa. 1986).

The Court of Appeals for the Third Circuit affirmed. . . .

II

Section 1404(a) states only that a district court may transfer venue for the convenience of the parties and witnesses when in the interest of justice. It says nothing about choice of law and nothing about affording plaintiffs different treatment from defendants. [The Court describes the facts and holding of *Van Dusen.*]

III

. . . *Van Dusen* reveals three independent reasons for our decision. First, §1404(a) should not deprive parties of state-law advantages that exist absent diversity jurisdiction. Second, §1404(a) should not create or multiply opportunities for forum shopping. Third, the decision to transfer venue under §1404(a) should turn on considerations of convenience and the interest of justice rather than on the possible prejudice resulting from a change of law. Although commentators have questioned whether the scant legislative history of §1404(a) compels reliance on these three policies, *see* Note, Choice of Law after Transfer of Venue, 75 Yale L.J. 90, 123 (1965), we find it prudent to consider them in deciding whether the rule in *Van Dusen* applies to transfers initiated by plaintiffs. We decide that, in addition to other considerations, these policies require a transferee forum to apply the law of the transferor court, regardless of who initiates the transfer. A transfer under §1404(a), in other words, does not change the law applicable to a diversity case.

A

The policy that §1404(a) should not deprive parties of state-law advantages, although perhaps discernible in the legislative history, has its real foundation in Erie R. Co. v. Tompkins, 304 U.S. 64 (1938). *See Van Dusen,* 376 U.S., at 637. The *Erie* rule remains a vital expression of the federal system and the concomitant integrity of the separate States. We explained *Erie* in Guaranty Trust Co. v. York, 326 U.S. 99, 109 (1945), as follows:

> In essence, the intent of [the *Erie*] decision was to insure that, in all cases where a federal court is exercising jurisdiction solely because of the diversity of citizenship of the parties, the outcome of the litigation in the federal court should be substantially the same, so far as legal rules determine the outcome of a litigation, as it would be if tried in a State court. The nub of the policy that underlies Erie R. Co. v. Tompkins is that for the same transaction the accident of a suit by a nonresident litigant in a federal court instead of in a State court a block away should not lead to a substantially different result.

In Hanna v. Plumer, 380 U.S. 460, 473 (1965), we held that Congress has the power to prescribe procedural rules that differ from state-law rules even at the expense of altering the outcome of litigation. This case does not involve a conflict. As in *Van Dusen,* our interpretation of §1404(a) is in full accord with the *Erie* rule.

The *Erie* policy had a clear implication for *Van Dusen.* The existence of diversity jurisdiction gave the defendants the opportunity to make a motion to transfer venue under §1404(a), and if the applicable law were to change after transfer, the plaintiff's venue privilege and resulting state-law advantages could be defeated at the defendant's option. 376 U.S., at 638. To allow the transfer and at the same time preserve the plaintiff's state-law advantages, we held that the choice-of-law rules should not change following a transfer initiated by a defendant. *Id.,* at 639.

Transfers initiated by a plaintiff involve some different considerations, but lead to the same result. Applying the transferor law, of course, will not deprive the plaintiff of any state-law advantages. A defendant, in one sense, also will lose no legal advantage if the transferor law controls after a transfer initiated by the plaintiff; the same law, after all, would have applied if the plaintiff had not made the motion. In another sense, however, a defendant may lose a nonlegal advantage. Deere, for example, would lose whatever advantage inheres in not having to litigate in Pennsylvania, or, put another way, in forcing the Ferenses to litigate in Mississippi or not at all.

We, nonetheless, find the advantage that the defendant loses slight. A plaintiff always can sue in the favorable state court or sue in diversity and not seek a transfer. By asking for application of the Mississippi statute of limitations following a transfer to Pennsylvania on grounds of convenience, the Ferenses are seeking to deprive Deere only of the advantage of using against them the inconvenience of litigating in Mississippi. The text of §1404(a) may not say anything about choice of law, but we think it not the purpose of the section to protect a party's ability to use inconvenience as a shield to discourage or hinder litigation otherwise proper. The section exists to eliminate inconvenience without altering permissible choices under the venue statutes. This interpretation should come as little surprise. As in our previous cases, we think that "[t]o construe §1404(a) this way merely carries out its design to protect litigants, witnesses and the public against unnecessary inconvenience and expense, not to provide a shelter for . . . proceedings in costly and inconvenient forums." Continental Grain Co. v. Barge FBL-585, 364 U.S. 19, 27 (1960). By creating an opportunity to have venue transferred between courts in different States on the basis of convenience, an option that does not exist absent federal jurisdiction, Congress, with respect to diversity, retained the *Erie* policy while diminishing the incidents of inconvenience.

Applying the transferee law, by contrast, would undermine the *Erie* rule in a serious way. It would mean that initiating a transfer under §1404(a) changes the state law applicable to a diversity case. We have held, in an isolated circumstance, that §1404(a) may pre-empt state law. *See* Stewart Organization, Inc. v. Ricoh Corp., 487 U.S. 22 (1988) (holding that federal law determines the validity of a forum selection clause). In general, however, we have seen §1404(a) as a housekeeping measure that should not alter the state law governing a case under *Erie*. *See Van Dusen, supra*; *see also Stewart Organization, supra*, at 37 (Scalia, J., dissenting) (finding the language of §1404(a) "plainly insufficient" to work a change in the applicable state law through pre-emption). The Mississippi statute of limitations, which everyone agrees would have applied if the Ferenses had not moved for a transfer, should continue to apply in this case.

In any event, defendants in the position of Deere would not fare much better if we required application of the transferee law instead of the transferor law. True, if the transferee law were to apply, some plaintiffs would not sue these defendants for fear that they would have no choice but to litigate in an inconvenient forum. But applying the transferee law would not discourage all plaintiffs from suing. Some plaintiffs would prefer to litigate in an inconvenient forum with favorable law than to litigate in a convenient forum with unfavorable law or not to litigate at all. The Ferenses, no doubt, would have abided by their initial choice of the District Court in Mississippi had they known that the District Court in Pennsylvania would dismiss their action. If we were to rule for Deere in this case, we would accomplish little more than discouraging the occasional motions by plaintiffs to transfer inconvenient cases. Other plaintiffs would sue in an inconvenient forum with the expectation that the defendants themselves would seek transfer to a convenient forum, resulting in application of the transferor law under *Van Dusen*. In this case, for example, Deere might have moved for a transfer if the Ferenses had not.

B

Van Dusen also sought to fashion a rule that would not create opportunities for forum shopping. Some commentators have seen this policy as the most important rationale of *Van Dusen, see, e.g.*, 19 C. Wright, A. Miller, & E. Cooper, Federal Practice and Procedure §4506, p. 79 (1982), but few attempt to explain the harm of forum shopping when the plaintiff initiates a transfer. An opportunity for forum shopping exists whenever a party has a choice of forums that will apply different laws. The *Van Dusen* policy against forum shopping simply requires us to interpret §1404(a) in a way that does not create an opportunity for obtaining a more favorable law by selecting a forum through a transfer of venue. In the *Van Dusen* case itself, this meant that we could not allow defendants to use a transfer to change the law. 376 U.S., at 636.

No interpretation of §1404(a), however, will create comparable opportunities for forum shopping by a plaintiff because, even without §1404(a), a plaintiff already has the option of shopping for a forum with the most favorable law. The Ferenses, for example, had an opportunity for forum shopping in the state courts because both the Mississippi and Pennsylvania courts had jurisdiction and because they each would have applied a different statute of limitations. Diversity jurisdiction did not eliminate these forum shopping opportunities; instead, under *Erie*, the federal courts had to replicate them. *See* Klaxon Co. v. Stentor Electric Mfg. Co., 313 U.S., at 496 ("Whatever lack of uniformity [*Erie*] may produce between federal courts in different states is attributable to our federal system, which leaves to a state, within the limits permitted by the Constitution, the right to pursue local policies diverging from those of its neighbors"). Applying the transferor law would not give a plaintiff an opportunity to use a transfer to obtain a law that he could not obtain through his initial forum selection. If it does make selection of the most favorable law more convenient, it does no more than recognize a forum shopping choice that already exists. This fact does not require us to apply the transferee law. Section 1404(a), to reiterate, exists to make venue convenient and should not allow the defendant to use inconvenience to discourage plaintiffs from exercising the opportunities that they already have.

Applying the transferee law, by contrast, might create opportunities for forum shopping in an indirect way. The advantage to Mississippi's personal injury lawyers that resulted from the State's then applicable 6-year statute of limitations has not escaped us; Mississippi's long limitation period no doubt drew plaintiffs to the State. Although *Sun Oil* held that the federal courts have little interest in a State's decision to create a long statute of limitations or to apply its statute of limitations to claims governed by foreign law, we should recognize the consequences of our interpretation of §1404(a). Applying the transferee law, to the extent that it discourages plaintiff-initiated transfers, might give States incentives to enact similar laws to bring in out-of-state business that would not be moved at the instance of the plaintiff.

C

Van Dusen also made clear that the decision to transfer venue under §1404(a) should turn on considerations of convenience rather than on the possibility of prejudice resulting from a change in the applicable law. *See* 376 U.S., at 636; Piper Aircraft Co. v. Reyno, 454 U.S. 235, 253-254, and n.20 (1981). We reasoned in *Van Dusen* that, if the law changed following a transfer initiated by the defendant, a district court "would at least be reluctant to grant transfers, despite considerations of convenience, if to do so might conceivably prejudice the claim of a plaintiff." 376 U.S., at 636. The court, to determine the prejudice, might have to make an elaborate survey of the law, including statutes of limitations, burdens of proof, presumptions, and the like. This would turn what is supposed to be a statute for convenience of the courts into one expending extensive judicial time and resources. Because this difficult task is contrary to the purpose of the statute, in *Van Dusen* we made it unnecessary by ruling that a transfer of venue by the defendant does not result in a change of law. This same policy requires application of the transferor law when a plaintiff initiates a transfer.

If the law were to change following a transfer initiated by a plaintiff, a district court in a similar fashion would be at least reluctant to grant a transfer that would prejudice the defendant. Hardship might occur because plaintiffs may find as many opportunities to exploit application of the transferee law as they would find opportunities for exploiting application of the transferor law. *See* Note, 63 Cornell L. Rev., at 156. If the transferee law were to apply, moreover, the plaintiff simply would not move to transfer unless the benefits of convenience outweighed the loss of favorable law.

Some might think that a plaintiff should pay the price for choosing an inconvenient forum by being put to a choice of law versus forum. But this assumes that §1404(a) is for the benefit only of the moving party. By the statute's own terms, it is not. Section 1404(a) also exists for the benefit of the witnesses and the interest of justice, which must include the convenience of the court. Litigation in an inconvenient forum does not harm the plaintiff alone. As Justice Jackson said:

> Administrative difficulties follow for courts when litigation is piled up in congested centers instead of being handled at its origin. Jury duty is a burden that ought not to be imposed upon the people of a community which has no relation to the litigation. In cases which touch the affairs of many persons, there is reason for holding the trial in their view and reach rather than in remote parts of the country where they can learn of it by report only. There is a local interest in having localized controversies decided at home. There is an appropriateness too, in having the trial of a diversity case in a forum that is at home with the state law that must govern the case, rather than having a court in some other forum untangle problems in conflicts of laws, and in law foreign to itself.

Gulf Oil Corp. v. Gilbert, 330 U.S. 501, 508-509 (1947). The desire to take a punitive view of the plaintiff's actions should not obscure the systemic costs of litigating in an inconvenient place.

D

This case involves some considerations to which we perhaps did not give sufficient attention in *Van Dusen.* Foresight and judicial economy now seem to favor the simple rule that the law does not change following a transfer of venue under §1404(a). Affording transfers initiated by plaintiffs different treatment from transfers initiated by defendants may seem quite workable in this case, but the simplicity is an illusion. If we were to hold that the transferee law applies following a §1404(a) motion by a plaintiff, cases such as this would not arise in the future. Although applying the transferee law, no doubt, would catch the Ferenses by surprise, in the future no plaintiffs in their position would move for a change of venue.

Other cases, however, would produce undesirable complications. The rule would leave unclear which law should apply when both a defendant and a plaintiff move for a transfer of venue or when the court transfers venue on its own motion. *See* Note, 63 Cornell L. Rev., at 158. The rule also might require variation in certain situations, such as when the plaintiff moves for a transfer following a removal from state court by the defendant, or when only one of several plaintiffs requests the transfer, or when circumstances change through no fault of the plaintiff making a once convenient forum inconvenient. True, we could reserve any consideration of these questions for a later day. But we have a duty, in deciding this case, to consider whether our decision will create litigation and uncertainty. On the basis of these considerations, we again conclude that the transferor law should apply regardless of who makes the §1404(a) motion.

IV

Some may object that a district court in Pennsylvania should not have to apply a Mississippi statute of limitations to a Pennsylvania cause of action. This point, although understandable, should have little to do with the outcome of this case. Congress gave the Ferenses the power to seek a transfer in §1404(a), and our decision in *Van Dusen* already could require a district court in Pennsylvania to apply the Mississippi statute of limitations to Pennsylvania claims. Our rule may seem too generous because it allows the Ferenses to have both their choice of law and their choice of forum, or even to reward the Ferenses for conduct that seems manipulative. We nonetheless see no alternative rule that would produce a more acceptable result. Deciding that the transferee law should-apply, in effect, would tell the Ferenses that they should have continued to litigate their warranty action in Pennsylvania and their tort action in Mississippi. Some might find this preferable, but we do not. We have made quite clear that "[t]o permit a situation in which two cases involving precisely the same issues are simultaneously pending in different District Courts leads to the wastefulness of time, energy and money that §1404(a) was designed to prevent." *Continental Grain*, 364 U.S., at 26.

From a substantive standpoint, two further objections give us pause but do not persuade us to change our rule. First, one might ask why we require the Ferenses to file in the District Court in Mississippi at all. Efficiency might seem to dictate a rule allowing plaintiffs in the Ferenses' position not to file in an inconvenient forum and then to return to a convenient forum though a transfer of venue, but instead simply to file in the convenient forum and ask for the law of the inconvenient forum to apply. Although our rule may invoke certain formality, one must remember that §1404(a) does not provide for an automatic transfer of venue. The section, instead, permits a transfer only when convenient and "in the interest of justice." Plaintiffs in the position of the Ferenses must go to the distant forum because they have no guarantee, until the court there examines the facts, that they may obtain a transfer. No one has contested the justice of transferring this particular case, but the option remains open to defendants in future cases. Although a court cannot ignore the systemic costs of inconvenience, it may consider the course that the litigation already has taken in determining the interest of justice.

Second, one might contend that, because no per se rule requiring a court to apply either the transferor law or the transferee law will seem appropriate in all circumstances, we should develop more sophisticated federal choice-of-law rules for diversity actions involving transfers. *See* Note, 75 Yale L.J., at 130-135. To a large extent, however, state conflicts-of-law rules already ensure that appropriate laws will apply to diversity cases. Federal law, as a general matter, does not interfere with these rules. *See Sun Oil,* 486 U.S., at 727-729. In addition, even if more elaborate federal choice-of-law rules would not run afoul of *Klaxon* and *Erie,* we believe that applying the law of the transferor forum effects the appropriate balance between fairness and simplicity.

For the foregoing reasons, we conclude that Mississippi's statute of limitations should govern the Ferenses' action. We reverse and remand for proceedings consistent with this opinion.

It is so ordered.

Justice SCALIA, with whom Justice BRENNAN, Justice MARSHALL, and Justice BLACKMUN join, dissenting.

The question we must answer today is whether 28 U.S.C. §1404(a) (1982 ed.) and the policies underlying *Klaxon*—namely, uniformity within a State and the avoidance of forum shopping—produce a result different from *Klaxon* when the suit in question was not filed in the federal court initially, but was transferred there under §1404(a) on plaintiff's motion. In Van Dusen v. Barrack, 376 U.S. 612 (1964), we held that a result different from *Klaxon* is produced when a suit has been transferred under §1404(a) on defendant's motion. Our reasons were two. First, we thought it highly unlikely that Congress, in enacting §1404(a), meant to provide defendants with a device by which to manipulate the substantive rules that would be applied. 376 U.S., at 633-636. That conclusion rested upon the fact that the law grants the plaintiff the advantage of choosing the venue in which his action will be tried, with whatever state-law advantages accompany that choice. A defensive use of §1404(a) in order to deprive the plaintiff of this "venue privilege," *id.*, at 634, would allow the defendant to " 'get a change of law as a bonus for a change of venue,' " *id.*, at 636 (citation omitted), and would permit the defendant to engage in forum shopping among States, a privilege that the *Klaxon* regime reserved for plaintiffs. Second, we concluded that the policies of *Erie* and *Klaxon* would be undermined by application of the transferee court's choice-of-law principles in the case of a defendant-initiated transfer, *id.*, at 637-640, because then "the 'accident' of federal diversity jurisdiction" would enable the defendant "to utilize a transfer to achieve a result in federal court which could not have been achieved in the courts of the State where the action was filed," *id.*, at 638. The goal of *Erie* and *Klaxon,* we reasoned, was to prevent "forum shopping" as between state and federal systems; the plaintiff makes a choice of forum law by filing the complaint, and that choice must be honored in federal court, just as it would have been honored in state court, where the defendant would not have been able to transfer the case to another State.

We left open in *Van Dusen* the question presented today, viz., whether "the same considerations would govern" if a plaintiff sought a §1404(a) transfer. 376 U.S., at 640. In my view, neither of those considerations is served—and indeed both are positively defeated—by a departure from *Klaxon* in that context. First, just as it is unlikely that Congress, in enacting §1404(a), meant to provide the defendant with a vehicle by which to manipulate in his favor the substantive law to be applied in a diversity case, so too is it unlikely that Congress meant to provide the *plaintiff* with a vehicle by which to appropriate the law of a distant and inconvenient forum in which he does not intend to litigate, and to carry that prize back to the State in which he wishes to try the case. Second, application of the transferor court's law in this context would encourage forum shopping between federal and state courts in the same jurisdiction on the basis of differential substantive law. It is true, of course, that the plaintiffs here did not select the *Mississippi* federal court in preference to the Mississippi state courts because of any differential substantive law; the former, like the latter, would have applied Mississippi choice-of-law rules and thus the Mississippi statute of limitations. But one must be blind to reality to say that it is the *Mississippi* federal court in which these plaintiffs have chosen to sue. That was merely a way station en route to suit in the *Pennsylvania* federal court. The plaintiffs were seeking to achieve exactly what *Klaxon* was designed to prevent: the use of a Pennsylvania federal court instead of a Pennsylvania state court in order to obtain application of a different substantive law. Our decision in *Van Dusen* compromised "the principle of uniformity within a state," *Klaxon, supra*, at 496, only in the abstract, but today's decision compromises it precisely in the respect that matters—*i.e.*, insofar as it bears upon the plaintiff's choice between a state and a federal forum. The significant federal judicial policy expressed in *Erie* and *Klaxon* is reduced to a laughingstock if it can so readily be evaded through filing-and-transfer.

The Court is undoubtedly correct that applying the *Klaxon* rule after a plaintiff-initiated transfer would deter a plaintiff in a situation such as exists here from seeking a transfer, since that would deprive him of the favorable substantive law. But that proves only that this disposition achieves what *Erie* and *Klaxon* are designed to achieve: preventing the plaintiff from using "the accident of diversity of citizenship," *Klaxon*, 313 U.S., at 496, to obtain the application of a different law within the State where he wishes to litigate. In the context of the present case, he must either litigate in the State of Mississippi under Mississippi law, or in the Commonwealth of Pennsylvania under Pennsylvania law.

[I]t seems to me that a proper calculation of systemic costs [of the Court's decision] would go as follows: Saved by the Court's rule will be the incremental cost of trying in forums that are inconvenient (but not so inconvenient as to prompt the court's sua sponte transfer) those suits that are now filed in such forums for choice-of-law purposes. But incurred by the Court's rule will be the costs of considering and effecting transfer, not only in those suits but in the indeterminate number of additional suits that will be filed in inconvenient forums now that filing-and-transfer is an approved form of shopping for law; plus the costs attending the necessity for transferee courts to figure out the choice-of-law rules (and probably the substantive law) of distant States much more often than our *Van Dusen* decision would require. It should be noted that the file-and-transfer ploy sanctioned by the Court today will be available not merely to achieve the relatively rare (and generally unneeded) benefit of a longer statute of limitations, but also to bring home to the desired state of litigation all sorts of favorable choice-of-law rules regarding substantive liability—in an era when the diversity among the States in choice-of-law principles has become kaleidoscopic.[2]

Thus, even as an exercise in giving the most extensive possible scope to the policies of §1404(a), the Court's opinion seems to me unsuccessful. But as I indicated by beginning this opinion with the Rules of Decision Act, that should not be the object of the exercise at all. The Court and I reach different results largely because we approach the question from different directions. For the Court, this case involves an "interpretation of §1404(a)," *ante*, at 524, and the central issue is whether *Klaxon* stands in the way of the policies of that statute. For me, the case involves an interpretation of the Rules of Decision Act, and the central issue is whether §1404(a) alters the "principle of uniformity within a state" which *Klaxon* says that Act embodies. I think my approach preferable, not only because the Rules of Decision Act does, and §1404(a) does not, address the specific subject of which law to apply, but also because, as the Court acknowledges, our jurisprudence under that statute is "a vital expression of the federal system and the concomitant integrity of the separate States," *ante*, at 523. To ask, as in effect the Court does, whether *Erie* gets in the way of §1404(a), rather than whether §1404(a) requires adjustment of *Erie*, seems to me the expression of a mistaken sense of priorities.

For the foregoing reasons, I respectfully dissent.

Questions and Comments

(1) If the dissent is correct that the issue is easily resolved by reference to the Rules of Decision Act, then wouldn't Van Dusen v. Barrack have to be overruled? How can the Act itself require a federal court to apply the same law as the state court across the street, when all it says is that "the laws of the several states . . . shall be regarded as rules of decisions," without saying which states? The notion that the relevant state is the one in which the

2. The current edition of Professor Leflar's treatise on American Conflicts Law lists 10 separate theories of choice of law that are applied, individually or in various combinations, by the 50 States. *See* R. Leflar, L. McDougall III, & R. Felix, American Conflicts Law §§86-91, 93-96 (4th ed. 1986). *See also* Kay, Theory into Practice: Choice of Law in the Courts, 34 Mercer L. Rev. 521, 525-584, 591-592 (1983).

federal court sits stems from *Erie,* not from the text of the Act, and *Erie* did not purport to be addressing matters such as choice of law after change of venue; indeed, if it had addressed such issues, its opinions could have been dismissed as dicta.

If *Klaxon* rests on constitutional principles, then why shouldn't it take precedence over the Rules of Decision Act, even assuming that the dissent is correct about what the Act requires? If section 1404(a) has equal standing to the Rules of Decision Act (both being statutes) then which one should govern in case of conflict?

(2) Doesn't the holding of the majority turn litigation into even more of an artificial game than it would otherwise be? Will the average person have any respect at all for the legal process if such things are allowed? Or was the average person's view of legal process already so low before *Ferens* that the *Ferens* result couldn't make things any worse?

(3) Both the majority and the dissent attempted to make it appear that their conclusions were compelled by the existing statutory scheme. If you were in charge of writing the statutes to govern federal venue, how would you draft them to avoid the *Ferens* problem?

2. *Erie* and Choice of Forum

Stewart Organization, Inc. v. Ricoh Corp.

487 U.S. 22 (1988)

Justice MARSHALL delivered the opinion of the Court.

This case presents the issue whether a federal court sitting in diversity should apply state or federal law in adjudicating a motion to transfer a case to a venue provided in a contractual forum-selection clause.

I

The dispute underlying this case grew out of a dealership agreement that obligated petitioner, an Alabama corporation, to market copier products of respondent, a nationwide manufacturer with its principal place of business in New Jersey. The agreement contained a forum-selection clause providing that any dispute arising out of the contract could be brought only in a court located in Manhattan. Business relations between the parties soured under circumstances that are not relevant here. In September 1984, petitioner brought a complaint in the United States District Court for the Northern District of Alabama. The core of the complaint was an allegation that respondent had breached the dealership agreement, but petitioner also included claims for breach of warranty, fraud, and antitrust violations.

Relying on the contractual forum-selection clause, respondent moved the District Court either to transfer the case to the Southern District of New York under 28 U.S.C. §1404(a) or to dismiss the case for improper venue under 28 U.S.C. §1406. The District Court denied the motion. It reasoned that the transfer motion was controlled by Alabama law and that Alabama looks unfavorably upon contractual forum-selection clauses. The court certified its ruling for interlocutory appeal, and the Court of Appeals for the Eleventh Circuit accepted jurisdiction.

On appeal, a divided panel of the Eleventh Circuit reversed the District Court. The panel concluded that questions of venue in diversity actions are governed by federal law, and that the parties' forum-selection clause was enforceable as a matter of federal law. The panel therefore reversed the order of the District Court and remanded with instructions to transfer the case to a Manhattan court. After petitioner successfully moved for rehearing en banc, the full Court of Appeals proceeded to adopt the result, and much of the reasoning, of the panel opinion. The en banc court, citing Congress' enactment or approval of several rules to govern venue determinations in diversity actions, first determined that "[v]enue is a matter of federal procedure." The Court of Appeals then applied the standards articulated in the admiralty case of The Bremen v. Zapata Off-Shore Co., 407 U.S. 1 (1972), to conclude that "the choice of forum clause in this contract is in all respects enforceable generally as a matter of federal law. . . ." We now affirm under somewhat different reasoning.

II

Both the panel opinion and the opinion of the full Court of Appeals referred to the difficulties that often attend "the sticky question of which law, state or federal, will govern various aspects of the decisions of federal courts sitting in diversity." A District Court's decision whether to apply a federal statute such as §1404(a) in a diversity action,[3] however, involves a considerably less intricate analysis than that which governs the "relatively unguided *Erie* choice." Our cases indicate that when the federal law sought to be applied is a congressional statute, the first and chief question for the District Court's

3. Respondent points out that jurisdiction in this case was alleged to rest both on the existence of an antitrust claim, *see* 28 U.S.C. §1337, and diversity of citizenship, *see* 28 U.S.C. §1332. Respondent does not suggest how the presence of a federal claim should affect the District Court's analysis of applicable law. The Court of Appeals plurality likewise did not address this issue, and indeed characterized this case simply as a diversity breach of contract action. Our conclusion that federal law governs transfer of this case, *see* Part III, *infra*, makes this issue academic for purposes of this case, because the presence of a federal question could cut only in favor of the application of federal law. We therefore are not called on to decide, nor do we decide, whether the existence of federal question as well as diversity jurisdiction necessarily alters a District Court's analysis of applicable law.

determination is whether the statute is "sufficiently broad to control the issue before the Court." This question involves a straightforward exercise in statutory interpretation to determine if the statute covers the point in dispute. *See* Walker v. Armco Steel Corp., *supra,* 446 U.S., at 750, and n.9.[4] *See also* Burlington Northern R. Co. v. Woods, (identifying inquiry as whether the Federal Rule "occupies [a state rule's] field of operation").

If the District Court determines that a federal statute covers the point in dispute, it proceeds to inquire whether the statute represents a valid exercise of Congress' authority under the Constitution. If Congress intended to reach the issue before the District Court, and if it enacted its intention into law in a manner that abides with the Constitution, that is the end of the matter; "[f]ederal courts are bound to apply rules enacted by Congress with respect to matters . . . over which it has legislative power." Prima Paint Corp. v. Flood & Conklin Mfg. Co., 388 U.S. 395, 406 (1967); *cf.* Hanna v. Plumer, *supra,* ("When a situation is covered by one of the Federal Rules . . . the court has been instructed to apply the Federal Rule, and can refuse to do so only if the Advisory Committee, this Court, and Congress erred in their prima facie judgment that the Rule in question transgresses neither the terms of the Enabling Act nor constitutional restrictions").[6] Thus, a District Court sitting in diversity must apply a federal statute that controls the issue before the court and that represents a valid exercise of Congress' constitutional powers.

III

Applying the above analysis to this case persuades us that federal law, specifically 28 U.S.C. §1404, governs the parties' venue dispute.

---

4. Our cases at times have referred to the question at this stage of the analysis as an inquiry into whether there is a "direct collision" between state and federal law. *See, e.g.,* Walker v. Armco Steel Corp., 446 U.S., at 749; Hanna v. Plumer, 380 U.S. 460, 472 (1965). Logic indicates, however, and a careful reading of the relevant passages confirms, that this language is not meant to mandate that federal law and state law be perfectly coextensive and equally applicable to the issue at hand; rather, the "direct collision" language, at least where the applicability of a federal statute is at issue, expresses the requirement that the federal statute be sufficiently broad to cover the point in dispute. *See* Hanna v. Plumer, *supra,* at 470. It would make no sense for the supremacy of federal law to wane precisely because there is no state law directly on point.

6. If no federal statute or Rule covers the point in dispute, the District Court then proceeds to evaluate whether application of federal judge-made law would disserve the so-called "twin aims of the *Erie* rule: discouragement of forum-shopping and avoidance of inequitable administration of the laws." Hanna v. Plumer, *supra,* 380 U.S., at 468. If application of federal judge-made law would disserve these two policies, the District Court should apply state law. *See* Walker v. Armco Steel Corp., 446 U.S. 740, 752-753 (1980).

A

At the outset we underscore a methodological difference in our approach to the question from that taken by the Court of Appeals. The en banc court determined that federal law controlled the issue based on a survey of different statutes and judicial decisions that together revealed a significant federal interest in questions of venue in general, and in choice-of-forum clauses in particular. The Court of Appeals then proceeded to apply the standards announced in our opinion in The Bremen v. Zapata Off-Shore Co., 407 U.S. 1 (1972),[7] to determine that the forum-selection clause in this case was enforceable. But the immediate issue before the District Court was whether to grant respondent's motion to transfer the action under 1404(a), and as Judge Tjoflat properly noted in his concurring opinion below, the immediate issue before the Court of Appeals was whether the District Court's denial of the §1404(a) motion constituted an abuse of discretion. Although we agree with the Court of Appeals that the *Bremen* case may prove "instructive" in resolving the parties' dispute; *but cf.* Texas Industries Inc. v. Radcliff Materials, Inc., 451 U.S. 630, 641-642, (1981) (federal common law developed under admiralty jurisdiction not freely transferable to diversity setting), we disagree with the court's articulation of the relevant inquiry as "whether the forum selection clause in this case is unenforceable under the standards set forth in *The Bremen.*" Rather, the first question for consideration should have been whether §1404(a) itself controls respondent's request to give effect to the parties' contractual choice of venue and transfer this case to a Manhattan court. For the reasons that follow, we hold that it does.

B

Section 1404(a) provides: "For the convenience of parties and witnesses, in the interest of justice, a district court may transfer any civil action to any other district or division where it might have been brought." Under the analysis outlined above, we first consider whether this provision is sufficiently broad to control the issue before the court. That issue is whether to transfer the case to a court in Manhattan in accordance with the forum-selection clause. We believe that the statute, fairly construed, does cover the point in dispute.

Section 1404(a) is intended to place discretion in the District Court to adjudicate motions for transfer according to an "individualized, case-by-case

---

7. In *The Bremen,* this Court held that federal courts sitting in admiralty generally should enforce forum selection clauses absent a showing that to do so "would be unreasonable and unjust, or that the clause was invalid for such reasons as fraud or overreaching." 407 U.S., at 15.

consideration of convenience and fairness." Van Dusen v. Barrack. A motion to transfer under §1404(a) thus calls on the District Court to weigh in the balance a number of case-specific factors. The presence of a forum-selection clause such as the parties entered into in this case will be a significant factor that figures centrally in the District Court's calculus. In its resolution of the 1404(a) motion in this case, for example, the District Court will be called on to address such issues as the convenience of a Manhattan forum given the parties' expressed preference for that venue, and the fairness of transfer in light of the forum selection clause and the parties' relative bargaining power. The flexible and individualized analysis Congress prescribed in §1404(a) thus encompasses consideration of the parties' private expression of their venue preferences.

Section 1404(a) may not be the only potential source of guidance for the District Court to consult in weighing the parties' private designation of a suitable forum. The premise of the dispute between the parties is that Alabama law may refuse to enforce forum-selection clauses providing for out-of-state venues as a matter of state public policy.[9] If that is so, the District Court will have either to integrate the factor of the forum-selection clause into its weighing of considerations as prescribed by Congress, or else to apply, as it did in this case, Alabama's categorical policy disfavoring forum-selection clauses. Our cases make clear that, as between these two choices in a single "field of operation," Burlington Northern R. Co. v. Woods, the instructions of Congress are supreme. *Cf.* 107 S. Ct., at 970 (where federal law's "discretionary mode of operation" conflicts with the nondiscretionary provision of Alabama law, federal law applies in diversity).

It is true that §1404(a) and Alabama's putative policy regarding forum-selection clauses are not perfectly coextensive. Section 1404(a) directs a District Court to take account of factors other than those that bear solely on the parties' private ordering of their affairs. The District Court also must weigh in the balance the convenience of the witnesses and those public-interest factors of systemic integrity and fairness that, in addition to private concerns, come under the heading of "the interest of justice." It is conceivable in a particular case, for example, that because of these factors a District Court acting under §1404(a) would refuse to transfer a case notwithstanding the counterweight of a forum-selection clause, whereas the coordinate state rule might dictate the

---

9. In its application of the standards set forth in *The Bremen* to this case, the Court of Appeals concluded that the Alabama policy against the enforcement of forum-selection clauses is intended to apply only to protect the jurisdiction of the state courts of Alabama and therefore would not come into play in this case, in which case this dispute might be much ado about nothing. Our determination that §1404(a) governs the parties' dispute notwithstanding any contrary Alabama policy makes it unnecessary to address the contours of state law. *See* n.4, *supra*.

opposite result.[10] But this potential conflict in fact frames an additional argument for the supremacy of federal law. Congress has directed that multiple considerations govern transfer within the federal court system, and a state policy focusing on a single concern or a subset of the factors identified in §1404(a) would defeat that command. Its application would impoverish the flexible and multifaceted analysis that Congress intended to govern motions to transfer within the federal system. The forum-selection clause, which represents the parties' agreement as to the most proper forum, should receive neither dispositive consideration (as respondent might have it) nor no consideration (as Alabama law might have it), but rather the consideration for which Congress provided in §1404(a). This is thus not a case in which state and federal rules "can exist side by side . . . each controlling its own intended sphere of coverage without conflict." Walker v. Armco Steel Corp., 446 U.S., at 752.

Because section 1404(a) controls the issue before the District Court, it must be applied if it represents a valid exercise of Congress's authority under the Constitution. The constitutional authority of Congress to enact section 1404(a) is not subject to serious question. As the Court made plain in *Hanna*, "the constitutional provision for a federal court system . . . carries with it congressional power to make rules governing the practice and pleading in those courts, which in turn includes a power to regulate matters which, though falling within the uncertain area between substance and procedure, are rationally capable of classification as either." Section 1404(a) is doubtless capable of classification as a procedural rule, and indeed, we have so classified it in holding that a transfer pursuant to §1404(a) does not carry with it a change in the applicable law. *See* Van Dusen v. Barrack, *supra*, 376 U.S., at 636-637 ("[B]oth the history and purposes of §1404(a) indicate that it should be regarded as a federal judicial housekeeping measure"). It therefore falls comfortably within Congress's powers under Article III as augmented by the Necessary and Proper Clause.

We hold that federal law, specifically 28 U.S.C. §1404(a), governs the District Court's decision whether to give effect to the parties' forum-selection clause and transfer this case to a court in Manhattan.[11] We therefore affirm the Eleventh Circuit order reversing the District Court's application of Alabama law. The case is remanded so that the District Court may determine

---

10. The dissent does not dispute this point, but rather argues that if the forum selection clause would be *unenforceable* under state law, then the clause cannot be accorded any weight by a federal court. Not the least of the problems with the dissent's analysis is that it makes the applicability of a federal statute depend on the content of state law. *See* n.4, *supra*. If a State cannot preempt a district court's consideration of a forum-selection clause by holding that the clause is automatically enforceable, it makes no sense for it to be able to do so by holding the clause automatically void.

11. Because a validly enacted Act of Congress controls the issue in dispute, we have no occasion to evaluate the impact of application of federal judge-made law on the "twin aims" that animate the *Erie* doctrine.

in the first instance the appropriate effect under federal law of the parties' forum-selection clause on respondent's §1404(a) motion.

It is so ordered.

Justice SCALIA, dissenting.

I agree with the opinion of the Court that the initial question before us is whether the validity between the parties of a contractual forum-selection clause falls within the scope of 28 U.S.C. §1404(a). I cannot agree, however, that the answer to that question is yes. Nor do I believe that the federal courts can, consistent with the twin-aims test of Erie R. Co. v. Tompkins, 304 U.S. 64 (1938), fashion a judge-made rule to govern this issue of contract validity.

I

When a litigant asserts that state law conflicts with a federal procedural statute or formal Rule of Procedure, a court's first task is to determine whether the disputed point in question in fact falls within the scope of the federal statute or Rule. In this case, the Court must determine whether the scope of §1404(a) is sufficiently broad to cause a direct collision with state law or implicitly to control the issue before the Court, *i.e.*, validity between the parties of the forum-selection clause, thereby leaving no room for the operation of state law. I conclude that it is not.

Although the language of §1404(a) provides no clear answer, in my view it does provide direction. The provision vests the district courts with authority to transfer a civil action to another district "[f]or the convenience of parties and witnesses, in the interest of justice." This language looks to the present and the future. As the specific reference to convenience of parties and witnesses suggests, it requires consideration of what is likely to be just in the future, when the case is tried, in light of things as they now stand. Accordingly, the courts in applying §1404(a) have examined a variety of factors, each of which pertains to facts that currently exist or will exist: *e.g.*, the forum actually chosen by the plaintiff, the current convenience of the parties and witnesses, the current location of pertinent books and records, similar litigation pending elsewhere, current docket conditions, and familiarity of the potential courts with governing state law. In holding that the validity between the parties of a forum-selection clause falls within the scope of §1404(a), the Court inevitably imports, in my view without adequate textual foundation, a new *retrospective* element into the court's deliberations, requiring examination of what the facts were concerning, among other things, the bargaining power of the parties and the presence or absence of overreaching at the time the contract was made.

The Court largely attempts to avoid acknowledging the novel scope it gives to §1404(a) by casting the issue as how much *weight* a district court should give a forum-selection clause as against other factors when it makes its determination under §1404(a). I agree that if the weight-among-factors issue were before us, it would be governed by §1404(a). That is because, while the parties may decide who between them should bear any inconvenience, only a court can decide how much weight should be given under §1404(a) to the factor of the parties' convenience as against other relevant factors such as the convenience of witnesses. But the Court's description of the issue begs the question: what law governs whether the forum-selection clause is a *valid* or *invalid* allocation of any inconvenience between the parties. If it is invalid, *i.e.*, should be voided, between the parties, it cannot be entitled to any weight in the §1404(a) determination. Since under Alabama law the forum-selection clause should be voided, *see* Redwing Carriers, Inc. v. Foster, 382 So. 2d 554, 556 (Ala. 1980), in this case the question of what weight should be given the forum-selection clause can be reached only if as a preliminary matter federal law controls the issue of the validity of the clause between the parties.*

Second, §1404(a) was enacted against the background that issues of contract, including a contract's validity, are nearly always governed by state law. It is simply contrary to the practice of our system that such an issue should be wrenched from state control in absence of a clear conflict with federal law or explicit statutory provision. It is particularly instructive in this regard to compare §1404(a) with another provision, enacted by the same Congress a year earlier, that *did* pre-empt state contract law, and in precisely the same field of agreement regarding forum selection. Section 2 of the Federal Arbitration Act, 61 Stat. 670, 9 U.S.C. §2, provides:

> A written provision in . . . a contract evidencing a transaction involving commerce to settle by arbitration a controversy thereafter arising

---

* Contrary to the opinion of the Court, there is nothing unusual about having "the applicability of a federal statute depend on the content of state law." We have recognized that precisely this is required when the application of the federal statute depends, as here, on resolution of an underlying issue that is fundamentally one of state law. *See* Commissioner v. Estate of Bosch, 387 U.S. 456, 457 (1967). Nor is the approach I believe is required undermined by the fact that there would still be some situations where the state-law rule on the validity of a forum-selection clause would not be dispositive of the issue of transfer between federal courts. When state law would hold a forum-selection clause invalid the federal court could nonetheless order transfer to another federal court under §1404(a), but it could do so only if such transfer was warranted without regard to the forum-selection clause. This is not at all remarkable since whether to transfer a case from one federal district court to another for reasons other than the contractual agreement of the parties is plainly made a matter of federal law by §1404(a). When, on the other hand, state law would hold a forum-selection clause valid, I agree with Justice Kennedy's concurrence that under §1404(a) such a valid forum-selection clause is to be "given controlling weight in all but the most exceptional cases." And even in those exceptional cases where a forum-selection clause is valid under state law but transfer is unwarranted because of some factor other than the convenience of the parties, the district court should give effect to state contract law by dismissing the suit.

> out of such contract or transaction, or the refusal to perform the whole or any part thereof, or an agreement in writing to submit to arbitration an existing controversy arising out of such a contract, transaction, or refusal, shall be valid, irrevocable, and enforceable, save upon such grounds as exist at law or in equity for the revocation of any contract.

We have said that an arbitration clause is a "kind of forum-selection clause," Scherk v. Alberto-Culver Co., 417 U.S. 506, 519 (1974), and the contrast between this explicit preemption of state contract law on the subject and §1404(a) could not be more stark. Section 1404(a) is simply a venue provision that nowhere mentions contracts or agreements, much less that the validity of certain contracts or agreements will be matters of federal law. It is difficult to believe that state contract law was meant to be pre-empted by this provision that we have said "should be regarded as a federal judicial housekeeping measure," Van Dusen v. Barrack, that we have said did not change "the relevant factors" which federal courts used to consider under the doctrine of forum non conveniens, Norwood v. Kirkpatrick, and that we have held can be applied retroactively because it is procedural, Ex parte Collett, 337 U.S. 55, 71 (1949). It seems to me the generality of its language—"[f]or the convenience of parties and witnesses, in the interest of justice"—is plainly insufficient to work the great change in law asserted here.

Third, it has been common ground in this Court since *Erie*, 304 U.S., at 74-77, that when a federal procedural statute or Rule of Procedure is not on point, substantial uniformity of predictable outcome between federal and state courts in adjudicating claims should be striven for. This rests upon a perception of the constitutional and congressional plan underlying the creation of diversity and pendent jurisdiction in the lower federal courts, which should quite obviously be carried forward into our interpretation of ambiguous statutes relating to the exercise of that jurisdiction. We should assume, in other words, when it is fair to do so, that Congress is just as concerned as we have been to avoid significant differences between state and federal courts in adjudicating claims. Thus, in deciding whether a federal procedural statute or Rule of Procedure encompasses a particular issue, a broad reading that would create significant disuniformity between state and federal courts should be avoided if the text permits. . . . As I have shown, the interpretation given §1404(a) by the Court today is neither the plain nor the more natural meaning; at best, §1404(a) is ambiguous. I would therefore construe it to avoid the significant encouragement to forum shopping that will inevitably be provided by the interpretation the Court adopts today.

II

Since no federal statute or Rule of Procedure governs the validity of a forum-selection clause, the remaining issue is whether federal courts may fashion a judge-made rule to govern the question. If they may not, the Rules of Decision Act, 28 U.S.C. §1652, mandates use of state law. . . .

In general, while interpreting and applying substantive law is the essence of the "judicial Power" created under Article III of the Constitution, that power does not encompass the making of substantive law. Whatever the scope of the federal courts' authority to create federal common law in other areas, it is plain that the mere fact that petitioner here brought an antitrust claim does not empower the federal courts to make common law on the question of the validity of the forum-selection clause. *See* Campbell v. Haverhill, 155 U.S. 610, 616 (1895) (Rules of Decision Act "itself neither contains nor suggests . . . a distinction" between federal question cases and diversity cases); *Del-Costello, supra,* 462 U.S., at 173, n.1 (Stevens, J., dissenting) (same); *cf.* Texas Industries, Inc. v. Radcliff Materials, Inc., 451 U.S. 630 (1981). The federal courts do have authority, however, to make procedural rules that govern the practice before them. . . .

In deciding what is substantive and what procedural for these purposes, we have adhered to a functional test based on the "twin aims of the *Erie* rule: discouragement of forum-shopping and avoidance of inequitable administration of the laws." Moreover, although in reviewing the validity of a federal procedural statute or Rule of Procedure we inquire only whether Congress or the rulemakers have trespassed beyond the wide latitude given them to determine that a matter is procedural, in reviewing the lower courts' application of the twin-aims test we apply our own judgment as a matter of law.

Under the twin-aims test, I believe state law controls the question of the validity of a forum-selection clause between the parties. The Eleventh Circuit's rule clearly encourages forum-shopping. Venue is often a vitally important matter, as is shown by the frequency with which parties contractually provide for and litigate the issue. Suit might well not be pursued, or might not be as successful, in a significantly less convenient forum. Transfer to such a less desirable forum is, therefore, of sufficient import that plaintiffs will base their decisions on the likelihood of that eventuality when they are choosing whether to sue in state or federal court. With respect to forum-selection clauses, in a State with law unfavorable to validity, plaintiffs who seek to avoid the effect of a clause will be encouraged to sue in state court, and nonresident defendants will be encouraged to shop for more favorable law by removing to federal court. In the reverse situation—where a State has law favorable to enforcing such clauses—plaintiffs will be encouraged to sue in federal court. This significant encouragement to forum shopping is alone sufficient to warrant application of state law.

I believe creating a judge-made rule fails the second part of the twin-aims test as well, producing inequitable administration of the laws. The best explanation of what constitutes inequitable administration of the laws is that found in *Erie* itself: allowing an unfair discrimination between non-citizens and citizens of the forum state. Whether discrimination is unfair in this context largely turns on how important is the matter in question. The decision of an important legal issue should not turn on the accident of diversity of citizenship or the presence of a federal question unrelated to that issue. It is difficult to imagine an issue of more importance, other than one that goes to the very merits of the lawsuit, than the validity of a contractual forum-selection provision. Certainly, the *Erie* doctrine has previously been held to require the application of state law on subjects of similar or obviously lesser importance. Nor can or should courts ignore that issues of contract validity are traditionally matters governed by state law.

For the reasons stated, I respectfully dissent.

Justice KENNEDY, with whom Justice O'CONNOR joins, concurring.

I concur in full. I write separately only to observe that enforcement of valid forum selection clauses, bargained for by the parties, protects their legitimate expectations and furthers vital interests of the justice system. Although our opinion in The Bremen v. Zapata Off-Shore Co. involved a federal district court sitting in admiralty, its reasoning applies with much force to federal courts sitting in diversity. The justifications we noted in *The Bremen* to counter the historical disfavor forum selection clauses had received in American courts should be understood to guide the District Court's analysis under §1404(a).

The federal judicial system has a strong interest in the correct resolution of these questions, not only to spare litigants unnecessary costs but also to relieve courts of time consuming pretrial motions. Courts should announce and encourage rules that support private parties who negotiate such clauses. Though state policies should be weighed in the balance, the authority and prerogative of the federal courts to determine the issue, as Congress has directed by §1404(a), should be exercised so that a valid forum selection clause is given controlling weight in all but the most exceptional cases.

Questions and Comments

(1) Should one assume that absent section 1404(a) the issue would have been decided under state law? What happens, for instance, when the alternative forum is one to which a transfer would be unavailable—for instance, the alternative forum is another nation or a state court in a state in which federal venue would not be appropriate? If *Reyno* had involved a contractual cause of action and the contract had a forum-selection clause, would state law apply? *Compare The Bremen,* at page 466 *supra.*

(2) Will federal law apply to all contract law aspects concerning the forum-selection clause? What if the state has a general doctrine about unconscionable clauses (for instance, invalidating clauses in fine print in adhesion contracts)? Should this doctrine be applied to determine whether an effective choice has been made, leaving to federal law the issue of how much

weight to give the parties' choice? What about the Parol Evidence Rule, under which state law might bar extrinsic proof of a contract clause not included in the written agreement?

(3) Red Bull Associates v. Best Western Intl. Inc., 862 F.2d 963 (2d Cir. 1988) was a post-*Ricoh* decision refusing transfer under section 1404(a) despite the presence of a forum-selection clause. The reason was in part that the substantive claim was one for racial discrimination, and there was a clear federal statutory policy of encouraging such claims. Does this rationale mean that if a claim of this sort were to be filed in a state court then its policy in favor of enforcing forum-selection clauses would be pre-empted?

(4) For a critical account of *Ricoh, see* Mullenix, Another Choice of Forum, Another Choice of Law: Consensual Adjudicatory Procedure in Federal Court, 57 Fordham L. Rev. 291 (1988). *See also* Borchers, Forum Selection Agreements in the Federal Courts after *Carnival Cruise:* A Proposal For Congressional Reform, 67 Wash. L. Rev. 55 (1992).

(5) Does *Van Dusen* apply after a change in venue pursuant to a forum-selection clause? If so, then hasn't the defendant been denied part of the bargained-for value of including a choice-of-forum clause? Note that the clause at issue in *Ricoh* stated that the selected forum was to be exclusive of any other forum. If the clause is respected by the parties and the case is initially brought in the chosen forum, then its choice-of-law rules, statute of limitations, and so forth will apply. But if the case is initiated somewhere else and transferred under section 1404(a)—and if *Van Dusen* is applicable—then the plaintiff will have gotten a fair amount of what he or she wanted, in violation of the exclusive choice-of-forum clause. *Compare* Brock v. Entre Computer Centers, 933 F.2d 1253 (4th Cir. 1991) which presented essentially this set of facts. The transferee court did not make clear whether it was applying the law of Virginia because that was what the transferor court would have done, or because it thought Virginia law was the correct law to apply under the circumstances.

Perhaps the best response to these concerns is that the court is not really enforcing the choice-of-forum clause when it transfers under *Ricoh,* but only taking the clause into account in deciding whether to transfer. Under this view, the fact that the defendant is not getting the entire benefit of his or her bargain does not matter. The defendant's real complaint is with the transferor state's disrespect for choice-of-forum clauses. But if this is the response, then a federal court faced with a request to honor a choice-of-forum clause should carefully phrase what it is doing. If the court is merely taking the clause into account in deciding a transfer motion—because it cannot enforce the clause directly, being situated in a state that does not enforce such clauses—then it should say so clearly, and *Van Dusen* will apply. If the court sits in a state that honors choice-of-forum clauses, however, and is only using section 1404(a) as a mechanism for enforcing the clause, then it should be clear that this is what the court is doing, because *Van Dusen* will not apply and the defendant will get the entire benefit of the forum-selection clause.

Forum non conveniens is a doctrine that gives courts discretion to dismiss a case within their jurisdiction if there is a more convenient forum elsewhere. 28 U.S.C. §1404 replaced the common law forum non conveniens doctrine with respect to federal court dismissals to other federal courts. But the doctrine of forum non conveniens retains validity in state court (because there is no general provision for transfer between state courts). It also applies in federal court if the forum of dismissal is a non-U.S. court. For example, in Piper Aircraft Co. v. Reyno, 454 U.S. 235 (1981), the Supreme Court ruled that a forum non conveniens dismissal to a Scottish court was appropriate in a case involving an airplane crash in Scotland.

Piper held that under the forum non conveniens doctrine, federal district courts have discretion to dismiss a case if they determine that there is an adequate alternate forum and various private and public interest factors weigh in favor of adjudicating the case in that forum. *See id.* 257-261. The court further held that in determining whether an alternate forum is "adequate," it was generally irrelevant that the laws or procedures in the alternate forum were less favorable to the plaintiff than those available in the United States. *Id.* 247-255. *Piper* did not address "whether under Erie v. Tompkins, state or federal law of forum non conveniens applies in a diversity case," *id.* at 249 n. 13, because the state and federal forum non conveniens laws in that case were identical. *See id.* They are not identical in the case that follows.

In re Air Crash Disaster Near New Orleans

821 F.2d 1147 (5th Cir. 1987)

HILL, Circuit Judge

These consolidated cases arise from the crash shortly after takeoff of Pan American World Airways Flight 759 near New Orleans, Louisiana. The plaintiffs are foreign citizens who sought recompense for their injuries in a Louisiana federal court. Pan American World Airways, Inc. (Pan American) invoked the doctrine of forum non conveniens, insisting that the plaintiffs' home country of Uruguay is the proper forum for the resolution of plaintiffs' claims. We took these cases en banc to decide whether the district court properly applied the doctrine of forum non conveniens. . . .

. . . We will address the following question[]: (1) In applying forum non conveniens in a diversity action, does a federal court apply the forum non conveniens law of the state in which it sits or federal forum non conveniens law [?] . . .

II

A

[S]ince these cases are based upon diversity jurisdiction, we are faced with the question of whether we are bound by Louisiana forum non conveniens law or federal forum non conveniens law under the teachings of Erie R.R. Co. v. Tompkins, 304 U.S. 64 (1938). Several courts, including the Supreme Court, have declined to decide whether, under *Erie,* state or federal law of forum non conveniens applies in diversity cases. *See* Piper Aircraft Co. v. Reyno, 454 U.S. at 248 n.13; Gulf Oil Corp. v. Gilbert, 330 U.S. at 509. On each of these occasions the courts reasoned that the issue need not be decided because the state and federal forum non conveniens law were virtually identical. In this case, however, Louisiana forum non conveniens law is substantially different than federal forum non conveniens law. We must therefore decide whether the district court in this case was obliged to apply either the federal or Louisiana law of forum non conveniens.

[Louisiana law does not permit a forum non conveniens dismissal to a foreign forum.] Thus, if we are bound to apply the Louisiana rule as a diversity court, our inquiry would end and the district court [denial of defendant's forum non conveniens motion] would be affirmed. . . . We cannot, however, under *Erie* take this expeditious avenue toward resolution of this appeal. We turn then to the difficult *Erie* question presented.

[O]ur task is to evaluate whether applying federal forum non conveniens in this case advances or hinders the "twin aims" of *Erie.* But first, two clarifications are in order. One, the "forum-shopping" concern is not really the problem of forum-shopping in itself. After all, the purpose of diversity jurisdiction is to *allow* a certain kind of forum-shopping. Rather, the "forum-shopping" concern for *Erie* purposes is the unfairness of giving one set of plaintiffs (those who can sue in federal court) some particular advantage unavailable to non-diverse plaintiffs who must proceed in state court. Two, the *Hanna* Court's second purpose—"inequitable administration of the laws"—is ambiguous. This purpose may refer either to extrinsic considerations of the fairness of the competing state and federal rules to the parties—"*inequitable* administration"—or to intrinsic considerations of the federal forum's own interests—"inequitable *administration.*" We conclude that *Hanna* intends the latter. The former interpretation would take federal courts into an analysis of the "fairness" of the state rule, in other words, its wisdom and propriety. This could only lead to normative assertions by federal courts that a given state law cannot be applied because to do so would be "inequitable." But it was precisely this normative role, this role of federal courts as prophets of a "brooding omnipresence," that *Erie* condemned. Therefore, *Hanna*'s second aim must refer to the federal courts' own interests in equitable self-administration.

Because almost any difference between the rules applied in state and federal courts can lead to different outcomes and "forum-shopping"—the ability of diversity plaintiffs to gain advantages denied to others—the first aim of *Erie* is always best satisfied by applying state law. To determine the importance of this aim for a particular issue, the question is always "how different will the outcomes be?" If Louisiana courts refuse to dismiss on forum non conveniens grounds, and if that doctrine does not apply to a Louisiana cause of action in a federal diversity court, there will be a tremendous disparity of result between trials in the two court systems. One case will proceed to judgment and the other will be dismissed to a foreign land.

Here we face a twist on the usual problem. The usual problem of forum-shopping in the *Erie* context is the ability of *plaintiffs* to choose an advantageous federal forum; there is an obvious inequity in allowing out-of-state plaintiffs advantages over local plaintiffs in suits under the same substantive law of the forum state. However, the occasional state courts that refuse to apply forum non conveniens—like Louisiana—become the advantageous forum for some relevant group of both local and non-resident plaintiffs. Thus, the differing state and federal rules contemplated by this case have no forum-shopping implications for plaintiffs. But there will be diversity between the parties in many such cases. Defendants in those cases will be able to remove the case to federal court, negating any plaintiff's advantage. Thus, our decision today will give some (arbitrary) set of *defendants* the ability to "forum-shop," *i.e.*, to receive an advantage in the federal court unavailable to the defendants who must remain in the state court. But this defendant-forum-shopping twist does not alter the unavoidable conclusion: The enormous difference between the outcomes of state and federal proceedings points forcefully toward applying state law under the first aim of *Erie*.

On the other hand, the interests of the federal courts in maintaining the federal doctrine even in a diversity case are powerful. We can describe those interests no better than has a panel of our colleagues on the Eleventh Circuit:

> The doctrine [of forum non conveniens] derives from the court's inherent power, under article III of the Constitution, to control the administration of the litigation before it and to prevent its process from becoming an instrument of abuse, injustice and oppression. . . . The Court's interest in controlling its crowded docket also provides a basis for the Court's inherent power to dismiss on grounds of forum non conveniens. . . . "Administrative difficulties follow for courts when litigation is piled up in congested centers instead of being handled at its origin. Jury duty is a burden that ought not to be imposed upon the people of a community which has no relation to the litigation." Gulf Oil Corp. v. Gilbert, 330 U.S. 501, 590-09 (1947). The forum non conveniens doctrine is "designed in part to help courts avoid conducting complex exercises in comparative law." *Piper Aircraft Co.*, 454 U.S. at 251.

Sibaja v. Dow Chemical Co., 757 F.2d 1215, 1218-1219 (11th Cir.). Federal forum interests in self-management point forcefully toward applying federal law under the second aim of *Erie*.

Our analysis of *Erie*'s twin aims in the context of selecting state or federal forum non conveniens law produces conflicting indications on how to resolve the issue. The aim of dissuading forum-shopping says apply Louisiana law in this diversity case. The other aim says apply federal law as a matter of internal consistency and administration. . . .

Thus we face a difficult *Erie*-doctrine choice. We must choose between maintaining important internal administrative and equitable powers of our courts at the cost of disuniformity of result between state and federal diversity courts, or uniformity at the cost of giving up part of our self-regulatory powers. It is fashionable to call a difficult choice between important objectives a "balancing" test, but we decline to resort to this metaphor. It is simply a matter of choice, and choose we must.

We hold that the interests of the federal forum in self-regulation, in administrative independence, and in self-management are more important than the disruption of uniformity created by applying federal forum non conveniens in diversity cases. . . . We therefore hold that a federal court sitting in a diversity action is required to apply the federal law of forum non conveniens when addressing motions to dismiss a plaintiff's case to a foreign forum.

[The court went on to hold that U.S. adherence to the Warsaw Convention (concerning international air transportation) does not require American courts to abstain from use of the doctrine.]

HIGGINBOTHAM, concurring in the judgment:

[W]ith deference, I am not persuaded by the analysis of the *Erie* question. I give greater weight to the interests favoring application of Louisiana law and less weight to the federal forum interest in self-administration.

Hanna involved a Federal Rule of Civil Procedure governed by the Rules Enabling Act; the *Hanna* court deferred to the Federal Rules, not because of federal forum interests inherent in article III, but because under the Rules Enabling Act, they were approved by Congress, the Advisory Committee, and the Supreme Court. Here we have a judge-made rule of forum non conveniens that displaces an arguably core decision of the state meant to assure its residents a forum in the United States.

Of course, federal courts have an interest in self-administration; they do in every *Erie* decision. But that interest must be viewed with caution when it lacks the support of the Rules Enabling Act mandate or an independent constitutional interest such as the seventh amendment; these are important, sometimes the dispositive, variables in an *Erie* analysis.

On the state side, it must not be forgotten that Louisiana has no doctrine of forum non conveniens. That is, Louisiana has not accepted the idea that its citizens may be denied the right to a court in the United States for reasons of efficiency or to otherwise husband judicially found resources. We are not choosing between a federal and state rule in circumstances where the federal formulation of a rule, while securing interests similar to a state rule, leads to a different result. Rather, we are asked to reject a decision by Louisiana that lies closer to substance on the spectrum of substance to procedure than would an adopted rule of forum non conveniens.

I

The twin aims of *Erie* are *not* competing aims. Indeed, they arise from the same source and serve related purposes. If a federal court in diversity applies a tort rule different from the state rule, and the federal rule requires a result opposite to what would be had in state court, then litigants will shop for the forum with the rule favoring their position, *and* a citizen of the state being sued in federal court will not have the same protection of the laws as he would had he been sued in his state's court. This says nothing of the "wisdom and propriety" of the tort rule. I take comfort from the *Hanna* Court's purpose in identifying the twin aims of *Erie:* to explain the contours of the "outcome-determinative" test. The fact that different federal and state rules result in conflicting outcomes matters only to the extent that it gives rise to forum shopping or unfair discrimination against citizens of the forum state.

I see *two* interests weighing in favor of applying state law—the twin aims of *Erie.* But . . . the majority drops away the related, second interest—avoidance of discrimination against citizens of the forum state.

In refusing to apply forum non conveniens, Louisiana has decided to provide greater protection against foreign actors, through access to local courts, than is available in federal courts. Application of the federal rule in diversity will have the potential of depriving the forum state's citizen of the material benefit of a convenient and friendly forum. Thus, although this case involves a twist on the typical *Erie* case—the nonresident defendants receive the benefits from the choice of forum—the attending discrimination against citizens of the forum state is no less real.

II

Just as the majority's interpretation of the twin aims of *Erie* places too *little* emphasis on the state law interests, it likewise places too *much* emphasis on the federal forum interests in self-administration. . . . *Hanna* does not give *federal courts* the power, beyond the mandate of the Enabling Act or other such statute, "to displace state laws on matters involving their basic competence as courts" without being subjected to the strictures of *Erie.*

The majority argues that such power is inherent in article III, but the Court in *Hanna* stated that the Constitution placed in the hands of Congress the primary power to make rules governing the practice and procedure in federal courts. I concede that a federal court possesses a *secondary* power of self-management under article III. But I do not think the forum non conveniens doctrine, which undoubtedly falls into the arguable area between substance and procedure, is entitled to the same presumption of validity in diversity as the Federal Rules of Civil Procedure.

Questions and Comments

(1) *In re Air Crash Disaster* was vacated by the Supreme Court on other grounds in light of the Supreme Court's ruling in Chan v. Korean Air Lines, Ltd., 490 U.S. 122 (1989), that the Warsaw Convention's damages limitations applied even if airline passengers failed to get actual notice. *See* 490 U.S. 1032 (1989).

(2) Isn't forum non conveniens an anti-forum shopping doctrine (*i.e.*, isn't it designed to redress the plaintiff's many forum shopping advantages)? Is this the type of state law that *Erie* or the Rules of Decision Act require federal courts to follow? What kind of regulatory preference does forum non conveniens represent? Who should craft the content of such a rule for federal courts?

(3) Both the majority and the concurrence in *In re Air Crash Disaster* agree that the differences between Louisiana and federal forum non conveniens law have no implications for *plaintiff* forum shopping. Do you see why? Is *Erie* meant to protect non-resident defendants from discrimination?

(4) In Sibaja v. Dow Chemical Co., 757 F.2d 1215, 1219 (11th Cir. 1985), the court reached the same conclusion as *In re Air Crash Disaster* through different reasoning:

> The forum non conveniens doctrine is a rule of venue, not a rule of decision. The doctrine provides "simply that a court may resist imposition upon its jurisdiction even when jurisdiction is authorized by the letter of [the law]." Gulf Oil Corp. v. Gilbert, 330 U.S. at 507. In contrast, "rules of decision" are the "substantive" law of the state, the "legal rules [which] determine the outcome of a litigation." Guaranty Trust Co. v. York, 326 U.S. 99 (1945). It is true that a judge-made rule may qualify as a rule of decision if it substantially affects the "character or result of a litigation." Hanna v. Plumer, 380 U.S. 460 (1965). But the trial court's decision, under the circumstances presented here, whether to exercise its jurisdiction and decide the case was not a decision going to the character and result of the controversy. Rather, it was a decision that occurred before, and completely apart from, any application of state substantive law. A trial court only reaches the state rule of decision, relating to the character and result of the litigation, once it has decided to try the case and determine whether the plaintiff has a valid claim for relief. We hold, accordingly, that the district court's application of the doctrine of forum

> non conveniens in this case did not operate as a state substantive rule of law and thus transgress *Erie*'s constitutional prohibition.

757 F.2d at 1219. Doesn't the Court's characterization of forum non conveniens as "procedural" beg the question? Can't forum non conveniens rules "determine the outcome of the litigation"? Doesn't the decision to litigate in the United States or abroad go to the "character and result of the controversy"? Isn't the analytical vacuousness of the substance/procedure distinction precisely why we have the "twin-aims" test? But is the "twin-aims" any better?

(4) Should state courts be bound by the federal forum non conveniens standards when they adjudicate international cases? The question only comes up in forum non conveniens cases involving dismissals to foreign fora. Scholars disagree about the answer. For the view that forum non conveniens should be treated as federal common law rule binding on the states, *see, e.g.*, Greenberg, The Appropriate Source of Law for Forum Non Conveniens Decisions in International Cases: A Proposal for the Development of Federal Common Law, 4 Int'l Tax & Bus. Law. 155, 156 (1986); Lowenfeld, Nationalizing International Law: Essay in Honor of Louis Henkin, 36 Colum. J. Transnat'l L. 121, 136-138 (1997). For two very different views about why the *Piper* standards do not trump state forum non conveniens law, *see* Goldsmith, Federal Courts, Foreign Affairs, and Federalism, 83 Va. L. Rev. 1617 (1997); Stein, *Erie* and Court Access, 100 Yale L.J. 1935 (1991). (The Stein article offers an excellent overview and analysis of the *Erie* issues implicated by various venue and related doctrines.)

The view that state forum non conveniens law survives in state court finds support in American Dredging Co. v. Miller, 510 U.S. 443 (1994), an admiralty case in state court between U.S. citizens. The Court concluded that, at least in the admiralty context, the federal forum non conveniens doctrine is a procedural rule and not one that trumps state law. It reasoned in part:

> At bottom, the doctrine of forum non conveniens is nothing more or less than a supervening venue provision, permitting displacement of the ordinary rules of venue when, in light of certain conditions, the trial court thinks that jurisdiction ought to be declined. But venue is a matter that goes to process rather than substantive rights—determining which among various competent courts will decide the case.

Id. at 453. Should this reasoning extend to non-admiralty cases? *Compare The Bremen,* page 446 *supra; Carnival Cruise*, page 451 *supra;* and Stewart Organization v. Ricoh Corp., page 600.

3. *Erie* and Judgments

Semtek Int'l Inc. v. Lockheed Martin Corp.

531 U.S. 497 (2001)

Justice SCALIA delivered the opinion of the Court.

This case presents the question whether the claim-preclusive effect of a federal judgment dismissing a diversity action on statute-of-limitations grounds is determined by the law of the State in which the federal court sits.

I

Petitioner filed a complaint against respondent in California state court, alleging breach of contract and various business torts. Respondent removed the case to the United States District Court for the Central District of California on the basis of diversity of citizenship, *see* 28 U.S.C. §§1332, 1441, and successfully moved to dismiss petitioner's claims as barred by California's 2-year statute of limitations. In its order of dismissal, the District Court, adopting language suggested by respondent, dismissed petitioner's claims "in [their] entirety on the merits and with prejudice." Without contesting the District Court's designation of its dismissal as "on the merits," petitioner appealed to the Court of Appeals for the Ninth Circuit, which affirmed the District Court's order. 168 F.3d 501 (1999) (table). Petitioner also brought suit against respondent in the State Circuit Court for Baltimore City, Maryland, alleging the same causes of action, which were not time barred under Maryland's 3-year statute of limitations. Respondent sought injunctive relief against this action from the California federal court under the All Writs Act, 28 U.S.C. §1651, and removed the action to the United States District Court for the District of Maryland on federal-question grounds (diversity grounds were not available because Lockheed "is a Maryland citizen," Semtek Int'l Inc. v. Lockheed Martin Corp., 988 F. Supp. 913, 914 (1997)). The California federal court denied the relief requested, and the Maryland federal court remanded the case to state court because the federal question arose only by way of defense. Following a hearing, the Maryland state court granted respondent's motion to dismiss on the ground of res judicata. Petitioner then returned to the California federal court and the Ninth Circuit, unsuccessfully moving both courts to amend the former's earlier order so as to indicate that the dismissal was not "on the merits." Petitioner also appealed the Maryland trial court's order of dismissal to the Maryland Court of Special Appeals. The Court of Special Appeals affirmed, holding that, regardless of whether California would have accorded claim-preclusive effect to a statute-of-limitations dismissal by one of its own courts, the dismissal by the California federal court barred the complaint filed in Maryland, since the res judicata effect of federal diversity judgments is prescribed by federal law, under which the earlier dismissal was on the merits and claim preclusive. After the Maryland Court of Appeals declined to review the case, we granted certiorari.

II

Petitioner contends that the outcome of this case is controlled by Dupasseur v. Rochereau, 21 Wall. 130, 135 (1875), which held that the res judicata effect of a federal diversity judgment "is such as would belong to judgments of the State courts rendered under similar circumstances," and may not be accorded any "higher sanctity or effect." Since, petitioner argues, the dismissal of an action on statute-of-limitations grounds by a California state court would not be claim preclusive, it follows that the similar dismissal of this diversity action by the California federal court cannot be claim preclusive. While we agree that this would be the result demanded by *Dupasseur*, the case is not dispositive because it was decided under the Conformity Act of 1872, 17 Stat. 196, which required federal courts to apply the procedural law of the forum State in nonequity cases. That arguably affected the outcome of the case. *See Dupasseur, supra,* at 135. *See also* Restatement (Second) of Judgments §87, Comment *a,* p.315 (1980) (*hereinafter* Restatement) ("Since procedural law largely determines the matters that may be adjudicated in an action, state law had to be considered in ascertaining the effect of a federal judgment").

Respondent, for its part, contends that the outcome of this case is controlled by Federal Rule of Civil Procedure 41(b), which provides as follows:

> "Involuntary Dismissal: Effect Thereof. For failure of the plaintiff to prosecute or to comply with these rules or any order of court, a defendant may move for dismissal of an action or of any claim against the defendant. Unless the court in its order for dismissal otherwise specifies, a dismissal under this subdivision and any dismissal not provided for in this rule, other than a dismissal for lack of jurisdiction, for improper venue, or for failure to join a party under Rule 19, operates as an adjudication upon the merits."

Since the dismissal here did not "otherwise specify" (indeed, it specifically stated that it *was* "on the merits"), and did not pertain to the excepted subjects of jurisdiction, venue, or joinder, it follows, respondent contends, that the dismissal "is entitled to claim preclusive effect."

Implicit in this reasoning is the unstated minor premise that all judgments denominated "on the merits" are entitled to claim-preclusive effect. That premise is not necessarily valid. The original connotation of an "on the merits" adjudication is one that actually "passes directly on the substance of [a particular] claim" before the court. Restatement §19, Comment *a,* at 161. That connotation remains common to every jurisdiction of which we are aware. *See ibid.* ("The prototypical [judgment on the merits is] one in which the merits of [a party's] claim are in fact adjudicated [for or] against the [party] after trial of the substantive issues"). And it is, we think, the meaning intended in those many statements to the effect that a judgment "on the merits" triggers the doctrine of res judicata or claim preclusion.

But over the years the meaning of the term "judgment on the merits" "has gradually undergone change," R. Marcus, M. Redish, & E. Sherman, Civil Procedure: A Modern Approach 1140-1141 (3d ed. 2000), and it has come to be applied to some judgments (such as the one involved here) that do *not* pass upon the substantive merits of a claim and hence do *not* (in many jurisdictions) entail claim-preclusive effect. That is why the Restatement of Judgments has abandoned the use of the term—"because of its possibly misleading connotations," Restatement §19, Comment *a*, at 161.

In short, it is no longer true that a judgment "on the merits" is necessarily a judgment entitled to claim-preclusive effect; and there are a number of reasons for believing that the phrase "adjudication upon the merits" does not bear that meaning in Rule 41(b). To begin with, Rule 41(b) sets forth nothing more than a default rule for determining the import of a dismissal (a dismissal is "upon the merits," with the three stated exceptions, unless the court "otherwise specifies"). This would be a highly peculiar context in which to announce a federally prescribed rule on the complex question of claim preclusion, saying in effect, "All federal dismissals (with three specified exceptions) preclude suit elsewhere, unless the court otherwise specifies."

And even apart from the purely default character of Rule 41(b), it would be peculiar to find a rule governing the effect that must be accorded federal judgments by other courts ensconced in rules governing the internal procedures of the rendering court itself. Indeed, such a rule would arguably violate the jurisdictional limitation of the Rules Enabling Act: that the Rules "shall not abridge, enlarge or modify any substantive right," 28 U.S.C. §2072(b). In the present case, for example, if California law left petitioner free to sue on this claim in Maryland even after the California statute of limitations had expired, the federal court's extinguishment of that right (through Rule 41(b)'s mandated claim-preclusive effect of its judgment) would seem to violate this limitation.

Moreover, as so interpreted, the Rule would in many cases violate the federalism principle of Erie R. Co. v. Tompkins, 304 U.S. 64, 78-80 (1938), by engendering "'substantial' variations [in outcomes] between state and federal litigation" which would "likely . . . influence the choice of a forum," Hanna v. Plumer, 380 U.S. 460, 467-468 (1965). With regard to the claim-preclusion issue involved in the present case, for example, the traditional rule is that expiration of the applicable statute of limitations merely bars the remedy and does not extinguish the substantive right, so that dismissal on that ground does not have claim-preclusive effect in other jurisdictions with longer, unexpired limitation periods. *See* Restatement (Second) of Conflict of Laws §§142(2), 143 (1969); Restatement of Judgments §49, Comment *a* (1942). Out-of-state defendants sued on stale claims in California and in other States adhering to this traditional rule would systematically remove state-law suits brought against them to federal court—where, unless otherwise specified, a statute-of-limitations dismissal would bar suit everywhere.

Finally, if Rule 41(b) did mean what respondent suggests, we would surely have relied upon it in our cases recognizing the claim-preclusive effect of federal judgments in federal-question cases. Yet for over half a century since the promulgation of Rule 41(b), we have not once done so.

We think the key to a more reasonable interpretation of the meaning of "operates as an adjudication upon the merits" in Rule 41(b) is to be found in Rule 41(a), which, in discussing the effect of voluntary dismissal by the plaintiff, makes clear that an "adjudication upon the merits" is the opposite of a "dismissal without prejudice":

> "Unless otherwise stated in the notice of dismissal or stipulation, the dismissal is without prejudice, except that a notice of dismissal operates as an adjudication upon the merits when filed by a plaintiff who has once dismissed in any court of the United States or of any state an action based on or including the same claim."

See also 18 Wright & Miller, §4435, at 329, n. 4 ("Both parts of Rule 41 . . . use the phrase 'without prejudice' as a contrast to adjudication on the merits"); 9 *id.*, §2373, at 396, n.4 ("'With prejudice' is an acceptable form of shorthand for 'an adjudication upon the merits'"). The primary meaning of "dismissal without prejudice," we think, is dismissal without barring the defendant from returning later, to the same court, with the same underlying claim. That will also ordinarily (though not always) have the consequence of not barring the claim from *other* courts, but its primary meaning relates to the dismissing court itself. Thus, Black's Law Dictionary (7th ed. 1999) defines "dismissed without prejudice" as "removed from the court's docket in such a way that the plaintiff may refile the same suit on the same claim," *id.*, at 482, and defines "dismissal without prejudice" as "[a] dismissal that does not bar the plaintiff from refiling the lawsuit within the applicable limitations period," *ibid.*

We think, then, that the effect of the "adjudication upon the merits" default provision of Rule 41(b)—and, presumably, of the explicit order in the present case that used the language of that default provision—is simply that, unlike a dismissal "without prejudice," the dismissal in the present case barred refiling of the same claim in the United States District Court for the Central District of California. That is undoubtedly a necessary condition, but it is not a sufficient one, for claim-preclusive effect in other courts.[2]

---

2. We do not decide whether, in a diversity case, a federal court's "dismissal upon the merits" (in the sense we have described), under circumstances where a state court would decree only a "dismissal without prejudice," abridges a "substantive right" and thus exceeds the authorization of the Rules Enabling Act. We think the situation will present itself more rarely than would the arguable violation of the Act that would ensue from interpreting Rule 41(b) as a rule of claim preclusion; and if it is a violation, can be more easily dealt with on direct appeal.

III

Having concluded that the claim-preclusive effect, in Maryland, of this California federal diversity judgment is dictated neither by Dupasseur v. Rochereau, as petitioner contends, nor by Rule 41(b), as respondent contends, we turn to consideration of what determines the issue. Neither the Full Faith and Credit Clause, U.S. Const., Art. IV, §1, nor the full faith and credit statute, 28 U.S.C. §1738, addresses the question. By their terms they govern the effects to be given only to state-court judgments (and, in the case of the statute, to judgments by courts of territories and possessions). And no other federal textual provision, neither of the Constitution nor of any statute, addresses the claim-preclusive effect of a judgment in a federal diversity action.

It is also true, however, that no federal textual provision addresses the claim-preclusive effect of a federal-court judgment in a federal-question case, yet we have long held that States cannot give those judgments merely whatever effect they would give their own judgments, but must accord them the effect that this Court prescribes. The reasoning of that line of cases suggests, moreover, that even when States are allowed to give federal judgments (notably, judgments in diversity cases) no more than the effect accorded to state judgments, that disposition is by direction of *this* Court, which has the last word on the claim-preclusive effect of *all* federal judgments:

> "It is true that for some purposes and within certain limits it is only required that the judgments of the courts of the United States shall be given the same force and effect as are given the judgments of the courts of the States wherein they are rendered; but it is equally true that whether a Federal judgment has been given due force and effect in the state court is a Federal question reviewable by this court, which will determine for itself whether such judgment has been given due weight or otherwise. . . .
>
> "When is the state court obliged to give to Federal judgments only the force and effect it gives to state court judgments within its own jurisdiction? Such cases are distinctly pointed out in the opinion of Mr. Justice Bradley in Dupasseur v. Rochereau [which stated that the case was a diversity case, applying state law under state procedure]." *Deposit Bank*, 191 U.S., at 514-515.

In other words, in *Dupasseur* the State was allowed (indeed, required) to give a federal diversity judgment no more effect than it would accord one of its own judgments only because reference to state law was *the federal rule that this Court deemed appropriate.* In short, federal common law governs the claim-preclusive effect of a dismissal by a federal court sitting in diversity. *See generally* R. Fallon, D. Meltzer, & D. Shapiro, Hart and Wechsler's The Federal Courts and the Federal System 1473 (4th ed. 1996); Degnan, Federalized Res Judicata, 85 Yale L.J. 741 (1976).

It is left to us, then, to determine the appropriate federal rule. And despite the sea change that has occurred in the background law since *Dupasseur* was decided—not only repeal of the Conformity Act but also the watershed decision of this Court in *Erie*—we think the result decreed by *Dupasseur* continues to be correct for diversity cases. Since state, rather than federal, substantive law is at issue there is no need for a uniform federal rule. And indeed, nationwide uniformity in the substance of the matter is better served by having the same claim-preclusive rule (the state rule) apply whether the dismissal has been ordered by a state or a federal court. This is, it seems to us, a classic case for adopting, as the federally prescribed rule of decision, the law that would be applied by state courts in the State in which the federal diversity court sits. *See* Gasperini v. Center for Humanities, Inc., 518 U.S. 415, 429-431 (1996); Walker v. Armco Steel Corp., 446 U.S., at 752-753; Klaxon Co. v. Stentor Elec. Mfg. Co., 313 U.S. 487, 496 (1941). As we have alluded to above, any other rule would produce the sort of "forum-shopping . . . and . . . inequitable administration of the laws" that *Erie* seeks to avoid, *Hanna,* 380 U.S., at 468, since filing in, or removing to, federal court would be encouraged by the divergent effects that the litigants would anticipate from likely grounds of dismissal. *See* Guaranty Trust Co. v. York, 326 U.S. at 109-110.

This federal reference to state law will not obtain, of course, in situations in which the state law is incompatible with federal interests. If, for example, state law did not accord claim-preclusive effect to dismissals for willful violation of discovery orders, federal courts' interest in the integrity of their own processes might justify a contrary federal rule. No such conflict with potential federal interests exists in the present case. Dismissal of this state cause of action was decreed by the California federal court only because the California statute of limitations so required; and there is no conceivable federal interest in giving that time bar more effect in other courts than the California courts themselves would impose.

Because the claim-preclusive effect of the California federal court's dismissal "upon the merits" of petitioner's action on statute-of-limitations grounds is governed by a federal rule that in turn incorporates California's law of claim preclusion (the content of which we do not pass upon today), the Maryland Court of Special Appeals erred in holding that the dismissal necessarily precluded the bringing of this action in the Maryland courts. The judgment is reversed, and the case remanded for further proceedings not inconsistent with this opinion.

It is so ordered.

Questions and Comments

(1) *Semtek* rejects defendant's interpretation of Rule 41 in part because it "would in many cases violate the federalism principle of Erie R. Co. v. Tompkins, 304 U.S. 64, 78-80 (1938), by engendering "substantial variations [in outcomes] between state and federal litigation which would

likely . . . influence the choice of a forum." *See Semtek, supra* page 621 (internal quotations removed). Is this the right test? Contrast *Semtek* with Hanna v. Plumer, 380 U.S. 460, 469-470 (1965), which stated that it is "incorrect [to assume] that the rule of Erie R. Co. v. Tompkins constitutes the appropriate test of the validity and therefore the applicability of a Federal Rule of Civil Procedure." *Compare also* Professor Ely's analysis, *supra* pages 575-576. Does *Semtek* portend closer judicial scrutiny under *Erie* of the Federal Rules of Civil Procedure? Or does this passage from *Semtek* simply state a canon of interpretation for federal rules of civil procedure that might clash with state law? Even if it is "merely" a canon, won't it lead to systemic underenforcement of the federal rules?

(2) *Semtek* holds that the federal common law rule for the claim-preclusive effects of dismissals by federal courts in diversity should incorporate the state-law preclusion rule unless "the state law is incompatible with federal interests." Does the Court ever offer a *reason* why judge-made federal common law should govern? Why doesn't the Court apply the "twin-aims" test to decide whether state law governs? Is *Semtek*'s rule of usually applying state law unless there is an important federal interest consistent with *Klaxon, supra* page 577, which holds that federal courts must (not may) apply state choice-of-law rules in diversity?

(3) How does the preclusion rule announced in *Semtek* comport with related preclusion rules under the full faith and credit clause and statute, discussed *infra* Chapter 6?

B. The Federal Common Law

Clearfield Trust Co. v. United States

318 U.S. 363 (1943)

Justice DOUGLAS delivered the opinion of the Court.

On April 28, 1936, a check was drawn on the Treasurer of the United States through the Federal Reserve Bank of Philadelphia to the order of Clair A. Barner in the amount of $24.20. It was dated at Harrisburg, Pennsylvania, and was drawn for services rendered by Barner to the Works Progress Administration. The check was placed in the mail addressed to Barner at his address in Mackeyville, Pa. Barner never received the check. Some unknown person obtained it in a mysterious manner and presented it to the J. C. Penney Co. store in Clearfield, Pa., representing that he was the payee and identifying himself to the satisfaction of the employees of J. C. Penney Co. He endorsed the check in the name of Barner and transferred it to J. C. Penney Co. in exchange for cash and merchandise. Barner never authorized the endorsement nor participated in the proceeds of the check. J. C. Penney Co.

endorsed the check over to the Clearfield Trust Co. which accepted it as agent for the purpose of collection and endorsed it as follows: "Pay to the order of Federal Reserve Bank of Philadelphia, Prior Endorsements Guaranteed." Clearfield Trust Co. collected the check from the United States through the Federal Reserve Bank of Philadelphia and paid the full amount thereof to J. C. Penney Co. Neither the Clearfield Trust Co. nor J. C. Penney Co. had any knowledge or suspicion of the forgery. Each acted in good faith. On or before May 10, 1936, Barner advised the timekeeper and the foreman of the W.P.A. project on which he was employed that he had not received the check in question. This information was duly communicated to other agents of the United States and on November 30, 1936, Barner executed an affidavit alleging that the endorsement of his name on the check was a forgery. No notice was given the Clearfield Trust Co. or J. C. Penney Co. of the forgery until January 12, 1937, at which time the Clearfield Trust Co. was notified. The first notice received by Clearfield Trust Co. that the United States was asking reimbursement was on August 31, 1937.

This suit was instituted in 1939 by the United States against the Clearfield Trust Co., the jurisdiction of the federal District Court being invoked pursuant to the provisions of §24(1) of the Judicial Code, 28 U.S.C. §41(1). The cause of action was based on the express guaranty of prior endorsements made by the Clearfield Trust Co. J. C. Penney Co. intervened as a defendant. The case was heard on complaint, answer and stipulation of facts. The District Court held that the rights of the parties were to be determined by the law of Pennsylvania and that since the United States unreasonably delayed in giving notice of the forgery to the Clearfield Trust Co., it was barred from recovery under the rule of Market Street Title & Trust Co. v. Chelten Trust Co., 296 Pa. 230, 145 A. 848. It accordingly dismissed the complaint. On appeal the Circuit Court of Appeals reversed. The case is here on a petition for a writ of certiorari which we granted because of the importance of the problems raised. . . .

We agree with the Circuit Court of Appeals that the rule of Erie R. Co. v. Tompkins does not apply to this action. The rights and duties of the United States on commercial paper which it issues are governed by federal rather than local law. When the United States disburses its funds or pays its debts, it is exercising a constitutional function or power. This check was issued for services performed under the Federal Emergency Relief Act of 1935. The authority to issue the check had its origin in the Constitution and the statutes of the United States and was in no way dependent on the laws of Pennsylvania or of any other state. The duties imposed upon the United States and the rights acquired by it as a result of the issuance find their roots in the same federal sources. In absence of an applicable Act of Congress it is for the federal courts to fashion the governing rule of law according to their own standards. United States v. Guaranty Trust Co. is not opposed to this result. That case was concerned with a conflict of laws rule as to the title acquired by a transferee in Yugoslavia under a forged endorsement. Since the payee's address was Yugoslavia, the check had "something of the quality of a foreign bill" and the law of Yugoslavia was applied to determine what title the transferee acquired.

In our choice of the applicable federal rule we have occasionally selected state law. But reasons which may make state law at times the appropriate federal rule are singularly inappropriate here. The issuance of commercial paper by the United States is on a vast scale and transactions in that paper from issuance to payment will commonly occur in several states. The application of state law, even without the conflict of laws rules of the forum, would subject the rights and duties of the United States to exceptional uncertainty. It would lead to great diversity in results by making identical transactions subject to the vagaries of the laws of the several states. The desirability of a uniform rule is plain. And while the federal law merchant, developed for about a century under the regime of Swift v. Tyson, represented general commercial law rather than a choice of a federal rule designed to protect a federal right, it nevertheless stands as a convenient source of reference for fashioning federal rules applicable to these federal questions. . . .

The *National Exchange Bank* case went no further than to hold that prompt notice of the discovery of the forgery was not a condition precedent to suit. It did not reach the question whether lack of prompt notice might be a defense. We think it may. If it is shown that the drawee on learning of the forgery did not give prompt notice of it and that damage resulted, recovery by the drawee is barred. The fact that the drawee is the United States and the laches those of its employees are not material. The United States as drawee of commercial paper stands in no different light than any other drawee. As stated in United States v. National Exchange Bank, "The United States does business on business terms." It is not excepted from the general rules governing the rights and duties of drawees "by the largeness of its dealings and its having to employ agents to do what if done by a principal in person would leave no room for doubt." But the damage occasioned by the delay must be established and not left to conjecture. Cases such as Market St. Title & Trust Co. v. Chelten Trust Co., *supra,* place the burden on the drawee of giving prompt notice of the forgery—injury to the defendant being presumed by the mere fact of delay. But we do not think that he who accepts a forged signature of a payee deserves that preferred treatment. It is his neglect or error in accepting the forger's signature which occasions the loss. He should be allowed to shift that loss to the drawee only on a clear showing that the drawee's delay in notifying him of the forgery caused him damage. No such damage has been shown by Clearfield Trust Co. who so far as appears can still recover from J. C. Penney Co. The only showing on the part of the latter is contained in the stipulation to the effect that if a check cashed for a customer is returned unpaid or for reclamation a short time after the date on which it is cashed, the employees can often locate the person who cashed it. It is further stipulated that when

J. C. Penney Co. was notified of the forgery in the present case none of its employees was able to remember anything about the transaction or check in question. The inference is that the more prompt the notice the more likely the detection of the forger. But that falls short of a showing that the delay caused a manifest loss. It is but another way of saying that mere delay is enough.

Affirmed.

Questions and Comments

(1) The *Clearfield* Court says "[t]he desirability of a uniform rule is plain." Is it? Since the United States will remain liable for failure to give notice in *Clearfield* situations when actual harm has been suffered for failure to give notice, federal officials will suffer no less burden on the notice issue under the harsher state law or the more relaxed federal common law. The behavior of federal officials, in other words, will not be affected by the choice of the controlling law. Only after-the-fact assessments of liability, which may be important on questions of settlement, trial strategy, or the like, will be affected. Is that enough federal interest to justify displacing federal law?

(2) In Miree v. DeKalb County, 433 U.S. 25 (1977), a number of actions were brought in the aftermath of the crash upon take-off of a Lear jet. One theory of liability was that the plaintiffs were third-party beneficiaries of the contract between the Federal Aviation Administration and the county, one provision of which was the county's undertaking to keep adjoining land compatible with normal airport operation. Plaintiffs alleged that the crash was caused by the aircraft's ingestion of birds attracted to a garbage dump adjoining the airport. In the lower courts there was disagreement about whether plaintiffs had claims under federal common law and state law and, if they had a claim under one but not the other, which was controlling. The asserted basis for federal common law was the *Clearfield* case, and the fact that the United States (through the FAA) was a party to the airport contract. The Supreme Court found no basis for creating any federal common law. Since the United States was not a party to the action, any federal interest was found to be too "speculative." Under such circumstances, only congressional directions to do so would justify creating federal law.

(3) Does the *Miree* decision indicate that federal common law is appropriate only when the United States is a party to the litigation? Undoubtedly not. Recall that under Textile Workers v. Lincoln Mills, 353 U.S. 448 (1957), the Court found a congressional intent to have the federal judiciary develop a federal common law of labor relations under §301 of the Taft-Hartley Act—apparently to save the constitutionality of the provision insofar as it granted jurisdiction to the federal courts without diversity.

(4) Is federal common law appropriate whenever the United States is a party to the litigation (and did not receive its rights by assignment)? Perhaps, but with a significant restriction. In United States v. Kimbell Foods, Inc., 440 U.S. 715 (1979), the presence of the United States as a holder of liens aris-

ing out of certain federal loan programs gave rise to federal common law, but the lack of a need for a uniform federal standard meant that the content of federal law was to be borrowed from state law.

(5) Many of these issues have come to the forefront in the Agent Orange litigation, described generally in Twerski, With Liberty and Justice for All: An Essay on Agent Orange and Choice of Law, 52 Brook. L. Rev. 341 (1986). This litigation against the United States and the chemical companies that had supplied the military with the herbicide Agent Orange during the Vietnam war was brought by individual veterans and their families. The district court initially concluded that the suit was governed by federal common law, but this finding was reversed by the Second Circuit. 635 F.2d 987 (2d Cir. 1980). This meant, of course, that the choice-of-law issue would have to be addressed. Since the individual claims had originally been filed all across the country and transferred to the Eastern District of New York, it was necessary under Van Dusen v. Barrack to ask what law would have been applied by the transferor courts. Note that this litigation implicated two arguments for federal common law: first, the fact that the United States was a party, and second, the need for uniformity.

The resulting choice-of-law nightmare was one that no judge ought to have been asked to address. Judge Weinstein opted for a "national consensus" approach, concluding that "under the special circumstances of this litigation, all transferor states would look to the same substantive law for the rule of decision on the critical substantive issues." In re "Agent Orange" Product Liability Litigation, 580 F. Supp. 690, 693 (E.D.N.Y. 1984). This required development of a multistate substantive rule that would compromise the interests of the competing states. But how is this different from developing a federal common-law rule of liability? Can there be any pretense that the court was simply deciding how the state courts would themselves have decided?

(6) One area in which it might be thought particularly appropriate to develop federal common law is the law of interstate relations, on the theory that where states are the disputants, it is unfair to allow the law of one of the involved parties to apply. This argument has been accepted in Hinderlider v. La Plata River and Cherry Creek Ditch Co., 304 U.S. 92 (1938), governing interstate water rights and decided the same day as *Erie Railroad.* How far should this reasoning be extended? Isn't it tempting to argue that *all* aspects of interstate relations should be a matter of federal law? But wouldn't this federalize the entire subject of conflict of laws?

Illinois v. City of Milwaukee

406 U.S. 91 (1972)

Justice Douglas delivered the opinion of the Court.

This is a motion by Illinois to file a bill of complaint under our original jurisdiction against four cities of Wisconsin, the Sewerage Commission of the City of Milwaukee, and the Metropolitan Sewerage Commission of the County of Milwaukee. The cause of action alleged is pollution by the defendants of Lake Michigan, a body of interstate water. According to plantiff, some 200 million gallons of raw or inadequately treated sewage and other waste materials are discharged daily into the lake in the Milwaukee area alone. Plaintiff alleges that it and its subdivisions prohibit and prevent such discharges, but that the defendants do not take such actions. Plaintiff asks that we abate this public nuisance.

I

Article III, §2, cl. 2, of the Constitution provides:

> In all Cases . . . in which a State shall be Party, the supreme Court shall have original Jurisdiction.

Congress has provided in 28 U.S.C. §1251 that

> (a) the Supreme Court shall have original and exclusive jurisdiction of:
>
> (1) All controversies between two or more States.

It has long been this Court's philosophy that "our original jurisdiction should be invoked sparingly." We construe 28 U.S.C. §1251 (a)(1), as we do Art. III, §2, cl. 2, to honor our original jurisdiction but to make it obligatory only in appropriate cases. And the question of what is appropriate concerns, of course, the seriousness and dignity of the claim; yet beyond that it necessarily involves the availability of another forum where there is jurisdiction over the named parties, where the issues tendered may be litigated, and where appropriate relief may be had. . . .

If the named public entities of Wisconsin may . . . be sued by Illinois in a federal district court, our original jurisdiction is not mandatory.

It is to that aspect of the case that we now turn.

II

Title 28 U.S.C. §1331(a) provides that

> [t]he district courts shall have original jurisdiction of all civil actions wherein the matter in controversy exceeds the sum or value of $10,000, exclusive of interest and costs, and arises under the Constitution, laws, or treaties of the United States.

The considerable interests involved in the purity of interstate waters would seem to put beyond question the jurisdictional amount provided in

§1331(a). The question is whether pollution of interstate or navigable waters creates actions arising under the "laws" of the United States within the meaning of §1331(a). We hold that it does; and we also hold that §1331(a) includes suits brought by a State.

Mr. Justice Brennan, speaking for the four members of this Court in Romero v. International Terminal Operating Co. (dissenting and concurring), who reached the issue, concluded that "laws," within the meaning of §1331(a), embraced claims founded on federal common law:

> The contention cannot be accepted that since petitioner's rights are judicially defined, they are not created by "the laws . . . of the United States" within the meaning of §1331. . . . In another context, that of state law, this Court has recognized that the statutory word "laws" includes court decisions. The converse situation is presented here in that federal courts have an extensive responsibility of fashioning rules of substantive law. . . . These rules are as fully "laws" of the United States as if they had been enacted by Congress.

(Citations omitted.)

Lower courts have reached the same conclusion. . . .

III

Congress had enacted numerous laws touching interstate waters. In 1899 it established some surveillance by the Army Corps of Engineers over industrial pollution, not including sewage. . . .

The 1899 Act has been reinforced and broadened by a complex of laws recently enacted. The Federal Water Pollution Control Act tightens control over discharges into navigable waters so as not to lower applicable water quality standards. By the National Environmental Policy Act of 1969, Congress "authorizes and directs" that "the policies, regulations, and public laws of the United States shall be interpreted and administered in accordance with the policies set forth in this Act" and that "all agencies of the Federal Government shall . . . identify and develop methods and procedures . . . which will insure that presently unquantified environmental amenities and values may be given appropriate consideration in decisionmaking along with economic and technical considerations." Congress has evinced increasing concern with the quality of the aquatic environment as it affects the conservation and safeguarding of fish and wildlife resources.

Buttressed by these new and expanding policies, the Corps of Engineers has issued new Rules and Regulations governing permits for discharges or deposits into navigable waters.

The Federal Water Pollution Control Act in §1(b) declares that it is federal policy

> to recognize, preserve, and protect the primary responsibilities and rights of the States in preventing and controlling water pollution.

But the Act makes clear that it is federal, not state, law that in the end controls the pollution of interstate or navigable waters.[3] While the States are given time to establish water quality standards, §10(c)(1), if a State fails to do so the federal administrator promulgates one. Section 10(a) makes pollution of interstate or navigable waters subject "to abatement" when it "endangers the health or welfare of any persons." The abatement that is authorized follows a long-drawn-out procedure unnecessary to relate here. It uses the conference procedure, hoping for amicable settlements. But if none is reached, the federal administrator may request the Attorney General to bring suit on behalf of the United States for abatement of the pollution. §10(g).

The remedy sought by Illinois is not within the precise scope of remedies prescribed by Congress. Yet the remedies which Congress provides are not necessarily the only federal remedies available. "It is not uncommon for federal courts to fashion federal law where federal rights are concerned." Textile Workers v. Lincoln Mills. When we deal with air and water in the ambient or interstate aspects, there is a federal common law, as Texas v. Pankey recently held.

The application of federal common law to abate a public nuisance in interstate or navigable waters is not inconsistent with the Water Pollution Control Act. Congress provided in §10(b) of that Act that, save as a court may decree otherwise in an enforcement action,

> [s]tate and interstate action to abate pollution of interstate or navigable waters shall be encouraged and shall not . . . be displaced by Federal enforcement action.

The leading air case is Georgia v. Tennessee Copper Co., where Georgia filed an original suit in this Court against a Tennessee company whose noxious gases were causing a wholesale destruction of forests, orchards, and crops in Georgia. The Court said:

> The caution with which demands of this sort, on the part of a State, for relief from injuries analogous to torts, must be examined, is dwelt upon in Missouri v. Illinois, 200 U.S. 496, 520, 521. But it is plain that some such demands must be recognized, if the grounds alleged are proved. When the States by their union made the forcible abatement of outside nuisances impossible to each, they did not thereby agree to submit to whatever might be done. They did not renounce the possibility of mak-

---

3. The contrary indication in Ohio v. Wyandotte Chemicals Corp., 401 U.S. 493, 498 n.3, was based on the preoccupation of that litigation with public nuisance under Ohio law, not the federal common law which we now hold is ample basis for federal jurisdiction under 28 U.S.C. §1331(a).

> ing reasonable demands on the ground of their still remaining *quasi*-sovereign interests; and the alternative to force is a suit in this court. Missouri v. Illinois, 180 U.S. 208, 241.

206 U.S., at 237.

The nature of the nuisance was described as follows:

> It is a fair and reasonable demand on the part of a sovereign that the air over its territory should not be polluted on a great scale by sulphurous acid gas, that the forests on its mountains, be they better or worse, and whatever domestic destruction they have suffered, should not be further destroyed or threatened by the act of persons beyond its control, that the crops and orchards on its hills should not be endangered from the same source. If any such demand is to be enforced this must be notwithstanding the hesitation that we might feel if the suit were between private parties, and the doubt whether, for the injuries which they might be suffering to their property, they should not be left to an action at law.

Id., at 238.

Our decisions concerning interstate waters contain the same theme. Rights in interstate streams, like questions of boundaries, "have been recognized as presenting federal questions.[6] Hinderlider v. La Plata Co., 304 U.S. 92, 110. The question of apportionment of interstate waters is a question of "federal common law" upon which state statutes or decisions are not conclusive.

In speaking of the problem of apportioning the waters of an interstate stream, the Court said in Kansas v. Colorado, 206 U.S. 46, 98, that "through these successive disputes and decisions this court is practically building up what may not improperly be called interstate common law." And *see* Texas v. New Jersey (escheat of intangible personal property), Texas v. Florida (suit by bill in the nature of interpleader to determine the true domicile of a decedent as the basis of death taxes).

Equitable apportionment of the waters of an interstate stream has often been made under the head of our original jurisdiction. The applicable federal common law depends on the facts peculiar to the particular case.

> Priority of appropriation is the guiding principle. But physical and climatic conditions, the consumptive use of water in the several sections of the river, the character and rate of return flows, the extent of established uses, the

---

6. Thus, it is not only the character of the parties that requires us to apply federal law. As Mr. Justice Harlan indicated for the Court in Banco Nacional de Cuba v. Sabbatino, where there is an overriding federal interest in the need for a uniform rule of decision or where the controversy touches basic interests in federalism, we have fashioned federal common law. Certainly these same demands for applying federal law are present in the pollution of a body of water such as Lake Michigan bounded, as it is, by four States.

> availability of storage water, the practical effect of wasteful uses on downstream areas, the damage to upstream areas as compared to the benefits to downstream areas if a limitation is imposed on the former—these are all relevant factors. They are merely an illustrative, not an exhaustive catalogue. They indicate the nature of the problem of apportionment and the delicate adjustment of interests which must be made.

325 U.S., at 618.

When it comes to water pollution this Court has spoken in terms of "a public nuisance." In Missouri v. Illinois the Court said,

> It may be imagined that a nuisance might be created by a State upon a navigable river like the Danube, which would amount to a casus belli for a State lower down, unless removed. If such a nuisance were created by a State upon the Mississippi the controversy would be resolved by the more peaceful means of a suit in this court.

It may happen that new federal laws and new federal regulations may in time pre-empt the field of federal common law of nuisance. But until that comes to pass, federal courts will be empowered to appraise the equities of the suits alleging creation of a public nuisance by water pollution. While federal law governs,[9] consideration of state standards may be relevant. Thus, a State with high water-quality standards may well ask that its strict standards be honored and that it not be compelled to lower itself to the more degrading standards of a neighbor. There are no fixed rules that govern; these will be equity suits in which the informed judgment of the chancellor will largely govern.

We deny, without prejudice, the motion for leave to file. While this original suit normally might be the appropriate vehicle for resolving this controversy, we exercise our discretion to remit the parties to an appropriate district court[10] whose powers are adequate to resolve the issues.

So ordered.

---

9. "Federal common law and not the varying common law of the individual States is, we think, entitled and necessary to be recognized as a basis for dealing in uniform standard with the environmental rights of a State against improper impairment by sources outside its domain. The more would this seem to be imperative in the present era of growing concern on the part of a State about its ecological conditions and impairments of them. In the outside sources of such impairment, more conflicting disputes, increasing assertions and proliferating contentions would seem to be inevitable. Until the field has been made the subject of comprehensive legislation or authorized administrative standards, only a federal common law basis can provide an adequate means for dealing with such claims as alleged federal rights. And the logic and practicality of regarding such claims as being entitled to be asserted within the federal-question jurisdiction of §1331(a) would seem to be selfevident." Texas v. Pankey, 441 F.2d 236, 241-242.

10. The rule of decision being federal, the "action . . . may be brought only in the judicial district where all defendants reside, or in which the claim arose," 28 U.S.C. §1391(b), thereby giving flexibility to the choice of venue.

Questions and Comments

(1) What was the source of authority in Illinois v. City of Milwaukee [*Milwaukee I*]? If it was congressional enactment in the area, should a violation of federal legislation be required? Was it shown in this case? Are some areas just "inherently federal"?

(2) Does the grant of original jurisdiction to the Supreme Court imply a grant of lawmaking power? See footnote 6 of the *Milwaukee I* opinion. Note that in *Milwaukee I*, unlike diversity cases, there is no grant of jurisdiction to the federal district courts unless it is first concluded that there is federal common law to support federal question jurisdiction.

(3) Is the *Milwaukee I* approach the one that should have been taken in State of Nevada v. Hall, page 402 *supra?* Does the fact that Nevada actually sent an agent into California adequately distinguish the two cases? Or is sending a person into California no more significant than sending pollution from Milwaukee into the water system of Chicago? Does the fact that Nevada's activity in *Hall* was commercial distinguish the cases, or should it be noted that private companies discharge pollution too, making the cases similar? Which way should a neutral federal court rule on the immunity of Nevada (immune under Nevada law, but not under California law) to damage actions?

(4) In City of Milwaukee v. Illinois, 451 U.S. 304 (1981) [*Milwaukee II*], the Court reviewed the decision that resulted when the state of Illinois (along with Michigan) took the Court's advice in the principal case and went to federal district court. Shortly after, however, Congress passed the Federal Water Pollution Control Act Amendments of 1972, 86 Stat. 816. Disagreeing with the courts below, the Supreme Court found that the 1972 amendments rendered unnecessary the creation or continued existence of any federal common law. (Note the first sentence of the penultimate paragraph in *Milwaukee* I).

Milwaukee II left open the question whether federal environmental statutes preempted state common law actions for injuries in one state caused by cross-border pollution originating in another. 451 U.S. at 310 n.4. The Supreme Court resolved the issue in International Paper Co. v. Ouellette, 479 U.S. 481 (1987). In *Ouellette*, property owners from the Vermont side of Lake Champlain brought a nuisance action for damages and injunctive relief under Vermont law against a New York paper mill that was discharging effluent into the lake. The Court held that savings provision in the Clean Water Act preempted nuisance actions under the affected state's law but not under the polluting state's law. The Court attributed to Congress a worry about the "chaotic regulatory structure" that would arise from inconsistent state pollution laws applying to a single pollution source. *Id.* at 496-497. *Compare* this concern with the concern about "inconsistent regulations" in the dormant commerce clause cases, *supra* pages 428-444.

How does cross-border pollution differ from any other cross-border tort that produces harm in multiple states? Would there be a good reason to prevent application of the law of the state of injury in a case involving multistate libel or an airplane crash? Won't *Ouellette* encourage upstream states to pollute at the expense of downstream states? But if downstream states can apply their laws, won't they clean up their water at the expense of upstream states? Is there any way around this problem?

(5) Many commentators believe that the Supreme Court in recent years has cut back on the scope of federal common law. *See, e.g.*, Lund, The Decline of Federal Common Law, 76 Bost. L. Rev. 895 (1996). A good example of this trend is O'Melveney & Myers v. Federal Deposit Ins. Co., 512 U.S. 79 (1994). In that case, the FDIC sued the law firm of O'Melveny & Myers for its work in connection with a failed thrift, alleging that the firm's negligence had contributed to the thrift's insolvency and to the resulting losses to the FDIC. In holding that state rather than federal law governed the defenses the law firm could raise to the federal agency's suit, the Court reasoned:

> [T]his is not one of those cases in which judicial creation of a special federal [common law] rule would be justified. Such cases are, as we have said in the past, "few and restricted," Wheeldin v. Wheeler, 373 U.S. 647, 651 (1963), limited to situations where there is a "significant conflict between some federal policy or interest and the use of state law." Wallis v. Pan American Petroleum Corp., 384 U.S. 63, 68 (1966). Our cases uniformly require the existence of such a conflict as a precondition for recognition of a federal rule of decision. *See, e.g.*, Kamen v. Kemper Financial Services, Inc., 500 U.S. 90 (1991). Not only the permissibility but also the scope of judicial displacement of state rules turns upon such a conflict. *See, e.g.*, *Kamen*, at 98. What is fatal to respondent's position in the present case is that it has identified *no* significant conflict with an identifiable federal policy or interest. There is not even at stake that most generic (and lightly invoked) of alleged federal interests, the interest in uniformity. The rules of decision at issue here do not govern the primary conduct of the United States or any of its agents or contractors, but affect only the FDIC's rights and liabilities, as receiver, with respect to primary conduct on the part of private actors that has already occurred. Uniformity of law might facilitate the FDIC's nationwide litigation of these suits, eliminating state-by-state research and reducing uncertainty—but if the avoidance of those ordinary consequences qualified as an identifiable federal interest, we would be awash in "federal common-law" rules. The closest respondent comes to identifying a specific, concrete federal policy or interest that is compromised by California law is its contention that state rules regarding the imputation of knowledge might "deplete the deposit insurance fund." But neither FIRREA nor the prior law sets forth any anticipated level for the fund, so what respondent must mean by "depletion" is simply the forgoing of *any* money which, under any *conceivable* legal rules, might accrue to the fund. That is a broad principle indeed, which would support not just elimination of the defense at issue here, but judicial creation of new, "federal-common-law" causes of action to enrich the fund. Of course we have no authority to do that, because there is no federal policy that the fund should always win. Our cases have previ-

> ously rejected "more money" arguments remarkably similar to the one made here. *See Kimbell Foods,* 440 U.S. at 737-738.
>
> Even less persuasive—indeed, positively probative of the dangers of respondent's facile approach to federal-common-law-making—is respondent's contention that it would "disserve the federal program" to permit California to insulate "the attorney's or accountant's malpractice," thereby imposing costs "on the nation's taxpayers, rather than on the negligent wrongdoer." By presuming to judge what constitutes malpractice, this argument demonstrates the runaway tendencies of "federal common law" untethered to a genuinely identifiable (as opposed to judicially constructed) federal policy. What sort of tort liability to impose on lawyers and accountants in general, and on lawyers and accountants who provide services to federally insured financial institutions in particular, "involves a host of considerations that must be weighed and appraised," *Northwest Airlines, Inc.,* 451 U.S. at 98, n.41—including, for example, the creation of incentives for careful work, provision of fair treatment to third parties, assurance of adequate recovery by the federal deposit insurance fund, and enablement of reasonably priced services. Within the federal system, at least, we have decided that that function of weighing and appraising "is more appropriately for those who write the laws, rather than for those who interpret them." *Northwest Airlines, supra,* at 98, n.41.

512 U.S. at 87-89; *see also* Atherton v. Federal Deposit Insurance Corp., 519 U.S. 213 (1996) (state law rather than federal common law sets the standard of conduct for officers and directors of federally insured savings institutions).

Would the Court have applied federal common law in *Clearfield Trust* and *Milwaukee I* under this standard?

6

Recognition of Judgments

"It is just as important that there be a place to end as there should be a place to begin litigation."* That is the principle underlying the concept of finality for judgments. And yet numerous considerations may militate against the finality of certain judgments. Most jurisdictions have a fairly elaborate system of law designed to give sufficient but not undue respect to judgments. Questions concerning this body of law generally arise in attacks on judgments. An attack may be either *direct* or *collateral*. A direct attack is an attempt to reopen or set aside the judgment itself. Rule 59 of the Federal Rules of Civil Procedure, for example, provides for the granting of a new trial for limited reasons and for a limited period of time (motions must be made within ten days after entry of judgment), and Rule 60 provides more limited grounds (such as fraud, newly discovered evidence, and the like) and a somewhat less limited time period for relieving a party of a final judgment. Such attacks on the original judgment are generally entertained only (or at least preferentially) in the court that rendered the original judgment.†

A more common concern is the collateral attack on a judgment, or, viewed from the opposite side, the binding effect of a judgment on subsequent litigation. Sometimes the entire question is labeled the problem of *res judicata*, but usually that term is reserved to describe the effect of a judgment itself on a subsequent case raising the same cause of action, while *collateral estoppel* refers to the effects of findings of fact actually contested in

---

* Stoll v. Gottlieb, 305 U.S. 165, 172 (1938).

† *See, e.g.*, Lapin v. Shulton, Inc., 333 F.2d 169 (9th Cir. 1964).

one lawsuit upon a subsequent piece of litigation which may involve a different cause of action but some of the same facts. Thus, for example, a default judgment may be given res judicata effect in a subsequent suit involving the same cause of action, but can be given no collateral estoppel effect because there is no actual contest over facts in a case terminated by a default judgment.

Res judicata, as narrowly defined, may further be broken down into two categories: *bar* and *merger*. "Bar" refers to the effect of the original judgment in preventing relitigation of the cause of action that was actually litigated. "Merger," on the other hand, refers to the effect of the original judgment in preventing litigation of matters that are considered so closely related to what was actually litigated that they should have been litigated all at once. The entire dispute, in other words, is said to have merged in the original judgment whether or not all parts of the dispute were actually litigated. To the extent that it is justified, bar is based on the idea that there is usually no good reason to litigate a matter twice, and that the chance that a second piece of litigation is likely to produce a better result is outweighed by the costs of relitigation. Merger, on the other hand, cannot be justified by a desire to avoid *re*litigation of matters, since it deals with matters that should have been but were not litigated originally. Instead it finds its justification in the concept of waiver and in a desire to protect the courts and the parties from needless fractionalization of disputes—from having to become involved in two lawsuits where one would do.

Collateral estoppel is limited to establishing, for purposes of the second piece of litigation, facts determined in previous litigation that were "(1) litigated by the parties; (2) determined by the tribunal; and (3) necessarily so determined."* It is somewhat more difficult to defend the role of collateral estoppel than that of res judicata. Although some time may be saved by refusal to reinquire into facts, the very complexity of the rules concerning collateral estoppel tends to consume a great deal of court time, and, since the cause of action is likely to be different if collateral estoppel rather than res judicata is at stake, it is probable that the parties will have to litigate at least some issues whether or not the doctrine is applied. On the other hand, the doctrine does preserve a certain seemliness about the law: it tends to guarantee that courts will not reach inconsistent conclusions, based on inconsistent factual findings, at least between identical parties.

Both res judicata and collateral estoppel require some identity of parties. Res judicata requires either absolute identity or *privity*—a legal connection with a party to the first action sufficient to make it fair that the nonparty be bound by or be able to take advantage of the former judgment. Collateral estoppel classically had the same requirements, but more recently there has been a relaxation of what is called the *mutuality* requirement. Mutuality requires that for *A* to take advantage of a factual finding in previous

---

* James, Hazard & Leubsdorf, Civil Procedure 704 (5th ed. 2001).

litigation against *B*, *B* must have been able to take advantage of the factual finding if it had gone the other way. A relaxation of the mutuality rule (which is also a relaxation of the identity-of-parties requirement) is seen in those jurisdictions that allow *A* to take advantage of a finding of fact against *B* in a previous suit pitting *C* against *B*. In other words, relaxation of the mutuality requirement allows a fact to be used against someone who *was* a party to previous litigation even though it is being so used by a person who was *not* a party to previous litigation. (A requirement that has not been relaxed is that the person against whom the finding is used must have been a party to the previous suit or in privity with one.)

None of the intricacies of the discussion above requires more than a single jurisdiction. Res judicata and collateral estoppel are common-law rules applicable within an individual court system. For present purposes, however, the chief interest in these two doctrines arises when the effect of a judgment or finding of fact from a court in State *X* is considered in a court in State *Y*. The broad outlines of State *Y*'s obligation to honor State *X*'s judgment are contained in the full faith and credit clause of the Constitution, and 28 U.S.C. §1738:

> [U.S. Const. art. IV, §1:] Full Faith and Credit shall be given in each State to the public Acts, Records, and judicial Proceedings of every other State. And the Congress may by general Laws prescribe the Manner in which such Acts, Records and Proceedings shall be proved, and the Effect thereof.
>
> [28 U.S.C. §1738:] State and Territorial statutes and judicial proceedings; full faith and credit.
>
> The Acts of legislature of any State, Territory, or Possession of the United States, or copies thereof, shall be authenticated by affixing the seal of such State, Territory or Possession thereto.
>
> The records and judicial proceedings of any court of any such State, Territory or Possession, or copies thereof, shall be proved or admitted in other courts within the United States and its Territories and Possessions by the attestation of the clerk and seal of the court annexed, if a seal exists, together with a certificate of a judge of the court that the said attestation is in proper form.
>
> Such Acts, records and judicial proceedings or copies thereof, so authenticated, shall have the same full faith and credit in every court within the United States and its Territories and Possessions as they have by law or usage in the courts of such State, Territory or Possession from which they are taken.

Commonly, full faith and credit questions arise in the United States when judgments from the courts of one state are presented for enforcement in the courts of another.* The statutory texts above, however, do little to answer many difficult problems in these cases, such as: What jurisdictional defects in the first judgment, if any, relieve the second court of the obligation

---

* Is there any basis in the full faith and credit clause or the implementing statute for requiring the states to give full faith and credit to the judgments of federal courts? If the full

to enforce a judgment; need the enforcing state respect a judgment contrary to its own deeply held substantive interests; and which state's laws apply as to mechanical or procedural issues of judgments enforcement? After examining these questions, this chapter takes a look at a special problem in the area of judgments enforcement, namely, domestic relations law.

A. Jurisdictional Requirements

Durfee v. Duke

375 U.S. 106 (1963)

Justice STEWART delivered the opinion of the Court.

The United States Constitution requires that "Full Faith and Credit shall be given in each State to the . . . judicial Proceedings of every other State." The case before us presents questions arising under this constitutional provision and under the federal statute enacted to implement it.

In 1956 the petitioners brought an action against the respondent in a Nebraska court to quiet title to certain bottom land situated on the Missouri River. The main channel of that river forms the boundary between the States of Nebraska and Missouri. The Nebraska court had jurisdiction over the subject matter of the controversy only if the land in question was in Nebraska. Whether the land was Nebraska land depended entirely upon a factual question—whether a shift in the river's course had been caused by avulsion or accretion.[1] The respondent appeared in the Nebraska court and through counsel fully litigated the issues, explicitly contesting the court's jurisdiction over the subject matter of the controversy.[2] After a hearing the court found the issues in favor of the petitioners and ordered that title to the land be quieted in them. The respondent appealed, and the Supreme Court of Nebraska affirmed the judgment after a trial de novo on the record made in the lower court. The State Supreme Court specifically found that the rule of avul-

---

faith and credit clause does not authorize such a rule, is there any other basis in the Constitution for requiring such recognition by the states? In fact, the Supreme Court has always required recognition of federal court judgments. *See, e.g.*, Metcalf v. Watertown, 153 U.S. 671 (1894). Would any other result be acceptable? *See generally* Burbank, Federal Judgments Law: Sources of Authority and Sources of Rules, 70 Tex. L. Rev. 1551 (1992).

1. Throughout this litigation there has been no dispute as to the controlling effect of this factual issue.

2. This is, therefore, not a case in which a party, although afforded an opportunity to contest subject-matter jurisdiction, did not litigate the issue. *Cf.* Chicot County Drainage Dist. v. Baxter State Bank, 308 U.S. 371.

sion was applicable, that the land in question was in Nebraska, that the Nebraska courts therefore had jurisdiction of the subject matter of the litigation, and that title to the land was in the petitioners. Durfee v. Keiffer, 168 Neb. 272, 95 N.W.2d 618. The respondent did not petition this Court for a writ of certiorari to review that judgment.

Two months later the respondent filed a suit against the petitioners in a Missouri court to quiet title to the same land. Her complaint alleged that the land was in Missouri. The suit was removed to a Federal District Court by reason of diversity of citizenship. The District Court after hearing evidence expressed the view that the land was in Missouri but held that all the issues had been adjudicated and determined in the Nebraska litigation, and that the judgment of the Nebraska Supreme Court was res judicata and "is not binding upon this court." The Court of Appeals reversed, holding that the District Court was not required to give full faith and credit to the Nebraska judgment, and that normal res judicata principles were not applicable because the controversy involved land and a court in Missouri was therefore free to retry the question of the Nebraska court's jurisdiction over the subject matter. We granted certiorari to consider a question important to the administration of justice in our federal system. For the reasons that follow, we reverse the judgment before us.

The constitutional command of full faith and credit, as implemented by Congress, requires that "judicial proceedings . . . shall have the same full faith and credit in every court within the United States . . . as they have by law or usage in the courts of such State . . . from which they are taken." Full faith and credit thus generally requires every State to give to a judgment at least the res judicata effect which the judgment would be accorded in the State which rendered it. "By the Constitutional provision for full faith and credit, the local doctrines of res judicata, speaking generally, become part of national jurisprudence, and therefore federal questions cognizable here." Riley v. New York Trust Co.

It is not questioned that the Nebraska courts would give full res judicata effect to the Nebraska judgment quieting title in the petitioners. It is the respondent's position, however, that whatever effect the Nebraska courts might give to the Nebraska judgment, the federal court in Missouri was free independently to determine whether the Nebraska court in fact had jurisdiction over the subject matter, *i.e.*, whether the land in question was actually in Nebraska.

In support of this position the respondent relies upon the many decisions of this Court which have held that a judgment of a court in one State is conclusive upon the merits in a court in another State only if the court in the first State had power to pass on the merits—had jurisdiction, that is, to render the judgment. As Mr. Justice Bradley stated the doctrine in the leading case of Thompson v. Whitman, 18 Wall. 457, "we think it clear that the jurisdiction of the court by which a judgment is rendered in any State may be questioned in a collateral proceeding in another State, notwithstanding the provision of the fourth article of the Constitution and the law of 1790, and notwithstanding the averments contained in the record of the judgment itself." The principle has been restated and applied in a variety of contexts.

However, while it is established that a court in one State, when asked to give effect to the judgment of a court in another State, may constitutionally inquire into the foreign court's jurisdiction to render that judgment, the modern decisions of this Court have carefully delineated the permissible scope of such an inquiry. From these decisions there emerges the general rule that a judgment is entitled to full faith and credit—even as to questions of jurisdiction—when the second court's inquiry disclosed that those questions have been fully and fairly litigated and finally decided in the court which rendered the original judgment.

With respect to questions of jurisdiction over the person,[3] this principle was unambiguously established in Baldwin v. Iowa State Traveling Men's Assn. There it was held that a federal court in Iowa must give binding effect to the judgment of a federal court in Missouri despite the claim that the original court did not have jurisdiction over the defendant's person, once it was shown to the court in Iowa that the question had been fully litigated in the Missouri forum. "Public policy," said the Court, "dictates that there be an end of litigation; that those who have contested an issue shall be bound by the result of the contest, and that matters once tried shall be considered forever settled as between the parties. We see no reason why this doctrine should not apply in every case where one voluntarily appears, presents his case and is fully heard, and why he should not, in the absence of fraud, be thereafter concluded by the judgment of the tribunal to which he has submitted his cause."

Following the *Baldwin* case, this Court soon made clear in a series of decisions that the general rule is no different when the claim is made that the original forum did not have jurisdiction over the subject matter. In each of these cases the claim was made that a court, when asked to enforce the judgment of another forum, was free to retry the question of that forum's jurisdiction over the subject matter. In each case this Court held that since the question of subject-matter jurisdiction had been fully litigated in the original forum, the issue could not be retried in a subsequent action between the parties.

The reasons for such a rule are apparent. In the words of the Court's opinion in Stoll v. Gottlieb, *supra*,

> We see no reason why a court, in the absence of an allegation of fraud in obtaining the judgment, should examine again the question whether the court making the earlier determination on an actual contest over juris-

---

3. It is not disputed in the present case that the Nebraska courts had jurisdiction over the respondent's person. She entered a general appearance in the trial court, and initiated the appeal to the Nebraska Supreme Court.

> diction between the parties, did have jurisdiction of the subject matter of the litigation. . . . Courts to determine the rights of parties are an integral part of our system of government. It is just as important that there should be a place to end as that there should be a place to begin litigation. After a party has his day in court, with opportunity to present his evidence and his view of the law, a collateral attack upon the decision as to jurisdiction there rendered merely retries the issue previously determined. There is no reason to expect that the second decision will be more satisfactory than the first.

To be sure, the general rule of finality of jurisdictional determinations is not without exceptions. Doctrines of federal pre-emption or sovereign immunity may in some contexts be controlling. Kalb v. Feuerstein [page 652 *infra*], U.S. v. U.S. Fid. Co., 309 U.S. 506.[4] But no such overriding considerations are present here.

It is argued that an exception to this rule of jurisdictional finality should be made with respect to cases involving real property because of this Court's emphatic expression of the doctrine that courts of one State are completely without jurisdiction directly to affect title to land in other States. This argument is wide of the mark. Courts of one State are equally without jurisdiction to dissolve the marriages of those domiciled in other States. But the location of land, like the domicile of a party to a divorce action, is a matter "to be resolved by judicial determination." Sherrer v. Sherrer. The question remains whether, once the matter has been fully litigated and judicially determined, it can be retried in another State in litigation between the same parties. Upon the reason and authority of the cases we have discussed, it is clear that the answer must be in the negative.

---

4. It is to be noted, however, that in neither of these cases had the jurisdictional issues actually been litigated in the first forum.

The Restatement of Conflict of Laws recognizes the possibility of such exceptions:

> Where a court has jurisdiction over the parties and determines that it has jurisdiction over the subject matter, the parties cannot collaterally attack the judgment on the ground that the court did not have jurisdiction over the subject matter, unless the policy underlying the doctrine of res judicata is outweighed by the policy against permitting the court to act beyond its jurisdiction. Among the factors appropriate to be considered in determining that collateral attack should be permitted are that
>
> (a) the lack of jurisdiction over the subject matter was clear;
>
> (b) the determination as to jurisdiction depended upon a question of law rather than of fact;
>
> (c) the court was one of limited and not of general jurisdiction;
>
> (d) the question of jurisdiction was not actually litigated;
>
> (e) the policy against the court's acting beyond its jurisdiction is strong.

Restatement, Conflict of Laws, §451(2) (Supp. 1948). *See* Restatement, Judgments, §10 (1942).

It is to be emphasized that all that was ultimately determined in the Nebraska litigation was title to the land in question as between the parties to the litigation there. Nothing there decided, and nothing that could be decided in litigation between the same parties or their privies in Missouri, could bind either Missouri or Nebraska with respect to any controversy they might have, now or in the future, as to the location of the boundary between them, or as to their respective sovereignty over the land in question. Either State may at any time protect its interest by initiating independent judicial proceedings here.

For the reasons stated, we hold in this case that the federal court in Missouri had the power and, upon proper averments, the duty to inquire into the jurisdiction of the Nebraska courts to render the decree quieting title to the land in the petitioners. We further hold that when that inquiry disclosed, as it did, that the jurisdictional issues had been fully and fairly litigated by the parties and finally determined in the Nebraska courts, the federal court in Missouri was correct in ruling that further inquiry was precluded. Accordingly the judgment of the Court of Appeals is reversed, and that of the District Court is affirmed.

It is so ordered.

Justice BLACK, concurring.

Petitioners and respondent dispute the ownership of a tract of land adjacent to the Missouri River, which is the boundary between Nebraska and Missouri. Resolution of this question turns on whether the land is in Nebraska or Missouri. Neither State, of course, has power to make a determination binding on the other as to which State the land is in. U.S. Const., Art III, §2; 28 U.S.C. §1251(a). However, in a private action brought by these Nebraska petitioners, the Nebraska Supreme Court has held that the disputed tract is in Nebraska. In the present suit, brought by this Missouri respondent in Missouri, the United States Court of Appeals has refused to be bound by the Nebraska court's judgment. I concur in today's reversal of the Court of Appeals' judgment, but with the understanding that we are not deciding the question whether the respondent would continue to be bound by the Nebraska judgment should it later be authoritatively decided, either in an original proceeding between the States in this Court or by a compact between the two States under Art. I, §10, that the disputed tract is in Missouri.

Fall v. Eastin

215 U.S. 1 (1909)

Justice MCKENNA delivered the opinion of the court.

The question in this case is whether a deed to land situated in Nebraska, made by a commissioner under the decree of a court of the State of Washington in an action for divorce, must be recognized in Nebraska under the due faith and credit clause of the Constitution of the United States.

The action was begun in Hamilton County, Nebraska, in 1897, to quiet title to the land and to cancel a certain mortgage thereon, given by E. W. Fall to W. H. Fall, and to cancel a deed executed therefor to defendant in error, Elizabeth Eastin.

Plaintiff alleged the following facts: She and E. W. Fall, who was a defendant in the trial court, were married in Indiana in 1876. Subsequently they went to Nebraska, and while living there, "by their joint efforts, accumulations and earnings, acquired jointly and by the same conveyance" the land in controversy. In 1889 they removed to the State of Washington, and continued to reside there as husband and wife until January, 1895, when they separated. On the twenty-seventh of February, 1895, her husband, she and he then being residents of King County, Washington, brought suit against her for divorce in the Superior Court of that county. He alleged in his complaint that he and plaintiff were bona fide residents of King County, and that he was the owner of the land in controversy, it being, as he alleged, "his separate property, purchased by money received from his parents." He prayed for a divorce and "for a just and equitable division of the property."

Plaintiff appeared in the action by answer and cross complaint, in which she denied the allegations of the complaint, and alleged that the property was community property, and "was purchased by and with the money and proceeds of the joint labor" of herself and husband after their marriage. She prayed that a divorce be denied him, and that the property be set apart to her as separate property, subject only to a mortgage of $1,000, which she alleged was given by him and her. In a reply to her answer and cross complaint he denied that she was the "owner as a member of the community in conjunction" with him of the property, and repeated the prayer of his complaint.

Plaintiff also alleges that the Code of Washington contained the following provisions:

> Sec. 2007 [now 4637]. In granting a divorce, the court shall also make such disposition of the property of the parties as shall appear just and equitable having regard to the respective merits of the parties and to the condition in which they will be left by such divorce, and to the party through whom the property was acquired, and to the burdens imposed upon it for the benefit of the children, and shall make provision for the guardianship, custody and support and education of the minor children of such marriage.

She further alleges that that provision had been construed by the Supreme Court of the State requiring of the parties to an action for divorce to bring into court all of " 'their property, and a complete showing must be made,' " and that it was decided that §2007 [now 4637] conferred upon the court " 'the power, in its discretion, to make a division of the separate property of the wife or husband.' "

She further alleges that a decree was entered granting her a divorce and setting apart to her that land in controversy as her own separate property forever, free and unencumbered from any claim of the plaintiff thereto, and that he was ordered and directed by the court to convey all his right, title and interest in and to the land within five days from the date of the decree.

She also alleges the execution of the deed to her by the commissioner appointed by the court, the execution and recording of the mortgage to W. H. Fall and the deed to defendant; that the deed and mortgage were each made without consideration and for the purpose of defrauding her, and that they cast a cloud upon her title derived by her under the decree of divorce and the commissioner's deed. She prays that her title be quieted and that the deed and mortgage be declared null and void.

. . . A decree was passed in favor of plaintiff, which was affirmed by the Supreme Court. Fall v. Fall, 75 Nebraska, 104; 106 N.W. Rep. 412. A rehearing was granted and the decree was reversed, Judge Sedgwick, who delivered the first opinion, dissenting.

The question is in narrow compass. The full faith and credit clause of the Constitution of the United States is invoked by plaintiff to sustain the deed executed under the decree of the court of the State of Washington. The argument in support of this is that the Washington court, having had jurisdiction of the parties and the subject-matter, in determination of the equities between the parties to the lands in controversy, decreed a conveyance to be made to her. This conveyance, it is contended, was decreed upon equities, and was as effectual as though her "husband and she had been strangers and she had bought the land from him and paid for it and he had then refused to convey it to her." In other words, that the decree of divorce in the State of Washington, which was made in consummation of equities which arose between the parties under the law of Washington, was "evidence of her right to the legal title of at least as much weight and value as a contract in writing, reciting the payment of the consideration for the land, would be."

The defendant, on the other hand, contends, as we gather from his petition for a rehearing in the Supreme Court of the State and from the opinions of the court, that "the Washington court had neither power nor jurisdiction to effect in the least, either legally or equitably," lands situated in Nebraska. . . .

In considering these propositions we must start with a concession of jurisdiction in the Washington court over both the parties and the subject-matter. Jurisdiction in that court is the first essential, but the ultimate question is, What is the effect of the decree upon the land and of the deed executed under it? . . .

The territorial limitation of the jurisdiction of courts of a State over property in another State has a limited exception in the jurisdiction of a court of equity, but it is an exception well defined. A court of equity having authority to act upon the person may indirectly act upon real estate in another State, through the instrumentality of this authority over the person. Whatever it may do through the party it may do to give effect to its decree respecting property, whether it goes to the entire disposition of it or only to effect it with liens or burdens. Story on Conflict of Laws, §544. . . .

But, however plausibly the contrary view may be sustained, we think that the doctrine that the court, not having jurisdiction of the res, cannot affect it by its decree, nor by a deed made by a master in accordance with the decree, is firmly established. [W]hen the subject-matter of a suit in a court of equity is within another State or country, but the parties within the jurisdiction of the court, the suit may be maintained and remedies granted which may directly affect and operate upon the person of the defendant and not upon the subject-matter, although the subject-matter is referred to in the decree, and the defendant is ordered to do or refrain from certain acts toward it, and it is thus ultimately but *indirectly* affected by the relief granted. In such case the decree is not of itself legal title, nor does it transfer the legal title. It must be executed by the party, and obedience is compelled by proceedings in the nature of contempt, attachment or sequestration. On the other hand, where the suit is strictly local, the subject-matter is specific property, and the relief when granted is such that it *must* act directly upon the subject-matter, and not upon the person of the defendant, the jurisdiction must be exercised in the State where the subject matter is situated. 3 Pomeroy's Equity, §§1317, 1318, and notes.

This doctrine is entirely consistent with the provision of the Constitution of the United States, which requires a judgment in any State to be given full faith and credit in the courts of every other State. This provision does not extend the jurisdiction of the courts of one State to property situated in another, but only makes the judgment rendered conclusive on the merits of the claim or subject-matter of the suit. "It does not carry with it into another State the efficacy of a judgment upon property or persons, to be enforced by execution. To give it the force of a judgment in another State it must become a judgment there; and can only be executed in the latter as its laws permit." M'Elmoyle v. Cohen, 13 Pet. 312.

Plaintiff seems to contend for a greater efficacy for a decree in equity affecting real property than is given to a judgment at law for the recovery of money simply. . . .

. . . There is, however, much temptation in the facts of this case to [grant effect to the Washington decree and conveyance]. As we have seen, the husband of the plaintiff brought suit against her in Washington for divorce, and, attempting to avail himself of the laws of Washington, prayed also that the land now in controversy be awarded to him. She appeared in the action, and, submitting to the jurisdiction which he had invoked, made counter-charges and prayers for relief. She established her charges, she was granted a divorce, and the land decreed to her. He, then, to defeat the decree and in fraud of her rights, conveyed the land to the defendant in this suit. This is the finding of the trial court. It is not questioned by the Supreme Court, but as the ruling of the latter court, that the decree in Washington gave no such equities as could be recognized in Nebraska as justifying an action to quiet title does not offend the Constitution of the United States, we are constrained to affirm its judgment.

So ordered.

Justice HARLAN and Justice BREWER dissent.

Justice HOLMES, concurring specially.

I am not prepared to dissent from the judgment of the court, but my reasons are different from those that have been stated.

The real question concerns the effect of the Washington decree. As between the parties to it that decree established in Washington a personal obligation of the husband to convey to his former wife. A personal obligation goes with the person. If the husband had made a contract, valid by the law of Washington, to do the same thing, I think there is no doubt that the contract would have been binding in Nebraska. So I conceive that a Washington decree for the specific performance of such a contract would be entitled to full faith and credit as between the parties in Nebraska. But it does not matter to its constitutional effect what the ground of the decree may be, whether a contract or something else. Fauntleroy v. Lum. (In this case it may have been that the wife contributed equally to the accumulation of the property, and so had an equitable claim.) A personal decree is equally within the jurisdiction of a court having the person within its power, whatever its ground and whatever it orders the defendant to do. Therefore I think that this decree was entitled to full faith and credit in Nebraska.

But the Nebraska court carefully avoids saying that the decree would not be binding between the original parties had the husband been before the court. The ground on which it goes is that to allow the judgment to affect the conscience of purchasers would be giving it an effect in rem. It treats the case as standing on the same footing as that of an innocent purchaser. Now if the court saw fit to deny the effect of a judgment upon privies in title, or if it considered the defendant an innocent purchaser, I do not see what we have to do with its decision, however wrong. I do not see why it is not within the power of the State to do away with equity or with the equitable doctrine as to purchasers with notice if it sees fit. Still less do I see how a mistake as to notice could give us jurisdiction. If the judgment binds the defendant it is not by its own operation, even with the Constitution behind it, but by the obligation imposed by equity upon a purchaser with notice. The ground of decision below was that there was no such obligation. The decision, even if wrong, did not deny to the Washington decree its full effect.

Questions and Comments

(1) Is Fall v. Eastin consistent with Durfee v. Duke? Does *Durfee* overrule *Fall?* Or is the difference that in *Fall* it was agreed that the land at issue was outside the forum, whereas in *Durfee* that was precisely the subject of the dispute?

(2) Several different interpretations of *Fall* are possible. The most immediately obvious is simply that a judgment rendered without jurisdiction is void and can be collaterally attacked elsewhere. In the alternative, *Fall* might mean that states have such a strong substantive interest in land within their borders that no other state can interfere. Or, possibly *Fall* hinges on the special nature of the system for recording interests in land; that although the rendering state might transfer a legal right to the property, this right would not become effective against third parties until properly recorded at the situs.

Which of these rationales best explains *Fall?* Which makes it the most consistent with *Durfee?* Note that if the judgment were a judgment for money or personal property, the prevailing party would still have to seek execution in the place where the property was located. Which state's laws would apply on the issue of the proper method of execution? Does the rendering state exceed its authority if it tries to execute the judgment directly? Does it infringe on the substantive interests of the state where the property was located? Does it infringe on the situs's interests in controlling the procedures by which judgments are enforced?

(3) Reception of the "land taboo" has not been warm among the commentators. *See, e.g.*, Baxter, Choice of Law and the Federal System, 16 Stan. L. Rev. 1, 15-17 (1963); Hancock, Equitable Conversion and the Land Taboo in the Conflict of Laws, 17 Stan. L. Rev. 1095 (1965), also Full Faith and Credit to Foreign Laws and Judgments in Real Property Litigation, 18 Stan. L. Rev. 1299 (1966), and Conceptual Devices for Avoiding the Land Taboo in Conflict of Laws, 20 Stan. L. Rev. 1 (1967); and Currie, Full Faith and Credit to Foreign Land Decrees, 21 U. Chi. L. Rev. 620 (1954). Currie suggests a number of end runs, including a careful arranging of the relief requested in the original action, with a request in the second court for a decree awarding title, the first decree to act as res judicata or to provide collateral estoppel effect.

(4) What was the nature of the action brought by the Nebraska plaintiff in *Durfee?* If you were the Nebraska plaintiff, would you be satisfied that you had completely "won" your case in light of Justice Black's concurring opinion? Is there any justification for suggesting, as Justice Black does, that a subsequent decision that the land was not in Nebraska should undercut the authority of the Nebraska judgment? Doesn't *Durfee* stand for the proposition that the land *was* in Nebraska, for purposes of this litigation, and that that fact can't be reexamined?

If the two states had previously litigated the question of sovereignty over the land in the Supreme Court, would the Court's determination of the issue be binding by way of res judicata, or merely by way of stare decisis? Would it matter? What if the states had agreed that one of them owned the land, without litigating the issue, before the private litigation in *Durfee* (but after the dispute had arisen). Should such an agreement affect the private litigation? Would it make any difference if it appeared that the agreement had been a compromise, with several parcels of land involved, and with each state giving up some claims it thought legitimate in order to get others?

(5) What would have happened if the Court in *Durfee* had come out the other way—that is, if it had granted the Missouri federal district court the right to determine, on its own, whether the Nebraska court had been correct in saying that the land was in Nebraska? If you had been the successful plaintiff in Nebraska, what would you have done as the federal marshal from Missouri entered the land to deliver it to your opponent? Would the federal marshal from Missouri and the sheriff from Nebraska have to shoot it out? Didn't the Supreme Court *have* to decide *Durfee* the way it did?

(6) Does *Durfee* guarantee that there won't be any shoot-outs between the sheriff and the marshal? What if the Missouri party had not appeared in the Nebraska proceedings, but the Nebraska court had claimed subject matter jurisdiction over the dispute by virtue of the land's presence within the state, and in rem jurisdiction for the same reason, thus binding all parties? Isn't that consistent with *Shaffer*, page 546 *supra?* Would *Durfee* make the Nebraska judgment binding under such circumstances? If not, and if the Nebraska party refuses to appear in a Missouri proceeding with jurisdiction based on the presence of the land in Missouri, who will keep the peace when sheriffs from the respective states show up to enforce the orders of their courts?

Kalb v. Feuerstein

308 U.S. 433 (1940)

Justice BLACK delivered the opinion of the Court.

Appellants are farmers. Two of appellees, as mortgagees, began foreclosure on appellants' farm March 7, 1933, in the Walworth (Wisconsin) County Court: judgment of foreclosure was entered April 21, 1933; July 20, 1935, the sheriff sold the property under the judgment; September 16, 1935, while appellant Ernest Newton Kalb had duly pending in the bankruptcy court a petition for composition and extension of time to pay his debts under §75 of the Bankruptcy Act (Frazier-Lemke Act), the Walworth County Court granted the mortgagees' motion for confirmation of the sheriff's sale; no stay of the foreclosure or of the subsequent action to enforce it was ever sought or granted in the state or bankruptcy court; December 16, 1935, the mortgagees, who had purchased at the sheriff's sale, obtained a writ of assistance from the state court; and March 12, 1936, the sheriff executed the writ by ejecting appellants and their family from the mortgaged farm.

The questions in both No. 120 and No. 121 are whether the Wisconsin County Court had jurisdiction, while the petition under the Frazier-Lemke Act was pending in the bankruptcy court, to confirm the sheriff's sale and to order appellants dispossessed, and, if it did not, whether its action in the absence of direct appeal is subject to collateral attack.

No. 120. After ejection from their farm, appellants brought an action in equity in the Circuit Court of Walworth County, Wisconsin, against the mortgagees who had purchased at the sheriff's sale, for restoration of possession, for cancellation of the sheriff's deed and for removal of the mortgagees from the farm. Demurrer was sustained for failure to state a cause of action and the complaint was dismissed. The Supreme Court of Wisconsin affirmed.

No. 121 is a suit in the state court by appellant Ernest Newton Kalb against the mortgagees, the sheriff and the County Court judge who confirmed the foreclosure sale and issued the writ of assistance. Damages are sought for conspiracy to deprive appellant of possession, for assault and battery, and for false imprisonment. As in No. 120, demurrer was sustained, and the Supreme Court of Wisconsin affirmed.

In its first opinion the Supreme Court of Wisconsin said: "It is the contention of the plaintiff [mortgagor] that this statute is self-executing—that is, that it requires no application to the state or federal court in which foreclosure proceedings are pending for a stay; in other words, that it provides for a statutory and not for a judicial stay. plaintiff's claims under the Bankruptcy Act present a question which clearly arises under the laws of the United States and therefore present a federal question upon which determination of the federal courts is controlling." Addressing itself solely to this federal question of construing the Frazier-Lemke Act, the Wisconsin court decided that the federal Act did not itself as an automatic statutory stay terminate the state court's jurisdiction when the farmer filed his petition in the bankruptcy court. Since there had been no judicial stay, it held that the confirmation of sale and writ of assistance were not in violation of the Act. . . .

[I]f appellants are right in their contention that the federal Act of itself, from the moment the petition was filed and so long as it remained pending, operated, in the absence of the bankruptcy court's consent, to oust the jurisdiction of the state court so as to stay its power to proceed with foreclosure, to confirm a sale, and to issue an order ejecting appellants from their farm, the action of the Walworth County Court was not merely erroneous but was beyond its power, void, and subject to collateral attack.

It is generally true that a judgment by a court of competent jurisdiction bears a presumption of regularity and is not thereafter subject to collateral attack.[7] But Congress, because its power over the subject of bankruptcy is plenary, may by specific bankruptcy legislation create an exception to that principle and render judicial acts taken with respect to the person or property of a debtor whom the bankruptcy law protects nullities and vulnerable collaterally. Although the Walworth County Court had general jurisdiction over foreclosures under the law of Wisconsin, a peremptory prohibition by Congress in the exercise of its supreme power over bankruptcy that no state court have jurisdiction over a petitioning farmer-debtor or his property, would

7. Chicot County Drainage District v. Baxter State Bank [page 656 *infra*].

have rendered the confirmation of sale and its enforcement beyond the County Court's power and nullities subject to collateral attack. The State cannot, in the exercise of control over local laws and practice, vest state courts with power to violate the supreme law of the land. The Constitution grants Congress exclusive power to regulate bankruptcy and under this power Congress can limit the jurisdiction which courts, state or federal, can exercise over the person and property of a debtor who duly invokes the bankruptcy law. If Congress has vested in the bankruptcy courts exclusive jurisdiction over farmer-debtors and their property, and has by its Act withdrawn from all other courts all power under any circumstances to maintain and enforce foreclosure proceedings against them, its Act is the supreme law of the land which all courts—state and federal—must observe. The wisdom and desirability of an automatic statutory ouster of jurisdiction of all except bankruptcy courts over farmer-debtors and their property were considerations for Congress alone.

We think the language and broad policy of the Frazier-Lemke Act conclusively demonstrate that Congress intended to, and did deprive the Wisconsin County Court of the power and jurisdiction to continue or maintain in any manner the foreclosure proceedings against appellants without the consent after hearing of the bankruptcy court in which the farmer's petition was then pending. . . .

Thus Congress repeatedly stated its unequivocal purpose to prohibit—in the absence of consent by the bankruptcy court in which a distressed farmer has a pending petition—a mortgagee or any court from instituting, or maintaining if already instituted, any proceeding against the farmer to sell under mortgage foreclosure, to confirm such a sale, or to dispossess under it. . . .

The mortgagees who sought to enforce the mortgage after the petition was duly filed in the bankruptcy court, the Walworth County Court that attempted to grant the mortgagees relief, and the sheriff who enforced the court's judgment, were all acting in violation of the controlling Act of Congress. Because that state court had been deprived of all jurisdiction or power to proceed with the foreclosure, the confirmation of the sale, the execution of the sheriff's deed, the writ of assistance, and the ejection of appellants from their property—to the extent based upon the court's actions—were all without authority of law. Individual responsibility for such unlawful acts must be decided according to the law of the State. We therefore express no opinion as to other contentions based upon state law and raised by appellees in support of the judgments of the Supreme Court of Wisconsin.

Congress manifested its intention that the issue of jurisdiction in the foreclosing court need not be contested or even raised by the distressed farmer-debtor. The protection of the farmers was left to the farmers themselves or to the Commissioners who might be laymen, and considerations as to whether the issue of jurisdiction was actually contested in the County Court,[18] or

18. Stoll v. Gottlieb [305 U.S. 165 (1938)].

whether it could have been contested,[19] are not applicable where the plenary power of Congress over bankruptcy has been exercised as in this Act.

The judgments in both cases are reversed and the causes are remanded to the Supreme Court of Wisconsin for further proceedings not inconsistent with this opinion.

Reversed.

Questions and Comments

(1) It is clear, isn't it, that Congress had the *right* to do what the Court claimed it did in *Kalb,* since the federal courts are not bound by the full faith and credit clause, and in any event, the full faith and credit clause provides for congressional implementation?

(2) But that leaves the question whether Congress actually had the intent attributed to it by the Court. The legislation in question was the result of the depression. Congress may have been especially solicitous of farmers. But where is the affirmative indication that it wished to go so far? Isn't the Court's verbiage about voidness and nullities a smoke screen to avoid discussion of the central issue, *i.e.,* what was the intent of Congress on this particular issue? Why would Congress want to give someone the protection of a statutory defense he didn't even raise if, as in *Chicot,* a defense of unconstitutionality cannot be so used even when raising it would have seemed futile (because the statute had not yet been declared unconstitutional)?

(3) The Supreme Court has been reluctant in the recent past to infer congressional intent not to abide by res judicata or collateral estoppel. Thus, in Allen v. McCurry, 449 U.S. 90 (1980), the Court held that a civil rights claim brought under 28 U.S.C. §1983, alleging an illegal search and seizure, was barred by an earlier state court ruling in a criminal prosecution that the search and seizure had been legal. And in Kremer v. Chemical Construction Corp., 456 U.S. 461 (1982), the Court ruled that full faith and credit was due to findings of nondiscrimination made by a state administrative agency and reviewed by state courts, thus barring a subsequent Title VII action in the federal courts.

(4) How true is it, as a general matter, that a jurisdictional defect renders a judgment subject to collateral attack? In Thompson v. Whitman, 85 U.S. 457 (1873), the Supreme Court held that lack of subject matter jurisdiction in one proceeding could allow a collateral attack in a later proceeding. There a ship had been seized in New Jersey waters under a statute that provided for seizure of ships operated by nonresidents raking clams in New Jersey waters. The statute provided for proceedings in the county of seizure to sell the ship. After Whitman's ship had been seized and he had been given notice of the pending forfeiture proceedings, his ship was sold. He then sued the sheriff in a New York state court. The action was

19. Chicot County Drainage District v. Baxter State Bank [page 656 *infra*].

removed to federal court by the sheriff, who interposed the defense of the previous adjudication. The jury found that the seizure had not occurred in the county in which the New Jersey proceedings took place, and that the ship operators had not been raking clams. The Supreme Court denied the sheriff's demand that the New Jersey proceedings be taken as conclusive on those two issues because they went to the jurisdiction of the New Jersey tribunal.

(5) Does a lack of Article III "case or controversy" jurisdiction render a judgment subject to attack? United States v. Swift and Co., 276 U.S. 311 (1928). What about lack of diversity of citizenship? McCormick v. Sullivan, 23 U.S. (10 Wheat.) 192 (1825).

(6) What if the party seeking to attack the jurisdiction of the first tribunal appeared in the original proceedings but failed to argue the jurisdictional issue, and the court consequently did not decide it? In Chicot County Drainage District v. Baxter State Bank, 308 U.S. 37 (1940), the opportunity to raise a jurisdictional issue was held sufficient to foreclose it later, even though the issue was *in fact* not raised.

(7) If the defendant objects to personal jurisdiction and fails to persuade the court, then this determination is binding even if some later court believes that there was in fact no personal jurisdiction. Baldwin v. Iowa State Traveling Men's Association, 283 U.S. 522 (1931). Most jurisdictions offer the device of the *special appearance* or its equivalent, to raise jurisdictional issues. One who appears *generally* is said to have acceded to the court's jurisdiction; one who appears *specially* raises only the jurisdictional issue as a preliminary matter. If she wins on that issue, the case is dismissed; if she loses, she has the option of arguing the merits or appealing on the basis of the court's jurisdictional decision. There are dangers, of course, in relying too strongly on the jurisdictional appeal—if it fails, one will have waived the defense on the merits. In the federal courts and states with similar rules, special appearances are unnecessary—the equivalent is provided for by the opportunity to make motions based on jurisdictional questions and provisions that jurisdictional issues are not waived by pleading to the merits if jurisdictional objections are also timely raised. *See* Federal Rules of Civil Procedure 12 and 13.

Should a state be required to offer the equivalent of the special appearance? In other words, should a state be allowed to give a litigant the choice between appearing and thereby waiving jurisdictional defenses, or staying away, with the danger that a later court will disagree with the jurisdiction defense and give effect to the default judgment rendered by the first court? In York v. Texas, 137 U.S. 15 (1890), the Supreme Court said Texas could pose that hard choice to litigants who believed that the Texas courts had no personal jurisdiction over them. The availability of collateral attack was said to be enough to satisfy due process. Texas amended its court rules in 1962 to allow special appearances. Texas Rule of Civil Procedure 120a.

B. Substantive Interests of the Enforcing State

Fauntleroy v. Lum

210 U.S. 230 (1908)

Justice HOLMES delivered the opinion of the court.

This is an action upon a Missouri judgment brought in a court of Mississippi. The declaration set forth the record of the judgment. The defendant pleaded that the original cause of action arose in Mississippi out of a gambling transaction in cotton futures; that he declined to pay the loss; that the controversy was submitted to arbitration, the question as to the illegality of the transaction, however, not being included in the submission; that an award was rendered against the defendant; that thereafter, finding the defendant temporarily in Missouri, the plaintiff brought suit there upon the award; that the trial court refused to allow the defendant to show the nature of the transaction, and that by the laws of Mississippi the same was illegal and void, but directed a verdict if the jury should find that the submission and award were made, and remained unpaid; and that a verdict was rendered and the judgment in suit entered upon the same. (The plaintiff in error is an assignee of the judgment, but nothing turns upon that.) The plea was demurred to on constitutional grounds, and the demurrer was overruled subject to exception. Thereupon replications were filed, again setting up the Constitution of the United States (Art. IV, §1), and were demurred to. The Supreme Court of Mississippi held the plea good and the replications bad, and judgment was entered for the defendant. Thereupon the case was brought here.

The main argument urged by the defendant to sustain the judgment below is addressed to the jurisdiction of the Mississippi courts.

The laws of Mississippi make dealing in futures a misdemeanor, and provide that contracts of that sort, made without intent to deliver the commodity or to pay the price, "shall not be enforced by any court." The defendant contends that this language deprives the Mississippi courts of jurisdiction, and that the case is like Anglo-American Provision Co. v. Davis Provision Co. No. 1. There the New York statutes refused to provide a court into which a foreign corporation could come, except upon causes of action arising within the State, etc., and it was held that the State of New York was under no constitutional obligation to give jurisdiction to its Supreme Court against its will. One question is whether that decision is in point.

No doubt it sometimes may be difficult to decide whether certain words in a statute are directed to jurisdiction or to merits, but the distinction between the two is plain. One goes to the power, the other only to the duty of the court. Under the common law it is the duty of a court of general jurisdiction not to enter a judgment upon a parol promise made without consideration; but it has power to do it, and, if it does, the judgment is unimpeachable, unless reversed. Yet a statute could be framed that would make the power, that is, the jurisdiction of the court dependent upon whether there was a consideration or not. Whether a given statute is intended simply to establish a rule of substantive law, and thus to define the duty of the court, or is meant to limit its power, is a question of construction and common sense. When it affects a court of general jurisdiction and deals with a matter upon which that court must pass, we naturally are slow to read ambiguous words, as meaning to leave the judgment open to dispute, or as intended to do more than to fix the rule by which the court should decide.

The case quoted concerned a statute plainly dealing with the authority and jurisdiction of the New York court. The statute now before us seems to us only to lay down a rule of decision. The Mississippi court in which this action was brought is a court of general jurisdiction and would have to decide upon the validity of the bar, if the suit upon the award or upon the original cause of action had been brought there. The words "shall not be enforced by any court" are simply another, possibly less emphatic, way of saying that an action shall not be brought to enforce such contracts. As suggested by the counsel for the plaintiff in error, no one would say that the words of the Mississippi statute of frauds, "An action shall not be brought whereby to charge a defendant," go to the jurisdiction of the court. Of course it could be argued that logically they had that scope, but common sense would revolt. . . . We regard this question as open under the decisions below, and we have expressed our opinion upon it independent of the effect of the judgment, although it might be that, even if jurisdiction of the original cause of action was withdrawn, it remained with regard to a suit upon a judgment based upon an award, whether the judgment or award was conclusive or not. But it might be held that the law as to jurisdiction in one case followed the law in the other, and therefore we proceed at once to the further question, whether the illegality of the original cause of action in Mississippi can be relied upon there as a ground for denying a recovery upon a judgment of another State.

The doctrine laid down by Chief Justice Marshall was "that the judgment of a state court should have the same credit, validity, and effect in every other court in the United States, which it had in the State where it was pronounced, and that whatever pleas would be good to a suit thereon in such State, and none others, could be pleaded in any other court of the United States." There is no doubt that this quotation was supposed to be an accurate statement of the law as late as Christmas v. Russell, where an attempt of Mississippi, by statute, to go behind judgments recovered in other States was declared void, and it was held that such judgments could not be impeached even for fraud. . . .

We assume that the statement of Chief Justice Marshall is correct. It is confirmed by the Act of May 26, 1790, c. 11, 1 Stat. 122 (Rev. Stat. §905), providing that the said records and judicial proceedings "shall have such faith and credit given to them in every court within the United States, as they have by law or usage in the courts of the State from whence the said records are or shall be taken." Whether the award would or would not have been conclusive, and whether the ruling of the Missouri court upon that matter was right or wrong, there can be no question that the judgment was conclusive in Missouri on the validity of the cause of action. A judgment is conclusive as to all the media concludendi, and it needs no authority to show that it cannot be impeached either in or out of the State by showing that it was based upon a mistake of law. Of course a want of jurisdiction over either the person or the subject-matter might be shown. But as the jurisdiction of the Missouri court is not open to dispute the judgment cannot be impeached in Mississippi even if it went upon a misapprehension of the Mississippi law.

We feel no apprehensions that painful or humiliating consequences will follow upon our decision. No court would give judgment for a plaintiff unless it believed that the facts were a cause of action by the law determining their effect. Mistakes will be rare. In this case the Missouri court no doubt supposed that the award was binding by the law of Mississippi. If it was mistaken it made a natural mistake. The validity of its judgment, even in Mississippi, is, as we believe, the result of the Constitution as it always has been understood, and is not a matter to arouse the susceptibilities of the States, all of which are equally concerned in the question and equally on both sides.

Judgment reversed.

Justice WHITE, with whom concurred Justice HARLAN, Justice MCKENNA and Justice DAY, dissenting.

. . . This court now reverses on the ground that the due faith and credit clause obliged the courts of Mississippi, in consequence of the action of the Missouri court, to give efficacy to transactions in Mississippi which were criminal, and which were against the public policy of that State. Although not wishing in the slightest degree to weaken the operation of the due faith and credit clause as interpreted and applied from the beginning, it to me seems that this ruling so enlarges that clause as to cause it to obliterate all state lines, since the effect will be to endow each State with authority to overthrow the public policy and criminal statutes of the others, thereby depriving all of their lawful authority. Moreover, the ruling now made, in my opinion, is contrary to the conceptions which caused the due faith and credit clause to be placed in the Constitution, and substantially overrules the previous decisions of this court interpreting that clause. My purpose is to briefly state the reasons which lead me to these conclusions. . . .

When the Constitution was adopted the principles of comity by which the decrees of the courts of one State were entitled to be enforced in another were generally known, but the enforcement of those principles by the several States had no absolute sanction, since they rested but in comity. Now it cannot be denied that under the rules of comity recognized at the time of the adoption of the Constitution, and which at this time universally prevail, no sovereignty was or is under the slightest moral obligation to give effect to a judgment of a court of another sovereignty, when to do so would compel the State in which the judgment was sought to be executed to enforce an illegal and prohibited contract, when both the contract and all the acts done in connection with its performance had taken place in the latter State. This seems to me conclusive of this case, since both in treatises of authoritative writers (Story, Conflict of Law §609), and by repeated adjudications of this court it has been settled that the purpose of the due faith and credit clause was not to confer any new power, but simply to make obligatory that duty which, when the Constitution was adopted rested, as has been said, in comity alone. . . .

No special reference has been made by me to the arbitration, because that is assumed by me to be negligible. If the cause of action was open for inquiry for the purpose of deciding whether the Missouri court had jurisdiction to render a judgment entitled to be enforced in another State, the arbitration is of no consequence. The violation of law in Mississippi could not be cured by seeking to arbitrate in that State in order to fix the sum of the fruits of the illegal acts. The ancient maxims that something cannot be made out of nothing, and that which is void for reasons of public policy cannot be made valid by confirmation or acquiescence, seem to my mind decisive.

I therefore dissent.

Questions and Comments

(1) Would there be any harm in limiting full faith and credit to judgments that themselves were not based on unconstitutional denial of full faith and credit to the laws of another state? That is what Missouri did, isn't it, when it failed to apply Mississippi law on the illegality of these contracts, with no apparent connection between the case and Missouri? Or, if that seems too daring a proposal, how about refusing full faith and credit whenever both of two factors are present: (a) denial of full faith and credit in arriving at the first judgment; and (b) violation of the criminal laws of the interested jurisdiction? Would that disrupt any rational scheme of federalism?

(2) Section 103 of the Restatement Second says:

> A judgment rendered in one State of the United States need not be recognized or enforced in a sister State if such recognition or enforcement is not required by the national policy of full faith and credit because it would involve an improper interference with important interests of the sister State.

The comment warns that the section has "an extremely narrow scope of application." It concedes, almost as an afterthought, that "[t]he Supreme Court of the United States has the final voice in determining what exceptions there are to full faith and credit, and the nature of these exceptions." The only case cited in the comment that failed to recognize a sister-state judgment is

Williams v. North Carolina, 325 U.S. 226 (1945). *Williams* came to the conclusion that a state could reexamine the supposed domicile of one party to ex parte divorce proceedings to see if the rendering court actually had jurisdiction (which is based upon domicile in divorce proceedings). Does that sound like an application of the principle set out above? The Reporter's Note cites a few other cases offering borderline support, including several concurring or dissenting opinions.

Professor Ehrenzweig, in The Second Conflicts Restatement: A Last Appeal for Its Withdrawal, 113 U. Pa. L. Rev. 1230, 1240 (1965), stated that there was "no authority whatsoever" for §103.

(3) *The penal exception.* In Huntington v. Attrill, 146 U.S. 657 (1892), the Supreme Court stated that one state need not enforce the "penal" claims of another, even if they were embodied in a judgment. Recall the discussion of that case in Paper Products Co. v. Doggrell, page 166 *supra.* Whether a law is penal "depends upon the question whether its purpose is to punish an offense against the public justice of the state, or to afford a private remedy to a person injured by a wrongful act." 146 U.S. at 657. *Compare* Heath v. Alabama, 474 U.S. 82 (1985), holding that the double jeopardy clause does not preclude a second prosecution in a second state. Does *Heath* suggest that the second state need not respect the criminal judgments of the first?

(4) Can a court order be penal? In Settle v. Settle, 25 Or. App. 579, 550 P.2d 445 (1976), the court, in dictum, indicated that a foreign decree would be considered punitive "only if it is clear that the court awarded or changed [child] custody because it was insulted by one parent disregarding its authority." 550 P.2d at 447. The mother had argued that an Indiana court had taken custody from her because she had left the state with the children, contrary to court order. The Oregon court found, however, that the basis for the Indiana action was her lack of fitness.

In Holbein v. Rigot, 245 So. 2d 57 (Fla. 1971), the Florida Supreme Court ruled that the punitive-damages portion of a Texas judgment was not exempt from full faith and credit enforcement in Florida on the grounds that it was a penal claim. "[O]ur holding is that plaintiff's Texas suit insofar as it sought to recover punitive damages was based on common law liability arising from fraud to redress a private wrong inflicted on plaintiffs and did not purport to redress a public wrong predicated on a statute that is penal in the international sense which may not be enforced in the courts of other states." *Id.* at 61. "*[M]ay* not be enforced"? Is it more important that a private wrong is being redressed, or that no statute is involved? And isn't one purpose of punitive damages to discourage future activity of the same kind directed against others? Isn't that an offense against the public justice?

(5) Milwaukee County v. M. E. White Co., 296 U.S. 268 (1935), laid to rest the old rule that one state does not have to enforce the tax judgments of another state. In light of that case, and *International Shoe,* isn't the tax area one where it would be rational to deny enforcement to another state's tax *law,* but honor its judgment, so that the dirty work of interpreting state tax

laws (without misinterpreting them) would fall on the courts of the states with the laws?

Thomas v. Washington Gas Light Co.

448 U.S. 261 (1980)

Justice STEVENS announced the judgment of the Court and delivered an opinion in which Justice BRENNAN, Justice STEWART, and Justice BLACKMUN join.

Petitioner received an award of disability benefits under the Virginia Workmen's Compensation Act. The question presented is whether the obligation of the District of Columbia to give full faith and credit to that award bars a supplemental award under the District's Workmen's Compensation Act.

Petitioner is a resident of the District of Columbia and was hired by respondent in the District of Columbia. During the year that he was employed by respondent, he worked primarily in the District but also worked in Virginia and Maryland. He sustained a back injury while at work in Arlington, Va., on January 22, 1971. Two weeks later he entered into an "Industrial Commission of Virginia Memorandum of Agreement as to Payment of Compensation" providing for benefits of $62 per week. Several weeks later the Virginia Industrial Commission approved the agreement and issued its award directing that payments continue "during incapacity," subject to various contingencies and changes set forth in the Virginia statute.

In 1974, petitioner notified the Department of Labor of his intention to seek compensation under the District of Columbia Act. Respondent opposed the claim primarily on the ground that since, as a matter of Virginia law, the Virginia award excluded any other recovery "at common law or otherwise" on account of the injury in Virginia, the District of Columbia's obligation to give that award full faith and credit precluded a second, supplemental award in the District.

The administrative law judge agreed with respondent that the Virginia award must be given res judicata effect in the District to the extent that it was res judicata in Virginia. He held, however, that the Virginia award, by its terms, did not preclude a further award of compensation in Virginia. Moreover, he construed the statutory prohibition against additional recovery "at common law or otherwise" as merely covering "common law and other remedies under Virginia law." After the taking of medical evidence, petitioner was awarded permanent total disability benefits payable from the date of his injury with a credit for the amounts previously paid under the Virginia award.

The Benefits Review Board upheld the award. Its order, however, was reversed by the United States Court of Appeals for the Fourth Circuit, which squarely held that a "second and separate proceeding in another jurisdiction upon the same injury after a prior recovery in another State [is] precluded by the Full Faith and Credit Clause." We granted certiorari and now reverse.

I

Respondent contends that the District of Columbia was without power to award petitioner additional compensation because of the Full Faith and Credit Clause of the Constitution or, more precisely, because of the federal statute implementing that Clause. An analysis of this contention must begin with two decisions from the 1940's that are almost directly on point: Magnolia Petroleum Co. v. Hunt, 320 U.S. 430, and Industrial Commission of Wisconsin v. McCartin, 330 U.S. 622.

In *Magnolia,* a case relied on heavily both by respondent and the Court of Appeals, the employee hired a Louisiana worker in Louisiana. The employee was later injured during the course of his employment in Texas. A tenuous majority held that Louisiana was not permitted to award the injured worker supplementary compensation under the Louisiana Act after he had already obtained a recovery from the Texas Industrial Accident Board: "Respondent was free to pursue his remedy in either state but, having chosen to seek it in Texas, where the award was res judicata, the full faith and credit clause precludes him from again seeking a remedy in Louisiana upon the same grounds."

Little more than three years later, the Court severely curtailed the impact of *Magnolia.* In *McCartin,* the employer and the worker both resided in Illinois and entered into an employment contract there for work to be performed in Wisconsin. The employee was injured in the course of that employment. He initially filed a claim with the Industrial Commission of Wisconsin. Prior to this Court's decision in *Magnolia,* the Wisconsin Commission informed him that under Wisconsin law, he could proceed under the Illinois Workmen's Compensation Act, and then claim compensation under the Wisconsin Act, with credit to be given for any payments made under the Illinois Act. Thereafter, the employer and the employee executed a contract for payment of a specific sum in full settlement of the employee's right under Illinois law. The contract expressly provided, however, that it would " 'not affect any rights that applicant may have under the Workmen's Compensation Act of the State of Wisconsin.' " The employee then obtained a supplemental award from the Wisconsin Industrial Commission; but the Wisconsin state courts vacated it under felt compulsion of the intervening decision in *Magnolia.*

This Court reversed, holding without dissent that *Magnolia* was not controlling. Although the Court could have relied exclusively on the contract provision reserving the employee's rights under Wisconsin law to distinguish the case from *Magnolia,* Justice Murphy's opinion provided a significantly different ground for the Court's holding when it said

> the reservation spells out what we believe to be implicit in [the Illinois Workmen's Compensation] Act—namely, that an award of the type here

> involved does not foreclose an additional award under the laws of another state. And in the setting of this case, that fact is of decisive significance.

Earlier in the opinion, the Court had stated that "[o]nly some unmistakable language by a state legislature or judiciary would warrant our accepting . . . a construction" that a workmen's compensation statute "is designed to preclude any recovery by proceedings brought in another state." The Illinois statute, which the Court held not to contain the "unmistakable language" required to preclude a supplemental award in Wisconsin, broadly provided:

> No common law or statutory right to recover damages for injury or death sustained by any employee while engaged in the line of his duty as such employee, other than the compensation herein provided, shall be available to any employee who is covered by the provisions of this act. . . .

The Virginia Workmen's Compensation Act's exclusive remedy provision is not exactly the same as Illinois'[s]; but it contains no "unmistakable language" directed at precluding a supplemental compensation award in another State that was not also in the Illinois Act. Consequently, *McCartin* by its terms, rather than the earlier *Magnolia* decision, is controlling as between the two precedents. Nevertheless, the fact that we find ourselves comparing the language of two state statutes, neither of which has been construed by the highest court of either State, in an attempt to resolve an issue arising under the Full Faith and Credit Clause makes us pause to inquire whether there is a fundamental flaw in our analysis of this federal question.

II

We cannot fail to observe that, in the Court's haste to retreat from *Magnolia,* it fashioned a rule that clashes with normally accepted full faith and credit principles. It has long been the law that "the judgment of a state court should have the same credit, validity, and effect, in every other court in the United States, which it had in the state where it was pronounced." Hampton v. McConnel, 3 Wheat. 234, 235 (Marshall, C.J.). This rule, if not compelled by the Full Faith and Credit Clause itself, is surely required by 28 U.S.C. §1738, which provides that the

> Acts, records and judicial proceedings . . . [of any State] shall have the same full faith and credit in every court within the United States . . . as they have by law or usage in the courts of [the] State . . . from which they are taken.

Thus, in effect, by virtue of the full faith and credit obligations of the several States, a State is permitted to determine the extraterritorial effect of its judgment; but it may only do so indirectly, by prescribing the effect of its judgments within the State.

The *McCartin* rule, however, focusing as it does on the extraterritorial intent of the rendering State, is fundamentally different. It authorizes a State, by drafting or construing its legislation in "unmistakable language," directly to determine the extraterritorial effect of its workmen's compensation awards. An authorization to a state legislature of this character is inconsistent with the rule established in Pacific Employers Ins. Co. v. Industrial Accident Commission [discussed at page 350 *supra*]: "This Court must determine for itself how far the full faith and credit clause compels the qualification or denial of rights asserted under the laws of one state, that of the forum, by the statute of another state." It follows inescapably that the *McCartin* "unmistakable language" rule represents an unwarranted delegation to the States of this Court's responsibility for the final arbitration of full faith and credit questions. The Full Faith and Credit Clause "is one of the provisions incorporated into the Constitution by its framers from the purpose of transforming an aggregation of independent, sovereign States into a nation." Sherrer v. Sherrer, 334 U.S. 343, 355. To vest the power of determining the extraterritorial effect of a State's own laws and judgments in the State itself risks the very kind of parochial entrenchment on the interests of other States that it was the purpose of the Full Faith and Credit Clause and other provisions of Art. IV of the Constitution to prevent. *See* Nevada v. Hall, 440 U.S. 410, 424-425.

Thus, a re-examination of *McCartin's* unmistakable language test reinforces our tentative conclusion that it does not provide an acceptable basis on which to distinguish *Magnolia.* But if we reject that test, we must decide whether to overrule either *Magnolia* or *McCartin.* In making this kind of decision, we must take into account both the practical values served by the doctrine of stare decisis and the principles that inform the Full Faith and Credit Clause.

III

The doctrine of stare decisis imposes a severe burden on the litigant who asks us to disavow one of our precedents. For that doctrine not only plays an important role in orderly adjudication; it also serves the broader societal interests in evenhanded, consistent, and predictable application of legal rules. When rights have been created or modified in reliance on established rules of law, the arguments against their change have special force.[18]

---

18. The doctrine of stare decises has a more limited application when the precedent rests on constitutional grounds. . . .

The full faith and credit area presents special problems because the Constitution expressly delegates to Congress the authority "by general Laws [to] prescribe the Manner in which [the States'] Acts, Records and Proceedings shall be proved, *and the effect thereof.*"

It is therefore appropriate to begin the inquiry by considering whether a rule that permits, or a rule that forecloses, successive workmen's compensation awards is more consistent with settled practice. The answer to this question is pellucidly clear.

It should first be noted that *Magnolia*, by only the slimmest majority, effected a dramatic change in the law that had previously prevailed throughout the United States. Of greater importance is the fact that as a practical matter the "unmistakable language" rule of construction announced in *McCartin* left only the narrowest area in which *Magnolia* could have any further precedential value. For the exclusivity language in the Illinois Act construed in *McCartin* was typical of most state workmen's compensation laws. Consequently, it was immediately recognized that *Magnolia* no longer had any significant practical impact. Moreover, since a state legislature seldom focuses on the extraterritorial effect of its enactments, and since a state court has even less occasion to consider whether an award under its State's law is intended to preclude a supplemental award under another State's workmen's compensation act, the probability that any State would thereafter announce a new rule against supplemental awards in other States was extremely remote. As a matter of fact, subsequent cases in the state courts have overwhelmingly followed *McCartin* and permitted successive state workmen's compensation awards. Thus, all that really remained of *Magnolia* after *McCartin* was a largely theoretical difference between what the Court described as "unmistakable language" and the broad language of the exclusive remedy provision in the Illinois Workmen's Compensation Act involved in *McCartin*.

This history indicates that the principal values underlying the doctrine of stare decisis would not be served either by attempting to revive *Magnolia* or by attempting to preserve the uneasy coexistence of *Magnolia* and *McCartin*. The latter attempt could only breed uncertainty and unpredictability, since the application of the "unmistakable language" rule of *McCartin* necessarily depends on a determination by one state tribunal of the effect to be given to statutory language enacted by the legislature of a different State. And the former would represent a rather dramatic change that surely would not promote stability in the law. Moreover, since *Magnolia* has been so rarely followed, there appears to be little danger that there has been any significant reliance on its rule. We conclude that a fresh examination of the full faith and credit issue is therefore entirely appropriate.

(Emphasis added.) Yet it is quite clear that Congress' power in this area is not exclusive, for this Court has given effect to the Clause beyond that required by implementing legislation. *See* Bradford Electric Co. v. Clapper. [T]he *Clapper* case rested on the constitutional Clause alone. *Carroll*, which for all intents and purposes buried whatever was left of *Clapper* after *Pacific Employers* . . . cast no doubt on *Clapper's* reliance on the Full Faith and Credit Clause itself.

IV

Three different state interests are affected by the potential conflict between Virginia and the District of Columbia. Virginia has a valid interest in placing a limit on the potential liability of companies that transact business within its borders. Both jurisdictions have a valid interest in the welfare of the injured employee—Virginia because the injury occurred within that State, and the District because the injured party was employed and resided there. And finally, Virginia has an interest in having the integrity of its formal determinations of contested issues respected by other sovereigns.

The conflict between the first two interests was resolved in Alaska Packers Association v. Industrial Accident Commission [discussed at page 349 *supra*], and a series of later cases. In *Alaska Packers*, California, the State where the employment contract was made, was allowed to apply its own workmen's compensation statute despite the statute of Alaska, the place where the injury occurred, which was said to afford the exclusive remedy for injuries occurring there. The Court held that the conflict between the statutes of two States ought not to be resolved "by giving automatic effect to the full faith and credit clause, compelling the courts of each state to subordinate its own statutes to those of the other, but by appraising the governmental interests of each jurisdiction, and turning the scale of decision according to their weight."

The converse situation was presented in Pacific Employers Insurance Co. v. Industrial Accident Commission of the State of California [also discussed page 350 *supra*]. In that case the injury occurred in California, and the objection to California's jurisdiction was based on a statute of Massachusetts, the State where the employee resided and where the employment contract had been made. The Massachusetts statute provided that the remedy afforded was exclusive of the worker's " 'right of action at common law or under the law of any other jurisdiction.' " Again, however, California was permitted to provide the employee with an award under the California statute.

The principle that the Full Faith and Credit Clause does not require a State to subordinate its own compensation policies to those of another State has been consistently applied in more recent cases. Nevada v. Hall, [page 402 *supra*]. Indeed, in the *Nevada* case the Court not only rejected the contention that California was required to respect a statutory limitation on the defendant's liability, but did so in a case in which the defendant was the sovereign State itself asserting, alternatively, an immunity from any liability in the courts of California.

It is thus perfectly clear that petitioner could have sought a compensation award in the first instance either in Virginia, the State in which the injury occurred, *Pacific Employers, supra*, or in the District of Columbia, where petitioner resided, his employer was principally located and the employment relation was formed, Alaska Packers Association v. Industrial Accident Commission of California, *supra.* And as those cases underscore, compensation could have been sought under either compensation scheme even if one statute or the other purported to confer an exclusive remedy on petitioner. Thus, for all practical purposes, respondent and its insurer would have had to measure their potential liability exposure by the more generous of the two workmen's compensation schemes in any event. It follows that a State's interest in limiting the potential liability of businesses within the State is not of controlling importance.

It is also manifest that the interest in providing adequate compensation to the injured worker would be fully served by the allowance of successive awards. In this respect the two jurisdictions share a common interest and there is no danger of significant conflict.

The ultimate issue, therefore, is whether Virginia's interest in the integrity of its tribunal's determinations forecloses a second proceeding to obtain a supplemental award in the District of Columbia. We return to the Court's prior resolution of this question in *Magnolia.*

The majority opinion in *Magnolia* took the position that the case called for a straightforward application of full faith and credit law: the worker's injury gave rise to a cause of action; relief was granted by the Texas Industrial Accident Board; that award precluded any further relief in Texas; and further relief was therefore precluded elsewhere as well. The majority relied heavily on Chicago, R.I. & P.R. Co. v. Schendel, 270 U.S. 611, for the propositions that a workmen's compensation award stands on the same footing as a court judgment, and that a compensation award under one State's law is a bar to a second award under another State's law.

But *Schendel* did not compel the result in *Magnolia.* In *Schendel,* the Court held that an Iowa state compensation award, which was grounded in a contested factual finding that the deceased railroad employee was engaged in intrastate commerce, precluded a subsequent claim under the Federal Employers' Liability Act brought in the Minnesota state courts, which would have required a finding that the employee was engaged in interstate commerce. *Schendel* therefore involved the unexceptionable full faith and credit principle that resolutions of factual matters underlying a judgment must be given the same res judicata effect in the forum State as they have in the rendering State. *See* Durfee v. Duke. The Minnesota courts could not have granted relief under the FELA and also respected the factual finding made in Iowa.

In contrast, neither *Magnolia* nor this case concerns a second State's contrary resolution of a factual matter determined in the first State's proceedings. Unlike the situation in *Schendel,* which involved two mutually exclusive remedies, compensation could be obtained under either Virginia's or the District's workmen's compensation statutes on the basis of the same set of facts. A supplemental award gives full effect to the facts determined by the first award and also allows full credit for payments pursuant to the earlier award. There is neither inconsistency nor double recovery.

We are also persuaded that *Magnolia's* reliance on *Schendel* for the proposition that workmen's compensation awards stand on the same footing as court judgments was unwarranted. To be sure, as we held in *Schendel*, the factfindings of state administrative tribunals are entitled to the same res judicata effect in the second State as findings by a court. But the critical differences between a court of general jurisdiction and an administrative agency with limited statutory authority forecloses the conclusion that constitutional rules applicable to court judgments are necessarily applicable to workmen's compensation awards.

A final judgment entered by a court of general jurisdiction normally establishes not only the measure of the plaintiff's rights but also limits of the defendant's liability. A traditional application of res judicata principles enables either party to claim the benefit of the judgment insofar as it resolved issues the court has jurisdiction to decide. Although a Virginia court is free to recognize the perhaps paramount interests of another State by choosing to apply that State's law in a particular case, the Industrial Commission of Virginia does not have that power. Its jurisdiction is limited to questions arising under the Virginia Workmen's Compensation Act. Typically, a workmen's compensation tribunal may only apply its own State's law. In this case, the Virginia Commission could and did establish the full measure of petitioner's rights under Virginia law, but it neither could nor purported to determine his rights under the law of the District of Columbia. Full faith and credit must be given to the determination that the Virginia Commission had the authority to make; but by a parity of reasoning, full faith and credit need not be given to determinations that it had no power to make. Since it was not requested, and had no authority, to pass on petitioner's rights under District of Columbia law, there can be no constitutional objection to a fresh adjudication of those rights.

It is true, of course, that after Virginia entered its award, that State had an interest in preserving the integrity of what it had done. And it is squarely within the purpose of the Full Faith and Credit Clause, as explained in *Pacific Employers*, "to preserve rights acquired or confirmed under the public acts" of Virginia by requiring other States to recognize their validity. Thus, Virginia had an interest in having respondent pay petitioner the amounts specified in its award. Allowing a supplementary recovery in the District does not conflict with that interest.

As we have already noted, Virginia also has a separate interest in placing a ceiling on the potential liability of companies that transact business within the State. But past cases have established that that interest is not strong enough to prevent other States with overlapping jurisdiction over particular injuries from giving effect to their more generous compensation policies when the employee selects the most favorable forum in the first instance. Thus, the only situations in which the *Magnolia* rule would tend to serve that interest are those in which an injured workman has either been constrained by circumstances to seek relief in the less generous forum or has simply made an ill-advised choice of his first forum.

But in neither of those cases is there any reason to give extra weight to the first State's interest in placing a ceiling on the employer's liability than it otherwise would have had. For neither the first nor the second State has any overriding interest in requiring an injured employee to proceed with special caution when first asserting his claim. Compensation proceedings are often initiated informally, without the advice of counsel, and without special attention to the choice of the most appropriate forum. Often the worker is still hospitalized when benefits are sought as was true in this case. And indeed, it is not always the injured worker who institutes the claim. This informality is consistent with the interests of both States. A rule forbidding supplemental recoveries under more favorable workmen's compensation schemes would require a far more formal and careful choice on the part of the injured worker than may be possible or desirable when immediate commencement of benefits may be essential.

Thus, whether or not the worker has sought an award from the less generous jurisdiction in the first instance, the vindication of that State's interest in placing a ceiling on employers' liability would inevitably impinge upon the substantial interests of the second jurisdiction in the welfare and subsistence of disabled workers—interests that a court of general jurisdiction might consider, but which must be ignored by the Virginia Industrial Commission. The reasons why the statutory policy of exclusivity of the other jurisdictions involved in *Alaska Packers* and *Pacific Employers, supra,* could not defeat California's implementation of its own compensation policies therefore continue to apply even after the entry of a workmen's compensation award.

Of course, it is for each State to formulate its own policy whether to grant supplemental awards according to its perception of its own interests. We simply conclude that the substantial interests of the second State in these circumstances should not be overridden by another State through an unnecessarily aggressive application of the Full Faith and Credit Clause, as was implicitly recognized at the time of *McCartin.*

We therefore would hold that a State has no legitimate interest within the context of our federal system in preventing another State from granting a supplemental compensation award when that second State would have had the power to apply its workmen's compensation law in the first instance. The Full Faith and Credit Clause should not be construed to preclude successive workmen's compensation awards. Accordingly, Magnolia Petroleum Co. v. Hunt should be overruled.

The judgment of the Court of Appeals is reversed.

Justice White, with whom The Chief Justice and Justice Powell join, concurring in the judgment.

I agree that the judgment of the Court of Appeals should be reversed, but I am unable to join in the reasoning by which the plurality reaches that result. Although the plurality argues strenuously that the rule of today's decision is limited to awards by state workmen's compensation boards, it seems to me that the underlying rationale goes much further. If the employer had exercised its statutory right of appeal to the Supreme Court of Virginia and that Court upheld the award, I presume that the plurality's rationale would nevertheless permit a subsequent award in the District of Columbia. Otherwise, employers interested in cutting off the possibility of a subsequent award in another jurisdiction need only seek judicial review of the award in the first forum. But if such a judicial decision is not preclusive in the second forum, then it appears that the plurality's rationale is not limited in its effect to judgments of administrative tribunals.

The plurality contends that unlike courts of general jurisdiction, workmen's compensation tribunals generally have no power to apply the law of another State and thus cannot determine the rights of the parties thereunder. Yet I see no reason why a judgment should not be entitled to full res judicata effect under the Full Faith and Credit Clause merely because the rendering tribunal was obligated to apply the law of the forum—provided, of course, as was certainly the case here, that the forum could constitutionally apply its law. The plurality's analysis seems to grant state legislatures the power to delimit the scope of a cause of action for federal full faith and credit purposes merely by enacting choice of law rules binding on the State's workmen's compensation tribunals. The plurality criticizes the *McCartin* case for vesting in the State the power to determine the extraterritorial effect of its own laws and judgments; yet it seems that its opinion is subject to the same objection. In any event, I am not convinced that Virginia, by instructing its industrial commission to apply Virginia law, could be said to have intended that the cause of action which merges in the Virginia judgment would not include claims under the laws of other States which arise out of precisely the same operative facts.

As a matter of logic, the plurality's analysis would seemingly apply to many everyday tort actions. I see no difference for full faith and credit purposes between a statute which lays down a forum-favoring choice of law rule and a common-law doctrine stating the same principle. Hence when a court, having power in the abstract to apply the law of another State, determines by application of the forum's choice of law rules to apply the substantive law of the forum, I would think that under the plurality's analysis the judgment would not determine rights arising under the law of some other State. Suppose, for example, that in a wrongful death action the court enters judgment on liability against the defendant, and determines to apply the law of the forum which sets a limit on the recovery allowed. The plurality's analysis would seem to permit the plaintiff to obtain a subsequent judgment in a second forum for damages exceeding the first forum's liability limit.

The plurality does say that factual determinations by a workmen's compensation board will be entitled to collateral estoppel effect in a second forum. While this rule does, to an extent, circumscribe the broadest possible implications of the plurality's reasoning, there would remain many cases, such as the wrongful death example discussed above, in which the second forum could provide additional recovery as a matter of substantive law while remaining true to the first forum's factual determinations. Moreover, the dispositive issues in tort actions are frequently mixed questions of law and fact as to which the second forum might apply its own rule of decision without obvious violation of the principles articulated by four Members of the Court. Actions by the defendant which satisfy the relevant standard of care in the first forum might nevertheless be considered "negligent" under the law of the second forum.

Hence the plurality's rationale would portend a wide-ranging reassessment of the principles of full faith and credit in many areas. Such a reassessment is not necessarily undesirable if the results are likely to be healthy for the judicial system and consistent with the underlying purposes of the Full Faith and Credit Clause. But at least without the benefit of briefs and arguments directed to the issue, I cannot conclude that the rule advocated by the plurality would have had such a beneficial impact.

One purpose of the Full Faith and Credit Clause is to bring an end to litigation. As the Court noted in Riley v. New York Trust Co., 315 U.S. 343, 348-349 (1941): "Were it not for this full faith and credit provision, so far as the Constitution controls the matter, adversaries could wage again their legal battles whenever they meet in other jurisdictions. Each state could control its own courts but itself could not project the effect of its decisions beyond its own boundaries." The plurality's opinion is at odds with this principle of finality. Plaintiffs dissatisfied with a judgment would have every incentive to seek additional recovery elsewhere, so long as the first forum applied its own law and there was a colorable argument that as a matter of law the second forum would permit a greater recovery. It seems to me grossly unfair that the plaintiff, having the initial choice of the forum, should be given the additional advantage of a second adjudication should his choice prove disappointing. Defendants, on the other hand, would no longer be assured that the judgment of the first forum is conclusive as to their obligations, and would face the prospect of burdensome and multiple litigation based on the same operative facts. Such litigation would also impose added strain on an already overworked judicial system.

Perhaps the major purpose of the Full Faith and Credit Clause is to act as a nationally unifying force. Sherrer v. Sherrer, 334 U.S. 343, 355 (1948). The plurality's rationale would substantially undercut that function. When a former judgment is set up as a defense under the Full Faith and Credit Clause, the court would be obliged to balance the various state interests involved. But the State of the second forum is not a neutral party to this balance. There seems to be a substantial danger—not presented by the firmer rule of res judicata—that the court in evaluating a full faith and credit defense would give controlling weight to its own parochial interests in concluding that the judgment of the first forum is not res judicata in the subsequent suit.

I would not overrule either *Magnolia* or *McCartin.* To my mind, Chief Justice Stone's opinion in *Magnolia* states the sounder doctrine; as noted. I do not see any overriding differences between workmen's compensation awards and court judgments that justify different treatment for the two. However, *McCartin* has been on the books for over 30 years and has been widely interpreted by state and federal courts as substantially limiting *Magnolia.* Unlike the plurality's opinion, *McCartin* is not subject to the objection that its principles are applicable outside the workmen's compensation area. Although I find *McCartin* to rest on questionable foundations, I am not now prepared to overrule it. And I agree with the plurality that *McCartin,* rather than *Magnolia,* is controlling as between the two precedents since the Virginia Workmen's Compensation Act lacks the "unmistakable language" which *McCartin* requires if a workmen's compensation award is to preclude a subsequent award in another State. I therefore concur in the judgment.

Justice REHNQUIST, with whom Justice MARSHALL joins, dissenting.

This is clearly a case where the whole is less than the sum of its parts. In choosing between two admittedly inconsistent precedents, Magnolia Petroleum Co. v. Hunt, 320 U.S. 430 (1943), and Industrial Commission of Wisconsin v. McCartin, 330 U.S. 622 (1947), six of us agree that the latter decision, *McCartin,* is analytically indefensible. The remaining three Members of the Court concede that it "rest[s] on questionable foundations." Nevertheless, when the smoke clears, it is *Magnolia* rather than *McCartin* that the plurality suggests should be overruled. Because I believe that *Magnolia* was correctly decided, and because I fear that the rule proposed by the plurality is both ill-considered and ill-defined, I dissent. . . .

One might support that, having destroyed *McCartin's* ratio decidendi, the plurality would return to the eminently defensible position adopted in *Magnolia.* But such is not the case. The plurality instead raises the banner of "stare decisis" and sets out in search of a new rationale to support the result reached in *McCartin,* significantly failing to even attempt to do the same thing for *Magnolia.*

If such post hoc rationalization seems a bit'odd, the theory ultimately chosen by the plurality is even odder. It would seem that, contrary to the assumption of this Court for at least the past 40 years, a judgment awarding workmen's compensation benefits is no longer entitled to full faith and credit unless, and only to the extent that, such a judgment resolves a disputed issue of fact. I believe that the plurality's justification for such a theory, which apparently first surfaced in a cluster of articles written in the wake of *Magnolia,* does not withstand close scrutiny.

The plurality identified three different "state interests" at stake in the present case: Virginia's interest in placing a limit on the potential liability of companies doing business in that State, Virginia's interest in the "integrity of its formal determinations of contested issues," and a shared interest of Virginia and the District of Columbia in the welfare of the injured employee. The plurality then undertakes to balance these interests and concludes that none of Virginia's concerns outweighs the concern of the District of Columbia for the welfare of petitioner.

Whenever this Court, or any court, attempts to balance competing interests it risks undervaluing or even overlooking important concerns. I believe that the plurality's analysis incorporates both errors. First, it asserts that Virginia's interest in limiting the liability of businesses operating within its borders can never outweigh the District of Columbia's interest in protecting its residents. In support of this proposition it cites Alaska Packers Association v. Industrial Accident Commission and Pacific Employers Insurance Company v. Industrial Accident Commission. Both of those cases, however, involved the degree of faith and credit to be afforded *statutes* of one State by the courts of another State. The present case involves an enforceable *judgment* entered by Virginia after adjudicatory proceedings. In *Magnolia* Mr. Chief Justice Stone, who authored *both Alaska Packers* and *Pacific Employers,* distinguished those two decisions for precisely this reason, chastising the lower court in that case for overlooking "the distinction, long recognized and applied by this Court . . . between the full faith and credit required to be given to judgments and that to which local common and statutory law is entitled under the Constitution and laws of the United States." This distinction, which has also been overlooked by the plurality here, makes perfect sense, since Virginia surely has a stronger interest in limiting an employer's liability to a fixed amount when that employer has already been haled before a Virginia tribunal and adjudged liable than when the employer simply claims the benefit of a Virginia statute in a proceeding brought in another State.

In a similar vein, the plurality completely ignores any interest that Virginia might assert in the finality of its adjudications. While workmen's compensation awards may be "nonfinal" in the sense that they are subject to continuing supervision and modification, Virginia nevertheless has a cognizable interest in requiring persons who avail themselves of its statutory remedy to eschew other alternative remedies that might be available to them. Otherwise, as apparently is the result here, Virginia's efforts and expense on an application's behalf are wasted when that applicant obtains a duplicative remedy in another State.

At base, the plurality's balancing analysis is incorrect because it recognizes no significant difference between the events that transpired in this case and those that *would* have transpired had petitioner initially sought his remedy in the District of Columbia. But there are differences. The Commonwealth of Virginia has expended its resources, at petitioner's behest, to provide petitioner with a remedy for his injury and a resolution of his "dispute" with his employer. That employer similarly has expended its resources, again at petitioner's behest, in complying with the judgment entered by Virginia. These efforts, and the corresponding interests in seeing that those efforts are not wasted, lie at the very heart of the divergent constitutional treatment of judgments and statutes. In this case, of course, Virginia and respondent expended very few resources in the administrative process. But that observation lends no assistance to the plurality, which would flatly hold that Virginia has absolutely no power to guarantee that a workmen's compensation award will be treated as a final judgment by other States.

In further support of its novel rule, the plurality attempts to distinguish the judgment entered in this case from one entered by a "court of general jurisdiction." Specifically, the plurality points out that the Industrial Commission of Virginia, unlike a state court of general jurisdiction, was limited by statute to consideration of Virginia law. According to the plurality, because the Commission "was not requested, and had no authority, to pass on petitioner's rights under District of Columbia law, there can be no constitutional objection to a fresh adjudication of those rights."

This argument might have some force if petitioner had somehow had Virginia law thrust upon him against his will. In this case, however, petitioner was free to choose the applicable law simply by choosing the forum in which he filed his initial claim. Unless the District of Columbia has an interest in forcing its residents to accept its law regardless of their wishes, I fail to see how the Virginia Commission's inability to look to District of Columbia law impinged upon that latter jurisdiction's interests. I thus fail to see why petitioner's election, as consummated in his Virginia ward, should not be given the same full faith and credit as would be afforded a judgment entered by a court of general jurisdiction.

I suspect that my Brethren's insistence on ratifying *McCartin's* result despite condemnation of its rationale is grounded in no small part upon their concern that injured workers are often coerced or maneuvered into filing their claims in jurisdictions amenable to their employers. There is, however, absolutely no evidence of such overreaching in the present case. Indeed, had there been "fraud, imposition, [or] mistake" in the filing of petitioner's claim, he would have been permitted, upon timely motion, to vacate the award. *See* Harris v. Diamond Construction Co., 184 Va. 711, 720, 36 S.E.2d 573, 577 (1946). In this regard, the award received by petitioner is treated no differently than any other judicial award, nor should it be. . . .

I fear that the plurality, in its zeal to remedy a perceived imbalance in bargaining power, would badly distort an important constitutional tenet. Its "interest analysis," once removed from the statutory choice-of-law context considered by the Court in *Alaska Packers* and *Pacific Employers,* knows no metes or bounds. Given the modern proliferation of quasi-judicial methods for resolving disputes and of various tribunals of limited jurisdiction, such a rule could only lead to confusion. I find such uncertainty unacceptable, and prefer the rule originally announced in Magnolia Petroleum Co. v. Hunt, a rule whose analytical validity is, even yet, unchallenged.

The Full Faith and Credit Clause did not allot to this Court the task of "balancing" interests where the "public Acts, Records, and judicial Proceedings" of a State were involved. It simply directed that they be given the "Full Faith and Credit" that the Court today denies to those of Virginia. I would affirm the judgment of the court below.

Questions and Comments

(1) Does the plurality answer satisfactorily *any* of the objections expressed in the concurring and dissenting opinions? In particular, isn't Justice Rehnquist right that the majority's rationale would operate at any time, in any kind of case, when a second forum would offer more (or different) damages on the same facts?

(2) What if State *A* offers a lump sum for the loss of a limb, with no compensation for pain and suffering and no punitive damages; State *B* gives no lump-sum compensation, instead requires proof of lost potential income, but does grant compensation for pain and suffering (but no punitive damages); and State *C* offers compensation for actual losses plus punitive damages? Is the injured worker with appropriate contacts with the three states entitled to the lump sum in State *A*, compensation for pain and suffering in State *B*, and punitive damages in State *C*? In other words, isn't it likely that the decision to grant one kind of damages is made at least in part because of the decision not to grant another? Wouldn't the total award collected above violate the policy of *each* state?

(3) What is the connection between *Thomas* and *Fauntleroy?* Doesn't the *Thomas* plurality allow the enforcing state to override the rendering state's finality interests with its own substantive interests? Isn't that contrary to *Fauntleroy*—or was there more "inconsistency" between the first and second resolutions in *Fauntleroy* than in *Thomas?*

(4) Why was the plurality so concerned that the *Magnolia/McCartin* rule rested interpretation of the federal statute upon state law—isn't that what the wording of the statute requires? *Compare* Marrese v. American Academy of Orthopedic Surgeons, 470 U.S. 373 (1984), in which the Court instructed the federal district courts to conduct a close reading of the preclusion rules of the rendering state, to determine how much preclusive effect was due. An excellent discussion of *Washington Gaslight* is Sterk, Full Faith and Credit, More or Less, to Judgments: Doubts about *Thomas v. Washington Gas Light Co.*, 69 Geo. L.J. 1329 (1981).

(5) In University of Tennessee v. Elliot, 478 U.S. 788 (1986), the Supreme Court held that 28 U.S.C. §1738 is not applicable to unreviewed state administrative fact finding, because section 1738 antedates the development of administrative agencies. It further held that application of a common-law preclusion rule would not be appropriate. Would it have been better in *Thomas* to rest the decision on the administrative nature of workers' compensation boards?

Baker v. General Motors Corp.

522 U.S. 222 (1998)

Justice GINSBURG delivered the opinion of the Court.

[Ronald Elwell worked for the Engineering Analysis Group of General Motors Corporation from 1959 until 1989. During this time he often aided GM lawyers defending GM against product liability actions. Between 1987 and 1991, the Elwell-GM employment relationship soured, resulting in failed negotiations over the terms of Elwell's retirement. In May 1991, Elwell appeared as a witness for the plaintiffs in a product liability against GM in Georgia and testified that the GM pickup truck fuel system was inferior to competing products. The next month Elwell sued GM in a Michigan state court, alleging wrongful discharge and other tort and contract claims. GM counterclaimed, contending that Elwell had breached his fiduciary duty to GM by disclosing privileged and confidential information and misappropriating documents. In August 1992, the parties entered into a settlement. Elwell received an undisclosed sum of money and agreed to the Michigan court's entry of a permanent injunction preventing him from disclosing GM's trade secrets and other confidential information, or from "testifying, without the prior written consent of General Motors Corporation, either upon deposition or at trial, as an expert witness, or as a witness of any kind, and from consulting with attorneys or their agents in any litigation already filed, or to be filed in the future, involving General Motors Corporation as an owner, seller, manufacturer and/or designer of the product(s) in issue." The injunction contained this exception that stated: "[This provision] shall not operate to interfere with the jurisdiction of the Court in . . . Georgia [where the litigation involving the fuel tank was still pending]." The injunction contained no other limitation, but a separate settlement agreement between the parties stated: "It is agreed that [Elwell's] appearance and testimony, if any, at hearings on Motions to quash subpoena or at deposition or trial or other official proceeding, if the Court or other tribunal so orders, will in no way form a basis for an action in violation of the Permanent Injunction or this Agreement." In the six years since the Elwell-GM settlement, Elwell testified against GM both in Georgia and in several other jurisdictions in which Elwell has been subpoenaed to testify.]

[Meanwhile, in September 1991, Kenneth and Steven Baker sued GM in Missouri state court to recover for the death of their mother in a highway accident in Missouri in a Chevrolet S-10 Blazer. After GM removed the case to federal court, the Bakers subpoenaed Elwell. GM objected to Elwell's appearance as a deponent or trial witness on the ground that the Michigan injunction barred his testimony. The district court allowed the Bakers to depose Elwell and to call him as a witness at trial on the grounds that (1) blocking Elwell's testimony pursuant to the Michigan injunction would violate Missouri's "public policy"; and (2) because a Michigan court could modify the Michigan injunction, so too could a Missouri federal court. Following GM's appeal from an $11.3 million jury award, the Eighth Circuit Court of Appeals reversed on the ground that Elwell's testimony should not have been admitted. The court reasoned that the trial court erroneously relied on Missouri's policy favoring disclosure of relevant, nonprivileged information because of Missouri's "equally strong public policy in favor of full faith and credit." The Eight Circuit also noted that the Michigan court "has been asked on several occasions to modify the injunction, [but] has yet to do so," and noted that, if the Michigan court did not intend to block Elwell's testimony in cases like the Bakers', "the injunction would . . . have been unnecessary." The Supreme Court granted certiorari "to decide whether the full faith and credit requirement stops the Bakers, who were not parties to the Michigan proceeding, from obtaining Elwell's testimony in their Missouri wrongful death action."]

II

A

Our [Full Faith and Credit Clause] precedent differentiates the credit owed to laws (legislative measures and common law) and to judgments. "In numerous cases this Court has held that credit must be given to the judgment of another state although the forum would not be required to entertain the suit on which the judgment was founded." Milwaukee County v. M. E. White Co., 296 U.S. 268, 277 (1935). The Full Faith and Credit Clause does not compel "a state to substitute the statutes of other states for its own statutes dealing with a subject matter concerning which it is competent to legislate." Pacific Employers Ins. Co. v. Industrial Accident Comm'n, 306 U.S. 493, 501 (1939); *see* Phillips Petroleum Co. v. Shutts, 472 U.S. 797, 818-819 (1985). Regarding judgments, however, the full faith and credit obligation is exacting. A final judgment in one State, if rendered by a court with adjudicatory authority over the subject matter and persons governed by the judgment, qualifies for recognition throughout the land. For claim and issue preclusion (res judicata) purposes, in other words, the judgment of the rendering State gains nationwide force.

A court may be guided by the forum State's "public policy" in determining the *law* applicable to a controversy. *See* Nevada v. Hall, 440 U.S. 410 (1976). But our decisions support no roving "public policy exception" to the full faith and credit due *judgments. See* Fauntleroy v. Lum, 210 U.S. 230, 237 (1908) (judgment of Missouri court entitled to full faith and credit in Mississippi even if Missouri judgment rested on a misapprehension of Mississippi law). In assuming the existence of a ubiquitous "public policy exception" permitting one State to resist recognition of another State's judgment, the District Court in the Bakers' wrongful-death action misread our precedent. "The full faith and credit clause is one of the provisions incorporated into the Constitution by its framers for the purpose of transforming an aggregation of independent, sovereign States into a nation." Sherrer v. Sherrer, 334 U.S. 343, 355 (1948). We are "aware of [no] considerations of local policy or law which could rightly be deemed to impair the force and effect which the full faith and credit clause and the Act of Congress require to be given to [a money] judgment outside the state of its rendition." Magnolia Petroleum Co. v. Hunt, 320 U.S. 430, 438 (1943).

The Court has never placed equity decrees outside the full faith and credit domain. Equity decrees for the payment of money have long been considered equivalent to judgments at law entitled to nationwide recognition. *See, e.g.*, Barber v. Barber, 323 U.S. 77 (1944) (unconditional adjudication of petitioner's right to recover a sum of money is entitled to full faith and credit); *see also* A. Ehrenzweig, Conflict of Laws §51, p.182 (rev. ed. 1962) (describing as "indefensible" the old doctrine that an equity decree, because it does not "merge" the claim into the judgment, does not qualify for recognition). We see no reason why the preclusive effects of an adjudication on parties and those "in privity" with them, *i.e.*, claim preclusion and issue preclusion (res judicata and collateral estoppel), should differ depending solely upon the type of relief sought in a civil action. *Cf.* Barber, 323 U.S. at 87 (Jackson, J., concurring) (Full Faith and Credit Clause and its implementing statute speak not of "judgments" but of " 'judicial proceedings' without limitation"); Fed. Rule Civ. Proc. 2 (providing for "one form of action to be known as 'civil action,' " in lieu of discretely labeled actions at law and suits in equity).

Full faith and credit, however, does not mean that States must adopt the practices of other States regarding the time, manner, and mechanisms for enforcing judgments. Enforcement measures do not travel with the sister state judgment as preclusive effects do; such measures remain subject to the evenhanded control of forum law. *See* McElmoyle *ex rel.* Bailey v. Cohen, 13 Peters 312, 325 (1839) (judgment may be enforced only as "laws [of enforcing forum] may permit"); *see also* Restatement (Second) of Conflict of Laws §99 (1969) ("The local law of the forum determines the methods by which a judgment of another state is enforced.").

Orders commanding action or inaction have been denied enforcement in a sister State when they purported to accomplish an official act within the exclusive province of that other State or interfered with litigation over which the ordering State had no authority. Thus, a sister State's decree concerning land ownership in another State has been held ineffective to transfer title, *see* Fall v. Eastin, 215 U.S. 1, although such a decree may indeed preclusively adjudicate the rights and obligations running between the *parties* to the foreign litigation, *see, e.g.*, Robertson v. Howard, 229 U.S. 254, 261 (1913) ("It may not be doubted that a court of equity in one State in a proper case could compel a defendant before it to convey property situated in another State."). And antisuit injunctions regarding litigation elsewhere, even if compatible with due process as a direction constraining parties to the decree, *see* Cole v. Cunningham, 133 U.S. 107 (1890), in fact have not controlled the second court's actions regarding litigation in that court. *See, e.g.*, James v. Grand Trunk Western R. Co., 14 Ill. 2d 356, 372, 152 N.E.2d 858, 867 (1958); *see also* E. Scoles & P. Hay, Conflict of Laws §24.21, p. 981 (2d ed. 1992) (observing that antisuit injunction "does not address, and thus has no preclusive effect on, the merits of the litigation [in the second forum]").[9] Sanctions for violations of an injunction, in any event, are generally administered by the court that issued the injunction. *See, e.g.*, Stiller v. Hardman, 324 F.2d 626, 628 (CA2 1963) (nonrendition forum enforces monetary relief portion of a judgment but leaves enforcement of injunctive portion to rendition forum).

B

With these background principles in view, we turn to the dimensions of the order GM relies upon to stop Elwell's testimony. Specifically, we take up the question: What matters did the Michigan injunction legitimately conclude?

As earlier recounted, the parties before the Michigan County Court, Elwell and GM, submitted an agreed-upon injunction, which the presiding judge signed. While no issue was joined, expressly litigated, and determined in the Michigan proceeding,[11] that order is *claim* preclusive between Elwell and GM. Elwell's claim for wrongful discharge and his related contract and tort claims have "merged in the judgment," and he cannot sue again to re-

9. This Court has held it impermissible for a state court to enjoin a party from proceeding in a federal court, *see* Donovan v. Dallas, 377 U.S. 408 (1964), but has not yet ruled on the credit due to a state court injunction barring a party from maintaining litigation in another State, see Ginsburg, Judgments in Search of Full Faith and Credit: The Last-in-Time Rule for Conflicting Judgments, 82 Harv. L. Rev. 798, 823 (1969); *see also* Reese, Full Faith and Credit to Foreign Equity Decrees, 42 Iowa L. Rev. 183, 198 (1957) (urging that, although this Court "has not yet had occasion to determine [the issue], . . . full faith and credit does not require dismissal of an action whose prosecution has been enjoined," for to hold otherwise "would mean in effect that the courts of one state can control what goes on in the courts of another"). State courts that have dealt with the question have, in the main, regarded antisuit injunctions as outside the full faith and credit ambit.

11. In no event, we have observed, can issue preclusion be invoked against one who did not participate in the prior adjudication. Thus, Justice Kennedy emphasizes the obvious in noting that the Michigan judgment has no preclusive effect on the Bakers, for they were not parties to the Michigan litigation. Such an observation misses the thrust of GM's argument. GM readily acknowledges "the commonplace rule that a person may not be bound by a judgment *in personam* in a case to which he was not made a party." But, GM adds, the Michigan decree does not bind the Bakers; it binds *Elwell* only. Most forcibly, GM insists that the Bakers cannot object to the binding effect GM seeks for the Michigan judgment because the Bakers have no constitutionally protected interest in obtaining the testimony of a particular witness. Given this argument, it is clear that issue preclusion principles, standing alone, cannot resolve the controversy GM presents.

cover more. Similarly, GM cannot sue Elwell elsewhere on the counterclaim GM asserted in Michigan.

Michigan's judgment, however, cannot reach beyond the Elwell-GM controversy to control proceedings against GM brought in other States, by other parties, asserting claims the merits of which Michigan has not considered. Michigan has no power over those parties, and no basis for commanding them to become intervenors in the Elwell-GM dispute. *See* Martin v. Wilks, 490 U.S. 755, 761-763 (1989). Most essentially, Michigan lacks authority to control courts elsewhere by precluding them, in actions brought by strangers to the Michigan litigation, from determining for themselves what witnesses are competent to testify and what evidence is relevant and admissible in their search for the truth. *See* Restatement (Second) of Conflict of Laws, §§137-139 (1969 and rev. 1988) (forum's own law governs witness competence and grounds for excluding evidence).

As the District Court recognized, Michigan's decree could operate against Elwell to preclude him from *volunteering* his testimony. But a Michigan court cannot, by entering the injunction to which Elwell and GM stipulated, dictate to a court in another jurisdiction that evidence relevant in the Bakers' case—a controversy to which Michigan is foreign—shall be inadmissible. This conclusion creates no general exception to the full faith and credit command, and surely does not permit a State to refuse to honor a sister state judgment based on the forum's choice of law or policy preferences. Rather, we simply recognize that, just as the mechanisms for enforcing a judgment do not travel with the judgment itself for purposes of Full Faith and Credit, see McElmoyle *ex rel.* Bailey v. Cohen, 13 Peters 312 (1839); and just as one State's judgment cannot automatically transfer title to land in another State, see Fall v. Eastin, 215 U.S. 1 (1909), similarly the Michigan decree cannot determine evidentiary issues in a lawsuit brought by parties who were not subject to the jurisdiction of the Michigan court.[12]

The language of the consent decree is informative in this regard. Excluding the then-pending Georgia action from the ban on testimony by Elwell without GM's permission, the decree provides that it "shall not operate to *interfere with the jurisdiction* of the Court in . . . Georgia." But if the Michigan order, extended to the Georgia case, would have "interfered with the jurisdiction" of the Georgia court, Michigan's ban would, in the same way, "interfere with the jurisdiction" of courts in other States in cases similar to the one pending in Georgia.

---

12. Justice Kennedy inexplicably reads into our decision a sweeping exception to full faith and credit based solely on "the integrity of Missouri's judicial processes." The Michigan judgment is not entitled to full faith and credit, we have endeavored to make plain, because it impermissibly interferes with Missouri's control of litigation *brought by parties who were not before the Michigan court.* Thus, Justice Kennedy's hypothetical, *see ibid.*, misses the mark. If the Bakers had been parties to the Michigan proceedings and had actually litigated the privileged character of Elwell's testimony, the Bakers would of course be precluded from relitigating that issue in Missouri.

In line with its recognition of the interference potential of the consent decree, GM provided in the settlement agreement that, if another court ordered Elwell to testify, his testimony would "in no way" render him vulnerable to suit in Michigan for violation of the injunction or agreement. The Eighth Circuit regarded this settlement agreement provision as merely a concession by GM that "some courts might fail to extend full faith and credit to the [Michigan] injunction." *Ibid.* As we have explained, however, Michigan's power does not reach into a Missouri courtroom to displace the forum's own determination whether to admit or exclude evidence relevant in the Bakers' wrongful-death case before it. In that light, we see no altruism in GM's agreement not to institute contempt or breach-of-contract proceedings against Elwell in Michigan for giving subpoenaed testimony elsewhere. Rather, we find it telling that GM ruled out resort to the court that entered the injunction, for injunctions are ordinarily enforced by the enjoining court, not by a surrogate tribunal.

In sum, Michigan has no authority to shield a witness from another jurisdiction's subpoena power in a case involving persons and causes outside Michigan's governance. Recognition, under full faith and credit, is owed to dispositions Michigan has authority to order. But a Michigan decree cannot command obedience elsewhere on a matter the Michigan court lacks authority to resolve. *See* Thomas v. Washington Gas Light Co., 448 U.S. 261, 282-283 (1980) (plurality opinion) ("Full faith and credit must be given to [a] determination that [a State's tribunal] had the authority to make; but by a parity of reasoning, full faith and credit need not be given to determinations that it had no power to make.").

Justice Scalia, concurring in the judgment.

I agree with the Court that enforcement measures do not travel with sister-state judgments as preclusive effects do. It has long been established that "the judgment of a state Court cannot be enforced out of the state by an execution issued within it." McElmoyle *ex rel.* Bailey v. Cohen, 13 Peters 312, 325 (1839). To recite that principle is to decide this case.

General Motors asked a District Court in Missouri to *enforce* a Michigan injunction. The Missouri court was no more obliged to enforce the Michigan injunction by preventing Elwell from presenting his testimony than it was obliged to enforce it by holding Elwell in contempt. The Full Faith and Credit Clause " 'did not make the judgments of other States domestic judgments to all intents and purposes, but only gave a general validity, faith, and credit to them, *as evidence.* No execution can issue upon such judgments without a new suit in the tribunals of other States.' " Thompson v. Whitman, 85 U.S. 457 (1874) (emphasis added) (quoting J. Story, Conflict of Laws §609). A judgment or decree of one State, to be sure, may be grounds for an action (or a defense to one) in another. But the Clause and its implementing statute

> "establish a rule of evidence, rather than of jurisdiction. While they make the record of a judgment, rendered after due notice in one State, conclu-

> sive evidence in the courts of another State, or of the United States, of the matter adjudged, they do not affect the jurisdiction, either of the court in which the judgment is rendered, or of the court in which it is offered in evidence. Judgments recovered in one State of the Union, when proved in the courts of another government, whether state or national, within the United States, differ from judgments recovered in a foreign country in no other respect than in not being reexaminable on their merits, nor impeachable for fraud in obtaining them, if rendered by a court having jurisdiction of the cause and of the parties." Wisconsin v. Pelican Ins. Co., 127 U.S. 265, 291-292 (1888) (citation omitted).

The judgment that General Motors obtained in Michigan " 'does not carry with it, into another State, the efficacy of a judgment upon property or persons, to be enforced by execution. To give it the force of a judgment in another State, it must be made a judgment there; and can only be executed in the latter as its laws may permit.' " Lynde v. Lynde, 181 U.S. 183, 187 (1901) (quoting McElmoyle, *supra,* at 325). *See, e.g.,* Watts v. Waddle, 6 Peters 389, 392 (1832), a case involving a suit to obtain an equity decree ordering the conveyance of land, duplicating such a decree already issued in another State.

Because neither the Full Faith and Credit Clause nor its implementing statute requires Missouri to execute the injunction issued by the courts of Michigan, I concur in the judgment.

Justice KENNEDY, with whom Justices O'CONNOR and THOMAS join, concurring in the judgment.

I concur in the judgment. In my view the case is controlled by well-settled full faith and credit principles which render the majority's extended analysis unnecessary and, with all due respect, problematic in some degree. This separate opinion explains my approach.

I

The majority, of course, is correct to hold that when a judgment is presented to the courts of a second State it may not be denied enforcement based upon some disagreement with the laws of the State of rendition. Full faith and credit forbids the second State from questioning a judgment on these grounds. There can be little doubt of this proposition. We have often recognized the second State's obligation to give effect to another State's judgments even when the law underlying those judgments contravenes the public policy of the second State.

My concern is that the majority, having stated the principle, proceeds to disregard it by announcing two broad exceptions. First, the majority would allow courts outside the issuing State to decline to enforce those judgments "purporting to accomplish an official act within the exclusive province of [a sister] State." Second, the basic rule of full faith and credit is said not to cover injunctions "interfering with litigation over which the ordering State had no authority." The exceptions the majority recognizes are neither consistent with its rejection of a public policy exception to full faith and credit nor in accord with established rules implementing the Full Faith and Credit Clause. As employed to resolve this case, furthermore, the exceptions to full faith and credit have a potential for disrupting judgments, and this ought to give us considerable pause. Our decisions have been careful not to foreclose all effect for the types of injunctions the majority would place outside the ambit of full faith and credit. These authorities seem to be disregarded by today's holding. For example, the majority chooses to discuss the extent to which courts may compel the conveyance of property in other jurisdictions. That subject has proven to be quite difficult. Some of our cases uphold actions by state courts affecting land outside their territorial reach. *E.g.*, Robertson v. Howard, 229 U.S. 254, 261 (1913) ("It may not be doubted that a court of equity in one State in a proper case could compel a defendant before it to convey property situated in another State"). Nor have we undertaken before today to announce an exception which denies full faith and credit based on the principle that the prior judgment interferes with litigation pending in another jurisdiction. As a general matter, there is disagreement among the state courts as to their duty to recognize decrees enjoining proceedings in other courts.

Subjects which are at once so fundamental and so delicate as these ought to be addressed only in a case necessarily requiring their discussion, and even then with caution lest we announce rules which will not be sound in later application. We might be required to hold, if some future case raises the issue, that an otherwise valid judgment cannot intrude upon essential processes of courts outside the issuing State in certain narrow circumstances, but we need not announce or define that principle here. Even if some qualification of full faith and credit were required where the judicial processes of a second State are sought to be controlled in their procedural and institutional aspects, the Court's discussion does not provide sufficient guidance on how this exception should be construed in light of our precedents. The majority's broad review of these matters does not articulate the rationale underlying its conclusions. In the absence of more elaboration, it is unclear what it is about the particular injunction here that renders it undeserving of full faith and credit. The Court's reliance upon unidentified principles to justify omitting certain types of injunctions from the doctrine's application leaves its decision in uneasy tension with its own rejection of a broad public policy exception to full faith and credit.

The following example illustrates the uncertainty surrounding the majority's approach. Suppose the Bakers had anticipated the need for Elwell's testimony in Missouri and had appeared in a Michigan court to litigate the privileged character of the testimony it sought to elicit. Assume further the law on privilege were the same in both jurisdictions. If Elwell, GM, and the Bakers were before the Michigan court and Michigan law gave its own injunction preclusive effect, the Bakers could not relitigate the point, if general principles of issue preclusion control. Perhaps the argument can be made, as the majority appears to say, that the integrity of Missouri's judicial processes demands a rule allowing relitigation of the issue; but, for the reasons given below, we need not confront this interesting question.

In any event, the rule would be an exception. Full faith and credit requires courts to do more than provide for direct enforcement of the judgments issued by other States. It also "requires federal courts to give the same preclusive effect to state court judgments that those judgments would be given in the courts of the State from which the judgments emerged." Kremer v. Chemical Constr. Corp., 456 U.S. 461, 466 (1982). Through full faith and credit, "the local doctrines of *res judicata,* speaking generally, become a part of national jurisprudence. . . ." Riley v. New York Trust Co., 315 U.S. 343, 349 (1942). And whether or not an injunction is enforceable in another State on its own terms, the courts of a second State are required to honor its issue preclusive effects.

II

In the case before us, of course, the Bakers were neither parties to the earlier litigation nor subject to the jurisdiction of the Michigan courts. The majority pays scant attention to this circumstance, which becomes critical. The beginning point of full faith and credit analysis requires a determination of the effect the judgment has in the courts of the issuing State. In our most recent full faith and credit cases, we have said that determining the force and effect of a judgment should be the first step in our analysis. "If the state courts would not give preclusive effect to the prior judgment, 'the courts of the United States can accord it no greater efficacy' under §1738." Haring v. Prosise, 462 U.S. 306, 313, n.6 (1983) (quoting Union & Planters' Bank v. Memphis, 189 U.S. 71, 75 (1903)). A conclusion that the issuing State would not give the prior judgment preclusive effect ends the inquiry, making it unnecessary to determine the existence of any exceptions to full faith and credit. We cannot decline to inquire into these state-law questions when the inquiry will obviate new extensions or exceptions to full faith and credit.

If we honor the undoubted principle that courts need give a prior judgment no more force or effect that the issuing State gives it, the case before us is resolved. Here the Court of Appeals and both parties in their arguments before our Court seemed to embrace the assumption that Michigan would apply the full force of its judgment to the Bakers. Michigan law does not appear to support the assumption.

The simple fact is that the Bakers were not parties to the Michigan proceedings, and nothing indicates Michigan would make the novel assertion that its earlier injunction binds the Bakers or any other party not then before it or subject to its jurisdiction. For collateral estoppel to apply under Michigan law, " 'the same parties must have had a full opportunity to litigate the issue, and there must be mutuality of estoppel.' " Nummer v. Treasury Dept.,

448 Mich. 534, 542, 533 N.W.2d 250, 253. Since the Bakers were not parties to the Michigan proceedings and had no opportunity to litigate any of the issues presented, it appears that Michigan law would not treat them as bound by the judgment. The majority cites no authority to the contrary.

It makes no difference that the judgment in question is an injunction. The Michigan Supreme Court has twice rejected arguments that injunctions have preclusive effect in later litigation, relying in no small part on the fact that the persons against whom preclusion is asserted were not parties to the earlier litigation.

[D]etermining as a threshold matter the extent to which Michigan law gives preclusive effect to the injunction eliminates the need to decide whether full faith and credit applies to equitable decrees as a general matter or the extent to which the general rules of full faith and credit are subject to exceptions. Michigan law would not seek to bind the Bakers to the injunction and that suffices to resolve the case. For these reasons, I concur in the judgment.

Questions and Comments

(1) The thrust of *Baker* is that a judgment from one state that purports to require an official act within the exclusive province of another state need not be given full faith and credit. Does the Court provide guidance about where the legitimate effect of the rendering court's judgment ends and the exclusive province of the other state begins? Is Justice Kennedy correct to claim that the majority in *Baker* creates a new exception to the bar on invoking local public policy to resist a foreign judgment?

(2) The *Baker* court says that the Michigan judgment "cannot reach beyond the Elwell-GM controversy," but it also confirms that the judgment is preclusive as between Elwell and GM. What if GM had brought a separate suit against Elwell in Missouri to enforce the injunction against him? Would the injunction be entitled to full faith and credit in this context? If so, what would happen if Elwell were nonetheless called to testify in the Bakers' case in federal court?

(3) The Restatement stated in 1971 that "the Supreme Court has not had occasion to determine whether full faith and credit *requires* a State of the United States to enforce a valid judgment of a sister State that orders the doing of an act other than the payment of money or that enjoins the doing of an act." Restatement (Second) of Conflict of Laws §102 cmt. C (1971) (emphasis added). Does *Baker* resolve this issue? On the one hand, it holds that the Michigan injunction need not be enforced in Missouri. On the other hand, the Court makes clear that, as a general matter, the full faith and credit clause applies to equity decrees. For an excellent analysis of Baker and its implications for how the full faith and credit clause applies to equity decrees, see

Price, Full Faith and Credit and the Equity Conflict, 84 Va. L. Rev. 747 (1998).

(4) What about antisuit injunctions that order parties not to litigate a case elsewhere? In Cole v. Cunningham, 133 U.S. 107, 134 (1890), the Court held that antisuit injunctions did not violate the full faith and credit clause. But the Supreme Court has never resolved whether antisuit injunctions must be given full faith and credit. Prior to *Baker,* most lower courts held that the full faith and credit clause does not compel recognition of an antisuit injunction. *See, e.g.*, Laker Airways v. Sabena, Belgian World Airlines, 731 F.2d 909, 934 (D.C. Cir. 1984) (dicta); James v. Grand T. W. R. Co., 152 N.E.2d 858 (Ill. 1958); *but see* Bard v. Charles R. Myers Ins. Agency, Inc., 839 S.W.2d 791 (Tex. 1992) (liquidation order issued by Vermont receivership court, prohibiting prosecution of any action against company in receivership which would interfere with receiver's conduct of company's affairs, given full faith and credit by Texas court). *James* reasoned that the antisuit injunction need not be respected because it operated upon the parties and not the court. What are *Baker*'s implications for antisuit injunctions?

Note: The Defense of Marriage Act

Article IV, §1 does more than obligate states to give "Full Faith and Credit . . . to the public Acts, Records, and judicial Proceedings of every other State." It also provides: "Congress may by general Laws prescribe the Manner in which such Acts, Records and Proceedings shall be proved, and the Effect thereof." Congress exercised this power in 1996 in enacting the Defense of Marriage Act ("DOMA"), 28 U.S.C. §1738C. DOMA was a response to the possibility that some states might legalize same-sex marriage (as Vermont subsequently did). It provides in pertinent part:

> No State, territory, or possession of the United States, or Indian tribe, shall be required to give effect to any public act, record, or judicial proceeding of any other State, territory, possession, or tribe respecting a relationship between persons of the same sex that is treated as a marriage under the laws of such other State, territory, possession, or tribe, or a right or claim arising from such relationship.

DOMA raises several interesting and novel questions. One is: Is DOMA necessary? We learned in Chapter 1, page 60 *supra,* that states sometimes deny recognition to marriages that violate local public policy. And *Baker* reaffirmed that the public policy exception is consistent with the full faith and credit clause. See *supra* page 678 (noting that it is consistent with the full faith and credit clause for "a court [to] be guided by the forum State's public policy' in determining the *law* applicable to a controversy"). Since (as Chapter 1 also showed) marriage recognition is generally viewed as a choice-of-law issue, DOMA at first glance seems unnecessary.

But although DOMA probably has no implications for choice-of-law questions involving same-sex marriages, it might well have bite with respect to judgments issues involving same-sex marriage. Consider this hypothetical:

> One member of a same-sex couple, long married and a resident in Hawaii, is negligently injured by a tourist from California. The uninjured spouse sues the California tourist in the Hawaii state courts for loss of consortium and wins a judgment. The California tourist does not pay, and the judgment creditor takes the Hawaii judgment to California to enforce it.

Borchers, *Baker v. General Motors*: Implications for Interjurisdictional Recognition on Nontraditional Marriages, 32 Creighton L. Rev. 147, 180-181 (1998). In the absence of DOMA, would California have an obligation under the full faith and credit clause to enforce this judgment? If so, does DOMA relieve California of this obligation?

If DOMA does relieve the states of a duty to enforce judgments related to same-sex marriages, is it constitutional? In other words, can Congress relieve the states of a full faith and credit obligation they would otherwise have? The answer depends on the meaning of the "effects" clause in Article IV, §1, reproduced above. There is remarkably little information about the original understanding of the clause, and there have been no definitive judicial interpretation of it. Scholars have reached a variety of conclusions. For the view that DOMA would in this circumstance be unconstitutional, see Kramer, Same-Sex Marriage, Conflict of Laws, and the Unconstitutional Public Policy Exception, 106 Yale L.J. 1965, 2003 (1997) ("Effects" clause cannot be read to "undermine or abolish" the full faith and credit obligation); Currie, Full Faith and Credit to Marriages, 1 Green Bag 2d 7, 8 (1997) ("If Article IV itself requires respect for Hawaii marriages, Congress cannot provide otherwise; like §5 of the fourteenth amendment, the 'effects' clause gives authority only to implement the constitutional provision, not to amend it."); Strasser, DOMA and The Two Faces of Federalism, 32 Creighton L Rev 457 (1998) (arguing that DOMA does not satisfy Article IV's requirement that Congress make "general Laws"). For views supporting a broad congressional power, see Rensberger, Same-Sex Marriages and the Defense of Marriage Act; A Deviant View of An Experiment in Full Faith and Credit, 32 Creighton L. Rev. 409, 450 (1998) (full faith and credit obligation under Article IV merely a default rule subject to congressional change under "effects" clause); Borchers, *supra,* at 183-184 (broad reading of DOMA consistent with Congress's power under Article IV); Whitten, The Original Understanding of the

Full Faith and Credit Clause and the Defense of Marriage Act, 32 Creighton L. Rev. 255 (1998) (originalist defense of Congress's power to enact DOMA).

C. The Enforcing State's Law of Judgments

Union National Bank v. Lamb

337 U.S. 38 (1949)

Justice DOUGLAS delivered the opinion of the Court.

Missouri has a statute which limits the life of a judgment to ten years after its original rendition or ten years after its revival. Missouri also provides that no judgment can be revived after ten years from its rendition. These provisions are applicable to all judgments whether rendered by a Missouri court or by any other court.

Petitioner has a Colorado judgment against respondent. It was obtained in 1927 and revived in Colorado in 1945 on personal service upon respondent in Missouri. Suit was then brought in Missouri on the revived Colorado judgment. The Supreme Court of Missouri, though assuming that the judgment was valid in Colorado, refused to enforce it because the original judgment under Missouri's law could not have been revived in 1945. It held that the lex fori governs the limitations of actions and that the Full Faith and Credit Clause of the Constitution, Art. IV, §1, did not require Missouri to recognize Colorado's more lenient policy as respects revival of judgments.

1. Petitioner sought to bring the case here by appeal. But we postponed the question of jurisdiction to the merits. Certiorari, not appeal, is the route by which the question whether or not full faith and credit has been given a foreign judgment is brought here. Hence we treat the papers as a petition for certiorari and grant it. . . .

3. Roche v. McDonald is dispositive of the merits. Roche had a Washington judgment against McDonald. He brought suit on that judgment in Oregon. He obtained a judgment in Oregon at a time when the original judgment had by Washington law expired and could not be revived. Roche then sued in Washington on the Oregon judgment. The Court reversed the Supreme Court of Washington which had held that full faith and credit need not be given the Oregon judgment since it would have been void and of no effect if rendered in Washington. The Court held that once the court of the sister State had jurisdiction over the parties and of the subject matter its judgment was valid and could not be impeached in the State of the forum, even though it could not have been obtained there. . . . For in those cases the Court had held that the State of the forum could not defeat the foreign judgment because it

was obtained by a procedure hostile to or inconsistent with that of the forum or because it was based on a cause of action which the forum itself would not have recognized.

Any other result would defeat the aim of the Full Faith and Credit Clause and the statute enacted pursuant to it. It is when a clash of policies between two states emerges that the need of the Clause is the greatest. It and the statute which implements it are indeed designed to resolve such controversies. There is no room for an exception, as Roche v. McDonald makes plain, where the clash of policies relates to revived judgments rather than to the nature of the underlying claims as in Fauntleroy v. Lum, *supra.* It is the judgment that must be given full faith and credit. In neither case can its integrity be impaired, save for attacks on the jurisdiction of the court that rendered it.

Cases of statute of limitations against a cause of action on a judgment (M'Elmoyle v. Cohen) involve different considerations as Christmas v. Russell long ago pointed out. They do not undermine the integrity of the judgment on which suit is brought. In this case it is the 1945 Colorado judgment that claims full faith and credit in Missouri. No Missouri statute of limitations is tendered to cut off a cause of action based on judgments of that vintage.

It is argued, however, that under Colorado law the 1945 Colorado judgment is not a new judgment and that the revivor did no more than extend the statutory period in which to enforce the old judgment. It is said that those were the assumptions on which the Missouri court proceeded. But we would have to add to and subtract from its opinion to give it that meaning. For when it placed revived judgments on the same basis as original judgments, it did so because of Missouri not Colorado law.

This is not a situation where Colorado law also makes that conclusion plain. The Colorado authorities which have been cited to us indeed seem to hold just the opposite. Thus La Fitte v. Salisbury holds that a revived judgment has the effect of a new one. We are referred to no Colorado authorities to the contrary.

But since the status of the 1945 judgment under Colorado law was not passed upon by the Missouri court, we do not determine the question. For the same reason we do not consider whether the service on which the Colorado judgment was revived satisfied due process. Both of those questions will be open on remand of the cause.

The suggestion that we follow the course taken in Minnesota v. National Tea Co. and vacate the judgment and remand the cause to the Missouri court so that it may first pass on these questions would be appropriate only if it were uncertain whether that court adjudicated a federal question. That course is singularly inappropriate here since it is plain that the Missouri court held that, whatever the effect of revivor under Colorado law, the Colorado judgment was not entitled to full faith and credit in Missouri. That holding is a ruling on a federal question and it cannot stand if, as assumed, the Colorado judgment had the force and effect of a new one.

Reversed.

[Dissenting opinions are omitted.]

Watkins v. Conway

385 U.S. 188 (1966)

Per Curiam.

This litigation began when appellant Watkins brought a tort action against Conway in a circuit court of Florida. On October 5, 1955, that court rendered a $25,000 judgment for appellant. Five years and one day later, appellant sued upon this judgment in a superior court of Georgia. Appellee raised §3-701 of the Georgia Code as a bar to the proceeding: "Suits upon foreign judgments.—All suits upon judgments obtained out of this State shall be brought within five years after such judgments shall have been obtained." The Georgia trial court gave summary judgment for appellee. In so doing, it rejected appellant's contention that §3-701 when read against the longer limitation period of domestic judgments set forth in Ga. Code §§110-1001, 110-1002 (1935), was inconsistent with the Full Faith and Credit and Equal Protection Clauses of the Federal Constitution. The Georgia Supreme Court affirmed, also rejecting appellant's constitutional challenge to §3-701. 221 Ga. 374, 144 S.E.2d 721 (1965). We noted probable jurisdiction under 28 U.S.C. §1257(2). 383 U.S. 941 (1966).

Although appellant lays his claim under two constitutional provisions, in reality his complaint is simply that Georgia has drawn an impermissible distinction between foreign and domestic judgments. He argues that the statute is understandable solely as a reflection of Georgia's desire to handicap out-of-state judgment creditors. If appellant's analysis of the purpose and effect of the statute were correct, we might well agree that it violates the Federal Constitution. For the decisions of this Court which appellee relies upon do not justify the discriminatory application of a statute of limitations to foreign actions.[1]

---

1. The case most directly in point, M'Elmoyle v. Cohen, 13 Pet. 312, upheld the Georgia statute with which we deal today. But the parties in that case did not argue the statute's shorter limitation for foreign judgments as the ground of its invalidity. Instead, the issue presented to this Court concerned the power of the States to impose any statute of limitations upon foreign judgments. *See* argument for plaintiff, 13 Pet., at 313-320. The language of Mr. Justice Wayne's opinion—"may not the law of a state fix different times for barring the remedy in a suit upon a judgment of another state, and for those of its own tribunals," 13 Pet., at 328—must be read against this argument. And, of course, that opinion cannot stand against an equal-protection claim, since it was written nearly 30 years before the Fourteenth Amendment was adopted.

Neither of the cases cited by the Georgia Supreme Court dictates the result of this case. The first, Metcalf v. Watertown, involved a Wisconsin statute which provided a shorter limitation for foreign, as opposed to domestic, judgments. But the holding of the case was merely that this statute should be construed as placing the same limitation on the judgment of a federal court sitting in Wisconsin as would apply to a judgment of a Wisconsin state court.

But the interpretation which the Georgia courts have given §3-701 convinces us that appellant has misconstrued it. The statute bars suits on foreign judgments only if the plaintiff cannot revive his judgment in the State where it was originally obtained. For the relevant date in applying §3-701 is not the date of the original judgment, but rather it is the date of the latest revival of the judgment. In the case at bar, for example, all appellant need do is return to Florida and revive his judgment. He can then come back to Georgia within five years and file suit free of the limitations of §3-701.

It can be seen, therefore, that the Georgia statute has not discriminated against the judgment from Florida. Instead, it has focused on the law of that State. If Florida had a statute of limitations of five years or less on its own judgments, the appellant would not be able to recover here. But this disability would flow from the conclusion of the Florida Legislature that suits on Florida judgments should be barred after that period. Georgia's construction of §3-701 would merely honor and give effect to that conclusion. Thus, full faith and credit is insured, rather than denied, the law of the judgment State. Similarly, there is no denial of equal protection in a scheme that relies upon the judgment State's view of the validity of its own judgments. Such a scheme hardly reflects invidious discrimination.

Affirmed.

Justice DOUGLAS dissents.

Questions and Comments

(1) Does the rule of M'Elmoyle v. Cohen, cited by a majority and dissent in *Union National Bank,* make sense? It allowed the forum state to apply its own statute of limitations to foreign judgments, viewing such an application as other than an attack on the merits of the foreign judgment. Is this because statutes of limitations are "procedural" and the enforcing state is the forum? *Compare* the discussion of *M'Elmoyle* in Sun Oil Co. v. Wortman, page 384 *supra.* But if the purpose of the statute of limitations is to protect either the parties or the courts (or both), isn't the domestic statute inappropriate on a foreign judgment because (a) the foreign judgment is supposed to be conclusive on the rights of the parties, including how much delay will be allowed, and (b) there is no intelligible forum procedural interest in limiting an action brought on a foreign judgment—an action that may be one of the simplest of all actions, since virtually no evidence need be taken?

(2) What other "procedural" rule might the enforcing state apply? What about its rules of jurisdiction? In Kenney v. Supreme Lodge of the World, 252 U.S. 411 (1920), the Court stated that phrasing a failure to enforce another state's judgments in terms of a lack of jurisdiction in the enforcing court is not an adequate explanation. The Illinois Supreme Court had held that since the original action could not have been brought in Illinois, there was no jurisdiction to enforce a judgment, either. Justice Holmes responded:

> It is plain that a State cannot escape its constitutional obligations by the simple device of denying jurisdiction in such cases to courts otherwise competent. Whether the Illinois statute should be construed [to deny jurisdiction, rather than to forbid the claim on substantive grounds] was for the Supreme Court of the State to decide, but read as that court read it, it attempted to achieve a result that the Constitution of the United States forbade.

Might there not be other, more traditionally "jurisdictional" rules as to which the enforcing state might apply its own law?

(3) The majority (and the omitted dissent) seem to assume in *Union National Bank* that it is critical whether the 1945 Colorado proceedings merely extended the statute of limitations on the original Colorado judgment or actually created a new judgment. The disagreement is in what to do about the uncertainty concerning that question. The distinction is significant because one may ignore a foreign statute of limitations, but not a foreign judgment. Doesn't this dichotomy point out the weakness of the analysis of both dissent and majority? Consider: (a) Why would Colorado ever find itself in a position to distinguish between the two views? Since Colorado will either enforce the new judgment if it is one, or enforce its own statute of limitations, if that is what the 1945 proceedings affected, there is no need to answer the question. Doesn't that mean that the opinion writers' theories demanded information about Colorado law that doesn't exist? (b) If it makes so little difference to Colorado, why should such great emphasis be placed on it in Missouri? Aren't the differences mere formalism, if they rise even to that level? (c) Is it clear that there should be such a clear line between the effect given to the statute of limitation on the judgment (it may be ignored) and the effect given to a finding that there is a new judgment (it must be implemented)? What is a rule concerning mandatory counterclaims—a law that can be ignored, or an effect of a judgment that must be honored? What is the proper category for a Virginia statute saying that once a worker compensation award has been made, no other action may be brought—a statute, that can be ignored, or a rule prescribing the effect of a judgment, that must be obeyed?

(4) Why the game-playing in *Watkins?* The Court purports to find, in the Georgia statue considered there, a kind of super full faith and credit because it makes the ability to enforce one's judgment in Georgia turn on whether it is still good where it was rendered. But why make the party with the judgment go back home to Florida? Why not simply refer to Florida law? And what if Florida requires new service of process, the defendant is absent, and the Florida courts don't have a continuing-jurisdiction theory that would allow them to consider that the jurisdiction from the first action continued for the second? What if the judgment is still good in Florida but it cannot be revived? Is it likely that Georgia really intended such extreme deference to the limitations of other states with statutes longer than five years (but shorter than

the plaintiff waited) and not to those states with statutes of less than five years (which would get ignored by Georgia, applying its own five-year statute)?

(5) If the reason that a state may apply its own statute of limitations is that such rules are considered "procedural" then what about other rules that might look procedural, such as compulsory counterclaim rules? If a counterclaim that was not raised in the original proceedings would have been compulsory in the rendering court but is not treated as compulsory in the enforcing court (or vice versa), which court's counterclaim rules apply?

In Chapman v. Aetna Finance, 615 F.2d 361 (5th Cir. 1980), it was held that section 1738 did not require the federal court to apply the rendering court's compulsory counterclaim rules (although the rules were ultimately applied, anyway, under a comity theory).

> The "intended function" of the full faith and credit clause, as applied to judicial proceedings, is to avoid "relitigation in other states of adjudicated issues." Fulfillment of that function plainly does not depend on extraterritorial application of essentially procedural res judicata rules. The Georgia compulsory counterclaim rule tracks Fed. R. Civ. P. 13(a), whose purpose is "to prevent multiplicity of actions." . . . Operating as it does to forfeit an unlitigated claim, Georgia's compulsory counterclaim rule is not unlike a statute of limitations, which . . . would not ordinarily be entitled to full faith and credit in foreign jurisdictions.

Chapman is commonly thought to have been overruled by Migra v. Warren City School Dist. Bd. of Education, 465 U.S. 75 (1984), holding federal courts to a more literal interpretation of section 1738, which states that the enforcing state must give the judgment "the same" effect as it would have in the rendering state. *See, e.g.*, Dubroff v. Dubroff, 833 F.2d 557 (5th Cir. 1987); McDougald v. Jenson, 786 F.2d 1465 (11th Cir. 1986). Does *Migra* dispense with the argument that the enforcing state may apply its own judgments law on "procedural" issues?

Because *Migra* dealt with federal deference to a state court judgment in the same state, and because it dealt with civil rights action (the plaintiff raised constitutional challenges to official actions), it might be thought that it is limited to that context, with its special federalism concerns. The argument would be that the Supreme Court was particularly interested in restricting relitigation in federal courts of politically sensitive issues that the local state courts had already addressed. However, the more literal interpretation of section 1738, requiring reference to the rendering state's compulsory counterclaim rules, has also been followed by state courts; *see, e.g.*, Nottingham v. Weld, 237 Va. 416, 377 S.E.2d 621 (1989) (involving a garden variety automobile accident). The increasing attention to the literal language of section 1738 (the "same effect" as in the rendering state) has also been manifested in the context of a subsequent antitrust action brought in federal court. *See* Marrese v. American Academy of Orthopaedic Surgeons, 470 U.S. 373 (1985).

(6) What happens when the enforcement court wants to give a judgment greater effect than the rendering court? Consider Hart v. American Airlines, 304 N.Y.S. 2d 810 (N.Y. Sup. Ct. 1969). Of various actions instituted following a plane crash in Kentucky, the first to be tried to conclusion was the one brought in Texas federal court that resulted in a jury verdict for plaintiffs based on a finding of defendant American Airline's negligence. *Hart* was a later action against American Airlines arising from the same accident but brought by different plaintiffs. The plaintiffs in *Hart* argued that the Texas judgment collaterally estopped the defendant from contesting liability. The defendant argued that the full faith and credit clause precluded the application of collateral estoppel in the New York action because Texas law required mutuality. The New York court disagreed:

> The State of Texas has no legitimate interest in imposing its rules on collateral estoppel upon these New York residents. . . . The fact that the plaintiffs herein involved are New York domiciliaries, as were their decedents, sufficiently establishes this State's superior interest in the issue of collateral estoppel. It may be observed that these plaintiffs occupy much the same relationship to the State of Texas as the nonresident *Hart* plaintiffs do to New York, and the unavailability of the New York rule on collateral estoppel to the *Hart* plaintiffs is equally relevant in holding the instant resident plaintiffs outside the scope of the Texas rule on that issue.
>
> Defendant's reliance on "full faith and credit" to defeat the application of collateral estoppel herein is misplaced. This is not a situation where the judgment, as such, of the Texas court is sought to be enforced. What is here involved is a policy determination by our courts that "One who has had his day in court should not be permitted to litigate the question anew," and, further, refusal "to tolerate a condition where, on relatively the same set of facts, one fact-finder, be it court or jury" may find a party liable while another exonerates him leading to the "inconsistent results which are always a blemish on a judicial system. It is in order to carry out these policy determinations in the disposition of cases in this jurisdiction that an evidentiary use is being made of a particular issue determination made in the Texas action.

Id. at 813-814. Is there any full faith and credit issue in this case at all? That is, is there anything in the principle of full faith and credit that would suggest that a state may not give *more* effect to a judgment than the rendering state would? Is it being too literal to reach a result under the full faith and credit clause's requirement that the second state give the "same" effect that the first state would give? *Compare* Columbia Casualty Co. v. Playtex FP Inc., 584 A. 2d 1214 (Del. 1991) (application of local collateral estoppel law in circumstance similar to *Hart* "is clearly at variance with the purpose and spirit of the full faith and credit clause"). On the general issue of which state's preclusion law to apply, see Shreve, Judgments from a Choice-of-Law Perspective, 40 Am J. Comp. L. 985 (1992).

(7) The Supreme Court has specifically held that a federal court may not give a judgment greater effect than would the state where it was rendered. Migra v. Warren City Sch. Dist. B. of Educ., 465 U.S. 75 (1984); Marrese v. American Academy of Orthopedic Surgeons, 470 U.S. 373, 384 (1984). Would this result in forum-shopping or *Erie* problems if a state court, in contrast, were allowed to give another state's judgment greater effect than would the rendering state?

Treinies v. Sunshine Mining Co.

308 U.S. 66 (1939)

Justice REED delivered the opinion of the Court.

This writ of certiorari was granted to review the action of the Court of Appeals for the Ninth Circuit in affirming a decree of the District Court of Idaho upon a bill of interpleader filed by the Sunshine Mining Company, a Washington corporation, against Evelyn H. Treinies and other citizens of the State of Washington, claimants to certain stock of the Sunshine Mining Company and the dividends therefrom, and Katherine Mason and T. R. Mason, her husband, and other citizens of the State of Idaho, adverse claimants to the same stock and dividends.

The occasion for the interpleader was the existence of inconsistent judgments as to the ownership of the Sunshine stock. The Superior Court of Spokane County, Washington, in administering the estate of Amelia Pelkes, adjudged that it was the property of John Pelkes, assignor of petitioner, Evelyn H. Treinies; and the District Court of Shoshone County, Idaho, adjudged that the same property belonged to respondent, Katherine Mason. They are the sole disputants. Other parties may be disregarded. On account of conflict between the judgments of the respective courts of sister states and the assertion of the failure to give full faith and credit to both in the interpleader action, we granted certiorari.

The alleged rights of the respective claimants arose as follows: Amelia Pelkes, the wife of John Pelkes, died testate in Spokane, Washington, in 1922, leaving her husband and one child, Katherine Mason, the offspring of a former marriage, as the beneficiaries of her will. As a part of her community estate, there were 30,598 shares of Sunshine Mining stock. It was considered valueless and was not inventoried or appraised. The order of distribution assigned a three-fourths undivided interest in these shares to Pelkes and a one-fourth to Mrs. Mason, an omnibus clause covering unknown property. The estate of Mrs. Pelkes was not distributed according to the order of distribution. Instead Pelkes and his stepdaughter, Mrs. Mason, divided the inventoried property between themselves in accordance with their wishes.

It is the contention of Pelkes and his assignee that this partition of the property was in consideration of the release by Mrs. Mason to Pelkes of all of her interest in the shares of the stock of the Sunshine Mining Company. On the other hand, Mrs. Mason asserts that Pelkes was to hold one-half of the amount owned, 15,299 shares, in trust for her.

In August, 1934, Mrs. Mason instituted a suit in the District Court of Idaho for Shoshone County against Pelkes, Evelyn H. Treinies, the Sunshine Mining Company, and others not important here, alleging that she was the owner of 15,299 shares of the stock, that these had been acquired by Miss Treinies from Pelkes with knowledge of Mrs. Mason's rights, and praying that the trust be established and the stock and dividends be awarded to her, Mrs. Mason. It was finally decreed by the District Court on August 18, 1936, after an appeal to the Supreme Court of Idaho, that the stock and dividends belonged to Mrs. Mason. Certiorari to the Supreme Court of Idaho was refused by this Court.

Before the entry of the first decree of the District Court of Idaho, Katherine Mason filed a petition in the Superior Court of Spokane County, Washington, in the probate proceedings involving Amelia Pelkes' will, to remove the executor, John Pelkes, for failure to file his report of distribution and for dissipation of the Sunshine stock. Pelkes by cross-petition claimed the stock. Thereupon Mrs. Mason applied to the Supreme Court of Washington for a writ of prohibition against further proceedings in the Superior Court on the ground of lack of jurisdiction in that court to determine the controversy over the stock. The writ was refused. On May 31, 1935, a judgment was entered in the Superior Court upholding in full the ownership of Pelkes.

After the Supreme Court of Idaho had decided the Idaho suit against Pelkes and Miss Treinies, they filed in August, 1936, a suit in the Superior Court of Washington against Katherine Mason and others alleging that they were the owners of the stock, further alleging that the Idaho decree was invalid for lack of jurisdiction, and asking that their title to the stock be quieted and the Sunshine Mining Company, a party to this and the Idaho suit, be compelled to recognize their ownership. It was at this point in the litigation that the Sunshine Mining Co. filed the bill of interpleader now under consideration. Further proceedings in the suit to quiet title were enjoined by the District Court in this action. [The Court first considered, sua sponte, its own jurisdiction in the case since there was no diversity between the interpleader plaintiff, Sunshine Mining Company, and the Washington defendants. The Court noted that the Interpleader Statute, 28 U.S.C. §1335, requires only minimal diversity—that at least one claimant be diverse in citizenship from at least one adverse claimant. The Court determined that the minimal diversity satisfied the requirement of §2, Article III of the Constitution granting jurisdiction to the federal courts over "Controversies . . . between Citizens of different States."]

Res Judicata of the Idaho Decree.—On the merits, petitioner's objection to the decree below is that it fails to consider and give effect to the Washington judgment of May 31, 1935, awarding the property in question to Pelkes, petitioner's assignor. It is petitioner's claim that the Washington judgment must be considered as effective in this litigation because the question of the jurisdiction of the Washington court was actually litigated before the Supreme Court of Washington and determined favorably to petitioner by the refusal to grant a writ of prohibition against the exercise of jurisdiction by the Washington Superior Court in probate. This failure to give effect to the judgment is said to infringe the full faith and credit clause of the Constitution. . . .[1]

The Court of Appeals correctly determined that the issue of jurisdiction vel non of the Washington court could not be relitigated in this interpleader. As the Idaho District Court was a court of general jurisdiction, its conclusions are unassailable collaterally except for fraud or lack of jurisdiction. The holding by the Idaho court of no jurisdiction in Washington necessarily determined the question raised here as to the Idaho jurisdiction against Miss Treinies' contention. She is bound by that judgment.

The power of the Idaho court to examine into the jurisdiction of the Washington court is beyond question. Even where the decision against the validity of the original judgment is erroneous, it is a valid exercise of judicial power by the second court.

One trial of an issue is enough. "The principles of res judicata apply to questions of jurisdiction as well as to other issues," as well to jurisdiction of the subject matter as of the parties.

Decree affirmed.

Questions and Comments

(1) It is clear, isn't it, that the enforcing state must address any arguments raised against the validity of a judgment it is called on to enforce? It must address questions such as whether there was personal jurisdiction in a default judgment, whether under prevailing law of collateral estoppel the first judgment involved sufficiently similar issues to be entitled to preclusive effect, whether there was adequate notice in the first suit, and the like.

---

1. It is unnecessary to consider whether the Idaho determination as to the jurisdiction of the Washington court was properly made. As the procedure by which a state court examines into the question of the jurisdiction of the court of a sister state is a matter within the control of the respective states (Adam v. Saenger, 303 U.S. 59, 63), it need only be added that such procedure is subject to question only on direct appeal.

It was stipulated by all parties to the Idaho cause that the Idaho courts might take judicial notice of the statutes and decisions of Washington. Some constitutional and statutory provisions relating to the jurisdiction of the Superior Court were pleaded and admitted. It has long been the rule in Idaho that its courts do not take judicial notice of the laws of another state and that without allegation and evidence it will be assumed the laws are the same as those of Idaho. While none of these cases involved a stipulation, the decision of the Supreme Court of Idaho declares the law of that jurisdiction. It follows from the Idaho court's refusal to look into the statutes of Washington that the jurisdiction of the Washington court was presumed to be governed by Idaho law. Under proper proof, the Idaho court would have been compelled to examine the jurisdiction of the Washington court under Washington law.

And on occasion, the enforcing court will decide that the prior judgment is unenforceable.

What if it decides wrongly? Doesn't the very authority to address such issues include the authority to make an occasional mistake? Why should such a mistake be entitled to less preclusive effect than a substantive error? If litigating a jurisdictional issue can foreclose later collateral attack (as we saw in Section A of this chapter), then why oughtn't we give the same effect to full and fair litigation of an issue of judgments law?

Is anything more than this involved in *Treinies?*

(2) On the other hand, won't the Court's decision encourage parties to attempt to have valid judgments undercut by the courts of other states because the last-in-time rule will make binding the ruling of the second state? Yet, isn't that better than the chaos that could be caused by a first-in-time rule under which subsequent courts could disagree about the existence or nonexistence of jurisdiction in the first court and, if they concluded there was such jurisdiction, could ignore the contrary rulings of other courts?

(3) If review had been sought from the final order of the Idaho district court, and it had been upheld by the Idaho Supreme Court with certiorari denied by the U.S. Supreme Court, would the result of this case have been any different? Should the Supreme Court be required to take cases that allege that the courts of one state have denied full faith and credit to the judgments of another?

(4) In Parsons Steel v. First Alabama Bank, 474 U.S. 518 (1986) a state court had (arguably, erroneously) refused to give sufficient res judicata effect to an earlier federal court judgment. After losing the res judicata argument in state court, the bank waited until the entire case was resolved and, on entry of judgment, returned to the federal court to request an injunction. The Supreme Court held that this avenue was foreclosed by the Anti-Injunction Act, 28 U.S.C. §2283, even though that Act allowed a federal court to issue injunctions "to protect or effectuate its judgments." The Court of Appeals had upheld the District Court's right to issue the injunction, but the Supreme Court disagreed:

> In reaching this holding, the majority explicitly declined to consider the possible preclusive effect, pursuant to the Full Faith and Credit Act, 28 U.S.C. § 1738, of the state court's determination after full litigation by the parties that the earlier federal-court judgment did not bar the state action. According to the majority, "while a federal court is generally bound by other state court determinations, the relitigation exception empowers a federal court to be the final adjudicator as to the res judicata effects of its prior judgments on a subsequent state action." . . .
>
> In our view, the majority of the Court of Appeals gave unwarrantedly short shrift to the important values of federalism and comity embodied in the Full Faith and Credit Act. As recently as last March, in Marrese v. American Academy of Orthopaedic Surgeons, 470 U.S. 373 (1985), we reaffirmed our holding in Migra v. Warren City School Dist. Bd. of Education, 465 U.S. 75 (1984), that under the Full Faith and Credit Act a

federal court must give the same preclusive effect to a state-court judgment as another court of that State would give. . . . The Full Faith and Credit Act thus "[allows] the States to determine, subject to the requirements of the statute and the Due Process Clause, the preclusive effect of judgments in their own courts."

In the instant case, however, the Court of Appeals did not consider the possible preclusive effect under Alabama law of the state-court judgment, and particularly of the state court's resolution of the res judicata issue, concluding instead that the relitigation exception to the Anti-Injunction Act limits the Full Faith and Credit Act. We do not agree. . . . We believe that the Anti-Injunction Act and the Full Faith and Credit Act can be construed consistently, simply by limiting the relitigation exception of the Anti-Injunction Act to those situations in which the state court has not yet ruled on the merits of the res judicata issue. Once the state court has finally rejected a claim of res judicata, then the Full Faith and Credit Act becomes applicable and federal courts must turn to state law to determine the preclusive effect of the state court's decision. . . .

We hold, therefore, that the Court of Appeals erred by refusing to consider the possible preclusive effect, under Alabama law, of the state-court judgment. Even if the state court mistakenly rejected respondents' claim of res judicata, this does not justify the highly intrusive remedy of a federal-court injunction against the enforcement of the state-court judgment. Rather, the Full Faith and Credit Act requires that federal courts give the state-court judgment, and particularly the state court's resolution of the res judicata issue, the same preclusive effect it would have had in another court of the same State. Challenges to the correctness of a state court's determination as to the conclusive effect of a federal judgment must be pursued by way of appeal through the state-court system and certiorari from this Court.

We think the District Court is best situated to determine and apply Alabama preclusion law in the first instance. Should the District Court conclude that the state-court judgment is not entitled to preclusive effect under Alabama law and the Full Faith and Credit Act, it would then be in the best position to decide the propriety of a federal-court injunction under the general principles of equity, comity, and federalism discussed in Mitchum v. Foster, 407 U.S. 225, 243 (1972).

D. Domestic Relations: A Special Problem of Judgments

Domestic relations law presents some peculiar legal problems because of the interplay between the rules of full faith and credit to judgments and the peculiar theoretical basis for jurisdiction in a divorce action. The theory says that a divorce action is an action in rem, the marriage relationship being the res. As with Harris v. Balk (discussed at page 545 *supra*), the problem lies in part in locating the res. Here, the theory indicates that the res is located where either party is domiciled. Thus, there are two states that can grant a divorce to a separated couple domiciled separately. But no more than two states should be available, since domicile, and not mere in personam jurisdiction, is a requisite for full faith and credit to the divorce decree.

This peculiar set of jurisdictional rules raises problems in the context of collateral attacks on judgments of divorce. The first major recent case was Williams v. North Carolina I, 317 U.S. 287 (1942), in which the State of North Carolina had prosecuted for bigamous cohabitation two North Carolinians who had run off to Nevada to get divorced from their stay-at-home spouses in ex parte Nevada proceedings, and had returned "married" to each other to live in the same small town. The Supreme Court reversed the conviction because it had not been established conclusively that the parties were not domiciled in Nevada. On retrial and conviction, the Supreme Court affirmed in Williams v. North Carolina II, 325 U.S. 226 (1945), because in the second trial the jury had been properly instructed that the Nevada divorce judgments could be found to be void only if the parties did not obtain bona fide domicile in Nevada. Justice Frankfurter's opinion stressed that North Carolina could not be bound by the ex parte conclusions of the Nevada court concerning the parties' domicile.

1. Ex Parte "Divisible Divorce"

Estin v. Estin

334 U.S. 541 (1948)

Opinion of the Court by Justice DOUGLAS, announced by Justice REED.

This case, here on certiorari to the Court of Appeals of New York, presents an important question under the Full Faith and Credit Clause of the Constitution. Article IV, §1. It is whether a New York decree awarding respondent $180 per month for her maintenance and support in a separation proceeding survived a Nevada divorce decree which subsequently was granted petitioner.

The parties were married in 1937 and lived together in New York until 1942 when the husband left the wife. There was no issue of the marriage. In 1943 she brought an action against him for a separation. He entered a general appearance. The court, finding that he had abandoned her, granted her a decree of separation and awarded her $180 per month as permanent alimony. In January 1944 he went to Nevada where in 1945 he instituted an action for divorce. She was notified of the action by constructive service but entered no appearance in it. In May, 1945, the Nevada court, finding that petitioner had been a bona fide resident of Nevada since January 30, 1944, granted him an absolute divorce "on the ground of three years continual separation, without cohabitation." The Nevada decree made no provision for alimony, though the Nevada court had been advised of the New York decree.

Prior to that time petitioner had made payments of alimony under the New York decree. After entry of the Nevada decree he ceased paying. Thereupon respondent sued in New York for a supplementary judgment for the amount of the arrears. Petitioner appeared in the action and moved to eliminate the alimony provisions of the separation decree by reason of the Nevada decree. The Supreme Court denied the motion and granted respondent judgment for the arrears. The judgment was affirmed by the Appellate Division, and then by the Court of Appeals.

We held in Williams v. North Carolina, 317 U.S. 287, 325 U.S. 226, (1) that a divorce decree granted by a State to one of its domiciliaries is entitled to full faith and credit in a bigamy prosecution brought in another State, even though the other spouse was given notice of the divorce proceeding only through constructive service; and (2) that while the finding of domicile by the court that granted the decree is entitled to prima facie weight, it is not conclusive in a sister State but might be relitigated there. The latter course was followed in this case, as a consequence of which the Supreme Court of New York found, in accord with the Nevada court, that petitioner "is now and since January, 1944, has been a bona fide resident of the State of Nevada."

Petitioner's argument therefore is that the tail must go with the hide—that since by the Nevada decree, recognized in New York, he and respondent are no longer husband and wife, no legal incidence of the marriage remains. We are given a detailed analysis of New York law to show that the New York courts have no power either by statute or by common law to compel a man to support his ex-wife, that alimony is payable only so long as the relation of husband and wife exists, and that in New York, as in some other states, a support order does not survive divorce.

The difficulty with that argument is that the highest court in New York has held in this case that a support order can survive divorce and that this one has survived petitioner's divorce. That conclusion is binding on us, except as it conflicts with the Full Faith and Credit Clause. It is not for us to say whether that ruling squares with what the New York courts said on earlier occasions. It is enough that New York today says that such is her policy. The only question for us is whether New York is powerless to make such a ruling in view of the Nevada decree.

We can put to one side the case where the wife was personally served or where she appeared in the divorce proceedings. The only service on her in this case was by publication and she made no appearance in the Nevada proceeding. The requirements of procedural due process were satisfied and the domicile of the husband in Nevada was foundation for a decree effecting a change in the marital capacity of both parties in all the other States of the Union, as well as in Nevada. But the fact that marital capacity was changed does not mean that every other legal incidence of the marriage was necessarily affected.

Although the point was not adjudicated in Barber v. Barber, the Court in that case recognized that while a divorce decree obtained in Wisconsin by a husband from his absent wife might dissolve the vinculum of the marriage, it did not mean that he was freed from payment of alimony under an earlier separation decree granted by New York. An absolutist might quarrel with the result and demand a rule that once a divorce is granted, the whole of the marriage relation is dissolved, leaving no roots or tendrils of any kind. But there are few areas of the law in black and white. The greys are dominant and even among them the shades are innumerable. For the eternal problem of the law is one of making accommodations between conflicting interests. This is why most legal problems end as questions of degree. That is true of the present problem under the Full Faith and Credit Clause. The question involves important considerations both of law and policy which it is essential to state.

The situations where a judgment of one State has been denied full faith and credit in another State, because its enforcement would contravene the latter's policy, have been few and far between. The Full Faith and Credit Clause is not to be applied, accordion-like, to accommodate our personal predilections. It substituted a command for the earlier principles of comity and thus basically altered the status of the States as independent sovereigns. Williams v. North Carolina. It ordered submission by one State even to hostile policies reflected in the judgment of another State, because the practical operation of the federal system, which the Constitution designed, demanded it. The fact that the requirements of full faith and credit, so far as judgments are concerned, are exacting, if not inexorable, does not mean, however, that the State of the domicile of one spouse may, through the use of constructive service, enter a decree that changes every legal incidence of the marriage relationship.

Marital status involves the regularity and integrity of the marriage relation. It affects the legitimacy of the offspring of marriage. It is the basis of criminal laws, as the bigamy prosecution in Williams v. North Carolina dramatically illustrates. The State has a considerable interest in preventing bigamous marriages and in protecting the offspring of marriages from being bastardized. The interest of the State extends to its domiciliaries. The State should have the power to guard its interest in them by changing or altering their marital status and by protecting them in that changed status throughout the farthest reaches of the nation. For a person domiciled in one State should not be allowed to suffer the penalties of bigamy for living outside the State with the only one which the State of his domicile recognizes as his lawful wife. And children born of the only marriage which is lawful in the State of his domicile should not carry the stigma of bastardy when they move elsewhere. These are matters of legitimate concern to the State of the domicile. They entitle the State of the domicile to bring in the absent spouse through constructive service. In no other way could the State of the domicile have and maintain effective control of the marital status of its domiciliaries.

Those are the considerations that have long permitted the State of the matrimonial domicile to change the marital status of the parties by an ex parte divorce proceeding, Thompson v. Thompson, considerations which in the *Williams* cases we thought were equally applicable to any State in which one spouse had established a bona fide domicile. But those considerations have little relevancy here. In this case New York evinced a concern with this broken marriage when both parties were domiciled in New York and before Nevada had any concern with it. New York was rightly concerned lest the abandoned spouse be left impoverished and perhaps become a public charge. The problem of her livelihood and support is plainly a matter in which her community had a legitimate interest. The New York court, having jurisdiction over both parties, undertook to protect her by granting her a judgment of permanent alimony. Nevada, however, apparently follows the rule that dissolution of the marriage puts an end to a support order. But the question is whether Nevada could under any circumstances adjudicate rights of respondent under the New York judgment when she was not personally served or did not appear in the proceeding.

Bassett v. Bassett, 141 F.2d 954, held that Nevada could not. We agree with that view.

The New York judgment is a property interest of respondent, created by New York in a proceeding in which both parties were present. It imposed obligations on petitioner and granted rights to respondent. The property interest which it created was an intangible, jurisdiction over which cannot be exerted through control over a physical thing. Jurisdiction over an intangible can indeed only arise from control or power over the persons whose relationships are the source of the rights and obligations.

Jurisdiction over a debtor is sufficient to give the State of his domicile some control over the debt which he owes. It can, for example, levy a tax on its transfer by will, appropriate it through garnishment or attachment (*see* Harris v. Balk, 198 U.S. 215), collect it and administer it for the benefit of creditors. But we are aware of no power which the State of domicile of the debtor has to determine the personal rights of the creditor in the intangible unless the creditor has been personally served or appears in the proceeding. The existence of any such power has been repeatedly denied. Pennoyer v. Neff, New York Life Ins. Co. v. Dunlevy.

We know of no source of power which would take the present case out of that category. The Nevada decree that is said to wipe out respondent's claim for alimony under the New York judgment is nothing less than an attempt by Nevada to restrain respondent from asserting her claim under that judgment. That is an attempt to exercise an in personam jurisdiction over a person not before the court. That may not be done. Since Nevada had no power to adjudicate respondent's rights in the New York judgment, New York need not give full faith and credit to that phase of Nevada's judgment. A judgment of a court having no jurisdiction to render it is not entitled to the full faith and credit which the Constitution and statute of the United States demand. Williams v. North Carolina.

The result in this situation is to make the divorce divisible—to give effect to the Nevada decree insofar as it affects marital status and to make it ineffective on the issue of alimony. It accommodates the interests of both Nevada and New York in this broken marriage by restricting each State to the matters of her dominant concern.

Since Nevada had no jurisdiction to alter respondent's rights in the New York judgment, we do not reach the further question whether in any event that judgment would be entitled to full faith and credit in Nevada. And it will be time enough to consider the effect of any discrimination shown to out-of-state ex parte divorces when a State makes that its policy.

Affirmed. . . .

Justice JACKSON, dissenting.

If there is one thing that the people are entitled to expect from their lawmakers, it is rules of law that will enable individuals to tell whether they are married and, if so, to whom. Today many people who have simply lived in more than one state do not know, and the most learned lawyer cannot advise them with any confidence. The uncertainties that result are not merely technical, nor are they trivial; they affect fundamental rights and relations such as the lawfulness of their cohabitation, their children's legitimacy, their title to property, and even whether they are law-abiding persons or criminals. In a society as mobile and nomadic as ours, such uncertainties affect large numbers of people and create a social problem of some magnitude. It is therefore important that, whatever we do, we shall not add to the confusion. I think that this decision does just that. . . .

The Court reaches the Solomon-like conclusion that the Nevada decree is half good and half bad under the full faith and credit clause. It is good to free the husband from the marriage; it is not good to free him from its incidental obligations. Assuming the judgment to be one which the Constitution requires to be recognized at all, I do not see how we can square this decision with the command that it be given *full* faith and credit. For reasons which I stated in dissenting in Williams v. North Carolina, I would not give standing under the clause to constructive service divorces obtained on short residence. But if we are to hold this divorce good, I do not see how it can be less good than a divorce would be if rendered by the courts of New York. . . .

May v. Anderson

345 U.S. 528 (1953)

Justice BURTON delivered the opinion of the Court.

The question presented is whether, in a habeas corpus proceeding attacking the right of a mother to retain possession of her minor children, an

Ohio court must give full faith and credit to a Wisconsin decree awarding custody of the children to their father when that decree is obtained by the father in an ex parte divorce action in a Wisconsin court which had no personal jurisdiction over the mother. For the reasons hereafter stated, our answer is no.

This proceeding began July 5, 1951, when Owen Anderson, here called the appellee, filed a petition for a writ of habeas corpus in the Probate Court of Columbiana County, Ohio. He alleged that his former wife, Leona Anderson May, here called the appellant, was illegally restraining the liberty of their children, Ronald, Sandra and James, aged, respectively, 12, 8 and 5, by refusing to deliver them to him in response to a decree issued by the County Court of Waukesha County, Wisconsin, February 5, 1947. With both parties and their children before it, the Probate Court ordered that, until this matter be finally determined, the children remain with their mother subject to their father's right to visit them at reasonable times.

After a hearing "on the petition, the stipulation of counsel for the parties as to the agreed statement of facts, and the testimony," the Probate Court decided that it was obliged by the Full Faith and Credit Clause of the Constitution of the United States to accept the Wisconsin decree as binding upon the mother. Accordingly, proceeding to the merits of the case upon the issues presented by the stipulations of counsel, it ordered the children discharged from further restraint by her. That order has been held in abeyance and the children are still with her. The Court of Appeals for Columbiana County, Ohio, affirmed. The Supreme Court of Ohio, without Opinion, denied a motion directing the Court of Appeals to certify its record for review, and dismissed an appeal on the ground that no debatable constitutional question was involved. . . .

The parties were married in Wisconsin and, until 1947, both were domiciled there. After marital troubles developed, they agreed in December, 1946, that appellant should take their children to Lisbon, Columbiana County, Ohio, and there think over her future course. By New Year's Day, she had decided not to return to Wisconsin and, by telephone, she informed her husband of that decision.

Within a few days he filed suit in Wisconsin, seeking both an absolute divorce and custody of the children. The only service of process upon appellant consisted of the delivery to her personally, in Ohio, of a copy of the Wisconsin summons and petition. Such service is authorized by a Wisconsin statute for use in an action for a divorce but that statute makes no mention of its availability in a proceeding for the custody of children. Appellant entered no appearance and took no part in this Wisconsin proceeding which produced not only a decree divorcing the parties from the bonds of matrimony but a decree purporting to award the custody of the children to their father, subject to a right of their mother to visit them at reasonable times. Appellant contests only the validity of the decree as to custody. *See* Estin v. Estin, recognizing the divisibility of decrees of divorce from those for payment of alimony.

Armed with a copy of the decree and accompanied by a local police officer, appellee, in Lisbon, Ohio, demanded and obtained the children from their mother. The record does not disclose what took place between 1947 and 1951, except that the children remained with their father in Wisconsin until July 1, 1951. He then brought them back to Lisbon and permitted them to visit their mother. This time, when he demanded their return, she refused to surrender them.

Relying upon the Wisconsin decree, he promptly filed in the Probate Court of Columbiana County, Ohio, the petition for a writ of habeas corpus now before us. Under Ohio procedure that writ tests only the immediate right to possession of the children. It does not open the door for the modification of any prior award of custody on a showing of changed circumstances. Nor is it available as a procedure for settling the future custody of children in the first instance. . . .

Separated as our issue is from that of the future interests of the children, we have before us the elemental question whether a court of a state, where a mother is neither domiciled, resident nor present, may cut off her immediate right to the care, custody, management and companionship of her minor children without having jurisdiction over her in personam. Rights far more precious to appellant than property rights will be cut off if she is to be bound by the Wisconsin award of custody. "[I]t is now too well settled to be open to further dispute that the 'full faith and credit' clause and the act of Congress passed pursuant to it, do not entitle a judgment in personam to extra-territorial effect if it be made to appear that it was rendered without jurisdiction over the person sought to be bound."

In Estin v. Estin and Kreiger v. Kreiger this Court upheld the validity of a Nevada divorce obtained ex parte by a husband, resident in Nevada, insofar as it dissolved the bonds of matrimony. At the same time, we held Nevada powerless to cut off, in that proceeding, a spouse's right to financial support under the prior decree of another state. In the instant case, we recognize that a mother's right to custody of her children is a personal right entitled to at least as much protection as her right to alimony.

In the instant case, the Ohio courts gave weight to appellee's contention that the Wisconsin award of custody binds appellant because, at the time it was issued, her children had a technical domicile in Wisconsin, although they were neither resident nor present there. We find it unnecessary to determine the children's legal domicile because, even if it be with their father, that does not give Wisconsin, certainly as against Ohio, the personal jurisdiction that it must have in order to deprive their mother of her personal right to their immediate possession.[8]

8. . . . The instant case does not present the special considerations that arise where a parent, with or without minor children, leaves a jurisdiction for the purpose of escaping process or otherwise evading jurisdiction, and we do not have here the considerations that arise when children are unlawfully or surreptitiously taken by one parent from the other.

The judgment of the Supreme Court of Ohio, accordingly, is reversed and the cause is remanded to it for further proceedings not inconsistent with this opinion.

Reversed and remanded. . . .

Justice JACKSON, whom Justice REED joins, dissenting.

The Court apparently is holding that the Federal Constitution prohibits Ohio from recognizing the validity of this Wisconsin divorce decree insofar as it settles custody of the couple's children. In the light of settled and unchallenged precedents of this Court, such a decision can only rest upon the proposition that Wisconsin's courts had no jurisdiction to make such a decree binding upon appellant.

A conclusion that a state must not recognize a judgment of a sister commonwealth involves very different considerations than a conclusion that it must do so. If Wisconsin has rendered a valid judgment, the Constitution not only requires every state to give it full faith and credit, but 28 U.S.C. §1738, referring to such judicial proceedings, commands that they "shall have the same full faith and credit in every court within the United States and its Territories and Possessions as they have by law or usage in the courts of such State, Territory or Possession from which they are taken." The only escape from obedience lies in a holding that the judgment rendered in Wisconsin, at least as to custody, is void and entitled to no standing even in Wisconsin. It is void only if it denies due process of law.

The Ohio courts reasoned that although personal jurisdiction over the wife was lacking, domicile of the children in Wisconsin was a sufficient jurisdictional basis to enable Wisconsin to bind all parties interested in their custody. This determination that the children were domiciled in Wisconsin has not been contested either at our bar or below. Therefore, under our precedents, it is conclusive. The husband, plaintiff in the case, was at all times domiciled in Wisconsin; the defendant-wife was a Wisconsin native, was married there and both were domiciled in that State until her move in December 1946, when the parties stipulate that she acquired an Ohio domicile. The children were born in Wisconsin, were always domiciled there, and were physically resident in Wisconsin at all times until December 1946, when their mother took them to Ohio with her. But the Ohio court specifically found that she brought the children to Ohio with the understanding that if she decided not to go back to Wisconsin the children were to be returned to that State. In spite of the fact that she did decide not to return, she kept the children in Ohio. It was under these circumstances that the Wisconsin decree was rendered in February 1947, less than two months after the wife had given up her physical residence in Wisconsin and held the children out of the State in breach of her agreement. . . .

The difference between a proceeding involving the status, custody and support of children and one involving adjudication of property rights is too apparent to require elaboration. In the former, courts are no longer concerned primarily with the proprietary claims of the contestants for the "res" before the court, but with the welfare of the "res" itself. Custody is viewed not with the idea of adjudicating rights *in* the children, as if they were chattels, but rather with the idea of making the best disposition possible for the welfare of the children. To speak of a court's "cutting off" a mother's right to custody of her children, as if it raised problems similar to those involved in "cutting off" her rights in a plot of ground, is to obliterate these obvious distinctions. Personal jurisdiction of all parties to be affected by a proceeding is highly desirable, to make certain that they have had valid notice and opportunity to be heard. But the assumption that it overrides all other considerations and in its absence a state is constitutionally impotent to resolve questions of custody flies in the face of our own cases. . . .

Questions and Comments

(1) Is there any sensible alternative to the holding in Estin v. Estin that Nevada could terminate the marriage of the parties but not the husband's obligation to support his former wife? Would *either* state grant a divorce without granting support if there had been full litigation with both parties present? If not, why should the Nevada decree be able to achieve that result by way of ex parte proceedings?

It is clear, isn't it, that domicile should provide enough of an interest for the state to grant the divorce? Think of the situation of the defendant spouse who cannot be found—should the other remain perpetually married? And if the state of domicile may grant a divorce, wouldn't it be intolerable for it not to be given full faith and credit, so that a person might be married in one place and not another?

(2) The conceptual framework for the doctrine of divisible divorce—that the basic divorce action is in rem, with the marriage relationship the res, located where either spouse lives, while other aspects of the action are in personam—received an interesting test in Carr v. Carr, 46 N.Y.2d 270, 385 N.E.2d 1234, 413 N.Y.S.2d 305 (1978). There, decedent Paul Carr had obtained an ex parte Honduran divorce from his wife Ann in 1967. At the time, Ann was living in New York. Later, Paul married Barbara, who at all relevant times lived in California. When Paul died and Ann learned that Barbara had applied for survivor benefits under the Foreign Service Retirement and Disability System (Paul had been with the Foreign Service), Ann brought an action in New York to invalidate the Honduran divorce and declare herself Paul's lawful surviving spouse. The New York court decided that it had no jurisdiction, despite the possibility of saying that the marital "res" was in New York. It pointed out that the real defendant was Barbara, and that she had never had any contacts with New York.

Along similar lines, California refused jurisdiction in a case brought by a California to have defendant declared his father. Hartford v. Superior Court,

47 Cal. 2d 447, 304 P.2d 1 (1956). Defendant was not domiciled in California, but plaintiff sought to analogize the father-son relationship to the marriage relationship and thus avoid the need for in personam jurisdiction. Justice Traynor said that the difference between divorce and establishing paternity was the difference "between the state's power to insulate its domiciliary from a relationship with one not within its jurisdiction and its lack of power to reach out and fasten a relationship upon a person over whom it has no jurisdiction." Is the distinction significant?

(3) Wasn't the result in May v. Anderson clearly wrong for the reasons stated by Justice Jackson? If the presence of real property within the state gives the state enough interest to determine the rights in it of those over whom it has no in personam jurisdiction, why can't the same be said when the "property" is a child—in whom the state presumably has a stronger interest? Wouldn't such reasoning work under *Shaffer*, page 546 *supra?* And even if it is considered necessary to obtain in personam jurisdiction over the wife in *May*, didn't Wisconsin have "minimal contacts" with her under the *International Shoe* standard? Isn't it strange that after *May* there is *no state* where either of the spouses can stay at home and sue? (Of course either can go to the domicile of the other, but at the risk of less favorable law.)

Is there anything in *Kulko, supra* page 527, that suggests a different result?

2. Bilateral Divorce

Johnson v. Muelberger

340 U.S. 581 (1951)

Justice REED delivered the opinion of the Court.

The right of a daughter to attack in New York the validity of her deceased father's Florida divorce is before us. She was his legatee. The divorce was granted in Florida after the father appeared there and contested the merits. The issue turns on the effect in New York under these circumstances of the Full Faith and Credit Clause of the Federal Constitution.

Eleanor Johnson Muelberger, respondent, is the child of decedent E. Bruce Johnson's first marriage. After the death of Johnson's first wife in 1939, he married one Madoline Ham, and they established their residence in New York. In August 1942, Madoline obtained a divorce from him in a Florida proceeding, although the undisputed facts as developed in the New York Surrogate's hearing show that she did not comply with the jurisdictional ninety-day residence requirement.

In 1944 Mr. Johnson entered into a marriage, his third, with petitioner, Genevieve Johnson, and in 1945 he died, leaving a will in which he gave his entire estate to his daughter, Eleanor. After probate of the will, the third wife filed notice of her election to take the statutory one-third share of the estate, under §18 of the New York Decedent Estate Law. This election was contested by respondent daughter, and a trial was had before the Surrogate, who determined that she could not attack the third wife's status as surviving spouse, on the basis of the alleged invalidity of Madoline's divorce, because the divorce proceeding had been a contested one, and "[s]ince the decree is valid and final in the State of Florida, it is not subject to collateral attack in the courts of this state." . . .

[U]nder our decisions, a state by virtue of the clause must give full faith and credit to an out-of-state divorce by barring either party to that divorce who has been personally served or who has entered a personal appearance from collaterally attacking the decree. Such an attack is barred where the party attacking would not be permitted to make a collateral attack in the courts of the granting state. This rule the Court of Appeals recognized. It determined, however, that a "stranger to the divorce action," as the daughter was held to be in New York, may collaterally attack her father's Florida divorce in New York if she could have attacked it in Florida.

No Florida case has come to our attention holding that a child may contest in Florida its parent's divorce where the parent was barred from contesting, as here, by res judicata. . . .

We conclude that Florida would not permit Mrs. Muelberger to attack the Florida decree of divorce between her father and his second wife as beyond the jurisdiction of the rendering court. In that case New York cannot permit such an attack by reason of the Full Faith and Credit Clause. When a divorce cannot be attacked for lack of jurisdiction by parties actually before the court or strangers in the rendering state, it cannot be attacked by them anywhere in the Union. The Full Faith and Credit Clause forbids.

Reversed.

[A dissenting opinion of Justice FRANKFURTER is omitted.]

Questions and Comments

(1) Would it be tolerable to allow the wholesale invalidation of parents' marriages by their children, or by anyone else, for that matter? Isn't this case explainable on the same basis as *Simons?*

(2) Didn't *Muelberger* and related cases give the go-ahead for the operation of divorce mills in the states? Was the Constitution actually intended to reach such a result? Aren't the parties' motivations entirely different in most bilateral divorce cases than they are in ordinary cases, such as Durfee v. Duke, page 642 *supra?* Remember that the rationale of *Durfee* was that one litigation of an issue was enough—but is it in a bilateral divorce situation in which the parties both intended to lie about domicile because both wanted a divorce and couldn't obtain it under the laws of their own domicile? Wouldn't an answer to the problem be to allow bilateral divorces to be granted on the basis of in personam jurisdiction, but require the law of the marital

domicile to be applied? Or would that just make the parties lie in order to get favorable law?

(3) Does the result in *Muelberger* prevent the state from prosecuting one or both of the parties later for bigamous cohabitation if they "remarry"? Can Florida law make the state of marital domicile a "stranger to the litigation" and conclude rights against it, in rem, by a judgment between the conspiring parties? Or can it prevent the state of marital domicile from establishing that it was such (rather than Florida) when it was not represented in the divorce proceedings and the Florida courts do not obtain jurisdiction over it? Isn't it clear that such prosecutions may go forward? Why haven't there been any?

(4) Does it make any more sense to allow strangers to try to attack the validity of a *marriage*, as in In re May's Estate, page 60 *supra*, than it does to attack their divorce? Note that the fact that a marriage is not a judgment, while a divorce is, gives the divorce more sanctity. Isn't that a pure accident of the fact that divorces are granted by way of the courts, and shouldn't a step back from the two require a reassessment of the current situation?

(5) Should the IRS be able to mount a collateral attack on a bilateral divorce? The principle of *Muelberger* presumably does not apply in the case of a bilateral divorce granted by another country, since the full faith and credit clause applies only to state judgments. In Boyter v. Commissioner of Internal Revenue, 668 F.2d 1382 (4th Cir. 1982), the Boyters had twice obtained year-end divorces, once in Haiti and once in the Dominican Republic. After filing separate tax returns (to avoid the "marital penalty"), they remarried. The Fourth Circuit ruled that under the Internal Revenue Code the IRS was bound by state law on the question of whether the Boyters were married. Without answering that question, the court remanded the case for a determination of whether the divorce was a "sham transaction" not deserving recognition under the Internal Revenue Code. Is it consistent to say that state law will be followed to determine whether the Boyters were validly divorced but that, even if they were, their divorce may be considered a "sham transaction"?

(6) Foreign country divorces will routinely be given comity if they appear regular and if the parties were actually domiciled in the foreign country at the time. The problem arises (not only in the tax context discussed in note (5) above) when the parties are American and attempt to get a foreign "quickie" divorce. Only New York seems to have recognized such divorces. In Rosenstiel v. Rosenstiel, 16 N.Y.2d. 64, 209 N.E.2d 709, 262 N.Y.S.2d 86 (1965), the New York Court of Appeals recognized (or at least protected from collateral attack) a Mexican divorce obtained by a one-day sojourn in Juarez. (A current "husband" was attacking the validity of his wife's divorce from her former husband in order to obtain an annulment of the present marriage.) The parties had obviously acted the way they did in order to avoid the strict divorce laws of New York, which have been somewhat modified and "liberalized." (The new statutes also make recognition of "quickie" divorces much more difficult.) The court justified its recognition in part by some legal "realism"—Nevada is no more the real domicile in most cases than is Mex-

ico. But isn't the fake domicile in Nevada a cost of implementing the full faith and credit clause, while the fake domicile in Mexico is not? Can the unsuccessful annulment plaintiff complain that recognizing such a divorce, the result of a sham proceeding, deprives him of due process? Or is it enough to observe that he was a stranger to the Mexican proceedings, so they deprived him of nothing that was his?

(7) One of the stranger cases of American jurisprudence is Alton v. Alton 207 F.2d 667 (3d Cir. 1953). Mrs. Alton had gone to the Virgin Islands from the couple's home in Connecticut. After six weeks and one day she filed for divorce, which her husband did not contest. Under Virgin Islands law, only the minimum residence period—not domicile—was required. The divorce was denied and the wife appealed. The husband did not respond. The Court of Appeals affirmed denial of the divorce on "due process" grounds, despite the fact that it is hard to find someone who is denied due process when both parties want the divorce. Would full faith and credit have made a more solid basis for the court's decision?

(The Supreme Court originally granted certiorari in the *Alton* case but dismissed the matter as moot and vacated the decision upon learning that the parties had obtained a divorce elsewhere. 347 U.S. 610 (1954).)

3. Modifications: Child Custody and Support

Yarborough v. Yarborough

290 U.S. 202 (1933)

Justice BRANDEIS delivered the opinion of the Court.

On August 10, 1930, Sadie Yarborough, then sixteen years of age, was living with her maternal grandfather, R. D. Blowers, at Spartanburg, South Carolina. Suing by him as guardian ad litem, she brought this action in a court of that State to require her father, W. A. Yarborough, a resident of Atlanta, Georgia, to make provision for her education and maintenance. She alleged "that she is now ready for college and is without funds and, unless the defendant makes provision for her, will be denied the necessities of life and an education, and will be dependent upon the charity of others."[1] Jurisdiction was obtained by attachment of defendant's property. Later he was served personally within South Carolina.

In bar of the action, W. A. Yarborough set up, among other defenses, a judgment entered in 1929 by the Superior Court of Fulton County, Georgia, in a suit for divorce brought by him against Sadie's mother. He alleged that

1. There was no suggestion that plaintiff would be destitute or become a public charge. Indeed, her grandfather testified that he was able and willing to provide $125 a month for her education and maintenance (the amount sought by plaintiff), if her father was unable to do so.

by the judgment the amount thereafter to be paid by him for Sadie's education and maintenance had been determined; that the sum so fixed had been paid; and that the judgment had been fully satisfied by him. He claimed that in Georgia the judgment was conclusive of the matter here in controversy; that having been satisfied, it relieved him, under the Georgia law, of all obligation to provide for the education and maintenance of their minor child; and that the full faith and credit clause of the Federal Constitution (Art. IV, §1) required the South Carolina court to give to that judgment the same effect in this proceeding which it has, and would have, in Georgia. The trial court denied the claim; ordered W. A. Yarborough to pay to the grandfather, as trustee, fifty dollars monthly for Sadie's education and support; and to pay $300 as fees of her counsel. . . .

For sometime prior to June, 1927, W. A. Yarborough, his wife and their daughter Sadie had lived together at Atlanta, Georgia, where he then was, and ever since has been, domiciled. In that month, Sadie's mother left Atlanta for Hendersonville, N. C., where she remained during the summer. Sadie joined her there, after a short stay at a camp. In September, 1927, while they were at Hendersonville, W. A. Yarborough brought, in the Superior Court for Fulton County, at Atlanta, suit against his wife for a total divorce on the ground of mental and physical cruelty. Mrs. Yarborough filed an answer and also a cross-suit in which she prayed a total divorce, the custody of the child and "that provision for permanent alimony be made for the support of the respondent and the minor child above mentioned [Sadie], and for the education of said minor child." An order, several times modified, awarded to the wife the custody of Sadie and, as temporary alimony, sums "for the support and maintenance of herself and her minor daughter Sadie." Hearings were held from time to time at Atlanta. At some of these, Sadie (and also her grandfather) was personally present. But she was not formally made a party to the litigation; she was not served with process; and no guardian ad litem was appointed for her therein.

[A] decree of total divorce, with the right in each to remarry, was entered on June 7, 1929; the wife was ordered to pay the costs; and jurisdiction of the case "was retained for the purpose of further enforcement of the orders of the court theretofore passed."[3] Among such orders, was the provision for the maintenance and education of Sadie here relied upon as res judicata. It was entered on January 17, 1929 (after the rendition of the first verdict). . . . It was contended below in the trial court, and there held, that the provision

3. Custody of Sadie had been awarded to the mother; and it had been ordered that the father be allowed the privilege of visiting his said minor daughter, and of having her with him, out of the presence of the defendant, on the second and fourth week-ends of each month, from the close of school hours Friday until Sunday night of said week ends, during school terms, and at like times during vacation; at which times the plaintiff shall be entitled to take said minor daughter on pleasure trips of reasonable distance returning her punctually at the conclusion of the allotted time.

of the decree of the Georgia court directing the payment to R. D. Blowers, trustee, of $1,750 to be "expended by him in his discretion for the benefit of the minor child, including her education, support, maintenance, medical attention and other necessary items of expenditure" was not intended to relieve the father from all further liability to support Sadie. This contention appears to have been abandoned. It is clear that Mrs. Yarborough, her husband and the court intended that this provision should absolve Sadie's father from further obligation to support her. That the term "permanent alimony" as used in the decree of the Georgia court, means a final provision for the minor child is shown by both the legislation of the State and the decisions of its highest court. The refusal of the South Carolina court to give the judgment effect as against Sadie is now sought to be justified on other grounds.

. . . The fact that Sadie has become a resident of South Carolina does not impair the finality of the judgment. South Carolina thereby acquired the jurisdiction to determine her status and the incidents of that status. Upon residents of that State it could impose duties for her benefit. Doubtless, it might have imposed upon her grandfather who was resident there a duty to support Sadie. But the mere fact of Sadie's residence in South Carolina does not give that State the power to impose such a duty upon the father who is not a resident and who long has been domiciled in Georgia. He has fulfilled the duty which he owes her by the law of his domicile and the judgment of its court. Upon that judgment he is entitled to rely. It was settled by Sistare v. Sistare, 218 U.S. 1, that the full faith and credit clause applies to an unalterable decree of alimony for a divorced wife. The clause applies, likewise, to an unalterable decree of alimony for a minor child. We need not consider whether South Carolina would have power to require the father, if he were domiciled there, to make further provision for the support, maintenance, or education of his daughter.

Reversed.

Justice STONE, dissenting.

I think the judgment should be affirmed.

The divorce decree of the Georgia court purported to adjudicate finally, both for the present and for the future, the right of a minor child of the marriage to support and maintenance, by directing her father to make a lump sum payment for that purpose. More than two years later, after the minor had become a domiciled resident of South Carolina, and after the sum paid had been exhausted, a court of that State, on the basis of her need as then shown, has rendered a judgment directing further payments for her support out the property of the father in South Carolina, in addition to that already commanded by the Georgia judgment.

For present purposes we may take it that the Georgia decree, as the statutes and decisions of the State declare, is unalterable and, as pronounced, is effective to govern the rights of the parties in Georgia. But there is nothing in the decree itself, or in the history of the proceedings which led to it, to suggest that it was rendered with any purpose or intent to regulate or control the relationship of parent and child, or the duties which flow from it, in places outside the State of Georgia where they might later come to reside. It would hardly be thought that Georgia, by judgment of its courts more than by its statutes, would attempt to regulate the relationship of parents and child domiciled outside of the State at the very time the decree was rendered; and, in the face of constitutional doubts that arise here, it is far from clear that its decree is to be interpreted as attempting to do more than to regulate that relationship while the infant continued to be domiciled within the State. But if we are to read the decree as though it contained a clause, in terms, restricting the power of any other state, in which the minor might come to reside, to make provision for her support, then, in the absence of some law of Congress requiring it, I am not persuaded that the full faith and credit clause gives sanction to such control by one state of the internal affairs of another.

Congress has said that the public records and the judicial proceedings of each state are to be given such faith and credit in other states as is accorded to them in the state "from which they are taken." But this broad language has never been applied without limitations. *See* McElmoyle v. Cohen, 13 Pet. 312. Between the prohibition of the due process clause, acting upon the courts of the state from which such proceedings may be taken, and the mandate of the full faith and credit clause, acting upon the state to which they may be taken, there is an area which federal authority has not occupied. As this Court has often recognized, there are many judgments which need not be given the same force and effect abroad which they have at home, and there are some, though valid in the state where rendered, to which the full faith and credit clause gives no force elsewhere. In the assertion of rights, defined by a judgment of one state, within the territory of another, there is often an inescapable conflict of interest of the two states, and there comes a point beyond which the imposition of the will of one state beyond its own borders involves a forbidden infringement of some legitimate domestic interest of the other. That point may vary with the circumstances of the case; and in the absence of provisions more specific than the general terms of the congressional enactment this Court must determine for itself the extent to which one state may qualify or deny rights claimed under proceedings or records of other states.

. . . The question presented here is whether the support and maintenance of a minor child, domiciled in South Carolina, is so peculiarly a subject of domestic concern that Georgia law can not impair South Carolina's authority. The subject matter of the judgment in each state is the duty which government may impose on a parent to support a minor child. The maintenance and support of children domiciled within a state, like their education and custody, is a subject in which government itself is deemed to have a peculiar interest and concern. Their tender years, their inability to provide for themselves, the importance to the state that its future citizens should be clothed, nourished and suitably educated, are considerations which lead all civilized countries to assume some control over the maintenance of minors.[12] The states very generally make some provision from their own resources for the maintenance and support of orphans or destitute children, but in order that children may not become public charges the duty of maintenance is one imposed primarily upon the parents, according to the needs of the child and their ability to meet those needs. This is usually accomplished by suit brought directly by some public officer, by the child by guardian or next friend, or by the mother, against the father for maintenance and support. The measure of the duty is the needs of the child and the ability of the parent to meet those needs at the very time when performance of the duty is invoked. Hence, it is no answer in such a suit that at some earlier time provision was made for the child, which is no longer available or suitable because of his greater needs, or because of the increased financial ability of the parent to provide for them, or that the child may be maintained from other sources.

In view of the universality of these principles it comes as a surprise that any state, merely because it has made some provision for the support of a child, should, either by statute or judicial decree, so tie its own hands as to foreclose all future inquiry into the duty of maintenance however affected by changed conditions.

Even though the Constitution does not deny to Georgia the power to indulge in such a policy for itself, it by no means follows that it gives to Georgia the privilege of prescribing that policy for other states in which the child comes to live. South Carolina has adopted a different policy. It imposes on the father or his property located within the state the duty to support his minor child domiciled there. . . .

The decision in Sistare v. Sistare lends no support to the contention that South Carolina can be precluded by a judgment of another state from providing for the future maintenance and support of a destitute child domiciled within its own borders, out of the property of her father, also located there. Here the Georgia decree did not end the relationship of parent and child, as a decree of divorce may end the marriage relationship. Had the infant continued to reside in Georgia, and had she sought in the courts of South Carolina to compel the application of property of her father, found there, to her further maintenance and support, full faith and credit to the Georgia decree applied to its own domiciled resident might have required the denial of any relief. *Cf.* Bates v. Bodie, 245 U.S. 520; Thompson v. Thompson, 226 U.S. 551. But when she became a domiciled resident of South Carolina, a new interest came into being,—the interest of the State of South Carolina as a measure of self-preservation to secure the adequate protection and maintenance

12. This control is particularly important in the case of the children of divorced couples. They are usually young; in Maryland over 60% are under ten years of age when divorce occurs. Divorces are often not contested and the intervention of a disinterested judge is frequently nominal. Allowances for children in the divorce court are typically small. Marshall and May, The Divorce Court, 31, 79-80, 82, 226-321, 323.

of helpless members of its own community and its prospective citizens. That interest was distinct from any which Georgia could conclusively regulate or control by its judgment, even though rendered while the child was domiciled in Georgia. The present decision extends the operation of the full faith and credit clause beyond its proper function of affording protection to the domestic interests of Georgia and makes it an instrument for encroachment by Georgia upon the domestic concerns of South Carolina.

Justice CARDOZO concurs in this opinion.

Questions and Comments

(1) Isn't there a striking resemblance between the dissenting opinion in *Yarborough* and the plurality opinion in Thomas v. Washington Gas Light, page 662 *supra?* Both suggest that the rendering state is overreaching if it attempts to define the continuing effect of its judgments in another state. Does that suggest that the *Thomas* plurality is inconsistent with the majority holding in *Yarborough?*

(2) *Yarborough* dealt with an unusual state law, which made awards of child support unmodifiable. If one takes seriously the text of the full faith and credit statute, then it seems clear that other states must treat the award as unmodifiable also. But conversely, the language of the statute offers enormous freedom to modify judgments from states with res judicata rules making such awards modifiable as a domestic matter.

(3) One related area in which this reasoning caused great problems was the modification of child custody awards. A disgruntled parent might simply take the child to another state and attempt to get a modification before some more sympathetic judicial forum. The problem of interstate child kidnapping grew to such serious proportions that 28 U.S.C. §1738 was amended, adding a new section in the effort to limit a state's power to modify awards rendered in other states. The current version of the statute provides:

§1738A. Full Faith and Credit Given to Child Custody Determinations

(a) The appropriate authorities of every State shall enforce according to its terms, and shall not modify except as provided in subsections (f), (g), and (h) of this section, any custody determination or visitation determination made consistently with the provisions of this section by a court of another State.

(b) As used in this section, the term—

(1) "child" means a person under the age of eighteen;

(2) "contestant" means a person, including a parent or grandparent, who claims a right to custody or visitation of a child;

(3) "custody determination" means a judgment, decree, or other order of a court providing for the custody of a child, and includes permanent and temporary orders, and initial orders and modifications;

(4) "home State" means the State in which, immediately preceding the time involved, the child lived with his parents, a parent, or a person acting as parent, for at least six consecutive months, and in the case of a child less than six months old, the State in which the child lived from birth with any of such persons. Periods of temporary absence of any of such persons are counted as part of the six-month or other period;

(5) "modification" and "modify" refer to a custody or visitation determination which modifies, replaces, supersedes, or otherwise is made subsequent to, a prior custody or visitation determination concerning the same child, whether made by the same court or not;

(6) "person acting as a parent" means a person, other than a parent, who has physical custody of a child and who has either been awarded custody by a court or claims a right to custody;

(7) "physical custody" means actual possession and control of a child;

(8) "State" means a State of the United States, the District of Columbia, the Commonwealth of Puerto Rico, or a territory or possession of the United States; and

(9) "visitation determination" means a judgment, decree, or other order of a court providing for the visitation of a child and includes permanent and temporary orders and initial orders and modifications.

(c) A child custody or visitation determination made by a court of a State is consistent with the provisions of this section only if—

(1) such court has jurisdiction under the law of such State; and

(2) one of the following conditions is met:

(A) such State (i) is the home State of the child on the date of the commencement of the proceeding, or (ii) had been the child's home State within six months before the date of the commencement of the proceeding and the child is absent from such State because of his removal or retention by a contestant or for other reasons, and a contestant continues to live in such State;

(B) (i) it appears that no other State would have jurisdiction under subparagraph (A), and (ii) it is in the best interest of the child that a court of such State assume jurisdiction because (I) the child and his parents, or the child and at least one contestant, have a significant connection with such State other than mere physical presence in such State, and (II) there is available in such State substantial evidence concerning the child's present or future care, protection, training, and personal relationships;

(C) the child is physically present in such State and (i) the child has been abandoned, or (ii) it is necessary in an emergency to protect the child because the child, a sibling, or parent of the child has been subjected to or threatened with mistreatment or abuse;

(D) (i) it appears that no other State would have jurisdiction under subparagraph (A), (B), (C), or (E), or another State has declined to exercise jurisdiction on the ground that the State whose jurisdiction is in issue is the more appropriate forum to determine the custody or visitation of the child, and (ii) it is in the best interest of the child that such court assume jurisdiction; or

(E) the court has continuing jurisdiction pursuant to subsection (d) of this section.

(d) The jurisdiction of a court of a State which has made a child custody or visitation determination consistently with the provisions of this section continues as long as the requirement of subsection (c)(1) of this section continues to be met and such State remains the residence of the child or of any contestant.

(e) Before a child custody or visitation determination is made, reasonable notice and opportunity to be heard shall be given to the contestants, any parent whose parental rights have not been previously terminated and any person who has physical custody of a child.

(f) A court of a State may modify a determination of the custody of the same child made by a court of another State, if—

(1) it has jurisdiction to make such a child custody determination; and

(2) the court of the other State no longer has jurisdiction, or it has declined to exercise such jurisdiction to modify such determination.

(g) A court of a State shall not exercise jurisdiction in any proceeding for a custody or visitation determination commenced during the pendency of a proceeding in a court of another State where such court of that other State is exercising jurisdiction consistently with the provisions of this section to make a custody determination.

(h) A court of a State may not modify a visitation determination made by a court of another State unless the court of the other State no longer has jurisdiction to modify such determination or has declined to exercise jurisdiction to modify such determination.

(4) The Parental Kidnapping Prevention Act (or "PKPA," as 28 U.S.C. §1738A is known) was in part a response to the perceived inadequacies in the Uniform Child Custody Jurisdiction Act "UCCJA"), 9 U.L.A. §116, which has been adopted in every state. For a valuable discussion of the history of the two laws, the way they fit together, and the many difficulties in their application, see Goldstein, The Tragedy of the Interstate Child: A Critical Reexamination of the Uniform Child Custody Jurisdiction Act and the Parental Kidnapping Prevention Act, 25 U.C. Davis L. Rev. 845 (1992). In 1997, the Commissioners on Uniform State Laws promulgated the Uniform Child Custody Jurisdiction and Enforcement Act ("UCCJEA"), a revision of the UCCJA designed to bring it in to conformity with the PKPA and to further clarify the jurisdictional and substantive law of interstate child custody. For analysis of the UCCJEA, see Spector, Uniform Child-Custody Jurisdiction and Enforcement Act, 32 Fam. L.Q. 301, 305 (1998); Hoff, The ABC's of the

UCCJEA: Interstate Child-Custody Practice Under the New Act, 32 Fam. L.Q. 267, 278 (1998). For cases applying both the PKPA and UCCJEA, see Jorgensen v. Vargas, 627 N.W.2d 550 (Iowa 2001); Seamans v. Seamans, 73 Ark. App. 27 (Ark. Ct. App. 2001); In re Marriage of Newsome, 68 Cal. App. 4th 949 (Cal. Ct. App. 1998).

(5) The Supreme Court has held that the P.K.P.A. does not create a federal cause of action. Thompson v. Thompson, 484 U.S. 174 (1988). Primary responsibility for enforcement of the act therefore rests with state courts, with appellate review to the United States Supreme Court.

(6) Is an Indian tribe a "State" within the meaning of the P.K.P.A.? *See* In re Larch, 872 F.2d 66 (1988), holding that tribal courts are bound by the act.

(7) International child custody cases are subject to a web of overlapping conventions, the primary one of which is the Hague Convention on the Civil Aspects of International Child Abduction (1980). For commentary, see Symposium, Symposium Issue Celebrating Twenty Years: The Past and Promise of the 1980 Hague Convention on the Civil Aspects of International Child Abduction, 33 N.Y.U. J. Int'l L. & Pol. 1 (2000); Harper, The Limitations of the Hague Convention and Alternative Remedies for a Parent Including Re-Abduction, 9 Emory Int'l L. Rev. 257 (1995); Finan, Convention on the Rights of the Child: A Potentially Effective Remedy in Cases of International Child Abduction, 34 Santa Clara L. Rev. 1007 (1994).

7

Conflicts in the International Setting

From one perspective, the preceding chapters are as much about conflicts in the international setting as about conflicts in the domestic setting. Choice-of-law issues, personal-jurisdiction issues, and judgment-enforcement issues arise in conflicts between a state and a foreign nation as well as in conflicts between the authority of two states. Why, then, is there any need to separate out conflicts in the international setting for special treatment?

The first reason is that when a state resolves an issue with international overtones, the resolution can have implications, sometimes adverse, for U.S. foreign policy. This raises the vertical conflicts question of which authority—state or federal—should control the issue. And this question, in turn, leads to a horizontal separation of powers question: Which branch of the federal government—the federal courts or the political branches—should decide the vertical conflicts question? We consider some of these issues in Section A below.

While Section A makes clear that states are in some respects not free to implement their own views of foreign policy, it is less clear what impact if any this has on typical conflict-of-laws problems. For example, in the international context, personal jurisdiction may be influenced by treaties regulating service of process abroad. *See, e.g.*, Volkswagenwerk Aktiengesellschaft v. Schlunk, 486 U.S. 694 (1988); Societe Nationale Industrielle Aerospatiale v. United States District Court, 482 U.S. 522 (1987). Moreover, Asahi Metal Industry Co. v. Superior Court of California, 480 U.S. 102 (1987), reprinted at page 534 *supra,* suggests that the due process clause demands heightened scrutiny of assertions of personal jurisdiction over defendants abroad. And, as we saw at page 544, *supra,* Federal Rule of Civil Procedure 4(k)(2) provides a somewhat different standard for personal jurisdiction in certain international cases heard in federal court.

In choice of law, one could argue that the identification and weighing of foreign state interests should be a matter for federal rather than state authorities. As we saw in Chapters 1 and 2, however, state courts have rarely been timid about applying their usual choice-of-law approaches to cases in which international elements are present.* However, international conflicts include not only conflicts between one of the 50 states and a foreign nation, but also conflicts between *federal* authority and another nation. The distinctive nature of the relationship between federal law and the law of other nations is the principal topic of Section B.

Section B's focus on the United States as one co-equal sovereign among many would seem to place it squarely into the realm of a traditional course on international law. Two characteristics of the discussion below, however, distinguish it from what might be expected in a standard course on international law. First, much of international law is concerned with relations between states. Commonly referred to as "public" international law, this topic involves questions about such issues as the proper conduct of war, the proper treatment of diplomats, and the demarcation of boundaries. While such issues concerning the horizontal relations between nation-states undoubtedly color the issues of "private" international law addressed below, they are not dealt with directly. Conflict of laws, even in the international arena, concerns itself primarily with questions of the reach of state authority in disputes involving private individuals.

Second, the cases and authorities discussed below adopt the perspective of an American court. International law belongs to all nations equally, but the American perspective on international conflicts is the only one investigated here. This is an important point, for the relationship between American law and international law is unclear and somewhat complicated. On the one hand, it is easy to find judicial assertions that, where a statute is ambiguous, it will be construed according to the presumption that Congress intended to act in accordance with the strictures of international law.** On the other, it is equally easy to find indications that where a clear inconsistency exists courts will honor a statute over an international norm.***

Another reason for difference in the international context is that constitutional limits might operate differently. Section C addresses whether and to what extent the Constitution limits congressional and presidential authority abroad. Finally, Section D addresses the consequences for the enforce-

---

* *See, e.g.*, Babcock v. Jackson, page 188 *supra;* Hurtado v, Superior Court, page 228 *supra.*

** *See* Schooner v. Charming Betsy, 6 U.S. 64, 80-81 (1804).

*** *See, e.g.*, The Chinese Exclusion Case, 130 U.S. 581 (1889) (Congress can violate treaties); Taveras-Lopez v. Reno, 127 F. Supp. 2d 598, 609 (M.D. Pa. 2000).

ment of foreign judgments of the fact that the full faith and credit clause imposes no obligation on states vis a vis foreign nations.

A. Act of State Doctrine and the Federal Common Law of Foreign Relations

Banco Nacional de Cuba v. Sabbatino

376 U.S. 398 (1964).

Mr. Justice HARLAN delivered the opinion of the Court.

[In July 1960, the Cuban government authorized the nationalization of the property of U.S. citizens in Cuba in response to an earlier U.S. reduction of Cuba's quota for sugar imports. Pursuant to this decree, the Cuban government expropriated sugar owned by a Cuban company, C.A.V., that was itself owned by U.S. residents. Farr, Whitlock & Co., a U.S. commodities broker, had previously contracted to purchase this sugar from C.A.V. on behalf of a client in Morocco. After the expropriation, Farr, Whitlock entered into a second purchase contract for the sugar with a Cuban governmental entity. The sugar was shipped and Farr, Whitlock received payment. Rather than transfer these proceeds to the Cuban government, Farr, Whitlock transferred them to Sabbatino, the New York court-appointed receiver of C.A.V.'s assets. Cuba transferred its rights in the sugar to Banco Nacional de Cuba, which sued to recover the sugar proceeds in federal court in New York. Sabbatino and Farr, Whitlock argued that Cuba never owned the sugar because its expropriation violated international law. Banco Nacional maintained in response that the act of state doctrine precluded the courts from inquiring into the validity of the Cuban expropriation. Both the district court and court of appeals ruled in favor of the defendants and declined to apply the act of state doctrine.]

The question which brought this case here, and is now found to be the dispositive issue, is whether the so-called act of state doctrine serves to sustain petitioner's claims in this litigation. . . .

IV

The classic American statement of the act of state doctrine, which appears to have taken root in England as early as 1674, and began to emerge in the jurisprudence of this country in the late eighteenth and early nineteenth centuries, is found in Underhill v. Hernandez, 168 U.S. 250, where Chief Justice Fuller said for a unanimous Court:

> Every sovereign State is bound to respect the independence of every other sovereign State, and the courts of one country will not sit in judgment on the acts of the government of another done within its own territory. Redress of grievances by reason of such acts must be obtained through the means open to be availed of by sovereign powers as between themselves.

. . . The outcome of this case . . . turns upon whether any of the contentions urged by respondents against the application of the act of state doctrine in the premises is acceptable: (1) that the doctrine does not apply to acts of state which violate international law, as is claimed to be the case here; (2) that the doctrine is inapplicable unless the Executive specifically interposes it in a particular case; and (3) that, in any event, the doctrine may not be invoked by a foreign government plaintiff in our courts.

V

Preliminarily, we discuss the foundations on which we deem the act of state doctrine to rest, and more particularly the question of whether state or federal law governs its application in a federal diversity case.[20]

We do not believe that this doctrine is compelled either by the inherent nature of sovereign authority, as some of the earlier decisions seem to imply, or by some principle of international law. If a transaction takes place in one jurisdiction and the forum is in another, the forum does not by dismissing an action or by applying its own law purport to divest the first jurisdiction of its territorial sovereignty; it merely declines to adjudicate or makes applicable its own law to parties or property before it. The refusal of one country to enforce the penal laws of another is a typical example of an instance when a court will not entertain a cause of action arising in another jurisdiction. While historic notions of sovereign authority do bear upon the wisdom of employing the act of state doctrine, they do not dictate its existence.

That international law does not require application of the doctrine is evidenced by the practice of nations. Most of the countries rendering decisions on the subject fail to follow the rule rigidly. No international arbitral or judicial decision discovered suggests that international law prescribes recognition of sovereign acts of foreign governments, and apparently no claim has ever been raised before an international tribunal that failure to apply the act of state doctrine constitutes a breach of international obligation. If international law does not prescribe use of the doctrine, neither does it forbid application of the rule even if it is claimed that the act of state in question violated international law. The traditional view of international law is that it

20. Although the complaint in this case alleged both diversity and federal question jurisdiction, the Court of Appeals reached jurisdiction only on the former ground. We need not decide, for reasons appearing hereafter, whether federal question jurisdiction also existed.

establishes substantive principles for determining whether one country has wronged another. Because of its peculiar nation-to-nation character the usual method for an individual to seek relief is to exhaust local remedies and then repair to the executive authorities of his own state to persuade them to champion his claim in diplomacy or before an international tribunal. . . . Although it is, of course, true that United States courts apply international law as a part of our own in appropriate circumstances, the public law of nations can hardly dictate to a country which is in theory wronged how to treat that wrong within its domestic borders.

Despite the broad statement in *Oetjen* [v. Central Leather Co., 246 U.S. 297 (1918)] that "The conduct of the foreign relations of our Government is committed by the Constitution to the Executive and Legislative . . . Departments," it cannot of course be thought that "every case or controversy which touches foreign relations lies beyond judicial cognizance." Baker v. Carr, 369 U.S. 186, 211. The text of the Constitution does not require the act of state doctrine; it does not irrevocably remove from the judiciary the capacity to review the validity of foreign acts of state.

The act of state doctrine does, however, have "constitutional" underpinnings. It arises out of the basic relationships between branches of government in a system of separation of powers. It concerns the competency of dissimilar institutions to make and implement particular kinds of decisions in the area of international relations. The doctrine as formulated in past decisions expresses the strong sense of the Judicial Branch that its engagement in the task of passing on the validity of foreign acts of state may hinder rather than further this country's pursuit of goals both for itself and for the community of nations as a whole in the international sphere. Many commentators disagree with this view; they have striven by means of distinguishing and limiting past decisions and by advancing various considerations of policy to stimulate a narrowing of the apparent scope of the rule. Whatever considerations are thought to predominate, it is plain that the problems involved are uniquely federal in nature. If federal authority, in this instance this Court, orders the field of judicial competence in this area for the federal courts, and the state courts are left free to formulate their own rules, the purposes behind the doctrine could be as effectively undermined as if there had been no federal pronouncement on the subject.

We could perhaps in this diversity action avoid the question of deciding whether federal or state law is applicable to this aspect of the litigation. New York has enunciated the act of state doctrine in terms that echo those of federal decisions decided during the reign of Swift v. Tyson, 16 Pet. 1. . . . Thus our conclusions might well be the same whether we dealt with this problem as one of state law, see Erie R. Co. v. Tompkins, 304 U.S. 64; Klaxon Co. v. Stentor Elec. Mfg. Co., 313 U.S. 487; . . . or federal law.

However, we are constrained to make it clear that an issue concerned with a basic choice regarding the competence and function of the Judiciary and the National Executive in ordering our relationships with other members of the international community must be treated exclusively as an aspect of federal law.[23] It seems fair to assume that the Court did not have rules like the act of state doctrine in mind when it decided Erie R. Co. v. Tompkins. Soon thereafter, Professor Philip C. Jessup, now a judge of the International Court of Justice, recognized the potential dangers were Erie extended to legal problems affecting international relations.[24] He cautioned that rules of international law should not be left to divergent and perhaps parochial state interpretations. His basic rationale is equally applicable to the act of state doctrine.

The Court in the pre-*Erie* act of state cases, although not burdened by the problem of the source of applicable law, used language sufficiently strong and broad-sweeping to suggest that state courts were not left free to develop their own doctrines (as they would have been had this Court merely been interpreting common law under Swift v. Tyson, *supra*). The Court of Appeals in the first *Bernstein* case, *supra,* a diversity suit, plainly considered the decisions of this Court, despite the intervention of *Erie,* to be controlling in regard to the act of state question, at the same time indicating that New York law governed other aspects of the case. We are not without other precedent for a determination that federal law governs; there are enclaves of federal judge-made law which bind the States. A national body of federal-court-built law has been held to have been contemplated by §301 of the Labor Management Relations Act, Textile Workers v. Lincoln Mills, 353 U.S. 448. Principles formulated by federal judicial law have been thought by this Court to be necessary to protect uniquely federal interests, D'Oench, Duhme & Co. v. Federal Deposit Ins. Corp., 315 U.S. 447; Clearfield Trust Co. v. United States, 318 U.S. 363. Of course the federal interest guarded in all these cases is one the ultimate statement of which is derived from a federal statute. Perhaps more directly in point are the bodies of law applied between States over boundaries and in regard to the apportionment of interstate waters.

In Hinderlider v. La Plata River Co., 304 U.S. 92, 110, in an opinion handed down the same day as *Erie* and by the same author, Mr. Justice Brandeis, the Court declared, "For whether the water of an interstate stream must be apportioned between the two States is a question of 'federal common law' upon which neither the statutes nor the decisions of either State can be conclusive." Although the suit was between two private litigants and the relevant States could not be made parties, the Court considered itself free to determine the effect of an interstate compact regulating water apportionment. The decision implies that no State can undermine the federal interest in equitably apportioned interstate waters even if it deals with private parties. This

23. At least this is true when the Court limits the scope of judicial inquiry. We need not now consider whether a state court might, in certain circumstances, adhere to a more restrictive view concerning the scope of examination of foreign acts than that required by this Court.

24. The Doctrine of Erie Railroad v. Tompkins Applied to International Law, 33 Am. J. Int'l L. 740 (1939).

would not mean that, absent a compact, the apportionment scheme could not be changed judicially or by Congress, but only that apportionment is a matter of federal law. *Cf.* Arizona v. California, 373 U.S. 546, 597-598. The problems surrounding the act of state doctrine are, albeit for different reasons, as intrinsically federal as are those involved in water apportionment or boundary disputes. The considerations supporting exclusion of state authority here are much like those which led the Court in United States v. California, 332 U.S. 19, to hold that the Federal Government possessed paramount rights in submerged lands though within the three-mile limit of coastal States. We conclude that the scope of the act of state doctrine must be determined according to federal law.[25]

VI

If the act of state doctrine is a principle of decision binding on federal and state courts alike but compelled by neither international law nor the Constitution, its continuing vitality depends on its capacity to reflect the proper distribution of functions between the judicial and political branches of the Government on matters bearing upon foreign affairs. It should be apparent that the greater the degree of codification or consensus concerning a particular area of international law, the more appropriate it is for the judiciary to render decisions regarding it, since the courts can then focus on the application of an agreed principle to circumstances of fact rather than on the sensitive task of establishing a principle not inconsistent with the national interest or with international justice. It is also evident that some aspects of international law touch much more sharply on national nerves than do others; the less important the implications of an issue are for our foreign relations, the weaker the justification for exclusivity in the political branches. The balance of relevant considerations may also be shifted if the government which perpetrated the challenged act of state is no longer in existence, as in the [Bernstein v. N. V. Nederlandsche-Amerikaansche Stoomvaart-Maatschappij, 173 F.2d 71 (2d Cir. 1949)], the political interest of this country may, as a result, be measurably altered. Therefore, rather than laying down or reaffirming an inflexible and all-encompassing rule in this case, we decide only that the Judicial Branch will not examine the validity of a taking of property within its own territory by a foreign sovereign government, extant and recognized by this country at the time of suit, in the absence of a treaty or

25. Various constitutional and statutory provisions indirectly support this determination, *see* U.S. Const., Art. I, §8, cls. 3, 10; Art. II, §§2, 3; Art. III, §2; 28 U. S. C. §§1251 (a)(2), (b)(1), (b)(3), 1332 (a)(2), 1333, 1350-1351, by reflecting a concern for uniformity in this country's dealings with foreign nations and indicating a desire to give matters of international significance to the jurisdiction of federal institutions. . . .

other unambiguous agreement regarding controlling legal principles, even if the complaint alleges that the taking violates customary international law.

There are few if any issues in international law today on which opinion seems to be so divided as the limitations on a state's power to expropriate the property of aliens. . . . The disagreement as to relevant international law standards reflects an even more basic divergence between the national interests of capital importing and capital exporting nations and between the social ideologies of those countries that favor state control of a considerable portion of the means of production and those that adhere to a free enterprise system. It is difficult to imagine the courts of this country embarking on adjudication in an area which touches more sensitively the practical and ideological goals of the various members of the community of nations.

. . . Following an expropriation of any significance, the Executive engages in diplomacy aimed to assure that United States citizens who are harmed are compensated fairly. Representing all claimants of this country, it will often be able, either by bilateral or multilateral talks, by submission to the United Nations, or by the employment of economic and political sanctions, to achieve some degree of general redress. Judicial determinations of invalidity of title can, on the other hand, have only an occasional impact, since they depend on the fortuitous circumstance of the property in question being brought into this country. Such decisions would, if the acts involved were declared invalid, often be likely to give offense to the expropriating country; since the concept of territorial sovereignty is so deep seated, any state may resent the refusal of the courts of another sovereign to accord validity to acts within its territorial borders. Piecemeal dispositions of this sort involving the probability of affront to another state could seriously interfere with negotiations being carried on by the Executive Branch and might prevent or render less favorable the terms of an agreement that could otherwise be reached. Relations with third countries which have engaged in similar expropriations would not be immune from effect. . . .

However offensive to the public policy of this country and its constituent States an expropriation of this kind may be, we conclude that both the national interest and progress toward the goal of establishing the rule of law among nations are best served by maintaining intact the act of state doctrine in this realm of its application.

VII

Finally, we must determine whether Cuba's status as a plaintiff in this case dictates a result at variance with the conclusions reached above. If the Court were to distinguish between suits brought by sovereign states and those of assignees, the rule would have little effect unless a careful examination were made in each case to determine if the private party suing had taken property in good faith. Such an inquiry would be exceptionally difficult, since the relevant transaction would almost invariably have occurred outside our borders. If such an investigation were deemed irrelevant, a state could always assign its claim.

Respondents offer another theory for treating the case differently because of Cuba's participation. It is claimed that the forum should simply apply its own law to all the relevant transactions. An analogy is drawn to the area of sovereign immunity, National City Bank v. Republic of China, 348 U.S. 356, in which, if a foreign country seeks redress in our courts, counterclaims are permissible. But immunity relates to the prerogative right not to have sovereign property subject to suit; fairness has been thought to require that when the sovereign seeks recovery, it be subject to legitimate counterclaims against it. The act of state doctrine, however, although it shares with the immunity doctrine a respect for sovereign states, concerns the limits for determining the validity of an otherwise applicable rule of law. It is plain that if a recognized government sued on a contract with a United States citizen, concededly legitimate by the locus of its making, performance, and most significant contacts, the forum would not apply its own substantive law of contracts. Since the act of state doctrine reflects the desirability of presuming the relevant transaction valid, the same result follows; the forum may not apply its local law regarding foreign expropriations.

Since the act of state doctrine proscribes a challenge to the validity of the Cuban expropriation decree in this case, any counterclaim based on asserted invalidity must fail. Whether a theory of conversion or breach of contract is the proper cause of action under New York law, the presumed validity of the expropriation is unaffected.

The judgment of the Court of Appeals is reversed and the case is remanded to the District Court for proceedings consistent with this opinion.

Mr. Justice White, dissenting

I am dismayed that the Court has, with one broad stroke, declared the ascertainment and application of international law beyond the competence of the courts of the United States in a large and important category of cases. I am also disappointed in the Court's declaration that the acts of a sovereign state with regard to the property of aliens within its borders are beyond the reach of international law in the courts of this country. However clearly established that law may be, a sovereign may violate it with impunity, except insofar as the political branches of the government may provide a remedy. This backward-looking doctrine, never before declared in this Court, is carried a disconcerting step further: not only are the courts powerless to question acts of state proscribed by international law but they are likewise powerless to refuse to adjudicate the claim founded upon a foreign law; they must render judgment and thereby validate the lawless act. Since the Court expressly extends its ruling to all acts of state expropriating property, however clearly inconsistent with the international community, all discriminatory expropriations of the property of aliens, as for example the taking of properties of persons belonging to certain races, religions or nationalities, are entitled to automatic validation in the courts of the United States. No other civilized country has found such a rigid rule necessary for the survival of the executive branch of its government; the executive of no other government seems to require such insulation from international law adjudications in its courts; and no other judiciary is apparently so incompetent to ascertain and apply international law. . . .

Questions and Comments

(1) At the time *Sabbatino* was decided, most courts would have applied the law of the place of the sugar at the time of transfer to determine ownership of the sugar. In *Sabbatino* this would presumably mean that Cuban law, including the Cuban expropriation decree, governed. Defendants in the lower courts in *Sabbatino* argued that giving effect to the allegedly illegal Cuban expropriation would violate local public policy. Since the act of state doctrine, as applied in *Sabbatino*, required U.S. courts to accept the validity of the foreign act of state, the doctrine can be viewed as "a special rule of conflicts denying the state of the forum its usual freedom to assert its own public policy and to refuse to apply the law of the state where a transaction 'occurred.' " Henkin, Foreign Affairs and the Constitution 413 n.33 (2d ed. 1996).

In this light, what are the implications of *Sabbatino* for choice of law generally? Does it require modification of *Klaxon*, reproduced *supra* page 577, in international cases? *See* Henkin, *id.* at 139 (*Sabbatino* authorizes federal courts to make federal choice-of-law rules in international cases); *see also* Chow, Limiting *Erie* in a New Age of International Law: Toward a Federal Common Law of International Choice of Law, 74 Iowa L. Rev. 165 (1988). In Day & Zimmerman, Inc. v. Challoner, 423 U.S. 3 (1975), the Supreme Court reaffirmed *Klaxon* in a diversity case involving an injury in Cambodia. The lower federal courts in Texas, sitting in diversity, had declined to apply Texas choice-of-law rules, which pointed to Cambodian substantive law. Instead, they applied a federal judge-made choice-of-law rule that selected Texas substantive law. The Supreme Court reversed, reasoning: "A federal court in a diversity case is not free to engraft onto those state rules exceptions or modifications which may commend themselves to the federal court, but which have not commended themselves to the State in which the federal court sits." 423 U.S. at 4.

Can *Sabbatino* be reconciled with *Challoner?* Is there room for federal choice-of-law rules in international cases after *Challoner?* Or is the act of state doctrine unique, perhaps because of the federal separation of powers issues it raises?

(2) *Sabbatino* holds that the act of state doctrine is a rule of federal common law binding on the states. What is the constitutional basis for this holding? What did the court mean when it said that although the "text of the Constitution" does not require the act of state doctrine, the doctrine nonethe-

less has " 'constitutional' underpinnings"? For analysis sympathetic to the federal common law of foreign relations announced in *Sabbatino,* see Brilmayer, Federalism, State Authority, and the Preemptive Power of International Law, 1994 Sup. Ct. Rev. 295; Clark, Federal Common Law: A Structural Reinterpretation, 144 Penn. L. Rev. 1245, 1292 (1996); Moore, Federalism and Foreign Relations, 1965 Duke L.J. 248. For critical commentary, see Goldsmith, Federal Courts, Foreign Affairs, and Federalism, 83 Va. L. Rev. 1617 (1997); Henkin, The Foreign Affairs Power of the Federal Courts: *Sabbatino,* 64 Colum. L. Rev. 805 (1964).

(3) Professor Henkin's treatise asserts that "*Sabbatino* establishes foreign affairs as a domain in which federal courts can make law with supremacy." *See* Henkin, Foreign Affairs and the Constitution, *supra,* at 139. But what precisely is the category of "foreign affairs"? As globalization proceeds apace, don't an increasing array of issues affect foreign affairs? Should international contracts be governed by a federal common law of foreign relations? International adoption? A tort case involving a foreign party? Should courts place special federal limits on the death penalty because it is so frequently the subject of foreign protests? If you answer "no" to any of these questions, how do you think courts should determine whether implications for U.S. foreign relations are sufficiently serious as to implicate the federal common law of foreign relations? And how do courts tell what federal rule will best serve U.S. foreign relations interests? Aren't the determinations required by the federal common law of foreign relations "of a kind in which the Judiciary has neither the aptitude, facilities nor responsibility and which has long been held to belong in the domain of political power not subject to judicial intrusion or inquiry," Chicago & Southern Airlines, Inc. v. Waterman Corp., 333 U.S. 103, 111 (1947)? How should courts resolve the tension between the federalism component of the federal common law of foreign relations (federal v. state authority) and the separation of powers component (federal political branch v. federal court authority)?

(4) Some courts have invoked *Sabbatino* in ruling that substantive law issues in international litigation implicate the federal common law of foreign relations. *See, e.g.,* Torres v. Southern Peru Copper Corp., 113 F.3d 540, 543 (5th Cir. 1997) (Peruvian citizens' state law tort suit against U.S. and alien corporations, including Peru's largest mining company, "raises substantial questions of federal common law by implicating important foreign policy concerns" and thus warrants removal to federal court); Republic of Phillippines v. Marcos, 806 F.2d 344, 354 (2d Cir. 1986) (common law conversion suit against Ferdinand Marcos and his associates "arises under federal common law because of necessary implications of such action for United States foreign policy"). *Torres* concluded that federal common law governed in order to remove a case from state court, only to dismiss it on grounds of forum non conveniens. *See also* Sequihua v. Texaco Inc., 847 F. Supp. 61, 62-63 (S.D. Tex. 1994); Kern v. Jepperson Sandersen, Inc., 867 F. Supp. 525, 532, 537-538 (S.D. Tex. 1994); *compare* Pacheco de Perez v. AT&T Co., 139 F.

3d 1368, 1377 (11th Cir. 1998) (noting that "where a state law action has as a substantial element an issue involving foreign relations or foreign policy matters, federal jurisdiction is present" but concluding that suit brought by Venezuelan citizens injured in a pipeline explosion did not affect American foreign policy); *but see* Patrickson v. Dole Food Co., 251 F.3d 795 (9th Cir. 2001) (criticizing this line of cases as misreadings of *Sabbatino* and inappropriate circumventions of the well-pleaded complaint rule).

(5) In Zschernig v. Miller, 389 U.S. 429 (1968), the Supreme Court invalidated an Oregon statute that denied inheritance to an East German who could not establish reciprocal inheritance rights for Americans under German law. The Court determined that the state statute had a direct impact upon foreign relations and may well adversely affect the power of the central government to deal with those problems, *id.* at 441, and concluded that it was an "intrusion by the state into the field of foreign affairs which the Constitution entrusts to the President and Congress," *id.* at 432. *Zschernig* is viewed as establishing a doctrine of "dormant foreign affairs preemption" in which federal courts preempt state law that intrudes on the exclusive federal foreign relations power even in the absence of affirmative federal legislation. What is the relationship between the federal common holding of *Sabbatino* and *Zschernig*'s dormant foreign affairs preemption doctrine? *Compare* Henkin, *supra,* at 139-140; 162-165 (federal common law created in *Sabbatino* is the exercise of a "legislative" power in the federal judiciary, while dormant foreign affairs preemption is a species of structural constitutional preemption) *with* Goldsmith, *supra,* at 1630 (the two decisions involve functionally identical judicial lawmaking powers because both decisions (a) assert that the Constitution's assignment of foreign relations powers to the federal government entails a self-executing exclusion of state authority; (b) justify preemption as needed to protect political branch prerogatives in foreign relations; and (c) are ultimately subject to congressional revision).

(6) In Barclays Bank PLC v. Franchise Tax Board of California, 512 U.S 298 (1994), the plaintiffs sought to invalidate California's method for taxing multinational corporations, arguing (in reliance on *Zschernig*) that the statute "impair[ed] federal uniformity in an area where federal uniformity is essential" by "preventing the federal government from speaking with one-voice in international trade." *Id.* at 320. The Court rejected the claim, reasoning in part that that courts have no authority to identify these effects and weigh them against the competing legitimate interests of states. *Id.* at 328 (plaintiffs claim of potential retaliation by trading partners "directed to the wrong forum" because "the judiciary is not vested with the power to decide how to balance a particular sovereign risk of retaliation against the sovereign right of the United States as a whole to let the States tax as they please.") Instead, the Court emphasized, it was the job of "Congress—whose voice, in this area, is the Nation's—to evaluate whether the national interest is best served by tax uniformity, or state autonomy." *Id.* at 331. Does the reasoning of *Barclay's Bank* undermine the federalism logic of *Sabbatino* and *Zschernig? Compare* Gold-

smith, *supra,* at 1701 (arguing that it does) *with* Koh, Is International Law Really State Law?, 111 Harv. L. Rev. 1824, 1848-1849 (1998) (arguing that it doesn't).

B. Extraterritoriality of Federal Statutes

1. Territorialism

EEOC v. Arabian American Oil Co.

499 U.S. 244 (1991)

Chief Justice REHNQUIST delivered the opinion of the Court.

These cases present the issue whether Title VII applies extraterritorially to regulate the employment practices of United States employers who employ United States citizens abroad. The United States Court of Appeals for the Fifth Circuit held that it does not, and we agree with that conclusion.

Petitioner Boureslan is a naturalized United States citizen who was born in Lebanon. The respondents are two Delaware corporations, Arabian American Oil Company (Aramco), and its subsidiary, Aramco Service Company (ASC). Aramco's principal place of business is Dhahran, Saudi Arabia, and it is licensed to do business in Texas. ASC's principal place of business is Houston, Texas.

In 1979, Boureslan was hired by ASC as a cost engineer in Houston. A year later he was transferred, at his request, to work for Aramco in Saudi Arabia. Boureslan remained with Aramco in Saudi Arabia until he was discharged in 1984. After filing a charge of discrimination with the Equal Employment Opportunity Commission (EEOC or Commission), he instituted this suit in the United States District Court for the Southern District of Texas against Aramco and ASC. He sought relief under both state law and Title VII of the Civil Rights Act of 1964, 42 U.S.C. §§2000e-2000e-17, on the ground that he was harassed and ultimately discharged by respondents on account of his race, religion, and national origin.

Respondents filed a motion for summary judgment on the ground that the District Court lacked subject-matter jurisdiction over Boureslan's claim because the protections of Title VII do not extend to United States citizens employed abroad by American employers. The District Court agreed and dismissed Boureslan's Title VII claim; it also dismissed his state-law claims for lack of pendent jurisdiction and entered final judgment in favor of respondents. A panel for the Fifth Circuit affirmed. After vacating the panel's decision and rehearing the case en banc, the court affirmed the District Court's dismissal of Boureslan's complaint. Both Boureslan and the EEOC petitioned for certiorari. We granted both petitions for certiorari to resolve this important issue of statutory interpretation.

Both parties concede, as they must, that Congress has the authority to enforce its laws beyond the territorial boundaries of the United States. Whether Congress has in fact exercised that authority in this case is a matter of statutory construction. It is our task to determine whether Congress intended the protections of Title VII to apply to United States citizens employed by American employers outside of the United States.

It is a longstanding principle of American law "that legislation of Congress, unless a contrary intent appears, is meant to apply only within the territorial jurisdiction of the United States." Foley Bros., Inc. v. Filardo, 336 U.S. 281, 285 (1949). This "canon of construction . . . is a valid approach whereby unexpressed congressional intent may be ascertained." *Ibid.* It serves to protect against unintended clashes between our laws and those of other nations which could result in international discord. *See* McCulloch v. Sociedad Nacional de Marineros de Honduras, 372 U.S. 10, 20-22 (1963).

In applying this rule of construction, we look to see whether "language in the [relevant Act] gives any indication of a congressional purpose to extend its coverage beyond places over which the United States has sovereignty or has some measure of legislative control." *Foley Bros., supra,* at 285. We assume that Congress legislates against the backdrop of the presumption against extraterritoriality. Therefore, unless there is "the affirmative intention of the Congress clearly expressed," *Benz, supra,* at 147, we must presume it "is primarily concerned with domestic conditions." *Foley Bros., supra,* at 285.

Boureslan and the EEOC contend that the language of Title VII evinces a clearly expressed intent on behalf of Congress to legislate extraterritorially. They rely principally on two provisions of the statute. First, petitioners argue that the statute's definitions of the jurisdictional terms "employer" and "commerce" are sufficiently broad to include United States firms that employ American citizens overseas. Second, they maintain that the statute's "alien exemption" clause, 42 U.S.C. §2000e-1, necessarily implies that Congress intended to protect American citizens from employment discrimination abroad. Petitioners also contend that we should defer to the EEOC's consistently held position that Title VII applies abroad. We conclude that petitioners' evidence, while not totally lacking in probative value, falls short of demonstrating the affirmative congressional intent required to extend the protections of Title VII beyond our territorial borders.

Title VII prohibits various discriminatory employment practices based on an individual's race, color, religion, sex, or national origin. *See* §§2000e-2, 2000e-3. An employer is subject to Title VII if it has employed 15 or more employees for a specified period and is "engaged in an industry affecting commerce." An industry affecting commerce is "any activity, business, or industry in commerce or in which a labor dispute would hinder or obstruct commerce or the free flow of commerce and includes any activity or industry 'affecting commerce' within the meaning of the Labor-Management Reporting and Disclosure Act of 1959 [(LMRDA)] [29 U.S.C. 401 et seq.]." §2000e(h). "Commerce," in turn, is defined as "trade, traffic, commerce, transportation, transmission, or communication among the several States; or between a State and any place outside thereof; or within the District of Columbia, or a possession of the United States; or between points in the same State but through a point outside thereof." §2000e(g).

Petitioners argue that by its plain language, Title VII's "broad jurisdictional language" reveals Congress's intent to extent the statute's protections to employment discrimination anywhere in the world by a United States employer who affects trade "between a State and any place outside thereof." More precisely, they assert that since Title VII defines "States" to include States, the District of Columbia, and specified territories, the clause "between a State and any place outside thereof" must be referring to areas beyond the territorial limit of the United States.

Respondents offer several alternative explanations for the statute's expansive language. They contend that the "or between a State and any place outside thereof" clause "provides the jurisdictional nexus required to regulate commerce that is not wholly within a single state, presumably as it affects both interstate and foreign commerce" but not to "regulate conduct exclusively *within* a foreign country." They also argue that since the definitions of the terms "employer," "commerce," and "industry affecting commerce" make no mention of "commerce with foreign nations," Congress cannot be said to have intended that the statute apply overseas. In support of this argument, petitioners point to Title II of the Civil Rights Act of 1964, governing public accommodation, which specifically defines commerce as it applies to foreign nations. Finally, respondents argue that while language present in the first bill considered by the House of Representatives contained the terms "foreign commerce" and "foreign nations," those terms were deleted by the Senate before the Civil Rights Act of 1964 was passed. They conclude that these deletions "[are] inconsistent with the notion of a clearly expressed congressional intent to apply Title VII extraterritorially."

We need not choose between these competing interpretations as we would be required to do in the absence of the presumption against extraterritorial application discussed above. Each is plausible, but no more persuasive than that. The language relied upon by petitioners—and it is they who must make the affirmative showing—is ambiguous, and does not speak directly to the question presented here. The intent of Congress as to the extraterritorial application of this statute must be deduced by inference from boilerplate language which can be found in any number of congressional Acts, none of which have ever been held to apply overseas.

Petitioners' reliance on Title VII's jurisdictional provisions also finds no support in our case law; we have repeatedly held that even statutes that contain broad language in their definitions of "commerce" that expressly refer to "*foreign* commerce" do not apply abroad.

The EEOC places great weight on an assertedly similar "broad jurisdictional grant in the Lanham Act" that this Court held applied extraterritorially in Steele v. Bulova Watch Co., 344 U.S. 280, 286 (1952). In *Steele,* we addressed whether the Lanham Act, designed to prevent deceptive and misleading use of trademarks, applied to acts of a United States citizen consummated in Mexico. The Act defined commerce as "all commerce which may lawfully be regulated by Congress." 15 U.S.C. §1127. The stated intent of the statute was "to regulate commerce within the control of Congress by making actionable the deceptive and misleading use of marks in such commerce." *Ibid.* While recognizing that "the legislation of Congress will not extend beyond the boundaries of the United States unless a contrary legislative intent appears," the Court concluded that in light of the fact that the allegedly unlawful conduct had some effects within the United States, coupled with the Act's "broad jurisdictional grant" and its "sweeping reach into 'all commerce which may lawfully be regulated by Congress,' " the statute was properly interpreted as applying abroad. *Steele, supra,* at 285, 287.

The EEOC's attempt to analogize these cases to *Steele* is unpersuasive. The Lanham Act by its terms applies to "all commerce which may lawfully be regulated by Congress." The Constitution gives Congress the power "to regulate Commerce with foreign Nations, and among the several States, and with the Indian Tribes." U.S. Const., Art. I, §8, cl. 3. Since the Act expressly stated that it applied to the extent of Congress' power over commerce, the Court in *Steele* concluded that Congress intended that the statute apply abroad. By contrast, Title VII's more limited, boilerplate "commerce" language does not support such an expansive construction of congressional intent. Moreover, unlike the language in the Lanham Act, Title VII's definition of "commerce" was derived expressly from the LMRDA, a statute that this Court had held, prior to the enactment of Title VII, did not apply abroad. *McCulloch, supra,* at 15.

Thus petitioner's argument based on the jurisdictional language of Title VII fails both as a matter of statutory language and of our previous case law. Many Acts of Congress are based on the authority of that body to regulate commerce among the several States, and the parts of these Acts setting forth the basis for legislative jurisdiction will obviously refer to such commerce in one way or another. If we were to permit possible, or even plausible, interpretations of language such as that involved here to override the presumption against extraterritorial application, there would be little left of the presumption.

Petitioners argue that Title VII's "alien exemption provision," 42 U.S.C. §2000e-1, "clearly manifests an intention" by Congress to protect United States citizens with respect to their employment outside of the United States. The alien-exemption provision says that the statute "shall not apply to an employer with respect to the employment of aliens outside any State." Petitioners contend that from this language a negative inference should be drawn that Congress intended Title VII to cover United States *citizens* working abroad for United States employers. There is "no other plausible explanation that the alien exemption exists," they argue, because "if Congress believed that the statute did not apply extraterritorially, it would have had no reason to include an exemption for a certain category of individuals employed outside the United States." Since "the statute's jurisdictional provisions cannot possibly be read to confer coverage only upon aliens employed outside the United States," petitioners conclude that "Congress could not rationally have enacted an exemption for the employment of aliens abroad if it intended to foreclose *all* potential extraterritorial applications of the statute."

Respondents resist petitioners' interpretation of the alien-exemption provision and assert two alternative *raisons d'etre* for that language. First, they contend that since aliens are included in the statute's definition of employee[1] and the definition of commerce includes possessions as well as "States," the purpose of the exemption is to provide that employers of aliens in the possessions of the United States are not covered by the statute. Thus, the "outside any State" clause means outside any State, but within the control of the United States. Respondents argue that "this reading of the alien exemption provision is consistent with and supported by the historical development of the provision." . . . Second, respondents assert that by negative implication, the exemption "confirms the coverage of aliens in the United States."

If petitioners are correct that the alien-exemption clause means that the statute applies to employers overseas, we see no way of distinguishing in its application between United States employers and foreign employers. Thus, a French employer of a United States citizen in France would be subject to Title VII—a result at which even petitioners balk. The EEOC assures us that in its view the term "employer" means only "American employer," but there is no such distinction in this statute and no indication that the EEOC in the normal course of its administration had produced a reasoned basis for such a distinction. Without clearer evidence of congressional intent to do so than is contained in the alien-exemption clause, we are unwilling to ascribe to that body a policy which would raise difficult issues of international law by imposing this country's employment-discrimination regime upon foreign corporations operating in foreign commerce.

This conclusion is fortified by the other elements in the statute suggesting a purely domestic focus. The statute as a whole indicates a concern that it not unduly interfere with the sovereignty and laws of the States. *See,*

---

1. Title VII defines "employee" as: "an individual employed by an employer, except that the term 'employee' shall not include any person elected to public office in any State or political subdivision of any State by the qualified voters thereof, or any person chosen by such officer to be on such officer's personal staff, or an appointee on the policy making level or an immediate adviser with respect to the exercise of the constitutional or legal powers of the office. The exemption set forth in the preceding sentence shall not include employees subject to the civil service laws of a State government, governmental agency or political subdivision." 42 U.S.C. §2000e(f).

e.g., 42 U.S.C. §2000h-4 (stating that the Act should not be construed to exclude the operation of state law or invalidate any state law unless inconsistent with the purposes of the Act); §2000e-5 (requiring the EEOC to accord substantial weight to findings of state or local authorities in proceedings under state or local law); §2000e-7 (providing that nothing in Title VII shall affect the application of state or local law unless such law requires or permits practices that would be unlawful under Title VII); §§2000e-5(c), (d), and (e) (provisions addressing deferral to state discrimination proceedings). While Title VII consistently speaks in terms of "States" and state proceedings, it fails even to mention foreign nations or foreign proceedings.

Similarly, Congress failed to provide any mechanisms for overseas enforcement of Title VII.

It is also reasonable to conclude that had Congress intended Title VII to apply overseas, it would have addressed the subject of conflicts with foreign laws and procedures. In amending the Age Discrimination in Employment Act of 1967 (ADEA), 29 U.S.C. §621 et seq., to apply abroad, Congress specifically addressed potential conflicts with foreign law by providing that it is not unlawful for an employer to take any action prohibited by the ADEA "where such practices involve an employee in a workplace in a foreign country, and compliance with [the ADEA] would cause such employer . . . to violate the laws of the country in which such workplace is located." §623(f)(1). Title VII, by contrast, fails to address conflicts with the laws of other nations.

Our conclusion today is buttressed by the fact that "when it desires to do so, Congress knows how to place the high seas within the jurisdictional reach of a statute." Argentine Republic v. Amerada Hess Shipping Corp., 488 U.S. 428, 440 (1989). Congress' awareness of the need to make a clear statement that a statute applies overseas is amply demonstrated by the numerous occasions on which it has expressly legislated the extraterritorial application of a statute. . . . Indeed, after several courts had held that the ADEA did not apply overseas, Congress amended § 11(f) to provide: "The term 'employee' includes any individual who is a citizen of the United States employed by an employer in a workplace in a foreign country." 29 U.S.C. § 630(f). . . . The expressed purpose of these changes was to "make provisions of the Act apply to citizens of the United States employed in foreign countries by U.S. corporations or their subsidiaries." S. Rep. No. 98-467, p.2 (1984). Congress, should it wish to do so, may similarly amend Title VII and in doing so will be able to calibrate its provisions in a way that we cannot.

Petitioners have failed to present sufficient affirmative evidence that Congress intended Title VII to apply abroad. Accordingly, the judgment of the Court of Appeals is

Affirmed.

Justice MARSHALL, with whom Justice BLACKMUN and Justice STEVENS join, dissenting.

Like any issue of statutory construction, the question whether Title VII protects United States citizens from discrimination by United States employers abroad turns solely on congressional intent. As the majority recognizes, our inquiry into congressional intent in this setting is informed by the traditional "canon of construction which teaches that legislation of Congress, unless a contrary intent appears, is meant to apply only within the territorial jurisdiction of the United States." Foley Bros., Inc. v. Filardo, 336 U.S. 281, 285 (1949). But contrary to what one would conclude from the majority's analysis, this canon is *not* a "clear statement" rule, the application of which relieves a court of the duty to give effect to all available indicia of the legislative will. Rather, as our case law applying the presumption against extraterritoriality well illustrates, a court may properly rely on this presumption only after exhausting all of the traditional tools "whereby unexpressed congressional intent may be ascertained." *Ibid.* When these tools are brought to bear on the issue in this case, the conclusion is inescapable that Congress *did* intend Title VII to protect United States citizens from discrimination by United States employers operating overseas. Consequently, I dissent.

I

Because it supplies the driving force of the majority's analysis, I start with "the canon . . . that legislation of Congress, unless a contrary intent appears, is meant to apply only within the territorial jurisdiction of the United States." *Ibid.* The majority recasts this principle as "the need to make *a clear statement* that a statute applies overseas." *Ante,* at 258 (emphasis added). So conceived, the presumption against extraterritoriality allows the majority to derive meaning from various instances of statutory silence—from Congress' failure, for instance, "to mention foreign nations or foreign proceedings," ante, at 256, "to provide any mechanisms for overseas enforcement," *ibid.*, or to "address the subject of conflicts with foreign laws and procedures," *ante,* at 256. At other points, the majority relies on its reformulation of the presumption to avoid the "need [to] choose between . . . competing interpretations" of affirmative statutory language that the majority concludes "does not speak *directly* to the question" of extraterritoriality. *Ante,* at 250 (emphasis added). In my view, the majority grossly distorts the effect of this rule of construction upon conventional techniques of statutory interpretation.

. . . The presumption against extraterritoriality is *not* a "clear statement" rule. Clear-statement rules operate less to reveal *actual* congressional intent than to shield important values from an *insufficiently strong* legislative intent to displace them. When they apply, such rules foreclose inquiry into extrinsic guides to interpretation, and even compel courts to select less plausible candidates from within the range of permissible constructions. The Court's analysis in *Foley Brothers* was by no means so narrowly constrained. Indeed, the Court considered the entire range of conventional sources "whereby *unexpressed* congressional intent may be ascertained." Subsequent applications of the presumption against extraterritoriality confirm that we have not imposed the drastic clear-statement burden upon Congress before giving effect to its intention that a particular enactment apply beyond the national boundaries.

II

A

Confirmation that Congress did *in fact* expect Title VII's central prohibition to have an extraterritorial reach is supplied by the so-called "alien exemption" provision. The alien-exemption provision states that Title VII "shall not apply to an employer with respect to the employment of aliens *outside any State*." 42 U.S.C. §2000e-1 (emphasis added). Absent an intention that Title VII *apply* "outside any State," Congress would have had no reason to craft this extraterritorial exemption. And because only discrimination against aliens is exempted, employers remain accountable for discrimination against United States citizens abroad.

The inference arising from the alien-exemption provision is more than sufficient to rebut the presumption against extraterritoriality.

Notwithstanding the basic rule of construction requiring courts to give effect to all of the statutory language, the majority never advances an alternative explanation of the alien-exemption provision that is consistent with the majority's own conclusion that Congress intended Title VII to have a purely domestic focus. The closest that the majority comes to attempting to give meaning to the alien-exemption provision is to identify without endorsement "two alternative *raisons d'etre* for that language" offered by respondents. Neither of these explanations is even minimally persuasive.

IV

In the hands of the majority, the presumption against extraterritoriality is transformed from a "valid approach whereby unexpressed congressional intent may be ascertained," *Foley Bros.*, 336 U.S., at 285, into a barrier to any genuine inquiry into the sources that reveal Congress' actual intentions. Because the language, history, and administrative interpretations of the statute all support application of Title VII to United States companies employing United States citizens abroad, I dissent.

Questions and Comments

(1) Note that the Court considers only whether or not U.S. law applies; it never considers application of Saudi Arabian law. This *unilateral* conflicts methodology contrasts with the *multilateral* approaches we saw in most of the

choice-of-law cases in Chapters 1 and 2, in which the court considers both local law and foreign law and chooses among them. Is there any reason why a court would invoke a unilateral methodology in cases involving federal law conflicts with foreign law? Is this phenomenon related to the penal law taboo discussed *supra* page 166? Does it have something to do with not wanting to offend a foreign sovereign by misapplying its law? Does the Court not consider Saudi Arabian law out of deference to the U.S. political branches? Is it better to resolve the applicability of American law unilaterally, or with reference to the laws and interests of other states?

For analysis of these issues see McConnaughay, Reviving the "Public Law Taboo" in International Conflict of Laws, 35 Stan. J Int'l L. 255 (1999); Dodge, Extraterritoriality and Conflict-of-Laws Theory: An Argument for Judicial Unilateralism, 39 Harv. Int'l L.J. 101 (1998); Weintraub, The Extraterritorial Application of Antitrust and Securities Laws: An Inquiry Into the Utility of a "Choice-of-Law" Approach, 70 Tex. L. Rev. 1799 (1992); Brilmayer, The Extraterritorial Application of American Law: A Methodological and Constitutional Appraisal, 50 Law & Contemp. Probs. 11 (1987); Lowenfeld, Public Law in the International Arena: Conflict of Laws, International Law, and Some Suggestions for Their Interaction, II Recueil des Cours 311 (1979).

(2) *Arabian American Oil* seems to rely on the same reasoning as the *Carroll* case, which stated at page 4 *supra*, that "universally recognized principles of private international or interstate law" hold that legislation applies only to local events. Is *Arabian American Oil* simply an artifact of outmoded territorialist thinking? Commentators who believe so include Born, A Reappraisal of the Extraterritorial Reach of U.S. Law, 24 Law & Pol'y Int'l Bus. 1 (1992); Kramer, Vestiges of Beale: Extraterritorial Application of American Law, 1991 S. Ct. Rev. 179 (1991). Professor Bradley disagrees. He maintains that the presumption against extraterritoriality is a legitimate approach to statutory construction grounded not (directly) in old territorial assumptions, but rather in separation of powers principles such as a judicial desire not to impinge on political branch prerogatives by violating international law or causing foreign relations controversy. *See* Bradley, Territorial Intellectual Property Rights in an Age of Globalism, 37 Va. J. Int'l L. 505, 550-561 (1997). Does this reasoning translate into domestic interstate cases like *Carroll?*

(3) The presumption against extraterritoriality has a distinguished history and continued relevance for many areas of federal substantive law. Consider the following cases:

(a) New York Central Railroad v. Chisholm, 268 U.S. 29 (1925), construing the Federal Employers Liability Act as "presumptively territorial." *See also* Boak v. Consolidated Rail Corp., 850 F.2d 110 (2d Cir. 1988).

(b) Foley Bros. Inc. v. Filardo, 336 U.S. 281 (1949), applying the eight-hour employment law territorially because: "The canon on construction which teaches that legislation of Congress, unless a contrary intent appears, is meant to apply only within the territorial jurisdiction of the United States, is a valid approach whereby unexpressed congressional intent may be ascertained. It is based on the assumption that Congress is primarily concerned with domestic conditions."

(c) McCulloch v. Sociedad Nacional de Marineros de Honduras, 372 U.S. 10, 19-22 (1963), holding that the National Labor Relations Act does not apply to the maritime operations of foreign-flag ships employing alien seamen. *See also* Benz v. Compania Naviera Hidalgo, S.A., 353 U.S. 138, 143-146 (1957).

(d) United States v. Palmer, 16 U.S. 610 (1818), ruling that a federal piracy statute did not to extend to robbery committed on the high seas by foreign citizens on board a foreign ship even though the statute purported to cover "any person or persons." Mere "general words" should not be construed to cover the conduct of foreign citizens outside U.S. territory.

(e) Smith v. United States, 507 U.S. 197 (1993), limiting the reach of the Federal Tort Claims Act in a case involving a tort that occurred in Antarctica. *But compare* Environmental Defense Fund v. Massey, 986 F.2d 528 (D.C. Cir. 1993), applying the National Environmental Policy Act's requirement of an environmental impact statement to the National Science Foundation's plan to incinerate waste in Antarctica.

(f) Amlon Metals, Inc., v. FMC Corp. 775 F. Supp. 668 (S.D.N. Y. 1991), interpreting the Resource Conservation and Recovery Act not to apply to toxic waste problem in Great Britain.

(g) Reyes-Gaona v. N.C. Growers Assn., 250 F.3d 861 (4th Cir. 2001), which held that the Age Discrimination in Employment Act did not apply to foreign nationals who apply in foreign countries for jobs in the United States.

(h) Twin Books Corp. v. Walt Disney Co., 83 F.3d 1162 (9th Cir. 1996), holding that the 1909 Copyright Act did not apply extraterritorially, and thus that a work first published outside of the United States was required under the 1909 Act to bear a copyright notice in order to claim copyright protection within the United States.

(4) The presumption against extraterritoriality is not irrebuttable. In Vermilya-Brown Co. v. Connell, 335 U.S. 377 (1948), the Court applied the Fair Labor Standards Act to employees of a contractor building a military installation on land in Bermuda held on a ninety-nine-year lease from the United Kingdom. And in Steele v. Bulova Watch Co., 344 U.S. 280 (1952), the Lanham Act was held applicable to the activities in Mexico of an American citizen. *Compare* Blackmer v. United States, 284 U.S., 421 (1932), which upheld federal subpoena power against an American residing abroad. *Steele* and *Vermilya-Brown* did not dispute the general validity of the territoriality

presumption, but rather found evidence of congressional intent sufficient to rebut it. And in *Steele,* some of the relevant activities had occurred in the United States, although the mark "Bulova" was not there affixed to the watches at issue.

2. Contacts and Effects

Lauritzen v. Larsen

345 U.S. 571 (1953)

Justice JACKSON delivered the opinion of the Court.

The key issue in this case is whether statutes of the United States should be applied to this claim of maritime tort. Larsen, a Danish seaman, while temporarily in New York joined the crew of the *Randa,* a ship of Danish flag and registry, owned by petitioner, a Danish citizen. Larsen signed ship's articles, written in Danish, providing that the rights of crew members would be governed by Danish law and by the employer's contract with the Danish Seamen's Union, of which Larsen was a member. He was negligently injured aboard the *Randa* in the course of employment, while in Havana harbor.

Respondent brought suit under the Jones Act on the law side of the District Court for the Southern District of New York and demanded a jury. Petitioner contended that Danish law was applicable and that, under it, respondent had received all of the compensation to which he was entitled. He also contested the court's jurisdiction. Entertaining the cause, the court ruled that American rather than Danish law applied, and the jury rendered a verdict of $4,267.50. The court of Appeals, Second Circuit, affirmed. Its decision, at least superficially, is at variance with its own earlier ones and conflicts with one by the New York Court of Appeals. We granted certiorari. . . .

Respondent does not deny that Danish law is applicable to his case. The contention as stated in his brief is rather that "A claimant may select whatever forum he desires and receive the benefits resulting from such choice" and "A ship owner is liable under the laws of the forum where he does business as well as in his own country." This contention that the Jones Act provides an optional cumulative remedy is not based on any explicit terms of the Act, which makes no provision for cases in which remedies have been obtained or are obtainable under foreign law. Rather he relies upon the literal catholicity of its terminology. If read literally, Congress has conferred an American right of action which requires nothing more than that plaintiff be "any seaman who shall suffer personal injury in the course of his employment." It makes no explicit requirement that either the seaman, the employment or the injury have the slightest connection with the United States. Unless some relationship of one or more of these to our national interest is implied, Congress has extended our law and opened our courts to all alien seafaring men injured anywhere in the world in service of watercraft of every foreign nation—a hand on a Chinese junk, never outside Chinese waters, would not be beyond its literal wording.

But Congress in 1920 wrote these all-comprehending words, not on a clean slate, but as a postscript to a long series of enactments governing shipping. All were enacted with regard to a seasoned body of maritime law developed by the experience of American courts long accustomed to dealing with admiralty problems in reconciling our own with foreign interests and in accommodating the reach of our own laws to those of other maritime nations.

The shipping laws of the United States, set forth in Title 46 of the United States Code, comprise a patchwork of separate enactments, some tracing far back in our history and many designed for particular emergencies. While some have been specific in application to foreign shipping and others in being confined to American shipping, many give no evidence that Congress addressed itself to their foreign application and are in general terms which leave their application to be judicially determined from context and circumstances. By usage as old as the Nation, such statutes have been construed to apply only to areas and transactions in which American law would be considered operative under prevalent doctrines of international law. Thus, in United States v. Palmer, 3 Wheat. 610, this Court was called upon to interpret a statute of 1790 (1 Stat. 115) punishing certain acts when committed on the high seas by "any person or persons," terms which, as Mr. Chief Justice Marshall observed, are "broad enough to comprehend every human being." But the Court determined that the literal universality of the prohibition "must not only be limited to cases within the jurisdiction of the state, but also to those objects to which the legislature intended to apply them" (p.631) and therefore would not reach a person performing the proscribed acts aboard the ship of a foreign state on the high seas.

This doctrine of construction is in accord with the long-heeded admonition of Mr. Chief Justice Marshall that "an act of congress ought never to be construed to violate the law of nations if any other possible construction remains. . . ." The Charming Betsy, 2 Cranch 64, 118. *See* The Nereide, 9 Cranch 388, 423; MacLeod v. United States, 229 U.S. 416, 434; Sandberg v. McDonald, 248 U.S. 185, 195. And it has long been accepted in maritime jurisprudence that ". . . if any construction otherwise be possible, an Act will not be construed as applying to foreigners in respect to acts done by them outside the dominions of the sovereign power enacting. That is a rule based on international law by which one sovereign power is bound to respect the subjects and the rights of all other sovereign powers outside its own territory." Lord Russell of Killowen in The Queen v. Jameson, [1896] 2 Q.B. 425, 430. This is not, as sometimes is implied, any impairment of our own sovereignty, or limitation of the power of Congress. "The law of the sea," we have had occasion to observe, "is in a peculiar sense an international law, but application of its specific rules depends upon acceptance by the United States." Farrell v. United States, 336 U.S. 511, 517. On the contrary, we are simply dealing with a problem of statutory construction rather commonplace in a federal system by which courts often have to decide whether "any" or "every" reaches to the limits of the enacting authority's usual scope or is to be applied to foreign events or transactions.

The history of the statute before us begins with the 1915 enactment of the comprehensive LaFollette Act, entitled, "An Act To promote the welfare of American seamen in the merchant marine of the United States; to abolish arrest and imprisonment as a penalty for desertion and to secure the abrogation of treaty provisions in relation thereto; and to promote safety at sea." 38 Stat. 1164. Many sections of this Act were in terms or by obvious implication restricted to American ships. Three sections were made specifically applicable to foreign vessels, and these provoked considerable doubt and debate. Others were phrased in terms which on their face might apply to the world or to anything less. . . . In 1920, Congress, under the title "An Act To provide for the promotion and maintenance of the American merchant marine . . ." and other subjects not relevant, provided a plan to aid our mercantile fleet and included the revised provision for injured seamen now before us for construction. 41 Stat. 988, 1007. It did so by reference to the Federal Employers' Liability Act, which we have held not applicable to an American citizen's injury sustained in Canada while in service of an American employer. New York Central R. Co. v. Chisholm, 268 U.S. 29. And it did not give the seaman the one really effective security for a claim against a foreign owner, a maritime lien.

Congress could not have been unaware of the necessity of construction imposed upon courts by such generality of language and as well warned that in the absence of more definite directions than are contained in the Jones Act it would be applied by the courts to foreign events, foreign ships and foreign seamen only in accordance with the usual doctrine and practices of maritime law.

Respondent places great stress upon the assertion that petitioner's commerce and contacts with the ports of the United States are frequent and regular, as the basis for applying our statutes to incidents aboard his ships. But the virtue and utility of sea-borne commerce lies in its frequent and important contacts with more than one country. If, to serve some immediate interest, the courts of each were to exploit every such contact to the limit of its power, it is not difficult to see that a multiplicity of conflicting and overlapping burdens would blight international carriage by sea. Hence, courts of this and other commercial nations have generally deferred to a nonnational or international maritime law of impressive maturity and universality. It has the force of law, not from extraterritorial reach of national laws, nor from abdication of its sovereign powers by any nation, but from acceptance by common consent of civilized communities of rules designed to foster amicable and workable commercial relations.

International or maritime law in such matters as this does not seek uniformity and does not purport to restrict any nation from making and altering its laws to govern its own shipping and territory. However, it aims at stability and order through usages which considerations of comity, reciprocity and long-range interest have developed to define the domain which each nation will claim as its own. Maritime law, like our municipal law, has attempted to avoid or resolve conflicts between competing laws by ascertaining and valuing points of contact between the transaction and the states or governments whose competing laws are involved. The criteria, in general, appear to be arrived at from weighing of the significance of one or more connecting factors between the shipping transaction regulated and the national interest served by the assertion of authority. It would not be candid to claim that our courts have arrived at satisfactory standards or apply those that they profess with perfect consistency. But in dealing with international commerce we cannot be unmindful of the necessity for mutual forbearance if retaliations are to be avoided; nor should we forget that any contact which we hold sufficient to warrant application of our law to a foreign transaction will logically be as strong a warrant for a foreign country to apply its law to an American transaction.

In the case before us, two foreign nations can claim some connecting factor with this tort—Denmark, because, among other reasons, the ship and the seaman were Danish nationals; Cuba, because the tortious conduct occurred and caused injury in Cuban waters. The United States may also claim contacts because the seaman had been hired in and was returned to the United States, which also is the state of the forum. We therefore review the several factors which, alone or in combination, are generally conceded to influence choice of law to govern a tort claim, particularly a maritime tort claim, and the weight and significance accorded them.

1. *Place of the Wrongful Act.*—The solution most commonly accepted as to torts in our municipal and in international law is to apply the law of the place where the acts giving rise to the liability occurred, the lex loci delicti commissi. This rule of locality, often applied to maritime torts, would indicate application of the law of Cuba, in whose domain the actionable wrong took place. The test of location of the wrongful act or omission, however sufficient for torts ashore, is of limited application to shipboard torts, because of the varieties of legal authority over waters she may navigate. These range from ports, harbors, roadsteads, straits, rivers and canals which form part of the domain of various states, through bays and gulfs, and that band of the littoral sea known as territorial waters, over which control in a large, but not unlimited, degree is conceded to the adjacent state. It includes, of course, the high seas as to which the law was probably settled and old when Grotius wrote that it cannot be anyone's property and cannot be monopolized by virtue of discovery, occupation, papal grant, prescription or custom. . . .

2. *Law of the Flag.*—Perhaps the most venerable and universal rule of maritime law relevant to our problem is that which gives cardinal importance to the law of the flag. Each state under international law may determine for itself the conditions on which it will grant its nationality to a merchant ship, thereby accepting responsibility for it and acquiring authority over it. Nationality is evidenced to the world by the ship's papers and its flag. The United

States has firmly and successfully maintained that the regularity and validity of a registration can be questioned only by the registering state.

This Court has said that the law of the flag supersedes the territorial principle, even for purposes of criminal jurisdiction of personnel of a merchant ship, because it "is deemed to be a part of the territory of that sovereignty [whose flag it flies], and not to lose that character when in navigable waters within the territorial limits of another sovereignty." On this principle, we concede a territorial government involved only concurrent jurisdiction of offenses aboard our ships. . . .

3. *Allegiance or Domicile of the Injured.*—Until recent times there was little occasion for conflict between the law of the flag and the law of the state of which the seafarer was a subject, for the long-standing rule, as pronounced by this Court after exhaustive review of authority, was that the nationality of the vessel for jurisdictional purposes was attributed to all her crew. . . . We need not, however, weigh the seaman's nationality against that of the ship, for here the two coincide without resort to fiction. Admittedly, respondent is neither citizen nor resident of the United States. While on direct examination he answered leading questions that he was living in New York when he joined the *Randa*, the articles which he signed recited, and on cross-examination he admitted, that his home was Silkeburg, Denmark. His presence in New York was transitory and created no such national interest in, or duty toward, him as to justify intervention of the law of one state on the shipboard of another.

4. *Allegiance of the Defendant Shipowner.*—A state "is not debarred by any rule of international law from governing the conduct of its own citizens upon the high seas or even in foreign countries when the rights of other nations or their nationals are not infringed." Skiriotes v. Florida, 313 U.S. 69, 73. Steele v. Bulova Watch Co., 344 U.S. 280, 282. Until recent times this factor was not a frequent occasion of conflict, for the nationality of the ship was that of its owners. But it is common knowledge that in recent years a practice has grown, particularly among American shipowners, to avoid stringent shipping laws by seeking foreign registration eagerly offered by some countries. Confronted with such operations, our courts on occasion have pressed beyond the formalities of more or less nominal foreign registration to enforce against American shipowners the obligations which our law places upon them. But here again the utmost liberality in disregard of formality does not support the application of American law in this case, for its appears beyond doubt that this owner is a Dane by nationality and domicile.

5. *Place of Contract.*—Place of contract, which was New York, is the factor on which respondent chiefly relies to invoke American law. It is one which often has significance in choice of law in a contract action. But a Jones Act suit is for tort, in which respect it differs from one to enforce liability for maintenance and cure. As we have said of the latter, "In the United States this obligation has been recognized consistently as an implied provision in

contracts of marine employment. Created thus with the contract of employment, the liability, unlike that for indemnity or that later created by the Jones Act, in no sense is predicated on the fault or negligence of the shipowner." But this action does not seek to recover anything due under the contract or damages for its breach.

The place of contracting in this instance, as is usual to such contracts, was fortuitous. A seaman takes his employment, like his fun, where he finds it; a ship takes on crew in any port where it needs them. The practical effect of making the lex loci contractus govern all tort claims during the service would be to subject a ship to a multitude of systems of law, to put some of the crew in a more advantageous position than others, and not unlikely in the long run to diminish hirings in ports of countries that take best care of their seamen. . . .

We do not think the place of contract is a substantial influence in the choice between competing laws to govern a maritime tort.

6. *Inaccessibility of Foreign Forum.*—It is argued, and particularly stressed by an amicus brief, that justice requires adjudication under American law to save seamen expense and loss of time in returning to a foreign forum. . . .

Confining ourselves to the case in hand, we do not find this seaman disadvantaged in obtaining his remedy under Danish law from being in New York instead of Denmark. The Danish compensation system does not necessitate delayed, prolonged, expensive and uncertain litigation. It is stipulated in this case that claims may be made through the Danish Consulate. There is not the slightest showing that to obtain any relief to which he is entitled under Danish law would require his presence in Denmark or necessitate his leaving New York. And, even if it were so, the record indicates that he was offered and declined free transportation to Denmark by petitioner.

7. *The Law of the Forum.*—It is urged that, since an American forum has perfected its jurisdiction over the parties and defendant does more or less frequent and regular business within the forum state, it should apply its own law to the controversy between them. The "doing business" which is enough to warrant service of process may fall quite short of the considerations necessary to bring extraterritorial torts to judgment under our law. Under respondent's contention, all that is necessary to bring a foreign transaction between foreigners in foreign ports under American law is to be able to serve American process on the defendant. We have held it a denial of due process of law when a state of the Union attempts to draw into control of its law otherwise foreign controversies, on slight connections, because it is a forum state. The purpose of a conflict-of-laws doctrine is to assure that a case will be treated in the same way under the appropriate law regardless of the fortuitous circumstances which often determine the forum. Jurisdiction of maritime cases in all countries is so wide and the nature of its subject matter so far-flung that there would be no justification for altering the law of a controversy just because local jurisdiction of the parties is obtainable.

This review of the connecting factors which either maritime law or our municipal law of conflicts regards as significant in determining the law applicable to a claim of actionable wrong shows an overwhelming preponderance in favor of Danish law. The parties are both Danish subjects, the events took place on a Danish ship, not within our territorial waters. Against these considerations is only the fact that the defendant was served here with process and that the plaintiff signed on in New York, where the defendant was engaged in our foreign commerce. The latter event is offset by provision of his contract that the law of Denmark should govern. We do not question the power of Congress to condition access to our ports by foreign-owned vessels upon submission to any liabilities it may consider good American policy to exact. But we can find no justification for interpreting the Jones Act to intervene between foreigners and their own law because of acts on a foreign ship not in our waters.

In apparent recognition of the weakness of the legal argument, a candid and brash appeal is made by respondent and by amicus briefs to extend the law to this situation as a means of benefiting seamen and enhancing the costs of foreign ship operation for the competitive advantage of our own. We are not sure that the interest of this foreign seaman, who is able to prove negligence, is the interest of all seamen or that his interest is that of the United States. Nor do we stop to inquire which law does whom the greater or the lesser good. The argument is misaddressed. It would be within the proprieties if addressed to Congress. Counsel familiar with the traditional attitude of this Court in maritime matters could not have intended it for us.[29]

The judgment below is reversed and the cause remanded to District Court for proceedings consistent herewith.

Reversed and remanded.

Justice BLACK agrees with the Court of Appeals and would affirm its judgment.

Justice CLARK, not having heard oral argument, took no part in the consideration or decision of this case.

Questions and Comments

(1) If *Arabian American Oil* is the international counterpart of the First Restatement, then are the seven factors in *Lauritzen* analogous to the factors listed in the various sections of the Restatement Second (*e.g.*, Section 188)?

(2) Why does the Court engage in a multilateral analysis in *Lauritzen* unlike the unilateral analysis in *Arabian American Oil? See supra* page 742 note 1.

29. *Cf.* The Peterhoff, 5 Wall. 28, 578: "In cases such as that now in judgment, we administer the public law of nations, and are not at liberty to inquire what is for the particular advantage or disadvantage of our own or another country."

(3) Would it be fair to say that "the usual doctrine and practices of maritime law" and international law play the same role in *Lauritzen* that the principles of territoriality did in *Arabian American Oil* (*i.e.*, to fill in a silent statute)? How should the Court construe a statute if Congress has given no guidance? Which is a more faithful method of statutory construction, to rely upon such general canons of interjurisdictional division of authority or to conduct a policy analysis of the sort that the modern domestic-policy analysts propose? Or are they the same?

(4) A serious effort to apply policy analysis to Jones Act cases is Symeonides, Maritime Conflicts of Law from the Perspective of Modern Choice of Law Methodology, 7 Mar. Law. 223 (1982). Among other things, the author collects the various American maritime statutes that actually contain choice-of-law limitations, hoping to glean some enlightenment about statutes as to which Congress has been silent.

(5) In Hellenic Lines v. Rhoditis, 398 U.S. 306 (1970), the Court applied the Jones Act to a Greek seaman employed under a Greek contract for injuries suffered in American waters on a ship of Greek registry. The vessel was owned by a Greek corporation, and more than 95 percent of the stock was owned by an American domiciliary who was a Greek citizen. The Court relied heavily on the fact of the American domicile of the owner, provoking an accusation by the dissent that it had departed both from the *Lauritzen* factors and from general maritime law.

3. Comity

Hartford Fire Insurance Co. v. California

509 U.S. 764 (1993)

Justice SOUTER announced the judgment of the Court and delivered the opinion of the Court with respect to Parts I, II(A), III, and IV, and an opinion with respect to Part II(B) in which Justice WHITE, Justice BLACKMUN and Justice STEVENS join.

The Sherman Act makes every contract, combination, or conspiracy in unreasonable restraint of interstate or foreign commerce illegal. 26 Stat. 209, as amended, 15 U.S.C. §1. These consolidated cases present questions about the application of that Act to the insurance industry, both here and abroad. The plaintiffs (respondents here) allege that both domestic and foreign defendants (petitioners here) violated the Sherman Act by engaging in various conspiracies to affect the American insurance market. A group of domestic defendants argues that the McCarran-Ferguson Act, 59 Stat. 33, as amended, 15 U.S.C. §1011 et seq., precludes application of the Sherman Act to the conduct alleged; a group of foreign defendants argues that the principle of international comity requires the District Court to refrain from exercising jurisdiction over certain claims against it. We hold that most of the domestic defendants' alleged conduct is not immunized from antitrust liability by the

McCarran-Ferguson Act, and that, even assuming it applies, the principle of international comity does not preclude District Court jurisdiction over the foreign conduct alleged.

I

The two petitions before us stem from consolidated litigation comprising the complaints of 19 States and many private plaintiffs alleging that the defendants, members of the insurance industry, conspired in violation of §1 of the Sherman Act to restrict the terms of coverage of commercial general liability (CGL) insurance available in the United States. Because the cases come to us on motions to dismiss, we take the allegations of the complaints as true.

A

According to the complaints, the object of the conspiracies was to force certain primary insurers (insurers who sell insurance directly to consumers) to change the terms of their standard CGL insurance policies to confirm with the policies the defendant insurers wanted to sell. The defendants wanted four changes.

First, CGL insurance has traditionally been sold in the United States on an "occurrence" basis, through a policy obligating the insurer "to pay or defend claims, whenever made, resulting from an accident or 'injurious exposure to conditions' that occurred during the [specific time] period the policy was in affect." In place of the traditional "occurrence" trigger of coverage, the defendants wanted a "claims-made" trigger, obligating the insurer to pay or defend only those claims made during the policy period. Such a policy has the distinct advantage for the insurer that when the policy period ends without a claim having been made, the insurer can be certain that the policy will not expose it to any further liability. Second, the defendants wanted the "claims-made" policy to have a "retroactive date" provision, which would further restrict coverage to claims based on incidents that occurred after a certain date. Such a provision eliminates the risk that an insurer, by issuing a claims-made policy, would assume liability arising from incidents that occurred before the policy's effective date, but remained undiscovered or caused no immediate harm. Third, CGL insurance has traditionally covered "sudden and accidental" pollution; the defendants and accidental" pollution; the defendants wanted to eliminate that coverage. Finally, CGL insurance has traditionally provided that the insurer would bear the legal costs of defending covered claims against the insured without regard to the policy's stated limits of coverage; the defendants wanted legal defense costs to be counted against the stated limits (providing a "legal defense cost cap").

[The Court then discussed the various allegations in the complaint.]

C

Nineteen States and a number of private plaintiffs filed 36 complaints against the insurers involved in this course of events, charging that the conspiracies described above violated §1 of the Sherman Act, 15 U.S.C. §1. After the actions had been consolidated for litigation in the Northern District of California, the defendants moved to dismiss for failure to state a cause of action, or, in the alternative, for summary judgment. The District Court granted the motions to dismiss. . . .

The Court of Appeals reversed. In re Insurance Antitrust Litigation, 938 F.2d 919 (9th Cir. 1991). . . .

We granted certiorari in No. 91-1111 to address two narrow questions about the scope of McCarran-Ferguson Act antitrust immunity,[8] and in No. 91-1128 to address the application of the Sherman Act to the foreign conduct at issue.[9] We now affirm in part, reverse in part, and remand.

[The Court first discussed the liability of the domestic insurance companies.]

III

Finally, we take up the question presented by No. 91-1128, whether certain claims against the London reinsurers should have been dismissed as improper applications of the Sherman Act to foreign conduct. The Fifth Claim for Relief of the California Complaint alleges a violation of §1 of the Sherman Act by certain London reinsurers who conspired to coerce primary insurers in the United States to offer CGL coverage on a claims-made basis, thereby making "occurrence CGL coverage . . . unavailable in the State of California for many risks." The Sixth Claim for Relief of the California Complaint alleges that the London reinsurers violated §1 by a conspiracy to limit coverage of pollution risks in North America, thereby rendering "pollution liability coverage . . . almost entirely unavailable for the vast majority of casualty insurance purchasers in the State of California." The Eighth Claim for

---

8. We limited our grant of certiorari in No. 91-1111 to these questions: "1. Whether domestic insurance companies whose conduct otherwise would be exempt from the federal antitrust laws under the McCarran-Ferguson Act lose that exemption because they participate with foreign reinsurers in the business of insurance," and "2. Whether agreements among primary insurers and reinsurers on such matters as standardized advisory insurance policy forms and terms of insurance coverage constitute a 'boycott' outside the exemption of the McCarran-Ferguson Act."

9. The question presented in No. 91-1128 is: "Did the court of appeals properly assess the extraterritorial reach of the U.S. antitrust laws in light of this Court's teachings and contemporary understanding of international law when it held that a U.S. district court may apply U.S. law to the conduct of a foreign insurance market regulated abroad?"

Relief of the California Complaint alleges a further §1 violation by the London reinsurers who, along with domestic retrocessional reinsurers, conspired to limit coverage of seepage, pollution, and property contamination risks in North America, thereby eliminating such coverage in the State of California.

At the outset, we note that the District Court undoubtedly had jurisdiction of these Sherman Act claims, as the London reinsurers apparently concede. *See* Tr. of Oral Arg. 37 ("Our position is not that the Sherman Act does not apply in the sense that a minimal basis for the exercise of jurisdiction doesn't exist here. Our position is that there are certain circumstances, and that this is one of them, in which the interests of another State are sufficient that the exercise of that jurisdiction should be restrained") Although the proposition was perhaps not always free from doubt, *see* American Banana Co. v. United Fruit Co., 213 U.S. 347 (1909), it is well established by now that the Sherman Act applies to foreign conduct that was meant to produce and did in fact produce some substantial effect in the United States. Restatement (Third) of Foreign Relations Law of the United States §415, and Reporters' Note 3 (1987) (hereinafter Restatement (Third) Foreign Relations Law). Such is the conduct alleged here: that the London reinsurers engaged in unlawful conspiracies to affect the market for insurance in the United States and that their conduct in fact produced substantial effect.[23] *See* 938 F.2d, at 933.

According to the London reinsurers, the District Court should have declined to exercise such jurisdiction under the principle of international comity.[24] The Court of Appeals agreed that courts should look to that principle in deciding whether to exercise jurisdiction under the Sherman Act. *Id.*, at 932. This availed the London reinsurers nothing, however. To be sure, the Court of Appeals believed that "application of [American] antitrust laws

23. Under §402 of the Foreign Trade Antitrust Improvements Act of 1982 (FTAIA), 96 Stat. 1246, 15 U.S.C. §6a, the Sherman Act does not apply to conduct involving foreign trade or commerce, other than import trade or import commerce, unless "such conduct has a direct, substantial, and reasonably foreseeable effect" on domestic or import commerce. 15 U.S.C. §6a(1)(A). The FTAIA was intended to exempt from the Sherman Act export transactions that did not injure the United States economy, *see* H.R. Rep. No. 97-686, pp. 2-3, 9-10 (1982); P. Areeda & H. Hovenkamp, Antitrust Law ¶236'a, pp. 296-297 (Supp. 1992), and it is unclear how it might apply to the conduct alleged here. Also unclear is whether the Act's "direct, substantial, and reasonably foreseeable effect" standard amends existing law or merely codifies it. *See id.*, ¶236'a, p.297. We need not address these questions here. Assuming that the FTAIA's standard affects this case, and assuming further that that standard differs from the prior law, the conduct alleged plainly meets its requirements.

24. Justice Scalia contends that comity concerns figure into the prior analysis whether jurisdiction exists under the Sherman Act. This contention is inconsistent with the general understanding that the Sherman Act covers foreign conduct producing a substantial intended effect in the United States, and that concerns of comity come into play, if at all, only after a court has determined that the acts complained of are subject to Sherman Act jurisdiction.

to the London reinsurance market 'would lead to significant conflict with English law and policy,' " and that "[s]uch a conflict, unless outweighed by other factors, would by itself be reason to decline exercise of jurisdiction." *Id.*, at 933 (citation omitted). But other factors, in the court's view, including the London reinsurers' express purpose to affect United States commerce and the substantial nature of the effect produced, outweighed the supposed conflict and required the exercise of jurisdiction in this case. *Id.*, at 934.

When it enacted the Foreign Trade Antitrust Improvements Act of 1982 (FTAIA), 96 Stat. 1246, 15 U.S.C. §6a, Congress expressed no view on the question whether a court with Sherman Act jurisdiction should ever decline to exercise such jurisdiction on grounds of international comity. See H.R.Rep. No. 97-686, p.13 (1982) ("If a court determines that the requirements for subject matter jurisdiction are met, [the FTAIA] would have no effect on the court['s] ability to employ notions of comity . . . or otherwise to take account of the international character of the transaction") (citing *Timberlane*). We need not decide that question here, however, for even assuming that in a proper case a court may decline to exercise Sherman Act jurisdiction over foreign conduct (or, as Justice Scalia would put it, may conclude by the employment of comity analysis in the first instance that there is no jurisdiction), international comity would not counsel against exercising jurisdiction in the circumstances alleged here.

The only substantial question in this case is whether "there is in fact a true conflict between domestic and foreign law." Société Nationale Industrielle Aérospatiale v. United States District Court, 482 U.S. 522, 555 (1987) (Blackmun, J., concurring in part and dissenting in part). The London reinsurers contend that applying the Act to their conduct would conflict significantly with British law, and the British Government, appearing before us as amicus curiae, concurs. They assert that Parliament has established a comprehensive regulatory regime over the London reinsurance market and that the conduct alleged here was perfectly consistent with British law and policy. But this is not to state a conflict. "[T]he fact that conduct is lawful in the state in which it took place will not, of itself, bar application of the United States antitrust laws," even where the foreign state has a strong policy to permit or encourage such conduct. Restatement (Third) Foreign Relations Law §415, Comment *j;*

No conflict exists, for these purposes, "where a person subject to regulation by two states can comply with the laws of both." Restatement (Third) Foreign Relations Law §403, Comment *e.*[25] Since the London reinsurers do not argue that British law requires them to act in some fashion prohibited by the law of the United States, or claim that their compliance with the laws of

---

25. Justice Scalia says that we put the cart before the horse in citing this authority, for he argues it may be apposite only after a determination over the foreign acts is reasonable. But whatever the order of cart and horse, conflict in this sense is the only substantial issue before the Court.

both countries is otherwise impossible, we see no conflict with British law. *See* Restatement (Third) Foreign Relations Law §403, Comment *e*, §415, Comment *j*. We have no need in this case to address other considerations that might inform a decision to refrain from the exercise of jurisdiction on grounds of international comity.

IV

The judgment of the Court of Appeals is affirmed in part and reversed in part, and the case is remanded for further proceedings consistent with this opinion.

It is so ordered.

Justice SCALIA delivered the opinion of the Court with respect to Part I, and delivered a dissenting opinion with respect to Part II, in which Justice O'CONNOR, Justice KENNEDY, and Justice THOMAS have joined. . . . With respect to the petition in No. 92-1128, I dissent from the Court's ruling concerning the extraterritorial application of the Sherman Act. . . .

II

The petitioners in No. 91-1128, various British corporations and other British subjects, argue that certain of the claims against them constitute an inappropriate extraterritorial application of the Sherman Act. It is important to distinguish two distinct questions raised by this petition: whether the District Court had jurisdiction, and whether the Sherman Act reaches the extraterritorial conduct alleged here. On the first question, I believe that the District Court had subject-matter jurisdiction over the Sherman Act claims against all the defendants (personal jurisdiction is not contested). The respondents asserted nonfrivolous claims under the Sherman Act, and 28 U.S.C. §1331 vests district courts with subject-matter jurisdiction over cases "arising under" federal statutes. As precedents such as Lauritzen v. Larsen, 345 U.S. 571 (1953), make clear, that is sufficient to establish the District Court's jurisdiction over these claims. . . .

The second question—the extraterritorial reach of the Sherman Act—has nothing to do with the jurisdiction of the courts. It is a question of substantive law turning on whether, in enacting the Sherman Act, Congress asserted regulatory power over the challenged conduct. *See* EEOC v. Arabian American Oil Co., 499 U.S. 244, 248 (1991) (*Aramco*) ("It is our task to determine whether Congress intended the protections of Title VII to apply to United States citizens employed by American employers outside of the United States"). If a plaintiff fails to prevail on this issue, the court does not dismiss the claim for want of subject-matter jurisdiction—want of power to adjudicate; rather, it decides the claim, ruling on the merits that the plaintiff has failed to state a cause of action under the relevant statute.

There is, however, a type of "jurisdiction" relevant to determining the extraterritorial reach of a statute; it is known as "legislative jurisdiction." This refers to "the authority of a state to make its law applicable to persons or activities," and is quite a separate matter from "jurisdiction to adjudicate." There is no doubt, of course, that Congress possesses legislative jurisdiction over the acts alleged in this complaint: Congress has broad power under Article I, §8, cl. 3 "[t]o regulate Commerce with foreign Nations," and this Court has repeatedly upheld its power to make laws applicable to persons or activities beyond our territorial boundaries where United States interests are affected. But the question in this case is whether, and to what extent, Congress *has* exercised that undoubted legislative jurisdiction in enacting the Sherman Act.

Two canons of statutory construction are relevant in this inquiry. The first is the "long-standing principle of American law 'that legislation of Congress, unless a contrary intent appears, is meant to apply only within the territorial jurisdiction of the United States.' " Applying that canon in *Aramco,* we held that the version of Title VII of the Civil Rights Act of 1964 then in force, 42 U.S.C. §§2000e-2000e-17 (1988 ed.), did not extend outside the territory of the United States even though the statute contained broad provisions extending its prohibitions to, for example, " 'any activity, business, or industry in commerce.' " We held such "boiler-plate language" to be an insufficient indication to override the presumption against extraterritoriality. The Sherman Act contains similar "boilerplate language," and if the question were not governed by precedent, it would be worth considering whether that presumption controls the outcome here. We have, however, found the presumption to be overcome with respect to our antitrust laws; it is now well established that the Sherman Act applies extraterritorially.

But if the presumption against extraterritoriality has been overcome or is otherwise inapplicable, a second canon of statutory construction becomes relevant: "[A]n act of congress ought never to be construed to violate the law of nations if any other possible construction remains." Murray v. The Charming Betsy, 2 Cranch 64, 118 (1804) (Marshall, C.J.). This canon is "wholly independent" of the presumption against extraterritoriality. *Aramco,* 499 U.S., at 292. It is relevant to determining the substantive reach of a statute because "the law of nations," or customary international law, includes limitations on a nation's exercise of its jurisdiction to prescribe. See Restatement (Third) §§401-416. Though it clearly has constitutional authority to do so, Congress is generally presumed not to have exceeded those customary international-law limits on jurisdiction to prescribe.

Consistent with that presumption, this and other courts have frequently recognized that, even where the presumption against extraterritoriality does not apply, statutes should not be interpreted to regulate foreign persons or conduct if that regulation would conflict with principles of international law. For example, in Romero v. International Terminal Operating Co., 358 U.S. 354 (1959), the plaintiff, a Spanish sailor who had been injured while working aboard a Spanish-flag and Spanish-owned vessel, filed a Jones Act claim against his Spanish employer. The presumption against extraterritorial application of federal statutes was inapplicable to the case, as the actionable tort had occurred in American waters. *See id.*, at 383. The Court nonetheless stated that, "in the absence of contrary congressional direction," it would apply "principles of choice of law that are consonant with the needs of a general federal maritime law and with due recognition of our self-regarding respect for the relevant interests of foreign nations in the regulation of maritime commerce as part of the legitimate concern of the international community." *Id.*, at 382-383. "The controlling considerations" in this choice-of-law analysis were "the interacting interests of the United States and of foreign countries." *Id.*, at 383.

Romero referred to, and followed, the choice-of-law analysis set forth in Lauritzen v. Larsen, 345 U.S. 571 (1953). As previously mentioned, *Lauritzen* also involved a Jones Act claim brought by a foreign sailor against a foreign employer. The *Lauritzen* Court recognized the basic problem: "If [the Jones Act were] read literally, Congress has conferred an American right of action which requires nothing more than that plaintiff be 'any seaman who shall suffer personal injury in the course of his employment.' " *Id.*, at 576. The solution it adopted was to construe the statute "to apply only to areas and transactions in which *American law would be considered operative under prevalent doctrines of international law.*" *Id.*, at 577 (emphasis added). To support application of international law to limit the facial breadth of the statute, the Court relied upon—of course—Chief Justice Marshall's statement in *The Charming Betsy* quoted *supra*, at 2919. It then set forth "several factors which, alone or in combination, are generally conceded to influence choice of law to govern a tort claim."

Lauritzen, Romero, and *McCulloch* were maritime cases, but we have recognized the principle that the scope of generally worded statutes must be construed in light of international law in other areas as well. More specifically, the principle was expressed in United States v. Aluminum Co. of America, 148 F.2d 416 (2d Cir. 1945), the decision that established the extraterritorial reach of the Sherman Act. In his opinion for the court, Judge Learned Hand cautioned "we are not to read general words, such as those in [the Sherman] Act, without regard to the limitations customarily observed by nations upon the exercise of their powers; limitations which generally correspond to those fixed by the 'Conflict of Laws.' " *Id.*, at 443.

More recent lower court precedent has also tempered the extraterritorial application of the Sherman Act with considerations of "international comity." The "comity" they refer to is not the comity of courts, whereby judges decline to exercise jurisdiction over matters more appropriately adjudged elsewhere, but rather what might be termed "prescriptive comity": the respect sovereign nations afford each other by limiting the reach of their laws.

That comity is exercised by legislatures when they enact laws, and courts assume it has been exercised when they come to interpreting the scope of laws their legislatures have enacted. It is a traditional component of choice-of-law theory. *See* J. Story, Commentaries on the Conflict of Laws §38 (1834) (distinguishing between the "comity of the courts" and the "comity of nations," and defining the latter as "the true foundation and extent of the obligation of the laws of one nation within the territories of another"). Comity in this sense includes the choice-of-law principles that, "in the absence of contrary congressional direction," are assumed to be incorporated into our substantive laws having extraterritorial reach. Considering comity in this way is just part of determining whether the Sherman Act prohibits the conduct at issue.[9]

In sum, the practice of using international law to limit the extraterritorial reach of statutes is firmly established in our jurisprudence. In proceeding to apply that practice to the present case, I shall rely on the Restatement (Third) of Foreign Relations Law for the relevant principles of international law. Its standards appear fairly supported in the decisions of this Court construing international choice-of-law principles (*Lauritzen, Romero,* and *McCulloch*) and in the decisions of other federal courts, especially *Timberlane.* Whether the Restatement precisely reflects international law in every detail matters little here, as I believe this case would be resolved the same way under virtually any conceivable test that takes account of foreign regulatory interests.

Under the Restatement, a nation having some "basis" for jurisdiction to prescribe law should nonetheless refrain from exercising that jurisdiction "with respect to a person or activity having connections with another state when the exercise of such jurisdiction is unreasonable." Restatement (Third) §403(1). The "reasonableness" inquiry turns on a number of factors including, but not limited to: "the extent to which the activity takes place within the territory [of the regulating state]," *id.,* §403(2)(a); "the connections, such as nationality, residence, or economic activity, between the regulating state and the person principally responsible for the activity to be regulated," *id.,* §403(2)(b); "the character of the activity to be regulated, the importance of regulation to the regulating state, the extent to which other states regulate such activities and the degree to which the desirability of such regulation is generally accepted," *id.,* §403(2)(c); "the extent to which another state may have an interest in regulating the activity," *id.,* §403(2)(g); and "the likelihood of

---

9. Some antitrust courts, including the Court of Appeals in the present case, have mistaken the comity at issue for the "comity of courts," which has led them to characterize the question presented as one of the "abstention," that is, whether they should "exercise or decline jurisdiction." Mannington Mills, Inc. v. Congoleum Corp., 595 F.2d 1287, 1294, 1296 (3d Cir. 1979); *see also* In re Insurance Antitrust Litigation, 938 F.2d 919, 932 (9th Cir. 1991). As I shall discuss, that seems to be the error the Court has fallen into today. Because courts are generally reluctant to refuse the exercise of conferred jurisdiction, confusion on this seemingly theoretical point can have the very practical consequence of greatly expanding the extraterritorial reach of the Sherman Act.

conflict with regulation by another state," *id.*, §403(2)(h). Rarely would these factors point more clearly against application of United States law.

The activity relevant to the counts at issue here took place primarily in the United Kingdom, and the defendants in these counts are British corporations and British subjects having their principal place of business or residence outside the United States.[10] Great Britain has established a comprehensive regulatory scheme governing the London reinsurance markets, and clearly has a heavy "interest in regulating the activity," *id.*, §403(2)(g). . . .

Considering these factors, I think it unimaginable that an assertion of legislative jurisdiction by the United States would be considered reasonable, and therefore it is inappropriate to assume, in the absence of statutory indication to the contrary, that Congress has made such an assertion.

It is evident from what I have said that the Court's comity analysis, which proceeds as though the issue is whether the courts should "decline to exercise . . . jurisdiction," *ante*, at 2910, rather than whether the Sherman Act covers this conduct, is simply misdirected. I do not at all agree, moreover, with the Court's conclusion that the issue of the substantive scope of the Sherman Act is not in the case. To be sure, the parties did not make a clear distinction between adjudicative jurisdiction and the scope of the statute. Parties often do not, as we have observed. . . . It is not realistic, and also not helpful, to pretend that the only really relevant issue in this case is not before us. In any event, if one erroneously chooses, as the Court does, to make adjudicative jurisdiction (or, more precisely, abstention) the vehicle for taking account of the needs of prescriptive comity, the Court still gets it wrong. It concludes that no "true conflict" counseling nonapplication of United States law (or rather, as it thinks, United States judicial jurisdiction) exists unless compliance with United States law would constitute a *violation* of another country's law. That breathtakingly broad proposition, which contradicts the many cases discussed earlier, will bring the Sherman Act and other laws into sharp and unnecessary conflict with the legitimate interests of other countries—particularly our closest trading partners.

In the sense in which the term "conflic[t]" was used in *Lauritzen*, 345 U.S., at 582, 592, and is generally understood in the field of conflicts of laws, there is clearly a conflict in this case. The petitioners here, like the defendant in *Lauritzen*, were not compelled by any foreign law to take their allegedly wrongful actions, but that no more precludes a conflict-of-laws analysis here than it did there. Where applicable foreign and domestic law provide different substantive rules of decision to govern the parties' dispute,

---

10. Some of the British corporations are subsidiaries of American corporations, and the Court of Appeals held that "[t]he interests of Britain are at least diminished where the parties are subsidiaries of American corporations." 938 F.2d, at 933. In effect, the Court of Appeals pierced the corporate veil in weighing the interests at stake. I do not think that was proper.

a conflict-of-laws analysis is necessary. *See generally* R. Weintraub, Commentary on Conflict of Laws 2-3 (1980); Restatement (First) of Conflict of Laws §1, Comment *c* and Illustrations (1934).

Literally the *only* support that the Court adduces for its position is §403 of the Restatement (Third) of Foreign Relations Law—or more precisely Comment *e* to that provision, which states:

> Subsection (3) [which says that a state should defer to another state if that state's interest is clearly greater] applies only when one state requires what another prohibits, or where compliance with the regulations of two states exercising jurisdiction consistently with this section is otherwise impossible. It does not apply where a person subject to regulation by two states can comply with the laws of both. . . .

The Court has completely misinterpreted this provision. Subsection (3) of §403 (requiring one State to defer to another in the limited circumstances just described) comes into play only after subsection (1) of §403 has been complied with—*i.e.*, after it has been determined that the exercise of jurisdiction by *both* of the two states is not "unreasonable." That prior question is answered by applying the factors (inter alia) set forth in subsection (2) of §403, that is, precisely the factors that I have discussed in text and that the Court rejects.

I would reverse the judgment of the Court of Appeals on this issue, and remand to the District Court with instructions to dismiss for failure to state a claim on the three counts at issue in No. 91-1128.

Questions and Comments

(1) *Hartford Fire* was decided against the backdrop of a long and varied history of U.S. courts applying the Sherman Act and related antitrust statutes in the international context. The Supreme Court originally construed the Sherman Act law to be strictly territorial. *See* American Banana Co. v. United Fruit Co., 213 U.S. 347 (1909). In 1927, the Court said the Sherman Act applied to "deliberate acts, here and elsewhere, [that] brought about forbidden results within the United States." United States v. Sisal Corp., 274 U.S. 268, 276 (1927). Eighteen years later, the Second Circuit, in a case referred to it because the Supreme Court lacked a quorum of disinterested Justices, held that U.S. antitrust law applies to agreements made abroad "if they were intended to affect imports and did affect them." United States v. Aluminum Co. of Am., 148 F.2d 416, 444 (2d Cir. 1945) (en banc). The Supreme Court appeared to endorse this "effects test" in later cases. *See* Matsushita Elec. Indus. Co. v. Zenith Radio Corp., 475 U.S. 574, 582 n.6 (1985); Continental Ore Co. v. Union Carbide & Carbon Corp., 370 U.S. 690, 704 (1962). In the 1970s and 1980s, lower courts applied the effects test aggres-

sively to regulate extraterritorial conduct, spawning controversy with some of our closest trading partners. Some lower courts modified the extraterritorial scope of the Sherman Act by engaging in comity analysis that balanced the interests of foreign nations and sometimes resulted in non-application of the Sherman Act even when the effects test was satisfied. *See, e.g.*, Mannington Mills v. Congoleum, 595 F.2d 1287 (3d Cir. 1979); Timberlane Lumber Co. v. Bank of America, 549 F.2d 597 (9th Cir. 1976); *but see* Laker Airways v. Sabena, 731 F.2d 909 (D.C. Cir. 1984). (granting virtually no deference to other states' interests). For an overview of this history, see Dam, Extraterritoriality in an Age of Globalization: The Hartford Fire Case, 1993 Sup. Ct. Rev. 289 (1993).

(2) If *Arabian American Oil* represents the traditional territorial approach, and *Lauritzen* adopts a more modern approach, would "comity" be the analog of Currie's vision of "restrained and moderate interpretation" in case of true conflicts, or Baxter's theory of "comparative impairment"?

(3) Why didn't *Hartford Fire* apply *Arabian American Oil*'s presumption against extraterritoriality? Because the Foreign Trade Antitrust Improvements Act of 1982 defeated the presumption? *See Hartford Fire, supra* page 755 and n.23. Because the allegedly illegal conduct produced substantial effects in the United States? Some other reason?

When should courts invoke the presumption? Lower courts do not appear to have a coherent answer to this question. For example, in the course of interpreting the National Environmental Policy Act, one court stated that the presumption does not apply when conduct or effects occur partially in the United States. *See* Environmental Defense Fund v. Massey, 986 F.2d 528, 531 (D.C. Cir. 1993). Another court, by contrast, applied the presumption in construing the Copyright Act even though acts abroad caused harmful local effects. *See* Subafilms Ltd. v. MGM-Pathe Communications Co. v. 24 F. 3d 1088, 1097 (9th Cir. 1994) (en banc). For a thorough analysis of the lower courts' post-*Hartford Fire* extraterritoriality decisions, see Dodge, Understanding the Presumption Against Extraterritoriality, 16 Berk. J. Int'l L. 85 (1998).

(4) Does *Hartford Fire* say that comity is only relevant if defendants face inconsistent obligations between U.S. and foreign law? If so, doesn't this portend a broad expansion of antitrust extraterritoriality, since "true conflicts" viewed this way will be rare? What do you think about the majority's definition of true conflicts? Is it consistent with the way that the phrase is used in state choice-of-law theory? Do you think the majority takes a balanced view of American and British interests? Would British courts accept this test as a way to define whether a British interest is at stake? Should that matter?

(5) The majority states at one point that "we have no need in this case to address other considerations that might inform a decision to refrain from the exercise of jurisdiction on grounds of comity." Why not? Is its lack of interest in other considerations caused by a failure of the parties to suggest what other considerations there might be, or to argue for them? Don't you

think that if such other considerations exist, then they should be taken into account? (It's not, after all, as though they would be superfluous or redundant; while a court need not reach issues that are unnecessary to its decision, in this case additional comity considerations might have changed the result.) Does the majority opinion's brush-off suggest that it does not think that any other considerations exist; that (in other words) the existence of a true conflict (as it defines the term) is the only basis for a grant of comity?

(6) What exactly is the nature of the presumptions at stake here? The dissent states that two different presumptions operate: first, the presumption against extraterritoriality, and second, the presumption against violation of international law. (Compare the dissent in *Arabian American Oil*, *supra* page 740.) It states that the operation of these two is not coterminous, and indeed, finds that they point in different directions in the present case. Admittedly, there are cases in which the presumptions operate independently; for example, as the dissent points out, where conduct takes place within U.S. territorial waters, the latter presumption may operate even if the former does not. But is the present set of facts one of these cases?

Note that to overcome the first presumption, one must apparently find that Congress intended the law to apply to the instant set of facts. (Or must one only find that Congress intended the law to apply to *some* sets of facts outside U.S. territory, but not necessarily this one?) But once that determination is made, shouldn't there be a sufficient indication of congressional intent to defeat the second? If Congress intends to have its law apply to cases in which application would violate international law, then doesn't it intend to violate international law? Or does the second presumption require some other sort of intent, in addition to the intent that the statute apply to the particular case (*e.g.*, a specific intent to disregard international law, per se)?

(7) The Federal Rules of Civil Procedure permit more extensive discovery than the rules of many foreign nations. They allow a party to discover, for example, relevant information that would not be admissible at trial. Fed. R. Civ. P. 26. This extensive discovery sometimes causes problems when the information or witness is in another country.

To facilitate international discovery, the United States ratified the Convention on the Taking of Evidence Abroad in Civil or Commercial Matters, The Hague, 1970, 23 U.S.T. 2555; T.I.A.S. No.7444, 847 U.N.T.S. 231. Congress implemented the Hague Evidence Convention in 28 U.S.C. §§1781-1782. Using the convention, a district court can issue a letter of request to the central authority of another contracting state, which in turn will take the requested evidence in accordance with its procedures.

Almost every contracting state has declared under Article 23 of the convention that it will not execute letters of request "issued for the purpose of obtaining pretrial discovery of documents" as known in common law countries. Some countries have gone further, passing "blocking statutes" that make it illegal to produce documents outside the country. Australia, Belgium, Denmark, France, India, Quebec, and Switzerland are among the states that have nondisclosure laws. *See* A. Lowe, Extraterritorial Jurisdiction, An An Collection of Legal Materials (1983).

In Société Nationale Industrielle Aerospatiale v. United States District Court, 482 U.S. 522 (1987), the Court unanimously held that the Hague Evidence Convention is not the exclusive means of obtaining evidence overseas from a foreign party who is a national of a contracting state. *Aerospatiale* involved a French defendant who claimed that French law forbade him from complying with a discovery order that was not issued through the convention. Five justices held that the convention is an alternative means of discovery to be used by the district court where reasonable, its appropriateness to be determined by the trial judge on a case-by-case basis.

How will the trial judge determine when resort to the convention will be reasonable? Only when the Federal Rules fail? What if a "blocking statute" does forbid compliance with a discovery order? Citing Fifth Amendment due process, Société Internationale Pour Participations Industrielles et Commerciales, S.A. v. Rogers, 357 U.S. 197 (1958), held that a plaintiff may not be sanctioned by dismissal of the case where the record showed a good-faith effort to comply with a discovery order blocked by foreign law.

(8) The *Hartford Fire* decision generated a great deal of commentary. *See* Dam, *supra;* Lowenfeld, Conflict, Balancing of Interests, and the Exercise of Jurisdiction to Prescribe: Reflections on the Insurance Antitrust Case, 89 Am. J. Int'l L. 42 (1995); Trimble, The Supreme Court and International Law: The Demise of Restatement Section 403, 89 Am. J. Int'l L. 53 (1995); Kramer, Extraterritorial Application of American Law After the Insurance Antitrust Case: A Reply to Professors Lowenfeld and Trimble, 89 Am. J. Int'l L. 750 (1995); Alford, Extraterritorial Application of Antitrust Laws: A Postscript on Hartford Fire Insurance Co. v. California, 34 Va. J. Int'l L. 213 (1993).

4. Universal Jurisdiction and Passive Personality

Filartiga v. Pena-Irala

577 F. Supp. 860 (E.D.N.Y. 1984)

NICKERSON, J.

Plaintiffs, Dolly M. E. and Dr. Joel Filartiga, citizens of Paraguay, brought this action against defendant Pena, also a Paraguayan citizen, and the former Inspector General of Police of Asuncion. They alleged that Pena tortured and murdered Joelito Filartiga, the seventeen year old brother and son, respectively, of plaintiffs, in retaliation for Dr. Filartiga's opposition to President Alfredo Stroessner's government. Plaintiffs invoked jurisdiction under, among other provisions, 28 U.S.C. §1350, giving the district court "original jurisdiction of any civil action by an alien for a tort only, committed in violation of the law of nations or a treaty of the United States."

This court followed what it deemed the binding precedents of IIT v. Vencap, Ltd., 519 F.2d 1001 (2d Cir. 1975) and Dreyfus v. von Finck, 534 F.2d 24 (2d Cir.), *cert. denied,* 429 U.S. 835 (1976), and dismissed for lack of jurisdiction on the ground that violations of the law of nations "do not occur when the aggrieved parties are nationals of the acting state," *id.* at 31.

The Court of Appeals reversed and remanded, concluding that the above quoted language from the *Dreyfus* opinion was "clearly out of tune with the current usage and practice of international law." Filartiga v. Pena-Irala, 630 F.2d 876, 884 (2d Cir. 1980). The Court of Appeals held that "deliberate torture perpetrated under color of official authority violates universally accepted norms of the international law of human rights, regardless of the nationality of the parties," and that 28 U.S.C. §1350 gave jurisdiction over an action asserting such a tort committed in violation of the law of nations. *Id.* at 878.

Following remand Pena took no further part in the action. This court granted a default and referred the question of damages to Magistrate John L. Caden for a report. The Magistrate, after a hearing, recommended damages of $200,000 for Dr. Joel Filartiga and $175,000 for Dolly Filartiga. Plaintiffs filed objections to the report, and the matter is now here for determination. . . .

II

The Court of Appeals decided only that Section 1350 gave jurisdiction. We must now face the issue left open by the Court of Appeals, namely, the nature of the "action" over which the section affords jurisdiction. Does the "tort" to which the statute refers mean a wrong "in violation of the law of nations" or merely a wrong actionable under the law of the appropriate sovereign state? The latter construction would make the violation of international law pertinent only to afford jurisdiction. The court would then, in accordance with traditional conflict of laws principles, apply the substantive law of Paraguay. If the "tort" to which the statute refers is the violation of international law, the court must look to that body of law to determine what substantive principles to apply.

The word "tort" has historically meant simply "wrong" or "the opposite of right," so-called, according to Lord Coke, because it is "wrested" or "crooked," being contrary to that which is "right" and "straight." Sir Edward Coke on Littleton 158b; *see also* W. Prosser, Law of Torts 2 (1971). There was nothing about the contemporary usage of the word in 1789, when Section 1350 was adopted, to suggest that it should be read to encompass wrongs defined as such by a national state but not by international law. Even before the adoption of the Constitution piracy was defined as a crime by the law of nations. As late as 1819 Congress passed legislation, now 18 U.S.C. §1651, providing for punishment of "the crime of piracy, as defined by the law of nations." Congress would hardly have supposed when it enacted Section 1350 that a "crime," but not the comparable "tort," was definable by the law of nations. Nor is there any legislative history of the section to suggest such a limitation.

Accordingly, there is no basis for adopting a narrow interpretation of Section 1350 inviting frustration of the purposes of international law by individual states that enact immunities for government personnel or other such exemptions or limitations. The court concludes that it should determine the substantive principles to be applied by looking to international law, which, as the Court of Appeals stated, "became a part of the common law *of the United States* upon the adoption of the Constitution." 630 F.2d at 886 (emphasis in original).

The international law described by the Court of Appeals does not ordain detailed remedies but sets forth norms. But plainly international "law" does not consist of mere benevolent yearnings never to be given effect. Indeed, the Declaration on the Protection of All Persons from Being Subjected to Torture, General Assembly Resolution 3452, adopted without dissent by the General Assembly, recites that where an act of torture has been committed by or at the instigation of a public official, the victim shall be afforded redress and compensation "in accordance with national law," art. 11, and that "[e]ach state" shall ensure that all acts of torture are offenses under its criminal law, art. 7.

The international law prohibiting torture established the standard and referred to the national states the task of enforcing it. By enacting Section 1350 Congress entrusted that task to the federal courts and gave them power to choose and develop federal remedies to effectuate the purposes of the international law incorporated into United States common law.

In order to take the international condemnation of torture seriously this court must adopt a remedy appropriate to the ends and reflective of the nature of the condemnation. Torture is viewed with universal abhorrence; the prohibition of torture by international consensus and express international accords is clear and unambiguous; and "for purposes of civil liability, the torturer has become—like the pirate and the slave trader before him—hostis humani generis, an enemy of all mankind." 630 F.2d at 884, 888, 890. We are dealing not with an ordinary case of assault and battery. If the courts of the United States are to adhere to the consensus of the community of humankind, any remedy they fashion must recognize that this case concerns an act so monstrous as to make its perpetrator an outlaw around the globe.

III

The common law of the United States includes, of course, the principles collected under the rubric of conflict of laws. For the most part in international matters those principles have been concerned with the relevant policies of the interested national states, and with "the needs" of the "international systems." Restatement (Second) of Conflict of Laws (1971) §6(2). The chief function of international choice-of-law rules has been said to be to further harmonious relations and commercial intercourse between states. *Id.*, comment d.

However, where the nations of the world have adopted a norm in terms so formal and unambiguous as to make it international "law," the interests of the global community transcend those of any one state. That does not mean that traditional choice-of-law principles are irrelevant. Clearly the court should consider the interests of Paraguay to the extent they do not inhibit the appropriate enforcement of the applicable international law or conflict with the public policy of the United States.

In this case the torture and death of Joelito occurred in Paraguay. The plaintiffs and Pena are Paraguayan and lived in Paraguay when the torture took place, although Dolly Filartiga has applied for permanent asylum in the United States. It was in Paraguay that plaintiffs suffered the claimed injuries, with the exception of the emotional trauma which followed Dolly Filartiga to this country. The parties' relationships with each other and with Joelito were centered in Paraguay.

Moreover, the written Paraguayan law prohibits torture. The Constitution of Paraguay, art. 50. The Paraguayan Penal Code, art. 337, provides that homicide by torture is punishable by an imprisonment for 15 to 20 years. Paraguay is a signatory to the American Convention on Human Rights, which proscribes the use of torture. Paraguayan law purports to allow recovery for wrongful death, including specific pecuniary damages, "moral damage," and court costs and attorney's fees. Thus, the pertinent formal Paraguayan law is ascertainable.

All these factors make it appropriate to look first to Paraguayan law in determining the remedy for the violation of international law. *See* Lauritzen v. Larsen; Restatement (Second) of Conflict of Laws (1971) §145(2). It might be objected that, despite Paraguay's official ban on torture, the "law" of that country is what it does in fact, Holmes, The Path of the Law, 10 Harv. L. Rev. 457, 461 (1897), and torture persists throughout the country. Amnesty International Report on Torture (1975) 214-216; D. Helfield and W. Wipfler, Mbarete: The Higher Law of Paraguay (The International League for Human Rights, 1980).

Where a nation's pronouncements form part of the consensus establishing an international law, however, it does not lie in the mouth of a citizen of that nation, though it professes one thing and does another, to claim that his country did not mean what it said. In concert with the other nations of the world Paraguay prohibited torture and thereby reaped the benefits the condemnation brought with it. Paraguayan citizens may not pretend that no such condemnation exists. If there be hypocrisy, we can only say with La Rochefoucauld that "hypocrisy is the homage which vice pays to virtue." Reflections; or Sentences and Moral Maxims 218 (1678).

To the extent that Pena might have expected that Paraguay would not hold him responsible for his official acts, that was not a "justified" expectation, Restatement (Second) of Conflict of Laws (1971) §6(2)(d) and comment g, so as to make unfair the application to him of the written law of Paraguay.

IV

Plaintiffs claim punitive damages, and the Magistrate recommended they be denied on the ground that they are not recoverable under the Paraguayan Civil Code. While compensable "moral" injuries under that code include emotional pain and suffering, loss of companionship and disruption of family life, Paraguayan Civil Code, arts. 1102, 1103, 1112, plaintiffs' expert agrees that the code does not provide for what United States courts would call punitive damages. Paraguayan law, in determining the intensity and duration of the suffering and the consequent "moral" damages, takes into account the heinous nature of the tort. However, such damages are not justified by the desire to punish the defendant. They are designed to compensate for the greater pain caused by the atrocious nature of the act.

Yet because, as the record establishes, Paraguay will not undertake to prosecute Pena for his acts, the objective of the international law making torture punishable as a crime can only be vindicated by imposing punitive damages. . . .

This court concludes that it is essential and proper to grant the remedy of punitive damages in order to give effect to the manifest objectives of the international prohibition against torture.

V

In concluding that the plaintiffs were entitled only to damages recoverable under Paraguayan law, the Magistrate recommended they be awarded $150,000 each as compensation for emotional pain and suffering, loss of companionship and disruption of family life. He also suggested that Dolly Filartiga receive $25,000 for her future medical expenses for treatment of her psychiatric impairment and that Dr. Filartiga receive $50,000 for past expenses related to funeral and medical expenses and to lost income. . . .

In determining the amount of punitive damages the court must consider a variety of factors. Pena's assets are pertinent. Brink's Inc. v. City of New York, 546 F. Supp. 403, 413 (S.D.N.Y. 1982), but the burden is on the defendant to show his modest means if he wishes them considered in mitigation. Zarcone v. Perry, 572 F.2d 52, 56 (2d Cir. 1978). The court has received no evidence on the subject.

The nature of the acts is plainly important. The court need not comment upon the malice that prompts one man to torture another in reprisal for the deeds of his father or to say to the dead man's sister as she left the corpse "Shut up. Here you have what you have been looking for and deserved." (Transcript at 16). Nor would any purpose be served by detailing Pena's conduct. Spread upon the records of this court is the evidence of wounds and of fractures, of burning and beating and of electric shock, of stabbing and whipping and of mutilation, and finally, perhaps mercifully, of death, in short, of the ultimate in human cruelty and brutality.

Chief among the considerations the court must weigh is the fact that this case concerns not a local tort but a wrong as to which the world has seen fit to speak. Punitive damages are designed not merely to teach a defendant not to repeat his conduct but to deter others from following his example. Zarcone v. Perry, *supra,* 572 F.2d at 55. To accomplish that purpose this court must make clear the depth of the international revulsion against torture and measure the award in accordance with the enormity of the offense. Thereby the judgment may perhaps have some deterrent effect. . . .

The record in this case shows that torture and death are bound to recur unless deterred. This court concludes that an award of punitive damages of no less than $5,000,000 to each plaintiff is appropriate to reflect adherence to the world community's proscription of torture and to attempt to deter its practice.

VI

Judgment may be entered for plaintiff Dolly M. E. Filartiga in the amount of $5,175,000 and for plaintiff Joel Filartiga in the amount of $5,210,364, a total judgment of $10,385,364. So ordered.

United States v. Yunis

681 F. Supp. 896 (D.D.C. 1988)

Barrington D. PARKER.

Defendant's motion to dismiss, presenting interesting and novel legal issues, challenges the authority for and the limits to which the United States government may extend its prosecutorial arm over certain crimes allegedly committed by a nonresident alien on foreign soil. . . .

I. Background

This criminal proceeding and indictment arise from the hijacking of a Jordanian civil aircraft, Royal Jordanian Airlines ("ALIA") Flight 402, on June 11, and 12, 1985. There is no dispute that the only nexus to the United States was the presence of several American nationals on board the flight. The airplane was registered in Jordan, flew the Jordanian flag and never landed on American soil or flew over American airspace.

On the morning of June 11, the aircraft was positioned at the Beirut International Airport, Beirut, Lebanon, for a scheduled departure to Amman, Jordan. As the 50-60 passengers boarded, several Arab men, one allegedly the defendant, stormed the plane and ordered the pilot to fly to Tunis, Tunisia where a meeting of the Arab League Conference was underway. The airplane departed from Beirut with all passengers, including the Americans, held hostage. The plane made a short landing in Larnaco, Cyprus where additional fuel was obtained. It then proceeded to Tunis where landing privileges were denied. The airplane flew to Palermo, Sicily, where it was allowed to replenish its fuel and food supply. Thereafter, it lifted off, destined once more for Tunis. Again, entry was denied and the pilot returned to Beirut. On the morning of June 12th, it took off for Damascus, Syria. However, the Syrian authorities also denied landing privileges. Thus after criss-crossing the Mediterranean Sea area for more than 30 hours, the hijackers were forced to return to Beirut, their point of initial departure.

After landing, the hostages were directed to exit the aircraft. The hijackers then called an impromptu press conference and the defendant Yunis allegedly read a speech, which he originally intended to give to the delegates of the Arab League Conference then meeting in Tunis. Following the speech, the hijackers blew up the Jordanian aircraft, quickly left the scene and vanished into the Beirut landscape.

Between June 11 and 12, 1985, ALIA flight 402 never landed on or flew over American space. Its flightpath was limited to an area within and around the Mediterranean Sea. Based on the absence of any nexus to United States territory, Yunis has moved to dismiss the entire indictment, arguing that no United States federal court has jurisdiction to prosecute a foreign national for crimes committed in foreign airspace and on foreign soil. He further claims that the presence of the American nationals on board the aircraft is an insufficient basis for exercising jurisdiction under principles of international law.

Defendant's motion raises several threshold inquiries: whether or not there is a basis for jurisdiction under international law, and if so, whether Congress intended to and had authority to extend jurisdiction of our federal courts over criminal offenses and events which were committed and occurred overseas and out of the territorial jurisdiction of such courts.

II. Analysis

A. Jurisdiction Under International Law

The parties agree that there are five traditional bases of jurisdiction over extraterritorial crimes under international law:

Territorial, wherein jurisdiction is based on the place where the offense is committed;

National, wherein jurisdiction is based on the nationality of the offender;

Protective, wherein jurisdiction is based on whether the national interest is injured;

Universal, wherein jurisdiction is conferred in any forum that obtains physical custody of the perpetrator of certain offenses considered particularly heinous and harmful to humanity;

Passive personal, wherein jurisdiction is based on the nationality of the victim.

These general principles were developed in 1935 by a Harvard Research Project in an effort to codify principles of jurisdiction under international law. *See* Harvard Research in International Law, Jurisdiction with Respect to Crime, 29 Am. J. Int'l L. 435, 445 (Supp. 1935). Most courts, including our Court of Appeals, have adopted the Harvard Research designations on jurisdiction. Several reputable treatises have also recognized the principles: L. Henkin, International Law Cases and Materials 447 (1980); A. D'Amato, International Law and World Order 564 (1980).

The Universal and the Passive Personal principle appear to offer potential bases for asserting jurisdiction over the hostage-taking and aircraft piracy charges against Yunis. However, his counsel argues that the Universal principle is not applicable because neither hostage-taking nor aircraft piracy are heinous crimes encompassed by the doctrine. He urges further, that the United States does not recognize Passive Personal as a legitimate source of jurisdiction. The government flatly disagrees and maintains that jurisdiction is appropriate under both.

1. UNIVERSAL PRINCIPLE

The Universal principle recognizes that certain offenses are so heinous and so widely condemned that "any state if it captures the offender may prosecute and punish that person on behalf of the world community regardless of the nationality of the offender or victim or where the crime was committed." M. Bassiouini, II International Criminal Law, Ch. 6 at 298 (ed. 1986). The crucial question for purposes of defendant's motion is how crimes are classified as "heinous" and whether aircraft piracy and hostage taking fit into this category.

Those crimes that are condemned by the world community and subject to prosecution under the Universal principal are often a matter of international conventions or treaties. *See* Demjanjuk v. Petrovsky, 776 F2d 571, 582 (6th Cir. 1985) (treaty against genocide signed by a significant number of states made that crime heinous; therefore, Israel had proper jurisdiction over nazi war criminal under the Universal principle).

Both offenses are the subject of international agreements. A majority of states in the world community including Lebanon, have signed three treaties condemning aircraft piracy: The Tokyo Convention,[2] The Hague Convention,[3] and The Montreal Convention.[4] The Hague and Montreal Conventions explicitly rely on the principle of Universal jurisdiction in mandating that all states "take such measures as may be necessary to establish its jurisdiction over the offenses . . . where the alleged offender is present in its territory." Hague Convention Art. 4 §2; Montreal Convention Art. 5 §2. Further, those treaties direct that all "contracting states . . . of which the alleged offender is found,. . . shall, be obliged, *without exception whatsoever and whether or not the offense was committed in its territory,* to submit the case to its competent authorities for the purpose of prosecution." Hague Convention Art. 7; Montreal Convention Art. 7 (emphasis added). These two provisions together demonstrate the international community's strong commitment to punish aircraft hijackers irrespective of where the hijacking occurred.

The global community has also joined together and adopted the International Convention for the Taking of Hostages,[5] an agreement which condemns and criminalizes the offense of hostage taking. Like the conventions denouncing aircraft piracy, this treaty requires signatory states to prosecute any alleged offenders "present in its territory."[6]

In light of the global efforts to punish aircraft piracy and hostage taking, international legal scholars unanimously agree that these crimes fit within the category of heinous crimes for purposes of asserting universal jurisdiction. In The Restatement (Revised) of Foreign Relations Law of the United States, a source heavily relied upon by the defendant, aircraft hijacking is specifically identified as a universal crime over which all states should exercise jurisdiction.

Our Circuit has cited the Restatement with approval and determined that the Universal principle, standing alone, provides sufficient basis for asserting jurisdiction over an alleged offender. Therefore, under recognized principles of international law, and the law of this Circuit, there is clear authority to assert jurisdiction over Yunis for the offenses of aircraft piracy and hostage taking.

---

2. Convention on Offenses and Certain Other Acts Committed on Board Aircraft, Sept. 14, 1963, T.I.A.S. No. 159.

3. Convention for the Suppression of Unlawful Seizure of Aircraft, Dec. 16, 1970, T.I.A.S. No. 7192.

4. Convention for the Suppression of Unlawful Acts against the Safety of Civil Aviation, Sept. 23, 1971, T.I.A.S. No. 7570.

5. 34 U.N. GAOR Supp. (No. 39) at 23, U.N. Doc. A/34/39 (1979), reprinted in 18 I.L.M. 1456 (1979) [hereinafter Hostage Taking Convention].

6. Art. V. §2 states "each state *shall* establish jurisdiction in cases where the alleged offender is present in its territory."

2. PASSIVE PERSONAL PRINCIPLE

This principle authorizes states to assert jurisdiction over offenses committed against their citizens abroad. It recognizes that each state has a legitimate interest in protecting the safety of its citizens when they journey outside national boundaries. Because American nationals were on board the Jordanian aircraft, the government contends that the Court may exercise jurisdiction over Yunis under this principle. Defendant argues that this theory of jurisdiction is neither recognized by the international community nor the United States and is an insufficient basis for sustaining jurisdiction over Yunis.

Although many international legal scholars agree that the principle is the most controversial of the five sources of jurisdiction, they also agree that the international community recognizes its legitimacy. . . . More importantly, the international community explicitly approved of the principle as a basis for asserting jurisdiction over hostage takers. As noted above, *supra* p. 9, the Hostage Taking Convention set forth certain mandatory sources of jurisdiction. But it also gave each signatory contrary discretion to exercise extraterritorial jurisdiction when the offense was committed "with respect to a hostage who is a national of that state if that state considers it appropriate." Art. 5(a)(d). Therefore, even if there are doubts regarding the international community's acceptance, there can be no doubt concerning the application of this principle to the offense of hostage taking, an offense for which Yunis is charged.

Defendant's counsel correctly notes that the Passive Personal principle traditionally has been an anathema to United States lawmakers. But his reliance on the Restatement (Revised) of Foreign Relations Laws for the claim that the United States can never invoke the principle is misplaced.[9] In the past, the United States has protested any assertion of such jurisdiction for fear that it could lead to indefinite criminal liability for its own citizens. This objection was based on the belief that foreigners visiting the United States should comply with our laws and should not be permitted to carry their laws with them. Otherwise Americans would face criminal prosecutions for actions unknown to them as illegal.[10] However, in the most recent draft of the Restatement, the authors noted that the theory "has been increasingly ac-

---

9. The Restatement provides that "A State does not have jurisdiction to prescribe a rule of law attaching a legal consequence to conduct of an alien outside its territory merely on the ground that the conduct affects one of its nationals." Restatement (Revised) of Foreign Relations Law §402.

10. The case most widely cited for the United States' rejection of the passive personality principle is known as the *Cutting* case, 1887 For. Rel. 751 (1888, reported in 2 J. B. Moore International Law Digest 232-240 (1906)). In that case, the Secretary of State protested the Mexican authority's assertion of jurisdiction over an American national seized while traveling in Mexico. The American was prosecuted for writing an article in a Texas newspaper criticizing a Mexican national. The Mexican authorities indicted him for criminal libel.

cepted when applied to terrorist and other organized attacks on a state's nationals by reason of their nationality, or to assassinations of a state's ambassadors, or government officials." Restatement (Revised) §402, comment g (Tent. Draft No. 6). The authors retreated from their wholesale rejection of the principle, recognizing that perpetrators of crimes unanimously condemned by members of the international community, should be aware of the illegality of their actions. Therefore, qualified application of the doctrine to serious and universally condemned crimes will not raise the specter of unlimited and unexpected criminal liability.

Thus the Universal and Passive Personality principles, together, provide ample grounds for this Court to assert jurisdiction over Yunis. In fact, reliance on both strengthens the basis for asserting jurisdiction. Not only is the United States acting on behalf of the world community to punish alleged offenders of crimes that threaten the very foundations of world order, but the United States has its own interest in protecting its nationals.[14]

B. Jurisdiction Under Domestic Law

Even if there is authority to assert jurisdiction over Yunis under International law, defendant's counsel argues that the Court has no jurisdiction under domestic law. He contends that Congress neither had the power nor the intention to authorize jurisdiction over the offenses of hostage taking and aircraft piracy committed "half way around the world."

But defendant's argument fails to recognize the power of the Congress to legislate overseas and to define and punish offenses committed on foreign soil. Article I section 8, Clause 11 of the Constitution gives Congress the power to "define and punish Piracies and Felonies committed on the High Seas and Offenses against the Law of Nations." As explained, *supra,* in the

---

14. The government also argues that a third doctrine, the Protective principle, offers grounds for asserting jurisdiction over Yunis. Because this principle gives states wide latitude in defining the parameters of their jurisdiction, the international community has strictly construed the reach of this doctrine to those offenses posing a direct, specific threat to national security. *See* Blakesley, United States Jurisdiction over Extraterritorial Crime, 73 J. Crim. L. & Criminology at 1136; Bassiouini, II International Criminal Law ch. 2 at 21. Recently, some academicians have urged a more liberal interpretation of the protective principle when applied to terroristic activities. Given "the increase in the number of terroristic threats against United States nationals abroad, there can be no doubt that the United States has significant security and protective interests at stake." Paust, Federal Jurisdiction over Extraterritorial Acts of Terrorism, 23 Va. J. of Int'l Law 191, 210 (1983).

In this case, the hijackers never made any demands upon the United States government nor directly threatened its security. Indeed, it was almost happenstance that three American nationals were on board the aircraft. Given the regional focus of the hijacking, a court would have to adopt an expansive view of the principle to assert jurisdiction over Yunis. Since jurisdiction is available under the Universality and Passive Personality principle, there is no reason to reach out and rely on the Protective principle as well.

discussion on the Universal principle, both hostage taking and aircraft piracy have been defined as offenses against the law of nations.

The two statutes under which the defendant was indicted, the Hostage Taking Act and the Aircraft Piracy Act, were part of a three bill package enacted by Congress in 1984 aimed at combating the rise of terrorism. Both were promulgated to extend jurisdiction over extraterritorial crimes and satisfy the country's obligations as a party to various international conventions. Because of the newness of the statutes, no court has been called upon to analyze the scope of the jurisdiction provisions. Therefore, the Court must rely on the recognized tools of statutory interpretation, the language of the statute along with the statutory history, to evaluate whether these provisions apply to the particular offenses charged in this indictment.

1. HOSTAGE TAKING ACT, 18 U.S.C. 1203

This statute imposes liability on any individual who takes an American national hostage irrespective of where the seizure occurs. Congress wrote the jurisdictional reach of the statute in clear and unambiguous language. Subsection (b)(1) provides that a defendant is properly chargeable for offenses occurring outside the United States if *any one* of the following circumstances exists:

> (A) the offender or the person seized or detained is a national of the United States;
>
> (B) the offender is found in the United States; or
>
> (C) the governmental organization sought to be compelled is the Government of the United States.

In the face of this unambiguous language, defendant nevertheless draws on the legislative history to argue that Congress did not intend to extend jurisdiction merely on the grounds that American nationals were seized. However, such reliance is misplaced. Our Circuit has stated time and again that "it is elementary in the law of statutory construction that, absent ambiguity or unreasonable result, the literal language of the statute controls and resort to legislative history is not only unnecessary but improper." . . .

Congress enacted the Hostage Taking Act to meet its obligations as a signatory state to the Hostage Taking Convention. Article 5 of that treaty required signatory states to extend jurisdiction over hijacking committed outside the United States when the offender was a citizen of the states, or "present" in the state. It also provided states with the discretion to assert jurisdiction when their nationals were taken hostage. Congress' voluntary decision to adopt this permissive basis of jurisdiction underscores its intent to exercise broad jurisdiction over any offender who threatens American nationals. Therefore, the plain language of the statute coupled with its legislative history and purpose clearly support a finding that Congress intended to assert extraterritorial jurisdiction over offenders such as Yunis who allegedly seized Americans hostage in foreign territory.

2. DESTRUCTION OF AIRCRAFT ACT, 18 U.S.C. 32

This statute imposes liability for willfully destroying an aircraft, assaulting passengers and crew on board an airflight, damaging an aircraft and placing a destructive device in the aircraft. 18 U.S.C. 32. Two subsections are included, 32(a) and 32(b). Subsection (a) applies to offenses committed against "any aircraft in the special aircraft jurisdiction of the United States or any civil aircraft used, operated, or employed in interstate, overseas, or foreign air commerce." Subsection (b) applies to acts of violence against any individual on board "any civil aircraft registered in a country other than the United States . . . if the offender is later found in the United States."

The subsections provide alternative bases for exercising jurisdiction. The operative provision of 32(a) is the location of the aircraft; the operative provision of 32(b) is the subsequent location of the offender. Together, the two impose a wide circle of liability. Defendant has been charged under each section. The Court will first discuss the application of 32(b) and then turn to the application of 32(a).

(a.) *Application of 32(b):* jurisdiction over offenders later "found" in the United States.

This provision expressly extends jurisdiction over an alleged saboteur who commits offenses against an aircraft located in foreign airspace and has no other nexus to the United States other than that he or she "is later found in the United States." 18 U.S.C. 32(b)(4). Defendant was charged with violating these provisions, in the superseding indictment of October 1, 1987 that was filed after Yunis was arrested and flown to this country aboard a naval plane.

Defendant's counsel argues that his client was not "found" in the United States within the meaning of the statute. He purports that the word "found" only pertains to individuals who voluntarily entered the United States and were later discovered by the government; the term was never envisioned to apply to defendants forcibly abducted and brought to the United States. Yunis did not voluntarily enter the country. To the contrary, he was lured through efforts and stratagem of FBI agents to international waters off the coast of Cyprus, where he was arrested and forcibly brought to the United States. Therefore, counsel argues that the government's forcible kidnapping of Yunis obviates any jurisdiction under this statute.

Defendant's attempt to limit the Court's jurisdiction is unavailing. Once a defendant is brought within the jurisdiction of the Court he is subject to prosecution for all federal offenses. Yunis was seized for alleged violation of the hostage taking statute. Physical presence in United States territory is not a necessary element for exercising subject matter jurisdiction over that offense. Only after he stepped onto American soil was the defendant charged with aircraft piracy. Indeed, once he was within the boundaries of the United States, the government was obligated by statute and the Montreal Convention to prosecute him for destroying the aircraft. As discussed earlier, both the Hague Convention and the Montreal Convention require all contracting states to exercise jurisdiction over individuals charged with seizing control of an aircraft. Any state that secures custody of the alleged hijackers is obligated to prosecute or extradite them. . . .

(b.) *Application of 32(a):* jurisdiction over aircraft in "overseas or foreign air commerce."

This provision imposes liability on individuals who damage and destroy an aircraft and/or perform acts of violence against passengers on board a civil aircraft that operates in "overseas or foreign air commerce." 18 U.S.C. §32(a). Yunis has been charged specifically in Count I with conspiracy to hijack and destroy an aircraft; Count III with destroying a civil aircraft; Count IV with placing a destructive device on a civil aircraft; and in Count V with performing acts of violence against passengers of a civil aircraft.

The 32(a) provision does not become operative unless the aircraft flies in "overseas or foreign air commerce." Defendant contends that the terms "overseas air commerce" and "foreign air commerce" require some nexus to the United States. Because the ALIA flight never landed on or even flew over American air space, he urges the Court to dismiss these counts. In turn, the government argues that Congress intended to regulate air commerce broadly and impose liability against alleged perpetrators of aircraft piracy irregardless of where the offense took place or which country operated the aircraft.

The Court agrees that Counts III, IV, and V must be dismissed. Section (a) of this provision is applicable only to aircraft operating in "interstate, overseas or foreign air commerce." The definitional provision of the Act, 18 U.S.C. §31, relies on the "meaning ascribed to those terms in the Federal Aviation Act of 1958, as amended." That statute provides:

> interstate air commerce, overseas air commerce, and foreign air commerce respectively, mean the carriage by aircraft of persons . . . or the operation or navigation of aircraft in the conduct or furtherance of a business or vocation, in commerce between, respectively,—
>
> (a) a place in any State of the United States . . . through the airspace over any place outside thereof; or between places in the same Territory or possession of the United States,
>
> (b) a place in any State of the United States and any place in a Territory or possession of the United States; and

(c) a place in the United States and any place outside thereof whether such commerce moves wholly by aircraft or partly by aircraft and partly by other forms of transportation.

49 U.S.C. §1301(23).

Although Congress could have expanded the jurisdictional net of subsection 32(a) by adopting a new, more expansive definition of "foreign air commerce," it deliberately chose to rely upon the definition of those terms already incorporated in the Federal Aviation Act. The government simply ignores a deliberate decision of Congress and urges a definition of foreign or overseas air commerce which directly contravenes the plain meaning and prevailing interpretation of these terms as defined in the Federal Aviation Act. The government's definition focuses on the cumulative travels of a passenger or piece of cargo rather than the flightpath of the particular aircraft. If the passenger or package *ever* landed or departed from American territory then the government urges that any flight taken by such passenger would be considered in "foreign air commerce." Because the American nationals must have departed from the United States some time in the past, the government asserts that any flight they boarded in the future, including ALIA flight 402, would be considered in the stream of "foreign air commerce" for purposes of liability under 18 U.S.C. §32(a).

By focusing solely on the passengers and their connection to United States soil no matter how remote, the government's definition makes almost every aircraft subject to regulation by the United States. Airline companies operating exclusively overseas which wanted to avoid such regulation would be forced to research the travel history of every potential passenger and then exclude any person who had every traveled to the United States. . . .

Questions and Comments

(1) *Filartiga* is better known for the Second Circuit's jurisdictional decision, of which this opinion is the remand. *Compare* Tel-Oren v. Libyan Arab Republic, 726 F.2d 774 (D.C. Cir. 1984) (dismissing for lack of subject matter jurisdiction a civil action concerning an attack by a Libyan against Israelis in Israel).

(2) If the *Filartiga* court was correct about a universal prohibition of torture, as a matter of international law, then why did it go on to inquire into the law of Paraguay? What would the court have done if there had been no official ban on torture in Paraguay? Given its disregard for the law of Paraguay on the issue of punitive damages, what was the point of asking about Paraguayan substantive law? What is the source of the court's punitive damages rule?

(3) Does the court in *Yunis* really need to rely on the principle of passive personality, which it recognizes as being the most tenuous of the bases for jurisdiction? Note that it hedges somewhat by applying the theory only to

heinous crimes such as hostage taking and terrorism, which might also qualify for universal jurisdiction as well.

(4) What is the connection between the theory of passive personality and the idea that a state may apply its law because of its legitimate interest in protecting its domiciliaries, a central tenet of modern choice-of-law theory? Why is the idea so much more controversial here than in the domestic choice-of-law context?

(5) Should *Yunis* have a constitutional complaint against application of American law? Does the fact that Article 1, section 8, clause 11, gives Congress power "to define and punish Piracies and Felonies committed on the High Seas and Offenses against the Law of Nations" mean that Yunis can have no due process objection? Would it mean that he has no due process right to a fair trial? When Congress legislates pursuant to its commerce clause powers, is it immune to challenges under the First Amendment?

Or is the answer that the due process clause applies, but is satisfied because universal jurisdiction poses no choice-of-law problems? The only activities punishable under universal jurisdiction, according to this rationale, are activities that are already illegal under the laws of all states.

Would you apply the passive personality principle in antitrust litigation? Why is it not relied upon more frequently in international civil litigation?

(6) Is the court suggesting, in footnote 24, that Congress could not constitutionally assert authority over global air traffic generally? How would such a suggestion fit with the remainder of the court's reasoning?

(7) Subsequent cases avoid the choice-of-law problem in *Filartiga* by applying international law directly or by recourse to federal common law. *See, e.g.*, In re Estate of Ferdinand Marcos, Human Rights Litigation, 25 F.3d 1467 (9th Cir. 1994); Beanal v. Freeport-McMoran, Inc., 197 F.3d 161 (5th Cir. 1999); Xuncax v. Gramajo, 886 F. Supp. 162 (D. Mass. 1995). In addition, in 1992, Congress passed the Torture Victim Protection Act (TVPA), which significantly minimizes choice-of-law problems with *Filartiga*-like litigation with respect to two causes of action. *See* Pub. L. No. 102-256, 106 Stat. 73 (1992), *codified at* 28 U.S.C. 1350 note. The TVPA created a federal cause of action against foreign officials who under color of state law commit torture or extra-judicial killings. Several plaintiffs have subsequently brought successful claims under the TVPA. *See, e.g.*, Kadic v. Karadzic, 74 F.3d 377 (2d Cir. 1996); Xuncax v. Gramajo, 886 F. Supp. 162 (D. Mass. 1995).

Substantial questions remain, however, in cases like *Filartiga* that fall outside the scope of the TVPA. First, plaintiffs cannot invoke the TVPA for customary international law violations such as slavery and genocide. Second, plaintiffs cannot use the TVPA against domestic officials because it applies only to individuals acting under color of foreign law. Third, the TVPA contains procedural rules including an exhaustion requirement and a statute of limitations. Problems in *Filartiga* thus remain for a wide array of potential lawsuits, and commentators have debated how the TVPA's enactment should bear on those cases. In some respects, the TVPA has complicated rather than narrowed the legal questions involved. For example, can the ATCA still provide causes of action for other customary international law violations such as slavery and genocide or does the TVPA restrict the permissible causes of action to torture and extra-judicial killing? Can a plaintiff sue under the ATCA for a claim of torture or an extra-judicial killing if the statute of limitations has expired under the TVPA? Should the TVPA's procedural limitations apply to other causes of action brought under the ATCA? More generally, does the TVPA endorse the choice-of-law answers courts had fashioned in ATCA cases, or does it instead show the need for specific federal enactments in this area. For a debate on the relationship between the TVPA and ATCA, *compare* Koh, Commentary, Is International Law Really State Law?, 111 Harv. L. Rev. 1824 (1998) and Goodman & Jinks, Filartiga's Firm Footing: International Human Rights and Federal Common Law, 66 Fordham L. Rev. 463 (1997) *with* Bradley & Goldsmith, Federal Courts and the Incorporation of International Law, 111 Harv. L. Rev. 2260 (1998) and Bradley & Goldsmith, The Current Illegitimacy of International Human Rights Litigation, 66 Fordham L. Rev. 319 (1997).

(8) As might be imagined given the contemporary concern with both international human rights violations and terrorism, there is substantial literature on the problems of universal jurisdiction. *See, e.g.*, Randall, Universal Jurisdiction Under International Law, 66 Tex. L. Rev. 785 (1988); Symposium, Universal Jurisdiction: Myths, Realities, and Prospects, 35 New Eng. L. Rev. 227 (2001); Aceves, Liberalism and International Legal Scholarship: The Pinochet Case and the Move Toward a Universal System of Transnational Law Litigation, 41 Harv. Intl. L.J. 129 (2000); Jordan, Universal Jurisdiction in a Dangerous World: A Weapon for All Nations Against International Crime, 9 MSU-DCL J. Intl. L. 1 (2000); Joyner, Arresting Impunity: The Case for Universal Jurisdiction in Bringing War Criminals to Accountability, 59 Law & Contemp. Probs. 153 (1996).

(9) Federal courts differ over whether universal jurisdiction applies in civil as well as criminal cases. *Compare* Xuncax v. Gramajo, 886 F. Supp. 162 (D. Mass. 1995) *with* Amerada Hess Shipping Corp. v. Argentine Republic, 638 F. Supp. 73 (S.D.N.Y. 1986), rev'd 830 F.2d 421 (2d Cir. 1987), rev'd on other grounds, 488 U.S. 428 (1989). In an *amicus curiae* brief submitted to the Supreme Court, a group of federal jurisdiction and international law professors' stated that "[i]t is a well-established principle of international law that all States have universal jurisdiction to provide criminal and civil redress for extraterritorial conduct that violates fundamental norms of the law of nations, such as genocide, piracy and torture." Brief of Amici Curiae in Support of Respondents in Karadzic v. Kadic, 20 Hastings Intl. & Comp. L. Rev. 686 (1997). The civil dimension of the issue has been the subject of recent academic attention. *See, e.g.*, Van Schaack, In Defense Of Civil Redress: The Domestic Enforcement of Human Rights Norms in the Context of the

Proposed Hague Judgments Convention, 42 Harv. Intl. L.J. 41 (2001); Bederman et al., The Enforcement of Human Rights and Humanitarian Law by Civil Suits in Municipal Courts: The Civil Dimension of Universal Jurisdiction, reprinted in Contemporary International Law Issues: New Forms, New Applications 156 (1998).

C. Extraterritoriality and the Constitution

United States v. Verdugo-Urquidez

494 U.S. 259 (1989)

CHIEF JUSTICE REHNQUIST delivered the opinion of the Court.

The question presented by this case is whether the Fourth Amendment applies to the search and seizure by United States agents of property that is owned by a nonresident alien and located in a foreign country. We hold that it does not.

Respondent Rene Martin Verdugo-Urquidez is a citizen and resident of Mexico. He is believed by the United States Drug Enforcement Agency (DEA) to be one of the leaders of a large and violent organization in Mexico that smuggles narcotics into the United States. Based on a complaint charging respondent with various narcotics-related offenses, the Government obtained a warrant for his arrest on August 3, 1985.

Following respondent's arrest, Terry Bowen, a DEA agent assigned to the Calexico DEA office, decided to arrange for searches of Verdugo-Urquidez's Mexican residences located in Mexicali and San Felipe. Bowen believed that the searches would reveal evidence related to respondent's alleged narcotics trafficking activities and his involvement in the kidnapping and torture-murder of DEA Special Agent Enrique Camarena Salazar (for which respondent subsequently has been convicted in a separate prosecution). Bowen telephoned Walter White, the Assistant Special Agent in charge of the DEA office in Mexico City, and asked him to seek authorization for the search from the Director General of the Mexican Federal Judicial Police (MFJP). After several attempts to reach high ranking Mexican officials, White eventually contacted the Director General, who authorized the searches and promised the cooperation of Mexican authorities. Thereafter, DEA agents working in concert with officers of the MFJP searched respondent's properties in Mexicali and San Felipe and seized certain documents. In particular, the search of the Mexicali residence uncovered a tally sheet, which the Government believes reflects the quantities of marijuana smuggled by Verdugo-Urquidez into the United States.

The District Court granted respondent's motion to suppress evidence seized during the searches, concluding that the Fourth Amendment applied to the searches and that the DEA agents had failed to justify searching respondent's premises without a warrant. A divided panel of the Court of Appeals for the Ninth Circuit affirmed. It cited this Court's decision in Reid v. Covert, 354 U.S. 1 (1957), which held that American citizens tried by United States military authorities in a foreign country were entitled to the protections of the Fifth and Sixth Amendments, and concluded that "[t]he Constitution imposes substantive constraints on the federal government, even when it operates abroad." Relying on our decision in INS v. Lopez-Mendoza, 468 U.S. 1032 (1984), where a majority of Justices assumed that illegal aliens in the United States have Fourth Amendment rights, the Ninth Circuit majority found it "difficult to conclude that Verdugo-Urquidez lacks these same protections." It also observed that persons in respondent's position enjoy certain trial-related rights, and reasoned that "[i]t would be odd indeed to acknowledge that Verdugo-Urquidez is entitled to due process under the fifth amendment, and to a fair trial under the sixth amendment, . . . and deny him the protection from unreasonable searches and seizures afforded under the fourth amendment." Having concluded that the Fourth Amendment applied to the searches of respondent's properties, the court went on to decide that the searches violated the Constitution because the DEA agents failed to procure a search warrant. Although recognizing that "an American search warrant would be of no legal validity in Mexico," the majority deemed it sufficient that a warrant would have "substantial constitutional value in this country," because it would reflect a magistrate's determination that there existed probable cause to search and would define the scope of the search.

Before analyzing the scope of the Fourth Amendment, we think it significant to note that it operates in a different manner than the Fifth Amendment, which is not at issue in this case. The privilege against self-incrimination guaranteed by the Fifth Amendment is a fundamental trial right of criminal defendants. *See* Malloy v. Hogan, 378 U.S. 1 (1964). Although conduct by law enforcement officials prior to trial may ultimately impair that right, a constitutional violation occurs only at trial. Kastigar v. United States, 406 U.S. 441, 453 (1972). The Fourth Amendment functions differently. It prohibits "unreasonable searches and seizures" whether or not the evidence is sought to be used in a criminal trial, and a violation of the Amendment is "fully accomplished" at the time of an unreasonable governmental intrusion. United States v. Calandra, 414 U.S. 338, 354 (1974); United States v. Leon, 468 U.S. 897, 906 (1984). For purposes of this case, therefore, if there were a constitutional violation, it occurred solely in Mexico. Whether evidence obtained from respondent's Mexican residences should be excluded at trial in the United States is a remedial question separate from the existence vel non of the constitutional violation.

The Fourth Amendment provides:

> The right of the people to be secure in their persons, houses, papers, and effects, against unreasonable searches and seizures, shall not be violated, and no Warrants shall issue, but upon probable cause, supported by Oath or affirmation, and particularly describing the place to be searched, and the persons or things to be seized.

That text, by contrast with the Fifth and Sixth Amendments, extends its reach only to "the people." Contrary to the suggestion of amici curiae that the Framers used this phrase "simply to avoid [an] awkward rhetorical redundancy," "the people" seems to have been a term of art employed in select parts of the Constitution. The Preamble declares that the Constitution is ordained and established by "the People of the United States." The Second Amendment protects "the right of the people to keep and bear Arms," and the Ninth and Tenth Amendments provide that certain rights and powers are retained by and reserved to "the people." *See also* U.S. Const., Amdt. 1 ("Congress shall make no law . . . abridging . . . *the right of the people* peaceably to assemble") (emphasis added); Art. I, §2, cl. 1 ("The House of Representatives shall be composed of Members chosen every second Year *by the People of the several States*") (emphasis added). While this textual exegesis is by no means conclusive, it suggests that "the people" protected by the Fourth Amendment, and by the First and Second Amendments, and to whom rights and powers are reserved in the Ninth and Tenth Amendments, refers to a class of a persons who are part of a national community or who have otherwise developed sufficient connection with this country to be considered part of that community. The language of these Amendments contrasts with the words "person" and "accused" used in the Fifth and Sixth Amendments regulating procedure in criminal cases.

What we know of the history of the drafting of the Fourth Amendment also suggests that its purpose was to restrict searches and seizures which might be conducted by the United States in domestic matters. . . . The available historical data show, . . . that the purpose of the Fourth Amendment was to protect the people of the United States against arbitrary action by their own Government; it was never suggested that the provision was intended to restrain the actions of the Federal Government against aliens outside of the United States territory.

There is likewise no indication that the Fourth Amendment was understood by contemporaries of the Framers to apply to activities of the United States directed against aliens in foreign territory or in international waters. Only seven years after the ratification of the Amendment, French interference with American commercial vessels engaged in neutral trade triggered what came to be known as the "undeclared war" with France. In an Act to "protect the Commerce of the United States" in 1798, Congress authorized President Adams to "instruct the commanders of the public armed vessels which are, or which shall be employed in the service of the United States, to subdue, seize and take any armed French vessel, which shall be found within the jurisdictional limits of the United States, or elsewhere, on the high seas." §1 of An Act Further to Protect the Commerce of the United States, ch. 68, 1 Stat. 578. This public naval force consisted of only 45 vessels, so Congress also gave the President power to grant to the owners of private armed ships and vessels of the United States "special commissions," which would allow them "the same license and authority for the subduing, seizing and capturing any armed French vessel, and for the recapture of the vessels, goods and effects of the people of the United States, as the public armed vessels of the United States may by law have." §2, 1 Stat. 579; *see* U.S. Const., Art. I, §8, cl. 11 (Congress has power to grant letters of marque and reprisal). Under the latter provision, 365 private armed vessels were commissioned before March 1, 1799, *see* G. Allen, Our Naval War with France 59 (1967); together, these enactments resulted in scores of seizures of foreign vessels under congressional authority. Some commanders were held liable by this Court for unlawful seizures because their actions were beyond the scope of the congressional grant of authority, *see, e.g.,* Little v. Barreme, 2 Cranch 170, 177-178 (1804); but it was never suggested that the Fourth Amendment restrained the authority of Congress or of United States agents to conduct operations such as this.

The global view taken by the Court of Appeals of the application of the Constitution is also contrary to this Court's decisions in the *Insular Cases,* which held that not every constitutional provision applies to governmental activity even where the United States has sovereign power. *See, e.g.,* Balzac v. Porto Rico, 258 U.S. 298 (1922) (Sixth Amendment right to jury trial inapplicable in Puerto Rico); Ocampo v. United States, 234 U.S. 91 (1914) (Fifth Amendment grand jury provision inapplicable in Philippines); Dorr v. United States, 195 U.S. 138 (1904) (jury trial provision inapplicable in Philippines); Hawaii v. Mankichi, 190 U.S. 197 (1903) (provisions on indictment by grand jury and jury trial inapplicable in Hawaii); Downes v. Bidwell, 182 U.S. 244 (1901) (Revenue Clauses of Constitution inapplicable to Puerto Rico). In *Dorr,* we declared the general rule that in an unincorporated territory—one not clearly destined for statehood—Congress was not required to adopt "a system of laws which shall include the right of trial by jury, and that *the Constitution does not, without legislation and of its own force, carry such right to territory so situated.*" 195 U.S., at 149 (emphasis added). Only "fundamental" constitutional rights are guaranteed to inhabitants of those territories. *Id.,* at 148; *Balzac, supra,* at 312-313. If that is true with respect to territories ultimately governed by Congress, respondent's claim that the protections of the Fourth Amendment extend to aliens in foreign nations is even weaker. And certainly, it is not open to us in light of the *Insular Cases* to endorse the view that every constitutional provision applies wherever the United States Government exercises its power.

Indeed, we have rejected the claim that aliens are entitled to Fifth Amendment rights outside the sovereign territory of the United States. In

Johnson v. Eisentrager, 339 U.S. 763 (1950), the Court held that enemy aliens arrested in China and imprisoned in Germany after World War II could not obtain writs of habeas corpus in our federal courts on the ground that their convictions for war crimes had violated the Fifth Amendment and other constitutional provisions. The *Eisentrager* opinion acknowledged that in some cases constitutional provisions extend beyond the citizenry; "[t]he alien . . . has been accorded a generous and ascending scale of rights as he increases his identity with our society." *Id.*, at 770. But our rejection of extraterritorial application of the Fifth Amendment was emphatic:

> Such extraterritorial application of organic law would have been so significant an innovation in the practice of governments that, if intended or apprehended, it could scarcely have failed to excite contemporary comment. Not one word can be cited. No decision of this Court supports such a view. *Cf.* Downes v. Bidwell, 182 U.S. 244 [(1901)]. None of the learned commentators on our Constitution has even hinted at it. The practice of every modern government is opposed to it.

Id., at 784. If such is true of the Fifth Amendment, which speaks in the relatively universal term of "person," it would seem even more true with respect to the Fourth Amendment, which applies only to "the people."

To support his all-encompassing view of the Fourth Amendment, respondent points to language from the plurality opinion in Reid v. Covert, 354 U.S. 1 (1957). *Reid* involved an attempt by Congress to subject the wives of American servicemen to trial by military tribunals without the protection of the Fifth and Sixth Amendments. The Court held that it was unconstitutional to apply the Uniform Code of Military Justice to the trials of the American women for capital crimes. Four Justices "reject[ed] the idea that when the United States acts *against citizens* abroad it can do so free of the Bill of Rights." *Id.*, at 5 (emphasis added). The plurality went on to say:

> The United States is entirely a creature of the Constitution. Its power and authority have no other source. It can only act in accordance with all the limitations imposed by the Constitution. When the Government reaches out to punish *a citizen* who is abroad, the shield which the Bill of Rights and other parts of the Constitution provide to protect his life and liberty should not be stripped away just because he happens to be in another land.

Id., at 5-6 (emphasis added; footnote omitted). Respondent urges that we interpret this discussion to mean that federal officials are constrained by the Fourth Amendment wherever and against whomever they act. But the holding of *Reid* stands for no such sweeping proposition: it decided that United States citizens stationed abroad could invoke the protection of the Fifth and Sixth Amendments. The concurrences by Justices Frankfurter and Harlan in *Reid* resolved the case on much narrower grounds than the plurality and declined even to hold that United States citizens were entitled to the full range of constitutional protections in all overseas criminal prosecutions. Since respondent is not a United States citizen, he can derive no comfort from the *Reid* holding.

Verdugo-Urquidez also relies on a series of cases in which we have held that aliens enjoy certain constitutional rights. These cases, however, establish only that aliens receive constitutional protections when they have come within the territory of the United States and developed substantial connections with this country. Respondent is an alien who has had no previous significant voluntary connection with the United States, so these cases avail him not.

Justice Stevens' concurrence in the judgment takes the view that even though the search took place in Mexico, it is nonetheless governed by the requirements of the Fourth Amendment because respondent was "lawfully present in the United States . . . even though he was brought and held here against his will." *Post,* at 279. But this sort of presence—lawful but involuntary—is not of the sort to indicate any substantial connection with our country. The extent to which respondent might claim the protection of the Fourth Amendment if the duration of his stay in the United States were to be prolonged—by a prison sentence, for example—we need not decide. When the search of his house in Mexico took place, he had been present in the United States for only a matter of days. We do not think the applicability of the Fourth Amendment to the search of premises in Mexico should turn on the fortuitous circumstance of whether the custodian of its nonresident alien owner had or had not transported him to the United States at the time the search was made.

The Court of Appeals found some support for its holding in our decision in INS v. Lopez-Mendoza, 468 U.S. 1032 (1984), where a majority of Justices assumed that the Fourth Amendment applied to illegal aliens in the United States. We cannot fault the Court of Appeals for placing some reliance on the case, but our decision did not expressly address the proposition gleaned by the court below. The question presented for decision in *Lopez-Mendoza* was limited to whether the Fourth Amendment's exclusionary rule should be extended to civil deportation proceedings; it did not encompass whether the protections of the Fourth Amendment extend to illegal aliens in this country. The Court often grants certiorari to decide particular legal issues while assuming without deciding the validity of antecedent propositions, and such assumptions—even on jurisdictional issues—are not binding in future cases that directly raise the questions. Our statements in *Lopez-Mendoza* are therefore not dispositive of how the Court would rule on a Fourth Amendment claim by illegal aliens in the United States if such a claim were squarely before us. Even assuming such aliens would be entitled to Fourth Amendment protections, their situation is different from respondent's. The illegal aliens in *Lopez-Mendoza* were in the United States voluntarily and presumably had accepted some societal obligations; but respondent had no voluntary connection with this country that might place him among "the people" of the United States.

Not only are history and case law against respondent, but as pointed out in Johnson v. Eisentrager, 393 U.S. 763 (1950), the result of accepting his claim would have significant and deleterious consequences for the United States in conducting activities beyond its boundaries. The rule adopted by the Court of Appeals would apply not only to law enforcement operations abroad, but also to other foreign policy operations which might result in "searches or seizures." The United States frequently employs Armed Forces outside this country—over 200 times in our history—for the protection of American citizens or national security. Application of the Fourth Amendment to those circumstances could significantly disrupt the ability of the political branches to respond to foreign situations involving our national interest. Were respondent to prevail, aliens with no attachment to this country might well bring actions for damages to remedy claimed violations of the Fourth Amendment in foreign countries or in international waters. . . . The Members of the Executive and Legislative Branches are sworn to uphold the Constitution, and they presumably desire to follow its commands. But the Court of Appeals' global view of its applicability would plunge them into a sea of uncertainty as to what might be reasonable in the way of searches and seizures conducted abroad. Indeed, the Court of Appeals held that absent exigent circumstances, United States agents could not effect a "search or seizure" for law enforcement purposes in a foreign country without first obtaining a warrant—which would be a dead letter outside the United States—from a magistrate in this country. Even if no warrant were required, American agents would have to articulate specific facts giving them probable cause to undertake a search or seizure if they wished to comply with the Fourth Amendment as conceived by the Court of Appeals.

We think that the text of the Fourth Amendment, its history, and our cases discussing the application of the Constitution to aliens and extraterritorially require rejection of respondent's claim. At the time of the search, he was a citizen and resident of Mexico with no voluntary attachment to the United States, and the place searched was located in Mexico. Under these circumstances, the Fourth Amendment has no application.

For better or for worse, we live in a world of nation-states in which our Government must be able to "functio[n] effectively in the company of sovereign nations." Perez v. Brownell, 356 U.S. 44, 57 (1958). Some who violate our laws may live outside our borders under a regime quite different from that which obtains in this country. Situations threatening to important American interests may arise halfway around the globe, situations which in the view of the political branches of our Government require an American response with armed force. If there are to be restrictions on searches and seizures which occur incident to such American action, they must be imposed by the political branches through diplomatic understanding, treaty, or legislation.

The judgment of the Court of Appeals is accordingly reversed.

Justice KENNEDY, concurring.

I agree that no violation of the Fourth Amendment has occurred and that we must reverse the judgment of the Court of Appeals. Although some explanation of my views is appropriate given the difficulties of this case, I do not believe they depart in fundamental respects from the opinion of the Court, which I join.

In cases involving the extraterritorial application of the Constitution, we have taken care to state whether the person claiming its protection is a citizen, *see, e.g.*, Reid v. Covert, 354 U.S. 1 (1957), or an alien, *see, e.g.*, Johnson v. Eisentrager, 339 U.S. 763 (1950). The distinction between citizens and aliens follows from the undoubted proposition that the Constitution does not create, nor do general principles of law create, any juridical relation between our country and some undefined, limitless class of noncitizens who are beyond our territory. We should note, however, that the absence of this relation does not depend on the idea that only a limited class of persons ratified the instrument that formed our Government. Though it must be beyond dispute that persons outside the United States did not and could not assent to the Constitution, that is quite irrelevant to any construction of the powers conferred or the limitations imposed by it. . . . The force of the Constitution is not confined because it was brought into being by certain persons who gave their immediate assent to its terms.

For somewhat similar reasons, I cannot place any weight on the reference to "the people" in the Fourth Amendment as a source of restricting its protections. With respect, I submit these words do not detract from its force or its reach. Given the history of our Nation's concern over warrantless and unreasonable searches, explicit recognition of "the right of the people" to Fourth Amendment protection may be interpreted to underscore the importance of the right, rather than to restrict the category of persons who may assert it. The restrictions that the United States must observe with reference to aliens beyond its territory or jurisdiction depend, as a consequence, on general principles of interpretation, not on an inquiry as to who formed the Constitution or a construction that some rights are mentioned as being those of "the people."

I take it to be correct, as the plurality opinion in Reid v. Covert sets forth, that the Government may act only as the Constitution authorizes, whether the actions in question are foreign or domestic. *See* 354 U.S., at 6. But this principle is only a first step in resolving this case. The question before us then becomes what constitutional standards apply when the Government acts, in reference to an alien, within its sphere of foreign operations. We have not overruled either In re Ross, 140 U.S. 453 (1891), or the so-called *Insular Cases* (*i.e.*, Downes v. Bidwell, 182 U.S. 244 (1901); Hawaii v. Mankichi, 190 U.S. 197 (1903); Dorr v. United States, 195 U.S. 138 (1904); Balzac v. Porto Rico, 258 U.S. 298 (1922)). These authorities, as well as United States v. Curtiss-Wright Export Corp., 299 U.S. 304, 318 (1936), stand for the proposition that we must interpret constitutional protections in light of the undoubted power of the United States to take actions to assert its legitimate power and authority abroad.

The conditions and considerations of this case would make adherence to the Fourth Amendment's warrant requirement impracticable and anomalous. Just as the Constitution in the *Insular Cases* did not require Congress to implement all constitutional guarantees in its territories because of their "wholly dissimilar traditions and institutions," the Constitution does not require United States agents to obtain a warrant when searching the foreign home of a nonresident alien. If the search had occurred in a residence within the United States, I have little doubt that the full protections of the Fourth Amendment would apply. But that is not this case. The absence of local judges or magistrates available to issue warrants, the differing and perhaps unascertainable conceptions of reasonableness and privacy that prevail abroad, and the need to cooperate with foreign officials all indicate that the Fourth Amendment's warrant requirement should not apply in Mexico as it does in this country. For this reason, in addition to the other persuasive justifications stated by the Court, I agree that no violation of the Fourth Amendment has occurred in the case before us. The rights of a citizen, as to whom the United States has continuing obligations, are not presented by this case.

I do not mean to imply, and the Court has not decided, that persons in the position of the respondent have no constitutional protection. The United States is prosecuting a foreign national in a court established under Article III, and all of the trial proceedings are governed by the Constitution. All would agree, for instance, that the dictates of the Due Process Clause of the Fifth Amendment protect the defendant. Indeed, as Justice Harlan put it, "the question of which specific safeguards . . . are appropriately to be applied in a particular context . . . can be reduced to the issue of what process is 'due' a defendant in the particular circumstances of a particular case." *Reid, supra,* at 75. Nothing approaching a violation of due process has occurred in this case.

Justice STEVENS, concurring in the judgment.

In my opinion aliens who are lawfully present in the United States are among those "people" who are entitled to the protection of the Bill of Rights, including the Fourth Amendment. Respondent is surely such a person even though he was brought and held here against his will. I therefore cannot join the Court's sweeping opinion.* I do agree, however, with the Government's submission that the search conducted by the United States agents with the approval and cooperation of the Mexican authorities was not "unreasonable" as that term is used in the first Clause of the Amendment. I do not believe the Warrant Clause has any application to searches of noncitizens' homes in foreign jurisdictions because American magistrates have no power to authorize such searches. I therefore concur in the Court's judgment.

Justice BRENNAN, with whom Justice MARSHALL joins, dissenting.

Particularly in the past decade, our Government has sought, successfully, to hold foreign nationals criminally liable under federal laws for con-

---

* The Court's interesting historical discussion is simply irrelevant to the question whether an alien lawfully within the sovereign territory of the United States is entitled to the protection of our laws. Nor is comment on illegal aliens' entitlement to the protections of the Fourth Amendment necessary to resolve this case.

duct committed entirely beyond the territorial limits of the United States that nevertheless has effects in this country. Foreign nationals must now take care not to violate our drug laws, our antitrust laws, our securities laws, and a host of other federal criminal statutes.

The Constitution is the source of Congress' authority to criminalize conduct, whether here or abroad, and of the Executive's authority to investigate and prosecute such conduct. But the same Constitution also prescribes limits on our Government's authority to investigate, prosecute, and punish criminal conduct, whether foreign or domestic. . . . The Court today creates an antilogy: the Constitution authorizes our Government to enforce our criminal laws abroad, but when Government agents exercise this authority, the Fourth Amendment does not travel with them. This cannot be. At the very least, the Fourth Amendment is an unavoidable correlative of the Government's power to enforce the criminal law.

A

. . . According to the majority, the term "the people" refers to "a class of persons who are part of a national community or who have otherwise developed sufficient connection with this country to be considered part of that community." The Court admits that "the people" extends beyond the citizenry, but leaves the precise contours of its "sufficient connection" test unclear. At one point the majority hints that aliens are protected by the Fourth Amendment only when they come within the United States and develop "substantial connections" with our country. At other junctures, the Court suggests that an alien's presence in the United States must be voluntary and that the alien must have "accepted some societal obligations." At yet other points, the majority implies that respondent would be protected by the Fourth Amendment if the place searched were in the United States.[7]

What the majority ignores, however, is the most obvious connection between Verdugo-Urquidez and the United States: he was investigated and is being prosecuted for violations of United States law and may well spend the

7. The Fourth Amendment contains no express or implied territorial limitations, and the majority does not hold that the Fourth Amendment is inapplicable to searches outside the United States and its territories. It holds that respondent is not protected by the Fourth Amendment because he is not one of "the people." Indeed, the majority's analysis implies that a foreign national who had "developed sufficient connection with this country to be considered part of [our] community" would be protected by the Fourth Amendment regardless of the location of the search. Certainly nothing in the Court's opinion questions the validity of the rule, accepted by every Court of Appeals to have considered the question, that the Fourth Amendment applies to searches conducted by the United States Government against United States citizens abroad. A warrantless, unreasonable search and seizure is no less a violation of the Fourth Amendment because it occurs in Mexicali, Mexico, rather than Calexico, California.

rest of his life in a United States prison. The "sufficient connection" is supplied not by Verdugo-Urquidez, but by the Government. Respondent is entitled to the protections of the Fourth Amendment because our Government, by investigating him and attempting to hold him accountable under United States criminal laws, has treated him as a member of our community for purposes of enforcing our laws. He has become, quite literally, one of the governed. Fundamental fairness and the ideals underlying our Bill of Rights compel the conclusion that when we impose "societal obligations," such as the obligation to comply with our criminal laws, on foreign nationals, we in turn are obliged to respect certain correlative rights, among them the Fourth Amendment.

By concluding that respondent is not one of "the people" protected by the Fourth Amendment, the majority disregards basic notions of mutuality. If we expect aliens to obey our laws, aliens should be able to expect that we will obey our Constitution when we investigate, prosecute, and punish them. . . .

Mutuality is essential to ensure the fundamental fairness that underlines our Bill of Rights. Foreign nationals investigated and prosecuted for alleged violations of United States criminal laws are just as vulnerable to oppressive Government behavior as are United States citizens investigated and prosecuted for the same alleged violations. Indeed, in a case such as this where the Government claims the existence of an international criminal conspiracy, citizens and foreign nationals may be codefendants, charged under the same statutes for the same conduct and facing the same penalties if convicted. They may have been investigated by the same agents pursuant to the same enforcement authority. When our Government holds these codefendants to the same standards of conduct, the Fourth Amendment, which protects the citizen from unreasonable searches and seizures, should protect the foreign national as well.

Mutuality also serves to inculcate the values of law and order. By respecting the rights of foreign nationals, we encourage other nations to respect the rights of our citizens. Moreover, as our Nation becomes increasingly concerned about the domestic effects of international crime, we cannot forget that the behavior of our law enforcement agents abroad sends a powerful message about the rule of law to individuals everywhere. . . . This principle is no different when the United States applies its rules of conduct to foreign nationals. If we seek respect for law and order, we must observe these principles ourselves. Lawlessness breeds lawlessness.

Finally, when United States agents conduct unreasonable searches, whether at home or abroad, they disregard our Nation's values. For over 200 years, our country has considered itself the world's foremost protector of liberties. The privacy and sanctity of the home have been primary tenets of our moral, philosophical, and judicial beliefs. Our national interest is defined by those values and by the need to preserve our own just institutions. We take pride in our commitment to a Government that cannot, on mere whim, break down doors and invade the most personal of places. We exhort other nations to follow our example. How can we explain to others—and to ourselves—that these long cherished ideals are suddenly of no consequence when the door being broken belongs to a foreigner?

B

In its effort to establish that respondent does not have sufficient connection to the United States to be considered one of "the people" protected by the Fourth Amendment, the Court relies on the text of the Amendment, historical evidence, and cases refusing to apply certain constitutional provisions outside the United States. None of these however, justifies the majority's cramped interpretation of the Fourth Amendment's applicability.

The majority looks to various constitutional provisions and suggests that " 'the people' seems to have been a term of art." But the majority admits that its "textual exegesis is by no means conclusive." *Ibid.*[9] One Member of the majority even states that he "cannot place any weight on the reference to 'the people' in the Fourth Amendment as a source of restricting its protections." (Kennedy, J., concurring). The majority suggests a restrictive interpretation of those with "sufficient connection" to this country to be considered among "the people," but the term "the people" is better understood as a rhetorical counterpoint to "the Government," such that rights that were reserved to "the people" were to protect all those subject to "the Government.". . . "The people" are "the governed."

The drafting history of the Fourth Amendment also does not support the majority's interpretation of "the people." First, the Drafters chose not to limit the right against unreasonable searches and seizures in more specific ways. They could have limited the right to "citizens," "freemen," "residents," or "the American people." The conventions called to ratify the Constitution in New York and Virginia, for example, each recommended an amendment stating, "That every freeman has a right to be secure from all unreasonable searches and seizures. . . ." W. Cuddihy, Search and Seizure in Great Britain and the American Colonies, pt. 2, p.571, n.129, 574, n.134 (1974). But the Drafters of the Fourth Amendment rejected this limitation and instead provided broadly for "[t]he right of the people to be secure in their persons, houses, papers, and effects." Second, historical materials contain no evidence

9. The majority places an unsupportable reliance on the fact that the Drafters used "the people" in the Fourth Amendment while using "person" and "accused" in the Fifth and Sixth Amendments respectively. The Drafters purposely did not use the term "accused." As the majority recognizes, the Fourth Amendment is violated at the time of an unreasonable governmental intrusion, even if the victim of unreasonable governmental action is never formally "accused" of any wrongdoing. The majority's suggestion that the Drafters could have used "person" ignores the fact that the Fourth Amendment then would have begun quite awkwardly: "The right of persons to be secure in their persons. . . ."

that the Drafters intended to limit the availability of the right expressed in the Fourth Amendment. The Amendment was introduced on the floor of Congress, considered by Committee, debated by the House of Representatives and the Senate, and submitted to the 13 States for approval. Throughout that entire process, no speaker or commentator, pro or con, referred to the term "the people" as a limitation.

The Court also relies on a series of cases dealing with the application of criminal procedural protections outside of the United States to conclude that "not every constitutional provision applies to governmental activity even where the United States has sovereign power." None of these cases, however, purports to read the phrase "the people" as limiting the protections of the Fourth Amendment to those with "sufficient connection" to the United States, and thus none gives content to the majority's analysis. The cases shed no light on the question whether respondent—a citizen of a nonenemy nation being tried in a United States federal court—is one of "the people" protected by the Fourth Amendment.

The majority mischaracterizes Johnson v. Eisentrager, 339 U.S. 763 (1950), as having "rejected the claim that aliens are entitled to Fifth Amendment rights outside the sovereign territory of the United States." In *Johnson,* 21 German nationals were convicted of engaging in continued military activity against the United States after the surrender of Germany and before the surrender of Japan in World War II. The Court held that "the Constitution does not confer a right of personal security or an immunity from military trial and punishment upon an *alien enemy* engaged in the hostile service of a government at war with the United States." 339 U.S., at 785 (emphasis added). As the Court wrote:

> It is war that exposes the relative vulnerability of the alien's status. The security and protection enjoyed while the nation of his allegiance remains in amity with the United States are greatly impaired when his nation takes up arms against us. . . . But disabilities this country lays upon the alien who becomes also an enemy are imposed temporarily as an incident of war and not as an incident of alienage.

Id., at 771-772. The Court rejected the German nationals' efforts to obtain writs of habeas corpus not because they were foreign nationals, but because they were enemy soldiers.

The *Insular Cases,* Balzac v. Porto Rico, 258 U.S. 298 (1922), Ocampo v. United States, 234 U.S. 91 (1914), Dorr v. United States, 195 U.S. 138 (1904), and Hawaii v. Mankichi, 190 U.S. 197 (1903), are likewise inapposite. The *Insular Cases* all concerned whether accused persons enjoyed the protections of certain rights in criminal prosecutions brought by territorial authorities in territorial courts. These cases were limited to their facts long ago, *see* Reid v. Covert, 354 U.S., at 14 (plurality opinion) ("[I]t is our judgment that neither the cases nor their reasoning should be given any further expansion"), and they are of no analytical value when a criminal defendant seeks to invoke the Fourth Amendment in a prosecution by the Federal Government in a federal court.[11]

C

The majority's rejection of respondent's claim to Fourth Amendment protection is apparently motivated by its fear that application of the Amendment to law enforcement searches against foreign nationals overseas "could significantly disrupt the ability of the political branches to respond to foreign situations involving our national interest." *Ante,* at 273-274. The majority's doomsday scenario—that American Armed Forces conducting a mission to protect our national security with no law enforcement objective "would have to articulate specific facts giving them probable cause to undertake a search or seizure," *ante,* at 274—is fanciful. Verdugo-Urquidez is protected by the Fourth Amendment because our Government, by investigating and prosecuting him, has made him one of "the governed." *See supra,* at 284, 287. Accepting respondent as one of "the governed," however, hardly requires the Court to accept enemy aliens in wartime as among "the governed" entitled to invoke the protection of the Fourth Amendment. *See* Johnson v. Eisentrager, *supra.*

Moreover, with respect to non-law-enforcement activities not directed against enemy aliens in wartime but nevertheless implicating national security, doctrinal exceptions to the general requirements of a warrant and probable cause likely would be applicable more frequently abroad, thus lessening the purported tension between the Fourth Amendment's strictures and the Executive's foreign affairs power. Many situations involving sensitive operations abroad likely would involve exigent circumstances such that the warrant requirement would be excused. Therefore, the Government's conduct would be assessed only under the reasonableness standard, the application of which depends on context.

In addition, where the precise contours of a "reasonable" search and seizure are unclear, the Executive Branch will not be "plunge[d] . . . into a sea of uncertainty," that will impair materially its ability to conduct foreign affairs. Doctrines such as official immunity have long protected Government agents from any undue chill on the exercise of lawful discretion. Similarly, the Court has recognized that there may be certain situations in which the offensive use

---

11. The last of the *Insular Cases* cited by the majority, Downes v. Bidwell, 182 U.S. 244 (1901), is equally irrelevant. In *Downes,* the Court held that Puerto Rico was not part of "the United States" with respect to the constitutional provision that "all Duties, Imposts and Excises shall be uniform throughout the United States," U.S. Const., Art. I, §8, cl. 1. 182 U.S., at 249. Unlike the Uniform Duties Clause, the Fourth Amendment contains no express territorial limitations.

of constitutional rights should be limited. In most cases implicating foreign policy concerns in which the reasonableness of an overseas search or seizure is unclear, application of the Fourth Amendment will not interfere with the Executive's traditional prerogative in foreign affairs because a court will have occasion to decide the constitutionality of such a search only if *the Executive* decides to bring a criminal prosecution and introduce evidence seized abroad. When the Executive decides to conduct a search as part of an ongoing criminal investigation, fails to get a warrant, and then seeks to introduce the fruits of that search at trial, however, the courts must enforce the Constitution.

Justice BLACKMUN, dissenting.

I cannot accept the Court of Appeals' conclusion, echoed in some portions of Justice Brennan's dissent, that the Fourth Amendment governs every action by an American official that can be characterized as a search or seizure. American agents acting abroad generally do not purport to exercise *sovereign* authority over the foreign nationals with whom they come in contact. The relationship between these agents and foreign nationals is therefore fundamentally different from the relationship between United States officials and individuals residing within this country.

I am inclined to agree with Justice Brennan, however, that when a foreign national is held accountable for purported violations of United States criminal laws, he has effectively been treated as one of "the governed" and therefore is entitled to Fourth Amendment protections. Although the Government's exercise of *power* abroad does not ordinarily implicate the Fourth Amendment, the enforcement of domestic criminal law seems to me to be the paradigmatic exercise of sovereignty over those who are compelled to obey. In any event, as Justice Stevens notes, *ante*, at 279, respondent was lawfully (though involuntarily) within this country at the time the search occurred. Under these circumstances I believe that respondent is entitled to invoke protections of the Fourth Amendment. I agree with the Government, however, that an American magistrate's lack of power to authorize a search abroad renders the Warrant Clause inapplicable to the search of a noncitizen's residence outside this country.

The Fourth Amendment nevertheless requires that the search be "reasonable." And when the purpose of a search is the procurement of evidence for a criminal prosecution, we have consistently held that the search, to be reasonable, must be based upon probable cause. Neither the District Court nor the Court of Appeals addressed the issue of probable cause, and I do not believe that a reliable determination could be made on the basis of the record before us. I therefore would vacate the judgment of the Court of Appeals and remand the case for further proceedings.

Questions and Comments

(1) Professor Neuman articulates four models regarding the proper reach of U.S. constitutional rights. First, a "universalist" approach "require[s] that

constitutional provisions that create rights with no express limitations as to the persons or places covered should be interpreted as applicable to every person and at every place." Second, a "membership" approach "legitimates government through the idea of an actual or hypothetical agreement embodying the consent of the governed who have established the state and empowered it to govern." On this view, "beneficiaries have rights based in the contract; nonbeneficiaries are relegated to whatever rights they may have independent of the contract." The only difficult issue is the identity of the parties to the contract. Third, under a "territorial" model, "the Constitution constrains the United States government only when it acts within the borders of the United States." Fourth, and finally, a "balancing" approach holds that "the government's reduced right to obedience [abroad] and reduced means of enforcement [abroad] may call for a reciprocal reduction in individual rights [abroad]." *See* Neuman, Whose Constitution?, 100 Yale L.J. 909, 916-921 (1991). Which of these four models does the majority opinion in *Verdugo* embrace? Which does Justice Brennan embrace? Which is normatively most attractive?

(2) Is the majority in *Verdugo* saying anything more than that there is an American "interest" in applying the Bill of Rights to citizens, and sometimes in applying substantive law to non-citizens, but no interest in applying the Bill of Rights to non-citizens (or, to non-citizens acting abroad)?

(3) In Sale v. Haitian Centers Council, Inc., 509 U.S. 155 (1993), eight members of the Supreme Court relied on the presumption against extraterritoriality to explain why a provision prohibiting the attorney general from deporting or returning aliens to a place where their lives or freedom would be threatened on account of race, religion, or political opinion should not apply to a return of Haitian boat people to Haiti. The boat people were mainly being picked up at sea, beyond the territorial jurisdiction of any state. In response to the argument that applying the law to protect the boat people would not offend any other nation, the Court cited Smith v. United States, page 744 *supra,* (concerning activities in Antarctica) for the proposition that this is not the presumption's sole purpose.

But should the same principles apply to restrict the reach of laws (or, as in *Verdugo,* constitutional provisions) that limit *government power* over noncitizens as apply to restrict the reach of laws that impose criminal punishment or civil damages on *individuals?* Presumably one of the reasons for the presumption in the latter situation is that individuals who act outside the United States should not ordinarily be subject to U.S. laws. How does this reasoning apply to U.S. government activities? Recall that there is ordinarily no problem with applying local law to the extraterritorial activities of local citizens; *see* Skiriotes v. Florida, page 349 *supra.* Doesn't it seem ironic that American criminal laws would reach Verdugo's activities, but American constitutional protections would not? *Compare Hartford Fire Insurance,* page 752 *supra.* Is there some reason that the Court is so stingy about extending the reach of protective rules but so generous about extending the reach of rules requiring outsiders to obey?

(4) United States v. Tiede, 86 F.R.D. 227 (1979), involved the trial of an East German hijacker before the United States Court for Berlin, a court authorized by an agreement amongst Germany and the Western Powers after the Second World War. The defendant requested a jury trial, to which he was not entitled (according to the prosecution) because the United States Constitution did not apply.

> The Court finds the Prosecution's argument to be entirely without merit. First, there has never been a time when United States authorities exercised governmental powers in any geographical area—whether at war or in times of peace—without regard for their own Constitution. Ex parte Milligan, 71 U.S. (4 Wall.) 2 (1866). Nor has there ever been a case in which constitutional officers, such as the Secretary of State, have exercised the powers of their office without constitutional limitations. Even in the long-discredited case of In re Ross, 140 U.S. 453 (1891), in which American consular officers were permitted to try United States citizens in certain "non-Christian" countries, the Court made its decision under the Constitution—not in total disregard of it. The distinction is subtle but real: the applicability of any provision of the Constitution is itself a point of constitutional law, to be decided in the last instance by the judiciary, not by the Executive Branch.
>
> This fundamental principle was forcefully and clearly announced by the Supreme Court more than a century ago in Ex parte Milligan, 71 U.S. (4 Wall.) 2 (1866):
>
>> [The Framers of the American Constitution] foresaw that troublous times would arise, when rulers and people would become restive under restraint, and seek by sharp and decisive measures to accomplish ends deemed just and proper; and that the principles of constitutional liberty would be in peril, unless established by irrepealable law. The history of the world had taught them that what was done in the past might be attempted in the future. *The Constitution of the United States is a law for rulers and people, equally in war and in peace, and covers with the shield of its protection all classes of men, at all times, and under all circumstances.* No doctrine, involving more pernicious consequences, was ever invented by the wit of man than that any of its provisions can be suspended during any of the great exigencies of government. Such a doctrine leads directly to anarchy or despotism, but the theory of necessity on which it is based is false; for the government, within the Constitution, has all the powers granted to it, which are necessary to preserve its existence; as has been happily proved by the result of the great effort to throw off its just authority. [Emphasis added.]
>
> Although the Supreme Court was reviewing the power of military commissions organized by military authorities in the United States during the Civil War, the wisdom of the principle set forth above is nowhere better

demonstrated than in this city, during this occupation, and before this Court.

The Prosecution's position, if accepted by this Court, would have dramatic consequences not only for the two defendants whom the United States has chosen to arraign before the Court, but for every person within the territorial limits of the United States Sector of Berlin. If the occupation authorities are not governed by the Constitution in this Court, they are not governed by the Constitution at all. And, if the occupation authorities may act free of all constitutional restraints, no one in the American Sector of Berlin has any protection from their untrammeled discretion. If there are no constitutional protections, there is no First Amendment, no Fifth Amendment or Sixth Amendment; even the Thirteenth Amendment's prohibition of involuntary servitude would be inapplicable. The American authorities, if the Secretary of State so decreed, would have the power, in time of peace and with respect to German and American citizens alike, to arrest any person with cause, to hold a person incommunicado, to deny an accused the benefit of counsel, to try a person summarily and to impose sentence—all as a part of the unreviewable exercise of foreign policy.

This Court does not suggest that the American occupation authorities intend to carry the Prosecution's thesis to its logical conclusion. Nonetheless, people have been deceived before in their assessment of the intentions of their own leaders and their own government; and those who have left the untrammeled, unchecked power in the hands of their leaders have not had a happy experience. It is a first principle of American life—not only life at home but life abroad—that everything American public officials do is governed by, measured against, and must be authorized by the United States Constitution.

As the Supreme Court made clear in Ex parte Milligan, *supra,* the Constitution is a living document to be applied under changing circumstances, in changing conditions and even in different places. The Court finds devoid of merit the suggestion that the Prosecution has no constitutional obligations or that this Court lacks the competence to inquire into those obligations. The Constitution of the United States manifestly applies to these proceedings.

86 F.R.D. 242-244.

(5) Reid v. Covert, 354 U.S. 1 (1956), involved the trials of two American military wives for capital offenses. Both because the defendants were citizens and because no opinion commanded the assent of a majority, its precedential strength on extraterritoriality generally had always been unclear. The plurality opinion urged strongly, however, that because the federal government was one of limited powers, bestowed by the Constitution, the restrictions contained within the Constitution necessarily applied as widely as the powers themselves did.

(6) As indicated in *Verdugo,* excludable immigrants are held to have no constitutional right to due process even if they are temporarily present in America. The theory is that technically they have not really "entered" the

United States. Note, The Measure of a Nation: Granting Excludable Aliens Fundamental Protections of Due Process, 73 Va. L. Rev. 1501 (1987); Note, The Constitutional Rights of Excludable Aliens: History Provides a Refuge, 61 Wash. L. Rev. 1449 (1986).

Why do excludable aliens have fewer due process rights than defendants in American civil suits, as to whom the United States Supreme Court has said "there has been no question in this country of excepting foreign nationals from the protection of the Due Process Clause"? Volkswagenwerk Aktiengesellschaft v. Schlunk, 486 U.S. 694 (1988).

(7) There is an interesting academic literature on the topic of the extraterritoriality of the U.S. Constitution. *See, e.g.*, Steinbock, The Fifth Amendment at Home and Abroad: A Comment on United States v. Balsys, 31 U. Tol. L. Rev. 209 (2000); Miller, The Limits of U.S. International Law Enforcement After *Verdugo-Urquidez:* Resurrecting *Rochin,* 58 U. Pitt. L. Rev. 867 (1997); Weisburd, Due Process Limits on Federal Extraterritorial Legislation?, 35 Colum. J. Transnatl. L. 379 (1997); Bentley, Toward an International Fourth Amendment: Rethinking Searches and Seizures Abroad After *Verdugo-Urquidez,* 27 Vand. J. Transnatl. L. 329 (1994); Neuman, Whose Constitution? 100 Yale L.J. 909 (1991); Stephan, Constitutional Limits on the Struggle Against International Terrorism: Revisiting the Rights of Overseas Aliens, 19 Conn. L. Rev. 831 (1987). *See generally* Brilmayer, Justifying International Acts (1989) (arguing that the legitimacy of international acts must be evaluated under the same terms as domestic acts).

United States v. Davis

905 F.2d 245 (9th Cir. 1989)

WIGGINS, Circuit Judge.

Peter Malcolm Davis appeals his convictions for possession of, and conspiracy to possess, marijuana on a vessel subject to the jurisdiction of the United States with intent to distribute in violation of the Maritime Drug Law Enforcement Act, 46 U.S.C. app. §§1903(a), 1903(j). The Coast Guard apprehended Davis on the high seas and he contests application of the Maritime Drug Law Enforcement Act to him. Furthermore, he alleges that the Coast Guard searched and seized his vessel in violation of the fourth amendment.

I. Facts and Proceedings

On June 15, 1987, the Coast Guard cutter *Cape Romain* encountered the *Myth of Ecurie ("Myth")*, approximately 35 miles southwest of Point Reyes, California. The *Myth* is a sailing vessel approximately 58 feet in length. The *Myth* was headed in the direction of San Francisco. The *Cape Romain* approached the *Myth* and Coast Guard personnel by radio requested permission to board. Peter Davis, the captain of the *Myth*, denied the request. He stated that the Coast Guard had no authority to board his boat because it was of British registry and was sailing on the high seas having departed from Hong Kong. Captain Davis announced his intention to alter his course for the Caribbean by way of Mexico.

The Coast Guard suspected the *Myth* of smuggling contraband. Factors leading to that suspicion were that the El Paso Intelligence Center had included the *Myth* on a list of vessels suspected of drug smuggling; the *Myth* was sailing in an area in which sailing vessels were infrequently found; and the *Myth* appeared to be carrying cargo.

The Coast Guard then requested permission from the United Kingdom to board the *Myth* in accordance with procedures in a 1981 agreement between the United States and the United Kingdom. The Coast Guard informed the British officials of the circumstances which led the Coast Guard to believe the *Myth* contained contraband material. By telex message, the United Kingdom gave the Coast Guard permission to board the *Myth* according to the terms of the 1981 Agreement.

On June 16, 1987, crew members from the *Cape Romain* boarded the *Myth*. By that time, the *Myth* had sailed to a location approximately 100 miles west of the California coast. The boarding officer smelled marijuana in the cabin of the *Myth*. Davis informed the boarding officer that he kept a shotgun below deck, and Davis and the boarding officer went below to obtain it. Below deck, the boarding officer saw numerous bales of material and smelled marijuana. Davis admitted that the bales were marijuana. The Coast Guard then arrested Davis and his crew and brought the *Myth* to the Coast Guard station on Yerba Buena Island in San Francisco. The Coast Guard there confiscated over 7,000 pounds of marijuana from the *Myth*.

Davis is not a citizen of the United States.

On September 2, 1987, Davis filed a motion to dismiss for lack of jurisdiction and a motion to suppress evidence obtained from the *Myth*. The district court denied both motions. On July 26, 1988, the district court found Davis guilty on stipulated facts. Davis timely appealed.

II. Discussion

A. Legislative Jurisdiction

Davis contends that the provisions of the statute under which he was convicted, the Maritime Drug Law Enforcement Act, 46 U.S.C. app. §§1903(a), 1903(j), do not apply to persons on foreign vessels outside the territory of the United States. The question of whether the United States may punish Davis' conduct involves three issues: 1) whether Congress has constitutional authority to give extraterritorial effect to the Maritime Drug Law Enforcement Act; if so, 2) whether the Constitution prohibits the United States from punishing Davis' conduct in this instance; and, if not, 3) does the Maritime Drug Law Enforcement Act apply to Davis' conduct?

1. CONGRESSIONAL AUTHORITY TO GIVE EXTRATERRITORIAL EFFECT TO THE MARITIME DRUG LAW ENFORCEMENT ACT

The Maritime Drug Law Enforcement Act, 46 U.S.C. app. §1903(a) and (j) state:

> (a) It is unlawful for any person on board a vessel of the United States, or on board a vessel subject to the jurisdiction of the United States, to knowingly or intentionally manufacture or distribute, or to possess with intent to manufacture or distribute, a controlled substance.
>
> (j) Any person who attempts or conspires to commit any offense defined in this Act [46 U.S.C. app. §§1904] is punishable by imprisonment or fine, or both, which may not exceed the maximum punishment prescribed for the offense, the commission of which was the object of the attempt of the conspiracy.

The United States Congress sits as a legislature of enumerated and specific powers. *See* Marbury v. Madison, 5 U.S. (1 Cranch) 137, 176, 2 L. Ed. 60 (1803). The Constitution gives Congress the power to "define and punish piracies and felonies on the high seas. . . ." U.S. Const. Art. I, sec. 8, cl. 10. The high seas lie seaward of the territorial sea, defined as the three mile belt of sea measured from the low water mark. We therefore find that the Constitution authorized Congress to give extraterritorial effect to the Act.

2. CONSTITUTIONAL RESTRICTIONS ON THE UNITED STATES' AUTHORITY TO PUNISH DAVIS' CONDUCT

We next examine what limitations exist on the United States' power to exercise that authority.

Contrary to Davis' assertions, compliance with international law does not determine whether the United States may apply the Act to his conduct. Only two restrictions exist on giving extraterritorial effect to Congress' directives. We require Congress make clear its intent to give extraterritorial effect to its statutes. And secondly, as a matter of constitutional law, we require that application of the statute to the acts in question not violate the due process clause of the fifth amendment.

In this case, Congress explicitly stated that it intended the Maritime Drug Law Enforcement Act to apply extraterritorially. 46 U.S.C. app. §1903(h) (Supp. IV 1986) ("This section is intended to reach acts of possession, manufacture, or distribution outside the territorial jurisdiction of the

United States"). Therefore, the only issue we must consider is whether application of the Maritime Drug Law Enforcement Act to Davis' conduct would violate due process.

In order to apply extraterritorially a federal criminal statute to a defendant consistently with due process, there must be a sufficient nexus between the defendant and the United States, *see* United States v. Peterson, 812 F.2d 486, 493 (9th Cir. 1987), so that such application would not be arbitrary or fundamentally unfair.

In the instant case, a sufficient nexus exists so that the application of the Maritime Drug Law Enforcement Act to Davis' extraterritorial conduct does not violate the due process clause. "Where an attempted transaction is aimed at causing criminal acts within the United States, there is a sufficient basis for the United States to exercise its jurisdiction." *Id.* The facts found by the district court in denying Davis' motion to dismiss for lack of jurisdiction support the reasonable conclusion that Davis intended to smuggle contraband into United States territory. At the time of its first detection, the *Myth* was 35 miles away from, and headed for, San Francisco. As the Coast Guard approached, the *Myth* changed its course for the Caribbean by way of Mexico, although the *Myth* was many miles from the Great Circle route from Hong Kong to Acapulco. The *Myth* is on a list of boats suspected of drug smuggling. It is unusual for a 58 foot sailing vessel to have sailed from the Myth's asserted point of departure, Hong Kong. The foregoing evidence is sufficient to establish a nexus between the *Myth* and the United States. We therefore find that the Constitution does not prohibit the application of the Marijuana Drug Law Enforcement Act to Davis.

3. APPLICATION OF THE MARITIME DRUG LAW ENFORCEMENT ACT TO DAVIS' CONDUCT

We must next determine whether the Maritime Drug Law Enforcement Act by its terms applies to Davis' conduct. We hold that it does. Section 1903(a) and (j) proscribe possession and conspiracy to possess marijuana with intent to distribute on board a vessel subject to the jurisdiction of the United States. Section 1903(c)(1)(D) defines vessels subject to the jurisdiction of the United States as vessels "located within the customs waters of the United States." In the case of a foreign vessel, 19 U.S.C. §1401(j) (1982) defines customs waters as follows:

> The term "customs waters" means, in the case of a foreign vessel subject to a treaty or some other arrangement between a foreign government and the United States enabling or permitting the authorities of the United States to board, examine, search, seize, or otherwise to enforce upon such vessel upon the high seas the laws of the United States, the waters within

> such distance of the coast of the United States as the said authorities are or may be so enabled or permitted by such treaty or arrangement.

Prior to boarding the *Myth,* the Coast Guard obtained permission to board from the United Kingdom in a telex which allowed the United States Coast Guard to board, search and seize the *Myth* in accordance with the terms of the 1981 Agreement.

Whether the consent given by the United Kingdom constitutes an arrangement pursuant to section 1401(j) presents a question of law subject to de novo review. We have held that informal arrangements can satisfy section 1491(j). *See, e.g., Peterson,* 812 F.2d at 493 (Panamanian consent by telex constituted an arrangement satisfying section 1491(j)). As long as the foreign government has made clear its indication of consent, the arrangement necessary to create customs waters around a specific vessel may be informal. An arrangement is simply a settlement or adjustment and contemplates no particular form. Thus, even verbal, ad hoc consent by a vessel's flag country is sufficient to bring the vessel within the definition of customs waters.

The telex sent by the United Kingdom stated:

> 1. HMG has verified registry of subj vessel and has authorized USG to board, search and seize, if evidence warrents [sic], under U.S. Law. HMG has indicated that the conditions and terms contained in 13 Nov 81 US/UK Agreemnt [sic] will be used in this case.
>
> 2. In view of the above, comdt has no objection to taking action against subj vessel under the terms of the US/UK Agreement.
>
> 3. Insure Amenbassy [sic] London is info addee on all related msc traffic.

We hold that the request for permission to board and the United Kingdom's reply telex constitutes an arrangement pursuant to section 1401(j). Therefore, Davis' vessel was located within the customs waters of the United States, and hence within its jurisdiction.

Davis argues that the Coast Guard failed to conduct its search pursuant to the terms and conditions of the 1981 Agreement, thereby vitiating the consent given by the United Kingdom. In order to board a vessel of British registry, the 1981 Agreement requires that authorities of the United States "reasonably believe that the vessel has on board a cargo of drugs for importation into the United States." Reasonable suspicion must be based upon "specific articulable facts, together with rational inferences from those facts." United States v. Reeh, 780 F.2d 1541, 1544 (11th Cir. 1986). Reasonable suspicion turns on the totality of particular circumstances. *Id.* We hold that the Coast Guard had reasonable suspicion to believe that the *Myth* was importing drugs. The listing of the *Myth* as a boat suspected of smuggling, the *Myth's* unusual location, its attempt to change course, and its lowered position in the water, indicating that it was carrying cargo, could reasonably lead a Coast Guard officer to believe the *Myth* was smuggling contraband. We thus find that the Coast Guard satisfied the conditions of the United Kingdom's consent.

B. The Validity of the Search and Seizure of the Myth

Davis . . . contends that the search and seizure of the *Myth* violates the fourth amendment. We hold that the protections of the fourth amendment do not extend to the search of the *Myth* on the high seas. *See* United States v. Verdugo-Urquidez, 494 U.S. 259 (1990). Although *Verdugo-Urquidez* only held that the fourth amendment does not apply to searches and seizures of nonresident aliens in foreign countries, the analysis and language adopted by the Court creates no exception for searches of nonresident aliens on the high seas. *See id.* (No indication that fourth amendment was intended to protect aliens in international waters).

III. Conclusion

We find that Congress had the authority to enact the Maritime Drug Law Enforcement Act and that it is constitutionally applied to defendant. Furthermore, because the fourth amendment does not extend to the search of nonresident aliens on the high seas, no fourth amendment violation occurred in the search of the *Myth*. Davis' convictions are Affirmed.

Questions and Comments

(1) Why does the Fifth Amendment potentially apply abroad to protect defendants against the federal government's overreaching, while the Fourth Amendment does not?

(2) United States v. Klimavicius-Viloria, 144 F.3d 1249 (9th Cir. 1998), followed *Davis* in imposing a due process "nexus" limitation on the application of the Maritime Drug Law Enforcement Act ("MDLEA"). It explained the requirement as follows:

> The MDLEA contains no nexus requirement. The nexus requirement is a judicial gloss applied to ensure that a defendant is not improperly haled before a court for trial. We have explained the need for the requirement this way: "A defendant [on a foreign flag ship] would have a legitimate expectation that because he has submitted himself to the laws of one nation [the foreign flag nation], other nations will not be entitled to exercise jurisdiction without some nexus." United States v. Caicedo, 47 F. 3d 370, 372 (9th Cir. 1995).

> The nexus requirement serves the same purpose as the "minimum contacts" test in personal jurisdiction. It ensures that a United States court will assert jurisdiction only over a defendant who "should reasonably anticipate being haled into court" in this country. World-Wide Volkswagen v. Woodsen, 444 U.S. 286 (1980).

Shouldn't the proper analogy be to due process limits on a state's application of its law to activities with which it has no connection, such as in *Dick, supra* page 343? How do the Fifth Amendment due process limits on federal extraterritorial authority compare with the Fourteenth Amendment due process limits on state authority? *See* Brilmayer and Norchi, Federal Extraterritoriality and Fifth Amendment Due Process, 105 Harv. L. Rev. 1217 (1992); Brilmayer, Extraterritorial Application of American Law: A Methodological and Constitutional Appraisal, 50 Law & Contemp. Probs. 11 (1987). For an argument that the due process clause of the Fifth Amendment does not limit the extraterritorial application of federal law, see Juenger, Constitutional Control of Extraterritoriality?: A Comment on Professor Brilmayer's Appraisal, 50 Law & Contemp. Probs. 39 (1987).

(4) It has been fairly universally assumed that the Fifth Amendment due process clause limits the reach of federal assertions of personal jurisdiction in the international context. *See, e.g.*, Amtrol, Inc. v. Vent-Rite Valve Corp., 646 F. Supp. 1168 (D. Mass. 1986), where the court applied the Fifth Amendment due process clause to 15 U.S.C. section 22, which provided worldwide service of process under the Clayton Act. In Volkswagenwerk Aktiengesellschaft v. Schlunk, 486 U.S. 694, 705 (1988), the Court observed that "there has been no question in this country of excepting foreign nationals from the protection of our Due Process Clause." While *Schlunk* involved the Fourteenth Amendment, the breadth of this language is suggestive. This does not mean, however, that the Fifth Amendment limits and the Fourteenth Amendment limits are identical. For one thing, it is entirely possible that where there is a federal long-arm statute, the Fifth Amendment requires contacts only with the nation as a whole. *See, e.g.*, Degnan and Kane, The Exercise of Jurisdiction over and Enforcement of Judgments Against Alien Defendants, 39 Hastings L.J. 799 (1988). Note that in establishing a nationwide contacts test for certain cases, Fed. R. Civ. P. 4(k)(2), cited at page 544, only purports to grant jurisdiction where consistent with the Constitution. In the alternative, it is arguable that Congress's plenary power over international affairs makes a federal long-arm statute less vulnerable to due process challenge than a state long-arm statute. *Compare* Damrosch, Foreign States and the Constitution, 73 Va. L. Rev. 483 (1987), arguing that by virtue of its foreign affairs power, Congress can dispense with the Fifth Amendment rights of foreign states.

(5) Might constitutional limits arise from the possibility that U.S. law would require an individual to undertake activity punishable in another state? Compare the theory of comity set forth in *Hartford Fire Insurance*, page 752 *supra*.

D. Recognition and Enforcement of Foreign Judgments

Matusevitch v. Ivanovich

877 F. Supp. 1 (D.D.C. 1995)

URBINA, J.

[Vladimir Matusevitch, currently a Maryland resident, worked in Europe from 1969-1992 as a journalist for Radio Free Europe. In 1984, he wrote a letter to the *Daily Telegraph*, a London newspaper, in response to an earlier article in the *Daily Telegraph* by Vladimir Telnikoff, an English citizen, concerning the appropriateness of cross-border radio broadcasts to Russia. Matusevitch's response letter accused Telnikoff of racism. After Matusevitch refused to apologize, Tenikoff filed a libel action against him and eventually won a £240,000 pound (approximately $360,000) judgment. Telnikoff later sought to have the judgment enforced in federal court in Maryland.]

I

B. NONRECOGNITION OF A FOREIGN JUDGMENT

[The Maryland Uniform Foreign-Money Judgments Recognition Act] lists mandatory and discretionary grounds for non-recognition. Section 10-704(b)(2) states that a foreign judgment need not be recognized if "the cause of action on which the judgment is based is repugnant to the public policy of the State."

Case law illustrates that United States courts have refused to recognize foreign judgments based on public policy grounds. In Laker Airways v. Sabena Belgian World Airlines, 731 F.2d 909, 931 (D.C. Cir. 1984), the court stated that it "is not required to give effect to foreign judicial proceedings grounded on policies which do violence to its own fundamental interests." In Tahan v. Hodgson, 662 F.2d 862, 864 (D.C. Cir. 1981), the court stated that the "requirements for enforcement of a foreign judgment expressed in Hilton [v. Guyot, 159 U.S. 113 (1895)] are that . . . the original claim not violate American public policy . . . that it not be repugnant to fundamental notions of what is decent and just in the State where enforcement is sought."

Although principles of comity, defined by the Supreme Court as "the recognition which one nation allows within its territory to the legislative, executive, or judicial acts of another nation, having due regard both to international duty and convenience, and to the rights of its own citizens or of other persons who are under the protection of its laws", are taken under consideration, the Supreme Court has ruled that comity "does not require, but rather forbids [recognition] where such a recognition works a direct violation of the policy of our laws, and does violence to what we deem the rights of our citizens." *Hilton*, 159 U.S. at 164, 193.

Two recent cases, Abdullah v. Sheridan Square Press, Inc. 154 F.R.D. 591 (S.D.N.Y. 1994) and Bachchan v. India Abroad Publications Inc., 585 N.Y.S.2d 661 (N.Y. Sup. Ct. 1992), illustrate decisions where courts have failed to recognize and foreign libel judgment grounded on public policy. In *Abdullah*, the court dismissed the claim for libel under English law, holding that "establishment of a claim for libel under the British law of defamation would be antithetical to the First Amendment protection accorded the defendants." In *Bachchan*, the court declined to recognize or enforce an English libel judgment on both constitutional and public policy grounds.

Although the court recognizes that there is case law rejecting arguments for non-recognition of a foreign judgment based on public policy grounds, those cases are distinguishable in that they concern minor differences in statutory law and in rules of civil procedure or corporate or commercial law. *See* Ackermann v. Levine, 788 F.2d 830, 842 (2d Cir. 1986) (noting that "mere variance with local public policy is not sufficient to decline enforcement").

In this case, libel standards that are contrary to U.S. libel standards would be repugnant to the public policies of the State of Maryland and the United States. Therefore, pursuant to section 10-704(b)(2) of the Recognition Act, this court declines to recognize the foreign judgment.

II

A. British Libel Law v. U.S. Libel Law

British law on libel differs from U.S. law. In the United Kingdom, the defendant bears the burden of proving allegedly defamatory statements true and the plaintiff is not required to prove malice on the part of the libel defendant. . . . As a result, a libel defendant would be held liable for statements the defendant honestly believed to be true and published without any negligence. In contrast, the law in the United States requires the plaintiff to prove that the statements were false and looks to the defendant's state of mind and intentions. In light of the different standards, this court concludes that recognition and enforcement of the foreign judgment in this case would deprive the plaintiff of his constitutional rights.

B. Protected Speech

Speech similar to the plaintiff's statements have received protection under the First Amendment to the Constitution and are thereby unactionable in U.S. courts. In Hustler Magazine. Inc. v. Falwell, 485 U.S. 46 (1988), the Supreme Court held that hyperbole is not actionable. Plaintiff contends that his statements were plainly hyperbolic because they were stated in an attempt to portray defendant's extremist position.

In addition, in the United States, courts look to the context in which the statements appeared when determining a First Amendment question. Moldea v. New York Times Co., 22 F.3d 310 (D.C. Cir. 1994), the most recent D.C. Circuit case concerning the First Amendment, confirmed the importance of context in a First Amendment analysis. In *Moldea,* the D.C. Court of Appeals reversed itself by admitting error and stated that "it is in part the settings of the speech in question that makes their hyperbolic nature apparent, and which helps determine the way in which the intended audience will receive them." *Id.* at 314.

In the case at hand, the court notes that the British judgment was based on jury instructions which asked the jury to ignore context. Therefore, this court finds that if the statements were read in context to the original article or statement and in reference to the location of the statements in the newspaper, a reader would reasonably be alerted to the statements' function as opinion and not as an assertion of fact.

C. Limited Public Figure

The Supreme Court in New York Times Co. v. Sullivan, 376 U.S. 254 (1964), explained that a public figure must show by clear and convincing evidence that the libel defendant published defamatory statements with actual malice. *See* New York Times Co., 376 U.S. at 279-280; Masson v. New Yorker Magazine, Inc., 501 U.S. 496 (1991). In Curtis Publishing Co. v. Butts, 388 U.S. 130 (1967) . . . the Supreme Court extended this standard to a nonpublic person who is "nevertheless intimately involved in the resolution of important public questions or, by reason of their fame, shape events in areas of concern to society at large."

The defendant in this case has described himself as a prominent activist for Human Rights in the Soviet Union since 1955 n.3. Therefore, for purposes of his article about the composition of Russian personnel hired by Radio Free Europe/Radio Liberty, the court finds that the defendant was a limited public figure. In light of defendant's status as a limited public figure, the plaintiff is entitled to all the constitutional safeguards concerning speech used against public figures.

During the trial in England, because of British libel standards for the defense of "fair comment", the court never looked to the degree of fault or the accused party's intentions. Also, although the British court determined that the plaintiff's use of inverted commas around certain words may have falsely mislead a reader to believe that the defendant actually wrote those words, the court in *Masson* concluded that "a deliberate alteration of the words uttered by a plaintiff does not equate with knowledge of falsity. . . . The use of quotations to attribute words not in fact spoken bears in a most important way on that inquiry, but it is not dispositive in every case." *Masson*, 501 U.S. at 517. As a result, since there appears to be no proof that the plaintiff made the statements with actual malice, the plaintiff enjoys the constitutional protection for speech directed against public figures.

For the reasons stated herein, the court grants summary judgment in favor of the Plaintiff.

Questions and Comments

(1) Is there a good reason to give foreign judgments less respect than the judgments of sister-states? Professors von Mehren and Trautman argue that there is, since (a) in the case of sister-state judgments there are federal policies present that are absent in the international context, (b) the legal systems of the states are more similar and founded on like principles, and (c) the judgments of sister states are subject to Supreme Court review if they show some serious excess. Von Mehren & Trautman, Recognition of Foreign Adjudications: A Survey and Suggested Approach, 81 Harv. L. Rev. 1601, 1607 (1968). Do you agree? Do these same reasons suggest that non-forum law should be given less respect in an international choice-of-law case than in a domestic one?

(2) Hilton v. Guyot, 159 U.S. 113 (1895), famously held that foreign judgments are generally enforceable but need not be enforced if the country from which they hail does not enforce U.S. judgments. Must state courts follow *Hilton*'s reciprocity requirement? Should federal courts apply state law on the enforcement of foreign judgments, or their own judge-made law? *Hilton* was decided before Erie v. Tompkins during the reign of Swift v. Tyson. After *Erie*, most federal courts sitting in diversity (including *Matusevitch*) hold that state rather than federal judge-made law governs the issue. *See, e.g.*, Choi v. Kim, 50 F. 3d 244, 248-250 (3d Cir. 1995); *see generally* Burbank, Federal Judgments Law: Sources of Authority and Sources of Rules, 70 Tex. L. Rev. 1551, 1577-1582 (1992).

Is this result consistent with *Sabbatino*'s federal common law of foreign relations? Many commentators think not. *See, e.g.*, Casad, Issue Preclusion and Foreign Country Judgments: Whose Law?, 70 Iowa L. Rev. 53 (1984); *but see* Goldsmith, Federal Courts, Foreign Relations, and Federalism, 83 Va. L. Rev. 1617 (1997) (arguing that state law should govern). Why is the act of state doctrine federalized while enforcement of judgments is not? Note the inversion from the domestic realm, where choice of law is governed by state law and enforcement of judgments is governed by federal law.

(3) The Maryland statute applied in *Matusevitch* is based on the Uniform Foreign Money Judgments Recognition Act, 13 U.L.A. 261 (1986 and supplement) ("UFMJRA"), which has been adopted by more than half the states. The Act provides that a foreign judgment that is "final and conclusive

and enforceable where rendered" is "conclusive between the parties to the extent that it grants or denies recovery of a sum of money," and is "enforceable in the same manner as the judgment of a sister state which is entitled to full faith and credit." *Id.* at §§2-3. The UFMJRA provides that a "foreign judgment *is not conclusive*" if it was "rendered under a system which does not provide impartial tribunals or procedures compatible with the requirements of due process of law," or if it was rendered by a court that lacked personal and subject matter jurisdiction. *Id.* at §4(a) (emphasis added). It further provides that a foreign judgment "*need not be recognized*" if (a) the defendant did not receive notice in the original proceeding, (b) the judgment was obtained by fraud, if the cause of action "on which the judgment is based is repugnant to the public policy of this state," (c) there is a conflict with another final and conclusive judgment, (d) there is inconsistency between the initial proceeding and a forum selection clause, or (e) in cases based on personal service, "the foreign court was a seriously inconvenient forum for the trial of the action." the "serious inconvenience" of the foreign court in cases based on personal service of process. *Id.* at §4(b) (emphasis added). How do these limitations on enforcement of foreign judgments compare with the limitations on the enforcement of domestic interstate judgments? Again, why the differences in the two contexts?

(4) In the European Union, the recognition and enforcement of foreign judgments is governed by an international treaty, the Brussels Convention. *See* Convention on Jurisdiction and the Enforcement of Judgments in Civil and Commercial Matters, Sept. 27, 1968, 3 Common Mkt. Rep. (CCH) P6003. Should we have a global treaty on the recognition and enforcement of judgments? In 1992, the United States proposed that the Hague Conference on Private International Law draft such a treaty for global adherence. There are many disagreement as to what the content of the treaty should include. For example, "transient" jurisdiction is accepted in the United States but generally prohibited in Europe. Also, Europeans worry about an international duty to enforce the large judgments that result from the United States' particular system of juries, contingency fees, and punitive damages. As of the summer of 2001, the Hague Conference has produced a draft treaty, but there is considerable uncertainty about whether it will be ratified. For up-to-date information on the treaty's progress, see *www.hcch.net/e/workprog/jdgm.html.* For various perspectives on the treaty's implications, see Symposium, A Hague Judgments Convention? 24 Brooklyn J. Intl. L. 111 (1998).

8

Conflicts and the Internet

The Internet (sometimes referred to as "cyberspace") is the transnational network of computer networks. Its many applications include the World Wide Web, electronic mail, usenet, chat rooms, and much more. The speed and ubiquity of Internet communications has sparked an explosion of interest in Internet-related conflict-of-laws issues.

Some commentators believe that it is impossible to regulate the Internet on the basis of territorial units of sovereignty. They suggest that we must rethink the field of conflict of laws:

> Cyberspace has no territorially based boundaries, because the cost and speed of message transmission on the Net is almost entirely independent of physical location. Messages can be transmitted from one physical location to any other location without degradation, decay, or substantial delay, and without any physical cues or barriers that might otherwise keep certain geographically remote places and people separate from one another. The Net enables transactions between people who do not know, and in many cases cannot know, each other's physical location. Location remains vitally important, but only location within a virtual space consisting of the "addresses" of the machines between which messages and information are routed. The system is indifferent to the physical location of those machines, and there is no necessary connection between an Internet address and a physical jurisdiction. . . .
>
> [E]fforts to control the flow of electronic information across physical borders—to map local regulation and physical boundaries onto Cyberspace—are likely to prove futile, . . . Individual electrons can easily, and without any realistic prospect of detection, "enter" any sovereign's territory. The volume of electronic communications crossing

territorial boundaries is just too great in relation to the resources available to government authorities. United States Customs officials . . . assert jurisdiction only over the physical goods that cross the geographic borders they guard and claim no right to force declarations of the value of materials transmitted by modem. Banking and securities regulators seem likely to lose their battle to impose local regulations on a global financial marketplace. And state attorneys general face serious challenges in seeking to intercept the electrons that transmit the kinds of consumer fraud that, if conducted physically within the local jurisdiction, would be easier to shut down.

Faced with their inability to control the flow of electrons across physical borders, some authorities strive to inject their boundaries into the new electronic medium through filtering mechanisms and the establishment of electronic barriers. Others have been quick to assert the right to regulate all online trade insofar as it might adversely affect local citizens. . . . [S]uch protective schemes will likely fail as well. First, the determined seeker of prohibited communications can simply reconfigure his connection so as to appear to reside in a location outside the particular locality, state, or country. Because the Net is engineered to work on the basis of "logical," not geographical, locations, any attempt to defeat the independence of messages from physical locations would be as futile as an effort to tie an atom and a bit together. And, moreover, assertions of law-making authority over Net activities on the ground that those activities constitute "entry into" the physical jurisdiction can just as easily be made by any territorially-based authority. If Minnesota law applies to gambling operations conducted on the World Wide Web because such operations foreseeably affect Minnesota residents, so, too, must the law of any physical jurisdiction from which those operations can be accessed. By asserting a right to regulate whatever its citizens may access on the Net, these local authorities are laying the predicate for an argument that Singapore or Iraq or any other sovereign can regulate the activities of U.S. companies operating in Cyberspace from a location physically within the United States. All such Web-based activity, in this view, must be subject simultaneously to the laws of all territorial sovereigns.

Nor are the effects of online activities tied to geographically proximate locations. Information available on the World Wide Web is available simultaneously to anyone with a connection to the global network. . . . A Web site physically located in Brazil . . . has no more of an effect on individuals in Brazil than does a Web site physically located in Belgium or Belize that is accessible in Brazil. Usenet discussion groups, to take another example, consist of continuously changing collections of messages that are routed from one network to another, with no centralized location at all. They exist, in effect, everywhere, nowhere in particular, and only on the Net.

The rise of an electronic medium that disregards geographical boundaries throws the law into disarray by creating entirely new phenomena that need to become the subject of clear legal rules but that cannot be governed, satisfactorily, by any current territorially based sovereign. For example, although privacy on the Net may be a familiar concept, analogous to privacy doctrine for mail systems, telephone calls, and print publications, electronic communications create serious questions regarding the nature and adequacy of geographically based privacy protections. Communications that create vast new transactional records may pass through or even simultaneously exist in many different territorial jurisdictions. What substantive law should we apply to protect this new, vulnerable body of transactional data? May a French policeman lawfully access the records of communications traveling across the Net from the United States to Japan? Similarly, whether it is permissible for a commercial entity to publish a record of all of any given individual's postings to Usenet newsgroups, or whether it is permissible to implement an interactive Web page application that inspects a user's "bookmarks" to determine which other pages that user has visited, are questions not readily addressed by existing legal regimes—both because the phenomena are novel and because any given local territorial sovereign cannot readily control the relevant, globally dispersed, actors and actions.

Because events on the Net occur everywhere but nowhere in particular, are engaged in by online personae who are both "real" (possessing reputations, able to perform services, and deploy intellectual assets) and "intangible" (not necessarily or traceably tied to any particular person in the physical sense), and concern "things" (messages, databases, standing relationships) that are not necessarily separated from one another by any physical boundaries, no physical jurisdiction has a more compelling claim than any other to subject these events exclusively to its laws.

Johnson & Post, Law and Borders—The Rise of Law in Cyberspace, 48 Stan. L. Rev. 1367, 1370-1376 (1996).

Consider these claims as you read the materials below.

A. Personal Jurisdiction

The Supreme Court has noted that "as technological progress has increased the flow of commerce between States, the need for jurisdiction has undergone a similar increase." Hanson v. Denkla, 357 U.S. 235, 250-251 (1958). The personal jurisdiction revolution initiated in *International Shoe*, discussed *supra* page 485, was a response to increased cross-border activity resulting from technological changes in travel (the railroad and automobile) and communication (the telephone and telegraph). Does the Internet require a similar revolution in personal jurisdiction thinking, or can it be accommodated by the personal jurisdiction framework developed during the past half century?

1. Activities-Based Jurisdiction

What does it mean for someone to purposefully avail herself of another forum via Internet contacts when Internet contacts can automatically appear in every state in the nation (not to mention every nation in the world)? If mere knowledge that the contacts may appear in another state constitutes purposeful availment, then every content provider can be exposed to *in personam* jurisdiction in every state where these contacts give rise to a cause of action. If something more than mere knowledge is needed, what is that something more?

Cybersell, Inc. v. Cybersell, Inc.

130 F. 3d 414 (9th Cir. 1997)

RYMER, Circuit Judge:

We are asked to hold that the allegedly infringing use of a service mark in a home page on the World Wide Web suffices for personal jurisdiction in the state where the holder of the mark has its principal place of business. Cybersell, Inc. [Cybersell AZ], an Arizona corporation that advertises for commercial services over the Internet, claims that Cybersell, Inc. [Cybersell FL], a Florida corporation that offers web page construction services over the Internet, infringed its federally registered mark and should be amenable to suit in Arizona because cyberspace is without borders and a web site which advertises a product or service is necessarily intended for use on a world wide basis. The district court disagreed, and so do we. Instead, applying our normal "minimum contacts" analysis, we conclude that it would not comport with "traditional notions of fair play and substantial justice" for Arizona to exercise personal jurisdiction over an allegedly infringing Florida web site advertiser who has no contacts with Arizona other than maintaining a home page that is accessible to Arizonans, and everyone else, over the Internet. We therefore affirm.

II

[The Court notes that the Arizona long-arm statute permits personal jurisdiction over parties to the maximum extent permitted by the U.S. Constitution.]

We use a three-part test to determine whether a district court may exercise specific jurisdiction over a nonresident defendant: (1) The nonresident defendant must do some act or consummate some transaction with the forum or perform some act by which he purposefully avails himself of the privilege of conducting activities in the forum, thereby invoking the benefits and protections; (2) the claim must be one which arises out of or results from the defendant's forum-related activities; and (3) exercise of jurisdiction must be reasonable.

A

Since the jurisdictional facts are not in dispute, we turn to the first requirement, which is the most critical. As the Supreme Court emphasized in *Hanson v. Denckla,* "it is essential in each case that there be some act by which the defendant purposefully avails itself of the privilege of conducting activities within the forum State, thus invoking the benefits and protections of its laws." 357 U.S. 235 (1958). We recently explained . . . that the "purposeful availment" requirement is satisfied if the defendant has taken deliberate action within the forum state or if he has created continuing obligations to forum residents. "It is not required that a defendant be physically present within, or have physical contacts with, the forum, provided that his efforts 'are purposefully directed' toward forum residents."

We have not yet considered when personal jurisdiction may be exercised in the context of cyberspace, but the Second and Sixth Circuits have had occasion to decide whether personal jurisdiction was properly exercised over defendants involved in transmissions over the Internet, see CompuServe, Inc. v. Patterson, 89 F.3d 1257 (6th Cir. 1996); Bensusan Restaurant Corp. v. King, 937 F. Supp. 295 (S.D.N.Y. 1996), *aff'd,* 126 F.3d 25 (2d Cir. 1997), as have a number of district courts. Because this is a matter of first impression for us, we have looked to all of these cases for guidance. Not surprisingly, they reflect a broad spectrum of Internet use on the one hand, and contacts with the forum on the other. As *CompuServe* and *Bensusan* seem to represent opposite ends of the spectrum, we start with them.

CompuServe is a computer information service headquartered in Columbus, Ohio, that contracts with individual subscribers to provide access to computing and information services via the Internet. It also operates as an electronic conduit to provide computer software products to its subscribers. Computer software generated and distributed in this way is often referred to as "shareware." Patterson is a Texas resident who subscribed to CompuServe and placed items of "shareware" on the CompuServe system pursuant to a "Shareware Registration Agreement" with CompuServe which provided, among other things, that it was "to be governed by and construed in accordance with" Ohio law. During the course of this relationship, Patterson electronically transmitted thirty-two master software files to CompuServe, which CompuServe stored and displayed to its subscribers. Sales were made in Ohio and elsewhere, and funds were transmitted through CompuServe in Ohio to Patterson in Texas. In effect, Patterson used CompuServe as a distribution center to market his software. When Patterson threatened litigation over allegedly infringing CompuServe software, CompuServe filed suit in Ohio seeking a declaratory judgment of noninfringement. The court found that Patterson's relationship with CompuServe as a software provider and marketer was a crucial indicator that Patterson had knowingly reached out to CompuServe's Ohio home and benefitted from CompuServe's handling of his software and fees. Because Patterson had chosen to transmit his product from

Texas to CompuServe's system in Ohio, and that system provided access to his software to others to whom he advertised and sold his product, the court concluded that Patterson purposefully availed himself of the privilege of doing business in Ohio.

By contrast, the defendant in *Bensusan* owned a small jazz club known as "The Blue Note" in Columbia, Missouri. He created a general access[5] web page that contained information about the club in Missouri as well as a calendar of events and ticketing information. Tickets were not available through the web site, however. To order tickets, web browsers had to use the names and addresses of ticket outlets in Columbia or a telephone number for charge-by-phone ticket orders, which were available for pick-up on the night of the show at the Blue Note box office in Columbia. Bensusan was a New York corporation that owned "The Blue Note," a popular jazz club in the heart of Greenwich Village. Bensusan owned the rights to the "The Blue Note" mark. Bensusan sued King for trademark infringement in New York. The district court distinguished King's passive web page, which just posted information, from the defendant's use of the Internet in *CompuServe* by observing that whereas the Texas Internet user specifically targeted Ohio by subscribing to the service, entering into an agreement to sell his software over the Internet, advertising through the service, and sending his software to the service in Ohio, King has done nothing to purposefully avail himself of the benefits of New York. King, like numerous others, simply created a Web site and permitted anyone who could find it to access it. Creating a site, like placing a product into the stream of commerce, may be felt nationwide-or even worldwide-but, without more, it is not an act purposefully directed toward the forum state. Given these facts, the court reasoned that the argument that the defendant "should have foreseen that users could access the site in New York and be confused as to the relationship of the two Blue Note clubs is insufficient to satisfy due process." *Benusan*, 937 F. Supp. at 301.

"Interactive" web sites present somewhat different issues. Unlike passive sites such as the defendant's in *Bensusan*, users can exchange information with the host computer when the site is interactive. Courts that have addressed interactive sites have looked to the "level of interactivity and commercial nature of the exchange of information that occurs on the Web site" to determine if sufficient contacts exist to warrant the exercise of jurisdiction. *See, e.g.*, Zippo Mfg. Co. v. Zippo Dot Com, Inc., 952 F. Supp. 1119, 1124 (W.D. Pa. 1997) (finding purposeful availment based on Dot Com's interactive web site and contracts with 3000 individuals and seven Internet access providers in Pennsylvania allowing them to download the electronic messages that form the basis of the suit).

Cybersell AZ points to several district court decisions which it contends have held that the mere advertisement or solicitation for sale of goods and

5. A general access site requires no authentication or access code for entry. Thus, the site is accessible to anyone who has access to the Internet.

services on the Internet gives rise to specific jurisdiction in the plaintiff's forum. However, so far as we are aware, no court has ever held that an Internet advertisement alone is sufficient to subject the advertiser to jurisdiction in the plaintiff's home state. Rather, in each, there has been "something more" to indicate that the defendant purposefully (albeit electronically) directed his activity in a substantial way to the forum state.

Inset Systems, Inc. v. Instruction Set, Inc., 937 F. Supp. 161 (D. Conn. 1996), is the case most favorable to Cybersell AZ's position. Inset developed and marketed computer software throughout the world; Instruction Set, Inc. (ISI) provided computer technology and support. Inset owned the federal trademark "INSET"; but ISI obtained "INSET.COM" as its Internet domain address for advertising its goods and services. ISI also used the telephone number "1-800-US-INSET." Inset learned of ISI's domain address when it tried to get the same address, and filed suit for trademark infringement in Connecticut. The court reasoned that ISI had purposefully availed itself of doing business in Connecticut because it directed its advertising activities via the Internet and its toll-free number toward the state of Connecticut (and all states); Internet sites and toll-free numbers are designed to communicate with people and their businesses in every state; an Internet advertisement could reach as many as 10,000 Internet users within Connecticut alone; and once posted on the Internet, an advertisement is continuously available to any Internet user.

Some courts have also given weight to the number of "hits" received by a web page from residents in the forum state, and to other evidence that Internet activity was directed at, or bore fruit in, the forum state. *See, e.g.*, Heroes, Inc. v. Heroes Found., 958 F. Supp. 1 (D.D.C. 1996) (web page that solicited contributions and provided toll-free telephone number along with the defendant's use on the web page of the allegedly infringing trademark and logo, along with other contacts, provided sustained contact with the District).

In sum, the common thread, well stated by the district court in *Zippo*, is that "the likelihood that personal jurisdiction can be constitutionally exercised is directly proportionate to the nature and quality of commercial activity that an entity conducts over the Internet." *Zippo*, 952 F. Supp. at 1124.

B

Here, Cybersell FL has conducted no commercial activity over the Internet in Arizona. All that it did was post an essentially passive home page on the web, using the name "CyberSell," which Cybersell AZ was in the process of registering as a federal service mark. While there is no question that anyone, anywhere could access that home page and thereby learn about the services offered, we cannot see how from that fact alone it can be inferred that Cybersell FL deliberately directed its merchandising efforts toward Arizona residents.

Cybersell FL did nothing to encourage people in Arizona to access its site, and there is no evidence that any part of its business (let alone a continuous part of its business) was sought or achieved in Arizona. To the contrary, it appears to be an operation where business was primarily generated by the personal contacts of one of its founders. While those contacts are not entirely local, they aren't in Arizona either. No Arizonan except for Cybersell AZ "hit" Cybersell FL's web site. There is no evidence that any Arizona resident signed up for Cybersell FL's web construction services. It entered into no contracts in Arizona, made no sales in Arizona, received no telephone calls from Arizona, earned no income from Arizona, and sent no messages over the Internet to Arizona. The only message it received over the Internet from Arizona was from Cybersell AZ. Cybersell FL did not have an "800" number, let alone a toll-free number that also used the "Cybersell" name. The interactivity of its web page is limited to receiving the browser's name and address and an indication of interest—signing up for the service is not an option, nor did anyone from Arizona do so. No money changed hands on the Internet from (or through) Arizona. In short, Cybersell FL has done no act and has consummated no transaction, nor has it performed any act by which it purposefully availed itself of the privilege of conducting activities, in Arizona, thereby invoking the benefits and protections of Arizona law.

We therefore hold that Cybersell FL's contacts are insufficient to establish "purposeful availment." Cybersell AZ has thus failed to satisfy the first prong of our three-part test for specific jurisdiction. We decline to go further solely on the footing that Cybersell AZ has alleged trademark infringement over the Internet by Cybersell FL's use of the registered name "Cybersell" on an essentially passive web page advertisement. Otherwise, every complaint arising out of alleged trademark infringement on the Internet would automatically result in personal jurisdiction wherever the plaintiff's principal place of business is located. That would not comport with traditional notions of what qualifies as purposeful activity invoking the benefits and protections of the forum state.

III

Cybersell AZ also invokes the "effects" test employed in Calder v. Jones, 465 U.S. 783 (1984), and Core-Vent Corp. v. Nobel Industries, 11 F.3d 1482 (9th Cir. 1993), with respect to intentional torts directed to the plaintiff, causing injury where the plaintiff lives. However, we don't see this as a *Calder* case. Because Shirley Jones was who she was (a famous entertainer who lived and worked in California) and was libeled by a story in the National Enquirer, which was published in Florida but had a nationwide circulation with a large audience in California, the Court could easily hold that California was the "focal point both of the story and of the harm suffered" and so jurisdiction in California based on the "effects" of the defendants' Florida conduct was proper. *Calder*, 465 U.S. at 789. There is nothing comparable about Cybersell FL's web page. Nor does the "effects" test apply with the same force to Cybersell AZ as it would to an individual, because a corporation "does not suffer harm in a particular geographic location in the same sense that an individual does." *Core-Vent*, 11 F.3d at 1486. Cybersell FL's web page simply was not aimed intentionally at Arizona knowing that harm was likely to be caused there to Cybersell AZ.

Starmedia Network, Inc. v. Star Media Inc.

2001 U.S. Dist. LEXIS 4870 (S.D.N.Y. 2001)

Cote, District Judge:

Plaintiff Starmedia Network, Inc. filed this action on June 22, 2000, alleging that Star Media Inc.'s domain name and corporate name infringe the plaintiff's trademark rights. Defendant moved to dismiss the complaint for lack of personal jurisdiction. . . . For the reasons stated below, defendant's motion is denied.

Plaintiff is a Delaware corporation with its principal place of business in New York. Plaintiff provides an Internet "portal" in the Spanish and Portugese languages. Through its website, which is named "starmedia.com," plaintiff provides a variety of information and services. Defendant, a Washington company with its principal place of business in the state of Washington, is a wholesale seller of software that recently launched a website called "starmediausa.com." Plaintiff claims that defendant's domain name infringes plaintiff's federally registered "STARMEDIA" marks.

The defendant's website includes a chart of shipping costs by time zone that comprises the entire continental United States. The site is interactive: although customers cannot purchase products through the site, they can register with the site and use the site to send comments to defendant. A company that wishes to sell the defendant's software can download a dealer application from the website. In a password protected area for registered users, product and pricing information is available to existing customers. Defendant estimates that only one out of 20 or 30 customers obtain a password.

While the defendant has sold goods in several states, including New Jersey, it has not sold goods in New York. The defendant has only two employees, and approximately 200 customers.

At the time defendant filed the motion to dismiss, it was disputing, inter alia, that it could reasonably expect its actions to have consequences in New York and that it derived substantial revenue from interstate commerce. Defendant has since stipulated that it receives substantial revenue from interstate commerce. The defendant also admits that it solicits business nationwide via the website and one of the purposes of its website is to attract new customers, including customers from New York. When the defendant registered "starmediausa.com" in 1999, it discovered that plaintiff's website existed, but did not check to see what was available at starmedia.com.

[After determining that the New York state long-arm statute is satisfied, the Court turns to the due process inquiry.]

The federal due process jurisdictional inquiry has two parts, the "minimum contacts" inquiry and the "reasonableness" inquiry. The minimum contacts analysis is governed by the Supreme Court case, International Shoe Co. v. Washington, 326 U.S. 310 (1945), and its progeny. Under the minimum contact analysis, "specific jurisdiction exists when 'a State exercises personal jurisdiction over a defendant in a suit arising out of or related to the defendant's contacts with the forum.' "

In cases involving Internet activity, courts have looked at the level and nature of the information exchange occurring over the Internet to determine the reasonableness of jurisdiction. Using these criteria, Internet activity has been classified using three categories: (1) "passive" websites, which make information available to visitors but do not permit an exchange of information; (2) "interactive" websites, which permit the exchange of information between the defendant and website viewers, but do not involve the actual conduct of business; and (3) websites in which the defendant clearly does business over the Internet, e.g., where a visitor may enter into a contract or purchase goods or services through the website. It is generally agreed that jurisdiction is not properly exercised in the first category, but is properly exercised in the last category. When considering the middle category, that is, sites which are interactive but are not used to conduct business, courts look to the " 'level of interactivity and commercial nature of the exchange of information that occurs on the Website' " to determine whether jurisdiction should be exercised. Mink v. AAAA Dev. LLC, 190 F.3d 333, 336 (5th Cir. 1999); *Cybersell*, 130 F.3d at 418.

In this case, defendant's website belongs in the second category. As discussed above, the website is interactive rather than passive. Furthermore, it is entirely commercial in nature. The level of interactivity, however, is limited. The defendant contends that it does not take online orders or sell any products directly over the Internet. It does, however, provide customers with access to certain confidential information through a password system, and does support an exchange of information through electronic mail.

Even with claims of trademark infringement arising in the context of interactive commercial websites, however, there is a serious question as to whether it would be reasonable to allow, in essence, jurisdiction over an alleged infringer "wherever the plaintiff's principal place of business is located." Thus, there are sound reasons to require some further connection between the defendant and the forum state. Here, the defendant has additional contacts with New York that make the exercise of personal jurisdiction appropriate. First, the defendant knew of plaintiff's domain name before it registered "starmediausa.com" as its domain name. Therefore, the defendant knew or should have known of plaintiff's place of business, and should have anticipated being haled into New York's courts to answer for the harm to a New York plaintiff caused by using a similar mark. *See* Panavision Int'l L.P. v. Toeppen, 141 F.3d 1316, 1322 (9th Cir. 1998). Coupled with this fact is the defendant's substantial income from interstate commerce and commercial use of the website to support its sales, including potentially to New York customers. In these circumstances, the plaintiff has shown prima facie evidence of "minimum contacts" with New York for purposes of specific jurisdiction under the Due Process Clause.

The second part of the due process personal jurisdiction test is determining the reasonableness of the exercise of jurisdiction. In undertaking this reasonableness analysis, the Supreme Court has identified the following factors:

> (1) the burden that the exercise of jurisdiction will impose on the defendant; (2) the interests of the forum state in adjudicating the case; (3) the plaintiff's interest in obtaining convenient and effective relief; (4) the interstate judicial system's interest in obtaining the most efficient resolution of the controversy; and (5) the shared interest of the states in furthering substantive social policies.

The only burden argued by defendant is the general inconvenience of litigating in New York. It has offered no evidence, however, to support an argument that this general burden presents any particular hardship to it. None of the other reasonableness considerations preclude the exercise of personal jurisdiction over defendant.

Questions and Comments

(1) Most courts agree with *Cybersell* and *Starmedia Network* that purely "passive" websites—Web sites that merely post information accessible to users in other jurisdictions—cannot be subject to personal jurisdiction in the places where they can be viewed. *But see* Telco Communication Group, Inc. v. An Apple a Day, Inc., 977 F. Supp. 404 (E.D. Va. 1997) (1997) (two press releases posted in Missouri give rise to jurisdiction for tort suit filed in Virginia because defendants "should have reasonably known that their press releases would be disseminated" in Virginia and knew that plaintiff was located in Virginia).

Does it make sense to decline jurisdiction when a passive Web site viewed in other states causes harm there? Consider Bailey v. Turbine Design, Inc, 86 F. Supp. 2d 790 (W.D. Tenn. 2000), in which a Florida corporation allegedly defamed Bailey, the owner of its Tennessee competitor, when it posted unflattering information about Bailey (arrest records, a mug shot, and damning information about his company) on its Web site located in Florida. Bailey argued that personal jurisdiction in Tennessee was proper because the publication was intended to cause injury in Tennessee. The Court dismissed the case for lack of personal jurisdiction simply because the web site was "passive." Isn't the "passive" label here a poor substitute for analysis? Aren't the defendant's contacts in an important sense directed toward Tennessee? Should the defendant receive immunity from jurisdiction in Tennessee simply because the publication could be viewed anywhere?

(2) The passive Web site holdings mean that, as *Cybersell* put it, "something more" than mere information on a Web page is needed to establish that a defendant "purposefully directed" its activities to another forum. There is substantial uncertainty about what more is needed, however. The easiest cases involve on-line dealings between a Web page operator in one state and residents of another jurisdiction, especially commercial dealings such as on-line contracts. *See, e.g.*, CompuServe, Inc. v. Patterson, 89 F. 3d 1257 (6th Cir. 1996) (personal jurisdiction in Ohio proper when Texas defendant knowingly contracts with Ohio party, transfers files to that party in Ohio, and collects revenue from related sale of software in Ohio); Zippo Mfg. Co. v. Zippo Dot Com, Inc., 952 F. Supp. 1119, 1125-1126 (W.D. Pa. 1997) (jurisdiction appropriate in Pennsylvania because defendant contracted with thousands of individuals and numerous Internet access providers in Pennsylvania).

Are these cases really different from the passive Web site cases? Would it make a difference if, as is quite possible, the defendants did not know *where* the plaintiffs they were doing business with were located? Can one purposefully avail oneself of a forum without knowing the identity of the forum? Must the out-of-state Web page operator take steps to learn the geographical location of Web page users?

(3) Sometimes non-Internet contacts constitute the "something more" needed to establish personal jurisdiction. Consider Blumenthal v. Drudge, 992 F. Supp. 44 (D.D.C. 1998), a suit by President Clinton's assistant against the owner of The Drudge Report, a popular Web page originating on a computer server in California, for allegedly defamatory remarks posted on the page. Drudge argued that his Web page was "passive," but the District court disagreed, noting that personal jurisdiction was justified in part because Drudge had solicited contributions and gossip from Washington, D.C., by telephone, e-mail, and postal mail, and had appeared personally there to promoted his web page. *Id.* at 54-56.

(4) What counts in determining the "something more"—the quantity of contacts, or their quality? *Compare* Tech Heads, Inc. v. Desktop Serv. Center, Inc., 105 F. Supp. 2d 1142, 1150 (D. Or. 2000) (noting that "quality" rather than "quantity" is what counts, and upholding jurisdiction based on "highly interactive website" that resulted in only one transaction in forum state) *with* Butler v. Beer Across America, 83 F. Supp. 2d 1261, 1267 (N.D. Ala. 2000) (declining jurisdiction in part because lawsuit was based on a single in-state sale, and defendants total sales in state amount to "significantly less that $100,000").

(5) The most difficult personal jurisdiction cases have been ones, like *Starmedia Network*, that involve "interactive" Web sites that allow a user to exchange information with the host computer. These cases are difficult be-

cause they involve "something more" than passive information, but (usually) less than clear evidence that the contacts were specifically aimed at the forum.

Is the distinction between passive and interactive Web sites helpful? Doesn't the distinction direct attention away from what's really important, namely, the defendant's conduct vis à vis the forum? Consider:

> The existence of a Web site, whether passive or interactive, does not rise to the requisite level of conduct [needed for personal jurisdiction]. Publishing a Web site requires no "deliberate" action within the forum state. Furthermore, a Web site is not automatically projected to a user's computer without invitation as are advertisements in a newspaper or on the television and radio. Rather, the user must take affirmative action to access either a passive or interactive Web Site. The user must turn on a computer, access the Internet and the Web, and browse the Web for a particular site. Thus, . . . information published on Web sites is not thrust upon users indiscriminately.

Millennium Enterprises, Inc. v. Millennium Music, LP, 33 F. Supp. 2d 907, 922 (D. Ore. 1999); *see also* GTE New Media Services Inc. v. BellSouth Corp., 199 F. 3d 1343, 1349-1350 (D.C. Cir. 2000) (similar critique of focus on interactivity). One response to this argument is that newspapers must be bought and televisions and radios must be turned on. But does the point about Web pages hold nonetheless?

(6) Many courts have analogized the problem of Internet contacts to the "stream of commerce" theory debated in *Asahi Metals,* reproduced *supra* 534. On this view, "[c]reating a site, like placing a product into the stream of commerce, may be felt nationwide—or even worldwide—but, without more, it is not an act purposefully directed towards the forum state." Bensusan Restaurant Corp. v. King, 937 F. Supp. 295, 301 (S.D.N.Y. 1996), *aff'd,* 126 F.3d 25 (2d Cir. 1997). This analogy may be apt, but is it helpful? After all, the *Asahi* Court divided 4–4 on the proper test in stream of commerce cases, and neither the plurality nor the dissenting opinions provided significant analytical guidance.

(7) As *Cybersell* suggests, courts sometimes use the "effects test" applied in Calder v. Jones, 465 U.S. 783 (1984), to find personal jurisdiction in intentional torts cases. *Calder* establishes jurisdiction if the defendant engages in "(1) intentional action (2) expressly aimed at the forum state (3) causing harm, the brunt of which is suffered, and the defendant knows is likely to be suffered, in the forum state." Panavision Intl. L.P. v. Toeppen, 141 F. 3d 1316, 1321 (9th Cir. 1998). Not surprisingly, courts have been inconsistent in determining when Internet contacts are expressly aimed at a forum state, "where" the harm is suffered, and whether the defendant likely knew it would be suffered there. Contrast *Cybersell* with *Panavision,* a similar domain name dispute in which the same Court held that the effects test was satisfied because a plaintiff in a domain name dispute suffers harm at its

principal pace of business, and thus that the defendant knew that its actions would cause harm in California. 141 F. 3d at 1321.

(8) The World Wide Web is only one of many Internet applications. How should personal jurisdiction operate when contacts are based on other applications, such as e-mail, chatrooms, bulletin boards, and usenet? *See* Blakey v. Continental Airlines, Inc., 164 N.J. 38 (2000) (electronic bulletin board contacts); Barrett v. Catacombs Press, 44 F. Supp. 2d 717 (E.D. Pa. 1999) (usenet contacts).

(9) No court to date has asserted general personal jurisdiction on the basis of Internet contacts. Why do you think this is so?

(10) There have been scores of articles written about the Internet and personal jurisdiction. Some of the better ones include Perritt, Economic and Other Barriers to Electronic Commerce, 21 U. Pa. J. Intl. L. Econ. Law 563 (2000); Stein, The Unexceptional Problem of Jurisdiction in Cyberspace, 32 Intl. Law. 1167 (1998); Perritt, Jr., Jurisdiction in Cyberspace, 41 Vill. L. Rev. 1, 100-103 (1996); Burk, Federalism in Cyberspace, 28 Conn. L. Rev. 1095 (1996).

2. Jurisdiction Based on Property

The Internet creates new forms of intangible property that implicate many difficult jurisdictional issues. This is especially true of Internet domain names, which are the unique verbal names—such as aol.com, or mcdonalds.com, or disney.com—that correlate with Web pages Internet addresses. From 1992-1998, during the early years of Internet growth, Network Solutions, Inc. ("NSI"), a private company in Virginia, held a contractual monopoly from the United States government to register and maintain domain name information. As a general matter, NSI doled out domain names on a first-come, first-serve basis. This led many to engage in "cybersquatting," a term that refers to the registration of domain names similar or identical to protected trademarks with the intent of intercepting Internet traffic intended for the mark owner or selling the domain name to mark owners for hefty fees. In 1999, Congress enacted the Anticybersquatting Consumer Protection Act ("ACPA"), 15 U.S.C. §1125 (d), which establishes civil liability for registering a domain name that is identical or confusingly similar to a trademark with the "bad faith intent to profit from that mark." The ACPA provides that a trademark holder may proceed against the cybersquatter not only in an *in personam* action, but also, in certain circumstances, against the domain name itself in an *in rem* action. This raises the questions (a) where is the property located?, and (b) is the assertion of *in rem* jurisdiction over domain names consistent with Shaffer v. Heitner?

Caesars World Inc. v. Caesars-Palace.com

112 F. Supp. 2d 502 (E.D. Va. 2000)

BRYAN, J.

On April 19, 1999, plaintiff brought this action against a multitude of domain names, alleging violations of the Lanham Act. An amendment to that act, the Anticybersquatting Consumer Protection Act, which allows an "owner of a mark" to bring an in rem action against domain names in certain circumstances, became law on November 29, 1999. 15 U.S.C. §1125(d).

Defendant Caesarcasino.com, like defendant Caesares.com, argues that the complaint should be dismissed on constitutional grounds and particularly, that it would violate due process for this court to exercise in rem jurisdiction over these defendants.

The Anticybersquatting Act allows for in rem proceedings by the owner of a mark against a domain name in the judicial district in which the domain name register, domain name registry, or other domain name authority that registered or assigned the domain name is located if (i) the domain name violates any right of the owner of a registered or protected mark; and (ii) the court finds that the owner either (I) is not able to obtain in personam jurisdiction over an allowed defendant:[3] or (II) through due diligence was not able to find a person who would have been an allowed defendant after meeting certain notice requirements set out in the Act. 15 U.S.C. §1125(d)(2)(A). With respect to the defendants whose motions are pending, (I) above applies. The question before this court, therefore, is whether in rem jurisdiction over defendants who are not subject to the personal jurisdiction of this court, or any other, meets the due process standards under the Constitution.

In this regard, defendant Casares.com argues that under Shaffer v. Heitner, 433 U.S. 186 (1977), in rem jurisdiction is only constitutional in those circumstances where the res provides minimum contacts sufficient for in personam jurisdiction. The court rejects this argument, and concludes that under *Shaffer*, there must be minimum contacts to support personal jurisdiction only in those in rem proceedings where the underlying cause of action is unrelated to the property which is located in the forum state. Here the property, that is, the domain name, is not only related to the cause of action but is its entire subject matter. Accordingly, it is unnecessary for minimum contacts to meet personal jurisdiction standards.

To the extent that minimum contacts are required for in rem jurisdiction under Shaffer, moreover, the fact of domain name registration with Network Solutions, Inc., in Virginia supplies that. Given the limited relief

3. Only those persons who meet specific criteria regarding their use of a domain name and regarding bad faith intentions can be liable to the owner of a mark in a civil action brought under this act. 15 U.S.C. §1125(d)(1), that is the "allowed defendants."

afforded by the Act, namely "the forfeiture or cancellation of the domain name or the transfer of the domain name to the owner of the mark," no due process violation occurs here as to defendants personally. 15 U.S.C. §1125(6)(2)(D). The court considers the enactment of the Anticybersquatting Consumer Protection Act a classic case of the distinction between in rem jurisdiction and in personam jurisdiction and a proper and constitutional use of in rem jurisdiction.

In further support of its constitutional challenge, defendant Casares.com argues that a domain name registration is not a proper kind of thing to serve as a res. In this regard, defendant contends, among other things, a domain name is merely data that forms part of an Internet addressing computer protocol and therefore, is not property. Defendant Casares.com contends further that even if it were property, it has no situs in Virginia. The court finds this line of argument unpersuasive. There is no prohibition on a legislative body making something property. Even if a domain name is no more than data, Congress can make data property and assign its place of registration as its situs.

Finally, in some form, both defendants argue that this ruling opens the floodgates for Internet litigation in Virginia. While this argument is a tempting one to adopt, it does not in this court's view furnish a reason to deny jurisdiction. For the above reasons, in rem jurisdiction under 15 U.S.C. §1125(d) does not violate due process as to these defendants.

Questions and Comments

(1) *Caesar's World* states the question before it as "whether in rem jurisdiction over defendants who are not subject to the personal jurisdiction of this court" satisfies due process. Isn't this confused? In rem jurisdiction is jurisdiction over property, not persons, even when the owners of the property challenge the jurisdiction.

(2) *Shaffer* stated that "[t]he fiction that an assertion of jurisdiction over property is anything but an assertion over the owner of the property supports an ancient form without substantial modern justification," and held that "all assertions of state-court jurisdiction must be evaluated according to the standards set forth in *International Shoe* and its progeny. . . ." Shaffer v. Heitner, 433 U.S. 186, 212 (1977). In this light, is *Caesar's World* correct to say that "under *Shaffer,* there must be minimum contacts to support personal jurisdiction only in those in rem proceedings where the underlying cause of action is unrelated to the property which is located in the forum state"? Does the court correct any possible error when it says that "[t]o the extent that minimum contacts are required for in rem jurisdiction under Shaffer, . . . the fact of domain name registration with Network Solutions, Inc., in Virginia supplies that"?

(3) *Shaffer* contemplated that certain forms of *in rem* jurisdiction were consistent with *Shoe's* minimum contacts analysis:

> [T]he presence of property in a State may bear on the existence of jurisdiction by providing contacts among the forum State, the defendant, and the litigation. For example, when claims to the property itself are the source of the underlying controversy between the plaintiff and the defendant, it would be unusual for the State where the property is located not to have jurisdiction. In such cases, the defendant's claim to property located in the State would normally indicate that he expected to benefit from the State's protection of his interest. It appears, therefore, that jurisdiction over many types of actions which now are or might be brought in rem would not be affected by a holding that any assertion of state-court jurisdiction must satisfy the International Shoe standard.

433 U.S. at 209. Does this passage have intangible property in addition to real property in mind? Does the analysis apply to domain names? In *Caesar's World,* did the owner of Caesarcasino.com purposefully avail itself of the benefits of Virginia when it registered its name on NSI's Web site? Does it matter whether it knew where NSI's headquarters were?

(4) Are there any limits to Congress's ability to define the situs of the domain name? In Fleetboston Financial Corp. v. Fleetbostonfinancial.com, 138 F. Supp. 2d 121 (D. Mass 2001), the plaintiff sued a domain name that a Brazilian resident had registered with Network Solutions, a Virginia company. Plaintiffs sued in a Massachusetts federal court under a provision of the ACPA providing that a domain name "shall be deemed to have its situs" not only where the domain name authority is located, but also in any judicial district in which "documents sufficient to establish control and authority regarding the disposition of the registration and use of the domain name are deposited with the court," 15 U.S.C. §§1125(d)(2)(c)(ii), which in this case was in Massachusetts, where plaintiff had an office. The court declined to assert in rem jurisdiction, reasoning in part that to do so would be unconstitutional:

> [I]t is an unusual case in which property exists in a state, but the owner of the property has no expectation that the property is within the protection of the state's laws. That, however, is precisely the instant case. The Anti-Cybersquatting Consumer Protection Act as read by plaintiff would allow an allegedly aggrieved copyright holder to file suit in the state of its choosing, and then compel the registrar of domain names to transfer a document that represents the domain name to that judicial district. The alleged cybersquatter will then have its property rights adjudicated in a forum that it has never been in, much less directed any purposeful action toward, and indeed could not have expected to be hailed into. When interpreted to achieve this result, the ACPA would permit a procedure that plainly offends traditional notions of fair play and justice [. . .] The logic of *Shaffer*'s limitations would appear to extend to actions in which the existence of the property in the state cannot fairly be said to represent meaningful contacts between the forum state, the defendant, and the litigation.

Id. at 134.

(5) Does the mere act of registering a domain name with NSI in Virginia establish enough contacts for *in personam* jurisdiction over the domain name's owner? *Compare* Lucent Technologies Inc. v. Lucentsucks.com, 95 F. Supp. 2d 528, 535 n.5 (E.D. Va. 2000) (answering in affirmative) *with* Heathmount A.E. Corp. v. Technodome.com, 106 F. Supp. 2d 860, 865-866 (E.D. Va. 2000) (answering in negative).

3. Jurisdiction Based on Consent

Caspi v. The Microsoft Network, LLC

732 A 2d 528 (N.J. App. 1999)

KESTIN, J.

[Plaintiffs brought this class action on behalf of 1.5 million members of the Microsoft Network ("MSN"), an Internet service provider, against The Microsoft Network, L.L.C. and Microsoft Corporation (collectively, "Microsoft"). The complaint alleged that Microsoft's overbilling practices constituted breach of contract, common law fraud, and consumer fraud. Microsoft moved to dismiss the case on the basis of a forum selection clause in paragraph 15.1 of the MSN membership agreement, which provided: "This agreement is governed by the laws of the State of Washington, USA, and you consent to the exclusive jurisdiction and venue of courts in King County, Washington in all disputes arising out of or relating to your use of MSN or your MSN membership." Before becoming MSN members, the plaintiffs had each scrolled through multiple computer screens of information and clicked "I Agree" on a page with a membership agreement containing the above clause.]

[Trial] Judge Fitzpatrick correctly discerned that

> New Jersey follows the logic of the United States Supreme Court decision in Carnival Cruise Lines v. Shute, 499 U.S. 585 (1991). In *Carnival*, cruise ship passengers were held to a forum selection clause which appeared in their travel contract. The clause enforced in Carnival was very similar in nature to the clause in question here, the primary difference being that the Carnival clause was placed in small print in a travel contract while the clause in the case sub judice was placed on-line on scrolled computer screens.
>
> The trial court opinion went on to analyze plaintiffs' contentions:
>
> Plaintiffs' consent to MSN's clause does not appear to be the result of fraud or overweening bargaining power. In New Jersey, fraud consists of (1) material misrepresentation of a past or present fact; (2) knowledge or belief by the declarant of its falsity; (3) an intention that the recipient rely on it; (4) reasonable reliance by the recipient; and (5) resulting damages. Plaintiffs have not shown that MSN's forum selection clause constitutes fraud. The clause is reasonable, clear and contains no material misrepresentation.

> Further, plaintiffs were not subjected to overweening bargaining power in dealing with Microsoft and MSN. The Supreme Court has held that a corporate vendor's inclusion of a forum selection clause in a consumer contract does not in itself constitute overweening bargaining power. *Carnival,* 499 U.S. 585. In order to invalidate a forum selection clause, something more than merely size difference must be shown. *Id.* A court's focus must be whether such an imbalance in size resulted in an inequality of bargaining power that was unfairly exploited by the more powerful party.
>
> Plaintiffs have shown little more than a size difference here. The online computer service industry is not one without competition, and therefore consumers are left with choices as to which service they select for Internet access, e-mail and other information services. Plaintiffs were not forced into a situation where MSN was the only available server. Additionally, plaintiffs and the class which they purport to represent were given ample opportunity to affirmatively assent to the forum selection clause. Like *Carnival,* plaintiffs here "retained the option of rejecting the contract with impunity." 499 U.S. 585, 595. In such a case, this court finds it impossible to perceive an overwhelming bargaining situation.

Judge Fitzpatrick opined that application of MSN's forum selection clause did not contravene public policy. . . . Finally, Judge Fitzpatrick held that enforcement of the forum selection clause would not inconvenience a trial. Given the fact that the named plaintiffs reside in several jurisdictions and that, if the class were to be certified, many different domestic and international domiciles would also be involved, "the inconvenience to all parties is no greater in Washington than anywhere else in the country."

After reviewing the record in the light of the arguments advanced by the parties, we are in substantial agreement with the reasons for decision articulated by Judge Fitzpatrick. We reject as meritless plaintiffs' arguments on appeal that the terms of the forum selection clause do not prevent plaintiffs from suing Microsoft outside of Washington or, alternatively, that the forum selection clause lacks adequate clarity. The meaning of the clause is plain and its effect as a limiting provision is clear. Furthermore, New Jersey's interest in assuring consumer fraud protection will not be frustrated by requiring plaintiffs to proceed with a lawsuit in Washington as prescribed by the plain language of the forum selection clause. As a general matter, none of the inherent characteristics of forum selection clauses implicate consumer fraud concepts in any special way. If a forum selection clause is clear in its purport and has been presented to the party to be bound in a fair and forthright fashion, no consumer fraud policies or principles have been violated. Moreover, as a matter of policy interest and apart from considerations bearing upon the choice-of-law provision in the forum selection clause, plaintiffs have given us no reason to apprehend that the nature and scope of consumer fraud protections afforded by the State of Washington are materially different or less broad in scope than those available in this State.

The only viable issues that remain bear upon the argument that plaintiffs did not receive adequate notice of the forum selection clause, and therefore that the clause never became part of the membership contract which bound them. . . . Defendants respond by arguing that 1) in the absence of fraud, a contracting party is bound by the provisions of a form contract even if he or she never reads them; 2) this clause met all reasonable standards of conspicuousness; and 3) the sign-up process gave plaintiffs ample opportunity to review and reject the agreement.

The holding in *Carnival Cruise* does not dispose of the notice question because the plaintiffs there had "essentially . . . conceded that they had notice of the forum-selection provision," by stating that they "[did] not contest . . . that the forum selection clause was reasonably communicated to [them], as much as three pages of fine print can be communicated." 499 U.S. at 590. The dissenting justices described the format in which the forum selection clause had been presented as "in the fine print on the back of the [cruise] ticket." *Id.* at 597 (STEVENS, J., dissenting).

The scenario presented here is different because of the medium used, electronic versus printed; but, in any sense that matters, there is no significant distinction. The plaintiffs in *Carnival* could have perused all the fine-print provisions of their travel contract if they wished before accepting the terms by purchasing their cruise ticket. The plaintiffs in this case were free to scroll through the various computer screens that presented the terms of their contracts before clicking their agreement.

Also, it seems clear that there was nothing extraordinary about the size or placement of the forum selection clause text. By every indication we have, the clause was presented in exactly the same format as most other provisions of the contract. It was the first item in the last paragraph of the electronic document. We note that a few paragraphs in the contract were presented in upper case typeface, presumably for emphasis, but most provisions, including the forum selection clause, were presented in lower case typeface. We discern nothing about the style or mode of presentation, or the placement of the provision, that can be taken as a basis for concluding that the forum selection clause was proffered unfairly, or with a design to conceal or de-emphasize its provisions. To conclude that plaintiffs are not bound by that clause would be equivalent to holding that they were bound by no other clause either, since all provisions were identically presented. Plaintiffs must be taken to have known that they were entering into a contract; and no good purpose, consonant with the dictates of reasonable reliability in commerce, would be served by permitting them to disavow particular provisions or the contracts as a whole.

The issue of reasonable notice regarding a forum selection clause is a question of law for the court to determine. We agree with the trial court that, in the absence of a better showing than has been made, plaintiffs must be seen to have had adequate notice of the forum selection clause. The resolution of this notice issue, at this stage of the litigation between plaintiffs and defendants must, of course, be seen to be without prejudice to any showing either party may have the opportunity to make in another jurisdiction in a plenary proceeding on the contract regarding issues apart from the validity and enforceability of the forum selection clause.

America Online, Inc. v. Superior Court of Alameda County

90 Cal. App. 4th 1, 108 Cal. Rptr. 2d 699 (1st App. Cal. 2001)

RUVOLO, J.

[This is a class action filed by former subscribers to America Online, Inc. ("AOL"), a Virginia Internet access provider, alleging that AOL continued to debit the class plaintiffs' credit cards for monthly service fees after termination of plaintiffs' AOL subscription. The complaint alleged violations of California's Unfair Business Practices Act, Bus. & Prof. Code, §§17200 et seq., California's CLRA, common law conversion/trespass, and common law fraud. AOL filed a motion to dismiss based on a forum selection clause contained in AOL's on-line "Terms of Service" (TOS) agreement. Paragraph 8 of the TOS, entitled "LAW AND LEGAL NOTICES," states:

> You expressly agree that exclusive jurisdiction for any claim or dispute with AOL or relating in any way to your membership or your use of AOL resides in the courts of Virginia and you further agree and expressly consent to the exercise of personal jurisdiction in the courts of Virginia in connection with any such dispute including any claim involving AOL or its affiliates, subsidiaries, employees, contractors, officers, directors, telecommunications providers and content providers. . . .

Additionally, paragraph 8 contained a choice of law provision designating Virginia law as being applicable to any dispute between the parties: "The laws of the Commonwealth of Virginia, excluding its conflicts-of-law rules, govern this Agreement and your membership." The lead plaintiff described the TOS provision on his home computer as a "densely worded, small-size text that was hard to read on the computer screen." The district court rejected AOL's motion to dismiss, and AOL filed this petition for writ of mandamus. After holding that AOL had the burden of proof on the enforceability of the forum selection clause, the Court turned to consider the enforcement issue.]

III. . . .

B. OVERVIEW OF FORUM SELECTION CLAUSE ENFORCEMENT

AOL correctly posits that California favors contractual forum selection clauses so long as they are entered into freely and voluntarily, and their enforcement would not be unreasonable. This favorable treatment is attributed to our law's devotion to the concept of one's free right to contract, and flows from the important practical effect such contractual rights have on commerce generally.

We agree with these sentiments, and view such clauses as likely to become even more ubiquitous as this state and nation become acculturated to electronic commerce. *See* Carnival Cruise Lines, Inc. v. Shute, 499 U.S. 585 (1991). Moreover, there are strong economic arguments in support of these agreements, favoring both merchants and consumers, including reduction in the costs of goods and services and the stimulation of e-commerce.

But this encomium is not boundless. Our law favors forum selection agreements only so long as they are procured freely and voluntarily, with the place chosen having some logical nexus to one of the parties or the dispute, and so long as California consumers will not find their substantial legal rights significantly impaired by their enforcement. Therefore, to be enforceable, the selected jurisdiction must be "suitable," "available," and able to "accomplish substantial justice." The Bremen v. Zapata Off-Shore Co., 407 U.S. 1 (1972). The trial court determined that the circumstances of contract formation did not reflect Mendoza's exercised free will, and that the effect of enforcing the forum selection clause here would violate California public policy by eviscerating important legal rights afforded to this state's consumers.

C. Enforcement of the Forum Selection Clause Violates Strong California Public Policy

California courts will refuse to defer to the selected forum if to do so would substantially diminish the rights of California residents in a way that violates our state's public policy. . . .

In Hall v. Superior Court, 150 Cal. App. 3d 411 (1983) (*Hall*), two California investors exchanged their interests in an oil and gas limited partnership in return for stock in one of their co-investors, Imperial Petroleum, Inc., a Utah corporation. Closer to the facts of this case, the contract embodying their exchange agreement contained *both* forum selection and choice of law provisions identifying Nevada as the selected forum and governing law. A dispute arose, and the two investors sued Imperial in California. *Id.* at 413-415. Imperial asserted the forum selection clause, and the trial court found the forum selection clause was enforceable.

In reversing the lower court's decision, the appellate court undertook an examination of both the choice of law clause as well as the forum selection clause noting that the enforceability of these clauses were "inextricably bound up" in one another. *Hall, supra,* at 416. The reason for considering them together was that absent a choice of law clause, the selected forum could apply California law to the dispute under the selected forum's conflict of laws principles. If so, there would be no risk that substantive law might be employed which would materially diminish rights of California residents in violation of California public policy. *Ibid.* However, where the effect of the transfer would be otherwise, the forum selection clause would not be enforced: "While California does not have any public policy against a choice of law provision, . . . an agreement designating [a foreign] law will not be given effect if it would violate a strong California public policy . . . [or] result in an evasion of . . . a statute of the forum protecting its citizens." *Hall,* 150 Cal. App. 3d at. 416-417.[6]

The *Hall* court determined that if the pending securities litigation were transferred to Nevada where Nevada law would be applied, the plaintiffs would lose the benefit of California's Corporate Securities Law of 1968 which would otherwise govern the transaction in question. This California law was designed to protect the public from fraud and deception in securities matters, by providing statutory remedies for violations of the California Corporations Code. *Hall,* 150 Cal. App. 3d at 417. For this reason, the remedial scheme, like the CRLA involved in this case, contains an anti-waiver provision. Corp. Code, §25701; *Hall,* 150 Cal. App. 3d at 417-418. The court concluded: "We believe the right of a buyer of securities in California to have California law and its concomitant nuances apply to any future dispute arising out of the transaction is a 'provision' within the meaning of [Corporations Code] section 25701 which cannot be waived or evaded by stipulation of the parties to a securities transaction. Consequently, we hold the choice of Nevada law provision in this agreement violates section 25701 and the public policy of this state [citation] and for that reason deny enforcement of the forum selection clause as unreasonable." *Id.* at p.418.

The CLRA parallels the Corporate Securities Law of 1968, at issue in *Hall,* insofar as the CRLA is a legislative embodiment of a desire to protect California consumers and furthers a strong public policy of this state. . . . Certainly, the CLRA provides remedial protections *at least* as important as those under the Corporate Securities Law of 1968. Therefore, by parity of reasoning, enforcement of AOL's forum selection clause, which is also accompanied by a choice of law provision favoring Virginia, would necessitate a waiver of the statutory remedies of the CLRA, in violation of that law's anti-waiver provision, Civ. Code, §1751, and California public policy. For this reason alone, we affirm the trial court's ruling.

This conclusion is reinforced by a statutory comparison of California and Virginia consumer protection laws, which reveals Virginia's law provides significantly less consumer protection to its citizens than California law provides for our own. [The court notes that remedies under the Virginia law are

---

6. At oral argument, counsel for AOL suggested for the first time that a Virginia court might apply California's consumer protection law to resolve this dispute. Not only was this suggestion legally unsupported, but we find it counter-intuitive to believe that a Virginia court would invoke California law to resolve a contract-based consumer dispute against a Virginia domiciliary where the parties agreed to have Virginia law applied, and where Virginia has a statutory consumer protection law of its own.

less favorable to consumers than under California law, and that the Virginia law is hostile to class actions while Class actions are an important consumer right under California law.] The unavailability of class action relief in this context is sufficient in and by itself to preclude enforcement of the TOS forum selection clause.

In addition to the unavailability of class actions and the apparent limitation in injunctive relief, neither punitive damages, nor enhanced remedies for disabled and senior citizens are recoverable under Virginia's law. More nuanced differences are the reduced recovery under the VCPA for "unintentional" acts, a shorter period of limitations, and Virginia's use of a Lodestar formula alone to calculate attorney fees recovery. Quite apart from the remedial limitations under Virginia law relating to injunctive and class action relief, the cumulative importance of even these less significant differences is substantial. Enforcement of a forum selection clause, which would impair these aggregate rights, would itself violate important California public policy. For this additional reason the trial court was correct in denying AOL's motion to stay or to dismiss.

In so holding we reject Mendoza's contention that the clause should not be enforced simply because it would be patently unreasonable to require him or other AOL customers who form the putative class to travel to Virginia to litigate the relatively nominal individual sums at issue. He points out that in 1998 and 1999, not a single suit by a non-Virginia resident appears to have been filed in AOL's Virginia home county, a development Mendoza suggests is directly related to the fact that the cost of prosecuting a claim in Virginia vastly exceeds the amounts normally at issue in individual claims against AOL.

But the additional cost or inconvenience necessitated by litigation in the selected forum is not part of the calculus when considering whether a forum selection clause should be enforced. . . . Yet Mendoza contends that [the California Supreme Court's] admonition not to consider convenience and cost in evaluating the validity of forum selection clauses applies only where there remains a "practical option [of travel to the selected forum] in terms of the expense and value of the controversy." As we understand it, Mendoza is arguing that expense in litigating in the selected forum can be considered if it exceeds the amount in controversy or at least renders the choice to litigate "impractical."

We disagree. . . . No case of which we are aware has interpreted this language as Mendoza suggests we should. Moreover, it is not at all clear what monetary amount was in dispute in that case, or whether it was "practical" to bring the litigation in the selected forum. Although the current dispute between Mendoza and AOL might make it impractical for Mendoza to pursue an individual claim in Virginia, there may be other potential disputes between Mendoza and AOL arising from their relationship which would have significantly greater value. Are we to parse the enforceability of the forum selection clause, then, based on the economic value of the particular claim in issue, so that the clause can be enforced some of the time (depending on the value of the claim), but not all of the time? If so, should trial courts use an objective standard, or consider the proclivities of the individual claimant who may not feel litigation in the selected forum is worth it? How should trial judges calculate the costs of litigation? Should they consider the extent to which the selected forum allows for the recovery of costs, including travel-related expenses? Should courts compute the extent to which extraordinary costs in enforcing contractual rights are included in the consideration paid for the goods or services purchased? . . . It was perhaps just such [concerns] that, in part, moved the Supreme Court to pronounce costs and convenience "[are] not the test of reasonableness [of forum selection clauses]."

Questions and Comments

(1) Because Internet communications and services can appear in literally every state and nation in the world, and because of the potential jurisdictional and choice-of-law confusion arising from these ubiquitous contacts, it is easy to understand why the Microsofts and AOLs of the world insist on forum selection clauses. But the ubiquity of contacts related to these services also raises the question whether consumers should have to litigate claims arising around the world from their use of the services in a single forum, especially when the value of the claims are often much less than the cost of travel to the distant forum. How should courts resolve this tension? Does the framework from *Carnival Cruise*, reproduced *supra* page 451, apply straightforwardly to the Internet context? What are the relevant differences between the forum selection clauses at issue in *Carnival Cruise* and the ones at issue in *Caspi* and *America Online?*

(2) The plaintiffs in *Caspi* actually clicked on, and thus in some sense affirmatively consented to, the MSN forum selection clause. In *America Online,* by contrast, it is unclear whether plaintiffs affirmatively consented to the AOL clause, or merely ran their eyes over the paragraph containing the clause as they clicked through pages of legal notices. Does affirmative consent to the clause matter to its enforcement?

Does one even need to see the forum selection clause to be bound by it? Consider the popular Internet portal Yahoo! If one scrolls to the bottom of the page at Yahoo.com and clicks on the tiny "Terms of Service," and then scrolls to the bottom of the TOS page, one finds the following:

> 24. GENERAL INFORMATION
>
> The TOS and the relationship between you and Yahoo shall be governed by the laws of the State of California without regard to its conflict of law provisions. You and Yahoo agree to submit to the personal and exclusive jurisdiction of the courts located within the county of Santa Clara, California. . . . You agree that regardless of any statute or law to the contrary, any claim or cause of action arising out of or related to use of the Service

> or the TOS must be filed within one (1) year after such claim or cause of action arose or be forever barred.

Have you ever visited Yahoo.com? Did you know you were consenting to litigate claims arising out of your use of its many Internet services—shopping, auctions, reference, personal advice, health, chat rooms, and much more—in Santa Clara, California, under California law? (Similar provisions can be found on most web pages with significant traffic.) Are these clauses enforceable if you've never seen them? Recall the analysis in Hill v. Gateway 2000, 105 F.3d 1147 (7th Cir. 1997), discussed *supra* page 458. A somewhat different view was expressed in Specht v. Netscape Communication Corp., 2001 U.S. Dist. LEXIS 2073 (2001), where the court held that an arbitration agreement contained in the unread License Agreement that accompanied downloaded Internet software was unenforceable. *Compare* Pollstar v. Gigmania Ltd, No. CIV-F-00-5671, 2000 WL 33266437 (E.D. Cal. 2000) (expressing concern about the enforceability of online "browse-wrap" license agreements).

What would happen to Internet activity if every user had to read and affirmatively consent to forum selection clauses on every Web page visited?

(3) The real concern in *America Online* seems to be not forum selection, but rather governing law. Would the *America Online* Court have enforced the forum selection clause if AOL's Terms of Service chose a Virginia forum but California governing law? Would AOL ever write such a clause? What does this suggest about the relationship between forum-selection clauses and choice-of-law clauses?

(4) *America Online* says the forum-selection clause must have "some logical connection to one of the parties or the dispute." *Compare* Restatement (Second) Conflict of Laws §187(2)(a) (1971) (*law* chosen by parties governs unless "the chosen state has no substantial relationship to the parties or the transaction and there is no other reasonable basis for the parties choice"). Virginia is presumably such a logical choice because it is the headquarters of AOL and the location of most of AOL's computer servers. In cases involving portals and related services that can be accessed on a worldwide basis, is every forum a logical choice? Is the defendant's headquarters the only logical choice? Do criteria of "logical choice" and "substantial relationship" make sense as applied to the Internet?

(5) Many have proposed that the controversies that arise out of the Internet are best resolved not by courts, but by a variety of private dispute resolution mechanisms. Professor Perritt summarizes this view well:

> Three characteristics of the Internet make traditional dispute resolution through administrative agency and judicial procedures unsatisfactory for many controversies that arise in Internet-based commerce and political interaction. The Internet's low economic barriers to entry invite participation in commerce and politics by small entities and individuals who cannot afford direct participation in many traditional markets and polit-

ical arenas. These low barriers to entry, and greater participation by individuals and small entities, also mean a greater incidence of small transactions. When dispute resolution costs are high, as they are for traditional administrative and judicial procedures, the transaction costs of dispute resolution threaten to swamp the value of the underlying transaction, meaning on the one hand that victims are less likely to seek vindication of their rights and, on the other hand, that actors and alleged wrongdoers may face litigation costs that outweigh the advantages of their offering goods and services in the new electronic markets. To realize the potential of participation by small entities and individuals and of small transactions, it is necessary to reduce the costs of dispute resolution.

Second, the geographic openness of electronic commerce makes stranger-to-stranger transactions more likely. The absence of informal means of developing trust, as when one shops regularly at the local bookstore, means that both merchants and consumers will be inhibited in engaging in commerce unless they have some recourse if the deal goes sour.

Third, the Internet is inherently global. Offering to sell goods on a web page published on a server physically located in Kansas is as visible to consumers in Kosovo as in Kansas. In other words, it is difficult to localize injury-producing conduct or the injury itself in Internet-based markets or political arenas. Traditional dispute resolution machinery depends upon localization to determine jurisdiction. Impediments to localization create uncertainty and controversy over assertions of jurisdiction. That uncertainty has two results. It may frustrate communities that resent being unable to reach through their legal machinery to protect local victims against conduct occurring in a far-off country. It also subjects anyone using the Internet to jurisdiction by any of nearly 200 countries in the world and, in many cases, to their subordinate political units.

Alternative dispute resolution, including not only arbitration and mediation but also a wider range of alternatives such as credit card chargebacks, escrow arrangements, complaint bulletin boards, and complaint aggregation services culminating in official enforcement activity, helps respond to these challenges in two ways. First, ADR can be designed to be much cheaper than traditional procedures. It also is inherently transnational when those agreeing to participate in the ADR process are in different countries.

Perritt, Dispute Resolution in Cyberspace: Demand for New Forms of ADR, 15 Ohio St. J. on Disp. Resol. 675, 676 (2000). Perritt goes on to discuss a variety of possible private dispute resolution mechanisms for the Internet, including a "virtual" magistrate program, credit card chargeback programs, escrow accounts, the Internet Corporation for Assigned Names and Numbers' Uniform Domain-Name Dispute Resolution Program, and much more. What is the relevance of the cases in this Section to these proposals? Would the notice and public policy limits on the enforcement of choice-of-law and choice-of-forum clauses apply to agreements for private dispute resolution? What does this suggest about the feasibility and scope of Perritt's proposals?

B. Choice of Law—Domestic and International

The Internet is believed by many to raise intractable choice-of-law puzzles. Consider this hypothetical:

> Whose substantive legal rules apply to a defamatory message that is written by someone in Mexico, read by someone in Israel, by means of an Internet server located in the United States, injuring the reputation of a Norwegian?

Perritt, Jurisdiction in Cyberspace, 41 Villanova L. Rev. 1, 3 (1996). And this one:

> Which of the many plausibly applicable bodies of copyright law do we consult to determine whether a hyperlink on a World Wide Web page located on a server in France and constructed by a Filipino citizen, which points to a server in Brazil that contains materials protected by German and French (but not Brazilian) copyright law, which is downloaded to a server in the United States and reposted to a Usenet newsgroup, constitutes a remediable infringement of copyright?

Post & Johnson, "Chaos Prevailing on Every Continent": Towards a New Theory of Decentralized Decision-Making in Complex Systems, 73 Chi.-Kent. L. Rev. 1055, 1056 (1998).

Are these problems significantly different than the ones analyzed throughout this casebook? Can the usual tools of conflict of laws resolve these problems, or must we develop new tools?

America Online, Inc. v. National Health Care Discount, Inc.

121 F. Supp. 2d 1255 (D. Iowa 2000)

ZOSS, Magistrate Judge.

[Plaintiff America Online, Inc. ("AOL"), a Delaware corporation, with its principal place of business in Virginia, is an Internet access provider that allows its subscribers to transmit electronic mail ("e-mail") to and from other AOL subscribers and across the Internet. Defendant National Health Care Discount, Inc. ("NHCD"), an Iowa corporation with its administrative offices in Sioux City, Iowa, and sales offices in Atlanta, Kansas City, Phoenix, Dallas, and Denver, is in the business of selling discount optical and dental service plans. Using contract e-mailers from all over the country (including, primarily, the services of Forrest Dayton of Marietta, Georgia), NHCD solicited business through large-volume, "unsolicited bulk e-mail" ("UBE"), sometimes known as "spam." Millions of these messages went to AOL users, at great expense to AOL. When AOL failed to persuade NHCD to stop sending such messages to its subscribers, it sued the company for common law conversion, trespass, and unjust enrichment, as well as violation of various state and federal statutes.]

A federal court exercising supplemental jurisdiction over state law claims in a federal question lawsuit must follow the choice-of-law rules of the forum state. Accordingly, the court looks to Iowa's choice-of-law rules to determine which state's law applies.

As both AOL and NHCD agree, Iowa follows the "most significant relationship" test expressed in section 145, Restatement (Second) Conflict of Laws ("Restatement"). The agreement ends there, however, as the parties differ on how the Restatement factors apply in the circumstances of this case.

The Restatement's "General Principle" set forth in section 145 provides:

> (1) The rights and liabilities of the parties with respect to an issue in tort are determined by the local law of the state which, with respect to that issue, has the most significant relationship to the occurrence and the parties under the principles stated in §6.
>
> (2) Contacts to be taken into account in applying the principles of §6 to determine the law applicable to an issue include:
>
> (a) the place where the injury occurred,
>
> (b) the place where the conduct causing the injury occurred,
>
> (c) the domicile, residence, nationality, place of incorporation and place of business of the parties, and
>
> (d) the place where the relationship, if any, between the parties is centered.
>
> These contacts are to be evaluated according to their relative importance with respect to the particular issue.

Restatement (Second) Conflict of Laws §145 (1971).

Section 145 must be read together with section 6, to which it refers:

> (1) A court, subject to constitutional restrictions, will follow a statutory directive of its own state on choice of law.
>
> (2) When there is no such directive, the factors relevant to the choice of the applicable rule of law include
>
> (a) the needs of the interstate and international systems,
>
> (b) the relevant policies of the forum,
>
> (c) the relevant policies of other interested states and the relative interests of those states in the determination of the particular issue,
>
> (d) the protection of justified expectations,
>
> (e) the basic policies underlying the particular field of law,
>
> (f) certainty, predictability and uniformity of result, and
>
> (g) ease in the determination and application of the law to be applied.

Restatement (Second) Conflict of Laws §6 (1971).

The parties only address the section 145 factors in their arguments concerning which state law applies here. As NHCD points out in its brief, none of those factors points conclusively to Virginia—nor, however, do those factors point clearly to Iowa or to any other state. The section 145 factors provide little in the way of resolving the choice-of-law issue. The court therefore turns to the principles set forth in section 6.

The principles in section 6(2) "underlie all rules of choice of law and are used in evaluating the significance of a relationship, with respect to the particular issue, to the potentially interested states, the occurrence and the parties." Restatement §145, comment (b). Subsections 6(2)(d), (e) and (f) are less important in the field of torts than they are in other areas such as contracts, property, wills and trusts. *Id.* "Because of the relative insignificance of the above-mentioned factors in the tort area of choice of law, the remaining factors listed in §6 assume greater importance . . . ," particularly the relevant policies of "the state with the dominant interest in the determination of the particular issue." *Id.* The court finds the factors in subsections (2)(b) and (c) to be controlling; *i.e.*, the relevant policies and interests of Iowa and Virginia.

As noted previously, NHCD is an Iowa corporation, doing business in Iowa. "[A] state has an obvious interest in regulating the conduct of persons within its territory. . . ." Restatement §6, comment d. Iowa's interest in regulating the actions of corporations doing business in Iowa is embodied in the Iowa Business Corporation Act, Iowa Code chapter 490. A corporation has no rights, including the right to do business, other than the rights conferred by the state's lawmaking power, and the state retains the right to amend the conditions under which corporations may do or continue to do business, and enforce those conditions by revoking a corporation's privileges for noncompliance. The state, therefore, has a vested interest in determining the rights and liabilities of domestic corporations as to actions arising within the state.

Here, however, the only actions by NHCD that appear to have arisen within Iowa are incorporation of the entity, maintenance of an office, and issuance of checks to pay the contract e-mailers. One could add to this list the receipt of NHCD's UBE by Iowa residents. Otherwise, all the actions giving rise to this lawsuit appear to have occurred elsewhere, in a number of states. AOL is incorporated in Delaware, and likely has members who received NHCD's UBE in all fifty states. Dayton's actions originated in Georgia. The record indicates NHCD contracted with other e-mailers from, *inter alia,* New York, California, Ohio, Florida, Missouri, Michigan, Tennessee, Kansas, Ohio and Maryland. NHCD's vice president Hermann Wilms, who, among other things, was responsible for contracting with Dayton, operated out of Overland Park, Kansas.

In addition to "regulating the conduct of persons within its territory," a state also has "an obvious interest . . . in providing redress for injuries that occurred there." Restatement §6, comment e. In the instant case, because there is no clearly demonstrable place where the alleged conduct occurred, "the place where the injury occurred is a contact that, as to most issues, plays an important role in the selection of the state of the applicable law." *Id.*

The only locale in which AOL's alleged injury is clearly demonstrable is Virginia. This is the site of AOL's hardware that it alleges was overburdened by NHCD's UBE. It also is the place where AOL allegedly sustained economic loss. Although no state has a clear relationship to the events giving rise to this action, Virginia's relationship appears to be the most significant. Accordingly, the court finds Virginia law shall control the non-statutory claims raised in this lawsuit.

Questions and Comments

(1) The Internet presents two general choice-of-law problems. The first is the problem of *complexity.* This is the problem of how to choose a single governing law for Internet activity that has multi-jurisdictional contacts. The second problem concerns *situs.* This is the problem of how to choose a governing law when the locus of relevant activity cannot easily be pinpointed in geographical space. Both problems raise similar concerns. The choice of any dispositive geographical contact or any particular law in these cases will often seem arbitrary because several jurisdictions have a legitimate claim to apply their law. Whatever law is chosen, seemingly genuine regulatory interests of the nations whose laws are not applied may be impaired.

These are genuine problems, but are they new to the Internet? Haven't we seen identical problems throughout this casebook? Indeed, aren't the problems of complexity and situs *the* problems in the conflict of laws? Are the hypotheticals in the introduction to this section, concerning copyright infringements and multistate libels on the Internet, more complex than the same issues in "real space"? Are they any more complex than similar issues presented by real-space events such as airplane crashes, mass torts, or multinational commercial transactions? Are they any more complex than a simple products liability suit arising from a two-car accident among residents of the same state? *Compare* Rutherford v. Goodyear Tire and Rubber Co, 943 F. Supp. 789, 790-791 (W.D. Ky. 1996), *aff'd,* 142 F. 3d 436 (6th Cir. 1998) (two car accident between residents of same state implicates the laws of the place of the accident, the states where the car and tire manufacturers are headquartered, the states where the car and tires were manufactured, and the state where the car was purchased).

(2) Is the real challenge of the Internet perhaps not the presence of new conflicts problems, but rather the dramatic increase in the number and percentage of intractable conflicts problems?

(3) The parties and events in *National Health Care Discount* (including the millions of UBE messages that formed the basis for the complaint) implicated contacts in every state in the union. But is every geographical contact equally significant? Why did the Court discount the state of the defendant's incorporation, the states where the UBE's were received, and the

states where the contract e-mailers were located? Why didn't it discuss the states where the routers and servers through which the UBE's traveled were located?

(4) Which conflicts of law methodology is best suited to Internet transactions? Consider:

> [C]yberspace transactions [need not] be resolved on the basis of geographical choice-of-law criteria that are sometimes difficult to apply to cyberspace, such as where events occur or where people are located at the time of the transaction. [These] are not the only choice-of-law criteria, and certainly not the best in contexts where the geographical locus of events is so unclear. Domicile (and its cognates, such as citizenship, principal place of business, habitual residence, and so on) are also valid choice-of-law criteria that have particular relevance to problems, like those in cyberspace, that involve the regulation of intangibles or of multinational transactions. [Moreover,] all choice-of-law problems [need not] be resolved by multilateral choice-of-law methodologies. A multilateral methodology asks which of several possible laws governs a transaction, and selects one of these laws on the basis of specified criteria. Multilateral methods accentuate the situs and complexity problems. But the regulatory issues that are most relevant to the cyberspace governance debate almost always involve unilateral choice-of-law methods that alleviate these problems. A unilateral method considers only whether the dispute at issue has close enough connections to the forum to justify the application of local law. If so, local law applies; if not, the case is dismissed and the potential applicability of foreign law is not considered. Unilateral choice-of-law methods make the complexity and situs problems less significant. They do not require a determination of which of a number of possible laws apply. Nor do they require a court of identify where certain events occurred. What matters is simply whether the activity has local effects that are significant enough to implicate local law.

Goldsmith, Against Cyberanarchy, 65 U. Chi. L. Rev. 1199, 1236-1237 (1998). Is this convincing? Did *National Health Care Discount* have any problem applying a multilateral choice-of-law method that selected a place of injury? Would interest analysis, which in many guises is a unilateral choice-of-law method, have provided a more satisfactory resolution?

(5) Because Internet communications usually cross many physical borders and thus give rise to difficult conflict of law problems, several commentators have suggested that Internet transactions be governed not by the law of any particular territorial government, but rather by a private law chosen by Internet users that will be uniform across particular Internet communities. Some of these commentators view the Internet as a separate "place" whose self-governance territorial governments should defer to:

> Many of the jurisdictional and substantive quandaries raised by border-crossing electronic communications could be resolved by one simple prin-

> ciple: conceiving of Cyberspace as a distinct "place" for purposes of legal analysis by recognizing a legally significant border between Cyberspace and the "real world." Using this new approach, we would no longer ask the unanswerable question "where" in the geographical world a Net-based transaction occurred. Instead, the more salient questions become: What rules are best suited to the often unique characteristics of this new place and the expectations of those who are engaged in various activities there? What mechanisms exist or need to be developed to determine the content of those rules and the mechanisms by which they can enforced? Answers to these questions will permit the development of rules better suited to the new phenomena in question, more likely to be made by those who understand and participate in those phenomena, and more likely to be enforced by means that the new global communications media make available and effective. . . .
>
> If the sysops and users who collectively inhabit and control a particular area of the Net want to establish special rules to govern conduct there, and if that rule set does not fundamentally impinge upon the vital interests of others who never visit this new space, then the law of sovereigns in the physical world should defer to this new form of self-government.

Johnson & Post, *supra,* at 1378-1379, 1393.

Is the Internet best thought of as a separate place? Are Internet activities self-contained? Consider this response:

> Cyberspace participants are no more self-contained than telephone users, members of the Catholic Church, corporations, and other private groups with activities that transcend jurisdictional borders. They are real people in real space transacting in a fashion that produces real-world effects on cyberspace participants and nonparticipants alike. Cyberspace users solicit and deliver kiddie porn, launder money, sexually harass, defraud, and so on. It is these and many other real-space costs—costs that cyberspace communities cannot effectively internalize—that national regulatory regimes worry about and aim to regulate.

Goldsmith, *supra,* at 1242. Keep this debate in mind as you read the following cases.

People of the State of New York v. World Interactive Gaming Corp.

714 N.Y.S.2d 844 (Sup. Ct. N.Y. 1999)

Ramos, J.

This proceeding is brought by the Attorney General of the State of New York pursuant to Executive Law §63 (12) and General Business Law article 23-A, to enjoin the respondents, World Interactive Gaming Corporation (WIGC), Golden Chips Casino, Inc. (GCC), and their principals, officers, and directors from operating within or offering to residents of New York State gambling over the Internet.

The central issue here is whether the State of New York can enjoin a foreign corporation legally licensed to operate a casino offshore from offering gambling to Internet users in New York. At issue is section 9(1) of article I of the New York Constitution which contains an express prohibition against any kind of gambling not authorized by the State Legislature. The prohibition represents a deep-rooted policy of the State against unauthorized gambling.

WIGC is a Delaware corporation that maintains corporate offices in New York. WIGC wholly owns GCC, an Antiguan subsidiary corporation which acquired a license from the government of Antigua to operate a land-based casino. Through contracts executed by WIGC, GCC developed interactive software, and purchased computer servers which were installed in Antigua, to allow users around the world to gamble from their home computers. GCC promoted its casino at its web site, and advertised on the Internet and in a national gambling magazine. The promotion was targeted nationally and was viewed by New York residents.

In February 1998, the Attorney General commenced an investigation into the practices of WIGC. . . . [The Attorney General's Office logged] onto respondents' web site, downloading the gambling software, and in July 1998, placed the first of several bets. Users who wished to gamble in the GCC Internet casino were directed to wire money to open a bank account in Antigua and download additional software from GCC's web site. In opening an account, users were asked to enter their permanent address. A user which submitted a permanent address in a State that permitted land-based gambling, such as Nevada, was granted permission to gamble. Although a user which entered a State such as New York, which does not permit land-based gambling, was denied permission to gamble, because the software does not verify the user's actual location, a user initially denied access could easily circumvent the denial by changing the State entered to that of Nevada, while remaining physically in New York State. The user could then log onto the GCC casino and play virtual slots, blackjack or roulette. This raises the question if this constitutes a good-faith effort not to engage in gambling in New York.

The Attorney General commenced this action pursuant to Executive Law §63 (12) and General Business Law article 23-A. Petitioner seeks: (1) to enjoin respondents from conducting a business within the State of New York until they are properly registered with the Secretary of State to conduct business in New York; (2) to enjoin respondents from running any aspect of their Internet gambling business within the State of New York; (3) to be awarded restitution and damages to injured investors.

Respondents contend that the transactions occurred offshore. . . . They claim that they were operating a duly licensed legitimate business fully authorized by the government of Antigua and in compliance with that country's rules and regulations of a land-based casino. They further argue that the Federal and State laws upon which the State relies either do not apply to the activities of WIGC or are too vague and ambiguous to criminalize the activity of Internet gambling, when such activity is offshore in Antigua.

[The Court finds personal jurisdiction over the defendants on the basis of their instate activities.]

Respondents argue that the court lacks subject matter jurisdiction, and that Internet gambling falls outside the scope of New York State gambling prohibitions, because the gambling occurs outside of New York State. However, under New York Penal Law, if the person engaged in gambling is located in New York, then New York is the location where the gambling occurred. *See* Penal Law §225.00 [2]. Here, some or all of those funds in an Antiguan bank account are staked every time the New York user enters betting information into the computer. It is irrelevant that Internet gambling is legal in Antigua. The act of entering the bet and transmitting the information from New York via the Internet is adequate to constitute gambling activity within New York State.

Wide range implications would arise if this court adopted respondents' argument that activities or transactions which may be targeted at New York residents are beyond the State's jurisdiction. Not only would such an approach severely undermine this State's deep-rooted policy against unauthorized gambling, it also would immunize from liability anyone who engages in any activity over the Internet which is otherwise illegal in this State. A computer server cannot be permitted to function as a shield against liability, particularly in this case where respondents actively targeted New York as the location where they conducted many of their allegedly illegal activities. Even though gambling is legal where the bet was accepted, the activity was transmitted from New York. Contrary to respondents' unsupported allegation of an Antiguan management company managing GCC, the evidence also indicates that the individuals who gave the computer commands operated from WIGC's New York office. The respondents enticed Internet users, including New York residents, to play in their casino.

The evidence demonstrates that respondents have violated New York Penal Law which states that "[a] person is guilty of promoting gambling . . . when he knowingly advances or profits from unlawful gambling activity." Penal Law §225.05. By having established the gambling enterprise, and advertised and solicited investors to buy its stock and to gamble through its online casino, respondents have "engage[d] in conduct which materially aids . . . gambling activity," in violation of New York law. Penal Law §225.00[4], which states "conduct includes but is not limited to conduct directed toward the creation or establishment of the particular game, contest, scheme, device . . . (or) toward the solicitation or inducement of persons to participate therein." Moreover, this court rejects respondents' argument that it unknowingly accepted bets from New York residents. New York users can easily circumvent the casino software in order to play by the simple expedient of entering an out-of-State address. Respondents' violation of the Penal Law is that they persisted in continuous illegal conduct directed toward the creation, establishment, and advancement of unauthorized gambling. The violation had occurred long before a New York resident ever staked a bet. Because all of respondents' activities illegally advanced gambling, this court finds that they have knowingly violated Penal Law §225.05.

Not only are respondents guilty of violating New York State's gambling laws but they have also violated several Federal laws. . . .

Because of the clear illegality present in respondents' actions, and the absence of any triable issue of fact, respondents are found liable under Executive Law §63 (12) for their State and Federal law violations.

REMEDIES

The Attorney General is entitled to injunctive relief which is routinely granted in special proceedings under Executive Law §63 (12). The requirement of a bond to assure future proper behavior on the part of an enjoined party traditionally accompanies such an injunction. This court finds the request for an injunction warranted, and directs fixing of the amount be incorporated in an order to be settled.

As for the Attorney General's request for restitution, penalties, and costs, which are available under Executive Law §63 (12) and General Business Law §353 (3), this court finds the circumstances warrant awarding them in this case.

Jeri-Jo Knitwear, Inc. v. Club Italia, Inc.

94 F. Supp. 2d 457 (S.D.N.Y. 2000)

OWEN, District Judge

Jeri-Jo requests this Court issue a contempt citation against the defendants for violating the Court's orders. On July 15, 1999, this Court granted Jerri-Jo's motion for summary judgment on its Lanham Act claims. The order specifically states, "Plaintiffs are entitled to injunctive relief based on my finding that defendant's have infringed plaintiffs' ENERGIE trademark." A judgment on consent was entered by the Court on December 3, 1999. That judgment permanently enjoined defendants, in the United States, from "advertising or promoting" apparel bearing Jerri-Jo's registered trademark ENERGIE or any colorable variation thereof or any confusingly similar trademark.

Defendants, Sixty S.p.A. ("Sixty") and Sixty U.S.A. (formerly known as Club Italia, Inc.), design, manufacture, sell, and distribute high price denim apparel under several labels, including the "ENERGIE" clothing label at issue in this case. All the clothing is designed in Italy and is sold worldwide. Sixty is the holder of valid trademarks for the ENERGIE mark in Italy, France, and Germany and has the right to sell ENERGIE apparel in numerous other countries, including Albania, Algeria, Armenia, Austria, Belgium, Bulgaria, Canada, China, Denmark, Finland, Ireland, Hong Kong, Israel, the Netherlands, North Korea, Portugal, Spain and the United Kingdom, among others.

Defendants are presently operating three Web sites at issue here, *www.misssixty.com, www.sixty.net,* and *www.energie.it.* Although the servers for all three sites are located in Italy, defendants had used a United States-based company to register its *www.misssixty.com* and *www.sixty.net* sites[1] one year before the consent judgment was entered for a substantial number of products (which are legitimately sold even today in the United States) including the ENERGIE line. The third site, *www.energie.it,* is registered in Italy[2] and permits the user to view defendants' 1999/2000 collection of ENERGIE apparel. The first two sites, *www.misssixty.com* and *www.sixty.net,* contain a hyperlink to defendants' ENERGIE apparel, but do not themselves display defendants' infringing apparel. A hyperlink is highlighted text or images that when selected by the user, permits him to view another related Web document. With regard to these two sites, the highlighted text that constitutes the hyperlink is the term "ENERGIE," and by selecting this linking term, the user is transported to defendants' *www.energie.it* Web site to view defendants' 1999/2000 collection of ENERGIE apparel.

Plaintiffs contend that this constitute "advertisement [and] promotion" within the United States, putting defendants in contempt of the consent judgment. A court has the power to hold a party in contempt where there is (1) a clear and unambiguous order, (2) clear and convincing proof of a party's noncompliance with that order, and (3) a failure to reasonably and diligently comply with the order.

With the foregoing as the law, plaintiffs argue that the Court's order clearly prohibits all advertisements and promotion of defendants' ENERGIE apparel in the United States. Plaintiffs contend defendants are in violation of the order because they continue to use *www.misssixty.com* and *www.sixty.net* sites to advertise and promote their entire line which includes the infringing ENERGIE apparel to United States consumers, and have not been reasonably diligent in complying with the Court's orders because they have taken no steps at all to restrict access or the likelihood of access to these sites by United States consumers for the ENERGIE line. Plaintiff assert defendants could have taken several steps to reduce the likelihood that a user in the United States would view their (U.S.) infringing ENERGIE collection. First, defendants could have changed the top level domain names from ".com" and ".net," which United States users are accustomed to using, to ".it," which

1. The end portion of a domain name, for example ".com," is called the top level domain. Internet addresses that end in ".com," ".net," ".org," and ".edu" are administered by a United States company, Network Solutions, Inc.

2. Addresses administered in other countries may have different top level domain names. The ".it" indicates an Italian Web site.

United States users are unaccustomed to using. Second, defendant could have removed the hypertext links from the *www.misssixty.com* and *www.sixty.net* Web sites to the *www.energie.it* Web site, which displays defendants' infringing ENERGIE collection. Third, defendant could restrict access to their Italian Web site by requiring a password, which would not be issued to United States users. Thus, plaintiffs argue that defendants cannot assert that they have been reasonably and diligently complying with the Court's orders.

Plaintiffs cite Playboy Enterprises, Inc. v. Chuckleberry Publishing, Inc., 939 F. Supp. 1032 (S.D.N.Y. 1996) to support their position. In Playboy, the Court had issued an injunction in 1981 against the use by an Italian company, Tattilo, of the mark PLAYMEN in connection with selling, offering for sale or distribution of English-language magazines in the United States. However, Tattilo was not prevented from selling Playmen magazines in Italy. Some years later, Playboy discovered that Tattilo had created an Internet site accessible by users from the United States which featured the Playmen name, *www.playmen.it.* Since users from the United States could download pictures and arrange subscription agreements from the site, Playboy moved to hold Tattilo in contempt for violating the injunction by offering for sale and distributing Playmen magazine in the United States. Finding Tattilo in contempt, the court ordered Tattilo to shut down the Web site or make it inaccessible to United States customers and awarded Playboy all of Tattilo's gross profits and its attorney's fees incurred in making the application. Plaintiffs argue that defendants' conduct here is no different from that described in Playboy. They argue that defendants are flouting the Court's orders by continuing to offer information about the infringing ENERGIE apparel, *i.e.*, promoting or advertising, through its Internet Web site which is accessible by United States consumers.

Defendants argue that the elements of contempt have not been satisfied. First, defendants argue that the Court's order is not "clear and unambiguous" since it does not expressly prohibit the operation of Sixty's internationally accessible Web sites. Second, defendants contend that they are in compliance with the consent judgment and that a Web site owner does not advertise or promote products simply by posting a Web site. In support of this second contention defendants cite Bensusan Restaurant Corp. v. Burger King, 937 F. Supp. 295, 299 (S.D.N.Y. 1996), *aff'd*, 126 F.3d 25 (2d Cir. 1997). Third, defendants argue that they have diligently complied the Court's orders because they investigated whether United States consumers could be blocked from their Web sites but found it was not possible to do so "conclusively." After so finding, defendants proposed to add a disclaimer to their sites indicating that the ENERGIE brand clothing from Sixty as presented on the Web sites is not available for sale or distribution in the United States and is not available for purchase by persons in the United States, and that plaintiffs' own the ENERGIE trademark in the United States and sell and distribute their own ENERGIE brand clothing in the United States. However, plaintiffs rejected this proposal.

While I agree with the plaintiffs that Chuckleberry provides guidance, and that defendant could be viewed as "advertising" in the United States in violation of the consent judgment, I can not, however, conclude on the total record before me that defendants' conduct is of that flouting wilfulness to have earned the denomination "contemnor." Defendants, one must keep in mind, do have world-wide rights in the mark outside the United States. Accordingly, while I direct the defendants to immediately delink its www .energie.it site from its *www.misssixty.com* and *www.sixty.net* sites, I do not conclude defendants should be required to delist its www.energie.it site from various search engines because I do not believe an adequate evidentiary foundation has been laid to require such broad relief where even plaintiff concedes 100% perfection is not possible, and, I repeat, defendants may legitimately advertise their mark over much of the rest of the globe, and there is no showing of damage to plaintiff from the failure to act with more dispatch. Plaintiffs did observe at oral argument that perfection is not possible, the Internet being what it is.

Licra and UEJF v. Yahoo! Inc.

Tribunal de Grande Instance de Paris, May 22, 2000

www.lapres.net/html/yahen.html (translation by Daniel Lapres)

GOMEZ, First Deputy Chief Justice.

[Yahoo! Inc. ("Yahoo!"), a U.S. corporation and one of the world's leading web portals, has an Internet auction site that offered for sale Nazi memorabilia such as flags, stamps, and military souvenirs. Persons at computers in France could access this site through links on the French-language portal of Yahoo!'s French subsidiary, Yahoo! France, or by accessing Yahoo!'s portal directly from France by typing *www.yahoo.com* into a computer browser. The International League Against Racism and Anti-Semitism (LICRA) and the Union of French Jewish Students (UEJF) sued Yahoo! And Yahoo! France, alleging violations of Article R. 645-2 of the French penal code, a World War II-era law criminalizing the exhibition or sale of racist materials. The plaintiffs asked the Court to force Yahoo! to block French users' access to Nazi objects for sale on Yahoo!'s U.S. auction site.]

Yahoo! Inc. has argued that our court is not territorially competent over the matter, because the alleged fault is committed on the territory of the United States. [It further argues for rejection of plaintiffs' claims on the ground that] the duties of vigilance and prior censure which the petitioners would seek to impose upon it are impossible obligations, first in terms of the law and the American constitution, in particular the First Amendment of the Constitution which institutes the liberty of expression and then in view of the technical impossibility of identifying surfers who visit the auction service, while recalling that in its charter it warns all surfers against using the service for purposes worthy of reprobation for whatsoever motive (incitement to hatred, racial or ethnic discrimination . . .).

Whereas it is not challenged that surfers who call up Yahoo.com from French territory may, directly or via the link offered by Yahoo.fr, see on their screens the pages, services and sites to which Yahoo.com gives access, in particular the auction service (Auctions) lodged by Geocities.com, the lodging service of Yahoo! Inc., in particular in its declension relating to Nazi objects;

Whereas the exposition for the purpose of sale of Nazi objects constitutes a violation of French law (article R.645-2 of the Criminal Code) as well as an offence against the collective memory of a country profoundly wounded by the atrocities committed by and in the name of a the Nazi criminal enterprise against its citizens and most importantly against its citizens of the Jewish religion;

Whereas while permitting the visualization in France of these objects and eventual participation of a surfer established in France in such an exposition/sale, Yahoo! Inc. thus has committed a wrong on the territory of France, a wrong, the unintentional nature of which is apparent, but which is the cause of harm to the LICRA as well as the UEJF which both have the mission of pursuing in France any and all forms of banalization of Nazism, regardless of the fact that the litigious activity is marginal in relation with the entire business of the auction sales service offered on its . . . Yahoo.com site;

Whereas Yahoo! Inc. claims that it is technically impossible to control access to its auction service or any other service, and that therefore it cannot prohibit any surfer from France from visualizing same on his screen;

Whereas it wishes nevertheless to emphasize that it warns all visitors against any uses of its services for purposes that are "worthy of reprobation for whatsoever reason," such as for purposes of racial or ethnic discrimination (*cf.* its user's charter);

But whereas Yahoo! Inc; is in a position to identify the geographical origin of the site which is coming to visit, based on the IP address of the caller, which should therefore enable it to prohibit surfers from France, by whatever means are appropriate, from accessing the services and sites the visualization of which on a screen set up in France, and in some cases teledischarging and reproduction of the contents, or of any other initiative justified by the nature of the site consulted, would be likely to be qualified in France as a crime and/or constitute a manifestly illegal nuisance within the meaning of articles 808 and 809 of New Code of Civil Procedure, which is manifestly the case of the exhibition of uniforms, insignia, emblems reminiscent of those worn or exhibited by the Nazis;

Whereas as regards surfers who navigate through sites which guarantee them anonymity, Yahoo! Inc. has fewer means of control except for example through refusing systematically access to such sites to all visitors who does not disclose their geographical origin;

Whereas the real difficulties encountered by Yahoo do not constitute insurmountable obstacles;

That [Yahoo!] will therefore be ordered to take any and all measures of such kind as to dissuade and make impossible any consultations by surfers calling from France to its sites and services in dispute the title and/or contents of which infringe upon the internal public order of France, especially the site selling Nazi objects;

That Yahoo will be given two months to enable it to formulate proposals of technical measures likely to lead to a settlement of this dispute;

Whereas, as regards Yahoo France, it bears mentioning that its site Yahoo.fr does not itself offer surfers calling from France access to the sites or series the title and/or the contents of which constitute infractions of French law; that therefore, it does not provide access to the site or services for auction sales of Nazi objects;

But whereas it offers surfers a link to Yahoo.com entitled "further research on Yahoo.com", without any particular warning;

Or whereas, knowing what are the contents of the services offered by Yahoo.com, and in this case the service of auction sales including in one of its declensions the sale of Nazi objects, it behooves it to warn surfers, by a banner, prior to the surfer's entry into the Yahoo.com site, that should the result of his search on Yahoo.com . . . point toward sites, pages or forums the title and or contents of which constitute a violation of French law, such as is the case of sites which, whether directly or indirectly, intentionally or unintentionally, make the apology of Nazism, it must interrupt the consultation of the site in question lest it incur the sanctions stipulated by French law or answer to legal actions which might be initiated against it;

NOW THEREFORE

At a public audience and rendering its judgment in first instance, after having heard all the parties, the Court: . . .

Orders Yahoo! Inc. to take such measures as will dissuade and render impossible any and all consultation on Yahoo.com of the auction service for Nazi objects as well as any other site or service which makes apologies of Nazism or questions of the existence of Nazi crimes;

Orders [a subsequent hearing] during which Yahoo! Inc. shall submit the measures which it intends to implement to end the harm and the nuisance suffered by the plaintiffs and to prevent any new incidents of nuisance;

Finds Yahoo! Inc. liable to pay to the LICRA an amount of 10,000 Francs [approximately $133] on the basis of article 700 of the New Code of Civil Procedure;

[Following this ruling, the Paris court convened a panel of Internet experts who prepared a report about the feasibility of Yahoo! blocking access in France to its U.S. auction site. The report concluded that Yahoo! could block French users from accessing its U.S. auction site with a 90% success rate through a combined process of (a) tracing the computer user's Internet Protocol address to its geographical source, and (b) conditioning access to the auction site on a declaration of nationality. The court embraced this conclusion, and also noted that Yahoo! had already been identifying French users to some degree because French users visiting Yahoo! auction site were greeted with French-language advertisements. On the basis of these findings, the Court affirmed its previous ruling, gave Yahoo! three months to comply, and ordered a fine of 100,000 francs (about $13,300) per day for noncompliance after that time. *See* Licra et UEJF v. Yahoo! Inc., Tribunal de Grande Instance de Paris, November 22, 2000, available at *www.lapres.net/html/yahen11.html* (translation by Daniel Lapres)].

Questions and Comments

(1) In January 2001, Yahoo! Inc. banned all Nazi paraphernalia from its U.S. auction sites but claimed that the move was not in response to the French decision. *See* Guernsey, Yahoo to Try Harder to Find Postings of Harmful Material, N.Y. Times, Jan. 3, 2001, Sec. 5, p.2.

(2) All three decisions—*World Interactive Gaming, Jeri-Jo Knitwear,* and *Yahoo!*—invoke "unilateral" methodologies that ask only whether local law applies or not. Why do these courts not consider the application of foreign law, and then choose between local and foreign law? Because the cases involve international as opposed to interstate conflicts? Because the laws at issue are "public" laws? Some other reason?

(3) All three cases involve Internet activity legal in one country that is deemed harmful in another country. An important issue in all three cases is whether the offshore content provider has taken adequate steps to keep the illegal content out of the nation where the content is deemed legal. In *World Interactive Gaming,* the court held that the offshore content provider had to do more than screen out on the basis of where users *said* they were from, because the user could falsify this information. In *Jeri-Jo Knitwear,* the court declined to force the offshore content provider to change domain names or require a geographical identification password, both of which would have kept some offending content out of the United States. And in *Yahoo!,* the court ordered Yahoo! to employ geographical identification and screening technology to block access in France to the U.S. auction site. *Compare* Statement of the Commission Regarding Use of Internet Web Sites to Offer Securities, Solicit Securities Transactions or Advertise Investment Services Offshore (March 23, 1998) (stating that to avoid U.S. securities liability, an unregistered offshore securities offeror must both (a) prominently disclaim that the offer is directed to countries other than the United States *and* (b) implement procedures that are reasonably designed to guard against sales to U.S. persons, such as ascertaining the purchasers geographical identification information (address or telephone number) prior to sale).

What steps should offshore content providers be required to take to keep out offending content? Does it depend on the cost of filtering? On its effectiveness? Does it depend on whether the content provider in some sense directs the content to the regulating nation? Should knowledge that the offending content is being accessed in a nation where it is illegal be enough? Compare, in this regard, the Internet personal jurisdiction cases above. *Compare also* the constitutional decisions in *Clay*, *Watson*, and *Hague*, reproduced *supra* pages 356, 354, and 359 respectively, where the Court imposed very weak notice requirements that were largely satisfied by knowledge of possible governing law.

A recent decision in Germany imposed significant duties on foreign Internet content providers. In the *Toben* case, 1 StR 184/00 (Bundesgerichtsh of December 12, 2000), Germany's highest court of civil affairs held that a German law prohibiting Nazi glorification applied to an Australian national who posted holocaust-denial information on an Australian Web site accessible in Germany. The defendant, who was arrested while visiting Germany, maintained that the Australian Web page was not directed toward Germany. The court rejected this argument, reasoning that holocaust-denial information was an inherent danger to public peace akin to other inherently dangerous activities (such as nuclear radiation and toxic waste) for which there was liability in Germany even if the source of the harm originated abroad and was not consciously directed to Germany. *Compare* Goldsmith, *supra*, at 1244 ("A manufacturer that pollutes in one state is not immune from the antipollution laws of other states where the pollution causes harm just because it cannot predict which way the wind blows. Similarly, a cyberspace content provider cannot necessarily claim ignorance about the geographical flow of information as a defense to the application of the law of the place where the information appears.").

(4) The *Yahoo!* Court ordered geographical screening of French users even though it was only 90% effective. By contrast, *Jeri-Jo Knitwear* court declined to order such screening, in part because "100% perfection is not possible." Must a screening mechanism be perfect to be useful? Professor Lessig thinks not:

> A regulation need not be absolutely effective to be sufficiently effective. It need not raise the cost of the prohibited activity to infinity in order to reduce the level of that activity quite substantially. If regulation increases the cost of access to this kind of information, it will reduce access to this information, even if it doesn't reduce it to zero. . . . If government regulation had to show that it was perfect before it was justified, then indeed there would be little regulation of cyberspace, or of real space either. But regulation, whether for the good or the bad, has a lower burden to meet.

Lessig, The Zones of Cyberspace, 48 Stan. L. Rev. 1403, 1405 (1996).

(5) Some worry that *Yahoo!* implies that all Internet communications can be regulated by all nations. A related worry is that if the *Yahoo!* approach prevails, Internet communications will bend to the requirements of the most restrictive nation. Are these concerns warranted? Can France enforce its laws against the vast majority of Internet users—E-commerce buyers and sellers, porn purveyors and consumers, chat room participants, Web-page owners and the like—who lack a physical presence or assets in France? As for companies like *Yahoo!*, don't all multinational firms face multiple regulatory burdens? One difference between Yahoo! and, say, McDonalds, might be that McDonalds can simultaneously comply with differing national health regulations around the world, but the architecture of the Internet precludes Yahoo! from knowing where in the world its content goes, making it impossible for them to comply with all local laws. Does the geographical filtering technology relied on in *Yahoo!* resolve this problem? Does it change the nature of the problem?

(6) Are the decisions in *World Interactive Gaming* and *Yahoo!* impermissibly extraterritorial? They both purport to regulate the local effects of offshore activity, but they both have profound consequences abroad. Couldn't one just as well say that in the absence of these decisions, the Antiguan gambling laws and the United States' First Amendment would have extraterritorial effect? So don't the extraterritorial effects run in both directions? Is either direction privileged? Or does the answer depend on which court you ask?

In answering this last question, consider the significance of the countersuit that Yahoo! brought against the La Ligue Contre Le Racisme et L'antisemitisme in federal court in California, seeking a declaration that the French court order was unenforceable in the United States. The district court rejected the French defendants' motion to dismiss for lack of personal jurisdiction. It reasoned that the defendants had purposefully availed itself of California by (a) sending a "cease and desist" letter to Yahoo!'s Santa Clara headquarters; (b) asking the French Court to require Yahoo! to perform specific physical acts in Santa Clara (such as re-engineering of its Santa Clara-based servers), and (c) utilizing United States Marshals to effect service of process on Yahoo! in California, all with the "conscious intent" of compelling Yahoo! to censor "constitutionally protected content on its U.S.-based Internet services." Yahoo! Inc. v. La Ligue Contre Le Racisme et L'antisemitisme, Case Number 00-21275 JF (N.D. Calif. June 7, 2001).

(7) The *Yahoo!* Case in the United States raises the possibility that the real conflict of laws problem presented by the Internet is not personal jurisdiction or choice of law, but rather enforcement of judgments:

> The real problem is turning a judgment supported by jurisdiction into meaningful economic relief. . . . If an old lady in Richmond, Virginia is the victim of fraud perpetuated through the Internet by someone located in Belgium, she has a reasonable chance of convincing a Virginia circuit

> court that it has jurisdiction over the Belgian actor. Unless the fraud is enormous, the Belgian actor is unlikely to appear and she is likely to get a default judgment. But what can she do with her default judgment? Even if the Belgian legal system, through its equivalent of the comity doctrine, will enforce the judgment, it is improbably that she will spend the money to get a Belgian lawyer to enforce the judgment in Belgium. The transaction costs dwarf the value of the claim.

Perritt, Will the Judgment-Proof Own Cyberspace?, 32 Intl. Lawyer 1121, 1123 (1998).

How serious a problem is this? What steps could Virginia take, in Virginia, to address the problem of fraudulent Internet activity originating from abroad? Is enforcement of judgments easier or harder in the domestic context? Why? For considerations of these issues, *see* Perritt, *id.;* Goldsmith, *supra,* at 1216-1221, 1224-1230.

(8) Note that the Internet provides a novel method of enforcing judgments. In the Fall of 2000, a Website located in Austria—voteauction.com—offered a service that enabled U.S. voters, including voters in Illinois, to buy and sell votes in the November 2000 election. The Chicago Board of Election Commissioners filed a civil lawsuit in the Circuit Court of Cook County against voteauction.com and its individual organizers and managers, arguing that voteauction.com threatened to corrupt or, at least, to undermine confidence in, the November 7, 2000, general election in Chicago. The court had jurisdiction over the defendants because the web site solicited voters in Illinois. But what remedy was available? The Election Board sought, and the trial court granted, an injunction against voteauction.com's domain name registry, Domain Bank. *See* Board of Election Commissioners of the City of Chicago v. Bernhard, No. 00-CE-031 (Cir. Ct. Cook Cty, Oct. 18, 2000). Domain Bank's standard domain name registration agreement prohibited the domain name use for "illegal purposes." In response to the injunction, which signified a judicial determination that the domain name was being used illegally, Domain Bank cancelled voteauction.com's domain name, shutting down voteauction.com all over the world. One week later, voteauction.com opened up under a new domain name, "vote-auction.com," and this domain name was registered in Switzerland with the International Council of Registrars ("CORE"). But CORE too had a prohibition against illegal use in its standard domain name registration agreement, and after extensive telephonic and email discussions between counsel for the Election Commissioners and counsel for CORE, CORE too cancelled the vote-auction.com domain name, once again shutting the site down. Vote-auction.com sought to publicize its IP address, the use of which would avoid the domain name system all together, but by then, the election had been held. For analysis of this type of remedy by the author who inspired the Chicago Board to seek it, see Perritt, Will the Judgment Proof Own Cyberspace?, 32 Intl. 1121 (1998).

C. Dormant Commerce Clause

American Library Association v. Pataki

969 F. Supp. 160 (S.D.N.Y. 1997)

PRESKA, L.

[The plaintiffs in this case are individuals and organizations who use the Internet to communicate, disseminate, display, and access a broad range of communications. The plaintiffs communicate online both within and outside the State of New York, and each plaintiff's communications are accessible from within and outside New York. The plaintiffs sue the Governor and the Attorney General of New York, alleging that N.Y. Penal Law §235.21, violates the dormant commerce clause. Section 235.21 makes it a crime for an individual

> Knowing the character and content of the communication which, in whole or in part, depicts actual or simulated nudity, sexual conduct or sado-masochistic abuse, and which is harmful to minors, [to] intentionally use[] any computer communication system allowing the input, output, examination or transfer, of computer data or computer programs from one computer to another, to initiate or engage in such communication with a person who is a minor.

The statute provides four regular defenses to prosecution: (a) The defendant made a reasonable effort to ascertain the true age of the minor and was unable to do so as a result of the actions taken by the minor; (b) The defendant has taken, in good faith, reasonable, effective and appropriate actions under the circumstances to restrict or prevent access by minors to materials specified in such subdivision, which may involve any appropriate measures to restrict minors from access to such communications, including any method which is feasible under available technology; (c) The defendant has restricted access to such materials by requiring use of a verified credit card, debit account, adult access code or adult personal identification number; or (d) The defendant has in good faith established a mechanism such that the labelling, segregation or other mechanism enables such material to be automatically blocked or screened by software or other capabilities reasonably available to responsible adults wishing to effect such blocking or screening and the defendant has not otherwise solicited minors not subject to such screening or blocking capabilities to access that material or circumvent any such screening or blocking.]

The Internet is a network of networks—a decentralized, self-maintaining series of redundant links among computers and computer networks, capable of rapidly transmitting communications without direct human involvement or control. No organization or entity controls the Internet; in fact, the chaotic, random structure of the Internet precludes any exercise of such control.

[P]erhaps the most well-known method of communicating information online is the Web; many laypeople erroneously believe that the Internet is co-extensive with the Web. The Web is really a publishing forum; it is comprised of millions of separate "Web sites" that display content provided by particular persons or organizations. Any Internet user anywhere in the world with the proper software can create a Web page, view Web pages posted by others, and then read text, look at images and video, and listen to sounds posted at these sites. Many large corporations, banks, brokerage houses, newspapers and magazines provide online editions of their reports and publications or operate independent Web sites. Government agencies and even courts use the Web to disseminate information to the public. At the same time, many individual users and small community organizations have established individual "home pages" on the Web that provide information to any interested person who "surfs by."

Regardless of the aspect of the Internet they are using, Internet users have no way to determine the characteristics of their audience that are salient under the New York Act—age and geographic location. In fact, in online communications through newsgroups, mailing lists, chat rooms, and the Web, the user has no way to determine with certainty that any particular person has accessed the user's speech. "Once a provider posts content on the Internet, it is available to all other Internet users worldwide."

The borderless world of the Internet raises profound questions concerning the relationship among the several states and the relationship of the federal government to each state, questions that go to the heart of "our federalism." . . . The unique nature of the Internet highlights the likelihood that a single actor might be subject to haphazard, uncoordinated, and even outright inconsistent regulation by states that the actor never intended to reach and possibly was unaware were being accessed. Typically, states' jurisdictional limits are related to geography; geography, however, is a virtually meaningless construct on the Internet.

[T]he New York Act . . . contravenes the Commerce Clause for three reasons. First, the Act represents an unconstitutional projection of New York law into conduct that occurs wholly outside New York. Second, the Act is invalid because although protecting children from indecent material is a legitimate and indisputably worthy subject of state legislation, the burdens on interstate commerce resulting from the Act clearly exceed any local benefit derived from it. Finally, the Internet is one of those areas of commerce that must be marked off as a national preserve to protect users from inconsistent legislation that, taken to its most extreme, could paralyze development of the Internet altogether.

B. New York Has Overreached by Enacting a Law That Seeks To Regulate Conduct Occurring Outside its Borders

In the present case, a number of witnesses testified to the chill that they felt as a result of the enactment of the New York statute; these witnesses refrained from engaging in particular types of interstate commerce. In particular, I note the testimony of Rudolf Kinsky, an artist with a virtual studio on Art on the Net's Website. Mr. Kinsky testified that he removed several images from his virtual studio because he feared prosecution under the New York Act. As described above, no Web siteholder is able to close his site to New Yorkers. Thus, even if Mr. Kinsky were located in California and wanted to display his work to a prospective purchaser in Oregon, he could not employ his virtual studio to do so without risking prosecution under the New York law.

Edgar v. MITE [Discussed *supra* page 443] teaches that for New York to attempt to strangle prospective interstate transactions between parties from states other than New York by this means offends the Commerce Clause. The "extraterritoriality" analysis of the Edgar opinion commanded only a plurality of the Court. Later majority holdings, however, expressly adopted the underlying principles on which Justice White relied in *Edgar*. [The Court discusses Healy v. The Beer Institute, discussed *supra* at 430, and Brown-Forman Distillers Corp. v. New York State Liquor Authority, reproduced *supra* at 428.] . . . The *Edgar/Healy* extraterritoriality analysis rests on the premise that the Commerce Clause has two aspects: it subordinates each state's authority over interstate commerce to the federal power of regulation (a vertical limitation), and it embodies a principle of comity that mandates that one state not expand its regulatory powers in a manner that encroaches upon the sovereignty of its fellow states (a horizontal limitation).

The nature of the Internet makes it impossible to restrict the effects of the New York Act to conduct occurring within New York. An Internet user may not intend that a message be accessible to New Yorkers, but lacks the ability to prevent New Yorkers from visiting a particular Website or viewing a particular newsgroup posting or receiving a particular mail exploder. Thus, conduct that may be legal in the state in which the user acts can subject the user to prosecution in New York and thus subordinate the user's home state's policy—perhaps favoring freedom of expression over a more protective stance—to New York's local concerns. New York has deliberately imposed its legislation on the Internet and, by doing so, projected its law into other states whose citizens use the Net. This encroachment upon the authority which the Constitution specifically confers upon the federal government and upon the sovereignty of New York's sister states is per se violative of the Commerce Clause.

C. The Burdens the Act Imposes on Interstate Commerce Exceed Any Local Benefit

Even if the Act were not a per se violation of the Commerce Clause by virtue of its extraterritorial effects, the Act would nonetheless be an invalid indirect regulation of interstate commerce, because the burdens it imposes on interstate commerce are excessive in relation to the local benefits it confers. The Supreme Court set forth the balancing test applicable to indirect regulations of interstate commerce in Pike v. Bruce Church. *Pike* requires a two-fold inquiry. The first level of examination is directed at the legitimacy of the state's interest. The next, and more difficult, determination weighs the burden on interstate commerce in light of the local benefit derived from the statute.

In the present case, I accept that the protection of children against pedophilia is a quintessentially legitimate state objective—a proposition with which I believe even the plaintiffs have expressed no quarrel. The defendants spent considerable time in their Memorandum and at argument asserting the legitimacy of the state's interest. Even with the fullest recognition that the protection of children from sexual exploitation is an indisputably valid state goal, however, the present statute cannot survive even the lesser scrutiny to which indirect regulations of interstate commerce are subject under the Constitution. The State cannot avoid the second stage of the inquiry simply by invoking the legitimate state interest underlying the Act.

The local benefits likely to result from the New York Act are not overwhelming. The Act can have no effect on communications originating outside the United States. As the three-judge panel that struck the federal analog of the New York Act, the Communications Decency Act, on First Amendment grounds concluded:

> [The Act] will almost certainly fail to accomplish the Government's interest in shielding children from pornography on the Internet. Nearly half of Internet communications originate outside the United States, and some percentage of that figure represents pornography. Pornography from, say, Amsterdam, will be no less appealing to a child on the Internet than pornography from New York City, and residents of Amsterdam have little incentive to comply with the [Act].

Further, in the present case, New York's prosecution of parties from out of state who have allegedly violated the Act, but whose only contact with New York occurs via the Internet, is beset with practical difficulties, even if New York is able to exercise criminal jurisdiction over such parties. The prospect of New York bounty hunters dragging pedophiles from the other 49 states into New York is not consistent with traditional concepts of comity.

Moreover, the State has espoused an interpretation of the Act that, if accepted, would further undermine its effectiveness. According to defendant, the Act reaches only pictorial messages that are harmful to minors and has no impact on purely textual communications. Were this interpretation adopted, Mr. Barlow, whose conduct supposedly motivated the supporters of the Act, would escape prosecution because his messages were verbal.

The Act is, of course, not the only law in New York's statute books designed to protect children against sexual exploitation. The State is able to protect children through vigorous enforcement of the existing laws criminalizing obscenity and child pornography. Moreover, plaintiffs do not challenge the sections of the statute that criminalize the sale of obscene materials to children, over the Internet or otherwise, and prohibit adults from luring children into sexual contact by communicating with them via the Internet. *See* N.Y. Penal Law §235.21(1); N.Y. Penal Law §235.22(2). The local benefit to be derived from the challenged section of the statute is therefore confined to that narrow class of cases that does not fit within the parameters of any other law. The efficacy of the statute is further limited, as discussed above, to those cases which New York is realistically able to prosecute.

Balanced against the limited local benefits resulting from the Act is an extreme burden on interstate commerce. The New York Act casts its net worldwide; moreover, the chilling effect that it produces is bound to exceed the actual cases that are likely to be prosecuted, as Internet users will steer clear of the Act by significant margin.

Moreover, as both three-judge panels that struck the federal statute have found, the costs associated with Internet users' attempts to comply with the terms of the defenses that the Act provides are excessive. Both courts that addressed the Communications Decency Act found that these costs of compliance, coupled with the threat of serious criminal sanctions for failure to comply, could drive some Internet users off the Internet altogether. While the defenses in the Act are not identical to those present in the CDA, the cost analysis undertaken by the ACLU and Shea courts is equally applicable to both statutes.

The severe burden on interstate commerce resulting from the New York statute is not justifiable in light of the attenuated local benefits arising from it. The alternative analysis of the Act as an indirect regulation on interstate commerce therefore also mandates the issuance of the preliminary injunction sought by plaintiffs.

D. The Act Unconstitutionally Subjects Interstate Use of the Internet to Inconsistent Regulations

Finally, a third mode of Commerce Clause analysis further confirms that the plaintiffs are likely to succeed on the merits of their claim that the New York Act is unconstitutional. The courts have long recognized that certain types of commerce demand consistent treatment and are therefore susceptible to regulation only on a national level. The Internet represents one of those areas; effective regulation will require national, and more likely global, cooperation. Regulation by any single state can only result in chaos, because at least some states will likely enact laws subjecting Internet users to conflicting obligations. Without the limitations imposed by the Commerce Clause, these inconsistent regulatory schemes could paralyze the development of the Internet altogether.

In numerous cases, the Supreme Court has acknowledged the need for coordination in the regulation of certain areas of commerce. [For example, in] Southern Pac. Co. v. Arizona ex rel. Sullivan, 325 U.S. 761 (1945), the Court addressed the constitutionality of an Arizona statute that limited the length of trains within the state to fourteen passenger and seventy freight cars. The lower court's findings demonstrated that 93% of the freight traffic and 95% of the passenger traffic in Arizona was interstate; moreover, the Court endorsed the findings that travel by trains of more than fourteen passenger cars and more than seventy freight cars over the main lines of the United States was standard practice, and that the Arizona law had the effect of forcing railroads to decouple their trains in Texas or New Mexico and reform the train at full length in California. Thus, the practical impact of the Arizona law was to control the length of trains, as the Court put it, "all the way from Los Angeles to El Paso." The Court concluded that the Arizona train limit law imposed a serious burden on interstate commerce, noting that various states had imposed varying limits. The Court stated:

> With such laws in force in states which are interspersed with those having no limit on train lengths, the confusion and difficulty with which interstate operations would be burdened under the varied system of state regulation and the unsatisfied need for uniformity in such regulation, if any, are evident.

In striking the Arizona law as an unconstitutional intrusion on interstate commerce, the Court relied on a long-established rule barring the states from regulating "those phases of the national commerce which, because of the need of national uniformity, demand that their regulation, if any, be prescribed by a single authority."

In Bibb v. Navajo Freight Lines, Inc., 359 U.S. 520 (1959), the Court examined an Illinois statute that required the use of contour mudguards on trucks in Illinois. The Court took note of the fact that straight or conventional mudguards were permissible in most other states and actually required in Arkansas. Recognizing the need for coordinated legislation, the Court stated that "the conflict between the Arkansas regulation and the Illinois regulation . . . suggests that this regulation of mudguards is not one of those matters 'admitting of diversity of treatment, according to the special requirements of local conditions.' " The Court struck the Illinois law as imposing an undue burden on interstate commerce, in part because Illinois was insisting upon "a design out of line with the requirements of almost all the other states."

The Internet, like the rail and highway traffic at issue in the cited cases, requires a cohesive national scheme of regulation so that users are reasonably able to determine their obligations. Regulation on a local level, by contrast, will leave users lost in a welter of inconsistent laws, imposed by different states with different priorities. New York is not the only state to enact a law purporting to regulate the content of communications on the Internet. Already

Oklahoma and Georgia have enacted laws designed to protect minors from indecent communications over the Internet; as might be expected, the states have selected different methods to accomplish their aims. Georgia has made it a crime to communicate anonymously over the Internet, while Oklahoma, like New York, has prohibited the online transmission of material deemed harmful to minors.

Further development of the Internet requires that users be able to predict the results of their Internet use with some degree of assurance. Haphazard and uncoordinated state regulation can only frustrate the growth of cyberspace. The need for uniformity in this unique sphere of commerce requires that New York's law be stricken as a violation of the Commerce Clause.

Washington v. Heckel

24 P.3d 404 (Wash. 2001)

OWENS, J.

The State of Washington filed suit against Oregon resident Jason Heckel, alleging that his transmissions of electronic mail (e-mail) to Washington residents violated Washington's commercial electronic mail act, chapter 19.190 RCW (the Act). . . . On cross-motions for summary judgment, the trial court dismissed the State's suit against Heckel, concluding that the Act violated the dormant Commerce Clause of the United States Constitution. This court granted the State's request for direct review. We hold that the Act does not unduly burden interstate commerce.

FACTS

As early as February 1996, defendant Jason Heckel, an Oregon resident doing business as Natural Instincts, began sending unsolicited commercial e-mail (UCE), or "spam," over the Internet. In 1997, Heckel developed a 46-page on-line booklet entitled "How to Profit from the Internet." The booklet described how to set up an on-line promotional business, acquire free e-mail accounts, and obtain software for sending bulk e-mail. From June 1998, Heckel marketed the booklet by sending between 100,000 and 1,000,000 UCE messages per week. To acquire the large volume of e-mail addresses, Heckel used the Extractor Pro software program, which harvests e-mail addresses from various on-line sources and enables a spammer to direct a bulk-mail message to those addresses by entering a simple command. The Extractor Pro program requires the spammer to enter a return e-mail address, a subject line, and the text of the message to be sent. The text of Heckel's UCE was a lengthy sales pitch that included testimonials from satisfied purchasers and culminated in an order form that the recipient could download and print. The order form included the Salem, Oregon, mailing address for

Natural Instincts. Charging $39.95 for the booklet, Heckel made 30 to 50 sales per month.

In June 1998, the Consumer Protection Division of the Washington State Attorney General's Office received complaints from Washington recipients of Heckel's UCE messages. The complaints alleged that Heckel's messages contained misleading subject lines and false transmission paths.[4] Responding to the June complaints, David Hill, an inspector from the Consumer Protection Division, sent Heckel a letter advising him of the existence of the Act. The Act provides that anyone sending a commercial e-mail message from a computer located in Washington or to an e-mail address held by a Washington resident may not use a third-party's domain name without permission, misrepresent or disguise in any other way the message's point of origin or transmission path, or use a misleading subject line.[6] RCW 19.190.030 makes a violation of the Act a per se violation of the Consumer Protection Act, chapter 19.86 RCW (CPA).

Responding to Hill's letter, Heckel telephoned Hill on or around June 25, 1998. According to Hill, he discussed with Heckel the provisions of the Act and the procedures bulk e-mailers can follow to identify e-mail addressees who are Washington residents. Nevertheless, the Attorney General's Office continued to receive consumer complaints alleging that Heckel's bulk e-mailings from Natural Instincts appeared to contain misleading subject

---

4. Each e-mail message, which is simply a computer data file, contains so-called "header" information in the "To," "From," and "Received" fields. When an e-mail message is transmitted from one e-mail address to another, the message generally passes through at least four computers: from the sender's computer, the message travels to the mail server computer of the sender's Internet Service Provider (ISP); that computer delivers the message to the mail server computer of the recipient's ISP, where it remains until the recipient retrieves it onto his or her own computer. Every computer on the Internet has a unique numerical address (an Internet Protocol or IP address), which is associated with a more readily recognizable domain name (such as "mysite.com"). As the e-mail message travels from sender to recipient, each computer transmitting the message attaches identifying data to the "Received" field in the header. The information serves as a kind of electronic postmark for the handling of the message. It is possible for a sender to alter (or "spoof") the header information by misidentifying either the computer from which the message originated or other computers along the transmission path.

6. (1) No person may initiate the transmission, conspire with another to initiate the transmission, or assist the transmission, of a commercial electronic mail message from a computer located in Washington or to an electronic mail address that the sender knows, or has reason to know, is held by a Washington resident that:

> (a) Uses a third party's internet domain name without permission of the third party, or otherwise misrepresents or obscures any information in identifying the point of origin or the transmission path of a commercial electronic mail message; or (b) Contains false or misleading information in the subject line.

(2) For purposes of this section, a person knows that the intended recipient of a commercial electronic mail message is a Washington resident if that information is available, upon request, from the registrant of the Internet domain name contained in the recipient's electronic mail address. RCW 19.190.020.

lines, false or unusable return e-mail addresses, and false or misleading transmission paths. Between June and September 1998, the Consumer Protection Division of the Attorney General's Office documented 20 complaints from 17 recipients of Heckel's UCE messages.

On October 22, 1998, the State filed suit against Heckel, stating three causes of action. First, the State alleged that Heckel had violated RCW 19.190.020(1)(b) and, in turn, the CPA, by using false or misleading information in the subject line of his UCE messages. Heckel used one of two subject lines to introduce his solicitations: "Did I get the right e-mail address?" and "For your review—HANDS OFF!" Clerk's Papers (CP) at 6, 92, 113. In the State's view, the first subject line falsely suggested that an acquaintance of the recipient was trying to make contact, while the second subject line invited the misperception that the message contained classified information for the particular recipient's review.

As its second cause of action, the State alleged that Heckel had violated RCW 19.190.020(1)(a), and thus the CPA, by misrepresenting information defining the transmission paths of his UCE messages. Heckel routed his spam through at least a dozen different domain names without receiving permission to do so from the registered owners of those names. For example, of the 20 complaints the Attorney General's Office received concerning Heckel's spam, 9 of the messages showed "13.com" as the initial ISP to transmit his spam. The 13.com domain name, however, was registered as early as November 1995 to another individual, from whom Heckel had not sought or received permission to use the registered name. In fact, because the owner of 13.com had not yet even activated that domain name, no messages could have been sent or received through 13.com.

Additionally, the State alleged that Heckel had violated the CPA by failing to provide a valid return e-mail address to which bulk-mail recipients could respond. When Heckel created his spam with the Extractor Pro software, he used at least a dozen different return e-mail addresses with the domain name "juno.com." . . . None of the Juno e-mail accounts was readily identifiable as belonging to Heckel; the user names that he registered generally consisted of a name or a name plus a number (*e.g.*, "Marlin 1374," "cindyt5667," "howardwesley13," "johnjacobson1374," and "sjtowns"). During August and September 1998, Heckel's Juno addresses were canceled within two days of his sending out a bulk e-mail message on the account. According to Heckel, when Juno canceled one e-mail account, he would simply open a new one and send out another bulk mailing. Because Heckel's accounts were canceled so rapidly, recipients who attempted to reply were unsuccessful. The State thus contended that Heckel's practice of cycling through e-mail addresses ensured that those addresses were useless to the recipients of his UCE messages. During the months that Heckel was sending out bulk e-mail solicitations on the Juno accounts, he maintained a personal e-mail account from which he sent no spam, but that e-mail address was not included in any of his spam messages. The State asserted that

Heckel's use of such ephemeral e-mail addresses in his UCE amounted to a deceptive practice in violation of RCW 19.86.020.

The State sought a permanent injunction and, pursuant to RCW 19.86.140 and .080 of the CPA, requested civil penalties, as well as costs and a reasonable attorney fee. . . . [The] trial court . . . found that the Act violated the Commerce Clause and was "unduly restrictive and burdensome." . . . Challenging the trial court's finding that the Act violated the Commerce Clause, the State sought this court's direct review.

Issue

Does the Act, which prohibits misrepresentation in the subject line or transmission path of any commercial e-mail message sent to Washington residents or from a Washington computer, unconstitutionally burden interstate commerce?

Analysis

Heckel's Challenge Under the Commerce Clause

The Commerce Clause grants Congress the "power . . . [t]o regulate commerce with foreign nations, and among the several states." Implicit in this affirmative grant is the negative or "dormant" Commerce Clause—the principle that the states impermissibly intrude on this federal power when they enact laws that unduly burden interstate commerce. *See* Franks & Son, Inc. v. State, 136 Wn.2d 737, 747, 966 P.2d 1232 (1998).

Analysis of a state law under the dormant Commerce Clause generally follows a two-step process. We first determine whether the state law openly discriminates against interstate commerce in favor of intrastate economic interests. If the law is facially neutral, applying impartially to in-state and out-of-state businesses, the analysis moves to the second step, a balancing of the local benefits against the interstate burdens:

> Where the statute regulates evenhandedly to effectuate a legitimate local public interest, and its effects on interstate commerce are only incidental, it will be upheld unless the burden imposed on such commerce is clearly excessive in relation to the putative local benefits. If a legitimate local purpose is found, then the question becomes one of degree. And the extent of the burden that will be tolerated will of course depend on the nature of the local interest involved, and on whether it could be promoted as well with a lesser impact on interstate activities. . . .

Id. at 754 (*quoting* Pike v. Bruce Church, Inc., 397 U.S. 137, 142, 90 S. Ct. 844, 25 L. Ed. 2d 174 (1970)).

The Act is not facially discriminatory. The Act applies evenhandedly to in-state and out-of-state spammers: "*No person*" may transmit the proscribed commercial e-mail messages "from a computer located in Washington or to an electronic mail address that the sender knows, or has reason to know, is held by a Washington resident." RCW 19.190.020(1) (emphasis added). Thus, just as the statute applied to Heckel, an Oregon resident, it is enforceable against a Washington business engaging in the same practices.

Because we conclude that the Act's local benefits surpass any alleged burden on interstate commerce, the statute likewise survives the *Pike* balancing test. The Act protects the interests of three groups—ISPs, actual owners of forged domain names, and e-mail users. The problems that spam causes have been discussed in prior cases and legislative hearings. A federal district court described the harms a mass e-mailer caused ISP CompuServe:

> In the present case, any value CompuServe realizes from its computer equipment is wholly derived from the extent to which that equipment can serve its subscriber base. . . . [H]andling the enormous volume of mass mailings that CompuServe receives places a tremendous burden on its equipment. Defendants' more recent practice of evading CompuServe's filters by disguising the origin of their messages commandeers even more computer resources because CompuServe's computers are forced to store undeliverable e-mail messages and labor in vain to return the messages to an address that does not exist. To the extent that defendants' multitudinous electronic mailings demand the disk space and drain the processing power of plaintiff's computer equipment, those resources are not available to serve CompuServe subscribers. Therefore, the value of that equipment to CompuServe is diminished even though it is not physically damaged by defendants' conduct.

CompuServe Inc. v. Cyber Promotions, Inc., 962 F. Supp. 1015, 1022 (S.D. Ohio 1997) (citations omitted) (granting preliminary injunction against bulk e-mailer on theory of trespass to chattels). To handle the increased e-mail traffic attributable to deceptive spam, ISPs must invest in more computer equipment. Operational costs likewise increase as ISPs hire more customer service representatives to field spam complaints and more system administrators to detect accounts being used to send spam.

Along with ISPs, the owners of impermissibly used domain names and e-mail addresses suffer economic harm. For example, the registered owner of "localhost.com" alleged that his computer system was shut down for three days by 7,000 responses to a bulk-mail message in which the spammer had forged the e-mail address "nobody at localhost.com" into his spam's header. Deceptive spam harms individual Internet users as well. When a spammer distorts the point of origin or transmission path of the message, e-mail recipients cannot promptly and effectively respond to the message (and thereby opt out of future mailings); their efforts to respond take time, cause frustration, and compound the problems that ISPs face in delivering and storing the bulk messages. And the use of false or misleading subject lines further hampers an individual's ability to use computer time most efficiently. When spammers use subject lines "such as 'Hi There!,' 'Information Request,' and 'Your Business Records,' " it becomes "virtually impossible" to distinguish spam from legitimate personal or business messages. Individuals who do not have flat-rate plans for Internet access but pay instead by the minute or hour are harmed more directly, but all Internet users (along with their ISPs) bear the cost of deceptive spam.

This cost-shifting—from deceptive spammers to businesses and e-mail users—has been likened to sending junk mail with postage due or making telemarketing calls to someone's pay-per-minute cellular phone. In a case involving the analogous practice of junk faxing (sending unsolicited faxes that contain advertisements), the Ninth Circuit acknowledged "the government's substantial interest in preventing the shifting of advertising costs to consumers." Destination Ventures, Ltd. v. F.C.C., 46 F.3d 54, 56 (9th Cir. 1995) (holding that the Telephone Consumer Protection Act's (47 U.S.C. §227) limitations on commercial speech did not violate the First Amendment). We thus recognize that the Act serves the "legitimate local purpose" of banning the cost-shifting inherent in the sending of deceptive spam.

Under the *Pike* balancing test, "[i]f a legitimate local purpose is found, then the question becomes one of degree." 397 U.S. at 142. In the present case, the trial court questioned whether the Act's requirement of truthfulness (in the subject lines and header information) would redress the costs associated with bulk e-mailings. As legal commentators have observed, however, "the truthfulness requirements (such as the requirement not to misrepresent the message's Internet origin) make spamming unattractive to the many fraudulent spammers, thereby reducing the volume of spam." Jack L. Goldsmith & Alan O. Sykes, *The Internet and the Dormant Commerce Clause,* 110 Yale L.J. 785, 819 (2001). Calling "simply wrong" the trial court's view "that truthful identification in the subject header would do little to relieve the annoyance of spam," the commentators assert that "[t]his identification alone would allow many people to delete the message without opening it (which takes time) and perhaps being offended by the content." *Id.* The Act's truthfulness requirements thus appear to advance the Act's aim of protecting ISPs and consumers from the problems associated with commercial bulk e-mail.

To be weighed against the Act's local benefits, the only burden the Act places on spammers is the requirement of truthfulness, a requirement that does not burden commerce at all but actually "facilitates it by eliminating fraud and deception." *Id.* Spammers must use an accurate, nonmisleading subject line, and they must not manipulate the transmission path to disguise the origin of their commercial messages. While spammers incur no costs in complying with the Act, they do incur costs for noncompliance, because they must take steps to introduce forged information into the header of their message. In finding the Act "unduly burdensome," the trial court apparently focused not on what spammers must do to comply with the Act but on what they must do if they choose to use deceptive subject lines or to falsify elements in the transmission path. To initiate *deceptive* spam without violating the Act, a spammer must weed out Washington residents by contacting the registrant of the domain name contained in the recipient's e-mail address. This focus on the burden of *non* compliance is contrary to the approach in the *Pike* balancing test, where the United States Supreme Court assessed the cost of compliance with a challenged statute. *Pike,* 397 U.S. at 143. Indeed, the trial court could have appropriately considered the filtering requirement a burden only if Washington's statute had banned outright the sending of UCE messages to Washington residents. We therefore conclude that Heckel has failed to prove that "the burden imposed on . . . commerce [by the Act] is *clearly excessive* in relation to the putative local benefits." *Id.* at 142 (emphasis added).

Drawing on two "unsettled and poorly understood" aspects of the dormant Commerce Clause analysis, Heckel contended that the Act (1) created inconsistency among the states and (2) regulated conduct occurring wholly outside of Washington.[14] The inconsistent-regulations test and the extraterritoriality analysis are appropriately regarded as facets of the *Pike* balancing test.[15] The Act survives both inquiries. At present, 17 other states have passed legislation regulating electronic solicitations. The truthfulness requirements of the Act do not conflict with any of the requirements in the other states' statutes, and it is inconceivable that any state would ever pass a law requiring spammers to use misleading subject lines or transmission paths. Some states' statutes do include additional requirements; for example, some statutes require spammers to provide contact information (for opt-out purposes) or to introduce subject lines with such labels as "ADV" or "ADV-ADLT." But because such statutes "merely create additional, but not irreconcilable, obligations," they "are not considered to be 'inconsistent' " for purposes of the dormant Commerce Clause analysis. Instructional Sys., Inc. v. Computer Curriculum Corp., 35 F.3d 813, 826 (3d Cir. 1994). The inquiry under the dormant Commerce Clause is not whether the states have enacted different anti-spam statutes but whether those differences create compliance costs that are "clearly excessive in relation to the putative local benefits." *Pike,* 397 U.S. at 142. We do not believe that the differences between the Act and the anti-spam laws of other states impose extraordinary costs on businesses deploying spam.

---

14. Jack L. Goldsmith & Alan O. Sykes, *The Internet and the Dormant Commerce Clause,* 110 Yale L.J. 785, 789 (2001).

15. *See* Goldsmith & Sykes, *supra* note 14, at 808 (concluding that "inconsistent-regulations cases, like extraterritoriality cases, should be viewed as just another variant of balancing analysis"); *see also* William Lee Biddle, *State Regulation of the Internet: Where Does the Balance of Federalist Power Lie?* 37 Cal. W. L. Rev. 161, 167 (2000) (suggesting that "[t]he burden placed on interstate commerce through inconsistent local regulation is more appropriately placed as part of the *Pike* balancing test, rather than its own, separate line of inquiry").

Nor does the Act violate the extraterritoriality principle in the dormant Commerce Clause analysis. Here, there is no "sweeping extraterritorial effect" that would outweigh the local benefits of the Act. Edgar v. MITE Corp., 457 U.S. 624, 642 (1982). Heckel offers the hypothetical of a Washington resident who downloads and reads the deceptive spam while in Portland or Denver. He contends that the dormant Commerce Clause is offended because the Act would regulate the recipient's conduct while out of state. However, the Act does not burden interstate commerce by regulating when or where recipients may open the proscribed UCE messages. Rather, the Act addresses the conduct of spammers in targeting Washington consumers. Moreover, the hypothetical mistakenly presumes that the Act must be construed to apply to Washington residents when they are out of state, a construction that creates a jurisdictional question not at issue in this case.

In sum, we reject the trial court's conclusion that the Act violates the dormant Commerce Clause. Although the trial court found particularly persuasive American Libraries Association v. Pataki, 969 F. Supp. 160 (S.D.N.Y. 1997), that decision—the first to apply the dormant Commerce Clause to a state law on Internet use—is distinguishable in a key respect. At issue in *American Libraries* was a New York statute that made it a crime to use a computer to distribute harmful, sexually explicit content to minors. The statute applied not just to initiation of e-mail messages but to all Internet activity, including the creation of websites. Thus, under the New York statute, a website creator in California could inadvertently violate the law simply because the site could be viewed in New York. Concerned with the statute's "chilling effect," *id.* at 179, the court observed that, if an artist "were located in California and wanted to display his work to a prospective purchaser in Oregon, he could not employ his virtual [Internet] studio to do so without risking prosecution under the New York law." 969 F. Supp. at 174. In contrast to the New York statute, which could reach all content posted on the Internet and therefore subject individuals to liability based on unintended access, the Act reaches only those deceptive UCE messages directed to a Washington resident or initiated from a computer located in Washington; in other words, the Act does not impose liability for messages that are merely routed through Washington or that are read by a Washington resident who was not the actual addressee.

Questions and Comments

(1) Does the logic of *American Libraries Assn.* leave room for any state regulation of the Internet? Don't state laws prohibiting Internet gambling, Internet computer crimes, Internet consumer protection, Internet libel, and the like have similar extraterritorial effects and similarly subject Internet users to inconsistent burdens?

(2) Several courts have followed *American Libraries Assn.*'s reasoning in invalidating statutes similar to New York's. *See, e.g.*, ACLU v. Johnson, 194

F.3d 1149 (10th Cir. 1999) (invalidating under the dormant commerce clause a New Mexico statute criminalizing dissemination of materials harmful to minors by computer). Other courts have distinguished *American Libraries Assn.* when a state prohibition on pornographic Internet communications with minors included an element of "luring" or "seducing" the minor into illicit sexual relations. *See* Hatch v. Superior Court, 94 Cal. Rptr. 2d 453, 471-472 (Ct. App. 2000); People v. Foley, 709 N.Y.S.2d 467, 477 (2000). These courts reason that the "luring" element eliminates any genuine commercial value in the regulated activity, *see Foley*, 709 N.Y.S.2d at 477, and that there is no reason to think state prosecutors will enforce the law against out-of-state seducers, *see Hatch*, 94 Cal. Rptr. 2d at 472-473. Are these convincing distinctions?

(3) *American Libraries Assn.* appears to assume that New York's criminalization of the sale of *obscene* materials to children over the Internet would survive the extraterritoriality prong of the dormant Commerce Clause. While New York's prohibition on pornographic communications with minors and its prohibition on the sale of obscenity to minors differ in substance, as applied to the Internet their extraterritorial effects are identical: Both regulations affect the pricing decisions of Web content providers in other states, and this influence on price may affect consumers in permissive jurisdictions outside of New York. Why, then, the differential treatment?

(4) An important premise in *American Libraries Assn.* is that "Internet users have no way to determine the characteristics of their audience that are salient under the New York Act—age and geographic location." Is this true? Many web page operators successfully condition access to content on the presentation of an adult personal identification number (PIN). *See* ACLU v. Reno, 31 F. Supp. 2d 473, 490 (E.D. Pa. 1999). They can also condition access to content of the presentation of geographical identification information, and as we learned in the *Yahoo!* case, *supra* page 851, firms have the ability to some degree to identify and screen users geographically. So the question is not the possibility of age and geographical identification, but rather their costs. When a state imposes these screening costs on out-of-state users, does it violate the dormant commerce clause?

Consider the analogous issue of a firm selling pornography in "real space." Such a firm must identify the restrictive "community standards" of each locality in the country, and tailor its content to that locality (which might entail barring the content from the community). *See* Miller v. California, 413 U.S. 15, 24-25 (1973). It must, in other words, incur costs in screening its content out of restrictive jurisdictions. Are these costs legitimate? In a First Amendment challenge to the regulation of a "real-space" "dial-a-porn" firm, the Supreme Court stated:

> [The content provider] is free to tailor its messages, on a selective basis, if it so chooses, to the communities it chooses to serve. While [it] may be forced to incur some costs in developing and implementing a system for

> screening the locale of incoming calls, there is no constitutional impediment to enacting a law which may impose such costs on a medium electing to provide these messages. Whether [the content provider] chooses to hire operators to determine the source of the calls or engages with the telephone company to arrange for the screening and blocking of out-of-area calls or finds another means for providing messages compatible with community standards is a decision for the message provider to make. . . . If [the firm's] audience is comprised of different communities with different local standards, [it] ultimately bears the burden of complying with the prohibition on obscene messages.

Sable Communications, Inc. v. FCC, 492 U.S. 115, 125-126 (1989). Is the analysis relevant to the dormant commerce clause as well? Do the costs that real-space pornography providers incur in keeping abreast of regulatory developments in different localities and in taking steps to comply with these regulations violate the dormant commerce clause? If not, why are "real-space" and Internet pornography providers treated differently?

(5) Are you convinced by *Heckel*'s attempt to distinguish *American Libraries Ass'n?* Can't a spammer "inadvertently violate" Washington's anti-spam law by sending messages to Washington recipients? Unlike the World Wide Web, which involves a two-way transmission between the content receiver and sender, e-mail transmissions are effectively one-way transmissions from the content sender to the receiver. When combined with the fact that e-mail addresses do not necessarily (or even usually) correspond with a geographic location, the result is that it is extraordinarily difficult for a spammer to identify and screen out persons in prohibited jurisdictions ex ante. Doesn't this make state regulation of e-mail more problematic (in terms of extraterritorial effects) than state regulation of web content?

(6) There is a growing literature on the Internet and the dormant commerce clause. *See* Goldsmith & Sykes, The Internet and the Dormant Commerce Clause, 110 Yale L.J. 785 (2001); Biddle, State Regulation of the Internet: Where Does the Balance of Federalist Power Lie? 37 Cal. W. L. Rev. 161, 167 (2000); Denning, Smokey and the Bandit in Cyberspace: the Dormant Commerce Clause, the Twenty-first Amendment, and State Regulation of Internet Alcohol Sales,—Const. Comm.—(forthcoming 2002); Burk, Federalism in Cyberspace, 28 Conn. L. Rev. 1095 (1996).

Table of Cases

Italic type indicates principal cases.

Table of Secondary Authorities

Aceves, Liberalism and International Legal Scholarship: The Pinochet Case and the Move Toward a Universal System of Transnational Law Litigation, 41 Harv. Intl. L.J. 129 (2000), 781

Adams, *World-Wide Volkswagen v. Woodson*—the Rest of the Story, 72 Neb. L. Rev. 1122 (1993), 524

Alexander, Unlimited Shareholder Liability Through a Procedural Lens, 106 Harv. L. Rev. 387 (1992), 563

Alford, Extraterritorial Application of Antitrust Laws: A Postscript on *Hartford Fire Insurance Co. v. California*, 34 Va. J. Intl. L. 213 (1993), 765

Audit, A Continental Lawyer Looks at Contemporary American Choice-of-Law Principles, 27 Am. J. Comp. L. 589 (1979), 238

Baldassare, Comment, Pandora's Box or Treasure Chest?: Circuit Courts Face 28 U.S.C. 1367's Effect on Multi-Plaintiff Diversity Actions, 27 Seton Hall L. Rev. 1497 (1997), 479

Bauer, The *Erie* Doctrine Revisited: How a Conflicts Perspective Can Aid the Analysis, 74 Notre Dame L. Rev. 1235 (1999), 575

Baxter, Choice of Law and the Federal System, 16 Stan. L. Rev. 1 (1963), 581, 651

Beale, A Treatise on the Conflict of Laws §332.2 (1935), 37

_____________, The Conflict of Laws (1935), 8, 55

Bederman et al., The Enforcement of Human Rights and Humanitarian Law by Civil Suits in Municipal Courts: The Civil Dimension of Universal Jurisdiction, reprinted in Contemporary International Law Issues: New Forms, New Applications 156 (1998), 782

Bentley, Toward an International Fourth Amendment: Rethinking Searches and Seizures Abroad After *Verdugo-Urquidez*, 27 Vand. J. Transnatl. L. 329 (1994), 800

Biddle, State Regulation of the Internet: Where Does the Balance of Federalist Power Lie? 37 Cal. W. L. Rev. 161 (2000), 873

Blumberg, The Increasing Recognition of Enterprise Principles in Determining Parent and Subsidiary Corporation Liabilities, 28 Conn. L. Rev. 295 (1996), 563

Borchers, *Baker v. General Motors:* Implications for Interjurisdictional Recognition on Nontraditional Marriages, 32 Creighton L. Rev. 147 (1998), 688

_____________, The Choice-of-Law Revolution: An Empirical Study, 49 Wash. & Lee L. Rev. 357 (1992)

_____________, Forum Selection Agreements in the Federal Courts *After Carnival Cruise*: A Proposal for Congressional Reform, 67 Wash. L. Rev. 55 (1992), 262, 333, 460, 611

_____________, Louisiana's Conflicts Codification: Some Empirical Observations Regarding Decisional Predictability, 60 La. L. Rev. 1061 (2000), 339

Kaye & Weissman, Interactive Judicial Federalism: Certified Questions in New York, 69 Fordham L. Rev. 373 (2000), 179
Kennedy, The Supreme Court Meets the Bridge of Frankenstein: *Phillips Petroleum Co. v. Shutts* and the State Multistate Class Action, 34 U. Kan. L. Rev. 255 (1985), 478
Kipp, Inferring Express Consent: The Paradox of Permitting Registration Statutes to Confer General Jurisdiction, 9 Rev. Litg. 1 (1990), 472
Kirgis, The Roles of Due Process and Full Faith and Credit in Choice of Law, 62 Cornell L. Rev. 94 (1976), 348, 400
Kobayashi & Ribstein, Choosing Law by Contract, The Fall and Rise of Freedom of Contract (1999), 303
Kogan, Toward a Jurisprudence of Choice of Law: The Priority of Fairness over Comity, 62 N.Y.U. L. Rev. 651 (1987), 354
Koh, Commentary, Is International Law Really State Law?, 111 Harv. L. Rev. 1824 (1998), 735, 781
Koppelman, Same-Sex Marriage, Choice of Law, and Public Policy, 76 Tex. L. Rev. 921 (1998), 72
Korn, The Choice-of-Law Revolution: A Critique, 83 Colum. L. Rev. 772 (1983), 789
Kramer, Extraterritorial Application of American Law After the Insurance Antitrust Case: A Reply to Professors Lowenfeld and Trimble, 89 Am. J. Intl. L. 750 (1995), 765
______________, Interest Analysis and the Presumption of Forum Law, 56 U. Chi. L. Rev. 1301 (1989), 236
______________, Rethinking Choice of Law, 90 Colum. L. Rev. 277 (1990), 236, 241
______________, Return of the Renovi, 66 N.Y.U. L. Rev. 979 (1991), 312
______________, Same-Sex Marriage, Conflict of Laws, and the Unconstitutional Public Policy Exception, 106 Yale L.J. 1965 (1997), 72, 401, 688
______________, Vestiges of Beale: Extraterritorial Application of American Law, 1991 S. Ct. Rev. 179 (1991), 743
Kreimer, The Law of Choice and Choice of Law: Abortion, the Right to Travel, and Extraterritorial Regulation in American Federalism, 67 Mich. L. Rev. 451 (1992), 393

Lando, New American Choice-of-Law Principles and the European Conflict of Laws of Contracts, 30 Am. J. Comp. L. 19 (1982), 239
Langevoort, The Supreme Court and the Politics of Corporate Takeovers: A Comment on *CTS Corp. v. General Dynamics Corp. of America*,101 Harv. L. Rev. 96 (1987), 443
Lasok & Stone, Conflicts of Laws in the European Community (1987), 238
Laycock, Equal Citizens of Equal and Territorial States: The Constitutional Foundations of Choice of Law, 92 Colum. L. Rev. 249 (1992), 353, 411
Laycock, Equality and the Citizens of Sister Slates, 15 Fla. St. L. Rev. 431 (1987), 411
Leathers, *Erie* and Its Progeny as Choice of Law Cases, 11 Hous. L. Rev. 791 (1974), 575
Leebron, Limited Liability, Tort Victims, and Creditors, 91 Colum. L. Rev. 1565 (1991), 96
Leflar, Choice-of-Law Statutes, 44 Tenn L. Rev. 951 (1977), 315
______________, Conflicts Law: More on Choice-Influencing Considerations, 54 Calif. L. Rev. 1584 (1996), 252
______________, Extrastate Enforcement of Penal and Governmental Claims, 46 Harv. L. Rev. 193 (1932), 173
Lessig, The Zones of Cyberspace, 48 Stan L Rev 1403 (1996), 855
Lorenzen, Selected Articles on the Conflict of Laws (1947), 8
Lowe, Extraterritorial Jurisdiction, An Annotated Collection of Legal Materials (1983), 765
Lowenfeld, Conflict, Balancing of Interests, and the Exercise of Jurisdiction to Prescribe: Reflections on the Insurance Antitrust Case, 89 Am. J. Intl. L. 42 (1995), 765
______________, Nationalizing International Law: Essay in Honor of Louis Henkin, 36 Colum. J. Transnatl. L. 121 (1997), 618

Table of Restatement Sections

Restatement (First) of Conflicts, on Penal Laws and Tax Claims

Restatement (Second) of Conflicts